GW00692265

——— **Which?** ———
# HOTEL GUIDE
——— 1992 ———

# Which?
# HOTEL GUIDE
## 1992

# Edited by Patricia Yates

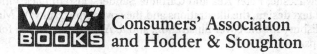 **Consumers' Association and Hodder & Stoughton**

Which? Hotel Guide 1992 was researched by *Holiday Which?*, part of the Association for Consumer Research, and published by Consumers' Association, 2 Marylebone Road, London NW1 4DX and Hodder & Stoughton, 47 Bedford Square, London WC1B 3DP

Copyright © 1991 Consumers' Association Limited
First edition September 1991

British Library Cataloguing in Publication Data
Which? hotel guide.
   1992–
   1. Great Britain. Hotels
   I. Consumers' Association
   647.944101

ISBN 0 340 55030 9

---

**Thanks for choosing this Guide . . .**

If you find it useful, we'd like to hear from you. Even if it doesn't live up to your expectations or do the job you were expecting, we'd still like to know. Then we can take your comments into account when preparing similar titles or, indeed, the next edition of the Guide. Address your letter to the Publishing Manager at Consumers' Association, FREEPOST, 2 Marylebone Road, London NW1 1YN. We look forward to hearing from you.

---

Typeset by Rowland Phototypesetting Ltd
Bury St Edmunds, Suffolk
Printed and bound in Great Britain by
BPCC Hazell Books Ltd,
Aylesbury, Bucks

Hoteliers do not pay for entries in *Which? Hotel Guide*, and the Editor and her inspectors accept no free hospitality. Consumers' Association does not permit hoteliers to mention their inclusion in *Which? Hotel Guide* in any advertising material.

Warm thanks to Deborah Buzan, Lorna Dean, Alison Leach, Andrew Leslie, Peter Rea and Caroline Sanders; also to Dick Vine for the text design, the illustrations and the cover typography; to Martin Salisbury for the cover illustration; and to Andrew Haughton for the maps.

# Contents

# Hotels – serving the consumer?

Here we are with the second edition of *Which? Hotel Guide*. Our first edition inspired many of you to put pen to paper – we've had hundreds of letters suggesting new hotels and commenting on our recommendations – and, indeed, on the Guide itself. Many of you also contributed enthusiastically to our list of likes and dislikes – of that, more later.

Reading your comments helped us to make various changes. For instance, we now list hotels alphabetically by town or village, echoing our sister publication, *The Good Food Guide*. If you know the name of a favourite hotel, but can't quite remember its location, refer to the index on page 801. If, on the other hand, you know the area you'll be in, and want to see the selection of hotels we've recommended, start with the maps at the back of the book.

Another improvement this year is that we asked all hoteliers to give us their prices *per room* (not per person) as well as specifying what they charge to individual guests occupying a double or twin room. We have included this information in the hotel's details, so that you can assess the situation before you ring to book.

As we did last year, we've included a broad range of places to stay – small B&Bs, friendly inns, plush country homes and streamlined business hotels. So, wherever you are, and whatever sort of place you like, there should be something in the Guide for you. We don't judge hotels on whether they have trouser presses or Jacuzzis in the room (though, of course, we tell you if they do). What we look for are hoteliers who work hard to put their guests first – who greet guests as if they are pleased to see them, keep their rooms warm and welcoming, and provide decent food decently served, comfortable bedrooms with good beds and clean bathrooms with plenty of hot water.

This year we've increased our geographical coverage, including for the first time hotels in the Channel Islands (so lots of reports on these, please), and our team of inspectors, often acting on tips from readers, have added to the number of hotels we can confidently recommend. To make the Guide even more useful we've added our selection of county round-ups in the **Visitors' Book**, hotels which are worth considering but which perhaps don't yet merit a full entry – see page 787. All in all, *Which? Hotel Guide 1992* covers nearly 1,000 of Britain's best places to stay. We must emphasise that we've inspected every single one and that there is absolutely no collusion with or payment from hoteliers.

Now for some fun. Last year we told you about our likes and dislikes. Many of you couldn't resist the temptation of adding your own contributions. Here are some of them.

# LIKES

## *Not just a number*

A warm welcome and some personal attention are winners every time: receptionists or owners who smile and greet you, someone who shows you to your room – and as much interest taken when you're leaving, not just indecent haste to get you to pay the bill. Guests like having their names remembered, rather than being 'the couple from number three'. Many of your letters said you'd go back to places that made you feel at home. 'The whole atmosphere is almost like visiting family and just picking up from where one left off the last time,' wrote one reader of Starlings Castle in Chirk, Clwyd. At the other end of the scale, the Blakeney Hotel in Blakeney, Norfolk was castigated: 'Never have we been made to feel so explicitly that an hotel was doing us a favour by letting us stay!'

## *Warm rooms and a warm welcome for out-of-season guests*

A number of people have mentioned their disappointment after spending sub-zero weekends away out-of-season. 'Our room was not large,' writes one reader of a stay at Killiecrankie Hotel in Scotland in October, 'but it was still cold as it was heated only by an electric fan heater controlled by a time switch and thermostat!' Another at Wasdale Head Inn, Gosforth, Cumbria says: 'The room temperature on 1 April was approximately 11 degrees Celsius with no heating on!' 'No central heating and the only warmth in the bedroom was via a single convector heater,' complains one guest of a February stay at the Crown Inn, Hopton Wafers, Shropshire. Where are the hoteliers? Huddled round the stove in the kitchen, we'll be bound. And often the lack of warmth isn't just in the temperature – it seems to be too much trouble to provide anything for the few winter guests who don't quite fill the hotel. Suddenly the menu is shortened, you're expected to decide on your dinner three hours in advance, it's 'a waste of money' to make proper coffee (instant will do), and the staff, in the only display of speed shown so far, strip the breakfast buffet if you're five minutes late.

## *Large(ish) bathrooms/hot water*

'Why is it that hotelkeepers believe that nobody wants to put anything in the bathroom except a toothbrush?' enquires our competition winner (see page 12). It sounds as if even he did rather better than the reader who stayed at the Manor Parc Country Hotel and Restaurant, Cardiff. 'Spoilt for me by minuscule washbasin in the bathroom. The only way to use the basin (fully occupied if you put your hands in) and look in the mirror was to sit sideways on the loo!' And we're getting rather bored reading about (and experiencing ourselves) British showers; it's about time hoteliers got away from the 'alternately freezing/scalding' variety and managed to provide constant hot water – even for early risers or when all the walkers return.

### Real milk and teapots

'They have got rid of the cow with the plastic teats and the UHT milk!' commented one reader on the return of real milk to bedroom tea-trays at the Royal Oak, Keswick, Cumbria. A pat on the back for hoteliers who offer it – and two pats for those who provide a proper teapot, avoiding the need for messy teabag-dunking.

### *'Do not disturb' signs*

No one wants their lie-in interrupted, or to have staff barging in at an inconvenient moment. Please can proper signs be provided – and their message heeded?

### *Flexible breakfast times*

'Unreasonable,' grumbled hoteliers, when we suggested this last year. 'We've got better things to do than make breakfast all day.' But there's no reason for banging in the kitchen when guests are ten minutes late. Early risers face similar problems. One visitor to an hotel in Ambleside, Cumbria wrote: 'On the day of departure, my husband asked a waiter at 8.10am if there would be any point in our coming down to breakfast before 8.30. In reply, he received the monosyllabic "no".' A gold star goes to Henry Phillips, at the Hundred House Hotel, Norton, Shropshire, who was on the scene at 6.30am to cater for one couple's request for an early start.

### *Good plain cooking*

Not every guest wants 'meat in cream sauce'. Particularly if they are staying for a few days, our readers clearly prefer the simple things done well.

One reader's comments on a stay at the Forte Hotel, Exeter, Devon was fairly typical: 'The restaurant produces really good plain food such as roast meat from the trolley, carved at your table, and a perfectly cooked lemon sole with lemon butter, on the bone but elegantly skinned.'

### *Proper coffee*

There is uniform outrage at instant coffee being served after dinner.

# DISLIKES

### *Meanness with the bedclothes*

We're still a nation of mixed habits at bedtime. Some of you comment, 'No duvets – hooray', while others welcome this Continental habit. But we are agreed that the increasingly frequent practice of using sheets under duvets needs to be stopped – some hoteliers like it because it saves the expense of blankets and, we reckon, alas, they don't necessarily change the duvet cover between guests. But, as one reader comments: 'One cannot wrap it round the body, it usually starts to slide off at the slightest movement and even if it doesn't an enormous amount of cold gets in round the sides of the bed where one has only the thickness of a sheet.' Please let's have duvet covers fresh for every new arrival – and why not splash out on king-sized duvets at the same time?

## Poor sound insulation

This peril of sub-dividing houses leaves guests with a far more intimate acquaintance with each other than they might wish. 'We could hear every sound from the room above – creaking floorboards, television, talking . . .'

## Bedside lights that are a fiddle

Who wants to get out of bed to switch off the light? So, a little more thought, please, even at Le Manoir aux Quat' Saisons at Great Milton, Oxfordshire. 'It was impossible to switch off the room lights from the bed without the bedside light going off as well.'

## Muzak

You hate it. 'Having unwanted music forced upon you is almost as bad as smoke.'

## Cheapskates

It started with those free sachets fanned out on the chest of drawers replacing flowers or ornaments. But some places go one better. One reader, who visited the Ilchester Arms, Abbotsbury, Dorset, found 'dirty soap under a new one in the bathroom, and complimentary bath lotions and shampoos which were in fact empty containers!'

## Drapes and dust

The inexorable march of the four-poster continues. Too often these big beds are crammed into rooms too small for them and even – horrors – bedecked (at the Mount Royal Hotel, York), with nylon-covered eiderdowns, one reader reports. Coming up on the inside track in the bedding 'Dislike' stakes are crown canopies surrounded by yards of draperies that aren't kept clean. 'The draperies above the bed (not a four-poster) had a layer of dust on them, and, as my husband suffers from asthma, we had to be careful not to disturb them. We think all those draperies are a bad idea, as they cannot be kept free of dust, however well the rest of the room is cleaned.' [Sopwell House, St Alban's, Herts.]

## Miserly vegetable portions

'Just three mange-tout,' gasped one would-be diner at Yalbury Cottage, Lower Bockhampton, Dorset. 'A dessertspoon of mashed potatoes, four french beans, two sprigs of broccoli and a dessert-spoon of turnip,' moaned another hungry eater at the King's Head, Cuckfield, West Sussex.

## Children

It is surely unacceptable that if you were travelling with a young child you would be barred from many of the hotels in this Guide. Of course, some children can be a nuisance, but then, for that matter, so can some parents. Many parents enjoy travelling with their children; they like talking to them, playing with them, taking them to new places. They would welcome cots in the room, reasonably priced family rooms, books and toys for rainy days, a high chair and high tea – and a peaceful dinner with other adults in the dining-room. Why are hoteliers' faces so firmly turned against younger visitors?

A letter we received from one reader may go some way towards answering this. 'We are constantly admonished for not welcoming children. The reason is that they are so vilely behaved; children used to adoration and unused to discipline can utterly ruin other people's expensive night out or weekend away.'

'Last weekend my husband and I went off to the Saracen's Head in Southwell, Nottinghamshire. At 8.30pm a 2-year-old was being fed, in a high chair, in the dining-room by two parents standing round the chair spooning food into its protesting mouth. It frequently spat it on to the carpet. The dining-room rang with the child's protests and the parents' distressed cooings. The waiting staff said this sort of thing was a frequent occurrence.'

## Hoteliers who can't handle complaints

It would be wise to forget the old adage 'the customer is always right' if you stay at some British hotels and, if you have any cause for complaint, be prepared to be told where to get off in no uncertain terms.

'When paying the bill (£60 for an attic/poor facilities), I complained of the cistern that had run all night overhead, overflowing drains and an entrance patio, and of the lack of friendliness. I was told: "Don't tell me how to run my business" and "Don't come back if you don't like it". I won't,' writes a visitor to the Vine House, Paulerspury, Northamptonshire.

Written complaints, even when couched in the calmest of terms, seem to meet a similar reaction, and the pay-off line used by hoteliers is so similar we're convinced hoteliers must pass it round at their association meetings. After the first two paragraphs explaining that this is the first complaint they've had in 20 years and arguing over whether the out-of-date muesli served for breakfast was actually unsafe, it invariably concludes: 'I am sorry you did not enjoy your stay and wish you luck in finding somewhere more suited to your taste.' I wonder what their repeat business is like?

## Discrimination against single travellers

'The person who answered the phone asked how many people I was booking for. I said: "Just myself." She said: "Sorry, we have no rooms" and promptly put the phone down.'

Is this experience typical of the single traveller? Oh yes, writes another single traveller. 'I accept the miserable logic that a single occupies more cubic feet than half a double and that I must therefore pay more. That does not mean that single rooms have to be the size of broom cupboards, located without a view on the back stairs, probably above the kitchen.' Except, of course, that they usually are, and if you are offered a double room at a slightly higher rate than the single, you can bet that it will be the poorest double in which there is barely space to move round the second unwanted bed.

Why should this be the case? Hoteliers tell us it is the law of supply and demand – there are very few single rooms around because it makes commercial sense to cater for couples. It seems to us, indeed, that the situation is worsening as hotels adopt the American habit of pricing by room so the single traveller occupying a double room has to pay the full double rate. And we suspect that many hotels bank on the fact that these inflated bills are often incurred by business travellers, who simply pass them on to their employers.

Perhaps hoteliers should be reminded that most of us probably travel on our own at some stage. We don't want to be treated as social misfits and be consigned to the worst rooms in the house. And in the current economic climate more and more business travellers don't have bottomless pits of expense accounts and are on the look-out for a comfortable, reasonably priced hotel.

Another much trumpeted development is the way business hotels are turning their attention to the 'lady executive', with specially designed bedrooms. A common assumption is that this lady executive requires pale pink/blue colour scheme – and an ironing-board, presumably in case she has got a week's supply of the family's laundry in the boot. One reader is not impressed: 'Very patronising. I should be able to borrow an iron whichever sex I am or room I use.'

## Tipping

We at *Which? Hotel Guide* dislike tipping as a practice and don't consider it warranted when people are simply doing their jobs.

Well, that's quite a list. But put it all together and you get the difference between the hotels on which you conclude: 'I wouldn't recommend this to my worst enemy' and 'Great. I would go back again – and tell my friends'. With finances likely to be tight again this year, the combination of your recommendations and our inspections means that our Guide can point you in the direction of the best hotels where you won't waste your money.

Finally, thank you to everyone who's written in with messages of support and tips, and to Morag Aitken of *Holiday Which?* who has handled all the correspondence and ensured that you have all had replies. Please do keep the letters coming – we like to get as many comments about hotels as possible. The forms, if you care to use these, are to be found at the back of the Guide and you can send them or letters to me using our Freepost address (printed on the forms).

We hope you enjoy using the Guide and very much look forward to hearing from you!

*Patricia Yates*

Patricia Yates, Editor

To celebrate our first edition last year we ran a competition to reward the writer of the most useful report on an hotel. All reports or letters received by 30 April 1991 were eligible. Thank you to everyone who wrote in, and many congratulations to our winner, Iain C. Baillie, a London reader. Mr Baillie's report on his Christmas stay at Amberley Castle Hotel near Arundel, Sussex wins him up to £500 to spend on a weekend break at the hotel of his choice. An eye for detail, and the ability to describe both the good and bad points, were the qualities that made Mr Baillie's report stand out. Here is a flavour of his comments:

*There are not many hotels, even country-house hotels, situated in major castles and certainly the approach to Amberley is impressive, up a drive, under a portcullis and into the courtyard of the castle. The main building in the castle walls (which more closely resembles an Edwardian mansion) is distinguished in appearance. Most of the rooms are modern inserts into one of the original walls. There are apparently two or three rooms within the main body of the house.*

*The rooms are well furnished and one of our rooms was of a reasonable size with good furniture and adequate wardrobe and drawers. Our second room on the first floor was on the small side with only just adequate wardrobe space and shelving. The furniture is on the whole good although the dressing room table turned out to be chipboard covered with good-quality chintz. The bathrooms are excellent although they badly need some extra shelving. Why is it that hotelkeepers believe that nobody needs to put anything in the bathroom apart from a toothbrush? There was no place for sponge bags, shaving cream and all the ancillary paraphernalia. Both bathrooms had a Jacuzzi and a good collection of soaps, shampoos, etc.*

*The dinners were extremely good. The Queen's Room Restaurant is an impressive room and the à la carte menu included such items as wild boar terrine and quail with mushrooms as appetisers; lamb with apricots and Scottish salmon with a crust of herbs as main courses; and a pleasant chocolate fantasy and almond biscuit ('praline parfait') dessert.*

*The breakfast was adequately cooked. There was a somewhat limited choice but they did offer a version of eggs benedict with smoked salmon instead of ham. Considering that they boast a 'breakfast chef' one was disappointed that there was no attempt to try a wider range of breakfast cooking including such classics as kedgeree. Unfortunately, the great English breakfast is rarely found in the English country hotel and those who praise the breakfasts at Amberley are probably not terribly well acquainted with the apotheosis of breakfast in Scotland. The kipper that I tried one morning must have been the smallest fish ever kippered: two might have been just about adequate, but one was ridiculous. However, the bread was baked on the premises and the croissants were reasonably good.*

Mr Baillie's comments also covered the friendly attitude of the staff and the quality of the service.

We hope he enjoys his prize (and writes to us with a report, of course!) and that the rest of you who contributed will by now have got used to dropping us a line.

# Your rights in hotels

A few days away at an hotel is a special treat for many of us, so we don't want anything to spoil it. And when we're travelling on business we don't want any hotel hassles that might distract us from clinching that important deal. But sometimes things do go wrong, and the hotel doesn't live up to expectations.

Below we set out your rights in dealing with hotels and answer some of the questions regularly asked by our readers. This should help you put things straight on the spot, but if it doesn't, we suggest ways to go about claiming your rights.

**When I arrived at the city-centre hotel where I'd booked a weekend break I was told that they had made a mistake and the hotel was full. Due to a popular conference, the only other room I could find was in a more expensive hotel at the other side of town, so I'm out of pocket. What are my rights?**

The hotel accepted your booking and was obliged to keep a room available for you. It is in breach of contract and liable to compensate you for the additional expenses arising out of that breach – the difference in cost between what you were expecting to pay and what you ended up having to pay, plus any travelling expenses. You should write first to the hotel manager explaining what happened, and enclosing copies of receipts for your additional expenditure. (See also Points 1–5 overleaf.)

**After booking I found that I had to cancel. I immediately wrote to advise the owners, but they refuse to return my deposit, and say they expect me to pay additional compensation.**

When you telephone to book a room and the hoteliers accept your booking you enter into a binding contract with them – they undertake to provide the required accommodation and meals for the specified dates at the agreed price, and you commit yourself to paying their charges. If you later cancel or fail to turn up, the hotel may be entitled to keep your deposit to defray administrative expenses, although it should be possible to challenge this if the deposited amount is a very high proportion of the total cost.

If an hotelier is unable to re-let the room you have booked – and he or she must try to do so – he or she can demand from you the loss of profit caused by your cancellation, which can be a substantial proportion of the total price. It's important to give as much notice as possible if you have to cancel: this increases the chances of your room being re-let. If after cancelling you find that the full amount has been charged to your credit card you should raise the matter with your credit card issuer, who will ask the hotel whether the room was re-let, and to justify the charge made.

**When I phoned to book a room the receptionist asked for my credit card number. I offered to send a deposit by cheque instead, but the receptionist insisted on taking the number.**

Hotels increasingly adopt this practice to protect themselves against loss when guests fail to turn up. It's reasonable for hotels to request a deposit, and where time permits a cheque should be acceptable.

*Your rights in hotels*

**After a long drive I stopped off at an hotel and asked for a room for the night. Although clearly not full the owners refused to give me a room. Can they do this?**

Hotels and inns are not allowed to refuse requests for food and shelter providing accommodation is available and the guest is sober, decently dressed and able to pay. If you meet these requirements and are turned away by an hotel with a vacancy you are entitled to sue for damages. If proprietors want to be able to turn away casual business, or are fussy about the sort of people they want in their establishment, they are likely to call it 'guesthouse' or 'private hotel'. In any event, it's illegal to exclude anyone on the grounds of race or sex.

**When I called to book they told me I would need to pay extra if I wanted to pay by credit card. Is this legal?**

Yes. Dual pricing was legalised early in 1991 and some hoteliers have elected to charge guests who pay by credit card extra to recover the commission payable to the card company. You can challenge this if you're not told when you book, or if it's not indicated on the tariff displayed in reception.

**I arrived at an hotel in winter and found I was the only guest. Both my bedrooms and the public rooms were distinctly chilly. I was uncomfortable throughout my stay and asked the management to turn up the heating, but things didn't improve.**

It's an implied term of the contract between you and the hotel that the accommodation will be of a reasonable standard, so it should be maintained at a reasonable temperature. You can claim compensation or seek a reduction of the bill. You were right to complain at the time. You are under a duty to 'mitigate your loss' – to keep your claim to a minimum. The most obvious way of doing this is to complain on the spot and give the management a chance to put things right.

**I was very unhappy when I was shown to my room. It hadn't been vacuumed, the wastebins were full, the towels hadn't been changed and I found dog hairs in the bed.**

You are entitled to a reasonable standard of accommodation having regard to the price paid. But no hotel, however cheap, should be dirty or unsafe. Ask for things to be put right, and if they're not, ask for a reduction of the bill.

**While I was in bed a section of the ceiling caved in. I was injured, but I could have been killed.**

Under the Occupiers' Liability Act hotel owners are responsible for the physical safety of their guests. You have a claim for compensation, and would be wise to seek legal advice to have it properly assessed.

**The hotel brochure promised floodlit tennis courts. When we arrived the lawns had been neglected and the nets were down. We couldn't play.**

A hotel must provide advertised facilities. If it doesn't you can claim compensation, or ask for an appropriate deduction from your bill in respect of the disappointment suffered. You might also want trading standards officers to consider bringing a case against the hotel under the Trade Descriptions Act.

**While I was staying at an hotel my video camera was stolen from my room.**
Hotel owners owe you a duty of care and must look after your property while it is on their premises. They are liable for any loss and damage as long as it wasn't your own fault – you would be unlikely to succeed if you left it clearly visible in a ground-floor room with the door and window unlocked. However, under the Hotel Proprietors Act, providing hotel owners display a notice at reception, they can limit their liability to £50 per item or £100 in total. They can't rely on this limit if the loss was caused by the negligence of their staff, although you will have to prove this.

**My car was broken into while parked in the hotel car park. I want compensation.**
The Hotel Proprietors Act doesn't cover cars. Your claim is unlikely to succeed.

**My dinner was inedible. Do I have to pay for it?**
The Supply of Goods and Services Act obliges hotels to prepare food with reasonable skill and care. The common law in Scotland imposes similar duties. If food is inedible, you should tell the waiter and ask for a replacement dish. If things aren't put right you can ask for a reduction of the billed amount. If you pay in full, possibly to avoid an unpleasant scene, write a note at the time saying that you are doing so under protest and 'reserving your rights'. This means that you retain your right to claim compensation later.

# Getting your rights

1 Always complain at the time if you're unhappy. It's by far the best way, and necessary to discharge your obligation to mitigate your loss.
2 If you reach deadlock you can deduct a sum from the bill in recognition of the deficient service received. Remember that the hotel might try to exercise its right of 'lien' by refusing to release your luggage until the bill is paid. It's probably easier to pay in full, but giving written notice that you are paying under protest and reserving your rights to claim compensation through the courts.
3 Legal advice is available from a number of sources. Citizens Advice Bureaux, Law Centres and Consumer Advice Centres give free advice on consumer disputes. In certain cases your local Trading Standards Department might be able to help. If instructing a solicitor be sure to sort out the cost implications at the outset. Or you can write to Consumers' Association's Legal Department at 2 Marylebone Road, London NW1 4DX.
4 Once you know where you stand, write to the hotel setting out your claim.
5 If this fails to get things sorted out and you feel you have a strong case, you can sue for sums of up to £1000 under the small claims procedure in the county court. In the Sheriff Court in Scotland the limit is £750. You shouldn't need a solicitor.

# Hotels of the Year

This year we thought we would like to pick out one hotel for each county that had particularly caught our eye. They are not necessarily the most luxurious or expensive – indeed there are several bed and breakfasts among them – but they all offer individual attention, comfort, a warm welcome – and something just a little bit unusual. Not all counties have an award winner.

## London

| | |
|---|---|
| *London* | Durrants |

## England

| | |
|---|---|
| *Avon* | Holly Lodge, Bath |
| *Berkshire* | The Royal Oak, Yattendon |
| *Buckinghamshire* | Hartwell House, Aylesbury |
| *Cambridgeshire* | Swynford Paddocks, Six Mile Bottom |
| *Cheshire* | Frogg Manor, Clutton |
| *Cornwall* | Manor Farm, Crackington Haven |
| *Cumbria* | Ees Wyke, Near Sawrey |
| *Derbyshire* | Hodgkinson's, Matlock Bath |
| *Devon* | The Nobody Inn, Doddiscombsleigh |
| *Dorset* | The Court, Frampton |
| *Co Durham* | Rose & Crown, Romaldkirk |
| *East Sussex* | Jeake's House, Rye |
| *Essex* | The Pier at Harwich, Harwich |
| *Gloucestershire* | Cusack's Glebe, Saintbury |
| *Hampshire* | Wykeham Arms, Winchester |
| *Hereford & Worcester* | The Haven, Hardwicke |
| *Hertfordshire* | Hanbury Manor, Thundridge |
| *Humberside* | Manor House, Walkington |
| *Isle of Wight* | Seaview Hotel, Seaview |
| *Kent* | Thruxted Oast, Chartham |
| *Lancashire* | The Victorian House, Thornton Cleveleys |
| *Leicestershire* | Stapleford Park, Stapleford |
| *Lincolnshire* | Hoe Hill, Swinhope |
| *Norfolk* | Stratton House, Swaffham |

| | |
|---|---|
| *Northumberland* | Breamish House, Powburn |
| *North Yorkshire* | Hob Green Hotel, Markington |
| *Oxfordshire* | Sugarswell Farm, Shenington |
| *Shropshire* | The Old Rectory, Hopesay |
| *Somerset* | Ashwick House, Dulverton |
| *Staffordshire* | Old Beams, Waterhouses |
| *Suffolk* | Hintlesham Hall, Hintlesham |
| *Warwickshire* | Pear Tree Cottage, Wilmcote |
| *West Sussex* | Gravetye Manor, East Grinstead |
| *West Yorkshire* | 42 The Calls, Leeds |
| *Wiltshire* | Priory Steps, Bradford-on-Avon |

## Scotland

| | |
|---|---|
| *Borders* | Cringletie House, Peebles |
| *Grampian* | Delnashaugh Inn, Ballindalloch |
| *Highland* | Glencripesdale House, Glencripesdale |
| *Lothian* | Forbes Lodge, Gifford |
| *Strathclyde* | The Town House, West George Street, Glasgow |

## Wales

| | |
|---|---|
| *Dyfed* | Tregynon Country House, Gwaun |
| *Gwent* | Abbey Hotel, Llanthony |
| *Gwynedd* | Ye Olde Bulls Head Inn, Beaumaris |
| *Powys* | Llangoed Hall, Llyswen |

## Channel Islands

| | |
|---|---|
| *Channel Islands* | La Sablonnerie, Sark |

# Finding your way round the Guide

We hope that you will find *Which? Hotel Guide* easy to use. It is arranged as follows: London, England, Scotland, Wales and the Channel Islands – and alphabetically by the name of the town or village within each region.

The best place to start is with the maps at the back of the Guide. Places with a recommended hotel are clearly marked by a solid triangle; more cautious recommendations that you might like to consider are denoted by an open triangle (see page 787). Further help can be had if you turn to the index on page 801 which lists each hotel by name.

# Symbols

There are three special symbols:

☺ This denotes somewhere where you can rely on *a good meal* – either the hotel features in the 1992 edition of *The Good Food Guide* or our inspectors were thoroughly impressed, whether by particularly competent home cooking or more lavish cuisine

£ This denotes that the hotel offers especially *good value* at whatever price level – though in fact they tend to be at the cheaper end

❀ This denotes that the hotel is in an *exceptionally peaceful situation* where you can be assured of a restful stay

Other symbols are used simply to organise our factual information:

❍ *Open and closing periods* of both the hotel and any restaurant

▣ *Directions* to help you find the hotel and details of *parking* facilities

↜ Details of the number and type (single, double, four-poster, etc.) of *bedrooms*; *bathrooms*; *shower-rooms and other facilities* in the rooms (all rooms have tea/coffee-making equipment unless we specify to the contrary)

◈ Details of the public rooms available and other *special facilities* including conference facilities (residential and non-residential), babysitting facilities, sports and games at the hotel or nearby. We give disabled readers as much information as we can about wheelchair access, but they should always telephone the hotel to check

● *Restrictions* of any kind – lack of wheelchair access, restrictions on children, dogs, smoking

▭ Details of *credit cards* accepted

▦ *Prices* that you can expect to pay in 1992 (if 1991 prices are quoted, we state for how long they will last). Unless specified otherwise we give prices *per room per night*, whether for one person in a single room, for one person alone in a twin or double room, or for two people sharing a double room. You will also find details of whether a deposit is required when you book as well as prices of meals in the restaurant, and of breakfast if it is *not* included in the room price. Room prices are rounded up to the nearest £1; meal prices to the nearest 50p

# LONDON

**LONDON**                                       **MAP 11**

# Abbey Court

20 PEMBRIDGE GARDENS, LONDON W2 4DU
TEL: 071-221 7518   FAX: 071-792 0858

*A private, well-detailed Victorian timepiece with lots of creature comforts. It will appeal.*

Just off Notting Hill Gate, one of London's more cosmopolitan melting pots, the Abbey Court stands discreetly inviting with neat plaque and window boxes in a street of large well-proportioned Victorian buildings. The big drawback is that there is only one public room – a gracious little lounge – and it doubles as the reception.

Pass the fine secretaire on the half-landing to the hotel's treasures. Take one of the three four-poster bedrooms: the bed is reproduction but there are antiques in the room (a chest of drawers and a dressing-table with a delicate wood-framed mirror). And what attention to detail: porcelain knick-knacks decorate a whatnot; on the chest of drawers you find a bowl of pot-pourri, still and fizzy mineral water, an old tin containing fresh shortbread and a wireless (too old-fashioned to be a radio). For comfort, the two armchairs are softened with extra cushions, and the rose marbled bathroom has a whirlpool bath and brass taps. Of course, smaller, lower-priced rooms are less lavish, and some have a piece of incongruous modern furniture and not so precious antiques, but all have the swanky bathrooms, comfortable armchairs and the decorative and consumable extras. Twenty-four-hour room service is available, providing light meals such as soups and salads.

| | |
|---|---|
| ◑ Open all year | ◈ Lounge |
| ⤢ Nearest tube station is Notting Hill Gate (Central, District and Circle lines). Parking difficult | ⊖ No wheelchair access; no children under 12; no dogs |
| 🛏 6 single, 6 twin, 7 double, 3 four-poster; all with bathroom/ WC, TV, room service, hair-dryer, trouser press; no tea/ coffee-making facilities in rooms | ▭ Access, Amex, Diners, Visa |
| | £ Single £82, twin/double £120, four-poster £150; deposit required. Continental B £8. (prices till Mar 92) |

# Abbey House

11 VICARAGE GATE, LONDON W8 4AG
TEL: 071-727 2594

*Top-rate budget accommodation in Kensington.*

This is a Victorian building housing a far less posh B&B than its salubrious location off Kensington Church Street, its marble-pillared portico and its grand hallway with original Edwardian black-and-white tiled floor and white wrought iron bannisters suggest.

It studiously avoids the kitsch or the garish: the bedrooms are simple, spacious (some large enough for families), decorated in white with synthetic carpets; all have washbasins. The shared bathrooms are pretty and floral. In the basement there is a cheerful breakfast room with red-painted chairs and a red carpet. A notice declaring that enquiries are dealt with only between 8.30am and noon seems to jar with the obvious efforts to make and keep the place so attractive.

◐ *Open all year*

⤤ *Nearest tube station is High Street Kensington (District and Circle lines). The hotel is off Kensington Church Street. Parking difficult*

🛏 *2 single, 9 twin/double, 4 family rooms; all with TV; no tea/ coffee-making facilities in rooms*

✥ *Breakfast room*

⊖ *No wheelchair access; no dogs; no smoking in public rooms*

▭ *None accepted*

£ *Single £28, single occupancy of twin/double £48, twin/double £48; family room £58 to £68; deposit required*

# Basil Street Hotel

BASIL STREET, LONDON SW3 1AH
TEL: 071-581 3311    TELEX: 28379 BASIL G
FAX: 071-581 3693

*Not the grandest hotel in London but roomy, tranquil and one of the most quintessentially English in town.*

Hidden behind what looks like a cinema façade next to the local fire station, the Basil Street Hotel enjoys a prime Knightsbridge location. It is surrounded by hotels and shops (two minutes' walk from Harrods) yet down a relatively quiet back street. It manages to be formal enough to entice the older generation (who remember when good service was always expected) and yet not so starchy as to deter the more relaxed visitor.

To the left of the main entrance is a snack bar sandwiched between a basement wine bar and 'Upstairs', a cheap carvery and salad bar, popular with shoppers and staff in the area. However, in the hotel itself you feel protected from the frantic world outside: rooms are set within its nether regions, well away from any bustle. In the Parrot Club, a club for ladies only (either members or hotel guests), there are clusters of sofas and chairs spread out over the large parquet floor. There's nearly as much room and quietude in the large lounge/bar where mid-afternoon the only sounds are ticking clocks and rustling newspapers.

Bedrooms are largely peaceful, too, in gentle floral patterns and with box armchairs. Bathrooms are grey marbled or Scandinavian style with cork floors and pine walls. Bedrooms without private bathrooms are a bargain. Regular visitors (Basilites) receive a discount.

◑ Open all year

⤢ Short walk from Knightsbridge tube station (Piccadilly line). Nearby car park

🛏 32 single, 28 twin, 17 double, 5 family, 1 suite; most with bathroom/WC, 8 public bathrooms; TV, room service, hair-dryer in all rooms; no tea/coffee-making facilities in rooms

◈ Restaurant, bar, air-conditioned wine bar, 3 lounges; conference facilities (max 60 people residential); babysitting

⬤ No wheelchair access; no dogs in public rooms

▭ Access, Amex, Diners, Visa

£ Single £55 to £103, single occupancy of twin/double £84 to £138, twin/double £84 to £138, family room £193, suite £222. Continental B £5, cooked B £9.50; set L £16; alc L, D £20 to £25

---

# The Beaufort

33 BEAUFORT GARDENS, LONDON SW3 1PP
TEL: 071-584 5252   TELEX: 929200
FAX: 071-589 2834

*One of the best and most expensive small private hotels in London; the interior design is personal, the service lavish.*

It is all about the extras. Included in the price of a room is breakfast (served in your room), a light evening meal, drinks from the honesty bar, use of a health club, dry-cleaning, extras in your room such as bathrobes, an umbrella, a Walkman, a shoeshine, TV and video recorder, videos and edibles and potables including shortbread, Swiss chocolates, a decanter of brandy . . . in sum, any hotel expenditure you might incur other than for the phone and personal laundry. The amount of favourable publicity the Beaufort has acquired from extending the freebie concept to its limit has probably paid many times over for any overly hedonistic customer.

The hotel prides itself on its quality of service, too: a constantly updated local restaurant guide in each bedroom indicates its efforts. All this, therefore, explains why the hotel is so expensive. (The director offers a 10 per cent discount for guests not wishing the extras.) It shares many of its physical characteristics with other London town house hotels, notably its shortage of public rooms and its peaceful position. It's set in a quiet Victorian cul-de-sac just round the corner from Harrods.

The interior has been personally designed by owner Diana Wallis. Somehow the handpainted pillars and uneven blue-washed walls of the sitting-room don't jar with the comfortable but ordinary sofas. Bedrooms are kitted out more conventionally in a variety of cool, fresh designs with fluffy carpets and attractive reproduction furniture. Bathrooms are spacious, some have wicker chairs.

○ Open all year, exc 22 Dec to 2 Jan

↗ Nearest tube station is Knightsbridge (Piccadilly line). Parking difficult

🛏 3 single, 5 twin, 13 double, 7 suites; all with bathroom/WC exc single rooms with shower/WC; TV, room service, hair-dryer, baby-listening, air-conditioning in all rooms; no tea/coffee-making facilities in rooms

◈ Lounge, bar; complimentary membership of local health club

● No wheelchair access, no children under 10 but babies welcome

▭ Access, Amex, Diners, Visa

£ Single £150 to £250, single occupancy of twin/double £160 to £250, twin/double £160 to £250, suite £250; deposit required. Special breaks available

# Blakes Hotel

33 ROLAND GARDENS, LONDON SW7 3PF
TEL: 071-370 6701　　TELEX: 8813500 BLAKES G
FAX: 071-373 0442

*Western sophistication and oriental decadence (or perhaps the other way round) in an utterly different, luxurious hotel.*

The foyer is decked out in bamboo-style seating, old, studded travelling trunks, a South American love bird and an outsize Venetian umbrella. The exotic atmosphere makes you feel you should have arrived by elephant, not taxi. Anouska Hempel Weinberg owns Blakes and is the creator of the hotel's startling design which uses a mixture of the oriental, the classical and the antique – and jet black.

On the first two floors the walls are decorated in black and gold, on the third and fourth grey and gold: both combinations of colours create an extraordinary sense of opulence. All the bedrooms are different: some have purple velvet walls, others have classical print-effect wallpaper, while there are framed prints in others. Mod cons (TVs and stereo tape recorders in some) are often hidden behind more drapes. Some rooms are possibly too offbeat to live in but are perfect for detaching the guest from reality.

In the basement is a very exclusive restaurant which boldly mixes east and west. Off it is the Chinese Room with a Chinese screen, silk cushions and a black and chrome cocktail bar.

○ Open all year

↗ Nearest tube station is Gloucester Road (Piccadilly, District and Circle lines). Parking difficult

🛏 13 single, 3 twin, 24 double, 12 suites; all with bathroom/WC, exc 4 singles with shower/WC,

TV, room service, hair-dryer, mini-bar, some rooms air-conditioned; no tea/coffee-making facilities in rooms

◈ Air-conditioned restaurant, bar, lounge

● No wheelchair access; no dogs

▭ Access, Amex, Diners, Visa

£ Single £120, single occupancy of
twin/double £150, twin/double
£180 to £295, suite £220 to

£600; deposit required.
Continental B £7.50, cooked B
£14; alc L £35, D £55

---

# Bryanston Court   ℒ

56/60 GREAT CUMBERLAND PLACE, LONDON W1H 7FD
TEL: 071-262 3141   TELEX: 262076 BRYCOR G
FAX: 071-262 7248

*A privately owned, old-fashioned place with modest bedrooms just
north of Marble Arch; stay at the Concorde next door to save a
few pounds.*

This is one of those hotels which proves that many travellers are better
served by an establishment which hasn't been thoroughly refurbished
and is thus more likely to be affordable and have more character. Its
peeling wallpaper may make it flawed for some, though. A Best Western
hotel which has been run by the Theodore family for fifteen years, it is
identical in style, down to the colour of the bedroom doors and corridors,
to its smaller sister the Concorde next door (see entry), except that the
Concorde is a bit more crumbly, smaller and consequently cosier.

The atmosphere inside is grander than you might expect: brown
leather chairs and oil portraits with picture lights adorn the large lounge
and bar. Upstairs, the bedrooms are simple, decorated with modern
furniture and pastel colours. Space is at a premium in the hotel and
consequently most of the bedrooms have a washbasin in the room, and
most but not all have old, tiled, pokey bathrooms with shower only. Get a
room overlooking the mews behind if traffic noise worries you as this is a
busy street. The Brunswick restaurant, decorated in a variety of pinks,
serves buffet breakfast, snacks and sandwiches.

◑ Open all year

🔁 Nearest tube station is Marble
Arch (Central line). On-street
parking

🛏 19 single, 24 twin, 7 double, 4
family; some with bathroom/WC,
most with shower/WC; all rooms
have TV, room service, hair-dryer

◇ Breakfast room, bar, lounge;
conference facilities (max 25
people)

⊖ No wheelchair access; no dogs in
bedrooms

▭ Access, Amex, Diners, Visa

£ Single £70, single occupancy of
twin/double £70, twin/double
£85; deposit required. Cooked
B £6

---

ℒ   *This denotes that the hotel offers especially good value at whatever price
level.*

# The Capital

BASIL STREET, LONDON SW3 IAT
TEL: 071-589 5171   TELEX: 919042 HOTCAP G
FAX: 071-225 0011

*This sumptuous hotel is under the same ownership as L'Hotel –
see that entry.*

◐ Open all year

🔁 Nearest tube station is
Knightsbridge (Piccadilly line).
Private car park

🛏 12 single, 9 twin, 13 double,
6 deluxe, 8 suites; all with
bathroom/WC, TV, room service,
hair-dryer, mini-bar, baby-
listening, air-conditioning

◈ Restaurant, bar (both air-
conditioned), lounge; conference
facilities (max 24 people

residential and non-residential);
tennis, riding nearby; babysitting

⊖ No wheelchair access; dogs at
manager's discretion

▭ Access, Amex, Diners, Visa

💷 Single £150, twin/double £175,
family room £200, suite £265;
deposit required. Continental B
£7.50, cooked B £10.50; set L
£18.50, £21.50; alc L, D £55.
(prices till Sept 91)

# Concorde Hotel

50 GREAT CUMBERLAND PLACE, LONDON W1H 7FD
TEL: 071-402 6169   TELEX: 262076 BRYCOR G
FAX: 071-724 1184

*This hotel is under the same ownership as the Bryanston Court –
see that entry.*

◐ Open all year, exc Xmas and
New Year

🔁 Nearest tube station is Marble
Arch (Central line). On-street
parking

🛏 9 single, 14 twin, 4 double, 1
family room; some with
bathroom/WC, most with
shower/WC; TV, room service,
hair-dryer in all rooms

◈ Breakfast room, bar, lounge

⊖ No wheelchair access; no dogs in
bedrooms

▭ Access, Amex, Diners, Visa

💷 Single £60 to £65, single
occupancy of twin/double £60 to
£65, twin/double £70 to £75,
family room £75 to £80; deposit
required. Cooked B £6

---

🌺   *This denotes that the hotel is in an exceptionally peaceful situation
where you can be assured of a restful stay.*

# The Connaught

CARLOS PLACE, LONDON W1Y 6AL
TEL: 071-499 7070   FAX: 071-495 3262

*Smaller, more dignified and restrained than its deluxe counterparts, it will continue to appeal to its elderly (and wealthy) clientele.*

Standing in the foyer of the Connaught, you can get a pretty accurate impression of the hotel. 'Could I see a brochure and a tariff?' 'We have neither, sir. We don't need to advertise and terms are available only on application.' Two attendants help an octogenarian awkwardly negotiating the problem of juggling handbag, walking stick and traversing at the same time the ten yards from sitting-room to lift. Many of the regular guests find it convenient to leave a suitcase of clothes permanently stored at the hotel, and have their bank accounts deducted by standing order.

The mahogany staircase leads to a treasure trove of fine antiques, both along the hotel corridors (where there are fine china displays too) and in the bedrooms. All the bedrooms have foyers but some doubles are still small. This should not be important: you're primarily paying for service and atmosphere. The bathrooms are narrow and ordinary (suites' bathrooms are in marble).

There's a choice of equally fine rooms downstairs: a maroon-coloured lounge with wing-chairs and large pictures of exotic birds and the Thames; the slightly fusty, beautifully proportioned sitting-room with oil paintings and chandelier where tea is served; a masculine oak-panelled bar with leather studded armchairs and a stag's head on the wall. The restaurant and grill have been praised for producing high-standard British and classical cuisine.

- ◑ Open all year
- ↗ Nearest tube station is Green Park (Piccadilly, Victoria and Jubilee lines). Parking difficult
- 🛏 30 single, 36 double, 24 suites; all with bathroom/WC, TV, room service, hair-dryer; no tea/coffee-making facilities in rooms
- ◈ Restaurant and grill room, bar,
- 2 lounges; babysitting; wheelchair access to hotel and restaurant, no ground-floor bedrooms but a lift
- ⊖ No dogs; no pipes in public areas
- ▭ Access, Visa
- £ Room prices only on application (from £150 in 1991). Alc L £30, D £35 plus 15% service

---

☕ *Denotes somewhere you can rely on a good meal – either the hotel features in the 1992 edition of our sister publication,* The Good Food Guide, *or our own inspectors thought the cooking impressive, whether particularly competent home cooking or more lavish cuisine.*

# Dorset Square

39/40 DORSET SQUARE, LONDON NW1 6QN
TEL: 071-723 7874    TELEX: 263964 DORSET G
FAX: 071-724 3328

*Exuberantly decorated Regency town house off Regent's Park.*

Opened in 1985 and elder sister to the Pelham (see entry), the Dorset Square is equally sumptuously furnished yet considerably cheaper. The elegant house stands on the corner of a beautifully preserved Regency square just off the south-western corner of Regent's Park. Until 1810 the square was site of Thomas Lord's first cricket ground after which it moved to St John's Wood. In memory of this sporting connection, male staff at the hotel wear white cricket sweaters, antique cricket bats stand in the hall, prints of famous cricketers adorn the walls, as does a cricketing mural in the restaurant.

Stripped pine doors lead through to boldly decorated bedrooms. Many have strong red and green flower schemes and a mix of antique and quality reproduction furniture. Small doubles are what they say they are.

The Dorset Square has the advantage of being considerably larger than most of its competitors, so you're not confined to your bedroom. You can opt instead for the rather disturbingly formal sitting-rooms, beautifully decorated with oil paintings, bright deep sofas and fine antiques, one of which houses an honesty bar. Otherwise, if you feel the hotel is really too plush to relax in, try the basement restaurant with its jolly checked tablecloths, and adjoining bar with rustic murals, plain tables and chairs and backgammon set ready for play.

◐ Open all year

↗ Nearest tube station is Baker Street (Circle, Jubilee, Metropolitan and Bakerloo lines). On-street parking

🛏 9 single, 28 double; most with bathroom/WC, some with shower/WC; TV, room service, mini-bar, valet service in all rooms; hair-dryer on request; half the rooms are air-conditioned

◇ Restaurant, bar, lounge (all air-conditioned); conference facilities (max 10 people residential)

⊖ No wheelchair access; no dogs

▭ Access, Amex, Visa

£ Single from £90, double £110 to £170; deposit required. Continental B £7.50, cooked B £9.50; alc L, D £30.50

---

*The 1993* Guide *will be published before Christmas 1992. Reports on hotels are most welcome at any time of the year, but are extremely valuable in the spring. Send them to* Which? Hotel Guide, *FREEPOST, 2 Marylebone Road, London NW1 1YN. No stamp is needed if reports are posted in the UK.*

# The Draycott

24–26 CADOGAN GARDENS, LONDON SW3 2RP
TEL: 071-730 6466   FAX: 071-730 0236

*Exclusive club-like atmosphere in luxurious, spacious, traditionally furnished Chelsea lodgings.*

On the door of this quiet, red-brick Victorian town house a notice says: 'Private club. Resident members and their guests please ring bell.' Have you arrived at the right place? 'It's not an hotel,' says the manageress, 'it's a residential club.' The actors and writers who stay here evidently prefer this air of exclusivity. If you can afford it, it's worth trying out for it represents flawless country house luxury at its best.

Your bedroom might have a four-poster or at least bed drapes, a large comfortable sofa, antiques, a bathroom of white marble, and a bath with an old-fashioned wooden base; and each is decked out with lots of plants and prints on the walls. Many also have big windows overlooking the square's gardens.

Most guests have breakfast in their rooms. There are piles of apples in large stone urns in the hall for the peckish. Downstairs, it's considerably roomier than other town house hotels in the area. There's a cosy light-panelled, smoking-room with a real fire and portraits on the walls; drinks are served from an antique waist-high round drinks bar. At the back overlooking the gardens to which the hotel has access, the spacious drawing-room, with a real open fire too, and comfortable, beautifully upholstered sofas, offers ideal surroundings for the most civilised afternoon tea. The atmosphere is rather idyllic.

- ◑ Open all year
- ⤴ Nearest tube station is Sloane Square (District and Circle lines). Parking difficult
- 🛏 6 single, 5 twin, 8 double, 1 four-poster, 4 suites; all with bathroom/WC, TV, room service, hair-dryer, mini-bar, baby-listening; no tea/coffee-making facilities in rooms
- ◈ Dining-room, bar, lounge;

- conference facilities (max 12 people residential)
- ⊖ No wheelchair access; no dogs
- 💳 Access, Amex, Diners, Visa
- £ Single £75 to £130, single occupancy of twin/double £175 to £225, twin/double £175 to £225, four-poster, family rooms and suites £250; deposit required. Continental B £7.50, cooked B £9.50

---

*See the inside front cover for a brief explanation of how to use the* Guide.

---

*Report forms are at the back of the book; write a letter if you prefer.*

# Durrants Hotel

GEORGE STREET, LONDON W1H 6BJ
TEL: 071-935 8131    TELEX: 894919 DURHOT G
FAX: 071-487 3510

*Best-value hotel of its type in London, offering traditional
Englishness in an old coaching-inn and a family home.*

'A home-from-home . . . enfolding friendliness and comfort . . . service
is as international as any London hotel but the manager's hand is felt
through it all . . . we don't know anywhere in London that can give the
same value and comfort.' Praise indeed to which a clutch of letters lends
credence. Other than the Goring (see entry), Durrants, a long, white and
brick-fronted Georgian building, is the only recommendable sizeable
London hotel which manages to convey a personalised family feel. The
Millers have run the hotel since the 1920s and the present, very English
Mr Miller remembers being here during the Blitz. He gives short shrift
to staff out of line, though you feel that their evident informality and
some less than spotless housekeeping means they get away with a few
liberties.

  Some quirks have remained, as one of our correspondents remarked:
'It would have been nice to have had tea/coffee-making facilities in the
room' (the owner is a self-confessed stickler for getting up and coming
down to eat breakfast). Bedrooms vary considerably, some being rather
small, others having extra space such as a walk-in cupboard, others
having extra style in the form of a brass bed. Many bathrooms look rather
dated but they're gradually being upgraded. Historical paraphernalia
such as old hotel bills and leases and oil portraits take up much of the
available wallspace throughout the building, whether along the creaky
corridors or downstairs in the dark panelled restaurant with private pews
and black leather seats, or in the residents' lounge or oak-panelled
lounge.

- Open all year
- Nearest tube station is Marble Arch (Central line). On-street parking
- 13 single, 38 twin, 29 double, 3 family, 3 suites, most with bathroom/WC; TV, room service, hair-dryer in all rooms; no tea/coffee-making facilities in rooms
- Restaurant, bar, 3 lounges; conference facilities (max 45 people residential). Wheelchair access to hotel (2 steps), restaurant, WC and lift, 7 ground-floor bedrooms
- No dogs
- Access, Amex, Visa
- Single £52 to £70, single occupancy of twin/double £79 to £95, twin/double £79 to £95, family room £130, suite £175; deposit required. Continental B £5.50; cooked B £8; alc L, D £25

---

*All reports are welcome on any hotel, whether or not it is in the* Guide.

# Ebury Court

24/32 EBURY STREET, LONDON SW1W 0LU
TEL: 071-730 8147  FAX: 071-823 5966

*A handwritten card greets you in your room in this cosy, old-fashioned, privately owned Victorian terrace hotel behind Victoria station.*

Ebury Court offers just about the cosiest lodgings in town and a considerable cut above all the other B&Bs in the street – though you wouldn't necessarily be able to tell from the turquoise railings and door outside. Even though space is at a premium and rooms have been stuffed into places where less daring architects would baulk at putting so much as a pot plant (a new room squashed in to a tiny courtyard, for example), it's too much of a warren of creaky stairs and low-ceilinged corridors to feel constricted.

Handed on to daughter and son-in-law in 1989 from the mother who had managed the hotel for fifty years, the place is undergoing some gradual changes but the owners seem sensitive to the importance of keeping to the hotel's original civilised simplicity, and they and their staff convey a genuine enthusiasm for their hotel.

There are fourteen unrefurbished singles – plain but all with a nice antique – none of which have private bathrooms, just washbasins, and robes in which to navigate the corridors. At the other end of the scale, two rooms have four-posters and others have canopies over the beds, armchairs and *en suite* bathrooms, though these are generally still small with shower only. Snugness is apparent in the public rooms too: the den of a bar with black leather armchairs used to be Ebury Court's private club until the owners realised they were losing valuable business by not allowing residents in. In the basement is a miniature-seeming breakfast room with pink-striped cushions and wall seats in tiny alcoves where Maureen and Noreen proudly serve a full English breakfast including a choice of six types of egg; upstairs, there is a similarly small but more formal restaurant serving from a short à la carte lunch and dinner menu.

◐ Closed Xmas and New Year; restaurant closed Sat eves Dec to Mar

↗ 3 minutes' walk from Victoria tube station (Victoria, District and Circle lines). On-street parking

🛏 18 single, 6 twin, 18 double, 2 four-poster, 1 family room; half rooms with bathroom/WC; TV, room service, hair-dryer in all rooms

◇ Restaurant, bar, lounge, drying room; conference facilities (max 12 people residential); babysitting

⊖ No wheelchair access

▭ Access, Diners, Visa

£ Single £65, twin/double £85 to £125, four-poster and family room £150; deposit required. Alc L, D £20

# Edward Lear

28/30 SEYMOUR STREET, LONDON WIH 5WD
TEL: 071-402 5401    FAX: 071-706 3766

*Though not particularly good value, an attractive B&B, cheaper than any other acceptable accommodation in spitting distance of Oxford Street.*

'To stay a night or two at the Lear
May not seem especially dear . . .'
Or cheap for that matter. Simple floral-decorated bedrooms have washbasins, four are *en suite* and over half the remainder have shower units. Take a room overlooking the mews behind the hotel to avoid street noise. As well as having more rooms than your normal B&B, it boasts lots of public space too: a light and attractive breakfast room and two lounges, one of which has a bookcase full of Edward Lear books to add to the illustrated limericks on the walls and the plaque outside in memory of the nonsense poet, who used to live here.

But despite highly successful efforts to personalise – and it doesn't just rely on poetry: a hallway wall is covered with framed pictures drawn by child guests – the fact that the owner does his managing from Australia means that the often evidenced passionate hospitality of many B&Bs may be less acute here.

- ◑ Open all year
- ⬛ Nearest tube station is Marble Arch (Central line). Parking difficult
- 🛏 14 singles, 8 twin, 4 doubles, 5 family rooms; some with bathroom or shower/WC; TV in all rooms
- ◈ Breakfast room, 2 lounges
- ⊖ No wheelchair access; no dogs
- ▭ Access, Visa
- £ Single £38 to £55, twin/double £50 to £60, family room £60 to £79; deposit required

# Egerton House

17 EGERTON TERRACE, LONDON SW3 2BX
TEL: 071-589 2412    FAX: 071-584 6540

*Posh and pricey new town house B&B with antiques and fine furnishings.*

'The Egerton is a godsend . . . this must undoubtedly be the best small hotel in London,' writes a businessman from Chicago. Pity the back-packer who turns up at these red-brick Victorian buildings down a quiet street just across from the V&A museum. This was once budget accommodation but recently converted to the smartest of town house hotels. Now, if dirty boots sullied even the pristine doormat, they might be shooed away by men in smart suits. But these men in suits also 'bring new meaning to the concept of friendliness and professionalism: no detail goes unnoticed or unattended here,' says a recent guest.

The brochure gets it about right in describing the hotel as having an 'aura of understated elegance'. In the sumptuousness of the drawing-room, you relax in plush red and green sofas and armchairs surrounded by oil paintings while green-liveried Brian the butler awaits your orders from the extensive honesty bar, its fine decanters on display. In the basement there is a light blue-toned breakfast room where tables are laid out with pretty Limoges china. Bedrooms vary considerably in size and cost, the smaller ones seeming better value ('charmingly decorated . . . Beautiful new marble bathrooms stocked with various toiletries are a wonderful treat'). The big pieces of furniture are antique; many bedrooms have elaborate plasterwork decorating white walls.

◑ *Open all year*

⤵ *Nearest tube station is South Kensington (Piccadilly, District and Circle lines). Private car park*

🛏 *12 single, 4 twin, 12 double, 1 four-poster, 1 suite; all with bathroom/WC, TV, room service, hair-dryer, mini-bar, air-conditioning*

◈ *Breakfast room, bar, lounge (all air-conditioned); conference*

*facilities (max 12 people non-residential)*

⊖ *No wheelchair access; no children under 8; no dogs*

▭ *Access, Amex, Visa*

£ *Single £98, single occupancy of twin/double £135, twin/double £135, four-poster £190, suite £230; deposit preferred. Continental B £7.50, cooked B £12.50; alc L, D £24*

---

# The Fenja

**69 CADOGAN GARDENS, LONDON SW3 2RB**
**TEL: 071-589 7333   TELEX: 934272 FENJA G**
**FAX: 071-581 4958**

*Tasteful, deluxe B&B off Sloane Square.*

Each of the 13 rooms is named after a writer or painter who lived in Chelsea, with a synopsis about the relevant artist in the room, and some appropriate prints. Turner once lived here and the grandest room, with a four-poster, is named after him. All the rooms differ but share an elegance which other hotels and their barrage of co-ordinated colour frequently fail to accomplish. All have soft-coloured wallpaper and antiques; most have attractive Victorian fireplaces. Instead of a standard mini-bar, each room has its own tray of cut-glass decanters and a bowl of fruit.

The owner's favourite bedroom is the green Rossetti room at the top of the house; draw back the blinds and the best of leafy Kensington can be seen through the window. Seemingly less formal than similar establishments in the area, it is unlikely to make you feel overpampered. There are light meals available on the room service menu, and, as with breakfast, you're encouraged to have this in your room as the only public area is a small lounge. The Fenja is located just round the corner from Sloane Square; it lies close to Cadogan Gardens to which it has access.

● Open all year

⚡ Short walk from Sloane Square tube station (District and Circle lines). On-street parking difficult

🛏 1 single, 7 twin, 4 double, 1 four-poster; most with bathroom/WC, some with shower/WC; TV, room service, hair-dryer, trouser press, mini-bar in all rooms; no tea/coffee-making facilities in rooms

◇ Lounge; conference facilities (max 12 people)

⊖ No wheelchair access; no dogs

▭ Access, Visa

£ Single £105, twin/double £145 to £205, four-poster £205; deposit required. Continental B £7.50, cooked B £11

---

# The Fielding                                  𝓛

4 BROAD COURT, BOW STREET, LONDON WC2B 5QZ
TEL: 071-836 8305   FAX: 071-497 0064

*A good-value, friendly hotel on a traffic-free street, right in the heart of Covent Garden.*

In the shadow of Bow Street Magistrates Court and a stone's throw from the Royal Opera House, this is a good central base convenient for the theatres and nightlife of central London. Over the last year some changes have been made to the hotel décor – new beechwood and mahogany chairs, for instance. Plans are in the offing to cheer up the pokey reception and bar.

The bedrooms, approached through a warren of narrow passages and staircases, are being gradually refurbished. The rooms are a miscellany of shapes and sizes, walls have been repainted, some in bold colours with spriggy floral cotton curtains and matching bedspreads and some new pine chests of drawers and bedside tables have been added. Rooms still retain their character, though, with vestiges of the old furnishings, a leatherette chair or a military-style chest and an assortment of pictures.

The basement restaurant is dark and dreary and under a separate franchise so you'd be better off in one of the Covent Garden cafés or restaurants. The Fielding's main advantage is that it is right at the heart of things, the welcome is friendly and personal and the prices are low. If you are going to be out and about in London and you're unconcerned about facilities this is a hotel that is definitely worth knowing about.

–The Fielding–

◑ Open all year, exc 24, 25 and 26 Dec

🚇 Nearest tube station is Covent Garden (Piccadilly line). Opposite Royal Opera House. Limited on-street parking

🛏 12 single, 10 twin, 9 double, 1 family room, 3 suites; some with bathroom/WC, some with shower/WC; TV, room service, hair-dryer, baby-listening in all rooms; tea/coffee-making facilities on request

◇ Restaurant, bar, lounge; babysitting

⊖ No wheelchair access; no dogs

▭ Access, Amex, Diners, Visa

£ Single £28 to £88, single occupancy of twin/double £59, twin/double £48 to £53, suite £53 to £99; family room £53 to £95; deposit required. Continental B £2.50, cooked B £4

*The hotel seemed snowbound and the staff told me that the electricity and other services had been cut off. My hopes of a decent breakfast faded. However, I was asked into the dining-room and the staff proceeded cheerfully to serve up a very good meal despite the difficult circumstances. When I asked for the bill afterwards, the management refused to accept any payment and apologised for the breakfast saying that it was not quite up to their usual standards due to the lack of electricity.* On an hotel in Wiltshire

# The Gore

189 QUEEN'S GATE, LONDON SW7 5EX
TEL: 071-584 6601   TELEX: 296244 GORTEL G
FAX: 071-589 8127

*Its restaurants, popular with smart Londoners, make this
Kensington hotel buzz; attractive rooms and a plethora of
paintings.*

Since April 1990 the Gore, a large Kensington house close to the Albert
Hall and sister to Hazlitt's (see below), has undergone an exciting
transformation under its new ownership. One of its directors is an art
dealer and he estimates there are 4,500 paintings and prints in the hotel;
many are on show in the hall, and they are also scattered on walls
throughout the corridors and bedrooms.

The Second Empire-style basement restaurant, One Ninety Queen's
Gate, is reserved for a modern collection to match the culinary art of chef
Antony Worrall-Thompson. The menus are highly praised for being
adaptable and inventive. Worrall-Thompson is also responsible for the
popular, informal and remarkably good-value food served in the modish
bistro on the ground floor. He owns the two restaurants, but they operate
in conjunction with the hotel.

Across the hallway is an inviting bar with sofas, its panelling giving it a
bit of a clubby feel. Upstairs, the bedrooms vary enormously in size but
are uniformly tasteful, with monochromatic walls, splashes of colour on
curtains and bedspreads and some antiques, especially in the larger
rooms – the more exclusive of which have expensive oils and tiled
frescoes.

- ◑ Open all year
- 🚇 Nearest tube station is Gloucester Road (Piccadilly, Circle and District lines). Parking difficult
- 🛏 27 single, 6 twin, 20 double, 5 deluxe; most with bathroom/WC, some with shower/WC; TV, room service, hair-dryer, mini-bar in all rooms

- ✇ 2 restaurants, bar, lounge; babysitting
- ⬤ No wheelchair access; dogs by prior arrangement
- ▭ Access, Amex, Diners, Visa
- £ Single £93 to £100, twin/double £114, deluxe £165, family room £134; deposit required. Continental B £5.50, cooked B £9.50; alc L, D £20

*If you are intending to make a lot of phone calls from your room, always
check what the hotel is going to charge you per unit. You may be so horrified
that you'll prefer to walk to the nearest phone box. Why let them get away
with excessive charges?*

# The Goring

15 BEESTON PLACE, LONDON SW1W 0JW
TEL: 071-834 8211   TELEX: 919166 GORING G
FAX: 071-834 4393

*A family-owned hotel for three generations – traditional and gentrified, showing a painstaking concern for high standards.*

A fine Edwardian building with few overt signs of grandeur or ostentation by which to justify charging that little bit more. But that's just it: understated Englishness needs careful and costly nurturing. It has that feeling of having become an institution. Built by O G Goring and opened as an hotel in 1910 (claimed to be the first in the world with private bathroom and central heating in every bedroom), it has been in the family ever since and directed by his grandson for the past twenty-five years.

George Goring takes pains to maintain high standards (including sleeping in all the bedrooms to see if they're comfortable). Many of the staff have been here for some time, and careful, personal management of highly trained staff is evidently one of the hotel's strongest trademarks. The formal restaurant, particularly popular at lunchtime, was busy with suited diners when we visited. In the large lounge, couples bag their favourite corner for a quiet natter in leather armchairs and sofas, perhaps opposite one of the skyscapes on the walls, or next to the life-size sheep in front of the fire (there are smaller versions in the bedrooms, and ducks in the bathrooms). The bar overlooks a private garden owned by the Duke of Westminster and rented out to Mr Goring for 1p a year – no access for guests unfortunately. Naturally, garden-facing bedrooms are preferable; many have original Edwardian brass beds and fitted furniture; walls are plain and colour schemes for curtains and bedspreads warm. Be wary of taking a Junior Suite: as just one large room, they are not what they sound.

- Open all year
- Nearest tube station is Victoria (Victoria, Circle and District lines). Small private car park and on-street parking
- 34 single, 24 twin, 17 double, 9 suites; all with bathroom/WC, TV, room service, hair-dryer, valet service; some rooms are air-conditioned
- Restaurant, bar, lounge;
- conference facilities (max 60 people residential)
- No wheelchair access; no dogs
- Access, Amex, Diners, Visa
- Single £135, twin/double £185, suite £210; deposit required. Continental B £7, cooked B £10; set L £19.50, D £25; alc L, D £40. Special breaks available

# Green Park Hotel

HALF MOON STREET, LONDON W1Y 8BP
TEL: 071-629 7522   TELEX: 28856
FAX: 071-491 8971

*A safe choice and cheap for Mayfair: a medium-size chain hotel in an attractive Georgian building.*

The Sarova Group has carefully converted seven Grade II-listed Georgian houses into one long, deceptively large hotel, and added old-fashioned street lamps to this attractive quiet street just off Piccadilly. Inside, long corridors stretch unbroken from one end to the other, with intermittent bumps indicating the original building divisions. Some guests may find the low-key attention and unintimidating décor easier to get along with than the ostentatious formality and/or grandeur of other hotels in the area. For example, staff may need calling over and soft piped music filters through the hotel (other establishments would regard this as very naff).

You can retreat anonymously into the shadowy recesses of the bar, which is decked out in a pleasant motley coloured collection of wing-chairs and sofas. Through the bar is Claude's Restaurant (named after Monet, who painted some scenes of Green Park and whose prints cover the walls), decorated in various floral blues and serving cheap two- or three-course meals. Both the bar and the restaurant have conservatory areas at the back which are used especially during the day.

The bedrooms were all refurbished in the summer of 1990 and are now more modern in style, in two-tone colour styles such as shades of pink, or aqua and peach. Deluxe rooms have a king-size bed, and bathrooms have bidet and Jacuzzi bath.

- ◑ *Open all year*
- ⤢ *Nearest tube station is Green Park (Piccadilly, Victoria and Jubilee lines). On-street parking*
- 🛏 *29 single, 48 twin, 69 double, 1 four-poster, 8 family rooms, 6 suites; most with bathroom/WC, a few with shower/WC; TV, room service, hair-dryer, trouser press and baby-listening in all rooms; no tea/coffee-making facilities in rooms*
- ✦ *Restaurant (air-conditioned), bar (air-conditioned), lounge; conference facilities (max 80 people residential); babysitting*
- ⊝ *No wheelchair access; no dogs*
- ▭ *Access, Amex, Diners, Visa*
- £ *Single £104, single occupancy of twin/double £114, twin/double £143, four-poster and family room £163, suite £174. Continental B £7, cooked B £10; set L, D £14.50; alc L, D £21*

---

*Prices are quoted* per room *rather than* per person.

# Hazlitt's

**6 FRITH STREET, LONDON W1V 5TZ**
**TEL: 071-434 1771 FAX: 071-439 1524**

*It more than achieves its understated aim of providing simple, civilised accommodation in Soho.*

You want to stay in Soho yet refuse to pay the earth for mediocre, impersonal accommodation for a large three-figure sum? Then Hazlitt's, built in 1718 and home to the eponymous essayist, is the place for you. All its rooms are named after historical characters who had a connection with the building, some well known such as Charles Lamb, others less so like the mysterious Prussian Resident. What attracts guests today is the hotel's position on trendy Frith Street with its popular wine-bars and restaurants.

As most people decorate their own home, Hazlitt's has acquired a cumulation of furniture and a remarkably large collection of sets of mainly Victorian prints, rejecting wholeheartedly the stylised interior design look so prevalent in many hotels. The owner (who also now owns the galleried walls of the Gore – see entry) has given the manager here virtually carte blanche to fill in any gaps on the walls as he sees fit. You'll find some of the loveliest bathrooms in London here: cork floors, freestanding Victorian baths and brass fittings; some have a bust (of which the house has many) staring at you while you're bathing.

Bedrooms vary from having chaises-longues, gilt mirrors, a dining table and chairs, to cottagey attic rooms with stripped pine furniture. Aesthetics outweigh functionality; taps may drip and drawers may be difficult to open, and the only concession to the usual hotel mod cons is a TV and telephone.

◑ Open all year, exc 6 days at Xmas

🡵 Short walk from Tottenham Court Road tube station (Northern and Central lines). Parking difficult

🛏 5 single, 7 twin, 10 double, 1 suite; all with bathroom/WC, TV, room service; no tea/coffee-making facilities in rooms

◈ Lounge

⊖ No wheelchair access; no dogs

▭ Access, Amex, Diners, Visa

£ Single £85, single occupancy of twin/double £85, twin/double £95, suite £145; deposit required. Continental B £5.50

---

*Warning to insomniacs, exercise freaks and late-night lovers: increasing numbers of hotels have infra-red triggered security lamps. To save being embarrassingly illuminated, check before you leave for your late-night or pre-dawn stroll.*

# Holland Park

6 LADBROKE TERRACE, LONDON W11 3PG
TEL: 071-792 0216   FAX: 071-727 8166

*Stay here if money matters as much as individual furnishings, and if mod cons are less important.*

A cheaper version of its nearby sister the Abbey Court (see above), its proprietors seem to have applied the same priorities, namely, to spend much of the hotel's budget on Victorian furnishings to decorate bedrooms and any public space, and to retain the building's character.

On the corner of one of Holland Park's salubrious tree-lined avenues just west of Notting Hill Gate tube, flower-beds with crocuses and daffodils surround a front lawn from which stone steps lead up to the front door. You don't know whether to expect a little B&B or palatial surroundings inside. The hotel somehow achieves both. In the hallway a leaflet stand competes for attention with large and well-framed Victorian prints.

The paceable lounge is wonderfully uncluttered: two large sofas face each other on a cream carpet under watercolour prints with picture lights, and there is a gas fire behind a brass fender. You can see the garden through the room's back window, neat and walled in, used for tea in summer. Smallish bedrooms present this hybrid of elegant simplicity too: one has a half-tester overhung by a little chandelier; many have worn antiques intermingled with less refined pieces, rugs on the floor and candlewick bedspreads. Bathrooms (seven rooms are not *en suite*) are old-fashioned with green tiles and cork floors.

- Open all year, exc 24 to 26 Dec
- Nearest tube station is Notting Hill Gate (Central, Circle and District lines). Parking difficult
- 10 single, 5 twin, 6 double, 2 family; some with bathroom/WC, some with shower/WC, 3 public bathrooms; TV in all rooms;

- baby-listening on request
- Lounge; babysitting
- No wheelchair access; no dogs
- Access, Amex, Visa
- Single £38 to £48, twin/double £48 to £65, family room £90 to £110; deposit required

# L'Hotel

28 BASIL STREET, LONDON SW3 1AT
TEL: 071-589 6286   TELEX: 919042 HOTCAP G
FAX: 071-225 0011 (attention L'Hotel)

*French country-style décor in a Knightsbridge B&B that's hard to fault.*

Stencilled walls and striking, naïve animal portraits on the walls of the stairs and corridors; simple wallpaper patterns and pine furniture in immaculate bedrooms, a wooden mini-bar, perhaps a rocking chair; prettily patterned tiled bathrooms with cork floors – there's a co-ordinated French country style throughout the house. Three bedrooms have fireplaces and are slightly larger than others.

Continuing the Gallic theme, in the basement is the chic wine-bar Le Metro. Popular with shoppers and businessmen, it offers several good wines by the glass, the food is fresh and sometimes imaginative and the service is attentive. Dark and convivial, it seems more suited to a lunchtime chat than a continental breakfast. You might expect to pay over the odds for staying in eyeshot of Harrods, but, by not being lavish with frills and service, L'Hotel can offer what it delightfully does at the price it does. (If you want 24-hour pampering, consider staying next door at the intimate Capital [see entry], under the same ownership. Its greater expense is also justified by *fin de siècle* decoration in the public rooms, designer fabrics in the bedrooms and a highly rated, very grand, haute cuisine restaurant.)

◗ Open all year; restaurant closed Sun

⬀ Nearest tube station is Knightsbridge (Piccadilly line). Private car park

🛏 11 twin, 1 suite, all with bathroom/WC, TV, hair-dryer, mini-bar

◈ Restaurant (air-conditioned), bar.

Wheelchair access to hotel (3 steps), one ground-floor room, no access to restaurant

⊖ None

▭ Access, Amex, Visa

£ Twin £110, suite £145. Alc L £15, D £18

---

# Hotel 167

167 OLD BROMPTON ROAD, LONDON SW5 0AN
TEL: 071-373 3221   FAX: 071-373 3360

*Different, modern and slightly bizarre B&B in South Kensington.*

This part green-painted, part brick Victorian corner house lies on the noisy Old Brompton Road, a ten-minute walk to South Kensington tube. Its modern style makes it quite unlike other B&Bs in the area. Large abstract paintings hang in the hallway and in the reception, which also doubles as a breakfast room with brown-and-white marble-topped tables.

Most of the bedrooms continue this offbeat vein. There are flowers in the bathrooms, and bedrooms are jazzy with venetian blinds, art posters, director's or black aluminium beach chairs. Some of the bedrooms have been furbished in more traditional reproduction wood and floral fabric styles; they are generally less interesting. All are double-glazed. One gripe: when we visited the service was alarmingly informal.

◑ Open all year

⤢ Short walk from South Kensington tube station (Piccadilly, District and Circle lines). Parking difficult

🛏 2 single, 7 twin, 10 double; most with bathroom/WC, some with shower/WC; TV, hair-dryer, mini-bar, baby-listening in all rooms

◈ Lounge

⊖ No wheelchair access; no dogs

▭ Access, Visa

£ Single £51, single occupancy of twin/double £61, twin/double £64 to £70, family room £76 to £82; deposit required. Cooked B £4.50

# Number Sixteen

16 SUMNER PLACE, LONDON SW7 3FG
TEL: 071-589 5232   TELEX: 266638 SXTEEN G
FAX: 071-584 8615

*A traditional, unpretentious South Kensington hotel with civilised furnishings and graceful public rooms.*

This is the most comfortable hotel of many on this perfectly proportioned early Victorian street with its rows of white porticoed fronts. Number Sixteen occupies four. Though refurbishment is gradually upgrading almost fusty timepieces to brighter, co-ordinated design showpieces, regular guests often ask for the plainer, more worn, older-styled rooms and bathrooms: Tapestry, for example (each room's name says something about its décor), hasn't been touched for fifteen years. Just over half of the bedrooms had been refurbished at the time of writing; all differ in size and décor and have antiques.

As there is no breakfast room in the hotel, each bedroom has a couple of cushioned cane chairs and table; and all have a mini-bar stocked with complimentary soft drinks. More than making up for the lack of dining facilities is the peaceful conservatory at the back, where you can sit in wicker chairs admiring the healthy walled garden. In the pair of elegantly furnished sitting-rooms with stuccoed ceilings, one bright, the other with deep red walls and shadowy corners, you can sip drinks from the 'honour bar'.

◑ Open all year

⤢ 100 yards from South Kensington tube station (Piccadilly, District and Circle lines). Parking difficult

🛏 9 single, 27 twin/double; most with bathroom/WC, some with shower/WC; TV, room service, hair-dryer, mini-bar in all rooms; no tea/coffee-making facilities in rooms

◈ Bar, 2 lounges, conservatory

⊖ No wheelchair access; no children under 12; no dogs in bedrooms

▭ Access, Amex, Diners, Visa

£ Single £60 to £100, single occupancy of twin/double £80 to £170, twin/double £80 to £170; deposit required. Cooked B £12

# Observatory House Hotel

37 HORNTON STREET, LONDON, W8 7NR
TEL: 071-937 1577    TELEX: 914972 OBSERV G
FAX: 071-938 3585

*More spacious and with more amenities than your average hole-in-the-wall B&B. Friendly and straightforward.*

Near Kensington Church Street, this beautiful late-Victorian red-brick and white-stone corner house, with pillared portico and florid cornices, stands on the site of an old observatory built in 1831 – it apparently used to house the world's largest telescope. Its more recent history is tantalising: a plaque in one of the suites says: 'In this room the King of Yugoslavia held a number of councils in exile'.

Despite the hotel's history and the impressiveness of the building's plasterwork on the ceilings and over door lintels, it's by no means grand. Its strength lies in the helpfulness and hospitality of Mr Meghji, the owner/manager, and his efforts to make the place attractive while still affordable.

Mr Meghji bought the hotel four years ago and has been upgrading it ever since. Two-thirds of the bedrooms have been refurbished now. However, both old and new rooms are functional and unexceptional, though their high ceilings make them seem large; the improved ones

-Observatory House-

have much better marble-floored and grey-tiled bathrooms. All but four
bedrooms have showers in their small bathrooms.

○ *Open all year*

▶ *Short walk from High Street
Kensington tube station (District
and Circle lines), on corner of
Hornton Street. Public car park
nearby*

🛏 *7 single, 5 twin, 8 double, 4
family rooms, 1 suite; some with
bathroom/WC, most with
shower/WC; TV, hair-dryer,
trouser press, mini-bar, baby-
listening, safe in all rooms*

◈ *Dining-room, lounge*

● *No wheelchair access; no dogs;
no smoking in public rooms*

▭ *Access, Amex, Diners, Visa*

£ *Single £50 to £60, single
occupancy of twin/double £50 to
£69, twin/double £64 to £80,
suite and family rooms £80 to
£100; deposit required. Alc L £7*

---

# One Cranley Place

1 CRANLEY PLACE, LONDON SW7 3AB
TEL: 071-589 7944   FAX: 071-225 3931

*Informal, upmarket B&B with expensively furnished bedrooms.*

Like so many smart establishments in the area, One Cranley Place aims
to appear quite unlike a hotel; it achieves it more than most. Just a black
No 1 on the Regency pillars of a white portico in this quiet, residential
South Ken street tells you you're in the right place. Inside, an absence of
overt colour and design co-ordination keeps up the private residential
feel, as does a cheery mix of old paintings and classical and modern prints
in the corridors.

The smaller bedrooms are worth booking; one, for example, quite big
enough, is furnished with a chandelier, delicate antiques and a walnut
bed. Bedrooms at the front are larger and lighter with tall bay windows
and high ceilings. All have an impressive array of furniture and are
decorated in pastel colours. Though it lacks a lounge proper – just
leather chesterfields in the reception area – it does have the advantage of
a really cheery breakfast room in blue country kitchen-style with
chequered tablecloths, festoon blinds and plate displays.

○ *Open all year*

▶ *Off Old Brompton Road. Nearest
tube station is South Kensington
(Piccadilly, District and Circle
lines). Parking difficult*

🛏 *4 twin, 4 double, 2 suites; most
with bathroom/WC; TV, room
service, hair-dryer in all rooms;
no tea/coffee-making facilities in
rooms*

◈ *Breakfast room, lounge; drying
room. Wheelchair access to
hotel (2 steps), one ground-floor
room*

● *No dogs*

▭ *Access, Amex, Diners, Visa*

£ *Twin/double £80 to £100, suites
£135; deposit required.
Continental B £5, cooked B £7*

# Pelham Hotel

15 CROMWELL PLACE, LONDON SW7 2LA
TEL: 071-589 8288   TELEX: 8814714 TUDOR G
FAX: 071-584 8444

*A thoroughly comfortable town house with lush furnishings.*

The Pelham's brochure gets it right by comparing the hotel to 'an English gentleman who sports jauntily coloured braces beneath his tweed suit': the place appears, and ostensibly is, a period town house, but it's been decorated with a gaiety that subverts its conventionality. Likewise, the staff go about their business formally, but with jovial enthusiasm too.

From the white late-Georgian façade outside you can see the Natural History Museum. It's on a noisy thoroughfare, but all the rooms are double glazed. One of the quirks of the hotel is that the owners, Kit and Tim Kemp, have specially acquired all the furniture, so even the eighteenth-century pine panelling in the drawing-room was bought at auction, and likewise all the antiques in it. In the basement, the cosy restaurant has fun, multicoloured fabrics, and the three-course traditional English menu offers good-value set lunches (though rather too many of the dishes listed have an additional supplement).

The air-conditioned bedrooms have antiques in them, too. Bold, striped wallpaper, or a rosette motif, or matching bed drapes and curtains (mini-bars hidden under more drapes) in strong floral patterns produce cheerful rooms. No expense has been spared in the quality of the fabrics, all the beds are queen- or king-size, and the bathrooms are in glazed granite.

- ◗ Open all year; restaurant closed Sat and Sun
- ⤢ Nearest tube station is South Kensington (Piccadilly, District and Circle lines). On-street parking
- 🛏 34 double, 3 suites; all with bathroom/WC, TV, room service, hair-dryer, mini-bar; trouser press in some rooms
- ◈ Restaurant, 2 bars, 2 lounges

(hotel has full air-conditioning); babysitting. Wheelchair access to hotel and restaurant, WC (M,F) and lift

- ⊖ Dogs at manager's discretion
- ▭ Access, Amex, Visa
- £ Twin/double £140 to £165, suite £265; deposit required. Continental B £7.50, cooked B £10.50; set L, D £15, £18; alc L, D £28

---

*The last morning, Monday, we had to leave at 7.30am and breakfast didn't begin on Mondays until 8am, no good for anyone wishing to go to work. The owners said they'd leave us 'something ready' in the dining-room, which turned out to be a bread roll, butter, cereal and marmalade, I think, only as they had omitted to tell us the whereabouts of the light switch it was very difficult to tell at 7am in the dark.* On an hotel in Blackburn

# Pembridge Court

34 PEMBRIDGE GARDENS, LONDON W2 4DX
TEL: 071-229 9977  TELEX: 298363 PEMCT G
FAX: 071-727 4982

*An unpretentious hotel enthusiastically run and individualistically decorated. Popular with musicians and antique dealers.*

At the far end of the same street as Abbey Court (see above), and in a similarly large free-standing Victorian building, the Pembridge Court is an altogether different proposition. It's been in the Capra family for twenty-odd years and its unique style reflects the tastes of the welcoming owner, Paul Capra. He is evidently an obsessive collector: throughout the hotel bedrooms, named after nearby areas of London, there are framed purses, fans and christening dresses livening up the walls. The rooms are comfortable rather than luxurious with a sparing use of colour; pine predominates in furniture and bedheads. Larger rooms have sofa beds; smaller singles, in a new extension, only have a shower. Bathrooms are good quality in salmon or grey tiling.

The new extension has been made as attractive as possible given it was built of exposed brick. It provides a residents' lounge which was being enlarged when we visited, and a wine-bar-style restaurant in the basement called Caps (Paul's nickname at school), open in the evenings only. Check out William's Room, named after a well-known prince who goes to school nearby, where you can find an eccentric collection of framed school and cricket caps. Food is inexpensive and the Thai chef always includes a couple of his national dishes on the menu.

- Open all year; restaurant eves only, closed Sun
- Short walk from Notting Hill Gate tube station (Central, District and Circle lines). Private parking for 2 cars
- 10 single, 2 twin, 1 four-poster, 3 family rooms, 9 suites; all with bathroom/WC, exc 8 singles with shower/WC; TV, room service, hair-dryer, trouser press, baby-listening in all rooms; no tea/coffee-making facilities in rooms
- Restaurant (air-conditioned), bar, lounge; conference facilities (max 20 people residential)
- No wheelchair access
- Access, Amex, Diners, Visa
- Single £81, single occupancy of twin/double £92, twin £100, four-poster £138; family room £150, suite £115 to £138; deposit required. Alc D £18. Special breaks available

---

*Dog lovers: some hotels not only welcome dogs, but they provide gourmet meals for them. Ask.*

# The Portobello

22 STANLEY GARDENS, LONDON W11 2NG
TEL: 071-727 2777   TELEX: 268349 PORT G
FAX: 071-792 9641

*It appeals to arty types who like the informal atmosphere, 24-hour service and sometimes cramped but very individual campaign-style bedrooms.*

Two tall Victorian houses back on to peaceful, tree-filled gardens (no access unfortunately). All but six of the bedrooms face the garden; some have big bay windows allowing its leafiness to invade the rooms. The rooms are entirely furnished with antiques, most of which have a military origin, stuff which 'could be thrown on the back of an elephant': desks, chests of drawers, breakfast trays, leather chairs, a footstool . . . The smaller rooms (and some are box-like, particularly the so-called 'cabins') have the advantage of summoning up this soldierly feel most vividly as the furniture's compactness becomes practical and not just decorative. 'Life-support systems' are hidden away in cupboards and constitute disappointing synthetic-looking continental breakfasts – Cellophane-wrapped croissants, for example. Some bedrooms are considerably bigger: four have four-posters and there are special rooms such as the 'Round Room' with circular bed and oriental furniture, and the 'Bath Room' with a bath a few feet from the bed.

Below the refined lounge, with balloon-backed chairs and pictures of cavalrymen on the walls, is an odd, out-of-keeping small basement restaurant and bar, with wicker chairs and sofas at one end and a few tables at the other. There's nothing too adventurous on the menu: full English breakfasts, pastas, baked potatoes, sandwiches and steaks.

◑ Open all year, exc 23 Dec to 2 Jan

⬀ Nearest tube station is Notting Hill Gate (Central, District and Circle lines). On-street parking

🛏 10 single, 3 twin, 5 double, 7 suites; all with shower/WC, suites with bath/WC; TV, room service, hair-dryer, mini-bar in all rooms

◈ Restaurant, bar, lounge; hotel partly air-conditioned

⊖ No wheelchair access; no dogs

▭ Access, Amex, Diners, Visa

£ Single £70, single occupancy of twin/double £109, twin/double £122, suite £166; deposit required. Cooked B £7.50; alc L £15, D £20

*If you make a booking using a credit card, and you find after cancelling that the full amount has been charged to your card, raise the matter with your credit card company. They will ask the hotelier to confirm whether the room was re-let, and to justify the charge they made.*

# The Savoy

THE STRAND, LONDON WC2R 0BP
TEL: 071-836 4343   TELEX: 24234 SAVOY
FAX: 071-240 6040

*Grand, late-Victorian hotel with many Art Deco touches. Famed as a meeting place for the rich and famous, for food, for style and for service.*

People of all ages, shapes and sizes seem to enjoy the Savoy: a couple of teenagers saunter in as if they own the place; businessmen finish entertaining their clients over a brandy; a trilby-attired gentleman greets his wife after an evidently busy shopping spree; an elderly lady occupies a succession of armchairs to take in the different scenes. What appeals? The Thames Foyer, more of a garden than a drawing-room, guarded by stags with a pagoda and a white piano in the middle and overlooked by pastoral murals and Art Deco mirrors with arboreal and floral designs, must be one of the most delightfully congenial places in London. Perhaps it's the variety of atmospheres but in a consonant style: the typically masculine, yew-panelled grill; the Art Deco cocktail bar, American in its idolisation of early screen legends; or the clean grey marble-topped tabled Chablis and oyster bar overlooking the hotel's busy entrance. The Savoy is a well-known meeting place for high-powered business breakfasts, political lunches and courtly teas.

If you do stay here, it will cost you less than it would at London's other leading hotels provided you elect not to have a river view. Many bedrooms have Art Deco features, such as metal-framed doors and mirrors and luggage racks and built-in cupboards; bathrooms are part marble (a few, very popular ones, in black) with gigantic old-fashioned shower heads. You're paying for elegance rather than outrageous luxury, and for service intended to be speedier and more intimate than normal room service. There's a bell by your bed with buttons for 'waiter', 'maid' and 'valet' and a cord by the bath.

- Open all year; grill closed Sun eve
- Between the Strand and the Embankment. Nearest tube station Charing Cross (Northern, Bakerloo and Jubilee lines). Private car park
- 57 single, 60 twin, 24 double, 11 triple, 48 suites; all with bathroom/WC, TV, room service, mini-bar, valet service; baby-listening, hair-dryer on request; no tea/coffee-making facilities in rooms
- 3 restaurants, 2 bars, lounge; conference facilities (max 450 people non-residential, 30 residential); air-conditioned public areas and some bedrooms; babysitting
- No wheelchair access; no dogs
- Access, Amex, Diners, Visa
- Single £170, single occupancy of twin/double £195, twin/double £195 to £260, triple £250, suite £280 to £600; deposit required. Continental B £11.50, cooked B £16; set L from £24.50, D £41.50; alc L £29, D £50 (prices till Sept 91)

# Woodville House

107 EBURY STREET, LONDON SW1W 9QU
TEL: 071-730 1048   FAX: 071-730 2574

*Best cheap B&B in the area if you don't want a private bathroom. Some might find it gaudy.*

Almost every other door in Ebury Street offers accommodation. This looks one of the most promising, even from a brief peek through the canopy-covered door of this three-storeyed Georgian terraced house. On a noticeboard, there is a plethora of information and a 'royalty of England family tree' and an historical map of England and Wales to entice visitors who like those sort of things.

Rachel Joplin, one of the owners, has described the bedrooms as 'camp': they're intended primarily to woo American visitors who make up 80 per cent of their trade. On each storey there's a double, a twin and a single, and a tiled bathroom to share. There are also two family rooms in the basement. All the bedrooms have extremely florid wallpaper and curtains, washbasins and diminutive armchairs, and net drapes embellish most beds. Bedrooms at the front have shutters which help reduce traffic noise.

Through the breakfast room lies an attractive small patio garden which guests can use during the summer. Another bonus is a kitchenette in the basement for making hot drinks and storing snacks or cold drinks.

◐ Open all year

🡢 Four minutes' walk from Victoria tube station (Victoria, District and Circle lines). Parking difficult

🛏 4 single, 3 twin, 3 double, 2 family rooms; none en suite, 4 bathrooms; TV, hair-dryer in all rooms; double rooms are air-conditioned

◇ Dining-room (air-conditioned), drying room

⊖ No wheelchair access; dogs in grounds only

▭ None accepted

£ Single £30, twin/double £45 to £48; deposit required

---

*When you telephone to book a room, and the hotel accepts your booking, you enter into a binding contract with them. This means they undertake to provide the specified accommodation and meals etc. for the agreed cost on the agreed dates, while you commit yourself to paying their charges. If you later have to cancel your booking, or fail to turn up, the hotel is likely to keep any deposit you have paid to defray administrative costs. If an hotel is unable to re-let the room you have booked – and it must try to do so – it is entitled to compensation for the loss of profit caused by your breach of contract. It can only claim a sum that is fair and reasonable – which can be up to two-thirds of the cost. It should not make a profit out of your failure to appear. It's important to give as much notice as possible when cancelling: this increases the chances of your room being re-let.*

# ENGLAND

**ABBOT'S SALFORD** WARWICKSHIRE **MAP 6**

# Salford Hall

ABBOT'S SALFORD, HEREFORD & WORCESTER WR11 5UT
TEL: EVESHAM (0386) 871300   TELEX: 336682 SALHAL G
FAX: (0386) 871301

*A smart Tudor mansion with comfortable rooms.*

Salford Hall, a Tudor mansion with seventeenth-century stone extension, opened as an hotel in 1989, thoroughly renovated after a period of
dereliction. This curious mix of styles dominates the gently sloping lawns
and fields surrounding it.

Inside, Tudor archways, stone walls and panelling give the hotel its
character, enhanced by a mix of reproduction and antique furnishings in
keeping with the style of the hotel. The high-ceilinged stone-walled
reception has a welcoming log fire in a massive arched fireplace, for
instance, and the restaurant deep red carpets and oak tables. There are
two areas to sit – the bright and summery glass-roofed courtyard or the
darker but relaxing club-style bar. Bedrooms vary in size but are
comfortable, with sumptuous chintz and some modern dark oak. Some
are in a separate stone and half-timbered annexe across the drive.

-Salford Hall-

◗ Open all year

⤢ On the A439, 8 miles west of Stratford-upon-Avon. Private car park

⛏ 2 single, 7 twin, 18 double, 8 four-poster; all with bathroom/WC, exc 1 double with shower/WC; TV, room service (limited), hair-dryer, trouser press, mini-bar, baby-listening in all rooms

◈ Restaurant, bar, lounge, snooker room, conservatory; conference facilities (max 50 people non-residential, 35 residential); tennis, croquet, sauna/solarium at hotel, other sports nearby

⊖ No wheelchair access; no children under 10 at dinner; no dogs; no smoking in restaurant

▭ Access, Amex, Diners, Visa

£ Single £80, single occupancy of twin/double £90, twin/double £100, four-poster £120; deposit required. Set L £15, D £22. Special breaks available

## ALDEBURGH SUFFOLK                                    MAP 7

# Austins

HIGH STREET, ALDEBURGH, SUFFOLK IP15 5DN
TEL: ALDEBURGH (0728) 453932   FAX: (0728) 453668

*Restaurant-oriented, personally run hotel. Away from the front but with plenty of visual pizazz to sustain your interest.*

The restaurant and bar take up most of the ground floor, but Austins has too many rooms to meet the definition of restaurant-with-rooms. The painted pink-brick house, with royal blue awnings and cast-iron railings, formerly two rows of back-to-back cottages, is not a typical seaside hotel, either. The beach is a street or two away; the entrance has a near-museum of Chinese pottery filling shelves to either side of the fireplace, and top-lit paintings, including one of co-owner Robert Selbie's great-grandfather, hang throughout the wide ground-floor rooms.

Furnishings blend plush modern with antique, so you are always comfortable but have interesting things to gaze upon. Signed photographs of actors and musicians, and posters of West End productions, testament to Robert Selbie's previous involvement in the theatre, cover the walls of the warmly lit bar. Framed celebrity photos also sit on the piano in the soft grey living-room. Mr Selbie's partner, Julian Alexander-Worster, creates the lunches and dinners – deep-fried artichoke hearts with herb mayonnaise, for instance, followed by tagine of lamb. Bedrooms at Austins deliver a less pronounced flavour but ample comforts and restful colour schemes. Three have sea views over rooftops.

◗ Open all year, exc 2 weeks late Jan/early Feb; restaurant closed Mon eve, and Tues lunch

⤢ At the south end of Aldeburgh High Street. On-street parking

⛏ 2 single, 2 twin, 3 double; most with bathroom/WC, some with shower/WC; TV, room service, baby-listening in all rooms; hair-dryer, trouser press on request

◈ Restaurant, bar, 2 lounges; golf, tennis, riding nearby

● No wheelchair access; children at owner's discretion; no dogs in public rooms

▭ Access, Amex, Visa

£ Single £51, single occupancy of twin/double £51, twin/double £73; deposit required. Set L £11.50; alc D £24.50. Special breaks available

---

**ALDERMINSTER** WARWICKSHIRE                    **MAP 6**

# Ettington Park

ALDERMINSTER, NR STRATFORD-UPON-AVON, WARWICKSHIRE CV37 8BS
TEL: STRATFORD-UPON-AVON (0789) 740740   FAX: (0789) 450472

*Splendidly restored Gothic mansion, efficiently run and deservedly popular for business conferences.*

The house stands at the end of a tree-lined driveway in forty acres of well-maintained park on the banks of the River Stour. And on a misty night, the first sight of this ornate neo-Gothic pile could cause faint hearts to skip a beat. But appearances are misleading because the atmosphere relaxes once you pass through the conservatory full of potted plants and palms.

Inside, the house is an impressive recreation of Victorian décor, with chocolate and cream colour schemes complemented by reproduction furniture, dark wood panelling and high-backed armchairs. Much thought has gone into the planning of this hotel and it shows in pleasing touches like the welcome basket of fruit and tin of sweets that await each guest in his/her room. An efficient and friendly set of staff set the tone for the stay, so it is easy to see why the hotel is a popular venue for business conferences. Check ahead if you don't want to feel like a gatecrasher at someone else's party. You can work up a fine dinner appetite in the swimming-pool or on the tennis court. Dinner is served in an elegant panelled room surrounded by hand-carved family crests with a fine rococo ceiling overhead. The menu is short but pricy, featuring dishes like salmon with pistachio to start, followed by veal with armagnac sauce. And if you over-indulge, there is a sauna to help you sweat it off.

◐ Open all year

🔁 5 miles south of Stratford-upon-Avon off the A3400. Private car park

🛏 6 twin, 33 double, 1 four-poster, 8 suites; all with bathroom/WC, TV, room service, hair-dryer, baby-listening; trouser-press in some rooms; no tea/coffee-making facilities in rooms

◈ Restaurant, 2 bars, lounge, conservatory; conference facilities (max 80 people non-residential, 48 residential); fishing, tennis, riding, sauna/solarium, heated indoor swimming-pool, clay-pigeon shooting at hotel, other sports nearby. Wheelchair access to hotel (ramp) and restaurant, no ground-floor bedrooms but lift

⊖  No dogs

▭  Access, Amex, Diners, Visa

£  Single occupancy of twin/double

£115, twin/double £145, four-
poster £165, suite £165; deposit
required. Set L £17.50, D £28;
alc L £25, D £35

---

**ALDWINCLE** NORTHAMPTONSHIRE                    **MAP 6**

# The Maltings

MAIN STREET, ALDWINCLE, KETTERING, NORTHAMPTONSHIRE NN14 3EP
TEL: CLOPTON (080 15) 233   FAX: (080 15) 326

*A lovely family home with a great garden and friendly hosts.*

On arrival you may find Margaret Faulkner gardening in the lovely back
garden (open to the public occasionally under the National Gardens'
Scheme). There's a sign on the front door saying if you get no answer, go
around to the back. The Maltings is where the malster for the Lilford
Estate once lived; the barn next door was formerly the malthouse for the
estate brewery. The long, attractive house is constructed from local
stone. 'It's like the Cotswolds without the number of people.'

Inside this stylish family house with lots of character, there are
flagstones and undulating floors (the corridor to the bedrooms). The
three bedrooms are all spacious and light. The dining-room is formal
with a large stone fireplace (in summer filled with pine cones) and a
central polished table, but if you're staying here alone you will probably
find yourself breakfasting in the warm kitchen with Margaret and Nigel.
There's also a large sitting-room with a TV and comfortable seats and
lots of room to relax. Margaret doesn't provide evening meals but she can
direct you to various eating places nearby.

○  Open all year

↗  In the centre of the village, on
the main street between the
garage and the village shop.
Private car park

🛏  1 single, 1 twin, 1 double; 2 with
bathroom/WC, 1 with shower/
WC; hair-dryer in all rooms; no
tea/coffee-making facilities in
rooms

◇  Dining-room, lounge, drying-
room; fishing, golf, riding nearby

⊖  No wheelchair access; no
children under 10; no dogs; no
smoking in bedrooms

▭  Access, Visa

£  Single £20, single occupancy of
twin/double £28, twin/double
£39; deposit required. Special
breaks available

---

*The* Guide *office can quickly spot when a hotelier is encouraging customers
to write a recommending inclusion – and sadly, several hotels have been
doing this in 1991. Such reports do not further an hotel's cause.*

**ALSTON** CUMBRIA                                                    **MAP 3**

# High Fell Hotel

ALSTON, CUMBRIA CA9 3BP
TEL: ALSTON (0434) 381597

*Comfortable farmhouse hotel in an unspoilt location.*

Lying well beyond the boundaries of the Lake District National Park, this restored seventeenth-century farmhouse is a good bet for exploring the parts of Cumbria most of the tourist hordes never reach.

Your much-travelled hosts, Peter and Val Dow, achieve an incongruous charm with a combination of the English rustic of stone walls and flagstones offsetting knick-knacks garnered from their earlier wanderings in Africa and the South Pacific.

Furniture ranges from antique to comfy-but-shabby. And one reader described the atmosphere as 'relaxed, and friendly and efficient at the same time'. Bedrooms are roomy and, while retaining period features such as beams, are decked out in modern fabrics with snazzy patterns, while the furniture reflects various eras and styles. Electric blankets plus real bedcovers ('no duvets – hooray,' report readers) help beat the winter's chill.

Food, served in the panelled and parquet-floored dining-room, is interesting and standards of cuisine are high. Try chicken liver and apple pâté, and boned chicken with hazelnut stuffing. Views of Cross Fell make the garden seating area an attractive place to linger.

- ◑ *Open all year*
- ⤤ *1¾ miles south of Alston on the A686 Penrith road, on a small driveway. Private car park*
- ⇌ *1 twin, 4 double; all with bathroom/WC, exc twin with shower/WC*
- ◈ *Dining-room, bar, lounge, golf, adventure sports, other sports nearby*

- ⊜ *No wheelchair access; no children under 14; no dogs; no smoking in dining-room*
- ▭ *Access, Amex, Visa*
- £ *Single occupancy of twin/double £20 to £28, twin/double £39 to £55; deposit required. Alc D from £16.50 (8pm) (prices till end 91). Special breaks available*

---

**AMBLESIDE** CUMBRIA                                              **MAP 3**

# Chapel House

KIRKSTONE ROAD, AMBLESIDE, CUMBRIA LA22 9DZ
TEL: AMBLESIDE (053 94) 33143

*Good food and old-fashioned hospitality at a sensible price.*

If you make your way up the brae to Duncan and Sandra Hamer's small hotel, you may well find the door opened by one of the many regulars who just can't imagine visiting the Lakes and staying anywhere else. But it's not clannish – new faces are soon made welcome. So what inspires such loyalty? It's not the bedrooms which although freshly decorated and nicely furnished are definitely on the small side. Forthright canny northerners tell you that the real magnet is Duncan's superb food and the no-nonsense value for money.

Front-facing rooms have views of the fells including Heron Pike, but are unfortunately plagued by daytime traffic noise, as drivers put their foot down to coax their cars up the steep brae. Dinner's a four-course no-choice affair, typically offering fare such as cocktail Japanese-style, purée of vegetable soup, grilled devilled chicken, and ginger and lemon pudding with butterscotch sauce. Coffee is taken afterwards in the homely lounge. The hearty breakfast will set you up for the day.

Since there's no television, entertainment is people-centred. One particularly enterprising contingent organised a fancy-dress party, but there's no pressure to join in if you just want to escape to your room. About ten o'clock Sandra and Duncan, bearing tea and biscuits, join the throng for a natter, and advise on routes for anyone planning a fell walk.

◑ Limited opening Nov, Dec; closed Jan, Feb

↗ To the north of Ambleside village. On-street parking

🛏 2 single, 2 twin, 5 double, 1 family room; some rooms with shower/WC; no tea/coffee-making facilities in rooms

◈ Dining-room, bar, lounge; drying facilities on request; water sports, other sports nearby

⊖ No wheelchair access; no dogs; no smoking in bedrooms

▭ None accepted

£ Single £27 to £33, twin/double £54 to £72; children £9 to £20; (rates inc dinner); deposit required. Set D £13 (7pm)

---

# Drunken Duck Inn

BARNGATES, AMBLESIDE, CUMBRIA LA22 0NG
TEL: HAWKSHEAD (096 66) 347

*Smashing country inn with comfortable rooms.*

Pubs with funny names sometimes disappoint. Not so the Drunken Duck; this venerable whitewashed hostelry is worthy of the tale that landed it with the colourful moniker – a chronicle retold on a panel in one of the cosy bars. Legend has it that a nineteenth-century landlady found what she believed to be a deceased duck, and started to pluck it for the oven. Whereupon the web-footed one, insensible from over-indulgence in the seepage from a wayward barrel, overcame its stupor and legged it with considerable speed. There's a happy ending: the relieved landlady got out her knitting needles and fashioned a jacket to keep the hapless bird warm. The present owners are just as concerned with creature comforts! Bedrooms are bright and well-furnished with chintzy curtains and a well-judged cottage feel. Bathrooms feature a stencilled duck motif and duck-shaped bubblebath sachets and soap.

The downstairs pub has three bars and lots of outdoor seating. Bar food, such as cheesy pasta with tuna and olives, is above average, and should be washed down with a well-kept pint of Theakston's, Jennings' or Murphy's stout, or one of the impressive array of malts. The four-course set dinner in the restaurant relies on traditional standards such as trout with almonds and chocolate sponge pudding. The fowl theme is further evident with model ducks from Donald to decoy, and a nifty sideline in duck T-shirts.

*Open all year; restaurant open Fri and Sat eves only but bar meals always available*

*Take the A593 out of Ambleside and turn left at Clappersgate on to the B5286 to Hawkshead. After 1 mile turn right immediately opposite the Outgate Inn. The inn is 1 mile up this road. Private car park*

*1 twin, 8 double, 1 annexe room; all with bathroom/WC, exc 1*

*double with shower/WC; TV, hair-dryer in all rooms*

*Dining-room, bar, darts-room; fishing at hotel, other sports nearby; drying facilities*

*No wheelchair access*

*Access, Visa*

*Single £40, twin/double £60 to £67; deposit required. Set D £25 (8pm, must book in advance); bar meals*

---

# Merewood Hotel

ECCLERIGG, WINDERMERE, CUMBRIA LA23 1LH
TEL: WINDERMERE (096 62) 6484    FAX: (096 62) 2128

*Comfortable country-house hotel in a good location.*

It's hard to believe that an hotel so close to the busy main Windermere to Ambleside road could be peaceful, but it is. The long, winding drive takes you over a series of sleeping policemen and past a thick wood of cypress and fir trees, delivering you at a solid Victorian mansion. Inside, the comforting smell of woodsmoke combines with the period interior to whisk you back in time. Calling in for afternoon tea on a cold April afternoon, one visitor was immediately ushered into the library by a friendly waiter who stoked up the fire and served the requested Darjeeling and a generous selection of biscuits and cakes in a jiffy (a happier experience than that of readers who wrote to complain of afternoon tea taking half an hour to arrive). It later transpired that the friendly northerner in the waxed jacket and chunky sweater who popped in to chat amiably was owner Norman Robinson. The library is a civilised room with ornate carved walnut fireplace, plush sofas and horsy prints. The neighbouring drawing-room is an elegant, feminine room in pretty pastels – a total contrast to the robustly masculine conservatory bar with its red leather chesterfields and mosaic floor.

The bedrooms are named after Romantic poets and other pre-Victorian writers and are stylishly furnished, juxtaposing pleasing period touches like wash-stands with contemporary comforts, though one reader complained that his room, Sheridan, was 'little larger than a cupboard, and I'm glad I was not sharing it'. Since we last reported, a new dining-room with views over Lake Windermere has opened, and dinner-dances are now held at weekends. The menu is 'franglais', offering classics like moules marinière, as well as robust English favourites. One niggle: the repetitive Clapton to Dionne Warwick Muzak, nostalgic as it is for thirtysomethings, is probably a mistake.

◑ *Open all year*

↗ *On the A591 Windermere to Ambleside road, opposite the Brockhole National Park entrance. Private car park*

🛏 *2 twin, 13 double, 2 four-poster, 3 suites; all with bathroom/WC, TV, room service, hair-dryer, baby-listening; trouser press on request*

◈ *Restaurant, bar, lounge, TV room, drying room, conservatory,*

*library/study; conference facilities (max 100 people non-residential, 20 residential); gym at hotel, other sports nearby. Wheelchair access to public rooms only*

⊖ *No dogs*

▭ *Access, Amex, Diners, Visa*

£ *Single occupancy of twin/double £72, twin/double £72, four-poster/suite £118; deposit required. Continental B £7, cooked B £7.50; alc L £9, D £26*

---

# Nanny Brow Hotel　　　　　⌘

AMBLESIDE, CUMBRIA LA22 9NF
TEL: AMBLESIDE (053 94) 32036　FAX: (053 94) 32450

*Well-run country house with careful management and cheerful staff.*

Come in search of a Cumbrian Mary Poppins and you'll be disappointed – there never was a nanny called Brow. The goats that used to scamper on the hotel's splendidly hilly site probably account for the name. The views, high above the Langdale valley, are priceless, and easily enjoyed from one of the white chairs on the trim little lawn with its flapping Union flag in front of the hotel. There are five more acres to explore if you have the energy.

The well-kept house is white stucco with black strapping. Inside, the general tone is comfortable but informal and unpretentious, with pretty fabrics to make even the large lounge feel cosy. Here you can opt for apposite country house games like *Cluedo*, or improve yourself with *Lorna Doone* and other classics that you never quite got around to reading.

The newish cocktail bar is a pleasant room with bamboo chairs, bright fabrics and a conservatory feel. Proprietor Michael Fletcher chats to guests while taking dinner orders. He's done his homework and addresses everyone by name. And he deserves brownie points for the large number of wines available by the glass – a canny way of coaxing guests away from French and German standards to less obvious treats like Californian white Zinfandel. Julio Iglesias follows Maurice Chevalier on the tape deck. Service in the dining-room is efficient and friendly. The six-course dinner menu offers three choices of both starter and main course and is traditional with flair – perhaps Arbroath smokie pâté with a julienne of salmon, followed by broccoli and Cheddar soup, sorbet and a Barnsley chop. Opt for the cheese – generous chunks of Huntsman or Truckle Cheddar.

Bedrooms range from rather uninspired standard rooms to bright new suites in the garden. All are comfortable. Good breakfasts include fresh pineapple, home-made croissants and pastries as well as the usual hearty grill. However, perhaps Michael should listen a little more sympathet-ically to complaints: one reader who received a cool welcome and a disappointing meal in the restaurant remarked: 'An understanding listening ear was all that was required, we didn't realise this was also out of season.'

◑ *Open all year*

↗ *On the A593 road from Ambleside to Coniston. Private car park*

🛏 *4 twin, 5 double, 2 four-poster, 7 garden suites (family rooms available); all with bathroom/ WC, TV, room service, hair-dryer, mini-bar, baby-listening*

◈ *Restaurant, bar, lounge, drying room, conference facilities (max 25 people non-residential, 18 residential); sauna, solarium at hotel, fishing, golf, other sports nearby*

⊖ *No wheelchair access; no children under 10 in restaurant; no dogs in public rooms; no smoking in restaurant*

▭ *Access, Amex, Visa*

£ *Single occupancy of twin/double £55 to £65, twin/double £90 to £130, four-poster £130 to £178, family room £130 to £150, suite £120 to £140 (rates inc dinner); deposit required. Set D £20; Sun L (Nov to Apr) £11. Special breaks available*

---

# Rothay Manor

**ROTHAY BRIDGE, AMBLESIDE, CUMBRIA LA22 0EH**
**TEL: AMBLESIDE (053 94) 33605   FAX: (053 94) 33607**

*Established country-house hotel that can still see off most of the upstart newcomers.*

With 25 years' experience, the Nixon family are old-hands at the country house hotel business, establishing and consolidating a considerable reputation for Rothay Manor before the recent explosion of numbers debased the genre. However, one reader detected an air of complacency and asked if the hotel was 'resting on its laurels', finding the welcome lacking warmth and the service 'unprofessional'.

Aiming to be comfortable and relaxing, Rothay Manor avoids the overblown excesses of some potential rivals, settling for gentility rather than designer modishness. The white Regency-style building sits at a busy road junction, and traffic noise somewhat mars enjoyment of the garden. Once you're indoors, the problem all but disappears. Rothay Manor's a favoured stop on the afternoon tea circuit, and a substantial buffet is set out for consumption in one of the sedate lounges. Non-smokers sit amid bold blue-striped Regency splendour, while smokers puff away in a more autumnal room with a *fleur-de-lys* print wallpaper, and a handsome grandfather clock.

The Regency theme continues in the restaurant. Diners can choose two or five courses from a short but well-judged menu that might range from Stilton, port and herb pâté through duck with orange to caramel mousse. One reader found that the breakfast was limited in scope and that an inedible sausage was served having been 'inadequately thawed'. Bedrooms are comfortable with modern furniture and soft furnishings in pastel shades.

◑ Closed Jan to early Feb

🔁 On the A593 south-west of Ambleside towards Coniston. Private car park

🛏️ 2 single, 3 twin, 5 double, 5 family rooms, 3 suites; all with bathroom/WC, TV, room service, hair-dryer, baby-listening

◈ Air-conditioned dining-room, bar, 3 lounges; conference facilities (max 30 people non-residential, 15 residential); croquet at hotel, other sports nearby. Wheelchair access to hotel (1 step), restaurant and WC (unisex), 3 ground-floor bedrooms, 2 specially equipped for the disabled

⊖ No dogs; no smoking in 1 lounge and dining-room

▭ Access, Amex, Diners, Visa

💷 Single £62 to £69, single occupancy of twin/double £72 to £79, twin/double £88 to £98, suite £124 to £138; children sharing parents' room £5 to £25 each; deposit required. Buffet L £5.50 to £9; set D £17, £23. Special breaks available

# Wateredge Hotel

BORRANS ROAD, AMBLESIDE, CUMBRIA LA22 0EP
TEL: AMBLESIDE (053 94) 32332   FAX: (053 94) 32332

*Charming lakeside inn on busy main road.*

As you drive past Waterhead Bay on the busy A591 there's little to suggest that these whitewashed seventeenth-century fishermen's cottages with the rowing boat motif that make up the Wateredge Hotel are anything special. Inside, it's another story. An irregularly shaped lounge, added in the 1930s, has picture windows. Order tea and watch the waterbound activity on Windermere, as swans glide and ducks paddle through the water. Small yachts, rowing boats and motor cruisers coast aimlessly while ferries head for Bowness. Rabbits scamper between the garden chairs on the trim lawns.

The building shows its age in the crooked beams, off-centre walls and slanting floors that confront you in the corridors radiating from the central hub. Antique knick-knacks from coffee grinders to rocking-horses lurk in interesting nooks and crannies. Bedrooms vary in size and furnishings, but all have cheerful modern fabrics to make them cosy. The superior lake and garden rooms in a recent addition are large and appealing, and some have stunning views. The dual-level dining-room is vista-less, but there's a sense of period style in its traditional inglenook fireplace, flagstone floor and low beams.

Choice at dinner is limited (except for dessert), but one reader observed that '[it] would have to be a very fussy guest who did not find something pleasing'. A typical menu might feature gravadlax, leek and fennel soup with home-made wholemeal bread, a sorbet, roast lamb or halibut, and a catalogue of desserts including hazelnut shortbread with cream and strawberries, as well as a good selection of British cheeses.

Closed mid-Dec to early Feb

On the A591 at Waterhead Bay, Ambleside. Private car park

3 single, 6 twin, 8 double, 1 family room, 5 half-suites; most with bathroom/WC, some with shower/WC; TV, hair-dryer; limited room service in all rooms

Air-conditioned dining-room, bar, 3 lounges, TV room, drying room; fishing, rowing (Apr to Oct), private jetty at hotel, other sports nearby

No wheelchair access; no children under 7; no dogs in public rooms and by arrangement in bedrooms; no smoking in dining-room

Access, Amex, Visa

Single £49 to £60, single occupancy of twin/double from £64 and £90, twin/double from £84 and £124, suite £116 to £140, family room £102 to £124 (rates inc dinner); deposit required. Set L from £9.50, D £21.50 (prices till end 91). Special breaks available

---

**ARNCLIFFE** NORTH YORKSHIRE                    **MAP 4**

# Amerdale House

ARNCLIFFE, LITTONDALE, NR SKIPTON, NORTH YORKSHIRE BD23 5QE
TEL: ARNCLIFFE (0756) 770250

*A place to go to be looked after, not in luxury but in friendly, comfortable surroundings.*

If you're looking for somewhere to have a peaceful, relaxing time, surrounded by beautiful scenery (tempting views down Littondale to the River Skirfare), this is the place for you. The house is very comfortable with an elegant and spacious drawing-room – pink is the predominant colour with sofas and satinised walls and a co-ordinated floral carpet. The dining-room is also a large room with the luxury of tables far enough apart for private conversations. Nigel Crapper is the chef and if you can close your eyes to the lambs gambolling outside the window you may enjoy cutlets of Dales lamb wrapped in filo pastry and some delicious local cheeses; there's always a vegetarian dish.

The bedrooms, both in the main house and the converted coach-house, are also comfortable, with hand-made pine furniture and good bathrooms. Five have particularly good views down the valley. Guests are well taken care of and the atmosphere is one of calm and friendliness. Be careful not to relax too much – you may never want to leave.

- ◑ Closed mid-Nov to mid-Mar
- ⤴ On the edge of the village of Arncliffe, 7 miles north of Grassington. Private car park
- ⇌ 3 twin, 7 double, 1 four-poster; most with bathroom/WC, some with shower/WC; TV in all rooms; hair-dryer, trouser press in most rooms
- ◇ Restaurant, bar, lounge; drying

facilities; fishing, riding, other sports nearby
- ⊖ No wheelchair access; no dogs; no smoking in restaurant
- ▭ Access, Visa
- £ Single occupancy of twin/double £59 to £61, twin/double/four-poster £97 to £101 (rates inc dinner). Set D £17 (prices till end 91). Special breaks available

---

**ARROW** WARWICKSHIRE                                      **MAP 6**

# Arrow Mill

ARROW, NR ALCESTER, WARWICKSHIRE B49 5NL
TEL: ALCESTER (0789) 762419   FAX: (0789) 765170

*A riverside setting, pretty views and pleasant accommodation.*

The Arrow Mill straddles the River Arrow in a pretty position amongst 55 acres of green fields. A drive from the road is bordered by daffodils in the spring, and ducks and swans waddle around close to the mill pond. The hotel was once the flour mill and was working until the 1960s. It's stone built and still has a working wheel, which you can see through a window from the restaurant.

Beams, exposed stone walls and whitewashed brick are typical of the building. There are two bars, the pub-like Gun bar and the Miller's bar, with squashy comfortable seating. The Millstream restaurant has a menu with lots of steaks. One February guest found the food good apart from one meat dish, and the staff 'helpful in finding us a repair garage for a car problem and a hairdresser for my wife!'. Bedrooms are spacious with plain décor and some beams that add character; there are few fripperies.

- ◑ Open all year, exc 2 weeks at Xmas
- ⤴ Just outside Alcester on the A435 Evesham road, opposite Ragley Hall. Private car park
- ⇌ 3 single, 5 twin, 3 double, 6 family rooms, 1 suite; most with bathroom/WC, singles with shower/WC; TV, room service in all rooms; hair-dryer on request

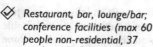 Restaurant, bar, lounge/bar;
conference facilities (max 60
people non-residential, 37
residential); fishing at hotel,
riding nearby; babysitting.
Wheelchair access to public
rooms only

● No dogs in public rooms

☐ Access, Amex, Diners, Visa

£ Single £60, single occupancy of
twin/double £65, twin/double
£72 to £84, suite £84, family
room £85 to £90; deposit
preferred. Sun L £11.50; alc D
£25; bar meals (room prices till
end 91). Special breaks available

## ASHBOURNE DERBYSHIRE                               MAP 4

# Callow Hall

MAPPLETON ROAD, ASHBOURNE, DERBYSHIRE DE6 2AA
TEL: ASHBOURNE (0335) 43403   FAX: (0335) 43624

*The Spencer family create a comfortable atmosphere and provide
very thoughtful service.*

Ashbourne, known as the 'Gateway to the Peak', is a busy market town
and yet after only about three minutes' drive you are in the peaceful
seclusion of Callow Hall. The building itself is a slightly forbidding,
turreted, grey stone Victorian hall which is owned and run by the
Spencer family. There's a reasonable-sized garden surrounding the
house, mainly neat lawns with some mature trees and shrubs, and plenty
of good walks nearby, with a stretch of trout fishing on Bentley Brook for
the less energetic.

The décor and atmosphere are surprisingly homely, given the grand
proportions of the rooms. A huge vase of flowers brightens the hall, large
rugs cover the stone floors both here and in the sitting-room, and the
atmosphere is welcoming. The sitting-room and bar are both cosy rooms
with open fires and an assortment of furnishings: a choice of studded
leather sofas and armchairs with a few tables and wooden chairs for those
keen on writing or playing cards.

The restaurant has a good reputation; Callow Hall began life more as a
restaurant-with-rooms than an hotel, and many diners are non-
residents. Now it feels much more like an hotel and is run in an extremely
efficient but unpretentious way. There's no snobbery about dress in the
evening and you're not made to feel awkward if you'd prefer a pint of beer
or a gin and tonic with your dinner rather than wine. David Spencer is the
chef and the food is delicious: perhaps moist salmon with a fine
cucumber sauce accompanied by celeriac, French beans, leeks and two
kinds of potatoes, all perfectly cooked. You can follow this either with a
choice from the trolley or from the excellent cheeseboard. The dining-
room is mainly red: red patterned wallpaper, a red carpet, red upholstered chairs and long red curtains.

The breakfast room and second dining-room, by contrast, is a very
light room with two large windows overlooking the hills. Light wooden

Habitat-style chairs and tables are simple but smart and the service is just as efficient as in the evening. The bedrooms are extremely comfortable with good modern bathrooms and high-quality, pretty fabrics. Some rooms are huge with fabulous views but a few of the smaller ones at the back can be a bit dark, light being somewhat obscured by a bank of earth. Children are welcomed – perhaps to reinforce this, the bedrooms are named after the Spencers' grandchildren.

○ *Open all year, exc 2 weeks Feb and 25, 26 Dec; restaurant closed Sun eve*

▣ *Follow the A515 Buxton road through Ashbourne and at the top of hill turn left at crossroads keeping the Bowling Green pub on your left. Take the first right into Mappleton Road. The hall entrance is on the right after the the humpbacked bridge. Private car park*

⇌ *3 twin, 7 double, 1 four-poster, 1 family room; all with bathroom/ WC, TV, room service, hair-dryer, trouser press, baby-listening*

◈ *2 dining-rooms, bar, 2 lounges, drying facilities; conference facilities (max 40 people non-residential, 12 residential); fishing at hotel, other sports nearby. Wheelchair access to restaurant and WC only*

⬤ *Dogs by arrangement only; no smoking in dining-rooms*

▭ *Access, Amex, Diners, Visa*

£ *Single occupancy of twin/double £63 to £78, twin/double £95 to £110, four-poster £115, family room £110; deposit required. Sun L £12 (other days by arrangement); set D £24; alc D £26. Special breaks available*

---

**ASHBURTON** DEVON　　　　　　　　　　　　　　　**MAP 8**

# Ashburton Hotel　　　

79 EAST STREET, ASHBURTON, DEVON TQ13 7AL
TEL: ASHBURTON (0364) 52784

*Small, refreshing hotel near the centre of town.*

The Ashburton, a Grade-II-listed Georgian town house, is small and neat. There is a little garden behind and a Victorian conservatory tacked on the side filled with plants and comfortable chairs. Most guests and the cat congregate in the small, artistically furnished lounge. Pictures are sparse but original and entertaining, the colours cool. Colour schemes stay refreshingly low-key in bedrooms as well, eschewing flowery and frilly fabrics, but rooms are cheerful, thanks to space, light and country antique furnishings.

Simple bathrooms are well arranged. Good smells waft upstairs during the early evening, so you may find you descend for a drink earlier than you'd planned. Chunky candles sit on the mantelpiece during dinner, a civilised affair in a handsome room. You can choose from several dishes at each stage on the à la carte menu which, with organic produce and talent, assures tasty food. Thin-sliced, port-cured pork salad to start, perhaps, then beef stroganoff and, to finish, hot chocolate and walnut brownie with fudge sauce. Just the job after a long walk on nearby Dartmoor.

◑ *Open all year, except Jan*

↗ *On the main road through Ashburton. Private car park*

🛏 *1 single, 1 twin, 4 double; most with bathroom/WC, 1 public bathroom; TV, room service in all rooms; hair-dryer on request*

◈ *Restaurant, lounge, drying room, library, conservatory, fishing,*

*golf, other sports nearby; babysitting*

⊖ *No wheelchair access; no dogs*

▭ *Access, Diners, Visa*

£ *Single £27, single occupancy of twin/double £33, twin/double £45 to £50; deposit required. Set D £18. Special breaks available*

# Holne Chase

**ASHBURTON, NEWTON ABBOT, DEVON TQ13 7NS**
**TEL: POUNDSGATE (036 43) 471   FAX: (036 43) 453**

*Family-run country-house hotel near Dartmoor National Park.*

'Holne Chase is romantic as well as peaceful', says the sign at the foot of the drive, but Hugh Bromage, who runs the hotel with his parents, is anxious to point out that children are also welcome. They certainly have space to run around and yet remain in view. The white gabled house is backed by woodland and looks out over four acres of lawns. Fishing is popular here. The hotel has over a mile stretch of the River Dart. A large fish pond is planned, but presumably for ornamental purposes only. Changes that have taken place during the last year include a new, business-hotel-style reception desk just beyond the entrance hall (convenient, perhaps, for its many business users, but jarring with an otherwise home-spun atmosphere), and a little alcove off the large, very comfortably furnished lounge is now lined with books, including useful guidebooks of the area.

Pleasing to look at are sepia photographs of Egypt in the dining-room, old cartoons in the lounge and watercolours in bedrooms. Darkwood bedroom furniture is balanced by soothing, co-ordinated pastel colour schemes. Rooms are a decent size and neatly arranged. Those at the front get uninterrupted views of the wooded countryside. New chef David Beazley's style of cooking is classical, with the likes of warm chicken liver salad in walnut dressing, roast poussin with reduced white wine vinegar, and lemon cheesecake. There are lots of half-bottles on the long wine list. You will remember your stay for a long time afterwards because guests are sent newsletters.

◑ Open all year

⤴ From Exeter take the second exit
(marked Ashburton) off the A38.
Follow signs to Two Bridges for 3
miles. Private car park

🛏 1 single, 4 twin, 9 double, 1
four-poster; most with bathroom/
WC, some with shower/WC; TV,
room service, hair-dryer, trouser
press, baby-listening; mini-bar in
some rooms

◈ Restaurant, bar, lounge, drying
room, library; conference
facilities (max 15 people
residential, 25 non-residential);

fishing, putting, croquet, cricket
facilities at hotel, other sports
nearby; babysitting. Wheelchair
access to hotel (ramp),
restaurant and WC (unisex), 1
ground-floor bedroom specially
equipped for the disabled

⊜ No smoking in restaurant

▭ Access, Amex, Diners, Visa

£ Single £59, single occupancy
twin/double £59, twin/double
£82 to £111; deposit preferred.
Set L £13.50, D £21.50. (Prices
till Apr 92.) Special breaks
available

---

**ASHFORD** DERBYSHIRE                                    **MAP 4**

# Riverside Country House

FENNEL STREET, ASHFORD, BAKEWELL, DERBYSHIRE
DE4 1QF
TEL: BAKEWELL (0629) 814275    FAX: (0629) 812873

*A very restful place with good food and gentle, efficient service.*

The L-shaped partially creeper-covered Georgian house is surrounded
by mature trees and gardens. Ashford is a very pretty village and the hotel
is in a romantic spot, slightly marred by the A6, which carries a fairly
constant whish of cars just the other side of the river, but once inside you
don't notice it.

The décor in the bedrooms is in good condition with variations of light
wallpaper and paintwork, and many have good views of the river. The
smallish, cosy bar/sitting-room is a very attractive room with some lovely
panelling and a heavy door reputed to be a cast-off from Chatsworth.
Look out for the particularly finely crafted set of chairs with cane backs.
The other sitting-room on the other side of the hall is quite a different
experience and strictly non-smoking. It has large low windows overlooking the garden and river with cushioned bench seats below them; it's
rather formal with Regency-style sofas and chairs, well spaced and a
couple of elegantly filled shelved alcoves. Drinks before dinner can be
taken in either room and then, depending on the number of guests and
visiting diners, you may be dining in the old kitchen – the old range has
been left but otherwise the patterned carpet and polished tables give no
hint of its previous usage – or the second dining-room. The Riverside
does a good Sunday lunch menu as well as dinner. A typical meal might
start with a crisp filo pastry basket filled with forest mushrooms, sautéed
in garlic with a cream sauce, continue with fresh local venison or the

chef's daily choice of fresh fish and seafood, and finish off with hot apple and spice crumble.

◐ *Open all year*

🔼 *2 miles north-west of Bakewell off the A6, in the centre of Ashford village. Private car park*

🛏 *6 twin, 6 double, 3 four-poster, 1 cottage (sleeps 5); most with bathroom/WC, some with shower/WC; TV, room service, hair-dryer, trouser press, baby-listening in all rooms*

◇ *2 dining-rooms, bar, lounge, drying room, conservatory; conference facilities (max 18 people residential, 20 non-residential); fishing, golf, other*

*sports nearby. Wheelchair access to hotel, restaurant and WC (disabled), 4 ground-floor bedrooms*

⊖ *No children under 12 (exc babies); dogs by arrangement only; smoking in bar only*

▭ *Access, Diners, Visa*

£ *Single occupancy of twin/double £79, twin/double £95, four-poster £105, cottage room £85; deposit required. Set L £14, D £29; alc L £18. Special breaks available*

---

## ASHTON KEYNES WILTSHIRE      MAP 6

# Two Cove House  

2 COVE HOUSE, ASHTON KEYNES, WILTSHIRE SN6 6NS
TEL: CIRENCESTER (0285) 861221

*Lovely seventeenth-century manor house in an appealing village near the source of the Thames.*

A narrow stream, which you may be interested to learn is the Thames, runs alongside the main road of this fetching little village, part of the Cotswold Water Park. Much more mature and imposing are the colourful gardens and mellow, pebble-dash house almost hidden behind One Cove House. A semi-detached with a difference: seventeenth-century for one thing, and having Civil War connections for another. Major and Mrs Hartland are happy to provide details of that as well as other points of interest about the house and sights within touring distance.

The Major's study, an attractively cluttered little room, has an alcove with a large map of the area plus stacks of tourist literature (and a television). Most of the rest of their handsomely furnished home, part of the Wolsey Lodge group, has been turned over to guests, and you will be made very welcome here. All around are large vases of flowers and polished sideboards and tables, plus family portraits. The bright green dining-room, the setting for traditional communal dinners (by arrangement only), looks out to the little back garden, a fine place to lounge on summer evenings. Bedrooms are brightly decorated, spacious, comfortable and very inexpensive. Not all have attached bathrooms, but several have washbasins (well-hidden in closets). A very English home, there is even a cat named Tiddles.

◗ Open all year, exc Xmas

⤴ Turn west off the A419 Swindon to Cirencester road towards Ashton Keynes. At the White Hart turn east and 100 yards on, turn left. Private car park

🛏 2 twin, 1 double, 1 family room; 2 with bathroom/WC, 1 with shower/WC; baby-listening in all rooms, hair-dryer on request

◈ Dining-room, 2 lounges, TV

room; fishing, riding, water sports nearby

⊖ No wheelchair access; no children at dinner; dogs by arrangement only

▭ None accepted

£ Single occupancy of twin/double £26 to £32, twin/double £36 to £46, family room £56; deposit required. Set D £15 (by arrangement only)

---

**ASPLEY GUISE** BEDFORDSHIRE                              **MAP 6**

# Moore Place

THE SQUARE, ASPLEY GUISE, MILTON KEYNES, BEDFORDSHIRE MK17 8DW
TEL: MILTON KEYNES (0908) 282000   FAX: (0908) 281888

*A fine Georgian house converted into a modern hotel catering to the business trade.*

Built by Francis Moore in 1786, Moore Place is the central feature of the village of Aspley Guise. The house overlooks the village square: mellow red brick, sparkling white porch and clipped lawn. Shame that the entrance to the hotel is round the back and the main entrance serves no other function rather than the purely decorative.

The approach from the car park takes in the modern additions to the house – a tail-like extension of new red brick linked to the house by a conservatory-style lobby containing the reception. The tail is wrapped around a contrived garden (floodlit at night) complete with waterfall. A second conservatory contains the restaurant draped with ample quantities of ruched pink and mint-green chintz. The food matches the surroundings: a little fussy and over-ambitious. The atmosphere is relaxed; single diners will feel comfortable and perfectly able to bring out the paper or novel to keep them company. Staff are professionally courteous rather than friendly but can seem more than unusually flustered. Bedrooms are business-neutral but all are a good size and have excellent facilities.

◗ Open all year

⤴ Leave the M1 at Junction 13 and follow signs to Aspley Guise. The hotel is in the centre of the village. Private car park

🛏 19 single, 6 twin, 28 double, 1 suite (some rooms in annexe); all with bathroom/WC, TV, room

service, hair-dryer, trouser press, baby-listening

◈ Restaurant, bar, 2 lounges, games room; conference facilities (max 50 people non-residential, 30 residential); golf, tennis, other sports nearby. Wheelchair access to hotel,

restaurant and WC (unisex), 4
ground-floor bedrooms

🌑 No dogs in public rooms

💳 Access, Amex, Diners, Visa

💷 Single £87, single occupancy of
twin/double £87, twin/double
£97, suite £150. Set L £17.50, D
£21; alc L, D £26. Special
breaks available

---

## ASTON CLINTON BUCKINGHAMSHIRE    MAP 6

# The Bell Inn

ASTON CLINTON, BUCKINGHAMSHIRE HP22 5HP
TEL: AYLESBURY (0296) 630252    FAX: (0296) 631250

*Famous for the food but it's well worth staying the night –*
*a sophisticated and stylish hotel-restaurant.*

The Bell Inn, shielded from the traffic on the A41 by a mature hedge, has
been run by the Harris family since 1940. The current Mr Harris, a
gentle and concerned host, confirms that the Bell is first and foremost a
place where people come to eat. Dining in the restaurant, scene of the
real action, takes place against the backdrop of murals running the length
of the curved inner wall, a vivid portrayal of a botanical paradise of
foodstuff, foliage and wildlife, in myriad shades of blue and green. The
restaurant is a substantial room but is divided by curtains and booths to
give diners a sense of privacy. For those either in a rush or on a tight
budget, the Bell does a 'one-plate lunch'.

One reader's report concentrates as much on the rooms as the food
and confirmed our impression that the hotel side of the business is as
worthy of attention as the culinary exploits: 'A memorable and wonderful
experience. The room was very large and comfortable and for someone
who judges the hotel by the appearance of the bathroom, I would give this
establishment a straight A.' Even for bathroom aficionados, the 'double
bath' in the 'Brewers House' is something a little special.

◑ Open all year

🔁 Aston Clinton is on the A41
between Tring and Aylesbury.
Private car park

🛏 10 twin, 3 double, 2 four-poster,
6 suites (most rooms in annexe);
all with bathroom/WC, TV, room
service, hair-dryer, mini-bar,
baby listening; trouser press in
suites; no tea/coffee-making
facilities in rooms

◈ Restaurant, bar, lounge, writing
room, smoking room; conference
facilities (max 300 people non-
residential); croquet at hotel,

other sports nearby; babysitting
by arrangement. Wheelchair
access to hotel and restaurant, 2
ground-floor bedrooms suitable
for the disabled

🌑 No dogs in public rooms; no
smoking in dining-room

💳 Access, Amex, Visa

💷 Single occupancy of twin/double
from £92, twin/double from
£107, four-poster from £133,
family room from £130, suite
from £189. Cooked B £5; set L,
D £17.50; alc L, D £35. Special
breaks available

# Tyrrells Ford

AVON, NR CHRISTCHURCH, HAMPSHIRE BH23 7BH
TEL: BRANSGORE (0425) 72646   FAX: (0425) 72262

*Affordable, friendly and modest country house in a rural location.*

Legend has it that on 1 August 1100 Sir Walter Tyrrell, after shooting
William Rufus, passed this way, crossing the River Avon on his escape to
the coast and France. The hotel, a large though unimposing two-storey
eighteenth-century cream-painted building, is set back from the road in
ten acres of unsculptured grounds. There are two large lawns running up
to the hotel, which is surrounded beyond by farmland and woodland.

Despite its high central hall with minstrels' gallery, its impressive
Y-shaped staircase opposite a huge hunting mural, and its panelled
dining-room with green button-back chairs (where you'll be competently served solid English fare – salmon, chicken, lamb and sole), the
furnishings and atmosphere are neither grand nor overpowering.

Owners Anna and Ivan Caplan make their presence felt. The latest
improvements are: a sparkling new ladies loo with pretty little floral
patterns and the stripping of the bar's panelling. Upstairs, most of the
light bedrooms command good views, the larger ones with bay windows,
some others a balcony; many have brass beds and reproduction
Renaissance-style dressing-tables.

- ◐ Open all year; restaurant closed
  Xmas night

- ◪ 4 miles north of Christchurch;
  take the B3347 from Ringwood
  or Christchurch. Private car park

- ⊨ 4 single, 4 twin, 8 double; most
  with bathroom/WC, some with
  shower/WC; TV, room service in
  all rooms; trouser press in 1
  room

- ◈ Restaurant, bar, lounge;
  conference facilities (max 40
  people non-residential, 16

residential); golf, riding, other
sports nearby. Wheelchair access
to restaurant only

- ⊖ No dogs

- ▭ Access, Visa

- £ Single £50 to £55, single
  occupancy of twin/double £60 to
  £65, twin/double £70 to £80;
  children under 12 in parents'
  room free; deposit required. Set L
  £12, D £17; alc D £25. Special
  breaks available

---

*I was a little surprised to see a notice at the foot of the stairs to the bedrooms*
*'Breakfast 8.30am: Saturday and Sunday 9am'. When I queried the*
*establishment's expectation that I would present myself for breakfast washed*
*and fully clothed at 9am on a holiday weekend I was told, 'we have to get*
*ready for Sunday lunches'. I made my point by coming down at 9.20.* On an
hotel in North Yorkshire

**AWRE** GLOUCESTERSHIRE                           MAP 6

# Old Vicarage

AWRE, NEWNHAM, GLOUCESTERSHIRE GL14 1EL
TEL: DEAN (0594) 510282

*A guesthouse that's slightly different; good home-produced meals served in a relaxed family atmosphere.*

Make sure you don't lose Nick and May Bull's handwritten directions on how to get to this lovely rambling Georgian house. The glasshouses give a clue to one of your hosts' activities – then you see the sheep, the ducks, the vineyard, the orchard, the herb garden. . . . If you thought self-sufficiency went out with *The Good Life*, come and see how close you can still get.

The Aga in the family kitchen is fuelled by coal from their own mine in the Forest of Dean, and the walls are hung with home-spun wool hangings and patchwork collages. Furniture is mostly antique, beds are high, washbasins have marble surrounds. The bath is freestanding. The atmosphere is relaxed and informal and family life is much in evidence.

Guests dine together on dishes such as home-produced lamb or Severn salmon (you can see the river from the window). Sauces often include home-made cider or wine, but the Bulls don't have a licence, so bring your own if you like a drink with your meal.

◗ Open all year, exc Xmas; restaurant open weekends only during school terms

🔌 1½ miles west of the A48 between Newnham and Blakeney, on the edge of the village of Awre. Private car park

🛏 1 twin, 3 double, 1 double with shower/WC, 2 public bathrooms; hair-dryer on request

◈ Dining-room, drawing-room, drying room; fishing, golf, other sports nearby

⊖ No wheelchair access; no children; no dogs; no smoking

▭ None accepted

£ Single occupancy of twin/double £20 to £22, twin/double £39 to £43; deposit required. Set D £13.50. Special breaks available

---

**AYLESBURY** BUCKINGHAMSHIRE                      MAP 6

# Hartwell House

OXFORD ROAD, AYLESBURY, BUCKINGHAMSHIRE HP17 8NL
TEL: AYLESBURY (0296) 747444   TELEX: 837108 HARTH G
FAX: (0296) 747450

*An impressive, elegant country house hotel. It's expensive but the prices are justified by the quality.*

Hartwell, a Grade-I-listed Jacobean and Georgian stately home, is one of three in the Historic House Hotels group, all of which easily merit inclusion in the Guide (see entries for Bodysgallen Hall and Middlethorpe Hall). Hartwell is perhaps the most lavish of the three, its sumptuousness summed up in corner rooms which are the size of city apartments. These have a superb double-aspect view out across the grounds which could take in the trout lake, the ha-ha, the obelisk, deconsecrated church or one of the statues or monuments that seem to strew the grounds and make an early-evening walk an essential part of any visit. Standards of service at Hartwell are enviably high.

The house was once home to the court of Louis XVIII in exile, and Lord Byron questioned why anyone would leave such a beautiful and peaceful spot, even if it was to ascend a throne.

The restaurant, named the Soane room after the architect of the Bank of England, is a restful, simple affair: creams, yellows and whites dominate. The rococo morning-room, drawing-room and library were all built around 1760 by the architect Henry Keene. The refurbishment of these grand rooms has concentrated on comfort and style, and the overall effect is one of stately but liveable luxury. The renovation and refurbishment took five years but the elevation of Hartwell to the top of the list as a choice for an indulgent weekend has been rather quicker.

○ Open all year

▣ On the A418 Oxford road, 2 miles west of Aylesbury. Private car park

🛏 4 single, 20 twin/double, 5 four-poster, 3 suites; all with bathroom/WC, TV, room service, hair-dryer, trouser press; no tea/coffee-making facilities in rooms

◈ 3 dining-rooms, bar, 4 drawing-rooms, library/study; conference facilities (max 30 residential and non-residential); fishing (lake), croquet, swimming pool and gym (from Oct 91) at hotel, other sports nearby. Wheelchair access to hotel (1 step), dining-rooms and WC (unisex), no ground-floor bedrooms but lift, 1 bedroom equipped for the disabled

● No children under 8; no dogs

▭ Access, Amex, Diners, Visa

£ Single £88, single occupancy of twin/double £105, twin/double £132, four-poster £175, suite £195; deposit required. Continental B £7.50, cooked B £10.50. Set L £19, D £32.50; alc L, D £45. Special breaks available

---

## BALSALL COMMON WEST MIDLANDS          MAP 6

# Haigs

KENILWORTH ROAD, BALSALL COMMON, NR COVENTRY, WEST MIDLANDS CV7 7EL
TEL: BERKSWELL (0676) 33004   FAX: (0676) 34572

*Friendly atmosphere and attentive service in this mid-price business hotel.*

Balsall Common stretches along the A452 and for those visiting the NEC, the hotel is well placed. It's run by Jean and John Cooper who have a regular business clientele. All available space at the front has been tarmacked to provide adequate parking, and the house itself extends back off the road with a small garden to the rear.

Rooms, including the single ones, are a good size, modern, with pale colours and all the basic gadgetry such as tea-making facilities, trouser press and shoe-cleaning extras. The public rooms are at the back of the hotel, with the dining-room overlooking the garden. Food is well presented, with strong flavours and some surprising dishes such as stuffed pigs' trotters. A fixed-price menu is good value and the service attentive. The bar is quiet and a comfortable spot for winding down after a day's business.

◐ Open all year, exc 24 Dec to 1 Jan

🔁 On the A452, 6 miles south of Junction 4 of the M6, 4 miles north of Kenilworth. Private car park

🛏 8 single, 5 twin; most with shower/WC, 1 public bathroom; TV, hair-dryer, trouser press in all rooms

◇ Restaurant, bar, lounge;

conference facilities (max 30 people non-residential); golf nearby. Wheelchair access to hotel (1 step) and restaurant, 2 ground-floor bedrooms

⊖ No children under 4; no dogs in public rooms

▭ Access, Visa

£ Single £27 to £49, twin £44 to £70; deposit required. Sun L £10; set D £15.50; alc D £22.50

## BANTHAM DEVON                                           MAP 8

# Sloop Inn

BANTHAM, NR KINGSBRIDGE, DEVON TQ7 3AJ
TEL: KINGSBRIDGE (0548) 560215/560489

*Simply furnished, cosy old pub close to a good beach and in a tiny, out-of-the-way village.*

Smugglers are implicated in the past life of this sixteenth-century inn; now it functions as an inexpensive holiday base. Three hundred yards over the sand-dunes is one of the best surfing beaches on the south coast.

The long, low, wiggly whitewashed inn with black trim is joined up to a string of thatched cottages, giving an initial false impression of its size. It is small. It is also very cosy and awash with boat-related paraphernalia. In keeping with the size and old character of the pub, bedrooms are small, cottagey, perhaps a mite poky. They are not expensive, though, and have television and tea-trays. Behind the pub, by the car park, are some modern cottages with self-catering facilities.

◐ Open all year, exc Jan (pub open all year)

🔁 From the A38, take the A381 to Totnes and Kingsbridge. From Kingsbridge, take Plymouth road

through Churchstow, at mini roundabout take Bantham road, follow for 2½ miles. Private car park

🛏 3 double, 2 family rooms; most

with bathroom/WC, I public
bathroom; TV, hair-dryer in all
rooms

 Restaurant, bar, lounge; laundry
facilities; fishing, water sports,
other sports nearby

 No wheelchair access

 None accepted

 Twin/double £21 to £25; deposit
required. Alc L £8 to £10, D £10
to £14

---

**BARNSTAPLE** DEVON                                    **MAP 8**

# Lynwood House

BISHOP'S TAWTON ROAD, BARNSTAPLE, DEVON EX32 9DZ
TEL: BARNSTAPLE (0271) 43695   FAX: (0271) 79340

*Down-to-earth, family-run restaurant with five bedrooms.
Caters well for business folk.*

Nobody can accuse John Roberts of not listening to his largely business
clientele. Indeed, when he decided to alter his well-established restaurant and add accommodation, he consulted local businessmen about
their ideal, user-friendly bedroom. Convenience, then, is the watchword
rather than atmosphere or beauty. Bedrooms in this sandy-brick Victorian house, overlooking the River Taw on the fringes of Barnstaple,
don't vary much. Here is what you'll find: twin beds with efficient
lighting, shelf space, two comfortable chairs (there is no lounge), low-key
colours (but frilly duvets), Teletext TVs, mirrors, built-in cupboards,
trouser presses that also handle skirts, home-made biscuits, proper
shoe-cleaning equipment, needle and cotton, a few stamps as well as
envelopes, and a large shower instead of a bath. (Light sleepers should
ask for 'Rumsdam', the quietest room.) Also on the first floor, and
another departure from most hotels, is the glitzy, black and pink
breakfast room, lined with padded benches and marble-topped café
tables, that also serves for small meetings.

The restaurant serves both business and local clientele with equal
attention. Everyone is warmly welcomed and shown to the small bar,
decorated in Victorian style with lamps and old photographs. Pot plants
and screens break up the large restaurant, set with polished wood tables.
John and sons Matthew and Christian run the restaurant; Ruth and
eldest son Adam are co-chefs. Good à la carte dinners make much of
local fish and are unfussy. Lemon sole mousse with lobster sauce,
scallops grilled in bacon, and orange bavarois are typical dishes.

 Open all year

From M5, take Junction 27 to
Barnstaple. At Barnstaple turn
left at Texas store and then turn
next right (follow Newport sign)
for 300 yards. Private car park

5 twin; all with shower/WC, TV,
room service, hair-dryer, trouser
press

Restaurant, bar; conference
facilities (max 100 people non-
residential); fishing, golf, other
sports nearby. Wheelchair access
to restaurant only

● No dogs; no smoking in public rooms

▭ Access, Visa

£ Single occupancy of twin £48, twin £68. Alc L, D £27; light meals

## BARROWFORD LANCASHIRE                                    MAP 4

# Oaklands House

CHURCH STREET, BARROWFORD, NELSON, LANCASHIRE BB9 6QU
TEL: NELSON (0282) 690655

*Comfortable, well-preserved Victorian house with an informal atmosphere.*

Nineteenth-century north country mill owners are easy to satirise, but it's hard to view the plutocrat who built this solid Victorian house as a villain. He felt no inhibitions about flaunting his 'brass' and the result is a legacy of intricately moulded ceilings, stained-glass and shallow archways, buttressed by fine Victorian furniture and fittings introduced by present owners Bob and Beryl Benson.

Despite the imposing scale, the style is informal with the Bensons dining with their guests from time to time. 'It's more of a family home than an hotel,' says Beryl. The four-course set dinners are traditional affairs often featuring English favourites such as smoked mackerel pâté, casseroled pork fillets and peach brûlée, followed by cheese and biscuits. Both bedrooms are spacious enough to accommodate solid Victorian furniture, complemented by appropriately dainty fabrics. Sloping lawns, a garden edged by tall trees, including two monkey puzzles, and an elegant fountain all add to the period grandeur.

◑ Open all year

⇗ Barrowford is 2 miles north-east of Nelson. Private car park

⇤ 2 twin; 1 public bathroom

◈ Dining-room, sitting-room; fishing, golf, other sports nearby

● No wheelchair access; no dogs; no smoking in bedrooms

▭ None accepted

£ Single occupancy of twin £20, twin £32; deposit required. Set D £12 (prices till end 91)

## BARWICK SOMERSET                                          MAP 9

# Little Barwick House

BARWICK, YEOVIL, SOMERSET BA22 9TD
TEL: YEOVIL (0935) 23902

*Personally run, urbane restaurant-with-rooms.*

Standing at the edge of a remote village and beneath tall beech, cypress and Scots pine trees, the white Georgian dower-house gives few clues, apart from some little signs directing you along country lanes, that it is anything other than a private home. The Colley welcome and pampering confirms the impression. A genial, civilised atmosphere prevails in this warmly furnished home, where modern prints and posters fit well into a mixture of old and antique furniture. For many guests the best thing about staying here is Veronica's cooking; for others it's the easy, unfussy but attractive style of bedrooms: warm but subtle hues, decorative touches and different art themes on the walls.

Christopher Colley serves drinks and canapés by the log-fire in the lounge and helps you decipher his scrawl on the shortish set menu of appealing choices. A high-ceilinged, warm, terracotta-coloured dining-room with oriental rugs on pine floors makes a pleasing setting for a dinner of, say, curried parsnip soup, salmon in butter, lime and dill, and old English trifle. 'When would you like breakfast?' makes a happy change from the usual 'Breakfast is at . . .'.

**◑** *Open all year, exc Xmas and New Year; restaurant open to residents only Sun eve*

**↗** *From Yeovil take the A37 Dorchester road. After 1 mile turn off left at the Red House pub; the house is ¼ mile on the left. Private car park*

**🛏** *2 twin, 4 double; most with bathroom/WC, some with shower/WC; TV in all rooms; hair-dryer, trouser press on request*

**◈** *Air-conditioned dining-room, 2*

*lounges; conference facilities (max 12 people non-residential); fishing, sailing, other sports nearby*

**⊖** *No wheelchair access; no dogs in public rooms; no smoking in dining-room*

**▭** *Access, Amex, Visa*

**£** *Single occupancy of twin/double £45, twin/double £56 to £70; deposit required. Set D £21; alc D £27 (prices till Mar 92). Special breaks available*

**BASLOW** DERBYSHIRE                                                **MAP 4**

# Cavendish Hotel

BASLOW, DERBYSHIRE DE4 1SP
TEL: BASLOW (0246) 582311   FAX: (0246) 582312

*A comfortable hotel with an unstuffy atmosphere but inconsistent service.*

History tells that there's been an inn here for centuries and until the 1970s it was known as the Peacock (you'll find a pictorial history hanging in the ground-floor corridor). It was then part of the Duke of Devonshire's estate and it was rebuilt as the Cavendish, sensitively preserving its original features. It has been kept in pristine condition and is a comfortable, tastefully decorated hotel. Due to the connections with the Devonshire estate, guests are allowed access to Chatsworth House across the fields which make a lovely 15-minute walk from the hotel. Part of the hotel fronts the main road but the bedroom and public rooms don't suffer from traffic noise as they all overlook the park. Most of the bedrooms both in the main part of the hotel and the newer Mitford wing are decorated and furnished to a very high standard with plenty of luxury extras, although one reader mentioned a few scruffy touches in one of the standard rooms and another thought they were too cluttered.

A recent addition to the public areas is the Garden Room – a casually smart conservatory room with simple tables and wicker chairs – the walls are of natural brick and the glass roof is softened by muslin drapes; it is very popular both with residents and passers-by. The comings and goings give the hotel an unstuffy and relaxed atmosphere even though the style of the surroundings is smart and civilised. The hall is light and immediately welcoming with generous informal flower arrangements. Pale blue and yellow are the predominant colours in the sitting-room and bar.

One reader felt that in this standard of hotel the finer points of etiquette should be observed – drinks carried in from the lounge, finger bowls supplied with the asparagus, and the wine topped up without being asked, for example, and that new customers should be pampered as much as regulars.

◑ *Open all year*

🚗 *9 miles west of Chesterfield on the A619. Private car park*

🛏 *13 twin, 9 double, 1 four-poster, 1 suite (air-conditioned); all with bathroom/WC, TV, room service, hair-dryer, mini-bar, baby-listening; binoculars in some rooms*

◈ *2 restaurants, bar, lounge; conference facilities (max 16 people residential); fishing at hotel, golf, other sports nearby*

⊖ *No wheelchair access; no dogs*

▭ *Access, Amex, Diners, Visa*

£ *Single occupancy of twin/double £70, twin/double £85, four-poster £95. Continental B £4.50, cooked B £9; set L, D £22.50; alc L, D £35 (prices till Mar 92). Special breaks available*

---

# Fischer's – Baslow Hall

CALVER ROAD, BASLOW, DERBYSHIRE DE4 1RR
TEL: BASLOW (0246) 583259

*A very comfortable place to stay with the assurance of a delicious dinner.*

The hall, built at the beginning of the century from mellow stone, isn't a beautiful house, but it has style. Set up above the main road, and approached by a curving drive through the trees, it stands in stately superiority over its near neighbours. There's a fountain in front of the house and the old entrance must have been quite grand. You now park and enter the house round the back. The Fischers had a number of plans when they bought the house a few years ago; some were dashed by the fire that swept through the place just before they were about to open for business. Miraculously, their fine furniture was still in store so they didn't lose everything.

The hotel finally opened in October 1989 and was worth waiting for. A restaurant-with-rooms is how it is billed and both aspects are exceptional. The spacious and comfortable bedrooms have been created with great care: each one is different, decorated with smart wallpapers and stylish fabrics, large beds and chic bathrooms. They are all named after places of local interest. Haddon is particularly special with a vast Victorian bath complete with huge shower-head. Max Fischer has had a passion for collecting furniture from a young age and the rooms are full of lovely pieces.

Downstairs, the original hall has become the sitting-room – a slightly odd shape and attractive with mullioned windows and cushioned window-seats matching the upholstered armchairs; the half-panelled walls and a large open fireplace help make the room cosy as well as chic. The two dining-rooms, one used for overspill or private functions, are smart without being austere, decorated with confidence in definite colour schemes. The quality of the food draws a faithful clientele: you might start with rösti with caviare and smoked salmon; gnocchi with spinach and tomato slipped in between this and a main course of roast monkfish, and lemon choux and a choice of desserts or cheese to follow.

- ◑ Open all year, exc 25, 26 Dec; restaurant closed Sun evenings
- ⤴ Follow the A623 through Baslow; the hotel is the last building on the right as you leave the village towards Calver. Private car park
- 🛏 I twin, 5 double; all with bathroom/WC, TV, room service, baby-listening; hair-dryer on request; no tea/coffee-making facilities in rooms
- ◈ 3 dining-rooms, I lounge; conference facilities (max 14 people non-residential); fishing, golf, other sports nearby. Wheelchair access to dining-rooms and WC (unisex) only
- ⊖ No children under 10; no dogs; no smoking in dining-rooms
- ▭ Access, Amex, Visa
- £ Single occupancy of twin/double £78, twin/double £88 to £108. Set L £18.50, D £31.50

---

## BASSENTHWAITE LAKE CUMBRIA      MAP 3

# Link House

BASSENTHWAITE LAKE, COCKERMOUTH, CUMBRIA CA13 9YD
TEL: BASSENTHWAITE LAKE (076 87) 76291

*Comfortable accommodation with flair.*

The cheerful, chubby Buddha who guards the landing sets the tone nicely. Inside May and Brian Smith's creamy white villa you'll find an idiosyncratic collection of antique curios (from toby jugs to embroidered samplers) that make this small hotel really feel like home. The cosy lounge is inviting with its log fire, framed tapestries, Tosca poster and a delightful collection of brass and china elephants, and the bright conservatory has rattan and wicker chairs with pastel-coloured cushions, wall-mounted plates and a profusion of plants – a stylish setting for afternoon tea. There are more personal bits and pieces in the dining-room where tables are set with Wedgwood china and Cumbria crystal goblets. A typical menu might offer pâté, carrot and lentil soup, pork chop cooked on stuffing with apple and onion rings, hot gingerbread with rum butter, and cheese. The bread is home-made.

The bedrooms have tasteful individual décor and *en suite* facilities. Upstairs rooms have spectacularly high ceilings and enchanting views of the lake and the peak of Skiddaw.

◐ Closed Dec, Jan

↗ On the A66 from Keswick to Cockermouth; turn right for Dubwath and then bear left. Private car park

🛏 2 single, 3 twin, 3 double; 1 with bathroom/WC, 2 public bathrooms; TV in all rooms

◈ 2 dining-rooms, bar, lounge, conservatory; fishing, golf, other

sports nearby

⊖ No wheelchair access; no children under 7; no dogs; no smoking in dining-room

▭ None accepted

£ Single £21 to £24, single occupancy of twin/double £28 to £31, twin/double £41 to £47; deposit required. Set D £12 (7pm). Special breaks available

---

# Pheasant Inn

**BASSENTHWAITE LAKE, NR COCKERMOUTH, CUMBRIA CA13 9YE**
**TEL: BASSENTHWAITE LAKE (076 87) 76234**

*A lovely genuine country pub with comfortable bedrooms.*

Breweries spend millions in trying to recreate the ambience of old English country pubs. The Pheasant is the real thing, situated in a quiet spot a couple of minutes from the A66. Originally a farm, the place was blessed with spring water that made good beer and metamorphosed into an inn where tempting victuals have been served since 1826. Even the most abstemious will feel tipsy as they encounter off-white walls and uneven floors that veer from the straight and narrow.

Public rooms are interesting with lots of knick-knacks – including a couple of stuffed pheasants, samplers and lots of brass and copper, and comfy chairs intended to be sat in rather than looked at. The oak-beamed dining-room has a display of Wedgwood plates and pheasant tapestries, while the lovely old low-ceilinged bar is washed in a nicotine-lacquer tint that predates the era of government health warnings and is stacked with hunting memorabilia. Melamine furniture has been banished from the bedrooms, which are bright and individual with pine and other good-quality furnishings. Room six is particularly splendid, as occupants get to sleep in a half-tester.

The food is mostly traditional, with extensive use of local produce and lots of choice in both the à la carte and set menus. Traditional roasts replace the à la carte menu on Sundays. There's also a good range of bar snacks.

◑ Open all year, exc 24 and 25 Dec

🔁 The inn is just off the A66, 7 miles west of Keswick on the west side of Bassenthwaite Lake. Private car park

🛏 4 single, 6 twin, 7 double, 3 rooms in bungalow annexe; most with bathroom/WC, 2 with shower/WC; room service, hair-dryer in all rooms; tea/coffee-making facilities in bungalow rooms; baby-listening on request

⟡ Dining-room, 3 lounges, drying room. Wheelchair access to hotel (no steps), restaurant and WC (M,F), 3 ground-floor bedrooms in bungalow annexe, I specially equipped for the disabled

⊖ No dogs in bedrooms; no smoking in dining-room, one lounge non-smoking

▭ None accepted

£ Single £48, single occupancy of twin/double £55, twin/double £61. Set L £10.50, D £23; alc L £12. Special breaks available

# Riggs Cottage     ℒ ❀

ROUTENBECK, BASSENTHWAITE LAKE, COCKERMOUTH, CUMBRIA
CA13 9YN
TEL: BASSENTHWAITE LAKE (076 87) 76580

*Great-value hillside guesthouse in a quieter part of the Lake District.*

You pitch in with the other guests at friendly Riggs Cottage, sharing both the bathroom and the dining-table. The advantages outweigh the draw-backs. The setting is bucolic, with woods and a nearly wild garden surrounding the small white seventeenth-century pebbledash cottage.

Inside, stone walls, beams, pine, cheerful colours and bird-oriented décor are the order of the day. Hazel Wilkinson is keen on self-sufficiency, so vegetables and herbs come from the garden, and trout from her pond or stream sometimes find their way on to the menu. Otherwise, a typical dinner, served at 6.30pm, might offer watercress soup, roast lamb with minted peas, new and roast potatoes and cour-gettes, then strawberry gateau or home-made ice-cream followed by cheese and biscuits. The aroma of new-baked bread wafts around the house.

Bedrooms are feminine and cosy with pretty fabrics. A tiny single is let only to children. Homesick Scots might find haggis on the breakfast menu – a rarity in these parts. Duck eggs also regularly appear.

◑ Closed Dec, Jan

⤴ From the A66 Keswick to Cockermouth road, follow signs to Wythop Mill. Look for the 'Riggs Cottage' sign on the right, ¾ mile after Pheasant Inn, cottage on left-hand side. Private car park

🛏 1 double, 1 family room (with shower/WC); 1 public bathroom

◈ Dining-room/lounge; fishing, water sports, other sports nearby

⊖ No wheelchair access; no children under 5; no dogs; no smoking

▭ None accepted

£ Single occupancy of twin/double £24 to £30, twin/double £34 to £40, family room £43 to £50; deposit required. Set D £10

## BATH AVON

# Cheriton House

9 UPPER OLDFIELD PARK, BATH, AVON BA2 3JX
TEL: BATH (0225) 429862

*Reliable, immaculate and welcoming bed and breakfast in residential outskirts. Great views of the city.*

Among Bath's many good bed and breakfasts are a few that stand out not so much for one particular attribute, but for being satisfyingly well rounded. Such is Cheriton House, efficiently run by Mike and Jo Babbage, who will greet you cheerfully and show you around. Their well-judged furnishings set off the house's late-Victorian character perfectly, whether in the lounge, with its carved walnut sideboard and Paisley-covered easy chairs, or in the simply furnished dining-room, done out in autumn colours, which looks out on to the well-kept back garden.

Old stripped pine as well as a little new pine furniture feature in the neat bedrooms. Room three, a greeny-grey twin, has only a shower and toilet, but its fireplace, sofa and *trompe-l'oeil* egg and dart border give it real pizazz. Room eight on the top floor has a slanted roof, so is less roomy, but you can see at least five of Bath's famous crescents from its window. Views of Bath come with room one on the ground floor, too.

◑ Open all year, exc Xmas and New Year

⤴ South of Bath, ½ mile up the A367 Wells Road. Upper Oldfield Park is first turning on right. Private car park

🛏 3 twin, 6 double; most with shower/WC, rest with bathroom/WC; TV, room service, hair-dryer in all rooms

◈ Dining-room, lounge; golf, tennis, other sports nearby

⊖ No wheelchair access; children at discretion of management only; no dogs

▭ Access, Visa

£ Single occupancy of twin/double £32 to £38, twin/double £45 to £56; deposit required

# Haydon House

**9 BLOOMFIELD PARK, BATH BA2 2BY**
**TEL: BATH (0225) 427351/444919  FAX: (0225) 469020**

*Prettily furnished, well-kept bed and breakfast in quiet suburbs.*

An octagonal white dovecote near the gate distinguishes this Edwardian house from the mostly private homes around it. A little entrance porch crammed with orchids tells you that at least one member of the household has green fingers and thumbs. Magdalene Ashman's way with plants and flowers is apparent throughout this neat and dapper home, and in springtime the split-level suntrap behind it brims with all the colours of the rainbow. Her light and breezy way with furnishings is also easy on the eyes.

This is a home to savour for comfort, too, whether you want to curl up with a newspaper in the pale pink lounge, watch television in the little study, or settle into your bedroom where a decanter of sherry awaits. Brightly patterned bedspreads, antiques (including a brass bed or two), lots of decorative touches and well-equipped, often colour co-ordinated/bath and shower-rooms are reasons enough to stay in your room. No dinners are served but guests get to know each other around the communal breakfast table. (If you are grumpy in the morning, Gordon will happily serve you breakfast in your room.)

- ◑ Open all year
- ⤢ From Bath centre follow signs for the A367 Exeter road and up Wells Road for ½ mile. The A367 turns right into a shopping area with the Bear pub on the right. At the end of a short dual carriageway, fork right into Bloomfield Road and second right into Bloomfield Park. On-street parking
- 🛏 1 twin, 3 double; most with shower/WC, 1 double with bathroom/WC; TV, trouser press in all rooms
- ◈ Dining-room, lounge, study; golf, tennis, other sports nearby
- ⊖ No wheelchair access; children by arrangement; no dogs; no smoking
- ▭ Access, Visa
- 💷 Single occupancy of twin/double £35 to £45, twin/double £50 to £60; deposit required. Special breaks available

# Holly Lodge

**8 UPPER OLDFIELD PARK, BATH, AVON BA2 3JZ**
**TEL: BATH (0225) 424042  FAX: (0225) 481138**

*Style, comfort and a warm welcome at a fair price.*

Having rescued the house from dereliction by sheer hard graft (a photo-album in the lounge tells the story), Carrolle Sellick and her partner

George Hall are determined to make sure everything at Holly Lodge is always 'just so'.

You can walk from the neat Victorian house down to the city centre in less than fifteen minutes, but you'll probably want to take the bus back – the steep hill would be good training for aspiring Sherpas! The views from the grounds are stunning, and the location peaceful.

Bedrooms are appealingly furnished, with fresh décor, co-ordinating curtains and bedding in modish patterns, and cosy touches like plump cushions, pot-pourri and resident soft toys. Some are distinctly feminine. Bath and shower rooms are modern and spotless with a subtle Art Deco theme. The lounge is comfortable and restful with carefully matched fabrics, snug sofas and an impressive chandelier. Personal memorabilia includes family photos, a collection of toby jugs, and a large elephant lamp.

The breakfast room is bright and airy with green and yellow décor, garden-style furniture and terrific views. And the food is just as good – a wide choice of cereals and fruit, an excellent traditional grill or a health-conscious fruit platter, limitless coffee or a range of designer teas and wonderful home-baked croissants.

◐ Open all year

⤢ ½ mile south-west of Bath city centre, off the A367 Wells Road. Private car park

🛏 1 single, 2 twin, 3 double; most with bathroom/WC, some with shower/WC; TV, hair-dryer, trouser press, baby-listening in all rooms

◈ Breakfast room, lounge; golf, tennis, other sports nearby; babysitting

⊖ No wheelchair access; no dogs; no smoking

▭ Access, Amex, Diners, Visa

£ Single £45, single occupancy of twin/double £55, twin/double £65; deposit required

# Paradise House

86-88 HOLLOWAY, BATH, AVON BA2 4PX
TEL: BATH (0225) 317723   FAX: (0225) 482005

*A handsome Georgian home and a good, mid-range B&B, not far from the town centre.*

Bath is beautiful, courtesy of its Georgian architects, and staying in an eighteenth-century house is a suitable way to round out a twentieth-century visit here. Paradise House, a fair trot up a steep hill, makes a good choice because of its out-of-the-way location, well-kept and smart furnishings and three-quarters of an acre of landscaped, pergola-dotted grounds. Excellent panoramic views take in the whole city.

You should be comfortable in the cheerfully decorated bedrooms, most of which have private bathrooms, and all of which are well equipped. Lots of advice on sightseeing and touring is provided in leaflet form and by David Cutting himself, but you are welcome to linger in his home all day should you like a change of pace. The lounge is welcoming, especially when a chill wind blows outside and the fire is lit. Come dinner time, though, you will have to tear yourself away: only breakfast is served. Parking isn't straightforward: double-yellow lines and, usually, other cars cover most of this cul-de-sac but a few garages are available within walking distance.

◑ *Open all year, exc Xmas week*

▨ *Follow A36 Bristol Road into Bath. Take A367 Exeter Road up hill. Holloway is third turning on left. Then take left fork downhill into cul-de-sac. On-street parking*

🛏 *4 twin, 4 double, 1 family room; most with bathroom/WC, some with shower/WC; TV, room service, hair-dryer in all rooms*

◈ *Dining-room, lounge; golf, fishing, other sports nearby*

⊖ *No wheelchair access; no children under 7; no dogs*

▭ *Access, Amex, Visa*

£ *Single occupancy of twin/double £42 to £58, twin/double £49 to £65, family room (3 people) £71 to £75; deposit required. Special breaks available*

---

# The Royal Crescent

---

16 ROYAL CRESCENT, BATH, AVON BA1 2LS
TEL: BATH (0225) 319090   TELEX: 444251 ROCRES G
FAX: (0225) 339401

*An aristocratic and fashionable place to indulge yourself, with the noisier parts of the city out of earshot.*

When in Bath, if finances permit, you may as well get into the swing of things and pamper yourself a bit. The entrance to the Royal Crescent Hotel isn't obvious (if it were, it would disrupt the sweep of this magnificent curving Georgian terrace). There is a degree of hush, but then this is one place still suited to high society. Afternoon tea in the formal drawing-room is an occasion to dress up for but you may be pleasantly surprised by the unstuffy atmosphere.

The lift is novel, being lined with spines of books. Less ingenuity has been applied to bedrooms, named after famous Bath inhabitants, but they've been kitted out in appropriately opulent style and do justice to the ceiling mouldings and stately dimensions. No two are alike, either. Some aren't even in the Royal Crescent. Stand (or sit) in the large patch of pretty garden behind the main hotel and you soon realise this is not the exclusive little residence you may have taken it for. As well as two houses of the Crescent, the hotel comprises the Dower House, large in its own right, and the Pavilion. George IV stayed in the Dower House when he was Prince Regent and regal portraits feature in the rather dark but comfortable dining-room where delicacies are commonplace on the menu.

◑ Open all year

↗ Close to Bath town centre, on the Royal Crescent. Private car park and on-street parking

🛏 4 single, 11 twin, 11 double, 5 four-poster, 13 suites; all with bathroom/WC (some suites with Jacuzzi), TV, room service, hair-dryer, trouser press, baby-listening; tea/coffee-making facilities on request

◈ Restaurant, bar, 3 lounges, conservatory; conference facilities (max 50 people residential and non-residential); croquet, heated plunge pool at hotel, golf, tennis, other sports nearby; babysitting. Wheelchair access to hotel (1 step) and restaurant, 4 ground-floor bedrooms, 1 specially equipped for the disabled

⊖ No children under 7 at dinner; no dogs

▭ Access, Amex, Diners, Visa

£ Single £90, twin/double £118 to £175, four-poster £140 to £175, suite £240 to £340; deposit required. Continental breakfast £8, cooked £10; set L £17, £21; alc L, D from £37 (prices till Apr 92). Special breaks available

---

# Sydney Gardens

---

SYDNEY ROAD, BATH, AVON BA2 6NT
TEL: BATH (0225) 464818/445362

*Non-smoking but otherwise easy-going B&B a short walk from the centre. Memorable for its well-furnished bedrooms and chummy hosts.*

Yet more evidence that Bath has as many fine places to stay at as to visit, Sydney Gardens has the advantage of being away from the bustle but within walking distance of main sights. A train runs past every so often, but the beautifully tended lawn, rockery and flower-beds that slope down from Diane and Stanley Smithson's tall Victorian house abut the large, tree-filled and peaceful Sydney Gardens.

Stanley Smithson's paintings and painted constructions (often clocks) hang about the cosily furnished downstairs rooms, ever-changing as they're bought by guests and replaced with new ones. The hospitality here is warm and bedrooms, though continually upgraded, become old friends to returning guests who cherish their individual, upbeat style. Pretty fabrics and lovely old furniture are common to all, as are firm mattresses and neat, traditional bathrooms. Patterns tend to be on the walls and ceilings rather than on the duvets. In room five (in the attic) you're enveloped by what seems like a blue and white engraving – a rather French room, this, with striped curtains and a chaise-longue. For breakfast there is fresh orange juice and home-made marmalade. 'Hosts charming and welcoming and the breakfast absolutely delicious,' one reader commented.

◑ Open all year, exc Xmas and 1 to 17 Jan

↗ On the A36 ring road in Bath. Private car park

✏ 3 twin, 3 double, all with bathroom/WC, TV, hair-dryer

◈ Breakfast room, lounge; tennis nearby

⊖ No wheelchair access; no children under 4; no dogs in

public rooms; no smoking

▭ Access, Visa

£ Single occupancy of twin/double £50 to £63, twin/double £59 to £69; deposit required. Special breaks available

**BATHFORD** AVON                                              **MAP 9**

# Eagle House

23 CHURCH STREET, BATHFORD, NR BATH, AVON BA1 7RS
TEL: BATH (0225) 859946

*Unpompous bed and breakfast, off the tourist beat yet within easy reach of Bath.*

Although Bath has lots of good, even quiet, places to stay, Bathford has out-of-the-way appeal and is pretty to boot. It also has Eagle House, the work of Georgian architect John Wood the Elder. A large stone wall separates the stately mansion from the narrow country lane that leads up to it past a few shops; only a small engraved stone sign tells you that you've arrived. John and Rosamund Napier have done the hotel interior proud, with antiques, oil portraits and aristocratic knick-knacks. The large drawing-room, white-carpeted and blessed with a high moulded ceiling and enormous columned and arched windows, is not in the least formal, perhaps because by the time you encounter it you'll already have tuned in to the casual style of the house.

The dining-room looks over one-and-a-half acres of garden and down to the town. So do all the bedrooms, which are good-sized and full of character. Some have more than one floor level: one has a platform bed; another has a bath on a dais. Each is named after the tree it faces. Frills are minimal, televisions quaint. Prices are fair, but note that cooked breakfast costs extra. Two rooms in a new but matching garden cottage have similar facilities and cost the same as those in the main building. For dinner you have a choice of two nearby pubs. Or Bath, of course.

◑ Open all year, exc 23 Dec to 3 Jan

⤴ Leave the A4 ¼ mile east of Batheaston on the A363 to Bradford-on-Avon. Stay only 150 yards on the A363, then fork left up Bathford Hill. After 300 yards turn first right into Church Street. Eagle House is 200 yards along on the right. Private car park

✏ 1 single, 2 twin, 2 double, 1 family room; 2 cottage rooms; all with bathroom/WC, TV, hair-dryer, baby-listening

◈ Breakfast room, lounge, drying room; conference facilities (max 12 people residential); croquet at hotel, other sports nearby

⊖ No wheelchair access; dogs discouraged in public rooms

▭ None accepted

£ Single £29 to £37, twin/double

£42 to £59, family room £50 to £59, suite £69 to £78, cottage room £42 to £59. Cooked B £2.50. Special breaks available

# The Orchard

80 HIGH STREET, BATHFORD, NR BATH, AVON BA1 7TG
TEL: BATH (0225) 858765

*Charming, peacefully sited guesthouse three miles from Bath. An easy-going place.*

A hundred yards up from the village shops, behind wrought-iron gates and surrounded by one and a half acres of beautiful quiet gardens, is where you'll find this listed Georgian house. Though they are seasoned hosts, John and Olga London are still delighted by the arrival of each new guest. Equally, you can easily appreciate the virtues of their carefully decorated home and unwind here more easily than you might in Bath.

Period antiques set the style; games and ornaments add homeliness. Elegantly proportioned downstairs rooms have cosy nooks, fires on cool evenings and views over the gardens. Much work has gone into each bedroom, all differently furnished and decorated. There are few concessions to convenience when it comes to breakfast (the only meal available): live yoghurt, proper orange juice and butter without the wrappings.

◑ Closed Nov to Feb

↗ Take the A4 to Bathford, go under bridge, and turn left up the hill at the Crown pub. The Orchard is 150 yards beyond the pub on the right-hand side. Private car park

🛏 2 twin, 2 double; all with bathroom/WC, TV; no tea/coffee-making facilities in rooms

◈ Breakfast room, lounge; tennis, riding, other sports nearby

⊖ No wheelchair access; no children under 11; no dogs; no smoking in bedrooms

▭ None accepted

£ Twin/double £48 to £60; deposit required

---

*Pure* Fawlty Towers, *from the manager who, on our arrival from a delayed flight from Germany, informed us that the last evening meal was in ten minutes and, later, that the roast beef we were eating was 'the best I have had in weeks and I hope there's some left for my supper', to the Italian Manuel. He was absolutely brilliant! One coffee, one tea became three orange juices. Scrambled egg was magically boiled. 'You sitta here for breakfast. Keepa same table for alla meals.' One couple ventured to sit near the window for breakfast and were promptly removed by a bowing waiter. 'Dat izza not your place – here iz your table.' On an hotel in Oxford*

# Little Hemingfold Farmhouse

TELHAM, BATTLE, EAST SUSSEX TN33 0TT
TEL: BATTLE (042 46) 4338

*A homely retreat in an idyllic position.*

An American correspondent who runs a small travel club claims Little
Hemingfold as the most enjoyable place she's stayed at in England
during the eight years she's been organising trips, and 'all five of my
fellow travellers continue to wax poetic about it'. She found the sur
roundings bucolic, the owners Peter and Allison Slater 'charming,
delightful people who treated us immediately as family, the accommodation roomy yet very cosy and the décor lovely'.

A half-mile-long rutted track takes you down, down and far away from
Hastings' suburbs to a picturesque and thoroughly unspoilt spot: a big
lake – on which you can fish for trout – an upturned rowing boat by its
shore, surrounded by gentle meadow and woodland, 40 acres of which
belongs to the farm. Just 30 yards from the water's edge stands a pinky-
cream-coloured development, a Victorian building with dripping eaves
adjoining the coach-house, an older cottage with little dormer windows.
It's surprisingly spacious inside. A big, light sitting-room, stocked with
books and games useful for rainy days, overlooks the lake. Past the pine
bar with rush matting on the floor, go through a smaller sitting-room to
the plainly furnished dining-room; you'll be seated communally unless
you say you want to eat alone. Expect fresh produce, decent wine and
some choice at every course. Four of the 13 bedrooms are in the main
building, the rest behind bright red doors in the coach-house annexe,
reached via a small inner courtyard with a goldfish pond and rose
pergolas. Most of the bedrooms here have quaint woodburning stoves.
Some of the furniture, a mixture of country pine and painted wood, can
verge on the makeshift, but the rooms are cheerful.

**●** Open all year

**⤢** 1 ½ miles south of Battle on the
A2100 look for road sign
indicating bend on left-hand side
of the road. This sign is at the
top of the farm lane. Private car
park

**⇌** 4 twin, 7 double, 1 four-poster, 1
family room (most rooms in
coach-house); most with
bathroom/WC, 2 public
bathrooms; TV, baby-listening in
all rooms; hair-dryer on request

**⬦** Dining-room, bar, 2 lounges,
drying room; conference facilities
(max 20 people non-residential,
13 residential); fishing, tennis,
boating, boules at hotel, other
sports nearby

**⊖** No wheelchair access; no dogs in
public rooms and in some
bedrooms only

**▭** Access, Visa

**£** Single occupancy of twin/double
£30 to £50, twin/double £60 to
£70, four-poster £60 to £70,

family room £90 to £105 (3
beds); deposit required. Set D

£18 (7.30pm). Special breaks
available

---

# Powdermills

---

POWDERMILL LANE, BATTLE, EAST SUSSEX TN33 0SP
TEL: BATTLE (042 46) 5511   FAX: (042 46) 4540

*An individual country house with elegant furniture, stylish
conversions and large grounds, but not at all awkwardly formal.*

Many features make this an unusual place. It used to be part of the Battle
Abbey estate and, in the eighteenth century, was the centre of a thriving
gunpowder industry during which time the Duke of Wellington came to
inspect it. Its 50 acres of farmland and woods are decorated with ponds,
statues and columns, and a gazebo, and serve as home to Soay sheep
('rare and primitive,' says the brochure), wildfowl, and carp in a seven-
acre lake. Despite all this, the bumpy drive and building works gave it a
less than country-house feel outside.

The Cowplands are antique dealers and they've furnished their white
Georgian manor interestingly and lavishly; some rooms, such as the
drawing-room, and bedrooms in the main building, have a traditional
Georgian feel and fine antiques. Some three years ago, a music room was
added to one side of the main house, with grand piano and harp, and an
accommodation wing where rooms have Georgian-styled windows,
white Venetian blinds, antique and cane furniture, and decadent beige or
black marble-styled bathrooms.

In November 1990, a second extension was completed to house a large
marble-floored restaurant, the Orangery, its french windows opening on
to a terrace at the side of the building overlooking the hotel's swimming
pool. The hotel has managed to bag chef Paul Webbe, formerly of the
Vieille Auberge in Battle, a *Good Food Guide* recommended restaurant
still under his direction that has been praised for direct and flavoursome
food. The menu offers an affordable set three-course menu (and
vegetarian alternative) and a considerably pricier à la carte selection.

◑ Open all year; restaurant closed
Sun eve

↗ Centrally located in Battle.
Powdermill Lane leads off the
A21 opposite Battle railway
station. Private car park

🛏 2 single, 7 twin, 4 double, 1
four-poster, 1 family room, 1
suite; all with bathroom/WC, TV,
room service, trouser press,
baby-listening; mini-bar and hair-

dryer in some rooms; no tea/
coffee-making facilities in rooms

◈ 2 restaurants, bar, lounge,
library; conference facilities (max
80 non-residential); fishing,
tennis, croquet, unheated
outdoor pool (in season) at hotel,
other sports nearby. Wheelchair
access to restaurant and WC
(unisex) only

⊖ No children in restaurant in eve

▦ Access, Visa

£ Single £40, single occupancy of twin/double £45, twin/double £55, four-poster £65, family

room £75, suite £80; deposit required. Set L £13, D £14.50; alc D £24. Special breaks available

---

**BEAMINSTER** DORSET　　　　　　　　　　　　　　　**MAP 9**

# The Bridge House

PROUT BRIDGE, BEAMINSTER, DORSET DT8 3AY
TEL: BEAMINSTER (0308) 862200

*Good food in relaxed, countrified surroundings.*

A priest lived in some part of this warm stone house in the thirteenth century, and in one room is his 'hole'. You'll find some endearing quirk or other in all of the bedrooms in the main house, but no shortage of modern comforts, good carpets and home-made shortbread. Chef/proprietor Peter Pinkster's jolly and well-run hotel has grown of late, in response to increased popularity, so there are now two annexes, a converted coach-house plus an entirely new one, finished in May 1991. New pine furniture, co-ordinated pastel colour schemes and modern bathrooms are perks of these newer rooms, but personality is sacrificed. The white stone bar and inter-connecting lounge, the latter with a real log fire in a large inglenook, have character to spare.

Hotel trappings such as signs and repeated flowery furnishings are almost non-existent; books by Thomas Hardy and vases of dried flowers sit happily in the country chic surroundings. The lovely peach-coloured, panelled dining-room, low lit by candles and a gas coal fire, is a quieter place to linger. The three-course dinners are good, unpretentious and competently cooked. A self-taught chef, Mr Pinkster is a stickler for ingredients, tapping local sources whenever possible. You may find West Bay scallops or Poole mussels amongst the several choices on the menu. Nutty wholemeal bread is baked on the premises. The house stands right on a main road, so light sleepers should remember to ask for a back room in the house, overlooking the walled garden, or one in an annexe.

◑ Open all year

🔁 In the centre of Beaminster, down the hill from the town square. Private car park

🛏 I single, 4 twin, 8 double, I family room; most with bathroom/WC, 2 with shower/WC; TV in all rooms; room service, hair-dryer on request

◈ Restaurant, bar, lounge, conservatory; conference

facilities (max 15 people residential); golf, tennis, other sports nearby. Wheelchair access to hotel (no steps) and restaurant, 4 ground-floor bedrooms, 2 specially equipped for the disabled

⊖ No dogs in public rooms; no smoking in restaurant

▦ Access, Amex, Visa

£ Single £34, single occupancy of

twin/double £46, twin/double
£62 to £92, deluxe room £107,
family room £36 per person;

deposit required. Alc L £15.50;
set D £22.50. Special breaks
available

# Hams Plot

6 BRIDPORT ROAD, BEAMINSTER, DORSET DT8 3LU
TEL: BEAMINSTER (0308) 862979

*Spacious, laid back and unfussy Wolsey Lodge. Near the town centre but well off the main road in extensive grounds.*

Though close to the town centre, the handsome white Regency house is well hidden from the road by greenery (and so are its swimming-pool and tennis court). Your lingering memory after a restful break at this Wolsey Lodge is likely to be of space as much as of peace and quiet. Says one reader, very satisfied with her roomy single: 'So often one pays a huge supplement and gets a converted broom cupboard.' You'll find dignity and order in the drawing-room, more casual comfort in the library.

Spacious and homely, often with Victorian pieces of furniture, the bedrooms are above typical B&B level. There are few modern touches apart from electric underblankets and duvets (televisions and phones are absent, and tea things hidden away), and some rooms could be called spartan. Bathrooms, also often large, are cheered up with milk-jug-shaped sachets of milk bath and animal-shaped soap. Since the Dear-loves don't serve dinner, your main chance to mingle with other guests is over breakfast, taken around one large table. (A little path leads you to the main road and to Bridge House, which is a good spot for dinner and gives Hams Plot residents a discount [see entry].) Giles and Judy are described as 'a friendly and charming couple' by one reader, but another was annoyed because a booking was first accepted by telephone but later cancelled.

- ◖ Closed end Oct to end Mar
- ⤢ Beaminster is on the A3066. Hams Plot is down the hill from the market-place, opposite the B3163 to Maiden Newton. Private car park
- 🛏 3 twin, 2 double; most with bathroom/WC, some with shower/WC; hair-dryer in all rooms
- ◈ Dining-room, bar/lounge, library;

- tennis, croquet, unheated open-air pool at hotel, other sports nearby
- ⊖ No wheelchair access; no children under 10; no dogs; no smoking
- ▭ None accepted
- £ Single occupancy of twin/double £36, twin/double £42 to £54; deposit required. Special breaks available

---

*The* Guide *is totally independent, accepts no free hospitality, and survives on the number of copies sold each year.*

# Montagu Arms

PALACE LANE, BEAULIEU, HAMPSHIRE SO42 7ZL
TEL: LYMINGTON (0590) 612324   FAX: (0590) 612188

*A civilised hotel situated in a picturesque village.*

Beaulieu is a village worthy of its name but its beauty seems a trifle artificial, with neat old red-bricked houses and lakes and perhaps a couple of New Forest ponies grazing at the edge of a garage forecourt. Its motor museum and thirteenth-century abbey attract many visitors. Taking its name from Lord Montagu's nearby estate, the hotel stands in the centre of the village, a listed building erected in 1925 in attractive mock-Tudor style and possessing beams and dark wooden panelling.

The formal dining-room has french windows opening on to a compact and trim tiered garden. You can choose from an excellent wine list and a formidable gourmet dinner menu. There are plenty of restful corners to anticipate or digest your meal: a commodious beamed sitting-room with open fire and plenty of soft seating, rattan and bentwood chairs in a conservatory extension and a dear little bar with armchairs and books. Across the front car park is the Wine Press, a very different, more modern affair where you can drink good beer and eat bar food at pew seats.

Bedrooms impress with gentle colour schemes, sofas or armchairs and gleaming new bathrooms.

○ Open all year

🡒 Leave the M27 at Junction 3 and follow signs for Beaulieu. The hotel is on the left as you enter the village. Private car park

🛏 4 single, 2 twin, 11 double, 4 four-poster, 3 suites; all with bathroom/WC, TV, room service, hair-dryer, trouser press, baby-listening; tea/coffee-making facilities on request

◈ Restaurant, 2 bars, 2 lounges, library, conservatory; conference

facilities (max 60 people non-residential, 24 residential); fishing, golf, other sports nearby. Wheelchair access to public rooms only

⊖ No dogs in public rooms

▭ Access, Amex, Diners, Visa

£ Single £68, single occupancy of twin/double £76, twin/double £96, four-poster/family room £130, suite £166. Set L from £12.50, D £22; alc D £35; bar meals (prices till end 91)

---

*See the back of the* Guide *for an index of hotels listed.*

---

*Hotels in our* Visitors' Book *towards the end of the* Guide *are additional hotels that may be worth a visit. Reports on these hotels are welcome.*

**BELFORD** NORTHUMBERLAND                    **MAP 3**

# Blue Bell

MARKET SQUARE, BELFORD, NORTHUMBERLAND NE70 7NE
TEL: BELFORD (0668) 213543   FAX: (0668) 213787

*A slightly stiff, creeper-covered village inn.*

The centre of Belford is much quieter now the A1 bypasses the village and the creeper-covered Blue Bell has a more peaceful situation. It is a mixture of the slightly stiff with the traditional: the dining-room with its red-patterned carpet, green curtains and matching wooden chairs together with the starched white linen cloths has an old-fashioned, slightly dowdy feel to it. The bar, too, could do with a bit of jazzing up; the lounge, though more formal, is brighter. It feels a bit cosier in winter when the fire's lit. Dinner consists of four courses, served by friendly if somewhat inexperienced staff.

Belford is a good base for visiting this part of the Northumbrian coast and visitors could have interesting days out discovering the Farne Islands and Holy Island, both only a short distance from Belford. The hotel has a three-acre garden behind and the quietest bedrooms, all refurbished to a high standard in Georgian style, overlook it.

◐ Open all year

⤴ Belford is 1 mile off the A1, 40 miles north of Newcastle upon Tyne. Private car park

🛏 1 single, 7 twin, 7 double, 1 four-poster, 1 family room (some in annexe); all with bathroom/WC, hair-dryer, trouser press

◈ Restaurant, 2 bars, lounge, games room; conference facilities (max 90 people non-residential, 17 residential); fishing, golf, other sports nearby. Wheelchair access to hotel (1 step), restaurant and WC (M,F),

2 ground-floor bedrooms, 1 specially equipped for the disabled

⊖ No children under 6; no dogs in public rooms and by arrangement only in bedrooms; no smoking in restaurant

▭ Access, Amex, Diners, Visa

£ Single £40, single occupancy of twin/double £50, twin/double £80 to £90, four-poster £90; children sharing parents' room free; deposit required. Bar meals from £6; set D from £16; alc D £19. Special breaks available

---

*To begin with, we were surprised that one could not order a simple pot of tea unless resident in the hotel, so we ordered two cream teas – these were described as containing 'scones, jam and cream'. Imagine my surprise, therefore, when a tray appeared with a small pot of tea, and only two scones in total – this for a total of £11! On an hotel in Suffolk*

# Belton Woods

BELTON, NR GRANTHAM, LINCOLNSHIRE NG32 2LN
TEL: GRANTHAM (0476) 593200   TELEX: 378508 BELTON G
FAX: (0476) 74547

*Expensive golfing and other sporting facilities in a newly opened hotel.*

At 618 yards the eighteenth hole on the Wellington golf course is the third longest in Europe – and that's not the only statistic worth noting about this recently opened hotel (January 1991). The enormous grounds, which include three golf courses, have been planted with 280,000 daffodil bulbs, 9,000 trees – and there is still space for tennis courts, a croquet lawn, an archery centre, a golf driving range and a planned equestrian centre. The facilities of the outdoor and indoor leisure centres are extensive and are the main reason for a visit to this large yellow-brick hotel.

Throughout the hotel there is pervasive Muzak – perhaps a Carpenters' Top 20 hit from the 1970s. The wood-panelled reception with a terracotta tiled floor leads through to a high-ceilinged lounge with wood-panelled pillars, studded club chairs and soft sofas. Upstairs, the cocktail lounge with a grand piano overlooks both the swimming-pool and the golf course. In the Manor restaurant by candlelight you can savour leek and basil bisque, perhaps, followed by sweet basil chicken. The more informal Plus Fours restaurant serves meals throughout the day.

Bedrooms are spacious and fine furnishings come in one of eight types of wood used throughout the hotel. Rich fabrics, bold checks, stripes and florals are all mixed cleverly and the overall effect is luxurious. The tariff for the hotel is not cheap, and for many of the facilities a further charge is made, but the weekend break rates are reasonable.

○ Open all year

↗ 2½ miles north of Grantham on the A607. Private car park

🛏 57 twin, 35 double, 4 suites; all with bathroom/WC, TV, room service, hair-dryer, trouser press, baby-listening; mini-bar in some rooms

◈ 2 restaurants, 3 bars, lounge, games room, drying room; conference facilities (max 300 people non-residential, 96 residential); fishing, golf, tennis, sauna, solarium, heated pool, gym, croquet, archery, snooker, squash at hotel; babysitting. Wheelchair access to hotel, restaurant and WC, 46 ground-floor bedrooms, 1 specially equipped for the disabled

⊖ No dogs in public rooms; no smoking in some bedrooms

▭ Access, Amex, Diners, Visa

£ Single occupancy of twin/double £98, twin/double £118, suite £185; deposit required. Set L £15, D £19.50; alc L, D £35. Special breaks available

**BENENDEN** KENT                                    **MAP 10**

# Crit Hall

CRANBROOK ROAD, BENENDEN, KENT TN17 4EU
TEL: CRANBROOK (0580) 240609   FAX: (0580) 241743

*Georgian farmhouse turned smart, upmarket guesthouse.*

Bill Sleigh, who came here with his wife Sara at the end of 1989, used to be in marketing, which no doubt accounts for the brochures, colour photos, maps, tariffs, a list of specialist nurseries in the area, guests' comments and so on with which we have been engulfed. It may also account for the size of the post we have received, abnormal for such a small and fledgling enterprise.

Separating the wheat from the chaff, we find a pleasant Georgian farmhouse set back a little from the road on the outskirts of a pretty village, with a civilised if rather formal atmosphere in elegant rooms. Readers write of a comfortable drawing-room with antiques and beautiful books, a large polished table and gleaming silver and glass and beautiful china in the dining-room. One describes the interior design-affected bedrooms thus: 'A very good size, enormous well-fitted bathroom, duvets on comfortable beds.'

Expect your bedroom to have fresh milk for morning tea, chocolate mints on the pillow at night, and flowers and plants in the bathroom. The four-course set dinner is by all accounts praiseworthy, but 'perhaps not for the hearty eater,' says one report. Expect 'simple home-cooked food – steak-and-kidney pie or chicken Cordon Bleu, and a choice of two red, two white wines at very reasonable prices'. Breakfast is served in the kitchen (Aga, pine table, beams, dried hops), the house's most relaxed, least starchy room.

◐ Open all year

▟ If you travel west on B2086 from centre of Benenden, Crit Hall is 1 mile on left. Parking available

🛏 3 twin; 2 with bathroom/WC, 1 with shower/WC; TV, room service, hair-dryer in all rooms

◈ Dining-room, drawing-room, drying room, conservatory; fishing, golf, other sports nearby

⊖ No wheelchair access; no children under 12; no dogs; no smoking in dining-room and bedrooms

▭ None accepted

£ Single occupancy of twin/double £22 to £25, twin/double £37 to £40. Set D £12 to £14 (prices till June 92). Special breaks available

---

*The text of entries is based on unsolicited reports sent in by readers and backed up by inspections. The factual details under the text are from questionnaires the* Guide *sends to all hotels that feature in the book.*

**BEPTON** WEST SUSSEX                                              **MAP 10**

# Park House

BEPTON, MIDHURST, WEST SUSSEX GU29 0JB
TEL: MIDHURST (0730) 812880   FAX: (0730) 815643

*An individualistic country house where you can participate in lots*
*of garden sports or visit local horsey events.*

A small Victorian country house down a sleepy Sussex lane with its own
pitch and putt, croquet lawn, two grass tennis courts, swimming-pool
and five-acre paddock, and the downs in the distance . . . It's hardly
surprising that the family of Ione Frances O'Brien, a charming and active
lady who has lived here all her life, won't let her sell up. In 1988, she
threw a big fortieth anniversary party for the hotel, and you can see many
fine ornaments celebrating the occasion, such as a horse's head statuette
from the Spanish team. The Spanish team? In the snug, help-yourself
bar, one wall is devoted to polo pictures and photos (Cowdray Park,
England's polo centre, is just up the road), and another to horse-racing
(Goodwood is only six miles away). If your only equestrian knowledge is
of the pantomime variety, you may find a soul mate: photos of Chichester
theatre actors who've stayed here cover another bar wall. And if you can
tell the difference between Red Rum and Laurence Olivier, better still,
as some socialising may be in order.

The house offers the comfort of a stylish hotel but with the size,
individuality and lack of design co-ordination of a private residence,
apparent in the parquet-floored sitting-room with subtle yellow walls,
deep sofas and an impressive library of modern hardback fiction, and the
bedrooms, furnished with a smattering of antique pieces, and perhaps a
chaise-longue or rattan chair. The large attic bedroom, facing out over
the fields, is the most obviously appealing. Ione does the cooking herself,
and serves the set meals in the more formal tomato-coloured dining-
room.

- ◑ Open all year
- ↗ Off the Midhurst to Bepton road. Private car park
- 🛏 1 single, 5 twin, 3 double, 2 in cottage annexe; most with bathroom/WC, some with shower/WC; TV, room service, trouser press in all rooms
- ◈ Dining-room, bar, lounge, TV room, drying room; putting course, tennis, croquet, heated outdoor pool at hotel, other sports nearby. Wheelchair access to hotel (1 step), dining-room and WC, 1 ground-floor bedroom
- ⊖ No dogs in public rooms
- ▭ Access, Visa
- £ Single £46 to £49, single occupancy of twin/double £46 to £49, twin/double £81 to £85. Prices for family and annexe rooms on application. Set L £12.50, D £15

*You will find report forms at the back of the Guide – please use them!*

**BETHERSDEN** KENT                              **MAP 10**

# Little Hodgeham

SMARDEN ROAD, BETHERSDEN, ASHFORD, KENT TN26 3HE
TEL: HIGH HALDEN (0233) 850323

*The vivacious hostess offers everything you'd expect in a 'proper' hotel, scaled down to fit in with her quaint, immaculately kept home.*

This is a picture-postcard, 500-year-old cottage with black beams, sandy plasterwork and roses round a red-painted door. At Little Hodgeham you're a guest in someone else's home and you'll undoubtedly enjoy yourself if you like socialising. The house and garden resound with the chat of engagingly eccentric, Australian-born owner Erica Wallace. She has strong ties with feathered friends, perhaps originating from her days as a *News of the World* journalist when she hatched a chick in her cleavage (a scrap-book provides the proof). Now Billy the duck, who waddles to the back door when called, keeps her company, and hens lay eggs for breakfast. Dinner is a bit more formal, beautifully prepared and presented; it is eaten communally round a polished yew table from Crown Derby china.

Erica loves her garden (a pretty half-acre with pond), and also reckons to spend freely decorating the house with flowers. Each highly personalised and comfortable bedroom has a striking colour scheme: the family four-poster room (with twin beds in improvised attic space) in pinks (walls, bedspreads, even radiators); another in periwinkle and lilac with towels to match; and her favourite in thick swirly oranges, greens and browns. To the side of the sitting-room is a clematis-covered conservatory leading through to the swimming-pool.

◑ Open Easter to end Aug

⤴ 10 miles west of Ashford on the A28 Bethersden road. Turn right at the Bull pub and go towards Smarden for 2 miles; the house is on the right. Private car park

🛏 1 twin, 1 four-poster, 1 family room; all with bathroom/WC, room service, hair-dryer

◈ Dining-room, lounge, TV room, conservatory; fishing, unheated pool at hotel, other sports nearby

⊖ No wheelchair access; no children under 6 (exc babies); no dogs in public rooms

▭ None accepted

£ Single occupancy price on application, twin/double/four-poster £89 (rates inc dinner); deposit required. Special breaks available

---

*The 1993 Guide will be published before Christmas 1992. Reports on hotels are most welcome at any time of the year, but are extremely valuable in the spring. Send them to* Which? Hotel Guide, *FREEPOST, 2 Marylebone Road, London NW1 1YN. No stamp is needed if reports are posted in the UK.*

# Bibury Court

BIBURY, NR CIRENCESTER, GLOUCESTERSHIRE GL7 5NT
TEL: BIBURY (028 5740) 337   FAX: (028 5740) 660

*Good-value country-house hotel with informal atmosphere and service.*

The 'elegant but well lived-in' Bibury Court stands on the outskirts of what William Morris called the most beautiful village in England. The warm yellow Cotswold stone has weathered well (considering its 350 years), softening the thrusting gables, turrets and chimneys. The interior is a mixture of styles, from the pink and white plaster ceilings to the gold on black pre-Raphaelite maidens on the wallpaper in the bar. One reader found the large panelled lounge 'a treat during January with its huge open fireplace and log fire and comfortable armchairs and sofas'. The feeling of country house rather than hotel is enhanced by the occasional rugs over boards rather than universal wall-to-wall carpeting, and there's a generous scattering of antiques, from Chinese cabinets to mahogany dressers filled with china.

Bedrooms are homely and comfortable rather than designer chintz, but there are almost frill-less four-posters for those who prefer them that way. Some of the grander bathrooms date from the last remodelling in 1922 – lots of marble and huge baths to wallow in. Guests no longer have to run the gauntlet of the elements to eat: the restaurant is now within the main building. Food is satisfying: one reader found the menu was 'a little heavy on butter and cream', but he was pleased to find several reasonably priced half-bottles on the wine list. He concludes: 'The worst thing to happen to this hotel would be a modernisation and upgrading programme which no doubt would produce a grander and swisher hotel but with a loss of some old world charm and a considerable uplift in prices.' Hear! Hear!

**◖** Open all year, exc 2 weeks at Xmas

**⏏** Bibury is on the B4425 between Burford and Cirencester. The hotel is behind the church, next to the river. Private car park

**⛟** 3 single, 4 twin, 4 double, 7 four-poster, 1 suite, family room; all with bathroom/WC, TV room service, hair-dryer, baby-listening

**◈** Restaurant, bar, lounge, TV room, games room, drying room; conference facilities (max 20 people residential); fishing, mini-golf at hotel, other sports nearby

**⊖** No wheelchair access; no dogs in restaurant

**▭** Access, Amex, Diners, Visa

**£** Single £41 to £47, twin/double £68, four-poster £68 to £88, family room from £80. Cooked B £4; alc L £11.50, D £18 (prices till end 91)

*Prices are quoted* per room *rather than* per person.

**BIGBURY-ON-SEA** DEVON                          **MAP 8**

# Burgh Island

BIGBURY-ON-SEA, DEVON TQ7 4AU
TEL: BIGBURY-ON-SEA (0548) 810514   FAX: (0548) 810243

*Harking back to the good old seaside holiday. An Art Deco
extravaganza in peaceful island setting.*

Now for something out of the ordinary that once upon a time was the
epitome of class and comfort. Burgh Island Hotel, about the only
building on this small off-shore 26-acre island, was born in the twenties
when living it up on holiday didn't begin with boarding an aeroplane.
Agatha Christie, Noël Coward, and the Prince of Wales and Wallis
Simpson (to name but a few) sought isolation in the massive, Art Deco
hotel.

Stark white, partly castellated, with turquoise trim, with a conservatory
here and a cupola there, it is once again appropriately fitted out with
Lloyd Loom wicker furniture and huge ferns and palms. The split-level
Palm Court is topped with a peacock dome ceiling. Every suite has a
separate sitting area; several have balconies. White walls, black curtains,
thirties sofas and fan uplighters take you back.

Activities, apart from exploring the island, include table and regular
tennis. You can also have a sauna. A public sea tractor or hotel jeep
whisks you across the narrow strip of water or low-tide sands to the
mainland. One visitor who booked ahead for afternoon tea found the
service less than satisfactory.

◐ Open all year

⤴ Follow signs to Bigbury-on-Sea.
At St Ann's Chapel call the hotel
from the phone box. Do not
drive across the beach to the
island. Private car park on
mainland

🛏 14 suites; all with bathroom/WC,
sitting room, TV, baby-listening;
room service and hair-dryer on
request

◇ 2 restaurants, bar, 2 lounges, 2
games rooms, drying room,

library, conservatory; conference
facilities (max 32 people
residential, 60 non-residential);
fishing, tennis, water sports,
sauna, solarium, natural tidal
pool, gym, croquet at hotel,
other sports nearby

⊖ No wheelchair access; no dogs

▭ Access, Amex, Visa

£ Suite £160 to £175 average
(rates inc dinner); deposit
required. Alc L £22; set D £28

---

*If you make a booking using a credit card, and you find after cancelling that
the full amount has been charged to your card, raise the matter with your
credit card company. They will ask the hotelier to confirm whether the room
was re-let, and to justify the charge they made.*

# Biggin Hall

BIGGIN, BUXTON, DERBYSHIRE SK17 0DH
TEL: HARTINGTON (0298) 84451

*A quiet, not too grand retreat. Very welcoming and oozing with old-fashioned comfort.*

If you're scared of geese this may not be the place for you. As you drive in and park in what must have been the farmyard, the geese appear as if from nowhere and 'greet' you. The Hall is at the prettiest end of the village and is a listed building. Dating from the seventeenth century with various sympathetically executed additions, it has remained a very attractive property. Right in the heart of the Peak District, Biggin isn't really on the way to anywhere. Most of the guests are drawn here for that reason and tend to be keen walkers and nature lovers. In deference to the often strenuous day's exercise, dinner is served promptly at 7pm.

Bedrooms are a mixture of styles and sizes depending on which part of the house they are in. All are comfortable and full of traditional touches: you may find yourself in a huge beamy room with sloping ceilings and a four-poster bed (one) or with brass beds and huge old chest-of-drawers (four). Number seven is very cosy with a half-tester bed and chintzy curtains over the mullioned windows. Across the courtyard, the eighteenth-century building has been converted into self-contained apartments. A triumphant feature, tirelessly sought out by the owner, are the silent fridges!

○ Open all year

⏏ At the end of Biggin village, ½ mile from the A515 mid-way between Ashbourne and Buxton. Private car park

🛏 Suite of 2 singles, 4 twin/double, 1 four-poster, 2 half-testers, 6 apartments; all with bathroom/WC, hair-dryer; tea/coffee-making facilities, TV, fridge, microwave in apartments

◈ Dining-room, lounge, TV room; conference facilities (max 40 people non-residential, 20 residential); fishing, riding nearby

● No wheelchair access; dogs in apartments only; no smoking in dining-room and 1 lounge

▭ Access, Visa

£ Single £25 to £29, single occupancy of twin/double £35, twin/double £45 to £65, four-poster £70 to £85, apartment £40 to £60; deposit required. Cooked B £4.50; set D £15

*Warning to insomniacs, exercise freaks and late-night lovers: increasing numbers of hotels have infra-red triggered security lamps. To save being embarrassingly illuminated, check before you leave for your late-night or pre-dawn stroll.*

**BILLINGSHURST** WEST SUSSEX                                    **MAP 10**

# The Old Wharf

WHARF FARM, NEWBRIDGE, BILLINGSHURST, WEST SUSSEX RH14 0JG
TEL: BILLINGSHURST (0403) 784096

*A canalside farmhouse B&B (with no rural odours) in a smart conversion.*

The name comes from the fact that the low square brick building, built in 1839, used to be a warehouse at the terminus of the Arun Navigation Company where in Victorian times coal, groceries and fertilisers were brought in, to be exchanged for grain and produce from the surrounding villages. Now, as then, it stands beside a short stretch of canal running along the meandering River Arun, surrounded by its own meadows, a striking contrast to the thundering traffic on the main road some hundred yards away.

The owners, Moira and David Mitchell, are farmers. Lambs totter, the lively sheepdog Max will give you a friendly welcome, and you'll be served free-range eggs for breakfast. Moira and David live in a separate attractive conversion. In the guests' part, the wharf's old hoist wheel dominates the open staircase. Bedrooms, all with views of the canal, are clean, neat and smart with pine furniture. Downstairs, the large and comfortable guests' lounge has a log fire blazing in winter. In summer, rather than take breakfast in the tile-floored breakfast room, you can sit outside in the small walled garden. Note that full English breakfast in low season is extra. Unfortunately, because of the proximity of the canal to the house, the Mitchells feel they can't take children under 12.

- ◑ Closed Xmas and New Year for 2 weeks
- ↗ Head west of Billingshurst on the A272 for 1½ miles. The house is on the south side, by the banks of the canal. Private car park
- 🛏 3 twin, 1 suite; all with bathroom/WC, TV
- ◈ Dining-room, lounge, TV room; fishing at hotel
- ⊖ No wheelchair access; no children under 12; no dogs; no smoking
- ▭ Access, Amex, Visa
- £ Single occupancy of twin £25 to £40, twin £30 to £50, suite £50 to £70; deposit required. Cooked B £5 in low season (inc in high season)

---

*My niece and her 14-year-old daughter were our guests for Sunday lunch – the latter in the normal rather outrageous dress, style and shoes of her generation and accent to match. I noticed a slight stiffness from the staff when we chose a sofa close to a large lunch party before lunch, and we were tabled at the far extremity of the dining-room well apart from the other guests; we had to ask for menus in the lounge and taking our order was delayed until long after guests arriving later, which seemed altogether a slovenly affair.* On an hotel in Chester

# Asquith House

19 PORTLAND ROAD, EDGBASTON, BIRMINGHAM, WEST MIDLANDS
B16 9HN
TEL: 021-454 5282/6699　FAX: 021-456 4668

*Friendly, homely house with pretty gardens.*

This solid, ivy-clad house with a pillared and porticoed entrance is about one and a half miles from the centre of Birmingham. It's unlike an hotel and has a warm feel to it; rich colours and wallpapers, a mix of furnishings, plus lots of decorative ornaments give it a Victorian feel.

The dining-room, with lace curtains and a fine display of china plates above the picture rail, has a mix of wooden chairs and tables. Margaret Gittens serves evening meals, by arrangement, using a variety of Cordon Bleu dishes. Unsurprisingly, the hotel gets a lot of return visitors wanting to stay in the bright rooms: cheerful flowery prints co-ordinate with flowery duvet covers; everything is immaculate. Rooms to the rear of the house have views over the lovely garden (weddings are held here sometimes in the summer), and there are tables and chairs set outside the second dining-room which also doubles as a function or conference room. It's a delightful place to stay both for tourists and business guests.

◑ *Closed Xmas and Easter*

🔁 *Off the main A456 Birmingham to Kidderminster road (Hagley Road), 1½ miles from the city centre. Private car park*

🛏 *2 single, 6 twin, 1 double, 1 family room; all with bathroom/ WC, TV, room service, hair-dryer*

◈ *2 dining-rooms, bar, lounge, TV room; conference facilities (max 40 people non-residential)*

⊖ *No wheelchair access; no dogs*

▭ *Access, Amex, Visa*

💷 *Single £51, single occupancy of twin/double £57, twin/double/ family room £62; deposit required. Set D £18.50*

# Copperfield House

60 UPLAND ROAD, SELLY OAK, BIRMINGHAM, WEST MIDLANDS B29 7JS
TEL: 021-472 8344　FAX: 021-472 8344

*Homely and friendly hotel close to the BBC and Birmingham University.*

This red-brick Victorian house stands on a corner of two leafy suburban roads close to the university and Pebble Mill. To the front is a gravelled car park, to the rear a lovely garden surrounded by mature trees and overlooked by several bedrooms.

The hotel is owned by the Bodycotes. It's a relaxed place with large airy rooms and a cheerful atmosphere created by affable hosts. In the hall is a small reception desk, off which is the high-ceilinged yellow lounge, with bright flower prints and velour sofas and chairs pushed back around the sides of the room. On a large wooden table is the honesty bar. In the evening there may be jazz playing through the music system.

The dining-room is the venue for meals from 7 to 8pm, with a set meal offering dishes such as mushroom and parsley soup followed by chicken stuffed with cambozola, peanuts and cucumber in a filo pastry in leek sauce. Cooked breakfasts are kept hot on a heated tray from which you help yourself. Bedrooms are light, decorated in pale colours and with white moulded units or pine, and there is an ironing-board on the landing – so help yourself.

◑ Open all year; restaurant closed Fri, Sat and Sun eves

⤢ 2 miles from Birmingham city centre. Travel south on the A38 and turn left just past Pebble Mill TV studios. Private car park

🛏 6 single, 5 twin, 4 double, 1 family; all with bathroom/WC, exc 2 singles with shower/WC; TV, room service, hair-dryer in all rooms

◇ Dining-room, lounge; conference facilities (max 20 people non-residential, 16 residential);

fishing, golf, other sports nearby. Wheelchair access to hotel (1 step) and restaurant, 2 ground-floor bedrooms, 1 specially equipped for the disabled

⊖ No dogs in public rooms; smoking in lounge only

▭ Access, Visa

£ Single £40, single occupancy of twin/double £40, twin/double £50, family room £60; deposit required. Set D £15 (prices till end Apr 92) Special breaks available

# Swallow Hotel

12 HAGLEY ROAD, FIVEWAYS, BIRMINGHAM B16 8SJ
TEL: 021-452 1144    TELEX: 333806 SWALLOW G
FAX: 021-456 3442

*Whilst the surroundings are less than peaceful the interior of this luxury hotel is a welcome reprieve from the traffic.*

When you drive up to this luxurious city-centre hotel you'll be greeted at the door by a chin-strapped capped bell-boy replete with gloves tucked under braided epaulettes. This Edwardian-style hotel opened in March 1990.

From the marble-floored reception you can see the uniformed wait-resses in long frilly white aprons serving morning coffee and tea in a drawing-room resplendent with chandelier, marble floor and polished surfaces. Furnishings are mostly modern but in keeping with the period, though there are a few antiques throughout the hotel. The small plush library is a quiet room in which to read the papers. The formal Edward Elgar restaurant is overpriced and 'too influenced by *nouvelle cuisine*,' reports one reader. The menu is inventive, the surroundings luxurious. There is also the Langtry Brasserie with the plaster decorations from a lately demolished Birmingham theatre. The menu is more varied and if you are there on a Friday lunchtime you may be offered fish and chips served up in paper. One reader reports that 'restaurant service showed some strain (especially at breakfast)'.

Bedrooms are sumptuous, relatively individual and with around twenty different designs throughout the hotel. Superior doubles have fine fabrics, are comfortable and of a good size and have some interesting prints of plants and flowers. The pretty Italian marble bathrooms are equally luxurious. The basement leisure centre is an added bonus with an Egyptian theme to the décor, a fair-sized pool and an impressive-looking gym.

○ Open all year

⊿ Near the centre of Birmingham, at Fiveways where the A456 crosses the A4540. Private car park

🛏 4 single, 38 twin, 51 double, 2 four-poster suites, 2 twin suites; all individually air-conditioned, with bathroom/WC, TV, room service, hair-dryer, trouser press, mini-bar, baby-listening

◇ 2 restaurants, bar, lounge, library; hotel air-conditioned

throughout; conference facilities (max 100 people); sauna/solarium, heated indoor pool, gym at hotel; babysitting. Wheelchair access to hotel, restaurants and WC, no ground-floor bedrooms but a lift

⊖ No dogs in public rooms; some bedrooms non-smoking

▭ Access, Amex, Diners, Visa

£ Single £98, twin/double £120, four-poster/suite £195. Set L, D from £17.50; alc L, D £50

---

**BISHOP'S TAWTON** DEVON                                    **MAP 8**

# Halmpstone Manor

BISHOP'S TAWTON, BARNSTAPLE, DEVON EX32 0EA
TEL: SWIMBRIDGE (0271) 830321    FAX: (0271) 830826

*A fine manor house in rural north Devon with first-rate service and well-stocked and comfortable bedrooms.*

As you drive along the muddy, straw-strewn drive, past tractors, barns and clucking chickens, you may well envisage a scene very different from the one that awaits you within the Stanburys' neat stone house, set in two hundred and fifty acres of fields and farmland. If you arrive in the morning, you may find staff in matching uniforms scurrying about the hallway, dusting a corner bar or rearranging guidebooks on tables.

Halmpstone Manor is more of an hotel than a farmhouse, but your hosts, Charles and Jane Stanbury, are an affable couple who will look after you as they might their friends. They have spent time and energy on the bedrooms. Some hotel gimmickry has crept in, such as new four-posters, crown canopies and packaged goodies; but comfort, space, antiques (especially Edwardian), and views of rolling hills should compensate. And look, no tea tray! Old-fashioned room service does very nicely, thank you, and both afternoon and morning tea are included in the room rate.

While you dine in the small pine-panelled dining-room (on cheese soufflé and lamb with a brioche and herb crust, perhaps), your bed will be turned down and towels replaced. Commendable breakfasts include fresh orange juice, kedgeree and home-made preserves.

◐ Open all year

⤴ Leave the M5 at Junction 27 and take the A377 Barnstaple road. At Bishop's Tawton, turn left at the garage and continue on this road for 2 miles, then turn right. Private car park

🛏 3 twin/double, 2 four-poster; some with bathroom/WC, some with shower/WC; TV, hair-dryer, room service, trouser press in all rooms; no tea/coffee-making facilities in rooms

◇ Restaurant, bar, lounge; conference facilities (max 12 people non-residential); golf, riding, other sports nearby

⊖ No wheelchair access; no children in restaurant; dogs in one bedroom only; no smoking in bedrooms

▭ Access, Amex, Visa

£ Single occupancy of double £66 to £69, double £88 to £92, four-poster £110 to £115. Set D £22; alc D £31. Special breaks available

**BLACKWELL** WARWICKSHIRE                    **MAP 6**

# Blackwell Grange

BLACKWELL, SHIPSTON-ON-STOUR, WARWICKSHIRE CV36 4PF
TEL: ILMINGTON (0608 82) 357

*A comfortable retreat on a real working farm which supplies home-grown produce.*

The farmhouse is an inviting seventeenth-century building in Cotswold stone, fronted by well-tended flowerbeds and lawns, but this is a real working farm. Mrs Vernon Miller strolls over to greet you from an adjoining paddock of sheep, removes her wellies before entering the flagstoned hall of the farmhouse, and shows you upstairs.

A pair of antlers above the stairwell is adorned with two hats. The two bedrooms are simply furnished but large and comfortable, with curving polished cabinets and decent-sized *en suite* bathrooms. The lounge, with its beamed ceiling, has soft sofas grouped round the open fireplace – a comfy spot to relax after dinner, which is available by prior arrangement only. The farm is a mixed venture, breeding cattle and racehorses as well as sheep, but home-produced lamb is the mainstay of the dinner menu, along with home-grown vegetables. The dining-room is cosy; in summer you can have dinner outside in the garden. There's no licence and no pub in the village, so bring a bottle if you like a drink with your meal.

⬤ Open all year

▣ In Blackwell take road towards Ilmington; the Grange is the last house on the right. Private car park

🛏 I twin, I double; both with bathroom/WC

◈ Dining-room, sitting-room; golf, riding nearby

⊖ No wheelchair access; no children under 10; no dogs; no smoking

▭ None accepted

£ Single occupancy of twin/double £30, twin/double £40; deposit required. Set D £9 to £15

---

**BLAKENEY** NORFOLK                                    **MAP 7**

# White Horse

4 HIGH STREET, BLAKENEY, NR HOLT, NORFOLK NR25 7AL
TEL: CLEY (0263) 740574

*Newly refurbished, no-nonsense old inn just up from the sea. Not the snazziest place to stay, but probably the best bet in town.*

This seventeenth-century Norfolk flint and brick inn (the first hotel in Blakeney) fits in well with its equally well-kept neighbours. New owners have spiced up the old inn formula with late twentieth-century prints (for sale) and a few modern furnishings.

The pub section, which is large but turns a corner around the bar at one end and extends into a quiet alcove at the other, is its best room, and a social hub in the evening. (A small lounge with comfortable armchairs and out-of-date magazines is the 'Residents' Sitting Area', according to a small sign on the mantelpiece, but being little more than an extension of the entrance hall, it's hardly conducive to a pre-dinner snooze.) The restaurant in the converted stables is a stark white room with few windows or embellishments, so, atmospherically speaking, it competes badly with the pub in the evenings. In the latter you can supplement the long snack menu with items from the restaurant list.

Bedrooms differ in size and outlook, with a sea view a bonus for several (the large Harbour Room to name but one). All have new but antique-finished pine furniture, and striped curtains and duvet covers in subdued colours. There is more designer consciousness in the smart bathrooms, notably Victorian-style brass taps and decorative tiling. A conservatory is planned, but the car park, into which it will extend, doesn't promise a pretty outlook.

⬤ Open all year

▣ Follow signs to Blakeney off the A149 between Cromer and Wells. Private car park

🛏 3 single, I twin, 4 double, I family; all with bathroom/WC exc I single with shower/WC;

TV in all rooms; hair-dryer and baby-listening on request

◈ Restaurant, bar, sitting-room; golf, fishing, other sports nearby. Wheelchair access to restaurant and WC (M) only

⊖ No dogs

⬜ Access, Amex, Visa

💷 Single £30, single occupancy of twin/double £60, twin/double £60, family room £75; deposit required. Bar meals from £4.50; alc D £17 (prices till Apr 92). Special breaks available

---

## BLANCHLAND NORTHUMBERLAND

**MAP 3**

# Lord Crewe Arms

BLANCHLAND, NR CONSETT, CO DURHAM DH8 9SP
TEL: BLANCHLAND (0434) 675251   FAX: (0434) 675337

---

*A twelfth-century building with a chequered past. The hotel offers comfortable rooms and good food.*

The Lord Crewe Arms is the heart of the village of Blanchland, acting as public tea-rooms, meeting place and watering-hole for locals and anyone who might happen to pass through this remote part of the Derwent Valley. The hotel was once the abbot's lodgings before the dissolution of Blanchland monastery. The Forsters, protagonists in the 1715 Jacobite rebellion, lived here for a while, Tom Forster evading Government forces by hiding in the priesthole in what is now a guests' sitting-room.

The hotel is full of historical items; not all of them are genuine but the overall impression works, and Americans especially love the heraldic artefacts and suits of armour. There are log fires in the reception area – a good start – and two more in the restaurant where an interesting menu offers mostly game birds and venison in light sauces. Enormous dark oil paintings of rather severe-looking former occupants look down on you as you eat. Bedrooms vary from flowery prettiness to perhaps more appropriate plainer décor and ancient furniture. All are a good size, warm and have welcoming sherry and chocolates on your arrival. If you dare, you could ask for the Bamburgh room which Dorothy Forster is reputed to haunt. Across the village square, a seventeenth-century coaching inn has been converted to provide another ten rooms.

◑ Open all year

🔁 On the B6306, south of Hexham

🛏 4 twin, 11 double, 1 four-poster, 2 family rooms; all with bathroom/WC, exc 2 doubles with shower/WC; TV, room service, hair-dryer, trouser press, baby-listening in all rooms

◈ Restaurant, bar, 4 lounges, library; conference facilities (max 18 people residential); fishing, tennis, other sports nearby

⊖ No wheelchair access; no dogs in public rooms

⬜ Access, Amex, Diners, Visa

💷 Single occupancy of twin/double £72, twin/double £96, four-poster £116, family room £96; deposit required. Alc D £30, Sunday L £13. Special breaks available

---

*All entries in the* Guide *are rewritten every year, not least because standards fluctuate. Don't trust an out-of-date* Guide.

# Appletree Holme

BLAWITH, NR ULVERSTON, CUMBRIA LA12 8EL
TEL: LOWICK BRIDGE (022 985) 618

*Rural charm and modern comforts in a peaceful setting.*

Pheasants strut about the five acres of land that surround this pretty pink-painted stone cottage. There's also a fair slice of well-preserved rustic charm in the stone walls, slate fireplace with open log fire, and low-beamed ceilings. But this is a sophisticated place and the fine antiques and careful colour schemes are more in the country house tradition.

Light and airy bedrooms combine old and modern furniture with an adventurous use of colour. Other memorable features include a couple of two-person baths, and the 'bubble' bath, where natural foam is created from water shooting through tiny holes along the bottom of the bath. This dominates an enormous boudoir-style carpeted chamber.

When it comes to food, Roy and Shirley Carlsen use good, seasonal, often local produce, simply prepared and cooked with inventive use of exotic spices. The no-choice dinners, served in the long, narrow dining-room overlooking the garden, often feature local fish or game. A recent menu offered grilled fillets of salmon with asparagus cream sauce and spinach vol-au-vent, lemon sorbet, then roast duckling with apple and calvados sauce and savoury herb stuffing. Cream, from a neighbour's dairy herd, could hardly be fresher, and breakfast jam is made from hedgerow berries.

**◑** Open all year

**⤴** Leave the M6 at Junction 36. Take the A590 to Greenodd, then the A5092 to Lowick Green and the A5084 to Blawith. Turn into the lane opposite Blawith church, through the farm, taking the first right and then first left at sign. Private car park

**🛏** 1 twin, 2 double, 1 annexe suite; most with bathroom/WC, twin with shower/WC; TV, room service, hair-dryer in all rooms

**◈** Restaurant, lounge, drying room, library/study; fishing, riding, other sports nearby

**⊖** No wheelchair access; children by arrangement only; no dogs; no smoking exc in 1 public room

**▭** Access, Amex, Visa

**£** Twin/double £98 to £106 (rates inc dinner); deposit required. Set D £18 (8pm) (prices till Easter 92)

---

*To find a double room with only one chair seemed strange. To have a room with no TV was no hardship since there was a sophisticated radio/intercom device by the bed; unfortunately, it was not in working order. To have an en suite bathroom without a window is quite common but unfortunately the fan triggered by the light made so much noise that every effort had to be made to avoid turning it on.* On an hotel in Inverness

# Crown Hotel

HIGH STREET, BLOCKLEY, NR MORETON-IN-MARSH, GLOUCESTERSHIRE
GL56 9EX
TEL: EVESHAM (0386) 700245    FAX: (0386) 700247

*Good pub accommodation in the heart of the touristy Cotswolds;
bathrooms are rather basic.*

Described by one reader as a 'secret' village in the Cotswolds, Blockley is
certainly overlooked compared with its more touristy neighbours of
Broadway and Chipping Campden. This sixteenth-century former
coaching-inn fronts directly on to the High Street, but this doesn't seem
to be a problem. According to the receptionist: 'The only complaint
we've had about noise was when the sign started squeaking in the wind.'

The bars and grill room are downstairs – dark beams, curved leather
chairs, wrought-iron circular tables – while the dining-room upstairs has
more natural light entering through large glass arched windows and
doors. Pyramidal displays of wine bottles and pink cloths and napkins
add to the 'very pleasant atmosphere and superb fresh food' commended
by readers. Fish is delivered from Cornwall two or three times a week.
From a menu written in both English and French, non-piscine dishes
might include breast of pigeon with tagliatelle, or chicken stuffed with
bacon mousse and served with cream and tarragon sauce.

Rooms in the original old building can be small, but are prettily
furnished, with stripped pine, floral fabrics, dried flowers and pot-
pourri. Fireplaces are painted white with details picked out in red and
yellow. Junior suites and de luxe doubles – newer conversions across the
way – are more spacious. Bathrooms are small and basic.

- **◑** Open all year
- **⤴** Off the main A44 Oxford to
  Evesham road, 1 mile past
  Moreton-in-Marsh, right turn
  down into village. Private car
  park
- **🛏** 1 single, 4 twin, 9 double, 4
  four-poster, 2 family rooms, 3
  suites; all with bathroom/WC
  exc 2 single with shower/WC;
  TV, room service, hair-dryer,
  baby-listening in all rooms
- **◈** 2 restaurants, 3 bars, 3 lounges,
  drying room; conference facilities

(max 20 people residential);
golf, fishing, other sports nearby.
Wheelchair access to hotel and
restaurants, 7 ground-floor
bedrooms
- **⊖** No smoking in restaurants; no
  dogs in public rooms
- **▭** Access, Amex, Visa
- **£** Single £50, single occupancy of
  twin/double £50, twin/double
  £67, four-poster £98, suite
  £106; deposit required. Set D
  £17, alc D £23 to £25. Special
  breaks available

*We mention those hotels that don't accept dogs; guide dogs, however, are
almost always an exception. Telephone ahead to make sure!*

# Devonshire Arms

BOLTON ABBEY, NR SKIPTON, NORTH YORKSHIRE BD23 6AJ
TEL: BOLTON ABBEY (075 671) 441    TELEX: 51218 DEVARM G
FAX: (075 671) 564

*A smart but welcoming hotel/coaching-inn. A good place to stay or stop for lunch in the Dales.*

The Duchess of Devonshire supervised the revamping of this coaching-inn, which reopened almost ten years ago, and has a continuing interest in it. Just outside the village of Bolton Abbey, it is strategically placed over Wharfedale. Lots of people use it as a lunch or tea stop while touring around but this doesn't lessen its elegance or comfort.

The cocktail bar is littered with Christies catalogues and the Dog Lounge gets more doggy by the year with two more pictures added since last year. The movement of pictures and furniture is at the whim of the Duchess: she might bring down a piece from Chatsworth for an airing or send a favourite back for a few months. Some of the bedrooms in the old part of the house are 'executive' rooms of an exceptional size and standard. One, the Mitford Room, is full of pictures of the Mitford girls; a new wing almost surrounds the croquet lawn and putting green at the back of the house and makes for quieter, if slightly smaller, bedrooms. Wherever they are, the bedrooms are very comfortable with all manner of thoughtful extras and full of interesting books and pictures. Dining is a smoothly-run operation, and game plays a large part on the menu.

- Open all year
- At the junction of the A59 and B6160, 5 miles north-west of Ilkley. Private car park
- 19 twin, 10 double, 8 four-poster, 2 family rooms, 1 suite; all with bathroom/WC, TV, room service, hair-dryer, trouser press, baby-listening
- Restaurant, 2 bars, 2 lounges, TV room, games room, conservatory, conference facilities (max 150 people non-residential, 80 residential); fishing, croquet, clay pigeon shooting at hotel, other sports nearby; babysitting. Wheelchair access to hotel, restaurant and WC (unisex), 19 ground-floor bedrooms, 2 specially equipped for the disabled
- No smoking in some bedrooms
- Access, Amex, Diners, Visa
- Single occupancy of twin/double £90, twin/double £110, four-poster £125, family room £140; deposit preferred. Set L £16, D £25; alc L £25, D £35. Special breaks available

---

⚱   *Denotes somewhere you can rely on a good meal – either the hotel features in the 1992 edition of our sister publication,* The Good Food Guide, *or our own inspectors thought the cooking impressive, whether particularly competent home cooking or more lavish cuisine.*

**BOLTON BY BOWLAND** LANCASHIRE                    **MAP 4**

# Harrop Fold

BOLTON BY BOWLAND, CLITHEROE, LANCASHIRE BB7 4PJ
TEL: BOLTON BY BOWLAND (020 07) 600

*Farmhouse hotel in remote location, offering comfortable and relaxing accommodation.*

Pay attention to the directions below. This working livestock farm, set amid 280 acres of rolling pastureland, is hard to find. Barns flank the old Norse-style house, whose beams might be pillage from Viking longships. Slightly more portable maritime memorabilia dominates the upstairs stable loft lounge where pride of place goes to the huge brass bell from the *Clacton Belle*. Views are gorgeous.

The Wood family are old hands at the hospitality game (even down to sending newsletters to their regulars), and have worked hard at cultivating the sort of relaxed atmosphere that appears effortless. The bar wavers between the sedate and the rustic, as horse-brasses rub shoulders with Victorian-style chairs. A traditional farmhouse dinner is served in the pleasant dining-room, always kicking off with home-made soup. Bedrooms are fresh, cheerful and comfortable without being stylish, although some of the bathrooms are noteworthy. Welcoming touches include a quarter bottle of wine in your room.

◑ Closed Jan

↗ From the A59 Clitheroe to Skipton road, take the turning to Bolton by Bowland. Bear left at the Spread Eagle hotel and continue to the Copper Nook hotel. Turn sharp left to Holden and Slaidburn. In Holden follow the sign to Harrop Fold and go left into the village. The hotel is first on the right. Private car park

🛏 2 twin, 6 double; all with bathroom/WC, TV, hair-dryer

◈ Dining-room, bar, 2 lounges; fishing, golf, other sports nearby

⊖ No wheelchair access; no children; no dogs; no smoking in bedrooms

▭ Access, Visa

£ Single occupancy of twin/double £46, twin/double £64; deposit required. Set D £16.50 (prices till end Dec 91). Special breaks available

---

ℒ    This denotes that the hotel offers especially good value at whatever price level.

---

🏵    This denotes that the hotel is in an exceptionally peaceful situation where you can be assured of a restful stay.

# Winterbourne

BONCHURCH, VENTNOR, ISLE OF WIGHT PO38 IRQ
TEL: ISLE OF WIGHT (0983) 852535   FAX: (0983) 853056

*A peaceful Victorian country house overlooking the sea and lovely grounds; Dickens once spent a summer here.*

Stand at the cliff edge of these beautiful grounds; only waves breaking far below and seagulls calling high above break the sound of silence. A short path takes you down to the shore; behind you lies a hide-and-seek garden with sloping lawns, meandering paths, a babbling stream, a heated outdoor pool, all overlooked by a delicate eleventh-century chapel – in short, an ideal summer retreat. Dickens found it so; arriving here in July 1849 he wrote to his wife: 'I think it is the prettiest place I ever saw in my life, at home or abroad.'

The stone manor, reached by a steep descent from the main road, looks across the garden against a backdrop of lush 'undercliff'. The Victorian interior doesn't match its beautiful surroundings, but the garden makes it palatable. The formal lounge with maroon damask-patterned sofas and armchairs has french windows opening on to the terrace. Though oppressively dark during the day, soft candle lighting, cut glass and classical music give the restaurant sophistication at night. During his three-month stay here, Dickens was working on *David Copperfield* (do press the present owner to read it – after all, he's been here for five years and has based most of his publicity around the writer), and bedrooms are named after characters in the book with appropriate drawings of each on the door. Over half the bedrooms face seaward and are obviously preferable; though mainly large they are also plain. A coach-house conversion houses five of them.

- ◐ Closed Nov to Mar
- ↩ Just off the A3055 Shanklin to Ventnor road, adjoining St Boniface church in Bonchurch. Private car park
- 🛏 3 single, 6 twin, 8 double, 1 suite; most with bathroom/WC, some with shower/WC; TV, room service, baby-listening in all rooms; tea/coffee-making facilities and hair-dryer on request
- ◈ Restaurant, bar, lounge, TV
- room; heated outdoor pool at hotel, other sports nearby; babysitting
- ⊖ No wheelchair access; no dogs or smoking in restaurant
- ▭ Access, Amex, Diners, Visa
- 💷 Single £55 to £61, single occupancy of twin/double £118 to £130, twin/double/suite £110 to £130 (rates inc dinner); deposit required. Alc L £7, D £25 (non-residents)

---

*Many hotels put their tariffs up in the spring. You are advised to confirm prices when you book.*

**BOSHAM** WEST SUSSEX                                **MAP 10**

# The Millstream

BOSHAM, CHICHESTER, WEST SUSSEX PO18 8HL
TEL: BOSHAM (0243) 573234   FAX: (0243) 573459

*A friendly unpretentious hotel in an attractive sailing village.*

Bosham, on the shores of one of the tributaries of Chichester's harbour, is the kind of village which is either very busy or very sleepy depending on the weather. On a fine day it can be inundated with trippers nosing in the shops and watching others playing about in boats. Out of season it's very quiet.

The Millstream can't boast a water's edge position or even sea view, but it's made the best of its resources. It has the feel and look of an outsize cottage with roses round the door, set in the heart of the village with a little stream running along the garden's edge; there are mallards everywhere, even in the flowerbeds. In summer, many punters will stop off here for a buffet lunch, and will make a beeline for the tables out on the lawn in front.

The house is arranged in an L-shape; one long, low-ceilinged open-plan room serves as a cane-chaired bar, a sitting-room with reproduction balloon backs and a grand piano, and a fresh, airy restaurant. Bedrooms are not flashy but are in a co-ordinated flowery style, and are either in the main building (some with small balconies overlooking the front garden), or in a newer clapboarded wing at the back. Hibernation Breaks in the winter months offer big reductions for two-night stays or longer.

◑ *Open all year*

🔼 *4 miles west of Chichester on A259, centrally located in Bosham on Bosham Lane, close to Old Bosham church. Private car park*

🛏 *5 single, 9 twin, 13 double, 1 four-poster, 1 family room; all with bathroom/WC, TV, room service, hair-dryer, trouser press, baby-listening*

◈ *Restaurant (air-conditioned), bar, lounge, TV room; conference*

*facilities (max 20 people residential); water sports, golf, other sports nearby. Wheelchair access to hotel, restaurant and WC (M,F), 4 ground-floor bedrooms*

⊖ *No dogs in public rooms*

▭ *Access, Amex, Diners, Visa*

£ *Single £59, single occupancy of twin/double £79, twin/double £106, four-poster £116; deposit required. Set L, D £16.50. Special breaks available*

---

*See page 787 for other hotels worthy of inclusion in our* Visitors' Book.

---

*Many hotels offer special rates for stays of a few nights or more. It is worth enquiring when you book.*

# Pethills Bank Cottage

BOTTOMHOUSE, NR LEEK, STAFFORDSHIRE ST13 7PF
TEL: ONECOTE (0538) 304277　FAX: (0538) 304575

*A very snug little B&B in a fairly wild, isolated spot. Your comfort is the hosts' prime concern.*

High up on a moor in the southern part of the Peak District National Park, Pethills is a small, white-painted cottage (with careful additions). It is isolated on the side of a single track road – a fairly windswept place compensated for by great views across the hills. The garden is incongruously neat in contrast to the rugged wildness of the surrounding scenery. It is very well planned with lovely shrubs and trees, and benches strategically placed to give the best views and maximum shelter.

Inside, everything is neat and compact. The sitting-room is tucked under a brick archway off the small hall. You can sit snug and safe, revelling in the warmth of the room with its neat, pale carpet with pink rugs, velveteen sofas while looking out across the wild countryside. The dining/breakfast room, three tables neatly laid, is light and roomy with some natural brick walls and windows overlooking the garden. Yvonne Martin prepares dinner only by arrangement but the breakfasts are a feast: lots of choice and always a delicious mixture of fresh fruits.

There's one bedroom on the ground floor – the largest – called the Garden Room; it has french windows opening on to its own private patio. The other two are upstairs, also of a good size, with room for a couple of comfortable chairs. All are very fresh and attractively decorated. Skylight windows give maximum light and the rooms and bathrooms are interesting shapes, cleverly fitted into the roof. You will certainly feel cosseted here.

◑ Open all year, exc Xmas

🔁 Close to the A523, 5 miles south-east of Leek, 10 miles north-west of Ashbourne. Turn into lane opposite the Little Chef restaurant and follow signs for ½ mile. Private car park

🛏 1 twin, 1 double, 1 suite; all with bathroom/WC, exc suite with shower/WC; TV, hair-dryer, baby-listening, ironing facilities in all rooms

◈ Dining-room, lounge; golf, riding nearby

⊖ No wheelchair access; no children under 5; no dogs; no smoking in public rooms and in 2 bedrooms

▭ None accepted

£ Single occupancy of twin/double £22 to £31, twin/double £33 to £38, suite £35 to £41; deposit required. Set D £15 by arrangement only

---

*If you have a small appetite, or just aren't feeling hungry, check if you can be given a reduction if you don't want the full menu.*

**BOUGHTON LEES** KENT                                                    **MAP 10**

# Eastwell Manor

EASTWELL PARK, BOUGHTON LEES, NR ASHFORD, KENT TN25 4HR
TEL: ASHFORD (0233) 635751   TELEX: 966281 EMANOR G
FAX: (0233) 635530

*A luxury manor house aimed at the conference trade.*

If the manor looks too perfect to be entirely true, it's because during the 1920s Sir John de Fonblanque Pennefather demolished the mansion and, mainly using the existing materials, rebuilt it as a low brick and stone building with lots of gables, mullion windows and amazing, out-of-proportion brick chimneys. It sits in 62 acres of grounds in the midst of a three-thousand-acre estate, a long drive through meadowland, daffodils and sheep.

As you enter the courtyard with its tubs of pansies, the keen staff of this Queen's Moat Houses hotel may have spotted your arrival and you're ushered into the large flagstoned hall. The scale, design and furnishings feel masculine: the billiard room (full-sized table, of course), the panelled bar with red leather chesterfields and 61 malt whiskies to choose from, or the similarly large sitting-room, panelled and strapworked, where games and a variety of chairs relieve any formal austerity.

Dining is very much a jacket-and-tie affair; expect cuisine that exceeds the aspirations of many company-owned country house hotels. Four bedrooms (the cheapest) face the courtyard, the rest look out over the splendid surrounding grounds – either farmland, or large formal gardens with paved walkways, a fountain surrounded by statues and chunky blocks of square-cut hedges.

◑ Open all year

▐ Take the A251 northwards from Ashford. Private car park

🛏 3 twin, 15 double, 5 suites; all with bathroom/WC, TV, room service, hair-dryer, trouser press, baby-listening; no tea/coffee-making facilities in rooms

◈ Restaurant, bar, lounge, games room; conference facilities (max 80 people non-residential, 23 residential); tennis at hotel,

fishing, golf, other sports nearby

⊖ No wheelchair access; no dogs in public rooms

▭ Access, Amex, Diners, Visa

£ Single £98, single occupancy of twin/double £130, twin/double £136 to £160, suite £174 to £255; deposit required. Set L £13, £16.50, D £24.50; alc L, D £42 (prices for 91). Special breaks available

---

*Prices are what you can expect to pay in 1992, except where specified to the contrary. Many hoteliers tell us that these prices can be regarded only as approximations.*

# Tanyard

WIERTON HILL, BOUGHTON MONCHELSEA, MAIDSTONE, KENT ME17 4JT
TEL: MAIDSTONE (0622) 744705

*A small personally run hotel in a wonderful house, where guests
can be as sociable as they wish.*

This fourteenth-century yeoman's house, partially brick, partially
timber-framed dividing soft sandy-coloured plasterwork, stands on a
rise with a long uninterrupted vista of the gently sloping countryside of
the Weald of Kent. Around the building there's a big pond with a stream
trickling into it, an orchard, sheep grazing in a field of kale and a wooden-
slatted cottage which dates from the 1600s.

Jan Davies lives here and she's been running Tanyard as an hotel since
1982. She also does the cooking: imaginative four-course set meals
served at 8pm in an intimate candlelit dining-room: perhaps quail's egg,
avocado, nut and bacon salad, followed by lemon sole fillets in smoked
salmon sauce, and amaretto soufflé for pudding. If guests get on, there
can be a house party atmosphere, but socialising is not *de rigueur*. Before
and after dinner, you can relax in the sitting-room in the traditional knole
settee or leather chesterfield. Two flights of steep stairs at either end of

-Tanyard-

the house take you to bedrooms confusingly named after colours that no longer match the design. Beams, 'mind your head' signs and mullion windows abound. Since last year a smart bathroom has been added to the spacious suite that takes up the top floor.

◗ *Closed mid-Dec to early Mar*

⏎ *From the B2163 at Boughton Monchelsea turn down Park Lane, opposite the Cock pub. Take the first right down Wierton Lane and fork right — Tanyard is on the left at the bottom of the hill. Private car park*

🛏 *1 twin, 3 double, 1 suite; all with bathroom/WC, exc twin with* *shower/WC; TV in all rooms; limited room service*

◈ *Dining-room, lounge*

⊖ *No wheelchair access; no children under 6; no dogs*

▭ *Access, Amex, Diners, Visa*

💷 *Single £50, single occupancy of twin/double £57, twin/double £71, suite £89; deposit required. Set D £19 (8pm) (prices till Dec 91)*

---

**BOUGHTON STREET** KENT                                    **MAP 10**

# Garden Hotel

167–169 THE STREET, BOUGHTON UNDER BLEAN, BOUGHTON STREET, NR FAVERSHAM, KENT ME13 9BH
TEL: CANTERBURY (0227) 751411   FAX: (0227) 751801

*Predominately a restaurant with much business trade; spruce and modern in style, it has no garden as such, but plant lovers will enjoy the décor.*

The hotel manages to be a retreat despite two important flaws: two busy roads. Lorries thunder along the A2 dual carriageway some two hundred yards behind the building's car park at the rear (largely concealed, visually anyway, by a bank of shrubs), and the hotel's front door opens on to the village high street which also bears a burden of traffic.

Sue and John Evans, who've been here since the end of 1989, couldn't have named the hotel more appropriately; even the lettering on the outside of the white, partially brick, partially boarded seventeenth-century building is wreathed in painted flowers. The interior is fresh and modern: the dining-room, a conservatory extension at the rear, drips with tumbling foliage everywhere; the split-level bar and sitting-room have green sofas and chairs and walls bedecked with more flowers and floral pictures.

Traffic noise does unfortunately intrude into the bedrooms, most of which continue the hotel's botanical theme, with apt motif on the door and strong green and cream floral co-ordination inside, along with modern pine furniture. Though some lack space they have all the expected mod cons. Good-value set menus of two or three courses might include asparagus in a hollandaise sauce or fried oysters and mushrooms in garlic, followed by guinea-fowl and William pear served with a brandy and game fumet, or navarin of fish on spinach and fennel with a saffron and watercress sauce.

| | | | |
|---|---|---|---|
| ◐ | Open all year | | conference facilities (max 16 people non-residential, 10 residential); public rooms air-conditioned; fishing, golf, other sports nearby. Wheelchair access to restaurant only |
| ⤴ | Leave the M2 at the end and turn right towards Canterbury, then next turn to Boughton. Take left at T-junction into village. The hotel is then ½ mile on the right-hand side. Private car park | | |
| 🛏 | 1 single, 7 twin, 2 double; all with bathroom/WC, TV, room service, hair-dryer, trouser press, baby-listening | ⊖ | No dogs |
| | | ▭ | Access, Amex, Diners, Visa |
| ◈ | Restaurant, bar, lounge; | ⊡ | Single £53, twin/double £70; children under 14 sharing parents' room free. Set L £13.50, D £17.50; alc L, D £24 |

---

**BOURNE** LINCOLNSHIRE                                    **MAP 4**

# Bourne Eau House

SOUTH STREET, BOURNE, LINCOLNSHIRE PE10 9LY
TEL: BOURNE (0778) 423621

*A formal house-party experience in a lovely old house with an attractive garden.*

Sited opposite the Memorial Gardens, the house is set back and hidden from the road by an old barn and is surrounded by a lovely lawned garden with borders and a gravel courtyard. The attractive stone house is part-Elizabethan and part-Georgian, and is owned by Dr and Mrs Bishop who retired to Bourne after working abroad for UNESCO.

'The welcome is entirely courteous, gentle and warm,' reports one reader. Inside, the house has fine antiques, is immaculately kept and very attractive. Each room is furnished from a particular period. Four-course meals, followed by coffee and mints, are all carefully prepared by Mrs Bishop. You eat in the flagstoned dining-room around the central polished table, and may be joined by your hosts. They are 'quietly gracious but not remotely stiff', reports one reader.

Afterwards, you can retire to the Georgian drawing-room (with a Jacobean fireplace), the library or the music room. The three bedrooms are all equally comfortable with fine furnishings, and the Master Suite additionally has a large bathroom and a dressing-room. 'It is difficult to fault the house,' concludes one reader, 'it was a privilege to stay here.'

| | | | |
|---|---|---|---|
| ◐ | Closed Xmas and Easter; restaurant closed Sun eve | | cenotaph in Bourne's Memorial Gardens, in South Street (A15). Private car park |
| ⤴ | The concealed entrance to the house is directly opposite the | 🛏 | 1 twin, 1 double, 1 suite; all with |

bathroom/WC, exc twin with
shower/WC; TV, room service,
hair-dryer in all rooms

✧ Dining-room, 2 lounges, library/
study; golf, fishing, other sports
nearby

⊖ No wheelchair access; children

by arrangement only; no dogs; no
smoking in bedrooms

▭ None accepted

£ Single occupancy of twin/double
£35 to £45, twin/double £50 to
£60, suite £60 to £70. Set D
£17 (7.30pm)

The hotel that was to have been listed here ceased trading as we went to press.

---

*When you telephone to book a room, and the hotel accepts your booking, you enter into a binding contract with them. This means they undertake to provide the specified accommodation and meals etc. for the agreed cost on the agreed dates, while you commit yourself to paying their charges. If you later have to cancel your booking, or fail to turn up, the hotel is likely to keep any deposit you have paid to defray administrative costs. If a hotel is unable to re-let the room you have booked – and it must try to do so – it is entitled to compensation for the loss of profit caused by your breach of contract. It can only claim a sum that is fair and reasonable – which can be up to two-thirds of the cost. It should not make a profit out of your failure to appear. It's important to give as much notice as possible when cancelling: this increases the chances of your room being re-let.*

# The Edgemoor

HAYTOR ROAD, BOVEY TRACEY, DEVON TQ13 9LE
TEL: BOVEY TRACEY (0626) 832466   FAX: (0626) 834760

*Friendly hotel sandwiched between dense woods and Dartmoor. A good all-rounder.*

The fabric might be brick or stone but so covered in every conceivable type of creeper is this fetching Victorian building that it's rather hard to tell. Little betrays its former role as a grammar school, either.

The small front garden with colourful parasols on picnic tables is an obvious setting for prolonged relaxation. What was once the assembly room, large and with high, Dutch barn ceiling and ministrels' gallery, is now a place for lingering: light and feminine, with soft, cheerful sofas and chairs, an open fire and lots of games and books. The bar is more cosy and old-fashioned. Although the dining-room is formal and ladylike, staff adopt an easy manner. As for bedrooms? Well there is little of the boarding school about them. Decorative frills and lots of brightly patterned fabrics make sure of that. Room ten has a ceiling very like the assembly hall lounge, so it can easily accommodate a pine four-poster bed.

◐ Open all year

🔁 Turn off the A38 onto the A382 Bovey Tracey road. Turn off the Bovey Tracey bypass on to the B3344 and follow signs for Widecombe – the hotel is ¼ mile along this road

🛏 3 single, 2 twin, 3 double, 3 four-poster, 1 family room; most with bathroom/WC, 2 singles with shower/WC; TV, room service, hair-dryer, trouser press, baby-listening in all rooms

◈ Restaurant, 2 bars, lounge; conference facilities (max 100 people residential, 12 residential); fishing, golf, other sports nearby. Wheelchair access to hotel (3 steps), restaurant and WC (M,F), 2 ground-floor bedrooms

⊖ No dogs in public rooms; no smoking in restaurant

▦ Access, Amex, Diners, Visa

£ Single £43, single occupancy of twin/double £50, twin/double £79, four-poster £85; deposit required. Set L £8.50 (by arrangement), D from £17. Special breaks available

*Are you aware of your rights as a consumer when you book into an hotel? Check them out on page 13.*

**BOWNESS-ON-WINDERMERE** CUMBRIA    **MAP 3**

# Lindeth Fell

BOWNESS-ON-WINDERMERE, CUMBRIA LA23 3JP
TEL: WINDERMERE (096 62) 3286

*A country-house hotel with heart – and possibly the best views of Windermere that you'll find.*

The union flag flapping in the breeze outside this Lakeland stone and pebbledash creeper-clad Edwardian house tells only part of the story. To be sure, Pat Kennedy and his wife Diana are ex-service personnel and proud of it, but they're also among the most unstuffy, least regimented people you're ever likely to meet. They love their house, and want you to enjoy it, too. There's just a hint of the Kennedys' RAF pedigree in the pervasive spick-and-span neatness, not to mention the tariff which advises with true Squadron Leader's precision that afternoon tea will be served '15.30–16.45 hrs'.

Lindeth Fell is a thoroughly comfortable place, furnished with a view to classic charm rather than designer chic, and makes the most of its oak panelling, antiques and Adam-style plaster ceilings. The Kennedys have led a globe-trotting life and public rooms such as the blue lounge display much-loved souvenirs – tribal carvings from Tanganyika, and photos of camel-racing in Oman. The recently extended dining-room has sensational views of Lake Windermere and the magnificent gardens, as does the terrace where drinks are served on summer evenings.

The bedrooms, most of which have lakeside views, are named after local villages and are comfortably rather than fashionably furnished. The five-course dinner, prepared by Diana and Sarah Churchward, changes nightly and is modern but unpretentious. A typical menu might include Morecambe Bay shrimps, salmon and parsley soup, as well as old favourites like roast beef with all the trimmings, and bread-and-butter pudding.

◐ Closed early Nov to early Mar

↗ I mile south of Bowness on the A5074 Lyth Valley to Lancaster road. Private car park

🛏 2 single, 4 twin, 6 double, 2 family rooms; most with bathroom/WC, some with shower/WC; TV, room service, hair-dryer, trouser press, baby-listening in all rooms

◈ 2 dining-rooms, 2 lounges; drying facilities; conference facilities (max 28 people residential); fishing, tennis, croquet, putting at hotel, other sports nearby.

Wheelchair access to hotel (ramp) and restaurant, I ground-floor bedroom specially equipped for disabled

⊖ No children under 7; no dogs; smoking discouraged in dining-rooms

▭ Access, Visa

£ Single £39, single occupancy of twin/double £54, twin/double £77 to £86; family room £96 (3 people); (rates inc dinner); deposit required. Set L £7.50, D £21

# Clos du Roy at Box House

BOX, WILTSHIRE SN14 9NR
TEL: BOX (0225) 744447   FAX: (0225) 743971

*A restaurant-with-rooms with a modern and adventurous
approach.*

'Roy' refers to Philippe Roy, chef/patron of this stylish restaurant-with-rooms, an eighteenth-century vicarage standing back from the A4. The restaurant moved from Bath in 1990 and has gained a sound reputation for creative modern cooking. Three-course dinners deliver unusual flavour combinations, and are as pretty as the dining-rooms in which they're served. A set dinner in spring included timbale of skate wing and red mullet with cucumber sauce, followed by venison with onion and kumquat confit, cheeses from Jacques Vernier of Paris and iced chocolate parfait with pistachios and orange sauce.

After that, you may well want to collapse into a deep, soft sofa, but most downstairs rooms at Box House are filled with pale yellow-clothed dining-tables and jazzy patterned padded chairs. Residents must make do with the bar and share it with non-residents, a drawback on Saturday evening, for instance. There are compensations upstairs, however. Though less adventurous than the food, the six bedrooms have been given more attention than the term 'restaurant-with-rooms' might lead you to expect. They are airy, light (thanks to big windows), extremely comfortable and fashionably decorated. Up-to-date bathrooms have separate showers. There is a heated swimming-pool in a quiet corner of the grounds and the gardens are exceptionally pleasant despite some road noise.

🌗 Open all year

↗ 5 miles from Bath east on the A4. Private car park

🛏 9 twin/double; all with bathroom/WC, TV, room service, hair-dryer, trouser press, baby-listening

◈ 3 restaurants, bar, lounge, drying room, nursery; conference facilities (max 30 people non-residential, 9 residential); swimming pool (heated) at hotel, other sports nearby. Wheelchair access to hotel (1 step), and restaurant and WC (unisex), no ground-floor bedrooms and no lift

⊖ No dogs in public rooms; no smoking in restaurant

▭ Access, Amex, Diners, Visa

£ Single occupancy of twin/double £70, twin/double £95 to £110, suite £130; deposit required. Cooked B £5; set L £15.50, D £29.50

*All entries in the* Guide *are rewritten every year, not least because standards fluctuate. Don't trust an out-of-date* Guide.

**BRADFORD** WEST YORKSHIRE                    **MAP 4**

# Restaurant Nineteen

NORTH PARK ROAD, HEATON, BRADFORD, WEST YORKSHIRE BD9 4NT
TEL: BRADFORD (0274) 492559

*A classy restaurant in a quiet part of town. Recently renovated rooms.*

In a leafy part of Bradford, opposite Lister park with its lawns and tennis courts, this established restaurant, well-known to *The Good Food Guide*, offers a handful of handsomely decorated bedrooms. The rooms are exotically named Carmelita, Ariadne or Ray after the bare-breasted women in the Russell Flint pictures on the wall. The rooms are plush with mottled pink or beige walls, thick quilts and modern tiled bathrooms. The lack of space in some is offset by plenty of cupboards and Roberts radios sit on bedside tables.

Yet more semi-clad women decorate the walls of the open-plan dining-room which is large, with mouldings like delicate cake icing. The green, peachy pink and white colour combination create a fresh, airy atmosphere contrasting with the rather fusty lounge with heavy fringed curtains, china ornaments and a ticking clock on the mantelpiece.

Robert Barbour calmly controls the front of house while Stephen Smith is in charge of the cooking. They are well aware that guests won't necessarily want to eat in-house every evening over a weekend stay, so will gladly suggest other restaurants to try nearby or in the city centre. If you decide to stay in, you shouldn't be disappointed. The four-course menu is a tempting line-up of creative flavours. Roast quail with sautéed polenta, wild mushrooms and Madeira sauce may be one of the four starters with a soup to follow, then perhaps loin of spring lamb. The wine list is shortish but well thought out.

◐ Open all year, exc 2 weeks Xmas and 2 weeks Sept; restaurant closed Mon and Sun eves

🔁 Follow the A650 Manningham Lane to the north of Bradford. North Park Road is a left turning just before Bradford Grammar School

🛏 2 twin, 2 double; all with bathroom/WC, TV, room service, hair-dryer, trouser press

◈ Restaurant, lounge; tennis, sauna/solarium, heated swimming pool, gym nearby

⊖ No wheelchair access; no dogs

▭ Access, Amex, Visa

💷 Single occupancy of twin/double £60, twin/double £70. Cooked B £7.50; set D £39

---

*Shame on you South Yorkshire, Tyne & Wear and Mid Glamorgan, the only counties without an hotel of merit in this year's* Guide.

# Bradford Old Windmill

4 MASONS LANE, BRADFORD-ON-AVON, WILTSHIRE BA15 1QN
TEL: BATH (0225) 866842

*Small and distinctly different hill-top guesthouse. Not for meat-eating smokers, and you must bring your own alcohol.*

Peter and Priscilla Roberts set up Distinctly Different, conversions of once-functional buildings from our industrial past, and created interesting places to stay. For financial reasons this hill-top windmill ceased functioning in 1817 less than ten years after it was built.

The curved walls of the four-storey, Cotswold-stone tower are three foot thick. There are exposed beams, stripped furniture, flowery fabrics and delightful 'flotsam and jetsam from beachcombing trips around the world'. Similar attention has been applied to the four bedrooms which are both romantic and comfortable. To say they come in all shapes is not to exaggerate; they are 'Round', 'Square', 'Oval' and 'Rectangular' (a family room with round bed; a double with waterbed and patchwork quilt; a twin and a single). Though rather small, bathrooms are modern and neat.

Good vegetarian dinners, taken communally, use lots of home-grown produce and travel the world for inspiration. Breakfasts might include sheep's yoghurt with fruit salad. The Roberts point out that as they run the establishment without extra staff, their time between ten in the morning and five in the evening is devoted to looking after the place, their vegetable garden and themselves.

◑ Open all year

🔁 In Bradford on the A363, find The Castle pub. Go down the hill towards the town centre. After 50 yards turn left into a private drive immediately before the first roadside house (no sign on road). Private car park

🛏 1 single, 1 twin, 1 double, 1 family room; double with bathroom/WC, 2 with shower/WC, 1 public bathroom; TV, hair-dryer on request

◈ Dining-room, lounge; clothes and boot drying; riding, tennis, other sports nearby

⊖ No wheelchair access; no children under 6; no dogs; no smoking

▭ None accepted

£ Single £30, single occupancy of twin/double £45 to £50, twin/double £50 to £60, family room (4 people) £80 to £90; deposit required. Set D (vegetarian) £18 (8pm)

---

*If you are intending to make a lot of phone calls from your room, always check what the hotel is going to charge you per unit. You may be so horrified that you'll prefer to walk to the nearest phone box. Why let them get away with excessive charges?*

# Priory Steps

NEWTOWN, BRADFORD-ON-AVON, WILTSHIRE BA15 1NQ
TEL: BRADFORD-ON-AVON (022 16) 2230

*An unusual home with excellent gardens that take in the whole of this charming and remarkably untouristy Cotswold town.*

The pavement narrows as you walk up from the town centre, making it hard to appreciate Priory Steps' grey stone façade without risking your neck. Inside, it is tranquillity itself, and from split-level, walled gardens you can appreciate not only the whole of the town and the Avon beneath, but also the gabled terrace of what in the seventeenth century were six weavers' cottages. Today, nicely joined up, they form the welcoming home of the young hosts, Carey and Diane Chapman.

The house is filled with entertaining family heirlooms arranged in a nonchalant manner. On the walls of the small entrance hall hang an enormous gilt mirror and a painting of Lord Byron. Nonchalant chic also describes the sitting-room downstairs. All five bedrooms have the same aspect, are furnished in an unfrilly, natural fashion and have bags of space. The blue room even has a separate sitting area. 'Charming, welcoming hosts, spacious rooms and bathrooms with nice pieces of furniture,' says a reader from Shropshire whose only niggles were that to use the tea-making facilities which are under the television, 'you'd have to be a contortionist'. He also commends the 'plain but beautifully cooked dinners' (home-made hummus, pork fillet with prunes and chocolate and cinnamon parfait, perhaps) served at around 7.30. Breakfast is just as jolly and more or less when you wish.

- ◑ Open all year
- ↗ Newtown is a left-hand turning, 200 yards to the north of the town-centre, off the A363 signposted Bath. Private car park
- 🛏 2 twin, 3 double; all with bathroom/WC, TV, hair-dryer
- ◈ Dining-room, lounge; conference facilities (max 12 people non-

residential); fishing, golf, other sport nearby
- ⊖ No wheelchair access; no dogs; no smoking in public rooms
- 💳 Access, Visa
- £ Single occupancy of twin/double £38 to £42, twin/double £54 to £58. Set D £15 (by arrangement)

---

*As we arrived, new owners were moving in. They were welcoming, but they (8 staff, who had little warning of the change) kept saying we must forgive them if things were not all as they should be. We became bored with this litany by the time were were told that most of the wines (on the excellent wine list) were unavailable.* On an hotel in North Yorkshire

**BRAITHWAITE** CUMBRIA    **MAP 3**

# Ivy House

BRAITHWAITE, KESWICK, CUMBRIA CA12 5SY
TEL: KESWICK (076 87) 78338    FAX: (076 87) 78338

*Good food and excellent value from an elegant family-run hotel.*

You won't miss this striking deep-green seventeenth-century house as you drive through the little village of Braithwaite. Nick and Wendy Shill's small hotel turns out to be a comfortable and stylish base with exceptional food and splendid value for money.

Décor varies between the countrified and the elegant. You'll find the former in the long, restful oak-beamed red lounge with its floral fabrics and a fire blazing at each end. The upstairs gallery-style restaurant is a rhapsody in green, and distinctly stylish. Food, though 'unashamedly traditional', is global in inspiration and might include pork satay with peanut sauce and cucumber, an enormous salmon steak in a dill sauce with prawns, ending up with a wicked sticky toffee pudding. Service is efficient and friendly, and candlelight is *de rigueur*. The wine list is good and sensibly priced but could benefit from a few more half-bottles. Bedrooms are smartly decorated and attractively furnished, some with antiques, others with good-quality modern furniture. One has an enormous four-poster draped in lace.

◐ Closed 2 weeks Dec and most of Jan

↱ Turn left off the A66 from Keswick on to the B5292 to Braithwaite village. The hotel is in the village centre. Private car park

🛏 2 single, 2 twin, 6 double, 2 four-poster; most with bathroom/WC, some with shower/WC; TV, hair-dryer in all rooms

⬥ Dining-room, bar, lounge, drying room; fishing, riding, other sports nearby

⊖ No wheelchair access; no dogs in public rooms; no smoking in dining-room

▭ Access, Amex, Diners, Visa

£ Single £39, single occupancy of twin/double £49, twin/double £78, four-poster £90 (rates inc dinner); deposit required (prices till Easter 92). Special breaks available

**BRAMPTON** CUMBRIA    **MAP 3**

# Farlam Hall

BRAMPTON, CUMBRIA CA8 2NG
TEL: HALLBANKGATE (06977) 46234    FAX: (06977) 46683

*Formal country house hotel with gracious hosts.*

Life was tough for the Roman garrisons of Hadrian's Wall. These days guests at the Quinion and Stevenson families' nearby seventeenth-to-nineteenth-century ivy-cloaked house have things rather easier. The antiques, floral arrangements and reading matter are in a classic country house style, and the modern reproduction artwork consequently sits somewhat uneasily. Drinks are served in the front lounge by formally dressed staff, prior to a theatrical procession to the formal dining-room. Both the smaller-scale original house and the high-ceilinged addition successfully conjure up the image of an upper-class Victorian house with lots of comfortable seating, decorative wallpaper, cases of ornate trinkets and fancy lamps.

Dinner is a four-course affair and the menu is modern and inventive. Changing nightly, it features dishes such as hot savoury ramekin of smoked trout, button mushrooms and smoked salmon with a puff pastry hat, saddle of hare marinated with caraway, set in a port and herb sauce, garnished with home-made noodles. Coffee is served in a grand but welcoming lounge, brimming with comfy sofas and easy chairs. Bedrooms are all of a decent size, some are enormous, and are decorated with plush fabrics and wallpapers. Finishing touches such as pictures and lampshades are less well judged. Ask for a large room if you're ready for heavy pampering: these have state-of-the-art bathrooms with separate shower cabinets and ritzy whirlpool baths.

- ◑ Open all year, exc Xmas to New Year and Feb

- ↗ 2½ miles along the A689 south-east of Brampton. Private car park

- 🛏 I single, 6 twin, 6 double, I four-poster; most with bathroom/WC, some with shower/WC; TV, room service, hair-dryer, trouser press in all rooms; no tea/coffee-making facilities in rooms

- ◈ Dining-room, 2 lounges; fishing, golf, other sports nearby

- ⊖ No wheelchair access; no children under 5; dogs by prior arrangement

- ▭ Access, Visa

- £ Single £100, single occupancy of twin/double £100, twin/double £170 to £190, four-poster £190 (rates inc dinner). Set D £26. Special breaks available

---

**BRANSCOMBE** DEVON                                      **MAP 8**

# The Look Out

BRANSCOMBE, SEATON, DEVON EX12 3DP
TEL: BRANSCOMBE (029 780) 262

*At odds with its seaside setting, but an entertaining and slick hotel with good bedrooms.*

As you approach the long white house, sitting on its own above the pebble beach and reached by fording a shallow stream, you may begin to visualise the inside of what were once six coastguard cottages. However, the low-beamed, open-plan lounge is not only chic, but has a distinctly French feel, with elaborately carved, French-style armchairs sitting on polished flagstones, huge sprays of dried flowers and arched stone fireplaces.

The restaurant panelling started life as ships' timbers; the partition that divides it from the lounge came from an old chapel house; the flagstones once lined the quay in Portsmouth; a heavily carved ancient French bible chest now holds drinks. Service might be likened to the French way, too, with formally dressed staff chatting casually to guests. A more British approach to accommodation ensures warmly furnished bedrooms with thick, quilted bedcovers and matching headboards, and space as well as comfort and convenience. All rooms face the sea. Old fireplaces, antiques, panelled walls and interesting artwork lift their character, though mini-bars holding television sets or acting as bedside tables detract. Bathrooms aren't all that large, even in the family rooms. New young chef Steven Hart eschews most things French on his menu, combining old English flavours in an enlightened, modern British style.

⦸ *Closed mid-Dec to mid-Jan; restaurant closed Mon eve*

↗ *Take the road in Branscombe all the way to the beach. Drive through the shallow ford between 'Private access to Look Out only' signs and continue straight ahead and up the cliffside driveway to the hotel. Private car park*

🛏 *2 twin, 2 double, 1 family room; most with bathroom/WC, some with shower/WC; TV, hair-dryer, mini-bar in all rooms*

◇ *Restaurant, bar, lounge; fishing, water sports, other sports nearby. Wheelchair access to restaurant only*

⊖ *No children under 6; no dogs in public rooms*

▭ *None accepted*

💷 *Single occupancy of twin/double £44 to £50, twin/double £72 to £80, family room £72 to £115; deposit required. Set D £23 to £25. Special breaks available*

---

**BRIGHTON** EAST SUSSEX                              **MAP 10**

# Topps

17 REGENCY SQUARE, BRIGHTON, EAST SUSSEX BN1 2FG
TEL: BRIGHTON (0273) 729334   FAX: (0273) 203679

*A small family hotel in a quiet, attractive position in the centre of town.*

Regency Square, a large grassy area surrounded by cream-coloured period buildings, many of them B&Bs and small hotels, must be one of the most ideal places to stay. Paul and Pauline Collins have given Topps, a conversion of two terraced houses, the feel of an upmarket B&B. It has a separate restaurant underneath. With little public space, the reception doubling up as a small sitting-room, it's fortunate that the rooms are so spacious and comfortable to live in. Many have built-in cupboards and big sofas, and all are decorated in a refreshingly uncluttered style with a variety of shades of solid reproduction wooden furniture; they all have a thick, Topps-monogrammed carpet. A couple have four-posters and small balconies, some have gas fires. Bathrooms, most with cork-tiled floors and vinyl walls, are equally large and have baths on raised platforms. What makes the rooms even less ordinary is the number of mod cons and little extras you get that are normally associated with far more expensive places including flowers, bath robes and slippers, a large collection of soaps and medicaments, and chocolates. A simple selection of snacks can be served in your room.

Bottoms, the basement restaurant where Mrs Collins prepares a small, good-value selection of bistro-type food, offers a varied wine list, and is popular with non-residents. Parking will cost you £5 in the Collins' garage, or a bit more in the car park underneath the square.

◖ *Open all year; restaurant closed Sun, Wed, and all Jan*

⬈ *Regency Square faces the seafront in Brighton, opposite West Pier and 200 yards from the Brighton Centre. Parking sometimes difficult, hotel has 2 spaces (£5)*

🛏 *I single, 3 twin, 8 double, 2 four-poster; all with bathroom/ WC, TV, room service, hair-dryer, trouser press, mini-bar*

◈ *Restaurant; golf, water sports, other sports nearby*

⊖ *No wheelchair access; no dogs*

▭ *Access, Amex, Diners, Visa*

£ *Single £45, single occupancy of twin/double £59, twin/double £79, four-poster £99; deposit required. Set D £18; alc D £22.50. Special breaks available*

---

**BRIMFIELD** HEREFORD AND WORCESTER     **MAP 6**

# Roebuck Hotel/Poppies

BRIMFIELD, LUDLOW, SHROPSHIRE SY8 4NE
TEL: BRIMFIELD (058 472) 230

*Excellent restaurant-with-rooms, with care and commitment applied equally to both.*

A pub and restaurant-with-rooms is really a more fitting description than an hotel, but the rooms here are a cut above your average pub. Carefully matching furnishings in bright pastels have been chosen and cafetières with real coffee and home-made cakes and biscuits are provided. Bathrooms are quite small, with not much space to spread things out.

But it's the restaurant and cooking that draw people in, with dishes like hot spinach soufflé with anchovy hollandaise sauce, and roast quail with wild mushroom and truffle stuffing and madeira sauce. The cheeseboard is particularly splendid, with a good range of British farmhouse cheeses. Carole Evans uses organic produce wherever possible, and also makes her own breakfast sausages, marmalade and honey – you can see the hive at the bottom of the garden, beyond John Evans' vegetable plot.

Locals and guests who prefer the comforting dark panelling of the lounge to the fresh pink cloths and cane chairs of the restaurant have an excellent choice of bar food (changed daily). Carole and John are both informal and welcoming: 'We leave the door to the stairs up to the rooms deliberately squeaky so that we can hear when guests come down and want their breakfast.'

🅘 *Open all year, exc 2 weeks Feb and 1 week Oct; restaurant closed Sun and Mon eves*

🔀 *Just off the A49, 4 miles south of Ludlow and 7 miles north of Leominster, in the village of Brimfield. Private car park*

🛏 *1 twin, 2 double; twin with bathroom/WC, doubles with shower/WC; TV, room service, hair-dryer, trouser press in all rooms*

✅ *Restaurant, bar, lounge, games room; golf, tennis, other sports nearby.*

⊖ *No wheelchair access; no dogs; no-smoking area in restaurant*

▭ *Access, Visa*

£ *Single occupancy of twin/double £35, twin/double £60; deposit required. Alc L, D £25 to £30; bar meals from £7*

---

**BRISTOL** AVON                                        **MAP 9**

# Berkeley Square

15 BERKELEY SQUARE, CLIFTON, BRISTOL, AVON BS8 1HB
TEL: BRISTOL (0272) 254000   FAX: (0272) 252970

*Comfortable mid-sized hotel in an elegant Regency square close to the centre of Bristol.*

With this elegant Georgian town house, the managers of the Berkeley Square Hotel have a head start in their search for style and individuality. Standing on one side of a quiet square just off Park Street shopping area, the hotel overlooks private gardens surrounded by beautiful Regency terraces. Bristol's museum and art gallery are two minutes' walk away.

Inside the building real efforts have been made to combat the ordinariness so many chain hotels fall victim to. Each of the 44 bedrooms is named after an 'interesting' Bristolian – Isambard Kingdom Brunel is inevitably represented, but so are many less well-known citizens – Elizabeth Blackwell for example, the world's first female doctor, and Kings Brennus and Belinus who founded the city in Saxon times. The bedrooms themselves are comfortable and smart with every facility, and there's generally lots of space in the spotless *en suite* bathrooms.

Continuing the historic city theme, there's a small exhibition of Bristol Blue glass in the reception area where Bizley the hotel cat usually stretches out. This is the only public room with easy chairs as there's no formal lounge. The hotel has a good-sized restaurant with fresh flowers on every table and unhurried professional staff. Down a spiral staircase to the basement there's a stylish cocktail bar where you might catch the barman practising his tray-spinning technique with erratic results.

Locals come here in the evenings which can make the front of the hotel rather noisy with chatter and car doors slamming, but by 11.30pm we found the square had become peaceful again.

◐ Open all year; restaurant closed Sun

🔲 In Bristol city centre. Private car park (limited) and on-street parking

🛏 25 single, 6 twin, 11 double, 1 suite; most with bathroom/WC, 3 singles with shower/WC; TV, room service, hair-dryer, trouser press, baby-listening in all rooms

◈ Restaurant, bar, TV room; conference facilities (max 12 people, residential); golf, tennis, other sports nearby

⊖ No wheelchair access; dogs by arrangement only; smoking in some bedrooms only

💳 Access, Amex, Diners, Visa

💷 Single £49 to £66, single occupancy of twin/double £59 to £76, twin/double £69 to £89, suite £89 to £99. Cooked B £7.50, Continental B £6 (inc in room price at weekends); set D £25.50, alc D from £25 (prices till Apr 92)

# Downlands

33 HENLEAZE GARDENS, BRISTOL BS9 4HH
TEL: BRISTOL (0272) 621639

*A comfortable B&B in a pleasant residential area of Bristol, a little way north of the city centre.*

This unspectacular, semi-detached house in Bristol's tree-lined suburbia dates from the turn of the century and has been run as a bed and breakfast for thirty years. What makes the guesthouse extraordinary is the thoughtfulness of the current owners, Ulla and Peter Newman. Each of the bedrooms has plenty of space and is comfortably furnished with the individuality of a family home. All rooms have TVs and most have armchairs. Facilities are otherwise very flexible – if you tire of Bristol's many restaurants the Newmans will cook an evening meal for you; and if you don't want to spend time alone in your room you are welcome to share the spacious ground-floor lounge with the family (they change the sign on the door from 'private' to 'lounge' whenever they feel there's a need). The lounge has double doors leading into the garden, and in summer you can sit outside.

◐ Open all year

🔲 From city centre head towards Westbury on Trym. On-street parking

🛏 2 single, 3 twin, 5 double, 1 family room; 3 public bathrooms; TV, hair-dryer in all rooms

◈ Dining-room, lounge; golf, tennis, other sports nearby. Wheelchair access to guesthouse, 1 ground-floor bedroom

⊖ No dogs or smoking in public rooms

💳 None accepted

💷 Single £20, single occupancy of twin/double £24, twin/double £36, family room £45

# St Vincent Rocks

8 SION HILL, CLIFTON, BRISTOL, AVON BS8 4BB
TEL: BRISTOL (0272) 739251   FAX: (0272) 238139

*Lovely views of the Avon Gorge and Clifton Suspension Bridge make this comfortable chain hotel quite special.*

St Vincent Rocks Hotel is a tall Regency town house with fancy wrought-iron balconies, very much like many of the other houses in the terrace which curves around Sion Hill. The hill is at the top of Clifton village, whose antique shops, wine cellars and restaurants are only a few minutes' walk away, and this Forte hotel's position, overlooking the gorge and the bridge, is quite special.

The restaurant has massive picture windows to make the most of the views which are particularly pretty at night when the bridge is lit up. This is perhaps the most attractive public room, with lots of fresh flowers and large decorated serving tables. The menu offers traditional home cooking: steaks, salmon, and roast chicken with sage and onion. Children are made to feel welcome: high chairs are provided and a children's menu. Bedrooms at the front of the hotel have the views and tend to be larger than those at the back, but all are comfortable, with smart reproduction furniture and, in the larger rooms, plenty of sitting space and desks, too. The atmosphere in the hotel is informal and friendly; staff, particularly at reception, are helpful and make an effort to avoid the anonymity of some chain hotels.

- ○ Open all year
- ↗ Follow signs from the M4 towards Clifton. Sion Hill is the last road on the left before the bridge. Private car park
- ⇌ 16 single, 10 twin, 19 double, 1 four-poster; most with bathroom/WC, some with shower/WC; TV, room service, baby-listening in all rooms; hair-dryer, trouser press in some rooms
- ◈ Restaurant, bar, lounge; conference facilities (max 50

people non-residential and residential); fishing, tennis, other sports nearby; babysitting
- ⊖ No wheelchair access; no dogs in public rooms; no smoking in restaurant
- ▭ Access, Amex, Diners, Visa
- £ Single £70, single occupancy of twin/double £80 to £90, twin/double £105, four-poster £115; deposit required. Set L £12, D £15; alc L, D £26. Special breaks available

---

*Report forms are at the back of the book; write a letter if you prefer.*

---

*The* Guide *is totally independent, accepts no free hospitality, and survives on the number of copies sold each year.*

**BROADWAY** HEREFORD AND WORCESTER                 **MAP 6**

# Collin House

COLLIN LANE, BROADWAY, HEREFORD AND WORCESTER WR12 7PB
TEL: BROADWAY (0386) 858354

*Good food and a friendly welcome at a smart but homely hotel just outside the Cotswolds' most popular tourist town.*

Set just off the road to Broadway, Collin House sits amid eight acres of gardens containing silver birches and fruit trees, and overlooks the Cotswold Hills. The crumbling gateposts are less imposing than some of the grand mansions around here, and so is the atmosphere. The emphasis is on relaxation and having a good time rather than stiff formality and swish elegance.

The bar, with its inglenook fireplace, chesterfield sofas and pewter tankards, is the place to eat a light lunch or to study the dinner menu, maybe choosing black pudding with Pomméry mustard sauce, or home-made damson ice-cream with almond meringue and cream. The separate restaurant has mullioned windows overlooking the garden and is decorated with fresh flowers, Victorian prints, and John Mills's collections of glass decanters and silver snuffboxes.

Bedrooms vary in size, are named after flowers, and are furnished accordingly, with Pimpernel being brighter than most. Those at the top of the house have most character, with dormer windows extending beyond the beams. Furnishings are not co-ordinated enough to be elegant, but are pretty and homely; bathrooms are well equipped.

◑ *Open all year, exc 24 to 28 Dec*

⤢ *One mile north-west of Broadway off the A44. Private car park*

🛏 *1 single, 4 twin, 2 four-poster; most with bathroom/WC, one with shower only; room service, hair-dryer in all rooms; TV on request*

◈ *Restaurant, bar, lounge; conference facilities (max 12 people residential); croquet, unheated outdoor swimming pool, golf, riding nearby*

⊖ *No wheelchair access; children under 7 by arrangement only, and no children under 10 in restaurant; no dogs*

▭ *Access, Visa*

£ *Single £44, single occupancy of twin/double £65, twin/double £85, four-poster £97; deposit required. Set L £14, bar L from £3.50; alc D from £16.50. Special breaks available*

---

*All rooms have tea/coffee-making facilities unless we mention to the contrary.*

# Dormy House

WILLERSEY HILL, BROADWAY, HEREFORD AND WORCESTER WR12 7LF
TEL: EVESHAM (0386) 852711   TELEX: 338275 DORMY G
FAX: (0386) 858636

*Smart farmhouse hotel with appealing, warren-like public rooms;*
*bedrooms have less character.*

'Dormy' is a golfing term meaning 'unbeatable'. Some of the bedrooms
of this high-quality farmhouse hotel overlook the greens of Broadway
Golf Club. Dormy House is a converted seventeenth-century farmhouse
with various additions: the public lounges are housed in an ivy-clad
Victorian building, with the restaurant in a modern conservatory to the
side. The walls have been left unplastered, the beams exposed, the
flagstones polished. Victorian engravings and ship prints look down on
the stone fireplaces, winged chesterfield chairs, and scroll-armed sofas
upholstered in duck prints.

Bedroom fittings are more modern, especially in the newer Danish
Court: high mansard ceilings, stripped pine, neutral colours, larger
bathrooms. Billowing white ceiling drapes in the conservatory restaurant
give a marquee effect. Perhaps conscious of the needs of some of their
lunching business clientele, dishes with a low cholesterol content are
indicated with a special heartbeat symbol on the à la carte menu – for
example, poached breast of chicken in a stock of leeks, prunes and
onions. For the less abstemious, a rendezvous of seafood in saffron sauce
had enough saffron in it to wipe out several beds of crocuses; home-
cured bresaola was pink and delicious. The well-annotated wine list
leans heavily towards France.

**◖** Open all year, exc 25, 26 Dec

**⟲** From Broadway, join the A44
signposted Moreton-in-Marsh;
travel up Fish Hill. Turn first left
at sign for 'Group 4', 'Dormy
House' and 'Broadway Golf
Club'. After ½ mile take the
right fork and approach a small
crossroads. Turn left, and the
hotel is on your left. Private car
park

**⛏** 7 single, 15 twin, 22 double, 2
four-poster, 3 suites (some
rooms in annexe); all with
bathroom/WC, TV, room service,
baby-listening; hair-dryer, trouser
press and mini-bar in suites only

**⟐** Restaurant, 3 bars, 2 lounges;
conference facilities (max 200
people non-residential, 49
residential); golf, tennis, other
sports nearby; babysitting

**⊖** No wheelchair access; dogs in
annexe rooms only

**▭** Access, Amex, Diners, Visa

**£** Single £54 to £70, single
occupancy of twin/double £70,
twin/double £98 to £108, four-
poster £130, suite from £135.
Set L £14.50, £16.50, D £25,
£32; alc L, D from £42. Special
breaks available

---

*You will find report forms at the back of the Guide – please use them!*

# The Old Rectory

CHURCH STREET, WILLERSEY, BROADWAY, HEREFORD AND WORCESTER
WR12 7PN
TEL: BROADWAY (0386) 853729

*Exceptionally friendly guesthouse, with home comforts and slap-up breakfasts.*

John and Helen Jones have come in for much praise from our readers for their eagerness to help their guests: for instance they 'went out of their way to assist us in finding excellent places for an evening meal'.

The seventeenth-century Old Rectory stands at the end of a cul-de-sac in the pretty village of Willersey, with immaculate gardens behind. Inside, it's comfortable rather than elegant, scattered with personal ornaments, trinkets and little extras – bathrooms have cotton-wool balls as well as the usual bath and shower sachets. Guests have access to their rooms at all times, but there is also a comfortable lounge, with a writing desk stacked with leaflets on local attractions. Helen does not serve evening meals, but John is a willing taxi-driver for guests wary of drinking and driving. Breakfasts are 'great, with non-stop tea/coffee and toast as well as cereal, fruit, and a cooked breakfast dish too. Just what you need!'

◐ Open most of the year

▣ One mile from Broadway on the B4632 Stratford Road. Turn right into Church Street at the Bell Inn. Private car park

⇌ 1 twin, 3 double, 1 four-poster, 1 four-poster suite; all with bathroom/WC, TV, hair-dryer, trouser press

◈ Dining-room, lounge, drying room, conservatory; golf, tennis, other sports nearby

⊖ No wheelchair access; no children under 8; no dogs; smoking in lounge only

▭ Access, Visa

£ Single occupancy of twin/double £39 to £49, twin/double/four-poster £60 to £75, four-poster suite £80 to £95; deposit required. Special breaks available

**BROCKTON** SHROPSHIRE                                    MAP 6

# Brockton Grange

BROCKTON, MUCH WENLOCK, SHROPSHIRE TF13 6JR
TEL: BROCKTON (074 636) 443

*A Victorian grange with beautifully kept rooms and friendly service.*

'Walk where buzzards soar above and the heron drops in for supper at the lake.' Brockton Grange's brochure reads rather dramatically but you get the idea that the house is surrounded by wildlife. The present owners have built a lake a stone's throw from the Grange, complete with island

and nesting boxes to help conserve wildlife in the dale. You can borrow a boat and catch your own fish here, gut it on the kitchen table and have it cooked in the Aga for your breakfast. Julia Russell's relaxed and friendly attitude towards guests also extends to the rest of your stay.

The bedrooms are each beautifully decorated in pretty or striking colours and there are lots of extras, like fresh flowers and chocolates, to make you feel welcome. There's a small sitting-room for guests, or you can linger over breakfast in the 'willow pattern' breakfast room. Among the Victorian lace, dried flowers and small antiques (many for sale), there is a wonderful breakfast of kippers, fruit salad, eggs and so on, served with lots of attention to presentation. Vegetarians and others with special dietary requests are catered for as a matter of course. Packed lunches are also available.

◐ Closed Dec

⤴ From Much Wenlock take B4378 signposted Craven Arms and Ludlow; go through Bourton to Brockton Crossroads, at Feathers Inn turn immediately right. House is ½ mile on left. Private car park

🛏 1 double, 1 family room; 1 with bathroom/WC, 1 with shower/ WC; both with TV; hair-dryer on request

◈ Dining-room, lounge, coarse and trout fishing at hotel

⊖ No wheelchair access; no dogs; no smoking

▭ None accepted

£ Single occupancy of double £30, double £40, family room from £45; deposit required

---

**BROMSBERROW HEATH** GLOUCESTERSHIRE                    **MAP 6**

# Grove House

BROMSBERROW HEATH, NR LEDBURY, HEREFORD AND WORCESTER HR8 1PE
TEL: BROMSBERROW (0531) 650584

*Comfortable, thoughtfully run farmhouse that will particularly appeal to equine fans.*

It's obvious from the moment that you park in front of the barn that horses are one of Ellen Ross's interests – a row of loose boxes overlooks part of the 13 acres where her horses graze. Inside, too, the red-brick creeper-clad house is hung with horse and hunting prints, as well as embroidered hangings and needlepoint.

The hotel has a well-loved, well lived-in farmhouse feeling, with dark beams and panelling set off by shining silverware and china, fresh flowers, country pursuit magazines and an interesting assortment of books. The spacious drawing-room allows guests more freedom, ensuring that they are not confined to their bedrooms. The bedrooms have decent-sized bathrooms and solid, often antique, furniture. Each room is individually decorated: the cosy deep pink walls of the twin set off the flowery bedspreads. Providing communal dinners in the panelled dining-room is a challenge faced with obvious relish by Ellen, who formerly ran a couple of much larger hotels in the area. Menus include lots of mousselines and fish: 'We get up at five in the morning to go to the central market in Birmingham – the sight and choice of all that fish makes you want to cook.'

◑ *Open all year, exc Xmas*

⚡ *Leave the M50 at Junction 2 and follow signs to Ledbury. Take first turning left to Bromsberrow Heath. In the village turn right by post office and go up the hill. Grove House is on the right. Private car park*

🛏 *1 twin, 2 four-poster; all with bathroom/WC, TV, hair-dryer; trouser press in twin room*

◈ *Dining-room, drawing-room; conference facilities (max 10 people non-residential); tennis at hotel, riding, other sports nearby*

⊖ *No wheelchair access; no dogs; no smoking in bedrooms*

▭ *None accepted*

£ *Single occupancy of twin/four-poster £45, twin/four-poster £68. Set D £21 (8pm)*

---

**BROMSGROVE** HEREFORD AND WORCESTER                    **MAP 6**

# Grafton Manor

---

GRAFTON LANE, BROMSGROVE, HEREFORD AND WORCESTER B61 7HA
TEL: BROMSGROVE (0527) 579007   FAX: (0527) 575221

---

*Family-run manor house hotel, refreshingly down-to-earth and serving good food.*

This grand Elizabethan manor house, with its star-shaped chimneys, stepped gables, and one-acre herb garden, once belonged to the Talbot family (whose coat of arms and furniture were at one stage removed from the manor because of the family's suspected involvement in the Gunpowder Plot). Their coat of arms is back in pride of place above the huge fireplace in the lounge, but it's very much John and June Morris's domain now.

A recurring motif is the Gothic arch, found in doors, alcoves, even shower suites. Rooms vary: standard doubles are rather small for the price – you get more space per pound in superior rooms. Bathrooms are a strange mix: modern avocado or white baths outnumber original Victorian cast-iron models. 'The ambience of this beautiful old house is very *Country Living* and *Horse and Hound*,' writes one reader, 'but the Morris family have none of the overbearing country image one might imagine in the owners of such a property.'

Dinner in the restaurant, with its gilt-embellished coving and shining silver, might include fresh oysters, cockles and mussels grilled with a Roquefort sabayon, or confit of duck with blackcurrant, kumquat and apricot sauce. A shortage of half-bottles on the wine list has been commented on. Continental or English breakfast is included in the tariff;

however, one early leaver felt that fresh coffee could have been delivered to his room at 7am: 'not that desperately early'.

◑ Open all year

⤢ 1½ miles south of Bromsgrove, off the B4091. Private car park

🛏 1 single, 2 twin, 3 double, 1 four-poster, 2 suites; all with bathroom/WC, TV, room service, hair-dryer, trouser press; no tea/coffee-making facilities in rooms

◈ Restaurant, lounge; conference facilities (max 9 people residential, 12 non-residential); golf, tennis, other sports nearby.

Wheelchair access to hotel and restaurant, 1 ground-floor bedroom

⊖ No dogs

▭ Access, Amex, Diners, Visa

£ Single £85, single occupancy of twin/double £85 to £95, twin/double £105, four-poster £125, suite £150; deposit required. Set L £15, D £28.50. Special breaks available

# Stakis Country Court

BIRMINGHAM ROAD, BROMSGROVE, HEREFORD AND WORCESTER B61 0JB
TEL: 021-447 7888   TELEX: 336976   FAX: 021-447 7273

*Highly computerised business hotel, with many facilities, that dares to be slightly different.*

The red-brick exterior looks like an out-of-town supermarket, with unpromising views of waste ground and housing estates. Inside, however, it's something else. If you're just a mite tired of bland, uniform business hotels, come and see how they can be jazzed up. The 'country court' concept apparently originated in Miami, and the lobby is a 1920s palm court, Miami-style. A tapering plaster and marble chimney centre-piece disappears through the ceiling, its whiteness set off by the emerald carpet with a raised pattern of deep pink roses, repeated in the upholstery of the surrounding sofas and chairs. Bronze horses, palms and brass-type light fittings complete the picture.

The restaurant and cocktail bar are in the more usual muted pinks and blues. The latest computer technology has been installed – waiting staff no longer traipse through to the kitchen but simply punch their orders into a keypad to be printed out in the kitchen to the chef. Even the piano is, rather unnervingly, operated by computer – look, no hands! Rooms have a standard business hotel layout, but in the hallmark white, pink and green. Special rooms have been designated for disabled people, women travelling on their own, and families.

◑ Open all year

⤢ Just off Junction 4 of the M5 and Junction 1 of the M42. Private car park

🛏 27 twin, 104 double, 10 suites; all with bathroom/WC, TV, room

service, hair-dryer, mini-bar, baby-listening

◈ Restaurant, bar, lounge; conference facilities (max 80 people non-residential) (all public areas air-conditioned);

sauna/solarium, heated swimming pool, gym, Jacuzzi, steam room all at hotel. Wheelchair access to hotel and restaurant/WC (M, F), 70 ground-floor bedrooms, 4 specially equipped for disabled people; babysitting

⊖ No dogs in public rooms; no smoking in upstairs bedrooms

▭ Access, Amex, Diners, Visa

£ Single occupancy of twin/double £80, twin/double £90, suite £101. Continental B £7; cooked B £8.50; set L £12.50, D £16; alc L, D on application (prices till Sept 91). Special breaks available

## BROXTED ESSEX                                   MAP 7

# Whitehall

CHURCH END, BROXTED, ESSEX CM6 2BZ
TEL: BISHOP'S STORTFORD (0279) 850603   FAX: (0279) 850385

*A smoothly run but slightly impersonal country hotel fifteen minutes from Stansted Airport.*

Standing on a hillside at the edge of the village, Whitehall is part-Elizabethan, multi-gabled and, yes, white. It looks established and is well adapted for business functions, especially since a second bedroom wing and conference hall in the converted barn were completed. This is all a far cry from the way it was in 1985, when the Keane family opened it with just four bedrooms.

We still think it could do with some personal touches, but commend it for comfort and service. Though you don't sink ankle deep into carpets, nor bump into many antiques, the furniture and cool colour schemes match and are decorative. Equally designer-conscious but warmer-tinted are the bedrooms. Rooms in the barn (two) and main house (five) have the sort of character only old houses can provide; those in the first extension (six) haven't the glamour or luxury of those in the latest extension (twelve) where you'll find separate showers, Teletext televisions and more space to sit. Prices are steepish but garden-view rooms are still worth the extra expense.

Another new feature is a second restaurant called the Grill which, though clearly intended for business lunches, is set with lady-like tall padded chairs. The larger restaurant is much more handsome, and here you can choose the likes of warm pigeon salad with hazelnut dressing, and hare stew with pickled red cabbage from the table d'hôte menu. (Or go for the 'menu surprise'.) Tall hedges break up the lovely large garden behind the house, and well-hidden behind that are the tennis court and swimming-pool.

◑ Open all year, exc 26 to 30 Dec

⤢ 10 minutes' drive from Junction 8 (Bishop's Stortford exit) of the M11. Broxted is two miles south-west of Thaxted. At Takeley take the left turning to Broxted. Private car park

🛏 4 twin, 21 double; all with

bathroom/WC, TV, room service, hair-dryer, trouser press; no tea/coffee-making facilities in rooms

 2 restaurants, bar, 2 lounges; conference facilities (max 120 people, 25 residential); tennis, unheated outdoor pool at hotel, other sports nearby. Wheelchair access to hotel (2 steps),

restaurant and WC (M,F), 2 ground-floor bedrooms

No children under 5; no dogs

Access, Amex, Diners, Visa

Single occupancy of twin/double £75, twin/double £95 to £155; deposit required. Set L £18.50, D £31.50 (prices till end 91)

---

**BROXTON** CHESHIRE　　　　　　　　　　　　　　　　**MAP 4**

# Broxton Hall

---

WHITCHURCH ROAD, BROXTON, CHESTER, CHESHIRE CH3 9JS
TEL: BROXTON (0829) 782321　FAX: (0829) 782330

---

*Beautiful Tudor house with excellent restaurant; some bedrooms are disappointing.*

Broxton Hall is perhaps at its most welcoming on a winter's evening when the darkness of local country roads is suddenly broken by a splendidly impressive floodlit half-timbered Tudor country house. While Broxton Hall's exterior may be imposing, the atmosphere becomes immediately more cosy in the intimate reception area and lounge. A large seventeenth-century log fireplace and dark oak tables scattered with *Country Living* magazines are waiting to greet you, and deep sofas and armchairs make it tempting for the tired traveller to curl up and relax, there and then.

The owners, George and Rosemary Hadley, are local antique dealers and throughout the house are examples of tasteful, unpretentious decoration: fine fabrics, paintings and porcelain mixing the best of antique and modern country styles. The dining-room is more modern in style but the atmosphere remains relaxed and convivial. The bar, where orders are taken, is full of locals as well as residents. The menu is a mix of English and French – pigeon breasts or crème Dubarry to start, loin of pork in mustard sauce or salmon en croûte for the main course. The cooking and service are first-class, the wine list extensive and the lighting and décor in keeping with the overall, relaxed impression. Afterwards, retire back to those deep armchairs to curl up in front of the log fire.

Perhaps the only disappointment is in the bedrooms, some of which fall short of the standards established elsewhere. A standard double was functional and somewhat impersonally furnished with surprisingly little of the attention to detail apparent elsewhere in the house.

Open all year, exc 25 Dec

8 miles from Chester on A41 towards Whitchurch. Situated at

the Broxton roundabout on the left. Private car park

3 single, 3 twin, 4 double, 1

four-poster, 4 family rooms; all with bathroom/WC, 1 public bathroom; TV, room service, hair-dryer, baby-listening in all rooms; trouser press in luxury rooms

 Dining-room, bar, drawing-room, library, conservatory; conference facilities (max 20 people non-residential, 15 residential); golf, riding nearby

No wheelchair access; no children under 12; no dogs in bedrooms

Access, Amex, Diners, Visa

Single £55, single occupancy of twin/double £70, twin/double £65, four-poster £85; deposit required. Set L £11.50, D £19.50; alc L from £2. Special breaks available

---

**BUCKLAND** GLOUCESTERSHIRE     **MAP 6**

# Buckland Manor

BUCKLAND, NR BROADWAY, HEREFORD AND WORCESTER WR12 7LY
TEL: BROADWAY (0386) 852626   FAX: (0386) 853557

*Stately country-house hotel in the best tradition – an expensive treat.*

The original lord of the manor was surely never so comfortable. This part-thirteenth-century, part-Elizabethan manor house, overlooked by the gargoyles of the adjoining church but little else, is now an extremely comfortable country-house hotel. Attention has been paid to the right sort of detail, with emphasis on tradition as well as comfort. The wood-panelled walls are hung with oil paintings of ancestors (though nobody knows whose), fabrics are heavy and not over-flowery, thick rugs cover polished creaking floors, and there's not a flounced blind in sight.

The restaurant has a lighter, more elegant feel, with white-painted panelling and blue velvet tasselled curtains. Tradition – French tradition, that is – also comes through in both the menu and wine list, with occasional nods to fashion: for example, terrine of duck foie gras and truffle with toasted brioche, beef fillet pan-fried with baby shallots and served with a cream sauce. Rooms are stately with a minimum of frilliness, except for the lacy tissue-box covers, and extras like open fires, fluffy bathrobes and a fruit bowl. The manor has its own natural spring: turn on the bath taps for a relaxing wallow or simply open the bottle provided in every bedroom.

Open all year

From Broadway, take the A46/B4632 towards Cheltenham; Buckland Manor is off to the left. Private car park

2 twin, 5 double, 2 four-poster, 1 family room; all with bathroom/WC, TV, room-service, hair-

dryer; no tea/coffee-making facilities in rooms

Restaurant, 2 lounges; conference facilities (max 10 people, residential); tennis, croquet, putting, heated outdoor swimming-pool at hotel, other sports nearby. Wheelchair access to hotel (1 step) and restaurant, 3 ground-floor bedrooms

● No children under 12; no dogs

▭ Access, Amex, Visa

£ Single occupancy of twin/double

£135 to £230, twin/double £145 to £240, four-poster £240; suite/family room £300 (4 people); deposit required. Sun L £17.50; alc L, D £35 (prices till Mar 92). Special breaks available

---

**BUCKNELL** SHROPSHIRE                                   **MAP 5**

# Bucknell House

BUCKNELL, SHROPSHIRE SY7 0AD
TEL: BUCKNELL (054 74) 248

*A very peaceful spot in beautiful countryside where the welcome is sincere and informal.*

In spring hundreds of daffodils line the long gravel drive leading to this rambling old vicarage where peacocks strut in the sunshine. Peter and Brenda Davies have placed a strategic notice in the bathroom which states: 'We do so hope you will relax and enjoy your stay in our home.' A home is just what it is. In one of the three guest bedrooms, their son's football and cricket team photos still cover part of the wall. In the hall are family wedding photos and the downstairs cloakroom houses three portraits of their now grown-up children. It is like staying at a friend's house: the welcome is friendly and courteous and everyone breakfasts at the same table. Brenda provides evening snacks only if required.

The bedrooms are comfortable with undistinguished but serviceable furniture and flowery duvets. From the 'Rose Room', there is a lovely outlook towards Bryant Park and Brenda will point out the line where three county boundaries – Shropshire, Herefordshire and Powys – meet, beyond the ha-ha in the garden.

The dining-room is quite formal with a long central table and large antique sideboards. In the living-room, local tourist information is set out for guests; the Davieses can give you ideas for walks.

○ Closed Dec, Jan, Feb

↗ Follow A4113 Ludlow to Knighton road, then B4368 towards Craven Arms. The house stands on B4367, on fringe of village. Private car park

⇌ 1 twin, 2 double; 1 bathroom, 2 toilets to share; all rooms have TV, hair-dryer and wash units

◇ Dining-room, drawing-room,

tennis at hotel, golf, fishing nearby

● No wheelchair access; no children under 12; dogs in bedrooms only; no smoking in bedrooms

▭ None accepted

£ Single occupancy of twin/double £18, twin/double £31

---

*See the inside front cover for a brief explanation of how to use the* Guide.

**BUILDWAS** SHROPSHIRE     **MAP 6**

# Bridge House     ℒ

BUILDWAS, TELFORD, SHROPSHIRE TF8 7BN
TEL: IRONBRIDGE (0952) 432105

*Good-value B&B in a lovely old house offering comfortable rooms and wacky collectors' items.*

It's a pity that this B&B is so close to the main road as otherwise its location would be ideal. Only two minutes' drive from the centre of Ironbridge, this seventeenth-century inn with its half-timbered façade and panelled rooms makes a comfortable base for exploring the nearby Ironbridge Gorge museums. Bridge House, the Hedges' family home up until a few years ago, is rather like a museum itself. From the collection of agricultural machinery in the garden to family mementoes and paraphernalia furnishing the cosy sitting-room, there is always something to attract your interest.

Over breakfast you can read about the property as it was in the 1960s before the present owners bought it for just a few hundred pounds. A full English breakfast is served by Mrs Hedges who will fill you in with more history of the house and local area.

The bedrooms are a good size and peaceful enough despite the main road. Some have quite ordinary, modern furniture, while others hold more luxurious antiques. Not all are *en suite*, but you will be entertained during the short stroll along the corridor by more family collections, this time bedwarmers and photographs from Mr Hedges' race horse owning days.

◑ Open all year, exc Xmas

↗ On the B4380 Shrewsbury road, 1½ miles out of Ironbridge. Private car park

🛏 1 single, 1 twin, 1 double, 1 four-poster, 1 family room; 1 room with bathroom/WC, 1 with shower/WC, 2 public bathrooms

◈ Dining-room, lounge, TV room;

fishing, tennis, sports nearby

⊖ No wheelchair access; no dogs

▭ None accepted

£ Single £16 to £18, single occupancy of twin/double £18 to £25, twin/double £20 to £36, four-poster £36 to £50, family room £52 to £60; deposit required

---

*We were offered no help with our luggage; when we came down to dinner, we looked into the residents' lounge and there sat two of the kitchen brigade, who neither got up nor even looked at us but rather stared at the television. Most of the bar had been taken over by the staff in the early evening, the majority of whom were off duty and getting tuned up for a staff birthday party later that night in a local night club.* On an hotel in Lancashire

# Old Vicarage

BURBAGE, MARLBOROUGH, WILTSHIRE SN8 3AG
TEL: MARLBOROUGH (0672) 810495

*A very comfortable and welcoming home in rural setting close to
Marlborough. Lovers of interesting bathrooms read on.*

Jane Cornelius and Robert Hector's brick and flint Gothic Victorian
rectory, a Wolsey Lodge in a rural village of thatched cottages and less
fetching modern homes, provides a relaxing retreat. High ceilings,
arches and tall windows are offset by warm, invigorating colour schemes;
fires crackle on cool evenings in several of the large downstairs rooms
where lots of books and magazines are provided. Or you can play croquet
in the lovely, tall tree-studded garden.

Robert serves and joins you for drinks before you are ushered into the
bright yellow-and-green dining-room where as many as twenty candles
are aglow. You might have quails' eggs, seasonal game (perhaps venison
with spicy sauce and juniper), cheeses, then rhubarb and orange mousse.
Everything is seasonal; organic vegetables often come from the garden.

You will be equally comfortable and cosseted in your bedrooms. All
three are roomy, prettily furnished and equipped with 'greedy tins' of
home-made shortbread, water, juice, fruit, chocolate truffles, sewing kits
and manicure sets. Bathrooms deliver a few surprises. The one in the
apricot room takes you right out of rural Wiltshire and transports you on
to an Italian balcony, with a vast mural of black columns breaking up sea
and sky. The blue room, a single, has an original Victorian loo. Breakfast
should not disappoint, with the likes of fresh dates, mango, melon and
organic bread to set you up for the day.

◑ Closed Jan, dining-room closed
Tues, Wed, Thur

🡶 From Burbage High Street, turn
east into Taskers Lane, take 3rd
turning on right into Eastcourt;
Old Vicarage is on the left.
Private car park

🛏 1 single, 1 twin, 1 double; all
with bathroom/WC; TV and hair-
dryer on request

◈ Dining-room, lounge; conference
facilities (max 10 people non-
residential); fishing, golf, other
sports nearby

⊖ No wheelchair access; no
children; no dogs; no smoking

▭ Access, Visa

£ Single £32, single occupancy of
twin/double £40, twin/double
£55; deposit required. Picnic
hamper £18, set D £25

---

*The text of entries is based on unsolicited reports sent in by readers and
backed up by inspections. The factual details under the text are from
questionnaires the* Guide *sends to all hotels that feature in the book.*

**BURFORD** OXFORDSHIRE     **MAP 6**

# Andrews Hotel

HIGH STREET, BURFORD, OXFORDSHIRE OX18 4RJ
TEL: BURFORD (099 382) 3151   FAX: (099 382) 3240

*An immaculate B&B in the centre of this bustling Cotswold village.*

Trevor Gibbons, a veritable bundle of entrepreneurial energy, runs Andrews Hotel in line with his own business philosophy: 'Find something that you're very good at and stick to it.' In the case of Andrews this means spotlessly clean and comfortable accommodation and a roaring line in cream teas.

Bedrooms are spacious, freshly emulsioned, constantly refurbished to ensure that no signs of tattiness creep in; with newly tiled bathrooms resplendent in natty blue and white.

Andrews is easily spotted on Burford's busy High Street, its Tudor black and white upper storeys in strong contrast to the Cotswold stone elsewhere. In the summer, hanging baskets add a splash of colour and provide something else for those queuing for tea to look at apart from the centre table in the front-room groaning under the weight of diet-destroying goodies.

| | |
|---|---|
| ◑ Open all year | ◈ Lounge, TV room; golf, tennis, other sports nearby |
| ⤴ The hotel is half-way along Burford High Street, beyond the traffic lights on the hill. On-street parking | ⊖ No wheelchair access; no dogs; no smoking in bedrooms and some public rooms |
| ⇌ I single, 6 double, 3 four-poster; some with bathroom/WC, rest with shower/WC; all rooms have TV; no tea/coffee-making facilities in rooms | ▭ Access, Amex, Diners, Visa |
| | ⊞ Single £50, single occupancy of twin/double £50, twin/double £72, four-poster from £82; deposit required |

# The Lamb Inn

SHEEP STREET, BURFORD, OXFORDSHIRE OX8 4LR
TEL: BURFORD (099 382) 3155

*Atmospheric Elizabethan inn with simple accommodation and a stylish restaurant.*

The Lamb Inn is made up of a number of fourteenth-century cottages, now knocked through, along Sheep Street – a quiet backwater away from the increasing bustle of Burford's High Street. The bar of the Lamb is a convivial, if cramped, spot for a drink and also does a lively lunchtime trade in ploughman's and other pub-fare. One reader comments that he 'can think of no more pleasant place to be, especially in the early evening'. A bar-hatch allows guests to order from the calmer side of the bar – a flagstone-floored lounge where there are ample comfy corners to retreat to with a drink and a good read. Familiar, slightly battered old armchairs surround the log fire and there's an overall sense of contented peace.

The restaurant is an interesting contrast to the grandparental cosiness elsewhere: a low-ceilinged elegant, candlelit, pillared room where ferns hanging from the ceiling provide a splash of verdant colour. The only problem is that the lights remain low at breakfast so reading the paper can cause severe eye strain. Roast quail stuffed with water-chestnut and chicken mousse was typical of the menu when we inspected, although the highlight was some exquisite sautéed Dublin prawns in lemon and chive butter. (There is only a buffet supper on Sundays, though.) Regulars retreat to the lounge and everyone chats easily over coffee. Down in the bar jovial laughter may disturb those who've gone to bed early.

Bedrooms, all except the singles now refurbished, are basic, floors a little uneven, so your chest of drawers may tip drunkenly. Reports on service are all complimentary and one in particular remarks: 'What a joy it is to find the same staff from one year's visit to the next – and what friendly and competent staff they are.'

◐ *Open all year, exc 25 and 26 Dec*

▱ *The inn is just off Burford High Street – turn by Tolesey Museum*

🛏 *3 single, 3 twin, 8 double, 1 four-poster; most with bathroom/WC, 1 with shower/WC, 3 rooms with shared facilities; room service, hair-dryer, baby-listening in all rooms; no tea/coffee-making facilities in rooms*

◈ *Restaurant, bar, 2 lounges, TV room, drying room; fishing, tennis, other sports nearby;*

*limited wheelchair access to hotel, (2 steps) restaurant and WC (M,F), 3 ground-floor bedrooms*

⊖ *No dogs in restaurant and by arrangement only in bedrooms*

▭ *Access, Visa*

£ *Single £36 to £40; single occupancy of twin/double £55 to £65; twin/double £67 to £75; four-poster £67 to £75. Set L £17, D £20 to £25; bar meals from £6.50. Special breaks available*

**BURLAND** CHESHIRE  **MAP 4**

# Burland Farm

WREXHAM ROAD, BURLAND, NR NANTWICH, CHESHIRE CW5 8ND
TEL: FADDILEY (0270 74) 210

*First-rate guesthouse on a working dairy farm.*

Various Allwoods have been farmers since the seventeenth century, and the present owners of this working dairy farm, Michael and Sandra, have got the countrified, chic effect down to a fine art. Family furniture takes its place with bought-in Victoriana; colours are subtle and well-chosen. Criss-crossed black beams huddle beneath the peaked roof, while windows are embellished with a delicate beehive pattern. The style is distinctly country house but the tariff reassuringly farmhouse.

Food is good and sometimes reflects Sandra's American heritage. One recent menu kicked off with lobster, avocado and bacon salad with lime sauce followed by Scotch sirloin steaks in a sauce of sesame oil, red wine and quince jelly. A boozy dessert might be strawberries in chardonnay with Cointreau and black pepper, served with little biscuits.

Bedrooms are very spacious, pretty and combine stripped pine, good antiques and painted brass bedsteads. Floral water colours and flowering pot-plants add a homely touch. New arrivals are welcomed with home-made cakes and biscuits, and a flask of fresh milk (the farm is green-top licensed). Traffic noise is clearly audible but enjoy the farmhouse sights and smells and you might just imagine yourself in Ambridge.

🕒 *Closed Xmas; restaurant closed Sun eve*

🏎 *4 miles west of Nantwich on the A534 Nantwich to Wrexham road. Private car park*

🛏 *2 twin, I double; I with bathroom/WC, 2 with shower/WC; TV, hair-dryer*

◈ *Dining-room, lounge, library; conference facilities (max 12*

*people non-residential); table tennis at hotel, other sports nearby*

⊖ *No wheelchair access; no children under 10; dogs in public rooms by arrangement only*

▭ *Amex*

£ *Twin/double £40 to £50; deposit required. Set L (by arrangement) £8, D £12.50 to £15*

## BURNHAM MARKET NORFOLK                              MAP 7

# Hoste Arms

THE GREEN, BURNHAM MARKET, KING'S LYNN, NORFOLK PE31 8HD
TEL: FAKENHAM (0328) 738257   FAX: (0328) 730103

*Successful application of new comforts to an old inn.*

Burnham Market is a smashing town, full of just the sort of unprecious old character most holiday-trippers go mad over. The Hoste is similarly low-key about its olde worlde charms, despite the fact '17th-Century Hotel' is more prominent on the sign than 'Hoste Arms'. Its well-maintained but wobbly-looking front is flesh-coloured, and it has a particularly fetching tile roof. Once inside, you're treated to a high level of taste and respect for the past. The theme is nautical, as it was in 1650 when local assizes were held here. Fires blaze in the huge hearth and the tile floor might well have been around for a few centuries.

Paul Whittome, a recent arrival, has stripped the pine, spruced up the furnishings and modernised without spoiling an inch of the inn's former glories. The restaurant is stylish without going overboard, and a seating area, away from the often crowded pub, has rattan chairs made comfortable with cushions. The chef is French, a departure from the Englishness you expect, but the food is in fact a mixture, tapping local produce (pheasant casserole, perhaps).

You leave the old world behind when you retire to your room. Ruched curtains in bold patterns hang at the windows, skirted tables stand by beds and there are jazzy decorative touches all about. All the rooms are reasonably sized, some are large. Two rooms have four-posters. Slick bathrooms are well stocked with toiletries.

◐ *Open all year*

▨ *10 miles north of Fakenham. Hoste Arms is on west side of Burnham Market. Private car park*

⇌ *2 twin, 4 double, 2 four-poster; all with bathroom/WC, TV, room service, hair-dryer, baby-listening*

◈ *2 dining-rooms, bar, lounge; conference facilities (max 20*

*people non-residential); golf, fishing, other sports nearby*

⊖ *No wheelchair access; no dogs; no smoking in one dining-room*

▭ *Access*

£ *Single occupancy of twin/double £33, twin/double £56, four-poster £76; deposit required. Alc L £9.50, D £13.50. Special breaks available*

## BURY ST EDMUNDS SUFFOLK                                    MAP 7

# The Angel

ANGEL HILL, BURY ST EDMUNDS, SUFFOLK IP33 1LT
TEL: BURY ST EDMUNDS (0284) 753926   TELEX: 81630 ANGEL G
FAX: (0284) 750092

*An institution in this historic, newly spruced-up square, and more casual than its imposing façade might suggest.*

Say 'The Angel' anywhere in East Anglia and most folk will immediately think of Bury's grand old hotel. Dickens stayed here (in Room 15, kept much as it was then), and had his Mr Pickwick enjoying a roast dinner here as well as hearing that Mrs Bardell's breach of promise action against him had begun. Locals are avid fans, knowing that an unstuffy hostelry resides behind the huge, ivy-clad front.

The basement Crypt, previously only a touch less formal than the elegant upstairs dining-room (which has lovely old portraits in oil, white tablecloths and serves good, more or less traditional meals), has now been refurbished into a more casual, all-day venue for quicker, snack meals. The entrance hall leads directly into a high-ceilinged reception area and lounge, but the sky-lit alcove off it and the leather-seated bar are more intimate and often quiet.

Less quiet are the front bedrooms though the ivy-framed windows are compensation. Most are luxurious and as comfortable as you'd expect at the price, with large antique wardrobes suiting the sizeable rooms. The suite is still worth the extra. Excellent bathrooms, even in singles.

◑ Open all year

� In the centre of Bury St Edmunds – follow signs for tourist information. Private car park

🛏 14 single, 10 twin, 11 double, 4 four-poster, 1 suite; all with bathroom/WC, TV, room service, hair-dryer, trouser press, baby-listening; tea/coffee-making facilities on request

◈ 2 restaurants, bar, lounge, drying room; conference facilities (max 150 people non-residential, 25 residential); golf, tennis, other sports nearby

⊖ No wheelchair access; dogs at manager's discretion; no smoking in restaurant and in some bedrooms

▭ Access, Amex, Diners, Visa

£ Single £70 to £80, single occupancy of twin/double £83, twin/double £100 to £115, four-poster £100 to £125, suite £155; deposit required. Continental B £6.50, cooked B £10; set L £12.50, D £20; alc L, D £26 (prices till Oct 91). Special breaks available

---

# Kingshott's

---

12 ANGEL HILL, BURY ST EDMUNDS, SUFFOLK IP33 1UZ
TEL: BURY ST EDMUNDS (0284) 704088   FAX: (0284) 763133

*Stylish town house hotel, now a B&B only.*

Gary and Dianne Kingshott's smart Georgian town house hotel has changed since we commented in last year's *Guide* that it was still finding its feet. Alas, they no longer offer dinner because of their involvement in another venture, the Beehive in Horringer (too far for most guests).

A new office block now looms over the Italianate garden behind the elegant terrace, more's the pity. Traffic is audible in front bedrooms, and you will probably be aware of idling commuter buses at breakfast. The small, very comfortable lounge also faces the square, but it is usually very quiet. Nevertheless, unlike the Angel over the way (see entry above), Kingshott's is not hotel-like, and antique furniture and swish paintings and porcelain set off by a bright colour scheme do their bit to set a gracious mood. Effective central heating keeps it cosy. Upstairs, via a curved staircase, there are good-sized bedrooms in whatever colour scheme you fancy, providing there's a wine in that colour. All have shiny chintz fabrics, antique furniture, plenty of goodies and not a speck of dirt. Those guests who lament the closure of the restaurant can at least look forward to fresh orange juice for breakfast.

◑ Open all year

▭ Part of a row of Georgian buildings on Angel Hill in the centre of Bury St Edmunds. Private car park

🛏 1 single, 3 double, 1 four-poster, 1 suite; some with bathroom/

WC, some with shower/WC; TV, room service, hair-dryer, trouser press in all rooms; no tea/coffee-making facilities in rooms

◈ Dining-room, bar, lounge; conference facilities (max 40 people non-residential); tennis,

golf, other sports nearby

 No wheelchair access; dogs by arrangement only

Access, Visa

£ Single £50, single occupancy of twin/double £55, four-poster £70, suite £75; deposit required

# Ounce House

NORTHGATE STREET, BURY ST EDMUNDS, SUFFOLK IP33 1HP
TEL: BURY ST EDMUNDS (0284) 761779/755192

*A classy home with many of the facilities of expensive hotels. As friendly and relaxed as you could wish for.*

The now-united pair of Victorian merchants' houses, not far from Bury's centre, are set back a little from a main road, providing space for cars and a buffer for sound. Simon and Jenny Pott's home is much more than a handy retreat for weary business people. Paintings of Pott ancestors, antiques, a grand piano, and sleek fabrics throughout the spacious and open ground-floor rooms might make it a formal place were it not for the easy-going Potts themselves.

The lower ground floor is broken up into three restaurants and a bar. It's a bit dark, but keep an eye out for detail. A local artist has painted cupboard doors with a magnificent *trompe-l'oeil*, making you think for an instant that there is a cornucopia of junk stacked on shelves behind glass doors. You should retain memories of your bedroom, too, for its attention to detail. Antique furniture, lots of light and a personal feel that confirms this really isn't an hotel are standard to otherwise completely individual rooms. There's a choice of simple rather than adventurous dishes on the set, four-course menu.

◑ Open all year; restaurant closed Sun, Mon

▰ Approaching Bury St Edmunds from east or west on the A45, leave by the second exit to the town. Turn left at the first roundabout into Northgate Street. The house is at the top of the hill on the right-hand side. Private car park

▨ I single, 2 twin, I double; most with bathroom/WC, I with shower/WC; TV, room service, hair-dryer, trouser press, baby-listening in all rooms

◈ Restaurant, 2 lounges, bar, library, TV; conference facilities (max 12 people residential); fishing, golf, other sports nearby

⬤ No wheelchair access; no dogs; no smoking

▭ Access, Visa

£ Single £35, single occupancy of twin/double £38 to £40, twin/double £60 to £70; deposit required. Alc L £8 to £12, D £15 to £20 (prices till Apr 92)

---

*£*    *This denotes that the hotel offers especially good value at whatever price level.*

**BUTTERMERE** CUMBRIA     **MAP 3**

# Bridge Hotel

BUTTERMERE, CUMBRIA CA13 9UZ
TEL: BUTTERMERE (059 685) 252/266

*Friendly and informal hotel/pub in a lovely setting.*

First licensed in 1735, the Bridge Hotel (aka the Bridge Inn, the Queen and the Victoria) has been in the business of supplying victuals for a long time. Much extended in the interim, it remains essentially a Lakeland stone house, rendered photogenic by the old bridge itself.

At its heart is an attractive traditional pub with low beams, exposed stone walls and tapestry-covered seating, where light meals are served. In contrast, the large, bright lounge impresses with pastel fabrics, dainty designs and good antiques. The restaurant's décor is uninspired but when it comes to food you can set off on a round-the-world package tour encompassing sardines portugaise grilled with a tomato, capsicum and garlic sauce, pork cutlet Normandy, served with spiced apple sauce, as well as traditional stand-bys like English lamb. Bedrooms are bright, though smallish, and are pleasantly furnished in cheerful colour schemes, though lacking television and radio due to poor reception. Two bigger rooms have four-posters. One welcome touch: residents can enjoy a home-baked afternoon tea included in the tariff.

- ◐ Open all year
- ⤴ Leave the M6 at Junction 40 and follow signs to Keswick. Bypass Keswick taking the turning to Buttermere. Private car park
- 🛏 2 single, 6 twin, 12 double, 2 four-poster; all with bathroom/WC; hair-dryer on request
- ◈ Restaurant, 2 bars, lounge, drying-room; conference facilities (max 20 people residential, 30 non-residential); fishing nearby
- ♿ No wheelchair access; no dogs in public rooms; no smoking in restaurant
- ▭ None accepted
- £ Single £40 to £48, single occupancy of twin/double £48 to £62, twin/double £64 to £82, four-poster £74 to £92 (rates inc dinner); deposit required. Set D £16.50; bar food at lunch. Special breaks available

---

*Prices are what you can expect to pay in 1992, except where specified to the contrary. Many hoteliers tell us that these prices can be regarded only as approximations.*

**BUTTERTON** STAFFORDSHIRE               **MAP 4**

# Black Lion Inn

BUTTERTON, NR LEEK, STAFFORDSHIRE ST13 7ST
TEL: LEEK (0538) 304232

*A welcoming, old-fashioned inn with most of the modern comforts.
Excellent touring base.*

The village of Butterton is in the south-eastern part of the Peak District
and, hidden off the main roads, is a very peaceful spot. Built in 1782, the
inn was probably two separate cottages before being joined together to
make an attractive, welcoming pub/hotel. It is a place of low ceilings,
beams and cosiness – old-fashioned and uncontrived, it's left to speak for
itself. The main rooms are really a series of different areas all with a bit of
the bar as their focal point. Most sections have an open log fire and all
have a selection of wooden tables and chairs with the occasional bench
seat either upholstered or scattered with pretty linen cushions. The plain
walls are covered with an assortment of old photographs, prints and
plates and the whole effect and atmosphere is very welcoming. The
Smith brothers who own and run it are an effective and unobtrusive
presence, providing everything their guests need.

    The comfortable bedrooms are all decorated differently, all with *en
suite* bathrooms and light pretty fabrics. Food is served in all the bar areas
both at lunchtime and in the evening. The thick home-made vegetable
soup is delicious and just the thing after a day tramping across the Peaks.
You also have the choice of eating in the marginally more formal
restaurant at the back of the hotel.

- ◑ Open all year, restaurant open
  Fri, Sat eves and Sun lunch

- ⤴ Opposite the church is Butterton
  village, 9 miles from Ashbourne,
  6 miles from Leek. Private car
  park

- ⤳ 2 double, 1 family room, all with
  bathroom/WC, TV, room service;
  hair-dryer

- ◈ Restaurant, 4 bars, lounge, TV

  room, games room, drying room;
  conference facilities (max 30
  people non-residential); riding,
  fishing, other sports nearby

- ⊖ No wheelchair access; no dogs in
  bedrooms

- ▭ None accepted

- £ Single occupancy of double £26,
  double £45. Set L £7, D £7; alc
  D £15

---

*So, when paying the bill (£60 for an attic room and poor facilities) I
complained of the cistern and lack of friendliness, to be told 'don't tell me how
to run my business' and 'don't come back if you don't like it'. (I won't.)* On
an hotel in Northamptonshire

**CALDBECK** CUMBRIA                                                          **MAP 3**

# High Greenrigg House

CALDBECK, CUMBRIA CA7 8HD
TEL: CALDBECK (069 98) 430

*Remote farmhouse with lots of activities to coax you away from the TV.*

If splendid isolation is what you're after this could be the one for you – a rambling house situated on a sheep-studded windswept moor. The warmth of the welcome from Robin and Fran Jacobs, and the open fire that greets you on arrival, banish any notion of chill. Slate floors, stone walls and beams confirm the house's seventeenth-century origins, and fabrics and furnishings are appropriately rustic, from an ancient original fireplace to a collection of pewter tankards.

A converted cow byre is a non-smoking lounge with television and drinks cupboard, while a sometime barn houses a bar and recreation area where you can test your skill at table tennis, snooker and darts. Compasses and maps are lent, and general advice given to help guests plan safe expeditions on the fells.

Bedrooms have pine furniture, smart duvet covers, fresh flowers and smashing views. The dining-room is bright, modern and homely with

-High Greenrigg House-

lots of pine including a Welsh dresser, and book-laden shelves. The four-course dinners use plenty of organic produce, with dishes such as lettuce soup, pork chop with mushrooms, and gooseberry fool. Sometimes, in deference to Fran's American roots, you'll find traditional stateside favourites like pecan pie.

◑ *Closed Nov to Feb; restaurant closed Tues, Fri eves*

⤵ *Take the B5299 west from Caldbeck for 3 miles. Turn left at a minor road signposted Greenhead, Branthwaite and Fellside. The house is ½ mile along on the left. Private car park*

🛏 *2 single, 2 twin, 3 double, 1 family room; most with bathroom/WC, some with shower/WC; no tea/coffee-making facilities in rooms*

◇ *Dining-room, bar, 2 lounges,*

*games-room; table tennis and snooker at hotel. Wheelchair access to hotel and restaurant (ramp), 2 ground-floor bedrooms, specially equipped for the disabled*

⊖ *No smoking in bedrooms and some public rooms*

▭ *None accepted*

£ *Single £20, single occupancy of twin/double £25, twin/double £40, family room £50; deposit required. Set D £12.50 (7pm); packed lunches available*

---

# Parkend Restaurant    ℒ ✿

CALDBECK, WIGTON, CUMBRIA CA7 8HH
TEL: CALDBECK (069 98) 494

*A small restaurant with comfortable rooms. A modernised farmhouse set in an unspoilt area.*

Do ye ken John Peel? The doyen of huntsmen, celebrated in traditional English folksong, and star of many a junior school concert, was born here. Today's owners, Neil and Dianne Richardson, are friendly hosts and have sensibly retained rustic and period features that even the famous pink-coated one would immediately recognise. The public areas comprise stone walls, low-beamed ceilings and narrow corridors, and a cosy, unfussy bar.

The dining-room is more urbane with pink scalloped cloths, candles and attractive place settings. Set dinners are hearty and English. The 'Parkend Challenge' mixed grill provides a talking point. Those of gargantuan appetite who can clear their plate, and handle both starter and pudding, win a place in the 'Parkend Book of Records'. Both the menu and the wine list offers good value.

Calling this just a restaurant is rather a misnomer. Bedrooms at this modernised seventeenth-century farmhouse certainly don't give the impression of being an afterthought. They offer pretty wallpaper and fabrics, pine furniture and a catalogue of goodies designed to make you feel at home. Early risers might stir the fox from his lair in the morning.

◑ Open all year

▱ Caldbeck is on the B5299, 1½ miles west of Caldbeck. Private car park

🛏 3 twin (family room available); all with bathroom/WC, TV, hair-dryer, baby-listening

◈ Dining-room, bar, lounge; tennis, riding, other sports nearby

⊖ No wheelchair access; no dogs in public rooms; no smoking in bedrooms

▭ Access, Amex, Diners, Visa

£ Single occupancy of twin/double £28, twin/double £42. Set L £6, D £12 to £15; alc L £3 to £10, D £10 to £20

---

**CALNE** WILTSHIRE                                               **MAP 9**

# Chilvester Hill House

CALNE, WILTSHIRE SN11 0LP
TEL: CALNE (0249) 813981/815785    FAX: (0249) 814217

*A Wolsey Lodge where you feel at home. A fine spot for a lethargic or an active weekend.*

Bath, Oxford, Salisbury and the Cotswolds are within striking distance but if you stay with the Dilleys in their large and spacious Victorian house, you may find inactivity comes easily. In any case exploring the house takes time, as there are collections all about: tins and china moulds, for instance. There are two sitting-rooms: a large and rather grand drawing-room decorated in soft pink and green, and a smaller, cosier room with TV, newspapers, magazines and videos galore. Should lethargy begin to pall, John will help you plan an itinerary. There are also guidebooks and maps in bedrooms to inspire.

This is a genuinely warm and welcoming home, and, as with most Wolsey Lodges, one where you will socialise with other guests as well as your hosts. You will also eat as you might with friends, at a set time, with no choice and at one table. (Unlike dinner parties, though, you get to express likes and dislikes before you arrive.) The seasons dictate the menu. In winter it is often a casserole, in summer fresh fish or Welsh lamb. Consideration for guests' comfort is evident in the three large bedrooms – which come in blue, pink and green. All are well furnished, quiet and equipped with remote control Teletext televisions and proper teapots. Bathrooms are modern. There is always fresh fruit and usually home-made preserves for breakfast.

◑ Open all year, exc 1 week in Spring or Autumn

▱ ½ mile from Calne on the A4 towards Chippenham. Take a right turn marked Bremhill and Ratford and immediately turn right again. Private car park

🛏 2 twin, 1 double, all with

bathroom/WC, TV; hair-dryer available on request

◈ Dining-room, drawing-room, sitting-room; conference facilities (max 16 people non-residential); outdoor heated pool in summer, fishing, golf, riding nearby

⊖ No wheelchair access; no

children under 12; no dogs; no smoking in the dining-room or bedrooms

Access, Amex, Diners, Visa

💷 Single occupancy of twin/double £40 to £50, twin/double £60 to £75, family room £81 to £90. Set D £18, £22 (8pm)

**CALSTOCK** CORNWALL　　　　　　　　　　　　　　**MAP 8**

# Danescombe Valley Hotel　

LOWER KELLY, CALSTOCK, CORNWALL PL18 9RY
TEL: TAVISTOCK (0822) 832414

*A cosy and sophisticated hotel in a beautiful setting.*

There are many aspects to this hotel that make it special. The position is stunning: on the bend of the tidal River Tamar with views stretching to the huge viaduct up-river and across to quiet pastures in the south. Then there is the house itself, a fine Georgian building tucked into the hillside. Try and book one of the spacious, high-ceilinged first-floor bedrooms from which french windows open out on to a fine Regency verandah. You can sit out and watch the morning mist rise from the river to shroud the viaduct and in the evening get hours of pleasure watching the fish rise. The corner room is particularly special as you can lie in bed and see both up- and down-river. Each room is different and has been decorated with taste and care; bathrooms are good, too – toys like mechanical swimming frogs will keep the young-at-heart happy.

Martin and Anna Smith have been running this small, personal hotel for six years. First-name terms are the norm here. Anna cooks a delicious set dinner from Friday to Tuesday evenings: perhaps her special tagliatelle with tomato sauce or marinated breast of duck served with a mustard and madeira sauce. West country unpasteurised farmhouse cheeses also feature. The three public rooms – bar, dining-room and sitting-room – are cosy and comfortable. Find time to visit the Cotehele estate just a short walk away through the woods.

◑ Closed Wed, Thurs; also closed Nov to Mar, exc 24 to 27 Dec; restaurant closed Wed, Thurs eves

🔼 ½ mile west of Calstock village along the river road. Private car park

🛏 2 twin, 3 double; all with bathroom/WC, hair-dryer; tea/coffee-making facilities on request

⬦ Dining-room, bar, lounge, drying room; fishing, golf, other sports nearby

⊖ No wheelchair access; no children under 12; no dogs; no smoking in dining-room

Access, Diners, Visa

💷 Twin/double £120, single occupancy by arrangement; deposit required. Set D £27.50 (8 pm)

*All reports are welcome on any hotel, whether or not it is in the* Guide.

**CAMPSEA ASH** SUFFOLK                                   **MAP 7**

# Old Rectory

CAMPSEA ASH, NR WOODBRIDGE, SUFFOLK IP13 0PU
TEL: WICKHAM MARKET (0728) 746524

*A very friendly hotel with laid-back atmosphere and good food.*

In four acres of garden in rural Suffolk, the Old Rectory has the feel of a cherished home. Its front is cheery in pink with violet window frames. Once inside, you will be welcomed by Stewart Bassett or one of his staff, or perhaps even Baron the boxer dog. Then you will be escorted to your room, stopping halfway to write down your preferences for breakfast in a book on the landing.

Bedrooms are decorated simply in warm colours. If you are lucky to get the room at the top of the house, you will be led through two doors and up a spiral staircase, like one in a medieval turret, which makes you feel as if the room is your own secret hideaway. Sloping roofs make it interesting and somehow cosy, although beware hopping in and out of the bath. Stewart Bassett likes people to feel relaxed: wander around and perhaps admire the statue of Hermes from his vantage point of the garden, or, if you arrive early for dinner, spend some time getting acquainted with the wine list – it has over 300 selections, one reason why many people come here. Stewart has an excellent description for each wine, including a welcome selection from the New World. He is also quite prepared to advise guests and has a good choice of half-bottles.

Around 8pm guests are coaxed into the conversatory-style dining-room where the first of four courses might be salmon and asparagus roulade, followed by chicken in a delicious white wine sauce and mushrooms. Then, if you have any room left, you might get an individual meringue with fresh raspberries, and finally the cheeseboard. Luckily the chairs are cane with plump cushions.

◑ *Open all year, exc Xmas; restaurant closed Sun eve*

⤴ *On the B1078, 1½ miles east of Wickham Market. Private car park*

🛏 *1 single, 2 twin, 1 double, 2 four-poster; all with bathroom/ WC; hair-dryer available on request*

◈ *Restaurant, bar, lounge, conservatory; conference facilities (max 16 people non-residential); fishing, golf, other sports nearby*

⊖ *No wheelchair access; no dogs; no smoking*

▭ *Access, Amex, Diners, Visa*

£ *Single £30, single occupancy of twin/double £30, twin/double £45, four-poster £47; deposit required. Set D £14*

---

*Many hotels put their tariffs up in the spring. You are advised to confirm prices when you book.*

# Cottage of Content

CAREY, HEREFORD AND WORCESTER HR2 6NG
TEL: CAREY (0432) 840242

*Pretty country pub with simple rooms and interesting food.*

Two fluffy white Samoyed dogs lie dozing on the flagstone floor of this fifteenth-century inn. Originally a set of labourers' cottages, the Cottage of Content sits beside a tributary of the River Wye behind walls banked up with cascading aubrietia.

The low beams are hung with dried flowers and miniature bales of hay, while a row of shiny tankards stands on the mantel shelf. You can drink your pint sitting on an old church pew as well as on more conventional wooden chairs and benches; there are a few tables outside for sunny days. The bar menu offers interesting variations, such as smoked oyster and bacon kebabs, and buckling and horseradish pâté, as well as old favourites like steak-and-kidney pie and lamb moussaka.

A set of ladder-like wooden steps leads up to the four bedrooms; all the rooms are creaky and nicely furnished. There's no separate residents' lounge and noise and cooking smells may be a bother on busy evenings, so the inn is probably best suited to the sociable who are happy to stay in the lounge until closing time.

⬤ Open all year, exc 25 Dec

⤵ Turn off the A49 towards Hoarworthy. The pub is 1½ miles from Hoarworthy village. Private car park

🛏 1 twin, 3 double; all with bathroom/WC, TV

◈ Dining-room, 2 bars, lounge, TV; golf, fishing, other sports nearby

⊖ No wheelchair access

▢ Access, Visa

£ Single occupancy of twin/double £30, twin/double £42; deposit required. Bar meals

---

*If you make a booking using a credit card, and you find after cancelling that the full amount has been charged to your card, raise the matter with your credit card company. They will ask the hotelier to confirm whether the room was re-let, and to justify the charge they made.*

**CARTMEL** CUMBRIA                                                    **MAP 3**

# Uplands

HAGGS LANE, CARTMEL, CUMBRIA LA11 6HD
TEL: CARTMEL (053 95) 36248

*Exceptional food and wine in an understated country house.*

This outpost of John Tovey's empire isn't coy about its distinguished antecedent – the sign outside confidently promises 'In the Miller Howe manner'. And that's what you'll find, notwithstanding the absence of Lakeside views. The house itself is modest, but overlooks several acres of pretty gardens and wooded land. Public areas are modern, spacious and stylish, with a distinctly feminine touch. Framed posters from New York's Metropolitan Museum of Art add a splash of colour to a lounge that's elegant without being plush. The dining-room also has a restrained style, combining neutral walls and pine tables with floral mats, cane-backed chairs and gas-style globe lamps on each table.

Bedrooms are small and individually furnished, comfortable and cheerful rather than characterful, but the food's the thing. Uplands is run by Tom and Diana Peter, formerly John Tovey's partners at Miller Howe. As one recent correspondent, a regular visitor, noted: 'Tom Peter never falters in the standards set and in the quality of the produce and the cooking.' The menu offers limited choice but is memorable. Dinner in April might include poached fresh asparagus in a puff pastry slice with smoked salmon and hollandaise sauce, courgette and rosemary soup, and pan-fried medallions of venison with blackcurrant and juniper sauce. There's a wider choice at the dessert stage where choices include banana, walnut and ginger farmhouse pie with warm butterscotch sauce.

◑ *Closed Jan, Feb; restaurant closed Mon eve*

▰ *From Cartmel village with the Pig and Whistle pub on your right, turn immediately left up Haggs Lane. The hotel is 1 mile up this road on the left. Private car park*

🛏 *3 twin, 2 double; some with bathroom/WC, some with shower/WC; TV, room service, hair-dryer; no tea/coffee-making facilities in rooms*

◈ *Dining-room, lounge, drying-room; golf, riding, other sports nearby*

⊖ *No wheelchair access; no children under 8; no dogs in public rooms; no smoking in dining-room*

▭ *Access, Amex, Visa*

£ *Single occupancy of twin/double £70 to £75, twin/double £116 to £124 (rates inc dinner). Set L £13.50, D £23.50. Special breaks available*

---

*If you are intending to make a lot of phone calls from your room, always check what the hotel is going to charge you per unit. You may be so horrified that you'll prefer to walk to the nearest phone box. Why let them get away with excessive charges?*

**CARTMEL FELL** CUMBRIA            **MAP 3**

# Lightwood Farm

CARTMEL FELL, CUMBRIA LA11 6NP
TEL: NEWBY BRIDGE (053 95) 31454

*Friendly farmhouse accommodation in a remote location.*

You'll find more than a few seventeenth-century Cumbrian farmhouses
in this *Guide*. Lightwood Farm lacks lake views, but owners Fideo and
Evelyn Cervetti offer good, comfortable accommodation at a very fair
price, and the one and a half acres of pretty gardens dotted with streams
are more than adequate compensation.

You'll find an original oak cupboard, inglenook fireplace, period doors
and enough exposed beams and rough walls to testify to the building's
age. There's a pleasant lack of gimmickry, and the bedrooms, two of
which are in a separate cottage, are cheerfully and thoughtfully furnished
in traditional style. The Cervettis have just finished converting a barn
into a further four *en suite* bedrooms, but the style remains the same. All
rooms have panoramic views and fresh flowers. The set dinners usually
offer a small choice of impressively simple but wholesome fare – tasty
soups, well-judged roasts and fresh vegetables often feature, with
vegetarian alternatives available. Coffee and mints are served in the
lounge. Follow the directions below or, unless you know the area well,
run the risk of getting well and truly lost.

- Open all year, exc Dec, Jan
- Follow signs for A590 to Newby Bridge, then take the A592 to Fell Foot. Turn right to Kendal; Lightwood is 2 miles on. Private car park
- 3 twin, 6 double; most with shower/WC, some with bathroom/WC; room service in all rooms; TV in some rooms

- Dining-room, 2 lounges; fishing, golf, other sports nearby
- No wheelchair access; no dogs; smoking in lounge only
- Visa
- Single occupancy of twin/double £20 to £28, twin/double £30 to £38; deposit required. Set D £9.50

---

*Dog lovers: some hotels not only welcome dogs, but they provide gourmet
meals for them. Ask.*

---

*Warning to insomniacs, exercise freaks and late-night lovers: increasing
numbers of hotels have infra-red triggered security lamps. To save being
embarrassingly illuminated, check before you leave for your late-night or
pre-dawn stroll.*

**CASTLE COMBE** WILTSHIRE                                    **MAP 9**

# Manor House

CASTLE COMBE, CHIPPENHAM, WILTSHIRE SN14 7HR
TEL: CASTLE COMBE (0249) 782206   TELEX: 449931 MANOR G
FAX: (0249) 782159

*Mostly Jacobean, entirely English manor in popular and, of course, pretty Cotswold town.*

Befitting this pretty English village, the creeper-clad Manor House is a splendid example of fine English architecture, in this case Jacobean. The exterior composition of turrets, gables, chimneys and leaded windows is almost as amazing as the interior of carved panelling, giant fireplaces (with fires usually lit) friezes and heraldic scrolls. The purity of design is naturally compromised for the sake of modern comforts, but the recent programme of improvements has been reasonably sympathetic. Warm and bright fabrics, soft sofas and good lighting, if not in keeping with seventeenth-century interior décor, make lounges easy places for pro-longed relaxation. There are several bars as well, plus a long, low, somewhat gloomy restaurant which specialises in formality, pomp and circumstance.

Breakfast is a more cheerful time and the food is better. It also costs extra, for shame. The Manor is a favourite venue for small business gatherings (there are three, variously sized meeting rooms). Bedrooms differ considerably in size, facilities and luxury, from smallish rooms in the Mews Cottage up the drive, to grand, totally unrestrained 'de luxe' rooms with half-testers and four-posters (some even antique), even an occasional television in the bathroom. The hotel has formal gardens looked on by mature trees, and 26 acres of parkland.

◑ *Open all year*

⤴ *10 minutes from Junction 17 of the M4. Follow signs to Chippenham, then take the A420 in direction of Bristol. Fork left on to the B4039 to Castle Combe. Private car park*

🛏 *30 twin/doubles, 3 four-poster, 3 suites (some rooms in cottages); all with bathroom/WC, TV, room service, hair-dryer, baby-listening; tea/coffee-making facilities, trouser press, mini-bar in some rooms*

◇ *Restaurant, bar, 3 lounges, conservatory; conference facilities (max 60 people non-residential, 36 residential);*

*fishing (Apr to Oct), tennis, croquet, heated outdoor swimming pool, bicycles at hotel, other sports nearby; babysitting. Wheelchair access to hotel (no steps) and 2 ground-floor bedrooms, 4 steps to restaurant*

⊖ *No dogs in public rooms*

▭ *Access, Amex, Diners, Visa*

£ *Single occupancy of twin/double from £100, twin/double from £100, four-poster from £165, suite £185, cottage £250; deposit required. Continental B £7, cooked B £9; set L £17, D £28; alc L £20, D £35. Special breaks available*

# Donington Thistle Hotel

EAST MIDLANDS AIRPORT, CASTLE DONINGTON, DERBYSHIRE DE7 2SH
TEL: DERBY (0332) 850700    TELEX: 377632 DONING G
FAX: (0332) 850823

*Attractively decorated airport hotel. Also convenient for the M1.*

On the corner of the entrance road to the airport and on a busy road, this modern, low red-bricked building is surprisingly attractive inside. With a refreshing Mediterranean flavour to the décor, red quarry tiles, white walls and bright woven wall hangings, the public areas have a cheering atmosphere on a wintry afternoon.

There are various function and conference rooms, and mid-week grey-suited businessmen cluster for coffee in one of the open-plan lounges with an open fire. The restaurant is light and airy, with white walls and pine and cane furnishings and large pots of dried flowers. The bar has a mix of alcove seating covered in striking woven cushions. Bedrooms are modern and more predictable but furnishings are of a good standard and the leisure centre is the answer for the evenings when any outing would mean a drive into nearby Castle Donington, or further afield (unless, of course, you're a plane spotter).

◗ *Open all year*

↗ *2 miles from Junction 24 of the M1, on the A453 at East Midlands Airport. Private car park*

🛏 *57 twin, 41 double, 4 family rooms, 4 suites; all with bathroom/WC, TV, room service, hair-dryer, trouser press, baby-listening; mini-bar in some rooms*

◈ *Restaurant, bar, lounge (public areas air-conditioned); conference facilities (200 people non-residential, 100 residential); sauna, solarium, heated indoor pool, gym, spa pool at hotel,*

*other sports nearby; babysitting by arrangement. Wheelchair access to hotel, restaurant and WC (unisex), 52 ground-floor bedrooms, 4 specially equipped for the disabled*

⊖ *No dogs in public rooms; some bedrooms and part of restaurant non-smoking*

▭ *Access, Amex, Diners, Visa*

£ *Single occupancy of twin/double from £73, twin/double/family room from £92, suite from £150. Continental B £7, cooked B £8.50; set L £13, D £17; alc L, D £25*

*See the back of the* Guide *for an index of hotels listed.*

*Hotels in our* Visitors' Book *towards the end of the* Guide *are additional hotels that may be worth a visit. Reports on these hotels are welcome.*

**CAWSTON** NORFOLK                          **MAP 7**

# Grey Gables

NORWICH ROAD, CAWSTON, NORFOLK NR10 4EY
TEL: NORWICH (0603) 871259

*This is a welcoming, down-to-earth guesthouse, well tucked away in rural Norfolk.*

It's not easy finding your way through the tangle of back roads, but persevere. The former rectory of Brandiston Church is the home of James and Rosalind Snaith; it makes a very pleasant rural retreat for around a dozen guests.

Entirely relaxed and homely, the house also boasts some style. A bow window, log fire and a collection of china dogs heighten the appeal of the Victorian-style sitting-room, decorated in soothing blues and greys. With its mahogany tables set with fine china and silver, and its walls decorated with plates, the dining-room is snazzier than the food ('nice straightforward English and French,' say the Snaiths). You can also have as many as five courses (or three or four) each with a short choice, and you'll find the likes of Norfolk ham with pease pudding (a house speciality), lovage soup and cassoulet of beef and beans in red wine. Then three sweets, all of which you're expected to try (though you can have just one and pay less). Wines, definitely above guesthouse calibre, number around 250.

There's less excess in the bedrooms but ample comfort. Hot-water bottles, and even a bath on legs in one, are perks of the bathrooms.

◑ Open all year, exc 24, 25 26 Dec

🅰 1 mile south of Cawston village, at Eastgate. Private car park

🛏 1 twin, 4 double, 1 family room; all with bathroom/WC, exc 1 double with shower/WC; TV, room service, hair-dryer in all rooms

◈ Dining-room, lounge; drying facilities; conference facilities (max 12 people non-residential, 6 residential); tennis at hotel, other sports nearby. Wheelchair

access to restaurant and WC (unisex) only

⊖ No children under 5 in restaurant eves; no dogs in public rooms; no smoking in dining-room

🗔 Access, Visa

£ Single occupancy of twin/double £42 to £43, twin/double £48 to £50, family room £52 to £54; deposit required. Set D £17; lunch by arrangement only. Special breaks available

---

*The* Guide *office can quickly spot when a hotelier is encouraging customers to write a recommending inclusion – and sadly, several hotels have been doing this in 1991. Such reports do not further a hotel's cause.*

# Chadlington House

CHAPEL ROAD, CHADLINGTON, OXFORDSHIRE OX7 3LZ
TEL: CHADLINGTON (060 876) 437

*A simple, friendly place to stay where you can be assured of amicable service and a good night's sleep.*

Chadlington is a rambling village largely by-passed by the coachloads of tourists in search of Cotswold cuteness. Chadlington House on the outskirts of the village was, so both brochure and owners remind you, once described as an architectural curiosity. Somewhere beneath the late Victorian, mock-Tudor exterior is a seventeenth-century two-bedroomed cottage. Don't spend too long pondering on the historic details, concentrate instead on the present in the form of a hotel run by Peter and Rita Oxford.

The Oxfords, devoted resident proprietors, are so unashamedly welcoming and downright pleasant as to reconfirm totally your faith in human nature. They've been in the business for over 30 years and Rita is full of hotelier's tales just waiting to be turned into a book. The best of the bedrooms, with sweeping views across rolling countryside, are at the front of the house but all are large and well maintained by Peter's tireless programme of redecoration.

The atmosphere is one of suburban cosiness: the Oxfords freely admit to catering for a slightly older clientele who appreciate peace and quiet, and the hotel's belief is that what people want, above all else, is an uninterrupted good night's sleep.

◑ *Closed Jan and Feb*

↗ *Turn off the A34 on to the B4022, or off the A361 from Burford. Chadlington is 2 miles south of Chipping Norton. Private car park*

🛏 *2 single, 2 twin, 6 double, 1 four-poster, 1 self-catering cottage/family room; most with bathroom/WC, rest with shower/WC; TV, hair-dryer, baby-listening in all rooms*

◇ *Restaurant, bar, lounge, drying room; conference facilities (max 30 non-residential, 10 residential); tennis, riding, other sports nearby. Wheelchair access to hotel, restaurant and WC, 1 ground-floor bedroom in cottage annexe*

⊖ *No children under 6 in restaurant; no dogs; no smoking in public rooms*

▭ *Access, Visa*

£ *Single £30 to £38, single occupancy of twin/double £35 to £45, twin/double £60 to £70, four-poster £60 to £80, cottage room £70 to £100; deposit required. Set D £16.50; alc D £18.50. Special breaks available*

---

🌿   *This denotes that the hotel is in an exceptionally peaceful situation where you can be assured of a restful stay.*

**CHAGFORD** DEVON                                        **MAP 8**

# Gidleigh Park

CHAGFORD, DEVON TQ13 8HH
TEL: CHAGFORD (0647) 432367 or 432225
TELEX: 42643 GIDLEY G   FAX: (0647) 432574

*Ultra-exclusive country-house hotel with wonderful croquet lawns.*

'Keep heart. You're still en route to Gidleigh Park,' says a sign some way along the tortuous, narrow country lane. Over a brook or two and you arrive at the large, mock-Tudor mansion. The scenery and tranquillity are impressive, but one reader commented: 'Not a particularly warm or friendly atmosphere,' in spite of the level of comfort inside the hotel.

The drawing-room is large but pretty, with antiques, decorative sofas and super views. The main, oak-panelled dining-room looks the part more than the underfurnished 'Lemon' dining-room. The map-lined bar and little, greenery-filled loggia are comfortable. The prices make more of an impression. One reader found the wine list expensive and prefaced by a statement justifying £20-plus per bottle. 'It would have been simpler to say that 26 acres of parkland cost money to maintain!' Clearly, though, the place attracts a clientele, especially from foreign parts.

The bedrooms, priced by aspect and size, are plushly decked out, no mistake, with chintz, crown canopies and bathrooms glitzed up with marble tiles and wood trimmings. If inherent character is missing, the quality of everything is superb. Whether these rooms are worth up to £180 per person per night is another matter, especially, if as readers have said, you get one of the smaller rooms which are rather cramped and suffer from cooking smells. If money is no object, then you could do worse than spend a week or two here, enjoying the wonderful countryside, playing on the best croquet lawns in the country and dining on red-wine risotto with asparagus, and grilled veal fillet and kidney with balsamic vinegar sauce. All our correspondents agree, Shaun Hill's cooking does indeed warrant the splurge.

◑ Open all year

🔁 In Chagford Square, turn right at Lloyds Bank into Mill Street. After 150 yards take the first fork to the right, and follow the lane for 1½ miles to its end. Private car park

🛏 12 double, 2 suites, 1 cottage; all with bathroom/WC, TV, hairdryer; no tea/coffee-making facilities in rooms

◈ Restaurant, bar, lounge; conference facilities (max 18 people non-residential, 16 residential); fishing, tennis, croquet at hotel, other sports nearby. Wheelchair access to restaurant only

⊖ No dogs in public rooms

▭ Access, Visa

£ Single occupancy of twin/double £180 to £275, twin/double £220 to £315, suite £290 to £340, cottage £400 to £500 (rates inc dinner); deposit required. Set L £33, £43, D £43, £50

# Mill End

SANDY PARK, CHAGFORD, NR NEWTON ABBOTT, DEVON TQ13 8JN
TEL: CHAGFORD (0647) 432282   FAX: (0647) 433106

*Fishing-oriented hotel in a converted flour mill that doesn't try to hide its modern-day appurtenances.*

On the edge of Dartmoor, standing close to a country road that fills with holiday traffic on sunny summer afternoons, the trim white hotel is very much a mix. Although bedrooms are comfortable and well-maintained, functional paraphernalia usually encountered in business hotels hardly adds to their quaintness; radios, tea-making gear and televisions are all wall-mounted and furniture is of the built-in variety. Fresh flowers help, and your bed may be nice and large.

Three downstairs rooms have access to a patio. There is more to admire in the public rooms. The old water-wheel, left from the days when this was a flour mill, still turns outside the traditionally-furnished dining-room (the menu is interesting and adventurous). Board games sit on a desk converted from an antique square piano in the spacious, black-beamed lounge, set with flowery sofas and warmed in winter by a log fire. A television room has books and magazines as well, but is rather a through-route. Those here for the fishing (a large percentage of guests), have their own little rooms for removing wellies, detailing their catch in the register and buying rods and flies. A pretty walled lawn is set in summer with lots of tables and chairs.

◑ Closed 12 to 22 Dec

⬈ From Exeter take the A30 Okehampton road. Turn south at Widdon Down on the A382 – do not turn into Chagford at Sandy Park. Private car park

🛏 2 single, 6 twin, 7 double, 2 family rooms; most with bathroom/WC, some with shower/WC; TV, room service, hair-dryer, baby-listening in all rooms

◇ Dining-room, bar, 2 lounges, TV room, drying room; conference facilities (max 28 people non-residential, 17 residential); fishing at hotel, other sports nearby. Wheelchair access to hotel and restaurant, 3 ground-floor bedrooms

⊖ No dogs in public rooms

▭ Access, Amex, Diners, Visa

£ Single £30, single occupancy of twin/double £45 to £60, twin/double £65 to £75; deposit required. Continental B £3.50, cooked B £8.50; set L £15 to £20, D £20 to £26.50. Special breaks available

---

*The* Guide *is totally independent, accepts no free hospitality, and survives on the number of copies sold each year.*

**CHALE** ISLE OF WIGHT                                          **MAP 9**

# Clarendon Hotel and Wight Mouse Inn

CHALE, ISLE OF WIGHT PO38 2HA
TEL: ISLE OF WIGHT (0983) 730431

*A seventeenth-century coaching-inn and lively country pub.*

In 1836 the Clarendon, a sailing ship, was wrecked off the coast; all but three of the passengers and crew died. Some four years later, the White Mouse (as it was then spelt) changed its name to the Clarendon. Just looking through all the promotional literature produced by present owners John and Jean Bradshaw is exhausting: reprinted excerpts from guides; a minibus service (the Mousemobile) for ferry collections, etc; a history of the hotel and its names; menus (every pub meal you can think of) and a list of its 365 whiskies; and you can leave with a Wight Mouse T-shirt, sweatshirt or hat.

Children are made welcome here. Extras for them include a special menu, indoor games rooms and a playground area on the big daisied lawns – beyond which lie the open downs and the white cliffs of Freshwater Bay. In fact, everyone's welcome, from daytime coach parties on island tours, to locals and young folk for the live music in the evening. The beams in the busy and noisy pub bar were rescued from the hotel's namesake ship; pleasant clutter – musical instruments, guns, antlers, oars – provide the decoration. The traditional red velveteen dining-room has lovely views, especially spectacular sunsets if you're lucky. Bedrooms, in modern white or pine fittings, are crisp and fresh; though not luxurious, they have good bathrooms. From some you can hear pub revelry.

🅞 Open all year

🄴 From Yarmouth take the A3055 Military Road west to Chale church and turn left. Private car park

🛏 2 twin, 3 double, 8 family rooms, 1 suite; some with bathroom/ WC, some with shower/WC, 3 public bathrooms; TV, room service, baby-listening in all rooms; hair-dryers in most rooms

◈ Dining-room, 2 bars, lounge, games room, drying room; conservatory; conference

facilities (max 14 people residential); fishing, sailing, other sports nearby; babysitting; play areas

⊖ No wheelchair access; no dogs in public rooms

▭ Access

£ Single occupancy of twin/double £35 to £39, twin/double £46 to £52, suite £67 (rates inc dinner); deposit required; children's rates. Set L £6, D £15; alc L, D £5 to £12.

---

*Prices are quoted* per room *rather than* per person.

# Charingworth Manor

CHARINGWORTH, NR CHIPPING CAMPDEN, GLOUCESTERSHIRE GL55 6NS
TEL: PAXFORD (038 678) 555   TELEX: 333444 CHARMA G
FAX: (038 678) 353

*Smart secluded manor house with thoughtful, unexpected touches.*

The approach is long and winding and negotiates a couple of cattle grids. At the rate at which Charingworth Manor is growing you wonder how long it will take to fill its empty 54 acres. In fact, the latest rooms have been converted from former pigsties, and these, together with an extension to the dining-room, are the limits of the expansionist plans for now.

The bedrooms in the original fourteenth-century manor house have the most character, with low beams and uneven floors and walls, but the newer conversions have swisher marble-floored bathrooms. All have welcoming glasses of unusual home-made wines and truffles. Public rooms are comfortable, with deep sofas and wing armchairs, antique furniture and strong colours. Dragged panelling in one of the sitting-rooms and bright green wicker chairs in the conservatory add a touch of the unconventional. The dining-room, in dark green, white and pink, is divided by arches into three sections so you don't feel too isolated if the house isn't full. An ambitious menu includes breast of squab in strudel leaves with wild mushroom mousseline, pan-fried squid with ratatouille, home-made noodles and red wine, and hot vanilla soufflé with banana ice-cream. Men are asked to wear a jacket and tie in the dining-room.

◐ Open all year

↗ 2½ miles east of Chipping Campden on the B4035. Private car park

🛏 8 twin, 12 double, 2 four-poster, 3 suites; all with bathroom/WC, TV, room service, hair-dryer, trouser press; baby-listening by arrangement; no tea/coffee-making facilities in rooms

◈ Restaurant, 3 lounges; conference facilities (max 34 people non-residential, 25 residential); babysitting by arrangement; tennis at hotel (sauna and pool from Feb 92), other sports nearby

⊖ No wheelchair access; no dogs in public rooms; no cigars or pipes in restaurant

▭ Access, Amex, Diners, Visa

£ Single occupancy of twin/double £85, twin/double from £105, four-poster £165, suite £200; deposit required. Set L £15.50, D £25; alc L, D £31 (prices till Apr 92)

---

*A long list was recited to us, ending with 'several goat cheeses'. I asked which goat cheeses, and our helpful waitress offered to bring a list. A Post-it note appeared on the table, eight or so cheeses listed, most misspelled, no unusual cheeses, and no goat cheeses at all.* On an hotel in North Yorkshire

**CHARTHAM** KENT                                              **MAP 10**

# Thruxted Oast

MYSTOLE, CHARTHAM, CANTERBURY, KENT CT4 7BX
TEL: CANTERBURY (0227) 730080

*A wonderful creation: a beautifully converted and decorated B&B
on a quiet Kentish back lane. Stay here as a base for Canterbury.*

'Tim and Hilary welcome you back with such enthusiasm you really do
feel like family,' remarked one returning guest. Tim and Hilary Derouet,
once farmers, bought Thruxted Oast on Valentine's Day 1986; after just
fourteen months they opened their home to guests. Look at the before-
and-after photos on the wall in the kitchen to realise what an achieve-
ment this was; the original oast house didn't even have any interior walls.
The house, in variegated grey and red brick with four white cowls atop its
roofs, is surrounded by fields of hop stakes and swathes of green cut by
tractor lines and has some of the most charmingly decorated bedrooms
you could imagine (cottagey fabrics and wallpaper, and stripped pine
furniture).

Bedrooms are named after Chaucer, the Wife of Bath and the Knight,
and have dried flowers, pictures and old bottles (largely rescued from
car-boot sales) jostling for space beneath high sloping ceilings with tie-
beams and trap doors. Every conceivable article of convenience and
comfort has been thought of, from hot-water bottles and bathroom scales
to a clothes-brush or an extra loo roll in an oast-house cosy. Along the
corridor beyond the bedrooms you come to the Derouets' picture-
framing workshop.

In the morning, a flower sprig in a napkin ring will decorate your place
at breakfast which is taken at the large communal table in the kitchen;
jams are home-made, eggs from their own chickens. In the evening,
guests can relax in sofas around the woodburning stove at the far end of
the enormous very habitable kitchen, or retire to the beautifully decorated sitting-room next door.

| | |
|---|---|
| ◑ Open all year, exc Xmas | 🛏 3 twin/double; all with shower/ WC, TV, hair-dryer |
| ↗ From Canterbury take the A28 Ashford road. After crossing the bypass, turn left into St Nicholas Road, then right at the T-junction. Continue on this road for 2 miles past the hospital and to a crossroads. Go straight over – the house is near the bottom of the hill, on the right. Private car park | ◈ Lounge; croquet at hotel, other sports nearby |
| | ⊖ No wheelchair access; no children under 8; no dogs; no smoking in bedrooms |
| | ▭ Access, Amex, Diners, Visa |
| | £ Single occupancy of twin/double £58, twin/double £68 |

*You will find report forms at the back of the Guide – please use them!*

# Chedington Court

CHEDINGTON, BEAMINSTER, DORSET DT8 3HY
TEL: CORSCOMBE (0935) 891265   FAX: (0935) 891442

*Elizabethan-style Victorian manor house in luscious grounds. A home rather than an hotel but with high-quality accommodation.*

Many readers have written to endorse last year's recommendation of Philip and Hilary Chapman's mellow stone Victorian hotel on the borders of Somerset and Devon. 'Quite the most enjoyable, self-indulgent weekend for ages. The bath towels were the largest and softest we have ever had the pleasure to be wrapped in.'

The Elizabethan-style house has been furnished in accordance with its grandeur, but is anything but staid, thanks to the Chapmans' easy style and maybe the fact that many guests are young. You'll not be at a loss for places to sit, books to read, or lovely views to look out to. As well as a lounge, there's a panelled library. Although they vary in size and décor, bedrooms are all light and spacious. 'Dorset', which has a bay window and five-star views you can also admire from your bed, is considered the best. Others have notable furniture: 'Devon' has an inlaid Dutch bed, and some of the furniture and carpet in 'Queen Mary' came from the eponymous liner.

Hilary Chapman's five-course dinners get similar commendation: 'Food *superb* and our need of a special diet unobtrusively adhered to, even with special canapés with our pre-dinner drinks'. 'Pleasant and unobtrusive service' can, according to one returning visitor, lean towards the amateurish. A stream, duck-pond, croquet lawn and putting green adorn the ten acres of gardens, with lots of paths to lead you from one to the other. The Chapmans have now opened a nine-hole, 3,000-yard golf course about a mile from the hotel for use by hotel guests.

- Closed from mid-Jan to mid-Feb
- Just off the A356 Crewkerne to Dorchester road, 4½ miles south-east of Crewkerne at Winyard's Gap. Private car park
- 2 twin, 2 twin/double, 4 double, 1 four-poster, 1 family room; most with bathroom/WC, 1 double with shower/WC; TV, room service, hair-dryer, baby-listening in all rooms; trouser press available on request
- Restaurant, dispense bar, lounge, drying room, library, billiard room, conservatory; conference facilities (max 20 people non-residential, 10 residential); golf, croquet at hotel, other sports nearby. Wheelchair access to restaurant, WC (unisex) only
- Children in restaurant at breakfast only; no dogs
- Access, Amex, Visa
- Single occupancy of twin/double £56 to £82, twin/double £96 to £138, four-poster £115 to £147; deposit required. Set D £28. Special breaks available

# Blossoms Hotel

ST JOHN STREET, CHESTER, CHESHIRE CH1 1HL
TEL: CHESTER (0244) 323186   TELEX: 61113 BLOSSM G
FAX: (0244) 346433

*Convenient location and pleasant bedrooms in a rather tired city-centre chain hotel.*

There are clear signs of wilting in this Forte bloom, though the place starts with several advantages, not least its location at the heart of the old walled city, a stone's throw from the famous timbered buildings of Old Chester. Too much poor taste has been allowed to intrude, detracting from the imposing staircase and genuinely grand reception area, with its display cases of trinkets and toffee. There's a slight air of desperation about the 'Nice things happen at Blossoms' board with its record of ruby weddings and reunion dinners, plus a letter from the Institute of Explosive Engineers' conference organiser.

Things improve in the bright bedrooms which have lots of facilities and bright duvet covers. Views in some, which overlook other rooftops, disappoint. Brooke's restaurant is light and airy with crisp table linen and fresh flowers. Other public areas are dreary; the Malt Shoppe bar carries an impressive range of malt whiskies, but is otherwise forgettable, and the coffee lounge with evidence of neglect, like spent light bulbs and inattentive service, has all the character of an ante-room. Food tends to the traditional with classics like celery and Stilton soup and game-keeper's pot. Both table d'hôte and à la carte menus are available. Downstairs the Snooty Fox offers bar food.

- Open all year

- On the main street in Chester by the East Gate clock. Limited on-street parking; free overnight parking provided in NCP car park nearby

- 5 single, 34 twin, 17 double, 1 four-poster, 2 family rooms, 5 suites; all with bathroom/WC, TV, room service, baby-listening; hair-dryer, trouser press in some rooms

- 2 restaurants, 2 bars, lounge; conference facilities (max 110 people non-residential, 64 residential); some public rooms air-conditioned; fishing, golf, other sports nearby

- No wheelchair access; no dogs in restaurants; some bedrooms non-smoking and no smoking in restaurants

- Access, Amex, Diners, Visa

- Single £70, single occupancy of twin/double £75, twin/double £90, four-poster/family room/suite £110; deposit required. Continental B £6.50, cooked B £8; set L £9, D £14; alc L, D £18 to £20. Special breaks available

# Castle House

23 CASTLE STREET, CHESTER, CHESHIRE CH1 2DS
TEL: CHESTER (0244) 350354

*Homely accommodation in ancient city-centre building.*

Guesthouses don't come much more discreet than this one, set in a quiet area of Chester's walled city, surrounded by professional offices and close to the military museum. A painted plaque confirms the name; otherwise there are no clues that this trim brick building, with window boxes adding a splash of colour, is open to guests.

At its heart is a marvellous sixteenth-century breakfast room and lounge with small kitchen off, the highlight of which is a carved wooden fireplace crowned by a plaster-sculpted coat of arms of the Virgin Queen. Brass and copper knick-knacks share space with a wireless that wouldn't disgrace a museum of broadcasting, and the overall effect is cosy.

Bedrooms are neat, clean and comfortable without being particularly stylish. One, known as 'the room with the funny wall', has an exposed section behind glass, while another has a cuddly resident Roland Rat. ing work was continuing as we inspected. Front-facing rooms may be affected by noise from a nearby pub.

- ◖ Open all year
- ▣ Within the city walls, next to the castle. On-street parking, can be difficult during day
- ▭ 2 single, 1 twin, 1 double, 1 family room; most with shower/WC, 1 public bathroom; TV in all rooms
- ◈ Lounge; fishing, golf, tennis,

other sports nearby
- ⊖ No wheelchair access; no dogs in public rooms
- ▭ Access, Visa
- £ Single £22, single occupancy of twin/double £32, twin/double £42, family room £50; deposit required

# Green Bough Hotel

60 HOOLE ROAD, CHESTER, CHESHIRE CH2 3NL
TEL: CHESTER (0244) 326241    FAX: (0244) 326265

*An inexpensive and comfortable base in a friendly guesthouse.*

There are a score or more hotels on this busy road which leads to Warrington and the motorway to Liverpool and Birkenhead. Green Bough is a solid, double-fronted house, as noise-scarred as the rest but with a lot of soul. The carved-oak fireplace in the lounge is older than the house, but sits easily with the chaise-longue, leather chesterfields and plants that create an authentic Victorian feel.

There's more carved oak in the bar. The dining-room is half-panelled, with modern leaf-pattern wallpaper and arches to divide it into cosy areas. Bedrooms include some in a next-door extension, and vary considerably in style and appeal, though all have interesting old furniture. Room eight has a four-poster and the extension room, number sixteen, is ideal for families. The newly refurbished bathrooms are now all *en suite*. Set dinners are traditional and freshly cooked. They offer a small choice, say, home-made soup followed by chicken and avocado in a white sauce, before ending up with ice-cream, cheese, or a sweet of the day.

◐ Closed Xmas and New Year

↗ Leave the M53 at the Chester junction. Travel along the A56 into Chester. The hotel is ½ mile from the M53 on the right-hand side. Private car park

⇌ 2 twin, 10 double, 1 four-poster, 5 family rooms, most with bathroom/WC, some with shower/WC; TV, room service, hair-dryer, baby-listening in all rooms

◇ Restaurant, bar, lounge, TV

room; conference facilities (max 12 people residential and non-residential); golf, tennis, other sports nearby. Wheelchair access to hotel (2 steps) and restaurant, 4 ground-floor bedrooms

● No dogs in public rooms

▭ Access, Visa

£ Single occupancy of twin/double £39 to £43, twin/double/four-poster £49 to £54; deposit required. Set L £8, D £11.50. Special breaks available

---

# The Redland

64 HOUGH GREEN, CHESTER, CHESHIRE CH4 8JY
TEL: CHESTER (0244) 671024

*High-Victorian Gothic guesthouse with surprising extras and a memorable host.*

It's a fair bet that this is the only hotel in the UK to boast a couple of figures of Lenin in its corridors. Glance at the name and you might suspect a statement of political commitment. In fact, the Bolshevik leader came to Britain in a suitcase along with other souvenirs from Theresa White's package trip to Moscow, and the name reflects the house's past life as home to the owner of the Redland Brick Company.

And a fine Victorian pile it is too, with a Gothic arched portico (within which a Wellington-booted suit of armour stands guard), and a baronial-style staircase and grand hall. Mrs White is a real character: energetic and enthusiastic, she has a sure eye for a period find to enhance the house (the aforementioned suit of armour came from an auction of costumes from a recent production of Robin Hood). Despite the macho entrance hall, with its portraits, wall-mounted swords and treacle-brown panelling with classical style doors, the place is never gloomy. Indeed, the adjacent drawing-room is a sedate place, with plush furnishings, ornate plasterwork and Wedgwood blue décor. The panelled and beamed breakfast room has pretty pastel curtains and table linen. With the exception of the rather austere single room, number eight, bedrooms are fabulous, combining stunning antiques with ritzy bathrooms. One boasts a splendid carved bed from Perth Castle. Still more surprises lurk downstairs, where you'll find a billiard room, sauna and solarium. Breakfast is hearty and cooked to order. Theresa eagerly provides suggestions on sightseeing, dining and getting the best out of the city. Front-facing rooms suffer from some traffic noise until about 11pm.

◐ *Open all year*

▶ *Leaving Chester take the A483 Wrexham road and then the A549 Saltney road for 200 yards. The hotel is opposite Westminster Park. Private car park*

🛏 *3 single, 2 twin, 5 double, 3 four-poster; most with bathroom/ WC, some with shower/WC; TV, hair-dryer, honesty bar in all rooms*

◈ *Breakfast room, lounge, sauna/ solarium at hotel, other sports nearby*

● *No wheelchair access; no dogs in public rooms*

▭ *Visa*

£ *Single £40, single occupancy of twin/double £40, twin/double £45 to £55, four-poster £60; deposit required*

---

**CHESTER-LE-STREET** CO DURHAM                           **MAP 3**

# Lumley Castle

CHESTER-LE-STREET, DURHAM, COUNTY DURHAM, DH3 4NX
TEL: 091-389 1111    TELEX: 537433
FAX: 091-387 1437

*A fourteenth-century castle with an extraordinary interior.*

A sign at the bottom of the drive warns you that Lumley Castle is 'no ordinary hotel', a common enough claim which in this case happens to be true. The building, bits of which date from the ninth century, is fairly unexceptional on the outside (a child's drawing of a castle), but the interior will astound you. Once your eyes are used to the half-light of authentic medieval gloom, you can begin to feast on the treasure trove which the present owner has gathered from all over the world.

The dining-room for example, supported by enormous pillars, is lined with folds of material and is crowded with antique carved screens, modern sculptured figures, statues straight out of an Arabian bazaar and ecclesiastical paraphernalia. Tables are well spaced despite the collection around them, and some are private enough for an intimate candlelit dinner. If you would prefer an Elizabethan banquet, you can have a pre-dinner drink in the dungeons before going up to take your place on one of several benches in the Baron's hall with its giant stone fireplace and minstrels' gallery. Banquets take place on Fridays and Saturdays only and the mead will leave you staggering back to your room. Each of the 50 or so 'sleeping chambers' is individually designed, most with a theme in mind, and varies from grand to spectacular. All are comfortable with luxury hotel facilities, though some are rather small and those in the courtyard slightly less intriguing. Bathrooms are all *en suite*, and basins and baths have been made especially for this hotel. There are lots more warm and comfortable public rooms for you to explore or retreat to if it all becomes a bit too much. Outside, the grounds slope down towards the River Wear.

◑ *Open all year, exc 25, 26 Dec and 1 Jan*

⤣ *Leave the A1(M) at the exit for Chester-le-Street and follow the A167 southwards for three miles. Private car park*

🛏 *13 single, 14 twin, 28 double, 7 four-poster, 2 family rooms, 1 suite; most with bathroom/WC, some with shower/WC; TV, room service, trouser press, baby-listening in all rooms; hair-dryer in some rooms*

◈ *Restaurant, private dining-room,*

*2 bars, 2 lounges, snooker room; conference facilities (max 150 people non-residential, 66 residential); fishing, golf, other sports nearby; babysitting*

⊖ *No wheelchair access; no dogs*

▭ *Access, Amex, Diners, Visa*

£ *Single £55, twin/double £80 to £98, four-poster £100 to £120, family room £90 to £108, suite £160. Set L £11.50, D £18; alc D £29.50. Special breaks available*

---

**CHIEVELEY** BERKSHIRE                MAP 9

# Blue Boar Inn

NORTH HEATH, CHIEVELEY, BERKSHIRE RG16 8UE
TEL: CHIEVELEY (0635) 248236

*A pleasant old pub on a windswept, isolated hilltop looking down on the M4.*

Accommodation at the Blue Boar is comfortably functional: it's a good spot for an overnight stop rather than a lengthy stay. Bedrooms are arranged around a courtyard of converted outbuildings at the back of the pub. The smallest are a little cramped but they all have good facilities, excellent bathrooms and quiet décor.

The pub is a sixteenth-century thatched affair – a knarled old tree is witness perhaps to Cromwell's stopover to plan the Battle of Newbury. There's a lively lunchtime trade, largely made up of suited businessmen eating in the bar from a menu on the chalkboard which stretches to fresh mussels and deep-fried Camembert. There seems little point in heading for the formality of the restaurant.

The Blue Boar is run with brisk efficiency by Mr Ebsworth who sums up his establishment by saying: 'All the rooms are clean, comfortable, and have got everything – and that's what's important.'

◑ Open all year; restaurant closed Sun eve

⤢ The inn is on the B4494 Newbury/Wantage road, 4 miles north of Newbury town centre. Private car park

🛏 2 single, 4 twin, 8 double, 1 four-poster; most with bathroom/ WC, some with shower/WC; TV in all rooms; room service, hair-dryer on request

◈ Restaurant, bar; fishing, golf, riding nearby. Wheelchair access to hotel and restuarant, 11 ground-floor bedrooms

⊖ No dogs

▭ Access, Amex, Diners, Visa

£ Single £37, single occupancy of twin/double £52, twin/double £65, four-poster £70. Alc L, D £17.50; bar meals

## CHIPPERFIELD HERTFORDSHIRE                                   MAP 10

# The Two Brewers

THE COMMON, CHIPPERFIELD, KINGS LANGLEY, WATFORD,
HERTFORDSHIRE WD4 9BS
TEL: WATFORD (0923) 265266   FAX: (0923) 261884

*A popular, characterful pub-turned-hotel let down by bland
bedrooms in need of refurbishment.*

Trainee managers doing the rounds of Forte properties must find their time at the Two Brewers a refreshing change from the normal diet of more substantial, less intimate hotels. Although the bedrooms in the modern extension are bland and in need of some attention, the older part of the hotel, freshly painted black and white cottages strung out alongside one side of the common, is a considerable improvement. The pub, once a training centre for prize fighters, is a bustling, popular spot but residents in search of something quieter can head for the next-door lounge. The restaurant offers good-value menus with choices adventurous enough to be interesting but not intimidating.

◑ Open all year

⤢ Leave the M25 at Junction 20. Follow signs to the A41. At the second zebra crossing in Kings Langley turn into Vicarage Lane and follow it for 3 miles until you reach a crossroads. Turn left; the inn is 100 yards on the right. Private car park

🛏 14 twin, 2 double, 4 family rooms; all with bathroom/WC, TV, room service, hair-dryer, trouser press, baby-listening

◈ Restaurant, bar, lounge; conference facilities (max 18 people non-residential and residential); fishing, tennis, other sports nearby. Wheelchair access to hotel (ramp), restaurant and WC, 10 ground-floor bedrooms

⊖ No dogs in restaurant; some public rooms and bedrooms non-smoking

▭ Access, Amex, Diners, Visa, THF Gold

£ Single occupancy of twin/double £85, twin/double £95; family room £110; deposit required. Continental B £6.50, cooked B £8; set L £15.50, D £17.50; alc L £28, D £32

**CHIPPING CAMPDEN** GLOUCESTERSHIRE     **MAP 6**

# Cotswold House

THE SQUARE, CHIPPING CAMPDEN, GLOUCESTERSHIRE GL55 6AN
TEL: EVESHAM (0386) 840330   FAX: (0386) 840310

*Highly original, stylish but comfortable hotel with relaxed atmosphere and a wide range of food.*

'Each room is highly individual,' runs the brochure blurb, and for once it's not kidding. Robert Greenstock, with his bow-tie and laid-back but helpful manner, disdains formal country house hotels: 'You can't relax in them.'

Guests reach the bedrooms via a grand wooden spiral staircase framed by Doric pillars. In the India Room a model tiger head above the bed grasps the overhead reading lights in its mouth, and the pelmets are shaped like the domes of Indian temples. The American Colonial Room has stencilled pineapples on the wall, sampler prints, and a four-poster bed, while the Garden Room is awash with poppies – on the bedspread and cushions, plus a whole bed of silk specimens above the wardrobe. 'We had a restrained military theme,' reports one reader, 'comfortable, pleasant and reassuring (a crocheted tin helmet on the loo roll would have spoiled it!).'

Public rooms have original touches too – four-way Ionic pillars in the dining-room and curving walls – that maintain the theatrical elegance. Greenstock's bar serves drinks and substantial snacks throughout the day; if you prefer more formal fare the restaurant menu includes dishes such as marinated goats' cheese with warm walnut and endive salad, and calves' liver, sweetbread and kidney gougère with oyster mushrooms.

◑ Closed 25 and 26 Dec

🔁 1 mile north of the A44 on the B4081 (between Broadway and Moreton-in-Marsh). Private car park

🛏 3 single, 5 twin, 6 double, 1 four-poster; all with bathroom/WC exc 1 single with shower/WC; TV, room service, hair-dryer in all rooms; no tea/coffee-making facilities in rooms

◈ Restaurant, bar, lounge, all-day café/bar; conference facilities (max 15 people residential and non-residential); croquet at hotel, other sports nearby

⊖ No wheelchair access; no children under 8; no dogs; no smoking in restaurant

▭ Access, Amex, Diners, Visa

💷 Single £55 to £68, single occupancy of twin/double £70 to £117, twin/double £85 to £117, four-poster £138. Set D £24.50, Sun L £17; light meals all day from £8 (prices till end 91). Special breaks available

*We mention those hotels that don't accept dogs; guide dogs, however, are almost always an exception. Telephone ahead to make sure!*

**CHITTLEHAMHOLT** DEVON                    **MAP 8**

# Highbullen

CHITTLEHAMHOLT, UMBERLEIGH, DEVON EX37 9HD
TEL: CHITTLEHAMHOLT (0769) 540561   FAX: (0769) 540492

*Defiantly different (and therefore possibly frustrating) country
hotel. Inexpensive, considering the good leisure facilities.*

Highbullen, run for many years by the Neil family, is in some ways
infuriatingly unconventional and in other ways charmingly crazy. Like it
or loathe it, you can't complain about the value; the price of the room
includes use of most of the hotel's many facilities.

The large house, high-Victorian with more than a hint of Gothic, isn't
half bad, either, nor is the rural, very peaceful spot. But, first you must
check in. On a table beneath the huge staircase in the wide, tiled entrance
hall sits a fat register. Next to it is an old cradle phone which you are
instructed to use. Staff and guests at Highbullen are usually downstairs
in the cavernous, vaulted basement bar and restaurant. The indoor pool
and gym are also downstairs. Only the billiard table is privileged enough
to warrant one of the handsome upstairs rooms. The drawing-room
deserves better than such relentlessly matching earthy-green velveteen
sofas and armchairs, but you get no sense you're in an hotel, even so.

There are fine antique beds in bedrooms, often plenty of space, and a
delightfully old-fashioned sense of design. You may note signs of wear
and tear, and not all rooms are conveniently laid out, but keep thinking of
the price and what it entitles you to. Many guests are here for the nine-
hole golf course – you may overhear more than one whinge about sand
pits during your stay – as well as swimming, tennis, baking in sauna or
steamroom, or having a massage.

- Open all year

- Leave the M5 at Junction 27 and take the A361 to South Molton. Here take the B3226 Exeter Road. After 5 miles, turn right up the hill to Chittlehamholt. The hotel is ½ mile beyond the village on the left. Private car park

- I single, 4 twin, 6 double in main house, 23 twin/double in annexes; all with bathroom/WC, TV, hair-dryer; room service in main house

- Restaurant, breakfast room, bar, 2 lounges, games room, drying room, library, conservatory; conference facilities (max 20 people non-residential and residential); fishing, golf, tennis, sauna, solarium, indoor and outdoor swimming pools, spa-bath at hotel, other sports nearby. Wheelchair access to hotel and restaurant, 4 ground-floor bedrooms

- No children under 8; no dogs; no smoking in restaurants and discouraged in bedrooms

- None accepted

- Single £60, single occupancy of twin/double £60, twin/double £100 to £140 (rates inc dinner). Cooked B £3.50; set D £17.50; light lunches

**CHOLMONDELEY** CHESHIRE  MAP 4

# Cholmondeley Arms

CHOLMONDELEY, MALPAS, CHESHIRE SY14 8BT
TEL: CHOLMONDELEY (0829) 720300

*Lively pub and restaurant in a converted schoolhouse.*

Victorian schools get a bad press. This 1982 conversion of a nineteenth-century schoolhouse could be just the thing to banish associations with Dotheboys Hall. Bright colours, scrubbed pine, fresh flowers and log fires all work to create a warm personality for this lively enterprise, and prevent the cathedral-like space from seeming institutional.

An imaginative menu is buttressed by daily specials from – you've guessed it – a blackboard. Nickelby and Smike never ate like this. Schoolboy fare like home-made pies and soups share the billing with devilled lambs' kidneys, a plethora of pancakes, omelettes and grills. Puddings are home-made and combine nursery favourites such as Bakewell pudding or hot baked syrup sponge and cream with distinctly sophisticated offerings such as iced soufflé Grand Marnier. High marks, particularly for the wine list and the real ale.

The bedrooms are in the former schoolmaster's house. Less inventive than the pub, they're comfortable and cheerful, with more gadgets than you would expect for the price. Soft furnishings and décor are floral-themed; the furniture is mostly white melamine. Rooms are on the small size, but so are the charges.

- ◑ Open all year, exc 25 Dec
- ⤤ On the A49 between Whitchurch and Tarporley, next to Cholmondeley Castle. Private car park
- 🛏 1 twin, 2 double, 1 family room; all with shower/TV, hair-dryer
- ◈ Bar/restaurant. Wheelchair access to hotel (1 step),

restaurant and WC, 1 ground-floor bedroom
- ⊖ None
- ▭ Access, Visa
- 💷 Single occupancy of twin/double £25, twin/double £30; children sharing parents' room £5 each. Continental B, cooked B £5; alc L, D £9 to £18; bar snacks (prices till end 91)

---

*L* *This denotes that the hotel offers especially good value at whatever price level.*

♨ *Denotes somewhere you can rely on a good meal – either the hotel features in the 1992 edition of our sister publication,* **The Good Food Guide,** *or our own inspectors thought the cooking impressive, whether particularly competent home cooking or more lavish cuisine.*

# The Plough at Clanfield

BOURTON ROAD, CLANFIELD, OXFORDSHIRE OX18 2RB
TEL: CLANFIELD (036 781) 222    FAX: (036 781) 596

*An attractive ivy-covered Elizabethan manor house where high
standards of comfort and service compensate for small rooms.*

'If you like good food, a comfortable atmosphere, charming and well-
fitted bedrooms and pleasant, attentive staff, then we believe you must go
a long way to better this.' The Plough is new to the Guide this year but
from the evidence of our inspection, readers' reports such as this appear
to be justified.

Of the six rooms, Bluebell and Clover are the smallest and generally
space is at a premium. Compensation in Bluebell is found in the form of a
double whirlpool bath. As you enter the rooms one of the first things to
catch the eye is the cuddly toy provided to keep you company.

The Plough is one of only four hotels in the Hatton Hotels group and
the atmosphere is very much that of a family- rather than corporately-run
establishment. The affable general manager could just as easily be
serving behind the bar or overseeing dinner as sitting in the office. Before
dinner everyone congregates in the lounge bar where the heavily laden
brandy table is both a topic of conversation and worthy of serious after-
dinner consideration. One reader writes: 'The menu is not extensive but
there were a number of special dishes available each evening, mainly fish
dishes dependent on local availability. To add to the enjoyment these are
lovingly described by the head waiter over pre-dinner drinks.' Dinner is
in one of two cosy, low-ceilinged, beamed rooms, ideal for winter dining
although possibly a bit short of natural light for lunch or summer eating.

○ *Open all year*

↗ *On the A4095 from Witney, 4
miles north of Faringdon. Private
car park*

🛏 *5 twin/double, 1 four-poster
suite; most with bathroom/WC,
some with shower/WC; TV, room
service, hair-dryer, trouser press,
baby-listening in all rooms; no
tea/coffee-making facilities in
rooms*

◈ *Restaurant, bar/lounge;
conference facilities (max 10
people non-residential, 6*

*residential); drying facilities;
fishing, golf, other sports nearby.
Wheelchair access to public
rooms only*

⊖ *No children under 7; no dogs; no
smoking in restaurant, 1
bedroom specifically no-smoking*

▭ *Access, Amex, Diners, Visa*

£ *Single occupancy of twin/double
£66, twin/double £86, four-
poster suite £105; deposit
required. Bar lunches; alc L £15,
D £23, £28. Special breaks
available*

*See page 787 for other hotels worthy of inclusion in our* Visitors' Book.

# Grey Friar Lodge

CLAPPERSGATE, AMBLESIDE, CUMBRIA LA22 9NE
TEL: AMBLESIDE (053 94) 33158

*Interesting knick-knacks, stunning views, and a very fair price.*

Tony Sutton stops for a couple of minutes every day just to look out of the window. Who can blame him? The views of the Brathay Valley, Park Fell and Weatherlam from this former bishop's residence at the foot of Loughrigg Fell are spectacular. And the Suttons are exceptional hosts, friendly and unpretentious, and they offer unstuffy northern hospitality, comfortable accommodation and agreeable food at a good price.

Knick-knacks abound. 'We're magpies,' says Sheila, cheerfully dusting a collection that embraces Victorian ornaments, wall-mounted muskets and a swordfish mandible. There are two lounges, one of which leads to the pretty garden. The accent is on comfort rather than designer style, and there's lots of homely brass and copper. Local caricatures by Wilks of *The Field* prove a talking point. The dining-room is a riot of Wedgwood plates.

Sheila prepares a five-course dinner that might include warm smoked trout mousse with almonds, roulade of turkey breast with spinach fettuccine, sticky toffee pudding, and cheeses served with celery and fruit. Most of the bedrooms are very large, with chintzy soft furnishings, lots of stripped pine and plenty of books. Bathrooms are good, though two top rooms with low water pressure have showers only.

◑ *Closed Nov to Feb*

↗ *On the A593, 1½ miles west of Ambleside. Private car park*

🛏 *2 twin, 5 double, 1 four-poster; all with bathroom or shower/ WC, exc 2 doubles with shower/ WC; TV, hair-dryer*

◈ *Dining-room, 2 lounges, drying-room; fishing, golf, other sports nearby*

⊖ *No wheelchair access; no children under 12; no dogs; no smoking in bedrooms*

▭ *None accepted*

💷 *Single occupancy of twin/double £40 to £42, twin/double £76 to £80, four-poster £82 to £86 (rates inc dinner, 7.30pm); deposit required. Special breaks available*

---

*Congratulations to Cumbria – our number 1 county with 53 full entries in this year's Guide.*

**CLAVERDON** WARWICKSHIRE                                    **MAP 6**

# Ardencote Manor

LYE GREEN ROAD, CLAVERDON, WARWICKSHIRE CV35 8LS
TEL: CLAVERDON (0926) 843111   FAX: (0926) 842646

*A business hotel making an effort to attract tourists with its pretty
position and well-equipped leisure centre.*

Surrounded by open fields and its own large garden with mature trees
and lots of daffodils in the spring, this is a peaceful place for a night or
two's stay. A rather ugly extension houses the leisure centre and a sign at
the entrance points out that the hotel is owned by private company. It's
regularly taken over for management training courses, and most of the
books in the library are related to them.

The Victorian house has well-proportioned rooms and large windows
overlooking the informal gardens but, in the bar at least, the décor is a
little uninteresting, with lots of dark wood reproduction furniture. More
imagination has been used in the dining-room – cosy with swathes of
peachy curtains and wood-panelled walls. Bedrooms are spacious and
well-equipped. The hotel is close to the village and handy for Birmingham, Coventry and the tourist sights of Warwickshire.

- Open all year
- 3 miles east of Henley-in-Arden, off the B4095 Warwick road. Private car park
- 9 single, 5 twin, 4 double; most with bathroom/WC, some with shower/WC; TV, hair-dryer, trouser press in all rooms
- Restaurant, bar, library; conference facilities (max 18

people, 120 non-residential); tennis, sauna/solarium, gym, indoor pool, squash at hotel
- No wheelchair access; no dogs
- Access, Amex, Diners, Visa
- Single £65, single occupancy of twin/double £85, twin/double £85; deposit required. Set L £11, D £16. Special breaks available

**CLEY** NORFOLK                                    **MAP 7**

# Cley Mill

CLEY NEXT THE SEA, HOLT, NORFOLK NR25 7NN
TEL: CLEY (0263) 740209

*Unusual and decorative base for the north Norfolk coast.*

Bird-watchers now wield binoculars along the north Norfolk coast where
once wool, grain and flour merchants plied their trade. Cley Mill, built in
the early eighteenth century, passed from milling to holiday-home use in
1921, and into the personally run guesthouse it is today in 1983. Two
rooms occupy the ground floor: the dining-room, into which you enter,

and a circular sitting-room with cottagey furnishings, open fire, television and sea views. From here a narrow staircase spirals up to an observation room (telescope provided).

Round and inward-slanting walls are naturally a feature of the comfortable and pretty bedrooms. There are not many rooms in the mill but the stables and boat sheds nearby have been turned into two self-catering units. A little garden on the River Glaven overlooks salt marshes and Cley bird sanctuary. It all feels very secluded, but you can see the mill from whichever direction you approach as it occupies an apron of land that sticks out from the town.

◑ *Closed Jan, Feb; restaurant closed Thur eve*

⤢ *On the A149 halfway between Wells and Cromer. Private car park*

🛏 *1 single, 2 twin, 3 double; most with bathroom/WC, 1 with shower/WC, 1 public bathroom; 2 self-catering flats*

◇ *Dining-room, lounge, drying room; conference facilities (max 12 people non-residential); golf, sailing, other sports nearby*

⊖ *No wheelchair access; no dogs in public rooms; no smoking in dining-room*

▭ *None accepted*

£ *Single £26, single occupancy of twin/double £34, twin/double £45 to £53; deposit required. Set D £14.50 (7pm). Special breaks available*

-Cley Mill-

# Bailiffscourt

CLIMPING, LITTLEHAMPTON, WEST SUSSEX, BN17 5RW
TEL: LITTLEHAMPTON (0903) 723511    TELEX: 877870 BLFSCT G
FAX: (0903) 723107

*Seaside medievalism achieved without suits of armour and serving wenches.*

This is an extraordinary folly on a grand scale: a medieval manor in 23 acres and set back from Climping's stony strand. It's a blatant fake – though the materials are entirely genuine, the assembly is latter-day. It was recreated in the 1930s by Lord Moyne (in a fit of expensive whimsy) from a magpie assortment of gleanings discovered in about-to-be-demolished houses all over southern England. As you enter the drive you see something resembling an architectural zoo, a group of ever-so-carefully reconstructed huts – the sort of thing you might find in a folk village preserved for tourists, all just a little too neat and tidy.

The larger gold-stone building is the main block, carefully medievalised with Gothic arches, mullioned windows and dark oak doorways. To one side is a further building topped with orderly thatch. Inside, the hotel's flagged passageways and stone stairwells lead through small lounges, bars and reception rooms furnished with period-style chairs, tapestries and embroidered wall hangings. Upstairs, the floor creaks and lurches unevenly underfoot. Bedrooms, named after local hamlets and fields lifted from a sixteenth-century map, vary; some are vast chapel-like spaces with soaring pitched rafters, others are cosy and charming with quaint leaded lights. Many have four-posters and log fires. One has an eccentric arrangement of two full-sized baths next to each other. Menus promise elaborate food: breast of chicken filled with Stilton and baked in Noilly Prat served with a port wine sauce. The hotel is professionally staffed rather than personally run.

○ Open all year

↗ At the roundabout in Arundel take the exit signposted Ford. After 3 miles turn right at the T-junction on to the A259, then first left towards Climping Beach. The hotel is a short way down this road on the right. Private car park

⇥ 2 single, 7 twin, 11 doubles (2 rooms in cottages, suites and four-posters available); all with bathroom/WC, TV, room service, hair-dryer; no tea/coffee-making facilities in rooms; baby-listening on request

◇ Restaurant, bar, 3 lounges, private dining-room, library, drying room; conference facilities (max 26 people non-residential, 20 residential); tennis, unheated pool, croquet, archery at hotel, other sports nearby

● No wheelchair access; no children under 8

▭ Access, Amex, Diners, Visa

£ Single £65 to £85, single occupancy of twin/double £85 to £110, twin/double £100 to £180, four-poster £120 to £180; deposit required. Set L £15.50, D £25. Special breaks available

# Birches Mill

CLUN, SHROPSHIRE SY7 8NL
TEL: CLUN (058 84) 409

*A warm welcome awaits at this hotel, deep in the heart of the countryside.*

Amid a web of country lanes and undulating hills, Birches Mill lies deep in the Welsh Marches and makes a good base for exploring Offa's Dyke. The hosts, Avis and Peter Ades, are nearly as welcoming as their black collie, Bobbie, who, tail wagging furiously, offers newly arrived guests presents of large sticks.

The Ades take great pride in the history of Birches Mill, which, in parts, dates back to around 1600. In its time the building has been a farmhouse as well as a mill. Flowing through the garden, a few yards from the ivy-covered façade of the house, is the River Unk, straddled by a rustic wooden foot bridge. Inside, the house is cosy, with old beams supporting low ceilings, an enormous fireplace and comfortable, faded armchairs. Guests eat together at a long polished oak table in the kitchen. 'There is only one sin I won't tolerate,' Avis admits, 'and that's someone turning up late for a meal.' As a former food writer she takes the subject very seriously and the menu reflects her passion for cooking. Dishes like pork with orange and ginger, or lamb chops with basil and garlic, are served with organically grown vegetables and followed by imaginative and tempting puddings. There are vegetarian and vegan dishes on the regular menu, but she is happy to provide more choice if guests warn her in advance.

The cottage-style bedrooms aren't spacious or luxurious but are well-heated and are brightened by flowery curtains and views over the river.

- Open all year
- Nearest main road is the A488 Clun to Bishop's Castle road. Private car park
- 1 twin, 1 double, 1 family room; 1 public bathroom; no tea/coffee-making facilities in rooms
- Dining-room, lounge, drying room; fishing, golf, riding nearby
- No wheelchair access; no children under 11; no dogs; no smoking in bedrooms
- None accepted
- Single occupancy of twin/double £26 to £28, twin/double £32 to £35. Set D £9 (7.30pm). Special breaks available

---

*The text of entries is based on unsolicited reports sent in by readers and backed up by inspections. The factual details under the text are from questionnaires the Guide sends to all hotels that feature in the book.*

# Old Post Office

9 THE SQUARE, CLUN, NR CRAVEN ARMS, SHROPSHIRE SY7 8JA
TEL: CLUN (058 84) 687

*Cosy rooms in an affectionately preserved post office, with an
excellent restaurant.*

A glance at 'Memories of Clun' in old photos, left out for guests in the
upstairs hall, confirms that the building has changed very little since
1907. The bottle-green façade of the original Victorian post office
(originally built in 1880) now houses a sorbet-orange restaurant with a
couple of bedrooms upstairs, one overlooking the Square, the other
enjoying a lovely view of the village. Richard and Anne Arbuthnot
provide books and board-games rather than television for their guests
and you'll find home-made biscuits, real coffee and herbal teas laid out
on arrival.

The bedrooms are simple: the small front one with a stripped pine
chest of drawers, the larger back one with an original fireplace. Although
there are plans to make one room *en suite* guests currently share a
spacious Scandinavian-style bathroom with pine-slatted walls.

The restaurant leads out to a terrace with wonderful views. In the
summer, tables are taken out here. A small bar and comfy seating area is
provided for a pre-dinner drink, while you pore over the tempting menu,
or a post-dinner coffee, while you recover. Menus change mid-month,
but one favourite is the twice-baked soufflé of Welsh goats' cheese on
lettuce with a hazelnut vinaigrette. You might try the roasted yellow
pepper soup with fresh Parmesan followed by roast guinea-fowl with a
celeriac and apple rösti. Puddings include such diet-busters as chocolate
slab with brandied prunes on a mango purée.

- ◑ *Closed Mon, Tue; 10 days Xmas*
- ⬈ *South of Shrewsbury on the A488
  via Bishop's Castle; north from
  Ludlow via A49 and B4368 to
  Clun. On-street parking*
- 🛏 *1 twin, 1 double; both rooms
  have hair-dryer*
- ◈ *Restaurant, lounge/bar, terrace;
  conference facilities (max 12*
- *people non-residential); fishing,
  golf, riding, other sports nearby.
  Wheelchair access to restaurant
  only*
- ⊖ *No dogs; no smoking in
  bedrooms*
- ▭ *Access, Visa*
- £ *Single occupancy of twin/double
  £26, twin/double £44; deposit
  required. Alc L £20, D £33*

---

☺    *Denotes somewhere you can rely on a good meal – either the hotel
features in the 1992 edition of our sister publication,* The Good
Food Guide, *or our own inspectors thought the cooking impressive,
whether particularly competent home cooking or more lavish cuisine.*

**CLUTTON** CHESHIRE                                    **MAP 4**

# Frogg Manor

FULLER'S MOOR, NANTWICH ROAD, BROXTON, NR CHESTER, CHESHIRE
CH3 9JH
TEL: BROXTON (0829) 782629

*Mild eccentricity and tremendous joie de vivre in friendly,
comfortable and stylish surroundings.*

The English produce eccentrics rather well, and John Sykes is a prime
specimen. Eschewing the classic country house formula he has transformed this Grade-II-listed white Georgian house into a celebration of
his idiosyncratic personality. Tributes from readers are many and
fulsome: 'superb' said two, 'quite delightful' another. It's easy to be
seduced by the charm of it all from the moment you encounter the man-
sized frog in polka dot tie pointing the way.

Beneath the jokiness there's a comfortable and pleasing hotel with
lavish Georgian and Victorian *objets d'art*, rich soft furnishings and
classy glass and china. Bedrooms, disappointingly not named after
Kermit or Jeremy Fisher, commemorate instead English historical
heavyweights plus Sherlock Holmes, and are beautifully furnished and
carefully thought out, with comfortable beds and good lighting. The
enormous Wellington Suite hides behind a bookcase in the sitting-room
and once inside you'll find the central bed bedecked with fine chintz and
a crown canopy, a pair of sofas and an 'undressing room'.

Food is unfussy and modern, with separate listings for vegetarian and
fat-free dishes, and lots of variations on a theme. The entertaining wine
list also impressed several readers, as has the house policy of flexibility
over breakfast time.

○ Open all year

⤴ Leave the M6 at Junction 16
towards Nantwich, and take the
A534 Wrexham road. The hotel
is 10 miles along this road on the
left. Private car park

🛏 5 double, 1 four-poster, 1 suite;
most with bathroom/WC, some
with shower/WC; TV, room
service, hair-dryer, trouser press,
baby-listening, ironing facilities in
all rooms

◈ Restaurant, bar, lounge,
conservatory; conference

facilities (max 24 people non-
residential, 6 residential); tennis
at hotel; babysitting

⊖ No wheelchair access; no
children under 4; no dogs in
public rooms; part of dining area
non-smoking

▭ Access, Amex, Diners, Visa

£ Single occupancy of twin/double
£40 to £76, twin/double £46 to
£96, four-poster £96, suite £96.
Continental B £4.50, cooked B
£7.50; set L £11, D £21; alc L,
D £28. Special breaks available

---

*All rooms have tea/coffee-making facilities unless we mention to the
contrary.*

# Red Lion

43 HIGH STREET, COLCHESTER, ESSEX CO1 1DJ
TEL: COLCHESTER (0206) 577986   FAX: (0206) 578207

*This genuine but not self-consciously quaint old inn in a busy town centre has been brought gracefully into the late-twentieth century.*

The Red Lion, which was enlarged and transformed into an inn in 1500, has retreated up a flight, and a busy arcade of shops now takes up the ground floor. This doesn't improve the Tudor façade, but how nice to leave the pace as well as the view of the High Street behind.

The carpeted bar and adjoining Alice Miller's Restaurant (she's a resident ghost), timber- and stucco-walled, are both very peaceful and spacious, a touch formal but jollied up by plenty of old English features such as wrought-iron standard lamps and wheel-backed or Windsor chairs. And beams, of course. Flowers and white tablecloths give freshness to the restaurant where mostly English cooking prevails.

A comfortable residents' lounge doesn't benefit from being a through-route to bedrooms. These are well-decorated and those in the original part have had much made of their handsome old features. You can see into the wattle and daub structure in room ten. The fourteen rooms in the Victorian wing are inevitably more anonymous, with pine furniture and smaller bathrooms. If you stay here, you at least needn't worry about having your sleep disturbed. Half of the old rooms face the front to be serenaded late into the night by music from the Hippodrome just over the road.

| | |
|---|---|
| ◑ Open all year, exc 24 Dec to 2 Jan | ◈ Restaurant, bar, lounge; conference facilities (max 40 people non-residential, 24 residential) |
| ⤢ Centrally located in Colchester High Street. Limited on-street parking, free overnight car park nearby | |
| | ⊖ No wheelchair access; no dogs |
| | ▭ Access, Amex, Diners, Visa |
| ⇴ 10 single, 7 twin, 6 double, 1 four-poster; most with bathroom or shower/WC, 2 singles with shower/WC; TV, baby-listening in all rooms; hair-dryer on request | ⊞£ Single £72, single occupancy of twin/double £72, twin/double £88, four-poster £95; deposit required. Set L £12, D £14; alc L, D £16. Special breaks available |

---

*Are you aware of your rights as a consumer when you book into an hotel? Check them out on page 13.*

**COLERNE** WILTSHIRE                                    **MAP 9**

# Lucknam Park

COLERNE, WILTSHIRE SN14 8AZ
TEL: BATH (0225) 742777   FAX: (0225) 743536

*On the contrived side, but providing unabashed luxury in plush
and stately surroundings.*

'Expensive luxury, but worth it,' comments one correspondent. Luck-
nam Park, a grand Georgian stone mansion sitting in 280 acres of
parkland, is plush throughout. Racehorses often share the long, beech-
lined drive with Mercedes and Bentleys, and the grand rooms throughout the main house show equally good breeding. Wonderful flower
arrangements and staff that temper the formality are all pluses. Some
formula furnishing has crept in, however, and you are unlikely to forget
you're in an hotel. The leisure centre is an attraction for many guests, of
course. Bedrooms hold no great surprises. There is some lovely old furniture, and design-conscious fabrics in vibrant, contrasting colours and
patterns happily avoid predictable pastels and flowers. De luxe suites,
getting on for £300 a night, aren't worth it, though you might enjoy
leafing through their guest books and finding names of famous former
inhabitants. The top-floor rooms in the converted stables (across the courtyard), have sloping ceilings and are fair value. Despite marble tiles and
monogramed robes, bathrooms never quite attain the decadence you
(or your company) are paying for. But we hear room service is excellent.
For decadence, the set menu does quite well. How about gâteau of
foie gras, truffle, chicken and pistachio followed by a galette of Cornish
crab and scallops on cream-braised onions? One reader reckoned the
restaurant was trying too hard, with waitresses on auto-smile.

◑ Open all year

⤢ Leave the M4 at Junction 17
onto the A429 Chippenham
road. Before Chippenham, turn
right for Bristol on the A420. At
Ford (3 miles) turn left to
Colerne, and right at the
crossroads for Colerne. The hotel
entrance is ¼ mile on the right.
Private car park

🛏 1 single, 11 twin, 18 double, 1
four-poster, 5 suites, 6 four-
poster suites; all with bathroom/
WC, TV, room service, hair-dryer;
baby-listening on request; no tea/
coffee-making facilities in rooms

◈ 2 restaurants, drawing-room,
library, laundry; conference

facilities (max 40 people non-
residential, 42 residential);
tennis, croquet, heated pool,
sauna, solarium, gym, whirlpool,
beauty room, snooker at hotel,
other sports nearby. Wheelchair
access to hotel (1 step),
restaurant and WC (M,F), 4
ground-floor bedrooms

⊖ No dogs

▭ Access, Amex, Diners, Visa

£ Single from £95, single
occupancy of twin/double from
£110, twin/double from £130,
suite from £215; deposit
required. Cooked B £5.50; alc L
£27, D £42.50. Special breaks
available

# Coleshill Hotel

HIGH STREET, COLESHILL, WARWICKSHIRE B46 3BF
TEL: COLESHILL (0675) 465527   FAX: (0675) 464013

*An ideal stopover for the business visitor to the NEC. Cheerful staff are an added bonus.*

The small town of Coleshill is just off the M42, on the edge of Warwickshire countryside. The hotel is on the high street and looks like two Georgian houses connected by a more modern addition, but it is actually little more than ten years old. It's in an ideal position for the NEC (a short drive away) and consequently it's a popular haunt of business clients.

The bar, with cheerful rustic décor, sofas and bench seating, is a good place to while away the evening, and the atmosphere gets quite jolly. The restaurant seems cluttered with busy patterns, country prints and decorative plates, but at the same time it's quite cosy for dinner with soft lighting. Service is friendly with the staff sparing time for a chat over dinner. Room four has a rather rickety four-poster that squeaks every time you turn over, and pink velour tub chairs and white fitted wardrobes. On our visit our telephone was broken and although the staff were very apologetic, they were unable to fix it.

◐ Open all year

↗ In the centre of Coleshill on the B4117, 1 mile north of the M6 (Junction 4). Private car park

🛏 2 single, 10 twin, 9 double, 2 four-poster; all with bathroom/WC, TV, room service, hairdryer, trouser press, babylistening

◈ Air-conditioned restaurant, bar; conference facilities (max 80 people non-residential, 24 residential); tennis, riding, other sports nearby. Wheelchair access to restaurant only

⊖ No children in restaurant after 8 pm; no dogs

▦ Access, Amex, Diners, Visa

£ Single £68, twin/double/four-poster £81; deposit required. Set L £8.50, £9.50, D £15; alc L, D £20. Special breaks available

# Coulsworthy House

COMBE MARTIN, DEVON EX34 0PD
TEL: COMBE MARTIN (0271) 882463

*A congenial family-run hotel with good facilities near Exmoor.*

Exmoor National Park stops at the hedge of this pretty white, mainly eighteenth-century house. 'Exmoor', says Mrs Anthony, 'is better tended and less spoilt than Dartmoor.' In any case, Coulsworthy House has a wonderful, sheep-dotted hillside situation with smashing views looking down on Combe Martin and a bit of the sea.

If the moor doesn't entice you, you can swim in the large heated pool, or play on the grass tennis court. The Anthonys with their daughter, Alison, and son-in-law, Mark, run a relaxed and jolly house that has a faithful following: one couple has been 22 times. In cool weather, you can curl up in front of the coal and log fire in the homely lounge; there are books and a TV here to amuse. A bar, decorated with whimsical Cecil Aldin watercolours, is just right for pre-dinner drinks, and the dining-room, cheerfully done up in pale green vineleaf wallpaper, makes an appealing venue for Alison's clever four-course dinners. The menu changes every night and amongst the many choices might be seafood crêpe, roast guinea-fowl with madeira sauce, and pear praline. Nicely embellished bedrooms come in all sizes, shapes and prices (and on two floors, with sloping ceilings a feature on the second floor). Room two, on the first floor, is an especially large and airy double with lace and satin trimmed pillow slips and cushions, lime wood bedside tables and a pretty, carpeted bathroom. There are duvets (or blankets) and every room has a bottle of Coulsworthy water from the house's own spring. Breakfasts are both healthy and indulgent. A bickering family of crows and an occasional Concorde might disrupt the peace just a little.

◑ *Closed 7 Dec to 7 Feb; restaurant closed Sun eve*

⤴ *Leave Blackmoor Gate on the A399 Combe Martin road. 2 miles from Blackmoor Gate take the right turning signposted Trentishoe and Hunters Inn – the house is 100 yards down this road. Private car park*

🛏 *2 single, 2 twin, 5 double, 1 family room; most with bathroom/WC, some with shower/WC; TV, baby-listening in all rooms; no tea/coffee-making facilities in rooms*

◈ *Restaurant, bar, lounge, TV room; tennis, croquet, heated outdoor swimming-pool (in season) at hotel, other sports nearby*

⊖ *No wheelchair access; no dogs or smoking in restaurant*

▭ *Access, Visa*

£ *Single £56 to £69, single occupancy of twin/double £84 to £118, twin/double £112 to £158, family room (4 people) £180 to £207 (rates inc dinner); deposit required. Sun L £16.50; set D £21.50. Special breaks available*

---

❀ *This denotes that the hotel is in an exceptionally peaceful situation where you can be assured of a restful stay.*

---

☕ *Denotes somewhere you can rely on a good meal – either the hotel features in the 1992 edition of our sister publication,* The Good Food Guide, *or our own inspectors thought the cooking impressive, whether particularly competent home cooking or more lavish cuisine.*

# Aydon Grange

CORBRIDGE, NORTHUMBERLAND NE45 5PW
TEL: HEXHAM (0434) 632169　FAX: 091-281 8430

*A large, elegant family home with extensive grounds and woodland.*

Aydon Grange is a large country manor house and still very much a family home. Derek Straker is your host, porter, butler and housekeeper. And, in his spare time, he looks after five acres of grounds and a kitchen garden, keeping up with the demand for fruit and vegetables from Angela Straker's kitchen. Evening meals are imaginative for an enterprise this small – carrot and orange soup, Snaffles mousse, pheasant breasts in apple and calvados sauce – and are served by candlelight at a mahogany table in the elegant dining-room.

Furnishings in the rest of the house are equally stylish but there's no intimidating formality or lack of comfort. The guests' sitting-room is comfortably large, with an open fire kept well supplied with logs; and there are books and magazines lying around (or board games if you ask) if television is not your idea of evening entertainment.

All the bedrooms are a good size with pretty prints, muted colours and some lovely pieces of furniture. Each has its own bathroom (generally enormous), a reflection of the care taken by the Strakers when converting their family home in 1989. Plenty of family photographs and other memorabilia remind you of the manor's former existence.

| | |
|---|---|
| ◑ *Open all year* | ⊖ *No wheelchair access; no children under 10; dogs by arrangement only; no smoking in bedrooms* |
| ↗ *Half a mile from the centre of Corbridge going north on the B6321 Aydon road. Private car park* | |
| | ▭ *None accepted* |
| ⇌ *2 twin, 2 double; all with bathroom/WC, hair-dryer; self-catering cottage (sleeps 7)* | ⊞£ *Single occupancy of twin/double £38 to £52, twin/double £60 to £70; cottage £125 to £285 per week. Set D £20 (8pm, by arrangement)* |
| ◈ *Dining-room, lounge with TV, drying room; tennis, croquet at hotel, other sports nearby* | |

---

*Perhaps a good example of the care taken was when my husband had to go to London one evening and arrived back at about 12.30am; the proprietor had waited up, although in fact he had given him a key, opened the door to welcome him back and offered him a cup of tea. On an hotel in Kent*

# Corse Lawn House

CORSE LAWN, GLOUCESTERSHIRE GL19 4LZ
TEL: GLOUCESTER (0452) 780 479/771   FAX: (0452) 780 840

*Stately rather than grand hotel, with good food and pleasant service.*

Denis and Baba Hine's success has resulted in a second extension to this gracious Queen Anne building. The newly laid gardens by the car park need time to develop, but the croquet lawn, tennis court and swimming-pool all seem in perfect order. The large attractive pond in front of the hotel, complete with ducks, once functioned as a coach-wash in pre-combustion engine days. Today, you can have lunch beside it when the weather allows.

Public rooms are decorated in restrained pastels: mostly greys, pinks and blues. The bar, in deep green and red stripes, is more striking. Beds all have corona drapes and rooms have been praised for having every comfort, though one reader found 'the bedside light rather inadequate for bedtime reading'. Set dinner in the elegant L-shaped dining-room might include dishes such as baked queen scallops with provençale stuffing, loin of veal with white wine and wild mushrooms, and mousse of three chocolates – one reader commented: 'Exquisite . . . excellent portions beautifully presented.' Denis, of cognac fame, looks after the wine list, which is particularly strong on claret. Breakfast is hearty enough 'to set you up for the day'. Service is courteous but not over-formal, 'friendly without being familiar'.

Open all year

From Tewkesbury take the A438 towards Ledbury for 4 miles. Turn left for Gloucester on the B4211 for 1 mile. The hotel is on the left. Private car park

5 twin, 10 double, 2 four-poster, 2 suites; all with bathroom/WC, TV, room service, hair-dryer, trouser press, baby-listening

Restaurant, bar, 3 lounges, TV room; conference facilities (max 40 people non-residential, 19 residential); tennis, croquet,

heated swimming-pool at hotel, other sports nearby. Wheelchair access to hotel, restaurant and WC (M,F), 5 ground-floor bedrooms including 3 equipped for disabled people

No dogs in restaurant

Access, Amex, Diners, Visa

Single from £65, single occupancy of twin/double from £65, twin/double £90, four-poster £100, suite £110. Set L £16, D £23.50; alc L, D £20/£35. Special breaks available

*Shame on you South Yorkshire, Tyne & Wear and Mid Glamorgan, the only counties without an hotel of merit in this year's* Guide.

# Crest Guesthouse

39 FRIARS ROAD, COVENTRY, WEST MIDLANDS CVI 2LJ
TEL: COVENTRY (0203) 227822

*Small guesthouse, central and friendly.*

Confusing to drive to by car but with easy access by footbridge from
Coventry railway station and the city centre, Mrs Harvey's immaculate
guesthouse is a useful find for those on a limited budget or those who
don't fancy the anonymity of a large chain hotel.

The turn-of-the-century house with bright blue paintwork is on a
quiet side-street. The lounge (with TV) and breakfast rooms are at either
end of a long room with a glass sliding door opening out on to the garden,
which gets lots of use on warm evenings. The bedrooms are all fresh and
bright with plumped-up duvets.

| | |
|---|---|
| ◑ Open all year | ✧ Dining-room, lounge; golf, tennis, other sports nearby |
| ⊿ In Coventry city centre, 3 minutes' walk from the railway station. Private car park | ⊖ No wheelchair access; no dogs |
| | ▭ None accepted |
| ⊨ 2 single, 2 twin, the twins with shower/WC en-suite and hair-dryer; 1 public bathroom; all rooms have TV | £ Single £19, single occupancy of twin/double £27, twin £40; deposit required |

# Hipping Hall

COWAN BRIDGE, KIRKBY LONSDALE, CUMBRIA LA6 2JJ
TEL: KIRKBY LONSDALE (052 42) 71187   FAX: (052 42) 72452

*Lovely secluded old house with house-party aspirations.*

Misanthropes beware. Guests at Jocelyn Ruffle and Ian Bryant's lovely
house are expected to join in. You'll soon get acquainted with the other
guests as you sit at a communal table in the Great Hall under its
minstrels' gallery quaffing wine. Put off? Don't be. 'Give it a try and
you'll love it,' promises Ian. 'So much more fun than seven couples
whispering to each other at separate tables.' Enter into the dinner-party
frame of mind and you'll get on just fine.

Period features such as uneven walls and off-centre door frames
accompany smart modern décor in autumn shades, and more rustic
touches survive in a log-burning stove and various antiques. Dinner
might include gravadlax with mustard sauce, courgette and rosemary
soup, breast of Landes duck with orange port sauce, excellent local
cheeses and plum and cinnamon flan. It's a no-choice affair, but if

anything offends your dietary or other sensibilities, given notice Jocelyn will prepare an agreeable alternative.

Bedrooms combine pine with Victorian and Edwardian furniture, and there are two cottage apartments. Fresh flowers and home-made cookies make them homely. Late risers will rejoice in the news that breakfast is available 'whenever you want it from 8.30am'. Converts to the *de rigueur* conviviality can assemble their own house-party and imitate their fore-fathers on forays into the surrounding countryside with flasks of Bull's Blood and an Edwardian champagne brunch, or, alternatively, organise croquet matches on the lawn.

◗ Closed Dec to Feb (exc for groups)

◿ On the A65, 3 miles east of Kirkby Lonsdale. Private car park

🛏 2 twin, 3 double, 2 suites; all with bathroom/WC, exc 1 double with shower/WC; TV, hair-dryer in all rooms

◇ Dining-room, bar, lounge, conservatory, breakfast-room; conference facilities (max 14

people residential); croquet at hotel, fishing, golf nearby

⊖ No wheelchair access; no children under 12; no dogs in public rooms; no smoking in dining-room

▭ Access, Visa

£ Single occupancy of twin/double £59, twin/double £69, suite £79; deposit required if more than 2 nights. Set D £18.50 (8pm)

## CRACKINGTON HAVEN CORNWALL                    MAP 8

# Manor Farm

CRACKINGTON HAVEN, BUDE, CORNWALL EX23 0JU
TEL: ST GENNYS (08403) 304

*House-party atmosphere in immaculate and beautiful homestead near the north Cornish coast.*

Camaraderie is cultivated by the Knights, so if you're the sort who likes to hide yourself away with a book before dinner, or dine and rise as the mood grabs you, then you shouldn't seek out this exquisitely sited old farmhouse. Many of Muriel Knight's guests have been coming for years and are by now familiar with the several left- and right-hand turns on by-roads and by-lanes that lead to the immaculate stone buildings (only several centuries old, though Crackington Manor was mentioned in the Domesday Book).

The gardens have the same cosseted appearance, as does the interior. Flagstoned floors, beams and low ceilings are respected; most of the furniture is antique. There are two comfortable sitting-rooms, one with television and books, another larger, where everyone congregates for drinks and coffee. You will convene at around 6.30pm, after serving yourself from a fully-equipped honesty bar in a nearby hallway. At seven sharp Muriel rings her bell, and you set off to find your place card on a lovely long mahogany table that seems to have been designed expressly for the room. John Tovey and Delia Smith are sources for Muriel's stylish four-course, no-choice dinners of fish ramekin, perhaps, pheasant in wine, garlic and onion cream sauce, then chocolate choux followed by cheese. Guests carry on animated conversations over coffee in the lounge (though some might retire to the magnificent snooker table over the way), before heading for their comfortable bedrooms, very 'ye olde', but simply furnished with modern as well as antique furniture. Remember to set your alarm; Muriel's bell will next ring at 8.30 in the morning.

◐ Open all year

🔁 From the A39 take the B3263 towards Crackington Haven. The farm is 2 miles along on the right. Private car park

🛏 1 single, 1 twin, 2 double, 2 annexe rooms; half with bathroom/WC, half with shower/WC; no tea/coffee-making facilities in rooms

◈ 2 dining-rooms, bar, 2 lounges, TV room, games room; fishing, tennis, water sports nearby

⊖ No wheelchair access; no children; no dogs; no smoking

▭ None accepted

£ Single £36 to £38, twin/double £72 to £84; annexe room £84 (rates inc dinner); deposit required

---

**CRANBROOK** KENT                                    **MAP 10**

# Kennel Holt

CRANBROOK, KENT TN17 2PT
TEL: CRANBROOK (0580) 712032   FAX: (0580) 712931

*A peacefully located Elizabethan manor house hotel popular for functions. Slightly disappointing bedrooms.*

This is somewhat larger than many of our other recommendations in Kent and big enough to cater for weddings and functions. Kennel Holt might suit those who don't like being swamped with attention but still want the experience of staying in a typical Kent country house. From the outside it seems perfect: an Elizabethan house with an amalgam of local styles (brick, tile-hung and weatherboarded). Next to it is an oast house, a willow pond and bird-shaped topiary hedges leading to a big lawn and woods beyond.

By comparison, the interior may disappoint. Bedrooms are light and well-equipped but a bit short on character. The hotel lacks a bar to sit in: drinks materialise from a small bar in the reception hall. There are two lounges, one with inglenook, the other (an Edwardian addition) with oak panelling, floral sofas and reproduction coffee tables. Happily, the owners have personalised the rooms with family photos and lots of china Old English Sheepdogs and stuffed toys. Operatic arias played through dinner make the beamed restaurant more atmospheric, as do silver candlesticks, cut glass and rolled napkins in flowered rings standing on deep blue cloths. Owner David Misseldine has taken over the cooking since we inspected last year: roast beef, veal escalope pizzaiola and noisettes of lamb appear on the menu; puddings might include chocolate fudge cake or raspberry Pavlova.

◑ *Open all year*

⬀ *Off the A262, I mile from its junction with the A229, north-west of Cranbrook. Private car park*

🛏 *I single, 4 twin, 3 double, 2 four-poster; most with bathroom/ WC, some with shower/WC; TV, room service, hair-dryer, baby-listening in all rooms*

◈ *Restaurant, bar, 2 lounges; conference facilities (max 40*

*people non-residential, 10 residential); croquet at hotel, other sports nearby. Wheelchair access to restaurant only*

⊖ *No children under 6*

▭ *Access, Amex, Diners, Visa*

£ *Single £50 to £85, single occupancy of twin/double £50 to £95, twin/double £68 to £85, four-poster £68 to £95; deposit required. Set L £17, D £23. Special breaks available*

---

# The Old Cloth Hall

CRANBROOK, KENT TN17 3NR
TEL: CRANBROOK (0580) 712220

*An exceptionally lovely fifteenth-century manor (Elizabeth I once had lunch here); now a family home.*

Situated on the outskirts of Cranbrook, this big, L-shaped timber-framed Tudor manor (part brick, part tile-hung) with soft creamy plasterwork, is mouthwateringly beautiful. A mature garden enhances the delightfulness of the house: rhododendrons, azaleas, japonica – and a grand old swimming-pool. Unsurprisingly, the interior is redolent of a grand family home: in the parquet-floored and beamed dining-room you can sit on antique chairs around a beautiful oval table; in the panelled and inglenooked drawing-room family photos stand on the piano. The owner Katherine Morgan cooks a set three-course dinner such as watercress soup, chicken and Dijon mustard and cream, and raspberry cheesecake (she's particularly into puddings). She'll probably eat with you and you may be offered seconds – just like staying with friends.

The lattice-windowed bedrooms feature pleasant surprises like books, a clothes-brush and an electric blanket, and there's a splendid four-poster master bedroom.

◑ *Open all year, exc Xmas*

⬀ *I mile out of Cranbrook on the Golford road to Tenterden. Turn right just before the cemetery. Private car park*

🛏 *I twin, I double, I four-poster; 2 with bathroom/WC, I with shower/WC; TV, room service, hair-dryer, trouser press, baby-listening; no tea/coffee-making facilities in rooms*

◇ Dining-room, lounge; tennis, unheated swimming-pool, croquet at hotel, other sports nearby

● No wheelchair access; no dogs; no smoking in bedrooms

▭ None accepted

£ Single occupancy of twin/double £45, twin/double £80, four-poster £90; deposit required. Set D £20

---

**CRANFORD** NORTHAMPTONSHIRE                                    **MAP 6**

# Dairy Farm

CRANFORD ST ANDREW, KETTERING, NORTHAMPTONSHIRE NN14 4AQ
TEL: CRANFORD (053 678) 273

*A peaceful B&B in a lovely Jacobean farmhouse.*

In the village of Cranford, down a quiet lane and a couple of hundred yards past the Woolpack pub, is Audrey Clarke's home. It's a lovely mellow yellow-stoned Jacobean house in a peaceful setting surrounded by a large garden and mature trees. There are no signs to indicate that Audrey offers B&B, but you'll get a friendly welcome.

The lemon-yellow-tiled hall with an oak chest leads through to the breakfast room with a central wooden table and arched stone fireplace. There's a massive sitting-room, with squashy armchairs and a settee grouped around the fireplace and an electric fire for chilly evenings. Beams and thick stone walls provide character, and from a window seat there's a good view through the leaded windows. The three bedrooms are all quite spacious, light and pretty and all have tea- and coffee-making facilities. It's perfect for a couple of nights' peace and quiet and Audrey is keen to sing the praises of the pretty villages in the area, likening them to the Cotswold villages but not so crowded. For evening meals, there is a pub in the village and a choice of other places nearby.

◐ Open all year

⤢ Cranford is just off the A1–M1 link road (A604). Dairy Farm is in the village at the end of St Andrew's Lane. Private car park

🛏 2 twin, 1 double; most with bathroom/WC, 1 public bathroom; hair-dryer, baby-listening in all rooms

◇ Dining-room, lounge; meetings facilities (max 10 people);

croquet at hotel, other sports nearby

● No wheelchair access; dogs by arrangement only; no smoking in bedrooms

▭ None accepted

£ Single occupancy of twin/double £18 to £20, twin/double £36 to £44; children under 10 half-price; deposit required. Set D £12 (7pm, must book)

---

*Hotels in our* Visitors' Book *towards the end of the* Guide *are additional hotels that may be worth a visit. Reports on these hotels are welcome.*

**CROSTHWAITE** CUMBRIA                          **MAP 3**

# Crosthwaite House

CROSTHWAITE, NR KENDAL, CUMBRIA LA8 8BP
TEL: CROSTHWAITE (044 88) 264

*Comfortable family-run guesthouse.*

Five miles from the bustle of Bowness, the Lyth Valley is astonishingly unspoilt, and Crosthwaite House is an ideal base from which to explore it. Robin and Marnie Dawson's three-storey Georgian house stands on a minor road. The smell of woodsmoke is instantly welcoming, and an air of family homeliness is effortlessly conveyed as the hesitant sound of recorder scales pipe through from the Dawsons' own quarters. Décor is simple but fresh: Robin redecorated the whole house in eight days on return from his annual expedition wintering in the Austrian ski resort of Söll where he plays the fiddle. Lucky guests might coax him into an impromptu performance, if he's not off jamming at some local hostelry.

Pre-dinner drinks are served in the cosy lounge, where amid the books and brasses you'll find a tapestry of a rural scene by Marnie's grand-mother. The dining-room is a handsome, countrified room with a stripped pine door, displays of plates and fresh flowers on wooden tables. Bedrooms are a reasonable size, and simply but comfortably furnished. Marnie's set dinners are good value, typically offering melon with fresh lime, spinach soup, chicken breasts in a mushroom cream sauce and a selection from the sweet trolley. A host of non-residents regularly descend for the very popular traditional Sunday lunch. One reader pronounced the food excellent and advised that 'the atmosphere that Mr and Mrs Dawson create is so friendly and welcoming we felt part of the family'.

- ◑ Closed mid-Nov to mid-Mar
- ⊠ Leave the M6 at Junction 36 on to the Kendal bypass (signed Barrow), then take the A590. Turn right on to the A5074 (signed Bowness and Windermere). Keep on this road and shortly after passing the Lyth Valley Hotel, turn right. Continue up this lane to the T-junction, turn left and the house is on the right. Private car park
- 🛏 1 single, 2 twin, 3 double; all with shower/WC, baby-listening;

- TV on request; 3 cottages (self-catering)
- ◈ Dining-room, lounge, drying facilities; fishing, golf, other sports nearby
- ⊖ No wheelchair access; no dogs in public rooms
- ▭ None accepted
- 💷 Single £22, single occupancy of twin/double £22, twin/double £22 to £44; children's rates; deposit required. Sun L £7; set D £12 (7.30pm)

---

*Dog lovers: some hotels not only welcome dogs, but they provide gourmet meals for them. Ask.*

**CROYDE** DEVON                                    **MAP 8**

# The Whiteleaf at Croyde

CROYDE, NR BRAUNTON, DEVON EX33 1PN
TEL: CROYDE (0271) 890266

*Small, homely guesthouse close to the sea. A good base if you like to eat well.*

The Whiteleaf is well established, well run and a good bet in an area overrun with impersonal hotels serving mediocre food. Here you will eat well. David Wallington's menus are neither short nor predictable. Might deep-fried seafood parcels with garlic mayonnaise, veal shin with white wine and anchovies, and apricot and custard tartlet tempt you?

The accommodation keeps pace. Wood-chip walled bedrooms, Flo Wallington points out, 'are not what you'd call large', but neither are they pokey. And you might be surprised to find mini-bars, hair-dryers, a proper teapot on the tea-tray, books and thermostatically controlled radiators. Room two, the pick of the bunch, boasts striking Balinese paintings. Prices are fair, especially for single guests. The sitting-room and dining-room are equally decorative and elaborately furnished, but are also comfortable. The Wallingtons are attentive to your needs. A small garden behind, overlooked by a cherry tree, makes a pleasant spot to sit. Croyde is a nice little village of thatched cottages and stone walls spilling over with flowers in spring. A short stroll over the dunes brings you to the beach.

● Closed part of Dec and Jan, 2 weeks in April/May and in July/Aug

🡒 South-west of Croyde on the B3231 Croyde to Braunton road. Private car park

🛏 1 twin, 3 double, 1 family room; all with bathroom/WC, exc 1 double with shower/WC; TV, hair-dryer, mini-bar, baby-listening in all rooms

✧ Restaurant, lounge; golf, water sports, other sports nearby

● No wheelchair access; no dogs in public rooms

▭ Access, Amex, Visa

£ Single occupancy of twin/double £29 to £32, twin/double £48 to £54, family room £59 to £65; deposit required. Set D £13.50, £19.50. Special breaks available

---

*The 1993* Guide *will be published before Christmas 1992. Reports on hotels are most welcome at any time of the year, but are extremely valuable in the spring. Send them to* Which? Hotel Guide, FREEPOST, 2 Marylebone Road, London NW1 1YN. *No stamp is needed if reports are posted in the UK.*

**CRUDWELL** WILTSHIRE                                          **MAP 9**

# Crudwell Court

CRUDWELL, NR MALMESBURY, WILTSHIRE SN16 9EP
TEL: CRUDWELL (066 67) 7194   FAX: (066 67) 7853

*Characterful old rectory that has been given the country-house
hotel treatment but remains refreshingly uncontrived and
unmodish.*

Brian and Susan Howe's creeper-clad hotel is a fine seventeenth-
century rectory with higgledy-piggledy additions. It is a spacious, light
and brightly decorated house, but one which, although designed rather
than haphazardly thrown together, never gets carried away with the
country-house hotel concept. Clean and tidy it certainly is, but worn
patches on carpets here and there, a bit of faded or chipped this and that,
and relaxed staff make it refreshingly unfussy. Hotel trappings aren't
obvious, either.

The front door opens into a narrow conservatory. Next comes a bright
yellow lounge and finally a large, flagstoned hall where a small desk holds
the register. Off this is a peach- and orange-coloured drawing-room
with very comfortable sofas and armchairs, antiques and large windows.
It is the big windows and varied design that make bedrooms here so
welcoming. They are on the whole roomy and though decoration is
restrained, they're never bleak. You'll find writing paper, pad and pencil,
magazines, solid mattresses, practical lighting, maybe even a colourful
window box or two.

Spaciousness is tempered in the dining-room, divided into three parts
and very low lit for intimacy. The nouvelle cuisine philosophy has been
adapted to satisfy large appetites. The lovely, formal walled gardens,
presided over by the imposing church, can easily be admired from within,
but deserve a walk around. For outdoor lounging, head for the walled
swimming-pool, a quiet and attractive retreat.

- Open all year
- On the A429, 3 miles north of Malmesbury heading towards Cirencester. Private car park
- 2 single, 13 twin/double; all with bathroom/WC, TV, room service, baby-listening; trouser press in some rooms; hair-dryer on request
- Restaurant, 2 lounges, conservatory; conference facilities (max 30 people non-residential, 15 residential); croquet, heated outdoor pool at hotel, other sports nearby. Wheelchair access to restaurant and WC (unisex) only
- No dogs in public rooms
- Access, Amex, Diners, Visa
- Single £40, single occupancy of twin/double £52, twin/double £77 to £100; deposit required. Set L £13, D from £17.50 (prices till end 91). Special breaks available

# Ockenden Manor

OCKENDEN LANE, CUCKFIELD, WEST SUSSEX RH17 5LD
TEL: HAYWARDS HEATH (0444) 416111   FAX: (0444) 415549

*Professionally run, country house hotel; bedrooms are excellent.*

Being at the end of a short lane off Cuckfield's town centre, Ockenden enjoys the best of both worlds: it is in the heart of a pretty village yet seemingly secluded, avoiding traffic noise and having expansive views across to the South Downs. The manor, overlooking well-kept hedged gardens, is an architectural hotch-potch: the oldest part is a cream and black-timbered Tudor building to which a large stone addition was made in the seventeenth century; a Victorian owner built a wing and stable block, and the present owners, Mr and Mrs Goodman (also of the Spread Eagle at Midhurst – see entry), completed a new bedroom wing in August 1990 along the south side of the hotel.

The older parts of the house have public rooms in the best of fine country house tradition: a large comfortable sitting-room, a spacious panelled bar and restaurant, with painted ceiling, stained-glass windows and fresh white tablecloths and flowers. Expect food of a nouvelle British tinge, often mixing fruit and meat, served formally from under silver dish domes.

Regardless of whether your bedroom is in the old house or in the new wing, it will be attractive – perhaps antique or stripped pine stencilled furniture, strong floral-patterned bedspreads, pretty china for tea – and very habitable. Some rooms in the old house have panelling, those in the new wing the views. After our complaint last year about having to pay over the odds for a newspaper you'll now be charged the face value.

○ Open all year

⤢ In the centre of Cuckfield, off the A272. Private car park

🛏 1 single, 4 twin, 13 double, 4 four-poster; all with bathroom/WC, exc single with shower/WC; TV, room service, hair-dryer, trouser press, baby-listening in all rooms

◈ Restaurant, bar, lounge, conservatory; conference facilities (max 50 people non-residential, 22 residential); golf, tennis, other sports nearby;

babysitting by arrangement. Wheelchair access to hotel, restaurant and WC (M,F), 4 ground-floor bedrooms

⊖ No dogs; no smoking in restaurant

▭ Access, Amex, Diners, Visa

£ Single £70, single occupancy of twin/double from £77, twin/double from £95, four-poster from £150; deposit required for 2-night stays. Cooked B £4.50; set L £18.50, D from £27.50. Special breaks available

---

*All reports are welcome on any hotel, whether or not it is in the* Guide

**CULLOMPTON** DEVON                                    **MAP 8**

# Manor House

2–4 FORE STREET, CULLOMPTON, DEVON EX15 1JL
TEL: TIVERTON (0884) 32281   FAX: (0884) 38344

*Solid, sympathetically furnished town-centre business hotel near the M5.*

Cullompton isn't a town you'd head for if you're looking for a picturesque Devonshire town; nor is it ugly. As aesthetics go, the Manor House Hotel fits into the same middle ground. Built in 1603 as a town house for a wool merchant, it has an attractive, multi-gabled and timbered façade; behind this extends a blander white stucco addition. Enter from the car park and you hit a cavernous pub and carvery, admirably furnished in country antiques and Persian-style rugs. Next comes a small, smart cocktail bar, a bit of a through-passage but well-furnished with Windsor chairs, a comfortable settle and what seem like very old paintings of rather fat animals. The posher restaurant, soft and spacious, is at the front, where you'd expect a lounge. (It serves for private functions, too.)

The configuration of bedrooms is more straightforward. All but a family room and a double face Fore Street, but prices are low. Recently refurbished with good-quality dark wood furniture and decent fabrics, they are well-equipped but, apart from one four-poster, devoid of gratuitous frills. Neat bathrooms have most personality; several have old plates or china ornaments as well as genuine old taps.

◑ Open all year

⤢ Leave the M5 at Junction 28. Follow signs to Cullompton. The hotel is in the centre of town. Private car park

🛏 2 twin, 5 double, 1 four-poster, 1 family room; all with bathroom/WC, TV, hair-dryer, trouser press, baby-listening

◈ Restaurant, bar, lounge; conference facilities (max 50 people, non-residential). Wheelchair access to restaurant only

⊖ No dogs

▭ Access, Visa

£ Single occupancy of twin/double £35, twin/double/four-poster £43, family room £55. Set L £9, D £9, £15; alc D £15, £18. Special breaks available

---

*The* Guide *office can quickly spot when a hotelier is encouraging customers to write a recommending inclusion – and sadly, several hotels have been doing this in 1991. Such reports do not further an hotel's cause.*

**DALLINGTON** EAST SUSSEX　　　　　　　　　　**MAP 10**

# Little Byres

CHRISTMAS FARM, BATTLE ROAD, WOODS CORNER, DALLINGTON, NR
HEATHFIELD, EAST SUSSEX TN21 9LE
TEL: BRIGHTLING (0424 82) 230

*A friendly welcome in a converted barn and stable block – and all
wrapped up in chic simplicity.*

The sign saying restaurant and motel must deter potential passing trade.
Never mind: their loss is your gain. Chris and Evelyn Davis have worked
on this rather isolated, windswept hill since 1986 and since May 1990 as
owners. An evident Francophile, Chris is offering affordable French-
style food and lodgings (so chickens and geese scattering as your car
enters the drive seem in keeping). His cooking has received high praise:
one reader describes a meal there as 'the ultimate eating experience . . .
all the other guests were clearly regulars, and as obviously happy with
their meal as we were – perfection.' From a five-course table d'hôte
menu with four or five choices at each stage you might be served home-
made lemon and dill fettuccine with mussels or marinated fresh salmon
with basil, lime and olive oil, followed by a fricassée of guinea-fowl with
garlic and cognac or sautéed calf's liver with apples and calvados, and
perhaps 'an amazing chocolate platter for dessert . . . and huge hand-
made truffles'.

　　The setting complements the food: a beautifully restored and converted old Sussex brick barn with lofty roof and black oak beams. A
woodburning stove and its lengthy flue take the nip out of the whistling
wind in winter, and in summer its large wooden doors, rescued from a
church ruin, can be opened to allow air to circulate. Behind the barn, a
black wooden-boarded and red-brick stable block has been converted in
identical fashion to make five chalet-style bedrooms, each with its own
front door. Virtually identical, they are small and simple but attractive,
with beams, simple floral patterns and wicker and bamboo furniture.

○ *Open all year; restaurant closed
Sun eve*

↗ *Situated on the B2096, mid-way
between Battle and Heathfield.
The hotel is not in Dallington
village. Private car park*

⊨ *1 twin, 4 double; all with
shower/WC, TV*

◇ *Restaurant; conference facilities
(max 30 people non-residential,
5 residential); golf, riding nearby.*

*Wheelchair access to hotel
(ramp), restaurant and WC, 5
ground-floor bedrooms, 2
specially equipped for the
disabled*

● *No dogs in public rooms*

▭ *Access, Visa*

£ *Single occupancy of twin/double
£20 to £40, twin/double £30 to
£40; deposit required. Set D
£22.50. Special breaks available*

*See the inside front cover for a brief explanation of how to use the* Guide.

**DARTMOUTH** DEVON                                                **MAP 8**

# The Royal Castle

11 THE QUAY, DARTMOUTH, DEVON TQ6 9PS
TEL: DARTMOUTH (0803) 833033   FAX: (0803) 835445

*Busy harbour-side location and a handsome, old, much-altered inn.*

Much has changed the look and demeanour of this harbour-side inn since it was born of two Tudor merchants' houses in the late-eighteenth century. By the early-nineteenth century it was sporting a new third floor with open wooden staircase and castellated façade. The Prince of Wales occasionally stayed, and in 1902 'Royal' was added to the name. Today, 'Royal Castle Hotel' in large gold letters grabs your attention from across the inner harbour.

Tourists and townsfolk crowd the downstairs Galleon Bar, once part of the original kitchens. There are plenty of quieter alcoves on the first floor, including a pleasant, windowless library and sedate sitting-room overlooking the harbour. The Adam restaurant, with embossed ceiling and formally set tables, enjoys the same views. A glass roof lets some light into the rather darker interior, illuminating a lovely collection of old ships' bells. Part of the old staircase and original Tudor fireplace are more fetching than the modern display case.

A reader writes: 'The library was particularly attractive, dining-room and lounge – good antique furnishings appreciated, the Charles II suite less good. Parking not easy.' Some bedrooms take the 'cosy concept' too literally but all are well furnished. Fish and seafood get top billing on the dinner menu but meat-lovers have Devonshire hogs' pudding (a kind of spicy sausage) to look forward to at breakfast.

◑ *Open all year*

🡥 *In the centre of Dartmouth overlooking the inner harbour. Limited private car parking and on-street parking facilities. Large local public car park*

🛏 *5 single, 3 twin, 4 double, 4 four-poster, 7 family rooms, 1 suite; most with bathroom/WC, some with shower/WC; TV, room service, hair-dryer, baby-listening in all rooms; 6 rooms air-conditioned*

◈ *Restaurant, 2 bars, 2 lounges, library/study, atrium area; conference facilities (max 120 people non-residential, 24 residential); fishing, riding, watersports nearby; babysitting*

⊖ *No wheelchair access*

▭ *Access, Visa*

£ *Single £39 to £48, single occupancy of twin/double £80 to £98, twin/double/four-poster £68 to £98; special rates for children; deposit required. Set L £9.50 (Sun), D £16, £20.50. Special breaks available*

*Congratulations to Cumbria – our number 1 county with 53 full entries in this year's Guide.*

# Dedham Vale/Terrace Restaurant

STRATFORD ROAD, DEDHAM, COLCHESTER, ESSEX CO7 6HW
TEL: COLCHESTER (0206) 322273   FAX: (0206) 322752

*Mix and match: somewhat impersonal luxury without a restaurant (Maison Talbooth) and more personality with food (Dedham Vale). Le Talbooth Restaurant, not too far away, makes another option for dinner wherever you choose to lay your head.*

The Milsom empire owns the Pier at Harwich (see entry) as well as this trio of eating and/or sleeping establishments. Le Talbooth has no bedrooms, Maison Talbooth (see below) no restaurant, while Dedham Vale/Terrace Restaurant has both.

Maison Talbooth, a not very imposing Victorian house by the road, has many fans for its sumptuous bedrooms which are equipped to the hilt and resplendent in fancy fabrics. The door of each bedroom sports the name of a British poet and on the occasionally bold-papered walls hangs a poem by him or her. You'll get great views, too, if you're lucky, and king-sized beds. Alas, all is not poetry to the eye. Mini-bars, though not the most fetching of *objets*, are surely more practical and preferable to these arrays of the little bottles, perhaps the first thing you focus on as you wake after a boozy dinner. You will have to look on them as you eat breakfast, too, since Maison Talbooth doesn't have a dining-room. Maybe you could balance your toast on your lap in the drawing-room. This is a pleasant, stately room, of plush armchairs, *Country Life* magazines, a grand piano, and french windows which open out on to a giant chessboard and croquet lawn.

Dedham Vale/Terrace Restaurant is a five- to ten-minute walk along the road. Here you get less luxury and pay far less. The ivy-clad house is further off the road, so sitting outside is more pleasant. Much of the décor is light and breezy, embodying outdoor images to give summery cheer. Certainly, the furnishings are more humble than at Maison Talbooth but character comes in larger helpings. An Italianate mural of trees, fields and balustrades covers the walls of the bar. The long, meandering Terrace Restaurant, decorated like an Edwardian conservatory, is light and plant-filled. It seats a crowd and is often bustling, especially when business lunches get into gear. A chef in tall hat performs at the rôtisserie while you load your plate from a large buffet table. Dedham Vale has an elegant boardroom, too. The Milsoms are in the process of replacing some of the older furnishings but aren't tampering with the mood.

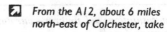

◗ *Open all year; restaurant closed Sun eve*          ⤢ *From the A12, about 6 miles north-east of Colchester, take*

the Stratford St Mary to Dedham road. After 1 mile take the second right-hand turning to Dedham. The hotel is 1 mile along this road on the right. Private car park

🛏 4 twin/double, 2 double, 1 family room; all with bathroom/WC, TV, room service, hair-dryer; no tea/coffee-making facilities in rooms

◈ Restaurant, bar, lounge;

conference facilities (max 16 people residential, 30 non-residential); fishing, golf, other sports nearby. Wheelchair access to restaurant only

⊖ No dogs

▭ Access, Amex, Visa

£ Single occupancy of twin/double £72, twin/double £87; family room (3 people) £112. Cooked B £6; buffet L £9.50; alc D £27.50. Special breaks available

---

# Maison Talbooth

STRATFORD ROAD, DEDHAM, COLCHESTER, ESSEX CO7 6HN
TEL: COLCHESTER (0206) 322367   FAX: (0206) 322752

◑ Open all year

⤢ Opposite the Dedham Vale Hotel (see above). Private car park

🛏 2 twin, 8 double, 1 family room, 1 suite; all with bathroom/WC, TV, room service, hair-dryer, mini-bar, baby-listening; tea/coffee-making facilities, trouser press on request

◈ Lounge, bar service, drying room, separate restaurant (Le Talbooth) nearby; conference facilities (max 16 people

residential); croquet at hotel, other sports nearby. Wheelchair access to hotel and restaurant, 5 ground-floor bedrooms

⊖ No children under 12 at dinner; no dogs

▭ Access, Visa

£ Single occupancy of twin/double £98, twin/double £118, family room £163, suite £138. Cooked B £5; set L £18.50, D £25, Sun L £20; alc D from £40. (Prices till Apr 92.) Special breaks available

---

**DENSTONE** STAFFORDSHIRE                                    MAP 4

# Stone House

COLLEGE ROAD, DENSTONE, UTTOXETER, STAFFORDSHIRE ST14 5HR
TEL: ROCESTER (0889) 590526   FAX: (0889) 591205

*An ordinary family house that has been turned into a welcoming B&B.*

You would be unlikely to venture into this sparsely residential lane unless you were on your way to Denstone College or already knew about Stone House – there is nothing particularly attractive about the immediate surroundings. The Moores have turned over their home to their guests and they themselves live across the yard, although they admit to sneaking back to their old bedroom for the occasional night when no one is staying. The three bedrooms are comfortable and quite cosy; two share a bathroom. The house has the feel of a private home: a grandfather clock ticks in the hall, hunting prints hang in the sitting-room and an old silver dish is now used for the cyclamen. An electric coal-effect fire brightens up the room on gloomy days and there's a mass of guidebooks for planning your tour of the Peak District.

Mrs Moore, helped by her husband, is happy to provide an evening meal but prefers twenty-four hours' notice. She's a fan of Cordon Bleu dishes so your dinner might be prawn salad, or carrot and coriander soup, followed by sauté of beef chasseur or chicken Vichy with a selection of vegetables, finishing off with a strawberry mousse or fresh pineapple.

🌓 *Open all year, exc Xmas and staff holidays*

🔀 *From Uttoxeter take the B5030 to Rocester. Go past the JCB factory then turn left to Denstone. Follow signs to Denstone College. The house is the only stone-built house on the road leading to Denstone College. Private car park*

🛏 *1 twin, 2 double (1 with bathroom/WC, 1 public bathroom); TV in all rooms; hair-dryer on request*

◇ *Dining-room, lounge*

⊖ *No wheelchair access; dogs by arrangement; no smoking in bedrooms*

▭ *None accepted*

💷 *Single occupancy of twin/double £23 to £26, twin/double £34 to £39. Set D £13.50 by arrangement only*

---

**DENT** CUMBRIA                                                      **MAP 3**

# Stone Close

MAIN STREET, DENT, NR SEDBERGH, CUMBRIA LA10 5QL
TEL: DENT (058 75) 231

*Friendly, rural B&B with a tea-room and restaurant.*

On the inland side of the M6 motorway, cobbled Dent sits amid lonely, hilly countryside. Two seventeenth-century farm cottages form Stone Close, a charming old-fashioned tea-shop with three comfortable bedrooms.

As befits its age, it's a riot of low beams, open fires in cast-iron stoves and wooden tables and chairs. Blackened pots and kettles add another period touch. Cooking, however, is modern British using good ingredients and some traditional allegiances – ham and pea soup, pork fillet with prunes and inventive pies and stews. Puddings are often creamy and boozy, and baking is a strong point. The cottage-sized bedrooms are cheerful but not at all lavish.

◑ Closed Jan and first half Feb; tea-shop closed mid-week from mid-Nov to Easter

⬈ From Sedbergh, Stone Close is the first building on the left on the cobbled street. On-street parking

⇔ 1 single, 1 double, 1 family room, 1 public bathroom

◇ Dining-room, tea-rooms; golf, riding, fishing nearby

⊖ No wheelchair access; no dogs in public rooms; no smoking in bedrooms and only after meals in dining-room

▭ None accepted

£ Single £15, twin/double £26, family room £32; deposit required. Meals, snacks all day; set D £10 (7.30pm, must be booked in advance)

---

**DIDDLEBURY** SHROPSHIRE                    **MAP 6**

# Glebe Farm

DIDDLEBURY, CRAVEN ARMS, SHROPSHIRE SY7 9DH
TEL: MUNSLOW (058 476) 221

---

*A pretty house in a lovely quiet setting. You'll have a delightful stay with very hospitable hosts.*

This is a lovely part of Shropshire and the quiet village of Diddlebury makes an excellent base from which to visit the numerous places of interest nearby: Ludlow and Ironbridge to name but two. The Glebe is next to the village church but in a large garden with its own organic vegetable patch. You can sit on the lawn and admire the proportions of the Norman tower. The house is over 400 years old with lovely old stone and half-timbering. It has been very well looked after since the Wilkes bought it over ten years ago. None of the charm has been lost even though improvements and modern facilities have been added.

The public rooms are large and warm with huge comfy sofas and other well-worn furniture. Uneven floors, the occasional rug – with or without dog resting on it – all add to the atmosphere. The dining-room is flagstoned with fine oak tables and leather-backed studded chairs; dinner is by arrangement and is straightforward home-cooking. The bedrooms are as crooked as the rest of the house and are pretty and home-spun with their own facilities. A cottage annexe offers a little more privacy but just as lovely views.

◑ Closed Nov to Mar; restaurant closed Mon, Tue, Thur, Sun eves

⬈ East of the B4368, 4 miles north-east of Craven Arms. Private car park

⇔ 1 single, 2 twin, 2 double (some rooms in cottage annexe); most with bathroom/WC, 1 public bathroom; TV, hair-dryer in all rooms; trouser press available

◇ Dining-room, bar, lounge; drying facilities; fishing, golf, riding nearby

⊖ No wheelchair access; no children under 8; dogs by arrangement only

🗔 None accepted

💷 Single £20 to £24, single
    occupancy of twin/double £22 to

£28, twin/double £36 to £52;
deposit required. Set D £13.50
(7.45pm)

---

**DISS** NORFOLK                                    **MAP 7**

# Salisbury House

84 VICTORIA ROAD, DISS, NORFOLK IP22 3JG
TEL: DISS (0379) 644738

*Well-known and popular restaurant with equally appealing
bedrooms.*

To many locals Salisbury House conjures up good food and wine but the
brochure comes closer to defining it: 'More a country home than a hotel'.
Barry and Sue Davies' early Victorian house stands close to the road but
bushes and the car park protect it somewhat from the sights and sounds
of traffic.

Readers have written enthusiastically of their visits here. 'Friendly and
welcoming – we felt at home', is typical of the praise. 'Greeted in a most
welcoming and friendly manner', writes another reader, who goes on to
praise the 'imaginative menus and outstanding food'. 'A relaxed atmosphere but very professional', is another comment. The character of
the hotel differs from room to room but the effect is always pleasing. The
leafy-green, L-shaped restaurant is elegant; the lovely Victorian parlour-
style front lounge very home-like. Good breakfasts, lunches and wine
tastings take place in the black-and-white tiled conservatory. Each
bedroom is very different. One has a brass bed, another lacquered
bamboo furniture, another an ornate gold mirror. There are Chinese
rugs, framed butterflies, stripped pine, borders around the ceilings and
honesty bars. The garden annexe room, 'a little on the small side but
extremely attractive', holds an Edwardian four-poster.

The only criticism has been that there is not enough wardrobe/
hanging space for two people. We agree that 'prices are very fair
considering the exceptionally high standards'. The food is modern
British and imaginative. Amongst the half-dozen or so choices at each
stage on the à la carte menu might be terrine of guinea-fowl and veal with
pistachios, red mullet with ratatouille, then white chocolate mousse with
dark chocolate sauce.

🔾 Open all year, exc 1 week at
   Xmas, 2 weeks in summer;
   restaurant closed Sun, Mon

🔁 Salisbury House is ½ mile from
   Diss town centre on the A1066
   heading towards Scole. Private
   car park

🛏 2 double, 1 four-poster annexe

room; all with bathroom/WC
(1 with whirlpool bath); TV,
room service, hair-dryer, mini-bar
in all rooms

◈ 2 restaurants, 2 lounges,
   conservatory, summer house;
   conference facilities (max 20
   people non-residential); croquet

at hotel, other sports nearby.
Wheelchair access to restaurant
and WC (unisex)

⊖ No dogs; no smoking

▭ Access, Visa

£ Single occupancy of double £46,
double/four-poster £62 to £64;
deposit required. Cooked B £3;
alc L, D £23

---

**DITTISHAM** DEVON                                                                                          **MAP 8**

# Fingals

OLD COOMBE, DITTISHAM, DARTMOUTH, DEVON TQ6 0JA
TEL: DITTISHAM (080 422) 398   FAX: (080 422) 401

*An unusual, easy-going and beautiful house in lovely countryside.*

The narrow, hedged-in lanes of the Dart River valley might prime you
for something very different from Fingals. No quaint thatched cottage
with B&B furnishings, this, but a sizeable sixteenth-century house with
delicate Queen Anne façade. It is also a supremely casual hotel. Long
after you've trundled home, you'll remember graceful rooms of warm
oak or pine panelling, a nice old collection of comfy furniture and varied
and intriguing art.

You will also remember Richard, an eager host who joins everyone at
the dinner table sometime around 8.30pm. Communal dinners are
merry rather than taxing, thanks to Richard's year as genial host at his
Fulham restaurant, also named after Fingal, his dalmatian. You can
choose what you eat, a fritto misto, say, then lamb in port and fruit glaze.
Although bedrooms come in various categories and many shapes and
sizes, they are uniformly excellent, with country antique furnishings and
original, mostly modern, art. You will find fewer uneven doors, ceilings
and walls in the new wing rooms, which are reached via a wooden
walkway that overlooks the grass tennis court. You won't be allowed to
forget Fingals, whatever your impressions; its newsletter will see to that,
telling you about the new sauna by the swimming pool, perhaps,
barbecues planned for Sunday and Monday nights, or the new art
gallery.

◑ Closed New Year to Easter;
restaurant closed Sun and Mon
eves

▨ From the B3207, take the left
turning to Dittisham 3 miles
before Dartmouth. Turn left by
Sportsman's Arms pub, then
follow signs to Fingals. Private
car park

🛏 1 twin, 5 double, 1 four-poster, 2
family rooms; all with bathroom/
WC, baby-listening; TV, hair-
dryer on request

◈ Restaurant, bar, lounge, TV
room, snooker room, library;
conference facilities (max 30
people non-residential, 9
residential); tennis, croquet,
table tennis, sauna/solarium,
heated outdoor pool at hotel,
other sports nearby

⊖ No wheelchair access; no dogs in
public rooms

▭ Amex, Visa

£ Single occupancy of twin/double
£45 to £50, twin/double £70 to

£80, four-poster £80 to £90,            deposit required. Set D £22.50.
family room £100 to £120;               Special breaks available

## DODDISCOMBSLEIGH DEVON                                    MAP 8

# The Nobody Inn

DODDISCOMBSLEIGH, NR EXETER, DEVON EX6 7PS
TEL: CHRISTOW (0647) 52394

*Cosy inn in rural Devon with a refreshingly untraditional
approach to catering.*

Nobody Inn soup has a traditional chicken stock base but delivers an
unexpected, fruity and spicy kick. The sixteenth-century Nobody Inn, as
old and dear (and unprecious) as you could wish for, and encircled by
perfectly kept little gardens, harbours a few surprises of its own. Most
concern food and drink.

Along with the usual pub offerings are traditionally brewed beers,
local ciders, five hundred wines and home-made mulled wine. You won't
be able to pronounce the name of this perfect English village if you
sample a tiny percentage of the whiskies on offer; at last count there were
132 varieties. Cheeses, of which around thirty are always on offer, also
rate highly. Look for cured venison and hot spiced bread pudding on the
suitably long dinner menu. Full-sized bottles of spirits standing out on a
tray are the only elements out-of-keeping with cottagey bedrooms, most
of which have private facilities. As with the downstairs, they are well-kept
and nicely mellow. Avoid room two, with a low dipping ceiling, if you're
tall. If noise bothers you or you're coming as a family, you can stay at
Town Barton, an eighteenth-century manor house a few minutes' walk
away.

- ◑ Open all year, exc 25 Dec and
  first 2 weeks Jan; restaurant
  closed Sun and Mon eves

- ◪ Leave the A38 at Haldon
  Racecourse (signposted
  Dunchideock) and follow signs to
  the Nobody Inn for 3 miles.
  Private car park

- 🛏 1 single, 1 twin, 2 double, 3
  annexe rooms; most with
  shower/WC; TV in all rooms;
  hair-dryer on request

- ◈ Restaurant, bar, lounge, drying
  room; conference facilities (max

25 people non-residential);
fishing, riding, other sports
nearby. Wheelchair access to inn
(1 step) and restaurant, 1
ground-floor bedroom

- ⊖ No children under 14; no dogs

- ▦ Access, Visa

- 💷 Single £23 to £32, single
  occupancy of twin/double £28 to
  £32, twin/double £44 to £53;
  deposit required. Bar lunches £6;
  alc D £13 (prices till Apr 92).
  Special breaks available

*If you have a small appetite, or just aren't feeling hungry, check if you can be
given a reduction if you don't want the full menu.*

**DORCHESTER-ON-THAMES** OXFORDSHIRE　　　**MAP 6**

# The George

HIGH STREET, DORCHESTER-ON-THAMES, OXFORDSHIRE OX10 7HH
TEL: OXFORD (0865) 340404　FAX: (0865) 341620

*Originally the barhouse to the abbey across the road, now a comfortable, characterful hotel with good food and convivial atmosphere.*

The George started life as a hostelry, inn and hotel around 1495. What was then barhouse to the abbey is now the old dining-room, a barn-like affair with exposed rafters, a style mirrored in the smaller additional dining-room next door. Life at the George centres around the bar with its wooden tables and high-backed benches, humpy ancient chairs and a couple of comfy sofas. A hotch-potch of tourists, locals in for a pint, and overnight guests mix easily, and there's a 'Potboys' menu if you'd like to eat in the thick of things. (Potboys traditionally served the food in a coaching-inn.)

Grander fare in the restaurant is introduced by a short but descriptive menu with plenty of sauces, and each dish has a suggested wine alongside although the prices of these recommendations aren't so openly proffered. Diners stay in the restaurant for coffee, the bar by now being too crowded and the residents' lounge to be avoided at all costs. It's a soulless, bleak room opposite the bar, only a few yards away but a million miles in terms of atmospheric change.

Avoid the single rooms in the stable suite — small and a little dingy. Elsewhere whitewashed walls, beamed ceilings, hidden steps and extra-ordinary angles make for interesting surroundings. A couple of rooms have the distinction of being approached along the minstrels' gallery in the courtyard, a rare architectural feature.

◑ *Open all year, exc 1 week at Xmas*

🔁 *Just off the A423 Henley to Oxford road, 8 miles south of Oxford*

🛏 *4 single, 5 twin, 7 double, 2 four-poster; all with bathroom/ WC, TV, room service (limited); hair-dryer, baby-listening, trouser press in 9 rooms*

◈ *Restaurant, bar, lounge; conference facilities (max 40*

*people non-residential, 18 residential); golf, riding nearby. Wheelchair access to hotel and restaurant (2 steps), 6 ground-floor bedrooms*

⊖ *No dogs in public rooms*

▭ *Access, Amex, Visa*

£ *Single £62, single occupancy twin/double £68, twin/double £75, four-poster £100. Alc L, D £23. (Prices till Apr 92.) Special breaks available*

---

*Many hotels offer special rates for stays of a few nights or more. It is worth enquiring when you book.*

# Country Friends

DORRINGTON, SHREWSBURY, SHROPSHIRE SY5 7JD
TEL: DORRINGTON (0743 73) 707

*A popular roadside restaurant with comfortable rooms to retire to
at the end of the evening.*

Bedrooms are a little way from the large half-timbered restaurant, but
near enough to stagger back to after dinner. There are three in the old
coach house which was opened at the beginning of 1989. Although
Charles and Pauline Whittaker's business is first and foremost a restaurant, the accommodation is a very comfortable extra.

The views from the bedrooms are not special. A fast road runs past
and the rumble of cars might disturb a light sleeper. But the rooms,
which come in pink and brown, orange and grey, and different blues, are
relaxing with carefully chosen furniture and chintzy quilts. They share a
bathroom which has lovely old brass bath fittings.

Charles does most of the cooking and the food is another good reason
for staying. Dinner is served in a beamed pink-and-brown restaurant,
glitzed-up with cut glass and candle lamps. Windows look out on to the
garden. A fixed-price three-course menu is available or an à la carte

- Country Friends -

menu which might offer crab ravioli served with a mild curry sauce, followed by duck breast with a corn syrup sauce and a mousse of coriander and shallot. There's more to tempt you in the morning too: bedroom prices include a breakfast of scrambled egg, smoked salmon and Buck's Fizz.

◐ Closed 2 weeks end July, 1 week end Oct, Xmas; restaurant closed Sun, Mon

⊖ No wheelchair access; no dogs; no smoking in restaurant

▣ 6 miles south of Shrewsbury on the A49. Private car park

▭ Access, Visa

▱ 1 twin, 2 double (1 with shower/WC)

£ Single occupancy of twin/double £35 to £37, twin/double £45 to £47; deposit required. Set L, D £17; alc L, D £27

◈ Restaurant, bar, lounge

---

**DOVER** KENT                                          **MAP 10**

# Number One Guesthouse

1 CASTLE STREET, DOVER, KENT CT16 1QH
TEL: DOVER (0304) 202007

*The experienced owners have tailored their B&B to the needs of early-morning ferry travellers; rooms are thoughtfully equipped.*

In an attractive creamy-orange and black-shuttered Georgian building on the corner of a fairly busy street near Dover's Eastern Docks, Adeline and John Reidy have been running this boldly designed Victorian-style B&B since 1976. Except for a small and apparently under-used lounge full of house plants, and a pleasant neat walled garden at the back, you're restricted to your room, so each room has a table laid with frilly white cloth and crockery ready for breakfast – chosen from a menu after you've arrived, and laid out by your door the night before if you're catching an early ferry.

Gold or brown velvet bedspreads give the bedrooms a certain style: Adeline believes that the comfort of beds is a neglected aspect in the B&B trade, and hers have velvet blankets (very popular apparently) and a choice of feather or Dunlopillows. All the rooms have armchairs, books, a 'fix it' box and a fat information file. Three rooms are family sized and have games and toys. Ask for a garden-facing room.

◐ Open all year

▣ Follow M20, A20 into central Dover. On-street parking

▱ 1 twin, 2 double, 2 family rooms; all with shower/WC, TV, room service, hair-dryer

◈ Lounge; fishing, golf, other sports nearby

⊖ No wheelchair access; no dogs; no smoking in public areas

▭ None accepted

£ Single occupancy of twin/double £20, twin/double £26 to £35, family room (4 people), £46 to £54; deposit required

# Ashwick House

NR DULVERTON, SOMERSET TA22 9QD
TEL: DULVERTON (0398) 23868

*Warm hospitality in an Edwardian country hotel blessed with a sublime position within Exmoor National Park.*

This small, Edwardian hotel sits in a gorgeous, startlingly fertile valley adjacent to wilder expanses of Exmoor. It takes a few minutes to adjust, but you soon look forward to the next hand-written informative sign, personalised menu, place card or little welcoming or instructive note. The bedrooms, named after trees, are good-sized, neat and comfortably furnished. Most have original fireplaces and stained-glass windows. Most also provide sublime views over the Barle River Valley and down to lovely lawns, conifers, ponds, maybe a deer or fox; but there is much to take in before your eyes reach the window. A mini-bar, a large free bottle of mineral water with sliced lemon, a lavish bowl of fruit, flowers, a remote control TV programmed with a film in the evening and exercise tape in the morning, a cassette radio with tapes provided, talking scales with instructions and conversion table, and a glass of Italian vermouth are but a few of the treats. The phone is in the cupboard since it is assumed you have come here to get away from it, and there is no drinks tray as Mr Sherwood brings loose leaf tea to your room as and when you want it. If that's not enough, there is a blood pressure gauge, first aid kit and binoculars in the hall. (There are further surprises, but we don't want to spoil the fun.) Mr Sherwood runs the place almost singlehandedly, but his enthusiasm, friendliness and energy level never seem to flag. He has extended the terrace, giving more space for fair weather afternoon teas and wonderful breakfasts that might include freshly pressed apple and mango juice. He also cooks and helps serve delicious, stylish four-course meals (you have a choice of starter and sweet). Most people convene in the galleried hall, where a log fire crackles in cool weather, but you may also retreat to the small cane-furnished library. The large drawing-room has strong black and red Chinese-style wallpaper and vivid plum-purple sofas: starkly different and impressively dramatic.

- **Open all year**
- **Take the B3223 from Dulverton by the post office. After 10 minutes, cross the cattle grid and take a left turn to Ashwick House**
- **2 twin, 4 double; all with bathroom/WC, TV, room service, hair-dryer, trouser press; mini-bar in 2 rooms**
- **Restaurant, bar, 2 lounges, drying room, library; conference facilities (max 20 people non-residential); solarium at hotel, fishing, riding nearby. Wheelchair access to restaurant only**
- **No children under 8; no dogs; no smoking in restaurant**
- **None accepted**

£ Single occupancy of twin/double
£50 to £53, twin/double £79 to
£86; deposit required. Set L (Sun

only) £14, D £18; packed
lunches. Special breaks available

---

**DUNCHURCH** WARWICKSHIRE                                          **MAP 6**

# The Dun Cow

THE GREEN, DUNCHURCH, NR RUGBY, WARWICKSHIRE CV22 6NJ
TEL: RUGBY (0788) 810233   FAX: (0788) 521243

*Ye olde traditional pub with lots of atmosphere.*

You can't easily miss this large seventeenth-century inn if you're passing
through the small village of Dunchurch. A rambling white-painted
building beside a road junction and traffic lights and opposite the village
shops, it's a popular place for lunch and dinner with its traditionally
English menu.

There are three dimly lit bars with lots of old world atmosphere,
flagstones, beams and fireplaces. From the cocktail bar you can see
through the massive fireplace to the dining-room with its starched white
tablecloths, candlelight and wooden settles.

Bedrooms are painted white with free-standing solid furniture. Some
bits are looking a bit tired but they are generally comfortable. Some
rooms lead out on to the courtyard where exits from the hotel to the large
potholed car park merge. Other bedrooms are above the Rampant Cat
Bistro (under the same ownership) across the road, or in the main
building above the bars and restaurant.

◐ Open all year

🔁 Leave the M1 at Junction 17 or
the M6 at Junction 1. The hotel
is in the centre of Dunchurch.
Private car park

🛏 3 twin, 13 double, 2 four-poster,
2 family rooms; some with
bathroom/WC, some with
shower/WC; TV, room service in
all rooms; hair-dryer on request;
no tea/coffee-making facilities in
rooms

◈ Restaurant, 2 bars, lounge;
conference facilities (max 60

people non-residential, 20
residential); fishing, golf, other
sports nearby. Wheelchair access
to hotel (1 step), restaurant and
WC (M,F), 4 ground-floor
bedrooms

⊖ No dogs in public rooms

▭ Access, Amex, Diners, Visa

£ Single occupancy of twin/double
£38 to £50, twin/double £50 to
£65, four-poster £60 to £70,
family room £65 to £70. Set L
£12, D £14; alc L, D from £18.
Special breaks available

---

*All entries in the* Guide *are rewritten every year, not least because standards*
*fluctuate. Don't trust an out-of-date* Guide.

**DURHAM** CO DURHAM                                      **MAP 3**

# Georgian Town House

10 CROSSGATE, DURHAM, CO DURHAM DH1 4PS
TEL: DURHAM 091-386 8070

*A listed eighteenth-century house in the centre of the medieval city, with views of the castle and cathedral.*

The Georgian Town House is a tall terraced building on a steep cobbled street in sight of the oldest, raised part of the city. The owners, an architect and an interior designer, have used lots of flair and yards of material to create a series of stylish and comfortable rooms. A stencilled ivy-leaf pattern runs throughout the house, and on each tiny landing there are hand-painted dressers, dried flower arrangements and pretty chairs (upholstered to match the curtains), reflecting Jane Weil's attention to detail.

Each of the bedrooms, some of which have views of the castle and cathedral, is individually decorated. The divide between bedroom and *en suite* bathroom is a curtain so you need to be feeling sociable with your room-mate. It pays to feel sociable at breakfast too, as the breakfast room is small and you will probably be sharing a table with other guests. Breakfast is beautifully presented, suits the health-conscious and there's no skimping on helpings.

🌓 Closed mid-Dec to Feb

🔃 Follow signs in Durham to Crook and Newcastle; go over traffic lights at St Margaret's Hospital and take first turning on right. Go down Allergate to junction with Crossgate. On-street parking

🛏 3 twin, 2 double, 1 family room; most with bathroom/WC, 1 double with shower/WC; TV in all rooms; hair-dryer on request

◈ Dining-room, lounge, conservatory

⊖ No wheelchair access; no dogs; no smoking in bedrooms

▭ None accepted

£ Single occupancy of twin/double £35 to £40, twin/double £40 to £45, family room £45 to £55; deposit required. Set D £10

**DUXFORD** CAMBRIDGESHIRE                                **MAP 7**

# Duxford Lodge

ICKLETON ROAD, DUXFORD, CAMBRIDGESHIRE CB2 4RU
TEL: CAMBRIDGE (0223) 836444   FAX: (0223) 832271

*What it lacks in pizazz, this country-house hotel makes up for in comfort and good food.*

The vintage aircraft from Duxford's famous air museum mark the exit off the M11. Motorway noise doesn't reach the small and pleasant village but some undistinguished modern housing and industry has encroached. The Georgian origins of the red-brick house have been similarly invaded by modern additions, the least delightful being the tarmac car park (for the many non-resident diners) which leaves little room for the garden. Inside, the décor is designer-smart but a touch deficient in personality and warmth. Relaxation might be taxing in the lounge, with its prim reproduction furniture; better to retire to the bar, where you'll find more comfort and less formal seating. Or, since food is the main event here, go straight into dinner in the pleasingly airy and peaceful restaurant.

You could start with a home-made soup or Mediterranean king prawns in a garlic and chive butter, and proceed to medallions of pork fillet sautéed with saffron, green peppercorns and cream served with an apple tartlet, or fillet of salmon stuffed with plums and thyme with a Pernod sauce. Each of the prettily furnished rooms comes in a different colour scheme. Rooms in the courtyard annexe are pokier (and less expensive).

◐ *Open all year, exc 25, 26 Dec and 1 Jan*

↗ *Duxford is just off Junction 10 of the M11. Private car park*

🛏 *4 single, 12 double; most with bathroom/WC, some with shower/WC; TV, hair-dryer, trouser press, mini-bar, baby-listening in all rooms*

◇ *Restaurant, bar, lounge; conference facilities (max 20*

*people non-residential, 16 residential)*

⊖ *No wheelchair access; dogs in annexe bedrooms only*

▭ *Access, Amex, Diners, Visa*

£ *Single £46 to £65, single occupancy of double £65, double £67 to £85. Set L £14.50, D £19.50; alc L, D £26 (prices till Apr 92). Special breaks available*

---

**EASINGTON** CLEVELAND                                    **MAP 3**

# Grinkle Park

EASINGTON, SALTBURN-BY-THE-SEA, CLEVELAND TS13 4UB
TEL: GUISBOROUGH (0287) 640515   FAX: (0287) 641278

*One of the Bass group of hotels trying to retain the country-house atmosphere while still attracting corporate trade.*

Grinkle Park was built in 1881 complete with castellated tower and is approached along a rhododendron-lined avenue. In 35 acres of grounds, strategically placed benches allow you to enjoy the view of the mature trees and small lake. Our inspection revealed that although not immaculate – a few patches of scuffed paintwork and thinning carpet – the hotel was, overall, comforting and very welcoming. The wear and tear might be the result of the frequent conferences and wedding parties and although you might find one of these in progress when you're staying the staff do try, often against the odds, and remember the personal touches.

The first-floor sitting-room is light and elegant with lovely views; the garden room, too, is pretty with bamboo and cane chairs and tables, and ruched curtains. The bar and dining-room are a bit more traditional. Bedrooms are named after flowers, local moors and birds in an attempt at originality. They are of a good size, with well planned bathrooms.

○ Open all year

↗ 1½ miles south of Easington, on Grinkle Lane which runs north from the A171. Private car park

🛏 7 single, 6 twin, 4 double, 2 four-poster; all with bathroom/WC, exc 6 singles with shower/WC; TV, room service, trouser press, baby-listening in all rooms; hair-dryer in some rooms

◇ Dining-room, bar, 2 lounges, snooker room, conservatory, sitting-room, drying room; conference facilities (max 60

people non-residential, 20 residential); tennis, snooker, croquet at hotel, other sports nearby. Wheelchair access to restaurant only

⊖ No dogs in public rooms

▭ Access, Amex, Diners, Visa

£ Single £60, single occupancy of twin/double £60, double/twin £78, four-poster £85; extra beds £12. Set L £10.50, D £15; alc D £18; bar snacks at lunch (Prices till Mar 92). Special breaks available

**EAST BUCKLAND** DEVON                                         **MAP 8**

# Lower Pitt Restaurant

EAST BUCKLAND, BARNSTAPLE, DEVON EX32 0TD
TEL: FILLEIGH (05986) 243 Changes at end October 91 to same number as fax
FAX: (0598) 760243

*Restaurant-with-rooms in charming sixteenth-century farmhouse. Out-of-the-way location but handy for Barnstaple or Exmoor.*

Cherry trees, wildflowers, 'some interesting shrubs', a dog, a cat and a whitewashed long farmhouse draped in honeysuckle: a pretty picture, especially in spring. As well as looking quaint and enjoying an isolated position on the edge of Exmoor, this restaurant-with-rooms is an urbane place where you can, if you feel like it, dress for dinner. (Top hats and high heels are not recommended because of the very low ceilings.) It's also a casual home.

Residents and non-residents mingle in the lounge whose white walls are bedecked with badger and owl plates or pictures and whose ingle-nook comes complete with log fire and bread oven. Another sitting-room with comfy loose-covered sofas has a gas log fire. Duck as you move into the old dairy, now the dining-room. Off this is a pretty new conservatory with further tables and great views of colourful trees and grazing cows.

Suzanne Lyons' à la carte dinners, which frequently draw on Eastern flavours and ingredients, have been praised; the well-chosen wine list, Jerome's department, is neither too long nor pricey and contains more than a token number of half-bottles. There are only three rooms and with the exception of those found on duvets, there are no frills. There are beams, of course, plus new pine and cane furniture, and little animal figurines to keep you company. Just B&B is available, but the Lyonses would rather you stayed for dinner.

◗ Open all year

⚡ 2 miles north of the A361, signposted East and West Buckland. The hotel is around the corner from the church. Private car park

🛏 1 twin, 2 double; twin with bathroom/WC, doubles with shower/WC; hair-dryer in all rooms

◈ Dining-rooms, bar, lounge, conservatory; fishing nearby

⊖ No wheelchair access; no children under 10; no dogs; no smoking in dining-rooms

▭ Access, Visa

£ Single occupancy of twin/double £35, twin/double £60; deposit required. Set D £20. Special breaks available

## EAST GRINSTEAD WEST SUSSEX                                    MAP 10

# Gravetye Manor

NR EAST GRINSTEAD, WEST SUSSEX RH19 4LJ
TEL: SHARPTHORNE (0342) 810567   TELEX: 957239 GRAVTY G
FAX: (0342) 810080

*A small hotel of exceptional quality in a splendid Elizabethan manor surrounded by lovely gardens.*

This Elizabethan stone mansion is set in a valley in extensive grounds, approached down a mile-long winding drive. Signs tell you to beware of the damage exhaust fumes inflict on plants. The hotel was once owned by William Robinson, an un-Victorian Victorian who cultivated the idea of the natural English garden. Though it was pouring with rain when we visited, a wander through the flower gardens under one of the large umbrellas provided in the porch proved irresistible; on finer days the trout-filled lake below would have been too.

Peter Herbert came to Gravetye in 1957 and created this country house hotel, hailed as a forerunner to now ubiquitous and often less successful imitations. The interior is a beautifully cared for Elizabethan manor (though Robinson has added many features): a flagstoned hall, a panelled sitting-room with knole settees, a large log fire and strapwork ceiling, two dining-rooms in similar style, and the Club Bar (Gravetye has a 'country club' which offers members events such as gourmet dinners) with a plethora of drinks on display.

Three of the bedrooms are panelled and the ones at the top of the house are beamed. All are entirely furnished in antiques and, perpetuating the horticultural theme indoors, are named after trees on the estate. The ambitious restaurant avoids pretension and the food achieves a good balance between plain British cooking and recipes with a more modern tilt. Serving staff are young and formal. A new extension for additional bedrooms is due to be completed in March 1992.

Open all year

Off the B2028 between Turners Hill and West Hoathly. Private car park

6 twin, 11 double, 1 four-poster; all with bathroom/WC, TV, room service, hair-dryer, trouser press; baby-listening by arrangement; no tea/coffee-making facilities in rooms

Restaurant, bar, 2 lounges, private dining-room; conference facilities (max 14 people non-residential); fishing, croquet at hotel, other sports nearby; babysitting by arrangement

No wheelchair access; no children under 7; no dogs; no smoking in restaurant

None accepted

Twin/double from £110, four-poster £175. Continental B £8, cooked B £12; set L £19, D £22; alc L, D £46

---

**EAST KNOYLE** WILTSHIRE                         **MAP 9**

# Milton Farm

EAST KNOYLE, SALISBURY, WILTSHIRE SP3 6BG
TEL: EAST KNOYLE (0747) 830247

*Small and fetching family home in lovely old, well-maintained farmhouse. Just right for a weekend retreat.*

The countryside hereabouts is lush and hilly with few sizeable towns. Milton is one of several hamlets that belong to East Knoyle and this well-kept, grey-stone farmhouse, which backs on to a seemingly endless field, has only a few neighbours. In other words, it's a good spot for a restful weekend or short holiday.

Rustic chic describes the style within the Hydes' largely Queen Anne house. The dining/sitting-room is stoned-walled but light from candles and the log fire is reflected in fine silver, glass and porcelain. Dinner might consist of salmon-wrapped eggs mollet with hollandaise sauce, lamb chops with Cumberland sauce and Normandy apple tart. Janice Hyde has put lots of decorative whimsy into the two bedrooms and co-ordinated fabrics and wallpaper make them alluring and interesting. There's ample space to move about in. Both bedrooms overlook the garden and have a private bathroom.

Closed Dec to Feb; dining-room closed Sun eve

¼ mile off the A350 at the north-west end of East Knoyle (signed Milton). Private car park

1 twin, 1 double; 1 with bathroom/WC, 1 with shower/WC; TV in both rooms

Dining-room; open-air swimming pool (May to Oct) at hotel, tennis nearby

No wheelchair access; no dogs

None accepted

Single occupancy of twin/double £36 to £40, twin/double £60 to £80; deposit required. Set D £12 to £14

**EAST PORTLEMOUTH** DEVON           **MAP 8**

# Gara Rock

EAST PORTLEMOUTH, NR SALCOMBE, DEVON TQ8 8PH
TEL: SALCOMBE (054 884) 2342/2341    FAX: (054 884) 3033

*Solitary, atop magnificent cliffs, a family-oriented hotel with
lively staff and good facilities.*

The winds may howl and the sea may roar, but take heart. On this wild
and jagged coast a fortifying oasis, equally welcoming to holidaying
families and solo walkers, awaits you. The self-catering units, canopied
façade and cluttered reception complete with gift shop do not look
immediately inviting, but from within the former coastguard station you
can enjoy the magnificent coastline as well as good old-fashioned
comfort.

Public rooms are down two flights from the reception: a large,
traditionally furnished panelled lounge, also warmed by a log fire when
needed, plus a small, passageway bar and a pine-floored dining-room
with extra large windows for surf-gazing. You can't quite see the
vegetable garden but evidence of it turns up in good-value set dinners.

Simply decorated bedrooms are light and airy, with candlewick
spreads and wicker furniture. Sea-facing rooms are the obvious ones to
go for; if you're lucky you'll get a bay window from which you can look
almost straight down to breaking waves. Young staff are chatty and eager
to help young families learn the ropes. Facilities for adults and children
alike are first-rate: outdoor pool, games room, wreck room, gym, plus
videos every night and organised entertainment most nights.

◑ *Closed Nov to Easter*

↗ *At Frogmore turn right, go over
bridge and follow signs for East
Portlemouth and Gara Rock.
Private car park*

🛏 *1 single, 5 twin, 5 double, 10
suites, 14 self-catering
apartments; most with
bathroom/WC, some with
shower/WC; TV, room service,
baby-listening in all rooms*

◇ *Restaurant, 2 bars, 2 lounges, TV
room, games room, drying room,
conservatory; conference
facilities (max 50 people non-
residential and residential);
fishing, tennis, croquet, sauna/
solarium, gym, bicycles, heated
outdoor pool at hotel, other
sports nearby; babysitting.
Wheelchair access to hotel,
restaurant and WC, 14 ground-
floor bedrooms*

⊖ *No children under 6 in
restaurant; no dogs in public
rooms; no smoking in restaurant*

▭ *Access, Visa*

£ *Single £24 to £41, single
occupancy of twin/double £36 to
£62, twin/double £48 to £90,
suite £62 to £165; self-catering
apartments £190 to £655 per
week (max 6 people); deposit
required. Set D £17; bar lunches
(prices till Nov 91)*

# St George Hotel

CASTLE STREET, ECCLESHALL, STAFFORDSHIRE ST21 6DF
TEL: ECCLESHALL (0785) 850300   FAX: (0785) 851492

*Jolly, popular inn with reasonable accommodation and a welcoming atmosphere.*

Slap in the centre of town, this seventeenth-century coaching-inn is a very popular meeting place, both at lunchtime and in the evenings. The bar area is divided into three sections: there's a snug little seating area a few steps up from the rest, making a quiet, private corner; a large inglenook fireplace gives a focal point to another part of the room and the rest is filled with a mixture of bench seats, stools and wooden and brass-topped tables. Décor is fairly traditional with reddish carpet and curtains, and the seats are covered in tapestry-style fabric. The whitewashed walls are decorated with small prints and old sepia photographs. Bar snacks are served throughout this bar area. For slightly more formal occasions you can try the Knights' Restaurant where white-clothed tables and wheel-backed chairs are neat but simple. When the fire's lit it's a cosy room.

The hotel reception is tucked in under the stairs at the back of the hotel. A thinly carpeted staircase leads up to the bedrooms. Pretty fabrics and plain wooden furniture are pleasant if not unusual and most of the rooms are a good size with pristine bathrooms. If you're a light sleeper try and get a room at the back.

⏻ Open all year; restaurant closed Sun eve

🅿 Leave the M6 at Junction 14 and follow signs for Eccleshall. Continue on this road for 5 miles and turn right at the T-junction. At the next crossroads turn right – the hotel is on one corner of the crossroads. Private car park

🛏 4 single, 1 twin, 4 double, 1 four-poster; most with bathroom/ WC, exc 2 singles with shower/ WC; room service, baby-listening in all rooms

♦ Restaurant, bar, lounge, drying room; conference facilities (max 30 people non-residential, 10 residential); fishing, golf, other sports nearby

⊖ No wheelchair access; no dogs in public rooms

▭ Access, Amex, Diners, Visa

£ Single £45, single occupancy of twin/double £45, twin/double £60, four-poster £60. Cooked B £5.50; alc D £15. Special breaks available

*If you make a booking using a credit card, and you find after cancelling that the full amount has been charged to your card, raise the matter with your credit card company. They will ask the hotelier to confirm whether the room was re-let, and to justify the charge they made.*

**ELLESMERE** SHROPSHIRE    **MAP 5**

# The Mount

ST JOHN'S HILL, ELLESMERE, SHROPSHIRE SY12 0EY
TEL: ELLESMERE (0691) 622466

*A beautifully kept guesthouse overlooking Ellesmere. Attentive hosts ensure a welcoming stay.*

The Mount is an elegant Georgian town house – tall and symmetrical, with a pretty latticework porch. As the name suggests, the house is on a hill, a former fortified promontory once occupied by the Knights of St John of Jerusalem. Despite its position it's tricky to find, so head for the church. Your first impression of the house at close quarters is the highly polished brass bell-pull at the front door; the polish continues inside.

Each room is beautifully decorated in fawns and greens, and is immaculately kept. The two Siamese cats, Kaimook and Rhama (meaning 'pearl' and 'Indian prince'), are typical of the elegance of the rest of the house. There are just two guest bedrooms, each with a private bathroom and incidental luxuries like fresh fruit and flowers. Breakfast is around the beautiful oak dining-table and includes freshly squeezed orange juice and tiny cottage loaves still warm from the bakery at the bottom of the hill.

- Open all year
- In Ellesmere, follow signs for Tetchill until the corner of Dell's estate agents, then sharp left up St John's Hill. 80 yards up the hill, turn left into an un-named lane. The Mount is the second house on the left at the top of the lane. Private car park
- 1 twin, 1 double; double with bathroom/WC, single with shower/WC; hair-dryer in all rooms; baby-listening on request
- Dining-room, lounge, drying room; laundry facilities; meetings facilities (max 8 people non-residential); fishing, golf, other sports nearby; babysitting
- No wheelchair access; no dogs; no smoking
- None accepted
- Single occupancy of twin/double £23, twin/double £40, reduced rates for children; deposit required. Special rates available

---

*Many hotels put their tariffs up in the spring. You are advised to confirm prices when you book.*

---

*Report forms are at the back of the book; write a letter if you prefer.*

# Black Hostelry

THE COLLEGE, FIRMARY LANE, ELY, CAMBRIDGESHIRE CB7 4DL
TEL: ELY (0353) 662612    FAX: (0353) 665658

*A B&B in a fascinating medieval building within Ely Cathedral's
grounds.*

Soak up some history, be centrally based and not spend a fortune:
it sounds a tempting package despite the spooky name. The Black
Hostelry, down a narrow alleyway right next to Ely Cathedral, gets its
name from the Black Monks (Benedictine) who used to live here.

You shouldn't be disappointed if you stay with Canon and Mrs Green.
Behind the heavy wooden door is a charmingly furnished home with
Norman-arched windows and doorways, and old fireplaces. There are
two guest rooms only: a large and comfortable apartment with double or
twin beds and a separate sitting-room which can be converted for family
use, and a large twin/double room. Both have TVs and tea-trays and
overlook pleasant meadows and gardens. The furnishings are a trifle
austere and better mattresses would be welcome. Single guests are
charged the full double rate. Breakfast only is available but includes
home-made wholemeal bread and kippers. It is served in the undercroft
of the original building which has a fine low-vaulted ceiling.

- Open all year, exc Xmas week
- Turn into Ely Cathedral grounds
  at the Porta Archway at the end
  of the Gallery, and follow the
  road round to the left to the
  Cathedral car park. Firmary Lane
  is in the right-hand corner of the
  car park and the Black Hostelry
  is second right in Firmary Lane.
  Private car park
- 1 twin/double, 1 apartment; both
  with bathroom/WC, TV, hair-
  dryer
- Breakfast room, lounge; golf,
  riding, other sports nearby
- No wheelchair access
- None accepted
- Single occupancy of twin/double
  £40, twin/double/apartment
  £40; children sharing parents'
  room £10 each; deposit required

---

*When you telephone to book a room, and the hotel accepts your booking, you
enter into a binding contract with them. This means they undertake to
provide the specified accommodation and meals etc. for the agreed cost on the
agreed dates, while you commit yourself to paying their charges. If you later
have to cancel your booking, or fail to turn up, the hotel may be entitled to
keep any deposit you have paid to defray administrative costs. If an hotel is
unable to re-let the room you have booked – and it must try to do so – it is
entitled to compensation for the loss of profit caused by your breach of
contract. It can only claim a sum that is fair and reasonable. It should not
make a profit out of your failure to appear. It's important to give as much
notice as possible when cancelling: this increases the chances of your room
being re-let.*

**ETTINGTON** WARWICKSHIRE                                    **MAP 6**

# Ettington Manor

ETTINGTON, STRATFORD-UPON-AVON, WARWICKSHIRE CV37 7SX
TEL: STRATFORD-UPON-AVON (0789) 740216

*Sociable, comfortable Wolsey Lodge in excellent location. Good
cooking and warm hospitality are pluses.*

A mellow Tudor building within striking distance of Stratford, Ettington
Manor is a welcoming Wolsey Lodge. Owner Julie Graham has beautifully renovated and modernised the interior while retaining original
features such as the Elizabethan fireplace and flagstones. Tapestries
adorn the walls, Persian carpets the floors.

The former chantry is now a bedroom, with a high-beamed ceiling,
four-poster bed, and window seats next to the mullioned panes. Other
rooms are smaller but equally well equipped with plenty of books, and
bottles of mineral water. Pink duvet covers have tatted decorations.
Excellent candlelit home-cooked dinners are eaten *en famille* in the
restful green dining-room; but a private table for two is available in a
smaller sitting-room if you ask. On summer days there's a small walled
rose garden where you can sit.

- Closed Nov, Dec, Jan
- Ettington village is on the A422 Banbury to Stratford road, 6 miles south-east of Stratford. In the centre of the village turn south into Rogers Lane. The manor is the first driveway on the right. Private car park
- 1 single, 1 twin, 1 double, 1 four-poster; all with shower/WC, TV, hair-dryer
- Dining-room, 2 lounges; conference facilities (max 24 people non-residential, 4 residential); croquet at hotel, other sports nearby
- No wheelchair access; no children under 12; no dogs; no smoking
- Access, Visa
- Single £38, single occupancy of twin/double £50, twin/double £65, four-poster £70; deposit required. Set D £8.50 (pre-theatre, 6pm) and £17.50 (7.30pm)

**EVERSHOT** DORSET                                          **MAP 9**

# Summer Lodge

EVERSHOT, DORSET DT2 0JR
TEL: EVERSHOT (0935) 83424   FAX: (0935) 83005

*Classic country-house hotel with a better than usual design sense.*

The drive past walls and big trees sets the magic working. Your first
encounter with this part off-white, part-brick Georgian house might,

however, induce tension. With so many additions and annexes, you might lug your bags to the wrong door. Even behind the right door you'll have trouble identifying a reception area. The restraint with signs and the impression, despite the size, of being a private home, add to the charisma of this former dower house of the Earls of Ilchester.

Margaret Corbett, a Constance Spry-trained designer, must have enjoyed doing up these nicely proportioned, bright rooms, some designed by Thomas Hardy. Good-quality furniture and the co-ordinating and contrasting of colours and patterns is sure-footed. The drawing-room is but one of several sitting areas, but rather over-filled with sofas and easy chairs. No such problem with bedrooms, being bright and breezy with cane furniture. Old cheese plates, a house speciality, brighten up window ledges and alcoves. Bathrooms, many with hand-painted tiles, are outstanding. If money is no problem, go for the master bedroom, as large as the drawing-room and with a gas coal fire. Several rooms in the Coach House annexe open out on to little terraces. Through almost every window are blissful garden and country views. (The two rabbits chasing each other are pets of the Corbetts.) An à la carte as well as set, five-course menu is now offered and there have been glowing reports this year for Roger Jones' cooking: oysters with avocado bavarois, for example, and Gressingham duck with ginger sauce. The wine list is also worthy.

◐ Open all year, exc first half Jan

↗ Evershot is 1 mile from the A37 mid-way between Dorchester and Yeovil. The entrance to the hotel is in Summer Lane. Private car park

🛏 3 single, 14 twin/double; all with bathroom/WC, TV, room service, hair-dryer

◈ Restaurant, bar, lounge, TV room; meetings facilities (max 10 people residential and non-residential); tennis, croquet, heated outdoor pool (May to Sept) at hotel, other sports nearby. Wheelchair access to hotel (ramp), restaurant and WC, 3 ground-floor bedrooms

⊖ No children under 8; no dogs in public rooms

▭ Access, Visa

💷 Single £85 to £115, single occupancy of double £100 to £150, twin/double £160 to £250 (rates inc dinner and cream tea). Set L £16.50, D £28; alc L £25, D £28. Special breaks available

---

**EVESHAM** HEREFORD AND WORCESTER　　　　　　　　　　**MAP 6**

# Evesham Hotel

COOPERS LANE, OFF WATERSIDE, EVESHAM, HEREFORD AND WORCESTER
WR11 6DA
TEL: EVESHAM (0386) 765566　FAX: (0386) 765443

*Wacky hotel with relaxed, friendly staff and thoughtful extras.*

Ownership of this modernised Tudor/Georgian building by the Jenkinson family 'does not guarantee high standards, concern, or relaxed hospitality', according to the brochure. Such disingenuousness is revealed for what it is as soon as you walk into the reception with its rows of teddies, some rather worn, hanging from the key fobs. These are only little brothers to the bigger bears which are present in every room, together with the plastic ducks.

The bedrooms up in the rafters, which are on two levels with sloping roofs and Snoopy telephones, are sure to appeal to children. The pretty walled garden with its gnarled old elms also has children's slides and a trampoline. Bedrooms in the new wing retain jokey touches but have less character overall. The jokiness extends to the menu notes and what must be one of the longest drinks lists in the world: 'Blue curaçao – looks as if you might clean the swimming pool with it(!)'.

Food is good and the menu is changed weekly. It always includes a vegetarian option, for example cabbage and hazelnut rissoles. The non-curaçao swimming pool is watched over by Coco the gorilla; there are also table tennis and table football facilities, and a red telephone box for Superman-style quick changers.

◖ Open all year, exc 25 and 26 Dec

⊿ Coopers Lane is off Waterside (A44) which runs along the River Avon in Evesham. Private car park

🛏 6 single, 11 twin, 22 double, 1 family room; most with bathroom/WC, a few with shower/WC; TV, room service, hair-dryer, iron and board, baby-listening in all rooms

◇ Restaurant, bar, lounge; conference facilities (max 12 people residential); croquet, table tennis, heated indoor pool at hotel, other sports nearby. Wheelchair access to public areas and restaurant only

⊖ No dogs in public rooms; no cigars, pipes in restaurant

▭ Access, Amex, Diners, Visa

£ Single £60 to £66, single occupancy of twin/double £60 to £66, twin/double £84 to £88, family room £100 to £110; deposit required. Buffet L £6.50; alc L £16 to £22, alc D £17 to £27. Special breaks available

---

**EXETER** DEVON                           **MAP 8**

# The Forte

SOUTHERNHAY EAST, EXETER, DEVON EX1 1QF
TEL: EXETER (0392) 412812   TELEX: 42717 THFEX G
FAX: (0392) 413549

*Solid and reliable city-centre hotel with style and good business and leisure facilities.*

'Easily the best Forte hotel I have stayed in,' enthuses one reader. 'Elegant and enjoyable interior décor and furnishing. My granddaughter calls it "post-modernist". The service was excellent, willing, friendly, helpful, *never servile*. The restaurant produces really good *plain* food such as roast meat from the trolley, carved at your table, and a perfectly cooked lemon sole. We liked, too, the apple pancakes and light raspberry cheesecake. Rooms small but well equipped. The fridge contained fresh milk, replaced every day.' What can we add? A few details, perhaps.

The Forte, not far from the Cathedral, is Georgian/Regency in style. It caters to business people and so specialises in efficiency and comfort rather than personality. It is not without style, however. Well-proportioned rooms with half-panelling and stepped ceiling mouldings are expensively and sensibly furnished with an assortment of antiques and modern furniture. Good-quality curtains and upholstery come in bright flowery patterns. If you've been in one of the one hundred and ten bedrooms you've more or less been in them all, but with some lavish and bold fabrics they're reasonably chic. The swimming-pool in the health and fitness club is almost as magnificent as the brochure claims, and is large enough to cope with crowds.

○ *Open all year*

⊿ *2 miles from Junction 29 of the M5. Follow signs for city centre. The hotel is 5 minutes from the railway station. Private car park*

⊨ *99 twin/double, 6 family rooms, 5 suites; all with bathroom/WC, TV, room service, hair-dryer, trouser press, mini-bar, baby-listening*

◇ *Restaurant, bar, lounge, terrace; conference facilities air-conditioned (max 120 people non-residential, 110 residential); gym, heated pool, sauna, solarium at hotel, other sports nearby; babysitting. Wheelchair access to hotel, restaurant and WC (unisex), 9 ground-floor bedrooms, 3 specially equipped for the disabled*

⊖ *No dogs in public rooms; some bedrooms non-smoking*

▭ *Access, Amex, Diners, Visa*

£ *Single occupancy of twin/double £85, twin/double £95, suite £130, family room £100; deposit required. Continental B £6.50, cooked B £9; set L £11.50, D £18.50; alc L £22, D £32 (prices till Feb 92). Special breaks available*

# The Oaksmere

BROME, NR EYE, SUFFOLK IP23 8AJ
TEL: DISS (0379) 870326   FAX: (0379) 870051

*Small old hotel brought to life by a splendid topiary garden and antique furniture.*

You encounter Oaksmere's most impressive feature even before you reach the end of the straight, tree-lined drive. Masses of immaculate topiary bushes, most of them vaguely humanoid and some appearing to hold hands, crowd the front lawns. A conservatory, in part 200 years old and complete with ancient vine and antique tile floor, is another surprise. Otherwise, the Oaksmere, a large, partly half-timbered, partly sixteenth-century house not far from Diss, is a predictably comfortable and user-friendly conversion.

'The whole atmosphere is warm, friendly, relaxing, quiet and with attentive service,' remarks one reader. The Oaksmere belongs to the Waveney chain and is pitched towards business use. Meeting rooms are more in evidence than sitting-rooms, but the conservatory is pleasant and fairly comfortable. So is the low-ceilinged, rambling bar in the original Tudor hall, though it's a pity the flagstones are now hidden beneath carpeting. Have a snack here or eat in the more formal restaurant. The set menu, priced by how many courses you manage (and with a ten per cent service charge), is adventurous, with the likes of deep-fried wedges of Camembert with port and orange sauce, and haunch of venison in red wine, juniper and herbs.

Bedrooms boast real antiques and modern trappings. Lovely old four-posters are shown off well in several rooms, and many rooms have large old fireplaces. Modern bathrooms have old-fashioned chunky basins and brass taps.

◑ *Open all year*

↵ *Turn off the A140 Norwich to Ipswich road on to the B1077 to Eye. The hotel is 30 yards on the left. Private car park.*

⇌ *1 twin, 6 double, 4 four-poster; most with bathroom/WC, some with shower/WC; TV, room service, hair-dryer, trouser press, mini-bar, baby-listening in all rooms*

◇ *Restaurant, bar, lounge, conservatory; conference*

*facilities (max 40 people non-residential, 11 residential); golf, swimming nearby*

⊖ *No wheelchair access; no dogs in public rooms or unattended in bedrooms*

▭ *Access, Amex, Diners, Visa*

£ *Single occupancy of twin/double £59, twin/double/four-poster £75, family room £10 extra per bed; deposit required. Set L, D £15; alc L, D £25. Special breaks available*

---

**FALMOUTH** CORNWALL                                    **MAP 8**

# Penmere Manor

MONGLEATH ROAD, FALMOUTH, CORNWALL TR11 4PN
TEL: FALMOUTH (0326) 211411   TELEX: 45608 PMHTL G
FAX: (0326) 317588

*Excellent leisure facilities in a quiet residential area. Somewhat unimaginative décor.*

'It is the leisure centre which makes the hotel,' writes a reader from Camelford, who also praises the 'lovely room', 'good food' and staff who are 'not at all snobbish'. The original Georgian house sits in five well-landscaped and leafy acres not far from the centre of town.

Inside are elegant spaces, large windows and ceiling decorations, but it looks like many a slick commercial country-house hotel (and, indeed, is publicised by Best Western): little ingenuity of design, repetitive furniture and few personal touches. It's not the cosiest or most informal of hotels, either, but is still popular with families which it genuinely welcomes. The facilities, including a handsome indoor pool with sauna, Jacuzzi and small gym, a large outdoor pool, billiards room and games room, are clearly the draw, but bedrooms, especially newly refurbished ones, can be recommended for fine value, good-quality furnishings and a sensible layout. The furniture is of blond wood and the matching bedspreads and curtains come in soft colours. Suites are the best value and the standards carry through to modern tiled bathrooms. More personal touches and something more on the walls wouldn't go amiss, but in some rooms you at least have Falmouth Bay to look at.

🕐 Open all year, exc 4 days over Xmas

🔼 From the A39 turn right on to Gweek and Constantine Road. Follow signposts for Budock Hospital, carry straight on for ¾ mile, turn left into Mongleath Road. Private car park

🛏 10 single, 7 twin, 7 double, 3 family rooms, 12 suites; most with bathroom/WC, some with shower/WC; TV, room service, hair-dryer, baby-listening in all rooms; trouser press, mini-bar in some rooms

◇ Restaurant, bar, 3 lounges (all with air-conditioning), 2 games rooms; conference facilities (max 40 people residential); sauna/solarium, 2 swimming-pools, gym, croquet at hotel, other sports nearby. Wheelchair access to hotel (ramp), restaurant and WC (M,F), 5 ground-floor bedrooms

⊖ No dogs in public rooms; no smoking in restaurant

▭ Access, Amex, Diners, Visa

£ Single £52 to £60, single occupancy of twin/double £67 to £75, twin/double/family room £78 to £87, suite £97 to £112; deposit required. Set D £19, alc L, D £26. Special breaks available

# Streets Hotel

THE STREET, FARMBOROUGH, NR BATH, AVON BA3 1AR
TEL: TIMSBURY (0761) 71452

*Small, likeable hotel, centrally placed for Bath and Bristol. Plenty of space to relax.*

Not streets ahead of the competition, perhaps, but a solid bet. On a side street, so fairly quiet, the mix of trim stone, seventeenth-century house, conservatory, lawns on different levels and outbuildings is a little ungainly. Once inside, you're quickly enveloped in old world surroundings: low ceiling and beams every which way. Furnishings are richly coloured and the furniture solid in an old English, largely Victorian tradition, but you'll probably note a few things Spanish, confirmed when your host greets you with a light Spanish accent.

The hotel is small, and knick-knacks, fresh flowers and family pictures give that all-important personal feel. You'll find more than the usual number of places to relax with a book or a pre-dinner drink, as well as a variety of décors, from the pale-furnished and bright conservatory to the masculine bar with Victorian settee and Spanish tapestry, to the traditional lounge with window seats and wood-burning stove. At the far end is the split-level restaurant. You may have to cross the courtyard to get to your room as most bedrooms are in the annexes. These are the largest, however, with yet more places to sit. Rooms vary considerably, though light furniture such as bentwood cane, and thick quilts, are typical. Bathrooms are spick and span. Soundproofing and lighting, however, aren't all they could be.

◑ *Open all year, exc Xmas; restaurant closed Sun eves*

🢅 *180 yards off the A39 Bath to Wells road, 7 miles from Bath, 13 miles from Wells. Private car park*

🛏 *3 twin, 4 double, 1 four-poster (some rooms in courtyard); all with bathroom/WC, TV, room service, hair-dryer*

◈ *Restaurant, bar, lounge, TV*

*room, conservatory; heated outdoor swimming-pool at hotel, other sports nearby*

⊖ *No wheelchair access; no children under 6; no dogs*

▭ *Access, Amex, Visa*

£ *Single occupancy of twin/double £42 to £48, twin/double £50 to £58, four-poster £57 to £63. Set D £14 (prices till Easter 92)*

---

**FERSFIELD** NORFOLK                                    **MAP 7**

# Strenneth Farmhouse

OLD AIRFIELD ROAD, FERSFIELD, DISS, NORFOLK IP22 2BP
TEL: BRESSINGHAM (0379 88) 8182   FAX: (0379 88) 8182

*Remotely sited old farmhouse with interestingly furnished bedrooms.*

Flat countryside and a collection of ugly cinderblock buildings near the old brick farmhouse don't augur well, but impressions change once you've walked under the arched hedge and into Ken and Brenda Webbs' cosy home. Lovers of uneven floors, beams and low ceilings will be well pleased. The main room of the house, into which the front door opens, is both sitting- and dining-room (though a new kitchen is planned which will allow the old one to become a proper dining-room). In winter it's warmed by a log fire and at most times makes a lively venue for meeting and chatting with other guests and the Webbs. You can also escape to a non-smoking sitting-room behind, done out as a Victorian parlour, where there is a TV but unfortunately only dried flowers in the fireplace.

The farmhouse is comfortable throughout, and bedrooms are very well furnished. Some have delightful antique beds. An 'executive suite' in a new, modern extension is not quite large enough for the old four-poster bed. You'll find space and homely touches in bathrooms as well as the occasional corner bath. Good, no-choice dinners, served at 7.30pm, might include pâté-stuffed mushrooms followed by lamb in wine and garlic, and meringue fruit baskets, and there's home-made jam for breakfast.

◐ Open all year, dining-room closed Wed eve

◈ Dining-room, 2 lounges; baby-sitting

🔁 Off A1066, 3 miles west of Diss. Approximately 2 miles through the village. Private car park

⊖ No wheelchair access; 1 lounge non-smoking

🛏 2 single, 2 twin, 2 double, 1 four-poster, 2 family rooms, some with bathroom/WC, some with shower/WC; baby-listening in all rooms; TV in some rooms; hair-dryer on request

▭ Access, Amex, Visa

£ Single £22 to £24, single occupancy of twin/double £32 to £36, twin/double £42 to £50, four-poster £54, family room from £46; deposit required. Set D £12

---

**FLAMBOROUGH** HUMBERSIDE                                    **MAP 4**

# Manor House

FLAMBOROUGH, BRIDLINGTON, HUMBERSIDE YO15 1PD
TEL: BRIDLINGTON (0262) 850943

*A stylish Wolsey Lodge on a very breezy bit of headland.*

Flamborough Head juts out into the North Sea just above Bridlington creating a series of chalk cliffs with smugglers' caves and secluded bays and inlets. The cliffs, good for wild walks and birdwatching, are one mile from Flamborough village. Flamborough manor house was recorded in the Domesday Book and has existed on the site ever since. The current building dates only from around 1800, and, after falling derelict in the 1970s, has been caringly restored by the present owners. The result is a house of some distinction – informal but luxurious.

Antiques, the overspill from Lesley Berry's antiques business which occupies the outbuildings, fill every room. Some are very curious, like the massive Portuguese double bed the owner picked up for £10. The house is not just an elegant showpiece however; there are books lying around and a log fire for a cosy afternoon if you're tired of braving windy headland walks. There are just two bedrooms, both with plenty of space and good-sized bathrooms. Outside, you can play croquet amongst the apple trees in a large garden, and to complete the scene, peacocks Noah and Priscilla will keep you company. Evening meals are available on request.

◑ Closed Xmas

🔁 Set back from road on the corner of Tower Street and Lighthouse Road, just past St Oswald's Church on road from Bridlington. Private car park

🛏 1 double, 1 four-poster; both with bathroom/WC, TV, hair-dryer

◈ Dining-room, lounge; fishing, golf, other sports nearby

⊖ No wheelchair access; no children under 8 (exc babies); no dogs; no smoking in bedrooms

▭ Access, Visa

£ Single occupancy of double £30, double £46, four-poster £56; deposit required. Set D £17.50

## FOWEY CORNWALL                                MAP 8

# Marina Hotel

THE ESPLANADE, FOWEY, CORNWALL PL23 1HY
TEL: FOWEY (0726) 833315

*A friendly hotel from which to observe the ever-changing harbour scene below.*

'An advantage and a disadvantage,' says David Johns about the novel way you are first likely to encounter this handsome Georgian house. Streets don't come much narrower than those in this lovely old town (pronounced Foy), and, although there is a tiny lay-by outside the Marina, it may be occupied so you have to whip out your luggage and plonk it inside the hallway, and then drive on up to the council car park, a good five minutes' walk away (a ferrying service is also available). Inconvenient, but certainly a conversation piece.

This is a traditionally furnished hotel, built in 1830 as a holiday retreat for the Bishop of Truro. Since arriving in the mid-eighties, David and Sheila have worked hard to make it an easy-going as well as comfortable place. Eat early to get a table near the large windows. The scene below the dining-room, which you can also enjoy close up from the hotel's little terrace and pier, is a fascinating traffic jam of tugs, yachts and tankers loaded with China clay.

A correspondent from Shropshire recites one particularly satisfying dinner (informal, despite lots of knives and forks): 'scallops marinated in ginger wine, seafood soup, grilled halibut with a white wine sauce, and a sumptuous dessert trolley'. But, she continues, 'the only dislike was the music at dinner – we prefer silence'. Ships' horns will serenade you in your room (hardly unpleasant), and harbour lights twinkle. Functional furniture, maybe new pine and industrial-wear carpets are balanced by dainty, wildflower patterns and light walls. Several harbour-facing rooms have small balconies.

◑ Closed Nov to end Feb

🔁 On the Esplanade in Fowey. Take the one-way system through the town and turn right

at the start of the shops. Cars are allowed to stop to unload; a public car park is nearby

🛏 5 twin, 6 double; most with

bathroom/WC, some with shower/WC; TV, baby-listening in all rooms; hair-dryer on request

◈ Restaurant, bar, 2 lounges, garden room; fishing at hotel, golf, riding, other sports nearby

● No wheelchair access; no children in restaurant eves; no

dogs in public rooms; no smoking in restaurant

▭ Access, Amex, Diners, Visa

£ Single occupancy of twin/double £38 to £55, twin/double £50 to £74; deposit required. Set D £15.50; alc D £23.50; bar lunches. Special breaks available

## FRAMPTON DORSET                                     MAP 9

# The Court

FRAMPTON, DORCHESTER, DORSET DT2 9NH
TEL: MAIDEN NEWTON (0300) 20242

*Easy-going country house with a well-travelled look and lots of space. Exceptionally good value.*

'Complete relaxation in a lovely country house,' goes Peggy Lazenby's brochure, and not without justification; but she offers lots more, and at terrific value. Her large, tall brick house was built in the thirties from centuries-old materials salvaged from nearby Frampton Manor House. Huge oak doors and a splendid oak staircase would stand out even more if it weren't for the fascinating artefacts, many from the Far East, that fill the spacious rooms along with European and British antiques and common-or-garden knick-knacks. You can spend a week just *looking*.

Thanks to plenty of homely furnishings and several cats and dogs, it is not in the least precious, so you really can unwind. During cooler weather the coal and log stove in the large mustard-coloured drawing-room is an attraction; in warmer weather the flagstone-floored conservatory which is crowded with huge and healthy-looking plants is the place to be. There is nothing fussy about bedrooms, but they have several notable features along with lots of space and light and fresh duvet covers. Room three, an enormous twin that spans the width of the house, has extraordinary pelmets over tall windows. Room one has a massive antique wardrobe plus a fireplace with electric log fire. The price includes a three-course dinner: timbale of chicken and mushrooms with Madeira sauce, say, followed by cod steaks with coriander, and Bavarian nut chocolate sponge with chocolate sauce. The Court is unlicensed, but you may bring your own wine.

◑ Closed end Sept to 1 May

⤢ Frampton is 4 miles from Dorchester on the A356. Turn left on to the Crewkerne road. Private car park

⇥ 1 single, 2 twin, 1 double; 2 public bathrooms

◈ Dining-room, lounge, conservatory

● No wheelchair access; no children; no smoking

▭ None accepted

£ Single £30, twin/double £60. Set D £15 (7pm)

**GAMLINGAY** CAMBRIDGESHIRE                          **MAP 7**

# The Emplins

CHURCH STREET, GAMLINGAY, SANDY, BEDFORDSHIRE SG19 3ER
TEL: SANDY (0767) 50581

*A thoroughly delightful place to stay, both for the fascinating
medieval house and for the warmth of the hospitality.*

The tan, fifteenth-century house is a gorgeous, ramshackle, half-
timbered affair on the fringes of a peaceful village. 'Warm welcome for
children especially,' writes one reader from London. 'Very nice bedrooms – you feel as if you were at your grandmother's house.'

The Emplins is large but broken into remarkably cosy rooms inside,
with low beamed ceilings, mellow antiques, oak panelling and warm
furnishings. Most rooms have open fires. The Gortons are always keen
to show you some hidden delight and relate their discovery of wall
paintings and superimposed fireplaces. The Gortons themselves are
entirely accommodating, which makes staying here a real treat.

Delicious, home-made dinners (taken at one table) and excellent
breakfasts are whenever you wish. Bedrooms are interestingly furnished:
the single, which looks out to the large herb garden, has murals as well as
linenfold panelling; the twin has a painted strip of wood. A twin and
double now combine to form a family room (price on application).
Electric blankets, flowers and fresh milk for your morning tea are but a
few of the considerate touches.

- ◑ Open all year
- ⤴ Gamlingay is between Potton
  and Eltisley, on the B1040, 5
  miles from the A1 and 6 miles
  from the A45. The hotel is beside
  the village church. On-street
  parking
- 🛏 1 single, 2 twin, 1 double; most
  with bathroom/WC; TV, hair-
  dryer available on request
- ◈ Dining-room, lounge, TV room,
  drying room; tennis, golf, riding
  nearby
- ⊖ No wheelchair access; no dogs in
  bedrooms; no smoking
- ▭ None accepted
- 💷 Single £25, single occupancy of
  twin/double £25, twin £50;
  deposit required. Set D from £9
  (residents only, must book in
  advance)

---

$\mathscr{L}$   *This denotes that the hotel offers especially good value at whatever price
level.*

---

🌸   *This denotes that the hotel is in an exceptionally peaceful situation
where you can be assured of a restful stay.*

**GILLINGHAM** DORSET                                    **MAP 9**

# Stock Hill House

WYKE, GILLINGHAM, DORSET SP8 5NR
TEL: GILLINGHAM (0747) 823626   FAX: (0747) 825628

*Beguiling and classy country house. Great fun for a decadent weekend.*

A long grand drive of beeches ends in exquisite grounds and gardens presided over by a stately Victorian manor house. Jacket and tie time, you think, but that's only part of the story. Yes, you are expected to dress for dinner, but no, this is not a stuffy country-house hotel. Nor will you find run-of-the-mill pastel chintz and reproduction grandfather clocks.

Peter and Nita Hauser's energies and dedication amaze. Artistic flower beds, delicious meals, immaculate housekeeping and up-to-date facilities are but a few of their achievements. One reader reports: 'From the moment we arrived until the final wave off (when nothing would deter them from standing in the pouring rain), everything was perfect and nothing too much trouble. A mere suggestion that we might play croquet found Peter Hausker raking autumnal leaves.' Says another reader: 'Top marks to Nita Hauser who, hearing a casual reference to a liking for Fernet Branca, got a bottle for our next visit.' Their ingenuity of design is what lifts this place above so many others. The furniture is always classy, almost always antique but rarely straightforward. India and China get more than a look-in. The chandeliers, moulded ceilings and opulent fabrics in rich tones seem almost conventional, but the whole works magnificently well. Tables are Venetian gilt or marble-topped; lamps are statues (or the other way around). Animals abound in every medium – a pair of bronze cats by the entrance, for instance. A zither (which Peter plays) sits on the desk in the spacious entrance hall, but your eye is drawn right away to two large ceremonial horses from India kicking out at you. The bedrooms also excel for their individual flair and richness of fixtures and fittings. Antiques are common to all, though some wardrobes are created of fabric to look like Arabian tents. Peter's set dinners show the same reverence for perfection and good ingredients, with a smidgen of flavour from his native Austria added for good measure.

◗ Open all year; restaurant closed Sun and Mon eves

▰ The hamlet of Wyke is on the B3081, 3 miles south of the A303. Private car park

▱ 2 single, 3 twin, 2 double, 1 four-poster; most with bathroom/WC, some with shower/WC; TV, room service, hair-dryer, trouser press in all rooms; tea/coffee-making facilities on request

✧ 2 dining-rooms, bar, lounge;

croquet, tennis at hotel, other sports nearby

⊜ No wheelchair access; no children under 7; no dogs; no smoking in dining-rooms

▭ Access, Visa

£ Single £75 to £85, single occupancy of twin/double £90 to £95, twin/double/four-poster £170; deposit required. Sun L £19, set D £28

**GISLINGHAM** SUFFOLK                                          **MAP 7**

# Old Guildhall

MILL STREET, GISLINGHAM, NR EYE, SUFFOLK IP23 8JT
TEL: MELLIS (037 9783) 361

*Fetching fifteenth-century thatched cottage with twentieth-century comforts.*

The Old Guildhall is easy to spot in this village of old and new houses. It takes up a good chunk of land, but is most distinctive for its pale pink walls and peaked, tidily thatched roof. The inside of the fifteenth-century, timber-framed structure, once the centre of local government and now a small hotel, is also notable. The low-beamed ceiling, open timber partitions and comfortable easy chairs provide all the cosiness you could want. Traditional furnishings and horse-brasses are offset by an assortment of ornaments including Italian porcelain figurines. There's also a fish tank. An open fire does its bit for atmosphere and a snooker table at one partitioned end should keep some guests entertained. Polished oak tables and chairs that look Austrian but were made by a local craftsman (and are more comfy than you might think) give the dining-room a modern look, but meals are traditional.

Ray and Ethel Tranter, who moved here from a larger hotel in the mid-eighties, have not gone mad putting mod cons in bedrooms, and therefore prices are reasonable. There are duvets, tasselled lamps and velour furniture as well as occasional antiques. Bathrooms, however, show a keenness for the ultra-modern: tiles, gold taps, even a corner bath.

◑ *Closed Jan*

⤴ *In the centre of Gislingham, opposite the village school. Private car park*

🛏 *3 twin, 1 double; all with bathroom/WC, TV; hair-dryer on request*

◈ *Restaurant, bar, lounge, games room; fishing, golf, swimming-*

*pool nearby*

● *No wheelchair access; dogs by arrangement; no smoking in bedrooms*

▭ *None accepted*

💷 *Single occupancy of twin/double £40, twin/double £50; deposit required. Set D £9.50; alc D £20. Special breaks available*

**GISSING** NORFOLK                                          **MAP 7**

# The Old Rectory

GISSING, DISS, NORFOLK IP22 3XB
TEL: TIVETSHALL (037 977) 575   FAX: (037 977) 4427

*An exuberantly furnished Victorian house in a peaceful hamlet.*

Protected behind a screen of trees at the edge of a remote hamlet, the Victorian brick rectory, standing in three acres of gardens and woodland, is handsome rather than flamboyant. The inside is much more lively: a spacious and well-furnished family home that reflects the cheerful and down-to-earth personalities of its owners.

Architectural drawings, collected by Ian Gillam, hang from the walls; vibrant colour schemes (peach and turquoise in the lounge, for instance) have been contributed by Jill. Open fires, books and magazines should keep you occupied in bad weather, as will the indoor swimming-pool. Guest bedrooms are good value, especially for single occupants, of whom there are many: the Gillam home is a favourite with business people visiting nearby Diss or even Norwich, half an hour to the north. Rooms are inviting; large, light, well-kept and filled with personal touches. Frills and borders make them romantic. Excellent bathrooms are well supplied with toiletries. Jill is a very capable cook but admits she often suggests that her guests visit the nearby pub for dinner.

○ *Open all year*

⬈ *From Diss take the road to Burston for 4 miles. At Burston, take the first left turn after the crossroads for 1 mile and turn right into Rectory Road, just before the church. Private car park*

🛏 *2 twin, 1 double; 2 with bathroom/WC, 1 with shower/WC; TV, hair-dryer, room service (limited) in all rooms*

◇ *Dining-room, drawing-room, conservatory, drying room;*

*conference facilities (max 12 people non-residential); indoor heated swimming-pool and croquet at hotel, other sports nearby; babysitting by arrangement*

⊖ *No wheelchair access; no dogs; smoking in drawing-room only*

▭ *None accepted*

£ *Single occupancy of twin/double £32 to £36, twin/double £44 to £48; deposit required. Set D £16 by arrangement. Special breaks available*

---

**GLEWSTONE** HEREFORD AND WORCESTER                    **MAP 6**

# Glewstone Court

GLEWSTONE, ROSS-ON-WYE, HEREFORD AND WORCESTER HR9 6AW
TEL: LLANGARRON (0989 84) 367   FAX: (0989 84) 282

*Spacious but homely family country house with genuinely warm owners and relaxed ambience.*

In spring it's a pretty sight with the surrounding acres of cherry trees all covered in frothy white blossom. But at any time of year Christine and William Reeve-Tucker make you feel warmly welcome at their part-Georgian, part-Victorian hotel. The rooms are spacious and well lit but the personal collections of knick-knacks such as a papier mâché pig or William's great-grandfather's doll's house encourage informality and knock pretensions of grandeur on the head.

Teapots are another feature: each bedroom has a differently shaped teapot, as well as a fluffy cat to be placed outside the door if you don't want to be disturbed in the morning. The Victoria Room, behind a curtain at the end of a passage, is huge, with views of the Wye Valley and Goodrich Castle. Other rooms are smaller, with stencilled walls created by Christine: 'I rather enjoy that sort of thing.' In winter the lounge is the place to relax in with either a drink before the log fire or a light lunch or supper. More formal meals are taken in the deep-pink restaurant, with pictures hung between *trompe l'oeil* ribbons. The menu might include smoked halibut with dill rémoulade, boned quail stuffed with rice and apricots, and brown-bread ice-cream.

◑ Open all year, exc Xmas

⤢ Glewstone is off the A40 between Ross-on-Wye and Monmouth. Private car park

🛏 6 double, 1 half-tester; most with bathroom/WC, 2 with shower/WC; TV, room-service, baby-listening in all rooms; hair-dryer on request

◈ Restaurant, bar, lounge, drying facilities; conference facilities (max 20 people non-residential,

7 residential); croquet at hotel, fishing, hot-air ballooning, canoeing and other sports nearby. Wheelchair access to restaurant and WC (unisex) only

⊖ No dogs in restaurant

▭ Access, Visa

£ Single occupancy of twin/double £50, twin/double £75, half-tester £88; deposit required. Set L £15, D £20; Sun L £13. Special breaks available

---

## GLOSSOP DERBYSHIRE                                    MAP 4

# The Wind in the Willows

DERBYSHIRE LEVEL, GLOSSOP, DERBYSHIRE SK13 9PT
TEL: GLOSSOP (0457) 868001   FAX: (0457) 853354

*A quiet, well-run hotel convenient for touring the Peak District.*

It's only a few minutes from the centre of town but you wouldn't know it as you look out east across the golf course and up towards Snake Pass. The Victorian stone house is no beauty but the five acres of garden are neat and pretty; there aren't as many willows as you might expect from the name but one droops dutifully over the stream at the bottom of the garden.

Inside is just as neat: a combination of staid and Victorian but managing to feel warm and welcoming. The drawing-room is large with modern windows providing a view up to the peaks. The furnishings in here are quite formal, softened somewhat by the patterned carpet and hairy rugs; the study, which can double as a small conference room, is panelled and much cosier. Anne Marsh, who runs the hotel with her son, is responsible for the food, while he takes care of the guests. Helped by a couple of young staff, dinner is served, as is breakfast, in a slightly dull dining-room: you may have asparagus mousse followed by neck of lamb with a honey and mint sauce and baked custard as a pudding. The emphasis is on 'home-cooking'. Anne aims to provide 'things you don't get in restaurants'. She has obviously trained her sons well – you can find her other son, Eric Marsh, running the Cavendish at Baslow (see entry).

Bedrooms are named after Mrs Marsh's grandchildren and are all decorated differently. They vary in size and price and have a mixture of furnishings.

◑ *Open all year; restaurant closed Xmas and New Year*

⬈ *1 mile east of Glossop town centre. Turn off the A57 opposite the Royal Oak pub. The hotel is 400 yards on the right just after the golf course. Private car park*

🛏 *3 twin, 3 double, 1 half-tester, 1 suite; some with bathroom/WC, most with shower/WC; TV, room service, hair-dryer, trouser press, baby-listening in all rooms*

◈ *Dining-room, lounge/bar; conference facilities (max 12 people non-residential, 8 residential); croquet at hotel, other sports nearby*

⊖ *No wheelchair access; no dogs*

▭ *Access, Amex, Visa*

£ *Single occupancy of twin/double £57 to £77, twin/double/half-tester £68 to £98, suite £98; deposit required. Set D £19*

---

**GOATHLAND** NORTH YORKSHIRE                            **MAP 3**

# Mallyan Spout

THE COMMON, GOATHLAND, WHITBY, NORTH YORKSHIRE YO22 5AN
TEL: WHITBY (0947) 86206

*A thoroughly agreeable place to spend a night or two. Well run by friendly, efficient owners.*

Although the hotel lies on the green in the centre of this popular village, you are still likely to find sheep munching the grass outside the entrance. The ivy-clad, stone building looks cosy from the outside and visitors are not disappointed once inside either. A number of bars and lounges give plenty of places to sit – they're certainly needed in high season.

The rooms are comfortingly old-fashioned: you may find a familiar hunting scene, an old warming pan hanging by the fire and a comfy armchair to sink into. No pretensions here – you can wear what you like and eat where you like in any of the public rooms. For more formal occasions, three- or four-course menus are offered in the dining-room. With Whitby so close, go for the fish.

Bedrooms have either heavy polished wood furnishings with suitable fabric or are more modern with paler wallpapers, new wood furniture and light, fresh chintzes. The Heslops have been running the hotel for over eighteen years and have many regulars. Their combination of competence and informality is irresistible.

◑ *Open all year*

⬈ *From Pickering take the A169 Whitby road. Turn left to*

*Goathland after Fylingdales. Private car park*

🛏 *1 single, 7 twin, 11 double, 2*

four-poster, 2 family rooms, 2 suites (some rooms in annexe); all with bathroom/WC, TV, room service, hair-dryer, trouser press; no tea/coffee-making facilities in rooms

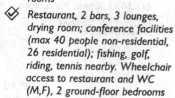 Restaurant, 2 bars, 3 lounges, drying room; conference facilities (max 40 people non-residential, 26 residential); fishing, golf, riding, tennis nearby. Wheelchair access to restaurant and WC (M,F), 2 ground-floor bedrooms

● No children in restaurant eves; no dogs in public rooms; I lounge non-smoking

▭ Access, Amex, Diners, Visa

£ Single £40 to £45, single occupancy of twin/double £45 to £50, twin/double £60 to £65, four-poster £75 to £80, suite £100, family room £70 (3 people); deposit required. Set L £10.50, D £18.50; alc L £17.50, D £30. Special breaks available

---

**GOSFORTH** CUMBRIA                    **MAP 3**

# Wasdale Head Inn

WASDALE HEAD, NR GOSFORTH, CUMBRIA CA20 IEX
TEL: WASDALE (094 67) 26229   FAX: (094 67) 26334

*Shangri-La for rock-climbers. It has adequate comfort and a memorable bar.*

Journey's end for many a weary but exalted climber fresh from conquering Scafell Pike is this rough and tumble inn at the end of a gorse-lined valley. Décor is in Victorian style, reminiscent of its early days as an inn, except in the smart, modern bar which is a feast of Jacobean oak-carved panelling with shiny copper and brass. The adjacent room is the popular and sometimes noisy billiards room.

The dining-room is panelled and carpeted, comfortable but unpretentious. Diners get a couple of choices throughout, with three main-course options, including one geared to non-meat-eaters. One springtime menu offered kiwi fruit and cashew-nut salad, cream of celery soup, roast guinea-fowl, various creamy desserts and cheese. One correspondent found the food disappointing but praised the freshly squeezed orange juice at breakfast.

Rooms are decorated with pine panelling, bright duvet covers, and comfy beds to help you recover from a hard day on the fells. Service is generally good. The tariff is not cheap and one reader, who found his room (number nine) chilly in April and affected by noise from the bar and wrought-iron fire escape outside used by the staff, thought it overpriced.

◑ Closed mid-Nov to 27 Dec and 13 Jan to mid-Mar

⚡ Follow signs for Wasdale Head from Gosforth or Santon Bridge. Private car park

🛏 2 single, 2 twin, 4 double, 2 family rooms; most with bathroom/WC, some with shower/WC; baby-listening in all rooms

Dining-room, 2 bars, lounge, pool room, drying room; fishing, riding, other sports nearby. Wheelchair access to restaurant only

No children under 8 at dinner; no dogs in public rooms; no smoking in dining-room

Access, Visa

Single £52, single occupancy of twin/double £59, twin/double £99, family room £143 (rates inc dinner); deposit required. Set D £16.50 (7.30pm); bar lunches (prices till end 91) Special breaks available

---

**GOUDHURST** KENT                                          **MAP 10**

# Star & Eagle

HIGH STREET, GOUDHURST, KENT TN17 1AL
TEL: GOUDHURST (0580) 211512/211338

*A striking ancient-timbered building with authentic old world public rooms.*

You don't expect much individual attention in a managed pub/hotel aimed, at least in part, towards the business trade, so it is a delightful surprise to be shown to your room, and when you come down for a drink to be extricated from the mêlée of a party and ushered to a quiet corner with the dinner menu. Other than that, it's the age and character of the building that makes the hotel recommendable.

The hotel is reputed to have been a monastery many years ago; its black-and-white timbered façade with lattice windows was recently damaged by fire but has been restored. The interior faithfully adheres to the fourteenth-century-inn-look: beams, brasses, leather-studded chairs, plain wooden tables. On either side of the bar are dining-rooms, the main one split-level, the other with an alarmingly sloping floor. A short à la carte menu offers appetising food in big portions. Breakfast may disappoint: carton orange juice, greasy bacon, packaged butter and jam. Bedrooms, with pine furnishings and light floral patterns, are large enough but bland; trouser presses and free videos are evidently geared to the needs of the businessperson.

The hotel, standing at the top of a typically attractive Kent village (old white weatherboarded and red-brick buildings), suffers from being on the corner of a busy main road, but front bedrooms have double glazing.

Open all year

Goudhurst is 2 miles off the A21, on the A262. Private car park

1 single, 4 twin, 4 double, 2 four-poster; most with bathroom/WC; TV, room service, hair-dryer, trouser press, baby-listening in all rooms

Restaurant, bar, lounge; conference facilities (max 25 people non-residential); golf, riding, other sports nearby

No wheelchair access; no dogs in public rooms and in bedrooms by arrangement only

Access, Amex, Visa

£ Single £50, single occupancy of twin/double £40 to £50, twin/ double £45 to £66, four-poster  £55 to £80; deposit required. Alc L, D £23 (prices till end 91). Special breaks available

---

## GRANGE-IN-BORROWDALE CUMBRIA                    MAP 3

# Borrowdale Gates Hotel

---

GRANGE-IN-BORROWDALE, KESWICK, CUMBRIA CA12 5UQ
TEL: KESWICK (076 87) 77204

*Comfortable family-run hotel in lovely surroundings.*

The short drive over the humpback bridge seems to leave the traffic of the main road a hundred miles behind. It's a stunning location, and this spruce little hotel, owned by Mr and Mrs Parkinson, is comfortable enough to help you make the most of it.

The white stucco and slate building with large windows has lots of facilities that wouldn't be out of place in a business hotel. The lounge sets the tone with its crackling fire, Welsh dresser, stag's head and hunting horn. The bright restaurant has huge picture windows to frame the spectacular views, and cane and rattan chairs with tapestry seats. A new restaurant is planned for 1992. Yards of ale are the focus of attention in the sloping-roofed bar. Bedrooms combine good Victorian furniture or mahogany-style repro, and chintzy fabrics add a sophisticated touch. 'Our top-floor room commanded beautiful views from two directions,' commented one reader. Rooms in the new wing are bigger, but those in the old house have more character. The set menu offers choice throughout, except at the soup stage, and might include terrine of chicken liver pâté, cream of celery and bacon soup, fillet of brill and Cumberland rum butter cheesecake with 'smiling waitresses who give prompt and expert service', according to one report.

○ Open all year (may close Jan, Feb 1992 for alterations)

↗ From Keswick follow the B5289 Borrowdale road for 3½ miles. Turn right over the double humpback bridge signposted Grange. The hotel is 100 yards past the village of Grange, on the right. Private car park

🛏 4 single, 8 twin, 9 double, 2 family rooms; most with bathroom/WC, some with shower/WC; TV in all rooms; hair-dryer, baby-listening on request

◇ Restaurant, bar, 3 lounges,

drying room; conference facilities (max 12 people residential only); golf, riding, other sports nearby. Wheelchair access to hotel (ramp), restaurant and WC (M,F), 6 ground-floor bedrooms

⊖ No dogs

▭ Access, Visa

£ Single £42 to £58, single occupancy of twin/double £42 to £68, twin/double £80 to £110 (family room price on application) (rates inc dinner); deposit required. Sun L £9.50; set D £18.50; light lunches. Special breaks available

# Graythwaite Manor

FERNHILL ROAD, GRANGE-OVER-SANDS, CUMBRIA LA11 7JE
TEL: GRANGE-OVER-SANDS (053 95) 32001/33755

*Friendly, relaxed and unpretentious hotel of character.*

Seaside resorts don't come much more traditional than Grange-over-Sands, and three generations of the Blakemore family have made Graythwaite Manor part of that tradition since before the war.

It's an attractive old creeper-clad house set amid eight acres of landscaped gardens, and is full of interesting furniture, paintings and curios. Open fires blunt the chill in the bar and lounge where there are comfy chairs to relax in, books and magazines to read and antiques to admire. Bedrooms vary in size and appeal, but few are small and some are huge. All have electric blankets. Some ground-floor rooms have traditional décor, rather shabby furniture and endearingly old-fashioned bathrooms. Plus points are imposing proportions and leaded and stained-glass windows that overlook the glistening sands of Morecambe Bay. Refurbished rooms have good quality modern furniture and bright, cheerful style.

Food is geared to the traditional, often elderly clientele, and eschews *nouvelle cuisine*. Hearty appetites are needed to tackle one of the six-course epic dinners – perhaps crispy duck pancake followed by cream of broccoli and almond soup, goujons of sole, roast leg of Cumbrian lamb, lemon meringue pie, and a cheeseboard or devils on horseback. The reasonably priced wine list has a decent selection of half-bottles. A mostly young staff offers efficient, helpful and genuinely friendly service. One innovation is a series of special interest weekend breaks for bridge, cookery and flower-arranging enthusiasts.

◖ *Closed Jan, Feb*

⤴ *Fernhill Road leads off the main esplanade road in Grange-over-Sands. Private car park*

🛏 *5 single, 11 twin, 4 double, 1 family room, 1 suite; all with bathroom/WC, TV, room service, baby-listening; hair-dryer on request*

◈ *Restaurant, bar, 2 lounges, conservatory; conference facilities (max 30 people non-residential, 22 residential);*

*tennis, billiards, putting at hotel, fishing, other sports nearby. Wheelchair access to hotel and restaurant, 5 ground-floor bedrooms*

● *No dogs*

▭ *Access, Visa*

£ *Single £35 to £55, single occupancy of twin/double from £40, twin/double £70 to £90, family room £70 to £110; deposit required. Set L £10, D £18.50. Special breaks available*

---

*Prices are quoted* per room *rather than* per person.

**GRANTHAM** LINCOLNSHIRE      **MAP 4**

# The Angel & Royal

HIGH STREET, GRANTHAM, LINCOLNSHIRE NG31 6PN
TEL: GRANTHAM (0476) 65816    FAX: (0476) 67149

*An old coaching-inn and recently refurbished town-centre hotel.*

Built over 750 years ago, the Angel claims to be the oldest coaching-inn in the country. It has just undergone some refurbishment and the medieval look is strictly confined to the King's Room restaurant and the bars. Unremarkable in many ways, this inn still provides a comfortable and friendly base in Grantham. The public Angel Bar is across the alley from the reception and is busy with locals, whilst the Falcon Bar with exposed stone walls, tapestries and pikes, and the connecting no-smoking lounge, are quieter, used more by the hotel guests.

The restaurant is in one of the oldest parts of the hotel, with oriel windows, elaborate stucco over the bays, and stone walls hung with tapestries – all rather impressive, but dulled by the standard furnishings. The menu is 'English Country Fayre' in style, with a choice of courses. Bedrooms are modern with repro furnishings. Superior twins or the larger executive bedrooms have armchairs and are pleasantly co-ordinated.

- ◑ Open all year
- ⏎ In Grantham's main street. Private car park
- ⮞ 11 single, 6 twin, 12 double, 1 suite; all with bathroom/WC, TV, hair-dryer, trouser press, baby-listening
- ◈ Restaurant, 2 bars, lounge; conference facilities (max 80 people non-residential, 30 residential); golf, swimming-pool nearby
- ⊖ No wheelchair access; no dogs in public rooms
- ▭ Access, Amex, Diners, Visa
- £ Single £75, twin/double £95; deposit required. Continental B £5.50, cooked B £8; set L £9, D £15; alc L, D £16

---

**GRASMERE** CUMBRIA      **MAP 3**

# White Moss House

RYDAL WATER, GRASMERE, CUMBRIA LA22 9SE
TEL: GRASMERE (096 65) 295; changes to (053 94) 35295 in 1992

*Excellent food in a comfortable hotel with literary associations.*

Wordsworth put his name to more than poems about daffodils. He also signed the indenture over water rights proudly displayed in the hall of White Moss House, which he once owned. Apparently, he spent little time here, although the views over Rydal Water are wonderful. These days Peter and Sue Dixon run the creeper-clad grey Lakeland stone villa as a restful hotel.

The style is cottagey and unpretentious with a cosy lounge where blue-tinged décor and chintzy furnishings provide a good place for quiet drinks, sociable coffee and pre-bedtime games of Scrabble. Bedrooms, including two in the hillside cottage (one of which has a four-poster), are individually decorated in various floral prints. Furniture might be antique or modern. Bathrooms run to thoughtful extras like nail brushes, cotton wool and classy toiletries.

The small dining-room is simple but elegant, and Wordsworthian daffodils often accompany the mats on the table. Peter Dixon's deftly produced real English food has won many plaudits. There's no choice till the pudding, but the consistent and confident use of fresh local ingredients cannot fail to impress. One menu offered spiced celeriac and chive soup, salmon and asparagus soufflé, rack of Westmorland Herdwick lamb roasted with parsley, sage, rosemary and thyme, desserts including banana toffee pie, and English cheeses with oat biscuits.

◑ *Closed Dec, Jan, Feb; restaurant closed Sun eve*

◪ *On the A591 at the north end of Rydal Water. Private car park*

🛏 *3 twin, 2 double, 1 cottage suite with four-poster; all with bathroom/WC, TV, room service, hair-dryer, trouser press; no tea/coffee-making facilities in rooms*

◈ *Dining-room, bar, lounge, drying*

*room; fishing at hotel, other sports nearby*

⊖ *No wheelchair access; no dogs; no smoking in dining-room*

▭ *Access, Visa*

£ *Single occupancy of twin/double £75 to £85, twin/double/four-poster £125 to £175 (rates inc dinner). Set D £26 (8pm)*

---

**GRASSINGTON** NORTH YORKSHIRE　　　　　　　　　　**MAP 4**

# Ashfield House

GRASSINGTON, NR SKIPTON, NORTH YORKSHIRE BD23 5AE
TEL: GRASSINGTON (0756) 752584

*A small, attractive seventeenth-century house close to the centre of the village.*

Grassington is an excellent centre from which to explore the Dales, and is a bustling, lively village. Ashfield House is only a couple of minutes from the hub of the action but manages to be quiet and secluded, cut off by a cobbled courtyard and a narrow lane. It is quite a small enterprise with only seven bedrooms, most having attractive pine furnishings and pretty fabrics.

The Harrisons took it over from the retiring owners a couple of years ago and are perpetuating the same friendliness and good atmosphere that had been established. Generally, the atmosphere is easy-going and relaxed, with only a few house rules governing smoking. Dinner is served promptly at 7pm in the simple dining-room. Straightforward English dishes appear on the menu, accompanied by home-grown vegetables whenever possible.

◑ *Closed Nov to early Feb*

▣ *A few yards off Grassington village square. Private car park*

🛏 *2 twin, 5 doubles; most rooms with shower/WC, 2 public bathrooms; TV in all rooms; hairdryer on request*

◈ *Dining-room, lounge/bar, 2 lounges, drying room; fishing, golf, other sports nearby*

⊖ *No wheelchair access; no children under 5; no dogs; smoking in one lounge only*

▭ *None accepted*

£ *Single occupancy of twin/double £23, twin/double £43 to £51; children sharing parents' room half-price; deposit required. Set D £12 (7pm)*

---

**GREAT HUCKLOW** DERBYSHIRE                                          **MAP 4**

# Hucklow Hall

---

GREAT HUCKLOW, TIDESWELL, BUXTON, DERBYSHIRE SK17 8RG
TEL: TIDESWELL (0298) 871175

*A peaceful, very relaxing retreat. Friendly, interesting hosts make your stay an experience you'll want to repeat.*

You definitely need directions to find the Hall. An old sign on the wall is just noticeable and even then it doesn't mention B&B. Anyway, the Whatleys don't really cater for passing trade. Word of mouth has done its stuff and Angela writes to everyone who books giving them details of how to get there and what to expect. It is a really lovely place in a tiny, isolated Peak village. Like most of the village houses it is of sandstone with mullioned windows; the large well-kept garden has a number of buildings and areas that the Whatleys have plans for, time permitting. Seek out the roofless summer house for a particularly good vantage point. John Whatley's mother is the main gardener and he has recently built her a greenhouse.

There are only three bedrooms: two very large double rooms that can also be used as family rooms and an ex-child's bedroom with an amusing raised bed – the experience is of staying in someone's home. Downstairs, a couple of comfortable sofas hug the fire and you don't have to move far to the dining-room table at one side of the room; this doesn't mean it's cramped: the room is large and homely with lots of books, rugs and other interesting pieces. Angela Whatley is an accomplished cook and regulars return again and again. You might have mushroom soup followed by chicken pie with herby mashed potato with cheese on top, ratatouille, and broccoli from the garden, then if you've got room a delicious crème brûlée decorated with fresh seasonal fruit. Dinner time is arranged to suit the guests and it's all a very genial affair. There's no licence but you are welcome to bring your own wine. Breakfast doesn't disappoint, either: cereals, muesli, stewed fruit and a cooked dish of, say, smoked bacon and mushrooms, will set you up for a hard day's walking.

○ Closed Dec to Feb

▨ Great Hucklow is signposted from the A623 Chapel-en-le-Frith to Baslow/Chesterfield road. The Hall is at the extreme east end of the village. Private car park

⤓ I single, I twin, I double; 2 public bathrooms; no tea/coffee-making facilities in rooms

◈ Dining-room/lounge; fishing, golf, other sports nearby

● No wheelchair access; no children under 5; no dogs or smoking in bedrooms

▭ None accepted

£ Single £17, single occupancy of twin/double £30, twin/double £34; deposit required. Set D £11 (7pm)

## GREAT LONGSTONE DERBYSHIRE                    MAP 4

# Croft Country House

GREAT LONGSTONE, NR BAKEWELL, DERBYSHIRE DE4 1TF
TEL: GREAT LONGSTONE (062 987) 278; changes to (0629) 640278 in 1992

*This well-kept hotel is an excellent base for touring the Peak District.*

The Macaskills took over the hotel at Easter 1991; it is their first hotel but Lynne was running an excellent B&B before, at the Old Vicarage at Alstonfield. So far, only a few changes will be noticed by the regulars. The Croft is in the heart of the village but also has four acres of garden so you feel quite secluded. Lots of walks can be taken nearby and the whole of the Peak District National Park is there for the more energetic. The house is very unusual: little of the Victorian exterior prepares you for the huge galleried main room with a lantern ceiling; flooded with light, it gratifies the original owner's love of Italian courtyards. Some of the furniture looks a bit lost in a room of these proportions but the large stone fireplace is a focus at one end and, now that the walls are covered with Victorian watercolours (Allan Macaskill has been collecting them for years and finally has the space for a display), the room feels less stark.

All the bedrooms lead off the galleried landing and vary in size. Neatly decorated, some rooms have pine furnishings, some Victorian, and unusually, most have fireplaces (not in use). Lynne has plans for the bedrooms, not drastic changes but cosier touches like fuller curtains and dried-flower arrangements. Dinner is at 7.30pm: everyone eats at the same time and there is a choice of starters and puddings but not main course. Let them know in advance if you have any special dietary needs.

○ Closed 4 Jan to end Feb

▨ 2 miles north-west of Bakewell. From Bakewell take the A6 Buxton road and turn right on to

the A6020. After I mile turn left towards Great Longstone. Private car park

⤓ I single, I twin, 7 double; some

with bathroom/WC, some with shower/WC, 2 public bathrooms; TV in all rooms; hair-dryer on request

◈ Restaurant, bar, 2 lounges, drying room; conference facilities (max 25 people non-residential, 9 residential); fishing, golf, other sports nearby. Wheelchair access to hotel, restaurant and WC, no ground-floor bedrooms but lift

and 2 bedrooms equipped for the disabled

⊖ No dogs; no smoking in restaurant

▭ Access, Visa

£ Single £50 to £55, single occupancy of twin/double £50 to £65, twin/double £62 to £82; deposit required. Set D £18.50 (7.30pm). Special breaks available

---

**GREAT MALVERN** HEREFORD AND WORCESTER     **MAP 6**

# The Red Gate

32 AVENUE ROAD, GREAT MALVERN, HEREFORD AND WORCESTER
WR14 3BJ
TEL: MALVERN (0684) 565013

*Good-value guesthouse in the Malverns for walkers and families.*

On a quiet tree-lined street this red-brick Victorian guesthouse is cared for, and goes in for bold use of large-print wallpaper, friezes and borders. The long dining-room has half a dozen small tables and a small brick terrace at the back overlooking the garden – mostly lawn with a few borders. The lounge is smaller, with deep red comfy armchairs and an ornate wooden mantelpiece that is reputed to have come from Corfe Castle.

The seven bedrooms each have different colour schemes and furnishings; five are *en suite*, most bathrooms being fairly basic with showers only. The single is rather small, but a large bay in the family room provides enough room for a table and chairs as well as a half-tester bed and a set of bunks. The four-course dinner is good value at £13, with local produce used wherever possible, and the soups and sweets are always home-made. Packed lunches can be provided on request.

◑ Open all year, exc Xmas and 2 weeks' annual holiday

� Close to Great Malvern Station and Malvern Girls' College, 10 minutes' walk from town centre. Private car park

⇌ 1 single, 2 twin, 3 double, 1 family room; most with shower or bathroom/WC; TV, room service in all rooms; hair-dryer on request

◈ Dining-room, lounge; drying facilities

⊖ No wheelchair access; no children under 8; no dogs; smoking in lounge only

▭ None accepted

£ Single £24 to £27, single occupancy of twin/double £25 to £40, twin/double £40 to £50; family room £58 to £66; deposit required. Set D £13

**GREAT MILTON** OXFORDSHIRE                              **MAP 6**

# Le Manoir aux Quat' Saisons

GREAT MILTON, OXFORDSHIRE OX9 7PD
TEL: GREAT MILTON (0844) 278881    TELEX: 837552 BLANC G
FAX: (0844) 278847

*Few doubt the quality of the food at this celebrated country manor house but readers are divided about the hotel.*

Raymond Blanc's restaurant has long been a talking point for foodies everywhere. Whether they leave ranting enthusiastically or a little disappointed, at some point the pilgrimage has to be made. But one couple from Scotland say that while certainly wanting to eat in the restaurant again they would not be staying. Their two-night weekend break cost over £1,000 and led them to remark: 'Being one of the world's great chefs does not equal being a great hotelier. We felt it was just a bed and breakfast place with very expensive room fittings.' Another reader, even after being woken at 3.15am by a fire alarm, couldn't rate the stay highly enough: 'Everything matters for Mr Blanc and his vast team.'

Raymond Blanc's undisputed strength is in the kitchen. The creation of tastes, textures and nostril-twitching aromas leaves guests amazed and filled with a wondrous curiosity as to just how these effects are achieved. One guest remarked: 'One of the characteristics of the food is certainly its lightness. Even after a number of courses I didn't feel in any way weighed down – but I certainly wasn't feeling hungry either.' Breakfast has come in for its share of criticism. 'Acid, tired-tasting orange juice', 'remarkably poor brioche', 'weak coffee and inattentive service'.

Décor in the hotel is in the classic country house ilk: heavy chintz curtains and drapes and comfortable sofas, while the bedrooms, each named after a flower, are more individual. Mermaid's Rose is perhaps the pick of the suites where the pink and white canopied bed is reached from below via a spiral staircase. Bathrooms are not always as big as you'd like – preparing for this sort of dinner needs space – and there have been murmurings from readers about problems with the plumbing, from erratic showers to water that was either very hot or very cold: 'you took your life in your hands to sit on the bidet with the wild fluctuations in temperature.'

Reports of minor disappointments and little mistakes are perhaps inevitable when expectations are so high but when all goes well Le Manoir is rarely bettered. 'Nothing is lacking; the grounds, rooms, lounges, kitchen and staff pull together to produce a quite extraordinary experience,' was how one reader summed up the stay.

◑ *Closed 3 weeks over Xmas and New Year*

↗ *Leave the M40 to Oxford at Junction 7. Turn left on to the A329, and second right,*

*signposted 'Great Milton Manor'. Private car park*

⬅ *1 twin, 12 double, 3 four-poster, 3 suites; all with bathroom/WC, TV, room service, hair-dryer,*

trouser press; no tea/coffee-
making facilities in rooms

◈ Restaurant (air-conditioned), 2
lounges, conservatory; laundry;
conference facilities (max 46
people non-residential, 19
residential); tennis, croquet,
outdoor heated swimming-pool
(summer only) at hotel, other
sports nearby; babysitting by
arrangement. Wheelchair access
to hotel (1 step) and restaurant,
5 ground-floor bedrooms, 1

specially equipped for the
disabled

⊖ No dogs; no smoking in part of
restaurant

▭ Access, Amex, Diners, Visa

£ Twin/double/four-poster from
£165, suite £375; deposit
required. Continental B £9.50,
cooked B £14.50; set L £26.50,
£29.50, D £59; alc L, D £75
(prices till Apr 92). Special
breaks available

---

**GREAT RISSINGTON** GLOUCESTERSHIRE                     **MAP 6**

---

# Lamb Inn

GREAT RISSINGTON, NR BOURTON-ON-THE-WATER, GLOUCESTERSHIRE
GL54 2LP
TEL: COTSWOLD (0451) 20388

*Pleasant, friendly country pub with interesting angular rooms but
pricey food.*

The Union flag flutters outside this 300-year-old village pub overlooking
the village green. Sloping gardens on the other side offer pretty views of
the Windrush Valley. The interior is as characterful as you'd expect in a
building of this age – lots of low beams, twisting passages, uneven
ceilings and awkward staircases and steps. As well as the buttery bar in
the pub itself, residents have their own lounge, with red velveteen wing
chairs and framed badger prints and country poems. There's also a
supply of magazines and board games.

The restaurant, in pale pink, feels lighter and more spacious than the
'duck or grouse' bar area, but food has disappointed in the past. Some
dishes on the menu seem expensive for what they are; vegetables or salad
are charged extra. Bedrooms are prettily decorated in floral fabrics (not
too frilly), with thoughtful supplies of tissues and bubble bath. Serving
staff are young and amiable.

◑ Open all year, exc 25, 26 Dec

↯ Leave the A40 for Burford. Turn
right out of Burford for the
Rissingtons. The inn is in the
centre of Great Rissington.
Private car park

⇌ 2 twin, 7 double, 2 four-poster, 1
suite; most with bathroom/WC,

some with shower/WC; hair-
dryer on request; TV in suite

◈ Restaurant, bar, lounge; heated
indoor swimming-pool (open
May to Sept), fishing, golf, riding
nearby

⊖ No wheelchair access; no dogs in
public rooms

Access, Amex, Visa

Single occupancy of twin/double £30 to £38, twin/double £40 to £46, four-poster £48 to £54,

suite £68 to £72; deposit required. Bar lunches, alc D £10 to £15. Special breaks available

## GREAT SNORING NORFOLK　　　　　　　　MAP 7

# Old Rectory

GREAT SNORING, FAKENHAM, NORFOLK NR21 0HP
TEL: FAKENHAM (0328) 820597　FAX: (0328) 820048

*Ornate Victorian rectory containing an unpompous household.*

Hedged-in lanes take you to Great Snoring – 'Little Sleepy' might be more apt, as the village has no shop or pub. The Old Rectory, William and Rosamund Scoles' home, probably dates from 1500. The large brick rectory is a splendid and unusual confection of arched and panelled octagonal turrets, round chimneys, terracotta tiles and mullioned windows, and it stands within a sheltered, two-acre garden.

The interior of beams, solid dark wood furniture and polished tile floors is lightened with bright colours, shiny silver and fresh flowers. Everyone gathers for pre-dinner drinks in the comfortable sitting-room. Staff are unobtrusive: 'good service rules,' remarks one reader 'and one can be as familiar or formal as one chooses in response.' Comfort applies to well-furnished bedrooms, too, but you may best remember the highly polished wood surfaces of tables and chests, or the window seat from which you can admire the lovely gardens. The Scoles have also put thought and money into the Shelton Suites, new self-catering facilities nearby. 'We give full marks on house, garden, cooking, attractive table appointments and charming family,' says a reader about a stay in spring. The dinners are resolutely English and there is no choice of main course. 'No garlic,' as Mrs Scoles puts it. One reader commended the 'queen of puddings, where a perfect marriage of eggs, lemon and raspberry brought long-lost childhood recollections of old delights'! 'However,' he added, 'the wine list is limited and could easily be extended in the same price range to give better variety.'

Open all year, exc 24 to 27 Dec

Great Snoring is 3 miles north-east of Fakenham, signposted from the A148. The Old Rectory is behind the church. Private car park

3 twin, 3 double, 5 cottages; all with bathroom/WC, TV, room service; no tea/coffee-making facilities in rooms

Dining-room, lounge; meeting facilities (max 12 people residential and non-residential)

No wheelchair access; no children under 12; no dogs; no smoking in dining-room

Amex, Diners

Single occupancy of twin/double £60, twin/double £82, cottage £125; deposit by arrangement. Set D £18.50

# Morritt Arms

GRETA BRIDGE, NR BARNARD CASTLE, CO DURHAM DL12 9SE
TEL: TEESDALE (0833) 27232/27392   FAX: (0833) 27570

*A traditional pub/hotel with a friendly atmosphere. Lots of places to visit nearby.*

Close to the confluence of the Rivers Tees and Greta, this is a very beautiful spot. It is also within easy reach of Barnard Castle and Bowes, where, as well as Dotheboys Hall of *Nicholas Nickleby* fame, there is an excellent museum. The Morritt Arms was built as a coaching-inn in the seventeenth century and this is more or less what it has remained.

Now it is run by twin brothers John and David Mulley in a traditional fashion: no background music and restricted private functions. A good welcome (extending to dogs and smokers) and decent food are the important factors. A number of bars on the ground floor provide you with a choice of public rooms. Get into a game of dominoes in the plainer bar room decorated with tankers or there's a more chintzy lounge-type room with armchairs and stuffed fish and animal heads as adornments. The atmosphere is enhanced by the strong Dickensian association – Gilroy's Pickwickian murals and various press cuttings are effective decoration. Over the last year the owners have completed their conversion work and all the bedrooms are now *en suite* – fairly plain and functional décor but adequately comfortable.

🌕 Open all year

⏩ On the A66(T) 10 miles north-west of Scotch Corner. Private car park

🛏 4 single, 5 twin, 7 double, 1 four-poster; all with bathroom/WC, TV, hair-dryer, trouser press; baby-listening by arrangement

◈ Restaurant, 2 bars, lounge, drying facilities; conference facilities (max 30 people non-residential, 17 residential); fishing, golf, riding nearby

⊖ No wheelchair access; no children under 6 in public areas eves

▭ Access, Amex, Diners, Visa

💷 Single £48, single occupancy of twin/double £48, twin/double £72, four-poster £72; extra beds £11 each. Set D £21; Sun L £12. Special breaks available

---

*The 1993 Guide will be published before Christmas 1992. Reports on hotels are most welcome at any time of the year, but are extremely valuable in the spring. Send them to* Which? Hotel Guide, FREEPOST, 2 Marylebone Road, London NW1 1YN. *No stamp is needed if reports are posted in the UK.*

**GRIMSTON** NORFOLK                                                    **MAP 7**

# Congham Hall

LYNN ROAD, GRIMSTON, KING'S LYNN, NORFOLK PE32 1AH
TEL: HILLINGTON (0485) 600250    TELEX: 81508 CHOTEL G
FAX: (0485) 601191

*Warm and civilised country house with first-rate service and good food. A treat for the senses.*

The eighteenth-century manor house, encircled by manicured gardens, makes an elegant country-house hotel, and has a loyal following from all over the world. Georgian reverence for light, space and graceful proportions is evident everywhere you look and is set off perfectly by rich, warm furnishings. You will be comfortable wherever you settle, be it in the long drawing-room with grand piano, cheerful canary-yellow bar, tiny conservatory or terrace. But your lasting memories will be as much olfactory as visual: bowls of scented petals, herbs sachets, lavish sprays of dried flowers, and pot-pourri fill the house with various perfumes. Herbs are Christine Forecast's passion, and you will find a table at the end of the long, wide hall with tempting goodies from her garden of more than 300 varieties.

Fresh herbs make their way into the hands of the five chefs, too, whether to end up in a trio of smoked fish mousses with oysters and truffle, or in the sauce of a fillet of beef with horseradish crust. The orangery extension in the dining-room is an especially pleasant spot. 'Winter snacks around the fire' and 'Summer lunch on the lawns' are welcome alternatives to dinner in the restaurant. And how about cocktails to piano music on Saturday evenings? The service, whether by the Forecasts themselves or their capable staff, is genuinely enthusiastic as well as professional.

Bedrooms should not disappoint. There are plenty of trendy touches such as crown canopies and skirted tables, and a bit of lightweight modern furniture, but jazzy patterns and inventive colour schemes more than compensate. Most rooms and most beds are large. From room four, the smallest double, to the supreme Garden Suite in the new wing, comfort is paramount.

**◖** Open all year

**⤴** Go to the A149/A148 interchange north-east of King's Lynn. Follow the A148 to Sandringham/Fakenham/Cromer for 100 yards. Turn right to Grimston. The hotel is 2½ miles further on the left-hand side. Private car park

**🛏** 1 single, 7 twin/double, 2 double, 2 four-poster, 2 suites; all with bathroom/WC, exc single with shower/WC; TV, room service, hair-dryer in all rooms; trouser press, mini-bar in some rooms; no tea/coffee-making facilities in rooms

**◈** Restaurant, bar, lounge, private dining-room, drying room; conference facilities (max 12 people residential and non-residential); tennis, croquet, heated outdoor pool (in season) at hotel, other sports nearby. Wheelchair access to restaurant only (2 steps)

● No children under 12; no dogs; no smoking in restaurant

▭ Access, Amex, Diners, Visa

£ Single £70, single occupancy of twin/double £80, twin/double £105, four-poster £120, suite £165; deposit required. Cooked B £2; set L £15, D £30. Special breaks available

**HADLEY WOOD** HERTFORDSHIRE                    **MAP 10**

# West Lodge Park

COCKFOSTERS ROAD, HADLEY WOOD, HERTFORDSHIRE EN4 0PY
TEL: 081-440 8311   TELEX: 24734
FAX: 081-449 3698

*A relaxing, unpretentious country-house hotel only 12 miles north of Piccadilly Circus.*

Stately, mature European lime trees line the driveway at West Lodge Park, an isolated haven of arboreal splendour within the orbital M25. Trees are important here. They are the passion of the hotel's owner, Mr Beale, and over the last 25 years a careful planting programme has established a celebrated collection in the grounds of the house. A brochure highlights some of the more unusual species to look for in a stroll around the grounds – the Swamp Cypress on the front lawn near the lake and an Antarctic Beech recovering from damage inflicted by the 1987 gales.

The hotel dates from the sixteenth century but the modern impression is of a substantial almost block-house like building, the product of substantial eighteenth-century modifications. Many of the bedrooms have window seats to make the best of the views and huge french windows in the ranch-style restaurant, a pleasantly informal place to eat, look out on to the lawns. West Lodge successfully manages to convince you that the bustle of the capital is considerably further than 12 miles away.

◑ Open all year

⤤ Leave the M25 at Junction 24; the hotel is 1 mile from the exit. Private car park

🛏 10 single, 20 twin, 16 double, 4 four-poster, 2 annexe rooms; all with bathroom/WC, TV, room service, hair-dryer, baby-listening, trouser press; mini-bar in some rooms

◈ Restaurant, bar, lounge; conference facilities (max 40

people residential and non-residential); putting, croquet at hotel, golf, tennis, riding nearby. Wheelchair access to restaurant only

● No dogs

▭ Access, Amex, Visa

£ Single £80, single occupancy of twin/double £95, twin/double £108, four-poster £143, suite £153. Set L, D £15

**HAMBLETON** LEICESTERSHIRE                                   **MAP 4**

# Hambleton Hall

HAMBLETON, NR OAKHAM, LEICESTERSHIRE LE15 8TH
TEL: OAKHAM (0572) 756991   FAX: (0572) 724721

*A luxurious country house in some fine countryside beside Rutland
Water.*

This peaceful, relaxed Victorian country mansion stands in beautiful and
well-cultivated grounds on a tongue of land jutting out into Rutland
Water. Built as a hunting lodge in 1881, it has for the last twelve years
been a country-house hotel run by Tim and Stefa Hart. The front of the
house is surrounded by mature cedars; the back has a terrace and formal
rose garden with lavender borders and the lake beyond. (One summer
visitor reported that the lake and trees meant 'horrendous hordes of
flying insects in the rooms'.)

In the entrance hall wellies and brollies stand ready for muddy walks.
You might prefer to curl up in a floral sofa in the comfortable drawing-
room or in one of the huge sofas in the bar. The elegant dining-room has
leaded windows, a lake view and a reputation for fine food. There is a
choice of a four-course table d'hôte menu or à la carte prepared by Brian
Baker, the head chef, who is keen on fish and shellfish dishes. Bedrooms
are all individually decorated with antiques and fine fabrics and bathrooms to match. However, one regular visitor commented: 'Our room
over the front door was small, stuffy, and noisy when people left in the
evening. We felt that the decorations are now beginning to show their
age.' More reports, please.

◑ *Open all year*

🔁 *3 miles east of Oakham, on a
peninsula in the middle of
Rutland Water. Private car park*

🛏 *14 double, 1 four-poster; all with
bathroom/WC, TV, room service;
hair-dryer, trouser press, baby-
listening on request; no tea/
coffee-making facilities in rooms*

◈ *Restaurant, bar, drawing-room;
laundry service; conference
facilities (max 30 people non-
residential, 15 residential);
tennis, heated swimming-pool,*

*bicycles at hotel, other sports
nearby; babysitting. Wheelchair
access to hotel and restaurant,
no ground-floor bedrooms but lift*

⊖ *No children under 9; no dogs in
public rooms; no pipes/cigars in
restaurant*

▭ *Access, Visa*

£ *Single occupancy of double
£105, double £105 to £225,
four-poster £150. Set L £17.50,
D £35; alc L, D £50. Special
breaks available*

---

🍲 *Denotes somewhere you can rely on a good meal – either the hotel
features in the 1992 edition of our sister publication,* The Good
Food Guide, *or our own inspectors thought the cooking impressive,
whether particularly competent home cooking or more lavish cuisine.*

**HAMSTERLEY FOREST** CO DURHAM          **MAP 3**

# Grove House

HAMSTERLEY FOREST, NR BISHOP AUCKLAND, CO DURHAM DL13 3NL
TEL: WITTON-LE-WEAR (038 888) 203

*A simple, welcoming guesthouse in a very peaceful forest location.*

Three miles into the mixed woodlands of Hamsterley Forest is this
peaceful stone-built guesthouse, once an aristocrat's shooting lodge.
Horses graze in the grounds, and the downstairs rooms reflect some of
the elegance of the lodge's heyday, with unusual cornices, friezes and
comfortable sofas.

Bedrooms are smaller and more modern, with washbasins but no
other *en suite* facilities. Some shooting still takes place in the forest –
Helene Close's fixed-price four-course menu often includes game such
as pheasant or venison as the main course. This may be sandwiched
between a mushroom roulade with watercress sauce and lemon mousse.
If you're planning to explore the surrounding forest, packed lunches can
also be arranged.

🄾 *Closed Aug and Xmas;
restaurant eves only*

🄾 *North of West Auckland off the
A68. Take the Hamsterley Forest
turning to Hamsterley village
and then the turning signposted
Hamsterley Forest. At Bedburn
fork left – the hotel is 3 miles
inside the forest on a tarmac
road. Private car park*

🛏 *2 twin, 2 double; 2 public
bathrooms; room service in all
rooms*

◈ *Dining-room, 2 lounges; golf,
riding, other sports nearby*

⊖ *No wheelchair access; no
children under 8; no dogs in
public rooms; no smoking*

▭ *None accepted*

£ *Single occupancy of twin/double
£24, twin/double £37. Set D £10
(7.30pm)*

**HANLEY CASTLE** HEREFORD AND WORCESTER          **MAP 6**

# Old Parsonage Farm

HANLEY CASTLE, HEREFORD AND WORCESTER WR8 0BU
TEL: HANLEY SWAN (0684) 310124

*Smart, spacious farmhouse with efficient but easy-going owners.*

It's easier to approach from Upton; from Malvern, you have to swing the
car almost back on itself up the drive. A couple of excitable spaniels rush
out to investigate your arrival, but they soon lose interest when Ann
Addison comes out to greet you.

The bedrooms are all in one wing of this L-shaped farmhouse and are very large. Despite their size, they're uncluttered almost to the point of sparseness – a double bed and a couple of armchairs seem to do little to fill the space. Lack of clutter doesn't equate with lack of facilities: tired walkers can watch TV downstairs in the deep-red sitting-room or relax in the elegant green drawing-room. Four-course dinners are served in the small dining-room next to the kitchen; the Addisons also run a wholesale wine business, so there's an extensive choice of bottles to accompany your meal. The Addisons' cooking and organisational skills make them a popular choice for 'functions', whether business or social, so it's wise to book in advance.

○ *Closed mid-Dec to mid-Jan*

↗ *Take the B4211 out of Upton upon Severn for 1½ miles towards Worcester. Turn left on to the B4209. The farm is 200 yards on the right. Private car park*

⇌ *1 twin, 1 double, 1 family room; all with shower/WC*

◇ *Dining-room, lounge, TV room/library, drying room; conference facilities (max 15 people, non-residential); golf, fishing, other sports nearby*

⊖ *No wheelchair access; no children under 10; no dogs in public rooms; no smoking in bedrooms*

▭ *Amex*

£ *Single occupancy of double £29, double £45, family room £53; deposit required. Set D £15 (prices till Apr 92)*

---

**HANWOOD** SHROPSHIRE                                     **MAP 6**

# White House

HANWOOD, NR SHREWSBURY, SHROPSHIRE SY5 8LP
TEL: SHREWSBURY (0743) 860414

*Lots of space to relax in comfort; warm hosts; and freshly laid eggs for breakfast.*

There are unusual goings on at this White House. Until recently, Raisa and Gorby were living here quite happily, then Gorby took off and left her with Omsk. What's more, Baldrick is in residence too. It seems a scandalous set-up, but ask for a tour around the garden and all becomes clear. Gill and Mike Mitchell look after a variety of feathered guests, as well as their human ones. There are Muscovy ducks, hens, geese and guinea-fowl on their one-and-a-half acres of garden which slopes gradually down to the Rea Brook and, as a result, breakfast eggs are freshly laid.

The Mitchells' aim is to ensure that their guests have space to feel relaxed and comfortable. Rather than create more bedrooms, they have recently opened up a large beamed lounge (formerly an abattoir), in addition to a cosy TV lounge and a brick-floored bar. Thankfully, its history has been completely exorcised by clever conversion, soft flowery sofas and an inviting central stove.

The bedrooms, named after inhabitants of the other famous White House, are crisply decorated, and throughout the guesthouse hang Gill's embroideries. The evening menu offers a good choice of meat and fish dishes, and one speciality is home-made crème caramel.

◐ *Open all year; restaurant closed Sun eve*

↗ *From Shrewsbury take the A488 Bishop's Castle road; the hotel is 3 miles away. Private cark park*

🛏 *1 single, 1 twin, 4 double; 1 with bathroom/WC, 1 with shower/WC; hair-dryer in all rooms*

◇ *Dining-room, bar, lounge, TV*

*room, drying room; fishing at hotel; golf, riding, other sports nearby*

⊖ *No wheelchair access; no dogs*

▭ *None accepted*

£ *Single £20, single occupancy of twin/double £30 to £38, twin/double £40 to £50. Set D £14. Special breaks available*

## HARDWICKE HEREFORD AND WORCESTER                    MAP 5

# The Haven

HARDWICKE, HAY-ON-WYE, HEREFORD AND WORCESTER HR3 5TA
TEL: CLIFFORD (049 73) 254

*Excellent-value and welcoming guesthouse with good food.*

This former Victorian vicarage was once the home of Thomas Webb, amateur astronomer and friend of Francis Kilvert. The current owners, Mark and Janet Robinson, have run special interest weekends on both Webb and Kilvert but if you're interested in more down-to-earth pursuits, like walking, you'll be equally welcome. It's also within handy book-throwing distance of Hay-on-Wye, if you fancy a browsing weekend. The Haven itself has a very tempting selection of books in the library, where pre-dinner introductions and exchanges of the 'And what did you do today?' type take place.

Dinner, at £11 for four courses plus coffee, is extremely good value. The menu is chalked up on a small blackboard in the hall and has at least two choices for each course, one of which is vegetarian. The cheese-board is diplomatically bipartisan – two English, two Welsh – and the limited selection of wines includes local Herefordshire examples. Mark and Janet join the guests in the sitting-room for after-dinner coffee and mints, their excitable whippet eventually falling asleep in Janet's arms.

Bedrooms are named after the views from their windows. The poshest is Radnor, with a four-poster bed and spacious sitting area. Glebe has twin beds, candlewick bedspreads, and a huge private bathroom across the corridor. Traffic noise is negligible; the biggest disturbance is likely to be the bleating sheep in the field to the front of the house: 'The field's ours, but not the sheep – it saves us having to cut the grass,' says Mark.

◐ *Closed Nov, Dec, Jan*

↗ *On the B4348, 2½ miles north-*

*east of Hay-on-Wye. Private car park*

▭ 1 single, 2 twin, 1 double, 1 four-poster, 1 family room; some with bathroom/WC, some with shower/WC, some public bathrooms; TV, hair-dryer, baby-listening in all rooms

◈ Dining-room, lounge, library; drying facilities; outdoor (unheated) swimming-pool at hotel, other sports nearby; babysitting. Wheelchair access to hotel (ramp) and dining-room, 1 ground-floor room

⊖ No dogs in public rooms; no smoking

▭ Amex

£ Single £18, single occupancy of twin/double £18, twin/double £40, four-poster £46, family room £40; deposit required. Set D £11 (7.30pm)

---

**HAROME** NORTH YORKSHIRE                                          **MAP 3**

# The Pheasant

HAROME, HELMSLEY, NORTH YORKSHIRE YO6 5JG
TEL: HELMSLEY (0439) 71241

*A family-run hotel in a very pretty village only three miles from the North York Moors National Park.*

Harome boasts six thatched cottages and that's a rarity in North Yorkshire, apparently. One, Holly Cottage, is part of the Pheasant Hotel. About three hundred yards from the main building, it is ideal for families, with a couple of twin rooms, bathroom and sitting-room. The Pheasant Suites are also detached but a bit nearer the main house, being just across the courtyard. Suitable for families or four friends, they have a double and twin bedroom in each with sitting-room, bath and extra loo. Some may relish the additional privacy of these two cottages but you do have to take all your meals at the hotel, so take an umbrella for rainy days.

In the main part of the hotel, you have a choice of places to linger: either the large outdoor terrace or the huge sitting-room with picture windows; both overlook the village green and pond. The cosy beamed bar and restaurant have large fireplaces which add warmth on chilly evenings. Expect good English cooking at dinner.

◑ Open all year, exc Xmas, Jan and Feb

⤢ Leave Helmsley on the A170 towards Scarborough. After ¼ mile turn right and follow signs to Harome. The hotel is near the church. Private car park

▭ 3 single, 6 twin, 6 double, 2 suites in cottage annexe; all with bathroom/WC, TV; limited room service; hair-dryer on request

◈ Dining-room, bar, lounge, drying room; fishing, golf, riding, other sports nearby. Wheelchair access to hotel (no steps), restaurant and WC (M,F), 4 ground-floor bedrooms

⊖ No children under 12; no dogs in public rooms and by arrangement only in bedrooms; no smoking in dining-room

▭ None accepted

💷 Single £49 to £55, twin/double
£98 to £110, suite/annexe £100
to £115 (rates inc dinner);

deposit required. Bar lunch £7;
set D £17.50. Special breaks
available

## HARTFIELD EAST SUSSEX                    MAP 10

# Bolebroke Watermill

EDENBRIDGE ROAD, HARTFIELD, EAST SUSSEX TN7 4JP
TEL: HARTFIELD (0892) 770425

*An interestingly converted watermill in a peaceful spot; tricky access to rooms.*

The existence of a watermill in this rural setting was first recorded in the Domesday Book. The present mill, weatherboarded and white painted, dates from 1740; it was last used as a working cornmill in 1948.

David and Christine Cooper have incorporated the mill's machinery into the rooms; one bedroom has the original pulleys somewhere above your bed, and the residents' lounge, secluded and cosy, has old grain hoppers and grinding wheels. The two delightful, cottagey-small split-level bedrooms, with sloping ceilings, plain walls and slanting doors, are unsuitable for the less nimble, reached as they are by ladder stairs and trapdoor or up the spiral staircase. Two newly finished rooms in the Elizabethan Miller's Barn are a four-poster (the 'honeymooners' hay-loft'), and a downstairs twin.

Christine Cooper produces delicious 'Sussex Suppers' on wicker trays: a choice of interesting soups (Sussex fish chowder, for one), a salad with smoked trout, chicken or Bolebroke Mill salt beef (from their own organically reared animals), home-made fruit pie, and a selection of obscure cheeses. Neither is breakfast run-of-the-mill, as it were, with freshly baked bread, a choice of jams and many interesting departures from the bacon and egg theme.

◑ Closed Dec, Jan, Feb; no eve meals Thurs and Sun

🚗 Take the A264 from East Grinstead towards Tunbridge Wells for 6 miles to a crossroads, and turn right to Hartfield on the B2026 for 1 mile. Turn left into an unmade lane just past Perryhill orchard. Private car park.

🛏 1 twin, 2 double, 1 four-poster, family accommodation available; all with bathroom/WC, TV, hair-dryer

◈ 2 dining-rooms, 2 lounges; conference facilities (max 12 people non-residential); fishing, golf, other sports nearby; babysitting

⊖ No wheelchair access; no children under 7; no dogs; no smoking

💳 Access, Amex, Visa

💷 Single occupancy of twin/double £40, double £40, twin/double £45, four-poster £50, family room from £80; deposit required. Set D £12.50

# The Pier at Harwich

THE QUAY, HARWICH, ESSEX CO12 3HH
TEL: HARWICH (0255) 241212   TELEX: 987083 LETALV G
FAX: (0206) 322752

*A duet of cheerful seafood restaurants with well-furnished and reasonably priced bedrooms attached. Go for the front rooms.*

Yet another Gerald Milsom venture (see Dedham Vale entry), and as much a maverick as the others. Luxury is not on the menu at this pair of restaurants and their half-dozen rooms, but comfort and value are dished out in generous quantities. You will eat well, too – informally in the ground-floor Ha'Penny Pier restaurant, a great favourite with families, or in the more peaceful though pricier restaurant above. The latter is more entertaining, with captain's wheel, navy blue carpet with the house anchor and fish motif, and railway posters. The long à la carte menu may consist of dressed crab, steamed plaice with fresh ginger, orange and spring onions, and apple and lemon cheesecake. Steak and chicken are also on offer.

There are more murals than windows on the harbour-facing wall, so why not stay the night and watch ships and ferries to-ing and fro-ing across the Stour and Orwell from your room? (Many guests, in fact, are

-The Pier-

bound to and from the North Sea ferry.) Colour schemes, pink with red for instance, are unconventional but rooms are tidy and homely, with crisp, patterned duvets and sparkling bathrooms – even a nautical touch or two.

◐ *Open all year, exc 25, 26 Dec*

↗ *On the quayside of Old Harwich. Private car park*

🛏 *6 double; all with bathroom/WC, TV, room service, hair-dryer*

◇ *2 restaurants, bar; sea fishing, watersports, golf, other sports nearby.*

⊖ *No wheelchair access; no dogs*

▭ *Access, Visa*

£ *Single occupancy of twin/double £45 to £60, twin/double £63 to £73. Cooked B £4; set L £12.50, D £16; alc L £18, D £20*

**HASSOP** DERBYSHIRE                                                   **MAP 4**

# Hassop Hall

HASSOP, NR BAKEWELL, DERBYSHIRE DE4 1NS
TEL: GREAT LONGSTONE (0629 87) 488   FAX: (0629 87) 577

*A fine country house in a lovely position.*

Surrounded by large and beautiful grounds, the hall itself has only five acres of gardens but guests are welcome to wander around the old estate. The ha-ha acts as the boundary in front of the house but the view is marvellous: rolling hills, mature trees and a tiny lake in the distance. There is very little to disturb you.

Inside, all is calmness and refined elegance. There's a room for every occasion and Hassop is often used for weddings, conferences, parties and private dinners. The rooms are adapted as required and all have grand proportions: high ceilings, long windows, decorated in excellent taste and style with antiques and fine pictures. The Blue sitting-room can either be intimately private or the no-smoking extension of the panelled bar. Dinner is taken in the double dining-room and is quite formal, with an unexceptional and awkwardly set out menu. About a third of the dishes carry an additional charge.

Bedrooms are huge and as well furnished as the rest of the house. You are encouraged to have breakfast (not included in the price) in your room and it's delivered and laid out on the table. It may be worth checking when you book if a function is planned during your stay.

◐ *Open all year, exc Xmas period; restaurant closed Sun eve*

↗ *2 miles north of Bakewell on the B6001. Private car park*

🛏 *8 twin/double, 2 four-poster, 2 family rooms; all with bathroom/ WC, TV, room service, hair-*

*dryer; no tea/coffee-making facilities in rooms*

◇ *3 restaurants, bar, lounge; conference facilities (max 60 people non-residential, 12 residential); tennis, croquet at hotel, other sports nearby.*

Wheelchair access to hotel
(2 steps), restaurant and WC
(M,F), no ground-floor bedrooms
but a lift

● No dogs in public rooms and in
bedrooms by arrangement; no
smoking in some public rooms

▭ Access, Amex, Diners, Visa

£ Single occupancy of twin/double
£59 to £89, twin/double £69 to
£99, four-poster £69 to £99,
family room £85 plus £10 for
each child. Continental B £6,
cooked B £9; set L £12, £13, D
£20, £24 (prices till end Mar
92) Special breaks available

---

**HASTINGLEIGH** KENT                                    **MAP 10**

# Woodman's Arms Auberge

HASSELL STREET, HASTINGLEIGH, ASHFORD, KENT TN25 5JE
TEL: ELMSTED (023 375) 250

*As the Guide went to press
this establishment closed.*

# Northleigh House

FIVE WAYS ROAD, HATTON, NR WARWICK, WARWICKSHIRE CV35 7HZ
TEL: WARWICK (0926) 484203

*A delightful and humorous hostess, and a stylish house set
amongst rich Warwickshire farmland.*

Sylvia's turn-of-the-century house is set back from the road and is
surrounded by farmland and a large flowering front garden. Sheep graze
in the small fields around the house; Sylvia has kept rare breeds of sheep
for some years. Two stone boars, retrieved from her childhood home,
stand on either side of the front door.

Inside, the house is relaxing and unfussy. Sylvia has designed each
bedroom in a restrained and subtle way. There's the Blue room with the
king-sized bed, a collection of books and a scallop border in a blue
bathroom. The Gold room has pictures of owls, an owl doorstop and rich
earthy-coloured fabrics. Sylvia is a self-confessed perfectionist, adjust-
ing pillows and towels as she moves through the rooms checking each
detail. She has slept in all the beds to check their comfort.

The sitting-room with wood panelling and a wood-burning stove ('I
can't use it as it sets off the fire alarms') is a laid-back room, with a lovely
collection of ornamental sheep on the mantelpiece. There are low seats
and several oil paintings by a favourite uncle on one wall, bookshelves on
another. The breakfast room is a relatively new addition to the house – on
each table is a toaster for hot toast. Sylvia's humour and enthusiasm for
welcoming guests to her house makes this a delightful place to stay.

◐ Open all year, exc 4 weeks
around Xmas

↗ Take the A4177 for 5 miles
north-west out of Warwick to
Five Ways Island, then turn left
towards Shrewley for ½ mile.
Private car park

🛏 1 single, 1 twin, 4 double; half
with bathroom/WC, half with
shower/WC; TV, room service,

fridge in all rooms

◈ Dining-room; lounge

⊖ No wheelchair access; no dogs in
public rooms; no smoking

▭ None accepted

£ Single £28, single occupancy of
twin/double from £28, twin/
double from £40. Supper trays
by arrangement

# Cockett's Hotel

MARKET PLACE, HAWES, NORTH YORKSHIRE DL8 3RD
TEL: WENSLEYDALE (0969) 667312

*Friendly hotel with simple rooms and a popular restaurant.*

Cockett's is right in the centre of Hawes village, a popular overnight stop
and a good base for walkers in this part of Yorkshire. This seventeenth-
century stone-built hotel is set back a few yards from the busy road so
there is plenty of space for cars just outside – is useful as the restaurant is
popular with non-residents and things can get a bit hectic, especially on
Tuesday (market day).

The food, which attracts people for miles around, is English and
French and includes rainbow trout, local lamb and duck, followed by a
range of Yorkshire cheeses. For hungry walkers the menu includes filling
puddings like ginger sponge. Because of the popularity of the restaurant
it's best to ask for one of the bedrooms at the back which are quieter and
have lovely views over Wensleydale. Bedrooms have simple modern
furniture, flowery wallpaper and are warm and comfortable, though
some are rather cramped. There's a small lounge downstairs, as well as a
bar for you to sit in after dinner either for planning the next day's walking
or for chatting to other guests.

- Open all year
- In the centre of Hawes, which is mid-way between Kendal and the A1, on the A684. On-street parking
- 2 twin, 4 double, 2 four-poster, some with bathroom/WC, some with shower/WC; TV, trouser press, baby-listening in all rooms; hair-dryer on request
- Restaurant, bar, lounge, drying room, library; fishing, riding nearby. Wheelchair access to hotel (1 step), restaurant and WC (M,F), 1 ground-floor bedroom, specially equipped for the disabled
- No children under 10; no dogs; no smoking in restaurant or bedrooms
- Visa
- Single occupancy of twin/double £25 to £30, twin/double £40 to £50, four-poster £60; deposit required. Set D £17; alc D £17

*You will find report forms at the back of the Guide – please use them!*

*All rooms have tea/coffee-making facilities unless we mention to the contrary.*

**HAWKRIDGE** SOMERSET                                    **MAP 8**

# Tarr Steps

HAWKRIDGE, DULVERTON, SOMERSET TA22 9PY
TEL: WINSFORD (064 385) 293

*Small hotel in the heart of Exmoor. Geared towards country
sporting types.*

Signs pointing to the Bronze Age Tarr Steps are nearly as common as
sheep on the many single track lanes that meander over this part of
Exmoor. Once you've twisted up the drive and entered the hallway that
stretches the length of this former Georgian rectory, you'll be in for a
thoroughly peaceful stay.

A whole valley stretches below the hotel, where many of the guests
have just spent a day in pursuit of game. In the half-panelled bar, the
Galileo thermometer or a multitude of springer spaniels might grab as
much attention as tales of yard-long trout. Also notable are the Jacobean-
style chairs. The window seat and fire compete as focal points, too. A
large lounge has another log fire, similarly spectacular views and plenty
of space to rest weary limbs on chintzy sofas. The olive green walled
dining-room is low-lit and almost formal, though jeans are acceptable.
Set dinners offer a short choice and might consist of devilled crab, then
guinea-fowl roasted with nuts and fruit, and ginger wine soufflé to
follow. Antique pine furniture and lacy bedspreads give the right
countrified look to bedrooms. Bathrooms are up-to-date. There are no
tea-making facilities and morning tea is a hefty £2.

◑ Closed Jan and Feb

↗ 7 miles from Dulverton. Leave
Dulverton on the road signposted
Hawkridge. Follow the road to
Hawkridge and then signs to
Tarr Steps and hotel. Private car
park

🛏 3 single, 4 twin, 4 double, 3
four-poster, all with bathroom/
WC, exc singles; room service,
hair-dryer in all rooms; no tea/
coffee-making facilities in rooms

◇ 2 restaurants, bar, lounge, drying
room; conference facilities (max
10 people residential); fishing
(Mar to Sept), clay pigeon and
rough shooting in grounds, other
sports nearby. Wheelchair access
to hotel, restaurant and WC
(M), 1 ground-floor room
specially equipped for the
disabled

⊖ No dogs in public rooms

▭ Access, Visa

£ Single £36, twin/double/four-
poster £72; deposit required. Set
L £16, D £20. Special breaks
available

---

*Prices are what you can expect to pay in 1992, except where specified to the
contrary. Many hoteliers tell us that these prices can be regarded only as
approximations.*

# Grizedale Lodge Hotel

GRIZEDALE, HAWKSHEAD, AMBLESIDE, CUMBRIA LA22 0QL
TEL: HAWKSHEAD (096 66) 532

*A comfortable, family-run hotel in quiet woodland.*

Don't let the address fool you. This smart, whitewashed former hunting lodge, tucked into Grizedale forest, seems to be a world away from the Hawkshead of clogged car parks and giant ice-cream cornets.

The hunting theme is evident in the décor, with stuffed deer heads and antlers bristling on the walls, and an abundance of hunting prints. Non-field sports enthusiasts will be consoled by the fact that there's a fair chance of encountering roe and red deer roaming free in the forest. The furnishing is cottagey, with low-slung bentwood armchairs and floral-patterned upholstery in the cosy lounge. This opens out on to the balcony where pretty white wrought-iron chairs provide an attractive spot for afternoon tea.

Bedrooms are comfortable rather than stylish and have solid old furniture. Margaret Lamb's traditional but inventive dinners have been justly acclaimed. Everything is home-made and the menu, which offers a reasonable choice, is changed every night: perhaps mushrooms in cream with garlic, grapefruit and peach sorbet, followed by Penrith peppered lamb, and warm chocolate fudge cake. Viennese coffee is served with chocolate mints and home-made fudge.

◑ Open all year, exc 2 Jan to mid-Feb

↗ 500 yards before reaching Hawkshead turn left (signposted Grizedale) and follow this road for 2 miles; the hotel is on the right. Private car park

🛏 2 twin, 3 double, I four-poster, I family room; some with bathroom/WC, most with shower/WC; TV in all rooms; hair-dryer on request

✧ Dining-room, bar, lounge, drying room; fishing, golf, water sports nearby. Wheelchair access to hotel (2 steps) and restaurant, I ground-floor bedroom

⊖ No children under 5; no dogs; smoking in bar and lounge only

▭ Access, Visa

£ Single occupancy of twin/double £38, twin/double £60, four-poster £68, family room £60; deposit required. Bar lunches available; set D £17. Special breaks available

---

*Congratulations to Cumbria – our number 1 county with 53 full entries in this year's Guide.*

# Highfield House

HAWKSHEAD HILL, AMBLESIDE, CUMBRIA LA22 0PN
TEL: HAWKSHEAD (096 66) 344; changes to (053 94) 36344 from Dec 91

*Friendly service and comfortable rooms in a splendid location and at a good price.*

Jim and Pauline Bennett get a lot of regular visitors to their traditional Lakeland-style villa perched high above the tourist-trap of Hawkshead. And no wonder. The staff are friendly, rooms are comfortable, the food is agreeable and the tariff very fair. All that, and the views are something to write home about as well.

It's a happy sort of house, full of plants, photographs and pictures. The lounge is a pleasant room in autumnal colours with chintzy curtains and rather too many comfy chairs grouped around a log fire. After dinner guests chat over coffee and mints or dip into *Wainwright* and plan the next day's walk. There are more muted colours in the dining-room, if you can tear your eyes away from the staggering views. Wines are lined up along a sideboard, a practice which alarmed one reader who was concerned about the corks drying out.

The short four-course menu may offer avocado mousse with prawns, followed by chicken breast with apricot and almond stuffing in a tarragon cream sauce. Cruelly, the Bennetts always encourage you to try more than one pudding, perhaps sticky toffee pudding and strawberry meringue gateau. All eleven rooms have pleasant décor – one reader was particularly pleased with room two, and with the fact that the ample supply of towels was changed daily.

◑ Open all year, exc Xmas

⤢ ¾ mile north of Hawkshead on the B5285 Coniston road, on the left-hand side. Private car park

⇌ 1 single, 3 twin, 5 double, 2 family rooms; most with bathroom/WC, some with shower/WC; TV, hair-dryer in all rooms; baby-listening on request

◇ Dining-room, bar, lounge, drying room; fishing, riding, water sports nearby.

⊜ No wheelchair access; no dogs in public rooms; no smoking in dining-room

▭ Access, Visa

£ Single £22 to £28, single occupancy of twin/double £24 to £33, twin/double £40 to £50, family room £57; deposit required. Set D £14. Special breaks available

---

*Hotels in our* Visitors' Book *towards the end of the* Guide *are additional hotels that may be worth a visit. Reports on these hotels are welcome.*

# Ivy House Hotel

MAIN STREET, HAWKSHEAD, NR AMBLESIDE, CUMBRIA LA22 0NS
TEL: HAWKSHEAD (096 66) 204

*Stridently coloured Georgian house with a memorable curving staircase.*

Its striking paintwork means that Ivy House stands out from the opposition – a leaf green façade grabs the attention when rivals are almost uniformly a testament to the durability of traditional Lakeland stone. Inside, a splendid curving staircase is equally eye-catching. It's difficult to know what to make of the group of child-sized padded chairs arranged around the sitting-room fire, as if in anticipation of an imminent visitation from the Seven Dwarfs. A collection of Christmas plates jazzes up the walls.

David and Jane Vaughan have an eye for the history of this one-time doctor's residence, and in the hall you'll find a photograph of Ivy House with a plus-foured proprietor, circa 1907. In the dining-room there are cottage-style chairs, ivy-green tablecloths and a collection of paperweights. The sideboard was made 'either by Mr Waring or Mr Gillow, we're not sure which'. Dinner, a four-course affair, is very traditional – cream of cauliflower and chive soup, perhaps, followed by steak and kidney pie. There's no choice until dessert, when from the eight on offer you might plump for gingerbread with rum butter and custard or chocolate mousse. Cheese and biscuits follow. Bedrooms are bright, but conventionally furnished, with those in the main house more attractive than those in the annexe rooms.

| | |
|---|---|
| ◑ Closed Nov to Feb | ⊖ No wheelchair access; no dogs in public rooms; no smoking in dining-room |
| ⮑ In the centre of the village. Private car park | |
| ⛵ 1 twin, 8 double, 2 family (some rooms in annexe); most with bathroom/WC, some with shower/WC | ▭ None accepted |
| | £ Single occupancy of twin/double £25 to £33, twin/double £50 to £65, suite £50 to £59; deposit required. Set D £8.50 |
| ◈ Dining-room, lounge, drying room; fishing, windsurfers for hire at hotel | |

---

*The text of entries is based on unsolicited reports sent in by readers and backed up by inspections. The factual details under the text are from questionnaires the* Guide *sends to all hotels that feature in the book.*

# Queen's Head Hotel

MAIN STREET, HAWKSHEAD, CUMBRIA LA22 0NS
TEL: HAWKSHEAD (096 66) 271; changes to (053 94) 36271 in late 1991

*Smashing old inn in touristy village.*

Good bar food makes the Queen's Head a popular choice in a village where you'll queue for a parking space even on a sunny April afternoon. It's a whitewashed seventeenth-century inn with black-painted Tudor-style additions. Inside, you'll find a real old English pub with oak beams, horse-brasses and a collection of plates that runs from Wedgwood through Christmas and cats to Charles and Di. It's a cosy, red velour realm with a snug for children and a line of toby jugs and tankards above the bar. Morbid curiosity will draw you to examine 'The Hawksid Girt Clog', a 20 inch by 16 inch monster dating from the early nineteenth century and made for the molecatcher John Watterson, so that he could continue to work after he contracted elephantiasis.

Bar meal options include crunchy garlic mushrooms, beef and mushroom pie and lots of open sandwiches. Puddings are designed to sabotage any diet – squidgy rum gateau, banana fool, hot apple cheesecake and a best-selling sticky toffee pudding. The slightly cramped oak-panelled dining-room is more sedate with ladderback chairs, chintzy curtains and lace-covered tables. Bedrooms are not large, but they're attractively decorated in modish prints and straightforward furniture.

◐ Open all year

🅿 The hotel is in the village square. Free parking at public car park

🛏 2 twin, 5 double, 1 four-poster, 2 family rooms, 1 with bathroom/WC, some with shower/WC, 2 public bathrooms; TV, hair-dryer, baby-listening in all rooms

◈ Restaurant, bar, lounge, drying room; fishing, golf, other sports nearby. Wheelchair access to restaurant only

⊖ No children under 8; no dogs; no smoking in restaurant or bedrooms

▭ Access, Amex, Visa

£ Single £26 to £36, single occupancy of twin/double £26 to £36, twin/double £42 to £51, four-poster £55 to £59, family room £70 to £74; deposit required. Set L from £4; alc D from £12

---

*If you make a booking using a credit card, and you find after cancelling that the full amount has been charged to your card, raise the matter with your credit card company. They will ask the hotelier to confirm whether the room was re-let, and to justify the charge they made.*

# Edwardian International

140 BATH ROAD, HAYES, MIDDLESEX UB3 5AW
TEL: 081-759 6311    TELEX: 23935
FAX: 081-759 4559

*Very comfortable, newly opened flagship hotel for the Edwardian Group.*

Seduced by the Edwardian Group's TV advertising? If you've got a plane to catch or a meeting to hold (and plenty of money – full rates make it one of Heathrow's most expensive hotels) visit its Heathrow flagship. Many people are doing so: there was a distinct buzz about the place when we inspected. And once inside you too will notice that this is a very different concept in airport hotels. Classical music greets you in the large marble-floored reception.

The public rooms are dominated by thick, strikingly coloured carpets, lending a sense of style and comfort. Henley's cocktail bar has strong-coloured Paisley-patterned furnishings, a stuccoed ceiling and repro-duction paintings; through it is the chandeliered, wood-panelled restaurant, serving an expensive à la carte menu in the evenings; or maybe you prefer to join the crowd for a cold buffet among murals, pillars and a sky-painted ceiling in the Brasserie. All the rooms surprise, none more so than the red wood-panelled Polo Bar where you can prop up the bar on saddles.

Blue and yellow handwoven carpets, bedspreads embossed with the hotel's crest, inlay and marquetry in the furniture, special cupboards for TVs and mini-bars, and marble bathrooms make bedrooms very plush, even when space is at a premium. But the hotel doesn't just look good – a professional welcome matches the quality of the hotel's furnishings. Expect a 30 per cent discount if it's your first stay or a weekend.

◑ Open all year

↗ On the main A4 Bath Road, on left-hand side heading towards London. Private car park

🛏 3 single, 260 twin, 175 double, 6 four-poster, 4 family rooms, 11 suites; all with bathroom/WC, TV, room service, hair-dryer, trouser press, mini-bar

◈ 2 restaurants, 2 bars, lounge; conference facilities (max 400 people residential), all air-conditioned; sauna/solarium, heated swimming-pool, gym at hotel. Wheelchair access to hotel, restaurants and WC (M,F), 81 ground-floor bedrooms

⬤ None

▤ Access, Amex, Diners, Visa

£ Single £153 to £184, twin/double £184 to £215, suite £434. Cooked B £10, continental B £8; set L £24.50, D £30, alc L, D from £35 (prices till end 91)

---

*See page 787 for other hotels worthy of inclusion in our* Visitors' Book.

**HAYLING ISLAND** HAMPSHIRE                                              **MAP 9**

# Cockle Warren Cottage

36 SEAFRONT, HAYLING ISLAND, HAMPSHIRE PO11 9HL
TEL: HAYLING ISLAND (0705) 464961

*Real effort and enthusiasm shown by a young couple in a small, individually run 'cottage hotel'.*

It's difficult to imagine on a bleak day who would voluntarily visit Hayling Island's seaside. It's got a steeply shelving shingle beach, the land around is mostly scrub, the shops with down-market resort offerings: amusements, bingo, fish and chips, fishing tackle.

David and Diane Skelton bought a plot of land here in 1980 and built a red and white brick cottage, now brought to life by canary yellow doors and a pretty garden. Later, a smart leafy conservatory was added, with chessboard tiled floor and five grey marble-topped tables. This overlooks an out-of-proportion swimming-pool, making up somewhat for the rather dull suburban-feeling living-room. The Skeltons like to think of the conservatory as a French café. Diane does all the cooking (for residents only), tailoring the number of courses to their individual appetites, while David puts his feet up waiting for a diner to press one of the tableside brass push-button bells for service (an ingenious d-i-y system devised by himself). Bedrooms are appropriately floral and cottagey, although two have four-posters. Tea on arrival and first thing in the morning, madeira and chocolates, as well as a host of other surprises, are unusual for so small a place.

◑ Open all year

⤴ From A3/M27 to Havant, go over bridge to Hayling Island, south to seafront, turn left ½ mile along front. Private car park

🛏 1 twin, 2 double, 2 four-poster, 1 annexe room; all with shower/WC, TV, room service, hairdryer, trouser press, babylistening; no tea/coffee-making facilities in rooms

◇ Restaurant, lounge, caféconservatory, heated swimming-pool (spring to autumn) at hotel, other sports nearby

⊖ No wheelchair access; no children under 7 (exc babies); no dogs; no smoking in lower lounge

▭ Access, Visa

£ Single occupancy of twin/double £35 to £50, twin/double £48 to £64, four-poster £64 to £78, annexe room £60 to £64; deposit required. Set D £23.50. Special breaks available

---

*If you are intending to make a lot of phone calls from your room, always check what the hotel is going to charge you per unit. You may be so horrified that you'll prefer to walk to the nearest phone box. Why let them get away with excessive charges?*

# The Bel Alp House

HAYTOR, NR BOVEY TRACEY, DEVON TQ13 9XX
TEL: HAYTOR (0364) 661217 FAX: (0364) 661292

*Gracious and immaculate country house near Dartmoor with kind hosts and a refined atmosphere.*

Deep in Devon and not far from Dartmoor, the lane leading to Bel Alp House passes several fancy dwellings almost hidden behind gates and pruned shrubbery. Roger and Sarah Curnock's stucco Edwardian house faces out over ravishing and unblemished hedged fields towards Torbay. Their hospitality is personal and attentive. The dining-room now has an extension and English dinner party cooking prevails on the five-course menu.

Graceful arches separate the public rooms. Harmonious colour schemes of greens and ochres, a profusion of plants, open fires, sofas and easy chairs you can easily doze off in, give warmth; antiques and family portraits abound. There are antiques in bedrooms as well, plus wild-flower prints, but room character is dictated more by vibrant chintz fabrics on crown or half-tester canopies, curtains and bedspreads. Double beds are king-sized as are two Victorian bathtubs that stand on marble plinths.

◑ Closed Dec to Feb

↗ 2½ miles west of Bovey Tracey off the B3387. Private car park

🛏 5 twin, 4 double; all with bathroom/WC, exc 1 double with shower/WC; TV, room service, hair-dryer, baby-listening in all rooms

✠ Dining-room, 2 lounges, games room, drying room; croquet, table tennis at hotel, other sports nearby. Wheelchair access to hotel (3 steps), dining-room and WC (M,F), 2 ground-floor bedrooms, lift

⊖ No dogs in public rooms; no smoking in dining-room and bedrooms

▭ Access, Visa

£ Single occupancy of twin/double £69 to £84, twin/double £126 to £144; deposit required. Set D £33. Special breaks available

---

*See the inside front cover for a brief explanation of how to use the* Guide.

---

*Report forms are at the back of the book; write a letter if you prefer.*

**HEACHAM** NORFOLK                                               **MAP 7**

# Holly Lodge

HEACHAM, NR KING'S LYNN, NORFOLK PE31 7HY
TEL: HEACHAM (0485) 70790

*An unusual and stylish home to stay at while visiting the north
Norfolk coast.*

The flint, stone and brick exterior of this listed Elizabethan house, with
decorative chimneys and gingerbread gables, sports no holly. It was once
Holy Lodge, having served as a dormitory for visiting monks and friars
during the Reformation. 'People sleep well here,' says Lesley Piper, the
owner.

Inside, you'll find a stylish synthesis of antiques, handsome old
portraits, modern prints and bold, often brightly coloured walls. There
are two lounges, each with open fire and one with television. The pea-
green and salmon dining-room with a mix of Victorian chairs manages to
balance refinement with informality. Dinners are carefully cooked and
draw on modern as well as traditional tastes. In winter, amongst the
several choices on the set menu, was a salad of grilled goats' cheese with
walnuts and apple, and fillet steak with spiced green peppercorns, brandy
and cream, a gratin of oranges and lime mousse.

New and old blend well in the excellent bedrooms, too. Most are very
spacious, a few have lovely antique beds, all at least some evidence of the
distant past such as a brick and timber wall or old fireplace. The twin we
complained about last year as being 'dull' is now a cheery bright yellow.
Bathrooms are simple.

◑ *Closed Jan, Feb; restaurant
closed Sun eve*

🔁 *From King's Lynn turn left off the
A149 into Heacham village at
the 'Norfolk Lavender' sign.
Holly Lodge is 900 yards down
the road on the right-hand side.
Private car park*

🛏 *1 twin, 3 double, 2 four-poster;
all with bathroom/WC, exc 1
double with shower/WC; room
service, hair-dryer in all rooms;
no tea/coffee-making facilities*

◈ *Restaurant, bar, lounge; golf,
tennis, other sports nearby.
Wheelchair access to restaurant
and WC only*

⊖ *No children under 5; no dogs; no
smoking in bedrooms*

▭ *Access, Visa*

💷 *Single occupancy of twin/double
£55, twin/double/four-poster
£85; deposit required. Set D
£19.50; alc D £22.50*

---

*Are you aware of your rights as a consumer when you book into an hotel?
Check them out on page 13.*

# Headlam Hall

HEADLAM, NR GAINFORD, DARLINGTON, CO DURHAM DL2 3HA
TEL: DARLINGTON (0325) 730238   FAX: (0325) 730790

*Good-value country-house hotel – cosy enough to enjoy if the weather turns nasty.*

Standing on the edge of a small, isolated village in rolling farmland outside Darlington, Headlam Hall can look a little foreboding at first. You drive in past the rows of stables round to the heavy entrance door at the back, overshadowed by the three-storey grey stone walls of the Jacobean country house. Once inside, the atmosphere is one of imposing solidity – flat-stoned carpeted passageways, lined with heavy oak antiques; massive stone pillars and an impressive carved fireplace.

The welcome is warm: a blazing log fire heats the wood-panelled hall and there are groups of high-backed chairs and chesterfield sofas to relax in, and a piano at one end. The lounge is all in sugary green, from the panelled walls to the ceiling. The seating here is more formal than comfortable but the windows open on to the lawns and immaculately trimmed beech and yew hedges which run down to the small stream at the bottom of the garden – beyond is open countryside. At the other end of the house, past the tiny red bar and the small reception desk tucked away near the stairs, is the dining-room. It's arranged in three parts: a conservatory looking on to the gardens, a breakfast room in a dark patterned wallpaper and the dining-room proper – just right for romantic evenings *à deux*.

Upstairs, the bedrooms vary from cavernous suites in sombre colours with four-poster beds and antiques, to smaller rooms with a lighter touch. There are some splendid bathrooms. Two words of warning – cooking smells may pervade the Green Room (which is above the kitchens) and some of the dividing walls between the rooms allow through noise from your neighbours rather too easily.

○ Open all year

◪ The Hall is signposted from the A67, 1½ miles north of Gainford. Private car park

🛏 7 twin, 5 double, 5 four-poster, 3 suites, 5 annexe rooms; all with bathroom/WC exc 2 twin rooms with shower/WC; TV, hair-dryer, baby-listening in all rooms, trouser press in some rooms

◈ 3 restaurants, bar, lounge, games room, conservatory; conference facilities (max 50 people non-residential, 30 residential); fishing, tennis, croquet, sauna/solarium, heated pool, gym at hotel. Wheelchair access to hotel and restaurant, 3 ground-floor bedrooms

⊖ No dogs in bedrooms; no smoking, exc in some public rooms

▭ Access, Amex, Visa

£ Single occupancy of twin/double £49, twin/double £61, four-poster £64, suite from £75; deposit required. Set L £10, D £14; alc D £17.50. Special breaks available

**HELFORD** CORNWALL                                    **MAP 8**

# Riverside

HELFORD, NR HELSTON, CORNWALL TR12 6JU
TEL: MANACCAN (032 623) 443   FAX: (032 623) 443

*A cosmopolitan restaurant-with-rooms in an outlying, unspoilt village. Tailor-made for walkers and gourmets.*

This tiny gem of a whitewashed village sits at the end of a long slender lane and spans a tidal creek.

Coming to the Darrells' restaurant-with-rooms, made up of four hillside cottages on various levels, is a good way to appreciate unspoilt Cornwall, with the bonus that you will also eat well. From much of the cosy, beamed restaurant you can take in the splendours of the terrace garden, tranquil village scene and creek. The atmosphere is decidedly cosmopolitan with a daily-changing, fixed-price menu that leans towards French provincial cooking, and good wines from a wide-ranging, reasonably priced list. David Rayner does good things with the freshest of fish and seafood, and Susie Darrell is no mean pastry chef. Given good weather, a drink on one of the four terraces surrounded by exotic tropical flora should set you up for such self-indulgence. If it is raining, you and non-resident diners can sit in the small, first-floor, cane-furnished lounge. To one side is a family room, to the other a small double. As with bedrooms in outside cottages, furniture is a mix of antique and modern. Furnishings are cool and fairly simple and cosiness rather than space is the rule. All rooms have radios and home-made shortbread, but no phones. Oddly for a food-oriented place, only continental breakfast is served, but then the croissants are home-made.

◑ Closed late Nov to early Feb

🅿 In Helford, the hotel car park is opposite the public car park

🛏 5 twin/double, 1 family room; all with bathroom/WC, TV, room service, hair-dryer, trouser press, mini-bar

◈ Restaurant, bar, lounge, drying room; fishing , golf, other sports nearby. Wheelchair access to hotel and restaurant, 5 ground-floor bedrooms

⊖ No children under 12 at dinner; no dogs

▭ None accepted

£ Twin/double £75 to £95, family room £110; deposit required. Cooked B £4.50; set D £28 (prices till Feb 92)

---

*We mention those hotels that don't accept dogs; guide dogs, however, are almost always an exception. Telephone ahead to make sure!*

# Hernes

GREYS ROAD, HENLEY-ON-THAMES, OXFORDSHIRE RG9 4NT
TEL: HENLEY-ON-THAMES (0491) 573245

*All that's good about a Wolsey Lodge: a comfortable, much-loved, interesting family home and genial hosts.*

Hernes has been home to the Ovey family for five generations and a sense of family history is rapidly conveyed to guests at this 400-acre estate a couple of miles outside the famous Thames valley town. Gillian Ovey describes her philosophy by saying: 'I don't want to run a hotel, I want guests who feel that they're coming to my house to enjoy it.' Readers agree that Gillian is very caring, happy to chat or to leave you to your own devices, and is full of advice on where to go and what to see.

The food, eaten communally with the Oveys surrounded by ancestral portraits has been particularly praised. If she's not cooking that night, or if you fancy eating out, Gillian will offer suggestions and book tables. Richard is Richard Ovey the seventh and will readily tell various versions of a chequered family history. Although the Oveys aren't licensed to sell alcohol Richard sometimes opens a bottle of wine for dinner, or you can bring your own.

The billiards room is a great place to relax. Despite its cavernous dimensions there is an intimate atmosphere around the wood stove in winter; in summer you can admire the view. On your way up the polished wooden staircase you can gaze at rowing photos of the Ovey succession at Eton. The guest rooms have a motley and enjoyable collection of furniture.

◑ Open all year, exc mid-Dec to mid-Jan

⤴ Telephone for directions. Private car park

🛏 1 twin, 1 double, 1 four-poster; 2 with bathroom/WC, 1 with shower/WC; hair-dryer on request

◈ Dining-room, lounge/hall, TV room, billiards room, drying room; conference facilities (max 10 people residential); croquet,

table tennis, outdoor heated pool (summer only) at hotel, other sports nearby

⊖ No wheelchair access; no children under 13; no dogs; no smoking

▭ None accepted

£ Single occupancy of twin/double £35 to £53, twin/double £60 to £65, four-poster £70; deposit required. Set D £18 to £20. Special breaks available

---

🍂    *This denotes that the hotel is in an exceptionally peaceful situation where you can be assured of a restful stay.*

# The Red Lion

HART STREET/RIVERSIDE, HENLEY-ON-THAMES, OXFORDSHIRE RG9 2AR
TEL: HENLEY-ON-THAMES (0491) 572161   FAX: (0491) 410039

*A solid, friendly hotel overlooking this famous stretch of the River Thames.*

An ivy-covered, red-brick fixture of the Henley scene, the Red Lion is nearing the end of a much-needed refurbishment undertaken by the new owners. The hotel is in a prime position opposite the Leander Club and just upstream from the finish of the regatta course, so if you wish to stay during Henley Regatta week (end of June/beginning of July) you will need to book a year in advance. Early-morning traffic may disturb you.

The Red Lion is thought to have been built in 1531, although there have been plenty of alterations and additions since then. The fourteenth-century Chantry Cottage, to one side of the original courtyard (now a car park), is used as staff accommodation. Décor in the bedrooms not yet reached by the refurbishment programme can be a colourful shock. New rooms are more muted but a definite improvement, with newly tiled bathrooms, floral bedcovers and curtains, and plain white or cream walls.

The service is excellent. The barman knows your name and room number before you've ordered and makes this seem a matter of course rather than anything unusual. Similarly, dinner in the Regency-style restaurant is served with care and a pleasant, though not aggressive, attentiveness by young staff. Pictures on the way up the creaking staircase tell tales of famous visitors of the coaching-inn past. A favourite recalls the Prince Regent's (soon to be George IV) consumption of 14 of the mutton chops for which the then cook, Mrs Dixon, was famous.

◐ Open all year

▨ Overlooks Henley Bridge and the River Thames. Private car park

🛏 6 single, 10 twin, 8 double, 1 four-poster, 1 family room; all with bathroom/WC (exc 3 singles), TV, room service; hair-dryer in 11 rooms

◈ Dining-room, 2 bars, lounge; conference facilities (max 100 people non-residential, 20 residential); golf, fishing, other sports nearby; babysitting.

Wheelchair access to dining-room only (1 step, through back entrance)

⊖ No dogs

▤ Access, Amex, Visa

£ Single £43 to £70, single occupancy of twin/double £70, twin/double £83 to £95, four-poster £95, family room £110. Cooked B £7.50, continental B £5; set L £19.50, D £22 (prices till May 92). Special breaks available

*Prices are quoted* per room *rather than* per person.

# Cleavers Lyng

CHURCH ROAD, HERSTMONCEUX, HAILSHAM, EAST SUSSEX BN27 1QJ
TEL: HERSTMONCEUX (0323) 833131

*A simple, cheap, well-run hotel in an old building occupying a rural position.*

Mother-and-son team Marylin and Neil Holden, who've lived here for over 30 years and have had paying guests for two-thirds of that time, reckon, unsurely, the name means something like 'a woodcutter's house on a hill rising from a marsh'. Down the bottom of a quiet, rural no-through road leading to the village church and Herstmonceux Castle and ending up in a farmyard stands this part tile-hung, part grey- and red-brick house dating from 1580. From its rear windows you look across the lawn and neat arrangements of white wrought-iron chairs out over the Pevensey Levels to the South Downs in the distance.

The main entrance takes you into the breakfast/dining-room which is low-ceilinged, beamed and with groups of plain wooden tables and chairs. At the back is a small bar and off it is a small TV lounge with comfy seating and magazines. Peace at breakfast – a limited choice on a short typed menu, capably cooked and presented – is disturbed by early risers navigating between tables with heavy loads en route from bedroom to car.

Evening meals take a similar approach: a limited choice of straightforward fare (prawn cocktail, pork in cider sauce) from a typed menu which changes every night. The bedrooms are up a steep flight of narrow stairs. Basic but cosy, they have old wooden furniture, a washbasin, a slab of soap, and a coarse towel. None is *en suite*; of the four bathrooms, two have shower and two bath; one gripe – a lack of hot water in the morning when we visited.

- Closed Xmas and New Year
- 2 miles off the A271 towards Herstmonceux church. Private car park
- 2 single, 4 twin, 2 double; 4 public bathrooms
- Dining-room, bar, lounge, TV room; conference facilities
- (max 8 people residential); fishing, golf, other sports nearby
- No wheelchair access
- None accepted
- Single £19, single occupancy of twin/double £23, twin/double £37. Set L £9, D £10; alc L £12.50

---

*Prices are what you can expect to pay in 1992, except where specified to the contrary. Many hoteliers tell us that these prices can be regarded only as approximations.*

**HERTFORD** HERTFORDSHIRE      **MAP 10**

# The Hall House

BROADOAK END, OFF BRAMFIELD ROAD, HERTFORD, HERTFORDSHIRE
SG14 2JA
TEL: HERTFORD (0992) 582807

*A comfortable, modern Wolsey Lodge set in secluded woodland
with caring, attentive hosts.*

Even with directions it's easy to whizz past a couple of times before
spotting the turning down to Broadoak End: a small cluster of buildings,
almost a hamlet in otherwise suburban Hertfordshire. Olive and Tim
Whiting are jovial, attentive hosts who take great pride in their house,
which is modern but rebuilt around fifteenth-century timbers.

There are only three rooms, the most attractive being in the main
house, whilst the other two, decked out in various shades of peach, are on
the far side of the swimming-pool in a bungalow annexe. Newly refurbished, with royal blue a favourite colour (for floors and silk flower
arrangements) and pot-pourri on shelves and sideboards, Hall House
can feel if anything, a little too perfect, leaving you, in the lounge in
particular, almost afraid to sit for fear of spoiling the effect.

Advance notice for vegetarian meals or other special requirements
makes life easier for all concerned. Bring your own drinks to have with
dinner as Hall House is not licensed.

◑ Open all year, exc 3 days at
Xmas

🡵 On the right-hand side,
¼ mile along the Bramfield
road, off the A119 Stevenage
road out of Hertford. Private car
park

🛏 3 double (2 in cottage annexe);
all with bathroom/WC, TV, hair-
dryer, trouser press

◈ Dining-room, lounge,

conservatory; conference
facilities (max 8 people); heated
outdoor swimming-pool (May to
Sept), other sports nearby

⊖ No wheelchair access; no
children under 14; no dogs; no
smoking

▭ Access, Visa

£ Single occupancy of double £45,
twin/double £60; deposit
required. Set D £18

**HIGHER BURWARDSLEY** CHESHIRE      **MAP 4**

# The Pheasant Inn

HIGHER BURWARDSLEY, TATTENHALL, CHESHIRE CH3 9PF
TEL: TATTENHALL (0829) 70434   FAX: (0829) 71097

*Fledgling hotel emerging from a traditional inn.*

David Greenhaugh's rural free house emerges transformed from pub to
hotel after a programme of renovation, refurbishment and revamping.

It's a seventeenth-century whitewashed and half-timbered, low-beamed building in a peaceful location; David is a genial host.

Two themes predominate: nautical touches reflect David's naval background; and the hunting theme gives rise to the usual surfeit of feather and fur and other 'sporting' memorabilia. Also featured are photos of David's shaggy Highland cattle – the 'Wha daur meddle wi' me' beasts, beloved of Scottish postcard vendors. You'll find Highland cattle (photos) displayed in the tartan-carpeted bistro dining-room, Highland beef on the menu, and the real thing alive and kicking in the pasture above the car park. A pleasant conservatory is part of the recent revamping. Bedrooms, most of which are in a converted sandstone barn, are stylish but cosy with functional built-in furniture and good bathrooms.

◐ Open all year

⤢ From A41 follow signposts for Tattenhall. From village follow signposts to Burwardsley. At top of hill bear left at the post office. Inn is at top of hill on left. Private car park

🛏 3 twin, 5 double; all with bathroom/WC, TV, hair-dryer, mini-bar

◈ Restaurant, bar, lounge, conservatory; fishing, golf, other sports nearby

⊖ No wheelchair access; no dogs

▭ Access, Amex, Diners, Visa

£ Single occupancy of twin/double £40, twin/double £50; deposit required. Alc L £8, D £15; bar snacks (prices till end 91). Special breaks available

---

**HINTLESHAM** SUFFOLK                                     **MAP 7**

# Hintlesham Hall

HINTLESHAM, IPSWICH, SUFFOLK IP8 3NS
TEL: HINTLESHAM (047 387) 334   FAX: (047 387) 463

*Plush, aristocratic country-house hotel now on a steady course. A favourite with foreign tourists and business clients alike.*

One of Suffolk's grandest houses, but a hotel with a varied career, Hintlesham Hall became famous during the 1970s when Robert Carrier ran it as a restaurant. The Watsons brought it in 1984 and opened four luxurious, designer-perfect bedrooms and capacity increased thereafter. New owners took over in June 1990, but general manager Tim Sunderland, who remained throughout the eighties, is still in command, and he and his team make sure that all guests – be they visiting Americans or business delegates up from London – are made to feel at ease in these grand and beautiful surroundings.

You can see the custard-coloured pile from the road, but shaved lawns and tall trees buffer it from passing traffic. Behind the stunning Georgian façade is a much older building, in part dating from the fifteenth century, but most of the hall has a Georgian grace with wide corridors and large windows. Unlike many stately homes converted into pleasure (or work) palaces, Hintlesham has class and plenty of variety. Furniture is mostly antique and soft furnishings are top quality. Some public rooms are intensely masculine, others demure and ladylike, and yet others in between – but all are similarly well designed. Sofas and armchairs promote the pursuit of unwinding. So, too, do the bedrooms, which, like the public rooms, are neither contrived nor crass. The price of dinners is sobering, though it includes canapés and service. Dishes such as duck liver pâté with truffles and Cumberland sauce, or calves' liver with sweet garlic, shallot and mushrooms in port sauce, tell of chef Alan Ford's accomplishments. Service is polished. Hintlesham Hall now has a new 18-hole golf course.

◐ Open all year; restaurant closed Sat lunch

➘ 4 miles west of Ipswich on the A1071 to Sudbury. Private car park

⇌ 1 single, 25 twin/double, 2 four-poster, 5 suites; all with bathroom/WC, TV, room service, hair-dryer, mini-bar

◈ 3 restaurants, bar, 2 lounges, games room, laundry service, library; conference facilities (max 100 people non-residential, 33 residential); fishing, golf, tennis at hotel; babysitting. Wheelchair access to restaurant (1 step) and WC (unisex) only

⊖ No children under 12 in restaurant; no dogs; no pipes or cigars in bedrooms

▭ Access, Amex, Diners, Visa

£ Single £85, single occupancy of twin/double £85 to £105, twin/double £97 to £160, four-poster £160, suites £178 to £300; deposit required. Cooked B £6.50; set L £18.50, D £29.50/£37.50 (prices till Mar 92). Special breaks available

---

**HINTON CHARTERHOUSE** AVON                                    **MAP 9**

# Green Lane House

1 GREEN LANE, HINTON CHARTERHOUSE, BATH, AVON BA3 6BL
TEL: LIMPLEY STOKE (0225) 723631

*Cosy, nicely furnished old cottage in a conservation village six miles from Bath.*

The eighteenth-century, browny-grey stone cottage sits on a little by-road just away from the centre of this conservation village. Bath is not far away and doubtless the focus of attention for many guests who stay with John and Lucille Baxter.

It shouldn't take you long to get your bearings once John (with a big smile) has opened the handsome elm door; to the right is the cosy lounge, to the left the breakfast room. The former comes complete with beamed fireplace (which the Baxters discovered), ginger jar and lots of Chinese rosewood furniture. It also has a television since the bedrooms don't. Rosewood furniture also sits in the small breakfast room (no dinner is served but restaurant advice supplied).

There are only four bedrooms but lots of variety, from the daffodil yellow double (room two), to the lilac *en suite* twin (room one). Room three has a small sitting area with more Chinese furniture and ginger jar lamp. All the bedrooms are simply but carefully furnished with fresh duvets and padded velveteen headboards.

| | | | |
|---|---|---|---|
| ◑ | *Closed Dec, Jan* | ⊖ | *No wheelchair access; no dogs; no smoking in breakfast room* |
| ⤴ | *Hinton Charterhouse is on the A36, approx 6 miles south-east of Bath. Turn left at Rose and Crown pub. Private car park* | ▭ | *Access, Visa* |
| | | £ | *Single occupancy of twin/double £24 to £35, twin/double £36 to £47; deposit required. Packed lunches available. Special breaks available* |
| 🛏 | *2 twin, 2 double; 2 with shower/ WC, 1 public bathroom; hair-dryer, baby-listening on request* | | |
| ◈ | *Breakfast room, lounge; golf, fishing, other sports nearby; babysitting* | | |

# Homewood Park

HINTON CHARTERHOUSE, BATH, AVON BA3 6BB
TEL: BATH (0225) 723731    FAX: (0225) 723820

*Suave country-house hotel not far from Bath, now in sensitive and capable new hands.*

Though set in a goodly patch of sloping lawns, this is still a rather ugly stone mansion with various extensions, but its character comes alive as soon as you step inside. Sleek surfaces and polished antiques alternate with plush but also interesting fabrics. The place has *personality*.

The rectangular drawing-room, with just the right number of beautifully upholstered sofas and armchairs, has a Chinese theme and a rotating collection of bronze sculptures. It's a good place for afternoon tea, especially if you bag the alcove. Framed Hermès scarves hang about the low-lit bar, which also has an open fire. The peachy restaurant is formally set and nouvelle-style dinners show new delicacy and invention. And as one reader reports: 'The service was impeccable, the staff extremely helpful and charming.'

Attention to both comfort and aesthetics make bedrooms as romantic as they are practical. Colour schemes, often two-tone, rely on soft pastel. Generous fabrics are draped at windows or over beds. There is solid new furniture along with the odd antique, original paintings on the walls and Persian rugs on carpets. Bathrooms are uniformly excellent and inviting, with embossed tiles, stencilled decoration and romantic lighting.

| | | | |
|---|---|---|---|
| ◑ | *Open all year* | 🛏 | *8 twin, 7 double; all with bathroom/WC, TV, room service, hair-dryer, baby-listening* |
| ⤴ | *Hinton Charterhouse is on the A36, approx 6 miles south-east of Bath. Private car park* | | |
| | | ◈ | *2 restaurants, bar, lounge;* |

-Homewood Park-

conference facilities (max 15 people residential); tennis at hotel, golf, riding nearby. Wheelchair access to hotel, restaurant and WC (unisex), 2 ground-floor bedrooms

 No dogs; no smoking in restaurants

Access, Amex, Diners, Visa

Single occupancy of twin/double £88, twin/double £99 to £138; deposit required. Cooked B £4 to £7.50; alc L £25, D £39 (prices till Apr 92)

---

**HOLDENBY** NORTHAMPTONSHIRE              **MAP 6**

# Lynton House

HOLDENBY, NORTHAMPTONSHIRE NN6 8DJ
TEL: NORTHAMPTON (0604) 770777

*Good Italian food is served and comfortable bedrooms are provided in a house surrounded by lovely gardens, and with fine views.*

Situated on the brow of a ridge, Lynton House has superb views over the Northamptonshire countryside. The house, just outside the pretty village of Holdenby, was reputedly once the home of Queen Victoria's chaplain and is surrounded by trees and a lovely garden. It's really a restaurant-with-rooms and the reasonable prices have made it popular in the area for lunches and evenings meals.

The long light restaurant with the large bay window and a conservatory extension has views on to the garden, and is pretty in soft pinks and reds. Carlo Bertozzi and his wife Carol came here about six years ago. At the time, on setting up the venture, they didn't want to have to pay vast sums on interior décor so they chose good-quality contract furnishings: wood with pink upholstery. These have stood the test of time, creating an attractive restaurant and a cosy bar. The wide hallway has a long pine bench and tiled floor and lots of black and white photographs.

The pale-coloured bedrooms, whilst by no means striking, have all mod cons and are comfortable; a couple have space for a sofa. The extensive four-course Italian menu is reasonably priced.

◑ *Open all year, exc Xmas, one week in spring and two weeks in the summer*

🔁 *The hotel is just to the east of Holdenby on the East Haddon to Church Brampton road. Private car park*

🛏 *2 single, I twin, 2 double, all with shower/WC, TV, room service, hair-dryer, trouser press; baby-listening*

◈ *Restaurant, bar, lounge,*

*conservatory; conference facilities (max 15 people non-residential); golf, tennis, riding nearby*

⊖ *No wheelchair access; no children under 6; no dogs; no cigars or pipes in restaurant*

▭ *Access, Visa*

£ *Single £62, single occupancy of twin/double £62, twin/double £75. Set L £14, D £20 (prices till Dec 91)*

---

**HOLMFIELD** WEST YORKSHIRE                           **MAP 4**

# Holdsworth House

HOLDSWORTH, HOLMFIELD, HALIFAX, WEST YORKSHIRE HX2 9TG
TEL: HALIFAX (0422) 240024    TELEX: 51574 HOLHSE G
FAX: (0422) 245174

*A Grade-II-listed building which is efficiently run without losing the feel of a family house.*

You would never believe this hotel has forty bedrooms – it doesn't look big enough. Built in 1633, this lovely house has a gabled front, mullioned windows and a heavy, studded front door set in a stone porch. Other bits have been added sensitively to the back. The Pearson family turned the house into an hotel over twenty years ago and it is still owned by them, although they have brought in management and staff. The bedrooms are all different and have been exceptionally well designed–comfortable but not over the top.

The public rooms, too, give visitors plenty of options. There is a large barrel-vaulted bar/sitting-room in addition to numerous other cosy alcoves dotted around the house. The dining-rooms/restaurant consist of three inter-connecting rooms; the atmosphere in here is enhanced by the lovely panelling, beamed ceilings and an array of china. The restaurant's reputation is spreading. One reader who stayed here with a party of eleven was well-pleased with the food but went further: 'Wine excellent. Welcome first-rate. Room comfortable. I had a slight stroke here and their care of me till I could leave was exemplary – the nicest place to be ill in.'

◑ Open all year, exc 25, 26 Dec; restaurant closed Sat and Sun lunch

↗ From Halifax, take the A629 towards Keighley. After 1½ miles turn right into Shay Lane, signposted Holmfield. The house is 1 mile on the right. Private car park

🛏 20 single, 2 twin, 9 double, 1 four-poster, 3 half-tester, 5 suites; all with bathroom/WC, exc 2 singles with shower/WC; TV, room service (limited), hair-dryer, mini-bar, baby-listening in all rooms; trouser press on request

◈ Restaurant, 2 bars, 2 lounges, breakfast room, drying facilities; conference facilities (max 94 people non-residential, 40 residential); golf, other sports nearby. Wheelchair access to hotel, restaurant and WC, 21 ground-floor bedrooms, 2 specially equipped for the disabled

⊝ No pipes or cigars in restaurant

▭ Access, Amex, Diners, Visa

💷 Single £74, twin/double/four-poster/half-tester £87, suite £100. Alc L, D £27 (prices till Mar 92). Special breaks available

---

**HOLYWELL** CAMBRIDGESHIRE                                      **MAP 7**

# The Old Ferry Boat Inn

HOLYWELL, ST IVES, CAMBRIDGESHIRE PE17 3TG
TEL: ST IVES (0480) 63227

*Classic riverside pub from the outside, less quaint inside but well-furnished. Newly decorated bedrooms have gone romantic.*

This is a classic riverside pub with thatched and tile roof that's listed in the *Guinness Book of Records* as the oldest in England. Since last year, bedrooms have gone ultra-feminine with modern fabrics, often ruched at the windows, pretty-pretty wallpaper trimmed with borders and new pine furniture. They are still the same, smallish size but they're well maintained, with bathrooms which are equipped with power showers.

The pub, meanwhile, which sits with its many picnic tables on the River Ouse, remains as before. One low-ceilinged, L-shaped bar is large but divided into cosy sitting areas and is furnished with tapestry-covered benches and wheelback and Windsor chairs. Behind this is Juliet's Restaurant, open at weekends only, named after the resident ghost. Bar snacks, of no particular merit, are always available. Weekends are busy times, especially in good weather when the Ferry Boat really sparkles. The conference room is being promoted so the atmosphere changes mid-week. More reports, please.

◐ Open all year

⤢ Near St Ives. Follow signs to Needingworth and then signs for Holywell and the inn. Private car park

🛏 1 twin, 4 double, 2 four-poster; all with shower/WC, four-posters with bathroom/WC; TV in all rooms

◈ Restaurant, air-conditioned bar; conference facilities (max 60

people non-residential, 7 residential); fishing, golf, other sports nearby. Wheelchair access to inn and restaurant only

⊖ No dogs

▭ Access, Amex, Visa

£ Single occupancy of twin/double £40, twin/double £50, four-poster £68; deposit required. Alc D £22.50; bar snacks. Special breaks available

---

**HOPESAY** SHROPSHIRE                                      **MAP 6**

# The Old Rectory

HOPESAY, CRAVEN ARMS, SHROPSHIRE SY7 8HD
TEL: LITTLE BRAMPTON (058 87) 245

*Gracious living in a mellow stone guesthouse surrounded by beautiful countryside.*

For those who crave 'tea-on-the-lawn Englishness' complete with cooing pigeons, carefully tended herbaceous borders, stately copper beeches and, of course, a croquet lawn, the Old Rectory may fit the bill. The pretty hamlet of Hopesay lies in an Area of Outstanding Natural Beauty and makes the Old Rectory a good base for walkers.

The high-ceilinged drawing-room is a comfortable place to rest tired limbs in the evening. Much thought has gone into making the bedrooms stylish: they are well co-ordinated and have fine antique furniture, but at the same time they aren't fussy. Amy and Graham Spencer make sure that their guests experience no niggling annoyances, by providing spare toothbrushes, razors, hot-water bottles, make-up mirrors, flannels, even paracetamol.

Everyone sits together in the dining-room, unless they specifically request separate tables. The menu is fairly traditional: a home-made soup, grapefruit or pâté starter, followed by a roast rib of beef, Welsh lamb or salmon, and tempting puddings such as 'chocolate surprise' or 'Boodle's orange fool', all cooked on an Aga. The guesthouse isn't licensed but residents can bring their own wine.

◐ Open all year, exc Xmas week and 2 weeks in Nov

⤢ Leave the A49 at Craven Arms. Take the B4368 signposted Clun. At Aston on Clun turn right over a small bridge for Hopesay. The Old Rectory is on the left, next to the church. Private car park

🛏 1 twin, 1 double, 1 suite; all with bathroom/WC, TV, hair-dryer

◈ Dining-room, lounge; croquet

⊖ No wheelchair access; no children under 12; no dogs; no smoking

▭ None accepted

⊞ Single occupancy of twin/double
£25 to £41, twin/double £50 to
£53, suite £58 to £62; deposit

required. Set D £15.50
(7.15pm). Special breaks
available

## HOPTON WAFERS SHROPSHIRE                    MAP 6

# Crown Inn

HOPTON WAFERS, CLEOBURY MORTIMER, NR KIDDERMINSTER, HEREFORD
AND WORCESTER DY14 0NB
TEL: CLEOBURY MORTIMER (0299) 270372   FAX: (0299) 271127

*A welcoming roadside coaching-inn with beamed bedrooms and a
cheery bar.*

Lying between two steep hills, the inn must have been a welcome sight to
tired horses in former centuries. To modern eyes its aspect may not
appear so inviting as it is now right on a fairly busy through-road, but
inside, the giant inglenook fireplace, long low bar and comfortable chairs
of the 'rent room' (so called because the Lord of the Hopton Estate
would collect tenants' rents there) offer ageless hospitality. Outside,
wooden benches and flower-filled tubs are set out on the lawn. The
bedrooms are interesting and characterful. They are mostly decorated in
modern pastel colours and the fresh, well co-ordinated design contrasts
effectively with the ancient beams. Room ten still has its original wood-
burning stove, although the new owner John Price admits it's more for
decoration now than use; and one chilly visitor found 'the only warmth in
the bedrooms was via a single convector heater'. Kerry Stanton super-
vises the cooking. Bar meals are served in the long, low bar with booths
upholstered in thick tapestry fabrics.

There is also a pretty country-style restaurant with yellow tablecloths.
For starters expect a terrine of field mushrooms or timbale of ratatouille,
then galette of local pheasant or noisettes of monkfish. For a dessert, you
may be offered a crêpe soufflé with passion-fruit cream or vacherin of
peaches.

John Price declares that he intends to retain the traditional olde-
worlde atmosphere, and so far alterations have happened mainly behind
the scenes. We await further reports.

◑ Open all year; restaurant closed
Sun and Mon eves, bar food
every evening

⚡ On the A4117 between Cleobury
Mortimer and Ludlow. Private
car park

🛏 2 twin, 6 double; all with
bathroom/WC, TV; room service,
hair-dryer and trouser press on
request

◈ Restaurant, bar; riding
nearby

⊖ No wheelchair access; no dogs

▭ Access, Visa

⊞ Single occupancy of twin/double
£38, twin/double £60; deposit
required. Set L, D £18.50; alc
bar meals from £8.50. Special
breaks available

# Chequers Thistle Hotel

BRIGHTON ROAD, HORLEY, SURREY RH6 8PH
TEL: HORLEY (0293) 786992    TELEX: 877550 CHQURS G
FAX: (0293) 820625

*More welcoming and homely than other hotels near Gatwick.*

You could safely predict that staying in a chain hotel near Gatwick airport
would be an anonymous affair, but the Chequers Thistle benefits from
relaxed and friendly service. Part of the building used to be a coaching-
inn dating from the sixteenth century and is now a popular pub/buttery
called the Halfway Halt (roughly halfway between London and
Brighton). The sign at the door asking for casual but smart dress,
and making plain that 'discourteous and unreasonable behaviour and
language will not be accepted', seems out-of-keeping with the informal
atmosphere and furnishings (wheelback chairs and black wrought-iron
tables).

   The reception is a far cry from the vast areas you find in other airport
hotels – instead, a few big sofas stand on thick carpets round a coffee
table laid out with the day's newspapers. There's a genteel restaurant and
bar. Modern bedrooms, though smallish, have smart and attractive
fabrics and new wooden furniture. Although the hotel is not directly on a
flight path, lack of double glazing and the subsequent noise may disturb
some.

◐ Open all year

🔁 On the A23, 2½ miles from
Gatwick Airport, off Junction 9 of
the M23. Private car park

🛏 I single, 44 twin, 33 double; all
with bathroom/WC, TV, room
service, hair-dryer, trouser press,
baby-listening

◇ 2 restaurants, 2 bars, lounge;
conference facilities (max 60
people residential and non-
residential); heated outdoor pool
(May to Sept) at hotel, other
sports nearby. Wheelchair access
to hotel and restaurant, 39
ground-floor bedrooms

⬤ No dogs; some bedrooms non-
smoking

▢ Access, Amex, Diners, Visa

💷 Single/single occupancy of twin/
double from £80, twin/double
from £90. Continental B £6.50,
cooked B £8.50; set L from £11,
D from £17; alc L, D £30.
Special breaks available

*The 1993* Guide *will be published before Christmas 1992. Reports on
hotels are most welcome at any time of the year, but are extremely valuable in
the spring. Send them to* Which? Hotel Guide, *FREEPOST, 2 Marylebone Road, London NW1 1YN. No stamp is needed if reports are posted in
the UK.*

**HORNDON ON THE HILL** ESSEX                          **MAP 10**

# Hill House

HIGH ROAD, HORNDON ON THE HILL, ESSEX SS17 8LD
TEL: STANFORD-LE-HOPE (0375) 642463   FAX: (0375) 361611

*Convenience and comfort in an attractive town.*

One end of the main street of this pleasant old market town stops abruptly not far from the half-timbered Bell pub. Two doors away is the brick, seventeenth-century Hill House, owned by Christine and John Vereker. As John manages the pub, anyone staying in Hill House can run up a bill at both places.

Hill House has an attractive restaurant and an adventurous menu but no lounge. Accommodation is geared to convenience and comfort since most guests are here on business, but trouser presses and fitted furniture are about the only things to detract from the rooms' quirky old character. One bed (in the new stable conversion behind) is reached via a spiral staircase, and one cupboard approached via several steps. Bright, chintzy furnishings and modern prints sum up the décor; room facilities include Teletext TVs and spa baths. Breakfast is extra, and disappointed one reader.

◐ Open all year, exc Xmas and New Year; restaurant closed Sun, Mon eves

🔁 The village is 5 miles south-west of Basildon. Private car park

🛏 3 twin, 7 double, most with bathroom/WC, some with shower/WC; TV, hair-dryer, trouser press in all rooms

◈ Restaurant; conference facilities (max 45 people non-residential,

14 residential); golf nearby. Wheelchair access to hotel, 3 ground-floor bedrooms

⊖ No dogs

▭ Access, Visa

£ Single occupancy of twin/double from £45, twin/double from £45; deposit required. Continental B £3, cooked B £5.50; set L £15, D £19

**HORNINGSHAM** WILTSHIRE                              **MAP 9**

# The Bath Arms

HORNINGSHAM, LONGLEAT, NR WARMINSTER, WILTSHIRE BA12 7LY
TEL: WARMINSTER (0985) 844308

*A friendly pub, convenient for Longleat.*

A simple, unassuming grey-stone pub, the Bath Arms was a priory house for Glastonbury Abbey before it was sold in 1763. The Twelve Apostles (gnarled lime trees) are reminders of the pub's holy connections.

More obvious today are the car park and nearby caravan site, but lunching on picnic tables is a popular activity. The usually busy bar, reached via a heavy wooden door, is long and low and furnished with log stove, brown velveteen upholstery and the quaintest tan wallpaper you're ever likely to see. Cottagey furnishings are right for the thick-walled bedrooms, from whose little windows you can look out over the garden or village green.

| | | | |
|---|---|---|---|
| ◑ | Open all year | | *fishing, golf, other sports nearby* |
| ⤢ | *Horningsham village is at the south side of Longleat Park, 5 miles south-west of Warminster. Private car park* | ⊖ | *No wheelchair access* |
| | | ▭ | *Access, Diners, Visa* |
| | | £ | *Single occupancy of twin/double £35, twin/double £58, family room £58 plus £10 per child; deposit required. Set L £7.50, D £8.50; alc L £15, D £17; bar meals. Special breaks available* |
| 🛏 | *4 twin, 3 double, 1 family room; all with bathroom/WC, TV, room service, hair-dryer* | | |
| ◈ | *Restaurant, bar, drying room;* | | |

---

**HUDDERSFIELD** WEST YORKSHIRE                    **MAP 4**

# Wellfield House

33 NEW HEY ROAD, MARSH, HUDDERSFIELD, WEST YORKSHIRE HD3 4AL
TEL: HUDDERSFIELD (0484) 425776

*Carefully preserved house with a relaxed, friendly atmosphere and highly praised breakfasts.*

The location is nothing special: halfway between the M62 and Huddersfield city centre, and on a busy A-road. But the anonymity of the setting makes the serene interior behind the austere Victorian façade all the more special. John and Polly Whitehead have local historians as well as hotel inspectors snooping around as many of the rooms are little changed since the last century. Surprises include the beautiful dark oak panelling in the breakfast room which was installed by Liberty in the early 1900s and is said to have been 'the talk of Huddersfield' at the time; and one of the bathrooms, in what used to be the servants' quarters, which has superb original Victorian fittings including a 'hooded' bath with a built-in spray shower.

Beaten copper inscriptions over the door and fireplace in the lounge speak of another age: 'man with the head, woman with the heart' and 'man for the field and woman for the hearth'. Affronted feminists can retire instead to the intimate bar next door, which overlooks the neat garden, and work through the bookcase of paperbacks provided for guests.

Stone and rubber hot-water bottles, lots of old magazines, delicious home-made ginger cake and John's 'well-judged informality' made one reader feel very much at home during her two-night stay. She reports that breakfast was as good as any she has had in any hotel. 'What was intended as a modest order of bacon and tomatoes produced three rashers and three tomatoes.' There's also home-made muesli, compôte of red fruits, stewed apple with honey, prunes, grapefruit and yoghurt – plus plenty of home-made wholemeal bread and marmalade. Dinners are cooked for guests on request and may include tomato and orange soup, followed by beef in ginger or grilled plaice in lemon and parsley butter, with a whisky and honey bombe to finish off the meal (not to mention the diner).

◐ *Open all year, exc 24 Dec to 2 Jan*

▨ *On the A640 between Huddersfield town centre and Junction 23 of the M62. Private car park*

🛏 *1 single, 2 twin, 1 double, 1 family room; all with bathroom/WC, TV, room service; hair-dryer on request*

◈ *Dining-room, bar, lounge; golf, tennis, other sports nearby*

⬤ *No wheelchair access; no dogs*

▭ *Access, Visa*

£ *Single £40, single occupancy of twin/double £40, twin/double £55, family room £65. Set L £12.50, D £13.50. Special breaks available*

---

**HUNGERFORD** BERKSHIRE                                                 **MAP 9**

# The Bear

CHARNHAM STREET, HUNGERFORD, BERKSHIRE RG17 0EL
TEL: HUNGERFORD (0488) 682512 TELEX: 477575 ref 202
FAX: (0488) 684357

*A stylishly renovated and hospitable town hotel handy for a weekend at Newbury races.*

According to the brochure blurb, the Bear 'is one of the oldest and most historic inns of England and is reputed to date back to the thirteenth century. Standing on what has been called "the crossroads of England", it has witnessed many famous events in our history.' Take such hyperbole with a substantial pinch of salt and be happy with the less dramatic facts that William of Orange and Charles I did stay here, one of Elizabeth I's coachmen is said to have died here during a royal visit to Hungerford and Samuel Pepys is also said to have been impressed by the quality of the fish!

There are two bedroom blocks in addition to the main building. One is a converted stables; the other (Bear Island) is on the far side of the car park – a new building with particularly well-fitted rooms, a four-poster room with huge windows and a chalet-style pine ceiling. A preservation order on the old inn rightly prevents structural alteration, so some rooms remain a little poky although the original beams are incorporated into modern refurbishment.

The restaurant is sombre, weighed down by the sheer quantity of ceiling beams. Most people head for the bar where things are a little lighter. The service is cheerful and obliging, in keeping with the general atmosphere of this comfortable no-frills place.

◗ *Open all year*

🔁 *The hotel is on the main A4 outside the centre of Hungerford. Private car park*

🛏 *4 single, 10 twin, 20 double, 2 four-poster, 3 family rooms, 2 suites; all with bathroom/WC, TV, room service, hair-dryer, trouser press, baby-listening*

◈ *Restaurant, bar, lounge; conference facilities (max 100 people non-residential, 41*

*residential); babysitting. Wheelchair access to restaurant only*

⊜ *No dogs in public rooms*

▭ *Access, Amex, Diners, Visa*

£ *Single £70 to £80, single occupancy of twin/double from £82, twin/double £80 to £90, four-poster £97, suite £97; Continental B £5.50, cooked B £7.50; set L £14, D £18; alc L, D £22*

# Marshgate Cottage

MARSH LANE, HUNGERFORD, BERKSHIRE RG17 0QX
TEL: HUNGERFORD (0488) 682307 FAX: (0488) 685475

*A pleasant, rural alternative to other M4 staging posts.*

Out beyond the modern housing estates that ring this Berkshire town is Marshgate Cottage: a small, family-run hotel on the edge of the town's Freeman's Marsh. The marsh, crossed by the Kennet & Avon canal just beyond the bounds of the hotel, is a Site of Special Scientific Interest notable for its wild flowers and bird life.

There are nine bedrooms – three in the original thatched cottage and six in the new, single-storey extension. Rooms are small and a little spartan, with simple pine furnishings and wooden, rug-covered floors. A tiny lounge and dining-room join new and old buildings together. Dinner is a simple affair: a couple of choices from the blackboard and eaten looking out across the marsh. The hotel is run by Mike and Elsebeth Walker, who are Scottish and Danish respectively, and these origins are reflected in the décor and style of the hotel: simple, straightforward and good value for money.

◗ *Closed 25 Dec to 25 Jan; restaurant closed Sun eve*

🔁 *From Hungerford High Street turn at Town Hall into Church Street, cross over stream (½ mile) and immediately right into Marsh Lane. Private car park*

🛏 *1 single, 3 twin, 2 double, 1*

*four-poster, 2 family rooms; most with shower/WC, 1 with bathroom/WC; TV in all rooms*

◈ *Dining-room, bar, lounge; conference facilities (max 10 people residential); golf, fishing, other sports nearby. Wheelchair access to hotel and restaurant, 7 ground-floor bedrooms*

- No children under 5; no dogs; smoking in some bedrooms only
- Access, Amex, Visa
- Single £26 to £35, single occupancy of twin/double £26 to £35, twin/double £35 to £49, four-poster £49, family room from £56; deposit required. Set D £17; alc D £21

---

**HUNMANBY** NORTH YORKSHIRE                                       **MAP 3**

# Wrangham House Hotel

10 STONEGATE, HUNMANBY, NORTH YORKSHIRE YO14 0NS
TEL: SCARBOROUGH (0723) 891333

*A very pretty house with comfortable accommodation and a very friendly atmosphere.*

Wrangham House, a Georgian vicarage, is part of 'The Old Rectory Experience' group. These are a collection of hotels/guesthouses that have been established in former rectories, vicarages, parsonages and manses from down the ages. Here, in about half an acre of well-kept gardens, you can have a very relaxing, comfortable stay. Mature trees surround the pretty gardens and at one end the neighbouring church spire rises up behind the garden wall.

Inside, most of the public rooms are cosy but with good proportions; the bar lounge has a cottagey feel. The sitting-room, with white-painted wood panelling and an open fire, is delightful. Archdeacon Wrangham's portrait hangs on one wall (he, a former owner) and on the coffee table is a stack of information on the house and its history, along with local information for those exploring the area. The dining-room has small circular polished tables and a mix of wooden chairs. A straightforward menu is served. The service is relaxed and very friendly.

The bedrooms are pretty, with matching curtains and bedspreads and pine furnishings; there's even room in some for a chintzy armchair.

- Open all year
- From the main A64 road follow the A1039 to Filey, turning right on to Hunmanby Road. The hotel is behind All Saints Church in Hunmanby village. Private car park
- 2 single, 4 twin, 7 double; most with bathroom/WC, some with shower/WC; TV, room service, hair-dryer in all rooms
- Restaurant, bar, lounge, drying room, conservatory; conference facilities (max 30 people non-residential); golf, riding, other sports nearby. Wheelchair access to hotel (no steps), restaurant and WC, 2 ground-floor bedrooms, 1 specially equipped for the disabled
- No children under 12; no dogs; smoking in bar only
- Access, Amex, Diners, Visa
- Single £31, single occupancy of twin/double £31, twin/double £62. Set D £12; alc D £18; bar lunches (prices till early 92). Special breaks available

# Hunstrete House

HUNSTRETE, CHELWOOD, NR BRISTOL, AVON BS18 4NS
TEL: HUNSTRETE (0761) 490490 FAX: (0761) 490732

*Stately, lavishly furnished and pricey country-house hotel that's kept much of its former family home feel.*

Hunstrete House, an eighteenth-century house in ninety-two acres of deer-park, has a solid English country-house pedigree. In 1989 the small Clipper Hotel group took it over from the Dupay family who had run it for more than a decade. Luckily, despite adapting to the needs and wishes of a business as well as leisure-minded clientele, they've maintained the trappings of a private home. Thea Dupay left a fine collection of antiques and some effervescent landscapes. Log fires still burn in the hall, library and drawing-room, even on summer evenings. Lovers of fine porcelain will be in seventh heaven: even the ashtrays are Limoges. Anyone wanting to be comfortable and well-looked-after should be equally satisfied.

A speciality menu of the day in late spring of 1991 ran thus: asparagus, smoked chicken and duck salad, wild mushroom consommé, salmon with a herb crust, brandysnap with fresh fruit and English cheese, a house speciality. Bedrooms vary in size: most are spacious but a small single might make a better deluxe broom cupboard. You might as well blow the inheritance, take a suite in the courtyard wing and enjoy a coal-effect gas fire, a huge bunch of flowers, fruit-bowl and welcoming decanter of sherry. Bathrooms, perhaps the most decadent feature at Hunstrete, will really make you feel spoiled. Not only is there a well-kept garden (with tennis court and swimming-pool), but also an Italianate courtyard filled with flowering shrubs and fine shell and horse fountain. Service by a mainly young, cheerful male staff is very good; you don't have to park your car or carry a single bag.

◑ Open all year

🔁 From Bristol, take the A37 (Wells road) to Chelwood village. Turn left at the traffic lights in Chelwood on to the A368. The hotel is 2 miles along this road on the left-hand side. Private car park

🛏 I single, 20 twin/double, 2 four-poster, I Suite; all with bathroom/WC, TV, room service, hair-dryer, trouser press; no tea/coffee-making facilities in rooms

◇ 2 restaurants, bar, 3 lounges, library; conference facilities (max 24 people residential); tennis, croquet, heated outdoor pool at hotel, other sports nearby. Wheelchair access to hotel (no steps), restaurants and WC (F), 7 ground-floor bedrooms

⊖ No children under 9; no dogs

▭ Access, Visa

£ Single £98, single occupancy of twin/double £125, twin/double £165, four-poster £175 to £250, suite £250; deposit required. Set L £16.50, D £32; alc L £35, D £40

**HUNTSHAM** DEVON                                    **MAP 8**

# Huntsham Court

HUNTSHAM, NR BAMPTON, DEVON EX16 7NA
TEL: CLAYHANGER (039 86) 365/210   FAX: (039 86) 456

*Convivial house-party operation in gorgeous old house. Bohemian
and slow-motion atmosphere will irritate some and please others.*

If you're bored with formula-plagued country-house hotels, a visit to
Huntsham Court should brighten your day. Unless, that is, you insist on
formal service, chintzy furnishings and a genteel atmosphere. Andrea
and Mogens Bolwig's huge Victorian Gothic mansion in deepest Devon
is composed of large, sometimes vast, panelled rooms, marble pillars, tall
stone fireplaces, stags' heads and parquet floors. Music echoes
throughout the house and pianos sit in every room. Billiards, table tennis,
board-games and sauna keep you happy on dull days.

   You're mostly left to your own devices in this laid-back household,
serving yourself from the excellent spread at tea or from the honesty bar.
Breakfast continues till mid-morning. No-choice, five-course dinners
are communal affairs eaten around a 24-seater table in the panelled
dining-room. You might have tomato coulis soup, home-smoked salmon
with herb quenelles, roast duckling, then cheese and a choice of desserts.
The young, casually dressed staff are mostly from the New World. They
or the Bolwigs will likely refer to you as Mr or Mrs Bach, Brahms, etc.,
after your bedroom (they also use first names). The size of bedrooms
should impress, as well as the pre-war wireless sets and mix of Victorian
and post-war furnishings. Beethoven has a piano and, in the middle of
the bathroom, two old cast-iron baths on legs. One reader, who visited in
February, thought the public rooms 'excellent', but complained of the
'old, uncomfortable bed' and cold rooms. Weddings, conferences or
groups of friends occasionally take over the house and special dos such as
Victorian melodramas are sometimes laid on.

◑ Open all year

⤴ Leave the M5 at Junction 27 and
take the exit to Sampford
Peverell. Turn right over the
bridge at Sampford Peverell.
Follow signs to Uplowman and
then to Huntsham. Private car
park

🛏 2 twin, 8 double, 1 half-tester, 3
family rooms; all with bathroom/
WC, hair-dryer; room service,
baby-listening on request; no
tea/coffee-making facilities in
rooms

◇ Dining-room, bar, 2 lounges,
music room, games room,
library, drying room; conference
facilities (max 20 people
residential and non-residential);
tennis, croquet, table tennis,
sauna, gym at hotel, other sports
nearby

⊖ No wheelchair access; no dogs

▭ Access, Amex, Visa

£ Single occupancy of twin/double
£60 to £70, twin/double/family
room £89 to £100; deposit
required. Set D £25. Special
breaks available

# Esseborne Manor

HURSTBOURNE TARRANT, ANDOVER, HAMPSHIRE SP11 0ER
TEL: HURSTBOURNE TARRANT (0264) 76444
FAX: (0264) 76473

*Stylish interior design and good food in a peaceful, small hotel.*

The local colours of nature on a windswept spring day – cream and yellow daffodils, light filtering across verdant rolling fields from a blue and grey sky – seem no more pleasing than the hues chosen by Michael and Frieda Yeo for their beautifully designed, cosy little country house. Standing independently among ploughed fields and sheep, the cream-painted Victorian house seems to promise nothing special, but the moment you've been shown to your room you'll see there's nothing heavily Victorian about the interior and that you're in for a treat. Sometimes striking but never grand, sometimes soothing but never dull, the colour schemes complement each other perfectly. Some bedrooms have special features: a private patio, an open-plan bedroom/bathroom; all are kitted out with flowers, fruit and chocolates to greet guests, and a couple of inflatable toys for the bath.

Highly praised food served in an intimate dining-room of feminine pinks receives equal attention to presentation, and has been described as being in a resolutely modern vein. Dinner comprises five courses, or an extremely fair-priced two or three. Retire afterwards to the homely but stylish bar in reds and blues or to the lounge in yellows and blues. The Yeos have created a distinctly grown-up and sophisticated atmosphere. Male diners should remember to bring a jacket.

- ◑ Open all year
- ⤢ On the A343 between Newbury and Andover. 1½ miles north of Hurstbourne Tarrant. Private car park
- ⇌ 5 twin, 6 double, 1 four-poster, 6 suites; all with bathroom/WC, TV, room service, hair-dryer; no tea/coffee-making facilities in rooms
- ◇ Dining-room, bar, lounge, drying-room; conference facilities (max 12 people residential); tennis, croquet at hotel, other sports nearby. Wheelchair access to hotel and restaurant, WC (M,F), 1 ground-floor bedroom specially equipped for the disabled
- ⊖ No children under 12; no dogs
- ▭ Access, Amex, Diners, Visa
- £ Single occupancy of twin/double £84, twin/double £108, four-poster £125; deposit required. Set L £15, D £35. Special breaks available

---

🌿 *This denotes that the hotel is in an exceptionally peaceful situation where you can be assured of a restful stay.*

**ILKLEY** WEST YORKSHIRE **MAP 4**

# Rombalds Hotel

WEST VIEW, WELLS ROAD, ILKLEY, WEST YORKSHIRE LS29 9JG
TEL: ILKLEY (0943) 603201  FAX: (0943) 816586

*You can be assured of a good dinner and a comfortable night's stay
in this well-kept Georgian hotel.*

A hundred yards from Rombalds and you're on the Yorkshire Moors; six
hundred yards in the other direction and you're in the centre of Ilkley.
You can experience the best of both worlds by staying at this comfortable
hotel with an excellent restaurant. Externally, it's an attractive Georgian
building with a town-size garden and enough room for a few people to sit
out. The public rooms are geared more towards the restaurant than the
hotel trade. Décor is intense both in colours and patterns, the result is
smart.

The owners are proud of their famous clientele, and press cuttings in
the bar show Edward Heath and Roy Hattersley dining at Rombalds
(though not together!). Apart from an à la carte dinner, they also offer a
good-value three-course buffet lunch. One of their specialities is the
Edwardian breakfasts, served from 9.30 to 1.30pm on Sundays, which
include steaks and smoked fish with the more usual breakfast com-
ponents, washed down with Buck's Fizz. It is quite a draw, so if you're
staying at a weekend, it's worth booking your breakfast place in advance.

◐ Open all year, exc 27 to 31 Dec

↗ From the A65 traffic lights in the
town centre, travel up Brook
Street, cross the Grove into
Wells Road; the hotel is 600
yards on the left. Private car
park

🛏 4 single, 2 twin, 4 double, 1
family room, 4 suites; some with
bathroom/WC, most with
shower/WC; TV, room service,
hair-dryer, trouser press, baby-
listening

◈ Restaurant, bar, lounge;
conference facilities (max 50
people non-residential, 15
residential); fishing, golf, other
sports nearby. Wheelchair access
to restaurant and WC (unisex)
only

● No dogs in public rooms

▭ Access, Amex, Diners, Visa

£ Single £60, single occupancy of
twin/double £80, twin/double
£90 to £110, family room £84,
suite £115 to £140; deposit
required. Set L £10.50, D £20;
alc D £25. Special breaks
available

---

🥣 *Denotes somewhere you can rely on a good meal – either the hotel
features in the 1992 edition of our sister publication,* The Good
Food Guide, *or our own inspectors thought the cooking impressive,
whether particularly competent home cooking or more lavish cuisine.*

# Manor House Farm

INGLEBY GREENHOW, NR GREAT AYTON, NORTH YORKSHIRE TS9 6RB
TEL: GREAT AYTON (0642) 722384

*An isolated farmhouse where you will be well treated and can find stabling for your horse.*

It's a far cry from Illinois, where Martin Bloom comes from, to this pretty northern farmhouse set in the middle of the North York Moors National Park. Tall stone gates and an avenue of trees lead you away from the village, but Manor House farm is actually less grand than this entrance-way suggests, though the duckpond and the collection of peacocks and Soay sheep provide suitably decorative surroundings.

The farmhouse is an eighteenth-century low-slung building with clean, austere lines and simple colours. There's a residents' lounge, a dining-room with a stone fireplace and a small study to escape to. All are comfortably if not luxuriously furnished. The three bedrooms share two bathrooms. The cooking is English in style and substantial, and there is a shortish wine list. Footpaths lead into the hills or you can explore the woods and fields.

- Open all year, exc Xmas
- Ingleby Greenhow is 10 miles south of Middlesbrough. Take the B1257 at Stokesley to Great Broughton, and turn off for Ingleby. The entrance to Manor House Farm is opposite the church in Ingleby. Private car park
- 2 twin, 1 double; 2 public bathrooms
- Dining-room, lounge, library/study, TV; fishing at hotel, other sports nearby
- No wheelchair access; no children under 12; no dogs; no smoking
- None accepted
- Single occupancy of twin/double £21, twin/double £42; deposit required. Set D £10.50 (7pm)

# Severn Lodge

NEW ROAD, IRONBRIDGE, SHROPSHIRE TF8 7AX
TEL: IRONBRIDGE (0952) 432148

*A lovely Georgian house with views of Ironbridge gorge.*

When Severn Lodge was built into the sheer sides of Ironbridge gorge, the architects thought it better to have no windows on the river side of the house to avoid overlooking the ugly industrial goings-on. Today, that's rather a pity as the bridge is an impressive sight and the village, with its antique shops and museums, is interesting enough in its own right.

There are still views from some of the bedrooms, however, and the terraced garden is a lovely vantage point, especially in summer.

Severn Lodge is the Reeds' family home, but now has three bedrooms reserved for guests. Each has plenty of space, is comfortably furnished and has its own private bathroom. There are mementoes of family travels on the walls, and the elegant blue sitting-room has lots of books and an open fireplace. The Reeds are excellent hosts who miss nothing and provide lots of extras, including a champagne bucket and ice should you need them, and home-grown strawberries with your breakfast in summer.

- Open all year
- A few minutes' walk from the Iron Bridge. With the bridge on your left, New Road is the right turn immediately before the Malthouse restaurant. Private car park
- 1 twin, 2 double; doubles with bathroom/WC, single with shower/WC; TV, hair-dryer in all rooms

- Dining-room, lounge, TV room, drying room
- No wheelchair access; no dogs; no smoking
- None accepted
- Single occupancy of twin/double £32, twin/double £40; deposit required

## ISLEY WALTON LEICESTERSHIRE                                      MAP 4

# Park Farmhouse

MELBOURNE ROAD, ISLEY WALTON, CASTLE DONINGTON,
LEICESTERSHIRE DE7 2RN
TEL: DERBY (0332) 862409

*Relaxed farmhouse hotel, convenient for Donington Park motor circuit.*

Within earshot of the Donington Park motor circuit, this farmhouse hotel offers good modest accommodation at a reasonable price. The atmosphere is relaxed and informal, with many of the visitors coming to watch a race or be involved with motor sport in some way.

The eighteenth-century black and white house has large windows at the front, which look out over the surrounding countryside. To the rear are outbuildings and a barn where occasional functions take place. Inside, there is a disproportionate amount of space in airy public rooms. The living-room has muted colours and some plain furnishings but also a grand piano and a fine walnut cabinet. Meals are taken in the stone-walled dining-room upon pine tables; a serving table blocks off the stone fireplace. A menu is written up behind the bar and the food is hearty and filling. John Shields ran a restaurant for twelve years before coming to Park Farmhouse; he doesn't want to repeat the experience, and prefers to keep the food simple. Bedrooms are unfussy with pine furniture and white walls and are all different sizes.

◐ Closed 10 days over Xmas and New Year

⤴ 7 miles north-east of Ashby de la Zouch. At Isley Walton on the A453, take the Melbourne turning. The house is ½ mile on the right, the only black and white building. Private car park

🛏 3 twin, 3 double, 2 family rooms; most with bathroom/WC, some with shower/WC; TV, hair-dryer, trouser press, baby-listening in all rooms

◈ Dining-room, bar, lounge; golf, swimming nearby. Wheelchair access to hotel (1 step), restaurant and WC, 2 ground-floor bedrooms

⊖ No dogs in public rooms; no smoking in dining-room

▭ Access, Amex, Diners, Visa

£ Single occupancy of twin/double £32 to £45, twin/double £42 to £55, family room £52 to £65; deposit required. Alc D £13.50

---

**JERVAULX** NORTH YORKSHIRE　　　　　　　　　　**MAP 3**

# Jervaulx Hall

JERVAULX, NR MASHAM, RIPON, NORTH YORKSHIRE HG4 4PH
TEL: BEDALE (0677) 60235  FAX: (0969) 24414

*A lovely country-house hotel in a peaceful setting.*

The ruins of Jervaulx Abbey just beside the hotel grounds are a romantic sight, particularly when covered with spring flowers. The monks from Jervaulx were apparently the first to start making Wensleydale cheese, originally using ewes' milk. Apart from the Abbey, the eight acres of grounds and gardens are lovely to wander around and Masham and Middleham, both attractive market towns, are within easy reach.

The hall is a great rambling stone house of mixed origins. There are french windows opening on to the gardens. The rooms are grand in size, full of comfortable armchairs and lots of fine pieces of furniture, including a grand piano. The owners have been clever in their renovations and modernisations and although all the bedrooms have their own bathrooms this has not interfered with the character of the house. All but one of the bedrooms are on the upper floor and are furnished with good-quality Victorian furniture and pretty fabrics.

◐ Closed mid-Dec to mid-Mar

⤴ On the A6108, mid-way between Masham and Middleham, next to Jervaulx Abbey. Private car park

🛏 5 twin, 5 double; all with bathroom/WC, hair-dryer

◈ Dining-room, self-service bar, 2 lounges, TV, drying room; croquet at hotel, other sports nearby. Wheelchair access to hotel (no steps), restaurant and WC (unisex), 1 ground-floor bedroom

⊖ None

▭ None accepted

£ Single occupancy of twin/double £75, twin/double £85 to £105 (rates inc dinner); deposit required. Set D £15 (8pm) (prices till Easter 92)

# Old Hall

JERVAULX, NR MASHAM, RIPON, NORTH YORKSHIRE HG4 4PH
TEL: BEDALE (0677) 60313

*An exceptional Wolsey Lodge. Stay in peace and comfort*
*surrounded by interesting things.*

Next door to Jervaulx Hall (see above), the Old Hall is where the
servants' quarters used to be. Now it has no connections with its next-
door neighbour and is run in a very different way. As it is one of the
Wolsey Lodge group, the experience is like going to stay at someone's
home – in this case, that of Angela and Ian Close. The atmosphere is
friendly and relaxing. You can chat to Angela as she prepares dinner, and
then all the family and guests eat together. As in any private house,
there's no choice and she serves whatever had looked good in the market
that day. Over the years the Closes have gathered together glass, china,
antiques and other unusual pieces which are scattered throughout the
house. The Hall is also interesting architecturally: look particularly at the
antique carved pine staircase and the huge black range in the kitchen.

There are three bedrooms in the main house and some in the nearby
cottage. As you'd expect in a private house, each one is individually done,
with as much style and taste as the rest of the house. Furniture is antique
and there may be a special piece of china or a collection of silver-handled
hairbrushes in your room. Flowers are very much a feature of the Old
Hall: Angela is a talented arranger as well as painter of flowers.

- Open all year
- On the A6108 between Masham and Leyburn. Private car park
- 1 single, 1 twin, 1 double; all with bathroom/WC; hair-dryer
- Dining-room, lounge; fishing, golf, riding nearby.
- No wheelchair access; no dogs in public rooms; no smoking in bedrooms
- None accepted
- Single £48, single occupancy of twin/double £48, twin/double £96 (rates inc dinner, 7.30 pm)

**KENDAL** CUMBRIA                                                                **MAP 3**

# Lane Head House

HELSINGTON, KENDAL, CUMBRIA LA9 5RJ
TEL: KENDAL (0539) 731283/721023

*Comfortable accommodation, friendly hosts and a convenient and*
*rural location.*

Tom Craig used to be a casino manager in London, but there's nothing
chancy about a stay here. You arrive via a half-mile lane and underpass
from the A66, delivered into a bucolic scene of shaggy sheep and

tractors. Next door's sheep dog comes up to say hello, and a couple of cats prowl around the grounds of this clotted-cream-coloured, mostly seventeenth-century pebbledash house with a 1920s extension.

Inside, the house is comfortable and unpretentious, and the panelled hallway with a barley twist staircase and Victorian prints is memorable. Carpets, curtains and wallpaper are distinctly non-designer. The lounge is simple with low cane-sided chairs, flocked wallpaper, an oriental doorstopper and a huge plant. The woodburning stove was struggling a little to beat the chill on the night of our springtime inspection. Large windows overlook the terrace, and a stone staircase leads to a 150-year-old knot garden. Despite the proximity of traffic, spend half an hour by the window and you'll see rabbits scamper on the lawn and chaffinches, magpies and finches swoop in and out of view.

Exposed beams form a cross in the oblong dining-room. There's no coherent style but it's comfortable and old-fashioned. Meals are tasty and filling with a reasonable choice at each stage – perhaps Morecambe Bay shrimps, followed by supreme of chicken in a Stilton and leek sauce and chocolate roulade. The wine list is short and conservative. Coffee (and Kendal mint cake) is a help-yourself affair in the lounge. Bedrooms are spacious, especially the suite-like room four. Fabrics are bright and cheerful, and towels are wonderfully fluffy.

🌓 *Open all year; restaurant closed Sun eve*

🡕 *Take the A6 southbound from Kendal to the town boundary. The house is up a country lane almost opposite the BP garage. Private car park*

🛏 *3 twin, 3 double, 1 suite; most with bathroom/WC, some with shower/WC; TV, room service in all rooms*

⬦ *Dining-room, lounge; golf, riding, other sports nearby*

⊖ *No wheelchair access; no children under 5; no dogs*

▭ *Access, Visa*

£ *Single occupancy of twin/double £35 to £40, twin/double £50 to £60, suite £55 to £65; deposit required. Set D £15 (7.30pm)*

**KENILWORTH** WARWICKSHIRE                              **MAP 6**

# Castle Laurels

22 CASTLE ROAD, KENILWORTH, WARWICKSHIRE CV8 1NG
TEL: KENILWORTH (0926) 56179   FAX: (0926) 54954

*Friendly Victorian family-run hotel with neat comfortable bedrooms.*

On a bend on a busy road close to Kenilworth Castle, the Glovers' Victorian house is a comfortable spot for a couple of nights' stay. The character of the house has been carefully preserved with original light fittings and stained-glass in the hallway, yet the bedrooms have mod cons.

Some are in the extension to the rear of the hotel and are smaller and have less character whilst rooms in the old part of the house have moulded ceilings. Room seven has beams and wood-panelling. All have duvets and shower rooms which are small, neat and adequate. The lounge is bright and homely with a fake log fire. In the dining-room unfussy traditional English meals are served.

◐ *Open all year, exc 10 days over Xmas*

⊟ *Opposite Kenilworth Castle and overlooking Abbey Fields Park in old Kenilworth. Private car park*

🛏 *3 single, 3 twin, 5 double, 1 family room; all with shower/ WC, TV*

◇ *Dining-room, lounge/bar, TV; tennis, swimming, other sports nearby*

⊖ *No wheelchair access; no dogs; no smoking in bedrooms*

▭ *Access, Visa*

£ *Single £26 to £28, single occupancy of twin/double £31 to £33, twin/double £41 to £44, family room £54 to £57 (3 people). Alc D £13.50; evening snacks*

**KESWICK** CUMBRIA                                          **MAP 3**

# Brundholme Hotel

BRUNDHOLME ROAD, KESWICK, CUMBRIA CA12 4NL
TEL: KESWICK (076 87) 74495

*Imposing family-run hotel in a rural setting; a stone's throw from bustling Keswick.*

Somehow, you don't expect to find an ochre-coloured Georgian Nash-style villa down a narrow country lane within sight and sound of the A66. Coleridge, when not waxing miserable about Ancient Mariners, described the location as 'delicious' and owners Lynn and Ian Charlton will fill you in on Brundholme (once called Old Windbrowe) and its other literary associations.

Indoors, proportions remain daunting, but despite high ceilings, tall windows, statuesque Victorian furniture, heavy curtains and solemn portraits the atmosphere is convivial. Décor is well judged, with appealing and classy flora and fauna wallpaper in the reception, anticipating the pastel walls and bright colour scheme that prevail in the rest of the house. The bar combines wall-mounted guns and a stuffed stag's head with Art Deco cast-iron tables with gold figures. Views of the valley will encourage you to dally with a drink. In the lounge solid mahogany furniture is offset by a pleasant salmon and green colour scheme. The main restaurant is spacious, stylish and ever so slightly formal, with brass candlesticks and a marble fireplace. The bright conservatory, where breakfast is served, pre-dates the house by a hundred years and is a pretty spot with prints and plates and hanging baskets of flowers. Bedrooms have attractive soft furnishings in bright, flowery patterns. Room five has a four-poster and a fine dressing-table inlaid with mother-of-pearl.

Dinner, for which there's a good choice, might offer smoked chicken with a salad of French lettuce with walnut vinaigrette, followed by soup or sorbet, then roast loin of Herdwick lamb with port and redcurrant sauce.

◐ *Closed Jan*

⤴ *Leave the A66 at the Crosthwaite roundabout and take the Keswick road. Turn left after Crosthwaite Garage for ½ mile, and left again down Brundholme Road. The hotel is ¼ mile on the right. Private car park*

🛏 *2 single, 2 twin, 6 double, 2 four-poster; all with bathroom/ WC, exc 2 singles with shower/ WC; TV, room service, hair-dryer in all rooms*

◈ *Restaurant, bar, lounge, drying room, conservatory; conference*

*facilities (max 20 people non-residential, 12 residential); bicycles at hotel, fishing, golf, other sports nearby. Wheelchair access to restaurant only*

⊖ *No children under 12; no dogs in public rooms; no smoking in restaurant*

▭ *Access, Visa*

£ *Single £41, single occupancy of twin/double £51, twin/double £82, four-poster £102; deposit required. Sun L £9; set D £19; alc L £12, D £20 (prices till Apr 92). Special breaks available*

---

# The Grange

MANOR BROW, KESWICK, CUMBRIA CA12 4BA
TEL: KESWICK (076 87) 72500

*Comfort and elegance close to Keswick town centre.*

Duncan Miller used to work in the financial sector. Wife Jane comes from a family of hoteliers. Together they run a comfortable, elegant hotel with a welcome emphasis on value for money. Manor Brow is a steep hill linking Keswick town centre with the Ambleside Road, and the Grange is near the top of it, screened from the road by trees. The elevated position gives it some stunning views.

The dining-room is a stylish, predominantly pink room with classic chairs and place settings of silver, Wedgwood, crystal and fresh flowers that would shame many a more expensive establishment. The adjacent lounge is similarly elegant with Queen Anne-style chairs and comfy floral print sofas, floral arrangements, and lots of magazines to browse through. There's also an outsize gong. The bar is cosier with sepia-tinted pictures, tapestry chairs and wall-mounted plates. Duncan is particularly proud of his range of malt whiskies.

Dinner is a five-course affair, with a limited choice available throughout. One weekday menu offered egg and prawn mayonnaise, cream of mushroom and walnut soup, breast of chicken with ginger and lemon, and chocolate and hazelnut meringues followed by cheese. Breakfast is

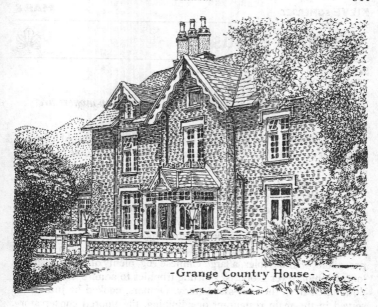

-Grange Country House-

unapologetically Scottish with porridge, Loch Fyne kippers and oatcakes featuring prominently.

Bedrooms vary in size but are individually designed; décor throughout is modern and chintzy, and furniture alternates between antique, white modern and pine. All are fresh, cheerful and attractive.

◑ Closed mid-Nov to mid-Mar

↱ From Keswick take the A591 towards Windermere for ½ mile. Take the first right – the hotel is 200 yards on the right. Private car park

🛏 3 twin, 5 double, 2 four-poster; half with bathroom/WC, half with shower/WC; TV, hair-dryer in all rooms

◇ Dining-room, bar, 2 lounges, drying room; fishing, golf, other sports nearby

⊖ No wheelchair access; no children under 5; no dogs in public rooms and in bedrooms by arrangement only; no smoking in dining-room

▭ Access, Visa

£ Single occupancy of twin/double £38 to £43, twin/double £60 to £69, four-poster £66 to £75; deposit required. Set D £15.50. Special breaks available

---

*Warning to insomniacs, exercise freaks and late-night lovers: increasing numbers of hotels have infra-red triggered security lamps. To save being embarrassingly illuminated, check before you leave for your late-night or pre-dawn stroll.*

# Meadow House

SEA LANE, KILVE, SOMERSET TA5 IEG
TEL: HOLFORD (0278 74) 546

*Tranquillity on tap in a lovely country home. New owners are carrying on as before.*

The Wyer-Roberts are now firmly ensconced in this lovely old hybrid of a house at the foot of the Quantocks, and though the welcome is as hearty and the accommodation as comfortable and attractive as before, their stamp is clear.

The mainly Georgian house was once a rectory and also a hiding-place for smugglers. Its setting of stunning gardens, meadows (naturally), wind-blown trees and distant sea views – not forgetting those quacking ducks over the road – is thankfully unchanged. The billiards room has turned into a smartly furnished and welcoming drawing-room with real fire, piano, walnut tables, a large Chinese rug, plenty of space to sit and lots of junior Wyer-Roberts' sporting trophies to admire. French windows open from the mid-sized study. Dinners, cooked by Judith and served in the main restaurant or adjoining, tile-floored conservatory, often draw on old English recipes: lobster soup followed by a King Charles purse (topside of beef stuffed with Exmoor pâté), perhaps, then pudding and superb English cheeses. Wines, Howard's domain, number over a hundred.

Pretty bedrooms are airy and partly furnished with antiques. Room four has the best view and two easy chairs from which to admire it. Suites in an L-shaped stable block have sitting areas and are more cottagey, with patchworks and old pine furniture.

● Open all year

� Take the A39 from Bridgwater. Once in Kilve turn right just before the Hood Arms pub into Sea Lane. Meadow House is ½ mile on the left. Private car park

▦ 3 twin, 2 double, 4 cottage suites/family rooms; most with bathroom/WC, some with shower/WC; TV, hair-dryer in all rooms

◈ Dining-room, 2 lounges, library/study, conservatory, drying room; conference facilities (max 30 people non-residential, 9 residential); croquet at hotel, other sports nearby; babysitting. Wheelchair access to 3 ground-floor bedrooms and dining-room only

● Dogs in cottages only; no smoking in public rooms

▭ Access, Amex, Visa

£ Single occupancy of twin/double £53, twin/double £76, cottage suite £76; deposit required. Set D £19; lunch by arrangement. Special breaks available

---

*All reports are welcome on any hotel, whether or not it is in the* Guide.

**KINTBURY** BERKSHIRE                                    **MAP 9**

# Dundas Arms

STATION ROAD, KINTBURY, BERKSHIRE RG15 0UT
TEL: KINTBURY (0488) 58263/58559   FAX: (0488) 58568

*A relaxed traditional inn by river and canal with an amiable
proprietor, good food and bedrooms.*

David Dalzell-Piper, owner and chef, describes himself as 'a cook first
and foremost and a businessman a poor fourth'. Second and third he's a
thoroughly pleasant bloke who works hard at ensuring that his guests feel
at ease. His culinary skills are renowned but guests who stay on Sundays
and Mondays when the restaurant is closed will not suffer unduly –
eating a steak in the bar perhaps, in one half of a cooper's barrel now
converted to an enveloping chair.

The view of water and weeping willows from the sage-green restaurant is restful and the food is similarly pleasing: set-price menus but with
plenty of choice, all excellently cooked and presented, with the gravadlax
consistently recommended.

The five bright bedrooms all in a row are in an extension beyond the
bar; a further attraction for guests is a secluded paved terrace on the
river's edge, a useful alternative if the crowds at the front have taken all
the seats overlooking the canal on busy summer days.

- Open all year, exc Xmas;
  restaurant closed Sun and Mon
  eves
- 1 mile off the A4 between
  Newbury and Hungerford.
  Private car park
- 2 twin, 3 double; all with
  bathroom/WC, TV
- Restaurant, bar; fishing, riding

- and swimming-pool nearby.
  Wheelchair access to hotel,
  restaurant and WC (M,F), 5
  ground-floor bedrooms
- Dogs by arrangement only
- Access, Amex, Visa
- Single occupancy of twin/double
  £55, twin/double £65, deposit
  required. Set L £16, D £25

**KIRKBY FLEETHAM** NORTH YORKSHIRE              **MAP 3**

# Kirkby Fleetham Hall

KIRKBY FLEETHAM, NORTHALLERTON, NORTH YORKSHIRE DL7 0SU
TEL: NORTHALLERTON (0609) 748711   FAX: (0609) 748747

*A country-house hotel in a grandly proportioned house but run in
an unstuffy, competent manner.*

The Hall dates from 1600 although the façade is more Georgian-
looking. It is a stately house with its own church ('Kirkby' means village
with a church) and over thirty acres of grounds and garden, so there's

very little to disturb the peace. The walled kitchen garden is very well
kept and its contents are used daily to produce mouth-watering dishes.

Inside, the Hall is all comfort and elegance. No scrimping on the
material for extravagant curtains and well-covered sofas with plenty of
cushions. There's nothing as vulgar as a bar: the drinks are stored in an
unobtrusive cupboard. The dining-room is a fairly formal room with
long windows overlooking the garden but the atmosphere throughout the
hotel is unstuffy.

The bedrooms are extremely comfortable and, like the rest of the
house, are decorated in high-quality fabrics. All the rooms are named
after birds and they vary in size and price. The owners are not always in
residence but the hotel is run efficiently by a friendly, competent
management and staff.

○ *Open all year*

⤴ *Leave the A1 at Catterick airfield. Then take the next left and next left again. The Hall is ½ mile further on. Private car park*

🛏 *7 twin, 10 double, 3 four-poster, 2 family rooms; all with bathroom/WC, TV, room service, hair-dryer; no tea/coffee-making facilities in rooms*

◇ *Restaurant, 2 lounges; conference facilities (max 30 people non-residential, 22*

*residential); fishing, clay pigeon shooting at hotel, other sports nearby*

⊖ *No wheelchair access; no children under 9 at dinner; no dogs in public rooms*

▭ *Access, Amex, Diners, Visa*

💷 *Single occupancy of twin/double £75, twin/double £120, four-poster £137 to £170, family room £134 to £154; deposit required. Set D £25. Special breaks available*

## KIRKBY LONSDALE CUMBRIA                                   MAP 3

# The Courtyard

5 FAIRBANK, KIRKBY LONSDALE, CUMBRIA LA6 2AZ
TEL: KIRKBY LONSDALE (052 42) 71613

*Welcoming guesthouse with large and cheerful bedrooms.*

Timothy and Gill Grey left Cambridge for this pretty Cumbrian town
four years ago, but they're enthusiastic propagandists for their new
northern whereabouts and happy to tell you about the local sights. The
Courtyard, a Georgian townhouse with a walled and peaceful garden,
makes a relaxing base from which to explore both the Yorkshire Dales
and the Lake District.

A strident burnt-orange hall subsides into more conventional décor
elsewhere, with an interesting mixture of modern and old prints and
paintings. The upstairs lounge is an elegant room furnished with
antiques, while the more casual grey-green breakfast room is cheerful
with fresh flowers, family photos and a large pine table which guests

share. Bedrooms are generously proportioned with gracious but comfortable, homely furnishings. The *en suite* twin room is a boon for forgetful packers with toothpaste, razor and plasters to take care of most eventualities. On the second floor, a room with a slanting roof houses an antique chest of drawers, lots of reading matter and a four-poster bed. The bathroom is shared with the Greys. They do not serve dinner but Kirkby has plenty of eating places.

- Open all year
- 100 yards from the church in Kirkby Lonsdale. Private car park
- 2 twin, 1 four-poster; 1 twin with bathroom/WC, room service; hair-dryer on request; 1 room with TV
- Breakfast room, lounge, drying room; fishing, riding, other

- sports nearby; babysitting
- No wheelchair access; no children under 10; no dogs; no smoking
- None accepted
- Single occupancy of twin/double £19, twin £30 to £35, four-poster £30; deposit required

## KIRKOSWALD CUMBRIA                                   MAP 3

# Prospect Hill

KIRKOSWALD, PENRITH, CUMBRIA CA10 1ER
TEL: LAZONBY (076 883) 500

*Out-of-the-way family-run hotel with cosy bedrooms and lots of rustic charm.*

Not many hotels can boast a resurrected engine room on the premises, but that's what you'll find in the Gin Case at Prospect Hill, where caramel-coloured splay out and down from the centre of a spacious semi-circular room with an open coal fire. Prospect Hill is a cosy place with rust-coloured stone walls, seventeenth-century antiques and décor that's heavy on warm reds and browns.

The large, low bar is a museum of rural life, with tractor seats, an old pump, scales, irons and antiquated farm tools. Muzak and candles are banned from the unpretentious rough-walled and beamed Hay Barn dining-room. Food is wholesome and varied: farmhouse soup, followed by beef with garlic, honey and Drambuie, or – from the separate vegetarian list – leek and lentil lasagne. Most bedrooms have fine views and successfully combine modern elements like wicker headboards with solid, old furniture.

- Open all year, exc 24, 25, 26 Dec
- The hotel is ½ mile north of Kirkoswald on the Armathwaite road. Private car park
- 3 single, 2 twin, 4 double, 1

- family room, 1 suite; some with bathroom/WC, 2 public bathrooms; TV in some rooms
- Restaurant, bar, lounge, TV room, drying room; conference facilities (max 40 people non-

residential, 11 residential);
croquet at hotel, fishing, other
sports nearby

⊖ No wheelchair access; no dogs

▭ Access, Visa

£ Single £19 to £42, single

occupancy of twin/double £28 to
£42, twin/double £41 to £52,
family room £62; deposit
required. Set D £17.50 (prices
till end 91). Special breaks
available

---

**KNIGHTWICK** HEREFORD AND WORCESTER                    **MAP 6**

# The Talbot

KNIGHTWICK, HEREFORD AND WORCESTER WR6 5PH
TEL: KNIGHTWICK (0886) 21235    FAX: (0886) 21060

*Pleasant pub with rooms – older ones have more character – and
ambitious menu.*

'Hotel' is perhaps overstating the case – the Talbot is simply a pub with
rooms. Next to the River Teme, this white fifteenth-century building
with its mossy stone tiles was supposed to be where Charles II holed up
after the Battle of Worcester. The old rooms are named with this in
mind: King Charles and Battlements I and II all have low ceilings and
beams, and occasionally alarmingly sloping floors. Furnishings are
simple. Rooms in the newer wing have numbers rather than names and
may be quieter, being further from the road. The walls are also
straighter, but the rooms are small and have little character.

Residents have their own lounge, but the lounge bar and dining area of
the pub are equally pleasant and cosy, although the public bar is scruffy
and unattractive. The menu is a cut above the usual pub fare. Daily
specials, chalked on a blackboard in the bar, might include pheasant
breast in filo pastry, smoked rabbit pie, or chicken satay. Lots of soups
and several vegetarian options are also included. Serving staff are young
and reasonably friendly, though not always forthcoming or knowledge-
able about the history of the place.

⊙ Open all year, exc 25 Dec eve

↗ Just off the A44 Worcester to
Bromyard road on the B4197 to
Martley. Private car park

🛏 3 single, 3 twin, 4 double, 1
family room; most with
bathroom/WC, some with
shower/WC; TV and room
service in all rooms

◈ Restaurant, bar, lounge;
conference facilities (max 100
non-residential, 10 residential);
fishing, sauna/solarium, squash

at hotel, other sports nearby

⊖ No wheelchair access; no dogs in
public rooms and by
arrangement in bedrooms

▭ Access, Visa

£ Single £23 to £29, single
occupancy of twin/double £23 to
£38, twin/double £39 to £53;
family room £49 to £63; deposit
required at peak times. Alc L
£12, D £15 (prices till end 91).
Special breaks available

**KNOWSTONE** DEVON                                    **MAP 8**

# Masons Arms

KNOWSTONE, SOUTH MOLTON, DEVON EX36 4RY
TEL: ANSTEY MILLS (039 84) 231/582

*An away-from-it-all, unprecious village pub near Exmoor with
bags of natural charm and gregarious resident owners.*

The best thing about this fine thirteenth-century inn, apart from its
chirpy owners (the Todds) and bearded collie (Charlie), is its lack of
pretence. No shiny new horse-brasses here. Television location scouts
must surely have discovered it; tourists certainly have. The outside is
stone and thatched, the inside old and weathered and apparently
untouched since a black and tan cost sixpence.

There are two small bars, the first with a great inglenook, uneven stone
floors, thick plank-topped tables, dusty old bottles hanging from the
ceiling and a fine array of rusty old farm tools on one wall. Behind is a
carpeted bar with another fire blazing and genuine bar billiards. The
restaurant is sweet and simple. So are the bedrooms which are well
endowed with black beams and uneven white walls. Room four is *en suite*
and has a brass bed, a Victorian sofa and an Edwardian cupboard. The
garden is wild and you can sit out on the terrace and revel in the smashing
views.

◑ Open all year, exc 24 to 26 Dec;
restaurant closed Sun, Tues eves

🔁 1½ miles off the A361 midway
between Tiverton and South
Molton. Turn right at signs for
picnic site Sidemoor. Private car
park

🛏 1 single, 1 twin, 3 double; some
with shower/WC; TV, room
service, hair-dryer, baby-listening
in all rooms; trouser press on
request

◈ Restaurant, bar, lounge;
conference facilities (max 12
people non-residential, 5
residential); fishing, riding nearby

⊖ No wheelchair access; no dogs or
smoking in restaurant

▭ None accepted

£ Single from £22, single
occupancy of twin/double from
£27, twin/double from £44. Set
D £11; bar meals (prices till end
91). Special breaks available

*All rooms have tea/coffee-making facilities unless we mention to the
contrary.*

# La Belle Epoque

60 KING STREET, KNUTSFORD, CHESHIRE WA16 6DT
TEL: KNUTSFORD (0565) 633060/632661　FAX: (0565) 634150

*Comfortable rooms, and good food served in an unusual restaurant.*

The plaudit-winning food has been the mainstay of this restaurant-with-rooms, modelled as a monument to the art nouveau movement. Indeed, your hosts prefer that bedrooms are let only to diners.

In contrast to the quasi-decadence of the *fin de siècle* restaurant, bedrooms are wholesomely cottagey with brass or carved wood bedsteads, and lots of pretty lace and chintz. But there hasn't been universal satisfaction. One reader found his bed poor, and snagged his finger on a protruding hook. Most bathrooms are good. Given that the place was originally built as King's Coffee House to commemorate Mrs Gaskell's Knutsford-inspired creation *Cranford*, one cannot help but wonder what that lady, wife and daughter of Unitarian ministers would make of its present incarnation. Dimly lit rooms, and walls and windows heavily draped with deep blue and green ruched and gathered fabrics, gave the right period feel when the restaurant starred as Palliards Restaurant in television's *Brideshead Revisited*. The overall effect is chic. Menu selections include langoustine salad, Lancashire duck with apricot sauce and creme brûlée. The wine list is long, enticing and predominantly French.

- ◐ Closed first week Jan and public holidays; restaurant closed Sun
- ⤵ In the centre of Knutsford. On-street parking
- 🛏 1 single, 2 twin, 4 double; all with bathroom/WC, TV
- ◈ Restaurant, bar; conference facilities (max 65 people non-residential); golf, tennis, other sports nearby
- ⊖ No wheelchair access; no children under 12; no dogs
- ▭ Access, Amex, Diners, Visa
- £ Single £35, single occupancy of twin/double £35 to £40, twin/double £45 to £50. Cooked B £5; alc D £30

# Longview Hotel

51–55 MANCHESTER ROAD, KNUTSFORD, CHESHIRE WA16 0LX
TEL: KNUTSFORD (0565) 632119　FAX: (0565) 652402

*Stylish guesthouse with lots of facilities and good food at a moderate cost.*

Tardis-like, the Longview is bigger on the inside than it appears from the outside. Outside, it's an ordinary, Victorian red-brick end-of-terrace house with a tacky red illuminated sign, inside it's a haven of elegance and style.

An old pulpit and mule cabinet function as reception desks, and there are lots of antiques and pieces of art nouveau sprinkled around the public rooms. The brick-walled cellar bar is well-stocked, though shabbily furnished, while the television lounge is cosy with a log fire and comfy seating. Bedrooms are comfortable with attractive, carefully co-ordinated soft furnishings in bold, modern colours. Facilities are on a par with many business hotels at a fraction of the price and include radio, remote-control television and trouser press. Service in the attractive restaurant is friendly and efficient, and the bold menu, characterised by literary allusions, offers a host of accomplished, well-presented dishes at very reasonable cost. Kick off with salmon and asparagus, and follow up with Gaskell Pork – pork fillets wrapped in foil parcels filled with peppers and salsa, and a choice from a selection of desserts, many with alcoholic oomph, or a good cheeseboard. There's a separate and inventive vegetarian menu.

◐ *Open all year, exc 24 Dec to 1 Jan; restaurant closed Sun eve*

↗ *Leave the M6 at Junction 19 and take the A556 towards Chester/Northwich. Just 20 yards along turn left into Tabley Lane, follow to end and turn right. Longview is 200 yards up on the left. Private car park*

⇌ *6 single, 7 twin, 9 double, 1 family, 2 self-catering cottages; all with bathroom/WC, TV, room service, hair-dryer, trouser press, baby-listening*

◈ *Restaurant, bar, lounge, drying room; conference facilities (max 16 people residential and non-residential); golf, tennis, other sports nearby; babysitting*

⊖ *No wheelchair access; no dogs in public rooms*

▭ *None accepted*

£ *Single £32 to £45, single occupancy of twin/double £42 to £50, twin/double £55 to £65, family room £65 to £75 (3 people); cottage £250 per week; deposit required. Set D £14.50; alc D £19.50. Special breaks available*

## LACOCK WILTSHIRE                    MAP 9

# At The Sign Of The Angel

6 CHURCH STREET, LACOCK, NR CHIPPENHAM, WILTSHIRE SN15 2LB
TEL: CHIPPENHAM (0249) 730230

*A medieval inn done out with élan. The pretty National Trust village takes you back in time, except in high season.*

The ancient wool village, including this fourteenth-century inn, belongs to the National Trust. It is coffee-table-book perfect. The town boasts a distinguished abbey and the Fox Talbot photography museum and is therefore crowded throughout the summer.

The half-timbered inn, on a little narrow side-street, has all the trappings: a moss-covered roof, rafters and beams, uneven floors, huge log fires, polished brass and silver and rich antique oak furniture. A popular watering-hole, you might assume, but in fact it has no bar. Non-residents come to dine, however, though one report about the meals this year was rather cool. Bedrooms won't disappoint fans of the crooked and askew. As one American reader put it: 'Those who want to feel the antiquity will be happy in the hotel. Those who want what we call "Kohler or Standard American" plumbing fixtures need to be in the new addition across the courtyard.' Good old furniture and cottagey prints come as standard. The upstairs residents' lounge, with land- and seascapes, and standard lamps doing their best to keep vertical on the sloping floor, is the place to relax, amongst surroundings of sagging armchairs, books, games and a friendly cat.

◑ Open all year, exc 22 Dec to 6 Jan

↯ Leave the M4 at Junction 17 and follow signs for Chippenham and Warminster. 3 miles south of Chippenham on the A350, Lacock is signposted on the left. Follow 'Local Traffic' signs into village. Church Street is at the bottom of the village. Private car park

🛏 2 twin, 6 double, 1 four-poster, 1 family (some in cottage annexe); all with bathroom/WC, TV, hair-dryer

◈ 3 restaurants, lounge; fishing, riding nearby

⊖ No wheelchair access; no children under 12; no dogs in public rooms

▭ Access, Amex, Visa

£ Single occupancy of twin/double £70, twin/double £93, four-poster £93; family room £120; deposit required. Set L £20 (Sun); alc L £25, D £32. Special breaks available

-At the Sign of the Angel-

**LANCASTER** LANCASHIRE                              **MAP 3**

# Edenbreck House

SUNNYSIDE LANE, LANCASTER, LANCASHIRE LA1 5ED
TEL: LANCASTER (0524) 32464

*Unusual, warm-hearted and entertaining B&B with lots of panache.*

As Victorian B&Bs go, Edenbreck starts off with one major handicap: it was built in 1984. None the less it looks the part with large gables and tile-roofed bay windows. The colourful garden (three-quarters of an acre of it) is dominated by a large pergola and creates a sense of seclusion. Inside, in dimension and style the house adopts nineteenth-century design patterns with tall windows and carved ceiling mouldings. That the illusion works is a tribute to the energy of proprietors Margaret and Barrie Houghton, who've created a memorable pastiche with astute antique purchases, a feel for the spirit of the age, and more than a pinch of Lancashire hospitality. The sitting-room has a handsome, tiled, cast-iron fireplace and rich velvet curtains, with books and games to while away the time. There's a conservatory off the large, beamed dining-room where breakfast is served. Bedrooms are individually styled and furnished, and include a garden family room, and one with a four-poster. One seems to come from another tradition altogether; with more shades of pink than a Barbara Cartland ensemble, an oblong Jacuzzi and a double bed on a raised dais, it's more LA than Lancaster, even if there's a sensible candlewick to keep out the northern chill.

◐ Open all year

🔼 From the city centre follow signs for the British Rail Castle station. Go past the station and turn left into Ashfield Avenue which leads to Sunnyside Lane. Private car park

🛏 2 twin, 2 double, 1 four-poster; all with bathroom/WC, exc four-poster with shower/WC; TV,

hair-dryer in all rooms

◈ Dining-room, lounge, conservatory; golf nearby

⊖ No wheelchair access; no smoking or dogs in public rooms

▭ Access, Diners, Visa

£ Single occupancy of twin/double £35, twin/double/four-poster £40; deposit required

---

*If you make a booking using a credit card, and you find after cancelling that the full amount has been charged to your card, raise the matter with your credit card company. They will ask the hotelier to confirm whether the room was re-let, and to justify the charge they made.*

# Langar Hall

LANGAR, NOTTINGHAMSHIRE NG13 9HG
TEL: HARBY (0949) 60559   FAX: (0949) 61045

*A lovely country house close to Nottingham and popular with
honeymooners.*

Hidden from the village of Langar behind the church, this lovely country
house, built in 1837 in the Vale of Belvoir, lies some eight miles east of
Nottingham. The house has been in Imogen Skirving's family for two
generations; her father used to entertain cricketers of the thirties here
when they came to play at Trent Bridge. Now the Hall has been
refurbished by Imogen and her husband (who are keen art dealers); you
will find pictures for sale hanging on the walls in the dining-room and
candelabras, statues and china all on display.

The house is relaxed and the hospitality charming. The *nouvelle cuisine*
English meal is served formally in the pillared dining-room, and afterwards you can retire to the white-walled sitting-room with its china on
display. Bedrooms are varied. You could end up with a vast room with a
four-poster bed, antiques and an old-fashioned bathroom, or, alternatively, one that is smaller and more intimate.

● Open all year

▨ Signposted off the A46 mid-way
between Leicester and Newark,
and off the A52 mid-way
between Grantham and
Nottingham. The hotel is behind
the church in Langar. Private car
park

⇔ 3 twin, 5 double, I four-poster, 2
family rooms; most with
bathroom/WC, some with
shower/WC; TV, room service in
all rooms; hair-dryer on request

◈ Restaurant, lounge, TV room,
library, private dining-room;

conference facilities (max 20
people non-residential, 10
residential); fishing at hotel,
other sports nearby

● No wheelchair access; dogs by
arrangement only; no smoking in
bedrooms

▭ Access, Amex, Visa

£ Single £25 to £48, single
occupancy of twin/double £48 to
£65, twin/double £65 to £70,
four-poster £95 to £100, family
room £90; deposit required. Set
D £20 to £25; alc L £15. Special
breaks available

*Many hotels offer special rates for stays of a few nights or more. It is worth
enquiring when you book.*

**LANGHO** LANCASHIRE                                                                          **MAP 4**

# Northcote Manor

NORTHCOTE ROAD, LANGHO, NR BLACKBURN, LANCASHIRE BB6 8BE
TEL: BLACKBURN (0254) 240555   FAX: (0254) 246568

*Good food in a pleasantly situated country-house hotel.*

Nineteenth-century cotton magnates didn't live near the dark satanic mills. Instead they built splendid, rural, half-timbered houses like this one, set in a couple of acres. Oak panelling, stained-glass windows, art nouveau door panels and a lovely carved oak staircase are helpful ingredients in the country-house mix.

Nigel Haworth and Craig Bancroft, who've worked at the Manor since the early eighties and bought it in 1989, have added friendly, attentive and professional staff and have adopted a policy of replacing incongruous furniture with Victoriana. Fresh flowers, attractive ruched curtains, chandeliers and open fires bolster the effect. Large, comfortable bedrooms have elegant Victorian wardrobes and bedsteads, colourful patterned wallpaper and contrasting curtains. Carpeted bathrooms are tiled, in one case with a Venetian glass mosaic.

Food in the two spacious candle- and chandelier-lit dining-rooms tends to the luxurious: smoked salmon and monkfish in a fennel butter followed by loin of veal wrapped in a cabbage leaf with a shortcrust lattice, and lemon-flavoured tuile with a lime sorbet. The wine list has some classy selections and a good choice of half-bottles.

- ◑ *Open all year, exc 26 Dec, 1 Jan*
- ↗ *Leave the M6 at Junction 31 and take the A59 Clitheroe road for 9 miles. The hotel is on the left-hand side before the 1st roundabout. Private car park*
- 🛏 *1 single, 1 twin, 4 double; most with bathroom/WC, some with shower/WC; TV, room service, hair-dryer, baby-listening in all rooms*

- ◈ *2 dining-rooms, bar, lounge; conference facilities (max 30 people non-residential); golf, tennis nearby; babysitting*
- ⊖ *No wheelchair access; no dogs*
- ▭ *Access, Amex, Diners, Visa*
- £ *Single £60, single occupancy of twin/double £60, twin/double £70; deposit required. Set L £12.50; alc L, D £25 to £30*

---

*Many hotels put their tariffs up in the spring. You are advised to confirm prices when you book.*

# Langley House

LANGLEY MARSH, WIVELISCOMBE, SOMERSET TA4 2UF
TEL: WIVELISCOMBE (0984) 23318    FAX: (0984) 24573

*A satisfying fusion of comfort, elegance, good food and wine in an intimate country-house setting.*

The cream-coloured and wistaria-clad house, on a secondary road in hilly, rural Somerset, has won interior and exterior design awards which shouldn't surprise you. A closely cropped lawn, ornamental trees, shrubs and picture-perfect flowerbeds make up the gardens. Some parts of the house are sixteenth century and quaint, the rest stately eighteenth century.

The design within is colourful yet subtle, assured yet experimental. The vibrant pink-walled drawing-room is set with deep sofas and easy chairs in salmon and grey-blue. A few steps down and you're in a smaller sitting area, all yellow and blue. Empty magnums and jeroboams of Lafite and Latour, enjoyed by winter shooting parties, line the shelves. Peter and Anne Wilson have had lots of experience in the hotel business, but this personal venture clearly suits them.

Peter's excellent four-course dinners served in a lovely sandy-orange dining-room of decoratively painted beams and ragged walls are testament to his continued enthusiasm. Dinners are modern in concept: warm quail salad, then turbot with leeks in vermouth sauce, perhaps, followed by lamb with onion and cassis purée. You're given a choice of desserts only.

Chintzes, flowery borders and crown canopies characterise the pretty but smallish bedrooms – *de rigueur* country-house hotel ingredients, perhaps, but here handled with flair. Less commonplace are the quilted spreads, fabric-backed wardrobe doors, stencilling and strong colours. Remodelling continues: Exmoor and Courtyard have had a face lift and a single has now grown into a fair-sized double. Double glazing helps against road noise.

- **◗** *Closed Feb*
- **⤴** *On an unclassified road signposted Langley Marsh that leads from the centre of Wiveliscombe. Private car park*
- **🛏** *1 single, 2 twin, 3 double, 1 four-poster, 1 family room; all with bathroom/WC, exc 1 double with shower/WC; TV, room service, hair-dryer, baby-listening in all rooms; no tea/coffee-making facilities in rooms*
- **◈** *Restaurant, bar, 2 lounges, drying room, conservatory; conference facilities (max 16 people residential and non-residential); croquet at hotel, other sports nearby; babysitting*
- **➖** *No wheelchair access; no dogs in public rooms; no smoking in restaurant*
- **▭** *Access, Amex, Visa*
- **💷** *Single £59, single occupancy of*

twin/double £64, twin/double £90, four-poster £100, family room £125; deposit required. Set

D £23.50, £26.50 (prices till Easter 92). Special breaks available

---

**LANGRISH** HAMPSHIRE                                    **MAP 9**

# Langrish House

LANGRISH, PETERSFIELD, HAMPSHIRE GU32 1RN
TEL: PETERSFIELD (0730) 66941   FAX: (0730) 60543

*Inexpensive country-house hotel in a fine position but rather bleak inside.*

Langrish House, a backwater of a place down a quiet country lane, has none the less seen a lot of action in its varied history. Its double wool pond was once used by sheepfarmers for cleaning raw wool; William Langrish enlarged the farmhouse to manor size in 1600 using mellow stone; and during the Civil War the Cromwellian-supporting family made Royalist prisoners extend it further by building a large cellar which was then used as a dungeon for the diggers themselves. A later teetotaller closed the nearby pub to put temptation out of his sons' reach. It was finally turned into an hotel in 1979.

One succinct letter received on Langrish sums it up well: 'Warm welcome. Pleasant room with lovely views. Lack of atmosphere however. Some log fires would help. Food disappointing.' Its position in a gentle verdant valley acts as its strongest point of recommendation; squirrels, deer, badgers and pheasant are said to visit its back lawn. Inexpensive compared to many country houses, it also has some lacklustre furnishings, such as thick-patterned pub-style carpets, and a lack of comfy chairs in the sitting-room. Interesting dining and bar areas are in the dungeons. Space, light and co-ordinated designs in fresh bedrooms are compensations.

Open all year, exc 24 Dec to 2 Jan; restaurant closed Sun eve

3 miles from Petersfield off the A272 Winchester road – turn left into East Meon Road. Private car park

6 single, 6 twin, 6 double; most with bathroom/WC; TV, room service, hair-dryer, trouser press, baby-listening in all rooms; tea/coffee-making facilities on request

Restaurant, 2 bars, lounge;

conference facilities (max 60 people non-residential); fishing, golf, other sports nearby. Wheelchair access to hotel (not restaurant), 4 ground-floor bedrooms

Dogs by arrangement

Access, Amex, Diners, Visa

Single £38 to £46, single occupancy of twin/double £45 to £49, twin/double £59 to £65. Cooked B £4; alc D £15 to £17. Special breaks available

# Lastingham Grange

LASTINGHAM, YORK, NORTH YORKSHIRE YO6 6TH
TEL: LASTINGHAM (075 15) 345/402

*A very peaceful spot in this Moors village. The style is old-fashioned complete with an attentive host.*

'Please keep this delightful hotel in the book with gold stars,' reports one reader. We are happy to be able to oblige. A lingering memory of a visit to Lastingham Grange must be the flowers: the garden is full of roses and so is the house. Carpets are flower-patterned, bedrooms have flowery wallpaper and there are plenty of fresh blooms in vases. You can add to that a generous and attentive host. Dennis Wood is the front-of-the-house man and is very much in evidence. He not only greets guests on arrival but also has time for a chat in the evening as he's taking orders for dinner and drinks.

The house was originally built in the seventeenth century as a farmhouse and it is the later additions that have made it into more of a manor house. The proportions remain quite homely and the public rooms though neat are not at all grand.

The bedrooms are a reasonable size and quite old-fashioned in their mixture of colours and styles. All have their own bathrooms and most have good views. One reader remarked: 'My room here was the prettiest imaginable – the ambience of the place was that of a monastery – with glorious gardens.'

● Open all year, exc Jan, Feb and Dec

⌐ 1½ miles east of Kirkbymoorside on the A170. Turn left where signposted Appleton-Le-Moors; the hotel is 3½ miles away, just the other side of Lastingham. Private car park

⇐ 2 single, 6 twin, 4 double, all with bathroom/WC; TV , room service, hair-dryer, trouser press, baby-listening

◇ Dining-room, lounge, drying room; fishing, golf, other sports nearby

⊖ No wheelchair access; no dogs; in public rooms and only in bedrooms by arrangement; no smoking in dining-room

▭ None accepted

£ Single £52, single occupancy of twin/double £52, twin/double £96; children under 12 free if sharing parents' room. Set L from £12, D from £19.50

---

*The text of entries is based on unsolicited reports sent in by readers and backed up by inspections. The factual details under the text are from questionnaires the* Guide *sends to all hotels that feature in the book.*

**LAVENHAM** SUFFOLK                                    **MAP 7**

# The Angel                                             ℒ

MARKET PLACE, LAVENHAM, SUFFOLK CO10 9QZ
TEL: SUDBURY (0787) 247388

*Comfort and excellent value. A jolly, civilised pub with above-average accommodation.*

Like both our other recommendations for this lovely medieval town, the good-value Angel has been around a while (it was first licensed in 1420), but unlike both, it is probably truer to its original self: a friendly and informal hostelry.

'Warm and friendly atmosphere. The proprietors and staff went out of their way to ensure that our stay was a most pleasant and enjoyable experience,' writes one reader. The large, U-shaped bar with impressive double inglenook Tudor fireplace has elements of a cultured home (Bach in the background, a bookcase, board games, plants, table lamps and comfortable seating); but with scrubbed wood tables, a games room and a boisterous clientele, it feels like a friendly local.

Food at the Angel is home-cooked and inexpensive. Snacks or fully fledged dinners from an à la carte menu, can, weather permitting, be taken almost anywhere: in the bar, in the enclosed garden behind, at picnic tables in the front or *even* in the small, informal restaurant at the far end of the bar. There is no lounge, but ample space for sitting in the decent-sized bedrooms. Character comes in the form of beams and exposed brick walls; furniture is old rather than antique.

◐ Open all year

⚡ On A1141, 2 miles east of A134 between Sudbury and Bury St Edmunds. Turn left from Lavenham High Street into Market Place. On-street parking and a public car park

🛏 1 single, 1 twin, 4 double, 1 family room; some with bathroom/WC, some with shower/WC; TV, room service, hair-dryer, baby-listening in all rooms

◇ Restaurant, bar, 2 lounges, TV

room, games room; fishing, golf, other sports nearby. Wheelchair access to hotel (ramp), restaurant and WC, 1 ground-floor room

⊖ Dogs in 1 bedroom only

▭ Access, Visa

£ Single £30 to £35, single occupancy of twin/double £30 to £35, twin/double £45 to £55, family room £55 to £65; deposit required. Alc L £12, D £16. Special breaks available

ℒ   *This denotes that the hotel offers especially good value at whatever price level.*

# The Great House

MARKET PLACE, LAVENHAM, SUFFOLK CO10 9QZ
TEL: LAVENHAM (0787) 247431

*Fine old English building but a very French atmosphere. A good restaurant.*

Suffolk's most resplendent medieval town and the town's finest square are the setting for what you might expect to be a very English establishment. The white house is mainly fifteenth century, like its neighbours, but is larger than most and has a Georgian façade. The real surprise lies behind the elegant wooden door. You'll probably be greeted with a cheerful 'Bonjour' from a formally dressed young man with limited English, and Edith Piaf might be heard in the background. The staff rather than the surroundings dictate the atmosphere here.

The bar, with its polished oak antique settle and tables, tapestry-covered armchair, coal fire and oriental carpet on dark wood floor, is faintly French. Across the small entrance hall and you're squarely back in England: wheelback chairs, wall-to-wall carpet and white tablecloths – a cosy restaurant, this, with low ceiling and another open fire below a carved Bessemer beam. In summer, meals are served in the lovely enclosed terrace behind. No prizes for guessing the style of cooking. Set lunches and dinners give a small choice and prices are kind. The cooking is classical with some modern nuances. The owner lives in Texas and one wonders if there is a connection between that fact and the size of the four bedrooms. They are enormous, with rugs on uneven floors and handsome half-timbered walls; two have separate sitting-rooms. Most furniture is antique but furnishings aren't smart.

○ Open all year

⤴ Lavenham is on the A1141, 2 miles east of the A134 between Bury St Edmunds and Sudbury. The hotel is in Lavenham's market place

🛏 2 twin, 1 double, 1 family room; most with bathroom/WC, exc 1 twin with shower/WC; TV, room service, hair-dryer, baby-listening in all rooms

◇ Restaurant, bar, lounge; conference facilities (max 15 people non-residential); tennis, riding, other sports nearby. Wheelchair access to restaurant only

⊖ No dogs in public rooms

▭ Access, Amex, Visa

£ Single occupancy of twin/double £50, twin/double £68 to £78; deposit required. Set L £13, D £14; alc L £9, D £18. Special breaks available

*See the inside front cover for a brief explanation of how to use the* Guide.

# The Swan

HIGH STREET, LAVENHAM, SUFFOLK CO10 9QA
TEL: LAVENHAM (0787) 247477   TELEX: 987198 SWANGHO G
FAX: (0787) 248286

*Large, well-known and expensive old inn in historic medieval town.*

If you're looking for an intimate and secluded old pub, give the Swan a miss. Its façade of several half-timbered frontages takes up a sizeable stretch of the high street of this much-visited town. It was probably an inn before America was discovered (and discovered by Americans some time later); its age makes it popular. On any Sunday afternoon its many interconnecting, low-ceilinged lounging areas teem with well-dressed tea-sippers and scampering children. Old features, such as narrow passageways and wobbly floors, haven't been obscured by too many modern trappings.

The restaurant, with high timber-roof and minstrels' gallery, is a grand place for a special occasion. The stamp of company ownership (in this case, Forte) is unmistakable, especially in predictably furnished bedrooms. They vary considerably; some abound with beams, some could be called dowdy; none get points for value. Guests on their own should request a double, which are not much more expensive than the rather boring superior singles. Staff can be a bit off-hand at busy times. More reports, please.

◐ Open all year

🔁 In Lavenham on the A1141. Private car park

🛏 9 single, 15 twin, 18 double, 2 four-posters, 3 suites; all with bathroom/WC, TV, room service, hair-dryer, trouser press, mini-bar, baby-listening

◈ Restaurant, 2 bars, 3 lounges; conference facilities (max 40 people residential and non-residential); golf, riding, other sports nearby; babysitting.

Wheelchair access to hotel, restaurant (2 steps) and WC, 5 ground-floor bedrooms (2 steps)

⊖ No dogs in public rooms

▭ Access, Amex, Diners, Visa

£ Single £75 to £80, single occupancy of twin/double £80 to £85, twin/double £95 to £105, four-poster £110 to £120, family room £95 to £105, suite £130 to £145. Continental B £6, cooked B £8; set L £14, D £20; alc L, D £30. Special breaks available

---

*The* Guide *is totally independent, accepts no free hospitality, and survives on the number of copies sold each year.*

# Flowerdale House

58 WARWICK ROAD, LEAMINGTON SPA, WARWICKSHIRE CV32 6AA
TEL: LEAMINGTON SPA (0926) 426002

*A homely B&B halfway between Leamington and Warwick.*

Bill and Barbara Powell run a neat and relaxed B&B on the edge of
Leamington. The Victorian house is spacious, with six rooms sharing the
disproportionally large public rooms. There is a sitting-room which
connects with the bar: both are comfortable rooms in which to lounge
around. Across the hall, the breakfast room leads through to the
conservatory with basket seating and plants.

Bedrooms are neat and airy, some in bright colours. They are simply
furnished with bright duvet covers and most have *en suite* facilities.
Flowerdale is popular with business folk and it often gets full when there
is a pig fair or other events at the nearby Stoneleigh Agricultural Centre.

◐ *Open all year*

⤤ *On the junction of Warwick New
Road (B4099) and Rugby Road,
opposite the headquarters of
Guide Dogs for the Blind. Private
car park*

🛏 *1 single, 3 twin, 2 double; most
with bathroom/WC, some with
shower/WC; TV in all rooms;
hair-dryer on request*

◈ *Breakfast room, bar, lounge,*

*conservatory; golf, fishing, other
sports nearby*

⊖ *No wheelchair access; no
children under 12; no dogs; no
smoking in public rooms*

▭ *Access, Visa*

£ *Single £21 to £25, single
occupancy of twin/double £28 to
£30, twin/double £36 to £40;
deposit required*

# The Lansdowne

87 CLARENDON STREET, LEAMINGTON SPA, WARWICKSHIRE CV32 4PF
TEL: LEAMINGTON SPA (0926) 450505   FAX: (0926) 420604

*There are attentive hosts and a warm convivial atmosphere in this
cosy town house hotel.*

This small town house hotel has a good reputation in Leamington. The
Regency-style building is warm and welcoming, and rooms are cosy and
the atmosphere relaxed. There's a mix of furnishings – some old and
some reproduction – but the overall feel is Victorian. Surfaces are
covered in lace and topped with pot plants and heavy curtains are draped
across windows. Bedrooms are plainer with stripped pine beds and large
wardrobes; the wallpapers are deep-coloured. Rooms at the back are
quieter than those at the front.

We've had good reports on meals: 'The boss takes great care to please his diners without overdoing the ostentation'; and 'having no half-bottles of the chosen wine, he straightaway put a full bottle on the table and invited us to help ourselves to half the bottle'. Another guest on a fourth visit to the hotel was disappointed in the caretaker service whilst Gillian and David Allen were away on holiday.

◑ *Open all year; restaurant closed to non-residents Sun*

🔁 *In the centre of Leamington Spa. Private car park*

🛏 *7 single, 5 twin, 3 double; some with bathroom/WC, most with shower/WC, 1 public bathroom; TV, hair-dryer, baby-listening on request*

◈ *Dining-room, bar, lounge; golf, tennis, other sports nearby.*

*Wheelchair access to hotel (1 step) and restaurant, 2 ground-floor bedrooms*

● *No children under 5; no dogs*

▭ *Access, Visa*

💷 *Single £25 to £48, single occupancy of twin/double £25 to £48, twin/double £39 to £58; deposit required. Set D £16. Special breaks available*

---

# York House

**9 YORK ROAD, LEAMINGTON SPA, WARWICKSHIRE CV31 3PR**
**TEL: LEAMINGTON SPA (0926) 424671**

*Small, family-run hotel of warmth and character.*

Close to the railway station on a quiet road facing on to a small park and the River Leam, this three-storey Victorian house is owned and run by Sue and Robert Davis. Over the past few years they have carefully created a hotel of character and warmth, reviving the house's period charm and filling it with Victoriana and knick-knacks.

The lounge, with a *chaise-longue* in the bay window, has pot plants, small polished tables with ornaments and a large fireplace with glazed tiles. The dining-room has a recently added dado rail and archway, and is adorned with family photographs, ornaments and a display of china in a glass cabinet. Sue Davis prepares set dinners which may include Parma ham and melon, followed by fillet steak in a brandy and peppercorn sauce and a selection of vegetables (but invariably including carrots).

Bedrooms are up the thickly carpeted stairs and are light and pretty.

◑ *Open all year*

🔁 *From main parade in Leamington Spa turn right into Dormer Place, left into Dale Street, then left into York Road. The hotel overlooks the River Leam. Private car park*

🛏 *2 single, 4 twin, 2 double, 2 family rooms, some with*

*bathroom/WC, some with shower/WC; TV, room service, hair-dryer, baby-listening in all rooms*

◈ *Dining-room, lounge; golf, tennis, other sports nearby; babysitting*

● *No wheelchair access; no dogs in dining-room and at hotel owner's discretion in bedrooms; no* smoking in dining-room and some bedrooms

▭ Access, Amex, Visa

£ Single £18 to £22, single

occupancy of twin/double £25 to £38, twin/double £33 to £50; family room £60; deposit required. Set D £13.50; alc D £21. Special breaks available

---

**LECK** LANCASHIRE                                      MAP 3

# Cobwebs

LECK, COWAN BRIDGE, KIRKBY LONSDALE, LANCASHIRE LA6 2HZ
TEL: KIRKBY LONSDALE (052 42) 72141  FAX: (052 42) 72141

*Small friendly country guesthouse with exceptional food.*

Lucky the fly that gets caught in this Cobweb! Just beyond the pleasant town of Kirkby Lonsdale you'll find a spick and span warm-coloured stone villa with a cobbled courtyard and pretty garden.

Food is at the heart of this enterprise, and Paul Kelly takes guests through the choices on the menu in the Victorian front parlour, before seating them in the small, modishly decorated restaurant. Split soups, perhaps chilled courgette and tarragon or sea trout and samphire, created by pouring from two ladles simultaneously, are a speciality here. Bread is home-baked and comes in three varieties. Sorbet precedes the main course – quail stuffed with wild rice and apricots, perhaps, followed by fruits marinated in Cointreau. Local cheeses round things off. The wine list is surprisingly comprehensive. The bedrooms are neat, chintzy and colour-themed, often with pine or good old furniture. Thoughtful touches include a wooden biscuit barrel full of nibbles and a hot-water bottle to beat the chill.

◑ Closed Jan to mid-Mar; restaurant closed Sun, Mon eves

▨ Leave the M6 at Junction 36 and travel east for 8 miles on the A65. Turn left at Cowan Bridge. Private car park

🛏 5 single, 2 twin, 3 double; most with bathroom/WC, some with shower/WC; TV, room service, hair-dryer in all rooms

◈ Restaurant, 2 lounges, drying

room, conservatory; fishing, golf nearby

⊖ No wheelchair access; no children under 12; no dogs; no smoking in restaurant

▭ Access, Visa

£ Single occupancy of twin/double £40, twin/double £60; deposit required. Set D £25. Special breaks available

---

*Shame on you South Yorkshire, Tyne & Wear and Mid Glamorgan, the only counties without an hotel of merit in this year's* Guide.

**LEDBURY** HEREFORD AND WORCESTER      **MAP 6**

# Hope End

HOPE END, LEDBURY, HEREFORD AND WORCESTER HR8 1JQ
TEL: LEDBURY (0531) 3613    FAX: (0531) 5697

*An unusual house in beautiful grounds; the kitchen garden is all-important.*

The name may spell doom and gloom, but the reality is totally different. A bumpy track leads over a mound and the house in the dip comes into view through the trees – an unusual red-brick Georgian building with idiosyncratic Eastern additions, like the minaret. Fancy fowl peck around the courtyard, but human visitors are less constrained: 20 acres of gardens and another 20 acres of parkland invite exploration. Banks of meadow flowers lead down to a landscaped water garden; Greek-style temples and stone statues clad in ivy or honeysuckle sit beneath the trees. The huge walled garden is Patricia and John Hegarty's pride and joy; here much of the organic fruit and vegetables used by Patricia in her cooking is grown. Tomatoes ripen in the glasshouse; sea kale is blanched beneath terracotta pots. From garden to table the transformation is excellent, with the emphasis, not surprisingly, on freshness. The menu has expanded since last year – a choice of three main courses is now offered, with at least one being vegetarian. Over 60 half-bottles are included on the extensive wine list, heavily biased towards France. The dining-room is simply furnished, hung with paintings of food.

The simplicity extends to the rest of the house, with lots of wood. Furniture is square and chunky; colours are plain and mostly natural tones, with scarcely a floral print in sight. Wood-burning stoves and log fires add cosiness to winter evenings, and picture frames surround original oils and sketches rather than prints. Bedrooms come in three sizes: best, medium and small. The best has beautiful views over the water garden and a huge bathroom with cork tiles and pine panelling.

◑ Open mid-Feb to mid-Dec; restaurant eves only, Mon, Tue eves residents supper only

▨ 2 miles north of Ledbury, just beyond Wellington Heath. Private car park

🛏 4 twin, 5 double, 1 annexe room, 1 cottage; all with bathroom/ WC, room service, hair-dryer

◈ Dining-room, 3 lounges, drying room; conference facilities (max 9 people residential)

⊖ No wheelchair access; no children under 12; no dogs; no smoking in dining-room

▭ Access, Visa

£ All rooms £90 to £135; deposit required. Set D £29

---

*Report forms are at the back of the book; write a letter if you prefer.*

# 42 The Calls

42 THE CALLS, LEEDS, WEST YORKSHIRE LS2 7EW
TEL: LEEDS (0532) 440099
FAX: (0532) 344100

*An exciting city hotel which shuns predictability and justifies its
high prices by careful attention to detail.*

Take four dilapidated grain warehouses by the River Aire in downtown
Leeds, add liberal amounts of glass and mirror (keeping the original
structure intact) and garnish with seemingly casual touches – a papier
mâché Thai duck in one corner, a bowl of oranges in another, original
sketches and prints on the walls. The result? An extremely stylish city-
centre hotel that is a world away from the usual functional but bland
business base.

It's a recipe concocted by the owner, Jonathan Wix, with the assistance
of a local interior designer, Juliet Jowitt, and it works well. With years of
experience in both running his own hotels and staying in other people's,
Jonathan has incorporated all his personal preferences and cut out the
things that make him mad. 'Breakfast always seems to arrive when I'm
getting into the shower,' he says, 'and I find myself opening the door
dripping wet.' Hence an ingenious hatch-cum-cupboard in which a
continental breakfast of fruit compôte, yoghurt and French pastries plus
a morning paper is left until you've dried off. Alternatively, cooked
breakfasts are served in the River Room below, its stark French furniture
contrasting with a striking red canvas. Another of Jonathan's grouses is
hotels that offer little more than a bed to sleep in: 'Having a bedroom is
third on the list of my priorities. I want a drawing-room first, then, if
necessary, an office.' As a result, the rooms are very well equipped, all
have CD players, filter-coffee machines and large desks (faxes and
secretarial services are also available). They are all differently decorated
and you'll find that the prices are dependent on their size. They don't
come cheap, but Jonathan has the sensible policy of automatically
upgrading guests to the best room available. One of the most popular
bedrooms is proving to be the slinky 307 with its black and grey 'glazed'
wallpaper and heavy beams. Other rooms are more colourful; most have
views on to the river and all are very quiet for a city centre. Because the
bedrooms are largely self-contained, the public rooms are more of an
afterthought. A small bar runs off the reception area with steps to a tiny
sitting area.

Friendly staff, rather self-consciously dressed in tail coats, are anxious
to please and, since there's no restaurant in-house, will book you a table
at the smart Brasserie Forty-Four, next door, which Jonathan co-owns
with Martin Hodgson. The food here is good, reasonably priced and
justifiably popular with locals.

◑ Open all year

↗ In the centre of Leeds; detailed instructions sent upon booking. Private car park and on-street metered parking

🛏 6 single, 24 twin/double, 6 double, 3 suites; all with bathroom/WC, TV, room service, hair-dryer, trouser press, mini-bar, baby-listening

◈ Breakfast room, brasserie, bar, lounge (all public areas air-conditioned); conference facilities (max 55 people non-residential, 43 residential); golf, riding, other sports nearby; babysitting. Wheelchair access to hotel and brasserie, 2 bedrooms specially equipped for the disabled

⊖ Dogs by arrangement only; some bedrooms non-smoking

▭ Access, Amex, Diners, Visa

£ Single £95, single occupancy of twin/double £115 to £125, twin/double £120 to £130, suite £140 to £185; deposit required. Cooked B £10, continental B £6; set L £10, D £11; alc L, D £20. Special breaks available

---

## LEICESTER LEICESTERSHIRE                    MAP 4

# Spindle Lodge

---

2 WEST WALK, LEICESTER, LEICESTERSHIRE LE1 7NA
TEL: LEICESTER (0533) 551380

*A friendly, family-run hotel ideal for university visitors.*

Tucked away down a quiet side street and in the midst of various university buildings, this Victorian house is a reasonably priced find in the centre of Leicester. The house, with an easy-going atmosphere, is owned and run by Angie and Trevor Cotton. They have recently laid new carpets in the hallway and stairs, refurbished the small bar and have applied for planning permission to build on five more rooms. 'It's like the Forth Bridge,' says Angie Cotton, 'with work always to be done'. In the tiled hallway you'll find a pay phone and information on the area.

The dining-room is appealing with lacy tablecloths, wooden chairs and a bold wallpaper with decorative straw hats displayed on the wall and ornaments on the mantelpiece. Evening meals are usually at 6.30pm by arrangement though Angie's flexible and, 'if someone wants a bowl of cornflakes at 10pm in the evening, then they can have it'. Bedrooms are plainer and less interesting but all are neatly kept and fresh and some have bathrooms.

◑ Open all year, exc Xmas and New Year; restaurant closed Fri, Sat and Sun eves

↗ From Leicester BR station, turn left onto the A6 London road and take the first turning right into De Montfort Street. Carry on to the traffic lights and turn left and first left again into West Walk. Private car park

🛏 5 single, 3 twin, 3 double, 2 family rooms, 1 with bathroom/WC, some with shower/WC, 2 public bathrooms; TV, room

service, baby-listening in all
rooms; hair-dryer, ironing
facilities on request

◈ Dining-room, bar, lounge;
babysitting

⬤ No wheelchair access; dogs in
bedrooms only, by arrangement;
no smoking in dining-room

▭ Access, Visa

£ Single £24 to £33, single
occupancy of twin/double £29 to
£33, twin/double £44 to £53;
family room £66; deposit
required. Alc D £12.50

---

## LEICESTER FOREST EAST LEICESTERSHIRE          MAP 4

# The Red Cow

HINCKLEY ROAD, LEICESTER FOREST EAST, LEICESTER, LEICESTERSHIRE
LE3 3PG
TEL: LEICESTER (0533) 387878   FAX: (0533) 387878 ext 259

*A thoroughly refurbished inn with a new separate accommodation block.*

Beside a busy road and fronted entirely by a large car park, the Red Cow
is an old thatched inn which has been thoroughly modernised on the
inside. Accommodation is in a separate building across the car park,
whilst the old building now houses a restaurant, a lounge bar, and, to the
rear, a conservatory for family use overlooking the garden.

In the early evening the lounge bar and conservatory are busy with
people dropping in for a drink after work. The atmosphere is sociable
and informal with children running around in the garden. The restaurant is decked out in the same country-style pine as the lounge bar and
serves an à la carte menu, or you can get bar snacks in the lounge bar.
Bedrooms are modern in pinks and blues and are reasonably priced. A
family room with two adults and two children under 14 years works out as
a bargain, particularly at weekends.

◐ Open all year

↗ On the A47 between Leicester
and Hinckley. Leave the M1 at
Junction 21 or 22 and follow
outer ring road. Private car park

🛏 4 twin, 27 double (family rooms
available); all with bathroom/
WC, TV, hair-dryer, trouser
press, baby-listening

◈ Restaurant, bar, conservatory,
family room; conference facilities
(max 10 people residential);
golf, heated swimming-pool

nearby. Wheelchair access to
hotel (ramp), restaurant and WC
(unisex), 16 ground-floor
bedrooms, 1 specially equipped
for the disabled

⬤ No dogs

▭ Access, Amex, Diners, Visa

£ Single occupancy of twin/double
£42, twin/double £50, family
room £50; deposit required. Bar
meals from £4; set L, D £8; alc
L, D £15. Special breaks
available

**LEIGHTON BUZZARD** BEDFORDSHIRE                **MAP 6**

# The Swan

HIGH STREET, LEIGHTON BUZZARD, BEDFORDSHIRE LU7 7EA
TEL: LEIGHTON BUZZARD (0525) 372148
FAX: (0525) 370444

*An efficiently run town-centre hotel with better food than most.*

Behind its attractively weathered façade, the Swan, opposite the market cross on the High Street, offers uncluttered comfort and genuinely attentive service from young staff. The hotel is a Georgian coaching-inn, but the age shows only in the creaking, uneven upstairs floors. The restaurant is newly refurbished: it's an inviting airy place with a conservatory extension out into the courtyard where once the coaches would have arrived.

Cooking is commendably simple but inventive. Vegetarians are exceptionally well catered for with their own menu – dishes such as crispy sesame pancakes filled with a spiced seasoning of pimento and shallots set on a madeira sauce.

A small lounge to the side of the entrance is screened from view by potted palms, and a separate entrance from the street gives access to the Hunters Bar, which bustles with lunchtime trade, particularly on Tuesday (market day). Bedrooms are large and comfortable enough to retreat to; those in the newer courtyard block have their own kitchenettes and are let as apartments.

- Open all year
- In the centre of Leighton Buzzard. Private car park
- 22 single, 4 twin, 10 double, 1 four-poster, 1 family; all with bathroom/WC, TV, room service, hair-dryer, trouser press, baby-listening
- Restaurant (air-conditioned), bar, lounge, conservatory; conference facilities (max 35 people, 16 residential); golf, tennis nearby
- No wheelchair access; no dogs
- Access, Amex, Diners, Visa
- Single from £75, single occupancy of twin/double from £80, twin/double from £80, four-poster from £85, family room from £80; deposit required. Alc L, D £20

---

*The cheese had seen better days, and wines on both evenings were not of the listed vintage (younger than advertised). No apology or explanation was offered for this aberration. We feel rather cowardly for not mentioning this latter point at the time, but having been dealt with at arm's length didn't think it would be worthwhile.* On an hotel in Cumbria

# Upper Buckton Farm

LEINTWARDINE, CRAVEN ARMS, SHROPSHIRE SY7 0JU
TEL: LEINTWARDINE (054 73) 634

*Peaceful, good-value farmhouse serving good food, run by friendly
family.*

'If the guide gave a classification for friendliness then Upper Buckton
would have it,' writes one satisfied reader. And, indeed, by the end of a
stay with the Lloyds, it's more like saying goodbye to old family friends
than to hotel proprietors.

Upper Buckton is a real working farm: in the morning Hayden boards
his tractor for a day ploughing the fields; in the evening he dons his green
gardening apron to act as head waiter and bottle-opener for the guests. If
you ask him nicely he might even divulge his secret method of wrapping a
napkin round the bottle to catch the drips! Guests eat dinner together at
7pm; although there are separate tables mealtimes are quite chatty.
Food, cooked by Yvonne, is appetising and down to earth: roast lamb
with home-made mint sauce, roast potatoes, courgettes, and a root
vegetable purée topped with chopped hazelnuts; and afterwards a cold
lemon soufflé. One reader describes meals as 'a sheer delight . . . I
always come away with a list of scribbled-down ideas'. Both Hayden and
Yvonne join the guests in the lounge for after-dinner coffee, still wearing
their gardening gear.

There is a large TV tucked away in the corner should conversation
ever start to flag, but one suspects that this is a rare occurrence.
Bedrooms are large, with solid wooden furniture and chintzy curtains.
Some overlook the garden with the millstream running along the bottom,
others look on to the yard.

🌓 *Open all year, exc Dec 25, 26,
31 and 1 Jan*

🔁 *Take the A4113 from Ludlow
towards Knighton. Turn right at
Walford crossroads for Buckton,
2nd farm on left. Private car
park*

🛏 *2 twin, 2 double; 4 public
bathrooms; tea/coffee-making
facilities, hair-dryer on request*

◈ *Dining-room, lounge, games
room, TV; croquet, table tennis
at farm*

⊖ *No wheelchair access; no dogs;
no smoking*

▭ *None accepted*

£ *Single occupancy of twin/double
£12 to £20; twin/double £24 to
£40; deposit required. Set D £12
(7pm, by arrangement)*

*You will find report forms at the back of the Guide – please use them!*

# The Farmhouse Hotel

UNIVERSITY FARM, LEW, NR BAMPTON, OXFORDSHIRE OX8 2AU
TEL: BAMPTON CASTLE (0993) 850297/851480

*An economical hotel on a working farm which offers comfortable accommodation and hearty meals.*

As you pull up in the farmyard you might notice the glistening snout of a Rolls-Royce poking, a little incongruously, out of one of the barn doors. It is often in use for weddings and special occasions, and Mrs Rouse, the homely proprietor, is also known to use it for a trip to the shops.

The hotel, like the outbuildings, is spruce but pleasantly worn. The sitting-room is clean but well-lived-in, with slightly battered settees and an inglenook fireplace with a cast-iron wood-burning stove. The bedrooms have a wide variety of décor. The best is Merton, in the attic, with exposed beams, pretty blue floral print coverings on bed, table and armchair, and freshly emulsioned walls. Queens, the largest of the rooms, with bed drapes, and walls and carpet the colour of fresh strawberry ice-cream, carries a higher tariff. Elsewhere the style is candlewick bedspreads and functional, uninspiring furniture.

The restaurant offers five different menus, the choice depending on how many courses you feel up to. The consistent elements are the hors d'oeuvre trolley, a tureen of soup and a choice of roasts. There's also a healthy eating choice: fish, chicken and salads. The conservatory extension is used for breakfasts.

○ Open all year, exc Xmas and New Year; restaurant closed Sun eve

↗ On the A4095 Witney to Bampton road. The hotel is set back from the road behind a range of stone farm buildings. Private car park

⇔ 2 twin, 3 double, 1 family room; half with bathroom/WC, half with shower/WC; TV, room service, hair-dryer in all rooms

◇ Restaurant (air-conditioned), bar, lounge, conservatory; conference facilities (max 30 people non-residential). Wheelchair access to hotel and restaurant, 1 ground-floor bedroom specially equipped for the disabled

● No children under 5; no dogs; no smoking in bedrooms and some public areas

▭ Access, Visa

£ Single occupancy of twin/double £35, twin/double £50; family room £60; deposit required. Set D £14.50

*See the back of the* Guide *for an index of hotels listed.*

# Lewtrenchard Manor

LEWDOWN, NR OKEHAMPTON, DEVON EX20 4PN
TEL: LEWDOWN (056 683) 256/222   FAX: (056 683) 332

*Fascinating stately home of grand proportions but cosy nature.*
*Haven for humans and ghosts alike.*

We'd like to apologise to Margaret Gould, resident ghost in this large, Elizabethan manor house, for exaggerating her non-existence in last year's Guide. With the imposing, high-ceilinged halls and rooms, weighty doors, dark and heavy panelling and embossed ceilings, Lewtrenchard might sound the perfect haven for ghosts. But perhaps a bit gloomy for humans? A few glances around and an encounter with your living hosts should soon exorcise any apprehensions. Since arriving in 1988, James and Susan Murray have refreshed, brightened and upgraded the furnishings. Stately antiques and modern fabrics go together; there are few dainty items about, so everything melds well. (The two leopard skins draped on the enormous chest by the grand staircase were once family pets and died a natural death.)

The Murrays' good-natured spirit and enthusiasm continue to impress many guests. Well-meaning rather than professional young staff take over at dinner, served in a majestic panelled dining-room lined with gilt-framed portraits of former residents. (A new chef arrived as we went to press.) Next morning, the Murrays will enquire how you slept. Very well, in all probability, and you may be remembering your grand Elizabethan-style four-poster bed, the white-carpeted bathroom, views through mullioned windows over formal gardens (by Gertrude Jekyll), the gentle sound of the fountain and tweeting of birds. The Murrays have been revamping bedrooms, seemingly with little regard for cost. Named after melodies of hymns by Sabine Baring-Gould, they're fine rooms, with antiques, window seats, carved fireplaces, bright walls and big beds. With its triple aspect, oak panelling, fabulous moulded and leather-trimmed ceiling, St Gertrude, theme of 'Onward Christian Soldiers', is the most striking. Mod cons and pampering extras are laid on, destined to please the many Americans who come to lap up the past and luxuriate in the present.

- Closed 3 weeks Jan and Feb
- Halfway between Okehampton and Launceston on the A30. At Lewdown turn left at the sign for Lewtrenchard and follow this road. Private car park
- 3 twin, 2 double, 2 four-poster, 1 suite; all with bathroom/WC, TV, room service, hair-dryer; no tea/coffee-making facilities in rooms
- 2 dining-rooms, bar, 3 lounges; conference facilities (max 40 people non-residential, 16 residential); fishing, croquet, clay pigeon shooting at hotel, riding, other sports nearby. Wheelchair access to dining-rooms and WC (unisex) only
- No children under 8; no dogs in

public rooms; no smoking in dining-room

🛏 Access, Amex, Diners, Visa

£ Single occupancy of twin/double

from £65, twin/double from £95, four-poster £125, suite £130; deposit required. Set L (Sun) £16, D £25; alc D £23 to £33. Special breaks available

## LICHFIELD STAFFORDSHIRE                          MAP 4

# Angel Croft

BEACON STREET, LICHFIELD, STAFFORDSHIRE WS13 7AA
TEL: LICHFIELD (0543) 258737   FAX: (0543) 415605

*A comfortingly old-fashioned and very efficiently run hotel near the cathedral.*

The hotel entrance is on the main road but you can sit in the large gardens stretching behind and forget the bustle of Lichfield. Both the main house and Westgate House, a bedroom annexe the other side of the car park, date from the mid-eighteenth century; even the railings are listed.

The Wharmby family have run the hotel for over twenty years and as soon as you enter there's a feeling of reliability. Portraits of the family hang in the hall and the general style of décor is old-fashioned but in good condition. A full lunch and dinner is served in the traditionally furnished dining-room and amounts to fairly plain English cooking. You can have lighter snacks in the bar downstairs or in the garden in summer. Bedrooms both in the main house and the annexe are comfortable if a little plain; if possible ask for one in the main house overlooking the garden: these rooms are large, very light and quiet.

◑ Open all year, exc 25, 26 Dec; restaurant closed Sun eve

⚡ On the main road running through Lichfield, opposite the cathedral. Private car park

🛏 12 twin, 5 double, 1 four-poster, 2 family rooms; most with bathroom/WC, some with shower/WC; TV, baby-listening in all rooms; hair-dryer on request

◈ Restaurant, bar, lounge; conference facilities (max 24

people non-residential, 20 residential); golf, tennis, other sports nearby. Wheelchair access to public rooms only

⊖ No dogs

🛏 Access, Amex, Diners, Visa

£ Single occupancy of twin/double £39 to £55, twin/double/ four-poster £55 to £67; suite £63 to £74, family room rate available on request. Set L £9.50 to £17, D £11 to £18.50. Special breaks available

# Old Rectory Cottage

21 GAIA LANE, LICHFIELD, STAFFORDSHIRE WS13 7LW
TEL: LICHFIELD (0543) 254941

*Neat little B&B within walking distance of the town centre.*

Gaia Lane runs off one of Lichfield's main streets and is a leafy, quiet
residential area. The cathedral, which you can see from one of the
bedrooms, is only a few minutes' walk away. Old Rectory Cottage is in
fact two cottages joined together with a bit added on one side; cream-
painted walls and mullioned windows come complete with ivy and
wistaria – it is a charming little place.

There are only two bedrooms, neither huge, but like everything else
here they are very neat. The double room is the largest, with attractive
wooden furniture, and the twin overlooks the garden. Both have washbasins as they share a bathroom. Flowery duvets and a collection of
personal objects and pictures give the bedrooms a homely feel.

Breakfast is whenever you want and served in the beamed, country-
style dining-room on a single pine table. The garden at the back is
beautifully kept and if guests are staying for a few days in summer the
Zavous are happy for them to use it. You are well looked after here but it's
strictly a B&B place – not a place to lounge around in on a rainy day.

- Open all year, exc Xmas and New Year
- In the centre of Lichfield, near the cathedral. Private car park
- 1 twin, 1 double (shared bathroom); both with TV
- Dining-room, laundry
- No wheelchair access; no
- children under 5; no dogs; no smoking in bedrooms
- None accepted
- Single occupancy of twin/double £19 to £20, twin/double £28 to £30; family room (1 child) £39; deposit required

# Swinfen Hall

SWINFEN, NR LICHFIELD, STAFFORDSHIRE WS14 9RS
TEL: LICHFIELD (0543) 481494   FAX: (0543) 480341

*An elegant house with an interesting history. Careful restoration
has left it feeling a little self-conscious but it should soften up.*

A manor house has been here since medieval times but the present hall
was completed only in 1757. It had been empty for years until the present
owners bought it and, after intensive restoration both externally and
internally, opened it as a hotel about two and a half years ago. They have
done a fine job with it – the stucco work is particularly flamboyant with
blue and cream ceilings in the hall and pink and white in the restaurant.

The drawing-room, also known as the cocktail lounge, is decorated in yellows and blues with french windows opening on to the terrace. When the owners have found the right pictures to fill areas of blank wall space it will probably look a lot more inviting. The bar was added on in 1857, as a games and music room. It was probably happier as that and feels slightly uncomfortable as a clubby bar with its reddish studded shiny leather armchairs and a jarring 'Gents' sign on the wall.

The bedrooms on the first floor are particularly large and high-ceilinged, and the fireplaces are grand. Furniture tends to be reproduction Regency with 'period furnishings' on this floor, while bedrooms on the second are smaller with pastel colours and light oak furniture. One of our readers was disappointed with the room he got: let out as a 'superior single', it was both small and lacking in facilities. All bathrooms are smart and functional with good-quality fittings. Don't miss the Grinling Gibbons panelling in the ballroom.

◑ Open all year

↗ 2 miles south of Lichfield, off the A38. Private car park

🛏 2 single, 11 double, 2 family rooms, 4 suites; all with bathroom/WC, TV, room service, hair-dryer, trouser press, baby-listening

◇ 2 restaurants, bar, 2 lounges; conference facilities (max 200 people non-residential, 19 residential); croquet at hotel, other sports nearby; babysitting. Wheelchair access to public rooms only

⊖ No dogs

▭ Access, Amex, Visa

£ Single £75, single occupancy of twin/double £85, twin/double £95, family room £115, suite £125; deposit required. Set L £18, D £26

---

**LINCOLN** LINCOLNSHIRE                    **MAP 4**

# D'Isney Place Hotel

EASTGATE, LINCOLN, LINCOLNSHIRE LN2 4AA
TEL: LINCOLN (0522) 538881   FAX: (0522) 511321

*If you're the sociable sort this may not be the place for you. But it's a stylish, central base.*

Close to Lincoln Cathedral, this eighteenth-century house describes itself as having an 'atmosphere of elegant luxury and quiet discretion'. Indeed, it does. It also offers stylish accommodation with special touches that make you aware you are being cosseted. There are no public rooms and breakfast only is served – in your room on Minton china – though there are plenty of places close by for an evening meal.

Rooms vary in size and are priced accordingly. They are fresh and pretty, some with bold floral fabrics and white cotton bedspreads. Some doubles are quite small and if you intend to be in a lot it's worth paying the extra for a larger room. Fresh flasks of milk for your tea-tray and soft white towelling robes are provided. Rooms on the ground floor suffer some noise in the mornings as breakfast trays are delivered to neighbouring rooms and the bell is rung in the hallway 'reception' to attract staff attention by guests departing early. We've also had good reports on the self-catering apartments. 'Marvellous sitting-room with views across the garden to the old cathedral.' 'Only one small quibble, which would certainly not deter us from a return visit, was that the minute shower room and toilet were situated off the twin-bedded room and the only washbasin was actually in the twin room.'

- ◐ Open all year
- ⤴ By the cathedral. Private car park
- 🛏 2 single, 3 twin, 12 double, 1 four-poster, 3 self-catering cottages; most with bathroom/ WC, some with shower/WC; TV, hair-dryer, baby-listening in all rooms
- ◈ Drying room; fishing, golf, other sports nearby; babysitting.

- Wheelchair access to hotel (ramp) and 8 ground-floor bedrooms
- ⊖ No dogs or smoking in public rooms
- ▭ Access, Amex, Diners, Visa
- £ Single £39, single occupancy of twin/double £48, twin/double £61, four-poster £70, cottage £188 per week; deposit required. Special breaks available

# The White Hart

BAILGATE, LINCOLN, LINCOLNSHIRE LN1 3AR
TEL: LINCOLN (0522) 526222   TELEX: 56304
FAX: (0522) 531798

*There's an old-fashioned feel to this ideally placed Forte hotel with elegant, well-kept rooms.*

You pay for the position here: the White Hart is two minutes' away from the cathedral and the castle and surrounded by small interesting shops. Inside, this old coaching-inn has been furnished in a comfortable style; there is an elegant, slightly old-fashioned feel with more than a smattering of antiques.

The old wooden revolving doors lead you into a hallway with a busy snug bar off to one side and a lounge area in front of you. Upholstered seats and sofas are gathered around low tables, with a mix of reading matter and newspapers for guests – though it's not ideal for peace and quiet with the reception desk off to one side and a door beyond it leading through to a elegant formal restaurant. There is a fair choice on the table d'hôte menu, plus more expensive selections. Lunches are served in the Orangery (site of the old courtyard), under a large skylight and decorated with ferns and a neo-classical mural. The hotel is popular with business guests and American tourists who appreciate, amongst other things, the power showers and thick towels in the bathrooms. Some bedrooms have antique furnishings and Chinese or strong floral patterns on fine fabrics; others have more standard fittings.

◑ Open all year

↗ Centrally situated in Lincoln, between the castle wall and the cathedral. Private car park

🛏 11 single, 11 twin, 15 double, 13 suites; all with bathroom/WC, TV, room service, hair-dryer, trouser press, baby-listening

◇ 2 restaurants, 2 bars, lounge; conference facilities (max 100 people non-residential, 50 residential); fishing, golf, other sports nearby; babysitting. Wheelchair access to hotel (1 step), restaurant and WC (M,F),no ground-floor bedrooms but a lift

⊖ No dogs in public rooms; some bedrooms non-smoking

▭ Access, Amex, Diners, Visa

£ Single £75, single occupancy of twin/double £85, twin/double £100 to £110; suite £115 to £135; deposit required. Continental B £6, cooked B £8.50, Set L £10.50, D £17.50; alc D from £32

## LINTON WEST YORKSHIRE                    MAP 4

# Wood Hall

LINTON, NR WETHERBY, WEST YORKSHIRE LS22 4JA
TEL: WETHERBY (0937) 587271   FAX: (0937) 584353

*Professionally run, relaxed country-house hotel. The sumptuous rooms overlook gorgeous countryside.*

Pause a moment as you round the final curve on the mile-long drive out of Linton and you will see a magnificent view of the hotel silhouetted by dark woods and facing the unspoilt fields of the Wharfe valley. The beautiful estate has a long and chequered history. Seized by William the Conqueror in 1070, it was bestowed on the French Vavasour family to whom it belonged for several centuries. You can still see their coat of arms in the main hall of the hotel, retrieved from the River Wharfe a long time after their mansion was destroyed by Cromwell. The present building was erected in 1750 and was used as a private house, then as a school, finally becoming an hotel in 1989.

Not surprisingly, it is a great hit with Americans and business people from Leeds wishing to escape to more peaceful surroundings at the end of the day. The personable manager has a policy of dressing casually and encouraging the staff to welcome all newly arrived guests at the door – a policy which seems to work, according to one reader, who praised the 'friendly service' she received. The style of interior is traditional without being fuddy-duddy and cleverly draws on colour schemes to achieve a sense of harmony. The 22 bedrooms are individually decorated but are all equipped with home-made biscuits, fresh fruit, shower robes and small teddies placed on pillows: 'It used to be sweets, until one terrible morning when a man came down to breakfast with a chocolate stuck to his head.'

The Oak Room has a very unusual bar made from the top of an old grand piano still with its ivories intact, and french windows open out on to a lawn with tables. Dinner is served in the Georgian Room, overlooking the valley, and has been praised as 'imaginative' by one reader. Main dishes may include roast rack of lamb on a bed of creamed spinach or pan-fried calf's liver with wild mushrooms.

◐ Open all year

🏧 From Wetherby take Harrogate road for ½ mile. Turn left to Sicklinghall and Linton. Cross bridge, turn left follow road to Linton. Turn right opposite the Windmill pub. Follow estate road for 1¼ miles. Private car park

🛏 21 doubles, 1 four-poster; all with bathroom/WC, TV, room service, hair-dryer, trouser press, baby-listening; tea/coffee-making facilities on request

◈ 3 restaurants, bar, lounge, games room, library; conference facilities (max 44 people non-residential, 22 residential);

fishing at hotel, other sports nearby. Wheelchair access to hotel (4 steps) and restaurant, 1 ground-floor bedroom specially equipped for the disabled

⊖ No children under 8 in restaurant eves; no dogs in public rooms; some public rooms non-smoking

▭ Access, Amex, Diners, Visa

£ Single occupancy of double £98, twin/double £108, four-poster £143, family room £143, suite £245; deposit required. Set L £15, D £20; alc L, D £35 (prices till Apr 92). Special breaks available

## LITTLEBURY GREEN ESSEX                                       MAP 7

# Elmdon Lee

LITTLEBURY GREEN, NR SAFFRON WALDEN, ESSEX CB11 4XB
TEL: ROYSTON (0763) 838237

*An old farmhouse but providing modern creature comforts and sociable dinners. All the right ingredients for a restful break.*

A rural idyll. This is a hill-top, eighteenth-century farmhouse coated in Virginia creeper, with walnut, oak and beech trees presiding over mature gardens. The 900-acre estate is farmed by Diana Duke's son Robert. She runs a small country crafts gift shop but her guests come first.

This is a fine place to stay, both for the homely comforts and the atmosphere, and, because it's a member of the Wolsey Lodge group, this means dining communally. Despite the occasional chandelier it is not a formal home, but it's nicely furnished and very conducive to relaxation. In the lounge, comfy, loose-covered chairs are grouped round a log fire and guests congregate over drinks to exchange tales of the day's events. Diana pops in now and again, then summons you for dinner. A log fire burns in the tan dining-room, a pleasant, elegant room with pine floor and horsey paintings.

Good, unfussy English home cooking is the order of the day, and you'll not go hungry. It's so much like eating with friends you'll be inclined to help clear up. And you'll find welcoming touches in your bedrooms such as fresh milk for your tea, mineral water, large fluffy towels and proper bars of soap. Antiques are mostly Victorian. Some rooms have large bay windows and comfortable chairs from which to admire the view.

◐ *Open all year, exc 25, 26 Dec*

⤢ *16 miles south-east of Cambridge. Travelling on the M11 from the north, leave at Junction 10; from the south, Junction 8. Elmdon Lee is on the outskirts of Littlebury Green. Private car park*

🛏 *1 single, 2 twin, 1 double; all with bathroom/WC, TV, hair-dryer*

◈ *Dining-room, lounge, breakfast room; conference facilities (max 14 people non-residential); fishing nearby*

⊖ *No wheelchair access; no dogs*

▭ *Access, Visa*

£ *Single £25, single occupancy of twin/double £30, twin/double £50; deposit required. Set D £15*

---

## LITTLE PETHERICK CORNWALL                                   MAP 8

# Molesworth Manor

LITTLE PETHERICK, NR PADSTOW, WADEBRIDGE, CORNWALL PL27 7QT
TEL: RUMFORD (0841) 540292

*A rare chance to stay in a fine old manor house and pay B&B prices.*

The large stone former rectory dates from the early seventeenth century. Various Molesworths have lived here but the Reverend Sir Hugh, resident in Victorian times, left the strongest mark. This is a fine manor with fine detail within, such as newel posts carved into lions' heads, Gothic arches, crests in tall glass windows and fancy mouldings around grandly proportioned rooms.

A drawing-room and library with parquet floor and gold mouldings are handsome indeed. For the privilege of staying in such blue-blooded surroundings you generally expect to pay dearly, but Peter Pearce and Heather Clarke's rooms, all with private facilities, start at £16. A lot of the furniture is Victorian. First-floor rooms have plenty of space for large wardrobes and tall dressers. The Cook's Bedroom, up a narrow staircase on the second floor, has a lovely old brass bed. Views of open countryside are common to all rooms, some have original fireplaces and one has a fine old bathtub on legs. Her Ladyship's Room is the tops – a corner double with a writing desk in the bay. Bathrooms are good-sized.

The drawing-room is the venue for pre-dinner drinks when there's a crowd, but the small, comfy morning room, with open fire, books, television and pine Welsh dresser is more in keeping with the casual home style. Oil paintings hang on the walls of the dining-room and the large table is lit by soft candlelight. The menu is à la carte, the food good franglais. You are well looked after throughout your stay and made to feel at home. 'Good 'morrow, good 'morrow,' chirps Peter as you come down to a breakfast of fresh fruits, yoghurts and muesli.

◑ Open all year; restaurant closed Sun eve

◪ On the A389 from Wadebridge to Padstow. Once through St Issey and Little Petherick you will find the manor 200 yards up the hill on the right. Private car park

⇌ I single, 7 double, I family room, I cottage; most with bathroom/WC, some with shower/WC; no tea/coffee-making facilities in rooms

◈ Dining-room, lounge, TV room, games room, drying room, library; fishing, golf, other sports nearby. Wheelchair access to dining-room only

⊖ No children under 12; no dogs; no smoking

▭ None accepted

£ Single £16, single occupancy of twin/double £23 to £30, twin/double £34 to £45, family room £44. Cooked B £3.50; alc D £15

## LITTLE SINGLETON LANCASHIRE                             MAP 4

# Mains Hall

MAINS LANE, LITTLE SINGLETON, NR BLACKPOOL, LANCASHIRE FY6 7LE
TEL: POULTON-LE-FYLDE (0253) 885130    FAX: (0253) 894132

*An historical house in quiet riverside setting, offering very good service.*

The Hall has been providing hospitality for travellers since it was built by monks in the sixteenth century. To the left of the library's fireplace, disguised by a bookcase, there's an intriguing secret hiding hole where the Catholic owners sheltered priests in times of persecution, and in the eighteenth century, during Bonnie Prince Charlie's campaign, a band of fugitives was given refuge in the house. Prince George (later George IV) was entertained here by his mistress Maria Fitzherbert throughout their nine-year love affair.

Today, the reception area, with deep leather sofas and ornate oak-panelling (carved with grinning figures telling tales of witchcraft), boasts Roger and Pamela Yeomans' own coat of arms alongside that of the previous owners'. Since taking over the hotel, Roger and Pamela seem to have upheld successfully the Hall's longstanding tradition of hospitality. One reader who visits every year reports that they provide 'excellent, personal, homely service' making it 'an oasis to be enjoyed by anyone, particularly business people wanting to "get away from it all"'.

The bar is a small cosy room, with a huge marble fireplace and exposed beams, and overlooks the bleak River Wyre. It is a good place for chatting to other guests. Alternatively, you can use the library, which doubles as an office during the day. The bedrooms are a good size, irregularly shaped and furnished with a mixture of antiques and repro-ductions. Some have original four-poster or half-tester beds. Evening meals are served with pampering attention in the tiny dining-room. There's a wide choice for breakfast with a traditional sideboard buffet, and kippers cooked to order.

⬤ Open all year; dining-room closed Sun eve

▣ From Junction 3 on M55, follow signs to Fleetwood (A585) for 5 miles. Ignore signs to Singleton; Mains Hall is ½ mile past second set of traffic lights. Private car park

⬤ 3 twin, 5 double, 1 four-poster, 1 family room; some with bathroom/WC, some with shower/WC; TV, room service, hair-dryer, trouser press, baby-listening in all rooms

⬙ 2 dining-rooms, bar, lounge, TV room, library, conservatory;

conference facilities (max 40 people non-residential, 10 residential); golf, fishing, other sports nearby. Wheelchair access to hotel and dining-rooms, 2 ground-floor bedrooms

⬤ No dogs in public areas; no smoking in bedrooms

▭ Access, Visa

£ Single occupancy of twin/double £45 to £65, twin/double £65 to £95, four-poster £120, family room £95; deposit required. Set D £22.50. Special breaks available

---

## LITTLE STRETTON SHROPSHIRE                  MAP 6

# Mynd House

LITTLE STRETTON, CHURCH STRETTON, SHROPSHIRE SY6 6RB
TEL: CHURCH STRETTON (0694) 722212   FAX: (0694) 724180

*Enthusiastic hosts welcome guests into their home to share their love of good living.*

The red-brick Edwardian house, backed by the beautiful hills of the Long Mynd, makes an excellent base to explore the Shropshire country-side. Janet and Robert Hill are used to welcoming walkers and among the local information left in bedrooms you'll find a copy of Robert's booklet, *Six Walks from Mynd House Hotel*.

The Hills' enthusiasm for their surroundings is also reflected in the titles given to the bedrooms – all named after the local hills. They are smartly done up and some have particular features. The curved 1820s bed in 'Ashbracken' is one of only three ever made. In 'Hazler' (a mini-suite) you'll find a four-poster, a double spa bath and a view of All Saints – 'the only thatched church in Shropshire,' claims Robert. Wine is another passion of the Hills and is revealed in an extensive wine list, running to 39 pages and over 240 labels. Wine experience weekends are offered, among other themed breaks.

In the evening, Robert dons a black tie, Janet an apron, and four-course table d'hôte or à la carte menus are served in the informal dining-room. Meals are accompanied by malty bread from the village bakery and rounded off by salty Shropshire Blue cheese. A newly decorated bar opens on to the garden and has cane chairs with a collection of French restaurant menus on the wall. Next door is a comfortable lounge, with chairs grouped around a large wood-burning stove.

◑ Closed Jan

🅰 On the B4370, 1¼ miles south-
west of Church Stretton. Private
car park

🛏 1 single, 2 twin, 3 double, 2
suites (1 four-poster); all with
bathroom/WC, TV, room service,
hair-dryer, baby-listening

◈ Restaurant, bar, 2 lounges;
conference facilities (max 12
people residential); fishing,
tennis, other sports nearby;
babysitting

⊖ No wheelchair access; no dogs in
public rooms and some
bedrooms; no smoking in
bedrooms

▭ Access, Amex, Visa

£ Single £35 to £40, single
occupancy of twin/double £50 to
£60, twin/double £65 to £75,
four-poster £75 to £80, suite
£80 to £85; deposit required. Set
L from £5, D £16; alc D £25.
Special breaks available

---

**LIVERPOOL** MERSEYSIDE                                    **MAP 4**

# Trials Hotel

52–62 CASTLE STREET, LIVERPOOL, MERSEYSIDE L2 7LQ
TEL: 051-227 1021
TELEX: 626125   FAX: 051-236 0110

*An hotel of style and character in Liverpool's financial district.*

Formerly a bank, Trials is a weighty neo-classical pile with tall arched
windows and balustrades. Inside is stylish luxury in grand country-house
manner: comfy sofas in bold prints, flowers and piles of magazines on
polished antique tables. The original banking hall, a grand and imposing
chamber, now houses Trials Brasserie. The exuberant, marble-
columned, split-level bar attracts a well-heeled clientele (still plenty of
bankers) who lounge in leather chesterfields and talk financial shop over
a soundtrack of loud pop music.

The plush first-floor restaurant is more sedate. The menu is French
and international, and the cuisine inventive but unfussy. Service is
friendly and professional. Bedrooms, designated 'suites' thanks to separate living areas with sofa, television, video and mini-bar, are enormous
and fashionably furnished. Lavish bathrooms feature corner whirlpool
baths.

◑ Open all year; restaurant closed
Sun eve

🅰 Castle Street runs between the
city hall and the law courts, near
the Pier Head. Private car park

🛏 20 suites; all with bathroom/WC,
TV, room service, hair-dryer,
trouser press, mini-bar, baby-
listening

◈ 2 restaurants, 2 bars, lounge;

conference facilities (max 120
non-residential, 20 residential);
golf, other sports nearby

⊖ No wheelchair access; dogs in
bedrooms by arrangement only

▭ Access, Amex, Diners, Visa

£ Suite rate £90 to £120. Cooked
B £7.50, continental B £6; set L
£9; alc L, D £26 (prices till Jan
92). Special breaks available

**LIVERSEDGE** WEST YORKSHIRE                    **MAP 4**

# Lillibet's Restaurant-with-Rooms

64 LEEDS ROAD, LIVERSEDGE, WEST YORKSHIRE WF15 6HX
TEL: HECKMONDWIKE (0924) 404911   FAX: (0924) 404912

*Improved accommodation in a new annexe gives a new lease of life to an excellent restaurant-with-rooms.*

Things have changed at Lillibet's since we last reported on it. It's still primarily a restaurant-with-rooms rather than an hotel, but the distinction is blurring. The creation of a new annexe means that six more rooms are available. Reports so far are good. One reader looks forward to returning to 'this lovely and comfortable hotel', adding that the staff were very 'friendly and willing to help with any minor problem'.

Changes have also occurred in the lounge and restaurant area. The original front door is no longer used; instead guests enter from the side of the house through a blue- and white-tiled ante-room. The restaurant has been enlarged and brightened, with cheerful yellow walls contrasting with the dark blue curtains and vases of artificial flowers that fill the alcoves. A prettily tiled fireplace is now open to public scrutiny in the newest section of the restaurant. Food is still good; one regular found the 'increased menus quite superb', offering a range of mouth-watering dishes: sliced lamb sweetbreads, medallions of venison, breast of guinea-fowl. There's also a separate menu for vegetarians. If you would rather not have the rich sauces they will cook things more simply for you and there's a cheaper menu for residents.

Some things don't change and, thankfully, there's one survivor of this alteration: the unique carpet with 'Lillibet's' picked out in a dull gold on a blue background that runs through most of the public areas.

● Closed Xmas, New Year, 2 weeks Aug; no accommodation Sat, Sun; restaurant closed Sun

▣ On the A62, halfway between Leeds and Huddersfield; near Junctions 25, 26 and 27 from the M62. Private car park

🛏 6 single, 2 twin, 5 double; most with bathroom/WC, some with shower/WC; TV, room service (limited), trouser press, baby-listening in all rooms; hair-dryer on request

◈ Restaurant, bar, lounge; conference facilities (max 20 people non-residential, 13 residential). Wheelchair access to hotel (1 step) and restaurant, 3 ground-floor bedrooms

⊖ No dogs

▭ Access, Amex, Visa

£ Single £49, single occupancy of twin/double £49 to £54, twin/double £65 to £70. Set L from £11, D £12.50/£17/£22.50

# Red Lion Inn

LLANFAIR WATERDINE, NR KNIGHTON, POWYS LD7 ITU
TEL: KNIGHTON (0547) 528214

*Snug backwater inn in beautiful countryside with appetising pub food and cottage-style bedrooms.*

Two bright red lions guard the entrance to this long whitewashed inn set with diamond-paned windows. Inside, locals sit by the bar quaffing beer from personal tankards. Smells of hops and cigarette smoke envelop the cosy bar, and you may find a fire burning in the stove. Piles of chopped wood lie in the spacious stone fireplace; the beams above are decorated with jugs and old glass bottles, the walls with harnesses. It feels as if little has changed for years. Bar meals are served in here, or in a small dining-room, with shelf-displays of toby jugs.

The menu consists of good basic pub fare. Suggestions include beef in beer, chilli con carne, scampi, or steak and kidney pie. For pudding, old favourites like crème caramel or fruit pies are offered. The three bedrooms are upstairs, opening out on to a broad hall with old military photos on the wall. The bedrooms are freshly painted, have low ceilings and small windows looking out on to the Shropshire Hills or the River Teme. It's wonderfully peaceful, the only disturbance the mooing of cows in the surrounding fields.

- ⏻ Open all year, exc 2 days at Xmas; closed Tue lunch, restaurant closed Sun eve in winter
- ↗ Leave Knighton on the B4355 signposted Newtown. After 3½ miles turn right to Llanfair Waterdine – the junction is opposite the Lloney Inn. Private car park
- 🛏 I twin, 2 double (I with bathroom/WC); I public shower; TV in I double
- ◈ Restaurant, 2 bars, lounge; golf, riding, fishing nearby
- ⊖ No wheelchair access; no children; no dogs
- ▭ None accepted
- £ Single occupancy of twin/double £23 to £30, twin/double £35 to £50; deposit required. Bar meals £1.20 to £8; alc D from £12.50

---

*If you are intending to make a lot of phone calls from your room, always check what the hotel is going to charge you per unit. You may be so horrified that you'll prefer to walk to the nearest phone box. Why let them get away with excessive charges?*

**LONGFRAMLINGTON** NORTHUMBERLAND  **MAP 3**

# Besom Barn

LONGFRAMLINGTON, NORTHUMBERLAND NE65 8EN
TEL: LONGFRAMLINGTON (0665) 570627

*This would make a reasonably priced motel-style stay in Coquetdale.*

This is more than just a barren pit-stop on the A697, for although the revolving sign, the painted cart in the yard and the piped Musak suggest a place that is folksy, Besom Barn is a skilfully put together operation.

Four pretty rooms with plenty of space and decent showers occupy converted farm buildings. The presence of three different eateries and a bar would seem a little excessive for the total number of guests, but of course a lot of people drop in for food, and you could do a lot worse, even if you don't want to stay the night. Full meals are served in the main restaurant where you eat surrounded by harnesses and horns, and a considerable variety of snacks is available. If you do stay, you will have your own key to the block as well as to your room and won't have to worry about when you come or go.

Bedrooms overlook the fields and are well sheltered from traffic noise, so you can eat the breakfast that is brought to you in tranquillity before setting off.

◑ Open all year, restaurant closed Sun, Mon eves in winter

🔁 On the A697, ½ mile north of Longframlington. Private car park

🛏 2 twin, 2 double; all with shower/WC, TV, room service, hair-dryer, mini-bar, baby-listening

◈ 3 restaurants, bar, lounge; conference facilities (max 40 people non-residential); fishing, golf, other sports nearby. Wheelchair access to hotel (3 steps), restaurant and WC (M,F), 4 ground-floor bedrooms

⊖ No dogs

▭ Access, Amex, Diners, Visa

£ Single occupancy of twin/double £40, twin/double £50; deposit required. Cooked B £4.50; alc L £17, D £22. Special breaks available

# Embleton Hall

LONGFRAMLINGTON, MORPETH, NORTHUMBERLAND NE65 8DT
TEL: LONGFRAMLINGTON (0665 570) 249

*This is a good-value country-house hotel in excellent countryside.*

Embleton Hall is stately rather than grand, though the entrance to the two-storey stone house and the fine oak staircase leading to the bedrooms suggest the sort of place that Jane Austen might have used as a setting if Northumberland had been her stamping ground.

As an hotel, it is a very comforting sort of place with endless little extras to cheer guests: books, toffees, fruit and bedtime chocolates are to be found in the flowery bedrooms named after previous generations of children who lived here. The bathrooms, too, are comforting, with large and fluffy towels and plenty of space to provide suitable resonance for those who like to sing.

Downstairs, there is plenty of sitting space, including a conservatory for when the sun shines, and a modern wooden bar for when it does not. Dining-rooms are very formal, with gleaming silver, lace and lots of frills. Dinners are set-price, four-course affairs, quite rich and with fine puddings. Breakfast takes place in the smaller of the dining-rooms, which overlooks the lovely gardens. For a relaxing stay in the country around the River Coquet, Embleton Hall is unlikely to disappoint.

● Open all year

🚗 On the A697 road from Morpeth to Coldstream, at the northern end of Longframlington village. Private car park

🛏 1 single, 3 twin, 4 double, 2 four-poster; all with bathroom/WC, exc 1 single with shower/WC; TV, room service, hair-dryer, trouser press, baby-listening in all rooms

◈ 2 dining-rooms, bar, lounge; games room, drying room;

conference facilities (max 30 people non-residential, 10 residential); tennis, croquet, table tennis at hotel, other sports nearby

● No wheelchair access; no dogs in public rooms

▭ Access, Amex, Diners, Visa

£ Single £45, single occupancy of twin/double £45, twin/double £60, four-poster £85, family room £70. Set L £9.50, D £18.50. Special breaks available

**LONGHORSLEY** NORTHUMBERLAND                                    **MAP 3**

# Linden Hall

LONGHORSLEY, MORPETH, NORTHUMBERLAND NE65 8XG
TEL: MORPETH (0670) 516611    TELEX: 538224 LINDEN G
FAX: (0670) 88544

*A country-house hotel with a booming business trade. Quite formal in parts with very comfortable bedrooms.*

Since the conversion of the barns into banqueting and conference rooms this has become quite a large operation. Even the Linden pub has been created within the stone-built granary. Linden Hall itself manages to keep a certain distance from this booming business trade although it spills over to an extent. The drawing-room is the lightest room in the house and is smartly decorated in yellows and blues with a mixture of antiques and high-quality contract furniture that works well together. A slight change of style is apparent in the hall where leather buttoned sofas and a couple of armchairs are carefully arranged under the skylight.

The Monck Cocktail Bar, with its large fireplace and bar built in at one end, is a pleasant place to have a drink and order dinner. Swagged curtains and fairly closely arranged tables in the Dobson Restaurant make for an intimate atmosphere in the evening but can be a bit formal at breakfast. The bedrooms are all different with no skimping on material: quilted bedcovers, skirted side-tables, co-ordinated armchairs are the norm here, and they are very comfortable.

◐ *Open all year*

🔃 *1 mile north of Longhorsley on the A697. Private car park*

🛏 *2 single, 5 twin, 17 double, 4 four-poster, 7 family rooms, 2 suites, 2 cottages; all with bathroom/WC, TV, room service, hair-dryer, trouser press, mini-bar, baby-listening*

◈ *2 restaurants, bar, lounge, games room, library/study, conservatory; conference facilities (max 250 non-residential, 47 residential); tennis, croquet, fishing, table tennis, sauna/solarium at hotel, other sports nearby; babysitting.*

*Wheelchair access to hotel (ramps), restaurant and WC (unisex), 10 ground-floor bedrooms, 2 specially equipped for the disabled*

⊖ *No dogs in public rooms and in bedrooms by arrangement only*

▭ *Access, Amex, Diners, Visa*

£ *Single £90, single occupancy of twin/double £110, twin/double £120, four-poster £160, family room £140, suite £180, cottage £315 to £525 per week; deposit required. Set L £17.50, D £21.50; alc L, D £30. Special breaks available*

---

**LONG MARSTON** WARWICKSHIRE                                   **MAP 6**

# King's Lodge

LONG MARSTON, STRATFORD-UPON-AVON, WARWICKSHIRE CV37 8RL
TEL: STRATFORD-UPON-AVON (0789) 720705

*Enthusiastic owners welcome you to their historic, well-restored house.*

Formerly known simply as the Manor House, King's Lodge takes its name from a fateful day in 1651, when the owner, John Tomes, gave shelter to Charles II after his defeat at the Battle of Worcester. The King, disguised as a manservant, was asked by a kitchen maid to wind up the roasting jack in the kitchen of the Great Hall – a task that was quite beyond him. Today, guests of George and Angela Jenkins can breakfast in what was once part of the Great Hall, still dominated by the inglenook fireplace at which Charles II struggled vainly. With its dark panelling, parquet floor, studded leather chairs and antique furniture, the dining-room is a good setting in which to visualise its historic past. If you prefer to see more concrete evidence – or rather, wattle and daub – go out into the flagstoned hall where a section of the original building structure is on show behind a glass panel. There's also a framed seventeenth-century demand for money and horses to help the King's cause.

Bedrooms continue the historical theme in rather more bipartisan mode, with pictures of Roundheads playing cards. There are beams a-plenty and the four-poster is made from the diseased elm trees that once grew in front of the house. Despite their loss, the four acres of grounds around the house are very pretty, with a duckpond and dovecote (though George admits he's not having much luck in attracting many doves), jasmine, honeysuckle and roses.

◐ *Closed Dec and Jan*

▨ *3 miles south of the A439 Stratford to Evesham road. Private car park*

🛏 *1 twin, 1 double (with bathroom/ WC), 1 four-poster, 3 public bathrooms; TV in double room; hair-dryer on request*

◈ *Dining-room, bar, TV room; fishing, golf, other sports nearby*

⊖ *No wheelchair access; no dogs in public rooms; no smoking in dining-room*

▭ *None accepted*

£ *Single occupancy of twin/double £23, twin/double £35, four-poster £38; deposit preferred. Set D £9 (7pm, by arrangement only)*

---

**LONG MELFORD** SUFFOLK                          **MAP 7**

# Black Lion/Countrymen Restaurant

THE GREEN, LONG MELFORD, SUFFOLK CO10 9DN
TEL: SUDBURY (0787) 312356   FAX: (0787) 74557

*Very agreeable family-run hotel with busy restaurant. Noisy corner location is not its best attribute.*

You will find the Green on the outskirts of this dignified old town. The old cream-coloured coaching-inn stands close to a busy corner. Window boxes, large divided windows and smart doorways are inviting, and the rustic interior wins full marks for being entertaining as well as casual and comfortable. Even the hallway is fun: old chests here, shelves of books there, and walls lined with prints and plates. Comings and goings of staff and townsfolk in for lunch do not make it the most peaceful of hotels and road noise will disturb light sleepers.

Except for the bunk-bedded room in the family suite which hasn't enough room to swing a teddy bear, bedrooms are spacious and very comfortable. Eye-pleasing colour schemes, stripped pine, excellent antique beds and pretty details are typical. The long but cosy lounge, a happy clutter of country antiques, breezy fabrics and hunting, racing and cricket prints, is also light and well placed for watching life on and beyond the Green. Non-resident diners and residents mingle here or next door in what, considering the collections, could be called either the

Toby Jug Bar or the Wine Regions of France Bar. Then to dinner in the
Countryman Restaurant and a choice of Country and Gastronomique
menus. Janet and Stephen Errington are amiable hosts, which further
adds to the enjoyment of staying here.

*Open all year, exc Xmas and
New Year; restaurant closed Sun
eve (and Mon eve in winter)*

*On the village green, 2 miles
north of Sudbury on the A134
towards Bury St Edmunds.
Private car park*

*2 twin, 3 double, 2 four-poster, 1
family room, 1 suite; all with
bathroom/WC, TV, hair-dryer,
baby-listening*

*Restaurant, bar, lounge;
conference facilities (max 16
people non-residential, 10*

*residential); golf, tennis, other
sports nearby. Wheelchair access
to restaurant only*

*No dogs in public rooms*

*Access, Visa*

*Single occupancy of twin/double
£45 to £55, twin/double £65 to
£75, four-poster £70 to £75,
suite £80 to £85, family room
£60 to £65; deposit required. Set
L £12, £17, D £18, £26; alc L
£17, D £25. Special breaks
available*

---

## LONGNOR SHROPSHIRE                                               MAP 6

# Moat House

LONGNOR, SHREWSBURY, SHROPSHIRE SY5 7PP
TEL: DORRINGTON (074 373) 434

*A lovingly restored medieval hall where atmosphere and history
combine with a warm welcome.*

The genuine enthusiasm which Peter Richards has for his family home
turned guesthouse is contagious. The moat, surrounding the old beamed
medieval manor house, is believed to date from the mid-thirteenth
century, and parts of the building are only a little younger. Although
neglected and even condemned earlier this century, it has been carefully
restored over the last thirty years and, as part of the Wolsey Lodge group,
it's a great favourite with history-hungry Americans.

A picture hanging in the large parlour shows how the building would
once have been a huge open hall with a central fireplace. Now, an extra
floor has been added and upstairs is an elegant dining-hall with old roof
timbers still tinged with medieval soot. Lit only by candles, dinner is
served on the long oak table and guests eat together with the Richards.
Two faces carved into beams, thought to be Edward D'Acton and
Eleanor Le Strange who lived in the house around 1390 as newlyweds,
make a conversation piece at dinner. Margaret cooks English dishes such
as lamb, followed by lemon syllabub or chocolate roulade. Bedrooms are
surprisingly modern in comparison with the public rooms and have
sensible twentieth-century comforts like electric blankets and carpeted
bathrooms.

◗ Closed Dec, Jan, Feb

↗ 8 miles south of Shrewsbury on
the A49, take east turn signed
Longnor. Go through village past
school and shop. Turn left into
lane signposted 'No Through
Road'. Where lane turns left the
Moat House is straight ahead.
Private car park

⇆ I twin, 2 double; all with
bathroom or shower/WC; no tea/

coffee-making facilities in rooms

◈ Dining-room, lounge; golf, tennis,
other sports nearby

⊖ No wheelchair access; no
children; no dogs; no smoking in
bedrooms

▭ Access, Visa

£ Single occupancy of twin/double
£36, twin/double £60; deposit
required. Set D £18 (8pm)
(prices till Dec 91)

**LOWER BOCKHAMPTON** DORSET                              **MAP 9**

# Yalbury Cottage

LOWER BOCKHAMPTON, DORCHESTER, DORSET DT2 8PZ
TEL: DORCHESTER (0305) 262382

*Thatched country cottage is a popular choice in the area.*

We have received plenty of support for this picturesque cottage, near
Hardy's Cottage and within shooting distance of Dorchester. Despite
the slightly small bedrooms, visitors commend the soundproofed walls,
furniture of different woods in otherwise similar rooms and provisions
such as ironing-boards, but our inspector was not impressed by a thin,
lumpy mattress. Bathrooms are decent and provided with robes.

Getting to the lounge and restaurant means crossing the courtyard,
though in foul weather you're allowed to nip past the kitchen. If this
annoys, the congenial pre-dinner drink gathering should not. The low,
beamed lounge where you gather for drinks is an inviting room with
antiques, comfortable sofas and chairs, log fire and soft lighting. Beyond
is the restaurant, again attractive and oozing character. Several readers
praise Yalbury for its five-course dinners, but one found the set meal
'rather expensive considering that there was no choice and that it was
possible to count the vegetables. Would you believe three mange-tout?'
Yet others mention the carrying of bags to your room, the washing of car
windows and immaculate service by German girls.

◗ Open all year, Dec or Jan by
arrangement only

↗ 2 miles east of Dorchester in
Lower Bockhampton, I mile
from the A35. Private car park

⇆ 2 twin, 6 double; all with
bathroom/WC, TV, room service,
hair-dryer, ironing facilities

◈ Restaurant, drawing-room; golf,

riding, other sports nearby

⊖ No wheelchair access; no
children; no dogs; no pipes,
cigars in restaurant

▭ Access, Visa

£ Single occupancy of twin/double
£55 to £62, twin/double £70 to
£88; deposit required. Set L £20,
D £22.50 (prices till Feb 92)

**LOWER SLAUGHTER** GLOUCESTERSHIRE                    **MAP 6**

# Lower Slaughter Manor

LOWER SLAUGHTER, GLOUCESTERSHIRE GL54 2HP
TEL: COTSWOLD (0451) 20456
FAX: (0451) 22150

*Lavish but slightly impersonal manor-house hotel with good facilities.*

The name derives not from some past massacre but from one Philippe de Sloitre, a Norman knight whose family was rewarded for its services to William the Conqueror by being granted land in this area in about 1070. Lower Slaughter Manor is rather younger: a stately seventeenth-century building complete with extravagant plasterwork and stone fireplaces.

Its refurbishment in 1986 has added the usual heavy swagged chintzes and flowery prints; bedrooms follow in much the same vein, sumptuous but unimaginative. Those in the converted coach-house are slightly more unusual, with extremely high ceilings, some with sloping beams. Of the four grades of double room, the 'standards' are the smallest – too small for the price. The lobby, with its deep-pink walls and Persian rug-covered sofas, is slightly more daring in its furnishings. Warmth of service seems to be inversely proportional to the staff's rank, if our inspector's experience is anything to go by.

Diners have a choice of a table d'hôte menu or the à la carte. Dishes range from classic dishes to more unusual combinations, such as turbot glazed with champagne and tarragon sabayon set on a beetroot sauce. Men are requested to wear a jacket and tie for dinner.

◑ Open all year

↗ Lower Slaughter is off the A429, 3 miles south of Stow-on-the-Wold. The Manor is on the right-hand side of the lane approaching the village centre. Private car park

🛏 2 single, 8 twin, 7 double, 2 four-poster; some rooms in coach-house; all with bathroom/WC, TV, room service, hair-dryer, trouser press; no tea/coffee-making facilities in rooms

◇ Dining-room, 3 lounges; conference facilities (max 36 people residential); fishing, tennis, croquet, heated swimming-pool, sauna/solarium at hotel, other sports nearby. Wheelchair access to coach-house, restaurant (7 steps to main house), 4 ground-floor rooms

● No children under 8

▭ Access, Amex, Diners, Visa

£ Single £92, single occupancy of twin/double £110, twin/double from £125, four-poster, £210; deposit required. Cooked B £7.50; set L £16.50, D £32; alc L, D £43. Special breaks available

---

*Prices are quoted* per room *rather than* per person.

**LOWICK** CUMBRIA          **MAP 3**

# Lowick House  

LOWICK, NR ULVERSTON, CUMBRIA LA12 8DX
TEL: LOWICK BRIDGE (022 985) 227

*Comfortable accommodation in an elegant family house set in large gardens.*

Lowick House, one of the first members of the Wolsey Lodge consortium, is not an hotel. That said, Dorothy Sutcliffe's sparkling white eighteenth-century home, set amid stunning large landscape gardens, is a very agreeable place to stay.

Personal touches such as silver toiletry sets, china ornaments and converted gas lamps make the bedrooms, where Victorian and Edwardian pictures hang on prettily papered walls. The bedrooms contain some stunning antiques, including finely inlaid Edwardian wardrobes and dressing-tables, and an early Victorian half-tester bed which still has its original silk embroidery and tassels. Bathrooms, though not *en suite*, are lovely.

Public rooms range from a comfortable lounge with a Persian-style carpet and a wall-mounted antelope's head to a very fine dining-room with a Sheraton sideboard and magnificent Edwardian bow-fronted display cabinet. Table settings are appropriately grand, with silver, cut and etched glass and good china. Six-course dinners combine home-grown vegetables and lots of traditional fowl and lamb with straightforward English cooking.

🌗 Open all year, exc Xmas and New Year

🔋 Leave the M6 at Junction 36 and take the A590 towards Barrow. At Greenodd turn right on to the A5092. Pass the Farmers Arms pub on the right, then fork on to the A5084 (signposted Coniston). Lowick House is 100 yards on the right. Private car park

🛏 I single, I twin, I double, I half-tester; some with bathroom/WC, some with shower/WC; no tea/

coffee-making facilities in rooms

◈ Dining-room, lounge, TV room; drying room, library/study; golf, riding, other sports nearby; babysitting

⊖ No wheelchair access; no children in dining-room; no dogs; no smoking

▭ None accepted

💷 Single £30, single occupancy of twin/double £30, twin/double/half-tester £60; deposit required. Set D £18 (7.30pm)

*All rooms have tea/coffee-making facilities unless we mention to the contrary.*

**LOXLEY** WARWICKSHIRE                          **MAP 6**

# Loxley Farm                                    ℒ 🦋

LOXLEY, WARWICKSHIRE CV35 9JN
TEL: STRATFORD-UPON-AVON (0789) 840265

*Picturesque cottage with lovely gardens and a friendly atmosphere.*

The Hortons have lived in this pretty half-timbered, thatched cottage
close to Stratford-upon-Avon for over twenty years. B&B is offered in
one of the beamed rooms in the house and in the Shieling, a barn
conversion about 60 yards from the house in large pretty gardens.

The cottage, which is part-thirteenth century, has masses of character
with low ceilings, uneven floors and a warm friendly feel. There is a smell
of fresh polish on shining flagstone floors and heavy-oak antique furnishings, plus vases of fresh flowers. The family dog pads about noise-
lessly. There's a cosy sitting-room with soft armchairs and an electric
fire; across the hall is the breakfast room with a selection of cereals and
home-made muesli and juices on the oak side-table – full English
breakfasts are served. By 1992 the room in the house will have a third bed
on the extra-wide beamed landing, shut off from the rest of the house
and with its own bathroom and staircase up to it. The thatched Shieling
with its two double bedrooms both have bathrooms *en suite* ('with Jacuzzi
tubs, really nice,' remarks one American reader) and share a small high-

– Loxley Farm –

ceilinged, exposed beamed sitting-room tastefully arranged, and a small kitchen, good for heating-up TV suppers. The privacy of the Shieling makes it ideal for a family or a small group of friends.

🌓 *Open all year, exc Xmas*

↗ *In Loxley village, 3½ miles south-east of Stratford-upon-Avon. Private car park*

🛏 *2 double, 1 family room; all with bathroom/WC*

◈ *Breakfast room, 2 lounges;*

*fishing, riding, other sports nearby*

⊖ *No wheelchair access; no dogs in public rooms*

▭ *None accepted*

💷 *Single occupancy of twin/double £24 to £26, twin/double £35 to £38; deposit required*

---

**LUDLOW** SHROPSHIRE                                          **MAP 6**

# Number Eleven

DINHAM, LUDLOW, SHROPSHIRE SY8 1EJ
TEL: LUDLOW (0584) 878584

*Smart town house run by very friendly hosts. Stylish rooms at a reasonable price.*

This guesthouse lies at the end of an elegant late-eighteenth-century listed Georgian terrace overlooking the ancient walls of Ludlow Castle. Inside, the house has been lovingly restored by Guy Crawley and Mike Martin who took much advice from the Georgian Society. The attention to detail is precise, even down to the brass door fittings, and false doors have been added upstairs to preserve the symmetry of the hallways. 'We are aiming for something that's not quite a B&B,' explains Guy mysteriously; 'we want people to feel it's the house they've always wanted to have themselves.'

The result is like walking into a page of one of the house-style magazines which are so carefully placed on coffee tables, and yet one which has a homely feel. The bedrooms are painted in relaxing pinks, greys and blues – Georgian colours – and have antique or painted furniture. They all face the castle except the top suite, nestling below the eaves, which overlooks the River Teme. Food is served in the spacious dining-room which is furnished with chunky antiques. Dinner is by request, and the cooking is plain but good. A typical menu could be a starter of fish pâté, pork cooked in tomato and ginger, followed by apple crumble, accompanied, if you're lucky, by Guy singing along to Sondheim in the kitchen. Coffee is served in the formal drawing-room which has an intriguing 'secret' door leading to a television room.

🌓 *Open all year*

↗ *Leave Castle Square along Dinham. The house is on the*

*dog-leg opposite the castle walls. Private car park*

🛏 *4 twin, 1 four-poster; most with*

bathroom/WC, some with shower/WC; TV, hair-dryer, tea/coffee-making facilities on request

Dining-room, drawing-room, TV room, drying room; fishing, golf, other sports nearby

No wheelchair access; no

children under 12; no dogs; smoking in drawing-room only

Access, Visa

Single occupancy of twin £22 to £25, twin £40 to £44, four-poster £50. Set D £10.50. Special breaks available

---

## LUSTLEIGH DEVON
MAP 8

# Willmead Farm

LUSTLEIGH, BOVEY TRACEY, NR NEWTON ABBOT, DEVON TQ13 9NP
TEL: LUSTLEIGH (064 77) 214

*Small picture-book cottage in a bucolic Dartmoor National Park setting. A treat for the senses and a place to recharge batteries.*

The ultimate escape from high-tech, twentieth-century life is neither impossible to find nor very far from a town. The undulating, fourteenth-century thatched cottage (combined from two singles since the days of Elizabeth I) is clad in thick creepers and sits in a broad field at the end of a hedged-in track. Ponds, stone walls, chickens, ducks and goats complete the untarnished picture of rustic country life. Americans lap it up for its Englishness, but all who visit are charmed by its spell – as well as by Hilary Roberts' welcome and hospitality.

The low and long interior of oak timbers and wobbly stone walls is made inviting with warm furnishings, log fires and all sorts of bits and bobs from bygone days. A minstrels' gallery is hung with guns, stags' heads and old photos. The three bedrooms, a twin with attached facilities, plus two doubles, have been gently upgraded over the years and are homely and larger than you'd expect. You can get cream tea and/or dinner at the Cleeve pub in Lustleigh, an easy fifteen-minute walk away. Breakfast is whenever you please. Smoking, out of respect for the thatched roof and other guests, is not permitted.

Open all year, exc Xmas and New Year

From Bovey Tracey, take A382 to Lustleigh, first left past telephone box. The farm is signposted. Private car park

1 twin, 2 double; 2 public shower rooms, 1 public bathroom

Dining-room, lounge

No wheelchair access; no children under 10; no dogs; no smoking

None accepted

Twin/double £38 to £43; deposit required

# Alexandra Hotel

POUND STREET, LYME REGIS, DORSET DT7 3HZ
TEL: LYME REGIS (0297) 442010

*Defiantly old-fashioned, friendly and well-run hotel with average facilities but a blissful, clifftop setting.*

Lyme Regis, holiday centre and home of the memorable Cobb of *French Lieutenant's Woman* fame, has a reasonable collection of hotels, though it is difficult to find one that stands out. This one, built in 1735 for a countess, is easy to miss – and turning the sharp angle into its forecourt is no fun.

A well-run and amiable hotel, it enjoys a wonderful setting above the sea. Tea on the broad lawn from where you can watch seagulls soar is an occasion. A long, plant-filled conservatory with cane and wood chairs and a fountain is the perfect place to linger over a drink and watch the sun disappear.

The main sitting-room is also well endowed with plants, and contains part of the hotel's impressive collection of ship models. Furnishings here are in fair condition but are dated. Then again, many guests admit to being pre-forties themselves and might feel out-of-place amongst pastel frills. Solid and attractive furniture is a feature of bedrooms: cherry veneer on the first floor, white pine on the second. Fabrics are modern and matching. There are few provisions but comfortable chairs from which to admire the view. Single rooms face the road. Your bed will be turned down while you dine, but the best thing about the staff is how welcoming and accommodating they are. Clawed, the cat, is equally friendly.

◖ Closed Xmas and Jan

↗ On the sea side of main street. Private car park

🛏 2 single, 6 twin, 11 double, 8 family rooms; all with bathroom/ WC, exc 1 single with shower/ WC; TV, room service, baby-listening

◈ Restaurant, bar, lounge, drying room, conservatory; golf, riding, other sports nearby. Wheelchair access to hotel (2 steps) only, 3 ground-floor bedrooms

⊖ No dogs

▭ Access, Amex, Diners, Visa

£ Single £46 to £52, single occupancy of twin/double £61, twin/double £92 to £104, family room £130 to £143; deposit required. Set L £10, D £15; alc L, D £25. Special breaks available

---

*All entries in the* Guide *are rewritten every year, not least because standards fluctuate. Don't trust an out-of-date* Guide.

**LYMINGTON** HAMPSHIRE                                      **MAP 9**

# Stanwell House

HIGH STREET, LYMINGTON, HANTS SO41 9AA
TEL: LYMINGTON (0590) 677123
FAX: (0590) 677756

*A safe choice: an upmarket but unremarkable town hotel with a
sailing clientele.*

Lymington, a charming little Georgian town with a ferry to the Isle of
Wight, and the New Forest just a couple of miles inland, makes a good
base for local explorers as well as being a Mecca for Solent yachtspeople.
The Stanwell, a much modernised Georgian building with a cream
exterior, is at the bottom of the high street, and is run, appropriately, by a
chain called Clipper Hotels. Railings Restaurant is its focal point, and it
is full of locals, business people and, of course, sailing enthusiasts.

A conventional menu receives ambitious presentation; some diners
have complained about the size of the portions – if you feel underfed,
breakfast offers a barrage of cooked choices. Last year we reported that
service could have done with 'a little spicing up'; this year it has been
highly professional and solicitous. Of the other public rooms, the cocktail
bar seems to work best, the little lounge's high coffee tables being the
wrong height for its deep flowery sofas, and the library, with leather
chairs and sets of bound books, is cramped and inauthentic.

Each bedroom is named after a Bordeaux château well-known for its
wine (Mouton Rothschild, for example). The rooms are refreshingly
light, with cream-coloured furniture and walls, and candlewick bedspreads. Those facing the street have double glazing, those at the back
have distant views of the sea, and yet more are situated in a new block at
the rear of the hotel beside a well-kept walled garden.

- Open all year
- In the centre of Lymington. On-
  street parking
- 6 single, 11 twin, 16 double, 1
  four-poster, 1 suite; all with
  bathroom/WC, TV, room service,
  hair-dryer, trouser press; baby-
  listening by arrangement
- Restaurant, bar, lounge, library;
  conference facilities (max 20

people residential); fishing, golf,
other sports nearby
- No wheelchair access; no dogs
- Access, Visa
- Single £68, single occupancy
  twin/double £78, twin/double
  £88. Set L £10.50, D £18.50; alc
  L, D £25 (prices till end 91).
  Special breaks available

*Are you aware of your rights as a consumer when you book into an hotel?
Check them out on page 13.*

# Chadwick House

55 BEECH LANE, MACCLESFIELD, CHESHIRE SK10 2DS
TEL: MACCLESFIELD (0625) 615558

*Town-centre hotel with attractive features and welcoming hosts.*

You'll pick out Chadwick House from its residential neighbours by its
white-columned portico, shutters and colourful window boxes. Inside,
rustic furniture and pretty fabrics and colours give it a rural demeanour,
and the various stabs at fakery – artificial flowers and phoney window-
pane dividers – somehow fail to annoy.

Bedroom décor is cheerful, crisp and clean with straw hats, fans and
baskets hung from the walls and an ever-present blue trim. Furniture is
modern pine. There's a lace-draped four-poster in the honeymoon
suite, and a couple of rocking chairs in the emphatically pink room ten.
The bar/dining-room is stylish with ruched curtains, and tiffany-style
lampshades. A budding teapot collection occupies the mantel over the
fireplace. Straightforward dinners are good value.

◑ Open all year; restaurant closed
Fri to Sun exc by arrangement

🔁 On the A523 north out of
Macclesfield, 200 yards from the
main junction with the A537.
Private car park

🛏 1 single, 2 twin, 8 double, 1
four-poster; most with bathroom/
WC, some with shower/WC; TV,
room service in all rooms; hair-
dryer, trouser press, baby-
listening on request

◈ Dining-room, bar, lounge, TV
room, drying room; conference
facilities (max 30 people non-
residential, 12 residential);
sauna, solarium at hotel, golf,
fishing, other sports nearby

⊖ No wheelchair access; no dogs;
smoking in lounge only

▭ Access, Diners, Visa

£ Single £23 to £40, single
occupancy of twin/double £30 to
£40, twin/double £44 to £55,
four-poster £65; deposit
required. Set D £8

# Madeley Court

MADELEY, NR TELFORD, SHROPSHIRE TF7 5DW
TEL: TELFORD (0952) 680068   FAX: (0952) 684275

*Experience medieval luxury in a faithfully restored manor house.*

In 1986, after centuries of neglect, Madeley Court stood derelict as the
previous owners waited for someone to tackle the huge restoration
project; someone who, they thought, would have to be daft to take on
such a massive, fund-swallowing enterprise. Finally Martin Ebelis

turned up, and selling everything he owned to achieve it, created a magnificent hotel from this sixteenth-century manor house.

Efforts to recreate the genuine character of a building, which dates in parts from the thirteenth century, include walls roughly washed rather than painted, rope matting floor covering, heavy oak doors (painstakingly tracked down where originals were missing), and materials whose designs are Elizabethan. It took a full two years just to acquire the appropriate furnishings, and now corridors and bedrooms are full of dark antique chests, tapestry wall-hangings and heavily-framed oil paintings. Bedrooms in the oldest part of the house are luxuriously furnished with medieval print fabrics, *fleur-de-lys* stencils and four-poster beds. Rooms at the top have heavy beams cutting across the room, and interesting nook-and-cranny bathrooms, which means you might find yourself sacrificing comfort for atmosphere. Not all rooms are historic, however; some, in an extension on the ground floor, though good sized and comfortable, are disappointingly reproduction.

You can eat in the brasserie in the undercroft or in the grand-scale restaurant. Formerly the Great Hall, the restaurant is large but not overwhelming. An enormous stone fireplace is kept well supplied with massive logs throughout your meal, and service is attentive and professional. The menu offers hare, wild duck with honey and ginger, pigeon, quail in port, wild mushrooms, and goose liver with truffles.

◑ Open all year; restaurant closed for lunch Sat and Mon, also Sun eve

🚗 4 miles from Junction 4 of the M54. Private car park

🛏 8 single, 3 twin, 16 double, 2 four-poster, 1 suite; all with bathroom/WC, TV, room service, hair-dryer, trouser press, baby-listening

◈ Restaurant, brasserie, 2 bars, 3 lounges; conference facilities (max 60 people non-residential, 30 residential); fishing in grounds, other sports nearby. Wheelchair access to hotel, restaurant and WC (unisex), 11 ground-floor bedrooms

⊖ No dogs; no smoking in restaurant

▭ Access, Amex, Diners, Visa

£ Single £75, single occupancy of twin/double £75, twin/double £90, four-poster £110, suite £180. Set L £10.50, D £19; alc L, D £35. Special breaks available

---

☕ *Denotes somewhere you can rely on a good meal – either the hotel features in the 1992 edition of our sister publication,* The Good Food Guide, *or our own inspectors thought the cooking impressive, whether particularly competent home cooking or more lavish cuisine.*

# Fredrick's Hotel

SHOPPENHANGERS ROAD, MAIDENHEAD, BERKSHIRE SL6 2PZ
TEL: MAIDENHEAD (0628) 35934   TELEX: 849966 FHOTEL G
FAX: (0628) 771054

*An overly expensive but excellently run hotel for the executive
unconcerned about the bill.*

Fredrick's is named after its founder, owner and creator. It is as Fredrick
Wolfgang Losel proudly announces in his brochure: 'The realisation of a
personal dream.' If the brochure is to be believed this even extends to
personally designing the kitchens. It would be fair to say that Mr Losel's
taste will not appeal to everyone: it's glitzy and lavish with glistening gold
pillars and the trickle of running water in the lobby, potted plants and
weathered statuettes in the 'winter garden'; a glassed-in terrace and a
general air of slightly overdone ostentation. But it is impressive in the
sheer amount of effort that has obviously gone into transforming this
large but rather ordinary turn-of-the-century house, on a boring suburban road, into an hotel.

The restaurant is as expensive as the hotel with a no-choice table
d'hôte menu costing £28.50 and main courses on the à la carte menu at
£18.50. Still, you can always admire the pale pink frescoes. Facilities in
the bedrooms are, as you'd expect, excellent throughout although the
rooms in the modest annexe lack character.

○ Open all year, exc 24 to 30 Dec;
restaurant closed Sat lunch

↗ Near the centre of Maidenhead,
close to the railway station.
Private car park

🛏 10 single, 13 twin, 9 double, 5
suites; most with bathroom/WC,
4 singles with shower/WC; TV,
room service, hair-dryer, mini-
bar; trouser press, ironing
facilities in most rooms; no tea/
coffee-making facilities in rooms

◇ Restaurant, bar, lounge (air-
conditioned), patio; conference
facilities (max 50 people non-
residential, 25 residential);
croquet at hotel, other sports
nearby. Wheelchair access to
hotel (ramp) and restaurant, 13
ground-floor bedrooms

● No dogs

▭ Access, Amex, Diners, Visa

£ Single £88 to £110, single
occupancy of twin/double £110
to £120, twin/double £145 to
£155, suite £155 to £220;
deposit required. Set L £19.50, D
£28.50; alc L, D £46.50

The hotel that was to have
been listed here was due to
be sold as we went to press.

---

*When you telephone to book a room, and the hotel accepts your booking, you enter into a binding contract with them. This means they undertake to provide the specified accommodation and meals etc. for the agreed cost on the agreed dates, while you commit yourself to paying their charges. If you later have to cancel your booking, or fail to turn up, the hotel may be entitled to keep any deposit you have paid to defray administrative costs. If an hotel is unable to re-let the room you have booked – and it must try to do so – it is entitled to compensation for the loss of profit caused by your breach of contract. It can only claim a sum that is fair and reasonable. It should not make a profit out of your failure to appear. It's important to give as much notice as possible when cancelling: this increases the chances of your room being re-let.*

---

*See page 787 for other hotels worthy of inclusion in our* Visitors' Book.

# The Cottage in the Wood

HOLYWELL ROAD, MALVERN WELLS, HEREFORD AND WORCESTER
WR14 4LG
TEL: MALVERN (0684) 573487   FAX: (0684) 560662

*Pretty country hotel with splendid views, excellent for walkers; some grumbles about service.*

Cottage by name but not by nature, this Georgian dower house stands halfway up one of the Malvern Hills itself. As a result, the views across the Severn plain as far as the Cotswolds are superb. Furnishings too would make for rather an upmarket cottage, with heavy curtains, a mixture of antique and reproduction furniture, and a table piled high with copies of *Period Interior* and *Antique Collector* magazines.

Rooms, both public and private, are not huge, but large enough to take this aspiring country-house style. For a room with a view, go for one at the front or in the Coach House. Greens and peachy pinks seem to be the most popular colours in the refurbished bedrooms, with tasselled bed-spreads and wallpaper patterned with flowers or birds of paradise. Each bathroom has a resident blue plastic dolphin. We've had one complaint about room size: a 'family room . . . would have been classed as small for a single room', and 'the bathroom . . . the smallest I have ever seen'. The bar is oddly downmarket, with drab brown pub-like banquettes that are not particularly comfortable; pre-dinner drinks and appetisers are served here. The L-shaped dining-room is prettier, with Indian paint-ings on the walls and candlelit tables. If you're lucky enough to get a table by the window you can watch the darkening valley below. Food can be variable: squid stewed in tomato and red wine was very good, but beef fillet with tomato and basil and the green salad were poor choices. A wide-ranging wine list includes such novelties as Texan Gewürztraminer. Service was pleasant enough when our inspector stayed, but one reader found it 'unhelpful, everything seemed to be too much trouble'. More reports, please.

○ Open all year

↗ Leave the M5 at Junction 8, taking the M50 to Junction 1. Follow the A38 towards Worcester but turn into Upton-on-Severn. Turn right over river bridge on to the B4211, then left on to the B4209 after 1 mile. Continue through Hanley Swan and on to T-junction in Wells Road (A449). Turn right and immediately left. Private car park

🛏 2 single, 4 twin, 11 double, 3 four-poster (some rooms in cottages); all with bathroom/ WC, TV, hair-dryer, baby-listening

◇ Restaurant, bar, lounge; conference facilities (max 14 people residential and non-residential); golf, riding, other sports nearby

⊖ No wheelchair access; no dogs in public rooms or some bedrooms; no smoking in restaurant

☐ Access, Amex, Visa

💷 Single £62, single occupancy of twin/double £74, twin/double

£87, four-poster from £110. Buffet L from £7.50; alc L, D £30. Special breaks available

# The Old Vicarage

HANLEY ROAD, MALVERN WELLS, HEREFORD AND WORCESTER WR14 4PH
TEL: MALVERN (0684) 572585

*Unassuming B&B in a pretty area not known for its bargain accommodation.*

Beagles and books abound at this solid Victorian B&B. A vicarage no longer, the house still has a slightly clerical feel, with its Gothic wooden door, robust cleanliness, and simple, understated décor. The comfortable lounge where ecclesiastical tea parties were once held now contains shelves of well-thumbed books, both literary and on local history (and nearly a whole shelf devoted to books on beagles), while the walls are adorned with hunting prints and canine photographs. The windows overlook the expansive lawns behind, where you may see a couple of canines in the flesh, tails wagging, anxious to be of help to Michael Gorvin in the relentless task of mowing the lawn. Bedrooms are jolly rather than formal.

Facilities vary: in one room the small bathroom is hidden behind a pair of white louvre doors; in another the electric shower cabinet is screened behind a curtain. The Gorvins no longer serve dinner, unless arranged in advance, but are quite happy to recommend local restaurants. Breakfast, in the pretty pink dining-room hung with eighteenth-century satirical prints, is a generous help-yourself affair from the sideboard, plus a choice of cooked dishes.

○ Open all year, exc Xmas; restaurant closed Sun

↗ From Malvern take the A449 Wells Road. Turn left down the B4209 Hanley Road to Upton-on-Severn. The hotel is close to the Three Counties Agricultural Showground. Private car park

🛏 2 twin, 3 double, 1 family room; half with bathroom/WC, half with shower/WC; TV in all rooms; room service, hair-dryer on request

◇ Dining-room, lounge; meetings

facilities (max 6 people residential, 10 non-residential); golf, riding, other sports nearby; babysitting by arrangement

● No wheelchair access; no dogs in public rooms

☐ None accepted

💷 Single occupancy of twin/double £28 to £32, twin/double £42 to £48, family room £52 to £56 (3 people); deposit required. Set D £14.50 by prior arrangement only. Special breaks available

# The Britannia

PORTLAND STREET, MANCHESTER M1 3LA
TEL: 061-228 2288   TELEX: 665007 RULBRI G
FAX: 061-236 9154

*Victorian flamboyance teamed with ultra-modern hi-tech leisure
facilities.*

It's hard to get away from the cotton industry and the industrial
revolution in these parts, and this hotel was converted from the swankiest
cotton warehause of all about ten years ago. The massive chandelier in
the royal blue foyer says traditional classic elegance, as do the lacy
balustrades of the grand central staircase and the flock wallpaper.
Though there's nowt more northern than mills, the raw materials came
from warmer climes, and the colonial legacy is imaginatively recalled in
the contemplative Buddhas and cherubs holding plant pots; the juxtaposition of a life-sized zebra among leather chesterfields is, however,
more Salvador Dali than ship canal.

It's a complex, multi-layered building, and the designers have given it
a battery of styles to match. So you'll find Jenny's restaurant, an outlet for
English food, looking like an upmarket pizzeria, and the actual pizzeria
looking like a pub. Bedrooms vary in size, style and price, though most
are large, and the split-level suites are enormous. For the most part less
dramatic than the public rooms, they none the less go in for some
startling soft furnishings and vibrant bathrooms in rust and cream. The
disco is predictably glitzy and the health club runs to sauna, solarium,
heated pool and gym for which you have to pay extra.

◗ *Open all year*

▞ *Centrally located in Manchester.
On-street parking (meters) and
NCP car park next to hotel*

🛏 *143 single, 77 twin, 91 double, 4
four-posters, 28 family rooms,
18 suites, 1 luxury suite; all with
bathroom/WC, TV, room service,
hair-dryer, trouser press, baby-
listening; some rooms air-
conditioned*

◈ *3 restaurants, 4 bars, lounge;
conference facilities (max 220
people non-residential, 180*

*residential); sauna, solarium,
heated pool, gym at hotel;
babysitting on request*

⊖ *No wheelchair access; dogs by
arrangement only*

▭ *Access, Amex, Diners, Visa*

£ *Single £30 to £75, single
occupancy of twin/double £40 to
£90, twin/double £50 to £100;
four-poster/family room/suite
£70 to £125, luxury suite £150
to £250. Continental B £9,
cooked B £9; Set L £7, £17; alc
L £12, D £20*

*All reports are welcome on any hotel, whether or not it is in the* Guide.

# Etrop Grange

OUTWOOD LANE, MANCHESTER AIRPORT, MANCHESTER M22 5NR
TEL: 061-499 0500   FAX: 061-499 0790

*Popular country-house hotel close to Manchester Airport.*

Airport hotels are all too often a bland mixture of concrete and international inoffensiveness, with little to recommend them but their proximity to the airport when you're due to depart at an ungodly hour. Etrop Grange is close enough to Manchester Airport to be convenient and far enough away to have a definite character of its own.

It's a listed Georgian house half-a-mile from the airport, and caters for a largely business clientele – hence the fax and photocopying service. A combination of the M56 and aircraft noise means that, double glazing notwithstanding, it could never be described as quiet. None the less it feels rural. The style is distinctly country house with Victorian and Edwardian antiques, floral-print curtains and borders and Persian rugs. The lounge is cosy, while there's more Victoriana in the candlelit dining-room which spills over into a small attractive conservatory.

Bedroom furniture is often Victorian with stripped pine, chintzy curtains, lots of lace and frills and more floral borders. Service is caring and professional. Dinner is a set five-course affair with good choice and the food is competently cooked and attractively presented.

◑ Open all year

⤵ Leave the M56 at Junction 5 and take the first left at the roundabout, signposted to the hotel which is 2 miles further on. Private car park

🛏 2 single, 26 double, 6 family rooms, 7 suites; all with bathroom/WC, exc 1 single with shower/WC; TV, room service, hair-dryer, trouser press, mini-bar, baby-listening in all rooms

◈ Restaurant, bar, lounge, conservatory; conference facilities (max 100 people non-residential, 41 residential);

fishing, golf, other sports nearby; babysitting. Wheelchair access to hotel (ramp), restaurant and WC, no ground-floor bedrooms

⊖ No smoking in some bedrooms

▭ Access, Amex, Visa

£ Single £55 to £115, single occupancy of twin/double £65 to £115, twin/double £65 to £125, four-poster £85 to £125, family room £85 to £135, suite from £105; deposit required. Continental B £6.50, cooked B £8.50; set L £12.50, £15.50, D £26.50. Special breaks available

---

*Prices are what you can expect to pay in 1992, except where specified to the contrary. Many hoteliers tell us that these prices can be regarded only as approximations.*

# Goldstone Hall

MARKET DRAYTON, SHROPSHIRE TF9 2NA
TEL: CHESWARDINE (0630 86) 202/487　FAX: (0630 86) 585

*A comfortable, beautifully furnished house with enjoyable dinners.*

Goldstone's profile may be on the up: the highly successful Clive of India and Candlemas dinners are not the only happenings at the Hall. There's Squire's Tiffin (lunch in the garden) in summer and a number of musical evenings during the year. The five acres of mature garden are being well looked after and development of the herb garden is under way.

The building, originally Elizabethan, gained a Georgian façade, a Victorian wing and, most recently, a conservatory in 1988. Parquet floors partially covered by Persian rugs, good antiques and stylish furniture are in evidence throughout the public rooms. Spacious and comfortable, there are plenty of places to sit and look out of the large windows. The golden retriever (Meg) lies peacefully snoring wherever the mood takes her (other dogs aren't allowed). The conservatory, with exposed original beams and new oak floor, has created a new large area of overspill from the main, Edwardian dining-room. Dinner is a serious affair and depending on your capacity can stretch to five courses. You might even be tempted by fresh salmon in filo pastry or home spiced beef at lunchtime, especially if you can have it in the garden. The bedrooms don't disappoint: furnished with lovely antiques and bright fabrics they also have luxury bathrooms.

- Open all year

- 4 miles south of Market Drayton off the A529, signposted Goldstone. Private car park

- 2 twin, 4 double, 1 four-poster, 1 suite; most with bathroom/WC, some with shower/WC; TV; room service, hair-dryer, baby-listening; trouser press in 1 room; no tea/coffee-making facilities in rooms

- Restaurant, bar, 3 lounges, snooker room, drying facilities, conservatory; conference facilities (max 60 people non-residential, 8 residential); croquet at hotel, other sports nearby; babysitting. Wheelchair access to hotel (1 step), restaurant and WC (unisex), 2 ground-floor bedrooms

- No dogs

- Access, Visa

- Single occupancy of twin/double £51, twin/double £65, four-poster £75, suite £97, family room £85. Alc L £19; set D £22, £27.50. Special breaks available

---

*We mention those hotels that don't accept dogs; guide dogs, however, are almost always an exception. Telephone ahead to make sure!*

**MARKINGTON** NORTH YORKSHIRE                    **MAP 4**

# Hob Green

MARKINGTON, HARROGATE, NORTH YORKSHIRE HG3 3PJ
TEL: HARROGATE (0423) 770031   FAX: (0423) 771589

*A competent hotel in beautiful countryside, well-placed for sightseeing.*

Flowers fill this hotel: there are colourful arrangements in the drawing-room, tubs by the entrance, brimming beds by the car park, sprigs on the wallpaper and bouquets on the bedspreads. Even the entrance hall, which doubles as a lounge, is gaily decorated with little bunches 'stencilled' on the wallpaper in lively strips of colour.

The hotel lies in over eight hundred acres of farm and woodland. Nearby sights include Fountains Abbey and Ripley Castle, with the Yorkshire Dales National Park close at hand. A very favourable report comes from a reader who was especially impressed by the well-stocked bathroom: 'Real bath sheets – fluffy, welcoming and two of them all for me. Hand cream, soap flakes, a face cloth, nailbrush and make-up-remover pads make this type of hotel a dream for a woman travelling alone.' The rooms have lovely views of rolling hills or of the neat vegetable and flower garden, looked after by two full-time gardeners who keep the kitchen (and the vases) replenished.

Three large sash windows overlook the garden and throw light on to the duck prints decorating the walls of the dining-room. Lacy covers smarten fresh green tablecloths, and sparkling cutlery and glassware lend an air of formality. Menus change a little every day but choices range from the Barnsley chop, to the rather more exotic-sounding banana-and-mango-filled supreme of chicken wrapped in bacon. Lunches, teas and drinks are served in the drawing-room, also formal, with a fine inlaid wooden cabinet and fine china displays. A sun room (half-lounge, half-conservatory) is also open to guests and has a jokey collection of Chinese hats arranged on trellis wallpaper and bamboo furniture.

◑ Open all year

🔋 Turn off the A61 Harrogate to Ripon road at Wormald Green and continue towards Markington. Hob Green is 1 mile through the village. Private car park

🛏 3 single, 5 twin, 3 double, 1 four-poster, 1 suite; all with bathroom/WC, TV, room service, hair-dryer, mini-bar

◈ Restaurant, lounge, conservatory;

conference facilities (max 12 people non-residential and residential); golf, riding nearby. Wheelchair access to restaurant and WC (unisex) only

⊖ No dogs in public rooms

▭ Access, Amex, Diners, Visa

£ Single £59 to £63, single occupancy of twin/double £70, twin/double £75, four-poster £93, suite £105. Alc D £25; Sun L £11. Special breaks available

# King's Head     𝓛

MARKET PLACE, MASHAM, NORTH YORKSHIRE HG4 4EF
TEL: RIPON (0765) 689295

*A popular inn in the centre of town, making an excellent base for touring the Dales.*

Masham is a popular centre for Wensleydale holidaymakers and they could do a lot worse than set up base at the King's Head. This well-kept, three-storey cream stone building commands the large market square, a place where guests may find it difficult to park on market days. A recent refurbishment has kept the traditional style and ensured a homely, welcoming atmosphere.

China plates line the picture rail, large fireplaces ensure cosiness in winter and there's plenty of room in the bars for locals, business travellers and holidaymakers. Bar meals are available at lunch but not in the evening. The dining-room seems rather formal after the relaxed jollity in the bar but in case the transition is too striking there is 'easy listening' music to keep diners company. The menu offers a reasonable choice of dishes with an emphasis on local recipes.

The bedrooms are fresh and comfortable with pine furnishings and light-coloured wallpaper and curtains and are well equipped with TVs, radios and a selection of bathroom goodies.

- ◑ Open all year
- ⤴ 15 minutes off the A1 from the Thirsk/Masham turn-off. The hotel is in Masham's market square. On-street parking
- 🛏 2 single, 1 twin, 6 double, 1 four-poster; most with bathroom/WC, some with shower/WC; TV, hair-dryer, trouser press in all rooms
- ✧ Restaurant, bar; conference facilities (max 50 people non-residential, 10 residential); fishing, golf, tennis, other sports nearby. Wheelchair access to restaurant only
- ⊖ No dogs
- ▭ Access, Amex, Diners, Visa
- 💷 Single £43, twin/double £60, four-poster £70; deposit required at peak times. Sun L £7.50; alc D £18 to £20; bar lunches. Special breaks available

---

𝓛   *This denotes that the hotel offers especially good value at whatever price level.*

**MATLOCK** DERBYSHIRE                                                    **MAP 4**

# Riber Hall

MATLOCK, DERBYSHIRE DE4 5JU
TEL: MATLOCK (0629) 582795   FAX: (0629) 580475

*A grand old hall with comfortable accommodation in the converted outbuildings.*

When Riber Hall first opened some twenty years ago it was only as a restaurant. Having established an excellent reputation, the owners branched out and built the bedrooms. Just a mile from the village of Tansley set up on the hill, it is quite a secluded spot in spite of the wildlife park behind the ruins of Riber Castle.

The hotel consists of a number of pinky-grey stone buildings set around a courtyard with the Hall commanding a prime position. To one side of this estate is a reasonable-sized walled garden; if it's too cold to go out you can sit in a slightly faded, comfortable chair in the conservatory and admire the garden. The bedrooms, all in the converted outbuildings, have whitewashed walls and beams – nine of the eleven have four-posters, most of which are antique. The rooms are all extremely comfortable, have good bathrooms and are individually decorated.

You approach the main house along a plant-filled covered way. A heavy oak door and a couple of steps lead inside and to the sitting-room. Having a heavily beamed ceiling and a blazing fire, it's a very cosy room in winter, maybe a little dark in summer. The main dining-room next door is traditional with plain décor and an assortment of tables; there's a lighter room upstairs which can double as a small conference room. Imaginative dishes and a good wine list make eating here a great pleasure.

- Open all year
- 1 mile off the A615; turn south at Tansley. Private car park
- 2 double, 9 four-poster; all with bathroom/WC, TV, room service, hair-dryer, trouser press, mini-bar; some rooms with whirlpool bath
- Dining-room, conservatory; conference facilities (max 14 people non-residential, 11 residential); tennis at hotel, other sports nearby
- No wheelchair access; no children under 10; no dogs
- Access, Amex, Diners, Visa
- Single occupancy of twin/double £76 to £90, double/four-poster £90 to £134; deposit required. Cooked B £7.50; set L £14; alc D £35 (prices till Apr 92). Special breaks available

*If you have a small appetite, or just aren't feeling hungry, check if you can be given a reduction if you don't want the full menu.*

**MATLOCK BATH DERBYSHIRE** **MAP 4**

# Hodgkinson's

150 SOUTH PARADE, MATLOCK BATH, DERBYSHIRE DE4 3NR
TEL: MATLOCK (0629) 582170

*A great place with lots of interesting touches. Exceptionally well renovated and comfortable.*

Matlock Bath is an unusual town and in a way it's not a surprise to find somewhere as original as Hodgkinson's here. It was built as a hotel in the 1780s and became Hodgkinson's about fifty years later when Mr Hodgkinson bought it; he had his brewery at the back where the present owners, Nigel and Malcolm, live. They're fascinated by the history of the house and whenever possible have preserved original elements, either left in place or repositioned to create an interesting and amusing focus. The restaurant/bar is quite small – six tables only – and they have only one sitting at dinner, so there's no rush and you can linger as long as you like. The other side of the mosaic hallway is one of the two sitting-rooms. Both this and the one upstairs (residents only) are Victorian in style. The compulsory print of 'Bubbles' is only a tiny element of the whole.

The six bedrooms are large and very comfortable with antique beds and lots of other interesting items. The shower rooms are small but smart and well-equipped. Look at the lights throughout the hotel – they're a remarkable collection. There's a free sauna for guests to use and a new addition is the hairdressing salon. It was to have been the second dining-room but beauty won. Try and arrive early and have your hair done before dinner. Nigel does the cooking, creates and writes out the menu. Cooking is definitely where his skills lie – you can hardly read the menu!

*Open all year; restaurant closed Sun eve*

*On the main A6 Derby to Manchester road, 1½ miles south of Matlock. Private car park*

*5 double, 1 half-tester; all with shower/WC, TV, room service, hair-dryer*

*Restaurant, bar, 2 lounges, drying room; sauna, hairdressing salon at hotel, fishing, riding, other sports nearby. Wheelchair access to restaurant only*

*No dogs in public rooms*

*Access, Amex, Visa*

*Single occupancy of twin/double £40 to £65, twin/double £45 to £75; deposit required. Set D £21. Special breaks available*

*Hotels in our* Visitors' Book *towards the end of the* Guide *are additional hotels that may be worth a visit. Reports on these hotels are welcome.*

**MAWNAN SMITH** CORNWALL                                    **MAP 8**

# Budock Vean

MAWNAN SMITH, NR FALMOUTH, CORNWALL TR11 5LG
TEL: FALMOUTH (0326) 250288   FAX: (0326) 250892

*Large, facility-rich hotel with a hunting lodge theme in an especially lush part of south Cornwall.*

No one on a budget chooses Budock Vean, and it gets no marks for being either intimate or lavish, but it does have plenty to offer. The 18-hole golf course brings in lots of business, as do the large indoor swimming-pool, beach, fishing and riding. The informal and friendly atmosphere also wins fans.

The early nineteenth-century, mansard-roofed building is itself large, with several additions. Inside, it's cavernous and done out like a hunting lodge with huge open fireplaces, stags' heads and high-beamed ceilings. Cocktail bar, conservatory and lounge are but a few of the many places to sit. Your bedroom may be in the original bit, the sixties block or the thirties block, but in any case you'll find ample space, comfortable rather than stylish furniture, dour rather than fresh colour schemes, and not much to interest the eye. Even newly refurbished rooms feel old-fashioned, but their bathrooms are tiled and have proper showers in baths.

◐ Closed 2 Jan to mid-Feb

↗ From Truro take the A39 for 7 miles, then the A394 for 1 mile. Follow signs to Mabe, Argal and Mawnan Smith. At the Red Lion pub fork right, signposted Budock Vean. Private car park

🛏 10 single, 29 twin, 16 double, 1 four-poster, 3 suites, 1 cottage; all with bathroom/WC, TV, room service, hair-dryer, baby-listening; ironing facilities

◈ Restaurant, 2 bars, 3 lounges, games room, conservatory;

conference facilities (max 25 people residential); fishing, golf, tennis, heated indoor pool at hotel, other sports nearby

● No wheelchair access; no dogs in public rooms

▭ Access, Amex, Diners, Visa

£ Single £55 to £85, single occupancy of twin/double £83 to £123, twin/double £110 to £170, four-poster/suite £130 to £190 (rates inc dinner); deposit required. Set D £20; alc D £28 to £35; bar lunches

---

*The 1993 Guide will be published before Christmas 1992. Reports on hotels are most welcome at any time of the year, but are extremely valuable in the spring. Send them to* Which? Hotel Guide, *FREEPOST, 2 Marylebone Road, London NW1 1YN. No stamp is needed if reports are posted in the UK.*

# Meudon Hotel

MAWNAN SMITH, NR FALMOUTH, CORNWALL TR11 5HT
TEL: FALMOUTH (0326) 250541   FAX: (0326) 250543

*A family-run hotel with extensive sub-tropical gardens, old-fashioned furnishings and first-rate service.*

You don't immediately see the original, turn-of-the-century Cornish mansion. Instead, you notice the forecourt, car park and characterless bedroom wing. Nor is your bedroom of restrained design and built-in furniture likely to enchant. What really grabs is the view, shared by all rooms, of a luscious sub-tropical wonderland of palms, camellias, azaleas rhododendrons (to name but a few), that dips out of view in a series of grassy terraces, then rises to be crowned by tall pines.

Take tea at round tables and listen to the cacophony of bird-song, then wander down to the sheltered, pebbly and sandy beach along one of several gorgeous paths. As well as being home to Cornish flora at its most exuberant, this is a very friendly, family-run hotel. Cheerful staff are formally dressed. Public rooms are a little severe, so young families may feel out of place. Best views over the garden are through the picture windows of the dining-room. Here, competent five-course dinners are served, but the high point of the evening for guests near the window is the nightly arrival of Henry the seagull – before or after the head waiter, Gabriel, puts out the scraps.

- Closed Jan, Feb
- From Truro take the A39 for 7 miles, then the A394 for 1 mile. Follow signs to Mabe, Argal and Mawnan Smith. Fork left at the Red Lion pub. The hotel is 1 mile on the right. Private car park
- 4 single, 22 twin/double, 3 double, 1 family room, 2 suites; all with bathroom/WC, TV, room service, hair-dryer, trouser press, baby-listening; tea/coffee-making facilities on request
- Restaurant, bar, 3 lounges, conservatory, drying room; fishing, riding, water sports, private beach at hotel, free golf, other sports nearby
- No wheelchair access; no children under 5; no dogs in public rooms
- Access, Diners, Visa
- Single £87, single occupancy of twin/double £105, twin/double £154, suite £210 (rates inc dinner); children half-price; deposit required. Set L £13, D £24; alc L £17, D £40 (prices till May 92). Special breaks available

*The* Guide *office can quickly spot when a hotelier is encouraging customers to write a recommending inclusion – and sadly, several hotels have been doing this in 1991. Such reports do not further an hotel's cause.*

# Nansidwell Country House

MAWNAN SMITH, FALMOUTH, CORNWALL TR11 5HU
TEL: FALMOUTH (0326) 250340   FAX: (0326) 250440

*Swish and artistically decorated country house in lush gardens. Good golfing nearby.*

Jamie and Felicity Robertson's home makes a neat, satisfying package in classical country-house hotel tradition: attractive house amidst sleek gardens (in this case sub-tropical), plush and comfortable surroundings, personal attention from resident owners and good food and wine.

The Edwardian stone house is covered in creepers, has mullioned windows and looks down to the sea through five acres of gardens. Plank floors, large fireplaces, window seats and elegantly proportioned rooms have been given just the right amount of dressing-up. Antiques are abundant; design-conscious fabrics and frills are out of *Homes and Gardens*. Felicity has decorated each bedroom differently. They are pretty rather than showy with good-quality, often striped fabrics, some antique furniture and a distinctly romantic feel.

The pale lemon restaurant, with fine views and dozens of colourful plates artistically placed on walls and pillars, is the setting for dinner. The area is rich in golf courses, but walking is popular and the Robertsons can supply you with a map of local footpaths.

◑ Closed 27 Dec to 31 Jan

🔁 From Truro take the A39 for 7 miles, then the A394 for 1 mile. Follow signs for Mabe, Argal and Mawnan Smith. At the Red Lion in Mawnan Smith fork left – the hotel is on the right. Private car park

🛏 12 twin/double; all with bathroom/WC, TV, room service (limited), hair-dryer; trouser press, baby-listening on request

🎿 Restaurant, bar, 2 lounges, drying room; tennis at hotel, other sports nearby; babysitting. Wheelchair access to hotel and restaurant, 2 ground-floor bedrooms

⊖ No children under 10 in restaurant eves; no dogs in public rooms

▭ Access, Visa

💷 Single occupancy of twin/double from £75, twin/double £81 to £140; deposit required. Cooked B £4; Sun L £15; set D £20; alc L, D £30. Special breaks available

---

*The text of entries is based on unsolicited reports sent in by readers and backed up by inspections. The factual details under the text are from questionnaires the Guide sends to all hotels that feature in the book.*

# Maxstoke Priory

MAXSTOKE, NR COLESHILL, WARWICKSHIRE B46 2QW
TEL: COLESHILL (0675) 462117

*Lovely old house offering B&B in rolling Warwickshire
countryside.*

The entrance to the priory is unmarked except for a 'Private' sign which
means that you drive through the old impressive gateway in trepidation.
Is it the right house? The fourteenth-century farmhouse with its black
studded door is intriguing. Horses peer out from the stable block or over
the wall from the small paddock, and behind the house you can see the
remains of the old priory. As well as being a keen horsewoman Mrs
Tyacke offers two rooms in the house for B&B. They are both spacious,
with *en suite* facilities, TVs and a mix of freestanding furnishings. One
has a display of prizewinning rosettes and great views of the priory
remains. Breakfast (as early as you like) is served in the oak-panelled
dining-room with its fantastic armorial painted ceiling and substantial
oak furnishings. The sitting-room is both comfortable and personal with
a massive open fireplace, loose-covered sofas and family photos. Next
door is a smaller room with a sofa and a desk, useful if you're doing a bit
of work after a day at the nearby NEC.

- ◑ Open all year
- ⏩ 2½ miles south-east of Coleshill.
  Private car park
- 🛏 2 twin; 1 with bathroom/WC, 1
  with shower/WC; TV, hair-dryer
  in both rooms
- ◈ Dining-room, lounge, study,
  drying room; swimming-pool and
- fishing at hotel, other sports
  nearby
- ⊖ No wheelchair access; no dogs in
  public rooms
- ▭ None accepted
- ⊞ Single occupancy of twin/double
  £26, twin/double £38

# Melbourn Bury

NR ROYSTON, HERTFORDSHIRE SG8 6DE
TEL: ROYSTON (0763) 261151    FAX: (0763) 262375

*A Victorian manor house with a formal atmosphere. You're
expected to be sociable here.*

This rambling white house stands well back from the road and is
protected by beech trees. The core dates from Tudor times, but what you
see from the outside is Victorian. Sylvia Hopkinson's ancestors arrived in

the middle of Victoria's reign, and there are antiques and heirlooms from former generations throughout the house.

Although the house now has a modern love for uncluttered spaces (and is airy and bright), you will not feel comfortable in trainers and jeans. The Hopkinsons often host conferences and receptions but let three very large and bright bedrooms only. As it's a Wolsey Lodge, you are expected to socialise with other guests before, during and after dinner. Set, no-choice dinners are served in grand style.

A reader writes: 'Really enchanting garden with lake, and civilised conversation with the lady of the house before and after dinner. Well-laid table – we were the only guests. Good smoked haddock mousse, bland chicken and boring vegetables. I think the food suffered because there had been a luncheon for 60 that day and there was to be another big one the next. Would stay again for a "one night stand".'

🌓 Open all year, exc Xmas, New Year and Easter

🔋 Leave Royston on the A10 northbound and take the first exit to Melbourn. The entrance to the house is 300 yards on the left after the turn. Private car park

🛏 1 single, 2 twin; all with bathroom/WC, exc 1 twin with shower/WC; TV, room service in all rooms; no tea/coffee-making facilities in rooms

🗹 Dining-room, lounge, billiard room, library, conservatory; conference facilities (max 50 people non-residential); croquet at hotel, golf nearby

⊖ No wheelchair access; no children under 8; no dogs

▭ Access, Amex, Visa

💷 Single £48, single occupancy of twin/double £48, twin £76; deposit required. Set D £14.50 (8pm)

---

**MELDRETH** CAMBRIDGESHIRE                **MAP 7**

# Chiswick House

MELDRETH, ROYSTON, HERTFORDSHIRE SG8 6LZ
TEL: ROYSTON (0763) 260242

*Quiet village setting and good B&B accommodation in historic farmhouse.*

The fifteenth-century, half-timbered house on the edge of the village is small in size and big on charm. James I may have used it as a hunting lodge in the early 1600s (his royal crest can be seen above the fireplace).

Chiswick House has been in the same family for almost 100 years and the present Elbourns have done much to show off its past and ensure its future. They've uncovered beams and furnished it appropriately, using lots of wood. The dining/sitting-room of dark oak panelling and beams has parquet floors. Against this, the polished oak furniture, including a refectory table and Jacobean-style chairs, looks just right. The Elbourns show respect to twentieth-century comforts, of course, and are very welcoming hosts. Around the coal fire are assembled a comfy leather sofa and studded leather chairs or you can enjoy the glassed-in, over-flow breakfast room which looks into the walled garden. The bedrooms in the house vary in shape but beams and cottagey furnishings are standard.

🔾 Open all year, exc Xmas week

🔁 Meldreth village is 1 mile west of the A10, 8 miles south of Cambridge and 3 miles north of Royston. Private car park

🛏 2 twin, 4 double (some rooms in stable annexe); 1 with bathroom/WC, most with shower/WC; baby-listening in all rooms; TV on request

◈ Breakfast room, lounge, drying room, conservatory; golf, tennis, riding nearby; babysitting. Wheelchair access to hotel (1 step), 4 ground-floor bedrooms

🔴 Babies and children over 12 only; no smoking

🔲 None accepted

£ Single occupancy of twin/double £33, twin/double £38; deposit required

---

**MELKSHAM** WILTSHIRE                                                        **MAP 9**

# Sandridge Park

MELKSHAM, WILTSHIRE SN12 7QU
TEL: MELKSHAM (0225) 706897   FAX: (0225) 702838

*A stately Victorian manor offering space, light and gracious living.*

Not an auspicious start: the sign at the bottom of the long, wooded drive warns of dog patrol security. The warm welcome comes from Annette Hoogeweegen (and Andrew when he's about, and maybe their menagerie of friendly dogs) as you pull up in front of their Victorian mansion. Annette's talents divide between gardening, interior decoration and cooking.

Inside the light and spacious house, a series of large, open rooms is decorated and furnished to a high standard (rich fabrics, collections of this and that, and unusual Austrian furniture). This is also a cultured household, with grand piano and zillions of books and modern prints that are not just there to cover walls. Space is a feature of all the bedrooms, but the ground-floor double, with a sofa and real fire, has most. Good bathrooms, not always *en suite*, have character too, perhaps an old bath on legs. Since 1990, Sandridge Park has been a part of the Wolsey Lodge group, so hospitality is of the convivial sort with communal drinks, dinners and coffee. The gardens, dovecote, bird-house, pond with wild ducks, cedars of Lebanon and 300-year-old chestnut tree are the perfect counterpart to indoor life at Sandridge Park.

🔾 Open all year, exc Xmas and New Year

🔁 From Melksham take the A3102 towards Colne. The hotel is 2 miles along this road on the left. Private car park

🛏 1 twin, 3 double; all with bathroom/WC, hair-dryer

◈ Dining-room, lounge, TV room, library; conference facilities (max 20 people non-residential, 4 residential); fishing, golf, other sports nearby

⬤ No wheelchair access; no children under 16; no dogs; no smoking in bedrooms

▭ None accepted

£ Single occupancy of twin/double £35, twin/double £70; deposit required. Set D from £18 (8pm, residents only). Special breaks available

# Shurnhold House

SHURNHOLD, MELKSHAM, WILTSHIRE SN12 8DG
TEL: BATH (0225) 790555

*A beautifully kept home-away-from-home, now a B&B only.*

The Meads' small Jacobean manor house as a broad appeal and also a wide clientele. Melksham brings in business folk and there are rich pickings for tourists not far away. The prices are low but the surroundings chic enough to make you feel you're treating yourself. Screened by trees but not far from the road, the Cotswold stone house is clad in wistaria, overlooked by a mighty yew tree and flanked by a split-level garden of formal flower beds and gravel-edged lawns.

The inside gives little impression of being other than a private home, and the Meads' jolly nature certainly confirms it. Solid Victorian furniture is balanced by a little frivolity, such as hedgehog doorstops, sentimental Pears children prints, a teapot collection and one Pooh Bear. The flagstoned bar, off the parquet-floored entrance hall, gets heavy use in the evenings, especially in winter when the log fire is lit. For a quiet retreat, the green and white lounge with a Victorian brocade three-piece suite should fit the bill. Dinner is no longer available, but good restaurants are to hand. Bedrooms are bright, spacious, pretty and supplied with good books and cold drinks. Carpeted bathrooms sparkle with white fittings.

◑ Open all year

▨ Shurnhold is just off the A365, 1 mile from Melksham, 10 miles from Bath. The driveway is well signposted. Private car park

⛏ 2 twin, 3 double, 1 four-poster, 1 family room, 1 annexe room; all with bathroom/WC, exc annexe room with shower/WC; TV, room service, hair-dryer, baby-listening in all rooms

◈ Dining-room, bar, lounge;

croquet at hotel, golf, tennis other sports nearby

⬤ No wheelchair access; dogs by arrangement in bedrooms only; smoking in bar only

▭ Access, Visa

£ Single occupancy of twin/double £45 to £48, twin/double £60 to £68, four-poster £68, family room £78, annexe room £42; deposit required. Cooked B £3

**MELLING** LANCASHIRE

MAP 3

# Melling Hall

MELLING, LANCASHIRE LA6 2RA
TEL: HORNBY (052 42) 21298

*First-class furniture and considerable comfort for a business
clientele.*

Recent legislation may lead owners Jim and Christine Ross to rethink the
sign that warns: 'The dog eats intruders'. Since taking over in the
mid-1980s, they've upgraded facilities and added lots of interesting and
beautiful old furniture that shows the Hall's natural features to best
effect. There's a carved mahogany staircase, graceful dark wood archways and a minstrels' gallery, as well as two ornate Chinese oak chairs
and an elderly lambing chair.

   Their guests are mainly business-oriented and the rather staid dining-
room serves Anglo-French food. The bar is more congenial, with arched
partitions, Lowry-like prints by Tom Dodson and a good choice of ales.
Bedroom furniture runs the gamut from Victorian and Edwardian
splendour to the occasional laminated headboard, but all are roomy and
cheerfully decorated. Room seven is the undoubted star – a showcase for
*fin de siècle* Hungarian ash furniture inherited from Jim's grandmother.
There's a bed with a tall rounded footboard, a marble-topped washstand, two round-backed chairs, a clothes-stand, and dressing-table
with swing mirror. Bold fabrics, Japanese prints and white carpet
complement the overall effect.

🌓 Open all year; restaurant closed
   Sun eve

🚗 On the A683, 5 miles south of
   Cowan Bridge. Private car park

🛏 2 single, 4 twin, 7 double, 1
   family room; most with
   bathroom/WC, some with
   shower/WC, 2 public bathrooms;
   TV, baby-listening in all rooms

◈ Restaurant, 2 bars, lounge,
   games room, drying room;
   conference facilities (max 100

people non-residential, 14
residential); fishing, golf, other
sports nearby. Wheelchair access
to restaurant and WC (M,F) only

🚫 No dogs in public rooms

▦ Access, Amex, Visa

💷 Single £20 to £38, single
occupancy of twin/double £20 to
£38, twin/double £30 to £55,
family room £41 to £60. Sun L
£7.50; set D £12.50; alc D £17.
Special breaks available

---

*All entries in the* Guide *are rewritten every year, not least because standards
fluctuate. Don't trust an out-of-date* Guide.

**MELTON MOWBRAY** LEICESTERSHIRE    **MAP 4**

# The Harboro

BURTON STREET, MELTON MOWBRAY, LEICESTERSHIRE LE13 1AF
TEL: MELTON MOWBRAY (0664) 60121    FAX: (0664) 64296

*Simple cheerful accommodation in the town centre. The hotel can
be good value for families.*

Most people, by now, recognise a Harvester Restaurant when they see
one. Waving figures of Aunt Sally and Worzel Gummidge welcome you
in to eat Gummidge Burgers or Aunt Sally's chicken nuggets. Well, this
one is no exception except that it has an hotel above it which offers
reasonable accommodation at a fair price and an atmosphere that would
appeal to any hamburger-loving child.

The Harvester chain belongs to the Forte group and this one is housed
in an old coaching-inn dating from the 1700s. Rooms are bright with a
mixture of tiny-patterned, purple and pink fabrics and wallpapers. The
hotel reception on the first floor is reached via the bar. The bar itself is
decorated with a country-style pine décor, and a mass of rustic objects
decorates walls and surfaces. Prices per room are fixed, making it a good-
value deal for a family room of three, though breakfast is not included in
the price and pushes up the final bill. Payment for an overnight stay is
also required on arrival – an unwelcome American habit.

○ Open all year

↗ On the A607 in Melton
Mowbray, opposite the church
and railway station. Private car
park

⊨ 7 single, 5 twin, 11 double, 3
family rooms; most with
bathroom/WC, some with
shower/WC; TV in all rooms;
hair-dryer, baby-listening on
request

◇ Restaurant, bar; fishing, golf,

other sports nearby. Wheelchair
access to restaurant only

⊖ No dogs in public rooms; no
smoking in some bedrooms

▭ Access, Amex, Visa

£ Single £25, twin/double £30,
family room £30; deposit
required. Continental B £3.50,
cooked B £5.50; alc L, D £14;
bar snacks (prices till end 91).
Special breaks available

---

*Hotels in our* Visitors' Book *towards the end of the* Guide *are additional
hotels that may be worth a visit. Reports on these hotels are welcome.*

# Chetcombe House

CHETCOMBE ROAD, MERE, WILTSHIRE BA12 6AZ
TEL: MERE (0747) 860219

*Small mid-range hotel on the edge of town. The gentle upgrading by new resident owners is welcome.*

The tan-coloured Chetcombe House, vintage 1937, has dubious architectural merit. The nearby car park is not the best introduction to a pleasant and friendly hotel that fills a gap between basic guesthouse and impersonal business hotel.

Inside, raspberry-coloured velveteen easy chairs just ask to be flopped into, and the log stove is welcoming. Pretty and tidy gardens (an acre in all) and fields beyond are visible through large windows, and even more so from the bench on the terrace. Pastel walls and big windows make the simple dining-room a cheerful place for inexpensive four-course dinners (no choice after the first course): carrot soup, maybe, then chicken in tarragon, and rhubarb Bakewell pudding before cheese. Wines from local merchant Robin Yapp are well-chosen. The owners have replaced velveteen padded headboards and dowdier items left from a previous era with smarter, less predictable furniture, so bedrooms are now appealing as well as comfortable. The basics are there and a family room is practical as well as roomy. More reports, please.

- Open all year
- Just off the A303 on the slip-road into Mere. Private car park
- 1 single, 1 twin, 2 double, 1 family room; some with bathroom/WC, some with shower/WC; TV in all rooms
- Dining-room, lounge
- No wheelchair access; no dogs in public rooms; no smoking in bedrooms
- Access, Amex, Visa
- Single £27, single occupancy of twin/double £27, twin/double £46, family room £60; deposit required. Set D £10 (7pm) (prices till Apr 92). Special breaks available

---

*See the inside front cover for a brief explanation of how to use the* Guide.

---

*Report forms are at the back of the book; write a letter if you prefer.*

# Forest of Arden

MAXSTOKE LANE, MERIDEN, COVENTRY, WARWICKSHIRE CV7 7HR
TEL: MERIDEN (0676) 22335   TELEX: 312604 FOA G
FAX: (0676) 23711

*Smart and stylish hotel with golf courses, a leisure centre and conference facilities.*

The modern brick building is approached via a long drive through some of the twelve thousand acres of grounds, woodland, lakes and golf courses. As many golf bags as pieces of luggage are unloaded out of car boots.

The interior has style. An open split-level space is divided into distinctive public areas where massive windows overlook the golf course and countryside beyond. The bar and lounge have exposed rafters and terracotta tiled floor; the upholstery, in soft colours, contrasts with the wall hangings on stark white walls. In the evening this area is warmed by pools of light and stays open until the last stragglers go to bed.

The restaurant overlooks an outdoor barbecue area and has high ceilings, and modern furnishings. Bedrooms are less original, decorated in muted blues and greens, but have everything you need, including immaculate bathrooms. The conference and leisure centres are self-contained and you have a choice of bars and restaurants by the golf course, in the leisure centre or the main hotel.

◗ Open all year

⤴ Take Junction 6 from the M42 and follow the A45 towards Coventry. Carry straight on to Stonebridge Island and after ¾ mile turn left into Maxstoke Lane. The hotel is 1½ miles on the left. Private car park

🛏 75 twin, 75 double, 2 suites; all with bathroom/WC, TV, room service, hair-dryer, trouser press, baby-listening

◇ 2 restaurants, 3 bars, lounge, games room, conservatory; conference facilities (max 150 people non-residential, 120 residential); all public areas air-conditioned; crèche facilities; fishing, golf, tennis, sauna/solarium, heated indoor swimming-pool, gym, beauty salon, spa bath, dance studio, snooker, squash at hotel. Wheelchair access to hotel (ramps), restaurant and WC (M,F), 50 ground-floor bedrooms, 2 specially equipped for the disabled

⊖ No dogs; no smoking in some public areas and some bedrooms

▭ Access, Amex, Diners, Visa

💷 Single occupancy of twin/double £105, twin/double £120, suite £175. Set L, D £19; alc L, D £35 (prices till Mar 92). Special breaks available

# Greystones

MARKET PLACE, MIDDLEHAM, NORTH YORKSHIRE DL8 4NR
TEL: WENSLEYDALE (0969) 22016

*A neat, friendly guesthouse in the centre of this historic town.*

A dignified Georgian house overlooking the market square is a good base when exploring this part of the Yorkshire Dales. The town is famous as both the home of Richard III and a major racehorse training centre.

Greystones is a small, four-bedroomed guesthouse run by a friendly couple who offer a good home-cooked evening meal and comfortable bedrooms. All the rooms are simply but brightly decorated with stylish modern fabrics. Every room has tea- and coffee-making facilities but guests wanting to watch TV must do so in the lounge downstairs and hope someone isn't playing the piano. The dining-room is full of pieces the Greenwoods have collected, and their engravings brighten the walls. An interesting menu includes such items as couscous of seafood and a swede pancake. The chef is happy to prepare some of the dishes in a plainer form as required. A number of courses, ranging from making sugar-paste flowers to yoga, are run at weekends.

Closed Dec and Jan, exc Xmas and New Year

From the A1 turn on to the B6267 to Masham and follow this road to Middleham. On-street parking

2 twin, 1 double, 1 family room; 1 with bathroom/WC, most with shower/WC; hair-dryer in all rooms

Dining-room, lounge, drying room; fishing, golf, riding nearby.

Wheelchair access to restaurant only

Dogs by arrangement only; no smoking in bedrooms or dining-room

None accepted

Single occupancy of twin/double £40, twin/double £50, family room £63; deposit required. Set D £12.50 (7pm). Special breaks available

# Miller's House

MARKET PLACE, MIDDLEHAM, NORTH YORKSHIRE DL8 4NR
TEL: WENSLEYDALE (0969) 22630

*A small well-run hotel. Friendly hosts delight in directing guests to the best of the Yorkshire Dales.*

Set slightly back from the market square, Miller's House is a fine-looking grey-stone Georgian house. The hotel has been stylishly decorated in keeping with the period of the house. The sitting-room is smart but cosy with a coal fire and comfortable reproduction furniture. There's a small bar at one end of this room and pictures and other figures remind guests of the proximity of Middleham's famous racing stables; the dining-room too has good-quality furnishings – no stinting on the curtains here, thick and heavy with swathes of cloth in both public rooms – and looks pretty when candlelit in the evenings. The wine list is good, complementing the well-presented dinners; the owners are interested in wine and have held a couple of wine-tasting weekends (among other special activity breaks). It's advisable not to over-eat in the evenings in order to have room for the full breakfast which will more than set you up for the day. Alternatively, you can settle for just fresh croissants, toast and coffee.

The bedrooms, named after individual Dales, are very comfortable and attractively decorated and furnished; all have their own bathrooms, some with free-standing Victorian baths. Judith and Crossley Sutherland are keen to help their guests get the best out of the area and keep folders of press cuttings, books, magazines and pamphlets lying around, as well as being on hand to give advice themselves.

◐ Closed Jan

↗ As Greystones entry above. Private car park

🛏 I single, 3 twin, 2 double, I four-poster; all with bathroom/ WC, TV, room service, hairdryer, mini-bar

◈ Dining-room, lounge/bar, drying room; croquet at hotel, other sports nearby

⊖ No wheelchair access; no children under 10; no dogs; no smoking in dining-room

▭ Access, Visa

£ Single £32, twin/double £64, four-poster £69; deposit required. Set D £18.50 (prices till Easter 92). Special breaks available

---

**MIDDLETON TYAS** NORTH YORKSHIRE        **MAP 3**

# Brook House

MIDDLETON TYAS, RICHMOND, NORTH YORKSHIRE DL10 6RP
TEL: DARLINGTON (0325) 377713

*A good spot for travellers on the A1 who prefer private houses to hotels.*

The Harrops' farmhouse, within minutes of Scotch Corner, is an excellent quiet hideaway from the stresses of journeys north or south. There are only two rooms, so it is wiser to book in advance than just drop in. The elegant Georgian proportions of the house are at their best in the huge drawing-room and the dining-room, and they are complemented by fine antique furniture, views across open fields and generally stylish comfort.

The bedrooms are also comfortable and have their own bathrooms

and views. Dinners are fairly formal and are eaten with the Harrops
round their oval mahogany table; breakfast is served in the farmhouse
kitchen. There's no licence, so bring your own tipples if you want.

○ *Open all year, exc Xmas*

↗ *Leave the A1 or A66 at Scotch Corner. Turn east through Middleton Tyas village and out on the Crofʹ road. After 1 mile at sharp left bend marked by black and white arrows, take lane to right for 500 yards. Private car park*

⇋ *1 twin, 1 double; both with bathroom/WC; no tea/coffee-making facilities in rooms*

◈ *Dining-room, drawing-room, sitting-room; tennis, golf, other sports nearby*

⊖ *No wheelchair access; young guests not encouraged; no dogs; smoking in drawing-room only*

▭ *None accepted*

£ *Single occupancy of twin/double £33, twin/double £56; deposit required. Set D £19.50 (7.30 to 8pm)*

**MIDHURST** WEST SUSSEX                                    **MAP 10**

# Spread Eagle

SOUTH STREET, MIDHURST, WEST SUSSEX GU29 9NH
TEL: MIDHURST (0730) 816911   TELEX: 86853 SPREA G
FAX: (0730) 815668

*A comfortable and interesting old coaching-inn.*

This wooden-framed tavern dates as far back as 1430 and was considerably added to in 1650. Its many centuries of history have left it with
medieval ships' timbers, Tudor bread ovens, a wig powder closet,
Flemish stained-glass windows, a window bricked-up to avoid tax,
creaking floors and sloping ceilings.

The restaurant, where pots of Christmas puddings hang from old oak
beams over a coppered inglenook fireplace, occupies the core of the
building, and suffers rather from being a thoroughfare. On one side lies
the original tavern, the large inviting Lounge Bar, with log-fire, windsor,
leather and upholstered armchairs; on the other is the main hotel
entrance where steps lead down to the Cellar Bar which is more basic,
with pews and seats built out of beer kegs.

You'll have to pay considerably more for one of the four-poster
bedrooms, some of which are enormous; alternatively, take a standard
room – the ones in the new block have good-quality reproduction
furniture, those in the main building some antiques, and the attic ones
are particularly inviting.

○ *Open all year*

↗ *On the edge of Midhurst village, overlooking South Pond. Private car park*

⇋ *2 single, 15 twin, 20 double, 3 four-poster, 1 four-poster suite; most with bathroom/WC, some with shower/WC; TV, room service, baby-listening in all rooms; hair-dryer, trouser press* in some rooms; no tea/coffee-making facilities in rooms

◈ 2 restaurants, 2 bars, lounge; conference facilities (max 45 people non-residential and residential); fishing, golf, other sports nearby; babysitting

● No wheelchair access

▭ Access, Amex, Diners, Visa

£ Single £68 to £72, single occupancy of twin/double £75 to £90, twin/double £85 to £110, four-poster from £130, suite £175; deposit required at peak times. Set L £17, D £25. Special breaks available

---

**MILDENHALL** SUFFOLK                                          **MAP 7**

# Riverside Hotel

MILL STREET, MILDENHALL, BURY ST EDMUNDS, SUFFOLK IP28 7EA
TEL: MILDENHALL (0638) 717274   FAX: (0638) 715997

*Useful and well-run hotel in the heart of East Anglia. Very popular for business meetings.*

The road runs right by, the river isn't immediately obvious, and a car park has eaten up the front garden. But take heart. Behind the Georgian brick façade resides a very pleasant hotel. High ceilings and colourful modern furnishings are compromised by some contrived homeliness: the books in the bar look like a job lot, and pictures might well have been bought by the yard. An ever-willing and cheerful staff is what makes this hotel – as well as efficiency, crucial to its many business clientele.

The restaurant side is clearly important; and the à la carte menus often venture beyond standard hotel cookery – oriental and Italian ingredients and flavours, in particular. Bedrooms, two of which are in an extension, have reasonable provisions and some inspiring fabrics of deep rather than pastel shades, which give them the edge over many commercial hotels. The extreme height of the first floor means smaller rooms here feel too vertical. Up another flight (by lift, if you wish) and the proportions improve; up yet again for cosier but darker rooms. A few four-posters and corner baths have crept in to please honeymooners. Back rooms are quietest and give a good view of the river. You can row to the next village in the hotel's boat if you fancy. Leisure facilities may soon be available for the less adventurous. More reports, please.

◑ Open all year

⤢ From the A11 Newmarket to Norwich road, take the A1101. The hotel is on the way out of Mildenhall going towards Barton Mills/Worlington. Private car park

⇚ 5 single, 5 twin, 7 double, 1 four-poster, 2 family rooms, 4 cottages; half with bathroom/WC, half with shower/WC; TV, room service, hair-dryer, trouser press, baby-listening in all rooms

◈ Restaurant, 2 bars, lounge, drying room; conference facilities (max 60 people non-residential, 26 residential); fishing, croquet, boat at hotel, other sports nearby

● No wheelchair access; no dogs in restaurant

▭ Access, Amex, Diners, Visa

£ Single £45 to £47, single occupancy of twin/double £52 to £54, twin/double £66 to £70,

four-poster/family room £78 to £82, cottage £40 to £82; deposit required. Sun L £10; alc L, D £19. Special breaks available

---

**MINEHEAD** SOMERSET                                        **MAP 8**

# Periton Park

MIDDLECOMBE, NR MINEHEAD, SOMERSET TA24 8SW
TEL: MINEHEAD (0643) 706885   FAX: (0643) 702698

*Spacious family home on the edge of Exmoor with all the comfort and quiet you could wish for.*

'Where time stands still,' proclaims the brochure, and, as you curve up the drive through rhododendrons and holly, past horse pastures and old walls, you can begin to believe it. The motto comes from the previous owners but even if new owners Richard and Angela Hunt, who arrived in September 1990, have bought a fresh look to this pale yellow Victorian house, their priority is still to offer good old-fashioned relaxation and comfort.

The airy salmon-coloured sitting-room with open fire and acres of bookshelves has gentle archways and large windows letting in plenty of light. Stylish chairs and settees replace many items of the former owners. The former billiard room, once a sombre maroon, is now salmon like the sitting-room and has been transformed into a very cheerful dining-room with modern prints and crisp tablecloths. There are several choices on the three-course dinner menu, perhaps cheese soufflé to start, Gressingham duck with plum sauce and spring onions, then crème brûlée.

From your bedroom you can look out over the 32 acres of woodland and garden. Old rather than antique furniture is standard. Good bathrooms have Victorian-style fittings. You may even find a decorated lavatory pan with wooden seat.

○ Closed Feb; restaurant closed Sun, Mon eves

⤢ On the south side of the A39 Minehead to Porlock road. Private car park

🛏 4 twin/double, 4 double (I with extra bed); half with bathroom/WC, half with shower/WC; TV, room service, hair-dryer in all rooms

◈ Restaurant, lounge, drying room; conference facilities (max 40 people non-residential, 8 residential); riding at hotel, other sports nearby. Wheelchair access to hotel (2 steps) and restaurant, I ground-floor bedroom specially equipped for the disabled

⊖ No children under 12; dogs in I bedroom only; no smoking in dining-room and I bedroom

▭ Access, Amex, Visa

£ Single occupancy of twin/double £57, twin/double £80; deposit required. Alc D £23. Special breaks available

**MOLLINGTON** CHESHIRE                              **MAP 4**

# Crabwall Manor

PARKGATE ROAD, MOLLINGTON, CHESTER, CHESHIRE CH1 6NE
TEL: GREAT MOLLINGTON (0244) 851666   TELEX: 61220 CRAWAL G
FAX (0244) 851400

*Stylish and grand country-house hotel set in large gardens.*

Crabwall Manor is a prime example of the neo-Gothic pile – a crenel-lated brick mansion complete with clock tower and stables and basking in eleven acres of lawns and gardens. The interior is a successful blend of antique and modern, with fine Georgian and Victorian pieces and up-to-date sofas. One of the three lounges is especially memorable with its walk-through inglenook, abundance of stylish fabrics and a Persian-style carpet. Décor in the Regency-style dining-room is soft-hued in pale peaches and greys; the tables are swathed in two layers of linen. There is also a new conservatory restaurant, plus a cocktail lounge.

Bedrooms, many of which have fine views from balconies, have good reproduction furniture with the occasional antique. Bathrooms are Hollywood-ritzy with double scallop-shaped basins, bidets and showers as well as bath, although one correspondent was unable to coax any hot water from the gilded taps for his morning ablutions. Food is in the modern international vein and has been much praised. One recent menu offered terrine of salmon and peppers with an orange vinaigrette, sorbet, then roast loin of pork with an apple and prune compôte on a thyme-flavoured sauce, then iced parfait of dark chocolate and coffee and a cheeseboard. Although the wine list is wide-ranging one buff wrote to us in disappointment at not being shown a bottle (which turned out not to be the chosen one) before it was poured. More reports, please.

◑ Open all year

⤴ On the A540 Chester to Hoylake road. Private car park

🛏 42 twin/double, 1 four-poster, 5 suites; all with bathroom/WC, TV, room service, hair-dryer, trouser press, baby-listening; no tea/coffee-making facilities in rooms

◈ Restaurant (air-conditioned), bar, 3 lounges, games room, conservatory; conference facilities (max 100 people non-residential, 48 residential); croquet at hotel, other sports nearby; babysitting. Wheelchair access to hotel (ramp), restaurant and WC (unisex), 19 ground-floor bedrooms, 1 specially equipped for the disabled

⊖ No dogs

▭ Access, Amex, Diners, Visa

£ Single occupancy of twin/double £95, twin/double £125, four-poster £185, suite £150. Continental B £5, cooked B £8; set L £13.50, D £23; alc L, D £37. Special breaks available

# Morston Hall

MORSTON, HOLT, NORFOLK NR25 7AA
TEL: CLEY (0263) 741041   FAX: (0263) 741034

*Comfortable and stylish accommodation in home-like atmosphere.
The proximity of the coast and the secluded gardens are bonuses.*

Although flat salt marshes are almost on the doorstep, the seventeenth-
century, flint and brick house is well enclosed in secluded gardens and its
entrance, obscured as you take the bend, is easy to miss. From the little
porch you enter straight into the wide lounge furnished with antiques,
chintz and dominated by an inglenook in which, whenever there's a hint
of chill, a fire blazes. A cat lounges on the long sofa. If it feels like a home
that's because it is, but the impression is consolidated since the Heatons
take only a few guests and because dinners are usually communal
(though sometimes staggered to accommodate outside diners). You'll
partake of home cooking, too. Fish and poultry turn up frequently.

High ceilings, good space and pretty antiques are common to all
bedrooms. Extras are minimal but the fundamentals are top quality.
There are lots of fat pillows, for instance, and good quilted bedcovers.
Lavender or bronze tiling jazzes up bathrooms. A double and twin make
an ideal family suite.

Open all year; restaurant closed
Thurs eve

On main A149 coast road, 2
miles west of Blakeney. Private
car park

I twin, 3 double; most with
bathroom/WC, I double with
shower/WC; TV, room service,
hair-dryer in all rooms

Restaurant, bar, lounge, drying
room; conference facilities (max
14 people non-residential);

fishing, golf, other sports nearby.
Wheelchair access to restaurant
only

No children under 8; no dogs

Access, Amex, Visa

Single occupancy of twin/double
£35 to £45, twin/double £60 to
£95; deposit required. Set L
£9.50, D £14, £18.50; alc L
£9.50, D £18.50. Special breaks
available

---

*The* Guide *is totally independent, accepts no free hospitality, and survives
on the number of copies sold each year.*

# Mosedale House

*SL*

MOSEDALE, MUNGRISDALE, CUMBRIA CA11 0XQ
TEL: THRELKELD (076 87) 79371

*Comfortably and sensitively restored farmhouse in a rural
location.*

Time seems to have stood still as sheep dogs gather their flocks and
horses clomp past. And Mosedale House is the real thing: a warm-hued
stone Victorian farmhouse with sheep, geese, ducks and hens.

All the guest bedrooms are bright and freshly decorated and very
comfortable with good-quality pine furniture and chintzy soft furnishings. The downstairs *en suite* twin room has been adapted for disabled
visitors with extra-wide doors and a specially designed shower room.
The Hayloft suite has a small sitting-room and kitchenette. The cosy
lounge boasts oak beams, exposed Lakeland stone walls and fabrics in
modern floral prints. The simple dining-room has farmhouse tables, a
lovely tiled fireplace and a wide selection of books on Cumbria and
mountaineering, and a charming picture of the house in appliqué and
embroidery. There are more books scattered throughout the house,
including some for children.

Typically, one of Lesley Smith's set dinners might offer celery soup,

- Mosedale House -

pork in cream, lemon cheesecake and cheese and biscuits. It's freshly
prepared and excellent value. Lesley is also happy to cater for vegetarians. The hearty English breakfast includes free-range eggs and
wonderful home-baked bread. Don't pass up the chance to take some
eggs home. Lesley is a friendly and caring hostess, and husband Colin
likes talking about walking with outward-bound guests.

| | | |
|---|---|---|
| ◑ | *Open all year* | *nearby. Wheelchair access to* |
| | | *hotel, dining-room and WC* |
| ⚡ | *From Penrith take the A66* | *(unisex), 1 ground-floor bedroom* |
| | *Keswick road for 9 miles and* | *specially equipped for the* |
| | *turn right at the sign for* | *disabled* |
| | *Mungrisdale/Caldbeck. The* | |
| | *house is 3½ miles along this* | ● *No dogs in public rooms; no* |
| | *road on the left. Private car park* | *smoking* |
| 🛏 | *2 twin, 3 double; most rooms* | ▭ *None accepted* |
| | *with shower/WC; TV, hair-dryer* | £ *Single occupancy of twin/double* |
| | *in all rooms* | *£22, twin/double £38 to £48;* |
| ◈ | *Dining-room, lounge, drying* | *deposit required. Set D £9.50* |
| | *room; fishing, golf, other sports* | *(7pm). Special breaks available* |

---

# Beetle & Wedge

MOULSFORD-ON-THAMES, OXFORDSHIRE OX10 9JF
TEL: CHOLSEY (0491) 651381   FAX: (0491) 651376

*Simple but comfortable accommodation in an attractive riverside
location are a successful formula for this popular small hotel.*

The greatest asset of the Beetle & Wedge is the superb riverfront
location. The Thames at Moulsford is beautifully rural, meandering its
way through the water meadows. Nine of the bedrooms have views of the
river (though rooms in the annexe look primarily on to the car park). The
Beetle & Wedge's other great attraction is the food; you can eat either in
the glassed-in restaurant adjoining the Victorian main house; in the
Boathouse on a conservatory-style terrace; or in a dark, warm and
welcoming bar. Food in the boathouse is a little simpler and considerably
cheaper. One part of the menu labelled 'From the Fire' refers to dishes
grilled in view by the aproned chef. Other choices are closer to the fare
served in the restaurant and there is a definite temptation to have two or
three starters, a habit encouraged by the lack of divisions on the menu.
The restaurant is a little more formal with cuisine and prices to match.

   The owners Richard and Kate Smith have recently sold the Royal Oak
at Yattendon (see entry), so perhaps no longer having this additional
diversion of their energies will produce a greater consistency to counter
reports of offhand service, dusty bedrooms and indifferent food. Our
recent inspection certainly found standards restored, with service informal but courteous and well timed. The bedrooms are simple and plainly

furnished – those in the annexe (a converted ferryman's cottage built around 1750) are a little larger than those in the main part. The hotel has the use of the St John's College barge.

◐ Open all year, exc 25 Dec; 1 restaurant closed Sun, Mon eves

🛇 On river; Moulsford is 8 miles north-west of Reading. Private car park

🛏 2 single, 9 twin/double, 1 four-poster (some rooms in annexe); all with bathroom/WC, TV, hair-dryer; baby-listening, room service on request

◈ 2 restaurants, bar, lounge, conservatory; drying facilities; conference facilities (max 20 people non-residential, 12

residential); fishing, watersports at hotel, other sports nearby; babysitting. Wheelchair access to hotel, restaurant and WC (unisex), 2 ground-floor bedrooms

⊖ Dogs by arrangement only

▭ Access, Amex, Diners, Visa

£ Single £60, single occupancy of twin/double £65, twin/double/four-poster £70 to £95. Sun L £20; alc L, D £35; bar meals (prices till Apr 92). Special breaks available

---

## MUNGRISDALE CUMBRIA                                          MAP 3

# The Mill Hotel

MUNGRISDALE, NR PENRITH, CUMBRIA CA11 0XR
TEL: THRELKELD (076 87) 79659

*The food's the thing at this relaxing small hotel in a quiet location.*

You are unlikely to stay in the actual mill but in the adjacent whitewashed stone cottage which, dating from 1651, has a considerable history of its own. The converted Mill Room is a two-bedroomed affair, with a large, slant-roofed lounge and interesting antique furniture. It's the best place to listen to the gurgle of the trout stream.

In the cottage, guests congregate in the small lounge. It's a rustic room with chintzy furnishings, horse-brasses and an open fireplace, and there's a bright sun lounge with attractive basketweave chairs. Bedrooms are cosy with floral print wallcoverings and pastel colour schemes. Furnishings, while adequate, are rather ordinary, though readers have welcomed the fresh flowers which add a touch of cheer. Most have bath or shower rooms, although rooms four and five share facilities.

A five-course dinner is served at 7pm in the dining-room which overlooks the fells. Décor is appropriately low-key with wheelback chairs, rush mats and candlelight. One springtime menu featured salad of pear slices with smoked ham and herbed mayonnaise, broccoli and lemon soup with the freshly baked soda bread that is a menu staple here ('memorable', wrote one reader), grilled rainbow trout with mustard and dill sauce, and English plum and almond tart followed by a cheeseboard.

One couple wrote to report an unhelpful attitude on the part of owner Richard Quinlan when they expressed dissatisfaction with their allocated room. More reports, please.

◖ *Closed Nov to Feb*

🔰 *From Keswick, the Mill is 2 miles north on the A66. The sign for Mungrisdale is mid-way between Penrith and Keswick. Private car park*

🛏 *4 twin, 5 double; most with bathroom/WC, some with shower/WC; TV, room service, hair-dryer in all rooms*

◈ *Dining-room, 3 lounges, TV room, games room, drying room, conservatory; fishing in grounds, other sports nearby; babysitting*

⊖ *No wheelchair access; no dogs in public rooms; no smoking in dining-room*

▭ *None accepted*

£ *Single occupancy of twin/double £30 to £41; twin/double £50 to £67; reduced rates for children; deposit required. Set D £17 (7pm)*

---

**NEAR SAWREY** CUMBRIA                                              **MAP 3**

# Ees Wyke

NEAR SAWREY, AMBLESIDE, CUMBRIA LA22 0JZ
TEL: HAWKSHEAD (096 66) 393; changes to (05394) 36393 from Dec 91

*A friendly family-run hotel in an excellent position.*

It takes more than good food, comfortable accommodation and a pleasant setting to make a really good hotel, though Ees Wyke has all of these. It also has friendly and unaffected hosts John and Margaret Williams.

The neat white Georgian house has a large garden bounded by a trout stream and is overlooked by a magnificent copper beech. A proper Victorian-style conservatory makes the most of terrific views of Esthwaite. It's a stylish spot to linger. Reading matter in the cane bookcase includes a set of Beatrix Potter books; she used to stay here as a child. Earnest Americans question John with academic intensity, anxious to identify the very lily pad on which Jeremy Fisher once sat. The neat coal-fired dining-room has a smart mirror, a carved wooden fireplace, a collection of china cottages and fresh flowers on the tables. The cosy lounge boasts reproduction Victorian sofas, comfy armchairs, lots of plants and a picture of the house commissioned from local artist Peter Oliver. The smart 'Blue' bedroom has corner views and a huge double-mirrored Edwardian wardrobe and dressing-table. 'Green' has an intricately carved and padded Victorian bedstead, while 'Blue Too' has a slanted and beamed ceiling, bright floral wallpaper and lots of space. Lake views from the bed in the 'White' room are among the best in the house. One reader wrote to praise the food, singling out the vegetables as 'superb'. Easter-time menus included moules marinière, escalope of veal with wholegrain mustard sauce, followed by a choice of home-made

sweets and the cheeseboard. The wine list is more cosmopolitan than
many and is competitively priced, with ten half-bottles.

◐ *Open all year (possibly closed for alterations Jan/Feb)*

↗ *1 mile to the west of Far Sawrey between Lake Windermere and Esthwaite Water. Private car park*

🛏 *3 twin, 5 double; some with bathroom/WC, most with shower/WC; TV, hair-dryer in all rooms*

◈ *Dining-room, 2 lounges;*

*conference facilities (max 20 people non-residential, 8 residential); fishing, golf, other sports nearby*

⊖ *No wheelchair access; no children under 10; no dogs in public rooms*

▭ *None accepted*

💷 *Single occupancy of twin/double £38 to £40, twin/double £56 to £60; deposit required. Set D £12. Special breaks available*

---

**NEEDHAM MARKET** SUFFOLK                                        **MAP 7**

# Pipps Ford

NEEDHAM MARKET, SUFFOLK IP6 8LJ
TEL: CODDENHAM (044 979) 208

*Casual and warm old farmhouse in pretty rural setting.*

This is a favourite with overworked business people who relish its twin
attributes of accessibility and rural peace. Only a minute off the busy A45
Ipswich to Bury St Edmunds road, along a peaceful river bank and
surrounded by pretty gardens and meadows, Pipps Ford is a half-
timbered Tudor farmhouse with various, casually scattered outbuildings.

Raewyn Hackett-Jones, who has run it as a guesthouse since the early
eighties, has enough energy and dedication to make most mums look like
layabouts. She and her one helper look after guests well, and the casual,
lived-in style of her home puts everyone in a holiday mood. In true
farmhouse style there are low, beamed ceilings, uneven floors, ingle-
nooks, and lots of cosy corners with soft easy chairs; also a pretty
conservatory with huge grapevine, lots of charming rustic detail and
china knick-knacks everywhere. Similarly, bedrooms are filled with
character (sagging floors a speciality) and show a natural design instinct
without suffering the overmatching syndrome. Pretty fabrics, patchworks, lovely old beds, bathrooms that match and bucolic scenes from
windows are typical. You are assumed to being having dinner unless you
specify otherwise. Given the quality of ingredients and home cooking we
suggest you eat in. Non-breakfast eaters should resolve to change their
ways or miss another of Pipps Ford's attractions.

◐ *Closed mid-Dec to mid-Jan*

↗ *Follow private road off*

*roundabout where A140 meets A45. Private car park*

–Pipps Ford–

 1 twin, 1 double, 1 four-poster, 4 annexe rooms; all with bathroom/WC, exc 1 annexe room with shower/WC; hair-dryer in all rooms

 Dining-room, 3 lounges, TV room, conservatory; conference facilities (max 16 people non-residential); fishing, tennis at hotel, other sports nearby. Wheelchair access to hotel and dining-room, 4 ground-floor bedrooms specially equipped for the disabled

● No children under 5 (exc babies); no dogs; no smoking in bedrooms

▭ None accepted

£ Single occupancy of twin/double £26, twin/double/four-poster £28; deposit required. Set D £17

---

**NETHERFIELD** EAST SUSSEX						**MAP 10**

# Netherfield Place

BATTLE, EAST SUSSEX TN33 9PP
TEL: BATTLE (042 46) 4455   FAX: (042 46) 4024

*Small country house run as smart, proper hotel.*

You can enjoy the 30 acres as you come up the long drive through meadowland, or by wandering around the compact Queen Anne-styled house that is in fact Edwardian. It is built from red and grey brick with what seems an excess of leaded casement windows. At the front stand ornamental cherry trees, a croquet lawn to one side, expertly trimmed hedges hiding a pond behind, and a prospering kitchen garden to the other side, your evening's vegetables laid out in neat rows.

Downstairs, a circuit takes you through the bar with low, round-backed leather seats and interesting bulging bar chairs, through to the more formal sitting-room with striped wing chairs and sofas on a parquet floor, and on to the light-panelled restaurant and thence a small conservatory. Bedrooms are named after knights at the Battle of Hastings (their coats of arms are on the doors) and have plain walls, floral co-ordinated soft furnishings, armchairs and wall-seats (for pleasant garden views). The food is very affordable by country-house prices, 'modern' in style with plenty of attention to presentation.

◐ *Open all year, exc last week Dec to mid-Jan*

⚡ *Take A2100 northwards from Battle for ¾ mile. Take right-hand turn towards Netherfield; the hotel is 1½ miles on the left. Private car park*

🛏 *4 single, 3 twin, 5 double, 1 four-poster, 1 family room; all with bathroom/WC, TV, room service, hair-dryer, baby-listening; no tea/coffee-making facilities in rooms*

◇ *Restaurant, bar, lounge; conference facilities (max 14 people residential, 50 non-residential); tennis at hotel, other sports nearby; babysitting. Wheelchair access to hotel (2 steps) and restaurant, WC only*

⊖ *No children in restaurant after 8pm; no dogs*

▭ *Access, Amex, Diners, Visa*

£ *Single £55, single occupancy of twin/double £75, twin/double £90 to £95, four-poster £120, family room £120 + £10 per child; deposit required. Set L £16.50, D £20; alc L, D £35, £40. Special breaks available*

---

**NETTLETON** WILTSHIRE                                    **MAP 9**

# Fosse Farmhouse

NETTLETON SHRUB, NETTLETON, NR CHIPPENHAM, WILTSHIRE SN14 7NJ
TEL: CASTLE COMBE (0249) 782286

*A happy and lively farmhouse hotel with tea-room and antique shop. A successful blend of English and French.*

Bath and the Cotswolds are within reach, and the mid-eighteenth-century stone farmhouse, right on the Roman Fosse Way, also provides entertainment, thanks to the hard work of Caron Cooper and her mother, June, in the form of a tea-room and an antiques shop. Many rustic features, beams and stone floors, for instance, have been resuscitated and are now set off by cheerful chintzes. The country antiques come from France, making the overall effect cross-Channel rather than ye olde English. There are some off-beat touches, too, such as the art nouveau terracotta busts which sit on the mantelpiece above a French, wood-burning stove in the cosy lounge.

White crocheted bedspreads, pine furniture and more chintzes decorate the bedrooms which are both pretty and countrified. The Pine Room, with brass and old lace as well as pine, works especially well. There are robes in bathrooms. France is also often evoked on the set dinner menu (fish soup à la provençale, salmon with hollandaise, for instance). Very un-French is the rule of no smoking in public rooms. Dogs are now welcome – with prior notice, however.

○ Open all year

↗ From Chippenham take the B4039 north-west until you reach the Gib village. Turn left opposite the village pub and continue for 1 mile – Fosse Farmhouse is the first farmhouse on the right. Private car park

⊨ 1 single, 2 twin, 1 double, 1 four-poster, 1 family room; half with bathroom/WC, half with shower/WC; TV, room service, hair-dryer, baby-listening in all rooms

◇ Dining-room, lounge; conference facilities (max 24 people non-residential); croquet at hotel, other sports nearby. Wheelchair access to restaurant only

● Dogs by prior arrangement only; no smoking in public rooms

▭ Access, Amex, Visa

£ Single £30 to £40, single occupancy of twin/double £35 to £45, twin/double £50 to £60, four-poster £75 to £85, family room £90 to £110; deposit required. Set L £18.50, D £20.50. Special breaks available

## NEWBURY BERKSHIRE · MAP 9

# Millwaters Hotel

LONDON ROAD, NEWBURY, BERKSHIRE RG13 2BY
TEL: NEWBURY (0635) 528838
FAX: (0635) 523406

*An attractive and stylish choice; conveniently located for an overnight stop off the M4 or for exploring southern England.*

Bathrooms are a feature at Millwaters. Huge bathtubs, whirlpools and even a sunken bath in a curtained alcove await those who love a good soak. The overall style of the hotel is clean-cut and uncluttered: the décor is simple pastels; furnishings are high quality and pleasant on the eye; most rooms have huge windows often looking out on to stunning gardens criss-crossed by the Rivers Kennet and Lambourn.

The hotel consists of three buildings: a Georgian manor house and two newer buildings – 'the Baker's Dozen' and the 'Miller's Tale'. The latter is a newly built barn-like extension. It houses the Oasis restaurant and has green beams draped with plastic foliage, green chairs and cloths, and also the lounge where all-enveloping leather sofas await tired executives or people returning from a day out at the races.

Rooms in the Baker's Dozen have balconies looking out on to the gardens and the burbling mill race is a quiet reminder of the water-filled gardens.

◑ Open all year

⤴ Leave the M4 at Junction 13 and take the A34. The hotel is 1 mile from the Robin Hood roundabout on the A4, opposite the Swan public house. Private car park

🛏 27 twin/double, 3 four-poster, 2 family rooms; all with bathroom/WC, TV, room service, hair-dryer, trouser press

◈ Restaurant, bar, lounge; conference facilities (max 72 people non-residential, 30 residential); fishing, croquet

at hotel, golf, other sports nearby. Wheelchair access to hotel, restaurant and WC, 11 ground-floor bedrooms, 1 specially equipped for the disabled

⊖ No children under 12; no dogs in public rooms

▭ Access, Amex, Diners, Visa

£ Single occupancy of twin/double £82, twin/double/four-poster/family room £104; deposit required. Cooked B £8.50; set L, D £15; alc L, D £25 (1991 prices)

---

**NEW MILTON** HAMPSHIRE                                        **MAP 9**

# Chewton Glen

CHRISTCHURCH ROAD, NEW MILTON, HAMPSHIRE BH25 6QS
TEL: HIGHCLIFFE (0425) 275341   TELEX: 41456 CHGLEN G
FAX: (0425) 272310

*One of Britain's most distinguished, luxurious hotels catering to a varied clientele.*

We reported last year on looming cranes and building site noises. All that is long finished. How impoverished it must have felt without the new accommodation wing and staggeringly showy health club with enormous classical-style indoor pool encased in pillars inside and out, and a sky-painted ceiling. If you don't know what to expect, driving up through the huge grounds to the long continuous row of buildings (which seems to grow from year to year) feels dauntingly like arriving back at boarding school. You've passed the newly erected indoor tennis court complex and the golf course. 'Got to keep the boys busy at all times', the headmaster's words din in your ears. The car park is newly tarmacked, the driveway signs clear and informative (to impress visiting parents). Everything suggests functionality rather than charm.   But inside, it feels like a very exclusive interior design shop with beautiful fabrics everywhere, and old croquet mallets, tennis rackets and golf clubs lie around ornamentally as in fashion pictures in glossy magazines. As for the bedrooms, ask for what you want and they can probably match your requirements, they claim (providing your prerequisite isn't that it should be cheap), be it a large room overlooking the croquet lawn, a two-floored suite in the coach-house at the rear of the hotel, or a standard room looking across the front lawns in the hotel's main building (generally the smallest but most charming). Dining in the famous Marryat Room restaurant provides outstanding epicurean treats.

◑ *Open all year*

🔁 *From the A35 take the turning to Walkford and Highcliffe (ignore signs to New Milton). Go through Walkford, then take the second turning on the left down Chewton Farm Road. The hotel entrance is on the right. Private car park*

🛏 *44 twin/double, I four-poster suite, 10 suites, I family room, 2 cottages; all with bathroom/WC, TV, room service, hair-dryer, trouser press; no tea/coffee-making facilities in rooms*

◈ *Restaurant, bar, 3 lounges, conservatory, sun lounge, games room; conference facilities (max*

*80 people residential); golf, tennis, croquet, sauna, solarium, heated indoor and outdoor swimming-pools, gym, treatment rooms, spa, hairdressing at hotel, other sports nearby*

⊖ *No wheelchair access; no children under 7; no dogs*

▭ *Access, Amex, Diners, Visa*

💷 *Single occupancy of twin/double £175 to £225, twin/double £175 to £225, four-poster £360, suite £295 to £360, cottage £295; deposit required. Continental B £9, cooked B £14; set L £20.50, D £38; alc L £23, D £43 (prices till Apr 92)*

---

**NORTHAMPTON** NORTHAMPTONSHIRE                    **MAP 6**

# The Swallow Hotel

EAGLE DRIVE, NORTHAMPTON, NORTHAMPTONSHIRE NN4 0HW
TEL: NORTHAMPTON (0604) 768700   TELEX: 31562 SWALLOW G
FAX: (0604) 769011

*Modern hotel on the outskirts of Northampton, convenient for the ring-road.*

Architecturally, there is little to distinguish this low-built red-brick hotel from many others throughout the country, but the décor is stylish with striking geometric patterns and spacious open-plan public areas.

The Spires restaurant serves good *nouvelle cuisine* meals. The lounge bar, with the grey, brown and orange colour scheme and triangular cushions arranged on dark bench seating, overlooks the leisure centre and the grounds (a gently sloping field with the Delapre lake beyond) and there is piped Muzak throughout. Springs restaurant serves a more informal reasonably priced menu of pasta, chicken, steaks and fish dishes. It is light and airy with trellis-partitioned booths and a buffet table for breakfast.

Spacious bedrooms have abstract prints which co-ordinate with the colour schemes of the modern furnishings. You can watch in-house movies and call for room service and if you've forgotten your toothbrush you can buy one from the dispensing machine in the corridor. Conference facilities and a leisure centre (small swimming-pool and saunas, etc.) make it attractive for the business traveller.

◗ Open all year

⤴ Leave the MI at Junction 15 and follow signs for Brackmills; the hotel is 3 miles from the motorway and I mile from the centre of Northampton. Private car park

🛏 50 single, 44 twin, 24 double, 4 suites; all with bathroom/WC, TV, room service, hair-dryer, trouser press, mini-bar, baby-listening

◈ 2 restaurants, bar, lounge; air-conditioned conference facilities (max 200 people non-residential, 120 residential); sauna/solarium, heated swimming-pool, gym, steam room at hotel, other

sports nearby; babysitting. Wheelchair access to hotel, restaurant and WC (unisex), 51 ground-floor bedrooms, 2 specially equipped for the disabled

⊖ No dogs in public rooms; smoking in some bedrooms only

▭ Access, Amex, Diners, Visa

£ Single £35 to £85, single occupancy of twin/double £35 to £85, twin/double/family room £70 to £100, suite £100 to £130; child's bed free. Set L £7 to £14, D £13 to £18; alc L, D £16 to £50. Special breaks available

## NORTH HUISH DEVON                                        MAP 8

# Brookdale House

NORTH HUISH, SOUTH BRENT, DEVON TQ10 9NR
TEL: GARA BRIDGE (0548 82) 402/415

*Good food and elegant comforts hidden away in a Devon valley. A most civilised and cosseting experience.*

Lacy gingerbread under the gables and vertically divided Gothic windows decorate this pale green Victorian house, tucked away in a little green valley just south of Dartmoor. Around it, a serene, well-tended garden is brightened by flowering shrubs and maybe a cat or two. Within is equally pleasing: space, graceful proportions and some stunning ceiling mouldings; plush furnishings, marble fireplaces, antiques and fine art to admire and comfortable sofas to sink into. Add to that smooth efficiency, personal attention and good food and you have this wholly satisfying country house.

'We're in the relaxation business,' says Charles Trevor-Roper. He and his wife Carol have not gone the frill-and-pastel route; deep, warm reds and oranges are their thing. Off the sitting-room is a little panelled bar with Victorian theme (cast-iron fireplace – American, in fact – stained glass, copper and brass). A gorgeous fruits-and-flowers ceiling moulding in the Regency-style dining-room has been painted in delicate oranges and greens to match the striped wallpaper. The four-course menu of five or so choices is prefaced with a blurb on suppliers and ingredients, but cooking also counts, of course. You might find pigeon and wild mushroom terrine, monkfish with crab and salmon quenelles in fennel sauce, Golden Saye cheese and sticky toffee pudding.

As with public areas, the eight bedrooms vary in character and size but not in degree of comfort, and Victorian antiques and fireplaces are the norm. Everything is provided from bathrobes to hot-water bottles (there are home-made biscuits to go with eight varieties of tea, for instance).

◐ *Closed 3 weeks Jan*

↗ *From the A38 Exeter to Plymouth road, follow signs into Avonwick village. Turn right opposite the Avon Inn and then first left at phone box. At the top of the hill turn right down the hill, and right again at the bottom. Brookdale House is the first gate on the left. Private car park*

⇌ *3 twin, 5 double; all with bathroom/WC, TV, hair-dryer, trouser press; room service during day*

◈ *Restaurant, bar, lounge, library/ study; conference facilities (max 8 people residential); fishing, golf, other sports nearby*

⊖ *No wheelchair access; no children under 10; no dogs; no smoking in restaurant*

▭ *Access, Visa*

£ *Single occupancy of twin/double £60 to £90, twin/double £75 to £110. Set D £28; snack lunches from £4. Special breaks available*

---

**NORTH ORMSBY** LINCOLNSHIRE                          **MAP 4**

# Abbey Farm

NORTH ORMSBY, LOUTH, LINCOLNSHIRE LN11 0TJ
TEL: GRIMSBY (0472) 840272

*Friendly farmhouse B&B in a lovely position.*

When guests arrive at the Findlays' arable farm situated in a pretty, secluded valley they are often surprised by the hills, expecting Lincolnshire flat lands rather than gently rounded horizons. The farm overlooks a small natural lake and some mature trees, and on the hillside is a rather ghostly white statue of a woman who is said to have died in a riding accident on that very spot. The Findlays have a copy of an article on the statue and a mass of other information on the area displayed on a table on the upstairs landing.

The house is homely, with large well-organised rooms; the dining-room and lounge overlook the garden, as do two of the guest bedrooms (ask for a room at the front). Each room has a washbasin and a mix of furniture. Beds have flowery duvet covers. Mrs Findlay prefers to give breakfast before 9am but is reasonably flexible. Evening meals are available by arrangement (or else she 'may not have food in the freezer!'). She is happy for guests to bring their own wine and a fridge is available (and fresh milk for making hot drinks in your room).

◑ Closed Nov, Xmas, New Year and owners' annual holiday

⬈ 5 miles north-west of Louth, 2 miles from the A16 and A18. Private car park

🛏 1 twin, 1 double, 1 family room; wash basin, hair-dryer in all rooms

◈ Dining-room, lounge, drying room; coarse fishing at farm, other sports nearby

⊖ No wheelchair access; no dogs in public rooms and in some bedrooms by arrangement only; no smoking in dining-room and bedrooms

▭ None accepted

£ Single £15, single occupancy of twin/double £15, twin/double £26, family room £26 plus £6.50 for children 5 to 12; deposit required. Set D £10.50 (7pm, must book)

**NORTON** SHROPSHIRE                                          **MAP 6**

# The Hundred House Hotel

BRIDGNORTH ROAD, NORTON, NR SHIFNAL, TELFORD, SHROPSHIRE
TF11 9EE
TEL: NORTON (0952 71) 353   FAX: (0952 71) 355

*A very welcoming inn. Great care, particularly in the bedrooms, has been taken to make guests feel at home.*

As its name suggests this hotel/inn takes its name from the days when the shires of England were divided into areas called 'hundreds' (for administrative purposes) and this area was part of the old Brimstone Hundred. The oldest part of the house is fourteenth century – the old timbered and thatched barn in the courtyard of the hotel that used to be the local court house. The main building is Georgian and bits have been added on as the hotel has been expanded over the years.

'This hotel was a very refreshing change from many that we have come across,' remarks one reader. 'The Phillips family have really made this hotel work.' Sylvia Phillips has planted the extensive herb garden and the pot-pourri and dried-flower arrangements throughout the house are all her creations. The bedrooms, full of pretty things, are decorated on a country patchwork theme and are all named after herbs and flowers.

Downstairs, the public rooms are less romantic but no less cosy. The quarry-tiled bars are quite dark but not gloomy and the family spirit of the Phillips makes the atmosphere jolly and welcoming. Dried herbs and hops hang from the ceiling and heavy oak settles compete with gourds and cast-iron pots. There's not much distinction between the bars and the carpeted restaurant and you can eat wherever you want. Food is served in the bars all day and a special menu is provided in the dining-room for breakfast, lunch and dinner. When a reader requested an early breakfast, Henry Phillips obliged by being on the scene at 6.30am.

◑ Open all year

▨ From the M6 take the M54 north of Birmingham. Exit at Junction 4 and follow signs to Kidderminster (A442). The hotel is in the village of Norton. Private car park

⇔ 2 double, 2 four-poster, 5 family rooms, 2 cottages; all with bathroom/WC, TV, room service, hair-dryer

◈ Restaurant, bar, games room; conference facilities (max 20 people, residential and non-residential); fishing, golf, other sports nearby

⊖ No wheelchair access; no dogs in public rooms and by arrangement only in bedrooms

▭ Access, Amex, Visa

£ Single occupancy of twin/double £59, twin/double £69, four-poster/family room £80; cottage £80 to £295 per week; deposit required. Alc L £11, D £18

---

**NOTTINGHAM** NOTTINGHAMSHIRE                          **MAP 4**

# Rutland Square

RUTLAND SQUARE, ST JAMES STREET, NOTTINGHAM, NOTTINGHAMSHIRE NG1 6FJ
TEL: NOTTINGHAM (0602) 411114   TELEX: 378504 RUTLAND G
FAX: (0602) 410014

*Smart city-centre hotel close to the castle.*

Squeezed in beside a multi-storey car park in central Nottingham, the tall red-brick modern hotel was opened in 1989 and has become popular with both business clients, 'with some quite substantial accounts', and locals who frequent the bar and restaurant. Slick interior design with gleaming surfaces, urns on podiums, columns and marble floors contrasts with Paisley patterns and bright checked fabrics; the décor is adventurous and fun. Uniformed staff are cheerful and the mood upbeat.

The bar and restaurant work well. Both are long and narrow and split-level with a partial glass roof. The restaurant (Elliot's – named after the owner) combines a garden theme with snug alcove seating on the lower level. The choice of food is varied and you pay a set price for two or three courses. Each of the six bedroom floors has a different colour scheme and limed oak modern furnishings, plus some interesting wall prints. Double rooms are reasonably sized, mini-doubles are just that but well equipped, and some of the rooms now have ironing-boards as opposed to the limitedly useful trouser press.

◑ Open all year

▨ Leave the M1 at Junction 25 and take the A52 to Nottingham. Follow signs to Nottingham Castle. Private car park (limited)

⇔ 73 single, 9 twin, 20 double, 1 four-poster, 2 family rooms, 1 suite; all with bathroom/WC, TV, room service, hair-dryer, mini-bar, baby-listening; trouser press available; ironing-boards in some rooms

◈ Restaurant, bar, lounge; some public areas air-conditioned;

conference facilities (max 500 people non-residential, 120 residential); golf, tennis, other sports nearby; babysitting. Wheelchair access to hotel, restaurant and WC, no ground-floor bedrooms but lift and 2 bedrooms specially equipped for the disabled

 No dogs in bedrooms

 Access, Amex, Diners, Visa

£ Single £65, single occupancy of twin/double £70, twin/double £80, four-poster £120, family room £95, suite £210. Continental B £7, cooked B £9; set L £14, D £16. Special breaks available

---

**NUNNINGTON** NORTH YORKSHIRE                                    **MAP 4**

# Ryedale Lodge

STATION ROAD, NUNNINGTON, NORTH YORKSHIRE YO6 5XB
TEL: NUNNINGTON (043 95) 246

*An unusual setting in sweeping farmland, where only tractors disturb the silence.*

There are a number of clues to the history of this hotel, although the first impression of the long low building isn't an immediate giveaway. Jon and Janet Laird will put your mind at rest by showing you a black and white photo of the building in its 1920s incarnation as Nunnington station. It's still deep in the heart of the countryside but now a great deal quieter, with nothing to disturb the peace except the occasional whirr of a tractor.

Although gutted and extended, the central core of the building remains essentially the same. The waiting-room and ticket office is now an elegant dining-room which attracts both locals and well-heeled parents treating their children to an evening out from a nearby boarding school. It's likely the station master would be surprised by the present state of his old upstairs quarters. One of the best bedrooms (room four) has a canopied bed, a plush bedspread, and bowls of fruit and Quality Street chocolates strategically placed for late-night snackers. The bathroom boasts a whirlpool bath and a loo with a window view. However, not all the bedrooms are as good and one reader found that his room was 'fairly spartan' for the price. 'The bed was also very small.'

Dinner comprises a set four courses prepared by Janet. Starters may include smoked salmon quiche followed by a delicious home-made soup. The main courses are substantial and tasty, whether duck en daube – tenderly cooked in a rich red wine sauce – or old-fashioned fish pie. We've had one report that food 'completely failed to live up to expectations' so more reports, please. Desserts are good, and the enigmatic 'coffee and something' (we quote the menu!) can be taken in the lounge or your bedroom.

○ Open all year, exc 3 weeks in Jan

 One mile west of Nunnington, towards Oswaldkirk. Pass

Nunnington Hall on the left, and after 400 yards turn right at the crossroads. Pass a church on your right, and the hotel is 1 mile further on the right. Private car park

🛏 2 twin, 6 double, 1 suite; all with bathroom/WC, TV, room service, hair-dryer, trouser press, minibar, baby-listening

◈ Restaurant, lounge, conservatory, drying room; fishing, golf, other sports nearby; babysitting. Wheelchair access to hotel (no steps), restaurant and WC (unisex), 1 ground-floor bedroom

⊜ No dogs; no smoking in restaurant

▭ Access, Visa

£ Single occupancy of twin/double £52 to £54, twin/double £79 to £84, suite £85 to £90; deposit required. Set D £25. Special breaks available

---

**OAKHAM** LEICESTERSHIRE                                          **MAP 4**

# Barnsdale Lodge

EXTON AVENUE, RUTLAND WATER, NR OAKHAM, LEICESTERSHIRE
LE15 8AH
TEL: OAKHAM (0572) 724678    FAX: (0572) 724961

*An example of Edwardian rusticity in a converted farmhouse with very comfortable bedrooms.*

Our first visit to this converted farmhouse hotel was in 1990, only a few days after it opened. Now, however, the teething troubles have been smoothed out and a couple of minor adjustments and additions to furnishings have taken place. The old cinema seats have gone from the restaurant (they looked good but were found to be uncomfortable), designer notepaper and pot-pourri have been put in the bedrooms and Robert Reid the manager has a new blazer which, complete with boater, he wears whilst overseeing lunches. Three enormous paintings, caricatures of the Edwardian English country house by Susan McCartney Snape, set the mood for this fun, comfortable hotel.

The thoroughly revamped farmhouse with extensive converted barns and an Edwardian theme combined with farmhouse rusticity is beside the road that runs along the north shore of Rutland Water. There are exposed stone walls and flagstoned floors, and a mixture of antiques and period furnishings. It attracts a good crowd of conference guests and fishermen. 'Elevenses', bar lunches and afternoon teas in the buttery are also a draw. There are three interconnecting dining-rooms serving traditional English dishes from the 'Edwardian Country Farmhouse Fare' menu.

Bedrooms, some with high-beamed sloping ceilings, are comfortable and have good-quality antiques and distinctive fabrics on half-testers or four-poster beds. In the barn conversion the triangular pigeon holes have been made into tiny windows which add more character to the immaculate bathrooms. In summer, the courtyard with enormous white umbrellas and sturdy wooden furniture is used for drinks and barbecues, and the barn, complete with a weather vane, can be booked for functions.

◑ Open all year

▣ On the A606 Oakham to Stamford road, 2 miles east of Oakham. Private car park

🛏 4 single, 6 twin, 2 double, 3 four-poster, 2 family rooms; most with bathroom/WC, some with shower/WC; TV, room service, hair-dryer, baby-listening in all rooms

◈ Restaurant, bar, drawing-room (air-conditioned), drying room; conference facilities (max 220

people non-residential, 17 residential); golf, water sports, other sports nearby. Wheelchair access to hotel (ramp), restaurant and WC, 4 ground-floor bedrooms

⊖ No dogs; no smoking

▭ Access, Amex, Diners, Visa

£ Single £46, single occupancy of twin/double £46, twin/double £66, four-poster £75, family room £73. Alc L £8, £15, D £12, £20. Special breaks available

# The Boultons

4 CATMOSE STREET, OAKHAM, LEICESTERSHIRE LE15 6HW
TEL: OAKHAM (0572) 722844   FAX: (0572) 724473

*An hotel with a relaxed atmosphere, cosy bar and well-equipped bedrooms.*

The creeper-clad house is owned by Debbie and Emad Saleeb. They have been with the hotel for the past six years and have added a large extension to the rear.

Once through the main front door, you have to walk along corridors past the bulk of the public rooms to a large empty modern reception area with exits to the rear car park. The Cobbler pub at the front has a cheering fireplace and beams and is used by residents as a place to relax in the evenings. The light and pretty restaurant, with an adjoining bar in deep reds, is approached through an arch and has fuchsia-patterned borders and wallpaper in reds and greens.

Bedrooms are cottagey in style though the extension rooms are resolutely modern with lots of facilities; those in the main body of the four-hundred-year-old house are a variety of shapes and sizes, some very plain, others refurbished in pine and cheerful fabrics. The atmosphere is relaxed and is popular with business clients and those on a weekend break. There is some lovely countryside all around.

◑ Open all year

▣ Centrally located in Oakham; the entrance to the private car park is in South Street

🛏 7 single, 4 twin, 12 double, 1 four-poster, 2 family rooms; most with bathroom/WC, 2 with

shower/WC; TV, room service, hair-dryer, trouser press, baby-listening in all rooms

◈ Restaurant, 2 bars, lounge, drying room; conference facilities (max 100 people non-residential, 26 residential); water sports,

tennis, other sports nearby.
Wheelchair access to hotel
(ramp) and restaurant, 8
ground-floor bedrooms, I
specially equipped for the
disabled

⊖ No dogs in public rooms

▭ Access, Amex, Diners, Visa

£ Single £40 to £60, twin/double
£55 to £70, four-poster £60 to
£80, family room £65 to £80.
Set L £8, D £14; alc L, D £20 to
£25; bar meals. Special breaks
available

# Whipper-In

THE MARKET PLACE, OAKHAM, LEICESTERSHIRE LE15 6DT
TEL: OAKHAM (0572) 756971   FAX: (0572) 757759

*A friendly hotel with stylish décor, and a relaxed bar.*

The Whipper-In was transformed several years ago from a pub into a
stylish and comfortable town house hotel. The owners also run a London
fabric shop, from which they have plundered the warm rich colours and
patterns that are used with style in these low-ceilinged rooms.

The hotel is well placed on the market square of this small town, and
the large bar with sofas and wing chairs is a popular meeting place for
locals as well as hotel guests. The atmosphere is relaxed and staff are
helpful. At the back of the hotel overlooking the courtyard is a small
elegant sitting-room with wicker chairs and a tiny conservatory extension. The restaurant walls are covered in hunting pictures and there are
fresh white tablecloths on round tables.

Some bedrooms are in the converted wing of the building. Lauderdale
is cosy with wild strawberry-patterned wallpaper and a sparkling
Victorian-style bathroom. Whilst used by business guests mid-week, this
hotel is also a good base for a weekend break. Rooms at the front of the
hotel may suffer from noise on Saturday and Wednesday market days.

◐ Open all year

⤒ In centre of Oakham. On-street
parking and nearby car park

⇌ 8 single, 6 twin, 8 double, 2
four-posters; all with bathroom/
WC, exc 2 singles with shower/
WC; TV, room service, hair-
dryer, baby-listening in all rooms

◇ Restaurant, bar, lounge,
conservatory; conference
facilities (max 45 people non-
residential, 24 residential); water

sports, riding, other sports
nearby; babysitting. Wheelchair
access to hotel and restaurant, 4
ground-floor bedrooms

⊖ None

▭ Access, Amex, Visa

£ Single £65, single occupancy
rate by arrangement, twin/
double £80, four-poster £90;
deposit required. Set L £8 to
£11, D £19; alc L, D £30 to
£35. Special breaks available

# George Hotel

100 HIGH STREET, ODIHAM, NR BASINGSTOKE, HAMPSHIRE RG25 1LP
TEL: BASINGSTOKE (0256) 702081    FAX: (0256) 704213

*A characterful well-run pub in a pretty village just a mile from
M3 (Junction 5)*

Moira and Peter Kelsey have made considerable efforts to raise their pub
to a cut above the average. They've made the most of the building's age
(fifteenth-century with an eighteenth-century frontage): during the
refurbishment of one of the bedrooms, a fascinating medieval wall-
painting of birds was discovered, believed to illustrate Chaucer's *Parle-
ment of Foules*; this has now been left exposed for occupants to view.

The focal point of the hotel is the beamed bar: one part decorated with
old sepia pictures of the village, another with brass musical instruments,
and another in agricultural theme with scythes and saws. Here you can
have popular and interesting bar meals – from tagliatelle to beef,
Guinness and mushroom pie. There is a congenial mix of locals,
businesspeople and passers-by, and the service is brisk. The restaurant
with pink tablecloths and a flagstone floor was once a ministerial court.

Double-glazed bedrooms, especially the larger ones, have solid pieces
of furniture and plenty of character, though the bathrooms need spruc-
ing up. The Kelseys are modernising and adding: in the last year they've
converted three bedrooms from the stable block overlooking the car park
at the back, which are quiet and modern in style and are made as
attractive as possible with flower baskets hanging outside to match those
in the adjacent coach-house. One reader found the service 'less than
polite' and the weekday room rates (higher than at the weekend)
somewhat high.

◐ Open all year; restaurant closed
Mon and Sun eves

⤴ Leave the M3 at Junction 5 and
take the Farnham road. Private
car park

🛏 6 single, 2 twin, 8 double, 2
four-poster; all with bathroom/
WC, TV, hair-dryer; limited room
service

◇ Restaurant, bar, lounge;
meetings facilities (max 10

people non-residential); fishing,
other sports nearby

⊖ No wheelchair access; no dogs in
public rooms; some bedrooms
are non-smoking

▭ Access, Amex, Diners, Visa

£ Single £58, twin/double £68,
four-poster £78; deposit
required. Sun L £13; (under-14s
£9); alc D £16 to £25. Special
breaks available

---

# Otley House

OTLEY, IPSWICH, SUFFOLK IP6 9NR
TEL: HELMINGHAM (0473) 890253

*A sociable country home where stylish furnishings, comfort and charming hosts make for a delightful stay.*

Lise and Michael Hilton do not take their role lightly, and many first-time visitors to their happy, elegantly furnished home (a Wolsey Lodge) quickly resolve to return again. It's tucked away in rural Suffolk and has a three-acre sprawl of lovely gardens, including a corker of a croquet lawn and wild duck pond.

The house is seventeenth century with a Georgian staircase, Tudor fireplace, even some Queen Anne features. There are antiques, oriental rugs on parquet floors, porcelain, and plants and flowers everywhere. Large windows let you appreciate the outdoors even in foul weather and there are log fires in winter for snuggling around. Of, if you wish, you can play the grand piano or take a turn at the full-sized billiard table.

Guests eat together beneath a chandelier in the Regency dining-room. Lise is Danish and some of her dishes are too – gravadlax, for instance. Bedrooms come in different colours but are spacious and uniformly welcoming. No doubt the best is Burgundy, a double with red walls, proper sitting area, rugs, plants and an eighteenth-century rocking cradle. The pine room has a four-poster but not such ravishing views.

◐ *Closed 1 Nov to 1 Mar; restaurant closed Sun eve*

⤢ *On the north side of Otley village, on the B1079. Private car park*

🛏 *2 twin, 1 double, 1 four-poster; all with bathroom/WC, TV, room service, hair-dryer; no tea/coffee-making facilities in rooms*

◈ *Dining-room, 2 lounges, billiard room; croquet at hotel, other sports nearby*

⊖ *No wheelchair access; no children under 12; no dogs; smoking in billiard room only*

▭ *None accepted*

💷 *Single occupancy of twin/double £34 to £38, twin/double £44 to £48, four-poster £48; deposit required. Set D £15 (7.30pm)*

*If you have a small appetite, or just aren't feeling hungry, check if you can be given a reduction if you don't want the full menu.*

> As we went to press, the hotel
> that was to have been listed
> here had to be dropped.

---

*All entries in the* Guide *are rewritten every year, not least because standards fluctuate. Don't trust an out-of-date* Guide.

---

*Hotels in our* Visitors' Book *towards the end of the* Guide *are additional hotels that may be worth a visit. Reports on these hotels are welcome.*

---

*Many hotels offer special rates for stays of a few nights or more. It is worth enquiring when you book.*

# The Talbot

NEW STREET, OUNDLE, PETERBOROUGH, CAMBRIDGESHIRE PE8 4EA
TEL: PETERBOROUGH (0832) 273621   FAX: (0832) 274545

*An old inn with some history, a ghost and modernised bedrooms.*

Sited in the prosperous market town of Oundle, the Talbot is just off the market square. The yellow-stone seventeenth-century inn with black paintwork has leaded windows and hanging baskets decorating the front arched entrance, which leads through to the long courtyard. The hotel was built from materials from Fotheringhay Castle and instead of the usual bed that Mary Queen of Scots *may* have slept in, the hotel contains the staircase from Fotheringhay that she *actually* walked down, directly before her execution. Room seven has a ghost – a framed newspaper cutting in the hall tells its story.

The bars are decorated in an appropriate manner with antique guns and crossed spears on the walls and the occasional oil portaits. Dark-wood pub-style furnishings and upholstered armchairs are in tune with the place. The spacious restaurant is simple and low-ceilinged and the lunch menu offers sirloin steaks, pork chops and chicken breasts with side salad and chips. Bedrooms are pretty and well furnished and have all mod cons.

◑ Open all year

🔼 In the centre of Oundle. Private car park

🛏 7 single, 9 twin, 20 double, 1 family, 3 suites, all with bathroom/WC, TV, room service, baby-listening; hair-dryer, trouser press, mini-bar in some rooms

◈ Restaurant, bar/lounge; lounge; conference facilities (max 90 people non-residential, 40 residential); golf, other sports nearby

⊖ No wheelchair access; no dogs in restaurant; no smoking in restaurant and some bedrooms

▭ Access, Amex, Diners, Visa

£ Single £65, single occupancy of twin/double £65, twin/double £85, suite £100, family room £120; deposit required. Continental B £6, cooked B £8; set L £10, D £16; alc L, D £22.50. Special breaks available

---

*The 1993* Guide *will be published before Christmas 1992. Reports on hotels are most welcome at any time of the year, but are extremely valuable in the spring. Send them to* Which? Hotel Guide, *FREEPOST, 2 Marylebone Road, London NW1 1YN. No stamp is needed if reports are posted in the UK.*

**OXFORD** OXFORDSHIRE                                    **MAP 6**

# Bath Place

4 & 5 BATH PLACE, OXFORD, OXFORDSHIRE OX1 3SU
TEL: OXFORD (0865) 791812   FAX: (0865) 791834

*Part of the Oxford tradition has been a lack of decent places at which to stay and eat; Bath Place rectifies this.*

Bath Place, a nest of beautifully restored seventeenth-century cottages, is squeezed into a crevice between the Turf Tavern, one of the city's most famous pubs and Hertford College, Evelyn Waugh's *alma mater*. Noise from the Turf can be a problem, especially in the summer when the courtyards echo to the sounds of student drinking. Parking is difficult but Bath Place is the more attractive because of this.

Somehow, ten bedrooms have been created out of the available space, a miracle of space-saving refurbishment although none of the resulting rooms can be described as palatial. Bath Place has rapidly established a reputation as one of the best places to eat in Oxford and the lack of competition shouldn't detract from the successful format of very reasonably priced à la carte and a no-choice flat rate table d'hôte menu. Given the size of the restaurant the tables are surprisingly well spaced and the style is informal, but pleasingly elegant.

Narrow, crooked staircases lead to small bedrooms where variations in the price are primarily the result of whether you have a bath or simply a shower cubicle. The quality of the furnishings is high, compensation for the lack of floor space.

◑ Open all year; restaurant closed Sun eve and Mon

⤴ Bath Place is a pedestrian lane off Holywell Street, between New College and Hertford College. Private car park and on-street parking

🛏 2 twin, 4 double, 2 four-poster, 2 suites; some with bathroom/WC, some with shower/WC; TV, room service, hair-dryer, mini-bar in all rooms

◈ Restaurant, bar (both air-conditioned), lounge; conference facilities (max 8 people non-residential and residential); fishing, tennis, other sports nearby

⊖ No wheelchair access; no dogs

▭ Access, Amex, Visa

£ Single occupancy of twin/double £75, twin/double £84 to £90, four-poster £100, suite £100 to £125; deposit required. Cooked B £7.50; set L £13, D £22; alc L, D £28. Special breaks available

---

*The text of entries is based on unsolicited reports sent in by readers and backed up by inspections. The factual details under the text are from questionnaires the* Guide *sends to all hotels that feature in the book.*

# Cotswold House

363 BANBURY ROAD, OXFORD, OXFORDSHIRE OX2 7PL
TEL: OXFORD (0865) 310558

*A modern, cheerful B&B on the outskirts of the city with exceptionally friendly hosts.*

You'd have to be feeling particularly down-in-the-mouth not to warm to Jim and Anne O'Kane, who run this fresh, immaculate B&B with a caring enthusiasm that is immediately conveyed to everyone who walks through the door. Cotswold House is a real favourite with parents who are in town to visit their student offspring and are looking for somewhere comfortable to stay that does not carry the price-tag that labels it as a special treat.

It's about a ten- or fifteen-minute bus ride into town, the bus stop is just opposite, and the O'Kanes are full of ideas on what to see, where to go and where to eat. The bedrooms are straightforwardly furnished and immaculate with dark wood reproduction Victorian furniture and fittings, and lacy frills around the floral pillows and loo roll covers.

Banbury Road is a busy arterial route but double glazing keeps the noise out and you're handily placed for escaping to the north of the city without having to battle with the traffic-clogged one-way system. Breakfasts, served in a small but cheery and functional breakfast room, can be traditional or vegetarian.

- ◑ Open all year, exc Xmas week
- ⓩ 2 miles north of Oxford city centre on the A423 Banbury road, inside Oxford ring road. Private car park
- ⇨ 1 single, 1 twin, 2 double, 2 family rooms; all with shower/WC, TV, hair-dryer, fridge
- ◈ Breakfast room/lounge; golf, tennis, swimming-pool nearby
- ⊖ No wheelchair access; no children under 6; no dogs; no smoking
- ▭ None accepted
- £ Single £28 to £32, single occupancy of twin/double £45, twin/double £46 to £53, family room £55 to £60

# Randolph Hotel

BEAUMONT STREET, OXFORD, OXFORDSHIRE OX1 2LN
TEL: OXFORD (0865) 247481   TELEX: 83446 RANDOF G
FAX: (0865) 791678

*A large traditional city-centre hotel with lively public rooms but some dowdy bedrooms.*

The Randolph, a grand hotel built when Britain ruled the world and Oxford was one of the lynchpins of British life, is in the midst of a much-needed refurbishment. The décor of bedrooms and corridors is to be brought up to the standard of the public rooms which exude a colonial calm. The Randolph is in the centre of the action, opposite the Ashmolean Museum and well placed for all the sights. This, combined with the standard of facilities, has convinced generations of American tourists that there really isn't anywhere else to stay in Oxford.

Inside, visitors from across the pond mix with shoppers who've popped in for coffee and students trying to impress their parents, providing that the parents are shelling out for the treat. The Randolph is also much used by corporate recruiters in town to tempt the brightest away with a little wining and dining. The dining-room located in the ground-floor corner of the building has recently had the ceiling raised which revealed the heraldic-like college coats of arms on the cornicing. The college crests reappear on the crockery. The public rooms and grand central staircase have Gothic pointed arches and carved stone ornaments which sit uneasily alongside the dated lurid orange wallpaper that covers some of the corridors (soon to vanish, we were told). Similarly, bedrooms not yet refurbished are functional but totally uninspiring and hard-pushed to justify the stiffish tariff. Some of the older staff have a sense of tradition apparent in their every gesture and movement. Fans of *Inspector Morse* will feel instantly at home – the hotel is a favourite location for the series as well as being the place where the stars stay when they're in town.

◑ Open all year

↗ In the centre of Oxford, opposite the Ashmolean Museum. Private car park

🛏 40 single, 29 twin, 32 double, 8 suites; all with bathroom/WC, TV, room service, hair-dryer, trouser press, baby-listening; mini-bar in suites

◇ Restaurant, bar, 2 lounges; conference facilities (max 300 people non-residential, 24 residential); fishing, golf, other sports nearby; babysitting. Wheelchair access to hotel (ramp), restaurant and WC (unisex), no ground-floor bedrooms but lift

⊖ No dogs in restaurant; no smoking in some bedrooms

▭ Access, Amex, Diners, Visa

£ Single £95, single occupancy of twin/double £100, twin/double £115, suite £140 to £250; deposit required. Cooked B £9.50; set L £16.50, D £22.50; alc L, D £25 to £60. Special breaks available

---

*If you make a booking using a credit card, and you find after cancelling that the full amount has been charged to your card, raise the matter with your credit card company. They will ask the hotelier to confirm whether the room was re-let, and to justify the charge made.*

# St Petroc's House

4 NEW STREET, PADSTOW, CORNWALL PL28 8EA
TEL: PADSTOW (0841) 532700

*A good welcome and good value in a smartly renovated hotel.*

At St Petroc's you are only a few minutes from the harbour, but in a quietish spot. It is said to be the fifth oldest building in the town, and dates from the seventeenth century. Only recently opened as an hotel, it has undergone much renovation. Its gleaming white front looks smart and welcoming. Inside, it is decorated simply but is comfortable. The dining-cum-breakfast room has whitewashed walls, black beams and a dark-wood floor. White and pink tablecloths and flowery china add to the neat cottagey ambience.

The little bar, its plain wood floor softened by a few rugs, has an old diver's decompression box and some ancient-looking diver's boots as decoration. The bedrooms are simple: dark-wood furniture, white woollen bedcovers and a rug or two on the floors.

○ Closed mid-Jan to end Feb

⊘ In Padstow, follow signs for routes out. Local public car park

⊨ 2 single, 3 twin, 4 double, 2 family rooms; most with shower/WC, some with bathroom/WC; TV in all rooms; hair-dryer, baby-listening on request

◇ Restaurant, bar, lounge; conference facilites (max 20 people non-residential, 10 residential); fishing, golf, other sports nearby

⊖ No wheelchair access; no dogs in public rooms and by arrangement only in bedrooms; no smoking in restaurant

▭ Access, Visa

£ Single £30 to £40, single occupancy of twin/double £35 to £50, twin/double £50 to £80, family room £88 to £100; deposit required. Special breaks available

# The Seafood Restaurant

RIVERSIDE, PADSTOW, CORNWALL PL28 8BY
TEL: PADSTOW (0841) 532485    FAX: (0841) 533344

*Sublime seafood for dinner in cosmopolitan surroundings, and modern, comfortable bedrooms.*

Everything about this harbour-side restaurant-with-rooms gets full marks. The ground floor of the former granary is now smart and modern, with a conservatory fronting a spacious, plant-filled room of parquet floors, large posters and prints, wicker furniture and crisp white nappery. Rick Stein's cooking gets the best from his excellent supplies and dinners rarely disappoint. Choose from a three-course menu or à la carte. Classic French fish soup makes a fine beginning, lemon sole with Beaujolais a good main course and chocolate marquise a satisfying finish. Well-chosen, mainly French wines, are fairly priced.

Though the emphasis is on food (there are no lounges here), bedrooms are more than an afterthought. As bright and cheerful as the restaurant, with pale walls and pastel fabrics, they provide plenty of space, are now all *en suite*, and have been carefully designed for practicality as well as aesthetics. Black beams, antiques and good wicker furniture combine well. Rooms five and six share an enormous terrace; the latter is perhaps the prettiest room of all. Tiled bathrooms also deserve a mention. You can take home a souvenir of your stay, namely *English Seafood Cookery* by one Richard Stein.

Closed mid-Dec to 1 Feb; restaurant closed Sun

On the quayside in Padstow. Private car park

10 twin, all with bathroom/WC, TV, hair-dryer, mini-bar, baby-listening

Restaurant, bar, conservatory; water sports, golf, other sports

nearby; babysitting by arrangement. Wheelchair access to restaurant and WC (M,F) only

No dogs in public rooms

Access, Visa

Single occupancy of twin £34 to £80, twin £55 to £105; deposit required. Set D £25.50; alc D £33. Special breaks available

**PAINSWICK** GLOUCESTERSHIRE        **MAP 6**

# Painswick Hotel

KEMPS LANE, PAINSWICK, GLOUCESTERSHIRE GL6 6YB
TEL: (0452) 812160    FAX: (0452) 814059

*Smart but relaxed hotel in an attractive village with good views; drive carefully.*

Legend has it that if a hundredth yew tree should ever start to grow in the churchyard of St Mary's Church in Painswick, the devil may start his work. Some might say that he has already had a hand in devising the narrow, twisting streets that a motorist has to negotiate to reach the Painswick Hotel, but at least there's reasonable parking when you arrive.

This stately Georgian building, with lovely views over the Severn Valley, was once the rectory of St Mary's but underwent refurbishment at the beginning of 1991 to celebrate 60 years as an hotel. As a result, good-quality standard furnishings in neutral colours are set off by unusual touches – two huge Chinese vases flanking the entrance, decoy ducks and Elizabethan troubadour dolls on bedroom mantelpieces, a set of bronze Thai instrumentalists in one of the lounges. One bedroom even has a carved banana tree standing in the corner of the bathroom. In the midst of this designer Oriental mix some of the original features remain: the white panelled ceiling in the bar has sunbursts and coats of arms picked out in green and gold, while the older part of the building retains its mullioned windows.

The menu, changed weekly, includes several fish dishes such as monkfish marinated in olive oil, basil, tarragon and garlic, but vegetarians who do not eat fish may have to put in a special request. Service is friendly and helpful.

◐ Open all year

🖥 Painswick is on the A46 between Stroud and Cheltenham. Private car park

🛏 2 single, 5 twin, 6 double, 5 four-poster, I family room; all with bathroom/WC, exc I single with shower/WC; TV, room service, hair-dryer, baby-listening in all rooms

◈ 2 restaurants, bar, 2 lounges, library; conference facilities (max

30 people non-residential); fishing, golf, other sports nearby

⬤ No wheelchair access; no dogs in public rooms and some bedrooms

▭ Access, Amex, Visa

£ Single £70, single occupancy of twin/double £80, twin/double £100, four-poster £125, family room £100; deposit required. Set L £17, D £30

---

**PANGBOURNE** BERKSHIRE                                    MAP 9

# The Copper Inn

CHURCH ROAD, PANGBOURNE, BERKSHIRE RG8 7AR
TEL: READING (0734) 842244  FAX: (0734) 845542

*A comfortably modernised hotel in a sleepy, contented Thames-side town.*

The Copper Inn, in an effort to rival the historical connections of some of the other hotels in the area, claims association with Admiral Nelson; apparently his coxswain stayed here and the beams may originate from one of his ships. There's no real need for this dredging for character – the modern-day attractions are sufficient. One reader's report, in particular, praises the attentiveness of the service. Our inspector was noticeably surprised by the quality of the food with a table d'hôte seeming excellent value and the food being interesting without being over-ambitious.

The best of the bedrooms are in the old house although those at the front may have a slight traffic noise problem. Modern half-tester and four-posters with pine furniture set the tone. Staff confide that the best room is definitely number seven. A stroll across the car park brings you to the garden wing – an uninteresting but perfectly functional bedroom annexe. All the bedrooms have ample creature comforts.

Sundays are busy as schoolboys from the college up the road sit dutifully having tea with relatives. Escape by taking a walk along one of the most attractive stretches of the Thames.

◐ Open all year

↱ Leave the M4 at Junction 12 and take the A340 to Pangbourne. Private car park

🛏 2 single, 8 twin, 10 double, 1 four-poster, 1 family room; all with bathroom/WC, TV, room service, hair-dryer, trouser press, baby-listening; mini-bar in some rooms

◇ Restaurant, bar, 2 lounges; conference facilities (max 60 people non-residential); fishing, golf, other sports nearby.

Wheelchair access to hotel (1 step) and restaurant (3 steps), one room specially equipped for the disabled

⊖ Dogs in bedrooms only

▭ Access, Amex, Diners, Visa

£ Single £70, single occupancy of twin/double £80, twin/double £80 to £90, four-poster £97, family room £90. Cooked B £7.50, continental B £5.50; set L £15, D £19; alc L, D £35 (prices till Apr 92). Special breaks available

---

## PARRACOMBE DEVON — MAP 8

# Heddon's Gate Hotel

HEDDON'S MOUTH, PARRACOMBE, BARNSTAPLE, DEVON EX31 4PZ
TEL: PARRACOMBE (059 83) 313

*Country house in a lovely and unusual setting, with off-beat furnishings and dedicated hospitality.*

The subheading on the brochure, 'An Exmoor hideaway', is appropriate. The custard-coloured former hunting lodge sits shrouded in thick forest with a very steep wooded valley spreading before it. Within, you'll be comfortable and made to feel special by surroundings as well as by Robert DeVille and his staff.

It's also a little quirky as you'll discover as soon as you spot Rose, a twenties-style store window dummy who presides over the entrance hall, dressed as a Christmas fairy or a hiker or golfer, or . . . You can hear the ticking of the clock here and finding a quiet nook for a read or a snooze is a doddle. There's a small library and macho bar as well as a more or less Edwardian lounge with a wide window and log fire. The long dining-room has a purer turn-of-the-century feel, with oval-backed chairs and lace cloths. The bedrooms are decorated with references to various nationalities or personalities: Chinese, Indian, Nursemaid's, Boy's, etc. Sometimes only a few items determine the theme (no futon in the Japanese room) but the level of comfort and furnishings is high and often appropriate to the late eighteenth-century age of the house.

Five-course dinners with minimum choices might run thus: mulligatawny soup; melon and Parma ham with nut vinaigrette; salmon baked in wholemeal pastry with onions and sultanas; crème brûlée; cheese; then coffee with home-made chocolates.

● Closed 1 Nov to Easter

▣ From the A39 4 miles west of Lynton, take the road signposted 'Martinhoe and Woody Bay'. Take the next left. Carry straight on at next crossroads and down a steep hill. The hotel drive is on the right. Private car park

🛏 1 single, 3 twin, 5 double, 1 four-poster, 1 suite, 3 cottage rooms; all with bathroom/WC, exc 1 double with shower/WC; TV, hair-dryer in all rooms

◈ Dining-room, bar, lounge, library, card room; fishing, riding nearby. Wheelchair access to dining-room only

● No children under 10; no smoking in dining-room

▭ None accepted

£ Single £44 to £52, single occupancy of twin/double £62 to £89, twin/double £88 to £104, four-poster £87 to £103, suite £95 to £114, cottage room from £91 to £120 (rates inc dinner). St D £18 (8pm). Special breaks available

---

**PENRITH** CUMBRIA          **MAP 3**

# North Lakes Hotel

ULLSWATER ROAD, PENRITH, CUMBRIA CA11 8QT
TEL: PENRITH (0768) 68111
FAX: (0768) 68291

*Modern business hotel with rustic flair and time for families.*

Business hotels don't need to be bland and unimaginative, as this example of the genre shows. Snap judgements are unlikely to be favourable: externally, the building is an uninspiring marriage of white pebbledash and black slate, and its location just off a busy roundabout on the A66 is unpromising. The pay-off is immediate access to the M6 – ideal for points north and south and excursions across the border.

Indoors, things improve. The main feature throughout the public areas is the peaked and raftered ceiling created from recycled local timber from old halls and churches, not to mention Preston railway station. The effect is hi-tech rustic with enormous chimney breasts, a warm colour scheme and slate, wooden or quarry-tiled floors judiciously used throughout a large open-plan area. The combination of textures works well. In the shadowy bar you'll find copper and brassware, stags' heads and a small eatery serving bar food.

The Martindale restaurant, visible through a latticed partition, is large and similarly rustic, but infinitely brighter. Both table d'hôte and à la carte menus are offered. A typical dinner might include smoked trout parfait, fillet of pan-fried pork Westmorland filled with smoked cheese, and chocolate and orange roulade. Bedrooms are comfortable and stylish with rich fabrics and lots of facilities. Non-smokers are rewarded with slabs of Kendal mint cake in place of ashtrays. The ritzy leisure club includes an inviting swimming-pool.

◑ Open all year

▣ 2 minutes from Junction 40 of the M6 on the A66. Private car park

⇌ 40 twin, 11 double, 4 four-poster, 6 family rooms, 10 suites, 14 executive rooms; all with bathroom/WC, TV, room service, hair-dryer, trouser press, baby-listening

◈ Restaurant, bar, 2 lounges, TV room, games room, drying room; conference facilities (max 200 people non-residential, 85 residential); leisure club, heated swimming-pool, 2 squash courts,

snooker at hotel, fishing, golf, other sports nearby; babysitting. Wheelchair access to hotel, restaurant, 23 ground-floor bedrooms and lift

⊖ No dogs in public rooms; no smoking in restaurant and some bedrooms non-smoking

▭ Access, Amex, Diners, Visa

£ Single occupancy of twin/double £88, twin/double/family room £105, four-poster/suite £125; deposit required. Set L £11, D £16; alc D £30. Special breaks available

---

**PENZANCE** CORNWALL                                    **MAP 8**

# The Abbey Hotel

ABBEY STREET, PENZANCE, CORNWALL TR18 4AR
TEL: PENZANCE (0736) 66906

*A good base for south Cornwall and a friendly home best remembered for its original and effervescent décor.*

The narrow street leading to the bold blue Abbey Hotel is unforgiving. Once you have managed it, you can relax – not hard to do in this *laissez-faire* house. Michael and Jean (Shrimpton) Cox call it an hotel, but you'll be hard put to see why. You can enter via the kitchens if you've got heavy cases, and the most direct way from the house to the small walled and cobblestoned garden is through the drawing-room window.

The building is mid-seventeenth century but the Gothic façade and staircase were added during the Regency period. The worldly collection of entertaining furnishings and *objets* arrived with the Coxes in the early 1980s. Planked floors and oriental carpets are common throughout the house but everything else is unique. A huge Chinese trunk, African carving, antique toys, Indian quilted tablecloth, an ancient croquet set, every conceivable form of frame-able art – and that's just the drawing-room. Traditional comforts haven't been overlooked: loose-covered flowery sofas that face the open fireplace are perfect for flopping into. A log fire burns in the dining-room, too, where assorted Victorian chairs surround polished tables. Set, three-course dinners are hearty, French-influenced and usually well-reported. Bedroom wall colours are vibrant (often a chalky Mediterranean blue) and patterns contrasting – Oriental rugs and patchworks, especially. The master bedroom is a favourite, not least because of its king-sized, pine-panelled bathroom.

◑ Open all year

🔃 On entering Penzance take the sea-front road. After 300 yards, just before the bridge, turn right. After 10 yards turn left and drive up slipway – the hotel is at the top. Private car park

🛏 2 single, 2 twin, 2 double, 1 suite; all with bathroom/WC, TV, baby-listening; limited room service, hair-dryer on request

◈ Dining-room, lounge; croquet at hotel, other sports nearby

⊜ No wheelchair access; no dogs in public rooms

▭ Amex, Visa

£ Single £60, single occupancy of twin/double £70 to £95, twin/double £80 to £105, suite from £120; deposit required. Set D £19.50. Special breaks available

---

**POOLE** DORSET                                    **MAP 9**

# Mansion House

THAMES STREET, POOLE, DORSET BH15 1JN
TEL: POOLE (0202) 685666    FAX: (0202) 665709

*Handsome Georgian house by the quay, with genteel, even staid atmosphere.*

Managing to find this elegant Georgian brick house tucked behind the quay on one of many narrow roads is difficult enough; parking can be a nightmare (beware of clampers). You might think you've missed the boat altogether: the words 'dining club' appear by the door next to Mansion House and an exclusive clubby aura hits you once inside. Graceful stairs lead up and down from the swish entrance lobby. Doors off corridors may well be closed – meetings in progress. Not an hotel for a relaxing weekend, perhaps, but one where you may fit in better than you'd thought.

Instant membership applies to overnight guests and the possibility of mingling with Poole luminaries is the perk of this serviceable hotel. Marbled columns, gilt candelabra and period furnishings mark the formal character of the place, but staff are hospitable. Jackets and tie are *de rigueur* in the windowless subterranean dining-room, which is a little claustrophobic despite warm lighting and pale walls. The snack bar, off the reception, is a bit more forgiving but the bar manages the most easy-going atmosphere with its captain's wheel, framed collection of knots, open fire and tall and padded settles. Traditional furnishings, a scattering of antiques to liven up the mostly reproduction furniture, reasonable space, good facilities and large windows typify bedrooms. Rooms in the rear wing, completed in early 1990, are as spacious as the rest.

◑ Open all year, restaurant closed Sun eve

🔃 In Poole, follow signs for 'Ferries'. Turn left on Poole Quay and first left again by the

Customs House. Private car park

🛏 8 single, 7 twin, 12 double, 1 suite; all with bathroom/WC, TV, room service, hair-dryer, trouser

press, baby-listening; no tea/
coffee-making facilities in rooms

◈ Restaurant (air-conditioned), 2
bars, lounge; conference facilities
(max 35 people non-residential,
28 residential); fishing, tennis,
other sports nearby; babysitting

⬤ No wheelchair access; no
children under 10 in restaurant;
no dogs

▭ Access, Amex, Diners, Visa

£ Single from £70, single
occupancy of twin/double from
£80, twin/double from £100,
suite from £140; deposit
required. Set L £12, D £19.50;
alc L £16, D £25. Special breaks
available

---

**POOL-IN-WHARFEDALE** WEST YORKSHIRE          **MAP 4**

# Pool Court

POOL BANK, POOL-IN-WHARFEDALE, OTLEY, WEST YORKSHIRE LS21 1EH
TEL: LEEDS (0532) 842288   FAX: (0532) 843115

*It's on the expensive side, but the food and bedrooms make it
worth the indulgence.*

Pool Court is close enough to the Leeds/Bradford airport to benefit from
considerable business trade, and its main appeal is likely to be to those on
expenses. This hotel is really a restaurant-with-rooms (and a classy
restaurant at that) where finely presented main courses with excellent
sauces are followed by memorable puddings, and accompanied by
excellent, if pricey, wines. The set dinner, very reasonably priced, is the
obvious option for those wishing to economise – they should also forego
the cooked breakfast which carries a fairly stiff add-on charge. The staff,
who manage to combine friendliness and efficiency with a clear definition of roles, greet you warmly, serve you as you might expect to be served
in grander places, and may even wave you goodbye when you leave.

Pool Court's rooms live up to the standard set in the restaurant, with
antiques, plenty of extras and comfortable beds. They are immaculate
and spacious. The sitting-room, by comparison, is something of a non-
event, emphasising Pool Court's main identity as a restaurant. But as a
good place to stay if you're on business, or to eat at while you're in the
area, Pool Court should be on your list.

◐ Closed 25 Dec for 2 weeks, and
2 weeks in July/Aug; restaurant
usually closed Sun, Mon. Private
car park

▰ 3 miles north of Leeds/Bradford
Airport, on the A658

🛏 1 single, 2 twin/double, 3 double;
all with bathroom/WC, exc
single with shower/WC; TV,
room service, hair-dryer, mini-

bar, baby-listening by
arrangement; no tea/coffee-
making facilities in rooms

◈ Air-conditioned restaurant, bar,
lounge, private dining-room;
conference facilities (max 30
people non-residential); fishing,
golf, other sports nearby.
Wheelchair access to public
rooms only

● No dogs; no cigars, pipes in restaurant

▭ Access, Amex, Diners, Visa

£ Single £70, single occupancy of twin/double £85 to £95, twin/

double £95 to £120; deposit required. Cooked B £7; set D £10; alc D £39 (prices till end 91). Special breaks available

---

**PORLOCK WEIR** SOMERSET      **MAP 8**

# Anchor Hotel & Ship Inn

PORLOCK WEIR, SOMERSET TA24 8PB
TEL: PORLOCK (0643) 862636    FAX: (0643) 862843

*Genuine old inn within walking distance of the shingle beach and moor. Accommodation is basic.*

Porlock Weir is a little out of the way, so you can escape most of the crowds that flock to Porlock. The nineteenth-century Anchor Hotel and the next door partly-thirteenth-century Ship Inn (a single concern) can't be accused of laying on a tourist-enticing atmosphere. Old features are genuine and fires are lit on cold evenings, but the furniture and décor are more homely than smart.

The low-beamed front bar of the Ship has lots of appeal because of its local clientele as well as its flagstoned floor and inglenook fireplaces at both ends. Bar food is available here and you can have full dinners in its dining-room. The Anchor dining-room is yet another possibility, not so quaint but just as friendly. Portions are generous in both restaurants, and the food is traditional and well cooked. You can also choose between cosy beamed bedrooms in the Ship or more frugal, old-fashioned rooms in the Anchor. In the latter, you might find a large bay window with comfy armchairs from which to take in sea views.

◐ Open all year (limited opening in Jan)

↗ Take the A39 to Porlock and then the B3225 to Porlock Harbour. Private car park

⇚ 2 single, 8 twin, 8 double, 1 four-poster, 3 family rooms, 4 annexe rooms; all with bathroom/WC, exc 1 double with shower/WC; TV, room service, baby-listening in all rooms

◇ Restaurant, 3 bars, 2 lounges, drying room; conference facilities

(max 40 people non-residential, 25 residential); fishing, golf, other sports nearby

● No wheelchair access; no dogs in public rooms

▭ Access, Amex, Visa

£ Single £40 to £70, twin/double £75 to £112, four-poster £85 to £95, family room £73 to £88, annexe room £60 to £69; deposit required. Set D £16; alc D £28.50; bar lunches. Special breaks available

**PORT ISAAC** CORNWALL                                  **MAP 8**

# Port Gaverne Hotel

PORTGAVERNE, NR PORT ISAAC, CORNWALL PL29 3SQ
TEL: BODMIN (0208) 880244   FAX: (0208) 880151

*A lively inn by the sea with better-than-average accommodation
and decent food.*

The unspoiled little pebble and shingle cove is National Trust property.
The Port Gaverne Hotel, an inn since 1608, has a similarly unaltered
look, though Iowan-born Fred Ross and his wife Midge, who have run
the place for over 20 years, have injected it with sophistication.

Its old-world charms of beams, exposed stone walls, log fires and
flagged floors are given pride of place, of course. There's a collection of
antique cruets as well as nautical instruments and old photographs. An
upstairs sitting-room, where you can get away from the inevitable
downstairs bustle, is crammed with velveteen sofas and chairs. The TV
room is more gloomy but the paintings of local scenes are at least
entertaining. A few ornate touches don't alter the basically simple nature
of bedrooms, decorated in fresh floral print fabrics. Some are in the
annexe, where the views are sublime, and some in the inn. Seven
renovated fishermen's cottages are also let on a self-catering basis.

The split-level dining-room is large and the scene at dinner is likely to
be animated, with Midge darting about taking orders. The set menu has
now been dropped, leaving the mid-length à la carte: straightforward and
fish-oriented.

- ◑ Closed 11 Jan to 22 Feb

- ◪ Port Gaverne is signposted from
  the B3314 south of Delabole via
  the B3267. Private car park

- ⊨ 3 single, 2 twin, 9 double, 4
  family rooms (some rooms in
  annexe); all with bathroom/WC,
  TV, hair-dryer, baby-listening;
  trouser press, room service on
  request; 7 self-catering cottages

- ◇ Dining-room, 3 bars, lounge, TV
  room, games room; drying
  facilities; conference facilities

  (max 50 people non-residential,
  34 residential); fishing, water
  sports at hotel, other sports
  nearby

- ⊖ No wheelchair access; no
  children under 7 at dinner; no
  dogs or smoking in dining-room

- ▭ Access, Amex, Diners, Visa

- £ Single £36 to £46, twin/double
  £72 to £92; deposit required;
  children's rates. Alc D £20;
  buffet lunch from £3.50

---

*Many hotels put their tariffs up in the spring. You are advised to confirm
prices when you book.*

# Sallyport

57–58 HIGH STREET, OLD PORTSMOUTH, HAMPSHIRE PO1 2LU
TEL: PORTSMOUTH (0705) 821860

*Simple rooms in an old, listed building above a busy pub in the most attractive part of the city.*

Much of Portsmouth was devastated in the Second World War and the modern city isn't very pretty. You may want to stay here, though, either to visit the historic ships (including the *Mary Rose* and the *Victory*) or as a stop-over prior to a cross-channel ferry trip. The Sallyport, a cream-coloured Georgian conversion using timbers from old wooden ships on a seventeenth-century oak frame, has an excellent position almost directly opposite the cathedral in the old town. Close by is the 'sally port', a gate in the sea wall where sailors used to 'sally forth'.

The ground floor is given over to a smartly furnished pub, a mix of leather and rattan chairs, and tables from which to eat good-quality pub food. Portraits and pictures of Nelson and a miniature model ship continue the naval theme. A cantilever Georgian staircase begins at the entrance doors and takes you to the hotel proper with its reception on the first floor and a small beamed and mahogany-panelled restaurant overlooking the cathedral. Named after famous seafaring or Portsmouth people, most bedrooms have gently sloping floors and beams. The candlewick bedspreads, plain dark furniture and lack of proper bathrooms (most have just a shower and washbasin with shared lavatories on each floor) mean they lack sophistication.

- Open all year, exc 25, 26 Dec; restaurant closed Sun eve
- Follow the signs for 'Historic Old Portsmouth'. On-street parking and public car park
- 3 single, 5 twin, 2 double; most with shower/WC, 4 public bathrooms; TV, baby-listening, room service in all rooms
- Restaurant, bar, lounge; conference facilities (max 40 people non-residential, 10 residential)
- No wheelchair access; dogs by arrangement only
- Access, Visa
- Single £38, single occupancy of twin/double £50, twin/double £60. Set D £9; alc D £16; bar lunches. Special breaks available

*All entries in the* Guide *are rewritten every year, not least because standards fluctuate. Don't trust an out-of-date* Guide.

**POUGHILL** CORNWALL                                    **MAP 8**

# Reeds

POUGHILL, BUDE, CORNWALL EX23 9EL
TEL: BUDE (0288) 352841

*A small, personally run country house near the coast with spacious accommodation.*

Reeds once grew all around the place, hence the name of this brick and white stucco Edwardian house. Lots of garden and a far-off view of the sea make it a pleasant spot for a long weekend break (Reeds is closed mid-week). Margaret Jackson, whose very personal project Reeds is, is ebullient and chatty.

The grand hall, from which most downstairs rooms and the staircase lead, seems formal but the two lounges, one with TV, the other with piano and record player, are smaller-scale and cosy. Some furniture is antique, some merely old. Everyone dines at 8 pm; there are four courses and no choice (but you're consulted when you book). The food is straightforward and usually good. Space is a feature of the three bedrooms which are well furnished, fresh and comfortable. Electric blankets are welcome, especially as heating in winter isn't all it could be. More reports, please.

◑ Open Fri to Mon; closed 25 Dec

⤴ Take Poughill Road from Bude. Turn left at the T-junction to Northcott Mouth. Reeds is 400 yards on the left next to the garden centre. Private car park

🛏 2 twin, 1 double; all with bathroom/WC, hair-dryer in all rooms; room service on request

◈ Restaurant, bar, lounge, drying room, TV room; fishing, golf, other sports nearby

⊖ No wheelchair access; no guests under 16; no dogs; smoking not encouraged

▭ None accepted

£ Single occupancy of twin/double £38, twin/double £65; deposit required. Set D £19.50 (8pm); light lunches

---

**POULTON-LE-FYLDE** LANCASHIRE                         **MAP 4**

# The River House

SKIPPOOL CREEK, THORNTON-LE-FYLDE, NR BLACKPOOL, LANCASHIRE
FY5 5LF
TEL: POULTON-LE-FYLDE (0253) 883497/883307    FAX: (0253) 892083

*Only a few miles from the bright lights of Blackpool is this secluded, individualistic hotel serving excellent food.*

The muddy banks of Skippool Creek, where fat-bottomed cruisers lean drunkenly against their rickety wooden moorings, could not seem further from the kiss-me-quick fun of Blackpool's Golden Mile, just down the road. Few people and even fewer cars venture down to this peaceful corner of Lancashire. The wistaria-clad house, built in the 1830s, is compact and contains a motley collection of bits and pieces oddly displayed in the hallways, on mantelpieces and sideboards.

It's not a hotel to suit everyone's taste or pocket. For a 'funny little hotel up the creek', rooms don't come cheap. Some might prefer to sample one of Bill and Carol Scott's famous meals and leave it at that. Bill is impassioned about food: mention the subject and he can talk for hours with unrestrained enthusiasm. Ingredients for meals are dependent on the season, and Bill picks his suppliers carefully, with fresh fish from Fleetwood and grouse from the Duke of Westminster's estate. 'Food should taste as it's meant to,' he says firmly; 'why smother things in marinade?' Guests can tuck into French-influenced courses of chateaubriand with béarnaise sauce or fish of the day. The intriguing 'ticky tacky' pudding is one of the River House specialities but there's usually a choice of eight others. There are many fine clarets on the wine list as well as such English offerings as gooseberry champagne or apple wine.

Bedrooms are comfortable and are awash with extras such as home-made shortbread and herbal toothpaste.

◑ Open all year, exc first 2 weeks in Aug; restaurant closed Sun eve

🅉 Take the A585 to Fleetwood and follow the road through 3 sets of traffic lights. At the roundabout take the third exit towards Little Thornton. As you leave the roundabout immediately on the left-hand side is Wyre Road leading to Skippool Creek. The house is at the end of this road on the left. Private car park

🛏 1 single, 2 double, 1 half-tester; all with bathroom/WC, exc single with shower/WC; TV,
room service, hair-dryer, trouser press in all rooms

◈ Restaurant, bar, lounge, conservatory; conference facilities (max 12 people non-residential); golf nearby

⬤ No wheelchair access; no dogs in public rooms

▭ Access, Visa

£ Single £55 to £65, single occupancy of twin/double £65 to £75, twin/double/half-tester £100 to £120. Alc L, D £35 to £40. Special breaks available

---

**POWBURN** NORTHUMBERLAND                                    **MAP 3**

# Breamish House

POWBURN, ALNWICK, NORTHUMBERLAND NE66 4LL
TEL: POWBURN (066 578) 266   FAX: (066 578) 500

*Former farmhouse and hunting lodge in a lovely setting.*

The elegant Georgian façade belies the hotel's earlier history: it was originally a seventeenth-century farmhouse, then converted to a hunting lodge in the 1880s before settling as a large gracious country house.

The drawing-room is elegant but quite cosy with flowery-patterned sofas and armchairs. Visitors gather in here before dinner. The menu is changed daily and although there isn't an enormous choice, the fairly traditional dishes are well cooked and the service pleasant. You might start with filo baskets filled with fresh salmon in a piquant sauce, followed by English lamb finished with a glaze of honey and orange. A delightful selection of local cheeses rounds the meal off.

The ten bedrooms are spacious and furnished in subtle colours according to their name, for example, Cedar, Oak and Chestnut. There are chocolates on the dressing-table, local mineral water and bowls of fresh flowers. Rooms at the back overlook a quaint courtyard with curving green staircases and a lawn beyond.

● *Closed Jan*

↗ *22 miles north of Morpeth on the A697 Coldstream road. There is a sharp right-hand bend as you enter Powburn; the hotel gates are on the left, approached by a long drive. Private car park*

🛏 *1 single, 3 twin, 6 double; most with bathroom/WC, some with shower/WC; TV, room service (limited), hair-dryer in all rooms*

◇ *Dining-room, 2 lounges, drying room; conference facilities (max 20 people non-residential, 11*

*residential); fishing, golf, riding nearby*

⊖ *No wheelchair access; children under 12 by arrangement only; no dogs in public rooms; no smoking in dining-room*

▭ *None accepted*

£ *Single £41 to £44, single occupancy of twin/double £40 to £60, twin/double £56 to £89; deposit required. Set L £12.50, D £19 (8pm) (prices till Feb 92). Special breaks available*

---

**QUORN** LEICESTERSHIRE                                    **MAP 4**

# Quorn Country Hotel

66 LEICESTER ROAD, QUORN, LOUGHBOROUGH, LEICESTERSHIRE LE12 8BB
TEL: QUORN (0509) 415050
FAX: (0509) 415557

*A smart hotel with friendly staff and comfortable rooms.*

This hotel was once a gentlemen's club. Even now, very occasionally, a prospective guest may drop in expecting the club still to be going strong.

Dating (in parts) from the sixteenth century, the stone buildings are now backed by a car park; beyond is a riverside garden and helipad. From the stone-floored reception, with a central polished table covered with glossy magazines, an oak staircase leads up past paintings of past inhabitants. The hotel aims to achieve a country-house style with a mix of dark wood, good-quality contract furnishings, deep, comfortable sofas and armchairs and the occasional oil or hunting picture.

There is a spacious lounge/bar and two restaurants: the Orangery, a conservatory with bamboo and wicker furnishings and garden scene murals along one wall; and the Shires, a snug restaurant, where deep-fried mushrooms followed by chicken with spinach and hazelnut stuffing with a wild mushroom sauce might be on offer. Bedrooms are spacious and smart. It's a comfortable base and the friendly staff add to the appeal.

◑ *Open all year, exc 1 Jan*

↗ *On the A6 between Leicester and Loughborough. Leave the M1 at Junction 23. Private car park*

🛏 *11 single, 5 twin, 3 suites; all with bathroom/WC, TV, room service, hair-dryer, trouser press, mini-bar, baby-listening*

◈ *Restaurant, bar, lounge, drying room, conservatory; conference facilities (max 50 people non-residential, 19 residential); fishing at hotel, golf nearby;*

*babysitting. Wheelchair access to hotel and restaurant, 1 ground-floor bedroom specially equipped for the disabled*

● *No dogs in public rooms*

▭ *Access, Amex, Diners, Visa*

£ *Single £70, single occupancy of twin/double £70, twin/double £84, suite £113. Continental B £5.50; cooked B £8; set D £18; alc L £12.50, D £19. Special breaks available*

---

**RAVENSTONEDALE** CUMBRIA                                    **MAP 3**

# The Black Swan

RAVENSTONEDALE, KIRKBY STEPHEN, CUMBRIA CA17 4NG
TEL: NEWBIGGIN-ON-LUNE (053 96) 23204

*Homely Edwardian hotel in unspoilt rural backwater.*

The welcome is somewhat off-hand. 'Phone 222 for attention,' orders a scribbled message on a pad. That done, things look up, and Norma Stuart appears in a flash, takes your luggage to your room and sees you settled in. Bedrooms vary in size but are comfortably furnished in a cheerful, unmodish way with a high level of facilities.

Bathrooms are utilitarian but extras include soap flakes and shower caps. The television lounge, though cosy with board games, books and magazines, otherwise resembles a spare room. Downstairs, pre- and post-dinner drinks and food orders are taken in a couple of pleasant parlour-style bars, where log-fires burn in winter and Thomas (a real tank engine of a cat) skulks, looking for someone to tickle his tummy. The main dining-room is simple but attractive with an ornate carved sideboard and an unusual representation of the *Last Supper*.

The four-course dinner menu changes nightly and offers choice at each stage except the soup, perhaps mushrooms in vermouth, celery soup, and salmon in a creamy cucumber sauce. Local cheeses or English sweets follow. One reader found sauces heavy on the cornflour and thought the cheeseboard had seen better days. Our inspector was addressed by name throughout, but we have had reports of guests being referred to as 'Room One'. More reports, please.

◐ Open all year

⬈ Leave the M6 at Junction 38 and take the A685 towards Brough. Ravenstonedale is less than 10 minutes from the motorway. Private car park

🛏 I single, 5 twin, 9 double; all with bathroom/WC, exc 2 doubles with shower/WC; TV, hair-dryer, baby-listening in all rooms

◇ Dining-room, 2 bars, 3 lounges, TV room, library, drying room; fishing, tennis nearby.

Wheelchair access to hotel (no steps), restaurant and WC, 3 ground-floor bedrooms specially equipped for the disabled

⊖ No dogs in public rooms; no smoking in dining-room

▭ Access, Amex, Visa

£ Single £38 to £41, single occupation of twin/double £38 to £41, twin/double £54 to £58; deposit required. Set L £8.50, D £18; alc L £9.50, D £12.50. Special breaks available

---

**READING** BERKSHIRE                                                        **MAP 9**

# Caversham Hotel

---

CAVERSHAM BRIDGE, RICHFIELD AVENUE, READING, BERKSHIRE RG1 8BD
TEL: READING (0734) 391818   TELEX: 846933 CAVSHM G
FAX: (0734) 391665

*A stylish business hotel in an attractive riverside location.*

The Caversham is a suave, sophisticated addition to the Thames Valley hotel scene, catering to the business trade generated by Reading's role as Britain's silicon city. It's perhaps not surprising that Japanese guests are much in evidence at the reception desk and that the staff actually have a fair crack at pronouncing the names.

The Caversham is unusual among Reading's hotels in actually having plentiful parking. The building itself is a low-rise red-brick building with the two-tier roof reminiscent of a new town headquarters of a building society. But inside it's spacious and coolly elegant. Reception steps lead down to a cocktail bar and then to a glass-roofed restaurant. Bookshelves in the cocktail bar break up the uniformity of marbled pink walls. The Three Men In a Boat tavern, its walls hung with old rowing photos, is absolutely packed in summer but it is a welcome alternative to the formal restaurant if you fancy a pint, a sandwich and a chance to unwind.

The hotel, possibly as the result of its location, seems more informal and relaxed than many of its type. Staff are young and openly friendly and there's a freshness that acts as an effective pick-you-up. Pale wood furniture, walls of pale blues, greens and pinks, and all the facilities you'd expect are found in all the rooms, although the pick of the bunch are eight suites overlooking the river with a premium to pay for the view.

◐ Open all year

⬈ Leave the M4 at Junction 10 and follow signs for Caversham. The hotel is next to Caversham Bridge overlooking the river. Private car park

🛏 1 single, 49 twin, 50 double, 8 suites; all with bathroom/WC, TV, room service, hair-dryer, trouser press, mini-bar

◈ Restaurant, 2 bars, lounge (all air-conditioned); conference facilities (max 200 people non-residential, 107 residential); sauna/solarium, heated swimming-pool, gym at hotel, other sports nearby; babysitting. Wheelchair access to hotel (ramps), restaurant and WC (unisex), no ground-floor bedrooms but large lift and 1 single bedroom equipped for the disabled

⊖ No dogs in public rooms and by prior arrangement only in bedrooms

▭ Access, Amex, Diners, Visa

£ Single occupancy of twin/double from £40, twin/double £40 to £98, suite £120 to £195. Continental B £6, cooked B £8.50 (inc in weekend price); set L £14.50, D £19; alc L, D £32.50. Special breaks available

# Ramada Hotel

OXFORD ROAD, READING, BERKSHIRE RG1 7RH
TEL: READING (0734) 586222   TELEX: 847785 RAMADA G
FAX: (0734) 597842

*An impressive, if ugly, business hotel with some unusual touches.*

Every room at the Reading Ramada comes complete with its own 'Duck in the Box' – quite literally a plastic bath duck complete with an easy-to-post box for mailing to friends, children, husband or wife. It's a gimmick that verges on the naff but is also a step up from the humdrum.

The Ramada sits alongside Reading's ring-road: a squat red-brick citadel-like building of little architectural distinction. It looks and is efficient. Rooms have all the facilities you'd expect, as well as plastic ducks. There's a well-equipped health club for expending any excess energy and a larger than hotel-norm swimming-pool. Each room also has sufficient selection of snacks to accompany a drink from the mini-bar. The décor throughout is functional, neutral pastels. As this is part of an American chain double beds are standard.

Non-smoking bedrooms and Lady Guest Rooms have both proved successful innovations and just in case you're weren't sure of the target market, fax machines are being installed in all rooms as standard. All in all, an impressive if impersonal stop for the busy executive.

◐ Open all year

↗ From Junction 10 on the M4 (west) take the A329(M) to Reading and follow signs to town centre. On-street parking plus parking in nearby car park

🛏 57 single, 129 twin/double, 9 executive rooms, 1 suite; all with bathroom/WC, air-conditioning, TV, room service, hair-dryer, mini-bar, trouser press; baby-listening on request

◈ Restaurant, buffet, 2 bars, lounge; conference facilities (max 220 people non-residential, residential by arrangement); air-

⊖ No dogs; some bedrooms non-smoking

▭ Access, Amex, Diners, Visa

£ Single £45 to £95, twin/double £105, suite £190; deposit required. Continental B £6, cooked B £8.50; set L, D £35; alc L, D £30; snacks, bar meals. Special breaks available

conditioning throughout; heated indoor swimming-pool, sauna, sunbeds, whirlpool, beautician, gym at hotel; babysitting. Wheelchair access to hotel (ramp), restaurant and WC (unisex); no ground-floor bedrooms but large lift and I bedroom specially equipped for the disabled

---

**REDMILE** LEICESTERSHIRE                                    **MAP 4**

# Peacock Farm

REDMILE, NOTTINGHAMSHIRE NG13 0GQ
TEL: BOTTESFORD (0949) 42475

---

*Cheerful rural haven, excellent for families and animal-loving business people alike.*

There are few hotels where you are likely to find sales executives going for a walk with a pet goat, but Peacock Farm is just the place to encourage this sort of healthy behaviour, and Tuppence the goat is usually co-operative. But there are dogs and cats too, plus swings, slides and a see-saw for children, and a huge garden to wander around. Who needs an expensive gymnasium?

Peacock Farm is a rambling sort of place with plenty of outbuildings, one containing bedrooms and another containing the pony. The farm used to belong to the Dukes of Rutland, and Belvoir Castle, on the horizon, is a reminder of feudal days. The ten-foot topiary peacock which marks the entrance is almost two hundred years old. The place, run by Nicky Reed, is happily informal, both in the bright residents' lounge and the lively small bar. The restaurant has a whitewashed farmhouse-look part and a more modern pine-panelled section, where a good-value set menu is supplemented by à la carte choices and daily specials. Food is home-cooked bistro-style. The bedrooms are all comfortable, spacious and simply decorated, as befits the tone of the place.

◑ Open all year

↗ Follow signs to Belvoir Castle. The farm is ½ mile out of Redmile village. Private car park

🛏 I single, 4 twin, 2 double, 3 family rooms; some with shower/WC, most with bathroom/WC; TV, baby-listening in all rooms

◇ Restaurant, bar, lounge, games room, drying room; conference facilities (max 30 people non-residential); unheated pool, croquet at hotel, other sports nearby; babysitting. Wheelchair access to hotel and restaurant, 2 ground-floor bedrooms, I specially equipped for the disabled

⊖ No dogs

▢ *Access, Amex, Visa*

⊞ *Single £18, single occupancy of
twin/double £22 to £27, twin/*

*double £30 to £37; special rates
for children; deposit required. Set
L, D £11.50; alc L, D £14.50;
bar lunches*

**REETH** NORTH YORKSHIRE　　　　　　　　**MAP 3**

# Arkleside Hotel

REETH, RICHMOND, NORTH YORKSHIRE DL11 6SG
TEL: RICHMOND (0748) 84200

*A small welcoming hotel in a lovely location.*

The views from this simple stone house over Swaledale are memorable.
It has long been an hotel but the Darbys have only recently taken it over.
Sylvia and Malcolm are friendly and very hospitable people and make
sure their guests are happy. With only eight bedrooms, there is plenty of
space for everyone in the two public rooms – the bar with groups of
fireside chairs and a lounge next door where you can browse comfortably
through one of the many books. A set five-course dinner in the cosy-
looking dining-room is well prepared and you get a chance to try one of
the traditional puddings as well as the selection of cheeses.

　　The bedrooms are all different, carefully furnished with a mixture of
pieces that all work well together. A reader sums up this hotel well:
'Small but pretty room. Pleasant and attentive hosts – they took your
comment about catering packs of marmalade to heart and even provided
local honey at breakfast. We enjoyed our stay immensely, particularly the
unstinting provision of soaps, shampoo, etc.'

◑ *Closed Xmas, Jan, Feb*

↱ *Turn off the A1 at the Catterick
and Richmond sign. Go into
Richmond and follow signs to
Reeth. The hotel is just off the
village green. Private car park*

🛏 *3 twin, 5 double; most with
shower/WC; TV, room service,
hair-dryer, baby-listening in all
rooms*

◈ *Restaurant, bar, lounge, drying
room; conference facilities (max*

*20 people non-residential, 8
residential); tennis, fishing, riding
nearby*

⊖ *No wheelchair access; no
children under 12; no dogs in
public rooms; smoking in bar
only*

▢ *Access, Visa*

⊞ *Single occupancy of twin/double
£35 to £38; twin/double £50 to
£55; deposit required. Set D £14
(8pm). Special breaks available*

---

*I requested poached eggs for breakfast. 'Sorry, only fried eggs' came the reply.*
On an hotel in Devon

**RHYDYCROESAU** SHROPSHIRE     **MAP 4**

# Pen-y-Dyffryn Hall

RHYDYCROESAU, NR OSWESTRY, SHROPSHIRE SY10 7DT
TEL: OSWESTRY (0691) 653700

*Comfortable family-run hotel; a relaxing venue for a couple of days in the Welsh Marches.*

Miles and Audrey Hunter are chartered surveyors by profession, both refugees from the south moving to the sheep-covered landscape of the marches on Black Monday. This Grade-II-listed former rectory is their first venture as hoteliers. The first to welcome you is the 15-year-old collie who optimistically brings a stick for suckers. Once you've escaped his silent entreaties, the entrance to the hotel leads straight into the small lounge and bar area. It is all very English and comfortable – a jumble of patterned armchairs around a log fire that guests settle into in their slippers to tell of their exploits that day. Miles works the bar at the other end of the room, making sure new guests are settling in. The open-plan breakfast room leads from the lounge, but dinner is served in the somewhat grander dining-room with tall windows overlooking the garden. There's a good-value set menu, or guests can choose from the à la carte. Audrey does the cooking: delicious starters (leek and potato soup with plenty of cream, pungent Guinness and Stilton pâté) and proper puddings (raspberry and apple crumble, hazelnut and treacle tart), though when we visited the meat was a touch chewy.

The bedrooms have all been redecorated and radiators put in, but there are still plans to update some of the bathrooms. Bedrooms all have lovely views and are solidly furnished with bright fabrics. The champagne room is a large family room in palest pink with a four-poster bed for the parents.

◖ Open all year

⤢ From Oswestry take the B4580 (Willow Street) out of town. The hotel is 3 miles west of Oswestry. Private car park

🛏 3 twin, 3 double, 1 four-poster/family room; some with bathroom/WC, some with shower/WC; TV, trouser press in all rooms; room service, hair-dryer, baby-listening on request

◈ 2 restaurants, bar, 2 lounges; conference facilities (max 30 people non-residential, 7 residential); fishing at hotel, other sports nearby; babysitting on request. Wheelchair access to restaurant only

⊖ No dogs in public rooms; no smoking in restaurants

▭ Access, Amex, Visa

£ Single occupancy of twin/double £37 to £39, twin/double £58 to £62, four-poster £70 to £74; deposit required. Set D £13; alc D £20. Special breaks available

---

*See the back of the* Guide *for an index of hotels listed.*

# Howe Villa

WHITCLIFFE MILL, RICHMOND, NORTH YORKSHIRE DL10 4TJ
TEL: RICHMOND (0748) 850055

*A very special small hotel where a good welcome, comfort and delicious food are all-important.*

Only about half a mile from the centre of Richmond but in lovely grounds and gardens, Howe Villa is in a peaceful, secluded spot. The house is Georgian and has been kept in all its finery. There's been no attempt to carve up large rooms to maximise revenue and the four bedrooms, all of which have their own excellent bathrooms, are extremely spacious with lovely proportions and furnished with delicacy and taste. Regulars all have their favourites: one reader is particularly fond of the Blue Room, not least because of its superb, large bathroom.

The public rooms are just as impressive, with high ceilings and views of the river. You can enjoy the same views from the dining-room while enjoying your meal: fresh tomato and mint soup, when our inspector called, followed by chicken breast with onion comfit and mustard sauce. Anita Berry, whose kind welcome and excellent food has been much praised by readers, aims to provide the facilities of a hotel with the comfort and attention given to a friend. One reader was so delighted by her breakfast platter that she felt moved to take a photo.

- ◑ *Closed Dec, Jan*
- ↯ *Howe Villa is half a mile from the centre of Richmond. Leave Richmond on the A6108 towards Leyburn. Turn left at the tyre service station and keep left, following the signs to Howe Villa. Private car park*
- ⊨ *3 twin, 1 double; half with bathroom/WC, half with shower/ WC; TV, room-service, hair-dryer in all rooms*
- ◈ *Dining-room, lounge; fishing, golf, riding, other sports nearby*
- ⊖ *No wheelchair access; no children under 12; no dogs; no smoking in bedrooms*
- ▭ *None accepted*
- £ *Single occupancy of twin/double £53, twin/double £80 to £92 (rates inc dinner); deposit required. Set D £18 (7.30pm)*

---

*Many hotels offer special rates for stays of a few nights or more. It is worth enquiring when you book.*

**RIPLEY** NORTH YORKSHIRE                                          **MAP 4**

# The Boar's Head

RIPLEY, HARROGATE, NORTH YORKSHIRE HG3 3AY
TEL: HARROGATE (0423) 771888   FAX: (0423) 771509

*All the warmth of a local village pub combined with interestingly furnished bedrooms.*

The opening of the Boar's Head in September 1990 wasn't only good news for travellers wanting to stay overnight in Ripley, but for the locals too, who had been without a pub for 71 years. In 1919, the estate owner and priest, Sir William Ingilby, banned the sale of alcohol on the Sabbath and, unable to survive without Sunday trading, the three pubs closed.

Sir Thomas Ingilby, the present owner, takes a more enlightened approach and has now completely revitalised the eighteenth-century coaching-inn, once the breakfast stop on the Leeds to Edinburgh route. The refurbishment seems successful. One couple told us they are planning to return there finding the hotel 'charmingly furnished to accord with the Georgian building' and the staff 'delightful and very efficient'. It's right at the hub of the solid brown-stone village (its unusual architecture inspired by another estate village in Alsace-Lorraine), and directly opposite the old market cross and village stocks. Not only is Ripley Castle a stone's throw away, but the hotel makes an excellent base for exploring Nidderdale and Fountains Abbey, with Harrogate close by.

There's an assortment of bedrooms, nine in the main house decorated with anything from Chinese fans to stars painted on the ceiling. Others face the grassy pub garden at the back and are smaller (you may well be side-stepping around your room-mate on the way to the bathroom), but brightly painted, with cane furniture; each is equipped with a copy of *James Herriot's Yorkshire*. A more spacious annexe with rooms named after local farms lies just across the road.

At a busy weekend, the number of tables and staff seems insufficient to cope with the 9.30am breakfast rush, but once it reaches you, the traditional fry-up makes any delay excusable. There are about six or seven choices per course at dinner. You may be offered a ravioli of sea scallops with a white truffle dressing, followed by a pan-fried breast of Gressingham duck. Sunday lunches are popular with day-trippers as well as hotel guests.

○ *Open all year*

⤢ *3 miles north of Harrogate on the A61. Private car park*

🛏 *23 double, 2 half-tester; most with bathroom/WC, some with shower/WC; TV, room service, hair-dryer, mini-bar, baby-listening in all rooms; trouser press on request*

 *Restaurant, bar, 2 lounges; conference facilities (max 80 people non-residential, 25 residential); fishing, tennis at hotel, other sports nearby. Wheelchair access to hotel (no steps), restaurant and WC, 5 ground-floor bedrooms, I specially equipped for the disabled*

⊖ No dogs in public rooms

▭ Access, Amex, Visa

£ Single occupancy of double £80,

double/half-tester £98; deposit required. Set L £11, D £25. Special breaks available

---

**ROCHFORD** ESSEX                                    **MAP 10**

# Hotel Renouf

BRADLEY WAY, ROCHFORD, ESSEX SS4 1BU
TEL: SOUTHEND (0702) 541334   TELEX: 995158 RENOUF G
FAX: (0702) 549563

*Food-oriented business hotel in handy if unfavourable location.*

The location of this purpose-built brick hotel, twixt railway line, town, car park and main road, is hardly inspiring. You may not warm to it once inside the windowless reception hall, either, but staff are friendly and capable, and the bar and restaurant, which show a fondness for lady-like padded chairs, are plush and comfortable. A pity there's no lounge.

In matters of food and accommodation, high priorities for the mainly business clientele, the hotel excels. Renouf's Restaurant, 200 yards up the road, and the hotel dining-room give two options. Monsieur Renouf, larger than life, is around and about at one or the other and will happily discuss wines or the menu, the former boasting some glitzy burgundies, the latter able to offer both light and rich French. Three versions of pressed duck are the house speciality. The busy executive will find the full range of practical goodies in bedrooms as well as handsome pine furniture. Suite facilities are self-indulgent, with bathrobes and Jacuzzis. Space, good-sized beds and comfort are guaranteed, but most of the singles face the busy road. Bathrooms are neat, compact and modern.

◑ Open all year, exc 26 to 30 Dec

⇗ Close to the railway station in Rochford. Private car park

🛏 7 single, 13 double/twin, 2 double, 1 suite, 1 family room; all with bathroom/WC, TV, room service, hair-dryer, baby-listening

◈ Restaurant, bar, function room; public rooms in hotel air-conditioned; conference facilities (max 40 people residential, 70 non-residential); fishing, golf, other sports nearby. Wheelchair access to hotel (1 step), restaurant and WC (unisex), 7 ground-floor bedrooms, 1 specially equipped for the disabled

⊖ No dogs in public rooms

▭ Access, Amex, Diners, Visa

£ Single £47 to £58, single occupancy of twin/double £68, twin/double £68 to £78, suite £88 to £98, family room £83 to £93. Set L £11.50, D £13.50; alc L, D £32 (prices till end 91)

---

*All reports are welcome on any hotel, whether or not it is in the* Guide.

**ROCKBOURNE** HAMPSHIRE                        **MAP 9**

# Shearings

ROCKBOURNE, FORDINGBRIDGE, HAMPSHIRE SP6 3NA
TEL: ROCKBOURNE (072 53) 256

*A pleasing absence of house rules makes this much-loved home
seem yours for the stay.*

Few places could summon up rural England more quintessentially than
Brigadier and Mrs Colin Watts' (or less formally Colin and Rosemary)
sixteenth-century, listed, timber-framed, thatched cottage. You approach the front door across a tiny bridge over a stream; at the back the
well-kept lawns slope up towards a footpath to the parish church. This
sleepy little village between Salisbury and the New Forest (its Roman
villa is its only claim to fame) provides it with an entirely appropriate
setting.

Inside, the house is lovingly furnished in cottagey style: pressed flower
pictures adorn the walls and chintzy chairs provide seating in the sitting-
room. If dining (say in advance), you'll be served pre-dinner drinks in the
drawing-room, and eat *en famille* in the candlelit dining-room. If not, and
many use Shearings just as a B&B, there are several good pubs within
easy reach. The bedrooms upstairs are reached along uneven floors.
With plain white walls criss-crossed by open beams and many welcoming
touches such as shelves of books, they have a charming simplicity. A self-
contained garden annexe unit has slightly more privacy. In summer,
breakfast, the *Daily Telegraph* by your plate, may be taken on the vine-
shaded patio in the garden.

◐  Closed mid-Dec to mid-Feb

▨  From Salisbury take the A354
Blandford road; 1 mile after
Coombe Bisset turn left to
Rockbourne. From Fordingbridge
take the B3078 towards
Damerham; before reaching
Damerham turn right to
Rockbourne. Private car park

🛏  1 single, 1 twin, 1 double; 1 with
private bathroom, 2 with shower
room; hair-dryer in all rooms

◈  Dining-room, lounge, TV, drying

room; laundry facilities; croquet
at hotel, other sports nearby

⊖  No wheelchair access; no
children under 12; no dogs; no
smoking

▭  None accepted

£  Single £20, single occupancy of
twin/double £27, twin/double
£40 to £42; deposit required. Set
D £12.50/£18 (8pm, by
arrangement only) (prices till
Apr 92). Special breaks available

# Mizzards Farm

ROGATE, PETERSFIELD, HAMPSHIRE GU31 5HS
TEL: ROGATE (0730) 821656

*Expect a good welcome at this large, well-furnished house set in acres of garden and fields.*

An ordinary AA accommodation sign leads you off a back road down a long pot-holed lane running parallel to the River Rother. It disguises well the anything-but-ordinary farmhouse at the end of it: a large stone and brick building, the earliest part dating from the seventeenth century, with acres of lawn running down to a pond with a willow and statue, and behind it a swimming-pool in a walled garden.

Mizzards Farm is more of a smallholding, really, and you might come across the Francis' small flock of sheep; otherwise, the animal you're most likely to meet is Barker the black retriever, who, when we visited, was still drying out after a walk with some guests that had involved a dip in the river.

The house was once owned by a glitzy pop star, who left his impression in an extraordinary bedroom, where the bed, behind white pillars, stands on a dais under a pink satin canopy, and the gaudy, marble bathroom has a double bath. The two other bedrooms are pretty and cottagey.

-Mizzards Farm-

Breakfast is taken on big bare wooden tables in a flagstoned hall-like room in the centre of the house. Guests also have the exclusive use of a large lounge with antiques, big sofas, open fire and grand piano.

◑ *Open all year, exc Xmas*

↗ *Travel south from the crossroads in Rogate, over the bridge and take the first road on the right. Private car park*

🛏 *2 twin, 1 four-poster; all with bathroom/WC, TV, hair-dryer*

◇ *Breakfast room, lounge, drying room; croquet, fishing, heated*

*pool (in season) at hotel, other sports nearby*

⊖ *No wheelchair access; no children under 7; no dogs; no smoking*

▭ *None accepted*

£ *Single occupancy of twin/double £27 to £32, twin/double £38 to £40, four-poster £42 to £44. Special breaks available*

---

**ROMALDKIRK** CO DURHAM           **MAP 3**

# Rose and Crown

ROMALDKIRK, BARNARD CASTLE, CO DURHAM DL12 9EB
TEL: TEESDALE (0833) 50213    FAX: (0833) 50828

*An eighteenth-century coaching inn with a friendly welcome.*

Where coaches and four horses used to drop off passengers, now arrivals use a BMW or a Volkswagen, but the function of the Rose and Crown hasn't changed. Built in 1733 as a coaching inn, it is still a great meeting place for locals and travellers. The Davys have been here for only a couple of years and although they've been carrying out some refurbishment, they are intent on preserving the character of the place.

This year has seen a new carpet in the hall, which complements a series of original watercolours. The bar is quite traditional with open fires, horse brasses and sepia photographs of old Romaldkirk. Bar food (well above average) is served here. It is unusual and delicious and might include large Greenland prawns served with a tomato-flavoured mayonnaise or smoked Loch Fyne salmon with a wedge of lemon. If you want a bit more formality choose the restaurant where there's a mouth-watering four-course menu with enough choice to satisfy most tastes, perhaps cauliflower soup with Gruyère croûtons to start, followed by guinea-fowl 'Rose and Crown style' – the legs casseroled in burgundy with shallots and smoked bacon and the breast sautéed with a calvados sauce. One satisfied visitor described the service as fast, efficient and very friendly.

Most of the bedrooms have now been redecorated and are comfortable and pleasantly furnished; some are spacious and have their own sitting-rooms.

◑ *Open all year, exc 25, 26 Dec; restaurant closed Sun eve*

↗ *Romaldkirk is 6 miles north-west of Barnard Castle on the B6277. Private car park*

🛏 1 single, 4 twin, 2 double, 1 four-poster, 1 family room, 2 suites (some rooms in annexe); all with bathroom/WC, TV, baby-listening; limited room service

◇ Restaurant, 2 bars, lounge, drying room; conference facilities (max 12 people non-residential and residential); fishing, golf, other sports nearby. Wheelchair access to hotel (no steps) and restaurant, 5 ground-floor bedrooms, 1 specially equipped for the disabled

⊖ No dogs in restaurant or lounge

▭ Access, Visa

£ Single £45, single occupancy of twin/double £45 to £64, twin/double £64, four-poster £64, suite £77, family room £70; deposit required. Set L £10, D £18 (prices till Mar 92). Special breaks available

---

## ROSEDALE ABBEY NORTH YORKSHIRE                    MAP 3

# Milburn Arms

ROSEDALE ABBEY, PICKERING, NORTH YORKSHIRE YO18 8RA
TEL: LASTINGHAM (075 15) 312   FAX: (075 15) 312

*A cheery pub/hotel in the centre of this pretty village on the North York Moors.*

There's been a change of ownership at this friendly hotel-cum-village pub. The Bentleys moved here in October 1990 and initial reports have been generally favourable (apart from one early one, bored by the frequent apologies). More recent visitors have found the place friendly and comfortable – and particularly liked the choice of half-bottles on the wine list. The informality of the place is evidenced by its popularity with the locals who come in for a game of dominoes or a chat, and visitors can glean useful advice on things to see in the locality.

   For those wishing to get away from the bustle at the bar there's a cosy, lived-in sitting-room with comfy, slightly faded armchairs, an open fire and plenty of games. The dining-room is the centre of the house and on two levels. Most of the bedrooms are in the converted stable block – decent size and well decorated and furnished. Bathrooms are good, too, with white tiles, cork floors and a selection of toiletries. Closing time noise may disturb early bedtimers.

○ Open all year

⤴ In the centre of Rosedale Abbey village, north of Pickering (10 miles), south of Guisborough (16 miles). Private car park

🛏 2 twin, 5 double, 1 four-poster, 3 family rooms; all with bathroom/WC, TV, room service, baby-listening; hair-dryer on request

◇ Restaurant, bar and bistro, lounge; conference facilities (max 11 people residential); golf, riding nearby. Wheelchair access to hotel (1 step) and restaurant, 4 ground-floor bedrooms

⊖ No children under 8 in restaurant at dinner; no dogs in

public rooms and some
bedrooms

▣ Access, Visa

£ Single occupancy of twin/double
£39 to £46, twin/double £69 to

£75, four-poster £74 to £80;
special rates for children; deposit
required. Set L (Sun) £8.50, D
£17; alc D £25; bar meals.
Special breaks available

## ROSTHWAITE CUMBRIA

MAP 3

# Hazel Bank

ROSTHWAITE, BORROWDALE, KEWSICK, CUMBRIA CA12 5XB
TEL: BORROWDALE (076 87) 77248

*Cheerful hosts make this unpretentious small hotel in a lovely
location a good place to relax.*

Many claim that Borrowdale is the loveliest valley in England; this fine
mid-nineteenth-century Lakeland stone villa is a good base from which
to explore it. You arrive via a humpback bridge and a long path. Gwen
Nuttall is a capable, cheerful and caring hostess who exudes northern
warmth. Her philosophy is simple: she aims to offer comfortable accommodation and good food at a reasonable cost. An army of regulars believe
that that is exactly what she and husband John, who's in charge of the
kitchen, do.

The house has an elevated position, and rooms are named after the
hills visible from the windows, such as Dale Head, Cat Bells and Great
Gable (the one with the four-poster). Décor is fresh and homely rather
than flashy. The small, neat dining-room is restful in pink and grey with
an impressive array of plates. The very comfortable lounge is quietly
stylish, with curtains and sofas in a co-ordinating dark pattern, ornate
plasterwork and a pretty dried-flower arrangement.

Bedrooms are comfortable rather than stylish and are decorated with
attractive modern prints. Furniture might be pine or melamine. The
tariff includes a four-course English dinner with no choice until dessert.
A typical May menu offered parsnip and lentil soup, roast lamb, old-
fashioned rice-pudding and a cheeseboard.

◑ Open 21 Mar to 1 Nov

🔁 From Keswick follow the B5289
signposted Borrowdale. Just
before Rosthwaite village, turn
left, crossing the river over the
humpback bridge. Private car
park.

🛏 1 single, 4 twin, 3 double, 1
four-poster; some with
bathroom/WC, most with
shower/WC; TV in some rooms

◈ Dining-room, bar, lounge, drying
room; water sports, other sports
nearby

⊖ No wheelchair access; no
children under 6; no dogs in
public rooms

▭ None accepted

£ Single £34, ⸱ ⸱/double £60 to
£72, four-poster £72 (rates inc
dinner, 7pm); deposit required

# Peacock Hotel

ROWSLEY, MATLOCK, DERBYSHIRE DE4 2EB
TEL: MATLOCK (0629) 733518   FAX: (0629) 732671

*A comfortable, jolly place run in traditional style, and much
frequented by tweedy locals.*

The Peacock is right in the centre of the village so some of the bedrooms
can suffer a bit from traffic noise, but behind the hotel there's a
narrowish garden by the River Derwent – a peaceful place to sit in the
summer, perhaps before or after the popular Sunday lunch.

The entrance hall opens out into a large welcoming sitting area. A
number of sofas, armchairs and old wooden tables, some heaped with
newspapers, jostle for space. Decoration throughout is simple and
unpretentious, with polished wood tables, plain carpets and chintzy
curtains. The bar is a very cosy, low-ceilinged room tucked around the
back and has little natural light. Plain brick walls suggest informality and
there are lots of little alcoves and secret corners with wooden benches
softened by linen cushions. You are reminded that this hotel is part of a
chain only by the bedrooms being priced as 'executive' and 'standard'.
You certainly get what you pay for: in the executive rooms bedcovers are
quilted and decoration is individual with nice pieces; in some of the
others you might get an older velveteen chair and a melamine side-shelf.

◑ Open all year

🔁 In the village of Rowsley, on the
A6, 3 miles south of Bakewell, 5
miles north of Matlock. Private
car park

🛏 2 single, 5 twin, 6 double, 1
four-poster; most with bathroom/
WC, some with shower/WC; TV,
room service, baby-listening,
trouser press, hair-dryer in all
rooms

◈ Restaurant, bar, lounge, drying
room; conference facilities (max
10 people non-residential and

residential); fishing in grounds,
other sports nearby

⊖ No wheelchair access; no
children in restaurant eve; no
dogs in public rooms and in some
bedrooms by arrangement only

▭ Access, Amex, Diners, Visa

£ Single £83, single occupancy of
twin/double £83 to £109, twin/
double £109, four-poster £114.
Continental B £6.50, cooked B
£8.50; set L £15, D £23; alc L,
D £23 to £28. Special breaks
available

---

**RUGBY** WARWICKSHIRE                          **MAP 6**

# Avondale Guest House

16 ELSE ROAD, RUGBY, WARWICKSHIRE CV21 3BA
TEL: RUGBY (0788) 578639

*A homely B&B which is convenient for the town centre.*

The Avondale is a large Victorian house on a quiet residential side-street close to the centre of Rugby. The house is owned by the Webbs who have lived here for 16 years and now that their children have left home they've let out five rooms to guests.

The hub of the house is the large light lounge-cum-breakfast room with tables covered in lace tablecloths by the bay window, and a settee and armchairs arranged around the fireplace with its electric fire. There are also a couple of tables on which you can play cards or gather around in the evenings.

Bedrooms are airy and pretty, all with a vanitory unit, some with old tiled fireplaces and pretty velour bedspreads with rosebud patterns. The Webbs get a lot of regular guests, including those attending courses in Rugby. They're also close to the headquarters of Relate so you may find yourself watching TV with a counsellor or two in the evenings. There is a pay phone in the hall and lots of leaflets on things to see and do.

| | | | |
|---|---|---|---|
| ◐ | Open all year | | other sports nearby |
| ⤴ | Off Moultrie road, close to Rugby public school. Private car park | ⊖ | No wheelchair access; no dogs; no smoking in public rooms |
| 🛏 | 3 twin, 1 family room; some with shower/WC, TV; hair-dryer on request | ▭ | None accepted |
| ◈ | Dining-room/lounge; fishing, golf, | £ | Single occupancy of twin/double £20 to £25, twin/double £34 to £38. |

**RUSPER** WEST SUSSEX                          **MAP 10**

# Ghyll Manor Hotel

HIGH STREET, RUSPER, NR HORSHAM, WEST SUSSEX RH12 4PX
TEL: RUSPER (0293) 871571   TELEX: 877557 GHYLL G
FAX: (0293) 871419

*One of the best Forte hotels, in a peaceful village close to Gatwick airport.*

Last year we reported on the resident peacocks but sadly after two were caught by a fox the rest have been whisked away to a peacock sanctuary. Never mind, this much restored Elizabethan manor with black timbers, herringbone pattern brick, big chimneys, beams and linenfold panelling exceeds the expectations of most Forte hotels.

In summer you can enjoy the lovely gardens from the flagged terrace, with lawns running down to a small lake with ducks and swans, and a pool and tennis court concealed behind walls; in winter, the cosy oak-panelled lounge, furnished in smart red-striped armchairs and sofas, has a roaring log fire. A regular frequenter of hotels says: 'Our weekend turned out to be one of the best we have enjoyed in recent years'. They stayed in Mahogany, one of the suites in the old manor house and 'four times the size of a normal hotel room with dressing-room, large walk-in wardrobe, and furniture of the massive mahogany variety with leather armchairs and antique items'.

The bedrooms in the main building have lattice windows and black-beamed rafters. Most of the rest are housed in a new brick block some hundred yards away from the main building and are generally smaller and far less interesting. High praise has been given to dinner, served in the light parquet-floored dining-room: 'The presentation and taste of each of our selections was near perfect . . . immaculately presented sweet dishes were almost a shame to disturb.'

| | |
|---|---|
| ◖ Open all year | (May to Sept), sauna, solarium hotel, other sports nearby; babysitting on request. |
| ⤢ In the centre of Rusper, 3½ miles east of the A24. Private car park | Wheelchair access to hotel and restaurant, 17 ground-floor bedrooms |
| 🛏 5 single, 2 twin, 10 double, 4 four-poster, 2 family rooms, 3 suites, 2 cottages; all with bathroom/WC, exc 1 single with shower/WC; TV, room service, hair-dryer, trouser press, baby-listening in all rooms | ⊖ No dogs in public rooms |
| | ▭ Access, Amex, Diners, Visa |
| ◈ Restaurant, bar, lounge, library; conference facilities (max 100 people non-residential, 28 residential); tennis, croquet, outdoor heated swimming-pool | £ Single £80, single occupancy of twin/double £85, twin/double £95, four-poster £115, family room/suite £130; deposit required. Continental B £6, cooked B £8.50; set L £16.50, £32, D £24, £32. Special breaks available |

---

**RYE** EAST SUSSEX                                                    **MAP 10**

# Jeake's House

MERMAID STREET, RYE, EAST SUSSEX TN31 7ET
TEL: RYE (0797) 222828   FAX: (0797) 222623

*One of the best-value and most stylish B&Bs in the South-East.*

'I never go wrong when I tell clients they must visit the town of Rye and spend a night or two at Jeake's House,' says an American correspondent. This listed building stands fittingly on one of the prettiest cobbled streets in town, along from old white-painted and red-tiled cottagey homes with names like 'House with two front doors' or 'House with a seat'.

Two plaques on the wall suggest an interesting history. One informs that Conrad Aiken, American poet and author, lived here; during his 23 years in the house many writers, T S Eliot and Malcolm Lowry among them, regularly visited. Francis and the articulate and friendly Jenny Hadfield, who does most of the B&B business and is a mine of information about the house's past, continue this artistic tradition: sounds of harp, flute or piano practice may reach your ears. The other plaque commemorates the laying of the foundation stone by Samuel Jeake in 1689 who used the building as a wool store and later a Baptist school. A galleried chapel was added in the following century which served as a Quaker meeting house and is now converted to a splendid breakfast room. Stand on the first-floor landing and look down on tables neatly laid with pink cloths and willow pattern crockery, and across at old sepia paintings and two large portraits of the Hadfields' grandparents

A sitting-room area, with a bar appropriately made from church pews, has just been added. The bedrooms are delightful, all very different but Victorian in style (but with no darkness or heaviness), with brass or mahogany beds and balloon-back period chairs. From attic rooms (watch out for the Lady in Blue!) you can enjoy the garden's magnolia tree, Rye's rooftops and the marshes leading to the sea.

- ◑ Open all year
- ⤢ Centrally located in old Rye. On-street parking nearby
- ⊨ 1 single, 1 twin, 6 double, 2 family rooms, 1 four-poster, 1 four-poster suite; most with bathroom/WC, some with shower/WC; TV, baby-listening in all rooms; hair-dryer on request
- ◈ Dining-room, bar, 2 lounges;
- golf, water sports nearby
- ⊖ No wheelchair access; no dogs in public rooms; no smoking in dining-room
- ▭ Access, Amex, Visa
- £ Single £21, single occupancy of twin/double £32 to £44, twin/double £38 to £50, four-poster £38 to £50, family room £63, suite £72; deposit required. Special breaks available

---

# Little Orchard House

---

WEST STREET, RYE, EAST SUSSEX TN31 7ES
TEL: RYE (0797) 223831

*B&B in a pleasant Georgian town house; lots of bonuses which are reflected in the room rates.*

Bank on an enthusiastic welcome from Sara Brinkhurst who took over Little Orchard House in October 1990. She claims her eighteenth-century grey and red brick building, down a cobbled street in the middle of Rye, has the second largest garden in town. An extraordinary (presently derelict) watchtower stands within its walls from which smugglers used to watch land and sea traffic in and out of town.

Guests take breakfast round a communal table in the light and modern open-plan pine breakfast room in an extension. You can eat as much as you can at whatever time, including a variety of special apple juices from a nearby orchard. From the lounge (large fire in winter, comfy sofas), where guests are cosseted on arrival with sherry and encouraged to look at menus for some recommended restaurants in town, stairs lead up to a minute and hideaway 'bookroom', and to three lovely bedrooms. As well as pretty floral designs, armchairs, books and lots of space, one has a tree mural in its bathroom painted by Sara; another a storm-oak four-poster built by her husband who's a furniture-maker. But B&B competition's hot in Rye and, even though this one successfully offers a superior degree of personal pampering and perks, our other recommendations beat it for value for money.

| | | | |
|---|---|---|---|
| ◑ | Open all year | | other sports nearby |
| ⤢ | Centrally located in Rye, off the High Street. Public parking close to hotel | ⊖ | No wheelchair access; no children under 13; no dogs; no smoking in some bedrooms |
| 🛏 | 1 twin, 1 double, 1 four-poster; all with bathroom exc double with shower/WC; TV, hair-dryer in all rooms | ▭ | Access, Visa |
| ◈ | Breakfast room, lounge, study, ironing service; fishing, tennis, | £ | Single occupancy of twin/double £35 to £50, twin/double £56 to £70, four-poster £70; deposit required (prices till Summer 92). Special breaks available |

---

# The Old Vicarage                                    ℒ

66 CHURCH SQUARE, RYE, EAST SUSSEX TN31 7HF
TEL: RYE (0797) 222119

*In a traffic-free position this is a straightforward B&B with good breakfasts and well-equipped bedrooms.*

'Strongly recommended,' advises a report. 'I particularly liked the very friendly welcome at all times during our stay.' A healthy modern-day job division means Paul Masters looks after the place while his wife goes out to work as an accountant. While sipping sherry in a yellow-patterned armchair in the small black-and-white vinyl-floored sitting-room you can peacefully watch groups of tourists on sightseeing tours round the closely packed old houses that hem in St Mary's Church at the top of the town, while an old lady sits on a sunny bench in the churchyard opposite eating chocolates. Do they notice the Masters' pink Georgian house, its two bay windows giving it a lovely proportion?

Bedrooms have a feminine, perhaps romantic, touch to them, a couple with four-posters, another a corona and drapes, in strong co-ordinated floral patterns, with wicker or reproduction balloon-back chairs. The large plainer basement bedroom has the only en suite bath. A thick file in each room contains a plethora of information on Rye, its restaurants and country walks. Breakfasts, served in a light dining-room of reproduction Victorian chairs and tables, 'were really good but slow', reports one reader. One of the family is in the tea trade, so you'll get a decent cuppa; you can buy packets of Central African Blend to take home with you.

◑ *Open all year, exc Xmas*

↗ *Go along Cinque Ports Street through Landgate Arch to High Street. Turn third left into West Street. By St Mary's Church. On-street parking (limited)*

🛏 *I twin, 2 double, 2 four-poster; I with bathroom/WC, I with shower/WC, 2 public bathrooms; TV, hair-dryer in all rooms*

◇ *Breakfast room, lounge; golf,*

*water sports, other sports nearby*

⊖ *No wheelchair access; no children under 10; no dogs; smoking in lounge only*

▭ *None accepted*

£ *Single occupancy of twin/double £26 to £40, twin/double £35 to £50, four-poster £48 to £50, family room £58 to £65; deposit required. Special breaks available*

---

**ST ALBANS** HERTFORDSHIRE                                    **MAP 10**

# Sopwell House

COTTONMILL LANE, SOPWELL, ST ALBANS, HERTFORDSHIRE AL1 2HQ
TEL: ST ALBANS (0727) 864477    TELEX: 927823 SOPWEL G
FAX: (0727) 44741

*A luxury country-house hotel aimed primarily at the business market but worth considering for a weekend break.*

A lengthy report propounding the merits of Sopwell House happily notes: 'We were taken to our room, which is as it should be, but a pleasant change in this day and age.' The hotel is a pleasant-looking subdued-pink Georgian building with modern accretions hidden round the back. It is run efficiently and the staff are courteous and attentive; the bedrooms are well furnished and lavishly decorated with metres of expensive cloth draped from beds and windows. One correspondent remarked that although most of the hotel was immaculately kept, the draperies above the bed had a layer of dust on them – a problem as her husband suffered from asthma. There's little benefit in being in the older part of the building as the rooms are remarkably uniform.

Magnolia trees stand amongst the diners in the conservatory restaur-ant; and food has been praised although some find the vegetables cooked just a shade too 'al dente'. Breakfasts, too, attract compliments for a particularly good cold table, including several exotic fruits. The best of Sopwell is undoubtedly the lounge: a fair representation of an old-fashioned club but with a modern lightness of touch. There's also a fairly decent library if you're caught short with nothing to read.

◐ Open all year

↗ From St Albans take the A1081
London Road south-east for 1
mile. Turn right at the traffic
lights by the 'Milehouse' pub and
across the mini-roundabout into
Cottonmill Lane. Private car park

🛏 12 single, 6 family, 18 twin, 15
double, 20 four-poster rooms; all
with bathroom/WC, TV, room
service, hair-dryer, trouser press,
baby-listening

◈ Restaurant (air-conditioned), bar,
lounge, library, conservatory,
restaurant; conference facilities
(max 350 people non-residential,

70 residential); sauna/solarium,
heated swimming-pool, gym,
other sports nearby; babysitting.
Wheelchair access to hotel
(ramp), restaurant, WC (M,F), 2
ground-floor bedrooms

⊖ No dogs in public rooms

▦ Access, Amex, Diners, Visa

£ Single £65 to £100, twin/double
£75 to £110, four-poster £70 to
£107, family room price on
application; deposit required.
Continental B £5.50, cooked B
£7.50; set L £15, £18.50, D
£18.50; alc L, D £24. Special
breaks available

## ST AUSTELL CORNWALL                                    MAP 8

# Boscundle Manor

TREGREHAN, ST AUSTELL, CORNWALL PL25 3RL
TEL: PAR (072 681) 3557   FAX: (072 681) 4997

*An attractive manor house with very friendly owners.*

The eighteenth-century house is quite close to the main road but acres of
grounds and gardens stretch out around it. Andrew Flint is busy
landscaping it, but it's a long job as he and his wife Mary are occupied
almost full time in the house. But when he does have a moment, he's
hacking through overgrown bushes to create another spot where guests
can sit and admire the surrounding countryside, or adding another hole
to his tiny golf course.

   Inside, it is decorated with the informality of a comfortable family
home, with a mixture of furnishings, some antiques and plenty of books
and pictures. The bar, tucked behind the sitting-room, is a mixture of
cosy and clubby and a great place to have a chat and a drink before
dinner. Guests can sit in the light sitting-room and peruse the menu.
Mary is the cook and an imaginative and experienced one: leave room for
one of her special puddings. One visitor was very impressed when, not
being able to manage one, the cost of it was deducted from the set dinner
charge. The Flints are natural, friendly hosts.

   Bedrooms vary in size and style but are generally homely and comfortable. Our inspector was rather disappointed by an ineffectual shower in
the single room. Breakfasts, cooked and brought to you by Andrew, are
eaten in the light, bright conservatory.

◐ Closed end Oct to Easter;
restaurant closed Sun to non-
residents

↗ 2 miles east of St Austell off the
A390, 150 yards up road signposted
Tregrehan. Private car park

2 single, 3 twin, 2 double, cottage with 3 bedrooms; all with bathroom/WC, exc singles with shower/WC; TV, room service, hair-dryer; trouser press, mini-bar, baby-listening in some rooms

Restaurant, bar, lounge, conservatory; golf, heated outdoor swimming-pool (May to mid-Sept), gym, croquet at hotel, other sports nearby; babysitting by arrangement

No wheelchair access; no dogs in public rooms

Access, Visa

Single £65, single occupancy of twin/double £80, twin/double £110, suite £150; deposit required. Set D £20

---

**ST BLAZEY** CORNWALL                                       **MAP 8**

# Nanscawen House

PRIDEAUX ROAD, ST BLAZEY, CORNWALL PL24 2SR
TEL: PAR (0726 81) 4488   FAX: (0726 81) 4488

*Lovely, spacious and intimate country house where you're entertained as friends.*

The Nanscawens moved away in 1520. Current residents, Keith and Janet Martin, arrived in late 1987 and discovered they liked entertaining what soon became a steady stream of weekend visitors. The creeper-clad stone house looks down over five multifarious acres of lovingly tended, often unusual, flowers, plants, mature trees and vegetable garden. The heated swimming-pool is large and deep, with proper diving-board, and there's a heated whirlpool bath nearby.

Despite family pictures and *Trivial Pursuit*, the substantial peachy beige and pale green drawing-room is a fairly formal room, but the sofas are the sort for collapsing into. Everyone eats together and the food certainly doesn't disappoint: smoked salmon, perhaps, then marinated chicken kebabs, cured pork sirloin in Cumberland sauce and crème brûlée. The bedrooms are bright, spotless and very comfortable. All three have pale, feminine colour schemes, decorative details and whirlpool baths. Prideaux, a double with white-painted four-poster, frilly pink valance and embroidered pillowcases, is vast but romantic. Breakfast is 'amazing', says one regular visitor. 'The atmosphere, welcome and service is second to none and the value for money is excellent,' says another.

Open all year, exc Xmas and New Year; restaurant closed Sun eve

From Plymouth on the A38, turn left at Dobwalls to A390 St Austell. In St Blazey turn right directly after railway, opposite the garage. The house is ¾ mile on the right. Private car park

1 twin, 1 double, 1 four-poster; all with bathroom/WC, TV, hair-dryer

Dining-room, lounge, conservatory; heated swimming-pool at hotel, fishing, other sports nearby

⊖ No wheelchair access; no children under 12; no dogs; no smoking

▭ Access, Visa

⊞ Single occupancy of twin/double £35 to £45, twin/double/four-poster £50 to £58; deposit required. Set D £18 (7.15pm). Special breaks available

## ST JOHN'S CHAPEL CO DURHAM                    MAP 3

# Pennine Lodge

ST JOHN'S CHAPEL, WEARDALE, CO DURHAM DL13 1QX
TEL: WEARDALE (0388) 537247

*A country guesthouse in lovely surroundings with good English cooking and a warm welcome.*

This stone farmhouse sits on the banks of the River Wear and visitors are lulled to sleep by the sound of water rushing over the rocks – they may even dream of the fish they might catch the next day. The friendly owners have taken great care to make their house warm and welcoming. The upstairs sitting-room is raftered which makes for a light, cheerful room with good views. Comfortable armchairs, a TV and plenty of books and local literature make it a great room in which to relax and get to know fellow guests.

The dining-room is another lovely old room with wide windowsills crammed with ornaments, plants and other items collected over the years. Dinner is described as 'traditional English fare' and is very well cooked and presented. You may start with a sardine salad followed by steak pie, creamed potatoes, carrots with parsley and broad beans, before a sweet or cheese and biscuits. The five bedrooms are small and cosy with pretty wallpapers and fabrics, fitted carpets and neat little shower rooms tucked under the roof timbers.

◐ Closed Oct to Mar

⤴ St John's Chapel is half-way between Alston and Stanhope on the A689. Private car park

🛏 2 twin, 2 double, 1 four-poster; some with bathroom/WC, some with shower/WC; hair-dryer on request

⊘ Dining-room, lounge; fishing at hotel, other sports nearby.

⊖ No wheelchair access; no children under 12; no dogs in public rooms; no smoking

▭ None accepted

⊞ Twin/double/four-poster £36; deposit required. Set D £9 (7 pm). Special breaks available

---

*Food/dinner very uninspiring – rather the impression of cooked at 7pm and served at 8.30pm!* On an hotel in the Highlands

**ST KEYNE** CORNWALL                                    **MAP 8**

# The Well House

ST KEYNE, LISKEARD, CORNWALL PL14 4RN
TEL: LISKEARD (0579) 42001

*Debonair country house in deepest Cornwall. Good food and wine are further pluses.*

Not quite the quaint and homespun hotel you might expect in this hidden corner of Cornwall. The pace slows and your horizons narrow as you wind along the single track lane. From the quiet setting – quacking ducks (quite tame as well as cute) and Victorian stone house – you might expect over-stuffed sofas with antimacassars and Axminster carpets. The original tiled floor entrance hall has a Victorian rocking chair and vases of dried flowers. A comfortable sitting-room, with subdued colours, log fire and bay windows looking over a timeless landscape, feels modern, as does the small panelled bar where Nick Wainford takes your order for dinner. The crisp, bright dining-room, with good views, well-spaced, stylishly set tables and large watercolours of appetising food, is even smarter. The cooking is suitably modern but not outlandishly so: tartare of smoked sea trout with cucumber and dill, scallops with spring onions and ginger, white chocolate truffle cake with rum and raisin sauce. The cheeseboard is worthy, the wine list fairly priced and interesting. Service is slick, as you'd expect. Solid furniture, good-quality furnishings and zappy modern prints are standard in bedrooms, most of which are good-sized. Goodies abound, especially in the modern bathrooms. A swimming-pool, good tennis court and croquet lawn more than justify the cost of staying here.

**◑** Open all year

**↗** From Liskeard take the B3254 to St Keyne. Pass through the village and past the church and carry straight on. The hotel is ½ mile from the church. Private car park

**🛏** 3 twin, 3 double, 1 family room; all with bathroom/WC, TV, room service, hair-dryer, trouser press, baby-listening; no tea/coffee-making facilities in rooms

**◈** Restaurant, bar, lounge; tennis, croquet, heated outdoor swimming-pool at hotel, other sports nearby. Wheelchair access to public rooms only

**⊖** No children under 8 in restaurant eves

**▭** Access, Amex, Visa

**£** Single occupancy of twin/double £60, twin/double £80 to £105, family room £125 to £140; deposit required. Cooked B £7.50; set L £21, D £25 and £30 (prices till Apr 92). Special breaks available

---

*See the inside front cover for a brief explanation of how to use the* Guide.

# The Lawyers Rest

UNDERCLIFF DRIVE, ST LAWRENCE, NR VENTNOR, ISLE OF WIGHT
PO38 1XF
TEL: ISLE OF WIGHT (0983) 852610

*Stylish and enthusiastically run hotel, with marvellous views from the southern tip of the island.*

A glowing reader's report on the hotel enthuses about the food and many personal touches, including a weather forecast supplied to each resident every morning. Ann Dex and Geoffrey Phillips' early-Victorian stone house looks out to sea over a strongly-sloping V-shaped terraced and walled garden with a collection of sub-tropical plants.

The owners seem to lead a startlingly full life. Once the breakfast rush is over, they actively woo passing trade with mid-morning coffee and cakes, light lunches, sandwiches, teas, only then to cook dinner (he the main course, she the starters and puddings). Meals consist of a nice mix of sensibly unfussy but interesting food with three choices for each course, accompanied by an imaginative wine list. And, meanwhile, Ann was in preparation for the London Marathon when we visited. Geoffrey is a solicitor, hence the hotel's name and logo depicting a contented, fat judge having a zizz, and the legal prints distributed throughout the hotel which used to adorn his office.

Two guests welcomed the absence of TVs as they sat reading to the sounds of ticking clocks in the comfortable Victorian-styled sitting-room, which has strong Chinese-patterned wallpaper, a coal fire in winter and period antiques. In contrast, the dining-room is in a small modern extension, with bamboo chairs and sliding glass windows. Bedrooms are furnished with floral patterns and wicker chairs, the larger ones boasting antiques (a mahogany wardrobe, walnut beds), some with splendid sea views, others the undercliff behind.

● *Closed Nov; open weekends only Dec to Feb*

▟ *On the main A3055 coast road on the south side of the island midway between Ventnor and Niton. Private car park*

⇌ *1 single, 2 twin, 5 double; half with bathroom/WC, half with shower/WC; hair-dryer on request; no tea/coffee-making facilities in rooms*

◈ *Dining-room, bar, lounge; conference facilities (max 20 people non-residential, 15 residential); sailing, golf, other sports nearby*

⊖ *No wheelchair access; no children under 10; no dogs in public rooms and by arrangement only in bedrooms; no smoking in dining-room*

▭ *Access, Amex, Visa*

£ *Single £45, single occupancy of twin/double £60 to £71, twin/double from £78 to £89 (rates inc dinner); deposit required. Alc L £15; set D £20.50 (7pm). Special breaks available*

# Wallett's Court

WEST CLIFFE, ST MARGARET'S AT CLIFFE, DOVER, KENT CT15 6EW
TEL: DOVER (0304) 852424   FAX: (0304) 853430

*Relaxed, family-run country-house hotel within an interesting old building.*

Don't be fooled by the address; though close to the coast, this white-painted black-window-framed manor house has a rural, inland position by a fairly quiet back road. Its porch dates it 1627, but cellars underneath, used for table tennis and snooker, originate from Norman times. It could serve as a base for a channel hop but it's attractive enough to justify a trip in its own right. For despite its evident age the building's smart and well kept.

To the left of the hall, which doubles as reception and bar, is the spacious sitting-room: you can flop onto an old sloping brown leather sofa or perch on a window seat admiring the ticking grandfather clock or the shining Steinway. The upright beams in the plainer, white-walled dining-room are intriguingly carved. Still, you probably won't want to be distracted from your food, cooked by owner Chris Oakley. You might be offered a combination of ingredients, such as a 'huntsman's platter' of game terrine and smoked goose breast in Cumberland sauce; or a fricassée of salmon and turbot in a mussel sauce with big prawns. A short, inexpensive set-price meal becomes a five-course gourmet affair on Saturday nights.

The characterful rooms in the main building are beamed, with sloping door frames, of a good size and with a large settee and gas fire in the fireplace. Four more functional fresh modern rooms with pine furniture and floral bedspreads are in the converted barn behind.

- Closed Xmas and 2 weeks Nov; restaurant closed Sun eve
- On the B2058 off the A258 Dover to Deal road, 5 minutes from Dover docks. Private car park
- 3 twin, 3 double, 1 family room; all with bathroom/WC, TV, baby-listening
- Restaurant, lounge, games room, conference facilities (max 20 people non-residential); tennis, table tennis, snooker at hotel, other sports nearby
- No wheelchair access; no dogs
- Access, Visa
- Single occupancy of twin/double from £37, twin/double £45; children sharing parents' room £5 to £10; deposit required. Set D £18, £24

*Warning to insomniacs, exercise freaks and late-night lovers: increasing numbers of hotels have infra-red triggered security lamps. To save being embarrassingly illuminated, check before you leave for your late-night or pre-dawn stroll.*

# St Martin's

ST MARTIN'S, ISLES OF SCILLY TR25 0QW
TEL: SCILLONIA (0720) 22092   FAX: (0720) 22298

*A beautiful spot. A modern hotel with lovely views, and comfort
for which you pay highly.*

It is probably difficult to find an unattractive position for an hotel in the
Scilly Isles and the Francis family certainly had no problems on St
Martin's. It has been designed to blend as well as possible into the
surroundings so as not to mar the view of the island. This has generally
been well achieved. From the outside the hotel looks like a series of low-
lying pitched-roof cottages. Inside, double-glazing minimises the glare
from the sun on good days and protects from the wind on bad ones. All
the public rooms have a view of the sea, and in the dining-room there are
prime spots but it's first come first seated, so get to breakfast early. The
table d'hôte menu may offer avocado, fennel and prawns, followed by
lobster St Martin's.

The sitting-room and bar are smartly but simply decorated and
although uniformed staff are at hand for your every request, the atmosphere is quite informal. One reader praised them as 'extremely helpful
and friendly, particularly to my children'. Bedrooms, decorated in the
same designer-style as the rest of the hotel, are comfortable and well
equipped but not huge. The hotel has its own launch which you can use
to visit other islands but beware – one reader was outraged to find he'd
been charged for a trip that he'd understood was free. One other
complaint from a reader, who was otherwise thrilled with the hotel,
concerned the 'poorly maintained swimming-pool and shoddy changing
rooms'.

◐ Closed Nov to Mar

🏎 There are helicopter/ferry
services from Penzance and a
Skybus service from Land's End.
There are no cars on the Scillies

🛏 14 twin/double, 2 double, 2 four-
poster, 4 family, 2 suites; all with
bathroom/WC, TV, room service,
baby-listening; hair-dryer and
trouser press on request; no tea/
coffee-making facilities in rooms

◈ Restaurant, bar, 2 lounges,
games room, drying room,
library/study; conference facilities
(max 24 people residential);
fishing, croquet, water sports,
snooker, indoor heated

swimming-pool at hotel, other
sports nearby

⊖ No wheelchair access; no dogs in
public rooms and in some
bedrooms by arrangement only;
no smoking in restaurant and 1
lounge

▭ Access, Amex, Diners, Visa

£ Single occupancy of twin/double
£86 to £130, twin/double/four-
poster/family room £130 to
£196, suite £150 to £206 (rates
inc dinner); deposit required. Set
D £20; alc L £13, D £25 (prices
till Nov 91). Special breaks
available

# Tregarthen's Hotel

ST MARY'S, ISLES OF SCILLY TR21 0PP
TEL: SCILLONIA (0720) 22540   FAX: (0720) 22089

*A relaxing hotel run with friendliness and efficiency.*

St Mary's is the main island of the Scillies and where the daily boat (except Sunday) docks from Penzance. Passengers don't have to worry about their luggage – as long as it's well-marked it will be delivered to the appropriate hotel by a tractor and trailer.

If you want to be near the harbour and the centre but not bothered by the noise, Tregarthen's is a good choice. The dining-room has lovely views down to the harbour and across to the other islands. White chairs and tables are lined up facing towards the window so the sooner you arrive for dinner the more likely you are to bag a front seat. Most of the staff are young and employed for the season but are willing and helpful. The sitting-room has recently been refurbished and is an attractive, comfortable room, though it's open-plan with the reception area so there's a fair amount of coming and going. The bar is separate and a great place to meet the locals.

The bedrooms are generally a good size, but our inspector found one of the small double rooms at the back dull and draughty and the bathroom old-fashioned.

◐ Closed from end of Oct to mid-Mar

⬈ Guests are met at the quay. The hotel is a 1-mile bus journey from the airport. There are no cars on the Scillies

🛏 6 single, 27 twin/double; most with bathroom/WC, some with shower/WC; TV, room service in all rooms; hair-dryer, baby-listening on request

◈ Restaurant, bar, lounge, drying room; fishing, golf, other sports nearby

⊖ No wheelchair access; no children under 5; no dogs in bedrooms

▭ Access, Amex, Diners, Visa

£ Single or single occupancy of twin/double £44 to £56, twin/double £84 to £111 (rates inc dinner); deposit required. Set D £18.50; bar lunches

---

*If you are intending to make a lot of phone calls from your room, always check what the hotel is going to charge you per unit. You may be so horrified that you'll prefer to walk to the nearest phone box. Why let them get away with excessive charges?*

# Hotel Tresanton

ST MAWES, TRURO, CORNWALL TR2 5DR
TEL: ST MAWES (0326) 270544    FAX: (0326) 270002

*A relaxing, well-run hotel overlooking a lovely estuary.*

Dominated by a castle built by Henry VIII to defend his lands against the French, St Mawes is a fashionable yachting resort on the fertile Roseland peninsula. You don't have to sail to appreciate the setting nor indeed this friendly hotel which has uninterrupted views of estuary and lighthouse. Bright white, with turquoise trim and many divided windows, it extends up the hill from the roadside, tropical plants dotting the split-level terrace.

Everyone looks after you with enthusiasm here and the mood is lighthearted. The décor alternates between smart and homely. A large, low sitting-room with log fire and good soft sofas and easy chairs hasn't the cheeriest of colour schemes. The cocktail bar and dining-room are smarter, the former also warmed in cool weather by an open fire, the latter having Chinese prints, and sea views through picture window. A fair choice on the four-course menu often includes lobster (extra but probably worth it). You don't need to specify a sea view when you book since every room is blessed with one, and two have balconies. Flowery quilts and curtains are good quality, but colours and decorative detail are conservative. Most rooms have attached bathrooms; the rest have wash-basins in rooms and private bathrooms across the hall.

| | |
|---|---|
| ◑ Closed Nov to Mar, exc Xmas to New Year | ◇ Restaurant, bar, lounge; fishing, tennis, water sports nearby |
| ⤳ From St Austell take the B3287 from Sticker to Tregony, then the A3078 from Tregony to St Mawes. Private car park | ⊖ No wheelchair access; no children under 10; no dogs in public rooms |
| ⇌ 4 single, 10 twin, 4 double, 3 suites; all with bathroom/WC, TV; hair-dryer on request; no tea/coffee-making facilities in rooms | ▭ Access, Visa |
| | £ Single £44, single occupancy of twin/double £83, twin/double £83 to £97, suite £145; deposit required. Set D £17.50; bar lunches. Special breaks available |

---

*The 1993* Guide *will be published before Christmas 1992. Reports on hotels are most welcome at any time of the year, but are extremely valuable in the spring. Send them to* Which? Hotel Guide, FREEPOST, 2 Maryle-bone Road, London NW1 1YN. *No stamp is needed if reports are posted in the UK.*

# Rising Sun

THE SQUARE, ST MAWES, NR TRURO, CORNWALL TR2 5DJ
TEL: FALMOUTH (0326) 270233

*A well-modernised, friendly pub with nicely furnished bedrooms.*
*Close to the harbour.*

You can people-watch from the benches and chairs in front of this pretty white pub, and also view the strip of beach and harbour. But roads on two sides and the sprawling town car park on another mar what must once have been a picturesque setting. The inside was quaint once, too, but in the hands of the previous owner and St Austell brewery (who took over in early 1990), it has gone up-market. Luckily, it's been sensibly done, leaving the little pubby bar more or less intact and bringing some chic to the rest. Handsome arrangements of fresh flowers sit all around. A small lounge in cerise and pale green has hessian wall-coverings and cosy seating. Young locals and visitors munch on hearty snacks in the jazzy pink and black cocktail bar, built on to the front. In the back is a peaceful dining-room with ceiling spotlights, hanging plants and comfy high-backed chairs; a civilised place for good and unexpectedly stylish set dinners of wild mushrooms in cream and tarragon sauce, perhaps, seafood in saffron sauce, and brandy snap baskets with strawberries and clotted cream. The bread is home-made and the service very friendly.

The standard of furnishings and range of facilities in bedrooms is excellent. Poppy-red and green curtains, pale walls and off-white quilted bedspreads are set off by new pine furniture. There are fresh as well as dried flowers, the latter hanging from the ceiling or draped over mirrors. Mattresses are high-quality. Five bedrooms overlook the harbour including a single room with a sweet cabin bed.

Closed Jan, Feb

Follow signs to Truro via the A39 when leaving Fraddon. Shortly after joining the A390 turn left on to the A3078 signposted St Mawes. The Rising Sun is by the harbour. Private car park

3 single, 5 twin, 4 double; most with bathroom/WC, some with shower/WC; TV in all rooms; hair-dryer on request

Restaurant, 2 bars, sitting-room, conservatory; fishing, riding, tennis, water sports nearby. Wheelchair access to restaurant and WC (disabled) only

No children under 5; no dogs in public rooms

Access, Visa

Single £26 to £35, single occupancy of twin/double £39 to £53, twin/double £52 to £70; deposit required. Sun L £9, set D £18. Special breaks available

---

*If you have a small appetite, or just aren't feeling hungry, check if you can be given a reduction if you don't want the full menu.*

# Cusack's Glebe

SAINTBURY, NR BROADWAY, HEREFORD AND WORCESTER WR12 7PX
TEL: BROADWAY (0386) 852210

*Lovely Cotswold B&B with friendly owners and rooms with both character and comfort.*

'Horses please shut the gate', reads the notice – perhaps they have particularly dextrous horses around here? Such a description could not apply to Ben, the painfully arthritic labrador who limps up to greet you after you close the gate. Owner Juliet Carro, however, has unstinting energy – with five horses and five acres of paddocks and gardens to look after she still manages a warm welcome to guests at her small fifteenth-century farmhouse.

The yellow Cotswold stone exterior with its neat kitchen and herb garden hides an interior of crooked floors and ceilings and low beams. Riding crops and various bits of tack hang on hooks behind the door as further evidence of Juliet's equine interests. The small landing has a display of ancient craft tools – spinning wheels and a glove donkey – and is hung with horseshoes. Part of the wall has been left unplastered to show the original wattle and daub construction. The two bedrooms in the main house have antique four-poster beds and shower/bathrooms. Breakfast includes croissants and home-made preserves in addition to the usual farmhouse fare. It's served in the drawing-room, a green, low-ceilinged room with pictures (for sale) of local villages painted by Juliet's mother.

◑ *Closed Xmas*

⤧ *Saintbury is between Broadway and Chipping Campden; Cusack's Glebe is one mile from Broadway Golf Club. Private car park*

🛏 *1 twin, 2 four-poster, 1 family room; 1 with bathroom/WC, rest with shower/WC; TV, hair-dryer, mini-bar in all rooms*

◈ *Lounge; golf, riding nearby*

⊖ *No wheelchair access; no children under 6; no dogs; no smoking in bedrooms*

▭ *None accepted*

£ *Twin £45, four-poster £50, family room (3 people) £60. Special breaks available*

---

*We mention those hotels that don't accept dogs; guide dogs, however, are almost always an exception. Telephone ahead to make sure!*

**SALCOMBE** DEVON                                    **MAP 8**

# Tides Reach

SOUTH SANDS, SALCOMBE, DEVON TQ8 8LJ
TEL: SALCOMBE (054 884) 3466   FAX: (054 884) 3954

*Unusual and out-of-the-way seaside hotel, with lots to do on rainy days.*

This is a deceptively large hotel across the road from a sandy bay in a remote and beautiful part of Devon. 'More than just a hotel' boasts the brochure, presumably referring to the leisure facilities which make good weather less vital to enjoyment. The interior design of Tides Reach is also unusual. A plant-filled entrance-way with a marble fountain leads into the cavernous ground floor which is decorated in deep blues and greens but is kept light by large windows looking across the bay. Reception/bar and sitting-room, with sea-blue velveteen chairs, merge into one another. These rooms are neither very homely nor peaceful, so you might prefer to lounge outdoors by the pool or on the beach.

Mrs Edwards has bypassed typical hotel bedroom design, favouring strong blues, variations on pink and snappy patterns; one all-blue room is so bright it might make you squint. More typical are the crown canopies, thick carpets and modern, built-in furniture. King-sized beds are welcome, though in some cases they've been put in pawn-sized rooms, and top-floor rooms have balconies with great views.

◑ Closed Nov to Feb

↗ Follow the A381 from Kingsbridge through Malborough to Salcombe. Turn right off the road into Salcombe signposted South Sands. Private car park

🛏 16 twin, 16 double, 3 family rooms, 4 suites; all with shower/WC, TV, room service, hairdryer, mini-bar, baby-listening; no tea/coffee-making facilities in rooms

◇ Restaurant, 2 bars, 3 lounges, games room, conservatory, drying room; hair and beauty salon; table tennis, sauna, solarium, heated swimming-pool, gym, water sports, squash at hotel, other sports nearby. Wheelchair access to restaurant only

⊖ No children under 8; no dogs in public rooms; no smoking in bedrooms

▭ Access, Amex, Diners, Visa

💷 Twin/double £104 to £158, family room £188 to £247, suite £138 to £169 (rates inc dinner); deposit required. Snack lunches; set D £23; alc D £34.50 (meal prices till Nov 91; room prices till Mar 92). Special breaks available

*Shame on you South Yorkshire, Tyne & Wear and Mid Glamorgan, the only counties without an hotel of merit in this year's* Guide.

# Brunel's Tunnel House

HIGH STREET, SALTFORD, BRISTOL, AVON BS18 3BQ
TEL: SALTFORD (0225) 873873

*Interesting smart and relaxed family-run hotel in a house once owned by the great engineer himself.*

Isambard Kingdom Brunel lived in this fine Georgian house, in Old Saltford, while working on the Great Western Railway (and may have had personal access to it via a staircase from the railway tunnel which runs directly below). The atmosphere inside is homely and there's a good line in knick-knacks. You can relax here, too, and be well looked after by the Mitchell family.

The pink damask three-piece suite and large bar in the bar/lounge look designed for a larger room. There is more space to move around and a fresh feel in bedrooms. Everything is co-ordinated, fabric over beds adds a touch of the romantic, but furniture and beige-flecked carpets are more functional than eye-catching. The local evening paper, fruit, sugared almonds, mineral water and fresh milk for tea are welcoming touches. The top-floor honeymoon suite, with lacy pelmet over a new brass bed, could be larger and has only a shower, but it costs no more. Dinner, not served at weekends, is three courses with no choice, but is good value. Saltford is a mostly picturesque village, an ideal base for tourists.

◐ *Open all year, exc Xmas; restaurant closed Fri, Sat, Sun eves*

🔁 *Saltford is mid-way between Bath and Bristol on the A4. In the centre of the village turn off the A4 by the side of Saltford Motor Services into Beech Road. The hotel faces the bottom of this road. Private car park*

🛏 *1 twin, 6 double; most with shower/WC, 1 double with bathroom/WC; TV, hair-dryer in all rooms*

◈ *Dining-room, bar/lounge; conference facilities (max 14 people non-residential, 8 residential); fishing, golf, other sports nearby*

⊝ *No wheelchair access; dogs in bedrooms only by arrangement; no smoking in dining-room*

▭ *Access, Amex, Visa*

💷 *Single occupancy of twin/double £40 to £47, twin/double £48 to £56. Set D £13 (7pm). Special breaks available*

---

*We had the misfortune of staying in the annexe which was sodden with damp. The bathroom was mouldy, as was the shower, towels, bed clothes and curtains.* On an hotel in the Yorkshire Dales

**SANDRINGHAM** NORFOLK     **MAP 7**

# Park House

SANDRINGHAM, KING'S LYNN, NORFOLK PE35 6EH
TEL: DERSINGHAM (0485) 543000

*Next door to Sandringham Country Park in pleasant grounds, a country-house hotel designed for disabled people. Excellent facilities and dedicated, cheerful staff.*

The Queen presented this Victorian House to the Leonard Cheshire Foundation in 1983. There can't be many such well-run and pleasant retreats for disabled people, nor many hotels which offer such a wide range of facilities and outings. Staff attend to everyone's needs with sensitivity and warmth. Disabled guests may bring their own carer or be looked after by the house SRN. Carers, friends and relatives are all welcome.

There are plenty of places to relax and be entertained: a large, bright courtyard conservatory, a library and music room, games room and proper drawing-room. Guests can play table tennis, snooker, bowls, the piano, cards, etc. The swimming-pool has a hoist, and Batricars take guests around wide garden paths. The terrace is perfectly placed for watching a cricket match. If that's not enough, outings and music festivals and painting weeks dot the calendar.

The furnishings of bedrooms are more traditional than modern, more low-key than cheery, but rooms, variously adapted, are fresh and very spacious. A few bed and bath hoists are available and Tendercare beds can be provided on request. Large singles have sit-down showers. Though the dining-room is arranged for convenience, it is done out with smart Scandinavian furniture and crisp nappery. Care is taken with meals, too. A good-value dinner menu in March offered cheese roulade, baked gammon with glazed peaches and Bakewell tart.

◑ Open all year, exc 14 to 21 Dec

◿ Turn right off the A149, 3 miles north of Knight's Hill roundabout, and follow hotel signs. Private car park

🛏 8 single, 8 twin, 1 suite; twins and suite with bathroom/WC, singles with shower/WC; TV in all rooms

◈ Dining-room, bar, 2 lounges, games room, library, conservatory, conference facilities (max 60 people non-residential); heated swimming-pool (Apr–Sept). Hotel designed specifically for use by disabled people, all bedrooms (exc suite) specially equipped

⊖ Guide dogs only; no smoking in bedrooms

▭ Access, Visa

£ Single £31 to £47, twin/double £44 to £76, family room £44 to £76; deposit required. Set L £6.50, D £11 (prices till Jan 92)

# Wrea Head Country Hotel

SCALBY, SCARBOROUGH, NORTH YORKSHIRE YO13 0PB
TEL: SCARBOROUGH (0723) 378211    FAX: (0723) 371780

*A comfortable Victorian hotel with well-decorated bedrooms.*

Fourteen acres of grounds and gardens separate the hotel from the surrounding suburbs of Scarborough. Built in the 1880s as a country retreat, it is solidly Victorian. The hall is light and comfortable with a huge window, half-panelling and shiny brown leather-studded sofas. The variety of colours and carpet patterns help brighten the public rooms along with the full-length windows. The sitting-room walls are half covered with bookshelves so there's plenty to read as well as a selection of games, and plush red chairs to curl up in.

The bar is bright too, half-panelled with white wood on which hang gilt-framed prints and oil paintings. There's no stinting on curtains in here with yards of bold striped material both at the side and above the windows; the atmosphere is busy and cheerful. The restaurant is traditional in style and the food is unremarkable.

The bedrooms are in the process of refurbishment and those that have been completed – the comfortable superior rooms – are quite rightly named: fat bedcovers match the curtains and everything else is smartly co-ordinated. Bathrooms, too, are large with modern facilities.

◑ Open all year, exc 23 to 28 Dec

🔁 From Scarborough follow the A171 north towards Whitby for 3 miles until hotel sign is seen on main road. Private car park

🛏 3 single, 6 twin, 9 double, 2 family rooms, 1 suite; all with bathroom/WC, exc singles with shower/WC; TV, room service, hair-dryer, baby-listening in all rooms; no tea/coffee-making facilities in rooms

◈ 2 restaurants, bar, lounge, library, conservatory; conference facilities (max 50 people non-residential, 20 residential); croquet at hotel, other sports nearby; babysitting

⊖ No wheelchair access; no dogs

▭ Access, Amex, Visa

💷 Single £35 to £50, single occupancy of twin/double £55 to £70, twin/double/family room £65 to £90, suite £125 to £150; deposit required. Set L £12.50, D £21.50. Special breaks available

---

*Prices are what you can expect to pay in 1992, except where specified to the contrary. Many hoteliers tell us that these prices can be regarded only as approximations.*

**SCOLE** NORFOLK                                            **MAP 7**

# Scole Inn

SCOLE, NR DISS, NORFOLK NR21 4DR
TEL: DISS (0379) 740481   FAX: (0379) 740762

*An odd mix of the practical and the decorative; a large
seventeenth-century inn geared towards business use.*

The Waveney Inns chain owns this large brick coaching-inn, built for a
wealthy wool merchant in 1655, and would be the first to admit that the
setting, in the dusty town of Scole, isn't its most enviable feature. The
Dutch-gabled front is very dignified but rises straight from a busy road.
Behind, a sea of company cars fills the space between stable extension
and inn, and glass doors into reception and restaurant have the allure of
two black eyes.

   Still, weathered timbers, leaded windows, huge oak doors, very high
ceilings and great beamed fireplaces have not been spoiled in turning this
Grade-I-listed building into a business hotel and upmarket hostelry.
Tapestry upholstery and handsome Jacobean furniture are especially
noteworthy. Historical links with Charles II, Lord Nelson and highway-
man John Belcher are cited. The latter was often in such a hurry to
escape the law that he forgot to dismount his horse before climbing the
huge oak staircase. (A gate now keeps guests from following in his
hoofsteps.)

   Although they are equipped to suit modern-day needs and are
comfortable, bedrooms could not be accused of having an up-to-date
look. Antiques, some fine beds included, are in considerable evidence,
however, and original features include lovely fireplaces. One room even
has a ghost. Twelve of the rooms are in the converted Georgian
stables. These are ghostless, shorter on character and more peaceful.
More reports, please.

◑ Open all year

⬈ On the A140 between Ipswich
and Norwich. Private car park

🛏 3 twin, 13 double, 5 four-poster,
2 family rooms; all with
bathroom/WC, TV, room service
(limited), hair-dryer, trouser
press

◇ Restaurant (air-conditioned), bar,
lounge; conference facilities
(max 40 people); golf, other
sports nearby. Wheelchair access
to restaurant and WC only

⊖ No dogs in public rooms

▭ Access, Amex, Diners, Visa

£ Single occupancy of twin/double
£46, twin/double £64, four-
poster £51 to £71, family room
£64; deposit required. Set L, D
£13; alc L, D £20. Special
breaks available

---

*Many hotels offer special rates for stays of a few nights or more. It is worth
enquiring when you book.*

# Seatoller House

SEATOLLER, BORROWDALE, KESWICK, CUMBRIA CA12 5XN
TEL: BORROWDALE (076 87) 77218

*House-party-style guesthouse with rugged clientele and cheerful,
unaffected hosts.*

The hamlet of Seatoller crouches at the foot of the Honister Pass, with
Fleetwith and Dale Head above. The road narrows dramatically and a
sign warns: 'No caravans'. This is serious walking and climbing country
and the motto here could well be: 'Real walkers don't watch TV'.
Instead, David and Ann Pepper give them what they want – a proper
drying room, a kitchen tea-bar with home-baking, and a picnic shop for
d-i-y packed lunches.

The three-hundred-year-old house is externally austere, but indoors
both smoking and non-smoking lounges are cosy, with beams, floral
prints and some fine antiques. Bedrooms, mostly big enough for families,
are simple but comfortable. All rooms have bathrooms. In keeping with
the natural camaraderie of the hiking brigade, the Peppers serve meals
communally at two large specially commissioned oak tables, in a slate
flagstoned room enlivened with hunting prints and a collection of toby
jugs. Food, prepared by Ann, is traditional English and designed to
satisfy hearty appetites worked up on bracing fell expeditions. A typical
May dinner offered cheese and prawn mousse, beef casserole with
potatoes, leeks and broccoli and lemon layer pudding.

- ◑ Closed Nov to Mar; restaurant
  closed Tues eve
- ⤢ 8 miles south of Keswick on the
  B5289. Private car park
- ⇌ 3 twin, 5 double, 1 annexe room;
  all with bathroom/WC
- ◈ Dining-room, lounge, library,
  drying room; fishing, water
  sports, other sports nearby

- ⊖ No wheelchair access; no
  children under 5; no dogs in
  public rooms; no smoking in
  bedrooms or some public rooms
- ▭ None accepted
- ⊞ Single occupancy of twin/double
  £32, twin/double/annexe £61
  (rates inc dinner); deposit
  required

# Seaview

HIGH STREET, SEAVIEW, ISLE OF WIGHT PO34 5EX
TEL: ISLE OF WIGHT (0983) 612711   FAX: (0983) 613729

*A family hotel with lots of maritime decorations and situated in a sailing village.*

Due to its deceptive size and the effective professional and personal management of Nicholas and Nicola Hayward who've been here for over ten years, the Seaview can accommodate all-comers. It's got a decent restaurant, atmospheric bars, comfortable rooms and, a rare combination, it welcomes and looks after children (special menus for example). Locals come to eat and drink all year round, and, with the surge of tourists in summer, restaurant, bar and hotel do get busy.

The hotel takes its name from the Victorian seaside resort, now a gentrified sailors' haunt. The Edwardian building is some hundred yards inland from the rocky and shingly coastline overlooking the Solent. There is a smart, small, closely packed restaurant with a gentle cacophony of ticking clocks. Pass along a corridor of nautical pictures and you get to the Pump Bar, a naval ward room with oars and rudders and ships' wheels, lying across from an inner courtyard with picnic tables.

Upstairs, there's a cosy residents' sitting-room with casual covers on old armchairs. The most atmospheric bedrooms are at the front and have some homely pieces of furniture; others have light colour schemes, and recently redecorated ones have smart bathrooms with large mirrors around the bath. Unsurprisingly, fish predominates on the restaurant's menu. Bar food includes staple stuff.

- **◑** Open all year; restaurant closed Sun eve
- **⤴** Take the B3330 from Ryde and follow signs to Seaview. The hotel is 25 yards from the sea front. Private car park
- **🛏** 12 twin, 4 double; all with bathroom/WC, exc 2 doubles with shower/WC; TV, baby-listening in all rooms; hair-dryer on request; no tea/coffee-making facilities in rooms
- **◈** Restaurant, 2 bars, 2 lounges; conference facilities (max 24 people non-residential, 16 residential); water sports, other sports nearby; babysitting by arrangement
- **⊖** No wheelchair access; no children under 3 at dinner; no dogs in public rooms; one lounge non-smoking; no smoking in restaurant
- **▭** Access, Amex, Visa
- **£** Single occupancy of twin/double from £44, twin/double from £65. Alc L, D from £21.50. Special breaks available

*Shame on you South Yorkshire, Tyne & Wear and Mid Glamorgan, the only counties without an hotel of merit in this year's* Guide.

**SEAVINGTON ST MARY** SOMERSET **MAP 8**

# The Pheasant

WATER STREET, SEAVINGTON ST MARY, NR ILMINSTER, SOMERSET
TA19 0QH
TEL: SOUTH PETHERTON (0460) 40502   FAX: (0460) 42388

*Extra comfort and a pleasant old-world atmosphere make this
hotel special.*

Once a seventeenth-century farmhouse, the Pheasant has been converted into the kind of thatched inn that combines a vision of old England
with some plusher modern-day comforts. Thus you have an old village,
grass and flowers, heavy wooden beams and inglenook fires, brass
bellows, decorative plates and oil paintings. But this is more than just the
traditional village pub, for as you wander through the hotel you notice the
care that has been taken over the co-ordination of furnishings and
decoration, and how neatly everything is kept.

By the time you reach the bedrooms you won't be so surprised to find
that they are individual in style. You may find yourself with a four-poster
or a brass bedstead, surrounded by cottagey decoration or a more formal
floral scheme. Families usually take the separate cottage, where there's
less worry about noise. The menu is extensive and there is something to
suit most tastes.

🌓 Closed 26 Dec to 10 Jan;
restaurant closed Sun eve

🏍 1 mile from the South Petherton
beginning of the A303 Ilminster
bypass; follow signs for 'Ilminster
local services' and Seavington St
Michael. Private car park

🛏 2 single, 3 twin, 4 double, 1
four-poster, 2 family rooms; all
with bathroom/WC, TV, hair-
dryer, trouser press; limited room
service

◈ Restaurant, bar, lounge;
conference facilities (max 20

people non-residential, 10
residential); fishing, golf, other
sports nearby. Wheelchair access
to hotel (1 step), restaurant and
WC, 5 ground-floor bedrooms

🚫 No dogs

💳 Access, Amex, Diners, Visa

💷 Single from £50, single
occupancy of twin/double £50,
twin/double/four-poster £70,
family room £105; 10% service
charge added to bills. Sun L £9
and £11; alc L £12.50, D
£17.50. Special breaks available

---

*Warning to insomniacs, exercise freaks and late-night lovers: increasing
numbers of hotels have infra-red triggered security lamps. To save being
embarrassingly illuminated, check before you leave for your late-night or
pre-dawn stroll.*

**SEDBUSK NORTH YORKSHIRE** **MAP 3**

# Stone House

SEDBUSK, NR HAWES, WENSLEYDALE, NORTH YORKSHIRE DL8 3PT
TEL: WENSLEYDALE (0969) 667571  FAX: (0969) 667720

*A cosy rural retreat with friendly, attentive hosts.*

The reception area of Stone House Hotel is crowded with armchairs, sofas and piles of books and magazines. And a motto above the door reads: 'The cares of tomorrow must wait while today is done.' It would be difficult not to find your stay here relaxing. Set in an English country garden, surrounded by sheep farms, and overlooking the foothills of the Pennines, this Yorkshire-stone 'gentleman's residence' was built in 1908 and was home for a while to Jeeves of P G Wodehouse fame. Jeeves worked as a gardener and played in the local Hawes cricket team, and it was as a cricketer that Wodehouse spotted him and borrowed the name for his soon-to-be-famous butler.

The oak-panelled guests' sitting-room with roaring log fire is ideal for curling up with a book, and there's a games room with three-quarters-sized snooker table, board-games and children's books. One reader reports visiting the hotel between Christmas and New Year: 'As we arrived the proprietors were, literally, picking up the last streamers hurled by the Xmas guests who had just left. Nevertheless our welcome was warm and spontaneous. Log fires burned in the bar and sitting-room, the place was immaculate and looked beautiful, and our bedroom most comfortable. Nothing was overlooked for our pleasure and quiet entertainment. An American couple longed for a signed copy of *James Herriot's Yorkshire*. At the beginning of dinner they asked how this might be done, since most Hawes shops were closed till January. By the time they had finished their meal our host had gone off in his car, found a signed copy of the book in question, and delivered it to their table. Their joy and amazement was worth a photograph.'

Bedrooms are simple but comfortable, some with four-posters; those on the ground floor have their own individual sun lounges. The restaurant, with its collections of all kinds of things from toy cars to bobbins, is the venue for unfussy traditional Yorkshire meals.

- ◗ *Closed Jan, open weekends only Dec and Feb*
- ⬈ *Take Muker Road from Hawes, at T-junction, turn right (signposted Askrigg); hotel is 500 yards on left. Private car park*
- ⇤ *2 single, 5 twin, 6 double, 2 four-poster; most with bathroom/WC, some with shower/WC; TV, baby-listening in all rooms*
- ✧ *Dining-room, bar, lounge, games room, drying room, library; conference facilities (max 28 people, residential); tennis at hotel, fishing nearby. Wheelchair access to hotel (2 steps) and restaurant, 4 ground-floor bedrooms*
- ⊜ *No smoking in dining-room*
- ▭ *Access, Visa*

*Single £27, single occupancy of twin/double £29 to £39, twin/double £43 to £54, four-poster*

*£65; deposit required. Set D £14. Special breaks available*

## SEVENOAKS KENT                                              MAP 10

# Royal Oak

UPPER HIGH STREET, SEVENOAKS, KENT TN13 1HY
TEL: SEVENOAKS (0732) 451109   FAX: (0732) 740187

*A boldly and appealingly designed town hotel, popular with business people.*

Sister to the Whipper-In in Oakham (see entry), the Royal Oak has just undergone a thorough refurbishment. The seventeenth-century brick, stone and slate-roofed hotel stands on a main road on the edge of town; the new buildings off the gravel car park at the back and lack of a garden might be offputting, but the strength of the hotel lies in the design within. Each bedroom has its own strong colour scheme, whether an agglomeration of plain colours or stripes, on walls, upholstery, bedspreads and curtains. Popular rooms at the top of the main building have sloping ceilings and diamond-shaped windows, perhaps matched by a bed with corona and drapes. Bathrooms are equally striking, with chequerboard vinyl floors and bright wallpaper.

The dining-room, in three intimate sections, harbours a feast of dashing upholstery and high-backed chairs. A wall at the far end displays a mural of Knole House, a National Trust property yards down the road. Good-value table d'hôte menus complement a charcoal grill on the à la carte. Alternatively, you could select something from the sophisticated bar food in the more informal adjacent wine-bar.

○ Open all year

⊠ In the old town. Private car park

⇌ 7 single, 11 twin, 20 double, 1 four-poster; all with bathroom/WC, exc 2 singles with shower/WC; TV, room service, hairdryer, trouser press, baby-listening in all rooms

◈ 2 restaurants, bar, lounge, drying room, conservatory; conference facilities (max 40 people non-residential and residential);

tennis at hotel, golf, other sports nearby. Wheelchair access to restaurant only

● No dogs in public rooms

▭ Access, Amex, Diners, Visa

£ Single £65, single occupancy of twin/double £75, twin/double/four-poster £80; deposit required. Set L £13.50, D £16.50; alc L, D £25. Special breaks available

---

*Report forms are at the back of the book; write a letter if you prefer.*

**SHAFTESBURY** DORSET                              **MAP 9**

# The Grosvenor

THE COMMONS, SHAFTESBURY, DORSET SP7 8JA
TEL: SHAFTESBURY (0747) 52282   FAX: (0747) 54755

*Efficiently run, town-centre hotel with a few points of interest and decent bedrooms.*

A few unusual features lift this town-centre hotel above the usual. The modernised coaching-inn formula is as unexciting as elsewhere: workable, with comfort taking precedence over natural old-world character and practicality counting more than beauty. A small room off the entrance hall is filled with tourist bumph rather than a reception desk and the usual smiling Forte staff. The set-up of two-part bar is predictable enough but the courtyard, filled with cast-iron furniture and plants, is really lovely.

Up a flight you get to the very large and long first-floor lounge with flowery sofas, matching swagged curtains at tall windows, fresh flowers and a corporate hotel's taste in art, not to mention the hotel's most distinguished asset: the Chevy Chase sideboard. This mammoth and heavily carved piece depicting the ballad of *Chevy Chase* in exacting detail is Victoriana at its best (or worst, depending on your taste). The previous landlord picked it up at auction in 1919 for £140. That's about what two people will spend in 1992 to stay the night in a superior double.

◑ *Open all year*

⤴ *In the centre of Shaftesbury – follow signs for town centre. Limited on-street parking*

🛏 *10 single, 15 twin, 10 double, 2 four-poster, 4 family rooms; all with bathroom/WC, exc 1 single with shower/WC; TV, room service, baby-listening in all rooms; hair-dryer, trouser press in four-poster rooms*

◈ *Restaurant, bar, lounge; conference facilities (max 150 people non-residential); riding, swimming-pool nearby*

⊖ *No wheelchair access; no dogs in public rooms*

▭ *Access, Amex, Diners, Visa*

£ *Single £55, twin/double/family room £130; deposit required. Cooked B £8; L £10, D £14.50. Special breaks available*

---

*If you are intending to make a lot of phone calls from your room, always check what the hotel is going to charge you per unit. You may be so horrified that you'll prefer to walk to the nearest phone box. Why let them get away with excessive charges?*

**SHENINGTON** OXFORDSHIRE                                      **MAP 6**

# Sugarswell Farm

SHENINGTON, BANBURY, OXFORDSHIRE OX15 6HW
TEL: TYSOE (029 588) 512

*A guesthouse notable for the care and concern shown by the owner
towards her guests.*

Rosemary Nunnely puts both her culinary prowess and love of antiques
to good use at Sugarswell, a 350-acre dairy farm approached along a
bumpy clay road lined in spring with drifts of daffodils. It's a comfortable
modern farmhouse but made of traditional stone; inside it's a pleasant
place benefiting greatly from the eye for quality of its owner. A hint to her
passion is found in the Sotheby's catalogues poking from among the
other magazines beside the blazing log fire, and more overtly in the
portraits lining the stairs, the Chippendale chairs in the dining-room, the
porcelain figures that grace occasional tables and other booty gleaned
from doing the rounds of the county's auction-houses.

   Rosemary's culinary expertise makes an early appearance: dinner is at
6.30pm and it's well worth ensuring that you've a healthy appetite as her
food is imaginative and excellently prepared and presented. The bedrooms while perhaps lacking the flair of the rest of the house are
attractively furnished, freshly decorated and all have *en suite* bathrooms
with extras such as foam bath and moisturiser.

| | |
|---|---|
| ◑ Open all year | ◈ Dining-room, lounge; conference facilities (max 15 people non-residential, 6 residential); fishing, riding nearby |
| ↗ From Banbury take the A422 Stratford-upon-Avon road. After 8 miles turn off left to Shenington and drive through the village. At the T-junction turn right, and right again at the crossroads. The farm is ¼ mile along this road. Private car park | ⬤ No wheelchair access; no children under 16; no dogs; no smoking |
| | ▭ None accepted |
| ⇔ 2 twin, 1 double; all with bathroom/WC, room service; TV on request | £ Single occupancy of twin/double £25 to £30, twin/double £38 to £46; deposit required. Set L (by arrangement) £9, D £16 (6.30pm) |

---

*The text of entries is based on unsolicited reports sent in by readers and
backed up by inspections. The factual details under the text are from
questionnaires the* Guide *sends to all hotels that feature in the book.*

**SHEPTON MALLET** SOMERSET                                    **MAP 8**

# Bowlish House Restaurant

WELLS ROAD, SHEPTON MALLET, SOMERSET BA4 5JD
TEL: SHEPTON MALLET (0749) 342022

*A characterful, good-humoured and easy-going restaurant-with-rooms on the edge of town.*

Bowlish House, on the outskirts of this ancient wool market town, has a foreboding Palladian façade with pedimented windows and a double door. You might still feel under-dressed inside the grand, flagstone-floored hall, but the grinning, casually garbed figure of Bob Morley soon deflates all worries.

Public rooms are high-ceilinged and often panelled, and the mostly Victorian furnishings are homely. The little bar with its squat, armless cerise-upholstered chairs, etchings and gas coal fire is even cosy. Across the hall, a larger sitting-room lets you spread out and get really comfy. Linda Morley cooks ('we couldn't afford anyone else') and her menus let you choose from around five choices at each of the three stages. Examples include courgette and green pepper soup, lamb's kidneys with sherry and mustard in puff pastry, and crème brûlée with fresh fruit. The wine list is long and tantalising. The dining-room is stately and hung with fine Victorian and pre-Victorian portraits; a pretty conservatory, 'the jungle', is all plants and bamboo furniture. Beyond it, a walled-in lawn is set with chairs in fair weather.

Upstairs are the four double bedrooms, also high-ceilinged and with painted panelling. They're characterful, with a happy assortment of antiques and old furniture. One has a sagging floor and a wide bathroom with entrances at either end. 'No supplement for single occupancy' is an amusing way of telling single guests they must pay full whack (but presumably they are only offered one breakfast).

◑ Open all year, exc between Xmas and New Year

↗ In Bowlish on the A371 Wells road, on the outskirts of Shepton Mallet. Private car park

🛏 I twin, 2 double; all with bathroom/WC, TV, hair-dryer

◈ Dining-room, bar, lounge, conservatory; conference facilities (max 25 people non-residential); fishing, golf, other sports nearby

⊖ No wheelchair access; no dogs in public rooms; limited smoking in restaurant

▭ Access, Visa

£ Single occupancy of twin/double £48, twin/double £48. Cooked B £3.50; set D £19.50 (prices till Easter 92)

# The Old Rectory

STRATFORD ROAD, SHERBOURNE, NR WARWICK, WARWICKSHIRE
CV35 8AB
TEL: BARFORD (0926) 624562

*Just off the M40, a relaxed friendly house convenient for Stratford and Warwick.*

Although this Georgian house lies next to a busy road, it's an informal, welcoming place to stay. The house is large and rambling and has a big walled garden with old outbuildings converted in 1991 into new bedrooms.

The house is liberally scattered with antiques (Martin and Sheila Greenwood are keen collectors), including fine iron and brass bedsteads. The living-room has an appealing smell of woodsmoke even when the fires are out. There are big chintzy sofas, and, if you would like a drink, you can help yourself from the honesty bar concealed in a wood-panelled cupboard. The breakfast room is equally attractive: with a large central oak table and display of china. There is nothing precious about the house and children are welcome. One of the bedrooms, with its own external entrance, is convenient for disabled visitors, as are the ground-floor rooms in the outbuildings. Bedrooms in the house mostly have their own facilities and are cheerfully colour co-ordinated.

○ Open all year, exc 24, 25, 26 Dec

⊅ On the A46, 3 miles south-west of Warwick. The hotel is at the junction of the A46 (heading towards Stratford) and Vicarage Lane. Private car park

⇚ 2 single, 3 twin, 7 double, 2 family rooms; most with bathroom/WC, some with shower/WC; TV in all rooms; hair-dryer on request

◇ Breakfast room, bar/lounge, drying room; conference facilities (max 10 people residential and non-residential); golf, tennis, other sports nearby. Wheelchair access to hotel and dining-room, 6 ground-floor bedrooms

⊖ No dogs or smoking in public rooms

▭ Access, Visa

£ Single £30, single occupancy of twin/double £30 to £38, twin/double £39 to £47, family room £50 to £65; deposit required

---

*The* Guide *is totally independent, accepts no free hospitality, and survives on the number of copies sold each year.*

**SHERIFF HUTTON** NORTH YORKSHIRE                    **MAP 4**

# Rangers House

SHERIFF HUTTON PARK, SHERIFF HUTTON, NORTH YORKSHIRE YO6 1RH
TEL: SHERIFF HUTTON (034 77) 397

*A very special place that is difficult to pigeonhole. A hotel without the formalities.*

As the name suggests, there is a connection between the house and hunting. It was built in 1639 as a brewhouse and stable for the royal hunting lodge. The park surrounding the house is peaceful and quiet; the gardens are fairly limited and enclosed by trees and the next door farm buildings. Guests are offered tea on arrival and shown to one of the six bedrooms. Each one is different, furnished with an interesting assortment of furniture and other original pieces; some have their own bathrooms; otherwise it's a short walk down the passage.

Downstairs, the sitting-room, known as 'the main hall', is where Laurence Sterne is said to have thrown the manuscript of *Tristram Shandy* in the fire in a fit of self-doubt, although he did retrieve it. A collection of eight ninepins can be found in here alongside a stag's head and lots of literature and maps giving information about the village's history. The dining-room has polished antique tables and chairs and silver toast racks at breakfast. Dorianne Butler runs the place with an informality that makes all visitors relax. Breakfast is when you want it. If it rains you can stay in all day. There is a drinks licence but guests may bring their own wine if they prefer – and there's no corkage charge.

- Open all year
- The house is just south of Sheriff Hutton on the road to York. A private drive leads to the house from the road. Private car park
- 1 single, 1 twin, 3 double, 1 family room; most with bathroom/WC, some with shower/WC; room service, hairdryer in all rooms
- Dining-room, 2 lounges, conservatory; golf, riding nearby; babysitting
- No wheelchair access; no dogs
- None accepted
- Single £32, single occupancy of twin/double £48, twin/double £60 to £64, family room £100; deposit required. Set D £18. Special breaks available

---

*Hotels in our* Visitors' Book *towards the end of the* Guide *are additional hotels that may be worth a visit. Reports on these hotels are welcome.*

# Shipdham Place

CHURCH CLOSE, SHIPDHAM, THETFORD, NORFOLK IP25 7LX
TEL: DEREHAM (0362) 820303

*Relaxed and homely country house and restaurant. Pleasantly quirky.*

On the outskirts of an unmemorable village and at the end of a short drive is where you'll find Tina and Alan Poultons' taupe-coloured house which is part seventeenth-century, part nineteenth-century, with a Georgian façade. The inside, spacious bright rooms and attractive panelled walls (in one case split bamboo), is a similar hybrid of periods. Quirky furnishings look as if they came together more by chance than design, and pictures look to have been chosen more for their ability to cover walls than for artistic merit. No matter. You should have no problem settling into this informal home, which, despite calling itself a country restaurant with rooms, turns over lots of space to residents.

There's a morning room (which gets no morning sun) as well as a very handsome pine-panelled lounge (with sun and open fire). Set three-course dinners, with a choice at each stage, incorporate good ingredients. Clam and samphire salad, saddle of lamb stuffed with herbs, and home-made ice-cream, are possible choices in summer.

You will find assorted furnishings in bedrooms and lots of character; two have four-posters. In the nineteenth-century part you'll have space and large sash windows. If you like it more intimate, ask for a seventeenth-century room. Cotton sheets and duvets are standard. Every bathroom has a cast-iron bath and a few also have marble-topped basins. A nearby airforce base is responsible for the occasional noise overhead and faint morning traffic can also be heard.

◑ Open all year

⤒ Midway between East Dereham and Watton, on the A1075. Opposite the church in Shipdham. Private car park

⇌ 2 twin, 3 double, 2 four-poster, 1 family room; all with bathroom/WC, TV, room service; no tea/coffee-making facilities in rooms

⬦ 2 restaurants, bar, 3 lounges, TV room; conference facilities (max 25 people non-residential, 8

residential); golf, tennis, other sports nearby

⊖ No wheelchair access; no dogs in public rooms; no smoking in restaurant

▭ Access, Visa

£ Single occupancy of twin/double £32 to £66, twin/double £45 to £85, four-poster £85, family room £95; deposit required. Set L £11.50, D £19 (prices till Easter 92). Special breaks available

SHIPHAM SOMERSET                                    MAP 8

# Daneswood House

CUCK HILL, SHIPHAM, NR WINSCOMBE, SOMERSET BS25 1RD
TEL: WINSCOMBE (0934 84) 3145/3945   FAX: (0934 84) 3824

*Extremely comfortable, family-run country hotel with adventurous furnishings and super-equipped bedrooms.*

A switchback drive rises dramatically from the country road to this substantial Edwardian house. A superb expanse of green valley and the Bristol Sound spread below; you can see Wales on a clear day. The house has many original features such as fancy ceiling mouldings and dark wood; period furniture and elaborately draped and bold furnishings look just right.

A spacious and comfortable lounge with a long bar and tall padded stools manages an Edwardian country house gentility. Here the affable David Hodges will serve you drinks and nibbles, pass round the dinner menu and wine list, and ask how your day went. The deep colours of the dark blue and tan dining-room make it a dramatic setting for the varied, accomplished and often adventurous cooking. Franglais with nouvelle presentation but English-sized helpings is the rule, though themes – Italian, for instance – make an occasional appearance.

Large windows and comfortable window seats are a feature in bedrooms, especially pleasant in front rooms where you can admire the view while you sip your tea. A prodigal use of striking, even daring, fabrics, good space, an excellent variety of modern and antique furniture and every hotel room goodie you've ever encountered (including satellite TV) confirm the impression that the Hodges are out to please. The three two-storey luxury suites in the new wing have masses of space and whirlpool baths, but their sitting-rooms are a bit clinical. Breakfasts, in the brightly furnished conservatory, offer plenty of choice. Several satisfied guests have written in on photocopied report forms provided in room folders. Very nice too, but we do prefer reports to be unsolicited.

🄯 Open all year, restaurant closed Sun eve

🔼 South of Bristol, 1½ miles off A38 towards Cheddar. Private car park

🛏 3 twin, 6 double, 3 suites; most with bathroom/WC, some with shower/WC; TV, room service, hair-dryer, trouser press, baby-listening in all rooms

◈ 3 restaurants, bar, lounge, conservatory, drying facilities; conference facilities (max 20 people non-residential); fishing, golf, other sports nearby. Wheelchair access to hotel (1 step), restaurant and WC (unisex), 3 ground-floor bedrooms

⊖ No dogs

 Access, Amex, Diners, Visa

 Single occupancy of twin/double £60, twin/double £80, suite £70 to £94; deposit required. Set L £17; alc L, D £32. Special breaks available

# Innsacre Country Restaurant

SHIPTON GORGE, BRIDPORT, DORSET DT6 4LJ
TEL: BRIDPORT (0308) 56137

*A friendly country restaurant with fairly plain rooms.*

There's been a change of ownership at Innsacre: Sydney and Leslie
Davies are new to hotelkeeping and have come fresh from hairdressing
in Winchester. They've kept the same kitchen team, though, so the food
is as good as ever.

Innsacre is tucked just off the busy A35 yet is still out of sight and
earshot behind a steep fold of hillside in a sheltered combe. The building
is a long low farmhouse with numerous additions and a few curious goats
scampering around outside. The entrance leads straight into a cosy
beamed bar with a welcoming log fire in an inglenook fireplace on chill
days and clusters of dark-wood chairs round tables. Curtained off to one
side is the restaurant with stone walls, ladderback chairs and good-sized
tables. There's a four-course dinner menu (if you're an oyster fan, try the
local Abbotsbury oysters – really thick and fleshy) that might include
venison in a rich bacon, shallots and cream sauce or rabbit served with
two sauces. Sydney Davies has moved away from the dessert trolley ('I
distrust them – you get left choosing the desserts that no one else
wanted') to plated puddings such as hot blueberry pancakes, or raspberry
and almond tartlet. Service is very friendly, except that everyone has a
tendency to disappear to the kitchen and reappear at the same time.
Sydney, however, makes sure he circulates and talks to all his guests.

The bedrooms are quite plain with heavy wooden furniture and light
walls. There are some nice welcoming touches – a dish of sweets, fresh
fruit and home-made biscuits (though they'd be better kept in a tin than
wrapped in clingfilm). The bathrooms, too, are plain, but expect to see
some upgrading here.

**◑** *Open all year*

**⤵** *2 miles east of Bridport. Just
south of the A35 Bridport to
Dorchester road, take the
turning signposted Shipton Gorge
and Burton Bradstock. Private
car park*

**🛏** *1 twin, 5 double, 2 family rooms;
all with bathroom/WC, TV, room
service, hair-dryer, baby-
listening; mini-bar available*

**◈** *Restaurant, bar, lounge, drying
room; conference facilities (max*
*20 people non-residential); golf,
riding, other sports nearby;
babysitting. Wheelchair access to
restaurant only*

**⊖** *No dogs in public rooms;
smoking in bar only*

**▭** *Access, Visa*

**£** *Single occupancy of twin/double
£45, twin/double £66, family
room £99; deposit required. Set
L £12.50, D £18.50 and £22.50;
light lunches from £2.50. Special
breaks available*

**SHIPTON-UNDER-WYCHWOOD** OXFORDSHIRE    **MAP 6**

# Shaven Crown

SHIPTON-UNDER-WYCHWOOD, OXFORDSHIRE OX7 6BA
TEL: SHIPTON-UNDER-WYCHWOOD (0993) 830330

*Once a fourteenth-century hospice to Bruern Abbey, now a characterful family-run hotel handy for Cotswold attractions.*

The pride of the Shaven Crown (a reference to the bald pates of the monks who once ate and drank here) is the fourteenth-century hall hung with eighteenth- and nineteenth-century tapestries and with the original double-collar braced wood ceiling in truly superb condition. You'll be relieved to know that the ladders that once led up out of the hall to the bedrooms have been replaced with more easily climbed staircases. Upstairs, all the rooms are simply and attractively furnished and the windowsills of highly polished elm set in thick walls are almost wide enough to serve as window seats. Number seven has an original fireplace (venerably old) while number eleven is the converted chapel and the largest room in the hotel.

The A361 from Banbury to Swindon is busy and the traffic does rumble past, but Mr Brookes assures guests that it's much quieter at night. The Brookes family run the Shaven Crown with generous doses of hearty bonhomie and all hands on deck. You can eat either in the small restaurant where the lovely, hefty elm tables are features in themselves, or on the other side of the pretty courtyard in the bar. Either way the food is plentiful and reasonably priced.

◖ Open all year

⤴ Four miles north of Burford on the A361, opposite the church and village green. Private car park

🛏 1 single, 2 twin, 4 double, 1 four-poster, 1 family room; most with bathroom/WC, some with shower/WC; TV in all rooms

◈ Restaurant, bar, lounge; bowls at hotel, golf, fishing, other sports nearby

⊖ No wheelchair access; no children under 5 in restaurant; no dogs

▭ Access, Visa

£ Single £31, single occupancy of twin/double £51.50, twin/double £67 to £69, four-poster £79, family room £116; deposit required (prices till Mar 92). Special breaks available

*If you have a small appetite, or just aren't feeling hungry, check if you can be given a reduction if you don't want the full menu.*

# Shrewley House

HOCKLEY ROAD, SHREWLEY, NR WARWICK, WARWICKSHIRE CV35 7AT
TEL: CLAVERDON (092 684) 2549

*Convenient for Stratford and the NEC, this is a relaxing, good-value guesthouse in an immaculately kept farmhouse.*

The Greens' immaculate Georgian farmhouse is a warm comfortable base for anyone who wants to explore this pretty area of Warwickshire. The welcome is genuine and the quality of the accommodation is high. As well as the three spacious rooms in the house, the Greens have converted the barn into self-catering cottages (which are let on a B&B basis when the rooms in the house are full). In either you'll have a comfortable stay.

In the house there are pine furnishings, pretty flowery fabrics and attractive bathrooms. Elizabeth Green makes many of the bedspreads and curtains herself. Each room has a tray of sherry, beer, nuts and fruit juices as well as tea and coffee. Sam's room (a four-poster room), has an adjoining room with two single beds which is ideal for a family, and there's a small collection of children's books for a bedtime story. The lounge is pale green with a lovely uninterrupted view of green fields from the large bay window. The dining-room is fresh and pretty with stripped wood floor and blue and white china on lace tablecloths. The two-storey cottage conversions each have two bedrooms and a sitting-room with kitchenette. They all open out on to the gravelled courtyard overlooking the well-kept gardens.

○ Open all year

🔁 5 miles north-west of Warwick on the B4439, which runs between the A41 Warwick road and the A34 Stratford road. Private car park

🛏 3 twin, 5 double, 1 four-poster, 1 family suite with four-poster (some rooms in cottages); all with bathroom/WC, TV, room service, hair-dryer, mini-bar; baby-listening on request

◈ Dining-room, lounge; drying facilities; conference facilities (max 10 people residential); croquet at hotel, other sports nearby; babysitting

⊖ No wheelchair access; no dogs in public rooms

▭ Access, Visa

£ Single occupancy of twin/double £25 to £35, twin/double £35 to £40, four-poster £45, cottage room £30 to £40, family room £45 to £65

---

*If you make a booking using a credit card, and you find after cancelling that the full amount has been charged to your card, raise the matter with your credit card company. They will ask the hotelier to confirm whether the room was re-let, and to justify the charge made.*

**SHREWSBURY** SHROPSHIRE                                         **MAP 6**

# Sandford House

ST JULIAN'S FRIARS, SHREWSBURY, SHROPSHIRE SY1 1XL
TEL: SHREWSBURY (0743) 343829

*A well-priced and well-placed bed and breakfast in an elegant
Grade-II-listed town house.*

Just off the main high street, Sandford House makes a good base for
exploring Shrewsbury. Look closer at some of the windows and you'll
realise they are *trompe-l'oeil*. The lively proprietors, Joan and Roy Jones,
had one elderly lady guest staying who remembered the place from when
it was a family house and had been proposed to in the breakfast room.
Other less romantic rumours suggest that, in the last century, it was once
a house for fallen women.

The present day reveals it as a cheerful (and very respectable) bed and
breakfast establishment with ordinary but relaxing bedrooms reached by
a circling staircase well. 'Guests are allowed to slide down the banisters,
if they wish,' assures Joan. Paddy the cat slinks around the pink lounge,
which has an ornate ceiling, a piano and fat sofa strewn with frilly
cushions. The breakfast room is very unusual. With cool blue walls,
delicate white-iced mouldings and lacy tablecloths set with willow-
pattern china, the impression is of sitting inside a Wedgwood vase. The
garden is a bonus for guests and in good weather is very popular.

◑ Open all year, exc Xmas and
New Year

↗ Cross over English Bridge
towards town centre; St Julian's
Friars is first on left. Private car
park

🛏 2 single, 3 twin, 4 double, 1
family room; 1 with bathroom/
WC, some with shower/WC, 2
public bathrooms; TV, room
service, hair-dryer in all rooms

◇ Dining-room, lounge, conference

facilities (max 10 people
residential); tennis, riding, other
sports nearby

⊖ No wheelchair access; no dogs in
public rooms

▭ None accepted

£ Single £19 to £25, single
occupancy of twin/double £23 to
£28, twin/double £33 to £38,
family room from £43; deposit
required (prices till Apr 92)

*The Guide office can quickly spot when a hotelier is encouraging customers
to write a recommending inclusion — and sadly, several hotels have been
doing this in 1991. Such reports do not further an hotel's cause.*

# The Greenway

SHURDINGTON, CHELTENHAM, GLOUCESTERSHIRE GL51 5UG
TEL: CHELTENHAM (0242) 862352    FAX: (0242) 862780

*Stylish, rather formal country-house hotel with pretty gardens in an area short of hotels of this calibre.*

'Greenway' once meant grove road or sheep road, and is the name of the pre-Roman path leading to an early burial site in the hills behind the hotel. The gardens around the hotel are quite green, too, with tall hedges in which arches have been clipped, a rose garden, and views of the sloping ridge and furrow pasture behind. Statues of cuddling cherubs and a pretty water garden complete the picture.

Inside, the public rooms are smart and formal, with large stone fireplaces, lots of antiques and fresh flowers, and chintzy print curtains surrounding mullioned windows. Unfortunately, the large bookshelves on the landing filled with interesting volumes are locked, for private use only. It's a shame, for details like this make the difference between country house and hotel. Bedrooms come in various shapes and sizes. Those on the first floor of the main house have plenty of space and large bathrooms; those on the second floor are cosier, with sloping beamed ceilings and smaller windows. The rooms in the former coach-house still retain parts of the old stall divisions, brick arches and unplastered walls.

Dinner is a formal affair, with men obliged to wear jackets after 7pm. The menu combines inspirations from various sources, with such dishes as braised goose with rosemary served with green lentils and shallots, and poached scallops and prawns in a butter pastry case with a coriander sauce. There's at least one vegetarian option at each course. The wine list majors on clarets.

○ Open all year, exc 25 Dec to 6 Jan; restaurant closed Sat lunch

⤤ 2½ miles south of Cheltenham town centre, off the A46. Private car park

🛏 2 single, 8 twin, 8 double; all with bathroom/WC, TV, room service, hair-dryer; no tea/coffee-making facilities in rooms

◇ Restaurant, bar, lounge; conference facilities (max 20 people residential); croquet at hotel, other sports nearby. Wheelchair access to hotel (ramp), restaurant and WC (M,F), 3 ground-floor bedrooms

● No children under 7; no dogs

▭ Access, Amex, Diners, Visa

£ Single £95, single occupancy of twin/double £105, twin/double from £130; deposit required. Set L £18, D £31. Special breaks available

---

*Dog lovers: some hotels not only welcome dogs, but they provide gourmet meals for them. Ask.*

**SIMONSBATH** SOMERSET                                          **MAP 8**

# Simonsbath House

SIMONSBATH, EXMOOR, SOMERSET TA24 7SH
TEL: EXFORD (064 383) 259

*A well-run and interesting hotel in the greenest part of Exmoor.*

Narrow lanes through forest bring you to this two-storey whitewashed
and weatherboarded house which looks like the hunting lodge it once
was. A six-page history traces Simonsbath House from its beginnings in
1654, when it was built by James Boevey (first owner of Exmoor), to
1985, when present owners, Sue and Mike Burns, took it over. The low-
ceilinged, side-by-side sitting- and dining-rooms should be illuminating
enough; there are plenty of reminders of long and not so long ago:
massive studded front door, heavy beams, family crests over log-burning
fireplaces and oak panelling. It's not gloomy thanks to warm colours,
generous flower arrangements and the Burns' cheerful natures.

There are old, comfy settees and Knole sofas in the burnt-orange
carpeted lounge. A combined library and bar at the far end is a clubby
room with lots of books and a coat of arms above the Edwardian fireplace.
You can dress for dinner and not feel out of place in the more designer-
conscious dining-room where tables are set with bone china and crystal.
Four-course, traditionally English menus change daily and give a small
choice.

Antique furniture and comfortable beds characterise the bedrooms
that lie off a creaky, bookshelf-lined corridor. Three have chintz-draped
four-posters but cost no more. Fine views take in the River Barle and a
beech forest. Exmoor Forest has wild red deer and game birds and is
good touring and walking country.

◑ *Closed Dec, Jan*

↗ *In Simonsbath village, on the
B3223. Private car park*

🛏 *3 twin, 1 double, 3 four-poster, 3
cottages; all with bathroom/WC,
TV, room service, hair-dryer; tea/
coffee-making facilities on
request*

◈ *Dining-room, bar, lounge, library,
drying room; fishing, riding nearby*

➖ *No wheelchair access; no
children under 10; no dogs; no
smoking in dining-room*

▭ *Access, Amex, Diners, Visa*

£ *Single occupancy of twin/double
£45 to £55, twin/double/four-
poster £80; cottage price on
request. Alc D £20. Special
breaks available*

---

*All entries in the* Guide *are rewritten every year, not least because standards
fluctuate. Don't trust an out-of-date* Guide.

# Singleton Lodge

LODGE LANE, SINGLETON, NR BLACKPOOL, LANCASHIRE FY6 8LT
TEL: POULTON-LE-FYLDE (0253) 883854

*A restful hotel tucked inside a noble manor house.*

Arriving via a cattle grid and a field of munching sheep, it's hard to believe that the bustle of Blackpool's Golden Mile is only fifteen minutes' drive away. Once upon a time this elegant eighteenth-century house served as Singleton's vicarage. Set amid five acres of parkland and garden, it must have been a much sought-after living. These days the interior remains rather grand although the décor is restrained with comfortable but rather commonplace furniture winning out over antiques. Knick-knacks and dried-flower arrangements add soul to the bright and comfortable lounge and bar.

Bedrooms are either cottagey with lots of pine, cane and wicker and cheery floral-print fabrics, or rather more formal Victorian. Up-to-date bathrooms have pretty wallpaper. Recently revamped four-course dinner menus provide choice throughout. A June menu included quails' eggs with smoked salmon, and seasonal salad and herb vinaigrette, home-made soup or sorbet, chicken breast stuffed with asparagus, herbs, garlic and mushrooms, and home-baked lemon and raspberry sponge.

○ Open all year, exc 25 to 27 Dec; restaurant closed Sun and Mon eves

⤢ Leave the M55 at Junction 3 and take the A585 Fleetwood road. Continue on this road for 4 miles to a set of traffic lights. Turn left, then left into Lodge Lane. The house is the third entrance on the left. Private car park

🛏 3 twin, 5 double, 1 four-poster, 1 family room; all with bathroom/WC, TV, hair-dryer, baby-listening

◈ Dining-room (air-conditioned), bar, lounge; golf, fishing, other sports nearby. Wheelchair access to restaurant and WC only

● No dogs in public rooms

▭ Access, Visa

£ Single occupancy of twin/double £43, twin/double £60, four-poster £60, family room £70. Sun L £8.50; alc D £20 (prices till Mar 92). Special breaks available

---

*If you have a small appetite, or just aren't feeling hungry, check if you can be given a reduction if you don't want the full menu.*

# Swynford Paddocks

SIX MILE BOTTOM, NEWMARKET, CAMBRIDGESHIRE CB8 0UE
TEL: SIX MILE BOTTOM (063 870) 234   FAX: (063 870) 283

*As sleek and graceful as a racehorse, with good breeding, spacious grounds and plenty of comforts.*

You don't have to love horses to appreciate this lovely 200-year-old mansion, though they are very much in evidence. Newmarket racing studs of flat lawns, neat white fences, tidy tracks and lean and shiny horses constitute the setting. If you're unmoved by Lord Byron or uninterested in his affair with Augusta, his half-sister, who once lived at Swynford, never mind. Conference and business use and company ownership notwithstanding, it oozes class and sophistication.

A reception desk in the hall matches the mellow oak doors and grand staircase that rises to a gallery. Uniformed staff tend to your every need. Lined with photographs of winners from the next door stud, and with tall, fancy drapes, window seats and a grand piano, the drawing-room is an elegant and genteel setting for afternoon tea and a study of the racing form. Three-course lunch and dinner menus are good value with several choices. There is even some ingenuity – for instance Stilton fritters with garlic yoghurt or seafood in creamy Benedictine sauce. Prices for rooms are lower when there's no racing. Standard doubles, though comfortable and well-stocked, are nothing to write home about. Superiors are far superior, with excellent bathrooms, lots of space and corner positions. The honeymoon suite has an Elizabethan-style four-poster and a split-level bathroom with Jacuzzi, twin basins, bidet and palm trees. Worth every hard-won penny.

- ○ Open all year, exc Xmas and New Year

- ⚡ On the A1304 between Cambridge and Newmarket. Private car park

- 🛏 3 single, 3 twin, 7 double, 2 four-poster; all with bathroom/ WC, TV, room service, hair-dryer, trouser press, mini-bar, baby-listening

- ◇ Restaurant, lounge/bar; conference facilities (max 25 people non-residential, 15 residential); tennis, croquet at hotel; babysitting

- ⊖ No wheelchair access; no dogs in public rooms; no smoking in restaurant

- ▭ Access, Amex, Diners, Visa

- £ Single £67, single occupancy of twin/double £82, twin/double £103, four-poster £123. Set L £14.50, D £20; alc L £25, D £28 (prices till Mar 92). Special breaks available

**SLAIDBURN** LANCASHIRE                                                  **MAP 4**

# Hark to Bounty Inn

TOWNEND, SLAIDBURN, CLITHEROE, LANCASHIRE BB7 3EP
TEL: SLAIDBURN (020 06) 246

*Cheerful, good-value accommodation in an historic inn.*

Once upon a time, when this old inn was known as the Dog, the local
squire broke off a day's fox hunting for a small libation with his friends.
Outside, the fox hounds, anxious to be on their way, set up a chorus of
wailing, above which could be heard the distinctive howl of the squire's
favourite dog. 'Hark to Bounty,' he said, and the name stuck. But,
whatever its name, this ancient inn has paid a curious dual role, and
upstairs you'll find a vast, vaulted courtroom, complete with dock and
judge's bench; the Upper Hodder Valley justices sat in judgment here as
recently as 1937.

It's a long stone building and most of the ground floor is given over to a
traditional beamed bar, with an open fire, off-kilter walls and lots of brass
and copperware. The connecting restaurant is decorated in a similar
vein. A recent menu, with lots of choice at each stage, included garlic
mushrooms, grilled Bowland trout with fresh lime sauce and lemon and
ginger crunch. The revamped residents' lounge is comfortable and
welcoming, having cheerful soft furnishings. The oak-beamed bedrooms echo the period flavour of the bar and have cottagey furnishings
with pastel colours and frilly touches. Room eight, in the eaves, and room
two have the most character. They're also especially large.

◐ *Open all year; restaurant closed*          ↗ *In Slaidburn village. Private car*
  *Mon eves in winter*                              *park*

-Hark to Bounty Inn-

1 single, 4 twin, 2 double, 1 family room; all with bathroom/WC, exc single with shower/WC; TV in all rooms

 Dining-room, bar, lounge, drying facilities; conference facilities (max 30 people non-residential, 8 residential); fishing, other sports nearby

No wheelchair access; no dogs in public rooms

Access, Amex, Diners, Visa

Single £20, single occupancy of twin/double £24, twin/double £40 to £44. Set D £14; bar snacks. Special breaks available

# Parrock Head Hotel

WOODHOUSE LANE, SLAIDBURN, NR CLITHEROE, LANCASHIRE BB7 3AH
TEL: SLAIDBURN (020 06) 614

*A modernised seventeenth-century farmhouse in a beautiful, remote location.*

The Forest of Bowland, a scenic corner of Lancashire tucked between the Lake District and the Yorkshire Dales, gets fewer visitors than it deserves. Many of those who make their way to Richard and Vicky Umbers' 'long' farmhouse turn into regulars, seduced by Slaidburn's position on a green and undulating plateau and by the fine cooking.

The décor is generally rustic with exposed stone walls, pine furniture and an open-plan pine staircase. There's a hint of sophistication in the upstairs lounge (converted from the hay-loft), with its antique tables, old family portrait and Act of Parliament clock. The seating is, somehow, less comfortable than it looks. The lounge shares fine views with the library, a place for books, magazines and information on local tourist sights. You can look through the narrow, railed opening through which the farmer tossed hay to his cattle in the milking parlour. This is now a smart but unstuffy beamed restaurant. The à la carte dinners are adventurous with a *nouvelle* slant. The menu changes daily, with an emphasis on fresh local produce, seasoned with herbs from the Parrock Head garden. One May menu offered hot mushrooms in a white wine and garlic cream, goujons of veal set on a red capsicum sauce, and chocolate salami on a melba sauce. The garden annexe bedrooms are cheaper, chintzier and have more modern bathrooms than the farmhouse ones. All are immaculately kept, comfortable and decorated in cheerful colour schemes.

Open all year, exc Xmas week

1 mile north-west of village. Private car park

4 twin, 5 double; all with bathroom/WC, TV, room service, hair-dryer, baby-listening

Restaurant, bar, 2 lounges; conference facilities (max 20 people non-residential, 9 residential); fishing nearby.

Wheelchair access to hotel and restaurant, 5 ground-floor bedrooms

No dogs

Access, Amex, Visa

Single occupancy of twin/double £36 to £38; twin/double £53 to £59; deposit required. Set L £11; alc D £19 (prices till Mar 92). Special breaks available

# The Bell

BELL LANE, SMARDEN, KENT TN27 8PN
TEL: SMARDEN (0233 77) 283

*A typical characterful old Kentish pub in rural countryside, with a
d-i-y breakfast.*

The Bell incorporates all the ingredients of a pleasant pub. The building
displays all local architectural styles: tile hanging, white clapboarding,
grey and red brick. Even the garden makes the most of Kentish
surroundings as picnic tables nestle among orchard trees. Inside, three
large bars in an L-shape happily offer much of what you might expect:
flagstone floors, panelling, beams (some decorated with dried hops),
inglenook fireplaces, brasses, copper pans and agricultural implements
on the walls, and seats fashioned from beer barrels. The pub's popular
with many different types: from the local gentry splitting a bottle of wine
and having a bite to eat, to local lads playing pool and fruit machines. Part
of the bar is reserved for families with children, and there's even a no-
smoking section. Good, sustaining food and drink best describes what
appears from behind the bar: Harvey's and Theakston's ales, elderflower
wine, and home-made soups and pâtés, steaks, pizzas, salads.

To reach the bedrooms, you need to go outside, and up a wrought-
iron fire escape; the bedrooms are simple and attractive. Three are small,
the fourth bigger with a large well-stocked bookcase. All face a road of
B-type proportions, so light sleepers may be aware of some traffic noise.
Continental breakfast in your room is a d-i-y job: help yourself to bread,
butter and jam portions and milk from the fridge in the corridor.

- ◑ *Open all year, exc 25 Dec*
- ⤣ *In the village of Smarden off the
  B2077 between Charing and
  Biddenden. Private car park*
- 🛏 *3 twin, 1 double; 2 public shower
  rooms; all with TV*
- ◈ *3 bars, games room; fishing, golf,*

- *other sports nearby*
- ⊝ *No wheelchair access; no
  smoking in 1 bar*
- ▭ *Access, Visa*
- ⊡ *Single occupancy of twin/double
  £18, twin/double £30; deposit
  required. Alc L, D £10*

---

*The food was simply awful – dinner especially – veg. so soggy a new-born
babe could have tackled them with ease and treacle tart as chewy as the sole of
a shoe.* On an hotel in Cornwall

**SOMERTON** SOMERSET                                    **MAP 9**

# The Lynch

4 BEHIND BERRY, SOMERTON, SOMERSET TA11 7PD
TEL: SOMERTON (0458) 72316   FAX: (0458) 74370

*Serene, carefully furnished Georgian house; a relaxing base for
this pretty and untrampled part of Somerset.*

This is a gorgeous and little-known patch of Somerset, and Somerton is
well placed for sights and walking. The off-white Grade-II-listed
Georgian house has ample, well-tended gardens and a lake complete
with black swans. Ray Copeland hasn't stinted on doing it up, recognis-
ing that the elegant framework of tall windows and moulded ceilings calls
for solid antiques and choice furnishings. That he used to be in textiles is
easy to believe.

Victorian rather than Georgian furniture is the rule, though if the
entrance is anything to go by (enormous dried-flower sprays on pedestals, ducks up the wall and Wedgwood on the sideboard), the rules aren't
rigid. Colours are warm; soft patterns restful. The drawing-room has an
inviting open fire. Low-slung chairs and settee are more comfortable
than they look but knowing guests will head for the deep, tapestry-
covered sofa, both soft and beautiful. In the dining-room you sit on
balloon-backed Victorian chairs and look out to the lake through floor-
to-ceiling windows. Alas, you'll enjoy the view in the mornings only, as
the Lynch is now a bed and breakfast venture. If that deters you, the
prices, which have dropped slightly, should entice.

Most bedrooms, named after villages, are large as are the good beds.
Excellent bathrooms have attractive old-style fittings.

- ◐ Open all year
- ⤢ On the north edge of Somerton, ¼ mile off the B3151 Yeovil to Street road. Private car park
- ⇌ 2 twin, 2 double, 2 four-poster, 2 cottages; all with bathroom/WC, exc 1 four-poster with shower/WC; TV, room service, hair-dryer, trouser press in all rooms
- ◇ Breakfast room, lounge; conference facilities (max 20 people non-residential, 6 residential)
- ⊖ No wheelchair access; no dogs in public rooms; smoking discouraged
- ▭ Access, Visa
- £ Single occupancy of twin/double £30, twin/double £55, four-poster £75; deposit preferred

*See the back of the* Guide *for an index of hotels listed.*

**SOURTON** DEVON                                    **MAP 8**

# Collaven Manor Hotel

SOURTON, NR OKEHAMPTON, DEVON EX20 4HH
TEL: BRIDESTOWE (083 786) 522   FAX: (083 786) 570

*A perfect base for Dartmoor and, with its comfort and centuries-old character, not half bad for hanging around in, either.*

The Buckleys are welcoming hosts and their fifteenth-century stone manor, abundantly clad in thick creeper and set in five acres of grounds, should fit the bill, whether you've come to hike on Dartmoor or just to hibernate. Smooth lawns, with a rockery, orderly flowering borders and a croquet lawn, blend into moorland. It is more a home than an hotel, despite having two restaurants.

The furnishing of the rural interior of low, beamed ceilings, stone fireplaces and white walls has been handled in an urbane manner. Chunky velveteen sofas blend well with the moss green in the Chinese carpet in the sitting-room, and antique and high-quality reproduction furniture meld well. Old china plates fill up spaces over mantels and door-frames here as in the Inglenook, the more countrified and informal of the two restaurants. The other, the Hamilton, serves a 'Gourmet Menu' which rather pompously calls nibbles a 'complimentary gesture from our chefs to commence your meal' but fulfils expectations with the likes of snails in a pastry tartlet, and chicken breast filled with sweet pepper, onion and cheese.

Woven and fringed bedspreads and dainty curtains fit the country style of bedrooms, most of which have copious honey-coloured beams, sloping ceilings and knotty pine doors. The furniture is both antique and reproduction. 'Absolutely superb. Welcome and attention were both warm but never intrusive. Food was magnificent, room splendid, comfortable and beautifully equipped. I will go back again.' Such are the waxings lyrical from a reader who points out one possible cause for annoyance: there are no locks on doors either to secure your belongings or yourself.

🌓 Closed 2 weeks Dec/Jan

🅿 On the A386 Tavistock to Okehampton road, 10 miles north of Tavistock, 4 miles south-west of Okehampton. Private car park

🛏 2 single, 3 twin, 3 double, 1 four-poster; most with bathroom/WC, some with shower/WC; TV, room service (limited), hair-dryer, baby-listening in all rooms

♦ 2 restaurants, bar, lounge; conference facilities (max 12

people non-residential); croquet, pitch and putt at hotel, other sports nearby

🚫 No wheelchair access; no children under 7 at dinner; no dogs; no smoking in restaurant

💳 Access, Visa

💷 Single £52, single occupancy of twin/double £67, twin/double £79 to £85, four-poster £95. Set L from £10, D from £15.50 (prices till Apr 92). Special breaks available

**SOUTHEND-ON-SEA** ESSEX                    **MAP 10**

# Mayflower Hotel

6 ROYAL TERRACE, SOUTHEND-ON-SEA, ESSEX SS1 1DY
TEL: SOUTHEND-ON-SEA (0702) 340489

*Simple and basic but also quiet, friendly and handy for the centre and the seafront.*

Frills are few, ditto facilities, and furnishings are reminiscent of a fifties seaside hotel. If that doesn't bother you, you should be well pleased with the Mayflower. Not far from the High Street, Royal Terrace is a picturesque cul-de-sac overlooking tree-filled public gardens and the estuary. The only Georgian terrace in Essex, claims Mrs Powell, and a fetching one at that; its lacy Regency balconies and columns are a delight.

For external displays, the Mayflower, comprising two houses, wins hands down. The inside is less beautiful. The lounge is also a pool room. A few chairs, old-fashioned TV, piles of magazines and a drinks machine hardly give a home-from-home look. You won't find much space to sit in bedrooms, either, but they're neither pokey nor dowdy. Candlewick bedspreads and old furniture give them the stamp of a traditional B&B. Several look out to the longest pier in the world; a couple have balconies and most are bright. Only a few have attached bathrooms and that's the way it will stay to preserve the character of the house. Mrs Powell and her son are happy, welcoming hosts, an important asset for their many guests. Breakfast only is served.

- Closed for 2 weeks at Xmas
- Head along the seafront towards the pier. At the roundabout turn up pier hill. On-street metered car parking
- 5 single, 18 twin/double; some with shower/WC; TV in all rooms; tea/coffee-making facilities in some rooms; hair-dryer on request
- Dining-room, lounge; golf, tennis, other sports nearby
- No wheelchair access; no children under 3
- None accepted
- Single from £19, single occupancy of twin/double £19 to £30, twin/double £30 to £40. Special breaks available

---

*Shame on you South Yorkshire, Tyne & Wear and Mid Glamorgan, the only counties without an hotel of merit in this year's* Guide.

**SOUTH MOLTON** DEVON

# Whitechapel Manor

SOUTH MOLTON, DEVON EX36 3EG
TEL: SOUTH MOLTON (0769) 573377  FAX: (0769) 573797

*A beautifully restored old house run by charming hosts.*

Since its total restoration and conversion, Whitechapel Manor has been upgraded to a Grade-I-listed house. The grey-stone manor house was originally built in 1575; the magnificent Jacobean oak screen that separates the entrance hall from the sitting-room was obviously added later and is a great feature. The panelling and the pictures date from Queen Anne, and William and Mary.

John Shapland carries your bags up to your room when you arrive. Until six years ago he was farming on the family farm nearby but fell in love with the house even though it needed an enormous amount doing to it. John and Patricia have carefully chosen each piece or picture to suit the period. A huge fireplace in the sitting-room is a perfect setting for two Knole sofas, a couple of antique side-tables and an attractive desk. Large baskets of dried flowers and pale patterned carpets are restful and stylish.

Dinner is expensive but very good, and is served in a smart, formal dining-room that is cleverly lit (mainly by candles) to give it an intimate atmosphere in the evenings. Starting with delicious canapés with your drink, dinner might include sea bass with fennel purée or a very delicate dish of halibut on a bed of spinach with a mousse of mushrooms and watercress. Back to the drawing-room for a generous cafetière of coffee and John comes and makes sure he's got the order for morning tea and a newspaper. The service from the owners and all their staff is faultless: friendly, efficient and courteous – very refreshing.

The bedrooms have been done with the same diligence and taste as the rest of the house, having smartly co-ordinated and well-fitted chintzy curtains and matching quilted bedcovers as well as neat well-equipped bathrooms.

- ◑ Open all year
- ⤢ Leave the M5 at Junction 27 and follow signs to Barnstaple. At the second roundabout turn right. The hotel is a further ¾ mile down an unmarked track. Private car park
- ⇜ 2 single, 5 twin/double, 2 double, 1 four-poster suite; all with bathroom/WC, TV, room service, hair-dryer, baby-listening; no tea/coffee-making facilities in rooms
- ◈ Restaurant, bar, lounge; drying facilities; conference facilities (max 19 people); croquet at hotel, other sports nearby
- ⊖ No wheelchair access; no dogs; no smoking in restaurant
- ▭ Access, Amex, Visa
- £ Single from £60, single occupancy of twin/double from £80, twin/double from £90, four-poster suite £170; deposit required. Set L from £25.50, D from £35.50 (prices till Autumn 91). Special breaks available

**SOUTHWOLD** SUFFOLK      **MAP 7**

# The Crown

HIGH STREET, SOUTHWOLD, SUFFOLK IP18 6DP
TEL: SOUTHWOLD (0502) 722275   TELEX: 97223 ADNAMS G
FAX: (0502) 724805

*Enjoyable, well-run inn with modest but attractive accommodation.*

'Decent simple accommodation,' says the brochure. 'This is an inn, not a grand hotel,' adds a note in the room. The Crown might not aspire to the luxuries or fame of the Swan, another Adnams hostelry just up the way, but it doesn't need to be so modest. Atmosphere comes in bigger dollops than at many fancier establishments and it's warmly welcoming and comfortable.

Behind the buff-painted brick façade is a large carpeted bar with green-grained panelling, unadorned wooden tables, a carved marble and wood fireplace and settles with red-vinyl seats – an informal and usually lively setting for a pint or, given that this is Adnams, a glass of wine. Imagination and variety typify bar snacks. Two- or three-course dinners (quail with mango and apple sauce, then lamb with mint butter, say) are served in the small restaurant off the bar, the tables covered in fresh white cloths. A small back bar with brass binnacle and navigation lamps is often quiet.

Simplicity is the by-word in bedrooms but they're far from sterile, with candlewick bedspreads and nice old pine and wicker furniture. One further example of modesty is welcome: the prices.

◑ Open all year, exc 1st week in Jan

↗ In the centre of Southwold. Private car park

🛏 2 single, 4 twin, 5 double, 1 family room, all with bathroom/WC, exc 1 twin with shower/WC; TV, hair-dryer in all rooms; limited room service; trouser press on request

◈ Restaurant (air-conditioned), 2 bars, lounge; conference facilities (max 20 people non-residential, 14 residential); fishing, golf, other sports nearby; babysitting

⊖ No wheelchair access; no dogs; no smoking in restaurant

▭ Access, Amex, Visa

£ Single £33, twin/double £52, family room £77. Cooked B £3.50; set L £13, £15, D £15.50, £18 (prices till Mar 92)

---

*Congratulations to Cumbria – our number 1 county with 53 full entries in this year's Guide.*

# The Swan

MARKET PLACE, SOUTHWOLD, SUFFOLK IP18 6EG
TEL: SOUTHWOLD (0502) 722186
FAX: (0502) 724800

*Well-known traditional inn and modern hotel. A popular venue for afternoon tea and small business meetings.*

Southwold's famous landmark, a well-preened brick and white inn with lacy railed balconies and small-paned windows, takes up most of one side of Market Place. It was rebuilt in 1660 after a fire wiped out most of the town, remodelled in the early 1800s, and during the twentieth century has grown into a stylish modern hotel, now owned by Adnams Brewery.

A low-ceilinged, dark green drawing-room, comfortable and sedately furnished with deep, solid colours and occasional flowery patterns, has original carved wood over doorframes, windows and fireplaces. The dining-room is formal: tall windows are fancily draped with brightly patterned curtains, appropriate for the classically English meals. More French is the welcome practice of offering menus of graduated prices. Many people come for business meetings and afternoon tea, though one reader considered the latter to be 'daylight robbery'.

The furnishings and maintenance of bedrooms is commendable if unexciting, and provisions are as you'd expect for the price. Standard bedrooms suffer from too little room; superior rooms are worth the supplement for the fine antique furniture as well as the extra space. One reader found the welcome warm and the atmosphere friendly, but

-Swan Hotel-

wouldn't recommend one of the garden rooms – 'very small and expensive for what it was. Our sleep was rudely shattered by a brewery lorry which stopped at the back of our room at 6.30 and left its engine running for half an hour. The whole room shuddered.' Apparently the brewery has a right of way through the hotel grounds – so, queries our correspondent – why wasn't he offered one of the rooms available away from the noise?

◑ *Open all year*

▣ *Centrally situated in Southwold's market square. Private car park*

🛏 *6 single, 21 twin, 16 double, 1 four-poster suite, 5 suites (inc 18 garden rooms); most with bathroom/WC, some with shower/WC; TV, room service, hair-dryer, baby-listening in all rooms; trouser press on request; no tea/coffee-making facilities in rooms*

◈ *2 dining-rooms, bar, lounge, reading room; drying facilities; conference facilities (max 50 people residential); golf, tennis,* *other sports nearby; babysitting on request. Wheelchair access to hotel, restaurant and WC (unisex), 18 ground-floor bedrooms*

⊖ *Dogs in garden bedrooms only; no smoking in dining-room.*

▭ *Access, Amex, Visa*

£ *Single £42 to £62, single occupancy of twin/double £77 to £128, twin/double £75 to £98, four-poster £128, suite £118 to £128; deposit required. Set L £12 to £19, D £17 to £27. Special breaks available*

---

**SOWERBY** NORTH YORKSHIRE                                      **MAP 3**

# Sheppard's

FRONT STREET, SOWERBY, THIRSK YO7 1JF
TEL: THIRSK (0845) 523655   FAX: (0845) 524720

*A good choice of accommodation and food in a friendly family-run business near the North York Moors.*

It's a true family concern. Sons Mark, Simon and Paul man the front-of-house, kitchen and bar, daughter Rachel helps out and Grandma cooks the apple pies and chocolate fudge pudding for the restaurant. Over fifteen years Roy and Olga Sheppard have expanded their business from the confines of the creeper-covered old farmhouse (where they still offer good-value B&B), across the courtyard to a converted stable block and granary which houses a restaurant and brasserie with bedrooms above.

The interior designer of the household is Olga who tours Yorkshire to find her chunky pine furniture. Her aim is clear: 'It's not a place that should be tarted up – we've tried to keep the country atmosphere.' With this in mind, she's kept the original stable manger in the restaurant, nailed horse-brasses on the beams and strung dried flowers from the ceiling of the flagstoned brasserie. The newest bedrooms were opened at the end of 1990. One of the nicest is 'the fat bedroom' (so-called because of its corpulent double bed), with its plumped cushions, elephant book-ends and a fine china display in the corner.

Guests can choose between the à la carte restaurant, offering choices such as supreme of salmon and rack of lamb, or the much cheaper brasserie with courses scribbled on the blackboard in the corner. Vegetarians are advised to declare themselves when they book. One reader described the food on both nights of his stay as 'outstanding' although he reports that he was alarmed by a prominent notice stating 'breakfast 8.30am: Saturday and Sunday 9.00am' saying: 'I made my point by coming down at 9.20.'

| | | |
|---|---|---|
| ◑ | Open all year | ⊖ No wheelchair access; no children under 10; no dogs; some bedrooms non-smoking |
| ↗ | ½ mile from Thirsk Market Square, take Sowerby Road from Castle Gate, Thirsk. Private car park | ▭ Access, Visa |
| ⊨ | 1 twin, 6 double, 1 four-poster; all with bathroom/WC, TV, room service, hair-dryer | £ Farmhouse: twin/double £40 to £50; elsewhere: twin/double £55 to £65, four-poster £75, single occupancy of twin/double from £40; deposit required. Sun L £10.50; alc D £16 (brasserie), £26 (restaurant). Special breaks |
| ◈ | 3 restaurants, bar, lounge, garden room; fishing, golf, other sports nearby | |

**SPREYTON** DEVON                                                    **MAP 8**

# Downhayes                                    ℒ

SPREYTON, CREDITON, DEVON EX17 5AR
TEL: BOW (0363) 82378

*Small country farmhouse in the heart of Devon with good-value accommodation and welcoming atmosphere.*

Stay with Tom and Prue Hines and you don't have to travel far to reach many of Devon's best gardens and National Trust houses as well as Dartmoor. This friendly and cheerful Wolsey Lodge, a cream-coloured, part-sixteenth-century Devon longhouse, on a narrow lane in unspoilt countryside, is made more picturesque by its vine-covered verandah and trim scree garden. There are several farm buildings nearby, one of which has been converted into games rooms with darts, table tennis and rowing machines.

The Hines no longer farm; their priority is their guests. The stairs, lined with hunting scenes, lead to two of the three bedrooms. They are immaculately kept and nicely furnished with pine and cane furniture and bright fabrics. Radios and books are provided, and the sweeping views from all three bedrooms are out of this world. One twin has a white woven bedspread, brass bed and good-quality pink carpet. The Hines share its bathroom. The downstairs twin is *en suite* and has doors to the garden. In the coral-coloured, beamed dining-room guests dine at two handsome elm tables. Apple and celery soup, roast lamb marinated in soya, ginger and sherry, and pear in fudge sauce, perhaps, and whatever wine you choose to bring.

◑ Open all year, exc 20 to 29 Dec

↗ Leave the A30 Exeter to Okehampton road at Whiddon Down ('Merrymeet' roundabout), 16 miles west of Exeter. Follow signs to Spreyton. Downhayes is on the left, 1½ miles north of Spreyton on the road to Bow. Private car park

🛏 2 twin, 1 double; 2 with bathroom/WC, 1 public bathroom

◈ Dining-room, lounge, games room; fishing, golf, other sports nearby

⊖ No wheelchair access; no children under 12; no dogs; no smoking in bedrooms

▭ Visa

⊞ Single occupancy of twin/double £27 to £32, twin/double £37 to £45; deposit required. Set L £6 (by arrangement only), D £12.50. Special breaks available

---

**STAMFORD** LINCOLNSHIRE                                    **MAP 4**

# The George of Stamford

71 ST MARTINS, STAMFORD, LINCOLNSHIRE PE9 2LB
TEL: STAMFORD (0780) 55171  TELEX: 32578 GEOSTA G
FAX: (0780) 57070

*A stylish old coaching inn, popular with business guests.*

This sixteenth-century inn is a popular place mid-week with functions and lunches attracting many guests. The bar, the Garden Lounge and the restaurant offer a variety of menus for different appetites and wallets, and the hotel has a lively air. The broad flagstoned entrance hall with a large oak chest, and an old portrait of one of the inn's larger guests (at almost 53 stone), leads past the cosy bar to the reception desk. On one side there is an open lounge with mellow exposed stone walls, a huge welcoming open fire and a mixture of inviting sofas and armchairs. Beyond, up several steps, there is another comfortable, warm bar.

The formal oak-panelled restaurant has upholstered high-backed chairs, candles and fresh flowers with dishes from a seasonal menu and roasts served off the wagon. The Garden Lounge has a central display of flourishing greenery and hanging plants, and white garden furnishings. Warm duck salad, soup and pasta are amongst the dishes on offer and it's a popular lunch stop. Bedrooms have comfortable reproduction furnishings and strong-patterned fabrics, and some overlook the lovely enclosed creeper-clad courtyard where drinks and meals are served.

◑ Open all year

↗ Exit from A1 marked Stamford; hotel is one mile from here in town centre. Private car park

🛏 12 single, 30 twin/double, 4

four-poster, 1 suite; all with bathroom/WC, exc 3 singles with shower/WC; TV, room service, hair-dryer, trouser press, baby-listening in all rooms; tea/

coffee-making facilities on
request

 2 restaurants, 2 bars, 2 lounges,
private dining-rooms, library,
conservatory; conference
facilities (max 50 people,
residential); business centre;
croquet at hotel, other sports
nearby; babysitting. Wheelchair
access to hotel, restaurant and
WC (unisex), no ground-floor
bedrooms and no lift

⬤ No dogs in public rooms

▭ Access, Amex, Diners, Visa

£ Single from £66 to £75, single
occupancy of twin/double £81 to
£92, twin/double £93 to £154,
four-poster £154, suite £118,
family room £256; deposit
required. Alc L, D £38. Special
breaks available

---

**STANTON WICK** AVON                                      **MAP 9**

# The Carpenters Arms

STANTON WICK, PENSFORD, BRISTOL BS18 4BX
TEL: COMPTON DANDO (0761) 490202   FAX: (0761) 490763

*Popular and well-run pub with modern cottagey bedrooms.*

The Carpenters Arms, off a by-road and overlooking the rolling Chew
Valley, is a low, tile-roofed inn comprising a string of seventeenth-
century mining cottages. It's inviting as soon as you spot it, and, as you'll
see by the rows of cars in the overspill car park at mealtimes, hardly
undiscovered. Thanks to good management and an efficient team who
serve up drink and large platters of home cooking at an impressive rate,
it's a first-rate pub for meals.

The cavernous bar of stone walls and heavy black beams has a log fire,
a large aquarium, copper bed-pans, padded red stools and wheelback
chairs. At one end, sturdy oak tables are used for civilised snacking and
proper meals. A dining-room with tapestry-covered chairs and crisp
linen, which takes up the other end, is pretty and comparatively quiet.
Residents shouldn't be disturbed by noise, either, once the pub has shut,
and bedrooms are reasonably sized, cheerful and decorated in a fresh
cottagey style. Modern bathrooms have full-sized baths. Three more
bedrooms are due to be finished in November 1991.

🅞 Open all year; restaurant closed
Sun eve

🔼 Turn off the A37 Wells to Bristol
road at Pensford; alternatively
turn off the A368 Bath to
Weston-super-Mare road.
Private car park

🛏 4 twin, 8 double; all with
bathroom/WC, TV, hair-dryer,
trouser press

◈ 2 restaurants, 2 bars, lounge;

conference facilities (max 20
people non-residential); fishing,
golf, tennis nearby

⬤ Wheelchair access to pub and
restaurant only; no dogs

▭ Access, Visa

£ Single occupancy of twin/double
£43, twin/double £50. Bar
meals; alc L, D £20. Special
breaks available

**STAPLEFORD** LEICESTERSHIRE                    **MAP 4**

# Stapleford Park

STAPLEFORD, NR MELTON MOWBRAY, LEICESTERSHIRE LE14 2EF
TEL: WYMONDHAM (057 284) 522   FAX: (057 284) 651

*A country-house hotel and 'sporting estate' with lots of style,
energy and a refreshingly unstuffy atmosphere.*

Before you are even out of the car, the door of the Paytons' yellow-stone
country house will open and you'll be welcomed into the wide entrance of
this Grade-I-listed building in the heart of rural Leicestershire. The
grounds are said to have been designed by Capability Brown; woods hide
a church and there is also a wonderful stable block saved from dilapida-
tion and now in use again, occasionally for the hunt meet. Bob and
Wendy Payton opened the hotel three years ago amidst some publicity.
They invited various designers in, and let them loose to create 'signature'
rooms.

Crabtree & Evelyn, Linda Cierach, David Hicks and Turnbull &
Asser are amongst those who contributed and rooms range from the
deluxe to the extraordinary. 'Crabtree & Evelyn' has walls covered in
flowering prints and a bathroom with a *trompe l'œil* of a country scene
above the bath, and a row of enormous bottles of bathtime goodies.
'Turnbull & Asser' has braces holding up pictures and shirt material
covering the walls. You may, however, prefer one of the more conventional, less expensive yet still luxurious rooms on the second floor, with
fine views over the gardens. The most refreshing thing about a stay at
Stapleford is the unstuffy atmosphere. Staff are down-to-earth and
friendly and the house has a lived-in feel to it. Beside the front door are
wellington boots to borrow and a large bowl of green apples. In the
library you can curl up in one of the deep clubby armchairs with the
papers. In the central saloon there's a *trompe l'oeil* which includes one of
the Paytons' dogs peering over the balcony though you are more likely to
find Gunther and Gus padding about downstairs with bright scarves
around their necks.

You can eat either in what were the old kitchens, a small dining-room
with high vaulted stone ceilings, or in the more elaborate carved Grinling
Gibbons dining-room. The American chefs, Rick Tramonto and Gale
Gand, produce old- and new-wave American cooking. From ham-
burgers on the 'casual' all-day menu to escalopes of veal with a wild
mushroom soufflé, couscous and a crispy sweetbread vinaigrette on the
dinner menu. Puddings stun with a choice of ice-creams and such dishes
as a frozen white chocolate soufflé with a chocolate fudge sauce or bread
and butter pudding with maple syrup.

🌓 *Open all year*

🔁 *Leave the A1 at the Colsterworth
roundabout and turn onto the
B676 towards Melton Mowbray.*

*The turn for Stapleford is 1 mile
past the village of Saxby, on the
left. Private car park*

🛏 *31 twin/double, 2 four-poster, 2*

suites; all with bathroom/WC, TV, room service, hair-dryer, trouser press, baby-listening; no tea/coffee-making facilities in rooms

Dining-room, bar, 4 lounges, library, drying room; conference facilities (max 300 people non-residential, 35 residential); fishing, tennis, riding, croquet, putting at hotel, other sports nearby. Wheelchair access to hotel (ramps), restaurant, WC

(unisex), no ground-floor bedrooms but lift

No children under 10; no smoking in dining-rooms

Access, Amex, Diners, Visa

Single occupancy of twin/double from £125, twin/double from £125, four-poster from £190, suite from £210; deposit required. Cooked B £8.50; set D £20; alc L £25, £43. Special breaks available

---

**STOKE-BY-NAYLAND** SUFFOLK　　　　　　　　　　**MAP 7**

# The Angel Inn　　

POLSTEAD ROAD, STOKE-BY-NAYLAND, NR COLCHESTER, ESSEX CO6 4SA
TEL: NAYLAND (0206) 263245

*Character and style in an old inn where you can eat well in formal or informal surroundings.*

The mostly eighteenth-century Angel has brick, stucco and weatherboard outside and heavy beams, brick walls and imposing huge fireplaces inside. Warm colours and posh country antiques lend sophistication, but, above all, it's an eating pub. If the Angel's food is popular with locals, locals might sometimes be more popular with the Angel than residents. One reader from West Sussex, having booked a room in advance, arrived to find the restaurant fully booked for dinner and a bar meal the only option; another reader who did manage to get a table remarks 'the food is worth running away from home for'. Even at lunch, the restaurant, a stylish room in the brick- and timber-walled converted barn, fills quickly. The cooking is mostly straightforward and shows off good, fresh ingredients, especially fish. Many restaurant dishes as well as excellent bar snacks are available in the brick-floored bar.

Staff are very capable and quick on their feet. A lounge with reception desk has a grandfather clock and nice old wing-back chairs around a log stove – a homely room indeed but, alas, also a through-route. Country décor carries through to bedrooms which are colourful, comfortable and nicely kept. Four look over the street; one takes in the garden. An outside cottage contains one self-contained double, similarly furnished. Bathrooms are simple.

Open all year, exc 25, 26 Dec and 1 Jan; restaurant closed Sun, Mon eves

2 miles off the A134 halfway between Colchester and Sudbury. Private car park

1 twin, 5 double; all with

bathroom/WC, TV, room service, hair-dryer

2 restaurants, 2 bars, lounge; fishing, golf, other sports nearby. Wheelchair access to restaurant only

No children under 8; no dogs

Access, Amex, Diners, Visa

Single occupancy of twin/double £41, twin/double £52. Alc L £14, D £23

---

**STOKE-ON-TRENT** STAFFORDSHIRE                        **MAP 4**

# Haydon House

HAYDON STREET, BASFORD, STOKE-ON-TRENT, STAFFORDSHIRE ST4 6JD
TEL: STOKE (0782) 711311
FAX: (0782) 717470

*An original and extremely well-run hotel with some outstanding bedrooms and very welcoming atmosphere.*

Bought as a family house during the late seventies, the Machin family turned Haydon House into an hotel in 1980. To describe it as a house is a misnomer – it has now expanded into over three houses. The bar and restaurant and other main rooms are all in the original building with a number of the bedrooms, Glebe Mews and 'No 2' as it's known, just across the road.

Its individuality strikes you as soon as you enter the reception. Beautiful clocks fill every available bit of wall space. The décor is Victorian, in keeping with the period of the building. The bar/ sitting-room which leads off the reception is on two levels. The upper part is a snug library area with books, hunting prints, other pieces of framed Victoriana and more clocks. A few steps bring you back down into the main part where wooden tables covered in lace cloths are surrounded by wheel-back chairs with little squab cushions. 'No 2' contains their new 'executive accommodation', finished in the spring of 1991: generously proportioned rooms with large windows and carefully chosen wallpapers and fabrics are casually chic. Planning has been careful and considered: hair-dryers close to mirrors, extra shaving mirrors and other thoughtful touches.

The hotel has recently started linking up with the local theatre and other cultural centres and one of their special evenings combines dinner and the theatre: you have your starter and main course at Haydon House, then go to the performance at the Victoria Theatre just down the road, and come back for pudding and coffee after the show.

Open all year, exc 1 week early Jan

Leave the M6 at Junction 16 or 15. Follow the A500 to the interchange with the A53. On the A53 head towards Newcastle-under-Lyme – the hotel is 100 yards along this road. Private car park

10 single, 5 twin, 6 double, 1 four-poster, 9 suites (some rooms in annexe); all with bathroom/WC, TV, room service, baby-listening; hair-dryer, trouser press, mini-bar in some rooms

Restaurant (air-conditioned), 2 bars, 2 lounges, conservatory; conference facilities (max 90 people non-residential, 30 residential); golf, tennis, other sports nearby

No wheelchair access; no dogs in public rooms

Access, Amex, Diners, Visa

Single £62, single occupancy of twin/double £66, twin/double £70, four-poster/suite £130. Continental B £4.50, cooked B £6; set L £14.50, D £16; alc L, D from £23

---

**STOKE UPON TERN** SHROPSHIRE         **MAP 4**

# Stoke Manor

STOKE UPON TERN, MARKET DRAYTON, SHROPSHIRE TF9 2DU
TEL: HODNET (063 084) 222

*Unusual and interesting farmhouse B&B in a quiet, rural setting.*

This is a three-bedroomed B&B with a difference. The Thomas family are fascinated by history and most of the things displayed in the house and outbuildings have been found in the 250 acres of farmland surrounding the manor. The foundations of Stoke Castle, which was destroyed in the Civil War, are being excavated and some of the finds are on show in the kitchen. If you'd like to wander around the farm, Mike has staked out a walk that takes you past the three-acre reservoir stocked with crayfish and tench.

The historical theme is continued in the bar where a few of Mike's collection of brightly painted horse-drawn farm vehicle seats are displayed to great effect on the walls. If you become interested, over a hundred more are displayed in one of the adjoining barns. On winter afternoons guests can relax in front of the open fire in the sitting-room and admire the beautiful views.

Bedrooms have lovelier views and are brightly furnished. There are plenty of thoughtful touches, like supplying blankets to guests who don't like duvets. Bathrooms are large and although one isn't *en suite*, robes are provided. Breakfast is served round the large dining-room table. Julie Thomas doesn't serve dinner but leaves folders in the room listing local pubs, several with restaurants.

Closed Dec

Between the A41 and A53 in village of Stoke upon Tern. Private car park

1 twin, 1 double, 1 family room; all with bathroom/WC, TV, hair-dryer, baby-listening

Dining-room, bar, lounge; fishing

at hotel, golf, riding nearby

No wheelchair access; no dogs; smoking in bar and lounge only

None accepted

Single occupancy of twin/double £25, twin/double £44, family room £66

**STON EASTON** SOMERSET                                      **MAP 8**

# Ston Easton Park

STON EASTON, BATH, SOMERSET BA3 4DF
TEL: CHEWTON MENDIP (0761) 241631   FAX: (0761) 21377

*Suave and classy Georgian manor. Hardly cosy but a top whack country-house experience.*

Ston Easton Park is both classic and extraordinary. The large Georgian mansion is austere but stately, the showpiece gardens and 30 acres of parkland exemplary; the comforts and elbow-room cosseting, the food and drink hard to fault, the service polished and very friendly. It doesn't look like an hotel but functions efficiently as one. Most remarkable is the purity of the décor. You won't find cost-cutting compromise or reproduction furniture, and the Smedleys (of canned food fame) continue to upgrade. You can now visit (and hire) the wonderful old basement kitchens, a near-museum of old stoves, pots and pans; and the gardens are being improved and will soon host a swimming-pool. All the antiques were brought in but look as if they belong in the grand rooms of 20-foot tall ceilings and fancy mouldings; curtains and upholstery are of the finest quality, the paintings and fires are real.

Set luncheons and dinners of many courses and several choices are expensive (feuilleté of smoked salmon, prawns and avocado with balsamic dressing; veal fillet in Parmesan crust with tomato and basil noodles; coconut cheesecake with ginger). All the furniture in the bedrooms is antique, some especially fine. It will cost you to stay in the Ludlow bedroom but how often do you sleep in a genuine Chippendale four-poster and hang your clothes in a Chippendale wardrobe? Marble bathrooms, in keeping with the rest of the house, are classy.

◐ Open all year

▨ On the A37 Bristol to Shepton Mallet road, 6 miles from Wells, 11 miles from Bath and Bristol. Private car park

🛏 13 twin/double, 6 four-poster, 2 air-conditioned cottage suites; all with bathroom/WC, TV, room service, hair-dryer; tea/coffee-making facilities, mini-bar in some rooms only; trouser press available

◇ 2 restaurants, 3 lounges, games room, library, drying room; conference facilities (max 24 people); tennis, hot-air ballooning, croquet at hotel, other sports nearby. Wheelchair access (2 steps) to public rooms only

⊖ No children under 12; no dogs in hotel (but free kennelling in grounds)

▭ Access, Amex, Diners, Visa

£ Single occupancy of twin/double £95 to £135, twin/double from £135, four-poster from £195, suite from £245. Cooked B £8, set L £24, D £35 (prices till Apr 92). Special breaks available

# Little Thakeham

MERRYWOOD LANE, STORRINGTON, WEST SUSSEX RH20 3HE
TEL: STORRINGTON (0903) 744416   FAX: (0903) 745022

*A fine Lutyens manor house with beautiful views and gardens,
unpretentiously run as a luxury hotel.*

On a small rise in the middle of rural Sussex and reached by a long drive
lined with walnut trees stands this golden stone building built by Edwin
Lutyens at the beginning of this century. 'Though it is not really a big
house, it has the air of one,' says the brochure accurately. It feels
Elizabethan, with its exposed stone walls, flagstones and floorboards,
mullioned windows, chunky fireplaces and oak doors. Yet it has been
gaily decorated in such a way as to make it feel very habitable (flowers
stencilled around the dining-room fireplace, a bowl of china fruit and a
flight of ornamental birds in the sitting-room, for example). The house
has been decorated in complementary contemporary furniture: to delight the inquisitive furniture buff, what about an upholstered chair in the
bar which could be described as a chaise-courte? The high-ceilinged
sitting-room has a minstrels' gallery and off it is the more intimate
dining-room with just nine tables covered in pink cloths.

Dinner is expensive. Southdown lamb is usually a fixture. Service can
let the meal down. The bar reveals the owners' equine passion with
photos of horses, jockeys and race cards on display. Bedrooms have oak
furniture and distinctive bathrooms with perhaps a sunken bath or one in
the middle of the room. Take a stroll in the gardens (a sea of daffodils
when we visited), through the paddock, orchard and along the stone and
wooden-trellised arbour; you'll probably meet Poppy the Jack Russell if
you haven't already.

◐ *Closed Xmas and New Year*

↗ *1½ miles north of Storrington off
the B2139, 400 yards down
Merrywood Lane. Private car
park*

🛏 *3 twin, 2 double, 2 four-poster, 2
suites; all with bathroom/WC,
TV, room service, hair-dryer,
trouser press; no tea/coffee-
making facilities in rooms*

◈ *Restaurant, bar, lounge;
conference facilities (max 14*

*people non-residential); tennis,
heated outdoor swimming-pool
at hotel, other sports nearby*

⊖ *No wheelchair access; children
by arrangement only; no dogs*

▭ *Access, Amex, Diners, Visa*

£ *Single occupancy of twin/double
£95, twin/double £150, four-
poster £150, suite £200; deposit
required. Set L £21.50, D
£32.50. Special breaks available*

**STOURBRIDGE** WEST MIDLANDS                                    **MAP 6**

# Talbot Hotel

HIGH STREET, STOURBRIDGE, WEST MIDLANDS DY8 1DW
TEL: STOURBRIDGE (0384) 394350   FAX: (0384) 371318

*This old coaching inn has charming accommodation and is
popular with locals.*

The handsome Georgian façade of the Talbot, originally an old
coaching-inn, is appealing and the position in the town centre away from
the ring-road is a convenient one. The hotel has undergone various
changes since the seventeenth century, although the structure and many
original features remain. It's a popular place for the locals with cosy,
atmospheric public rooms with beams, low lighting, and comfy chesterfields or wing armchairs.

There's a glass extension to the rear with an exit to the car park and a
coffee shop en route to the restaurant which are less relaxing places for a
drink. However, Foley's restaurant with windows draped in netting is a
cheerful room, and an à la carte menu or a set menu are on offer.

Upstairs, the bedrooms are mostly furnished in bright matching
fabrics and light pine furnishings. The honeymoon suite is special, with
dark mahogany Victorian furniture and frilly flowery fabrics. Rooms are
all spacious though bathrooms tend to be on the small side. Even so, it's
an hotel that offers comfort at reasonable rates.

◐ Open all year

⤢ Centrally located in Stourbridge's
High Street. Private car park

🛏 7 single, 18 twin/double; most
with bathroom/WC, some with
shower/WC; TV, room service,
hair-dryer, trouser press, baby-
listening in all rooms

◇ Restaurant, bar, lounge,
conservatory; conference
facilities (max 150 people non-
residential, 25 residential);

tennis, golf, other sports nearby.
Wheelchair access to restaurant
only

⊖ None

▭ Access, Amex, Visa

£ Single £56, single occupancy of
twin/double £56, twin/double
£70, four-poster £82, suite
£165; deposit required. Set L
£3.50, D £13; alc L, D £19
(prices till Sept 91). Special
breaks available

---

*The* Guide *office can quickly spot when a hotelier is encouraging customers
to write a recommending inclusion – and sadly, several hotels have been
doing this in 1991. Such reports do not further an hotel's cause.*

# Wyck Hill House

BURFORD ROAD, STOW-ON-THE-WOLD, GLOUCESTERSHIRE GL54 1HY
TEL: COTSWOLD (0451) 31936
FAX: (0451) 32243

*Comfortable manor-house hotel with good views and attractive
public rooms; bathrooms functional rather than luxurious.*

This eighteenth-century manor house, with glorious views over the
Windrush Valley, has changed hands several times over the past few
years; the latest owners have plans to develop another 15 bedrooms and
conference facilities. The large entrance hall, relatively gloomy even on a
sunny day, contains antiques and assorted chinoiserie collected by
previous Texan owners on their jaunts round the world. It's the most
interesting part of the hotel, its tapestries vying with a framed hunting-
pink for attention, and deep sofas arranged round the large fireplace.
The bar has a clubby feel, with curving leather armchairs and a large
window-seat with tapestry cushions. A conservatory extension to the
restaurant allows you to admire the views while you eat, though the
original dining-room is more intimate, with dark red wallpaper and
extravagant pelmets.

The dinner menu gives full descriptions: 'Three flavours of chicken –
oak smoked, a chilled mousse and warm collops of maize-fed breast set
around a crisp feuilleté case filled with truffled scrambled egg.' This has
been described as excellent, as have goujons of sole surrounding crab
meat with baked oyster and soufflé. Breakfast is 'above average', with
croissants 'fresh but rather doughy in the centre'. Bedrooms in the main
building are a good size and continue the country-house style, but
bathrooms look rather cheaply furnished by comparison; there are plans
to refurbish these soon. We've received comments on the 'eccentric'
lighting system and draughts in the bathroom – 'particularly notable one
night when the house was hit by a gale'. Soundproofing has also been
judged less than adequate. Rooms in the coach-house are cosier, with
lower ceilings and smaller windows adorned with both net curtains and
flounced blinds. Service is 'very pleasant and helpful'.

**◑** Open all year

**↗** Wyck Hill is on the west side of
the A424, 2 miles from Stow.
Private car park

**🛏** 1 single, 28 twin/double; all with
bathroom/WC, TV, room service,
hair-dryer, trouser press, baby-
listening

**◈** 2 restaurants (one air-
conditioned), bar, 2 lounges,
library; conference facilities (max

18 people residential); croquet
at hotel, other sports nearby;
babysitting by arrangement

**⊖** No wheelchair access; no dogs;
no smoking in restaurant

**▭** Access, Amex, Diners, Visa

**£** Single £75, single occupancy of
twin/double £75, twin/double
£95 to £170. Set L £15; alc D
£37. Special breaks available

# Caterham House

58/59 ROTHER STREET, STRATFORD-UPON-AVON, WARWICKSHIRE
CV37 6LT
TEL: STRATFORD-UPON-AVON (0789) 267309/297070

*Inexpensive, spacious guesthouse where you may rub shoulders
with theatre folk.*

'Quite splendid. Good to have showers that work, a bed that's comfortable, a cheerful host, decent breakfast and a smashing atmosphere.
We're going again.' Praise indeed, from one satisfied reader. This
attractive terracotta-orange Georgian house close to the centre of
Stratford is an ideal place for a weekend break.

Dominique and Olive Maury have created an elegant guesthouse with
a cosmopolitan feel. Rooms are light and airy with some striking hand-
printed wallpapers, flagstone and wooden floors and scattered antiques.
Each room is individually decorated. The charm of the place is increased
with the absence of trouser presses and tea- and coffee-making facilities.
Dominique sadly acknowledges that even in France tea-making facilities
are becoming universal but he thinks they're messy and is keen to serve
his guests with tea and coffee when they want it (with no extra charge).

There is a TV in the lounge which has black squashy seating, but it's a
room little used by guests. The breakfast room with the blue iris
wallpaper and the polished communal tables is more appealing. The
Maurys don't serve evening meals but there are plenty of places to eat at
nearby. There is a limited parking area to the rear and side of the house.

◑ Open all year

🔁 In the centre of Stratford,
opposite the police station.
Private car park

🛏 4 twin, 6 double, 1 family room;
two rooms with shower/WC; no
tea/coffee-making facilities in
rooms

◈ Breakfast room, lounge with TV;
babysitting

⊖ No wheelchair access; no dogs in
public rooms

▭ Access, Visa

💷 Single occupancy of twin/double
£29 to £44, twin/double £33 to
£48, family room from £45

# Victoria Spa Lodge

BISHOPTON LANE, STRATFORD-UPON-AVON, WARWICKSHIRE CV37 9QY
TEL: STRATFORD-UPON-AVON (0789) 267985

*Cheerful hosts and immaculate accommodation feature in an old
Victorian house with lots of character.*

Bill and Dreen Tozer have lived in their early Victorian House for over
ten years and they have been offering B&B for over three. It's a cheerful

home, sitting beside a humpback bridge over the canal with a tow path that leads to Stratford-upon-Avon in one direction and to Mary Arden's House in Wilmcote in the other. The Tozers' friendly welcome puts you at ease at once.

They have decorated the light long breakfast room, a room with high windows, with a collection of ornaments. On a polished sideboard are various glass decanters, on the other side a collection of Wedgwood. Polished tables are laid out for breakfast whilst at one end of the lovely wood-floored room amongst the pot plants is a red velvet buttoned sofa and chairs to lounge on in the evenings, although most guests venture out.

Bedrooms are decorated in pale colours and are light and pretty with flowery ceramic door knobs, old fireplaces and the occasional chandelier. There are lots of personal ornaments, a few fake flowers, flowery curtains and plumped up duvets. Most have their own bathrooms. Those on the second floor have sloping ceilings.

| | |
|---|---|
| ◗ Open all year | golf, tennis, other sports nearby |
| ⤴ 1½ miles north of Stratford on the A3400. Private car park | ⊖ No wheelchair access; no dogs; no smoking in public rooms |
| 🛏 3 twin, 4 double, 2 family rooms; most with shower/WC, 1 with bathroom/WC; TV in all rooms; hair-dryer, trouser press on request | ▭ Access, Visa |
| | £ Single occupancy of twin/double £33 to £38, twin/double £41 to £46; deposit required. Set pre-theatre D £15 by arrangement |
| ◈ Dining-room (air-conditioned); | |

---

# The Swan Diplomat

HIGH STREET, STREATLEY-ON-THAMES, BERKSHIRE RG8 9HR
TEL: GORING-ON-THAMES (0491) 873737    TELEX: 848259 SWANTL G
FAX: (0491) 872554

*An upmarket, well-run riverside hotel where high standards of food, comfort and facilities carry a stiffish price-tag.*

An overall air of executive sophistication permeates the Swan. 'Diplomat' is a reference to the Swedish owners who bought the hotel in 1988.

Any Victorian origins are well hidden by a mélange of additions that extend upstream from the bridge and Goring weir. The great challenge, if unescorted, is to find your room, especially in the older part of the house. The room numbering system seems to defy logic but looking out on to the river rather than the gleaming corporate motors in the car park makes obvious sense. If you don't manage to get a riverside room you can take some consolation playing with the panoply of equipment in the rooms which are all spacious and excellently designed.

The location is classical Thames: everything you'd expect, with suitably weeping willows, low-lying drifting mists and, yes, even some swans. The hotel also has use of an Edwardian saloon launch for trips up river. If you fancy water-borne entertaining remaining firmly fixed to the bank, the Magdalen College barge has been overhauled, with private parties and meetings in mind, and is moored at the garden's edge.

The public rooms make good use of the setting with river view picture windows. Service is formal and marked by effusive thanks. The food is well presented and proficiently cooked; breakfast in yet another of the interlocking rooms consists of a well-stocked buffet.

◑ *Open all year, exc 2 to 8 Jan*

↗ *From Junction 12 on the M4 take the exit to Theale, then the A340 to Pangbourne and the A329 to Streatley. The Swan Diplomat is just before the river bridge. Private car park*

🛏 *9 single, 12 twin, 23 double, 1 four-poster, 1 suite; all with bathroom/WC, TV, room service, hair-dryer, mini-bar*

◈ *Restaurant, bar, lounge, TV room, games room; conference facilities (max 90 people non-residential, 46 residential); croquet, sauna, heated swimming-pool, rowing boat hire at hotel, other sports nearby; babysitting. Wheelchair access to hotel, restaurant and WC (unisex), 16 ground-floor bedrooms, 2 specially equipped for the disabled*

⊖ *No dogs in public rooms*

▦ *Access, Amex, Diners, Visa*

£ *Single £82, single occupancy of twin/double £97, twin/double £110, four-poster £125, suite £187; deposit required. Cooked B £9; set L £18.50, D £21.50; alc L £30, D £35 (prices till April 92). Special breaks available*

---

**STRETTON** LEICESTERSHIRE                                                 **MAP 4**

# Ram Jam Inn

GREAT NORTH ROAD, STRETTON, OAKHAM, LEICESTERSHIRE LE15 7QX
TEL: STAMFORD (0780) 410776   TELEX: 342888

*Civilised pit-stop on the A1 where you can recharge your batteries. Large comfortable bedrooms.*

This old coaching-inn has been converted into an American-style eatery with rooms. It stands on the west side of the A1, but is signposted for travellers heading north or south and is a good place to stop for a bite to eat or an overnight stay.

It's creatively decorated, efficiently staffed and sparkling clean. The American motif is most apparent in the restaurant and snack bar where waitresses dressed in striped shirts, bow-ties and aprons serve up tasty grills and French fries. In the restaurant you might have something like home-made burger and salad or barbecued pork rib. The snack bar is less formal, with stools arranged around a serving hatch, but the sandwiches and coffee are very good. As you would expect, the roadside location means there is some traffic noise, but the quality of the eight bedrooms is such that you should still be comfortable. They are furnished with whitened and carved pine furniture, jazzy tartan curtains and watercolours. Ceiling mouldings and leaded windows stand as a reminder of the building's age, while the huge cork and tile bathrooms are modern.

- ◑ *Open all year, exc 25 Dec*
- ↗ *On the A1, 9 miles north of Stamford. Private car park*
- 🛏 *6 twin, 1 double, 1 family; all with bathroom/WC, TV*
- ◈ *Restaurant, bar, coffee bar; conference facilities (max 40 people non-residential, 8 residential); riding nearby. Wheelchair access to restaurant*

*and WC (M,F) only*
- ⊖ *No dogs in public rooms*
- ▭ *Access, Amex, Visa*
- £ *Single occupancy of twin/double £39, twin/double £49, family room £62; deposit required. Continental B £2, cooked B £4.50; alc L £15, D £17; bar snacks available*

## STURMINSTER NEWTON DORSET      MAP 9

# Plumber Manor

STURMINSTER NEWTON, DORSET DT10 2AF
TEL: STURMINSTER NEWTON (0258) 72507    FAX: (0258) 73370

*A restaurant-with-rooms in a large family mansion that's deep in Hardy country.*

The drive takes you over a brook, past horse pastures and paddocks and finally to the large Jacobean house. Prideaux-Brunes have lived in it since the early seventeenth-century, which makes it even more surprising that most of the public rooms are surprisingly devoid of homely touches. (The three labradors, father, son and grandfather, help somewhat.) Someone could spend more thought on decoration, too. You'll find it an easy-going home, even so, where staff and space and comfortable places to lounge encourage you to relax.

The restaurant is handsome and Brian Prideaux-Brune takes food seriously. Ingredients are good and the cooking honest and unfancy. A wide gallery hung with family portraits leads to six bedrooms which are decent-sized, furnished with antiques and hunting scenes but look dated rather than elegant. Six more, found in the converted stone barn, are larger and more successful. Four more, completed in 1990, are in 'The Courtyard'. Hardy country draws some guests, as do the tennis court, croquet lawn, shooting and hunting (stabling is free). There is also a trout stream running through the grounds. More reports, please.

- ◑ *Closed Feb*
- ↗ *2 miles south of Sturminster Newton, on the road to*

*Hazelbury Bryan. Plumber Manor is 1¼ miles from the A357. Private car park*

🛏 14 twin/double, 2 double; all with bathroom/WC, TV, hair-dryer; trouser press in some rooms

◈ Restaurant, bar, lounge; conference facilities (20 people non-residential, 16 residential); tennis, croquet at hotel, other sports nearby. Wheelchair access to hotel and restaurant, 10

ground-floor bedrooms, 2 specially equipped for the disabled

⊖ No children under 12; no dogs

▭ Access, Amex, Diners, Visa

⊞ Single occupancy of twin/double £60 to £80, twin/double £80 to £120. Set D £19 and £24. Special breaks available

---

**SUTTON** CHESHIRE                                          **MAP 4**

# Sutton Hall

---

BULLOCK'S LANE, SUTTON, MACCLESFIELD, CHESHIRE SK11 0HE
TEL: SUTTON (026 05) 3211   FAX: (026 05) 2538

*A friendly old inn in a remote location. There's an abundance of four-poster beds.*

When a hostelry boasts a history that goes back to 1093 the effect can be quite daunting, as reverence for age hijacks all other considerations. In fact, Sutton Hall, a jumble of stone buildings mostly dating from the sixteenth century, is a resolutely unstuffy and pleasant hotel. It certainly has its grand side: a long private drive, a gatehouse and several fountains.

Thick timbers divide the pub-like bar into more intimate seating areas, but despite the beams, brasses, open fire and rustic tables it manages to be less predictable than most renditions of the olde-worlde inn. An inglenook is flanked on one side by an elegant longcase clock, on the other by a reproduction suit of armour. The cane and veneer fans suspended from the high ceilings are pure Somerset Maugham. Atmospheric bedrooms are grand in scale and eschew the current mania for flowery fabrics. Instead, they rely on a restrained colour scheme and good Victorian and Edwardian furniture for their appeal. Except for the single, each has a lace-trimmed four-poster. Practitioners of the art of one-upmanship should opt for room eight; it has two four-posters.

The four-course dinner, served in an inviting dining-room, is quintessentially English: perhaps mushrooms with bacon in garlic butter, then cream of chicken and leek soup and roast venison served with a redcurrant and port sauce, with dessert or a cheeseboard to follow.

◑ Open all year

↗ Off the A523 Macclesfield to Leek road. Private car park

🛏 1 single, 8 four-poster; all with bathroom/WC, exc single with shower/WC; TV, room service, trouser press, baby-listening, hair-dryer on request

◈ 2 restaurants, bar, lounge, library; laundry/drying facilities; conference facilities (max 30 people non-residential, 10 residential); fishing, golf, other sports nearby. Wheelchair access to restaurant, WC only

⊖ No dogs in public rooms

▭ Access, Amex, Visa

£ Single £65, single occupancy of twin/double £65, four-poster

£80; deposit required. Set L from £10, D from £18

## SWAFFHAM NORFOLK

MAP 7

# Stratton House

ASH CLOSE, SWAFFHAM, NORFOLK PE37 7NH
TEL: SWAFFHAM (0760) 23845    FAX: (0760) 23845

*A very happy, personally run hotel providing a warming, romantic, pampering experience.*

Everything about Strattons comes as a pleasant surprise. It's close to Swaffham market but hidden in a green, almost rural oasis with wide circular drive and mature trees. The large, part-seventeenth-, part-eighteenth-century brick house with pointed gables and rounded windows is striking, and the interior is effervescently decorated in romantic country style. You're greeted with a broad smile and a 'Hello! I'm Vanessa', shown the original butler's pull should she or Les be out of earshot at any time, and given a tour.

The two-part Villa lounge is set with fat-cushioned sofas upon which sit cat-shaped cushions and probably one of the two real cats. China cats smile out at you too, from the mantel over the coal fire, from the pine dresser and window ledges. There are masses of dried flowers, Victorian furniture, flowery prints, lace at the windows, plus toys and books. The bedrooms, too, are filled with antiques, good fabrics and pretty detail such as lace and ribbons, and interesting pictures. All are fair-sized, have nice views and are quiet. Good lighting and comfortable beds are standard, as are televisions, telephones and tea trays. Modern but old-fashioned style bathrooms match perfectly. The Louis room, once the nanny's quarters, has a Louis XV walnut bed covered in white lace and cotton, and overlooks the rose trellis. If you take the Venetian room, with splendid walnut Renaissance bed and red chesterfield, you're offered a celebration package with bubbly and flowers. Breakfast, lunch and dinner take place in the basement 'Rustic'. Vanessa's good, freshly cooked English meals come in generous helpings, especially her fine breakfasts. 'No portion control here', as one reader puts it. 'That's what I call breakfast, one that will stick by me until dinner.' Dinner is three courses but can be adjusted to two if you prefer. Vanessa and Les might join you for coffee.

◑ Open all year

↗ At north end of market place, behind shop fronts. The entrance to Ash Close is between estate agents William Brown and

Express Cleaners. Private car park

🛏 2 single, 1 twin, 3 double, 1 family room; some with bathroom/WC, some with shower/WC; TV, room service,

hair-dryer, baby-listening in all rooms

✧ Restaurant, bar, drawing-room, TV room, drying room, conference facilities (max 7 people residential, 40 non-residential); golf, fishing, other sports nearby; babysitting

⊖ No wheelchair access; no dogs in public areas; no smoking in restaurant or bedrooms

▭ Access, Amex, Visa

£ Single from £45, single occupancy of twin/double from £46, twin/double from £60, family room £68; deposit required. Set D £16.50 (prices till Jan 92). Special breaks available

---

## SWINHOPE LINCOLNSHIRE                    MAP 4

# Hoe Hill

SWINHOPE, NR BINBROOK, LINCOLNSHIRE LN3 6HX
TEL: BINBROOK (047 283) 206   Changes to (0472) 398206 in Autumn/Winter 91

*Good food at a welcoming B&B.*

When you look into Erica Curd's elegant sitting-room with its sofa, polished tables and small bar, you can't quite imagine a cooking demonstration for forty cookery enthusiasts taking place here, but it does happen. Not only that but Erica also runs an immaculate B&B and serves popular three-course evening meals.

The late-eighteenth-century farmhouse (once the warren bailiff or rabbit catcher's cottage) is on a country road near the small village of Binbrook. It has spacious rooms with light fresh décor and there is both a shower and a separate bathroom with bright cloud-papered sloping ceiling and a Paddington bear and golliwog in a cradle.

Breakfast offers lots of variety with a choice of Lincolnshire sausages or kippers or a full English breakfast, and kedgeree or a baked Lincolnshire platter at weekends. Bread is home-made, as is the marmalade, and the coffee is freshly ground. Evening meals should be ordered in advance: Erica offers a glass of sherry and wine with the meal and chocolates with your coffee.

◑ Open all year, exc owners' holidays

↗ On the B1203 Market Rasen to Grimsby road, 1 mile from Binbrook north towards Grimsby. Private car park

⇌ 2 twin, 1 family room; 2 public bathrooms; hair-dryer, trouser press, baby-listening in all rooms

✧ Dining-room, lounge, drying room; croquet at hotel, other sports nearby

⊖ No wheelchair access; no dogs; no smoking in bedrooms

▭ None accepted

£ Single occupancy of twin/double £13 to £15, twin/double £24 to £26; deposit required. Set D £10 (7 to 7.30pm, must book). Special breaks available

# Talland Bay

NR LOOE, CORNWALL PL13 2JB
TEL: POLPERRO (0503) 72667   FAX: (0503) 72940

*A country hotel with more comfort than style. Sublime sub-
tropical setting and good facilities are reasons to seek it out.*

This is an old, partly sixteenth-century Cornish manor house that has
stayed behind the times. It could be considered dated or refreshingly
immune to crass modernisation. Flock, shiny moulded or woodchip
wallpaper – you will find them all, but there is also some pleasing
attractive panelling. No one can refute that the setting, high up and
overlooking the coastal path and bay, is perfect, or that the gardens, a
beautiful mix of stately pines and sub-tropical exotica, are anything other
than wonderful.

From the chairs and umbrella-topped tables on the flagstoned terrace,
you can take it all in, sip morning coffee or take a long drink, then slip into
the swimming-pool. French windows lead from the terrace to both
sitting-rooms, one prim and formal, the other more comfortable and
traditional. The studded dining-room chairs and tired pictures do
nothing for this potentially elegant part-panelled and wood-floored
room, but set dinner menus work hard at bringing in some trendy
flavours and ingredients.

Hot-water bottles, soap powder and good toiletries are welcome extras
in pale-walled bedrooms which have dainty fabrics. Special interest
holidays such as landscape painting, bridge and yoga are on offer.

◑ *Closed Jan*

▨ *From Looe take the A387 and
turn left at hotel sign. Follow this
lane for I mile. The hotel is on
the left. Private car park*

🛏 *4 single, 11 twin, 2 double, 2
four-poster, 2 family rooms, 2
suites, 1 cottage suite; all with
bathroom/WC, TV, room service,
hair-dryer, baby-listening; trouser
press in some rooms*

◈ *Restaurant, bar, 2 lounges,
games room; conference
facilities (max 50 people non-
residential, 24 residential);
croquet, putting green, table
tennis, sauna, solarium, heated
outdoor swimming-pool (May to*

*Sept) at hotel, other sports
nearby. Wheelchair access to
hotel (2 steps) and restaurant, 2
ground-floor bedrooms, 1
specially equipped for the
disabled*

⊖ *No children under 5 in
restaurant; no dogs in public
rooms*

▭ *Access, Amex, Diners, Visa*

£ *Single £50 to £72, twin/double
£102 to £153, four-poster £115
to £172, family room £102 to
£223 (4 people), suite £102 to
£223 (rates inc dinner); deposit
required. Set L £8, D £18; alc D
£35. Special breaks available*

**TANTOBIE** CO DURHAM                                    **MAP 3**

# Oak Tree Inn

TANTOBIE, NR STANLEY, CO DURHAM DH9 9RF
TEL: STANLEY (0207) 235445

*An unusual pub in an area where there is little else to charm.*

The gutted ex-steel town of Consett and the clutter of old mining villages on the south-western fringes of Newcastle may suggest industrial decline, but there is nothing declining about the Oak Tree Inn, where a combination of French bourgeois cooking and pleasant bedrooms ensure that the rooms are often full. Sylvia, from Alsace-Lorraine, is an unlikely person to find running a northern inn and is responsible for turning this one into something rather out of the ordinary.

There is a plain, no-frills bar downstairs sure enough, but a rather magnificent Victorian dining-room upstairs, where French cooking is served. The bedrooms have tiled fireplaces and are a pleasant and comfortable surprise. Some are in an annexe in an old terraced mining cottage, and the coach-house conversion we mentioned last year has been completed. The house predates most of the industrial clutter and was once an eighteenth-century manor house. The Oak Tree makes a good alternative to staying in central Newcastle and is within easy reach of Hadrian's Wall and the Beamish Industrial Museum.

○ Open all year

🔼 The inn is 1¾ miles north-west of Stanley, and ½ mile from the A692 Gateshead to Consett road – turn off at the Pickering Nook garage. Private car park

🛏 2 single, 2 twin, 1 double, 1 four-poster, 1 suite, 1 family room (some rooms in annexe); some with bathroom/WC, some with shower/WC; TV, room service in all rooms; hair-dryer on request

✥ Restaurant, breakfast room, 2 bars, lounge, games room; conference facilities (max 20 people non-residential, 8 residential); golf, riding, other sports nearby; babysitting by arrangement. Wheelchair access to inn and 4 ground-floor bedrooms; restaurant not ground-floor but guests may dine in breakfast room

⊖ Dogs in bar only and in bedrooms by arrangement only; no smoking in some public rooms

▭ Access, Amex, Diners, Visa

£ Single £16 to £22, single occupancy of twin/double £22 to £26, twin/double £30 to £40, four-poster £44 to £50, family room £40 (3 people), suite £44 to £50; deposit required. Set D £8; alc D £15; bar meals; lunch by arrangement. Special breaks available

*Many hotels put their tariffs up in the spring. You are advised to confirm prices when you book.*

# Willington Hall

TARPORLEY, CHESHIRE CW6 0NB
TEL: KELSALL (0829) 52321   FAX: (0829) 52596

*Grand but unstuffy manor house in splendid parkland.*

This early Victorian house, a classic example of baronial style with pitched roofs, rows of chimneys and neo-classical pillars, was built with the spoils of the Peninsular War. The surrounding two thousand acres of parkland and a split-level Italianate garden add to the air of opulence. It is, however, a traditional-style hotel in the country rather than a member of the new school of designer country-house hotels, and décor is sometimes, like the prices, more guesthouse than mansion house.

Locals gather for bar snacks in public rooms which are decorated with homely velour furniture and rather less homely gold-framed family portraits. The three interlinking dining-rooms manage informality despite linen-dressed tables and candlelight. The à la carte menu is traditional English 'but very good', one reader reports; 'it's always fully booked for meals.' A typical meal might include home-made smoked mackerel pâté followed by rack of lamb with tender vegetables. Pudding or cheese rounds things off. There's also a wider-than-average range of bar snacks served at lunchtime and in the evenings. Bedrooms are large, comfortable and well furnished, with a smattering of antiques. One reader particularly recommends room one, which has windows on two sides, bright fabrics and a lace-draped bed, 'plus a lovely view when sitting on the loo'. Spick and span bathrooms are old-fashioned but spacious.

- ◐ Open all year, exc 25 Dec; dining-room closed Sun eve
- ↗ Tarporley is off the A51 mid-way between Nantwich and Chester. Private car park
- ⇔ 2 single, 5 twin, 3 double (family room available); all with bathroom/WC, TV, room service, hair-dryer
- ✧ Dining-room, 2 bars, 2 lounges, drying room; conference facilities

- (max 20 people non-residential, 9 residential); tennis at hotel, other sports nearby; babysitting
- ⊖ No wheelchair access; no dogs in public rooms
- ▭ Access, Diners, Visa
- £ Single £49, single occupancy of twin/double £68, twin/double/family room £68. Cooked B £6, continental B £4; set L £12.50; alc L, D £17 to £18; bar meals

---

*All rooms have tea/coffee-making facilities unless we mention to the contrary.*

**TAUNTON** SOMERSET                                    **MAP 8**

# Castle Hotel

CASTLE GREEN, TAUNTON, SOMERSET TA1 1NF
TEL: TAUNTON (0823) 272671   TELEX: 46488
FAX: (0823) 336066

*An historical castle, but uneven as an hotel. Comfortable and professionally run.*

The site goes back to AD 710, so they say, and the castle had a spell as a Norman fortress. Added to, burnt, rebuilt, it was finally dismantled in the late 1680s and turned into an hotel, which is how it has remained for the last three hundred years.

A couple of owners have come and gone since then, the current one being Kit Chapman and family. Modern shops and vast town car park have crept up on the grand wistaria-covered building and do little to set it off. You should still find some peace in the Norman garden, excavated and restored in the 1930s. The Castle is geared to business and overseas tourist clientele and is professionally run. The numerous public rooms vary; often they're a trifle dour, but are comfortable and decorated and equipped with relevant medieval hues and trappings plus lots of modern chintz. The Rose Room is popular for tea, drinks and after-dinner coffee. The large and fancy restaurant has a reputation for good food and is a popular place for locals on a spree. The surroundings might be too grandiose and formal for many guests, however, and dinner is long-winded and expensive.

If you stay in one of the newly refurbished bedrooms, you can expect high-quality furnishings (heavy quilted bedcovers, fat lamps and co-ordinated curtains, for instance. Others can be drab, with run-down bathrooms. Smaller rooms don't warrant the price, either.

◑ Open all year

⤢ From Taunton town centre, follow signs for the Castle. Private car park

🛏 11 single, 12 twin, 7 double, 1 four-poster, 4 suites; all with bathroom/WC, TV, room service, baby-listening; hair-dryer, trouser press, tea/coffee-making facilities on request

◇ Restaurant, 2 bars, 2 lounges, drying room; conference facilities (max 75 people non-residential,

35 residential); fishing, golf, other sports nearby; nanny service

⊖ No wheelchair access; no dogs or smoking in restaurant

▭ Access, Amex, Diners, Visa

£ Single £75, single occupancy of twin/double £110, twin/double/four-poster £125, family room £143, suite £180; deposit required. Set L £15, D £22.50; alc L, D £40 (prices till end 91). Special breaks available

# The Horn of Plenty

GULWORTHY, TAVISTOCK, DEVON PL19 8JD
TEL: TAVISTOCK (0822) 832528

*A restaurant with views in a tranquil and pretty spot. Well-arranged bedrooms are a bonus.*

This creeper-clad stone Georgian mansion, once owned by the Duke of Bedford, is set in four lovely acres on the lower slopes of Dartmoor. It looks like a typical country-house hotel but in reality is a country restaurant with detached rooms.

Dining-tables seem to cover much of its open ground floor and overflow outside beneath a vine-covered arbour. Even indoors, you're likely to have great views of the Tamar Valley, especially from the bright extension. A scalloped pine ceiling gives the impression of side-by-side railway carriages. The décor is, otherwise, unmemorable, but Royal Worcester china, linen and delicate glasses do their bit to lend class. The drawing-room, decorated in mellow tones, has a collection of old sofas and an open fire. Elaine and Ian Gatehouse, who arrived in the summer of 1990, have spruced up the décor, created a private dining-room for functions and hired a good chef. Set lunches and dinners give a limited choice but are good value. On the pricier carte you might find home-made cannelloni stuffed with artichokes, mushrooms and asparagus; loin of lamb with brioche crumb crust; and passion fruit bavarois.

The coach-house, some yards behind the house, is the location of all but one of the letting bedrooms. They are almost identical with narrow beams, white walls, pine furniture, nondescript flowery fabrics on curtains and padded headboards, small matching but bland pastel pictures, and an odd arrangement of lace and quilts over bedspreads. The wonderful views of the walled garden and hills (from balconies, in some cases) remain the best feature, and tables and chairs set by large windows are ideal for good continental breakfasts of croissants, fruit – and porridge.

- Open all year, exc 25, 26 Dec

- Take the A390 from Tavistock towards Liskeard. When 3 miles from Tavistock turn right at Gulworthy Cross. After ½ mile turn left – the hotel is 500 yards on the right. Private car park

- 7 twin/double; most with bathroom/WC, some with shower/WC; TV, room service, hair-dryer, mini-bar, baby-listening in all rooms

- Restaurant, lounge, drying-room, private dining-room; conference facilities (max 16 people non-residential, 7 residential); fishing, golf, other sports nearby. Wheelchair access to hotel, restaurant and WC (M,F), 4 ground-floor bedrooms, 2 specially equipped for the disabled

- No children under 13 (none under 5 for Sun lunch); no dogs in bedrooms; smoking discouraged in bedrooms

▭ *Access, Amex, Visa*

£ *Single occupancy of twin/double £48 to £58, twin/double £58 to £78; deposit required. Cooked B*

*£8.50; set L £17, D £22.50; alc L £25, D £30. Special breaks available*

## TEIGNMOUTH DEVON                                                    MAP 8

# Thomas Luny House

TEIGN STREET, TEIGNMOUTH, DEVON TQ14 8EG
TEL: TEIGNMOUTH (0626) 772976

*Luxurious but informal and sociable home in beautiful Georgian house with imaginatively furnished, good-value bedrooms.*

Teignmouth, one of Devon's oldest seaside resort towns, fishing and shipping centre, hasn't the dramatic setting of Torquay just down the coast, nor does it have its wall-to-wall hotels and crowds. This Wolsey Lodge, well-hidden behind a stone wall in the old quarter, was built by marine artist Thomas Luny. The very handsome white-and-black trimmed Georgian house has been refurbished and furnished to a high standard by new, young owners Alison and John Allan.

Beautiful curtains, swagged and tailed or pleated, are a feature throughout, and so are the antiques. Double doors stand open between the two halves of the sitting-room, a nicely proportioned room with log fire, family photographs, *National Geographic*s going back to 1959, and frilled chairs in stripes and neat patterns. French windows lead to a fair-sized walled garden where you can sit out and be serenaded by seagulls and ships' sirens.

Dinner, though informal, is a civilised occasion. Everyone eats together at the polished oval table and there's no choice: herby eggs, lamb with grainy mustard and tomato sauce, perhaps, then maybe lemon meringue pie. There's a short wine list. The frills are from the old school – tea and cake when you arrive, early morning tea brought to your room (with a newspaper). The four, good-sized bedrooms show a modern and inventive sense of design. They are themed and detail carries through to pictures and fabrics. The ugly warehouses between the house and harbour are being dismantled, so back rooms may once again look over the sea.

◑ *Open all year exc early Jan*

↗ *In Teignmouth follow signs for the quay, then for Teign Street. Private car park*

🛏 *2 twin, 1 double, 1 four-poster; most with bathroom/WC, double with shower/WC; TV, room service in all rooms; hair-dryer on request; no tea/coffee-making facilities in rooms*

◈ *Dining-room, 2 lounges; meetings facilities (max 4 people residential); fishing, golf, other sports nearby*

⊖ *No wheelchair access; no children under 12; no dogs; no*

smoking in dining-room

🚭 None accepted

💷 Single occupancy of twin/double
£28, twin/double/four-poster

*£55. Set D £13.50 (8pm, residents only). Special breaks available*

---

**TELFORD** SHROPSHIRE                    **MAP 6**

# Holiday Inn

ST QUENTIN GATE, TELFORD, SHROPSHIRE TF3 4EH
TEL: TELFORD (0952) 292500    TELEX: 359126 HITEL G
FAX: (0952) 291949

*A stylish business hotel which is also popular with users of the nearby racket ball centre.*

From the outside you might well wonder why we've recommended this hotel: a standard modern low-level brick-built construction on a round-about. But go inside and things should become clearer. The open-plan design is stylish and welcoming with Japanese touches to the décor that clearly find favour with the visiting Japanese businessmen. There's a small, quiet lounge area with big settees for reading the papers, and a bar where groups of businessmen cluster around small round tables. The restaurant is smart and minimalist in design, with flowers on pedestals used throughout the public rooms.

All the bedrooms are similarly modern and stylish. The standard double has two large beds and light wood and black furniture. The executive suite has a slightly different colour scheme, with amber and black furniture plus additional extras such as bathrobes. The Lady Executives are furnished in pastel beige and pinks and get an ironing-board (just in case you didn't have time to do the week's housework!). In one there's no wardrobe, just a hanging space behind a curtain. If you intend doing some work there's a study room in grey with black furniture including a full-sized working desk and a programmable telephone, or if you need to unwind there's a large spa bath. As well as attracting business users, the hotel says it is doing well at the weekends with visitors to the racket ball centre (free entrance to guests).

🌓 Open all year

↗ ½ mile south-east of Telford town centre, just off the St Quentin roundabout. Private car park

🛏 50 twin, 50 double (inc 12 executive suites); all with bathroom/WC, TV, room service, hair-dryer, trouser press, mini-bar, baby-listening; ironing facilities in some rooms or on request

◇ Restaurant, bar, lounge (all air-conditioned), children's playroom; conference facilities (max 250 people non-residential, 100 residential); sauna, steam room, swimming-pool, gym at hotel, other sports nearby. Wheelchair access to hotel, restaurant and WC, 30 ground-floor bedrooms, 2 specially equipped for the disabled

⊖ None

▢ Access, Amex, Diners, Visa

£ Single occupancy of twin/double £87, twin/double £98, suite £117; deposit required.

Continental B £8, cooked B £9; set L £11, D £16; alc L, D £20. Special breaks available

## TETBURY GLOUCESTERSHIRE

MAP 6

# Calcot Manor

TETBURY, GLOUCESTERSHIRE GL8 8YJ
TEL: TETBURY (0666) 890391  FAX: (0666) 890394

*A friendly welcome in a modernised farmhouse hotel. Popular for business conferences, it also has luxurious bedrooms.*

The original fourteenth-century farm buildings are gradually being converted into luxurious bedrooms as Calcot Manor expands. Only the crumbling tithe barn that once belonged to the monks of Kingswood Abbey vaguely retains something of the agricultural purpose for which it was built.

The current owners, the Ball family, are neither monastic nor country bumpkins: their main aim is to make people feel at home. The public rooms in the main building, in pale peaches and greens, do in fact feel like a family home, and Sheena the labrador snoozing by the open fire adds to the effect. All bedrooms are well equipped; fruit is provided on tables in the corridors. The newer rooms in the stable blocks, with their undulating mossy roofs, show a touch more imagination than the normal 'sumptuous but safe' school of interior design. For example, the Highland Room has tartan cushions and Scottish prints and curving brick pillars as well as a sunken whirlpool bath and exposed beams. One reader warns: 'Don't wear open-toed shoes to cross the gravel drive to the main house for dinner.'

Dinner is pricey but the food is good. No surprises either: the menu may be a mouthful in itself, but at least you know what you're getting, as in 'Boned quail filled with chicken livers and fresh truffle served on wild mushrooms and grapes complemented by a smooth Madeira sauce'. Alternatively, you can opt for a simpler, cheaper menu with a choice of three, four, or five courses.

● Open all year; restaurant closed to non-residents Sun

⚡ 3 miles west of Tetbury on the A4135. Private car park

🛏 11 double/twin, 4 double, 1 four-poster (some rooms in annexe); all with bathroom/WC, TV, room service, hair-dryer; no tea/coffee-making facilities in rooms

◇ Restaurant, 2 lounges, drying facilities; conference facilities (max 25 people non-residential, 18 residential); croquet, heated open air swimming-pool (May to Sept) at hotel, other sports nearby. Wheelchair access to hotel (ramp), restaurant and WC (unisex), 7 ground-floor bedrooms, 1 specially equipped for the disabled

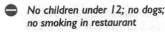

● No children under 12; no dogs;
  no smoking in restaurant

▭ Access, Amex, Diners, Visa

£ Single occupancy of twin/double
  £85 to £105, twin/double £97 to

£133, four-poster £143. Set L
£13 to £18, D £29 to £36
(prices till end 91). Special
breaks available

---

# The Close

---

8 LONG STREET, TETBURY, GLOUCESTERSHIRE GL8 8AQ
TEL: TETBURY (0666) 502272    FAX: (0666) 504401

*Comfortable town-house hotel with a lot of style and friendly
service.*

This 400-year-old, flat-fronted hotel with attractive lawns and an
elegant pond is on the main road through Tetbury, but secondary double
glazing in the front rooms means that the traffic noise isn't too noticeable. Peter Reeves has used both energy and imagination to turn this into
a very comfortable town-house hotel. Unusual additions like a corner
turret might be thought to be overdoing it at other establishments, but it
works here. The most spectacular bedroom is the Deco Room, with a
deep blue carpet, reproduction furniture and a superb original circular
mirror. Others also show imaginative touches, like painted marbled
arches; the smaller rooms with insufficient space for baths have power
showers. All are well equipped, with home-made fudge, sparkling
mineral water and miniature bottles of sherry.

Public rooms are also occasionally fanciful: the atrium in the drawing-
room is painted with clouds, while the white Adam ceilings in the two-
part dining-room are complemented with sunburst mirrors. The menu is
not extensive, with a choice of about five dishes at each stage, including
one vegetarian main course. Occasionally descriptions run wild, just like
the venison 'stalked from the valleys surrounding Exmoor', but mostly
they are a model of restraint. The Close also serves light lunches in the
small sitting-room beside the residents' bar: Gressingham duck terrine
with Cumberland sauce was pleasing, but surely light lunchers as well as
formal diners should be entitled to proper napkins rather than flimsy
paper affairs in a hotel of this calibre?

◑ Open all year, exc early Jan

↗ Situated in the main street of
  Tetbury, 10 miles from the M4
  and M5. Private car park

🛏 6 twin, 6 double, 3 four-poster;
  all with bathroom/WC, exc 2
  doubles with shower/WC; TV,
  room service, hair-dryer, trouser
  press in all rooms; baby-listening

by arrangement; no tea/coffee-
making facilities in rooms

◈ 2 dining-rooms, bar, 2 lounges;
  conference facilities (max 36
  people non-residential, 15
  residential); golf, tennis, other
  sports nearby

● No wheelchair access; no
  children under 10; no dogs; no

smoking in dining-room

▢ Access, Amex, Diners, Visa

£ Single occupancy of twin/double
£55 to £120, twin/double £75 to
£140, four-poster £140 to £155;

deposit required. Cooked B
£7.50; alc L £18.50 to £21.50,
D £29.50 to £34.50. Special
breaks available

**TEWKESBURY** GLOUCESTERSHIRE                                   **MAP 6**

# Puckrup Hall

PUCKRUP, NR TEWKESBURY, GLOUCESTERSHIRE GL20 6EL
TEL: TEWKESBURY (0684) 296200   FAX: (0684) 850788

*Elegant Regency building, occasionally over-prettified but with
comfortable rooms, in an area sadly lacking in good
accommodation.*

The first impression of Puckrup Hall (formerly Tewkesbury Hall) is of a
christening cake, thanks to the pale pink highlighting of parts of the
elegant Regency façade.

Inside, the sugared almond effect is continued in the elaborate coving,
but the rest of the décor takes the plunge into bolder colour schemes,
particularly the newly decorated restaurant in deep green and white. The
orangery is also inviting, with stencilled walls and natural light. The 16
bedrooms are named after the 12 months of the year and the four
seasons, with interior designs 'to catch the colours of the year'. Certainly
Spring and May give the impression of more colour and freshness than,
say, Winter and January. Furniture is mostly modern reproduction.
Bathrooms, too, have modern fittings and are a decent size, though don't
seem to offer much in the way of extras.

Food has been praised as 'excellent'; the daily dinner menu includes at
least one vegetarian option, such as aubergine fritters with leeks and
Somerset brie, shallot marmalade, and hazelnut salad. The cheeseboard
is mostly British, the exception being a French goats' cheese, served
toasted with salad. Service is polite and friendly.

◑ Open all year

⤢ 2 miles north of Tewkesbury on
the A38. Private car park

🛏 3 twin, 10 double, 2 four-poster,
1 family room; all with
bathroom/WC, TV, room service,
hair-dryer, trouser press; no tea/
coffee-making facilities in rooms

◈ Restaurant, bar, lounge,
conservatory; conference
facilities (max 16 people
residential, 200 non-residential);
babysitting; fishing at hotel, other
sports nearby. Wheelchair access

to restaurant and WC (unisex)
only

⊖ No children in restaurant after
7.30pm; no dogs in public rooms;
no smoking in restaurant

▢ Access, Amex, Diners, Visa

£ Single occupancy of twin/double
£78 to £83, twin/double £99 to
£110, four-poster £125 to £135,
family room £110 to £120;
deposit required. Set L £17, D
£24.50; alc L £23, D £30.
Special breaks available

# Abingworth Hall

THAKEHAM ROAD, STORRINGTON, WEST SUSSEX RH20 3EF
TEL: WEST CHILTINGTON (0798) 813636   FAX: (0798) 813914

*An unimposing Edwardian house with an attractive garden.*

Perhaps it proved difficult to know how to advertise the history of an
hotel when the first owners of the hall, built in 1910, were the Mosley
family. Shortly after the Second World War it became an hotel; in 1983
Philip and Pauline Bulman took it over. Evidenced by their newsletter,
they have successfully made the hall part of the community and host
musical evenings and wine tastings.

The black and white building with pronounced grey slate roofs stands
on the edge of the village of Thakeham separated from the main road by a
smooth lawn running down to cedar trees around an ornamental lake.
The rest of the eight acres of land includes less formal gardens, a tennis
court and pitch and putt, and a hedged-in small pool at the back. Public
rooms present a contrast of styles: a cosy, oak-panelled drawing-room
with books and wing-chairs (you may have to turf out Poppy and Footsie,
the hotel's cats, to get a seat); a 'cocktail bar' with grand piano and dainty
coffee tables, and a well-positioned conservatory overlooking the
garden; and at the rear of the building a traditional, white tableclothed
restaurant where jacket and tie are required for men.

Though claiming to be *nouvelle*, the food reflects traditional country-
house fare: bread, croissants, ice-cream and preserves are made on the
premises. Bedrooms in the main house, especially those overlooking the
front garden, are the most popular. Other bedrooms are in the later
Garden Wing, supposedly very quiet and in pleasant pastel colours, but
less stylish.

**◑** *Closed first half Jan*

**⤴** *2 miles north of Storrington on
the B2139. Private car park*

**🛏** *2 single, 4 twin, 14 double, 1
suite; all with bathroom/WC, exc
1 double with shower/WC; TV,
room service, hair-dryer in all
rooms; trouser press in some
rooms; no tea/coffee-making
facilities in rooms*

**◈** *Restaurant, bar, lounge,
conservatory; conference
facilities (max 30 people non-*

*residential, 21 residential);
fishing, tennis, heated swimming
pool (May to Sept) in grounds,
other sports nearby. Wheelchair
access to restaurant only*

**●** *No children under 10; no dogs*

**▭** *Access, Visa*

**£** *Single £64, single occupancy of
twin/double £75, twin/double
£87, suite £153; deposit
required. Set L £17, D £28; alc L
£23, D £35 (prices till Apr 92).
Special breaks available*

**THAME** OXFORDSHIRE     **MAP 6**

# Thatchers Hotel

29–30 LOWER HIGH STREET, THAME, OXFORDSHIRE OX9 2AA
TEL: THAME (084 421) 2146/3058   FAX: (084 421) 7413

*An unusual, slightly quirky hotel with a few entertaining surprises
hidden behind a conventional thatched façade.*

Oscar the parrot sits in the corner of the bar watching the jovial suited
businessmen quaff wine in the glow of the burning fire. Next door is a
four-poster bedroom with a separate room to one side containing a Californian hot-tub ringed by candles and empty champagne bottles.
Conventional Thatchers probably isn't, but stylish and comfortable and
with a real sense of personality, it most definitely is.

The restaurant, a low-ceilinged room with cream walls and brown-
painted beams, is more straightforward. The food is delicious and the
pricing of the table d'hôte menu makes allowance for those not looking
for the full repast. On the lunchtime menu the sauté of lamb with basil
and tomato proved an excellent choice: beautifully tender, light and
delicate but with a fullness of flavour in the sauce.

Thatchers is run by Terry Connor, a retired ad-man/bon viveur who
dislikes personal publicity. So, apologies for the mention, but Thatchers
is very much his creation. The single rooms are tiny with thin walls but
they have been effectively furnished. In the cottage the sloping double
lives up to its name with walls and floors seemingly all at sea. Number
seven requires a degree of agility to enter as the door is a little hatchway
halfway up the stairs. The surprise of finding a four-poster is therefore
all the greater. All-in-all Thatchers is good entertainment.

- ◐ Open all year; restaurant closed Sun eve
- ⤢ In the centre of Thame. Private car park
- ⇌ 4 single, 1 twin, 1 double, 4 four-poster; some with bathroom/WC, most with shower/WC; TV, room service, hair-dryer, baby-listening in all rooms; no tea/coffee-making facilities in rooms
- ⬦ Restaurant, bar; sauna/solarium at hotel, fishing, golf, other sports nearby; babysitting
- ⊖ No wheelchair access
- ▭ Access, Visa
- ⊞ Single £49 to £63, single occupancy of twin/double £63, twin/double £70, four-poster £75 to £85. Set L, D £9.50 to £17.50; alc L, D £25 to £30

---

*Dog lovers: some hotels not only welcome dogs, but they provide gourmet
meals for them. Ask.*

**THORNBURY** AVON  **MAP 9**

# Thornbury Castle

THORNBURY, NR BRISTOL, AVON BS12 1HH
TEL: THORNBURY (0454) 281182   FAX: (0454) 416188

*Luxurious hotel within a fine medieval castle with magnificent bedchambers which win it many American fans.*

Business people from Bristol come regularly to wallow in history over a good lunch, and Americans seek it out for its definitive old English atmosphere. The huge, grey-stone, crenellated Thornbury Castle delivers the goods: a history that goes back to 1511, a sleek walled garden complete with vineyard, a high-ceilinged interior of stone and mullioned windows, crest-emblazoned oak panelling and intricately carved Tudor fireplaces.

In the large sitting-room, convincing electric candelabras, mellow antique furniture and old portraits in oil integrate well with soft upholstered sofas and chairs. The dining-room, divided into two, manages to be cosy, elegant and medieval. No boars' heads here. Modern English cooking is on offer and the set menu allows you to take two or three courses. If the menu is effusive and lavish, the cooking is honest and talented. Service is polished but more deferential than friendly. Our main gripe is about the fake fires; if any fireplaces demanded the real thing, they're these. The fake coal fires in several bedchambers offend less. Named after famous visitors or residents, eight bedchambers are in

-Thornbury Castle-

the main castle. These are decorated in light frilly, co-ordinated fabrics
with pale carpets. The rest, across the courtyard in an annexe cleverly
constructed from old walls and stairs, are more castle-like with bays and
arched windows. It's really worth splashing out on one of the superiors,
which have masses of space befitting the ancient bulbous-legged four-
posters, and stone walls and lovely carved panelling.

◐ Open all year, exc 2 to 12 Jan

↗ Leave the M4 or M5 motorway
and take the A38 towards
Thornbury. Turn off this road on
to the B4061 and continue to the
monumental water pump. Bear
left and continue for 300 yards –
the entrance to the castle is to
the left of the parish church in
Thornbury. Private car park

🛏 2 single, 4 twin, 3 double, 8
four-poster, 1 suite; all with
bathroom/WC, TV, room service,
hair-dryer, trouser press; tea/
coffee-making facilities on
request

◈ Dining-room, 2 lounges, library;
conference facilities (max 24
people non-residential, 18
residential); croquet, archery at
hotel, other sports nearby;
laundry facilities

⊖ No wheelchair access; no
children under 12; no dogs; no
smoking in dining-room

▭ Access, Amex, Diners, Visa

£ Single £75 to £80, single
occupancy of twin/double from
£85, twin/double from £90, four-
poster from £145, suite £165 to
£190. Cooked B £7.50; set L
£18, D £29.50. Special breaks
available

---

**THORNTON CLEVELEYS** LANCASHIRE                    **MAP 4**

# The Victorian House

TRUNNAH ROAD, THORNTON CLEVELEYS, LANCASHIRE FY5 4HF
TEL: CLEVELEYS (0253) 860619   FAX: (0253) 865350

*A vigorous evocation of Victorian style in a comfortable
restaurant-with-rooms.*

Half-hearted re-creations of Victorian splendour are ten-a-penny. This
one's the real thing: a veritable temple of Victoriana on the suburban
fringes of Blackpool. On taking over in 1988 Louise and Didier Guerin
found much that was authentically Victorian and have since worked on
appositely rich colour schemes to make some rooms less gloomy, making
it easier to admire the wealth of period detail. Deep-green Paisley
pattern wallpaper covers the small lounge and bar. An abundance of
delicate furniture (some reproduction) gives the characteristic cluttered
feel, complete with ornate gilt-framed mirrors, sepia-tinted prints, fresh
and dried flowers and clusters of assorted knick-knacks on little tables.
Windows are draped with fine lace and heavy brocade, and doyleys, lace
tablecloths and antimacassars conjure up the spirit of that fastidious age.

A large restaurant in rust and green is attended by cheerful and
capable waitresses in period costume. Lavish is the best way to describe

Didier's four-course dinners: perhaps, asparagus and quail eggs encased in puff pastry with hollandaise sauce, spinach and coconut cream soup and roast loin of lamb on a rosemary cream sauce, followed by dessert. Lunches are served in a conservatory extension. The large bedrooms are less flamboyant than the public rooms, but have mellow colours, solid furniture and more heavyweight fabrics. Each has a resident doll, a copper kettle and a grand, brass-tapped bathroom. Good breakfasts include freshly squeezed orange juice.

◐ *Open all year, exc 2 weeks Feb, 2 weeks Nov; dining-room closed Sun eve*

▣ *3 miles to the north of Blackpool. Private car park*

🛏 *2 double, I four-poster; all with bathroom/WC, TV, room service, hair-dryer, trouser press*

◈ *2 dining-rooms, bar, lounge, conservatory; conference*

*facilities (max 40 people non-residential); golf, tennis, other sports nearby*

⊖ *No wheelchair access; no children under 6; no dogs in public rooms*

▭ *Access, Visa*

💷 *Single occupancy of twin/double £40, twin/double £65, four-poster £70. Set D £18; alc L £10*

---

**THORPE MARKET** NORFOLK                                    **MAP 7**

# Green Farm

NORTH WALSHAM ROAD, THORPE MARKET, NORWICH, NORFOLK
NR11 8TH
TEL: SOUTHREPPS (0263) 833602

*Not the home-like feel you might be after, but the welcome is genuine and it's fair value if you land a large room.*

The brochure's claim of 'Unusual, exciting, exquisite' is mildly outrageous. The crow-stepped flint and brick house, which stands well back from the road, is typical of the area, and the décor within is neither provocative nor very special. Simple furniture, some rather lightweight cane, is the rule, and more homely touches would not go amiss. Despite the claims, the atmosphere is unpretentious and informal, and the Lomaxes will look after you well.

The pub, done out like a country kitchen, is jolly, and meals are fair value. A barely more formal restaurant serves for set dinners. The cost of rooms fluctuates according to size. Some are too small for their four-posters, others have plenty of space for their attractive old pine, brass or half-tester beds. Antiques and flowery fabrics lift the décor and bathrooms are well equipped. Fruit, chocolate and flowers are laid on to justify prices. More reports, please.

◐ *Open all year, exc 25, 26 Dec*

▣ *Green Farm is on the A149, 4*

*miles from Cromer. From Norwich take the A140 towards*

Cromer as far as Roughton, and turn right for Thorpe Market. Private car park

🛏 1 single, 1 twin, 3 double, 2 four-poster (some rooms in annexe); all with bathroom/WC, TV, room service, baby-listening

◇ Restaurant, bar, lounge, drying room; conference facilities (max 12 people residential and non-residential); tennis, riding, other sports nearby; babysitting by

arrangement. Wheelchair access to hotel (2 steps), restaurant and WC, 2 ground-floor bedrooms

⊖ No children under 6 at dinner; smoking in bar only

▭ Access, Visa

£ Single £42 to £46, single occupancy of twin/double £42 to £46, twin/double/four-poster £80; deposit required. Set L £14, D £16.50; alc L, D £25. Special breaks available

---

## THUNDRIDGE HERTFORDSHIRE                                MAP 10

# Hanbury Manor

THUNDRIDGE, NR WARE, HERTFORDSHIRE SG12 0SD
TEL: WARE (0920) 487722   TELEX: 817515 HANMAN G
FAX: (0920) 487682/487692

*Think up a good excuse for a night of pure indulgence and head for this lavish, extensive and expensive new hotel.*

The conversion of Hanbury Manor from convent school to luxury hotel was completed only in October 1990, too late for inclusion in last year's Guide. The hotel is the first British venture for the American Rock Resorts group whose other hotels are in the Caribbean and Hawaii. Thundridge lacks the climatic appeal of these locations but Hanbury Manor does its best to make up for a rather uninspiring location in this rather bland bit of Hertfordshire.

It's an imposing red-brick building, bristling with chimneys and looking out across acres of parkland that have been sculpted into the first nine holes of a golf course designed by Jack Nicklaus II of Golden Bear Design Associates, the company run by his famous father. It is no exaggeration to say that no expense has been spared; from the tiled and marbled splendour of the health club's generous pool to the recruitment of Albert Roux to oversee culinary affairs, money has apparently not been a problem. No surprise therefore that prices are high to recoup this sort of investment.

The efforts of Mr Roux are best sampled in the Zodiac dining-room where the planetary signs are suitably featured in the ceiling moulding. The Oak Hall, with carved dragons either side of the fireplace, is the heart of the hotel and the oldest part of the building. Adjoining wings include 1934 additions and a new, sympathetic extension housing the health club.

A feature of the rooms, especially those looking out across the golf course, are the huge windows which fill the rooms with light. The extra extravagance of paying for a suite is almost worth it given the leap in size gained from a standard double. If you're going to splash out you might as well get soaked! American ownership has ensured that service is less formal but no less efficient than the smart uniforms would suggest.

◑ Open all year; 1 restaurant closed Sun eve

⚡ On the A10. Leave the M25 at Junction 25. Private car park

🛏 4 single, 47 twin, 32 double, 3 four-poster, 10 suites (some rooms in annexe); all with bathroom/WC, TV, room service, hair-dryer, trouser press, mini-bar; no tea/coffee-making facilities in rooms

◈ 3 restaurants, 2 bars, lounge, snooker room, library/study; conference facilities (max 112 people non-residential and residential); crèche; golf, tennis, sauna, solarium, heated swimming-pool, health spa, gym,

dance studio, squash at hotel, other sports nearby. Wheelchair access to hotel (2 steps), restaurant and WC, 2 ground-floor bedrooms, 1 specially equipped for the disabled

⊖ No dogs; some bedrooms non-smoking

▭ Access, Amex, Diners, Visa

£ Single from £135, single occupancy of twin/double from £145, twin/double from £145, four-poster £195, suite from £200; deposit required. Set L from £15, D from £17.50; alc L £20, D £40. Special breaks available

**TITCHWELL** NORFOLK                          **MAP 7**

# Titchwell Manor

TITCHWELL, NR BRANCASTER, KING'S LYNN, NORFOLK PE31 8BB
TEL: BRANCASTER (0485) 210221   TELEX: 32376 ANGTEL G (ref. 060)
FAX: (0778) 424461 (ref. 060)

*A birdwatchers' base and a very comfortable English hotel.*

Twitchwell might be more like it: birdwatching is a major pastime for the guests at this family-run hotel. A main road runs right in front of the solid Victorian house, but across it lies the bird reserve, the beach and the sea, visible from most public rooms and several bedrooms. A small, sheltered garden behind the hotel is well kept.

For a traditional, friendly and unpretentious place, the décor is both old-fashioned and fashionable: some things are mis-matched, others over-co-ordinated. The sitting-room, a clutter of nice old Victoriana, birdwatching magazines and books, is a fine and relaxing room. The bar is rather overly decorated in buttoned blue velveteen but is warmed by a coal fire. The curtains and carpet in the prim dining-room make a strange match; the cottagey 'pine room' extension is less formal and more cohesive, a pleasant, bright room where high teas and early suppers as well as regular dinners are served. Buttoned and padded headboards, chairs, dainty fabrics and fringed lampshades are typical of bedrooms. Four rooms in the quiet rear annexe are self-contained. More reports, please.

◐ Open all year

↗ On the A149 between Thornham and Burnham Market. Private car park

🛏 3 single, 6 twin, 5 double, 2 family rooms; most with bathroom/WC, some with shower/WC; TV, room service, hair-dryer, trouser press, baby-listening in all rooms

◈ Restaurant, bar, lounge; fishing, golf, other sports nearby;

babysitting. Wheelchair access to hotel and restaurant, 5 ground-floor bedrooms

⊖ No dogs in public rooms

▭ Access, Amex, Diners, Visa

£ Single £31 to £36, single occupancy of twin/double £36 to £41, twin/double/family room £62 to £72; deposit required. Set L £10, D £16. Special breaks available

---

**TREGONY** CORNWALL                    **MAP 8**

# Tregony House

TREGONY, TRURO, CORNWALL TR2 5RN
TEL: TREGONY (087 253) 671

*Easy to like and easy on the wallet; a guesthouse with a village setting and caring hosts.*

Tregony House sits on the wide and quiet high street of an attractive village. It has an eighteenth-century front and a charming beamed, seventeenth-century back, originally a dairy and dairyman's lodging. Should that not provide enough variety, the rest is mid-nineteenth century. Since early 1990, ex-dental surgeon Barry Sullivan and his wife Judith (a draughtswoman and house chef) have let out five, prettily decorated bedrooms, preferably on dinner, bed and breakfast terms. A self-contained Cottage Suite (two doubles and private bathroom) is reached by a separate staircase. Hospitality and comfort are high priorities, and one of many uniformly favourable reports described the Sullivans' concern to please: a complaint about instant coffee brought the real thing the next day, albeit rather weak. The guests' lounge may be a little dated but has solid and firm sofas, fashion and interior design magazines and books and games to keep you occupied. You can sit in the garden, too.

Four-course dinners are served in the old dairy, now a rustically decorated white-walled and beamed room, with antique lamps and a wine rack constructed from cut-off clay pipes. The little bar at one end is a little too cosy to accommodate everybody at once. Providing good food is another Sullivan forte. Fresh local produce including herbs from the walled garden (plus energy and flair) go into Judith's cooking; carbonnade of beef, plaice rolled and stuffed with prawns, and lamb cutlets in a redcurrant sauce have been described as 'excellent'.

◐ Closed Nov to Feb

↗ Leave St Austell on the A390

Truro road. After Sticker and Hewas Water, fork left on the

B3287 and follow signs to St Mawes and Tregony. The hotel is in Tregony's main street, opposite the King's Arms. Private car park

✉ 1 single, 2 twin, 1 double, 1 suite; some with bathroom/WC, some with shower/WC, 1 public bathroom; hair-dryer on request

◇ Dining-room, bar, lounge; fishing, tennis, riding, bowls nearby

⊜ No wheelchair access; no children under 7; no dogs; no smoking in dining-room

▭ None accepted

£ Single £28, twin/double £55 to £61 (rates inc dinner, 7pm); deposit required

**TRING** HERTFORDSHIRE                                    **MAP 10**

# Rose & Crown

HIGH STREET, TRING, HERTFORDSHIRE HP23 5AH
TEL: TRING (0442 82) 4071    TELEX: 826538 RSCRO G
FAX: (0442) 890735

*An unfussy town-centre hotel with all the essentials and down-to-earth, friendly staff.*

This substantial mock-Tudor hotel in the middle of a busy Hertfordshire town, is a good choice for an uncomplicated overnight stop. One of the Lansbury Hotels group, the Rose & Crown is particularly notable for the chatty, almost motherly, staff who are intent on getting a smile out of their guests come what may. Bedrooms suffer from an overdose of yellow but otherwise the décor is simple and inoffensive.

Upper-floor rooms have sloping ceilings, nooks and crannies and more character although it may be a squeeze to get past the bed. Downstairs rooms have disabled access but are otherwise less preferable. Since last year both restaurant and menu have been overhauled. Oak bookshelves, topped with riding boots, saddles and hats, provide the backdrop to a menu that when we visited included a dish called Chicken Rothschild, a tribute to the multi-millionaire who built the original house for his private guests. There has been some local resistance to the banishing to history of the steakhouse past but hotel guests are definitely better served by the improvements. Light sleepers should ask for a room at the back of the hotel.

● Open all year

⚡ In the centre of Tring. Private car park

✉ 10 single, 5 twin, 8 double, 2 four-poster, 2 family; most with bathroom/WC, 1 with shower/WC; TV, hair-dryer, room service, trouser press, baby-listening in all rooms

◇ Restaurant, bar; conference facilities (max 80 people non-residential, 27 residential); fishing, golf, other sports nearby. Wheelchair access to hotel, restaurant, WC (unisex), and 1 ground-floor bedroom suitable for the disabled

⊜ No dogs; some bedrooms and public rooms non-smoking

▭ Access, Amex, Diners, Visa

💷 Single £68, single occupancy of twin/double £75, twin/double £80, four-poster £93, family room £93; deposit required. Set

L £9, D £14.50; alc L £18.50, D £22; bar meals (prices till Aug 1991). Special breaks available

---

**TRISPEN** CORNWALL  MAP 8

# Laniley House

---

NR TRISPEN, TRURO, CORNWALL TR4 9AU
TEL: TRURO (0872) 75201

*Flamboyantly decorated Victorian country house three miles from Truro.*

The Victorian pebbledash house was built around 150 years ago by a mine owner. Now it's the home of Jacqueline Gartner, who moved here from Surrey in the early eighties. You might pass her near the end of the long drive, as she feeds her goats in a little paddock.

The two acres of gardens are partly wild, but plenty of attention has been paid to the house. Some people might consider the bold colour scheme to be equally wild, but no one can say it's not cheerful. (And it all rather matches Jackie's bright personality.) Ceilings are tall and the lighting is good, so the heavy Victorian furniture fits in well. There are attractive tiled floors and oriental carpets. A huge walnut sideboard dominates the homely lounge, a place to linger thanks to comfortable, floppy sofas, books, videos and records. The breakfast room, the only small room in the house, is bright pink and a lattice covers one wall. Bedroom accommodation isn't luxurious and apart from TVs, radios and tea-making facilities, it's basic; the rooms, all giant-sized doubles, aren't dull, however. The house is licensed but provides bed and breakfast only.

🌓 Open all year, exc Xmas and New Year

🇿 3 miles north of Truro on the A3076 Newquay road. Turn off right at the Frogmore/Trehane turning. Private car park

🛏 3 double; 1 with bathroom/WC; TV in all rooms

◈ Dining-room, lounge

⊖ No wheelchair access; no children under 16; no dogs; no smoking in bedrooms

▭ None accepted

💷 Single occupancy of double £22 to £25, double £30 to £34

---

*You will find report forms at the back of the Guide – please use them!*

# Lane Head Farm

TROUTBECK, PENRITH, CUMBRIA CA11 0SY
TEL: THRELKELD (076 87) 79220

*A comfortable, friendly farmhouse with genial hosts.*

As Lakeland farmhouses go, this one, visible from the A66, is refreshingly easy to find. It's a spruce whitewashed building with a neat
black trim and floral borders and tubs of plants to add a splash of colour.
Elegant white garden furniture sits on the lawn, ready for afternoon
cream teas.

Indoors, the theme is rustic. Dinner is served on an old altar table in an
oak-beamed room. Watercolours of Tewin, Herts, where friendly hosts
Tony Bew and wife Mary used to live, decorate the walls. Of the two
sitting-rooms, the larger television lounge is pleasantly decorated in a
modern blue country-style print. A collection of Wedgwood calendar
plates and an antelope head line the walls. Two bedrooms have four-
posters and all are quietly stylish with high-quality furnishings and
cheerful floral print curtains and duvet covers. Hearty English dinners
are available on request and might offer prawn cocktail, individual steak,
kidney and smoked oyster pies, rum nicky and Stilton cheese.

- ◑ Open all year
- ↗ 9 miles east of Keswick on the left-hand side of the A66. Private car park
- 🛏 I twin, I double, 2 four-poster, I family room; some with bathroom/WC; TV in some rooms
- ◈ Dining-room, bar, 2 lounges, TV room; golf, riding nearby. Wheelchair access to hotel (I step) and dining-room, I ground-floor bedroom
- ⊖ No dogs; no smoking in bedrooms
- ▭ None accepted
- £ Single occupancy of twin/double £18 to £22, twin/double/four-poster £35 to £42, family room £55; deposit required. Set D £11 (7pm, by arrangement)

---

*When you telephone to book a room, and the hotel accepts your booking, you
enter into a binding contract with them. This means they undertake to
provide the specified accommodation and meals etc. for the agreed cost on the
agreed dates, while you commit yourself to paying their charges. If you later
have to cancel your booking, or fail to turn up, the hotel is likely to keep any
deposit you have paid to defray administrative costs. If a hotel is unable to
re-let the room you have booked – and it must try to do so – it is entitled to
compensation for the loss of profit caused by your breach of contract. It can
only claim a sum that is fair and reasonable – which can be up to two-thirds
of the cost. It should not make a profit out of your failure to appear. It's
important to give as much notice as possible when cancelling: this increases
the chances of your room being re-let.*

**TROUTBECK (WINDERMERE) CUMBRIA**            **MAP 3**

# Mortal Man Hotel

TROUTBECK, WINDERMERE, CUMBRIA LA23 1PL
TEL: AMBLESIDE (053 94) 33193

*Delightful old inn in a pastoral location.*

'They have a different tempo of life up there,' wrote one enthusiastic regular visitor to this popular country inn. Upon reaching your destination you'll find a spruce white pebbledash house in an enviable position with views over the fells and down to Lake Windermere at the foot of the valley. Hosts Chris and Annette Poulsom offer traditional Lakeland hospitality, and furnishings remain simple and rustic, with lots of dark beams, thick walls and a smattering of tankards and horse-brasses.

A fire blazes in the residents' lounge, which is a cosy, beamed room with green and russet sofas and chairs. The pub-like bar serves good meals, avoids twee phoney rusticity and is justifiably popular. In comparison, the brightly lit but comfortable dining-room is rather a dull place. The five-course dinners change nightly, offer a reasonable choice and are very good value. Offerings might include smoked mackerel fillet, wrapped in bacon, grilled and served with an apple sauce, cream of spring onion soup, poached rainbow trout plus choices from the sweet trolley and cheeseboard. The wine list is well chosen. The twelve bedrooms have fine views and are very comfortable. Some have very good old furniture. Bathrooms may be a little on the small side. One reader regrets the switch to duvets, but is otherwise fulsome in his praise. Breakfast, served at the languid hour of 9am, is worth waiting for. Parents might like to note that as well as a labrador called James, the hotel is home to Roki the rottweiler.

- ◑ Closed mid-Nov to mid-Feb
- ⤢ Troutbeck is on the A592, 3 miles north of Windermere. Private car park
- ⇌ 2 single, 6 twin, 4 double; all with bathroom/WC, TV, hairdryer, trouser press; room service by arrangement
- ◈ Dining-room, bar, lounge, drying room; fishing, golf, other sports
  nearby. Wheelchair access to restaurant only
- ⊖ No children under 5
- ▭ None accepted
- £ Single £45 to £52, single occupancy of twin/double £45 to £52, twin/double £90 to £104 (rates inc dinner). Set L £11, D £17.50; bar meals from £1.50. Special breaks available

---

*All reports are welcome on any hotel, whether or not it is in the* Guide.

**TRURO** CORNWALL                                          **MAP 8**

# Alverton Manor

TREGOLLS ROAD, TRURO, CORNWALL TR1 1XQ
TEL: TRURO (0872) 76633   FAX: (0872) 222989

*A fine setting and impressive exterior, but fundamentally a business hotel.*

The hilltop setting and the proximity to the centre of Truro are in this hotel's favour. The lovely rambling Victorian sandstone manor, home to the Bishop of Truro in the 1880s and later a convent, has plenty of intrigue.

It has a slate roof, arched and mullioned windows and, within, good examples of arched doorways and hardwood staircases. It is a well-maintained, plush and comfortable place, but to be avoided if you are expecting intimacy and personal service. Though it may be going after the country-house hotel image, Alverton Manor is clearly an out-and-out business hotel. The main corridor is stately but, with many doors along it often closed for meetings, can be dark and unwelcoming.

The restaurant is a fine, formal room, all apricot and cream, and the dinners, nouvelle in style and elaborate, are worthy. Individually decorated and mostly good-sized bedrooms show a keen talent for interior design but could do with some homely touches. Promotional rates can be good value. More reports, please.

◐ Open all year

🚗 On the A390 (Tregolls Road) from St Austell leading into Truro. Private car park

🛏 6 single, 4 twin, 9 double, 6 suites; most with bathroom/WC, some with shower/WC; TV, room service, hair-dryer, trouser press, baby-listening in all rooms; no tea/coffee-making facilities in rooms

◈ Restaurant, bar, lounge, billiard room, drying room, library/study; conference facilities (max 220 people non-residential, 25

residential); golf, water sports, other sports nearby. Wheelchair access to hotel, restaurant and WC (M,F), 3 ground-floor bedrooms

⊖ No children under 12; no dogs

▭ Access, Amex, Diners, Visa

£ Single £45 to £55, single occupancy of twin/double £55 to £65, twin/double £65 to £75, suite £100 to £110; deposit required. Set D £13.50; alc D £25 (prices till end Sept 91). Special breaks available

---

*Congratulations to Cumbria – our number 1 county with 53 full entries in this year's Guide.*

**TUNBRIDGE WELLS** KENT                    **MAP 10**

# Spa Hotel

MOUNT EPHRAIM, TUNBRIDGE WELLS, KENT TN4 8XJ
TEL: TUNBRIDGE WELLS (0892) 20331   TELEX: 957188 SPATEL G
FAX: (0892) 510575

*Large, traditionally styled, family-owned hotel trying to cater for all sorts.*

Visiting virtually empty hotels out of season can prove dispiriting. Not so here. The Goring family, who also own the eponymous London hotel (see entry) welcome functions and conferences and offer enticingly reduced rates for weekend breaks throughout the year. So on a cold Friday morning in early spring the hotel was buzzing with its fresh, professional staff administering to business people and couples, and while other guests were swimming in the indoor pool and using the Jacuzzi, new arrivals were booking in and a wedding reception was in full flow.

What looks from the road like a typical Georgian pile-of-an-hotel has a much better rear aspect looking over splendid landscaped gardens with lakes and rhododendrons. The large reception/lounge, with pillars, and sofas and chairs grouped around low tables, acts as the hotel's hub: guests take morning coffee or afternoon tea here. One corridor leads to a spruce health club and the Equestrian bar, the other way to the enormous, chandeliered restaurant. Bedrooms let the hotel down, being plain and dowdy; refurbished ones have little more sparkle other than in their new white-and-green tiled bathrooms with wooden bath surrounds.

◐ Open all year

⤵ The hotel is a short drive from the centre of Tunbridge Wells, off the A264 East Grinstead road. Private car park

🛏 33 single, 24 twin, 14 double, 5 suites (family rooms available); all with shower/WC, TV, room service, hair-dryer, baby-listening; trouser press in some rooms

◇ Restaurant, bar, lounge, study; conference facilities (max 300 people non-residential, 76 residential); tennis, leisure centre with sauna, solarium, pool, jogging track, Jacuzzi, gym at hotel, other sports nearby; hair

and beauty salon; babysitting by arrangement. Wheelchair access to hotel (1 step) and restaurant, 2 ground-floor bedrooms, 1 specially equipped for the disabled

⊝ No dogs in public rooms

▭ Access, Amex, Diners, Visa

£ Single £69, single occupancy of twin/double £74, twin/double £84 to £97, suite £97; children sharing parents' room free; deposit required. Continental B £5, cooked B £7.50; set D £20, £23; alc L £15, D £25 (prices till end Mar 92). Special breaks available

# Mill House

CORNMILL LANE, TUTBURY, NR BURTON-ON-TRENT, STAFFORDSHIRE
DE13 9HA
TEL: BURTON-ON-TRENT (0283) 813300/813634

*Immaculate B&B with comfortable smart bedrooms and excellent bathrooms. Restaurants and pubs half a mile away.*

The setting beside the river is almost picture-book. The Chapmans are in the sheepskin business and the outlying buildings are devoted to this. Elizabeth Chapman runs the B&B as a sideline, most of her time being taken up with the clothes shop next to the car park. However, this is not reflected in the standard of B&B.

The house has been extremely well renovated and decorated with good-quality materials. There's a neat sitting-room which isn't really for guests' use although they may gather there or meet friends before going out for dinner. There are three exceptionally light and comfortable bedrooms, decorated with subtle co-ordination of wallpapers, bedcovers and paintwork. The bathrooms are as smart as the rest of the place; if you're particularly keen on bathrooms ask for the bedroom and bathroom that overlook the river – the bathroom is huge with a parquet floor and a large window.

Breakfast is the only meal on offer and is served at one table in an attractive, quite clubby, breakfast room. Elizabeth encourages guests to stagger their breakfast times and this tends to work very well; you can have whatever you want and it's cooked to order.

| | |
|---|---|
| ◑ *Closed Xmas and New Year* | *other sports nearby* |
| 🔼 *3½ miles off the A38, mid-way between the villages of Rolleston and Tutbury. Private car park* | ⊖ *No wheelchair access; no children under 12; no dogs; no smoking* |
| 🛏 *3 twin; 1 with bathroom/WC, 2 with shower/WC; TV in all rooms; hair-dryer on request* | ▭ *None accepted* |
| | £ *Single occupancy of twin £30 to £35, twin £45 to £48* |
| ◈ *Breakfast room; fishing, golf,* | |

---

*We mention those hotels that don't accept dogs; guide dogs, however, are almost always an exception. Telephone ahead to make sure!*

**UFFINGTON** OXFORDSHIRE                                          **MAP 9**

# The Craven

FERNHAM ROAD, UFFINGTON, OXFORDSHIRE SN7 7RD
TEL: UFFINGTON (036 782) 449

*An appealing and inviting thatched cottage in a sleepy village in
quiet countryside with easy-going and personable hosts.*

First to greet you on arriving at the Craven may well be Humphrey, an
immensely lovable and characterful Old English sheepdog who weighs
up guests from beneath hair-covered eyes. Running a close second will
be Carol Wadsworth, a charming and amiable host who runs the Craven
with the help of a couple of girls from the village.

It's a small cottage, dating from 1650, and contains more rooms than
you'd think but no dining-room, so dinner – simple and made from fresh
produce – and breakfast are eaten around the kitchen table with
Humphrey wrapped around your feet. There's a wide variety of bedroom
sizes and furniture types; a much slept-in pretty elm single bed, a half-
tester with muslin drapes, and a four-poster squeezed into one of the
downstairs rooms.

Uffington is a quiet rural backwater with little traffic and is well placed
for exploring the Oxfordshire countryside and walking up to the
Uffington White Horse cut into the hillside above.

◐ Open all year; no meals Sat eve

↵ Take the A420 from Oxford to
Swindon, and after 15 miles turn
left to Fernham. At Fernham turn
left. Drive through the village
and take the first right on
leaving the village. The hotel is
1½ miles down the hill on the
right. Private car park

🛏 3 single, 2 twin, 2 double, 1
four-poster, 1 family room; some
with bathroom/WC; room
service, hair-dryer, baby-listening
in all rooms; no tea/coffee-
making facilities in rooms

◇ Lounge, TV room, drying room;
golf, tennis, other sports nearby.
Wheelchair access to house and
WC, 2 ground-floor bedrooms, 1
specially equipped for the
disabled

⊖ No dogs; no smoking in
bedrooms

▭ None accepted

£ Single £20, single occupancy of
twin/double £25 to £30, twin/
double from £35, four-poster
£50. Set D £10.50

*Are you aware of your rights as a consumer when you book into an hotel?
Check them out on page 13.*

# Sharrow Bay

LAKE ULLSWATER, HOWTOWN, NEAR PENRITH, CUMBRIA CA10 2LZ
TEL: POOLEY BRIDGE (07684) 86301/86483    FAX: (07684) 86349

*The* doyen *of Lakeland country house hotels. Formal yet relaxing and a haven for lovers of good food.*

Country house hotels come and go, but Sharrow Bay goes on and on, as sure-footed as ever. In March 1992 Francis Coulson and Brian Sack will be opening for their 44th season, and still the plaudits flood in. Doing the rounds of our Cumbrian inspection, we discovered from rival hoteliers that Sharrow Bay is the hotel they would most like to emulate. And no wonder. The secluded position on the banks of Ullswater, one of the least spoilt lakes, is enviable, and the mature gardens are magnificent.

The early-Victorian house is crammed full of antiques, mainly Regency Victorian and Edwardian. This is the sort of place that makes you very glad that you don't have to do the dusting, as antiques, ornaments and *objets d'art* crowd every available space. Fat cherubs in gilt and porcelain seem to peep out from everywhere. Flowers, books and magazines are in abundance. The absence of bar and reception helps to foster the illusion that this is a welcoming private house, and the staff are efficient and discreetly professional. A recently added conservatory helps relieve the crush in the cramped drawing-rooms when non-resident hordes descend for the Sharrow Bay afternoon tea. Window seats with a lake view are the most sought-after. One word of warning; forego lunch if you want to do justice to the relays of toast, sandwiches, scones, preserves, cakes and biscuits that will be brought to your table. The elaborate dinners also follow a long-standing and successful formula, with a formal and tempting display of desserts described to each guest on entering the lakeside dining-room. The choice on the six-course menu is bewildering – a dozen or more starters, main courses and desserts, with the agony of decision-making relieved at the no-choice fish and sorbet courses. One evening in May diners might have chosen duck foie gras served with spinach and orange curaçao and brandy sauce, fillets of Aberdeen halibut with salmon mousseline, served with beurre blanc sauce. Pineapple sorbet was followed by roast lamb, and lemon steamed sponge with creamy egg custard preceded well-cared for cheeses. Four chefs work towards a house style, with the emphasis on excellence rather than innovation.

Bedrooms at Sharrow Bay might be in the main house or one of the assorted and scattered annexes. Many have marvellous lake views. There are antiques, lavish fabrics and books and games in profusion, though the overall effect, while enormously pleasing, is less ritzy than you might expect: this is no temple of antiseptic regimented co-ordination. As one reader said: 'These bedrooms are definitely not put together by a top designer. They're much too friendly!' Residents in the seventeenth-century Bank House, a mile along the shore, breakfast in the magnificent converted barn with grand stone fireplace scavenged from Warwick Castle.

◑ Closed Dec, Jan, Feb

↗ Leave the M6 at Junction 40 and follow the signs for Ullswater. At Pooley Bridge take a right-hand turn to Howtown. Follow this road for 2 miles to the lakeside. Private car park

🛏 5 single, 7 twin, 10 double, 6 suites; most with bathroom/WC, some with shower/WC; TV, limited room service, hair-dryer, trouser press in all rooms; half with mini-bar; 6 with tea/coffee-making facilities

◈ 2 dining-rooms, 5 lounges,

conservatory; conference facilities (max 12 people residential); fishing at hotel; golf, other sports nearby. Wheelchair access to hotel and restaurant, 4 ground-floor bedrooms

⊖ No children under 13; no dogs; no smoking in dining-rooms and bedrooms

▭ None accepted

£ Single £82 to £113, twin/double £160 to £270, suite £256 to £270, cottages from £226 (rates inc dinner). Set L £29.50, D £39.50

---

**ULVERSTON** CUMBRIA                                                    **MAP 3**

# Trinity House                                              𝓛

---

PRINCES STREET, ULVERSTON, CUMBRIA LA12 7NB
TEL: BARROW-IN-FURNESS (0229) 57639

*A comfortable Georgian home with agreeable hosts, but in a slightly inauspicious location.*

There aren't many hotels where you're likely to find a fireplace in your room with fire laid in the grate, just waiting to be lit. That's one of the bonuses at this Grade-II-listed former Georgian rectory in the pleasant market town of Ulverston, about half-an-hour's drive from the central lakes.

The drawback is the proximity of a busy road. Double glazing filters out most of the traffic noise and the hotel has many compensating features. Period character has been respected in the sensitive restoration by Fleet Street refugee Stephanie Thompson and her partner Keith Sutton. Fat armchairs and a chaise-longue are grouped around the fireplace in the vivid green rag-rolled bar/lounge. Balloon-backed Victorian chairs set the tone in the popular wood-panelled dining-room, where the emphasis is on fresh, local produce. One springtime menu offered fish soup with a pastry lid, chicken and tarragon, Cumberland rum nicky and a cheeseboard. Bread is home-baked.

The bedrooms, mostly large and high-ceilinged combine Victorian and Edwardian antiques with modern bamboo. Décor is alternately handsome or feminine, with voguish colours, and some wallpaper has stencilled patterns. Duvet covers are frilled and satin-trimmed, and there's a brass bedstead in the extra-large room two. Several of the large bathrooms have old-fashioned bath surrounds and pictures on the walls.

◐ *Open all year, exc Jan; dining-room closed Sun eve*

⬈ *Approaching Ulverston on the A590, the hotel is on the left of the main road after the second set of traffic lights. Private car park*

🛏 *1 single, 2 twin, 3 double, most with bathroom/WC, some with shower/WC; TV in all rooms*

◈ *Dining-room, bar/lounge; golf, riding, other sports nearby; babysitting. Wheelchair access to*

*hotel (ramp), restaurant and WC (F), 1 ground-floor bedroom specially equipped for the disabled*

⊖ *No dogs in public rooms*

▭ *Access, Amex, Visa*

£ *Single £33 to £35, single occupancy of twin/double £36 to £38, twin/double £45 to £56, family room £56; deposit required. Set D £13; alc D £16. Special breaks available*

---

**UPPINGHAM** LEICESTERSHIRE                                         **MAP 4**

# The Lake Isle

16 HIGH STREET EAST, UPPINGHAM, LEICESTERSHIRE LE15 9PZ
TEL: UPPINGHAM (0572) 822951   FAX: (0572) 822951

*A well-run town house and restaurant (with a notable wine list) with prettily decorated rooms.*

It is the restaurant that receives most of the attention at this smart eighteenth-century town house in the centre of the market town of Uppingham. This is a shame because the eleven bedrooms are far from basic. Each is differently decorated with co-ordinating wallpapers and carpets in pastel shades. A decanter of sherry awaits newly arrived guests in their rooms. The influence of alcohol hangs (metaphorically!) in the air. All the bedrooms are named after French wine regions, apart from one which takes its name from a malt whisky. Wine is obviously a great love of the host David Whitfield, and his cellar boasts over three hundred bins. Wine evenings are held four times a year. Light drinkers will be pleased to see there is an extensive range of half-bottles.

The restaurant's cuisine is French, making use of fresh supplies, some of which are imported directly from the Paris Rungis market, although some reports suggest the quality of the dishes that result from such promising ingredients can vary. The decoration in the restaurant, which is at the front of the house, is cheerful and informal with scrubbed pine tables and sideboard. There is also a bar and, upstairs, a comfortable lounge.

◐ *Open all year*

⬈ *In Uppingham's High Street, reached via Reeves Yard. Private*

*car park*

🛏 *1 single, 2 twin, 7 double, cottage suite; most with*

bathroom/WC, some with shower/WC; TV, room service, hair-dryer, trouser press in all rooms

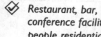 Restaurant, bar, lounge; conference facilities (max 10 people residential and non-residential); fishing, water sports nearby. Wheelchair access to restaurant only

● No dogs in restaurant; smoking discouraged in restaurant

▭ Access, Amex, Diners, Visa

£ Single £41 to £47, twin/double £60 to £68, suite/family room £72 to £78; deposit required. Set L £11, D £18.50 to £22.50. Special breaks available

# Rutland House

61 HIGH STREET EAST, UPPINGHAM, LEICESTERSHIRE LE15 9PY
TEL: UPPINGHAM (0572) 822497

*A basic guesthouse in the centre of town with few facilities but friendly hosts.*

This Victorian double-fronted sandstone guesthouse is situated past the shops in the High Street; the row of colourful hanging baskets on the outside wall makes it easy to find. It's a good place for parents and friends visiting pupils at Uppingham school, and attractions like Rutland Water and Rockingham Castle are also within striking distance.

Jenny and Ken Hitchen, who have been in the business all their working lives, are the friendly owners. There is no communal sitting-room, but the sheer size of the bedrooms, with their high ceilings and bay windows, compensates for that. Room three, the double, is the gayest. Decoration is simple and understated, relying on earthy colours supplemented by potted plants.

◐ Open all year

↱ Centrally located in Uppingham. High Street East is approached via the market square. Private car park

⇔ 1 single, 1 twin, 1 double, 1 family room; all with bathroom/WC, TV, hair-dryer; trouser press on request

◇ Breakfast room, drying room;

fishing, golf, other sports nearby. Wheelchair access to hotel and breakfast room, 1 ground-floor bedroom

● No dogs or smoking in public rooms

▭ None accepted

£ Single £27, twin/double £37, family room £45; deposit required

---

*See page 787 for other hotels worthy of inclusion in our* Visitors' Book.

# Curdon Mill

VELLOW, WILLITON, SOMERSET TA4 4LS
TEL: STOGUMBER (0984) 56522

*Lovely farm hotel in a beautifully preserved water mill.*

The drive leads through the farmyard: cows peer out from Dutch doors, chickens scurry around. More amusement follows, for Curdon Mill has turned many interesting vestiges of its working past into decoration. The stream contributes its gentle gurgle; grinding stones lean against one end of the long, tall, reddish stone building, and you'll see bits of the waterwheel and mechanism here and there. All very atmospheric, but Richard and Daphne Criddle's hospitable natures also add to your stay.

The narrow hallway functions as the reception; the rest of the hotel is upstairs. The sitting-room is cheerful, with floor-to-ceiling windows and comfy armchairs in light-coloured loose covers. The second-floor dining-room which stretches the width of the mill allows ample space for non-resident diners. It's carpeted but rustic, with a fine, very old oak Welsh dresser, and the original wheel shaft at ceiling level. The best hillside views, complete with beams and slanting ceilings, are features of the four second-floor bedrooms. All the bedrooms are imaginatively and individually furnished. The Stag Room is so called because you supposedly have good views of the beasts (and because of the brand name of the furiture). The Walnut Room is the largest. 'Six nights in the Walnut Room turned out a wonderfully relaxing and refreshing break and the Mill a perfect base for exploring Somerset churches with minimal contact with August holiday traffic,' writes a reader. 'The end-of-harvest field work, dogs, cats, ferrets, pheasant chicks, ponies and 6am cockcrow was a stimulating background to a very comfortable mill by the stream. Mrs Criddle is an excellent manager and welcoming hostess.'

○ Open all year

▣ Leave Taunton on the A358 towards Williton. Just before Williton take the left turning for Vellow – the mill is 1 mile on the left. Private car park

🛏 3 twin, 3 double; all with shower/WC, exc 1 twin with bathroom/WC; TV, room service, hair-dryer

◈ Restaurant, bar, lounge; conference facilities (max 20 people non-residential); fishing,

croquet, heated outdoor swimming-pool (Apr to Sept) at hotel, other sports nearby

● No wheelchair access; no children under 10; no dogs; no smoking

▭ None accepted

💷 Single occupancy of twin/double £25, twin/double £39 to £60; deposit required. Alc D £15; Sun L £10.50

**VENTNOR** ISLE OF WIGHT                                    **MAP 9**

# Hillside

151 MITCHELL AVENUE, VENTNOR, ISLE OF WIGHT PO38 1DR
TEL: ISLE OF WIGHT (0983) 852271

*An inexpensive hotel with lovely views, large gardens and friendly hosts (especially to dogs).*

'The best thing about this hotel was the warmth of the reception by the owners, who were so friendly and kind we did not want to leave,' reported one reader. We found Brenda Hart and her husband Peter (much happier since they started up here in 1988 than in his previous existence as a Surrey-based lorry driver) relaxed and cheerful. 'They are animal lovers and there are two dogs resident as well as guests' dogs who are always welcome,' continues the letter. We were greeted by three four-legged residents: a golden retriever, golden labrador and a border collie (the first to welcome us, a barking tumble of fur and old bedspread).

A thatched house built in 1801, it's set a little back from the main road at the top of the town under a steep bluff, with panoramic views of Ventnor's rooftops and the sea beyond. Well-kept bedrooms have simple, co-ordinated floral patterns, and all but three have a view. To the sound of Musak in the yellow dining-room, expect to taste some of Brenda's home cooking: a five-course meal of remarkable value, including cheese and coffee, with a fish, meat and vegetarian selection, served between 6.30 and 7pm. Guests can relax in the 'dry lounge' (no late-night drinkers to spoil the peace and quiet), or in the small pine-panelled bar which Peter will man till midnight. Pride of place, however, must go to the long conservatory with prime views, decked out attractively with bamboo chairs and hanging flower baskets. From here guests can also watch a family of badgers who come up to dine in the garden.

◑ *Open all year*

⤴ *A few minutes' drive from the centre of Ventnor. Private car park*

🛏 *1 single, 2 twin, 7 double, 1 family room; some with bathroom/WC, some with shower/WC; TV, room service in all rooms; hair-dryer on request*

◈ *Dining-room, bar, lounge, library, conservatory; golf, tennis, bowls nearby*

⊖ *No wheelchair access; no children under 5; no dogs in public rooms*

▭ *Access, Amex, Visa*

£ *Single £25, single occupancy of twin/double £25 to £28, double £50, family room £50 (rates inc dinner); deposit required*

---

*We mention those hotels that don't accept dogs; guide dogs, however, are almost always an exception. Telephone ahead to make sure!*

# The Nare Hotel

CARNE BEACH, VERYAN, NR TRURO, CORNWALL TR2 5PF
TEL: TRURO (0872) 501279   FAX: (0872) 501856

*A modern and comfortable hotel with a prime beach-side location and wide-ranging facilities.*

You can hardly beat this location: on the wide crescent of Gerrans Bay, one of the Roseland peninsula's several prime spots. The Nare, just up from the beach, is a large sprawling hotel. Space, light from floor-to-ceiling windows, fresh flowers, open fires and soft seating make public rooms exceedingly pleasant and comfortable. Some odd combinations of patterns and colours notwithstanding, high-quality antiques, china and decent artwork put the Nare into the classy league.

You'll be hard put to find any pomp from the Grays, owners since early 1989, or their staff, who cope well with the diverse clientele. There's a playroom and an outdoor play area as well as outdoor swimming-pool, tennis court and billiard room. The restaurant is a low extension with elaborately draped curtains at fat arched windows. Well-cooked and filling four-course dinners become special occasions with an hors d'oeuvre table, fattening dessert trolley and much in between. Ties and low voices are expected. You can have light lunches and cream teas in a smaller and simpler Gwendra room (where children's teas are served) or outdoors on one of the garden or pool terraces. Improvements continue, the most recent being new deluxe 'Sea View' twins with balcony or terrace. Rooms, many with floor-to-ceiling windows, vary in size and are harmoniously furnished with dark-wood antiques, plain pale carpets and walls, and bold, flowery curtains.

A reader writes: 'Our stay with our daughter and her two young children was most enjoyable. The setting and tranquillity can't be overstated. Staff exceptionally friendly and very helpful, cases carried to your room, etc. The charm of the Grays is much in evidence. Hotel needs a good odd-job man and management should see that everything works. Will return again as, indeed, do many of the guests.'

◖ Open all year

◪ 1 mile west of Veryan, on Carne Beach. Private car park

🛏 4 single, 17 twin, 17 double, 3 family rooms; most with bathroom/WC, some with shower/WC; TV, room service, hair-dryer, baby-listening in all rooms

◈ 2 restaurants, 2 bars, 4 lounges, games room, conservatory; tennis, billiards, sauna, solarium, outdoor swimming-pool (heated Easter to Oct) at hotel, other sports nearby; babysitting (small fee). Wheelchair access to hotel, restaurant and WC (M,F), 7 ground-floor bedrooms, 2 specially equipped for the disabled

● No children under 7 at dinner; no dogs in public rooms

▭ Access, Visa

£  Single £40 to £95, twin/double          deposit required. Sun lunch
   £80 to £160; children's rates;          £11.50; alc D from £23

---

**VOWCHURCH** HEREFORD AND WORCESTER                              **MAP 6**

# Croft Country House

VOWCHURCH, HEREFORD AND WORCESTER HR2 0QE
TEL: PETERCHURCH (0981) 550226

*Friendly, homely family guesthouse with hearty food.*

This is a pleasant guesthouse rather than the grand mansion that might
be implied by the name. Croft Country House dates largely from the
eighteenth century with later additions. The grounds would do anyone
proud: six and a half acres of lawns, orchards, borders packed with
flowering shrubs, and a grass tennis court. The Molinarys took over in
1990; their excitable red setter and more staid spaniel greet you.

The small dining-room was once the consulting room of a previous
doctor owner. The lounge is spacious, with comfortable armchairs, an
open fire, and bookshelves loaded with board games. There are a few
antiques and a fair sprinkling of stripped pine.

The Croft Room is the largest bedroom, with drapes above the bed
and a lovely bathroom with a bay window overlooking the garden. The
smallest double also has a large bathroom decorated in peach and pine.
Further bedrooms available in two annexes – the Coach House and the
Mews – are plainer but still comfortable. Food comes in generous
portions, with at least three choices at each course at dinner. It is fairly
traditional stuff: leek and potato soup, sirloin of beef in red wine, sticky
toffee pudding with butterscotch sauce.

◐ Open all year

↗ From Hereford take the A465
  Abergavenny road for 4 miles,
  turn right at petrol station and
  follow road through to
  Vowchurch. Private car park

🛏 1 twin, 3 double, 1 four-poster
  (2 rooms in annexes); most with
  bathroom/WC, some with
  shower/WC; TV, room service,
  hair-dryer in all rooms

◇ Restaurant, dining-room, bar,
  lounge, conservatory; tennis at

hotel, fishing, golf, riding nearby.
Wheelchair access to hotel and
1 ground-floor bedroom

⊖ No children under 10; no dogs;
  smoking discouraged

▭ Access, Visa

£ Single occupancy of twin/double
  £32, twin/double £42, suite £53;
  deposit required. Set L (Sun)
  £10, D £15, £19; alc D £21.
  Special breaks available

# The Manor House

NORTHLANDS, WALKINGTON, NR BEVERLEY, HUMBERSIDE HU17 8RT
TEL: HULL (0482) 881645   FAX: (0482) 866501

*The desire to pamper both with food and comfort is sometimes overwhelming but the intention is genuine.*

This is a very sybaritic place with the main emphasis on the food. Derek and Lee Baugh, directors and chefs-patrons, defy the 'too many cooks' maxim and produce an elaborate menu, both in content and description. A meal may start with traditional mussel soup with cream, saffron and wine served with deep-fried seaweed, followed by roast rack of lamb filled with a rosemary seasoning and presented with a fritter basket of glazed vegetables. After a mouthwatering range of desserts, you can finish up with an interesting selection of cheeses, some local. Drinks before dinner (and coffee after) are taken in the drawing-room – not really a place for flopping in. Muzak (light classics and popular songs) pursues you throughout the public rooms.

The bedrooms are the place to find respite. There may only be five but the Baughs have lavished everything on them: huge beds prettified with a cluster of small cushions, lots of elegant fitted cupboard space, skirted tables, china, fresh flowers.

Open all year; restaurant closed Sun

In Walkington turn left at traffic lights and left at first crossroads. The Manor House is 1/4 mile further on the left. Private car park

5 double; all with bathroom/WC, TV, hair-dryer, mini-bar

Restaurant, lounge, bar, conservatory; conference facilities (max 20 people non-residential); croquet at hotel, golf, riding nearby

No wheelchair access; no children under 12; dogs by arrangement only; no smoking in bedrooms

Access, Visa

Single occupancy of double £70; double £90; deposit required. Cooked B £7.50; alc D £30

# New Hall

WALMLEY ROAD, WALMLEY, SUTTON COLDFIELD, WEST MIDLANDS B76 8QX
TEL: 021-378 2442   TELEX: 333580 NEWHAL G
FAX: 021-378 4637

*Historic castle with luxurious accommodation, at a price.*

Somehow the signposts saying 'Squirrels crossing' on the drive leading to the hotel and the numerous matching signs saying 'private' give the impression you are about to enter a contrived theme park-style castle. The Union Flag flying from the castellated tower and the sentry box in the car park both strengthen this impression. Once you're inside this thirteenth-century castle, surrounded by a moat filled with water lilies, this impression begins to fade. Instead, you are enveloped in a luxurious hotel.

In each room you'll get a hint of the castle's history: fine stained-glass and leaded windows, stonework, coats of arms, the Earl of Warwick's family tree, fine hunting prints and a collection of prints decorating hushed corridors. Oil paintings and tapestries cover the walls and the cosy bar and elegant dining-room are all furnished in keeping with the period. Suites, all individually designed, are in the oldest parts of the castle: some have sloping ceilings and beams and can be massive and sumptuous. Many of the bedrooms are in the sympathetic extension built to one side; bathrooms are equally luxurious. In the wood-panelled dining-room, starched tablecloths are laid with silverware and shining glassware. The set menu may feature a duet of Brixham crab and glazed pineapple to start followed by escalope of Dutch veal on a classic bonne femme sauce with a pudding menu offering maybe iced gooseberry and stem ginger soufflé to finish. The wine list is extensive.

🌓 *Open all year*

⤴ *Leave M6 at Junction 5 and follow A452 signposted Sutton Coldfield. At the 3rd roundabout turn right, continue on B4148 through Walmley village; after 1 mile turn left to New Hall. Private car park*

🛏 *4 single, 16 twin, 32 double, 3 four-poster, 3 family rooms, 4 suites; all with bathroom/WC, TV, room service, hair-dryer, trouser press*

◇ *Restaurant, bar, 2 lounges; conference facilities (max 40 people residential), helipad, golf driving net, croquet, putting at hotel; babysitting. Wheelchair access to hotel, restaurant and WC (unisex), 22 ground-floor bedrooms, 1 specially equipped for the disabled*

⊖ *No children under 8; no dogs; no smoking in public rooms*

▭ *Access, Amex, Diners, Visa*

£ *Single £89, single occupancy of twin/double £89 to £105, twin/double £105 to £130, four-poster from £160, family room from £175, suite from £170; deposit required. Cooked B £9.50, continental B £7.50; set L £16.50, D £24; alc D £37.50 (prices till Dec 91). Special breaks available*

---

*Although in our 40s we suspect we were 25 years short of their target age range – older residents seeming to be favoured with conversation.* On an hotel in Cumbria

# The Priory

CHURCH GREEN, WAREHAM, DORSET BH20 4ND
TEL: WAREHAM (0929) 551666/552772   TELEX: 41143 PRIORY G
FAX: (0929) 554519

*Small luxurious hotel within an ancient priory. Some hotel
excesses in bedrooms but otherwise refined.*

Church green is one of several leafy enclaves in a splendid old market
town, and is dominated by Lady St Mary's tower. The sixteenth-century
priory, which abuts the tower, is a mellow assembly of stone walls, gables
and wavering rooftops. You have to look hard to pick out the entrance.

Doors lead off to various public areas from a long narrow corridor.
Antiques and high-quality furnishings in medieval-style colours and
fabrics set off these four-hundred-year-old stone rooms. As well as a
large, plush lounge with beams, real fire and grand piano, there is a small
dining-room for breakfasts and weekday lunches, a snug bar and a
second lounge upstairs. Small windows mean they're never flooded in
daylight, but views stretch over four acres of sloping garden to the river
bank. A visitor in early spring reported: 'The gardens were in excellent
order and still a blaze of colour. The gardener told us that in January he
had 39 different flowers and shrubs in bloom. All the staff were helpful
and the overall atmosphere in the hotel was a delight.'

The main dining-room, in the vaulted cellars, is both cosy and formal,
with pink napery and tall-backed, tapestry-covered chairs. Expect to find
the likes of chicken breast stuffed with sweetbreads, pimentos and dry
sherry on the menu. In the otherwise good bedrooms, provisions and
goodies have been assigned the ridiculous role of decoration: bitty
sachets of shoe polish and matching sewing kits sit fanned out on tops of
chests of drawers; tissues burst, bouquet style, from ugly boxes and hotel
menus and brochures sit propped up on tables. The bedrooms come in
interesting shapes and sizes, have sloping roofs and the odd fireplace and
low door-frame. The designer touch is obvious in the chic matching
fabrics, and antiques chosen to mix with modern furniture. Singles tend
to be small; best take a double room if you're on your own and pay the
surcharge. Bathrooms come in all sizes, too, with various degrees of
luxury.

○ Open all year

🔁 150 yards from Wareham's main
street (South Street), on the
banks of the River Frome. Private
car park

🛏 3 single, 4 twin/double, 8 double,
2 four-poster, 2 suites; all with
bathroom/WC, exc 2 doubles
with shower/WC; TV, room

service, hair-dryer, mini-bar;
trouser press, tea/coffee-making
facilities on request

◇ 2 dining-rooms, bar, 2 lounges,
TV room; conference facilities
(max 19 people residential);
fishing, croquet at hotel, other
sports nearby. Wheelchair access
to hotel, restaurant and WC, 4
ground-floor bedrooms

No dogs

 Access, Amex, Diners, Visa

Single £70, single occupancy of twin/double £60 to £100, twin/double £75 to £170, four-poster

£140 to £150, suite £175. Set L £10 to £15, D £22.50 to £26.50; alc L, D £30; light lunches (prices till end 91). Special breaks available

## WARMINSTER WILTSHIRE                                                MAP 9

# Bishopstrow House

WARMINSTER, WILTSHIRE BA12 9HH
TEL: WARMINSTER (0985) 212312   TELEX: 444829 BISHOP G
FAX: (0985) 216769

*A grand, business-oriented hotel near Longleat that manages not to overwhelm and is lavish with its facilities.*

The large, creeper-clad grey house, built in 1817 by John Pinch of Bath, wasn't exactly humdrum to begin with, but furnishings now do justice to the grand-scale framework. It is light and airy and, of course, modernised for comfort. Lounging, dining and conferences take place in plush surroundings where antiques mingle with good reproduction furniture, and artistic bunches of greenery from the garden make a refreshing change from flowers.

In bedrooms, too, a few of which are in the newly converted stable block around the courtyard, convenience and comfort reign. Features that Americans, especially, appreciate include a round, pillared bathtub in an alcove with a pleated silk ceiling, and antique four-posters. The Grecian-style indoor pool has a touch of the decadent about it, too.

Eating at Bishopstrow can also be classed as indulgent. Chris Suter, 'Young Chef of the Year in 1990', reworks French classics to good, if complex, effect. Weekends, when businessmen are absent, are the best times to relax around the place. The facilities, not to mention the graceful gardens and grounds with statues, cypress trees and flower beds, are impressive.

Open all year

Approaching Warminster on the B3414, after a sharp left-hand bend take a right turn into the hotel's drive. Private car park

2 twin, 23 double, 1 four-poster, 3 family rooms, 3 suites; all with bathroom/WC, TV, room service, hair-dryer, baby-listening; trouser press in some rooms; no tea/coffee-making facilities in rooms

Dining-room, 3 lounges, conservatory; conference facilities (max 70 people non-residential, 32 residential); fishing, tennis, water sports, sauna/solarium, indoor and outdoor swimming-pools at hotel, other sports nearby; babysitting

No wheelchair access; no dogs in public rooms

Access, Amex, Diners, Visa

Single £110, single occupancy of twin/double £112, twin/double £127, four-poster £203, family room £127, suite £277; deposit required. Set L £15.50, D £33. Special breaks available

**WATERHOUSES** STAFFORDSHIRE                              **MAP 4**

# Old Beams Restaurant

WATERHOUSES, STAFFORDSHIRE ST10 3HW
TEL: LEEK (0538) 308254

*An extremely good restaurant with very comfortable, well-designed rooms and a friendly, relaxed atmosphere.*

The only bad thing about this restaurant-with-rooms is its proximity to the main Leek to Ashbourne road. Unless you're an acutely sensitive sleeper this should not be a reason to pass it by. The pretty stone house has a tiny front garden with a neat lawn and a wonderful scent of hyacinths and lavender.

The restaurant has an excellent reputation. You might dine in the main part of the building or in the conservatory extension. Here the windows overlook the garden and the whole of one wall is a mural painted by Tim Plant, appropriately so as the rest of the area is full of plants and flowers. The beamed ceiling, creamy walls and reddish carpet are a very restful setting for the carefully chosen and well presented food. Ann Wallis is a perfectionist with the housekeeping and it shows: the scent of fresh flowers mixes with roasting pine logs and greets you as you enter the reception and tiny, but atmospheric bar of Old Beams. Orders and bookings are staggered so there's enough room for everyone to sit down before and after dinner at the bar or beside the double-sided fire.

All the bedrooms (except one) are in the modern building, 'Les Chambres', across the main road and all named after a local china manufacturer. Wedgwood is predominantly sky blue with pale ash furnishings and a grey marble bathroom, Royal Stafford has hand-embroidered cotton sheets – everything is of the highest standard. In bathrooms, all the china is from the relevant pottery. Breakfast is served in the conservatory or you can have a light breakfast in your room. You will feel spoilt and charmed after a stay here.

◑ *Open all year, exc 3 weeks from Sat before Xmas; restaurant closed Sun eve, Sat lunch and Mon*

▰ *From Ashbourne take the A52 and continue on this road to Leek. On passing through Waterhouses the hotel is on the right (A523). Private car park*

⇤ *5 double, 1 four-poster; all with bathroom/WC, TV, room service, hair-dryer, baby listening; no tea/coffee-making facilities in rooms*

◈ *Restaurant, bar, lounge, conservatory, laundry/drying*

*facilities; meetings facilities (max 16 people non-residential); fishing in grounds, other sports nearby. Wheelchair access to hotel, restaurant and WC, 1 ground-floor bedroom, specially equipped for the disabled*

⊖ *No children under 8; no dogs; no smoking*

▭ *Access, Amex, Diners, Visa*

£ *Single occupancy of double £53 to £73, double/four-poster £68 to £87; deposit required. Set L £16.50, D £29.50*

**WATERMILLOCK** CUMBRIA                    **MAP 3**

# The Old Church

WATERMILLOCK, ULLSWATER, PENRITH, CUMBRIA CA11 0JN
TEL: POOLEY BRIDGE (076 84) 86204   FAX: (076 84) 86368

*Upmarket country-house hotel in a super lakeside position.*

Lovers of ancient churches, searching for Gothic arches or Romanesque tracery will be disappointed. The long path that leads you through open pastureland to the shores of Lake Ullswater delivers you at a spruce and stately white country house built in 1745. Nothing remains of the original twelfth-century church that gives the hotel its name. The lakeside position is stunning.

Kevin and Maureen Whitemore run a well-groomed country-house hotel with all the necessary ingredients: polished antiques, fresh flowers, open fires and lots of books and magazines. A fire blazes in the grate of a carved wooden fireplace in the deep-red entrance hall. An impressive, creaking staircase sweeps to the bedrooms upstairs. Bold green and pink floral wallpaper co-ordinates with bright pink bookcases in the lounge. The bar is similarly exuberant in a blue and pink décor, with the bottles stashed in a discreet cupboard. Both rooms are comfortable and tall windows give glorious views.

The elegant dining-room which overlooks the lake is rather more restrained, affecting the atmosphere at dinner. This is a five-course affair with choice throughout except at the soup stage. A May menu offered gravadlax with mustard and dill dressing, cream of potato, ginger and watercress soup, supreme of chicken with pesto filling and red peppers, followed by raspberry crème brûlée and a cheeseboard. Bedrooms, named after birds, are airy and immaculately kept. Peregrine Falcon, a corner room, has windows on two sides and views over the marina and garden. Colours are generally more muted than in public rooms, although the same careful use of fabrics is evident. Square chintz canopies hang over several beds. There are fresh flowers and good toiletries, but fewer frills than you might expect at the price. Service is 'outstanding and most insistent. I've been taught to carry my own case rather than let a lady do the work but the pretty young lady here virtually wrestled me to the ground for the privilege,' advised one guest.

◑ *Closed Dec, Jan, Feb*

⬆ *3 miles south of Pooley Bridge on the A592, 15 minutes from Junction 40 of the M6. Private car park*

🛏 *3 twin, 7 double; all with bathroom/WC, hair-dryer, baby-listening, limited room service; TV on request; no tea/coffee-making facilities in rooms*

◈ *Restaurant, bar, lounge, TV room; drying facilities; conference facilities (max 15 people non-residential, 10 residential); fishing, water sports, sailing, rowing boat at hotel, other sports nearby; babysitting*

⊖ *No wheelchair access; no children in restaurant eves; no dogs; no smoking in restaurant*

*England*

⬜ Access, Visa (subject to 4% charge)

💷 Single occupancy of twin/double £75 to £165, twin/double £150

to £210 (rates inc dinner). Set D £27.50; alc L £15.50 (prices till end 91)

---

**WATER YEAT** CUMBRIA

**MAP 3**

# Water Yeat

WATER YEAT, NR ULVERSTON, CUMBRIA LA12 8DJ
TEL: LOWICK BRIDGE (022 985) 306

*Outstanding guesthouse with lots of comfort and cheerful Anglo-French hosts.*

Pierre and Jill Labat are a cosmopolitan pair and this seventeenth-century Cumbrian farmhouse combines traditional English elements with a hint of the exotic. So you'll find the classic beams, stone walls and flagstone floors accompanied by a collection of less familiar objects, assembled from China, Peru, India and the Middle East from when the Labats worked for Cunard Lines. Guessing the use of some of the less-familiar objects makes for an interesting after-dinner diversion.

They've successfully created an informal atmosphere in a house with rustic appeal but more than a dash of flair. Bedrooms often have beams and original fireplaces, and most have fine views. They vary in size and style, but all are cheerful and clean and feature frilled duvet-covers and delicate floral patterns with borders. The Edwardian-themed room three has (with apologies to E M Forster) a loo with a view. Jill's cooking is an *entente cordiale* of English heartiness and French flair. There's an alternative at each stage of dinner: perhaps watercress, wild garlic and orange soup followed by roast guinea-fowl in cucumber and rosé wine and nutty chocolate fudge pie and a cheeseboard. The wine list is short but well chosen.

◑ Closed Jan to mid-Feb; dining-room open most eves

🔁 On the A5084, 7 miles south of Coniston, 7 miles north of Ulverston, on the western side of Coniston Water. Private car park

🛏 2 single, 2 double, 2 twin, 1 family room; some rooms with shower or bathroom/WC, 3 public bathrooms; TV on request

⬦ Dining-room, lounge; bicycles, table tennis, sailing at hotel, other sports nearby

⊖ No wheelchair access; no children under 5; no dogs; no smoking in bedrooms

⬜ None accepted

💷 Single £19 to £20, single occupancy of twin/double £26 to £35, twin/double £35 to £50, family room £48 to £55; deposit required. Set D £14.50 (8pm). Special breaks available

**WATH** NORTH YORKSHIRE    MAP 4

# Sportsman's Arms

WATH-IN-NIDDERDALE, PATELEY BRIDGE, HARROGATE, NORTH
YORKSHIRE HG3 5PP
TEL: HARROGATE (0423) 711306

*A coaching-inn/restaurant-with-rooms in a particularly beautiful
location.*

Wath is a tiny village near Pateley Bridge surrounded by fields and
beautiful countryside. The main focus of this inn is on food and drink;
there's no formal reception – you just knock on the kitchen door to get in.
Residents have a couple of cosy sitting-rooms; one has a huge tiled
fireplace with horse shoes and hunting prints, and silver jugs hanging
from old beams. The bar, more recently decorated than the rest of the
establishment, is distinctly more modern in style but the whole place has
a great atmosphere, assisted by the locals who are very friendly to the odd
outsider who stumbles upon Wath: two old men play dominoes every
night and the only disturbance is likely to be the arrival of another man
with his whippet.

The bedrooms are functional but adequate and neatly decorated in
cottagey style. The main draw is the food which features such dishes as
feuilleté of langoustine and asparagus in a minted orange sauce, or fresh
pasta with sautéed cabbage and garlic for starters, followed by roast
breast of duckling in a beetroot and orange sauce or fresh Nidderdale
trout with mushrooms and capers. One reader described his meal as
'imaginative, well cooked and presented with good portions' and he was
as impressed with the large cooked breakfast.

◑ Open all year, exc 25 Dec, and
26 Dec and 1 Jan eves

↗ From Harrogate take the A61 to
Ripley and the B6165 to Pateley
Bridge. At Pateley Bridge follow
signs for Ramsgill but turn off at
Wath after 1½ miles. Private
car park

🛏 2 twin, 5 double; 2 rooms with
shower/WC, 2 public bathrooms;
TV, room service in all rooms

◇ Restaurant, bar, 2 lounges;

conference facilities (max 20
people non-residential, 7
residential); fishing at hotel,
other sports nearby

⊖ No wheelchair access; no
smoking in bedrooms

▭ Access, Amex, Diners, Visa

£ Single occupancy of twin/double
£27 to £29, twin/double £45 to
£48. Sun L £11.50, bar lunches
all week; set D £11.50, £17.50;
alc D £15 to £25

---

*See the inside front cover for a brief explanation of how to use the* Guide.

# Well House

34–40 HIGH STREET, WATLINGTON, OXFORDSHIRE OX9 5PY
TEL: WATLINGTON (049 161) 3333　FAX: (049 161) 2025

*A reasonably priced hotel in a region where overpricing is the norm.*

Having consulted the menu on the wall outside which might include such mouthwatering propositions as mousseline of sole in a turban of smoked salmon and marinated venison steak with juniper berry sauce and having been further encouraged by the price, don't be put off by the slightly drab beige entrance hall or the oil-paintings in the otherwise attractive dining-room which are strikingly bright.

Well House is actually three houses joined together at the bottom end of a narrow slumbering high street. The restaurant and sitting-room are in the oldest of the buildings: a wealthy merchant's house built around 1400. Beams reappear in some of the bedrooms where attractive fabrics, rush-seated chairs and chunky tables are found. Rooms in the newer wing include a spacious family suite. The hotel is a popular spot and the Crawfords have a band of loyal regulars.

**◑** Open all year; restaurant closed Sun, Mon to non-residents

**⤢** In the centre of Watlington village, 2 miles from Junction 6 of the M40. Private car park

**⇌** 1 single, 4 twin, 5 double; most with bathroom/WC, some with shower/WC; TV in all rooms; hair-dryer, baby-listening on request

**◈** Restaurant, bar, lounge; conference facilities (max 12 people non-residential, 10 residential); tennis nearby. Wheelchair access to hotel (special door) and restaurant, 2 ground-floor bedrooms

**⊖** No dogs

**▭** Access, Amex, Diners, Visa

**£** Single £40, single occupancy of twin/double £47, twin/double £62. Cooked B £3; set L, D £17; alc L, D £24

---

*We hadn't even started our meal when the proprietress was asking if everything was all right – but even worse was her attitude the next morning at breakfast – she looked really terribly hung-over, it's true – but perhaps she could have tried to be less offputting about what she thought we should have. 'Well, IF YOU CAN FACE IT, we can cook you a full English breakfast.'*
On an hotel in Staffordshire

# Crossroads

HIGH STREET, WEEDON, NORTHAMPTONSHIRE NN7 4PX
TEL: WEEDON (0327) 40354   FAX: (0327) 40849

*Just off the M1, Crossroads is good for an overnight stop having comfortable rooms and friendly staff.*

You'd almost expect it to be the Crossroads Motel of television notoriety – after all, it is roughly in the right part of the world – but fortunately this Crossroads experience is less monotonous, and the characters far more exciting.

The old toll house that has been swallowed up by the hotel was used by the Daventry and Southern Turnpike Company in the nineteenth century. Today, the junction on the A45 is still a busy one and the building looks more like an hotel with the Garden House bedroom blocks across the car park.

The main building, which incorporates the old toll house, houses the main reception area, bar and restaurant. There are some fine decorative touches in these cheerful snug rooms: in the bar an apothecary's counter has been beautifully restored and has gleaming brass foot rails and a showcase of miniatures; in the restaurant is a collection of antique clocks. Bedrooms are spacious and brightly decorated with thoughtful extras like hot-water bottles. Those in the Garden House blocks are quieter.

○ Open all year, exc 25, 26 Dec

↗ 4 miles south-east of Daventry, at the junction of the A5 and A45, 3 miles from Junction 16 of the M1. Private car park

⇌ 8 single, 23 twin, 10 double, 3 four-poster, 4 family rooms; all with bathroom/WC, TV, hair-dryer, trouser press, mini-bar, baby-listening; cottage in grounds

◇ Air-conditioned restaurant and bar, lounge; conference facilities

(max 50 people non-residential and residential); tennis, fishing, heated swimming-pool at hotel, other sports nearby

⊖ No wheelchair access; no dogs

▭ Access, Amex, Diners, Visa

£ Single £70, single occupancy of twin/double £70, twin/double £80, four-poster £95, family room £99; deposit preferred. Alc L, D £20. Special breaks available

---

*Many hotels offer special rates for stays of a few nights or more. It is worth enquiring when you book.*

# Holdfast Cottage

WELLAND, NR MALVERN, HEREFORD AND WORCESTER WR13 6NA
TEL: HANLEY SWAN (0684) 310288

*Snug, friendly hotel with all home comforts; avoid a small single room.*

Larger than your average country cottage with roses round the door, Holdfast Cottage nevertheless manages to retain the compact cosiness associated with such dwellings. The long drive, lined with daffodils in spring, leads past landscaped lawns and up to the extended, wistaria-clad building. Through the attractive conservatory, filled with greenery surrounding the cane furniture, is the exceptionally low-beamed hall. The lounge is less oppressive, with ancient leather armchairs on casters and a modern comfy sofa, and views of the gardens.

Bedrooms are named after the nearby Malvern Hills. Tinker is painted a pretty blue, the teddy's bow-tie matching the soft furnishings. The unfortunately named Hangman, a small single, hasn't even enough room to swing a cat, particularly in the bathroom with its half-size basin. The dining-room is whimsical, with cases of mounted butterflies and a stuffed owl and duck. Diners have a choice of two menus; the quality of the food varies. When our inspector dined, home-made lovage and potato soup was good, and quail came stuffed with a tasty pâté but was undercooked. Service is amiable and obliging.

- ◑ Open all year
- 🔁 On the A4104 halfway between Little Malvern and Welland. Private car park
- 🛏 2 single, 2 twin, 4 double; all with bathroom or shower/WC, exc 1 single with shower/WC; TV, hair-dryer in all rooms
- ◈ Dining-room, bar, lounge, conservatory; conference facilities (max 8 people residential, 12 non-residential);

croquet at hotel, other sports nearby
- ⊖ No wheelchair access; no smoking in dining-room and bedrooms
- ▭ Access, Visa
- £ Single £34 to £44, single occupancy of twin/double £48 to £52, twin/double £66 to £74; deposit required. Set D £14; alc D £23.50. Special breaks available

---

*I found the atmosphere in the dining-room rather pretentious and felt that the set meal was rather expensive considering that there was no choice and that it was possible to count the vegetables – would you believe three mange-tout?!* On an hotel in Dorset

**WELLINGBOROUGH** NORTHAMPTONSHIRE                                **MAP 6**

# The Hind

SHEEP STREET, WELLINGBOROUGH, NORTHAMPTONSHIRE NN8 1BY
TEL: WELLINGBOROUGH (0933) 222827   FAX: (0933) 441921

*Popular for business guests: a sixteenth-century inn with cosy rooms.*

Within the one-way system in the centre of town, the Hind is situated between the pedestrianised shopping centre and the municipal car park.

The hotel relies on its age for its style. Over four hundred years old, yet thoroughly refurbished since then, the public rooms have dark wood panelling and there are beams in the Commons restaurant. It's a popular place for business guests, having newly redecorated bedrooms, a couple of them syndicate rooms for small meetings. Several open out on to a courtyard used for parking, and the rooms on the lower floor tend to be a little dark though brightly furnished.

- ◑ Open all year
- ⤵ In Wellingborough town centre, on the one-way system. Private car park plus free parking behind hotel
- 🛏 10 single, 10 twin, 11 double, 1 four-poster, 2 family rooms; all with bathroom/WC, TV, room service, hair-dryer, trouser press, baby-listening
- ◇ Air-conditioned restaurant, 2 bars, lounge; conference facilities (max 40 people non-residential, 20 residential); golf, riding, other sports nearby. Wheelchair access to restaurant and WC (unisex) only
- ⊖ No dogs in public rooms and some bedrooms; some bedrooms non-smoking
- ▭ Access, Amex, Diners, Visa
- £ Single £70, single occupancy of twin/double £75, twin/double £87, four-poster £97, family room £112. Set L £10, D £12; alc L, D from £15

**WELLS** SOMERSET                                                **MAP 8**

# Worth House

WORTH, WELLS, SOMERSET BA5 1LW
TEL: WELLS (0749) 672041

*A cosy, jolly hotel and restaurant where relaxing comes easy and paying is no hardship*

This pale green cube-shaped hotel stands by a minor road near Wells. Behind is an acre of pretty garden with seating around the base of a weeping willow tree, a rock garden and a hillside of contented-looking cows. Parts of the house are sixteenth-century and owners Nicholas Potts, his wife, Penny and brother Stephen, who arrived in the spring of

1990, have endowed it with a nice mix of old country furniture, a good restaurant and friendly vibes.

With small rooms and homely furnishings, it is very cosy. The lounge, near the little entrance hall, has a massive oak-beamed inglenook with wood stove. The restaurant, 'Tyler's', has an attractive rustic look and another log stove in an inglenook – hardly formal, but jackets and ties are encouraged. Nicholas produces a blend of French and English meals, with around half a dozen courses at each stage, perhaps fried Camembert with apple and cranberry sauce, then braised noisettes of lamb with root vegetables and port sauce, followed by brown-bread ice-cream with a raspberry coulis.

The simple and homely bedrooms have been brightened up with borders and colourful wallpaper, sometimes making the old furniture look dowdy. They are all reasonably sized and all but one face the garden. Prices are low, especially for single guests who pay just half the double rate.

| | |
|---|---|
| ◐ Open all year | fishing, golf, other sports nearby |
| ⤤ 2 miles west of Wells on the B3139 Wedmore/Burnham road. Private car park | ⊖ No wheelchair access; no dogs; no smoking in restaurant and 1 lounge |
| 🛏 1 single, 3 twin, 2 double, 2 family rooms; some with bathroom/WC, some with shower/WC; room service, hair-dryer, trouser press, baby-listening in all rooms | ▭ Access, Visa |
| | £ Single £28, single occupancy of twin/double £28, twin/double £56; children under 12 sharing parents' room £7 each; deposit required. Set L £7.50; alc D £21. Special breaks available |
| ◈ Restaurant, bar, 2 lounges; | |

---

**WEST BEXINGTON** DORSET             **MAP 9**

# The Manor

BEACH ROAD, WEST BEXINGTON, NR DORCHESTER, DORSET DT2 9DF
TEL: BURTON BRADSTOCK (0308) 897616/897785    FAX: (0308) 897035

*An agreeable mix of country pub and mid-range hotel. Plenty of character and fine views over Chesil Beach.*

The road to the village and Chesil Beach is lined with caravan parks and holiday cottages, and finding the ancient stone manor house of Bessington (now West Bexington) at the end of the road, comes as a surprise. Despite its name, the Manor is a down-to-earth, friendly, pub-like hotel.

Character comes in good measure: stone walls, oak panelling, some heavy carving (mentioned in the Domesday Book), real fires everywhere, and an unconventional arrangement of rooms. You reach the Victorian-style conservatory by going downstairs, through the dimly-lit stone-walled bar which was the original cellar, then upstairs again into the light.

Filled with amazingly convincing fake plants, this is a good place from which to admire the sea out of the rain or wind. There's also a residents' lounge with comfy old-fashioned heavy sofas. It looks over the pretty flower garden, which, with its swings, climbs and slides, will please younger guests.

The dining-room is especially attractive with stone-flagged floor and racing and hunting pictures that express the family's love of horses. And the food is satisfying, with the likes of mushrooms in garlic, cream and basil sauce, and scallop and monkfish kebabs with chilli sauce. Bedrooms are simply decorated, cottagey and small. Many have endless sea views. The Childs and their staff look after you well, enquiring how your day went and listening to the answer.

◐ *Open all year*

⚡ *5 miles south-east of Bridport on the B3157. Private car park*

🛏 *1 single, 3 twin, 8 double, 1 family room; most with bathroom/WC, some with shower/WC; TV, room service, hair-dryer, baby-listening in all rooms*

◈ *Restaurant, bar, 2 lounges, conservatory; conference facilities (max 70 people non-*
*residential, 13 residential); golf, water sports, other sports nearby*

⊖ *No wheelchair access; dogs in bar only*

▭ *Access, Amex, Diners, Visa*

💷 *Single £39 to £45, single occupancy of twin/double £39 to £45, twin/double £65 to £75; children under 10 sharing parents' room half-price; deposit required. Set L £15, D £18.50. Special breaks available*

---

**WESTDEAN** EAST SUSSEX                          **MAP 10**

# The Old Parsonage

WESTDEAN, ALFRISTON, NR SEAFORD, EAST SUSSEX BN25 4AL
TEL: ALFRISTON (0323) 870432

*What does it feel like to be a spoilt monk? Stay here, reputedly the oldest, continuously inhabited small medieval house in the country, and find out.*

Many villages on the coastal side of the South Downs have either suffered the ravages of development or are scarred by hordes of visitors. The quiet hamlet of Westdean escapes both, protected from the onslaught of housing estates by the surrounding Friston Forest, and from the masses by being up a cul-de-sac off the main tourist track.

Backing on to the twelfth-century church's graveyard, the Parsonage is only marginally younger – built, by the monks of Wilmington Priory in 1280, with monumentally thick flint walls and narrow, randomly placed diamond lattice windows. The Victorians added an extension so in keeping that from the outside it would fool all but the most acute architectural eye. Raymond and Angela Woodhams, civilised and welcoming, took over the building from an uncle who used to open the house to visitors. A tour now would take you to the three bedrooms: the Hall, a splendid room on the first floor with carved four-poster, and the Solar, adjoining the Hall and once its ante-room – both have beautiful timber roofs and their own spiral staircases; and the Hidden Room (so called because prior to the Victorian addition there would seem to have been no way into it), a simpler twin. Exposed flint and chalk blocks, black-painted shutters, wooden floorboards and a candle give an impression of medieval austerity; daffodils, mineral water, pretty china and tins for tea/coffee and an unsolicited hot-water bottle offer actual comfort suffused with the utmost care. Each room has its own similarly imaginatively decorated bathroom.

On winter evenings you can tuck up in the knole settee in front of a blazing fire, while in the morning you breakfast off individually laid tables. It's faultless: freshly squeezed orange juice; grapefruit segments cut for you; an English breakfast with double portions of everything; butter and marmalade . . .

- ◐ Closed Xmas and New Year
- ⤢ Off the A259 Brighton to Hastings coast road, east of Seaford. Private car park
- ⊫ 1 twin, 1 double, 1 four-poster; all with bathroom/WC, hairdryer
- ◈ Lounge, library/study; fishing,

- golf, other sports nearby
- ⊖ No wheelchair access; no children under 12; no dogs; no smoking in bedrooms
- ▭ None accepted
- £ Single occupancy of twin/double £30 to £40, twin/double £45 to £55, four-poster £60

---

**WEST DOWN** DEVON                                          **MAP 8**

# Long House

THE SQUARE, WEST DOWN, NR ILFRACOMBE, DEVON EX34 8NF
TEL: ILFRACOMBE (0271) 863242

*Delightful country cottage with more than a little sophistication, in addition to eager hosts and pretty bedrooms.*

The village is far enough away from the beach to be off the tourist beat, and pretty enough to make up for the lack of sea views. Four times a day a farmer parades his cows right past this neat and picturesque white long house en route to and from milking. Once home to a smithy and village shop, in the spring of 1989 it turned into what Rob and Pauline Hart call a country cottage hotel.

First, you encounter a cosy tearoom where dried flowers festoon white or rough stone walls and hang in baskets from the ceiling. Wheels from a hay rake stand about and home-made cakes sit on a pine dresser. It becomes intimate in the evening: curtains are drawn and tables dressed with linen cloths and napkins. Pauline's set dinners (with no choice for the main course) might run: crabbie courgettes, honey chicken with wild rice, and crème brûlée. Wines are far from *ordinaires* and more than just Rob's hobby: he's a Master of Wine. He also makes a jolly front-of-house. The rest of the ground floor is a low-ceilinged and rustic but stylishly furnished home with handsome country antiques. Through a little bar lounge, with a door to a little garden, you reach the main lounge, with large inglenook fireplace, mullioned windows, sparkling copper and brass, modern and Victorian family photographs and quality daily news-papers. Just as comfy and inviting are the bedrooms with beams, occasional slanting roofs, crisp and cheerful fabrics and rustic antiques. There are blankets if you don't like duvets. Room one is a smallish double with an old brass bed and a shower. Room two is more spacious and has a large, beamed bathroom with an Edwardian two-seater lavatory.

🌓 Open all year, exc mid-Nov to mid-Mar

🔋 Situated ½ mile off the A361 Barnstaple to Ilfracombe road, 4 miles from Woolacombe Bay. On-street parking

🛏 1 twin, 3 double; most with bathroom/WC, 1 double with shower/WC; TV, room service, hair-dryer in all rooms

◈ Dining-room, bar/lounge, lounge, drying room; conference facilities (max 10 people non-residential); fishing, golf, other sports nearby; babysitting

⊖ No wheelchair access; no dogs; no smoking in dining-room

▭ Access

💷 Single occupancy of twin/double £26, twin/double £47; deposit required. Set D £12.50; alc L £10.50

---

*When you telephone to book a room, and the hotel accepts your booking, you enter into a binding contract with them. This means they undertake to provide the specified accommodation and meals etc. for the agreed cost on the agreed dates, while you commit yourself to paying their charges. If you later have to cancel your booking, or fail to turn up, the hotel may be entitled to keep any deposit you have paid to defray administrative costs. If an hotel is unable to re-let the room you have booked – and it must try to do so – it is entitled to compensation for the loss of profit caused by your breach of contract. It can only claim a sum that is fair and reasonable. It should not make a profit out of your failure to appear. It's important to give as much notice as possible when cancelling: this increases the chances of your room being re-let.*

The hotel that was to
have been listed here changed
hands as we went to press.

---

**WEST MALVERN** HEREFORD AND WORCESTER            **MAP 6**

# One Eight Four

184 WEST MALVERN ROAD, MALVERN, HEREFORD AND WORCESTER
WR14 4AZ
TEL: MALVERN (0684) 566544

*Smart, deceptively large bed and breakfast with lovely views and
friendly hosts. Good for a walking weekend.*

With its blue canopies and neat exterior fronting directly on to the road,
Dennis and Jan Kellett's bed and breakfast looks more like a restaurant.
It's only when you go in that you realise that the building is bigger than it
seems: five floors as opposed to the two which are apparent from the
road. The slope it's built on drops sharply enough to allow additional
floors and a car park to be added below – and provides glorious views of
the Malvern countryside. The small seating area in the lobby, with its
baize green carpet and walking magazines, is the only public area besides
the dining-room, but one gets the feeling that guests who come here are
likely to prefer an active weekend in the hills rather than one lounging
beside Alfie the Burmese cat.

The breakfast room, with excellent views and an old gun cupboard full of books, is separated by a small screen from the kitchen where Jan makes her famed muffins. The largest of the five bedrooms is at the top of the house, with a sunken Victorian bath, brass bed and tiled washstand. The other rooms are smaller but also nicely furnished, with hand-carved mirrors and Georgian finger plates. Dennis also makes his own finger plates in Edwardian designs out of miraculously aged leather ('I can't tell you how – it's a trade secret').

| | | | |
|---|---|---|---|
| ◑ | Open all year | ◈ | Dining-room, lounge; golf, tennis, other sports nearby |
| ⤢ | On the B4232, I mile from the junction with the A449 Malvern to Worcester road (1½ miles from the centre of Great Malvern). Limited private parking, also on-street parking | ⊖ | No wheelchair access; no children under 12; no dogs; smoking in lounge only |
| | | ▭ | Access, Visa |
| 🛏 | I twin, 4 double; some with bathroom/WC, some with shower/WC; TV in all rooms; hair-dryer on request | £ | Single occupancy of twin/double £25, twin/double £35 to £41; deposit required. Light snacks only. Special breaks available |

---

**WEST MERSEA** ESSEX                                            **MAP 7**

# Blackwater Hotel

---

20–22 CHURCH ROAD, WEST MERSEA, COLCHESTER, ESSEX CO5 8QH
TEL: COLCHESTER (0206) 383338/383038

*A good French restaurant with simple bedrooms.*

The harbour is not very quaint but good food and accommodation in cheerful surroundings can be found chez Mme Chapleo. Her ivy-clad restaurant-with-rooms is by the church within a Victorian coaching-inn composed of three cottages. The white-walled and multi-beamed restaurant is informal, jolly and dressed up with horse-brasses and copper; there is little, in fact, apart from red-checked tablecloths and strings of onions that looks foreign.

French bistro cooking is the main drift of the carte that only occasionally slips out of gear with prawn cocktail or smoked mackerel pâté. Daily specials provide most interest. At lunchtime there is a set menu. Pre-dinner drinks and coffee are taken in a civilised manner in the small lounge, set with velvety chairs and made homely with knick-knacks.

Brightly furnished bedrooms have candlewick bedspreads and flowery curtains. They're simple but welcoming, and private bathrooms across the corridor are immaculate.

| | | |
|---|---|---|
| ◑ | Closed last 3 weeks Jan and first week Feb; restaurant closed Sun eve | of Mersea Island. Drive through the village until you reach the church on your left and the White Hart pub on your right; |
| ⤢ | West Mersea is at the west end | |

turn right into Church Road. Private car park

🛏 3 twin, 4 double; most rooms with bathroom/WC; TV in all rooms

◈ Restaurant, bar, lounge, breakfast room; golf, riding, other sports nearby. Wheelchair access to restaurant and WC (M,F) only

⊖ Dogs by arrangement only

▭ Access, Amex, Visa

£ Single £28 to £48, single occupancy of twin/double £28 to £48, twin/double £40 to £65; deposit required. Alc L, D £27. Special breaks available

---

**WESTON-UNDER-REDCASTLE** SHROPSHIRE     **MAP 4**

# The Citadel

WESTON-UNDER-REDCASTLE, NR SHREWSBURY, SHROPSHIRE ST4 5JY
TEL: HODNET (063 084) 204

*A lovely setting for this elegant, unusual house with large stylish rooms.*

Built when the passion for mock-Gothic architecture was at its height, the Citadel is an archetypal castle. Castellated turrets and round towers are just like the castles of children's picture-books.

The style is continued inside. Walls are hung with tapestries, and a fine inlaid octagonal table acts as a centrepiece. The sitting-room, warmed by a roaring fire in winter, is a fairly plain but comfortable room with Regency furniture and a grand piano for anyone inclined to play. The dining-room, where guests gather for dinner at 7.30pm, is a fine

-The Citadel-

example of the mock-Gothic with its coffered ceiling adorned with plaster vines. Of the three bedrooms, the turreted one is the most unusual but all are a good size and decorated with fine attention paid to the period features. Furniture is old-fashioned but somehow it all suits the atmosphere of the place.

◑ *Closed Nov to Mar, exc for parties of 4 to 6 people staying 2 nights min*

🚗 *On the A49, 12 miles north of Shrewsbury, 8 miles south of Whitchurch; follow signs to Weston/Hawkstone Park. The hotel is 1/4 mile out of the village of Weston, on Hodnet road. Private car park*

🛏 *2 twin, 1 double; 2 with bathroom/WC, 1 with shower/WC; hair-dryer in all rooms; TV in some rooms; tea/coffee-*

*making facilities on request*

◈ *Dining-room, lounge, games room; table tennis at hotel, golf nearby*

⊖ *No wheelchair access; no children; no dogs; no smoking in bedrooms*

▭ *None accepted*

£ *Single occupancy of twin/double £35, twin/double £50 to £55; deposit required. Set D £15 (7.30pm). Special breaks available*

---

**WEST WITTON** NORTH YORKSHIRE                              **MAP 3**

# The Wensleydale Heifer

WEST WITTON, WENSLEYDALE, NORTH YORKSHIRE DL8 4LS
TEL: WENSLEYDALE (0969) 22322  FAX: (0969) 24183

*Pretty village pub in the Dales, used by holidaymakers and honeymooners alike.*

This pretty whitewashed village inn lies in the Yorkshire Dales National Park and offers a surprisingly large number of rooms in relation to its apparent size.

Inside, it's as cosy as you'd expect an inn to be, although, since last year's edition, a great deal of refurbishment has taken place. The 'comfortably sagging chintz armchairs' in the lounge have been replaced by newly upholstered green and tangerine settees with not a sag in sight. Look closely and you see the colour scheme subtly matched in the carpet. The restaurant has also been extended and, like the Seafood Bistro, offers a range of fish dishes such as battered Whitby haddock and pan-fried scallops with spinach and chive butter as well as a good selection of meat dishes.

The bedrooms, named after local areas like Lady Hill and The Gallops, range from the ordinary to the rather more elaborate. One of the four-poster beds (to attract honeymooners) was crammed into a smallish room. There are more bedrooms in a quiet annexe, further from road and pub noise. One reader's reaction to these was not favourable. Visiting on a wet November day she also found that 'hotel guests were not encouraged to spend afternoons in the public seating areas and you had to struggle to get tea and coffee at these times'. More reports, please.

- *Open all year*
- *West of the village of West Witton, on the A684 Leyburn to Hawes road. Private car park*
- *6 twin, 9 double, 2 four-poster, 1 family room, 1 suite (some in annexe buildings); all with bathroom/WC, exc 3 doubles with shower/WC; baby-listening in all rooms*
- *Restaurant, bistro, bar, lounge; fishing, riding nearby*
- *No wheelchair access*
- *Access, Amex, Visa*
- *Single occupancy of twin/double £45, twin/double £62, four-poster £72, family room £72, suite £82; deposit required. Set L £11, D £20. Special breaks available*

**WHAPLODE** LINCOLNSHIRE **MAP 4**

# Guy Wells

WHAPLODE, SPALDING, LINCOLNSHIRE PE12 6TZ
TEL: HOLBEACH (0406) 22239

*Attractive and friendly farmhouse B&B in an area starved of good accommodation.*

Surrounded by flat fenland, this lovely Queen Anne farmhouse, backed by large glasshouses, is surrounded by a pretty garden and protected from the wind by trees all around.

The Thompsons run a friendly B&B and offer comfortable and stylish accommodation on their arable and horticultural farm. If Richard has time, he is happy to take interested guests round the glasshouses to see the marvellous array of blooms. Only three bedrooms are let, each with some fine furnishings including a half-tester in one. There is a wash-basin in each, plus a spacious shared bathroom in the corridor.

Downstairs, the beamed dining-room with its display of blue pottery and the sitting-room with its wood-burning stove are both attractive rooms in which to relax. Evening meals are available only at the weekends, when you might be offered home-grown vegetables and organic beef followed by fruit crumbles. For breakfast you can try their fresh free-range eggs.

- *Open all year, exc Xmas*
- *2 miles west of Holbeach on the A151, the farm is the first house on the left down Eastgate in Whaplode. Private car park*
- *1 twin, 1 double, 1 half-tester; 1 public bathroom*
- *Dining-room, lounge; fishing, golf, other sports nearby*
- *No wheelchair access; no children under 12; no dogs; no smoking*
- *None accepted*

£ Single occupancy of twin/double
£20, twin/double £32, half-tester
£30, family room (extra bed)

£42; deposit required. Set D £10
(by arrangement only). Special
breaks available

## WHEDDON CROSS SOMERSET

MAP 8

# Raleigh Manor

WHEDDON CROSS, NR DUNSTER, SOMERSET TA24 7BB
TEL: TIMBERSCOMBE (0643) 841484

*A country house high up on Exmoor. Despite some formal décor,
there is a relaxed tone.*

The village of Wheddon Cross is one of the highest on Exmoor, and from
this small hotel, on a wooded hillside outside the village, you can gaze
over miles of valleys and hills. The 102-year-old house has personality:
brick, weatherboard and stone with white trim without, and parquet
floors, stripped pine doors and open fires within. And it's been decorated
with good furnishings, some antiques, stripped pine and plenty of
comfortable seating.

The lounge is a little formal: square pelmets over large windows and
not many personal touches. You may feel more at home in the library
which has a built-in pine dresser filled with games, books and china, and
a wood-burning stove. Set four-course dinners are straightforward and
unpretentious. The house *tour de force* is to be found in the Squire's
bedroom: a turn-of-the-century walnut half-tester bed. Antiques turn
up in other bedrooms, also decorated in light floral patterns. There
aren't many facilities and carpeted bathrooms are old-fashioned.

○ Closed Nov to mid-Mar

⤴ Turn left 200 yards north of
Wheddon Cross down a private
road. Raleigh Manor is 800 yards
past Watercombe farm, across
the fields. Private car park

🛏 1 single, 2 twin, 3 double, 1 half-
tester; most with bathroom/WC,
some with shower/WC; TV in all
rooms; baby-listening on request

◈ Dining-room, lounge, library,
conservatory; fishing, riding,
water sports nearby

● No wheelchair access; no dogs in
public rooms

▭ Access, Visa

£ Single £28, single occupancy of
twin/double £38, twin/double
£56, half-tester £66; deposit
required. Set D £14

---

*Our sleep was rudely shortened by a brewery lorry which stopped at the back
of our room at 6.30am and left its engine running for half an hour. The
whole room shuddered. The manager was friendly but dismissive, as if to say
that lorries are a fact of life.* On an hotel in Suffolk

**WHIMPLE** DEVON                                    **MAP 8**

# Woodhayes

WHIMPLE, NR EXETER, DEVON EX5 2TD
TEL: WHIMPLE (0404) 822237

*A pampering country-house hotel close to Exeter.*

Woodhayes is a country-house hotel on the edge of a peaceful village and
has all the classic ingredients: a co-ordinated scheme of warm, soft
colours, plump sofas, paintings and prints, gilt mirrors and high-quality
furnishings – not to mention the tennis court and croquet lawn.

Unwind in either of the lounges, which are decorated in peaches and
pinks. Like the snug stone-flagged bar, they have coal-effect gas fires
(phoney but with genuine glow). The restaurant has one too, and a gilt-
framed mirror above its mantelpiece. Candelabra, antique sideboard and
fancy settings on linen cloths are as elegant as the good set dinners of
many courses: courgette mousse, lettuce and mint soup, sorbet, sole with
salmon mousseline, roast chicken with tarragon, then a choice of
desserts and cheese. After that, most people could sleep well on cold
floorboards. You will, of course, find comfort in the bedrooms, where the
chic décor of the downstairs gives way to a homelier, more old-fashioned
look. A reader who has stayed thrice and plans three further visits before
the year is out, writes: 'There are not many hotels that make you feel you
are coming home but this one does thanks to its wonderful owners.' Take
the all-in package and feel really cosseted: dinner, bed and breakfast; a
newspaper; tea and coffee whenever you like and, in the afternoon, tea
with home-made cakes.

- ◐ Open all year
- 🔼 8 miles east of Exeter off the A30 Exeter to Honiton road. Take the turning for Whimple and the hotel is just before the village. Private car park
- 🛏 2 twin, 4 double; all with bathroom/WC, TV, room service, hair-dryer; no tea/coffee-making facilities in rooms
- ◈ Dining-room, bar, 2 lounges;

- meetings facilities (max 6 people residential); tennis, croquet at hotel, other sports nearby
- ⊖ No wheelchair access; no children under 12; no dogs
- ▭ Access, Amex, Diners, Visa
- £ Single occupancy of twin/double £75, twin/double £110 (rates inc dinner). Set L £14, D £22.50

*Many hotels put their tariffs up in the spring. You are advised to confirm
prices when you book.*

**WHITEWELL** LANCASHIRE                                    **MAP 4**

# The Inn at Whitewell

WHITEWELL, FOREST OF BOWLAND, NR CLITHEROE, LANCASHIRE BB7 3AT
TEL: DUNSOP BRIDGE (020 08) 222

*Antiques and hi-fis in an inviting country inn.*

This long stone inn, full of character and imagination, straddles the rural inn/country-house hotel divide with some aplomb. The stylish entrance lounge is warm and welcoming with a profusion of polished brass, antiques, fresh flowers and a log fire. The handsome dining-room overlooks the River Hodder and a classically beautiful English land-scape. Wooden tables, ladderback chairs, sporting prints and hunting knick-knacks place the bar firmly in the country-inn tradition.

The long hall doubles as a receptacle for decorative whimsy – old leather suitcases, golf bags, toppers and a stuffed fox resplendent in batsman's pads – and a storeroom for Richard Bowman's other interests as wine merchant and art dealer. You're likely to find cases of wine stacked at random, and walls hung with a variety of pictures. Bedrooms are splendid, spacious, light and decorated with the confidence that suggests the hand of a professional interior designer: a combination of beautiful curtains, modern fabrics and antique furniture. In room five you'll find a real fire and a carved wood and brass bedstead. Several bathrooms have splendid Victorian or Edwardian fittings. Mr Bowman has another innovation he calls his 'wildcard'; all the rooms have video players and Bang and Olufsen sound systems. Food has been described as adequate, rather than exciting. A recent menu offered several choices including a chicken and pigeon terrine set in a basil and yoghurt sauce, and roast fillet of pork served with a dark ale sauce. One correspondent whose visit coincided with a staff birthday party reported that service let the side down: 'We were offered no help with our luggage . . . we had to ask for a dinner menu, ask for the order to be taken, ask for a wine list and eventually go to our table because no one showed us there.'

◐ *Open all year*

⤴ *Whitewell is 6 miles north-west of Clitheroe. Private car park*

🛏 *4 twin/double, I four-poster, 3 half-tester, I suite (family rooms available); all with bathroom/ WC, TV, baby-listening, room service; hair-dryer, trouser press on request; no tea/coffee-making facilities in rooms*

◇ *Restaurant, dining-room, 2 bars, lounge, games room, drying room; conference facilities (max 50 people non-residential, 9 residential); fishing at hotel in season, other sports nearby. Wheelchair access to restaurant only*

⊖ *None*

▭ *Access, Amex, Diners, Visa*

£ *Single occupancy of twin/double £47, twin/double/half-tester/ four-poster £62, suite £98; children sharing parents' room £9; deposit required. Set D £19.50; alc L £14, D £29; bar meals*

# The Old House

THE SQUARE, WICKHAM, HAMPSHIRE PO17 5JG
TEL: WICKHAM (0329) 833049   FAX: (0329) 833672

*A well-furnished Georgian town house with expensive, good regional French food.*

The medieval houses around Wickham's preserved square predate the Old House, for Richard and Annie Skipworth's hotel, a listed building, was built in 1715. Exposed rafters in bedrooms, an ornately carved oak bar, polished wood floors and panelling in lounges and tie-beams in the dining-room dictate the interior's style. Patio windows at the far end overlook a secluded garden of rose pergolas and clematis.

Furnishings complement the house's style: antiques, red velvety armchairs and candlesticks in the small reception rooms; and period furniture and comfortable armchairs in bedrooms. The restaurant has a high reputation and is costly as there's no table d'hôte menu. The à la carte is short but imaginative, using fresh and high-quality produce. The all-round priciness of the Old House may stem from its being predominantly used by business people. Bedrooms are not available on Sundays, and guests are evidently expected to be up and about by 9am, by which time cleaning is well under way.

◑ Closed 2 weeks Xmas, 2 weeks Easter, 2 weeks July/Aug; restaurant closed Sun

▣ 3 miles north of Fareham in the village square, at the junction of the A333 and A32. Private car park

⇤ 3 single, 3 twin, 5 double, 1 family room (some rooms in annexe); most with bathroom/WC, some with shower/WC; TV, room service, hair-dryer, trouser press, baby-listening in all rooms; tea/coffee-making facilities in annexe rooms only

◈ Restaurant, bar, 2 lounges; conference facilities (max 14 people non-residential, 12 residential); golf, tennis, other sports nearby. Wheelchair access to restaurant only

⊖ No dogs

▭ Access, Amex, Diners, Visa

£ Single from £80, twin/double from £95, family room from £105; deposit required. Alc L, D from £30

*On the day of our departure, my husband asked a waiter at 8.10am if there would be any point in our coming down to breakfast before 8.30am (the earliest time breakfast was available in the dining-room). In reply he received the monosyllabic – 'No.'* On an hotel in the Lake District

**WILLERBY** HUMBERSIDE                          **MAP 4**

# Willerby Manor

WELL LANE, WILLERBY, NR HULL, HUMBERSIDE HU10 6ER
TEL: HULL (0482) 652616   TELEX: 592629 TOWN G ref. Willerby
FAX: (0482) 653901

*An efficiently run hotel in a Victorian house near Hull which is
mainly geared towards the business trade.*

It takes only ten minutes to reach the centre of Hull so the hotel has
wisely geared itself to the business trade. The choice of eating venues
within the hotel attracts a wider range of visitor. You can choose between
'Lafite', the formal restaurant with smartly set tables and gliding waiters
serving from the French-inspired menu, or, less grand in the basement,
'Raffaele's', which concentrates on pasta and pizzas. There's also
'Everglades', where a quick and takeaway service dispenses pizzas and
baked potatoes.

The bedrooms were redecorated in the recent refurbishment and are
very comfortable. Some are in Regency-style with striped wallpaper,
heavy curtains and co-ordinating contract furniture; others, the cheaper
ones without the garden view, have smart, bright curtains and matching
covers with fitted bamboo-style furniture. Bathrooms and general facilities are all up to standard.

- ◑ Open all year; restaurant closed
  Sun eve

- ▦ From the A63 head for Willerby
  town centre. Private car park

- ⇌ 4 single, 10 twin, 22 double; all
  with bathroom/WC, exc 1
  double with shower/WC; TV,
  room service, hair-dryer, baby-
  listening in all rooms; trouser
  press in some rooms

- ◈ Restaurant, bistro, bar, lounge/
  conservatory; conference

- facilities (max 400 people non-
  residential, 36 residential); golf,
  riding, other sports nearby

- ⊖ No wheelchair access

- ▭ Access, Amex, Visa

- £ Single £25 to £59, single
  occupancy of twin/double £28 to
  £65; twin/double £40 to £82;
  deposit required. Continental B
  £4.50, cooked B £7.50; set L
  £9.50, D £12.50; alc L, D
  £19.50 to £22.50

*Warning to insomniacs, exercise freaks and late-night lovers: increasing
numbers of hotels have infra-red triggered security lamps. To save being
embarrassingly illuminated, check before you leave for your late-night or
pre-dawn stroll.*

# Pear Tree Cottage

CHURCH ROAD, WILMCOTE, STRATFORD-UPON-AVON, WARWICKSHIRE
CV37 9UX
TEL: STRATFORD-UPON-AVON (0789) 205889

*Good-value B&B in quiet cul-de-sac, providing a high standard
of accommodation.*

The Manders' home is tucked away off the road in this quiet village close
to Stratford-upon-Avon. It's just what you would expect a sixteenth-
century cottage to be, half-timbered with stone, plus the addition of a
sympathetic modern extension. The pretty garden has flowering
borders, fruit trees and smooth lawns – soothing surroundings after a day
on the road or sightseeing in busy Stratford. From one of the rooms (and
a bathroom), depending on your height, you can peer out of the windows
across the fields to Mary Arden's Cottage; though the day-trippers come
and go they're far enough away not to intrude on your peace and quiet.

The cottage has two small, neat lounges. Between the two is the stone-
flagged breakfast room with a large antique oak and elm sideboard and
blue and white china on polished tables. The cottagey style is continued
in the bedrooms (named after flowers), all of which are well furnished
and have *en suite* facilities. They are refreshingly 'un-twee' with plain
walls and carpets. The Manders are enthusiastic hosts and as well as a
warm welcome you'll get lots of suggestions for touring the surrounding
area.

- ◑ Open all year, exc Xmas to 2 Jan
- ⤢ 3½ miles north-west of Stratford off the A3400. Private car park
- 🛏 2 twin, 3 double, 1 family room; half with bathroom/WC, half with shower/WC; TV, hair-dryer in all rooms
- ◈ Dining-room, 2 lounges, TV
- room; golf, riding, other sports nearby
- ⊖ No wheelchair access; no children under 2; no dogs or smoking in public rooms
- ▭ None accepted
- £ Single occupancy of twin/double £28, twin/double £38, family room £48

*The* Guide *office can quickly spot when a hotelier is encouraging customers
to write a recommending inclusion – and sadly, several hotels have been
doing this in 1991. Such reports do not further an hotel's cause.*

**WINCANTON** SOMERSET                              **MAP 8**

# Holbrook House

HOLBROOK, NEAR WINCANTON, SOMERSET BA9 8BS
TEL: WINCANTON (0963) 32377

*Even fifty-somethings might find it dated, but a country-house
hotel to cherish for its solidity, comfort and hospitality.*

A short winding drive from the A303 brings you to the large, dour stone
house with cedars towering over it. Open the front door and walk back
through time into a vast and high-ceilinged hall/sitting-room with an
open fire and fat, thirties-style armchairs in bright yellow loose covers
(the sort where your knees end up higher than your shoulders). You'll be
greeted with a big smile, perhaps by Mr or Mrs Taylor, who arrived in
the early forties, enchanted by the space and Spanish mahogany doors.
In 1946 they turned it into an hotel and thus, mostly unchanged, it has
remained.

  This is a cheerful house with plenty of daylight streaming through big
windows, large, formal sprays of fresh flowers, open fires, a piano, lots of
books and very friendly hosts and staff. There are comfortable places
everywhere for a quiet read. If you want to watch television, you'll find
the appropriate lounge on the first floor. Bedrooms are large, high-
ceilinged, light, neat and, of course, old-fashioned. Several rooms with
washbasins and bathrooms are disappointing for the price which, alas, is
rather up-to-date. Sporting facilities are excellent and there is good
seating around and about the pretty and well-kept grounds where the
occasional deer wanders at dusk.

◑ Open all year

⤢ 1½ miles off the A303 on the
A371 towards Castle Cary.
Private car park

🛏 4 single, 5 twin, 9 double, 2
family rooms; most with
bathroom/WC, some with
shower/WC; baby-listening in all
rooms; TV, hair-dryer on request

◈ Dining-room, 2 lounges, lounge/
bar, TV room, games room;
conference facilities (max 25
people non-residential, 20
residential); tennis, heated

outdoor swimming-pool (May to
Sept) at hotel, other sports
nearby

⊖ No wheelchair access; no dogs in
public rooms

▭ Access, Visa

💷 Single £30 to £40, single
occupancy of twin/double £40 to
£48, twin/double £65 to £72,
family room £108 (4 people);
deposit required. Set L £11, D
£15; alc L £25, D £30 (prices till
end 91). Special breaks available

---

*Prices are quoted* per room *rather than* per person.

# Wykeham Arms

75 KINGSGATE STREET, WINCHESTER, HAMPSHIRE SO23 9PE
TEL: WINCHESTER (0962) 853834   FAX: (0962) 854411

*An idiosyncratic and most welcoming pub serving interesting food.*

Do you remember those old desks at school with bolted-on chair and
flip-up lid? Did you get into trouble for engraving your name on them
with your compass, or for dropping marbles through the ink well and
making a terrible racket? Well, you can relive your youth in the Wykeham
Arms, whose bar-side desks used to be presided over by Winchester
College scholars. It isn't just the desks that give this pub, ideally
positioned in a quiet, narrow street a short stroll from the cathedral and
just across from the College, a scholastic air. You'll find at one end of the
building an assortment of old sporting accessories, and at the other, on
the mantelpiece above one of the log fires, a collection of books including
dictionaries and thesaurus ready to settle lexical disputes. Tankards and
pictures cover almost every inch of wallspace in the bar; the first-floor
breakfast room and all the bedrooms are similarly smothered in paintings
and prints. When we visited, owner Graeme Jameson had been sorting
out a newly acquired batch, looking for blank spaces to fill – he reckons
the pub has 600 pictures and 1,000 tankards on display.

From some bedrooms you can see the cathedral if you lean out into the
street. They vary considerably, furnished in country pine and a liberal
smattering of antiques; Nelson (the admiral was reputed to have slept
here) has sloping floors and a sofa, Hamilton a pair of high Victorian
single beds once belonging to Graeme's grandparents. Two more have
odd bathrooms, one with a V-shaped ceiling, the other a red velvet chair.
The bar is comfortably split into four separate areas, one of which is set
aside for eating and designated no-smoking (no cigarettes are sold in the
pub). Food rates importantly here. Look forward to adventurous stuff
such as guinea-fowl, venison, spinach and Stilton soup, and baked goats'
cheese.

**◖** *Open all year; restaurant closed
Sun, also Mon eve*

**↗** *Immediately south of the
cathedral by Kingsgate at the
junction of Canon Street and
Kingsgate Road. Private car park*

**🛏** *3 twin, 4 double; all with
bathroom/WC, TV, hair-dryer,
mini-bar*

**◈** *Breakfast room, 4 bars; sauna at*

*hotel, fishing nearby. Wheelchair
access to restaurant only*

**⊖** *No children under 14; no
smoking in breakfast room, one
dining area and some bedrooms*

**▭** *None accepted*

**£** *Single occupancy of twin/double
£60 to £65, twin/double £70 to
£80. Alc L £17, D £22*

**WINDERMERE** CUMBRIA                                                                                     **MAP 3**

# The Archway

13 COLLEGE ROAD, WINDERMERE, CUMBRIA LA23 1BY
TEL: WINDERMERE (05394) 45613

*A memorable guesthouse in a central but quiet corner of
Windermere.*

Viewed from the outside this small Victorian stone terrace house is
unremarkable, yet letters have flooded in from well-satisfied readers.
Indoors, it is true, you'll find a guesthouse of exceptional flair, run by
capable, concerned and companionable hosts. Décor is in the traditional
rural vein, with lots of splendid period pieces. Solid Victorian furniture
sets the tone in the salmon-coloured lounge, and the accompanying lace
curtains, ceiling borders, paintings and drawings are all in keeping with
the mood. An interesting collection of books makes this a pleasant spot to
linger.

The stripped pine dining-room is an appropriate setting for the
health-conscious meals. Aurea Greenhalgh uses local organic produce
whenever possible. A lighter two-course supper has been introduced to
replace the traditional dinner – perhaps home-made chicken and ham
pie served with English new potatoes tossed in yoghurt and mint, a crisp
summer salad and corn bread, followed by summer pudding with fresh
cream, and home-made lemonade with a dash of fresh lime. Bread and
pasta are also home-made using organic flour, and vegetarian dishes
are always available. Breakfast has been much-praised: 'Absolutely
amazing,' wrote one correspondent of the array of cereals, muesli, dried
and fresh fruits, yoghurts, fruit and vegetable juices that complement a
traditional farmhouse grill or kippers. Fresh pancakes and spicy apple
griddle cakes bring a taste of the USA to Cumbria.

Bedrooms are cosy, pretty and comfortable with attractive antique
furniture, delicate modern wallpaper and good armchairs. All but one
have genuine Victorian patchwork quilts. The Greenhalghs are happy to
give advice on walks and drives.

◑ *Open all year, exc 10 to 30 Jan;
restaurant closed Sun eve*

⤤ *Close to the centre of
Windermere village, a short
walk from the tourist information
centre. Limited private parking;
on-street parking available*

🛏 *1 single, 2 twin, 2 double; all
with shower/WC, exc 1 twin with
bathroom/WC; TV, room service
in all rooms; hair-dryer on
request*

◇ *Dining-room, lounge; bicycles at
hotel, fishing, golf nearby*

⊖ *No wheelchair access; no
children under 10; no dogs; no
smoking*

▭ *None accepted*

£ *Single £20 to £24, single
occupancy of twin/double £30 to
£36, twin/double £40 to £48;
deposit required. Set D £10.50
(6.45pm). Special breaks
available*

# Holbeck Ghyll

HOLBECK LANE, WINDERMERE, CUMBRIA LA23 I LU
TEL: AMBLESIDE (05394) 32375   FAX: (05394) 34743

*A personally run hotel that attains high standards of comfort.*

This Victorian lodge is set in an elevated position with fine lake views
from the public rooms and some of the bedrooms. What gives it its edge,
however, is the sheer hard work and dedication put in by its owners,
David and Patricia Nicholson. As one American guest enthused: 'The
proprietor . . . is marvellous and reminded us of our Dudley Moore. He
wears different hats for different chores: you'll see him in the restaurant
waiting at table as well as behind the front desk.'

All the rooms are comfortable, though prices vary – it's worth
splashing out on the best room to get the wonderful views. Furnishings
include soft florals, heavy wood wardrobes, sometimes an old fireplace,
and a couple of chairs for lounging in. Downstairs, the house has some
lovely Art Deco touches, a couple of comfortable lounges and a fine
wood-panelled hall with an open fireplace. The restaurant is large, with
well-spaced tables, and the set menu has been praised as 'sophisticated
and very good'. Those with a sweet tooth can ponder over the display of
desserts at the entrance. Service is professional, only slightly marred on
inspection by the waiter's refusal to display the cheeseboard. It was 'too
heavy', but somehow the neighbouring waitress seemed to manage.
Breakfast is a treat with home-made preserves beautifully served on fine
china, and plenty of hot coffee and toast.

◗ Closed Jan

⤴ 3 miles north of Windermere on
the Ambleside road. Turn right to
Troutbeck after Brockhole
Visitors' Centre. The hotel is ½
mile on the left. Private car park

🛏 3 twin, 9 double, I four-poster, I
family room; all with bathroom/
WC, exc I double with shower/
WC; TV, hair-dryer, room
service, baby-listening in all
rooms

◈ Restaurant, bar, 2 lounges,
billiard room; conference
facilities (max I4 people

residential, 30 non-residential);
putting green at hotel, fishing,
golf, other sports nearby;
babysitting by arrangement

⊖ No wheelchair access; no
children under 8 in restaurant
eves; no dogs in public rooms; no
smoking in bedrooms

▭ Access, Visa

£ Single £67, twin/double £106 to
£140, four-poster £140 (prices
inc dinner); deposit required. Sun
L £14; set D £25; alc D £30.
Special breaks available

# Miller Howe

RAYRIGG ROAD, WINDERMERE, CUMBRIA LA23 1EY
TEL: WINDERMERE (096 62) 2536   FAX: (096 62) 5664

*Self-confident flamboyance and food of legendary magnificence.*

Not many people get to be legends in their own lifetime but John Tovey
has done just that, as the battery of certificates and 'Freedoms' bestowed
by various cities around the globe (and prominently displayed in the
entrance hall) testify. There's nothing particularly distinguished about
the turn-of-the-century white pebbledashed building, though its position high above Lake Windermere is enviable, and the broad, neat
sloping lawns dotted with statues are classically beautiful. Interior décor
in the public rooms is a mix of the clubby (dark carpets and walls and
leather chesterfields) and the exuberant (a veritable choir of fat cherubs).
The recently added conservatory is lighter and offers wonderful panoramic views. On fine days the chairs on the terrace are an alternative
spot to linger.

Dinner, however, is what Miller Howe, is all about. At 8.30pm, when
everyone is seated (and some gib at this regimented routine) the lights are
dimmed and choreographed waiters purvey a procession of plates. Food
enthusiasts are divided as to the subtlety of the cuisine; many applaud it
as Anglo-French at its best. Others, confused by the complexity of
entangled flavours that characterise a Tovey creation, accuse it of
following the décor over the top. There's no dispute over the flamboyance of the no-choice-till-dessert repast, the attention to detail or the
quality of the ingredients. One May evening diners were offered pasta
with cheese and brandy sauce served with deep-fried lightly curried
apple, followed by chilled cucumber soup and cubed salmon, chopped
fennel, prawn and garden herbs in a wine aspic on dressed lettuce with
brown bread. And this was but an overture for roast local farm chicken
stuffed with cheese herb pâté, basted with lemon and honey and served
on a basil and tomato sauce, and accompanied by seven elaborately
treated and distinctly flavoured vegetables. After such sensory overload
the simplicity of a fresh raspberry cheesecake is doubly refreshing. The
menu leaves you in no doubt as to who is the star of the show. If not off
lecturing, performing cookery demonstrations or overseeing his other
ventures, Mr Tovey, who designs but no longer cooks, takes a curtain call
during the main course. For all his showmanship, he seemed genuinely
touched when one reader asked him to autograph a menu.

Most bedrooms have magnificent views, and the décor, while in
traditional country-house style, is less ritzy than you might expect. They
are, however, supremely comfortable with extras that range from rubber
ducks and bathrobes to a stereo sound system, Hunter Davies' *Lake
District Quiz Book*, and several games. A first-rate Buck's Fizz awaits you
as you troop down for a characteristically comprehensive breakfast.

◑   Closed Dec to Mar

⤢   On the A592 between
     Windermere and Bowness.
     Private car park

🛏   9 twin, 4 double; most with
     bathroom/WC, 2 with shower/
     WC; room service (limited), hair-
     dryer, trouser press in all rooms;
     TV on request; no tea/coffee-
     making facilities in rooms

◈   Restaurant (air-conditioned), 4
     lounges, conservatory, drying
     room; limited conference
     facilities (details on request);

watersports, other sports nearby

⊝   No wheelchair access; no
     children under 12; no dogs in
     public rooms; no smoking in
     restaurant

▭   Access, Amex, Diners, Visa

£   Single occupancy rate on
     application, twin/double £130 to
     £240 (rates inc dinner); deposit
     required if late booking; 12½%
     service charge added to bills. Set
     D £30 (prices till end 91).
     Special breaks available

---

**WINDSOR** BERKSHIRE                        **MAP 9**

# Sir Christopher Wren's House

THAMES STREET, WINDSOR, BERKSHIRE SL4 1PX
TEL: WINDSOR (0753) 861354   TELEX: 847938 WRENSH G
FAX: (0753) 860172

*A hotel of considerable historic interest. While not without
inconsistencies, it still leaves a favourable impression.*

Beneath the walls of Windsor Castle and looking across the Thames to
the boathouses of Eton: you can't get much more English than that. The
house, crowded slightly by recent accretions, was built and lived in by the
great man himself in 1676. Inside, even allowing for attempts to create a
period feel, the décor is a little fussy, the style overblown and slightly
cluttered. Similarly odd are the signs hanging from the railings outside
touting teas and meals at discount rates, not really what you'd expect
from an establishment that advertises itself as one of the 'Premier Hotels
on the Thames'.

   Signs aside, dinner in the Orangerie Restaurant is a success; the food
tends towards the nouvelle but is not overly messed about and the
atmosphere is relaxed and enjoyable, created in large part by thoughtful
and intelligent service.

   Over-emphasis on the frills has, in the bedrooms, resulted in a few
problems with the basics: there's a shortage of space for writing and ugly,
antiquated heating/air-conditioning units. But the bathrooms with gold
taps, his and hers basins and efficient plumbing, and the attention
lavished on matching pastel fabrics, more than compensates – these are
agreeable, comfortable rooms.

◑   Open all year

⤢   In the centre of Windsor, close

to Windsor Riverside station.
Private car park

🛏 7 single, 10 twin, 16 double, 5 four-poster, 2 family rooms; all with bathroom/WC, TV, room service, hair-dryer, trouser press; mini-bar in 2 rooms

◈ Restaurant, bar, 2 lounges, library, conservatory; air-conditioned conference facilities (max 100 people non-residential, 40 residential); fishing, golf, other sports nearby

⊖ No wheelchair access

▭ Access, Amex, Diners, Visa

💷 Single £68, £78, single occupancy of twin/double £95, twin/double £105, four-poster £105, family room £110; deposit required. Continental B £5.50, cooked B £7; set L £9.50, D £12.50; alc L £21, D £22.50 (prices till Mar 92). Special breaks available

---

**WINSFORD** SOMERSET                          **MAP 8**

# Royal Oak

WINSFORD, MINEHEAD, SOMERSET TA24 7JE
TEL: WINSFORD (0643 85) 455   FAX: (0643 85) 388

*A classic inn in a perfect Exmoor village.*

If you're coming from Withypool you will enter Winsford by fording a stream: it's your first glimpse of this particularly lovely pint-size Exmoor village and its decorative inn. Baskets of flowers hang from the long, eight-hundred-year-old inn the colour of buttermilk. On top is a delightful reed thatch, with first-floor windows peering out from beneath wavy arches like eyes from beneath heavy lids.

The sleepy image continues inside the low, oak-beamed inn: locals pass the time of day in the bar, and out-of-towners cat-nap in front of the sitting-room fire. Comfortable and cosy, the sitting-rooms have decorative extras: stones and pebbles gaily painted with portraits of cats, owls or pigs, plus pottery figures, filling shelves, window ledges, everywhere.

Back to the traditional in the restaurant, where another fire glows and candlelit lamps stand on crisp tablecloths. Gold-trimmed, cream-coloured furniture is standard in bedrooms, as are plain walls and dainty prints. Apart from the beams and slanting ceilings, the best features of the bedrooms under the eaves (others are in an annexe) are the little windows with their thick awnings of thatch.

⊙ Open all year

🡒 4 miles north of Dulverton, 10 miles south of Minehead, off the A396. Private car park

🛏 2 twin, 11 double, 1 family suite (some rooms in annexe); all with bathroom/WC, TV, room service (limited), hair-dryer

◈ Dining-room, 2 bars, 3 lounges, drying room; fishing at hotel,

riding, other sports nearby

⊖ No wheelchair access

▭ Access, Amex, Diners, Visa

💷 Single occupancy of twin/double £60 to £65, twin/double £89 to £99, suite £120; deposit required. Sun L £12.50; set D £20; alc D £27.50. Special breaks available

**WINSTER** DERBYSHIRE                                         **MAP 4**

# The Dower House

MAIN STREET, WINSTER, DERBYSHIRE DE4 2DH
TEL: WINSTER (0629) 650213   FAX: (0629 88) 894

*A prettily decorated and extremely comfortable B&B. An ideal
base for the southern part of the Peak District.*

At the west end of Winster, you would drive straight into the Dower
House if you failed to follow the main street as it twists out of the village.
Grade-II-listed Elizabethan with parts added in later centuries, it has a
small gravelled area in front of the house – just big enough for three or
four cars to park. That's plenty as there are only three rooms. Decorated
with smart, fresh matching duvet covers and white wicker chairs with co-
ordinating cushions, all the bedrooms are beautifully kept. Each room
has its own handbasin and shares a separate shower, loo and bathroom.

You walk straight into a welcoming hall/sitting-room, part-parquet,
part-carpeted, with comfortable chairs grouped around a large open
fireplace. The owners have their own sitting-room but are close by if you
need them. The dining-room is for breakfast only, served at the one table
and cooked to order. There are a couple of pubs in the village that serve
food in the evenings and plenty of restaurants in the area.

- ◑ Open Mar to Oct
- ⤴ Turn off the A6 Matlock to
  Bakewell road on to the B5057
  to Winster. The hotel is at the
  end of the main street. Private
  car park
- 🛏 2 twin, 1 double, 2 public
  bathrooms; TV in all rooms
- ◈ Dining-room, lounge, drying
  room; fishing, golf, other sports
  nearby
- ⊖ No wheelchair access; no
  children under 10; no dogs in
  dining-room
- ▭ None accepted
- £ Single occupancy of twin/double
  £16, twin/double £32; deposit
  required

**WINTERINGHAM** HUMBERSIDE                                   **MAP 4**

# Winteringham Fields

WINTERINGHAM, SOUTH HUMBERSIDE DN15 9PF
TEL: SCUNTHORPE (0724) 733096   FAX: (0724) 733898

*A restaurant-with-rooms possessing plenty of character.*

One reader complains that they had 'a heck of a time' finding this hotel –
needing to ask several different people before eventually finding the way.
It is worth finding though, for the general pleasantness of the rooms and
the added bonus of good food (though we have heard a disappointed
muttering about the latter – more reports, please). Winteringham Fields

is a Swiss/Yorkshire combination, run by Germain and Annie Schwab, though it is largely Annie who is responsible for the Victorian character of the public rooms, with a multiplicity of different textures, colours and ornaments. The lounge (parlour?) is particularly good at transporting you backwards in time, and you earnestly expect sing-songs in front of the upright piano.

Bedrooms are also interestingly furnished (with good modern beds) and each has the unusual and welcome attribute of a small dressing-room. One of the bathrooms is reached down a flight of stairs to what used to be an apple store – 'delightful, but you have to take care in the middle of the night'. The restaurant is garnished with columns, whose combination of blue, pink and gold leaf lends a surprising air of modern formality to the place. Dinners are not notably cheap. A nice small hotel, as one reader comments, though they add that the price may prevent them from returning.

◐ Closed Xmas, first half Jan, first week Aug; restaurant closed Sun

↗ Winteringham is on the south bank of the Humber estuary, 6 miles west of the Humber Bridge, off the A1077. Hotel is at crossroads in centre of village. Private car park

🛏 3 twin, 2 double, 1 four-poster; most with bathroom/WC, some with shower/WC; TV, room service, hair-dryer in all rooms; no tea/coffee-making facilities in rooms

◈ Restaurant, bar, lounge, library, conservatory; fishing, golf, riding nearby. Wheelchair access to restaurant only

⊖ No children under 10; no dogs; no smoking in bedrooms

▭ Access, Visa

£ Single occupancy of twin/double £65, twin/double £80 to £85, four-poster £95. Cooked B £6; set L £14, D £28 to £38; alc D £38 to £50

---

**WITHERSLACK** CUMBRIA                                    **MAP 3**

# The Old Vicarage

---

CHURCH ROAD, WITHERSLACK, GRANGE-OVER-SANDS, CUMBRIA LA11 6RS
TEL: WITHERSLACK (044 852) 381
FAX: (044 852) 373

*Stylish and sophisticated Georgian retreat in pleasant rural backwater, with swish new garden extension.*

The hordes that invade the Lake District somehow don't make it to this lovely spot in the Winster Valley. The Burrington-Brown and Reeve families have capitalised on the fine location of the old house, adding an all-weather tennis court and a suite of five upmarket bedrooms in the extensive garden. In the original house, the atmosphere is restrained and simply elegant, with classic good taste all around. Two smallish lounge/bars provide plenty of seating in cane and wicker chairs, and comfy round-backed padded armchairs. They're appealing places to sit and read or set up the various board games to hand. Bedrooms combine cast-iron fireplaces, Victorian taps and wooden basin surrounds with the modern floral-print fabrics, oak and cane furniture and potted ferns that make them feel light and airy.

When the grandfather clock in the hall strikes 8pm, Mr Burrington-Brown escorts you into the elegant, formal dining-room, where wine is racked in the fireplace, and an array of spirits and liquers is arranged across a Welsh dresser. The set five-course dinner offers no choice until the dessert stage (when you're prevailed upon to try both). Stanley Reeve is an enlightened chef and weaves local and home-grown ingredients into his menus. One April night guests were offered fresh halibut cooked in a cream and wine sauce with fresh tomato, home-made celery and apple soup followed by roast leg of Highland lamb served with fresh mint sauce and a rich gravy. Dessert options preceded a cheeseboard.

Bedrooms in the new Orchard House wing are decidedly chic and combine cheerful modern fabrics, with bamboo headboards, stripped pine desks and stereo systems incorporating compact disc players. Bathrooms are stylish.

○ Open all year

↗ Leave the M6 at Junction 36, following the signs to Barrow-in-Furness. Turn off the A590 into Witherslack and 50 yards past the telephone box, turn left. The hotel is ¾ mile along this lane on the left. Private car park

🛏 1 single, 4 twin, 7 double, 1 four-poster; all with bathroom/WC, exc single with shower/WC; TV, room service, hair-dryer in all rooms; mini-bar in some rooms

◇ Restaurant, breakfast room, 2 lounges, drying room; tennis at hotel, other sports nearby.

Wheelchair access to hotel (3 steps) and restaurant, 5 ground-floor bedrooms, one specially equipped for the disabled

● No children under 12 in restaurant; no dogs in public rooms or unattended in bedrooms; no smoking in public rooms

▭ Access, Amex, Diners, Visa

£ Single £40, single occupancy of twin/double from £57, twin/double from £102, four-poster £144; deposit required. Set D £26 (8pm) (prices till Apr 92). Special breaks available

---

**WITHINGTON** GLOUCESTERSHIRE                                    **MAP 6**

# Halewell Close

---

WITHINGTON, NR CHELTENHAM, GLOUCESTERSHIRE GL54 4BN
TEL: WITHINGTON (0242) 89238

*Stylish Wolsey Lodge with beautiful grounds; just right for getting away from it all.*

Be sure to get clear directions about how to find this Wolsey Lodge – Withington spreads itself enough to cause frustration after several

U-turns. The brisk Elizabeth Carey-Wilson is accustomed to the tan-trums of the travel-worn: 'People arrive all hot and bothered but come down a few hours later after a good rest with their good humour amazingly restored.' And it would be difficult to remain grouchy for long in this lovely part-fifteenth-century house, formerly a small farming monastery.

The cloisters have been glassed in – Mrs Carey-Wilson has plans for a sunken garden in the middle – and the remains of original frescoes can be seen on one of the dining-room walls. Also in this room is some beautiful linenfold panelling, a long polished table for communal din-ners, and a small 'snug' screened off by Edwardian scrap screens standing on the flagstone floor. There are several sitting-rooms, the most impressive of which has a high sloping ceiling with an elaborate system of beams, a crown-like wrought-iron chandelier, and mullioned stained-glass windows. Bedrooms are informal and relaxing, with more beams and antiques, and good-sized bathrooms, though we have had a report about weak water pressure on one occasion. The 50 acres of grounds surrounding the house include a trout lake fed by natural springs and pretty terraced gardens.

◖ Open all year; dinner by arrangement

🚗 Leave the A40 south on the A436 Andoversford road, and take the first left to Withington. Private car park

🛏 2 twin, 4 double (2 with separate children's rooms); all with bathroom/WC, TV; baby-listening, hair-dryer on request

◈ Dining-room, bar, lounge, TV room, library, drying facilities; meetings facilities; fishing at hotel Apr to Oct, also heated

outdoor swimming-pool May to Sept, riding nearby. Wheelchair access to hotel, dining-room and WC, 1 ground-floor bedroom equipped for the disabled

⊖ No children under 8 at dinner; no dogs in public rooms or in some bedrooms; no smoking in dining-room

▭ Access, Visa

£ Single occupancy of twin/double £48, twin/double £75; family rate by arrangement; deposit required. Set D £17.50 (8pm)

**WITHYPOOL** SOMERSET           **MAP 8**

# Royal Oak Inn

WITHYPOOL, SOMERSET TA24 7QP
TEL: EXFORD (064 383) 506    FAX: (064 383) 659

*A comfortable inn in the heart of Exmoor that combines cosiness and sophistication.*

You can feel that this is a popular place as soon as you walk in. The beams and panelling tell of its sixteenth-century origins and the decoration and furnishings have been sensibly and sympathetically done. You are immediately made to feel at home and the staff are friendly and good-humoured.

In one bar you can eat or drink settling back into the cushioned bench seats. Lots of hunting trophies adorn the walls and reinforce the country-inn atmosphere; the other bar is a lot more fun if you're in the mood for joining in local chat and the odd song or two. There's also a rather sophisticated dining-room. Decorated in blues and a mustardy yellow, it can be cosy on a winter's evening with a lit fire and candles. The menu has starters like deep-fried Brie with gooseberry conserve or smoked haddock with cream and Pernod sauce; the main dishes might include grilled fillet of sole with chives.

The bedrooms, approached via a creaky old staircase, are a good size, decorated with pretty unfussy chintz, nice pieces of period furniture and have lattice panes in the heavy stone-framed windows. Bathrooms are perfectly adequate. Breakfast is taken in the dining-room: delicious strong cafetière coffee and a well-cooked breakfast.

○ Open all year, exc 25 and 26 Dec

↗ From Bampton take the B3222, then the B3223 north-west towards Withypool. Private car park

🛏 1 twin, 5 double, 1 four-poster, 1 family room; some with bathroom/WC, some with shower/WC, 2 public bathrooms; TV, room service, hair-dryer, baby-listening in all rooms

✦ Dining-room, bar, lounge, drying room; fishing, riding, clay pigeon shooting, other sports nearby

● No wheelchair access; no children under 10

▭ Access, Amex, Diners, Visa

£ Single occupancy of twin/double £32 to £42, twin/double £56 to £68, four-poster £68, family room £84; deposit required. Set D £19; alc D £25; bar lunches

---

**WOODSTOCK** OXFORDSHIRE                                    **MAP 6**

# The Bear Hotel

PARK STREET, WOODSTOCK, OXFORDSHIRE OX7 1SZ
TEL: WOODSTOCK (0993) 811511    TELEX: 837921 BERTEL G
FAX: (0993) 813380

*A pleasantly atmospheric sixteenth-century coaching-inn whose location goes some way towards justifying the tariff.*

The entrance to Blenheim, the Duke of Marlborough's stately home, is a few hundred yards down the road and it's fair to say that the popularity of the Bear is in part due to the proximity of this major tourist attraction. In the summer, visitors flow steadily along Park Street. But the Bear is worthy of attention in its own right. Crooked doorways, labyrinthine stairways, creaking floors and battered tapestries give the hotel a genuine atmosphere and character that Forte have, so far, left intact.

The bar and restaurant, both with blackened beams – the first cosily pub-like, the second elegantly candlelit – fit in well with the overall scheme of things. In the bar the 1734 'Rules and Orders of Cocking' are given pride of place. In the restaurant, starters are more imaginative than the main courses. Service is totally professional yet there are definite hints of a relaxed and genuine approach emanating from behind the uniforms.

The Blenheim Suite is said to have been a favourite retreat of Liz Taylor and Richard Burton, but all the rooms are a good size and individually decorated and furnished. Attic rooms pose a threat to the heads of taller guests.

◑ *Open all year*

↗ *8 miles north of Oxford on the A34 Stratford road, in the town centre. Private car park*

🛏 *5 single, 19 twin, 13 double, 4 four-poster, 1 family room, 3 suites; all with bathroom/WC, TV, room service, hair-dryer, trouser press, baby-listening*

◈ *Restaurant (air-conditioned), bar, lounge; conference facilities (max 70 people non-residential, 45 residential), tennis, golf, other sports nearby; babysitting by arrangement. Wheelchair access*

*to hotel, restaurant and WC (unisex), 6 ground-floor bedrooms*

⊖ *No dogs in public rooms; some bedrooms non-smoking*

▭ *Access, Amex, Diners, Visa*

£ *Single £80, single occupancy of twin/double £83, twin/double £100, four-poster/family room £127, suite £160; deposit required. Continental B £6, cooked B £8; set L £17.50, D £22.50; alc L, D £30. Special breaks available*

---

# The Feathers

MARKET STREET, WOODSTOCK, OXFORDSHIRE OX7 1SX
TEL: WOODSTOCK (0993) 812291   FAX: (0993) 813158

*Popular with old and young alike – a privately owned hotel with an excellent restaurant where the approach is informal and welcoming.*

The Feathers is nearing the end of a refurbishment that has involved a reduction in the number of rooms (not a regular phenomenon, that). Only one single survives but that is soon to go, converted into a sitting-room for a suite. The straightforward red-brick exterior of the hotel hides a maze of passages and stairways but once you've found your room you're well rewarded: quality furnishings and no little flair have gone into rooms that encourage lounging.

Downstairs, while there have been criticisms of the service in the restaurant, the food itself has received nothing but praise. The formula revolves around a menu of half a dozen choices for each course where simple descriptions belie the effort and culinary skill of Nick Gill. An appetite and time are essential as the set dinner spreads over five courses, followed by coffee taken upstairs in the drawing-room in one of two clusters of plumped-up sofas. The restaurant itself is an effective combination of blue and yellow with chairs arranged in matching pairs to complement the colour scheme.

◐ *Open all year*

⤴ *Centrally located in Woodstock. If you come from the south, Market Street is the second turning on the left. On-street parking*

⇌ *1 single, 7 twin, 6 double, 3 suites; most with bathroom/WC, 1 public bathroom; TV, hair-dryer, baby-listening in all rooms; no tea/coffee-making facilities in rooms*

◇ *Restaurant (air-conditioned), bar, 2 lounges; conference facilities*

*(max 17 people residential, 25 non-residential); golf, tennis, other sports nearby. Wheelchair access to restaurant and WC (M) only*

⊖ *No dogs in bar or restaurant*

▭ *Access, Amex, Diners, Visa*

£ *Single £75, single occupancy of twin/double £85, twin/double £90 to £125, suite £145; deposit required. Cooked B £5.50; set L £16.50, D £19.50; alc L, D £26*

**WOODY BAY** DEVON                                          **MAP 8**

# Woody Bay Hotel

WOODY BAY, PARRACOMBE, DEVON EX31 4QX
TEL: PARRACOMBE (059 83) 264

*Sublime and dramatic setting on the edge of Exmoor. The hotel doesn't quite match up but is comfortable.*

A 1-in-4 road zigzags its way to the steep, wooded hillside and this 1890s hotel enveloped by woods. The rocky coastline and bay lie below, a view you'll enjoy from most public rooms and a good many bedrooms. The Scott family works hard to make your stay pleasant. 'A G&T on the terrace watching the sun go down behind the headland and the water below is truly restful,' writes one reader. You can enjoy the amazing panorama from the lounge, or help yourself to a novel or reference book from the bookshelf which clads one wall. If, that is, you can keep yourself from dozing in the big, soft easy chairs.

Sunsets are a feature from the dining-room, and the food is more than adequate: chilled cucumber soup, braised venison, and 'deliciously fresh' fruit salad, for instance. After dinner, the Scotts may invite you to join in a sing-song and later meet a live owl from their small sanctuary. Should you decline, you may not entirely escape the strains of 'Que sera, sera' which will probably continue past eleven. Recently decorated bedrooms ('very bright, cheerful and fresh') have light and uplifting colour schemes and are simply furnished. Bathrooms are of a reasonable standard.

◐ *Closed early Jan to mid-Feb*

⤴ *The hotel is well signed from the A39 and is 2 miles west of*

*Barbrook. Private car park*

⇌ *1 single, 4 twin, 6 double, 2 four-poster, 1 family room; most*

with bathroom/WC, some with
shower/WC, 1 public bathroom;
TV, hair-dryer on request

◇ Restaurant, bar, lounge; fishing,
riding, water sports nearby

⊖ No wheelchair access; no
children under 8; dogs in bar
only

▭ Access, Visa

£ Single £26 to £39, twin/double
£46 to £78, four-poster £58 to
£84; deposit required. Set D
£16.50; alc L £11, D £24; bar
lunches

## WOOLACOMBE DEVON                                MAP 8

# Little Beach

THE ESPLANADE, WOOLACOMBE, DEVON EX34 7DJ
TEL: BARNSTAPLE (0271) 870398

*A medium-sized beach hotel, capably run and with very friendly hosts.*

Neither the beach nor the hotel is little, especially the former which stretches for three miles. The latter, one of several places to stay along the Esplanade, was an Edwardian gentleman's country house and took up as an hotel in the twenties. Nola and Brian Welling changed professions too, previously dealing in antiques. As hoteliers they've attracted letters of praise: 'Brian and Nola are very unobtrusive but efficient. They are always there if you need them or for a chat.'

In the dining-room, polished cabinets of china, one of Brian's main interests, are compensation for diners not lucky enough to bag a window seat. A TV lounge has been turned into a small antique shop specialising in wooden boxes. Peaceful and spacious ground-floor rooms boast some antiques but have been furnished for comfort. Plants and a well-stocked bookshelf share the large, sea-facing bay of the drawing-room with its excellent easy chairs, settees and writing desk. A sun lounge with wicker chairs functions as a bar. You can also take your pre-dinner drink and enjoy the panorama of beach, the Isle of Lundy and Baggy Point cliffs from the split-level terrace. Striped wallpaper and flowery or Paisley print bedspreads are decorative touches of essentially basic bedrooms. Readers have commented on the pleasure of having early-morning tea brought to their room. Bathrooms are simple and small. Dinners are traditional but show some invention. One report concludes: 'A stress-free holiday. We could have stayed for weeks.'

◐ Closed Nov to Feb

🄼 From Barnstaple take the A361 to Ilfracombe. After 10 miles turn left at Mullacott Cross roundabout, signposted Woolacombe 3 miles. Private car park

🛏 2 single, 1 twin, 7 double; some with bathroom/WC, some with shower/WC, 1 public bathroom; TV in all rooms; room service, hair-dryer, ironing facilities on request

◈ Dining-room, bar, 2 lounges,
drying room; golf, water sports,
other sports nearby

⊖ No wheelchair access; no
children under 7; no dogs in
public rooms; no smoking in
dining-room

▭ Access, Visa

£ Single £35, single occupancy of
twin/double £35, twin/double
£62 to £86 (rates inc dinner);
deposit required. Bar lunches.
Special breaks available

**WOOLLEY GREEN** WILTSHIRE                          **MAP 9**

# Woolley Grange

BRADFORD-ON-AVON, WILTSHIRE BA15 1TX
TEL: BRADFORD-ON-AVON (022 16) 4705   FAX: (022 16) 4059

*A serene and plushly furnished Jacobean manor in perfect English
countryside.*

Woolley Grange is an august, many-gabled Jacobean manor just outside
the medieval town of Bradford-on-Avon. Gardens are both formal and
dramatic, the car park is tucked out of view, and the intimate interior is
rich in deep panelling, moulded ceilings and swish antiques, many of
them Edwardian and Victorian. Hotel paraphernalia is low-key and
comfort and service top-class. Best of all, it manages to avoid being
precious.

None of the several sitting-rooms is very large, and intimate corners
are plentiful, but it feels very grand. Log fires contribute warmth and
atmosphere and there are exotic features here and there. A sphinx-like,
blue and gold figure poses demurely at the top of the stairs, and one of the
bedrooms has an elephant foot table. Glass and beams, replacing a
collapsed roof, extend from the dining-room to an exterior wall, creating
a conservatory-like room: a lovely and impressive setting for afternoon
tea. Set, four-course lunches and dinners are pricey but as elegant and
polished as the restaurant. For dinner, amongst the several choices, you
might find smoked lamb salad, turbot with leeks and tomatoes, and hot
caramel soufflé. Though less interesting than the setting or public
rooms, bedrooms, if on the small side, should fulfil most people's
perception of a sybaritic country-house hotel. They are less luxurious
and more countrified than the downstairs, with summery colours,
patchwork quilts and pine or brass beds. Bathrooms are ordinary and
several small doubles have showers only.

◑ Open all year

🔁 On the B3109, 1 mile north-east
of Bradford-on-Avon. Private car
park

🛏 1 single, 17 double, 2 suites;
most with bathroom/WC, some
with shower/WC; TV, room

service, hair-dryer, baby-listening
in all rooms; no tea/coffee-
making facilities in rooms

◈ Restaurant, 3 lounges, games
room, supervised nursery, library/
study, conservatory; conference
facilities (max 35 people non-

residential, 20 residential);
tennis, croquet, badminton,
heated outdoor swimming-pool
(Easter to Oct) at hotel, other
sports nearby; babysitting

● No wheelchair access; no dogs in
restaurant

▭ Access, Amex, Diners, Visa

£ Single £80, single occupancy of
double £80, double £89 to £125,
family room £135, suite £158;
deposit required. Set L £10 to
£30, D £27 to £40. Special
breaks available

## WOOLSTASTON SHROPSHIRE                                    MAP 6

# Rectory Farm

WOOLSTASTON, LEEBOTWOOD, CHURCH STRETTON, SHROPSHIRE
SY6 6NN
TEL: LEEBOTWOOD (069 45) 306

*Homely comfort and good views in a farmhouse B&B offering
good value for money.*

The gleaming white, half-beamed house in the tiny village of Woolstaston looks long enough to be an entire row of cottages. It faces miles of
unspoilt Shropshire countryside with good views towards the Wrekin,
and lies on the slopes of the Long Mynd hills. John Davies, who was born
here, still runs the beef farm, while his wife Jeanette runs the bed and
breakfast side of the business. She is well versed in the art of hospitality
as she used to be an inspector of B&Bs all over the country and feels the
most important way of making people feel at home is by letting them
wander.

The house is filled with personal touches: Jeanette's grandmother was
responsible for most of the embroidery and even a carved chair, while her
mother painted some of the oil paintings in the bedrooms. In the hall
hangs an austere portrait of her great, great grandfather: 'I believe he sat
52 times for the painting, so he deserves a bit of wall space.'

The bedrooms are spacious, especially the pink room which is light
and airy, with a sofa and copies of *Country Life* magazine. The tiled
bathrooms are small but adequate. Downstairs, there is old oak panelling
in the hall and an ancient bread oven. Breakfast is served in a high-
ceiling dining-room, formerly a stable.

◑ Closed Dec to Feb

⤢ Leave the A49 Shrewsbury to
Hereford road at Leebotwood.
Continue for 1¾ miles to
Woolstaston. The farm is to the
right of the village green. Private
cark park

🛏 2 twin, 1 double; all with
bathroom/WC, room service,
hair-dryer, tea/coffee-making

facilities on request

◈ Lounge, TV room; golf, tennis,
riding nearby

● No wheelchair access; no
children under 12; no dogs;
smoking in lounge only

▭ None accepted

£ Single occupancy of twin/double
£20 to £22, twin/double £32

**WORFIELD** SHROPSHIRE                                    **MAP 6**

# Old Vicarage Hotel

WORFIELD, BRIDGNORTH, SHROPSHIRE WV15 5JZ
TEL: WORFIELD (074 64) 497   FAX: (074 64) 552

*A neat, comfortable hotel with efficient, willing hosts.*

The setting for this Edwardian hotel is quite bleak – on an exposed
hillside in two acres of garden – but the benefit is the lovely views. If
you're lucky you might see a red-legged partridge sitting on the drive as
you approach. Everything is very neat: closely mown grass, well-spaced
plant pots outside, formal flower arrangements, polished floors inside,
and nothing out of place.

Christine and Peter Iles aim for an 'air of efficient informality' in the
running of their hotel. Some might find it a bit stiff and uncosy, with
highly polished tables and red leather chairs in the dining-room, but the
mixture of antique and repro pieces forms a coherent whole in these
warm and decent-sized rooms. The conservatory for drinks before and
after dinner offers lovely views. Dinner might be a three-course 'supper',
or a more formal dinner of five carefully prepared dishes.

The bedrooms are named after the local villages you can see from the
windows and are very comfortable with luxuries including bath robes and
electric blankets. The recently adapted stables incorporate a well-
thought-out suite for disabled visitors.

- Open all year
- 1 mile from the A454 and 2 miles from the A442, to the east of Bridgnorth. Private car park
- 4 twin, 8 double, 1 four-poster, 1 suite; most with bathroom/WC, some with shower/WC; TV, room service, hair-dryer, trouser press, mini-bar, baby-listening
- Restaurant, bar, lounge, conservatory; conference facilities (max 30 people non-residential, 14 residential); golf, tennis, other sports nearby; babysitting. Wheelchair access to hotel (2 steps) and restaurant, 2 ground-floor bedrooms, 1 specially equipped for the disabled
- No dogs in public rooms; some bedrooms non-smoking and no smoking in restaurant
- Access, Amex, Diners, Visa
- Single occupancy of twin/double £62, twin/double £77, four-poster £85, suite £85; deposit required. Set L £13.50, D £16.50, £25 (prices till end 91). Special breaks available

---

*Many hotels offer special rates for stays of a few nights or more. It is worth
enquiring when you book.*

**WORLESTON** CHESHIRE                **MAP 4**

# Rookery Hall

WORLESTON, NR NANTWICH, CHESHIRE CW5 6DQ
TEL: NANTWICH (0270) 610016   FAX: (0270) 626027

*Superior, recently extended country-house hotel offering lavish comfort at a price.*

Most visitors don't make use of the helipad. None the less, you'll be in no doubt that this is a top-of-the-range country-house hotel with lots of drive and ambition. Thirty acres of garden, classical statues and a lake surround this nineteenth-century revamping of a Georgian house with château-style slate pitched roof. It now has 34 new bedrooms and a conference centre.

Standards of service reflect the ethos of an earlier time: someone will greet you before you park on the gravel forecourt, and your bags will be whisked to your room while you check in. Indoors, the scale is grand and the ambience formal, with fine antiques, plush carpets and drapes and imposing paintings. A grand wooden staircase leads to the lavish, bright, uniformly excellent bedrooms, furnished with antiques and blessed with splendid views. Marbled bathrooms are spacious and mildly decadent.

There's more Victorian splendour in the oak-panelled dining-room, where guests are seated at antique walnut and mahogany tables and chairs. Cuisine is modern British in style, relies on seasonal local ingredients and is artistically presented. You might choose ravioli of lobster and broccoli with a fricassée of wild mushrooms, grilled saddle of rabbit on a port wine and thyme sauce with glazed chestnuts, and a hot soufflé of orange and milk chocolate. The lengthy wine list is particularly strong on clarets and burgundies, with choice weighted away from the budget end of the list.

◐ *Open all year*

⤢ *Off the B5074 at Worleston. Private car park*

🛏 *2 single, 35 twin/double, 1 four-poster, 5 suites (some rooms in annexe); all with bathroom/WC, TV, room service, hair-dryer, trouser-press; no tea/coffee-making facilities in rooms*

◇ *3 dining-rooms, 2 bars, 2 lounges; conference facilities (max 80 people non-residential, 45 residential); fishing, tennis, croquet, putting at hotel, other sports nearby; babysitting by arrangement. Wheelchair access to hotel, restaurant, WC (unisex) and lift, 1 bedroom specially equipped for the disabled*

⊖ *No dogs; no smoking in dining-room and some bedrooms*

▭ *Access, Amex, Diners, Visa*

£ *Single £87, single occupancy of twin/double £97, twin/double from £112, four-poster £245, suite from £155. Set L £16.50, D £30; alc L £30, D £40. Special breaks available*

# Bradley Hall

WYLAM, NORTHUMBERLAND NE41 8JL
TEL: WYLAM (0661) 853821

*An opportunity to stay in a fine Palladian house and feel like a guest of the family.*

Roderick and Virginia Simpson emphatically do not run an hotel. Staying at their Wolsey Lodge is intended to feel 'like being at a house-party' so you are treated as guests of the family in every way except that you pay for the treat rather than leave a box of chocolates.

The house is magnificent. An eighteenth-century Palladian mansion built by the Simpsons' ancestors, it is surrounded by fifty acres of parkland. Three bedrooms are let to guests who have to share a bathroom, but that is more than made up for by the standard of furnishings and the size of the rooms. Downstairs, guests are made welcome in the south-facing drawing-room which is elegant and comfortable. Everywhere you look in Bradley Hall there is something to admire: the Chinese Chippendale staircase and the gold leaf, rococo ceiling to name but two. A four-course dinner is available by arrangement and if there aren't many people staying, you may find yourself eating in the delightful kitchen.

- ◑ Closed Oct to Mar
- ⤢ 1½ miles south of the River Tyne and Wylam village; approach by the A695 between Prudhoe and Crawcrook. Private car park
- 🛏 1 twin, 2 double (one with shower), public bathroom; hairdryer, trouser press on request; no tea/coffee-making facilities in rooms
- ◈ Dining-room, lounge, TV room, drying room, study; conference facilities (max 12 people non-residential); croquet at hotel, other sports nearby
- ⊖ No wheelchair access; no children under 10; no dogs; no smoking in bedrooms
- ▭ None accepted
- £ Single occupancy of twin/double £35, twin/double £60; deposit required. Set D £18 (7.30pm, by arrangement only)

*If you have a small appetite, or just aren't feeling hungry, check if you can be given a reduction if you don't want the full menu.*

**YATTENDON** BERKSHIRE                          **MAP 9**

# Royal Oak

THE SQUARE, YATTENDON, NR NEWBURY, BERKSHIRE RG16 0UF
TEL: HERMITAGE (0635) 201325   FAX: (0635) 201926

*An appealing combination of pub, restaurant and hotel in a ideal
location for overnight stays and weekends away.*

The Royal Oak was, up until March 1991, owned by Richard and Kate
Smith but they have now, it would appear, decided to concentrate their
efforts on the larger Beetle & Wedge up the road in Moulsford (see
entry). Regulars will be pleased to know that little will change as the new
owners are the former manager, Julie Huff, and chef, Dominique Orizet.

The Royal Oak is marked by a pub-style black and gold sign in the
centre of this Berkshire village, a short but sinuous drive from the M4.
But inside it is much more than just a pub. Certainly the majority of the
noise comes from the bar to the right of the lounge, and although the beer
is good, most people come here for the bar menu and efficient informal
service that would shame many restaurants. The intention, admirably
achieved, is to provide an excellent quick lunch or dinner in convivial
comfort. Back through the lounge, which around meal times is something of a thoroughfare, the efforts of Mr Orizet find a more formal
setting: the restaurant with Regency-style dining chairs and an enveloping pale orange glow. The food is more expensive and a little more
ambitious, although on the day our inspector ate there, dishes such as
ballantine of foie gras with Sauternes aspic appeared on both menus.

Upstairs, there are five rooms furnished in country-house style with
floral chintzes and antique furniture, a polished corner wardrobe being a
particularly eye-catching but practical piece. A garden at the rear awaits
sunny weather and it's particularly necessary to book at weekends when
London migrates along the M4 in search of peace and quiet.

◑ Open all year; restaurant closed
  Sun eve

↗ In centre of Yattendon village.
  Private car park

🛏 5 twin/double; some with
  bathroom/WC; TV, room service,
  hair-dryer, baby-listening in all
  rooms

◈ Restaurant, bar, lounge, private
  dining-room; conference facilities
  (max 8 people non-residential);
  golf, tennis, riding nearby;

  babysitting by arrangement.
  Wheelchair access to restaurant
  only

⊖ No dogs in public rooms

▭ Access, Amex, Diners, Visa

£ Single occupancy of twin/double
  from £60, twin/double from £70.
  Alc L, D £25 to £30 (restaurant),
  £17 to £20 (bar); bar snacks
  (prices till 92). Special breaks
  available

*Congratulations to Cumbria – our number 1 county with 53 full entries in
this year's Guide.*

# Middlethorpe Hall

BISHOPTHORPE ROAD, YORK, NORTH YORKSHIRE YO2 1QB
TEL: YORK (0904) 641241
FAX: (0904) 620176

*Just next to the racecourse just south of York. If you stay here
you'll have backed a winner.*

In 1980 the future of Middlethorpe Hall was looking bleak. After a series
of owners, one of whom turned it into a nightclub, the fabric of the
building was threatened through lack of maintenance. Historic House
Hotels saw the potential of the building and have restored it to its present
glory. If you've been to Bodysgallen Hall or Hartwell House (see entries)
you will know the standard to expect. The front of the house shows off to
best advantage its fine William III lines, and walking in the walled garden
and grounds beyond the ha-ha gives plenty of opportunities to appreciate
the scene.

Inside, careful restoration and preservation has created a very beautiful house. It's grand and a bit austere at first impression but once you've
sunk into the incredibly soft sofas and gazed around, the place begins to
exude warmth. Service is impeccable and unobtrusive as with all hotels in
this group. Dinner is a grand affair and needs a good few hours of serious
reading to get the best from the wine list alone. A fairly short carte is
supplemented by a daily menu, maybe oak-smoked Loch Fyne salmon,
followed by breast of Lunesdale duck with braised lentils on a potato
scone, then a hearty selection of puddings or cheeses.

There's a choice of bedrooms between the ones in the main house or
those in the skilfully converted outbuildings. The ones in the main
building are grandly proportioned rooms, beautifully done and furnished
with antiques. The annexe rooms are slightly more informal in style but
fitted out with the same care as the rest of the house. It's a great treat to
stay here but it doesn't come cheap.

🌓 Open all year

🔀 The Hall is 1½ miles south of
York, beside York racecourse.
Private car park

🛏 5 single, 10 twin, 8 double, 1
four-poster, 4 suites, 2 cottage
suites; all with bathroom/WC,
TV, room service, hair-dryer,
trouser press; tea/coffee-making
facilities in cottage suites
only

◈ Restaurant, grill, 2 lounges,
library; conference facilities (max
63 people non-residential, 30

residential); croquet at hotel,
other sports nearby

➖ No wheelchair access; no
children under 8; no dogs

🏧 Access, Amex, Diners, Visa

💷 Single £83, single occupancy of
twin/double £99, twin/double
£115 to £129, four-poster £159,
suite £189, cottage suite £165;
deposit required. Continental B
£6.50, cooked B £9.50; set L
£15 to £17, D £29.50; alc L, D
£39 (prices till Apr 92). Special
breaks available

**ZEALS** WILTSHIRE                              **MAP 9**

# Stag Cottage                                   ℒℒ

FANTLEY LANE, ZEALS, WILTSHIRE BA12 6NX
TEL: BOURTON (0747) 840458

*A pretty and inexpensive place for bed, breakfast and cream teas.*

Seventeenth-century, whitewashed and thatched, Stag Cottage sits on a side lane by the village post office. Wooden tables and chairs are set out on a little patch of green across the lane. Not the most tranquil spot for cream teas (the Marie and Peter Boxall speciality) – it's better to be indoors where the thick walls keep out road noise. The charming cottagey surroundings suit this most English of traditions as much as blobs of clotted cream suit home-baked scones. The scones here aren't just the plain version but include bacon and cheese ones, too. They are accompanied by home-made cakes, all served in the beamed, inglenook dining-room under the watchful eye of a black cat.

You need to climb a steep flight of stairs to the bedrooms. Though there are only four, they come in many configurations and are as quaint, pretty and cosy as can be, with more wavy than straight lines and little space. If you ask for the largest room, you'll sleep in a four-poster. Secondary glazing blocks out traffic noise. The Boxalls don't serve dinner but can arrange it for you at the village inn.

- ◑ Open all year
- ↗ Zeals is on the A303 London to Exeter road, 2 miles west of Mere. The cottage is next door to the village post office. Private car park
- 🛏 I single, I twin, I double, I four-poster
- ◈ Dining-room, TV; golf, fishing,

other sports nearby; babysitting
- ⊖ No wheelchair access; dogs at Boxalls' discretion; no smoking
- ▭ None accepted
- 💷 Single £13, single occupancy of twin/double £18, twin/double/four-poster £24; deposit required

---

*I was surprised to find on arrival that there was no one in the hotel to receive guests. The front door was open to the street and in the hall was a telephone, with a notice inviting guests to dial a number for instructions. I did this and was told by a voice that my room was the one in the hall, just beside the front door. The door of this room was wide open too, so I went in. There was no washbasin in the room and I searched in vain on the ground floor for a bathroom. I dialled the number again and said that I had been told there would be a bathroom next door to my room. After about 20 minutes, the proprietor came down and showed me the bathroom, which was on the first floor. I said that this was an unacceptable arrangement and that I would not be able to stay for a second night, when my wife was to have joined me. The proprietor accepted this with ill grace.* On an hotel in Kingston-on-Thames

# SCOTLAND

**ABERFELDY** TAYSIDE **MAP 1**

# Farleyer House

ABERFELDY, PERTHSHIRE PH15 2JE
TEL: ABERFELDY (0887) 20332   FAX: (0887) 29430

*A spot of luxury in the middle of the Perthshire Highlands.*

Aberfeldy is an excellent place to stay if you want to be well-positioned to explore the southern Highlands, or to escape the crowds which throng Pitlochry. Once you've crossed General Wade's splendid bridge over the Tay, Farleyer House is discreetly signposted and lies surrounded by wood and parkland, while the gardens are being gradually developed.

It's a curious house, looking more like a large farmhouse than a conventional sporting lodge, with an arch into the yard behind and green surrounds to the windows. The sitting-rooms are upstairs, in best Scottish tradition, to take advantage of the light, and the principal one, with its window seat, is especially good. The bar is more of an alcove, while the dining-room downstairs is green and formal, an excellent setting for Frances Atkins' modern and appetising food, which includes sorrel soup and brioche. The bedrooms are furnished with attractive antiques like most of the rest of the house.

◑ *Open all year, exc 1st 3 weeks in Dec and Feb*

*— the hotel is 1 mile on the right. Private car park*

⤴ *From Aberfeldy take the B846 to Kinloch Rannoch through Weem*

🛏 *1 single, 3 twin, 5 double, 2 suites; all with bathroom/WC,*

-Farleyer House-

TV, hair-dryer, room service; no tea/coffee-making facilities in rooms

 Restaurant, bar, lounge, library/study, drying room; conference facilities (max 20 people non-residential, 11 residential); golf at hotel, other sports nearby. Wheelchair access to restaurant and WC (unisex) only

⊖ No children under 10; no dogs; no smoking in restaurant

▭ Access, Amex, Diners, Visa

£ Single £75 to £90, single occupancy of twin/double from £85, twin/double £80 to £85, suite £100 to £120 (rates inc dinner); deposit required. Set L £17.50, D £27.50. Special breaks available

## ACHILTIBUIE HIGHLAND                                         MAP 1

# Summer Isles

ACHILTIBUIE, BY ULLAPOOL, ROSS-SHIRE IV26 2YG
TEL: ACHILTIBUIE (085 482) 282   FAX: (085 482) 251

*A simple hotel in an extended crofting township by the sea.*

There's nothing especially grand about the Summer Isles Hotel, but for a combination of remoteness and fine views, it is ideal. Achiltibuie is a straggling collection of houses on a flattish area of land, with an unrivalled view of sea and islands, and some of Scotland's most attractive mountains in the neighbourhood.

The hotel is very much a local centre – and the public bar is usually full of chatty locals. It has a small lounge and fresh, well-appointed bedrooms (some in an annexe, but none the worse for that). The food is extremely good for such a remote spot, with fresh fish, in particular, a strong point. The packed lunches are also memorable. Boat trips to the Summer Isles, fishing on nearby lochs, or expeditions to climb the nearby peaks are the obvious activities, but the Summer Isles is also a good spot for a couple of days hiding away from a more stressful existence.

● Closed mid-Oct to Easter

▣ 10 miles north of Ullapool on the A835 turn left on to a single-track road to Achiltibuie. The village is 15 miles along this road, and the hotel 1 mile further on the left. Private car park

⇌ 1 twin, 2 double, 1 cottage, 7 annexe rooms; most with bathroom/WC, 3 public bathrooms; hair-dryer in all rooms; no tea/coffee-making facilities in rooms

⬦ Dining-room, 2 bars, lounge, drying room, study, coffee shop (May to Sept); fishing nearby

⊖ No wheelchair access; no children under 8; no dogs in public rooms; no smoking in dining-room

▭ None accepted

£ Single occupancy of twin/double £44 to £53, twin/double £57 to £79, annexe room £66 to £77, cottage £102. Set D £29 (room prices till Oct 91). Special breaks available

**ARDRISHAIG** STRATHCLYDE                                    **MAP 2**

# Fascadale House

TARBERT ROAD, ARDRISHAIG, BY LOCHGILPHEAD, ARGYLL PA30 8EP
TEL: LOCHGILPHEAD (0546) 3845

*A bed and breakfast with standards belonging to the country-house bracket in an elegant house beside Loch Fyne.*

The village of Ardrishaig lies at the eastern end of the Crinan Canal, and this elegant Victorian villa stands on the southern outskirts, with views out over Loch Fyne. Michael and Monica Farka started their bed and breakfast business in 1990, and have done up three of the best bedrooms comfortably and with restrained good taste. They are all big rooms – of the sort you might expect in a country-house hotel rather than a B&B – and have excellent bathrooms to go with them, one boasting a replica 1908 handbasin as made for the Savoy.

Down the imposing carved staircase, the drawing-room doubles as a dining-room, but is quite large enough for both functions. Drawings of Prague adorn the walls, reflecting Michael's Czech origins. A list of local restaurants is on hand for those needing evening meals.

| | |
|---|---|
| ◑ *Closed Nov to Feb inclusive* | ✧ *Dining-room, lounge, drying room; fishing, golf, other sports nearby* |
| ↗ *From Glasgow take A82 Loch Lomond road to Tarbert, then A83 signposted Campbeltown. Continue through Lochgilphead and Ardrishaig on the A83; Fascadale House is one mile from centre of Ardrishaig. Private car park* | ⊖ *No wheelchair access; no dogs; no smoking* |
| | ▭ *None accepted* |
| | £ *Single occupancy of twin/double £20 to £22, twin/double £36 to £40, family room £45, cottage £90 to £250 per week; deposit required* |
| ⇰ *1 twin, 1 double, 1 family room, 3 cottages; all with bathroom/WC; hair-dryer on request* | |

**ARDUAINE** STRATHCLYDE                                    **MAP 2**

# Loch Melfort Hotel

ARDUAINE, BY OBAN, ARGYLL PA34 4XG
TEL: KILMELFORD (085 22) 233   FAX: (085 22) 214

*Spectacularly situated to catch the views, this hotel is becoming increasingly comfortable as refurbishment continues.*

On a clear day you can just see the twin peaks of the Paps of Jura above the intervening tree-clad islands lining Loch Melfort. Philip and Rosalind Lewis's hotel stands at the foot of the loch, with a meadow running down to the shore. The dignity of the solid white house is somewhat undermined by the 1960s chalet-style 'Cedar Lodge' extension; the short walk from here to the main building can be draughty. But the interior of the hotel is warm and comforting, especially in the chartroom bar with its telescope, or in the small panelled library. The cocktail bar has been recently refurbished in a pleasant mix of pastel colours, and plans are in hand to reshape the dining-room to allow more tables to take advantage of the view.

Bedrooms continue to be upgraded, with pine and fresh fabrics replacing the dated fittings in the Cedar Wing. Bathrooms here are on the small side. Philip Lewis's cooking makes the most of the local seafood: lobster from Luing, scallops from Jura, oysters from Seil. The hotel makes a comfortable and good-value base for exploring Knapdale.

○ *Open all year, exc 3 Jan to 1 Mar*

▱ *19 miles south of Oban on the A816 to Lochgilphead. Private car park*

🛏 *1 single, 18 twin, 7 double, 1 family room; all with bathroom/WC, exc single with shower/WC; TV, room service, baby-listening in all rooms; hair-dryer on request*

◈ *Restaurant, bar, lounge, library, drying room; conference facilities*

*(max 20 people residential and non-residential); fishing, riding, water sports nearby. Wheelchair access to hotel (ramp), restaurant and WC, 10 ground-floor bedrooms*

● *Dogs in some bedrooms only; no smoking in dining-room*

▭ *Access, Visa*

£ *Single occupancy of twin/double £30 to £60, twin/double £60 to £90. Set D from £20; bar meals. Special breaks available*

---

**ARISAIG** HIGHLAND                                    **MAP 1**

# The Arisaig Hotel

ARISAIG, INVERNESS-SHIRE PH39 4NH
TEL: ARISAIG (068 75) 210

*An unpretentious hotel on the West Highland coast; food here is more important than luxury.*

The Arisaig Hotel's location is slightly marred by the road and clutter of the small harbour which separates it from the sea, but the surrounding coast is attractive enough. It is a simple place, doubling as the local pub, and the décor is on the dull side, with the traditional patterned carpets and velveteen sofas of the rather old-fashioned Highland hotel. We've also heard of non-functioning bedside radios and noisy fans in the bathrooms. But George and Janice Stewart have an enthusiastic following – especially for their food – the seafood in particular drawing praise: 'The climax of our week's holiday was cold fresh lobster, caught that day, and with the flavour that only absolutely fresh lobster can give.'

Breakfasts are held to be equally good and substantial. The service, by friendly local staff, is praiseworthy. The bedrooms, like the public rooms, are simple, varying in size and their views, but perfectly adequate for most people. Some are in a modern annexe. The public bar is pretty basic but locals and guests mix happily with the Stewarts' active encouragement.

**◑** Open all year

**↗** Take the A830 from Fort William towards Mallaig. Arisaig is 10 miles before Mallaig. The hotel is in central Arisaig. Private car park

**⊨** 2 single, 7 twin, 2 double, 4 family; most with bathroom/WC, 5 public bathrooms; baby-listening in all rooms; TV, room service, hair-dryer on request

**◈** Dining-room, 2 bars, lounge, TV

room; fishing, golf nearby. Wheelchair access to public areas only, with assistance

**⊖** No dogs in public rooms or unattended in bedrooms; no smoking in dining-room

**▭** Access, Visa

**£** Single £25 to £34, single occupancy of twin/double £31 to £47, twin/double £52 to £83. Set D £23.50; alc L £4 to £10. Special breaks available

# Arisaig House

BEASDALE, BY ARISAIG, INVERNESS-SHIRE PH39 4NR
TEL: ARISAIG (068 75) 622    TELEX: 777279 ARISAI G
FAX: (068 75) 626

*A grand, slightly stiff country-house hotel.*

This is a big Victorian mansion surrounded by woodland and rhododendrons about three miles east of Arisaig itself. From the house you can stroll down to the shore of Loch nan Uamh and imagine Bonnie Prince Charlie landing here in 1745 full of hope, and skulking on the shore a year later as a refugee after the failure of his uprising. He would probably have enjoyed Arisaig House, for the service is efficient and the food is competent. He might have found the bedrooms a little less than princely in their furnishings, though they are light, airy and spacious. Those with views of the loch are by far the nicest and it is worth asking for one if you can.

Flowers bedeck the magnificent sitting-rooms; these are relaxing, if rather formal rooms. The dining-room too can be a bit hushed but the friendly waitresses don't stand on ceremony unduly. The hotel's gardens make for pleasant strolls, while the rough woodland and hill tracks leading off into the country provide some excellent, more strenuous walking.

**◑** Closed mid-Nov to early Mar

**↗** 2 miles north of Fort William, take the A830, signposted Mallaig. Arisaig House is 32 miles on, just after Beasdale

station, 3 miles before village of Arisaig. Private car park

**⊨** 2 single, 7 twin, 6 double; all with bathroom/WC, TV, room service, hair-dryer; no tea/coffee-making facilities in rooms

◈ Restaurant, bar, 2 lounges, games room, drying room; fishing, other sports nearby. Wheelchair access to restaurant only

● No children under 10; no dogs;

no smoking in restaurant

▭ Access, Visa

💷 Single £55, single occupancy of twin/double from £143, twin/double from £135 (rates inc dinner); deposit required. Set D £35. Special breaks available

## AUCHENCAIRN DUMFRIES & GALLOWAY                    MAP 2

# Balcary Bay Hotel

AUCHENCAIRN, BY CASTLE DOUGLAS, KIRKCUDBRIGHTSHIRE DG7 1QZ
TEL: AUCHENCAIRN (055 664) 217/311

*Friendliness and a good location rather than outstanding character are the hallmarks of this hotel.*

Balcary Bay looks out towards the Solway Firth, an area rich in smuggling associations, birdlife and ancient remains. The hotel itself, like many old buildings near the sea, has smuggling legends directly associated with it. Contraband was stored behind the fireplace in the old cellar, and no doubt was landed on the nearby beaches.

Now the old house has been modernised inside, making it rather more anonymous than the white-painted exterior suggests. The bedrooms are plain and functional with nothing outstanding by the way of furniture – those which overlook Balcary Bay are far the nicest, and there are curious touches, such as shoe-cleaning machines and trouser presses, which make you speculate whether there's a flock of refugee businessmen somewhere among the wildlife on this isolated coastline. The public rooms, which have lovely views, are again lacking in character, though they are very comfortable. The anonymous atmosphere of the hotel certainly does not extend to the staff who are eminently friendly and hospitable as they bustle here and there, and you are unlikely to be unable to find someone to chat to or to answer questions. The food is unambitious but substantial.

◐ Closed Dec to end Feb

↗ Off the A711 Dumfries to Kirkcudbright road, 2 miles out of Auchencairn on the shore road. Private car park

🛏 3 single, 7 twin, 5 double, 1 four-poster, 1 family room; all with bathroom/WC, exc 1 single with shower/WC; TV, room service, hair-dryer in all rooms

◈ Dining-room, bar, 2 lounges, snooker room, drying room;

fishing, water sports at hotel; babysitting. Wheelchair access to dining-room and bar only

● No children under 8 in dining-room eves; no dogs in public rooms

▭ Access, Visa

💷 Single £46, twin/double £75 to £90; deposit required. Set D £17; alc L, D £24. Special breaks available

**AUCHTERARDER** TAYSIDE

**MAP 2**

# Auchterarder House

AUCHTERARDER, PERTHSHIRE PH3 1DZ
TEL: AUCHTERARDER (0764) 63646   FAX: (0764) 62939

*A grand baronial pile with plenty of space and an easy-going atmosphere.*

An American guest at Auchterarder warns that, to transatlantic eyes, the hotel is brushing the upper limits of an acceptable tariff: 'We did feel that for Americans whose dollar does not go very far in Britain, this was a very, very expensive hotel.'

Run by the same family who own the Roman Camp at Callander, Auchterarder House is a grand Victorian building with all the appropriate trimmings of panelling, high ceilings and spacious rooms. If the hotel is nearly empty, you will feel that you are rattling around in it, while if it is full you will hardly notice the fact. Luckily, there's absolutely nothing stiff or over-formal about this hotel, and it is this, rather than its grandeur, which gives it a place in this Guide. In fact, it has a pleasantly relaxed and comfortable feeling about it, which encourages you to take advantage of the warm conservatory, full of plants and places to sit, or the cosy bar. The food is traditional (one reader thought this better described as unimaginative), but excellently presented, while the wine list contains some fine old rarities (a quick way of adding further to the size of your bill). Bedrooms vary from the cosy to the grand – all are well furnished.

- Open all year
- On the B8062, 1½ miles north of Auchterarder. Private car park
- 10 twin, 2 double, 3 suites; all with bathroom/WC, TV, room service, hair-dryer, trouser press/iron; no tea/coffee-making facilities in rooms
- Dining-room, lounge, library, conservatory; conference facilities (max 50 people non-residential, 15 residential); fishing, golf, other sports nearby.

- Wheelchair access to hotel and restaurant, 1 ground-floor bedroom
- No children under 11; no dogs in public rooms; no smoking in dining-room
- Access, Amex, Diners, Visa
- Single occupancy of twin/double £70 to £100, twin/double £110 to £185, suite £160 to £185; deposit required. Set L £15, £25, D £28.50, £50. Special breaks available

---

*One hotel leaves welcoming small teddy bears on pillows. 'It used to be sweets, until one terrible morning when a man came down to breakfast with a chocolate stuck to his head.'* On an hotel in Yorkshire

# Gleneagles

AUCHTERARDER, PERTHSHIRE PH3 1NF
TEL: AUCHTERARDER (0764) 62231    TELEX: 76105 GHPLC G
FAX: (0764) 62134

*Gleneagles continues to measure up to the luxury standards it set more than half a century ago.*

Since 1924, when it opened as a luxury hotel to tempt people into travelling by the Caledonian Railway, Gleneagles has become a byword for Scottish hotelkeeping. In an age of increasing diversity and magnificence among Scottish luxury hotels, Gleneagles is still up there with the best of them. Its guests may go there for the name, the golf, or simply because they have happy memories from long ago, but they are unlikely to be disappointed.

Of course much of the trade is international – Harvey Nichols or Burberry will provide suitable souvenirs on the premises – but the appeal of Gleneagles is wider than this. With five bars and five restaurants, it may seem as though the hotel is simply enormous, but in fact the public rooms are kept small to preserve the atmosphere, and it is worth choosing where you want to eat in advance, and booking to make sure you have a place. The leisure side of the hotel is constantly expanding, with top names behind the golf, tennis, riding and shooting, but one suspects that it is as much for the high standards of service, and for the fact that regulars are recognised and welcomed, that make many visitors continue to return. These days it cannot be said that the Ochil Hills are quite such an adventure as they may have been in 1924, but the hotel remains as well positioned as ever, within easy reach of Edinburgh and Glasgow, and surrounded by lovely countryside.

◐ Open all year

⤢ Just off the A9 mid-way between Stirling and Perth. Private car park

🛏 28 single, 58 twin, 122 double, 8 four-poster, 20 suites; all with bathroom/WC, TV, room service, hair-dryer, trouser press, mini-bar; no tea/coffee-making facilities in rooms

◈ 5 restaurants, 5 bars, lounge, games room, library/study, conservatory; conference facilities (max 360 people); golf, tennis, riding, croquet, sauna, solarium, heated swimming-pool, gym, squash, bowls, health spa, shooting school, fishing at hotel; babysitting. Wheelchair access to hotel (ramp), restaurant and WC (unisex), 13 ground-floor bedrooms, 2 specially equipped for the disabled

● None

▭ Access, Amex, Diners, Visa

 Single £125, twin/double £185 to £235, suite £370 to £750; deposit required. Set L £21.50, D £34; alc D £45 (prices till Mar 92). Special breaks available

**AUCHTERHOUSE** TAYSIDE                                    **MAP I**

# Old Mansion House

AUCHTERHOUSE, BY DUNDEE, ANGUS DD3 0QN
TEL: AUCHTERHOUSE (082 626) 366   FAX: (082 626) 400

*A highly satisfactory hotel in a very old house indeed. Well placed for Perth or Dundee.*

This is a beautiful house, surrounded by even more beautiful gardens. Parts of the building go back to the fifteenth century, and you get a taste of those insecure times when you find that you must climb from the vaulted entrance (which would once have been a storeroom) to reach the old hall on the first floor.

The Old Mansion House is as much a restaurant as an hotel, and the sitting-rooms and dining-rooms are geared more to this side of the operation. One dining-room is especially magnificent, with ornate plaster ceiling and seventeenth-century fireplace. Dinners are à la carte and lavish. The bedrooms, even further up in the old house, are spacious and comfortable, with a mixture of furnishings and many antiques. The bathrooms are anything but fifteenth century. A swimming-pool and grass tennis court provide recreation for the active.

◑ Open all year, exc first week Jan

🔁 Take the A923 Coupar Angus road out of Dundee, cross the Kingsway and fork right at Muirhead. The hotel is on the left 2 miles on. Private car park

🛏 2 twin, 2 four-poster, 2 family rooms; all with bathroom/WC, TV, room service, hair-dryer, mini-bar, baby-listening

◈ 2 dining-rooms, 2 bars, 2 lounges, library; conference facilities (max 20 people non-residential); tennis, croquet, swimming-pool, squash at hotel, other sports nearby. Wheelchair access to restaurant and WC (M,F) only

⊖ No children in dining-rooms eves; no dogs in public rooms; no smoking in dining-rooms

▭ Access, Amex, Diners, Visa

£ Single occupancy of twin/double £65, twin/double £90, four-poster/family room £100. Set L £14; alc L, D £25. Special breaks available

*The 1993 Guide will be published before Christmas 1992. Reports on hotels are most welcome at any time of the year, but are extremely valuable in the spring. Send them to Which? Hotel Guide, FREEPOST, 2 Marylebone Road, London NW1 1YN. No stamp is needed if reports are posted in the UK.*

# Ballachulish House

BALLACHULISH, ARGYLL PA39 4JX
TEL: BALLACHULISH (085 52) 266

*A pretty eighteenth-century family home close to Glencoe. Lots of space inside and out.*

John and Liz Grey are creating four new bedrooms out of one wing of their white, beautifully proportioned home to add to their existing accommodation. It is too soon to say what effect this will have on the easy-going atmosphere of the place – probably very little.

The house, set back from the road but visible from it, looks just the sort of place you hope will prove to be open to guests, with its small garden, its sunny position and the hills behind. Inside, the drawing-room is long, with armchairs grouped together near the windows and a piano at the darker end. A central table and plenty of surrounding space make the dining-room an elegantly cool place. There's a mixture of interesting furnishings and family clutter.

The bedrooms at the front with views of the loch are massive and have good big beds; those behind are smaller and a little darker. Liz Grey's dinners use plenty of local seafood and are five-course affairs, with a choice of main course.

○ Open all year

⤴ From Crianlarich take the A82 to Ballachulish, at the roundabout before Balluchulish Bridge. The hotel is 200 yards on left. Private car park

🛏 1 twin, 1 double, 2 family rooms; all with bathroom/WC; hair-dryer, baby-listening on request

◈ Dining-room, drawing-room, drying room; fishing, golf, other

sports nearby

⊖ No wheelchair access; no dogs in public rooms and by arrangement only in bedrooms; smoking in drawing-room only

▭ Access, Visa

£ Single occupancy of twin/double £25 to £40, twin/double £20 to £35; deposit required. Set D £18.50 (7.30 pm)

---

*Shame on you South Yorkshire, Tyne & Wear and Mid Glamorgan, the only counties without an hotel of merit in this year's* Guide.

---

*If you are intending to make a lot of phone calls from your room, always check what the hotel is going to charge you per unit. You may be so horrified that you'll prefer to walk to the nearest phone box. Why let them get away with excessive charges?*

# Craigendarroch Hotel

BRAEMAR ROAD, BALLATER, DEESIDE AB3 5XA
TEL: BALLATER (033 97) 55858   TELEX: 739952
FAX: (033 97) 55447

*An hotel and timeshare complex which makes up in facilities what it lacks in atmosphere.*

Ballater is an old spa resort which was founded by a Jacobite reprieved from execution, who found out that a local woman had cured herself of scrofula by bathing in a nearby peat bog. Although it doesn't have quite the cachet of Braemar or Banchory, Ballater makes an excellent Deeside base, and if what you are after is a comfortable hotel with masses of facilities on site, then the Craigendarroch is worth considering.

The complex is based around an old house a short distance outside Ballater, but most of it is modern. No fewer than three restaurants cater for most pockets – with the family fare in the 'Café Jardin' being good value and good quality. There's a jolly open-plan sitting area around the pool and a quiet little study and bar tucked away in the bowels of the hotel if you want to escape from the noise. The bedrooms are bland sorts of places, but with all the extras. The facilities range from snooker to swimming with plenty in between. None of this comes especially cheap but you can guarantee that you'll find something to entertain you, even on the most dismal of days.

○ *Open all year*

↗ *½ mile outside Ballater on the A93 Braemar road. Private car park*

🛏 *21 twin, 21 double, 1 four-poster, 6 family rooms, 1 suite; all with bathroom/WC, TV, room service, hair-dryer, trouser press, mini-bar, baby-listening*

◇ *3 restaurants, 2 bars, snooker room, laundry facilities, study; conference facilities (max 100 people residential and non-residential); tennis, sauna/solarium, swimming-pool, gym, clay pigeon shooting at hotel,*

*other sports nearby; crèche, adventure playground for children; babysitting. Wheelchair access to hotel (ramp), restaurant and WC (unisex), 1 bedroom specially equipped for the disabled*

⊖ *No dogs; no smoking in specified areas*

▭ *Access, Amex, Diners, Visa*

£ *Single occupancy of twin/double £87, twin/double £118, four-poster £155, suite £170; deposit required. Set L £15.50, D £17.50; alc L £30, D £35*

# Tullich Lodge

BY BALLATER, ABERDEENSHIRE AB3 5SB
TEL: BALLATER (033 97) 55406   FAX: (033 97) 55397

*A place for addicts of Victoriana, with a strong style and a strong sense of continuity.*

Tullich Lodge is one of those places where the owners have placed an idiosyncratic stamp on everything from furniture to the small everyday rituals. Hector Macdonald and Neil Bannister have been in partnership here for over two decades, so the stamp is virtually indelible – and guests who don't know what to expect may feel a little constrained. What you should be expecting is a love of the Victorian period – manifested in all sorts of details from the bath taps to the heavy draping of the curtains – combined with the excellent food.

The granite baronial house, on a lumpy hill outside the old spa town of Ballater, is ideally suited to both – for there are spacious public rooms (the first-floor sitting-room is especially attractive) which were made for precisely the kind of furniture which now fills them, while the fish and game of Deeside provide first-class ingredients for the four-course dinners. These usually include one of the hotel's famous soups. The bedrooms, again Victorian in tone, right down to the knobbly beds (the framework, that is, certainly not the mattresses), are pretty and comfortable. Both hosts work hard to make sure your stay will be enjoyable.

◐ Closed end Nov to end Mar

◩ 1½ miles east of Ballater on the A93 Aberdeen to Braemar road. Private car park

🛏 3 single, 5 twin, 2 double; most with bathroom/WC, some with shower/WC; hair-dryer, baby-listening in all rooms; trouser press in some rooms; no tea/coffee-making facilities in rooms

◈ Dining-room, bar, 2 lounges, drying room; fishing, golf, other sports nearby. Wheelchair access to restaurant only

⊖ No dogs in public rooms; no smoking in dining-room

▭ Access, Amex, Diners, Visa

💷 Single £77, single occupancy of twin/double £114, twin/double £144; deposit required. Set L £6.50, D £24. Special breaks available

---

*Many hotels offer special rates for stays of a few nights or more. It is worth enquiring when you book.*

**BALLINDALLOCH** GRAMPIAN **MAP 1**

# Delnashaugh Inn

BALLINDALLOCH, BANFFSHIRE AB37 9AS
TEL: BALLINDALLOCH (080 72) 255   FAX: (080 72) 389

*A very comfortable inn, impeccably managed and with excellent home cooking.*

This small Speyside inn lies in the middle of a steep bend on the A95. It is a place to hearten all hoteliers toiling for a large impersonal company, for David Ogden, who leased and renovated Delnashaugh in 1990, is a refugee manager from the bed-factory world, determined to enjoy his own way of doing things.

Certainly the standard of service at Delnashaugh would not disgrace hotels charging twice the price, while the same hotels would be most unlikely to produce food of the quality which emerges from Marion Ogden's kitchen. There's nothing too fancy about it, but if, say, a roast leg of lamb, cooked *au point* and served with a proper Scots gravy and lashings of vegetables, followed by a fresh fruit salad where fresh is the operative word, appeals more than jazzed-up sauces and carrots cut to look like rosebuds, then this is the place to head for.

The ground floor of the inn is mostly taken up by the bar: a bright, warm room furnished in primary red and green, with a smaller lounge opening out of it. The bedrooms are medium-sized, comfortably furnished with modern, sensible hotel furniture and have brightly lit, good-sized bathrooms attached. Although it doubles as a sporting hotel (fishing on the Avon and shooting on the nearby Ballindalloch estate), this is an excellent hotel to know about if you simply want to spend a few days exploring Speyside, or even if you are just looking for a bed for the night.

◐ Closed Dec, Jan

⤴ On the A95, 15 miles north-east of Grantown-on-Spey. Private car park

🛏 1 single, 8 twin; all with bathroom/WC, TV, room service, hair-dryer, baby-listening

◈ Dining-room, bar, lounge; fishing, shooting at hotel. Wheelchair access to hotel (ramp), dining-room, specially adapted WC (unisex) and 5 ground-floor bedrooms

⊖ No dogs

▭ Access, Visa

£ Single £45 to £50, single occupancy of twin/double £55 to £75, twin/double £100 to £120 (rates inc dinner). Set £18.50; bar lunches

---

*Congratulations to Cumbria – our number 1 county with 53 full entries in this year's Guide.*

# Banchory Lodge

BANCHORY, KINCARDINE & DEESIDE AB31 3HS
TEL: BANCHORY (033 02) 2625   FAX: (033 02) 5019

*Comfortable hotel on Deeside; prime territory for anglers.*

The Jaffrays have run this rambling Georgian house for getting on for
thirty years now, and have built up a formidable number of regulars, most
of whom come for the fishing, but who also appreciate the sort of friendly
atmosphere where no one bats an eyelid if you saunter to the washing
machines with a bundle of damp fishing gear under your arm.

The hotel is situated at the confluence of the Rivers Dee and Feugh,
convenient also for Banchory itself, which is only a short stroll away. It is
a maze of passages leading to bedrooms or lounges and is a much bigger
place than it appears at first glance. All the bedrooms are different; the
nicest ones overlook the Dee. Some are rather heavily decorated in
Edwardian-style, some more recently doneup and brightly modern.
There is a high proportion of family rooms among them. The food is
hearty and traditionally Scottish in its use of fish and game. Service is
friendly and efficient.

○ *Closed mid Dec to Jan*

◿ *18 miles inland from Aberdeen
on the A93, 2 minutes from
centre of Banchory. Private car
park*

🛏 *5 twin, 6 double, 2 four-poster, 9
family rooms, 2 suites; all with
bathroom/WC, exc 1 double
with shower/WC; TV, room
service, hair-dryer, baby-listening
in all rooms*

◈ *2 restaurants, bar, 2 lounges,
games room, drying room;
conference facilities (max 20*

*people residential, 30 non-
residential); fishing, sauna,
solarium at hotel, other sports
nearby*

⊖ *No wheelchair access; no dogs in
bedrooms*

▭ *Access, Amex, Diners, Visa*

£ *Single occupancy of twin/double
£60, twin/double £85, four-
poster/family room £100, suite
£120; deposit required. Set L
£10.50, D £22; alc L £6.50
(prices till Dec 91). Special
breaks available*

---

*We mention those hotels that don't accept dogs; guide dogs, however, are
almost always an exception. Telephone ahead to make sure!*

# Invery House

BRIDGE OF FEUGH, BANCHORY, KINCARDINE & DEESIDE AB31 3NJ
TEL: BANCHORY (033 02) 4782　TELEX: 73737
FAX: (033 02) 4712

*An exceptionally pleasant country-house hotel with just the right indulgent atmosphere.*

Ignore all the stuff in the brochure about chauffeur-driven cars and helicopter landing pads; Invery House is very much nicer than these images of an executive playground suggest. It is a well-proportioned white house – not quite plush enough to be called a mansion – positioned in the middle of a green lawn beside the River Feugh outside Banchory.

The hall is green-wellie and salmon-rod territory; the lounge fairly formal, but with plenty of space among the sofas, and the dining-room – complete with 'hugger' armchairs – more formal still. Yet there is a satisfactory air of relaxed indulgence about the house – Walter Scott, after whose works the bedrooms are named, would feel perfectly at home. It is partly the light shed through the high windows, partly the scattering of antiques, partly the freshness of the place.

Bedrooms are excellent, but less interesting than the bathrooms, where a touch of happy eccentricity has infected the design: one is palatially brassy; another has touches of Imperial Rome, with tiles and a step up; while one, remarkably, seems to vanish deep into the wall so that you plunge in over the shallow end and swim for the taps. Before your bath, you can fish the Dee or the Feugh, or play croquet on the lawn.

- Open all year

- Take the A93 Aberdeen to Banchory road, then the B974 south for 1 mile towards Fettercairn. Private car park

- 1 single, 6 twin, 4 double, 1 four-poster, 2 suites; all with bathroom/WC, TV, room service, hair-dryer

- 2 dining-rooms, bar, 2 lounges, games room, drying room, library; conference facilities (max 30 people non-residential); fishing, putting, croquet at hotel; golf, other sports nearby. Wheelchair access to dining-room and WC (unisex) only

- No children under 8; no dogs (kennel facilities available)

- Access, Amex, Diners, Visa

- Single £75 to £80, single occupancy of twin/double £85 to £95, twin/double £100 to £125, four-poster £120 to £175, suite £185 to £245; deposit required. Set L £17.50, D £34.50. Special breaks available

*All rooms have tea/coffee-making facilities unless we mention to the contrary.*

# Kinloch House

BY BLAIRGOWRIE, PERTHSHIRE PH10 6SG
TEL: ESSENDY (025 084) 237    FAX: (025 084) 333

*A very relaxing family-run hotel in a splendid baronial house.*

Whether it is the Highland cattle in the extensive grounds, the kennels for gun-dogs, or the splendidly baronial hall with its flickering fire, comfortable old armchairs, dog and magazines, there is something about Kinloch House which makes you instantly feel you have been invited for a sporting holiday in Edwardian Scotland. It even takes a little time to notice that the turreted extension to the old ivy-covered house is actually quite modern.

David Shentall plays the concerned host, explaining the menus carefully, making sure you are well looked after, and generally creating the relaxed atmosphere which is one of the chief charms of this hotel. After a fine meal of beautifully presented food, majoring on fish and game, and with a supplementary page of more elaborate concoctions, you traverse the beautiful gallery overlooking the hall before heading for the bedrooms, which are cosy with pine and antique furniture. The large conservatory, with its comfortable be-cushioned wickerwork sofas, is an excellent spot in which to enjoy the sun and admire the goldfish.

- Open all year, exc 15 to 30 Dec
- On the A923, 3 miles west of Blairgowrie. Private car park
- 5 single (including 2 four-poster), 8 twin, 1 double, 5 four-poster, 2 suites; all with bathroom/WC, exc 4 singles with shower/WC; TV, room service (limited), hair-dryer, trouser press, baby-listening in all rooms
- Dining-room, bar, lounge, TV room, conservatory, drying room; conference facilities (max 20 people residential and non-residential); fishing at hotel, other sports nearby. Wheelchair access to hotel (ramp), restaurant and WC, 4 ground-floor bedrooms
- No children under 7 in dining-room; dogs in some bedrooms only; no smoking in dining-room
- Access, Amex, Diners, Visa
- Single £70, single occupancy of twin/double £112, twin/double/four-poster £132, suite £165 (rates inc dinner). Set L £13.50, D £21

---

*Prices are what you can expect to pay in 1992, except where specified to the contrary. Many hoteliers tell us that these prices can be regarded only as approximations.*

# Busta House

BRAE, SHETLAND ZE2 9QN
TEL: BRAE (0806 22) 506    TELEX: 9312100218
FAX: (0806 22) 588

*A compromise between business hotel and holiday hang-out, which works thanks to the old house, relaxed atmosphere and interesting food.*

The hotel is a hybrid – part country-house retreat in a house whose rambling white-painted exterior speaks of history and age, and part business hotel with contract furnishings and trouser presses in the bedrooms. A great deal of the hotel's trade comes from nearby Sullom Voe oil terminal, but this should in no way detract from the pleasures of the place as it is about the only spot in the wilds of northern Shetland which will pamper you in style.

Under the management of Peter and Judith Jones, a pleasant relaxation has been brought to Busta – trays are brought into the 'Long Room' before a peat and wood fire, and a spinning wheel sits in the corner for the instruction of puzzled helicopter pilots and others. The Gifford library, a non-smoking room tucked well away on the first floor, is an alternative source of relaxation and peace. Outside, there are a few stunted trees (a fine wood in local terms), and a miniature harbour with a boat for pottering about the Voe (sea loch) when the wind lets up.

Dinner in the restaurant is a formal affair, with beautifully laid tables and a tantalising menu drawing on the best of Shetland's produce. In the bar, the food is just as good, though inevitably more limited in choice. In Shetland, where good hotels are hard to come by, Busta House is an obvious choice, and not desperately expensive either, and now that it benefits from a less taut management style than in previous years, is becoming an ever better place to stay.

- ◑ Open all year, exc 22 Dec to 3 Jan
- ⤢ From Lerwick take the A970 north to Brae. Bear left and take the left turn for Busta. Private car park
- ⇋ 2 single, 8 twin, 9 double, 1 four-poster; most with bathroom/ WC, some with shower/WC; TV, room service, hair-dryer, trouser press, baby-listening in all rooms
- ◈ Restaurant, bar, 2 lounges, library, drying room; laundry service; conference facilities (max 25 people residential); hotel fishing boat and cabin cruiser, loch fishing free to guests. Wheelchair access to restaurant only
- ⊖ No children under 6 in restaurant; no dogs in public rooms; no smoking in restaurant or library
- ▭ Access, Amex, Diners, Visa
- £ Single £56, single occupancy of twin/double £56 to £66, twin/ double £70 to £73, four-poster £80. Set D from £19; bar meals. Special breaks available

# Bunchrew House

BUNCHREW, INVERNESS-SHIRE IV3 6TA
TEL: INVERNESS (0463) 234917   FAX: (0463) 710620

*Outside Inverness on the sea's edge and in an old mansion, this hotel is both smart and homely.*

The Kessock bridge across the Beauly Firth now takes most of the heavy traffic which used to crawl along the shoreline west of Inverness, leaving the area around Bunchrew House to the seabirds and the yachts. Bunchrew House is a pinkish baronial creation, with an old tower at its heart – a place that doubtless has tragic stories to tell of Culloden and its bloody aftermath.

But now it is genial country hotel, yet close enough to Inverness to be an obvious haven for business people wishing to avoid more predictable places to stay. The entrance hall is baronial and grand, as are the panelled bar and sitting-room, but this is counteracted by the family-run feel of the place, emphasised by photographs, *Spitting Image* models, and the geniality of your hosts, Alan and Patsy Wilson. The set dinner has a lot going for it – a good-value four-course meal served briskly in a dining-room which has beautiful views over the sea. Bedrooms are stylish and the bathrooms are excellent. Most of the rooms also have good views.

○ Open all year

⤤ 2 miles from Inverness on the A862 Inverness to Beauly road. Private car park

🛏 4 twin, 2 double, 2 four-poster, 1 family room, 3 suites; all with bathroom/WC, TV, room service, hair-dryer, mini-bar, baby-listening; trouser press in some rooms; tea/coffee-making facilities on request

◈ 2 dining-rooms, bar, lounge, drying room; conference facilities (max 80 people non-residential,

12 residential); fishing at hotel, other sports nearby; babysitting. Wheelchair access to dining-rooms only

⊖ No dogs in public rooms; no smoking in dining-rooms

▭ Access, Amex, Visa

£ Single occupancy of twin/double £55 to £65, twin/double £75 to £90, four-poster £90 to £120, family room £75 to £110, suite £90 to £115; deposit required. Set L £9.50, D £19.50. Special breaks available

---

☕ *Denotes somewhere you can rely on a good meal – either the hotel features in the 1992 edition of our sister publication,* The Good Food Guide, *or our own inspectors thought the cooking impressive, whether particularly competent home cooking or more lavish cuisine.*

**CALLANDER** CENTRAL                                                 **MAP 2**

# Roman Camp

CALLANDER, PERTHSHIRE FK17 8BG
TEL: CALLANDER (0877) 30003   TELEX: 9312132123
FAX: (0877) 31533

*A quiet hideaway from the tourist throngs; an ideal base for exploring the Trossachs.*

These days, Callander is not the quiet little village on the edge of the unknown that daring nineteenth-century travellers experienced – Sir Walter Scott and Dr Finlay between them have turned the village into a thriving tourist centre. The Roman Camp lies just outside the village, and once you are inside the pretty pink building, which was built as a shooting lodge for the Duke of Perth, the tour coaches can safely be forgotten.

The sitting-room with its golden walls and the library with its panelling and ornate ceiling exude peace, and there are further nooks and crannies to curl up in. The dining-room is not so romantic: bench seating rules here, but the bedrooms are again cosy and comfortable, with chintz or fresh cotton fabrics and plenty of extras. 'Super rooms' is the verdict of one visitor. The hotel is in *The Good Food Guide* (hence its tureen award) but one reader twice encountered cold, overcooked vegetables and dishes that he felt were not worthy of the price. More reports on this side of the hotel would be welcome. But no one quarrels with the comfort, the seclusion or the beautiful grounds.

◑ Open all year

⤴ Head north on A84 from Stirling to Oban, turn left off Callander main street down 200-yard driveway to hotel. Private car park

🛏 4 single, 5 twin, 4 double, 1 four-poster, 3 suites; all with bathroom/WC, exc 2 singles with shower/WC; TV, room service, hair-dryer, baby-listening in all rooms

◇ Dining-room, bar, drawing-room, library, conservatory, drying room; conference facilities (max 45 people non-residential, 14 residential); fishing at hotel, other sports nearby. Wheelchair access to hotel, restaurant and WC (M,F), 7 ground-floor bedrooms, 1 specially equipped for the disabled

⊖ No children in dining-room during dinner; no dogs in public rooms; no smoking in dining-room

▭ Access, Amex, Diners, Visa

£ Single occupancy of twin/double £60 to £80, twin/double £70 to £125, four-poster £70 to £90, suite £105 to £155; children sharing parents' room £25; deposit required. Set L £18.50, D £34. Special breaks available

**CANONBIE** DUMFRIES & GALLOWAY                    **MAP 2**

# Riverside Inn

CANONBIE, DUMFRIESSHIRE DG14 0UX
TEL: CANONBIE (038 73) 71512/71295

*Those in the know break their northward journey at this well-positioned inn to the north of Carlisle.*

Canonbie, in years gone by, used to lie at the heart of the 'Debateable Land' – a no-man's land between the warring countries of England and Scotland, populated only by thieves and outlaws. You wouldn't guess this from the peaceful appearance of the village by the River Esk today, nor from the appearance of the Riverside Inn, where it seems that nothing more drastic than a power cut (of which there are plenty, for some reason) has ever disturbed the peace.

The inn revolves around the consumption of food – whether in the restaurant with its brick fireplace and its three-course menu (a new wine list was introduced for 1991), or in the split-level bar, where even the numerous tables cannot prevent the build-up of the odd lunchtime queue. Away from all this activity, the small residents' lounge is comfortably simple, as are the bedrooms – though they have everything you need, and space to sit in as well. The bathrooms are up-to-date and functional without being in the least dreary. 'We had an excellent breakfast in the morning and left feeling greatly inspired for the future,' wrote one guest, who runs an hotel himself. What better accolade could there be?

- ◑ Closed 2 weeks Nov, 2 weeks Feb; also Xmas and New Year; restaurant closed Sun eve

- ⤢ Leave the M6 at Junction 44 and take the A7 Edinburgh road for 13 miles, then follow signs to Canonbie. Private car park

- ⇌ 3 twin, 2 double, 1 four-poster; all with bathroom/WC, exc doubles with shower/WC; TV, hair-dryer in all rooms

- ⬙ Dining-room, bar, 2 lounges; fishing, golf, other sports nearby

- ⊖ No wheelchair access; no children under 10; no dogs; no smoking in dining-room

- ▭ Access, Visa

- £ Twin/double £69, four-poster £82; deposit required. Set D £21. Special breaks available

---

*Warning to insomniacs, exercise freaks and late-night lovers: increasing numbers of hotels have infra-red triggered security lamps. To save being embarrassingly illuminated, check before you leave for your late-night or pre-dawn stroll.*

**CREETOWN DUMFRIES & GALLOWAY** **MAP 2**

# Hill of Burns

CREETOWN, BY NEWTON STEWART, WIGTOWNSHIRE DG8 7HF
TEL: CREETOWN (067 182) 487

*A small, very friendly hotel in a quiet village overlooking the Cree estuary.*

Creetown is the sort of coastline village where nothing much ever seems to have happened, and it is only when you start delving into the local history that you find that Neolithic cairns lie nearby, and that the Mersey docks were built from local stone. Hill of Burns does indeed stand on the top of a hill above the village.

The house was extended in the nineteenth century to give it the appearance of a grander place than it is at heart. This is mostly achieved by the heavy portico. Now it makes for a very fine hotel, with big, comfortable public rooms, and no trace of superficial jazzing up. That essential piece of Edwardian country-house design – the billiard room – has been retained here to the advantage of guests. Furnishings are simple on the whole, with stripped pine and plain carpets doing nothing to detract from the spaciousness of the bedrooms. Food is simple and straightforward, without a great deal of choice, and the owners, Stephen and Mrs Moore, as friendly as you could wish. For an hotel in a house of this style, the tariff is good value.

◐ Open all year, exc Jan and beginning Nov

⤴ Take the road opposite the clock tower in the centre of Creetown village and continue up the hill – the hotel entrance gates are at the top of the hill on the right. Private car park

🛏 2 twin, 3 double, 1 suite; all with bathroom/WC, TV, room service, hair-dryer

◇ Dining-room, lounge, billiard room, drying room; croquet at hotel, fishing, golf nearby. Wheelchair access to hotel and dining-room, 1 ground-floor bedroom

⊖ No dogs in public rooms; no smoking in dining-room

▭ Access, Visa

£ Single occupancy of twin/double £35 to £41, twin/double £50 to £62, suite £72; deposit required. Set D £16.50. Special breaks available

---

*The text of entries is based on unsolicited reports sent in by readers and backed up by inspections. The factual details under the text are from questionnaires the Guide sends to all hotels that feature in the book.*

**CRINAN** STRATHCLYDE    **MAP 2**

# Crinan Hotel

CRINAN, ARGYLL PA31 8SR
TEL: CRINAN (0546 83) 261   FAX: (0546 83) 292

*A haunt for yachting enthusiasts and canal lovers in a beautiful spot at the edge of the sea.*

The Crinan Hotel is as popular with those who come for a meal and to watch the boats passing through the locks into the Crinan Canal as it is with those who stay longer. The Ryan family have been running the hotel for some years and are accustomed to the whims of yachting folk and holidaymakers alike. They offer lovely bright bedrooms (decorated with pine and vivid fabrics), all of which have a view either of the sea or of the canal basin, and they offer food – either in the upstairs Lock 16 seafood restaurant, with its blue and white decoration and its view of the sea, or in the more conventional Telford room on the ground floor. One reader complained that although dinner was served between 8 and 9pm, the menu was not available until 8.30pm, although 'the wait was enlivened by a high-volume conversation between the chef and a companion; the kitchen seemed to act as an echo chamber'. He also found that half the listed wines were unavailable – but all are agreed that the food is delicious. Fresh flowers and nautical paintings are scattered throughout the hotel, and there is plenty of room to relax in the sitting-rooms.

◑ Open all year; 1 restaurant open May to Sept only, closed Sun, Mon eves

▨ Crinan village is at the north end of the Crinan Canal – follow the A841 from Cairnbaan. Private car park

🛏 2 single, 14 twin, 6 double, 1 family room; all with bathroom/WC, TV, room service, hairdryer; no tea/coffee-making facilities in rooms

◇ 2 restaurants, 3 bars, lounge, drying room; conference facilities

(max 100 people non-residential); watersports at hotel, fishing, other sports nearby. Wheelchair access to hotel, restaurant and WC, no ground-floor bedrooms but a lift

⊖ None

▭ Access, Visa

£ Single £50 to £70, single occupancy of twin/double £80 to £85, twin/double £80 to £110; deposit required. Alc L £8.50; set D £25

---

*The* Guide *office can quickly spot when a hotelier is encouraging customers to write a recommending inclusion – and sadly, several hotels have been doing this in 1991. Such reports do not further an hotel's cause.*

**CROMARTY** HIGHLAND                                                    **MAP 1**

# Royal Hotel                                                                  $\mathcal{SL}$

MARINE TERRACE, CROMARTY, ROSS-SHIRE IV11 8YN
TEL: CROMARTY (038 17) 217

*A seashore hotel in an old Scottish port. Out-of-the-way but very civilised.*

This is a genuinely friendly, comfortable hotel in one of the east coast of Scotland's loveliest and most historic old towns. It's out on a limb – perched on the end of the Black Isle – but well worth tucking yourself into for a few days of seaside strolling and gentle exploration.

At the front of the hotel, a glass verandah looks straight over the Cromarty Firth – you can eat here and enjoy the sunset or bask in the sunshine. There's a restaurant, but the bar meals are ample and satisfying enough for most people, particularly since the service is attentive and happy to please, whether you are a resident or just dropping in for a snack. Upstairs, the bedrooms, most with views out over the Firth, have been carefully decorated with restrained good taste, and are well maintained and spacious. The only thing likely to disturb your dreams is the throb of propellers as a ship slips into the Nigg fabrication yard on the other shore.

- Open all year; dining-room, closed Sun eve
- From the A9 turn right 1 mile north of Inverness on to the A832. Private car park
- 3 single, 2 twin, 3 double, 2 family rooms; most with bathroom/WC, 1 family room with shower/WC; TV, hair-dryer, baby-listening in all rooms
- Dining-room, 2 bars, 2 lounges,
- TV room, conservatory; conference facilities (max 30 people non-residential); shooting, bird-watching, other sports nearby. Wheelchair access to dining-room only
- No dogs in public rooms
- Access, Amex, Visa
- Single £25, single occupancy of twin/double £30, twin/double £49. Set L £9.50, D £15

**DERVAIG** STRATHCLYDE                                                  **MAP 1**

# Druimard Country House

DERVAIG, ISLE OF MULL, ARGYLL PA75 6QW
TEL: DERVAIG (068 84) 345

*A neat and comfortable hotel with theatrical overtones.*

The Mull Little Theatre is well known, both on and off the island, as the smallest public theatre in Britain. The Murrays own both the theatre and the Druimard Hotel, so it is not surprising to find prints of Shakespeare or playbills adorning the walls. On theatre nights, cars cram the driveway as people gather for pre-performance dinners (there aren't too many alternatives in this isolated corner of Mull), and there's a happy babble of anticipation in the restaurant.

Bedrooms are well equipped with sensible, solid furnishings. The residents' lounge is on the small side, but there's a pleasant conservatory which functions as bar and breakfast room too. One guest writes that he was pleasantly surprised by the food and that the juxtaposition of hotel and 'sophisticated' theatre folk made this an unusual discovery.

○ Open Apr to Oct, limited opening Nov to Mar

↗ 8½ miles west of Tobermory on the B8073. Turn left after Dervaig church – the hotel is on the left, on the village outskirts. Private car park

⇌ 2 twin, 3 double, 1 suite; some with bathroom/WC, some with shower/WC; TV in all rooms; hair-dryer, trouser press on request

◇ 2 restaurants, lounge, conservatory; conference

facilities (Nov to Mar by arrangement, max 40 people non-residential, 7 residential); fishing, water sports, other sports nearby. Wheelchair access to restaurant only

⊖ No dogs in public rooms; no smoking in restaurants

▭ Access, Visa

£ Single occupancy of twin/double £45, twin/double £60 to £70, suite £115; deposit required. Set D £9.50, £12; alc D £20

# Druimnacroish Country House

DRUIMNACROISH, DERVAIG, ISLE OF MULL, ARGYLL PA75 6QW
TEL: DERVAIG (068 84) 274

*A most comfortable outpost in a converted farmhouse.*

There are flowers everywhere at this old stone farm, about a mile outside the small village of Dervaig. The garden is usually a blaze of colour but, even in the early part of the year, the conservatory with its camellias, orange tree and grape vine gives a foretaste of things to come and cheers the souls of those who find the Mull landscape a little too bleak.

The conservatory runs into the lounges and dining-room in a sort of open-plan green and red living space, which feels spacious and airy. Silver candlesticks stand on the dark tables, and dinners have a touch of formality about them. Everyone sits down to Wendy McLean's traditional food, roast lamb, perhaps, at the same time. There's no choice but your preferences are, of course, taken into account if you make them known. The bedrooms are spacious and well equipped and the bathrooms well up to country-house standards.

○ Closed mid-Oct to mid-Apr

↗ From the Craignure ferry landing

take the A849 Tobermory road. North of Salen fork left towards

Dervaig for 8 miles. Private car park

4 twin, 2 double; all with bathroom/WC, TV, room service, hair-dryer

Dining-room, bar, 2 lounges, conservatory, drying room; fishing nearby. Wheelchair access to hotel, restaurant and WC, 2 ground-floor bedrooms

No children under 12; no dogs in public rooms; no smoking in dining-room and 1 lounge

Access, Amex, Diners, Visa

Single occupancy of twin/double £48, twin/double £96; deposit required. Set D £20 (8pm). Special breaks available

---

## DRUMNADROCHIT HIGHLAND       MAP 1

# Polmaily House

DRUMNADROCHIT, INVERNESS-SHIRE IV3 6XT
TEL: DRUMNADROCHIT (045 62) 343   FAX: (045 62) 813

*A comfortable, unelaborate country hotel near Loch Ness, providing monstrously good food.*

Drumnadrochit, rather more than halfway up the western shore of Loch Ness, has shops stuffed full of model 'Nessies', not to mention the self-styled Official Loch Ness Monster Exhibition. So there's no doubt what drives the village's tourist life, but don't let the inevitable tat put you off finding Polmaily, a couple of miles west of Drumnadrochit and well away from the hubbub.

This is a simple family hotel in a white-painted house, extended over the years in various directions to leave a warren of passages; also an unheated swimming-pool (often populated by ducks rather than by swimmers), a small library, nine pretty bedrooms and a host and hostess whose approach to life is efficient but informal. Nick and Alison Parsons have filled their house with books, rugs and stripped pine rather than silver and polished mahogany, but Alison produces food worthy of far grander enterprises and offers a remarkably flexible choice of menus – three, four or five courses at will. Most of her food is simple in conception but extremely good in flavour and execution.

Closed Nov to Easter

2 miles west of Drumnadrochit on the A831 Cannich road. Private car park

2 single, 2 twin, 3 double, 1 four-poster, 1 family room; most with bathroom/WC; room service in all rooms; hair-dryer on request; no tea/coffee-making facilities in rooms

Dining-room, bar, lounge, TV room, library/study; tennis, croquet, unheated swimming-pool at hotel, other sports nearby. Wheelchair access to restaurant and WC (unisex) only

No dogs; no smoking in dining-room

Access, Visa

Single £45, single occupancy of twin/double £60 to £95, twin/double/four-poster £100; deposit required. Set D £20 to £25

**DUNKELD** TAYSIDE  **MAP I**

# Kinnaird

KINNAIRD ESTATE, BY DUNKELD, PERTHSHIRE PH8 0LB
TEL: BALLINLUIG (0796) 82440   FAX: (0796) 82289

*Sumptuous luxury on Tayside.*

Kinnaird stands alone beneath a crag on the unfrequented right bank of the Tay a short way north of Dunkeld. The ground drops steeply in front to the flood plain of the river, and you look out from the dining-room over the fields to the distant scurrying cars on the A9. The eighteenth-century house is a curious Z-shape, of grey stone, creeper-covered in parts. Under the ownership of Constance Ward and the management of John Webber, it opened as an hotel in the summer of 1990, after some years as a restaurant. It is primarily a luxury sporting hotel, with shooting and fishing on the estate, but doubles as a country-house retreat.

The luxury is most apparent in the bedrooms, which benefit from a combination of the best British and American design. This means massive triple beds, dressing-tables, work table, comfortable armchairs before the fire, swathes of bright fabric, half a decanter of sherry and all the trimmings. The bathrooms are even better: 'You can live in them,' as one guest reports – deep bathtubs complete with a mirror for shaving attached to the soap rack, acres of fluffy towels and bathrobes, plus endless bottles and sachets.

Downstairs, you'll find the drawing-room furnished in more conventional shooting-lodge style, with deep sofas and armchairs and a crackling wood fire. Drinks are brought to you here along with the menu. The dining-room lies at the far end of the passage which runs along the ground floor. The food is *nouvelle cuisine* – absolutely beautifully presented (little strips of courgette come wrapped as parcels), but with the odd weak spot. When we inspected we tasted two virtually identical sauces with the starter and main course, and the cheese could have been better kept. But there are good touches: a choice of coffees for breakfast, for example. The management style is quietly efficient; some might prefer it to be more extrovert, since a rarified atmosphere can reign if the hotel isn't full. But these are niggles: we leave the last word to a satisfied guest: 'Magic – I can't wait to go back.'

○ Closed Feb

↗ After passing Dunkeld village on your right, turn left on to the B898 signposted Dalguise and Balnaguard. After 4 miles Kinnaird's main gates are on the right. Private car park

🛏 8 twin/double, 1 suite; all with bathroom/WC, TV, room service, hair-dryer, trouser press, baby-listening; no tea/coffee-making facilities in rooms

◇ 2 dining-rooms, lounge, billiard room, drying room, study; conference facilities (max 20 people non-residential); fishing, tennis, shooting at hotel, golf, other sports nearby. Wheelchair access to hotel (ramps) and dining-rooms (unisex disabled

WC), I ground-floor bedroom
and lift

━ No children under 12; no dogs
(kennel facilities available)

▭ Access, Amex, Visa

£ Single occupancy of twin/double
£85 to £150, twin/double £120
to £165, suite £210. Set L £17
to £21, D £34.50 (prices till Mar
92). Special breaks available

**EASSIE** TAYSIDE                                          **MAP I**

# Castleton House

BY GLAMIS, FORFAR, ANGUS DD8 ISJ
TEL: GLAMIS (030 784) 340   FAX: (030 784) 506

*A bright, cheerful hotel with ambitious food.*

Castleton House stands in the great fertile lowland valley of Strathmore
within easy reach of Perth and Dundee, and a stone's throw away from
Glamis Castle. Shielded from the Forfar to Blairgowrie road by its
gardens, the grey Edwardian house stands on the site of an older
fortification, of which traces of the moat remain.

The freshly redecorated interior is warmly welcoming, as are William
and Maureen Little, the proprietors. William's pride is his food: a
competitively priced main dinner menu, with a seafood night once a week
and a gourmet dinner once a fortnight. Even the bar lunch allows a three-
course blow-out: maybe mussels, strips of beef fillet and orange and
gingerbread sticky pudding. The hotel's lounge, which is a little small
and sparse, is put in the shade by the two dining-rooms: one in the
conservatory, where green-stained wooden chairs add to the impression
of dining *al fresco*; the other, more formally decorated in dusky pink at the
back of the house. The bar, long and light, is the place to relax before or
after your meal. The bedrooms are all different, all spacious and
furnished with flowery or patterned modern fabrics, while the bathrooms
have good showers and gleaming fittings.

◑ Open all year

🔁 On the A94 between Coupar
Angus and Forfar. Private car
park

🛏 5 twin, I double; all with
bathroom/WC, TV, room service,
hair-dryer

◇ Restaurant, bar, lounge,
conservatory; fishing, golf nearby.

Wheelchair access to restaurant
and WC (unisex) only

━ No dogs

▭ Access, Amex, Visa

£ Single occupancy of twin/double
£55, twin/double £85; deposit
required. Set L £10.50, D £19.50
(prices till Easter 92). Special
breaks available

---

*See page 787 for other hotels worthy of inclusion in our* Visitors' Book.

# The Albany

39–43 ALBANY STREET, EDINBURGH EH1 3QY
TEL: 031-556 0397   TELEX: 727079 ALBANY G
FAX: 031-557 6633

*A town house at the quieter end of the New Town; whose comfort
and general elegance make up for a little datedness.*

The Albany is something of a staple for those in search of somewhere
quiet and comfortable to stay within easy reach of the centre of Edinburgh. One reader was well pleased, finding the service discreet but
thorough and the staff very welcoming.

The hotel stands in a terrace of late-Georgian houses at the less
fashionable eastern end of Edinburgh's New Town, down the hill, a little
away from the action, but well positioned for all that. Three adjacent
houses make up the hotel and they have retained their original grace,
with lovely staircases, balustrades and cupolas. The bedrooms, as you
would expect, vary from the corniced high-windowed master bedrooms
to the smaller rooms at the top, which were maybe once the nursery wing.
Some of the furnishings are dated and so are some of the colour
schemes, but the rooms are comfortable enough, while the drawing-
room is a most pleasant place to relax in. The basement restaurant is
bright and airy, with plenty of space and a much newer feel to it; the bar is
cosy and friendly.

- ◑ Open all year, exc 25, 26 Dec
  and 1, 2 Jan

- ↗ Albany Street runs parallel to
  Princes Street, near the bus
  station and St Andrew's Square.
  On-street parking and public car
  park nearby

- ⇌ 5 single, 14 twin, 1 double, 2
  family rooms; some with
  bathroom/WC, some with
  shower/WC; TV, room service in
  all rooms

- ◈ Restaurant, bar, lounge;
  conference facilities (max 18
  people residential and non-
  residential); golf, tennis, other
  sports nearby; babysitting

- ⊖ No wheelchair access; no dogs in
  public rooms; no smoking

- ▭ Access, Visa

- £ Single £55 to £65; twin/double
  £65 to £85; children under 12
  free; deposit required. Alc D
  from £25; bar lunches

# The Howard

36 GREAT KING STREET, EDINBURGH EH3 6QH
TEL: 031-557 3500   FAX: 031-557 6515

*A luxurious private hotel close to the centre of Edinburgh.*

Great King Street always was one of the posher bits of Edinburgh's New
Town, so it is no surprise to find a luxury hotel like the Howard taking

advantage of the street's fine position and splendid architecture. Discretion is the hallmark of this hotel, as befits its price and surroundings. Once past the brass plate by the doorway, you find yourself inside a town house, or rather three town houses joined together, of sumptuous splendour.

The drawing-room, with its heavy curtains effectively excluding the outside world, is a place where you can sink into the deep chairs with a sigh of relief. The restaurant runs across the entire basement area of the three houses, and is formal and elegant, with brisk and attentive service and ambitious, good food. The bedrooms are something of a bit of a mixture in size – singles come off worst here, as they do in so many other places. But all the bedrooms are furnished with great comfort, and a lot of trouble has been taken to supply the things that need supplying, such as mineral water, fruit and magazines, as well as the things that don't, such as your own personalised teddy.

- Open all year
- Centrally located, off Dundas Street. Private car park
- 4 single, 4 twin, 6 double, 2 four-poster; all with bathroom/WC, TV, room service, hair-dryer, trouser press; no tea/coffee-making facilities in rooms
- Restaurant, drawing-room, drying facilities; conference facilities (max 18 people non-residential, 16 residential); golf, tennis, other sports nearby
- No wheelchair access; no dogs
- Access, Amex, Diners, Visa
- Single £97, twin/double £148 to £189, suite £225. Set L £10.50, D £25 (prices till end Sept 91)

# Scandic Crown

80 HIGH STREET, THE ROYAL MILE, EDINBURGH EH1 1TH
TEL: 031-557 9797   TELEX: 727298 SCHEDH G
FAX: 031-557 9789

*Still the best option among Edinburgh's modern business hotels. Fine position, good design and some idiosyncratic touches.*

The Scandic Crown occupies a prime position in Edinburgh's Old Town, right in the middle of the famous Royal Mile between the castle and Holyrood Palace. For such a sensitive site, it was essential that the architecture should fit in, and it does.

First impressions are of a stone town house, with a tower at one angle, backed by two higher tenements. In fact it is all one complex, internally linked by corridors and lifts – the only disadvantage being a rather long trudge if your room is right at the back. The open-plan ground floor can become rather discordant as different types of music and voice meet and mingle, but you can escape either to the hushed formality of the Jewel restaurant, or to the more relaxed, but rather conventional piano bar. A brightly lit downstairs bistro doubles as the breakfast room. Scandinavian touches are subtle but serve to make the hotel distinctive. There are Danish or Swedish serving staff among the British, smorgasbord lunches, proper gravadlax in the seafood salad and even underfloor heating in the bathrooms to warm your toes while you are brushing your teeth.

The bedrooms are again distinguished by small instances of good sense – a convenient plug for computers, proper space for open suitcases, and supremely comfortable beds. The service stretches beyond efficiency towards friendliness (the receptionists make efforts to remember your name, for example). The food in the restaurant is extremely competent without being flashy, and it is also worth mentioning the car park – a massive advantage in Edinburgh's notoriously congested centre.

◑ Open all year

⤢ From Waverley Station, cross North Bridge to the first set of traffic lights. The hotel is on the left on the Royal Mile. Private car park

🛏 22 single, 126 twin, 72 double, 8 family rooms, 10 suites; all with bathroom/WC, TV, room service, hair-dryer, trouser press, mini-bar

◈ 2 restaurants, 2 bars, lounge, laundry facilities; conference facilities (max 200 people residential and non-residential); sauna, solarium, indoor swimming-pool, gym at hotel, other sports nearby; babysitting. Wheelchair access to hotel, restaurant and WC, 3 bedrooms specially equipped for the disabled

⊖ Dogs by arrangement; some bedrooms non-smoking

▭ Access, Amex, Diners, Visa

£ Single from £81, single occupancy of twin/double from £97, twin/double from £118, suite from £210; deposit required (prices till end Mar 92). Cooked B £8.50; set L £10, D £14; buffet L, D £13 (1991 prices)

---

# Sibbet House

26 NORTHUMBERLAND STREET, EDINBURGH EH3 6LS
TEL: 031-556 1078   FAX: 031-557 9445

---

*A guesthouse in the Georgian New Town. A rare example of a first-class, medium-priced place to stay in the city centre.*

Sibbet House is the sort of place that Edinburgh should be full of, but isn't. It is a large town house in one of the less extravagant of Edinburgh's Georgian streets, halfway down the steep slope that plunges towards the Forth, but only a few minutes' panting climb away from the shops of George Street and the city centre (there are buses for the unfit).

Before their new incarnation as providers of accommodation, the Sibbets were antique dealers, and the decoration of the house reflects their love of fine things. But they have managed to retain the atmosphere of a family home – in fact you will be sleeping in what were once the children's bedrooms. The book-lined front lounge with its two tables is now used as the dining-room, while the drawing-room is on the first floor, as is usual in many of the New Town's houses. This is a cosy place, with family photographs and many lovely objects to look at. There are three bedrooms: the blue room is the nicest, with its sofa, stripy wallpaper and exercise bicycle in the bathroom. The surrounding streets contain a good choice of places to eat in the evenings. Sibbet House is the sort of place which led one satisfied businessman-refugee to write that it had saved his company £200 in one month by staying there. Its popularity means that it is worth booking well in advance.

- ◑ *Open all year*
- ⤢ *Northumberland Street runs parallel to Princes Street, four streets north. On-street parking*
- ⛵ *1 double, 2 family rooms; double with bathroom/WC, family rooms with shower/WC; TV, hair-dryer, trouser press, baby-listening in all rooms*
- ◇ *Dining-room, drawing-room,*

- *library; golf, tennis, other sports nearby; babysitting*
- ⬤ *No wheelchair access; no dogs; smoking in bedrooms only*
- ▭ *Access, Visa*
- £ *Single occupancy of twin/double £39, twin/double £46, family room £60; children sharing parents' room half-price; deposit required*

---

**ERISKA** STRATHCLYDE                                                   **MAP 1**

# Isle of Eriska

---

LEDAIG, BY OBAN, ARGYLL PA37 1SD
TEL: LEDAIG (063 172) 371    TELEX: 777040 ERISKA G
FAX: (063 172) 531

*Peace and quiet reign in this backwater where the civilised atmosphere is backed by competent service and good cooking.*

Eriska is an island, though you would hardly notice the bridge that leads on to it if it were not for the speed ramps. At the edge of the island stands a granite and sandstone mansion, built in 1884 and a curious mixture of appealing frontages and undistinguished clutter.

This is now the home of the Buchanan-Smith family and feels definitely more like home than hotel – the home possibly of a generous country uncle of the sort who is happy to have your wellie boots in his hall but likes you to change for dinner. This is a role which Robin Buchanan-Smith fulfils well: good conversation, books, local knowledge and politics are all grist to his mill. And dinner is well worth changing for: a formal six-course affair with a couple of choices at the main stages, all immaculately cooked and presented.

The bedrooms, reached by the staircase from the panelled hall, are named after the Hebrides, and vary as much in size as do those islands. They have a mix of furnishings and a mix of views. The library (with a bar in the corner) has an equally interesting variety of books, while the drawing-room contains plenty of deep sofas to read them in. It is obvious that people get hooked on this hotel and return to it again and again.

◑ Closed Nov to Feb

⤵ Take the A85 Crianlarich road over Connel Bridge. Isle of Eriska is signposted from Benderloch. Private car park

🛏 2 twin, 14 twin/double; all with shower/WC, TV, room service, hair-dryer, trouser press; baby-listening on request

◈ Dining-room, drawing-room, drying room, library; conference facilities (max 16 people residential); tennis, riding,

croquet, putting green, water sports at hotel, fishing, golf nearby. Wheelchair access to hotel (ramp) and dining-room, 2 ground-floor bedrooms specially equipped for the disabled

⊖ No children in dining-room eves; no dogs in public rooms

▭ Access, Visa

£ Single occupancy of twin £154, twin/double £154; deposit required. Set D £37. Special breaks available

## ETTRICKBRIDGE BORDERS                                        MAP 2

# Ettrickshaws

ETTRICKBRIDGE, NR SELKIRK, SELKIRKSHIRE TD7 5HW
TEL: SELKIRK (0750) 52229

*A slightly eccentric hotel in beautiful countryside.*

This house was built in 1891, apparently by a successful sheep farmer returned from down-under, and it is possible that its architecture has Australian overtones. There's nothing Australian about the hallway, with its flat wooden arch and its baronial touches, nor about the beautiful light drawing-room, with comfortable sofas looking down through the high windows towards the River Ettrick. These belong firmly to the Scottish Edwardian tradition.

The bedrooms at Ettrickshaws are a curious mixture, with their fittings ranging from the plain and the old-fashioned, through Art Deco to chinoiserie, and the same variations can be found in the bathrooms. All are comfortable, however, though not luxurious. The restaurant, with a strange metallic wallpaper, is square and a little cramped if the hotel is full. The food is plain, honest and reasonably priced. For residents there is free fishing on two miles of the River Ettrick, with the chance of a salmon if the water and the season are right. For non-fishers, this section of the Ettrick Valley is one of the most beautiful spots in the Borders.

◑ Closed Dec and Jan

⤵ 1½ miles west of Ettrickbridge on the B7009. Private car park

🛏 3 twin, 3 double, 1 family room; all with bathroom/WC, exc 1 twin with shower/WC; TV in all rooms; hair-dryer on request;

limited room service

◈ Restaurant, bar, lounge; drying facilities; fishing at hotel, other sports nearby

⊖ No wheelchair access; no children under 9; no dogs or smoking in public rooms

▭ Access, Diners, Visa

£ⷦ Single occupancy of twin/double
£45 to £60, twin/double £60 to

£75; deposit required. Set D
£13; alc D £18.50; bar lunches.
Special breaks available

**FETTERCAIRN** GRAMPIAN                MAP 1

# Ramsay Arms

FETTERCAIRN, KINCARDINESHIRE AB30 1XY
TEL: FETTERCAIRN (056 14) 334   FAX: (056 14) 500

*A good-value pub in a tiny village.*

Queen Victoria once stayed at the Ramsay Arms and the inhabitants of
this tiny village took the extraordinary step of building a triumphal arch to
celebrate the fact that someone famous had noticed them. This
ridiculous but touching folly still dominates the place and means that you
approach the hotel rather as if you were driving into a ducal palace.

The Ramsay Arms is a village pub with a little added class – notably its
rather fine panelled nineteenth-century dining-room, called the
Gladstone Room in honour of that Prime Minister, whose childhood
home is nearby. It also has a surprising sauna and Jacuzzi tucked away
beyond its very nicely refurbished bedrooms. There's a lively public bar
and a more genteel lounge bar. The food isn't bad either and there's a
refreshingly welcome atmosphere from the staff. The secret of the place
of course lies in the fact that the owners are still relatively new and
determined to make a go of things.

🄾 Open all year

🄰 Take the B974 from the A94
Forfar to Aberdeen road. Private
car park

🛏 3 single, 3 twin, 4 double, 1
four-poster, 1 family room; most
with bathroom/WC, some with
shower/WC; TV, room service,
hair-dryer, baby-listening in all
rooms

◈ Dining-room, 2 bars, lounge,
drying room, library, residents'
lounge; sauna, gym, Jacuzzi at
hotel, other sports nearby

⊖ No wheelchair access

▭ Access, Visa

£ⷦ Single £31, single occupancy of
twin/double £31, twin/double
£45, four-poster £50, family
room from £45; deposit required.
Alc L £10, D £16 (prices till end
91)

---

*If you are intending to make a lot of phone calls from your room, always
check what the hotel is going to charge you per unit. You may be so horrified
that you'll prefer to walk to the nearest phone box. Why let them get away
with excessive charges?*

# The Factor's House

TORLUNDY, FORT WILLIAM, INVERNESS-SHIRE PH33 6SN
TEL: FORT WILLIAM (0397) 705767   TELEX: 776229
FAX: (0397) 702953 (these are the same numbers as for Inverlochy Castle – see next entry)

*If Inverlochy Castle is beyond your purse, try this very different, unpretentious chip off the same block.*

The Factor's House is run by Peter Hobbs, the son of the owners of Inverlochy Castle, and stands at the foot of one of the avenues which lead from the A82 to that famed hotel. 'We would strongly recommend it for its combination of unpretentious charm, very good service and good food,' writes one guest.

It is a small hotel in a modern-looking building but probably not the place for large rumbustious families. The atmosphere is certainly conducive to making friends: this is partly to do with the size, partly to do with the hail-fellow-well-met approach to guests, and partly to do with the presence of yarn-encouraging objects such as the much-mentioned walrus's penis bone.

There was a change of chef in 1991 but the menu remains much as it used to be. One reader writers that sound insulation is poor and that the combination of road noise, chatter from the living-room and other guests' snores can counteract the soporific West Highland air.

| | |
|---|---|
| ◑ Closed mid-Nov to mid-Mar; dining-room closed Sun, Mon eves | ◈ Dining-room, 2 lounges, drying room; fishing, golf, other sports nearby |
| ⤴ 3 miles north of Fort William, just off the A82 Inverness road. Private car park | ⊖ No wheelchair access; no children under 6; no dogs in public rooms |
| ⇌ 1 single, 2 twin, 4 double; most with bathroom/WC, some with shower/WC; TV, hair-dryer, trouser press in all rooms; no tea/coffee-making facilities in rooms | ▭ Access, Visa |
| | ⊞ Single £59 to £65, single occupancy of twin/double £65 to £76, twin/double £65 to £85; deposit required. Set D £20 |

---

*If you make a booking using a credit card, and you find after cancelling that the full amount has been charged to your card, raise the matter with your credit card company. They will ask the hotelier to confirm whether the room was re-let, and to justify the charge they made.*

# Inverlochy Castle

TORLUNDY, FORT WILLIAM, INVERNESS-SHIRE PH33 6SN
TEL: FORT WILLIAM (0397) 702177   TELEX: 776229
FAX: (0397) 702953 (these are the same numbers as for Factor's House – see
previous entry)

*This remains one of Scotland's premier hotels, with red carpet
treatment and prices to match.*

It is hard to know (before you pay the bill) whether you are in an
extremely good hotel, or whether you are a guest at the country house of
some fabulous Edwardian grandee. For Inverlochy Castle successfully
manages to recreate that dreamworld of elegant country luxury which
many lesser hotels witter on about but never manage to achieve.

Grete Hobbs, who continues to supervise the running of the place, has
avoided over-stuffing the public rooms with expensive modern furnishings. What you find in the expansive hall, lounge and billiard room are
carefully chosen period pieces to go with the extravagant fresco-and-
cornice elaborations of the house, such as rugs, chandeliers, a chess
table, embroidery, carved sideboards and heavy dark tables. The
drawing-room is relaxing and comfortable and overlooks the loch. The
service might be by a servants-hall full of gentlemen's gentlemen – the
staff shimmer, as Jeeves did, and your mind hardly forms a request
before there is someone at your elbow to answer it. The food is delicate
and precise, with plenty of local fish and game.

Bedrooms are in much the same style as the rest of the castle, but with
plenty of concessions to modernity, such as superb bathrooms and plenty
of luxuries. They vary considerably in size, and are charged for accordingly (though none could be described as cheap). The squat baronial
mock-castle is surrounded by extensive grounds – a maze of avenues
carving their way through rhododendron jungles and past lakes. Ben
Nevis looms in the background.

◑ Closed mid-Nov to I Mar

🔼 On the A82 Glasgow to
Inverness road, 3 miles north of
Fort William. Private car park

🛏 I single, 15 twin/double, I
family room, I suite; all with
bathroom/WC, TV, room service,
hair-dryer; no tea/coffee-making
facilities in rooms

◇ 2 dining-rooms, 2 lounges,
billiard room, library, laundry

facilities; fishing, tennis, billiards
at hotel, golf, other sports
nearby; babysitting

⊖ No wheelchair access; no
children under 12; hotel has
kennels for dogs

▭ Access, Visa

£ Single from £120, twin/double
£150 to £220, suite £250;
deposit required. Set L £17.50 to
£30, D £39

# Woodlands Country House

WINDYKNOWE ROAD, GALASHIELS, SELKIRKSHIRE TD1 1RQ
TEL: GALASHIELS (0896) 4722

*The surroundings may be suburban, but the style is Gothic and the standards are high.*

Woodlands lies halfway up a steep back road out of Galashiels and is a Victorian mansion of precisely the type that mill owners built to impress their neighbours. The exterior is dourly imposing, enlivened by the pelargoniums which cram the windows of the dark wood conservatory.

But going inside is like entering a Gothic chapel, with an elaborate stone archway leading from the hall to the dining-room, a set of bare stone steps with a central rail leading, not to an altar, but towards the bedrooms, and carved pillars on the fringes. It is like being inside a Romantic poem – the *Eve of St Agnes*, or *Christabel*, perhaps. This impression is dispelled by the bar, which is bright, warm and cheery, and by the dining-room, where the pink coverings go well with the streaky marble fireplace. Alas, the airy lounge has been downgraded to a conference room and over-filled with furniture. 'With the conservatory and the bar, no one ever sat here,' explains Kevin Winsland. A pity all the same. The bedrooms, apart from the small singles, are large and well equipped; the old panelled billiard room at the top of the house is especially nice. Bar meals have been upgraded since last year, and now provide a substantial alternative to the fairly traditional food in the restaurant.

◗ Open all year

🚫 Off the A7 from Edinburgh or Carlisle, through Galashiels. The hotel is on the back road towards Peebles. Private car park

🛏 2 single, 2 twin, 5 double (family rooms available); all with bathroom/WC, exc 1 single with shower/WC; TV, room service, trouser press, baby-listening in all rooms; hair dryer on request

◈ Restaurant, bar, lounge, billiard room, drying room, conservatory;

conference facilities (max 30 people non-residential, 9 residential); golf, tennis, other sports nearby

⊖ No wheelchair access; no dogs in public rooms

▭ Access, Visa

£ Single £42, single occupancy of twin/double £47, twin/double £65, family room £90. Set L £9.50; alc L, D £12 to £16; bar meals

---

*All entries in the* Guide *are rewritten every year, not least because standards fluctuate. Don't trust an out-of-date* Guide.

**GIFFORD** LOTHIAN                                       **MAP 2**

# Forbes Lodge

GIFFORD, EAST LOTHIAN EH41 4JE
TEL: GIFFORD (062 081) 212

*A tranquil Wolsey Lodge in a pretty East Lothian village.*

Lady Marioth Hay's family used to inhabit the nearby Yester House,
whose resplendent gates stand at the end of the village. The beautiful
family portraits which line the walls of Forbes Lodge originally hung
there, and you can tell that they were designed for a much bigger place.
Not that Forbes Lodge is small. It is a substantial stone house, so
successfully tucked away in its gardens that the nearby village might not
exist. The gardens, beautifully designed, run along the edge of a small
river, and contain much to delight, being one of Lady Marioth's most
obvious enthusiasms.

Inside, Forbes Lodge is a mix of elegance and informality, with the
drawing-room and library feeling cosy and lived-in; the latter has an
open fire and TV. The dining-room is rather more formal, with its bird-
pattern fabrics and crisp table settings. The bedrooms are spacious and
comfortable, and there are interesting features, such as the single four-
poster bed, the *chaise percée* and the extraordinary 'box bath' – set into the
wall and curtained from the draughts. The dinners are by arrangement
only, and often include fruit and vegetables from the garden. They are
straightforward and good value.

- ◑ Open all year; dining-room open
  by arrangement only

- ↗ Take the road to Haddington
  and follow the signs to Gifford.
  Turn towards Edinburgh and
  Forbes Lodge is the first house on
  the right, beyond the bridge over
  the stream

- 🛏 2 single (1 four-poster room), 1
  twin; some with bathroom/WC;
  all with hair-dryer

- ◈ Dining-room, drawing-room,
  drying room, library

- ⊖ No wheelchair access; no
  children; no dogs; no smoking in
  bedrooms

- ▭ None accepted

- £ Single £30, single occupancy of
  twin/double £60, twin/double
  £60; deposit required. Set D £16
  (by arrangement, 8pm)

**GIGHA** STRATHCLYDE                                       **MAP 2**

# Gigha Hotel

ISLE OF GIGHA, ARGYLL PA41 7AD
TEL: GIGHA (058 35) 254   FAX: (058 35) 282

*An island hotel, perfect for an isolated holiday.*

The island of Gigha, which lies off the western coast of the Mull of
Kintyre, is a place where everything is in miniature, from the small sandy

beaches to the golf course and the tiny trout loch. A small ferry chugs across the sound and will carry you to within a five-minute walk of the hotel (if you want to bring your car, it's well worth booking in advance as the ferry is very small). The hotel will pick you up if you don't want to walk from the landing stage.

The hotel is an old white farmhouse, imaginatively converted, retaining stone walls in the dining-room and a range of pretty, medium-sized bedrooms, whose decoration smacks of the floral 1970s and is utterly soothing. The bar is by far the liveliest spot in the hotel and most people congregate there, although the lounge with its fire and sofas is more relaxing, especially during a spell of sea-mist. The food comes in ample quantities, and may be a little on the heavy side. Bicycling up and down Gigha's narrow roads is by far the best way to explore the island. Most people make for the renowned gardens at Achamore, but there are plenty of other hidden spots.

🌓 *Open all year*

🔁 *Take the car ferry from Tayinloan and then follow the road from the ferry landing to a T-junction. Turn left and the hotel is 100 yards down this road. Private car park*

🛏 *7 twin, 6 double, 3 self-catering cottages; most with bathroom/ WC, some with shower/WC*

◇ *Restaurant, bistro, bar, lounge; conference facilities (max 40*

*people non-residential, 15 residential); fishing, golf nearby. Wheelchair access to restaurant only*

⊜ *No dogs (kennels available)*

▭ *Access, Visa*

£ *Single occupancy of twin/double £35 to £39, twin/double £70; cottages £295 to £375 per week; deposit required. Set L £11, D £19. Special breaks available*

---

**GLASGOW** STRATHCLYDE                                    **MAP 2**

---

# Babbity Bowster

---

16–18 BLACKFRIARS STREET, GLASGOW G1 1PE
TEL: 041-552 5055

*Lively café/bar/restaurant with no-frills rooms offering a crash course in modern Glasgow culture.*

Fraser Laurie's much-imitated winning formula continues to delight, and is as popular as ever. The sensitive restoration of a derelict Robert Adam house, in the now-trendy Merchant City area, walked off with an armful of awards, and the cheerful, uncontrived atmosphere of robust Glasgow *bonhomie* is just as well judged. This being Glasgow, the bar's the heart of the matter, and the diverse clientele includes wine-quaffing young professionals, arty real-alers and woolly-hatted, shopping-bag-laden ladies putting their feet up with a cappuccino and the *Glasgow Herald*.

The simple, predominantly grey décor is enlivened by a pretty stencilled beam that runs below the high ceiling, while well-known Glasgow worthies gaze down from striking monochrome photographs. Folk and jazz artists make regular appearances, and poetry readings give a platform to local writing talent. Soothing live music sets the tone at the 'Sunday morning hangover cure' which quickly became a local institution. The all-day food in the café/bar ranges from filled rolls and baked potatoes to vegetarian haggis and lamb stovies, as well as daily specials such as Gigha scallops in creamy cider sauce. There's more choice in the upstairs restaurant (less noisy, less atmosphere), and all the bread and pastries served are now home-baked. Mouthwatering Carradale kippers are a good bet at breakfast time.

The bedrooms have been redecorated since we expressed reservations last year, but remain ascetic. The philosophy is understandable – who needs a television when there's so much going on downstairs? One reader found the simple, pine-and-pastel rooms just too spartan, and decamped to a chain hotel in search of greater comfort. But if you're prepared to forgo trouser presses, kettles and the like, and ready to join in the boisterous fun, there's no better introduction to Glasgow.

- ◑ Open all year, restaurant closed Sun eve
- ⤤ In the city centre. Private car park
- ⇚ 1 single, 4 twin, 1 double; all with shower/WC
- ◈ Restaurant, café/bar
- ⊖ No wheelchair access; no dogs;

no smoking in bedrooms

- ▭ Access, Amex, Visa
- £ Single £36, single occupancy of twin/double £36, twin/double £56. Continental B £1.50, cooked B £3.50; light meal (L, D) from £3.50

# One Devonshire Gardens

1 DEVONSHIRE GARDENS, GLASGOW G12 0UX
TEL: 041-334 9494/339 2001   FAX: 041-337 1663

*Sumptuous, innovative hotel with a distinctly individual style.*

Ken McCulloch's maverick venture continues to consolidate its position as one of Britain's most memorable hotels. These days the hotel spans numbers one, two and three Devonshire Gardens, with each house, while retaining individual characteristics, displaying the imaginative flair that makes the place extra-special.

There's a theatrical self-confidence about the whole enterprise, evident from the moment a poised young lady welcomes you into the midnight-blue hall of house number one. Suddenly you feel aeons away from the traffic thundering along Great Western Road, as you're engulfed by a triumph of interior design and swept into an ambience that owes more to the eighteen- than to the nineteen-nineties. The dining-room is equally dramatic with its heavy curtains, wood panelling and ribbon-bowed napkins.

The huge drawing-rooms are bright and airy with acres of heavy-weight fabric, and comfortable sofas. A small, black figure perches on a much-travelled trunk in house two, ready to make up the numbers when guests would otherwise be thirteen at table. There's a similar 'extra man' somewhere in each house.

Bedrooms are fiercely individual and unapologetically opulent: all have magnificent fireplaces and magisterial sofas, chic wallcoverings and elegant carpets and drapes, often with stripes and polka dots. Each room has an 'entertainment centre' with television and compact disc player tucked away discreetly in antique-style armoires. Bathrooms are similarly grand in style, although one reader who found the hotel otherwise 'delightful' was disappointed to be allocated one of the three rooms with a shower only, 'and not a particularly efficient one' at that.

The menu relies extensively on fresh Scottish ingredients, and is more traditional than previously, with offerings such as Loch Fyne mussels and roasted loin of lamb with a thyme jus.

○ Open all year, exc 25 Dec; dining-room closed Sat L

▤ From the M8 take the A82 Dumbarton/Kelvinside turn-off. Turn right into Great Western Road. At the ninth set of traffic lights turn left into Hyndland Road, then first right to Devonshire Gardens. On-street parking

🛏 3 twin, 15 double, 9 four-poster, 2 suites; most with bathroom/WC, some with shower/WC; TV, room service, hair-dryer, mini-bar, full valet service in all

rooms; no tea/coffee-making facilities in rooms

◈ Dining-room, bar, 2 lounges, drying room; conference facilities (max 25 residential); babysitting

● No wheelchair access; no children in dining-room; no dogs in public rooms

▭ Access, Amex, Diners, Visa

💷 Single occupancy of twin/double £110, twin/double £140, four-poster £140, suite £165; deposit required. Cooked B £7; set L £18, D £30 (1991 prices)

---

# The Town House

4 HUGHENDEN TERRACE, GLASGOW G12 9XR
TEL: 041-357 0862   FAX: 041-339 9605

*Good-value accommodation in a smart West End location.*

A neighbour's cat has adopted Bill and Charlotte Thow's homely yet elegant Town House as a sort of home-from-home, and it's easy to sympathise with her feline instinct. This is a splendid late-Victorian house in a residential Kelvinside terrace, carefully restored to show off its period features to best advantage. The public areas have dizzily high ceilings and wonderfully ornate cornices. A plant bedecked top-floor gallery, flooded with natural light, has a restful conservatory-like feel and an imposing staircase. The civilised lounge has an impressive fireplace (complete with the obligatory Glaswegian mantelpiece fixture, 'the wally dug'), prints of Dundee and comfy leather sofas – just the sort of place to kick your shoes off and relax.

The bright dining-room has beige walls, embroidered samplers and modern works by local artist Maria Mulhern. Breakfast is traditional Scottish, on porridge and kipper lines, while the sensibly short dinner menu sticks to accepted standards like lasagne and sirloin steak.

All bedrooms are well proportioned, while several are huge and some have views over the garden (currently the focus of the Thows' improvement plans). Most have a pink and grey colour scheme and good-quality modern furniture.

◑ *Open all year*

⬈ *From the A82 Great Western Road, turn right at the Hyndland signpost and then first right into Hughenden Road. On-street parking*

🛏 *2 twin, 6 double, 2 family rooms; all with shower/WC, TV, baby-listening*

◇ *Dining-room, lounge; conference facilities (max 20 people residential); golf, tennis, other sports nearby*

⊖ *No wheelchair access; no dogs; no smoking in dining-room*

▭ *None accepted*

£ *Single occupancy of twin/double £42, twin/double £54; family room £60 to £70; deposit required. Alc D £20*

---

# Town House

54 WEST GEORGE STREET, GLASGOW G2 1NG
TEL: 041-332 3320   FAX: 041-332 9756

*Expense-account comfort in Glasgow's city centre, with good-value weekend breaks if you're picking up the tab yourself.*

They don't do things by halves in the former City of Culture: and, to prove the point, there are now two establishments by the name of The Town House. There's no connection between them, and they could scarcely be more different. The newcomer gives Glasgow something previously sorely missed – a medium-sized city-centre business hotel with a sense of style and flair.

You'll find this Town House close to Queen Street Station in a splendid, refurbished Victorian building which was once the city's Liberal Club. Something of the character of that era, when Glasgow was the Second City of the Empire, is retained in the public rooms with their lofty ceilings, ornate plasterwork and period fireplaces (the electric fan heater seen in the Gordon Room on our inspection was somewhat incongruous).

The Music Room restaurant, where guests dine on French-influenced dishes assembled from fresh local ingredients, has particularly striking plasterwork, and a central fountain provides a focus of attention. There's welcome relief from the grating Muzak, when a piano and violin duo rip through standards from the 'A nightingale sang in Berkeley Square' era. The menu is particularly strong on fish and seafood, and is well presented. Service is friendly, and the accents owe more to Partick than to Paris. The traditional Scottish breakfast disappoints – the absence of porridge and potato scones on our inspection was (in local parlance) 'a scunner'.

The bedrooms are bright and decent-sized with pastel décor and modern soft furnishings in well-co-ordinated modish colours. Lots of lamps and just about every conceivable pampering extra, as well as glitzy bathrooms, make this a thoroughly comfortable central base.

◑ Open all year, exc 26 Dec

⤢ At the George Square end of West George Street, in the city centre. Parking difficult

🛏 3 single, 11 twin, 16 double, 2 four-poster, 2 suites; all with bathroom/WC, TV, room service, hair-dryer, trouser press, mini-bar

◈ Restaurant, bar, lounge; conference facilities (max 65 people residential); golf, tennis, other sports nearby; babysitting

⊖ No wheelchair access; no dogs in public rooms

▭ Access, Amex, Diners, Visa

💷 Single £88, twin/double £100, four-poster £110, family room £135, suite £135; deposit required. Continental B £4.50, cooked B £8.50; set L £10.50/£12.50, D £19; alc L, D £25. Special breaks available

---

**GLENBORRODALE** HIGHLAND                    **MAP 1**

# Glenborrodale Castle

GLENBORRODALE, ACHARACLE, ARGYLL PH36 4JP
TEL: GLENBORRODALE (097 24) 266   TELEX: 778815
FAX: (097 24) 224

*A luxurious but unstuffy hotel in isolated surroundings.*

Ardnamurchan is a long flat peninsula thrusting out from Scotland's west coast into the Atlantic. Glenborrodale lies on the southern shore, looking across Loch Sunart to the hills of Morven and to Mull beyond. The castle is a red sandstone Victorian Gothic affair, built by a mining magnate in questionable taste but in unashamed splendour. Peter de Savary bought it and spent more than two million pounds turning it into a sort of super-hotel for those who like to be pampered in the wilderness.

The money has not gone to waste either, for the good taste shown by Mrs de Savary and interior designer Cathleen Seymour is evident everywhere. They have managed to create public rooms which are furnished in keeping with the castle's grandeur, but without any hint of stuffy formality. This is also true of the bedrooms, where heavy fabrics and comfortable beds are the rule – backed up by superb bathrooms. The food is in keeping with the rest of the hotel: inventive without being over-elaborate. Activities from tennis to water sports are on hand and there is a golf course 45 minutes' away by private launch.

◑ *Closed from 31 Oct to Easter*

🡕 *41 miles west of Fort William on the Ardnamurchan peninsula. Private car park*

🛏 *4 twin, 7 double, 5 four-poster; all with bathroom/WC, TV, hair-dryer, limited room service in all rooms*

◈ *Dining-room, bar, lounge, games room, drying room, conservatory; conference facilities (max 30 people non-residential, 8*

*residential); fishing, putting, tennis, croquet, clay pigeon shooting, gym, water sports, sauna/solarium at hotel*

⊖ *No wheelchair access; no dogs; no smoking in dining-room*

▭ *Access, Amex, Visa*

£ *Single occupancy of twin/double £100, twin/double £150, four-poster £200; deposit required. Set D £27.50; alc L £15 (prices till Nov 91)*

---

**GLENCRIPESDALE** HIGHLAND            **MAP 1**

# Glencripesdale House

LOCH SUNART, ACHARACLE, ARGYLL PH36 4JH
TEL: SALEN (0967 85) 263

*For absolute isolation, few hotels beat this.*

It is an eight-mile drive from the main road down a rough forestry track, and it takes an hour. Halfway down there's a gate with a coded lock. This is not a game of dungeons and dragons – it's the normal method of arrival at Glencripesdale. The moral is clear: there's little point in turning up without warning. If you try, you would be lucky ever to arrive. But, armed with instructions from the Hemmings, the persistent traveller is amply rewarded by a sojourn in what is probably the most isolated hotel in Britain. The scenery too is rewarding, for the converted farmhouse stands by the very shores of Loch Sunart.

This is more of a guesthouse than a hotel, but the four bedrooms are full of character, the sitting-room is full of books and the small dining-room is rather sweet. It's a good place for families especially, since there is a separate playroom in the outbuildings with a dressing-up box. The tariff, which at first glance may seem pricey for a small hotel in the middle of nowhere, suddenly reveals itself as excellent value when you realise it includes dinner, packed lunch and afternoon tea as well as your room.

◑ *Closed Nov to Feb, exc Xmas and New Year*

🡕 *Archaracle is the postal address only; the hotel is 35 miles away on the south side of Loch Sunart. Take the A861 from the Corran ferry towards Strontian and fork*

*left on to the A884. Follow signs for 'Laudale 2' – the hotel is 8 miles along on a forestry track through the Laudale Estate. Hosts will supply detailed directions. Private car park*

🛏 *2 twin, 2 double; half with*

bathroom/WC, half with shower/
WC; no tea/coffee-making
facilities in rooms

 Dining-room, library/lounge,
games room, drying room,
conservatory; fishing, table
tennis, water sports at hotel

⊖ No wheelchair access; no dogs;
no smoking in dining-room

⊟ None accepted

£ Rates from £55 per person
(rates inc dinner, packed lunch
and afternoon tea); deposit
required

---

**GLENELG** HIGHLAND      **MAP 1**

# Glenelg Inn

GLENELG, BY KYLE OF LOCHALSH, ROSS-SHIRE IV40 8AG
TEL: GLENELG (059 982) 273

*An isolated but sophisticated inn, with decorative furniture and a
charming host.*

The old military road over the pass to Glenelg is much less dramatically
steep than it used to be before improvements were made, but it is still
sufficiently minor to be ignored by the tourists heading for Skye. The
Glenelg Inn is, both physically and metaphorically, at the centre of the
little village which lies on the far side.

It looks a typical pub, with fine views out towards Skye, and a large
warm bar with hard benches, dartboard and billiard table. But stay the
night here and you will be impressed by the food, the furnishings, and the
manner in which Christopher Main runs a professional business beneath
a disguise of outward-going bonhomie and all-embracing charm. The
bedrooms are quiet and simple but elegantly put together with a mix of
practical furnishings, and antiques which have probably been in the
family for many years. There is a small morning room for residents with
comfy chairs and a drinks cabinet if you don't want to join in at the bar,
and other extras, such as a games room, which you are unlikely to need
unless you hit a long wet spell. The menu is straightforward and
unpretentious; the food is excellently cooked and served in friendly
fashion.

◑ Hotel open Easter to Oct (inn
open all year)

⤴ From Fort William/Inverness
take the A87 towards Kyle of
Lochalsh. Turn left at Shiel
Bridge. Follow road over hill for
9 miles to Glenelg village.
Private car park

⇌ 3 twin, 3 double (family rooms
available); all with bathroom/
WC, TV, hair-dryer

 Dining-room, bar, lounge, games

room, study; solarium, water
sports at hotel, other sports
nearby. Wheelchair access to
hotel and restaurant, 1 ground-
floor bedroom

⊖ No dogs or smoking in dining-
room

⊟ Access, Visa

£ £40 to £60 per person (rates inc
dinner); deposit required. Set L
from £1.50, D £18.50

**GLENSHIEL** HIGHLAND                                    **MAP 1**

# Kintail Lodge

GLENSHIEL, BY KYLE OF LOCHALSH, ROSS-SHIRE IV40 8HL
TEL: GLENSHIEL (059 981) 275   FAX: (059 981) 226

*An inexpensive base at the foot of Glenshiel.*

With the impressive peaks of the Five Sisters of Kintail rising nearby, and the waters of Loch Duich almost lapping up against the building, the location of Kintail Lodge could only be bettered if the building were a little further away from the main A87 road – but at least this makes it easy enough to find.

There are plenty of comfortable places to sit in the hotel: both the conservatory and another sitting-room on the far side of the hall have splendid views down the loch. There is some dated furniture around, and what one guest described as 'the green paint of yesteryear', while the food has been rated as uninspiring. Bedrooms are mostly light and comfortable and priced according to size and view. The staff are very friendly and the atmosphere easy-going and welcoming. More reports, please.

◐ *Open all year, exc 24 Dec to 2 Jan*

🡒 *On the A87 Inverness to Kyle of Lochalsh road, at the head of Loch Duich. Private car park*

🛏 *3 single, 4 twin, 5 double (family rooms available); most with bathroom/WC, some with shower/WC; TV in all rooms*

◈ *Dining-room, bar, lounge, drying room, conservatory; fishing, riding nearby*

⊖ *No wheelchair access; no dogs in public rooms; no smoking in dining-room*

▭ *Access, Visa*

£ *Single £23 to £34, single occupancy of twin/double £33 to £44, twin/double £46 to £68; reduced prices for children sharing parents' room; deposit required. Set D £17. Special breaks available*

---

**GULLANE** LOTHIAN                                    **MAP 2**

# Greywalls

GREYWALLS, MUIRFIELD, GULLANE, EAST LOTHIAN EH31 2EG
TEL: GULLANE (0620) 842144   FAX: (0620) 842241

*The house is Lutyens, the gardens Jekyll, the view overlooks Muirfield championship golf course and the sea is nearby.*

Half-hidden behind its sand-coloured walls, the beauty of the Lutyens house only gradually dawns on you. It's easy to become confused by the shape of the low, rambling building, for the entrance is at the angle of a kind of X. Everything about Greywalls speaks of quiet good taste, and quiet good service too – and the golfing connection, with photographs, autographs and cuttings of, by and about famous champions, comes almost as an afterthought. The polished sward of Muirfield runs past the windows – far too sacred for hotel guests to disport themselves on. But there is tennis and croquet to make up for that, and nine other golf courses nearby, while Gertrude Jekyll's garden, with its careful divisions and hedged-in paths, makes a secret spot to wander in away from the sea breezes.

Inside, the library is by far the most original room, with a fire and racks of books, while the dining-room bustles with enterprise. Paul Baron's modern cooking is unfussy and his breakfasts hearty. Bedrooms in the main house are decorated with colourful birds, trees and flowers and many look out on the golf course. In the new wing they are standardised and therefore feel a lot more functional.

◗ *Closed Nov to Mar*

⿻ *From the A1 take the North Berwick turn-off and the A198 to Gullane. From Edinburgh take the A198 to Gullane. Private car park*

🛏 *4 single, 13 twin, 1 four-poster, 1 lodge, 4 gatehouses; all with bathroom/WC, TV, room service, hair-dryer, baby-listening*

◈ *Dining-room, bar, 3 lounges, drying room, library, conservatory; conference facilities (max 15 people*

*residential and non-residential); tennis, croquet at hotel, fishing, golf, riding nearby; babysitting. Wheelchair access to dining-room and WC (M,F) and 1 lodge only*

⊖ *No dogs in public rooms*

▭ *Access, Amex, Diners, Visa*

£ *Single £80, single occupancy of twin/double £127, twin/double £135, four-poster and gatehouse £135; deposit required. Set L £15, D £32. Special breaks available*

---

## INNERLEITHEN BORDERS　　　　　　　　　　MAP 2

# The Ley

INNERLEITHEN, PEEBLESSHIRE EH44 6NL
TEL: INNERLEITHEN (0896) 830240

---

*It's worth knowing about this excellent guesthouse if you are spending time in the Tweed Valley.*

The Ley is tucked away up the unfrequented road which runs over the hills from Innerleithen to Edinburgh. When you arrive at the golf course you know you are nearly there. This is a Victorian house with a more recent tower-like extension added to it. The Ley is set on the hillside above the Leithen Water and hidden away in the trees, with a rock garden tumbling around and behind it. Doreen McVicar runs it as part of the Wolsey Lodge consortium (not thick on the ground in Scotland, perhaps because of the 'Englishman's home' motto).

The Ley's three bedrooms and overflow room are beautifully furnished, and named after trees which are visible from the window. Ask for Larch if you fancy a study in pink and white, or for Scots Pine if living in a dark-green voluptuous tent, with the best shower in the house, appeals. The drawing-room is large and comforting, the dining-room formal and gleaming. Mrs McVicar's home cooking is normally for guests only, but is available to non-residents on Fridays and Saturdays.

◐ *Closed Dec and Jan*

↗ *Take the A72 from Galashiels to Innerleithen, turn right on to the B709 for Heriot, continue for 2 miles through the golf course, then turn left across a white bridge for the Ley. Private car park*

🛏 *1 single, 2 twin, 1 double; half with bathroom/WC, half with shower/WC; hair-dryer, trouser press in all rooms; TV on request*

◈ *Dining-room, lounge, TV room, drying room; croquet at hotel, fishing, golf, other sports nearby*

⊖ *No wheelchair access; no children under 12; no dogs; no smoking in bedrooms*

▭ *None accepted*

£ *Single £27, single occupancy of twin/double £35 to £39, twin/double £60 to £68; deposit required. Set D £16.50 (8pm)*

---

## INVERNESS HIGHLAND                                        MAP I

# Dunain Park

NR INVERNESS, INVERNESS-SHIRE IV3 6JN
TEL: INVERNESS (0463) 230512   FAX: (0463) 224532

*A comfortable hotel near Inverness, welcoming both tourists and business people.*

A couple of miles south of Inverness, just off the main A82 road to Fort William, this unremarkable-looking building houses a very pleasant and relaxed hotel, good for business people and holidaymakers alike.

The indoor pool and sauna are a major bonus if the weather is wet, while there are large grounds to wander in if it is dry. But the chief charm of the hotel is the friendliness of its staff and the warmth of the welcome extended to the traveller. Two large sitting-rooms, with views across the hills, provide just about enough space to relax in, though you may find it more peaceful to stay in one of the suites if the hotel is full.

The food is good without being over-ambitious and is well prepared and presented, down to the home-made chocolates that come with the coffee. Furnishings are a mixture of the new and the old, with some reproduction pieces thrown in too. There are plenty of books in the light bedrooms.

◐ *Open all year*

↗ *2½ miles south-west of Inverness, just off A82 Fort William road. Private car park*

🛏 *1 twin, 1 double, 2 four-poster, 6 suites, 2 garden suites; all with bathroom/WC, TV, room service, hair-dryer, trouser press; tea/coffee-making facilities on request*

Dining-room, 2 lounges;
conference facilities (max 10
people residential and non-
residential); sauna, heated indoor
swimming-pool at hotel, other
sports nearby. Wheelchair access
to hotel and restaurant, 3
ground-floor bedrooms, 1
specially equipped for the
disabled

⊖ No dogs in public rooms and in
bedrooms by arrangement; no
smoking in dining-room and
bedrooms

▭ Access, Amex, Diners, Visa

£ Single occupancy of twin/double
£75, twin/double £110, four-
poster £120, suite £140; deposit
required. Alc L £16, D £25.
Special breaks available

## IONA STRATHCLYDE                                            MAP 1

# Argyll House

ISLE OF IONA, ARGYLL PA76 6SJ
TEL: IONA (068 17) 334

*This hotel provides everything you need for a stay on a special island.*

The tour coaches roll in convoys down the lonely roads of Mull to the
ferry for Iona, for this island, for many centuries the centre of Chris-
tianity in Scotland and burial place of Scottish kings, is now a place of
modern-day pilgrimage. For all that, those who love the island swear that
to stay on once the last coach has left reveals the tranquillity of the spot.

Argyll House lies a few hundred yards from the ferry pier, so there's
no trouble in finding it, and it can accommodate a substantial number of
people. It is a simple hotel, but very much more than just a convenient
overnight stop. Coal fires in the lounges, interesting paintings all over the
hotel and a bright, plant-scattered sun lounge add the necessary homeliness. Add to this the simple but well-thought-out food, heavily reliant on
the hotel's own organic garden, and always with a vegetarian option, and
you have a place worth coming to in its own right. The bedrooms vary in
size: some are definitely small, with an unusually large proportion of
single rooms. All are furnished in a simple manner.

○ Closed mid-Oct to Easter

↗ 200 yards from the ferry jetty on
Iona. Cars parked (free of
charge) at Fionnphort, Isle of
Mull

🛏 10 single, 4 twin, 3 double, 2
family rooms; some with
bathroom/WC, some with
shower/WC, 4 public bathrooms;
hair-dryer, baby-listening on
request

◇ Dining-room, 2 lounges,
conservatory, drying room;
conference facilities (max 12

people residential); fishing, golf
nearby. Wheelchair access to
restaurant (1 step) and WC
(unisex) only

⊖ No dogs in dining-room; no
smoking in dining-room and 1
lounge

▭ Access, Visa

£ Single £24 to £31, single
occupancy of twin/double £44 to
£58, twin/double £44 to £58,
family room £55 to £73; deposit
required. Set D £14 (7pm); alc L
£9

**JEDBURGH** BORDERS                                                    **MAP 2**

# Hundalee House

JEDBURGH, ROXBURGHSHIRE TD8 6PA
TEL: JEDBURGH (0835) 63011

*An ebulliently run guesthouse in an old Borders house.*

Hundalee is a large grey-stone house dating largely from the eighteenth century. It stands on a tranquil plateau of farmland high above the Jed Water. The turning to it is easily missed, so keep your wits about you. Mrs Whittaker, whose welcome is of the variety which sets you instantly at ease, added another room to her guest accommodation in 1991. As in all the bedrooms, her professional knowledge of fabrics has been put to good use. The 'blue room' is still the nicest, however, and even though she has put another bed into it for family use, you hardly notice the diminution of space. The dining-room at Hundalee is magnificently Georgian, with views out over the lawn or rockery down to the little gazebo by the pond – plenty to gaze at while you anticipate the breakfast.

- ◑ Closed Nov to Mar
- ⤢ 1 mile south of Jedburgh off the A68. Private car park
- 🛏 1 twin, 2 double, 1 four-poster, 1 family room; 1 with bathroom/ WC, 1 with shower/WC, 2 public bathrooms; TV in all rooms
- ◈ Breakfast room, lounge; fishing, golf, other sports nearby; babysitting. Wheelchair access to house and dining-room, 1 ground-floor bedroom specially equipped for the disabled
- ⊖ No dogs; no smoking
- ▭ None accepted
- £ Single occupancy of twin/double £20 to £25, twin/double £28 to £34, four-poster £25 to £36; deposit required

# The Spinney

LANGLEE, JEDBURGH, ROXBURGHSHIRE TD8 6PB
TEL: JEDBURGH (0835) 63525

*A neat modern B&B surrounded by a neat modern garden.*

Big changes are planned at the Spinney, with a whole new accommodation block to be built – carefully planned so as not to disrupt the garden too badly. But for the time being it remains a three-room bed and breakfast with everything you need: a warm welcome from Mrs Fry, space to spread yourself in the bedrooms and plenty of comfort upstairs and down. The modern house is on the edge of the A68 where it begins its final descent to Jedburgh from the south, but is well shielded from the road (very light sleepers should ask for a room on the far side). The drive leads through immaculately kept rockeries to a sweep of pinkish gravel in front of the house – an excellent sun trap on fine days.

| | |
|---|---|
| ◑ Closed Nov to Feb | ⊖ No wheelchair access; no children under 5; no dogs |
| ↗ 2 miles south of Jedburgh on the A68. Private car park | ▭ None accepted |
| ⇌ 1 twin, 2 double; all with shower/WC | £ Twin/double £33; deposit required |
| ◇ Breakfast room, lounge | |

**KELSO** BORDERS                                                    **MAP 2**

# Ednam House

BRIDGE STREET, KELSO, ROXBURGHSHIRE TD5 7HT
TEL: KELSO (0573) 24168   FAX: (0573) 26319

*A fishing hotel in a lovely Georgian house with an atmosphere of peaceful, if old-fashioned gentility.*

We omitted Ednam House last year on the grounds that some of its bedrooms were pretty cramped, its food in need of a rethink and its character rather old-fashioned. Our readers hastened to tell us we were wrong, and that it was precisely Ednam House's continuity (the current owners are the third generation of owners) and unchanging character, not to mention Mrs Brooks' sweetness to her guests, that is much valued by readers.

It is a beautiful Georgian house, right in the centre of Kelso, with lawns stretching down to the Tweed behind. It is chiefly a fishing hotel and much of its routine is geared to keeping both anglers and their non-fishing spouses happy. The two lounges, with fine ceilings and original woodwork, have clusters of chairs and tables designed for sitting at with quiet cups of coffee, while the dining-room is in a glassy extension jutting out on to the lawn. Paintings, usually with a fishing theme, decorate the lounges and spacious hall. The main bar is newly redecorated with claret and cream Chinese-style wallpaper; the cocktail bar has yet to be redone. Most of the bedrooms are small, although those in the oldest part of the house where the stairway rises to an impressive cupola are anything but, but they are more expensive. The family's youngest son took charge of the kitchens in 1991 and aims to improve the cooking, service and presentation of the food, without doing anything radical to a fairly plain menu.

| | |
|---|---|
| ◑ Closed 24 Dec to 9 Jan | suite; most with bathroom/WC, some with shower/WC; TV, room service, hair-dryer, trouser press, baby-listening in all rooms |
| ↗ 100 yards from the town square in Kelso – the main gate is on the right of Bridge Street. Private car park | |
| ⇌ 9 single, 15 twin, 6 double, 1 | |

Restaurant, 2 bars, 3 lounges, drying room; fishing, golf, other sports nearby; babysitting

 No wheelchair access

Access, Visa

 Single £38, single occupancy of twin/double £38, twin/double/four-poster £56 to £77, suite £75. Sun L £9; set D £16; bar lunches (prices till end 91)

---

**KENTALLEN** HIGHLAND            **MAP 1**

# Ardsheal House

KENTALLEN, APPIN, ARGYLL PA38 4BX
TEL: DUROR (063 174) 227   FAX: (063 174) 342

*A pretty house in hushed surroundings on the edge of Loch Linnhe, given lots of character by its American owners.*

Like so many in the Highlands, the original house belonging to the Stewarts of Appin was burnt during the repressions following the 1745 Jacobite rising. But the site is so impressive that it was quickly rebuilt. What you find today is in many ways a typical West Highland mansion, set in a patch of startling green at the end of a narrow avenue sandwiched between hillside and sea, and surrounded by specimen trees. Views westward are stunning.

Inside, there are all manner of delights, from the strange barrel window overlooking the loch to some massive pieces of American furniture, including a nineteenth-century sleigh bed. Watercolours of the area by local artist Phoebe Barron decorate many of the walls. What used to be the narrow butler's pantry is now the bar. 'It gets unbelievably full,' says Mrs Taylor, 'but people don't seem to mind.' Over the billiard table hang massive antique brass lamps. The dining-room is half in the conservatory, and half in a more formal interior room. The food, maybe roulade of hare, followed by grilled halibut with vermouth and spinach sauce, rounded off with baked peach and brandy tart, is excellent.

○ Closed early Nov to Easter

▣ On the A828, 5 miles south of the Ballachulish Bridge. Private car park

⇔ 1 single, 4 twin, 8 double, most with bathroom/WC, some with shower/WC; hair-dryer, baby-listening in all rooms; no tea/coffee-making facilities in rooms

◇ Dining-room, bar, 2 lounges, TV room, games room, drying room, conservatory, conference facilities (max 12 people residential and non-residential);

tennis at hotel, other sports nearby. Wheelchair access to restaurant only

● No dogs or smoking in dining-room; cigarette smoking only in bedrooms

Access, Visa

£ Single £82, single occupancy of twin/double from £98, twin/double £120 to £165, children sharing parents' room £30 (rates inc dinner); deposit required. Set L £16.50, D £31 (8.30pm)

# The Holly Tree

KENTALLEN, APPIN, ARGYLL PA38 4BY
TEL: DUROR (063 174) 292   FAX: (063 174) 345

*A deservedly popular hotel in an old railway station, with
wonderful views and a good-hearted atmosphere.*

The old railway station at Kentallen makes a good hotel – the more so
because it is blessed with a superb westward view across Loch Linnhe to
the mountains of Ardgour. It is hard to imagine a more pleasant
sensation than sitting in the dining-room watching the rain clouds
brewing over the mountains in the last rays of the sun and preparing to
tuck into something from Alasdair Robertson's handwritten menu,
which grows ever more illegible from year to year (but then he enjoys
explaining it to guests).

Much of the old railway station remains buried inside the hotel: the old
tea-room is now the bar and the fire, around which generations of
passengers huddled, is still there. The frontage, ticket office and so forth,
now form one wall of the entrance passage, while the dining-room with
its central, enclosed fire inhabits what were once the platforms.

The upstairs bedrooms have the same view over the loch and are
modern and comfortable with just about enough space to relax in, while
the ones downstairs facing the road lack the view but may be cheaper.
Shelves of books and racks of newspapers in the loch-facing lounge cater
for the inevitable wet day or two.

◖ Closed Jan and Feb, exc by
   arrangement

⤢ On the A828, 3 miles south of
   Ballachulish Bridge. Private car
   park

🛏 6 twin, 6 double (family rooms
   available); all with bathroom/
   WC, exc 1 twin with shower/
   WC; TV, hair-dryer, baby-
   listening in all rooms

◈ Dining-room, bar, lounge, drying
   room; conference facilities (max
   20 people non-residential, 12
   residential); fishing at hotel,
   riding, water sports nearby;

babysitting. Wheelchair access to
hotel, restaurant and WC
(unisex), 2 ground-floor
bedrooms specially equipped for
the disabled

⊖ No dogs in public rooms; no
   smoking in dining-room

▭ Access, Amex, Visa

£ Single occupancy of twin/double
   £65, twin/double £122, extra
   bed for children £10, children
   under 5 free (rates inc dinner);
   deposit required. Set L £12.50, D
   £26. Special breaks available

---

*Many hotels put up their tariffs in the spring. You are advised to confirm
prices when you book.*

# Kildrummy Castle

KILDRUMMY, BY ALFORD, ABERDEENSHIRE AB3 8RA
TEL: KILDRUMMY (097 55) 71288   FAX: (097 55) 71345

*A 'new' castle beside the ruins of a much older one in a pretty part of the Don Valley.*

Colonel Ogston built this Scottish baronial-style castle in 1901, did a lot to stabilise the ruins of the thirteenth-century stronghold which lie virtually next door, and called in a firm of Japanese designers to create a water garden in the 'back den' underneath its walls. If you stay in what was once his home, you are greeted by the usual fine trappings of the turn-of-the-century 'big hoose', from the stone porch and the panelled hall to the lions guarding the fine oak staircase.

It makes a good hotel, without being pretentious in design or furnishings. The drawing-room is spacious and bright, with plenty of places to sit, while the dining-room is Victorian in feel. Bedrooms contain a mixture of old and new furniture and vary considerably in size. Bathrooms are modern and neat. The food is a straightforward mix of British and French. You have to pay to visit the gardens, which are run by a separate trust, but they make a lovely spot for a quiet walk, especially when the azaleas are out.

- ◖ *Open all year, exc Jan*
- ⬇ *Off the A97 Huntly to Ballater road, 35 miles west of Aberdeen. Private car park*
- 🛏 *2 single, 6 twin, 5 double, 2 four-poster, 2 family rooms; all with bathroom/WC, exc 1 twin with shower/WC; TV, room service, hair-dryer, trouser press in all rooms*
- ◇ *Dining-room, bar, lounge, billiard room, drying room, library; conference facilities (max 20 people non-residential, 17 residential); fishing, riding nearby; babysitting by arrangement*
- ⊖ *No wheelchair access; no dogs in bedrooms; no smoking in dining-room*
- ▭ *Access, Amex, Visa*
- £ *Single £60, twin/double £96, four-poster/family room £110. Set L £13, D £24; alc L, D £30*

---

*Hotels in our* Visitors' Book *towards the end of the* Guide *are additional hotels that may be worth a visit. Reports on these hotels are welcome.*

# Kilfinan Hotel

KILFINAN, NR TIGHNABRUAICH, ARGYLL PA21 2EP
TEL: KILFINAN (070 082) 201    FAX: (070 082) 205

*A coaching-inn in the unspoilt countryside of the Cowal
Peninsula.*

'Totally delightful. Warm welcome, excellent food and a large and very
comfortable bedroom,' comments one reader. Another report describes
the welcome as polite rather than effusive and the bedrooms glacial when
they arrived for a stay in May. However, all agree that the pretty
bedrooms, with their spriggy wallpaper and good-quality carpets are
immaculate. One couple didn't like 'the old-fashioned wardrobe which
did not make for pleasant disposal of our suits and dresses – a crush hung
from central and side hooks'.

The food draws praise. The smoked salmon comes in generous
portions, while the kippers, here at the heart of Loch Fyne kipper-land,
are good quality. The old inn is in the middle of the tiny village of
Kilfinan, and the cellars suggest it is a place of great antiquity. The
dining-room, with its huge fireplace and beams, still manages to suggest
the days when stage-coaches rumbled their slow way around the banks of
Loch Fyne, while the rest of the hotel is bright and modern. It is short on
places to sit and relax, the lounge bar being fairly small, but there is a
pleasant paved area outside for when the weather is fine.

- ◐ Open all year
- ⤢ On the east side of Loch Fyne, 4 miles north-west of Tighnabruaich. Private car park
- 🛏 7 twin, 4 double, 1 cottage room; all with bathroom/WC, TV, room service, baby-listening; no tea/coffee-making facilities in rooms
- ◈ Dining-room, bar/lounge, games room, drying room; conference facilities (max 50 people non-residential, 13 residential); fishing at hotel, other sports nearby. Wheelchair access to restaurant only
- ⊖ None
- ▭ Access, Amex, Visa
- £ Single occupancy of twin/double £37, twin/double £54, cottage room £80; deposit required. Continental B £4, cooked B £8; set D £21; alc D £25; bar lunches

---

*The* Guide *is totally independent, accepts no free hospitality, and survives
on the number of copies sold each year.*

# KILMORE STRATHCLYDE

# Glenfeochan House

KILMORE, BY OBAN, ARGYLL PA34 4QR
TEL: KILMORE (063 177) 273

*A luxurious experience – a privately owned elegant baronial mansion surrounded by fine gardens.*

Glenfeochan is a grey, turreted mansion in best Scottish baronial style, built in 1875 – its slightly dour exterior is softened by the blaze of rhododendrons and azaleas which surrounds it in May. It lies back from the Oban to Campbeltown road at the end of a typical highland avenue; for guests there is free fishing in the river which runs through the grounds.

David and Patricia Baber rescued the house just before decay became terminal, saving the beautiful and unusual plasterwork on the ceilings of drawing-room and landing. The carved American pine staircase is another unusual feature. The drawing-room is huge, lit by windows on two sides and is comfortably, if formally, furnished. In the dining-room a long dark oak table takes pride of place; silver gleams; the dark charcoal curtains impress. The three bedrooms are large, furnished in best country-house style, and with beds of ample size. Patricia, Cordon Bleu-trained, cooks the dinners herself using produce from the estate

-Glenfeochan House-

wherever possible. She cooks more or less what she feels her guests would like – after consulting them of course.

○ *Open Mar to Nov*

▨ *5 miles south of Oban on the A816. Private car park*

🛏 *1 twin, 2 double; all with bathroom/WC, TV, room service, hair-dryer*

◈ *Dining-room, drawing-room, TV room, drying room; fishing, clay pigeon shooting at hotel, other*

*sports nearby*

⊖ *No wheelchair access; no children under 10; no dogs; smoking in drawing-room only*

▭ *None accepted*

£ *Twin/double £112; deposit required. Set D £25.50; packed lunches £5. Special breaks available*

---

**KINBUCK** CENTRAL                    **MAP 2**

# Cromlix House

KINBUCK, DUNBLANE, PERTHSHIRE FK15 9JT
TEL: DUNBLANE (0786) 822125   TELEX: 779959 CLXHSE G
FAX: (0786) 825450

*An ideal place to savour, on a five-thousand-acre Scottish estate.*

Cromlix House was built in 1874 and extended in Edwardian times, but the surrounding lands have remained in the hands of the Drummonds, Hays and Edens for 500 years. As you might expect in a house of this period, Cromlix is a mixture of labyrinthine corridors and staircases, bedrooms of all sizes, and elegant reception rooms, while the mellow pinkish-grey sandstone exterior overlooks spacious lawns and a newly renovated rockery.

The interior is lavishly scattered with family treasures assembled over the centuries: family portraits gaze down on you as you ascend the stair, and there is a constant temptation to stop and examine this or that unusual piece of furniture. Not every bedroom is spacious (Edward Eden continues the work of transforming them) but they are all comfortable. The fine wooden ceilings in the library and dining-room are part of the original fabric of the house, while the enormous conservatory is just the place to savour a sunny day. Dinner is formal and six-course, using much produce from the estate: notably lamb from the flock of Jacob sheep. Opportunities for sport on the estate, especially fishing, abound.

○ *Open all year, exc 2 Jan to 28 Feb*

▨ *The hotel lies 4 miles north of Dunblane, ¼ mile north of Kinbuck on the B8033. Leave the A9 Dunblane bypass at the B8033 Kinbuck/Dunblane exit. Private car park*

🛏 *3 twin, 3 double, 8 suites; all with bathroom/WC, TV, room service; hair-dryer, baby-listening on request; no tea/coffee-making facilities in rooms*

◈ *Dining-room, 2 lounges, library,*

---

conservatory; conference facilities (max 32 people non-residential, 14 residential); fishing, tennis, croquet at hotel, other sports nearby; babysitting

⊖ No wheelchair access; no dogs in public rooms; no smoking in dining-room

▢ Access, Amex, Diners, Visa

£ Single occupancy of twin/double £100, twin/double £140, suite £210; deposit required. Set L £8.50, D £32

---

## KINGUSSIE HIGHLAND                                          MAP 1

# The Cross

25–27 HIGH STREET, KINGUSSIE, INVERNESS-SHIRE PH21 1HX
TEL: KINGUSSIE (0540) 661166   FAX: (0540) 661080

*A restaurant-with-rooms – but first-class rooms.*

Tony Hadley's restaurant in Kingussie is well-known locally, and draws people in search of a good dinner. It is not hard to find: a green frontage on Kingussie's High Street, with a little sitting area inside the door and tables scattered away towards the back of the room, some in little alcoves.

If you are happy to eat here, you can stay in one of Mr Hadley's three rooms. It is the quality of these which gets the Cross a mention here. They are peaceful, gentle rooms with magnificent home-designed half-tester beds and imaginative use of pine and soft fabrics. Bathrooms are small but contain decent showers. There is a tiny sitting area for residents on the landing – just a coffee table and a couple of armchairs, but you don't really need more. Early bedders should perhaps avoid the ground-floor bedroom, where noise from the restaurant may filter through. This is a good place to know about if you are heading up the A9 and need a meal and a place to rest your head.

◑ Closed 3 weeks in May and 5 weeks Nov/Dec; restaurant closed Sun, Mon eves

⤢ In the centre of Kingussie village, on the main street. On-street parking

⇌ 1 twin, 2 double; all with shower/WC, hair-dryer; no tea/coffee-making facilities in rooms

◇ Restaurant, lounge; fishing, golf, other sports nearby. Wheelchair access to restaurant only

⊖ No children under 8; no dogs; no smoking in restaurant or bedrooms

▢ Access, Visa

£ Single occupancy of twin/double £60 to £70, twin/double £100 to £120 (rates inc dinner). Set D £23.50, £29.50 (prices till Mar 92)

# Kinlochbervie Hotel

KINLOCHBERVIE, BY LAIRG, SUTHERLAND IV27 4RP
TEL: KINLOCHBERVIE (097 182) 275   FAX: (097 182) 438

*On a hill above the busy fishing harbour, this is a useful haven for those who want to combine comfort with exploration of wild country.*

Kinlochbervie used to be in the middle of nowhere, but it has now turned into one of Scotland's bigger fishing ports as the fleet has shifted to north-western waters. The hotel stands high above the modern harbour buildings, allowing you a bird's eye view of the trawlers creeping in under a cloud of gulls.

It is a curious combination of a rather genteel hotel, jolly bar and bistro, and hostel – for the unrefurbished cheap rooms in the annexe are fairly basic. (If you stay in them, by the way, you probably won't be able to be fitted into the main dining-room and will have to make do with the bistro – no real hardship unless you can't face steaks or fish and chips.)

In the main hotel, bedrooms are comfortable rather than pretty, while the dining-room and the residents' lounge, with their fine views of the harbour, are good places to sit of an evening. The food here is straight-forward, well cooked and nicely presented, with the emphasis on seafood. If the atmosphere is too stiff, try the public bar beyond the bistro. This is full of boisterous locals and much of the talk is of fish and fishing.

◑ Open all year (restricted services Nov to Mar)

↗ The hotel is above the fishing harbour in Kinlochbervie. Private car park

🛏 5 twin, 4 double, 5 family rooms; 8 twin/doubles in annexe; most rooms with bathroom/WC, some with shower/WC; TV, room service, hair-dryer, trouser press in all rooms

◈ Restaurant, bistro, 2 bars, 2 lounges, drying room; fishing, golf, riding nearby; babysitting. Wheelchair access to annexe only

⊖ No dogs in public rooms; no smoking in restaurant

▭ Access, Amex, Diners, Visa

£ Single occupancy of twin/double £50, twin/double £70 to £80, annexe room £40 to £50, children sharing parents' room free; deposit required. Set D £27; alc L £12. Special breaks available

---

*Dog lovers: some hotels not only welcome dogs, but they provide gourmet meals for them. Ask.*

**KIRKWALL** ORKNEY ISLANDS                                    **MAP 1**

# Foveran Hotel

ST OLA, KIRKWALL, ORKNEY KW15 1SF
TEL: KIRKWALL (0856) 2389

*Still the best place to stay on Orkney's mainland, although the
new management has yet to prove itself.*

Choosing the right road out of Kirkwall to reach the Foveran is not that
easy, and it's also easy to miss the low-slung modern building on the edge
of Scapa Flow. Persevere, though, for this small relaxed hotel remains
the best place to stay on the mainland of Orkney. New management took
over the hotel in the autumn of 1990, but no major changes are planned
apart from staying open all year and upgrading the small bedrooms.

The lounge and restaurant are pleasant rooms in Scandinavian style,
with decorations of corn dollies and straw fans from the Orient on the
walls. The food remains good, with local fresh fish and meat, home-
made desserts, imaginative starters and an extensive choice for vegetarians. The service is friendly, efficient and chatty. Lots of families from
Kirkwall come to eat in the evenings and sit over coffee in the lounge
afterwards. Children are welcome. We would welcome reports on
whether the hotel continues to measure up to its previous high standards.

🌓 *Open all year; restaurant closed
Sun eve*

🔁 *From Kirkwall take the A3964 to
Orphir for 2 miles. Take the left
turning signposted for the hotel.
Private car park*

🛏 *3 single, 3 twin, 2 double, 1
family room; some with
bathroom/WC, most with
shower/WC; TV, room service,
hair-dryer, baby-listening in all
rooms*

❖ *Restaurant, lounge, TV room,
drying room; fishing, golf, other
sports nearby. Wheelchair access
to hotel, restaurant and WC
(M,F), 9 ground-floor bedrooms*

⊖ *No dogs in public rooms*

▭ *Access, Visa*

£ *Single £38, single occupancy of
twin/double £43, twin/double
£62; children sharing parents'
room £10; deposit required. Alc
D £18 (prices till end 91)*

---

**KIRN** STRATHCLYDE                                            **MAP 2**

# Enmore Hotel

MARINE PARADE, KIRN, DUNOON, ARGYLL PA23 8HH
TEL: DUNOON (0369) 2230    FAX: (0369) 2148

*A pleasant Victorian resort hotel with unexpected luxuries.*

Dunoon was and is a favourite 'doon the watter' resort for Glaswegians.
It lies on the western shore of the Firth of Clyde and most people still get

there by ferry, although the days of the steamboats which shuttled down from Glasgow are gone.

The Enmore, a mile outside the town, is separated from the sea by the road and the promenade, and looks, in all respects, a solid, respectable seaside hotel. But under the management of David and Angela Wilson guests are treated with outgoing friendliness, and there is no need to fear meeting the traditional purse-lipped seaside hotelier here. The residents' lounge is large, with plenty of relaxing sofas, the bar is small, the dining-room formal. Bedrooms are lovely, individual and pretty. One has a queen-sized heated waterbed and an *en suite* whirlpool bath for the adventurous, another has a four-poster for the romantic. The food is fresh, not over-ambitious, well presented and served by cheery staff.

○ Closed 2 weeks in Jan

⤴ On the seafront at Kirn, north of Dunoon on the A815. Private car park

🛏 2 single, 2 twin, 3 double, 4 four-poster, 1 family room; most with bathroom/WC, some with shower/WC; TV, room service, hair-dryer, baby-listening in all rooms

◇ Dining-room, bar, 2 lounges, games room, drying room, conservatory; conference

facilities (max 35 people non-residential, 12 residential); squash at hotel, other sports nearby; babysitting

● No wheelchair access; no dogs or smoking in dining-room

▭ Access, Visa

💷 Single £40, single occupancy of twin/double £48, twin/double/family room £76, four-poster £110; deposit required. Set L £10, D £18. Special breaks available

**LAIRG** HIGHLAND                                                    **MAP 1**

# Achany House

BY LAIRG, SUTHERLAND IV27 4EE
TEL: LAIRG (0549) 2172/2433   FAX: (0549) 2433

*A quite exceptional guesthouse. Highest standards, genuine family friendliness and not a scrap of pretentiousness.*

Places like this aren't supposed to exist, least of all in the remoter parts of the Scottish Highlands, where all too often the more imposing the exterior of the building, the worse the draughts, the damp, the food and the welcome. Not here. This is a towered mansion restored to its glory, turned into a family home, and positively glowing with a new lease of life after a slow decline since the days when the Mathesons (of Jardine Matheson) disported themselves here. What curiosity or quirkiness led Erika Havers-Strong decide to take in guests, we can only guess at, but it may have something to do with the urge which drove her to gain a pilot's licence because she was frightened of flying, or to take up stalking so that she could understand how to improve what she was offering to her sporting clients. Whatever the case, the guests can only gasp.

On offer are spacious and beautiful bedrooms, a five-course dinner (maybe venison pâté and wild salmon if you are lucky, served on a huge, newly crafted mahogany table so immaculate that you hardly dare breathe), and plenty of living-room space of varying degrees of informality. And, above all, a genuine, unforced house-party atmosphere, which evolves naturally from the relaxed style of the household and is aided by Margaret the cook's laughter ('She came with the house,' explains Erika.) Quite how all this is achieved without apparent effort is not easily discerned, but the effect is that you rapidly forget that you are a guest at all. Erika regularly receives thank-you letters from those who have stayed with her – a hotelier can be paid no greater compliment.

◑ Closed early Nov to end Mar

⤵ From Inverness take the A9 to Bonar Bridge and turn north on to the A836. North of Invershin, turn on to the A837 and follow signs to 'Falls of Shin' on the B864. The house is 2 miles north of 'Falls of Shin'. Private car park

🛏 2 twin, I double; 3 private bathrooms; hair-dryer in all rooms

◈ Dining-room, drawing-room, TV room, drying room; fishing, golf, riding nearby

⊖ No wheelchair access; children by arrangement; no dogs; smoking in TV room only

▭ Access, Amex, Visa

£ Single occupancy of twin/double £55 to £70, twin/double £110 to £140 (rates inc dinner). Packed L and set L £6, D £25. Special breaks available

---

# Sutherland Arms Hotel

**LAIRG, SUTHERLAND IV27 4AT**
**TEL: LAIRG (0549) 2291   FAX: (0549) 2261**

*A traditional fishing hotel, with old-fashioned touches.*

The village of Lairg, famous for its lamb sales and centre for the network of post buses which wind their way over some of Scotland's most desolate roads, makes a good place to hole up for a week's peace. The Sutherland Arms has been catering for holidaymakers, especially anglers, for a long time, and is also a lively centre for locals.

There's a certain lived-in feeling to some of the furniture – as comfortable as a well-worn slipper – but the hotel gets the essentials right. The lounges are cosy, the food reasonable and the bedrooms have everything required, including a video system to make up for the occasionally dodgy television reception. There's nothing luxurious about the Sutherland Arms – it's not in the character of the place – but if you are happy with a simple Scottish hotel, this is a good example.

◑ Closed Nov to Mar

⤵ Leave the A9 at Bonar Bridge and take the A836 to Lairg. Private car park

🛏 I single, 16 twin, 7 double, 2 family; most with bathroom/WC, some with shower/WC, 4 public bathrooms; TV, room service in all rooms

◇ Dining-room, 2 bars, lounge, drying room; fishing, water sports nearby. Wheelchair access to hotel and restaurant, 6 ground-floor bedrooms

⊖ No dogs in public rooms

▭ Access, Amex, Diners, Visa

£ Single £37, single occupancy of twin/double £49, twin/double £74 to £80; children under 12 sharing parents' room free; deposit required. Set D £16 to £20; bar lunches (prices till Oct 91)

---

**LARGS** STRATHCLYDE                                    **MAP 2**

# Brisbane House

---

14 GREENOCK ROAD, ESPLANADE, LARGS, AYRSHIRE KA30 8NF
TEL: LARGS (0475) 687200    FAX: (0475) 676295

*A sparkling, new seaside hotel – Italianate, palatial and with excellent ice-cream!*

Largs is one of the nicest seaside resorts on the Ayrshire coast, a summer holiday spot for generations of Glaswegians. Part of its draw has always been the ice-creams of Nardini's café on the esplanade – now the Nardini family have an hotel too.

It was opened in 1990 after a five-year conversion and refurbishment of a Georgian house, and the famous ice-cream is of course on the menu. This is not the hotel's only virtue, for it is a modern and expansive enterprise, as you can see the minute you go into the entrance hall. It is marbled throughout, with twin brass-railed staircases curving upwards towards the bedrooms. The bedrooms, some large, some not, are furnished with mahogany, cherrywood and softly coloured fabrics. The honeymoon suite is extra palatial, with views to suit. The food in the ground-floor restaurant is straightforward. You are unlikely to run across a new gourmet experience, but you will go to bed well satisfied. For a few days by the sea, this makes an excellent base.

◑ Open all year

🡒 On the Clyde Estuary on the A78. Private car park

🛏 6 single, 5 twin, 6 double, 2 suites, 2 family rooms; all with bathroom/WC, exc 6 singles with shower/WC; TV, room service, hair-dryer, trouser press, baby-listening in all rooms

◇ Restaurant, bar/lounge; conference facilities (max 40 people non-residential, 23 residential); fishing, golf, other sports nearby. Wheelchair access to public rooms only

⊖ No dogs

▭ Access, Amex, Diners, Visa

£ Single £50, single occupancy of twin/double £60, twin/double £80, suite £110, family room £90; deposit required. Set D £20; alc L £13, D £26; bar lunches. Special breaks available

**LESLIE** GRAMPIAN                                          **MAP 1**

# Leslie Castle

LESLIE, BY INSCH, ABERDEENSHIRE AB52 6NX
TEL: INSCH (0464) 20869   FAX: (0464) 21076

*A guesthouse in a castle restored from a ruin, providing a curious
mixture of recreated authenticity and homely modernity in a
cheerful family atmosphere.*

It has taken the Leslies ten years and more than half a million pounds to
return the ruined castle which once belonged to the family to its original
appearance. The effort involved can best be judged by looking at their
before-and-after photographs. Their persistence has resulted in a recreated seventeenth-century tower house, which still looks incongruously new, but will soon bed down to resemble its ancient neighbours.
There's still a little to be done round the edges by way of a garden.

Downstairs, a flagstone floor and the retention of a huge fireplace
make an atmospheric breakfast room, while the old great hall upstairs
and the living quarters off it are turned into comfortable rooms. The
furniture, in dark oak, is modelled on seventeenth-century patterns, but
is considerably more comfortable than the originals are likely to have
been. A new set of family portraits is beginning to line the hall above the
fireplace. Everywhere the castle's slight austerity is set off by greenery
and homely knick-knacks. The bedrooms are spacious, modern (despite
the low entries to some) and extremely comfortable. Two have four-

-Leslie Castle-

posters, again in modern dark oak. All in all this is a guesthouse full of interest.

◐ Open all year

↗ From Aberdeen/Inverness A96 road, 7 miles north of Inverurie, take B9002 signposted Insch. After 2 miles turn left to Auchleven/Clatt. At Auchleven crossroads, go straight over and follow signposts to Leslie for 2 miles. The castle is on the right, just before hamlet of Leslie. Private car park

⇌ 2 twin, 1 double, 2 four-poster; all with bathroom/WC, TV, room service, hair-dryer, trouser press,

baby-listening

◇ Dining-room, lounge, drying room; conference facilities (max 40 people non-residential); golf, fishing, other sports nearby

⊖ No wheelchair access; no dogs; no smoking in bedrooms

▭ Access, Amex, Visa

£ Single occupancy of twin/double £74 to £82, twin/double £98 to £113, four-poster £108 to £123; deposit required. Set L £17.50, D £22.50

---

**LICKISTO** WESTERN ISLES                                          **MAP 1**

# Two Waters Guesthouse

LICKISTO, ISLE OF HARRIS, OUTER HEBRIDES PA8 3EL
TEL: MANISH (085 983) 246

*An excellent guesthouse in an extremely remote area of Harris.*

There are times, as you drive the narrow single-track road which winds down the east coast of Harris, when you wonder if the landscape of broken rock and innumerable small lochs is all there is in the world, and whether towns and motorways are just a distant dream. Just when you are beginning to believe it, you arrive at Two Waters, a small modern bungalow with a boat drawn up on the shore. The sight of the garden full of vegetables is wonderfully reviving, and you will revive still further under the friendly hospitality of John and Jill Barber.

The guesthouse is small and you certainly won't be able to avoid fellow guests in the cosy sitting-room or at the communal table, and there is not a lot of space in the pretty, flowery bedrooms. But that is not the point. The point is to feast on the seafood, fresh or smoked, supplied by John and to sample Jill's baking and her fresh vegetables. The point is also to relax, explore, or potter about in the boat – an extremely good place for a get-away-from-it-all day or two.

◐ Closed Oct to Apr

↗ From Tarbert ferry point travel south on the A859 towards Rodel for 5 miles. Turn left on the C79 (Rodel via east) for 2 miles. Two

Waters is on the left-hand side past the second bridge. Private car park

⇌ 2 twin, 2 double; most with shower/WC; hair-dryer, baby-listening in all rooms

◇ Dining-room, lounge, drying
room; fishing nearby, boat
available. Wheelchair access to
hotel (2 steps) and 4 ground-
floor bedrooms

⊖ No children under 12; no dogs in
public rooms

▭ None accepted

£ Single occupancy of twin/double
£25, twin/double £40; deposit
required. Set D £12 (7pm).
Special breaks available

---

**LOCHINVER** HIGHLAND                                    **MAP 1**

# Inver Lodge Hotel

LOCHINVER, SUTHERLAND IV27 4LU
TEL: LOCHINVER (057 14) 496    FAX: (057 14) 395

*A modern purpose-built hotel in a beautiful area. It lacks
character but is comfortably furnished.*

The Inver Lodge Hotel is something of an oddity in this area of starkly
beautiful countryside. Indeed, the building, completed in 1988, might
stick out like a sore thumb if it were not quite carefully positioned on top
of a hill overlooking Lochinver harbour.

Inside, you will find very much what you might expect from the
somewhat anonymous frontage – a good-quality, rather bland hotel of
the sort that is as common on the shores of Spain or Greece, but very rare
in the west highlands of Scotland. The advantages of the Inver Lodge are
its views, which are tremendous, its comfort, which is considerable, and
its facilities. The furnishings, too, are of good quality and are well co-
ordinated throughout. The dinners are set five-course affairs. In common with many other hotels up here, this one has access to fishing on
nearby rivers and lochs. If you happen to hit a bad spell of weather, you
will be grateful for the hotel's space and slickness. At other times you
might find it lacking in character.

◗ Closed from Nov to Apr

⤴ Take the A837 to Lochinver. In
the village, take the first left
after the village hall. Private car
park

🛏 11 twin, 9 double; all with
bathroom/WC, TV, room service,
hair-dryer, trouser press, mini-
bar

◇ Dining-room, bar, 2 lounges,
games room, drying room; sauna
at hotel, fishing, other sports

nearby. Wheelchair access to
hotel, restaurant and WC
(unisex), 11 ground-floor
bedrooms

⊖ No children under 7 in dining-
room eves; no dogs in public
rooms

▭ Access, Amex, Diners, Visa

£ Single occupancy of twin/double
£67 to £76, twin/double £103 to
£113; deposit required. Set D
£26; Sun L £16.50

**LYBSTER** HIGHLAND                               **MAP 1**

# The Portland Arms

LYBSTER, CAITHNESS KW3 6BS
TEL: LYBSTER (059 32) 208   FAX: (059 32) 208 ext 200

*A well-run inn in the far north; tasty food in large quantities,*
*and many virtues besides.*

Beyond Inverness, where the A9 winds up the coast towards John
o'Groats, there are few places of any quality to stay at for the traveller
venturing this far north. The Portland Arms, beside the main road at
Lybster, is all the more welcome for being a good-value haven in a desert.

It's a traditional coaching-inn inside and out, but warm, welcoming
and blessed with above-average food which comes in the quantities
necessary for gale-proofing the guest. There's good local venison,
salmon and fresh prawns, plus some fine sticky puddings – and all at the
sort of price which would only stretch to a few rounds of sandwiches in
London. Bedrooms are spacious (a couple have four-posters), and there
are bathrooms with bidets. One word of warning: the hot water was
rather unpredictable when we inspected. If you intend to bath early or
late, check that the boiler will be on!

- ◑ Open all year
- ↗ On the main A9 trunk road, 12 miles south of Wick. Private car park
- 🛏 5 single, 5 twin, 4 double, 2 four-posters, 1 half-tester, 3 family rooms; some with bathroom/WC, most with shower/WC; TV, room service in all rooms; hair-dryer on request
- ◈ Dining-room, 2 bars, 2 lounges, conservatory; golf, other sports nearby
- ⊖ No wheelchair access; no dogs in dining-room
- ▭ Access, Visa
- £ Single £31, single occupancy of twin/double £31, twin/double/four-poster £46, family room £46 (children charged for meals only). Set D £16; alc L from £4. Special breaks available

---

**MOFFAT** DUMFRIES & GALLOWAY                       **MAP 2**

# Beechwood

HARTHOPE PLACE, MOFFAT, DUMFRIESSHIRE DG10 9RS
TEL: MOFFAT (0683) 20210  FAX: (0683) 20889

*A very friendly hotel in this popular small town, offering*
*everything you need.*

Beechwood stands on a hill overlooking the small one-time spa town of
Moffat – much like many of the other Victorian and Edwardian villas
which line the streets. It is peaceful and dignified and studded by the
splendid trees which stand beside its small lawn. Beechwood's quality

lies in the thoughtfulness of its management, in the persons of Jeff and Linda Rogers.

The bedrooms are certainly not lavishly furnished, and bathrooms are rather tucked away in corners, but are equipped with all sorts of extras, from hot-water bottles to cotton-wool buds. Decoration is conventional, which means tapestry-upholstered chairs, velveteen sofas and tasselled wall lamps, but there is ample space to sit, and you can lunch in the sunshine of the conservatory. You are unlikely to be disappointed by the food, either. At breakfast real orange juice is served. As one reader summed up: 'I am not a "second-time-round person" for any occasion or place, no matter how excellent it is at first, but both my husband and myself will find ourselves going back to the Beechwood.'

◗ *Closed Jan*

⤢ *At the north end of Moffat. Turn off the main road into Harthope Place and follow the road round to the left for 200 yards. Private car park*

🛏 *3 twin, 3 double, 1 family room; all with bathroom/WC, exc 1 double with shower/WC; TV, room service, hair-dryer, baby-listening in all rooms*

◈ *Restaurant, bar, lounge, library, conservatory, drying room;*

*conference facilities (max 20 people non-residential, 7 residential); fishing, golf, other sports nearby. Wheelchair access to restaurant and WC (M,F) only*

⊖ *No smoking in restaurant*

▭ *Access, Amex, Visa*

£ *Single occupancy of twin/double £47, twin/double £67, family room £67; deposit required. Set L £11.50, D £17.50. Special breaks available*

---

**NAIRN** HIGHLAND                    MAP 1

# Clifton House

VIEWFIELD STREET, NAIRN, NAIRNSHIRE IV12 4HW
TEL: NAIRN (0667) 53119   FAX: (0667) 52836

*A comfortable and unusual outpost for theatrical types on the shores of the Moray Firth.*

No thespian can afford to miss this. You can dine on a stage; the drawing-room is full of albums of the drama productions which take place here during the winter; and the serving staff are marshalled like actors in the crowd scene awaiting their cue. Clifton House marries hotel to stage and if your fellow guests fail to greet you with cries of 'Darling', it is their fault, not the fault of the setting.

The hotel is the creation of J Gordon Macintyre, and it is clear that the talents which are useful to him in stage direction have been equally valuable in designing and running his hotel. To start with, there is the arresting use of pictures and mirrors. The former span a huge range, from watercolours of local scenery, through striking oils of cattle in snow to engravings of elephants in Tsavo. All hang densely on corridor and room walls, but are placed with considerable care. The mirrors down-stairs add considerably to the light and space.

Underneath this superabundance of colour and brightness, lots of crimsons and reds, lies the fabric of a really rather ordinary, positively institutional building. But the skilful transformation of rooms (no 21 for example has a mirror-tiled pillar running down the centre, behind which lurks a modern loo and solidly old-fashioned washbasin) has turned it into a place with just a hint of decadence. The drawing-room is comfortable and arty and leads straight to the dining-room, where the food arrives in a sequence of delicious scenes, with the emphasis on very fresh seafood.

**◐** Closed Dec and Jan

**↗** Entering Nairn on the A96, turn west at the only roundabout in the town, down Marine Road. The hotel is ½ mile on the left. Private car park

**🛏** 6 single, 2 twin, 6 double, 2 four-poster (family rooms available); all with bathroom/WC, exc I single with shower/WC; room service in all rooms; no tea/coffee-making facilities in rooms

**◈** 2 dining-rooms, drawing-room,

sitting-room, TV room, drying room; golf, tennis, other sports nearby

**⊖** No wheelchair access; no dogs in dining-rooms; one dining-room is non-smoking

**▭** Access, Amex, Diners, Visa

**£** Single £46 to £51, single occupancy of twin/double £88 to £96, twin/double £88 to £96, four-poster/family room £96; deposit preferred. Alc L, D £25. (prices till Nov 91)

---

# Ard-na-Coille

KINGUSSIE ROAD, NEWTONMORE, INVERNESS-SHIRE PH20 IAY
TEL: NEWTONMORE (0540) 673214   FAX: (0540) 673453

*A good-value, fairly plain hotel which is well placed for exploration of the Spey Valley.*

The house of Ard-na-Coille is set well above the road running from Newtonmore towards Kingussie, giving it commanding views across the Spey Valley towards the Cairngorms which rise on the far side. It is a modestly sized place and far enough away from the village to give the impression of being out on its own.

The bedrooms, many of which share the wonderful outlook over to the mountains, are the best part of Nancy Ferrier and Barry Cottam's hotel, being bright, modern and extremely comfortable. Downstairs, the dining-room is a quiet, plain, rather stark room, with a pair of antlers above you as you eat. The sitting-room is cosy, with books about the

Cairngorms to tempt you into an excursion. The food is praised and the wine list is long and interesting.

◑ Open all year, exc mid-Nov to late Dec and 1 week Apr, 1 week Sept

🔁 On the A86 Newtonmore to Kingussie road at the north-east end of Newtonmore. Private car park

🛏 1 single, 3 twin, 2 double, 1 family room; most with bathroom/WC, some with shower/WC; hair-dryer, baby-listening in all rooms; no tea/coffee-making facilities in rooms

◈ Dining-room, 2 lounges, TV

room, drying room; fishing, golf, other sports nearby

⊖ No wheelchair access; no dogs in public rooms and in bedrooms by arrangement only; no smoking in dining-room

▭ Access, Visa

£ Single £50, single occupancy of twin/double £50 to £70, twin/double £100; reduced rates for children (rates inc dinner); deposit required. Set D £25 (7.45pm). Special breaks available

---

## NEWTON STEWART DUMFRIES & GALLOWAY          MAP 2

# Kirroughtree Hotel

NEWTON STEWART, WIGTOWNSHIRE DG8 6AN
TEL: NEWTON STEWART (0671) 2141   FAX: (0671) 2425

*A friendly hotel with eccentric and not always convincing rococo decoration.*

Flamboyance is the name of the game here. The chocolate and cream house gives you a taste as you approach: towered and spiked like a rich man's folly.

Inside, it drips with gilded pictures, ornate plasterwork and curling greenery. Burns stood on the staircase here, reciting his poems to his friends, the Herons, backed by a huge stained-glass window. It is intriguing to speculate whether he would have enjoyed a short break in the hotel of today. Two dining-rooms with curly-whirly ceiling plaster-work flank the lounge, identical except that one is red and contains smokers and the other is blue and does not.

Food is described flamboyantly enough on the menu, but is actually fairly simple and straightforward. The lounge itself perhaps has too many plants in it to be entirely relaxing. Bedrooms, despite rococo overtones such as gilded dressing-tables and sculpted mirrors, are a little bit old-fashioned in places. The service is eminently good-natured.

◑ Closed 2 Jan to 8 Feb

🔁 1 mile east of Newton Stewart – follow signs for hotel from the A75. Private car park

🛏 3 single, 7 twin, 9 double, 2 family rooms, 1 suite; all with

bathroom/WC, TV, room service, hair-dryer; no tea/coffee-making facilities in rooms

◈ 2 dining-rooms, bar, lounge, drying room; conference facilities (max 20 people non-residential and residential); tennis, croquet, pitch and putt, bowls, clay pigeon shooting at hotel, other sports nearby

⊖ No wheelchair access; no children under 10; dogs in annexe bedrooms only; no smoking in 1 dining-room

▭ Access, Amex, Diners, Visa

£ Single £76, twin/double £152, suite £178, family room £228 (rates inc dinner); deposit required. Set D £27; alc L £18 (prices till Jan 92). Special breaks available

## OBAN STRATHCLYDE                                              MAP 1

# Knipoch Hotel

OBAN, ARGYLL PA34 4QT
TEL: KILNINVER (085 26) 251   FAX: (085 26) 249

*Neither country-house hotel nor modern pub: standards of welcome and cooking in the first category; some of the furnishing in the second.*

A reader perfectly sums up the conflicting impressions which Knipoch is likely to give its new guests. 'First impression – a pub with mass-produced furniture with heat-resistant sealer; bare floors; walls with rather commonplace, mass-produced pictures; identical bedrooms; tiny bathrooms with noisy fans . . . Second impression – this was the Scottish equivalent of the French *auberge* with extremely efficient and discreet service, wonderful breakfasts, an outstanding wine list and very good five-course dinners cooked by Mrs Craig, the owner's mother.'

Knipoch stands looking out over Loch Feochan – with an old house buried inside the modern extensions and conversions. It is true that the décor is a bit stark, but the polished wood floors with their rugs and the uncluttered walls are rather restful, giving an air of monastic peace not usually found in hotels. No attempt is made to disguise the modernity, but there are some nice touches – the fireplace is modelled on a common medieval pattern, for example. The weatherbeaten traveller is well served: 'What a wonderful way to be greeted at 11pm – hot cocoa Pernod with home-baked shortbread.' A typical dinner might comprise shellfish in puff pastry, spring chicken with creamy mushroom sauce, cheeses served with pecan bread, followed by whisky crêpes.

● Closed mid-Nov to mid-Feb

↗ 6 miles south of Oban on the A816. Private car park

⇌ 4 twin, 11 double, 2 family rooms; all with bathroom/WC, TV, room service, hair-dryer, baby-listening; tea/coffee-making facilities on request

◈ Restaurant, bar, lounge; fishing, golf, other sports nearby

⊖ No wheelchair access; no dogs

▭ Access, Amex, Diners, Visa

£ Single occupancy of twin/double £59, twin/double £118. Set D £36; lunch by arrangement

**OLDMELDRUM** GRAMPIAN                    **MAP I**

# Meldrum House                    $\mathscr{L}$ ❀

OLDMELDRUM, ABERDEENSHIRE AB5 0AE
TEL: OLDMELDRUM (065 12) 2294

*An old family seat in a slightly barren part of Aberdeenshire.
Comfortable and good value.*

A winding avenue through a theatrical archway entrance and past a small
lake brings you to this venerable family home outside the small village of
Oldmeldrum. What Meldrum House will be like without the forceful
personality of Robin Duff (who sadly died in 1990) behind it, only time
can tell. But the house remains in the family, as well managed and as
comfortable as ever.

It is a large grey-stone pile, which looks firmly Victorian until you
come to the bar, which used to be the vaulted kitchen of a far older house.
The rough stone ceiling and dim lighting make you feel you are sitting in
a sea cavern. To move from here past the tiger in the hall to the beautiful
drawing-room with its six long windows overlooking the grounds is to
pass through six centuries in a flash. The house contains many mementoes of Robin Duff's adventurous career as a foreign correspondent –
from the tiger to photographs and an ancient slide projector. The
bedrooms, like the drawing-room, are enormous, with huge comfortable
beds and antique furniture. Food is British, with maybe a curry thrown in
in honour of the Duffs' Indian connections and a French dish or two.
Seafood and venison are prominent on the menu. The grounds are huge,
from where you can watch the Highland cattle and the hundreds of
rabbits.

◑ Closed mid-Dec to Mar

🔁 18 miles north-west of Aberdeen
on the A947 Banff road. The
main entrance to the hotel is at
the junction of the A947 and the
B9170. Private car park

🛏 5 twin, 2 double, 2 four-poster, 1
suite; most with bathroom/WC,
some with shower/WC; TV, room
service in all rooms; hair-dryer
on request; no tea/coffee-making
facilities in rooms

◇ 2 dining-rooms, bar, lounge,
library; conference facilities (max
10 people residential); fishing,
golf, riding nearby. Wheelchair
access to hotel, restaurant and
WC, 1 ground-floor bedroom

⊖ No dogs in public rooms; no
cigars or pipes in dining-rooms

▭ Access, Amex, Diners, Visa

£ Single occupancy of twin/double
£65, twin/double £95, four-
poster £105, suite £150. Bar
lunches; set D £26

# Kinloch Lodge

SLEAT, ISLE OF SKYE IV43 8QY
TEL: ISLE ORNSAY (047 13) 214/333   FAX: (047 13) 277

*Prices are on the high side. You are paying for cachet and competence rather than for brilliance.*

If you choose to stay at Kinloch Lodge, you must be prepared to pay quite a lot for the cachet of staying in the home of Lord Macdonald, of dining among his family portraits, and of eating the food devised, if not actually cooked, by Lady Macdonald, author of the *Harrods Book of Entertaining* and other cookery books to be found on top people's kitchen shelves up and down the country. For it has to be said that the prices that Kinloch Lodge is now charging are not otherwise justified.

  The house itself occupies a first-class position in the south of Skye, with the fine views and the remoteness from tedious urban existence which are what you might expect from a holiday in this most romantic of Hebridean islands. And it's a pretty house with its Edwardian shooting lodge solidity, its patch of green lawn (plus sheep) and its fresh white ex⸱ ⸱rior. The two lounges with roaring fires, and the large, stately dining-room in dark green with softly lit ancestors on the walls are comforting and restful. But it's not really a practical hotel. Some bedrooms are notoriously small and more space to move in or to put things on could be created without too much trouble. There is no room for a spacious hall or reception area either, and you virtually have to stumble up the staircase to the bedrooms the moment you are through the door. The electric fires in the bedrooms and the gas fire in the dining-room have to work hard in inclement weather. None of this would perhaps matter in the least, and the high charge would be justified, were it not that the hotel is beginning to feel weary. When we inspected, the welcome was a bit perfunctory, the service correct and willing rather than friendly, and the food competent and pleasant rather than exquisite. Kinloch Lodge needs to look to its laurels: fine hotels in this part of Scotland are no longer the rarity they once were.

- ◑ Open mid-Mar to end Nov
- ↗ From the Kyleakin ferry take the A850 for 7 miles and turn left on to the A851 for another 7 miles. The hotel is signposted on the left. Private car park
- ⇌ 5 twin, 5 double; all with bathroom/WC, hair-dryer
- ◈ Dining-room, 2 drawing-rooms, drying room; conference facilities (max 20 non-residential, 10 residential); fishing, golf, shooting nearby
- ⊖ No wheelchair access; no children under 8 at dinner; no dogs in public rooms and by arrangement only in bedrooms; smoking not encouraged in bedrooms
- ▭ Access, Visa
- ⊞ Single occupancy of twin/double £25 to £95, twin/double £50 to £150; deposit required. Set D £25 to £30 (8pm). Special breaks available

**PEAT INN** FIFE                                    **MAP 2**

# The Peat Inn

PEAT INN, BY CUPAR, FIFE KY15 5LH
TEL: PEAT INN (033 484) 206   FAX: (033 484) 530

*Lavish accommodation and excellent food. A rare treat.*

If a village is to be named after an inn, it helps if the inn is a good one. The Peat Inn certainly is. From the outside it looks a traditional homely sort of pub, white-painted and scarcely thrusting itself into prominence. But the reality is rather different. To call the Peat Inn a restaurant-with-rooms is to do it a disservice, for although the restaurant is without doubt the most important feature of the place, the accommodation is luxurious and extremely spacious. A restaurant-with-suites might be a better way of describing the place.

It gets crowded in the evenings, with the happy buzz of people looking forward to a great meal. The dining area which stretches over three separate rooms is not in the least formal but has everything arranged just so. You can eat à la carte, or from a four- or six-course set menu (the six-course version is available only for whole tables) and there is a wide-ranging wine list (David Wilson's special love) to go with the superbly presented food, which makes the most of the fish brought ashore on the Fife coast.

The bedrooms are really split-level suites, with masses of space in both sections and grey marbled bathrooms. Breakfast is brought to your sitting-room, together with the morning paper.

◑ Closed Sun, Mon; also 2 weeks Nov, 2 weeks Jan

↗ At the junction of the B940 and B941, 6 miles south-west of St Andrews. Private car park

🛏 8 suites; all with bathroom/WC, TV, room service, hair-dryer; no tea/coffee-making facilities in rooms

◈ Dining-room, lounge, bar; fishing, golf, other sports nearby.

Wheelchair access to hotel, dining-room and WC (unisex), I ground-floor bedroom specially equipped for the disabled

⊖ No children under 12; no dogs; no smoking in public rooms

▭ Access, Amex, Diners, Visa

£ Single occupancy of suite £95, suite £115 to £125; deposit required. Set L £17.50, D £30; alc D £38

---

*If you have a small appetite, or just aren't feeling hungry, check if you can be given a reduction if you don't want the full menu.*

**PEEBLES** BORDERS                                    **MAP 2**

# Cringletie House

PEEBLES, PEEBLESSHIRE EH45 8PL
TEL: EDDLESTON (072 13) 233   FAX: (072 13) 244

*Relaxing and traditional Borders hotel in lovely grounds.*

Perhaps even before checking in you should take a stroll round
Cringletie's walled vegetable garden, buttonholing Nick the gardener ('I
wanted to be a farmer and this was the next best thing') if you see him.
For the immaculate rows of green delicacies and the fragrant green-
houses presage what awaits you inside the hotel – attention to detail,
thoughtful design and a love of good things to eat. The panegyrics we
received from one couple on their bathroom – 'Very new, luxurious, with
cream and mushroom tiling, orange towels and lavish bottles of shampoo'
– reveal that humbler matters are not neglected either.

Cringletie is a red sandstone baronial mansion, compact as such
buildings go, but with plenty of room for frills such as turrets and
dormers. Stanley Maguire continues to capitalise on its quirks, finding
space for those luxurious bathrooms without ruining the fabric of the
place. The cooking and the decoration are under Aileen Maguire's
careful eye, and there's Cringletie honey for breakfast too. Bedrooms are
scattered all over the place (a couple tucked in behind the kitchen), but
are universally comfortable. The food is a treat: parsnip soup, chicken
with chestnut purée, meringues perhaps, plus those vegetables from the

-Cringletie-

garden. Public rooms are comfortable and club-like with views of the lovely grounds.

◑ Closed 2 Jan to 7 Mar

⤧ 2½ miles north of Peebles on the A703. Private car park

🛏 1 single, 8 twin, 4 double (family rooms available); all with bathroom/WC, TV, room service, hair-dryer, trouser press, baby-listening; no tea/coffee-making facilities in rooms

◈ 2 restaurants, bar, 2 lounges,

drying room; tennis, croquet, putting green at hotel, other sports nearby

⊖ No wheelchair access; no dogs in public rooms; 1 lounge non-smoking

▭ Access, Visa

£ Single £44, single occupancy of twin/double £55, twin/double £80. Sun L £13.50, set D £22.50

# Tweedbridge House

CHAMBERS TERRACE, PEEBLES, PEEBLESSHIRE EH45 9DZ
TEL: PEEBLES (0721) 20590   FAX: (0721) 22793

*A merchant's house which once saw life as a showpiece for an interior design company and is now run privately.*

You can't miss Tweedbridge House, for it stands high above the bridge on the south bank of the Tweed in the centre of Peebles. Getting to it is another matter (see directions below).

Sharon and Fraser Leddie bought the hotel in 1990 from a firm of interior designers who used it as a showpiece. So you now have an excellent combination of a family-run hotel with high-quality reproduction antiques and a range of interesting fabrics. Even one of the smaller bedrooms manages to find space for three ceramic lamps, and there are interesting chests-of-drawers and bookcases. But this is not the only surprise. The dining-room, which used to be the billiard room where the original owner Mr Roger took on his neighbours, is entirely panelled in Indian laurel, shipped home from a tea plantation. With its three flattened arches and a deep alcove where a gas fire roars, this is a splendid formal room to eat in. Unfortunately, instead of the pastoral countryside which once lay beyond the windows, you now overlook an estate of bungalows.

The food is straightforward and well cooked, while the menu is sensibly divided into 'light' and 'more substantial'. After the magnificence of the restaurant, the lounge is on the ordinary side, apart from a turret alcove. One word of warning – the plumbing can be idiosyncratic and possesses a banshee wail.

◑ Open all year

⤧ In Peebles, cross Tweedbridge, take the first right, then first left and follow the road into

Chamber Terrace. Private car park

🛏 1 single, 1 twin, 2 double, 1 four-poster; some with

bathroom/WC, some with
shower/WC; TV, hair-dryer in all
rooms

◈ Restaurant, bar, lounge, private
dining-room; conference facilities
(max 12 people non-residential,
5 residential); fishing, golf, other
sports nearby. Wheelchair access

to restaurant and WC (M) only

⊜ No dogs; no smoking in
restaurant

▭ Access, Amex, Diners, Visa

£ Single £40, single occupancy of
twin/double £48, twin/double
£70, four-poster £80. Alc L £12,
D £18

---

**PETERHEAD** GRAMPIAN                                    **MAP 1**

# Waterside Inn

FRASERBURGH ROAD, PETERHEAD, ABERDEENSHIRE AB42 7BN
TEL: PETERHEAD (0779) 71121   TELEX: 739413 WATIN G
FAX: (0779) 70670

*A business hotel in the coastal wilderness of Aberdeenshire –*
*something of a necessary haven.*

Peterhead's busy fishing harbour and its nearness to oil and gas installa-
tions of St Fergus and Cruden Bay mean that it is a town a lot of business
people have to come to, however briefly. This hotel, a couple of miles
north of the town and within earshot of the North Sea crashing on the
beaches, is their best haven. It's a classic business hotel in an unlikely
environment of treeless countryside and sand dunes, but despite the
onslaught of the weather it still manages to look fresh and clean on the
outside, and is cheerfully warm within.

Rooms are in two large blocks and there's a large swimming-pool, a
sauna, and a bevy of exercise bicycles if you need to get warm in a hurry.
A grill room, a restaurant, two bars and a couple of snooker tables
complete the scene. The menu is carefully designed to suit most tastes –
nothing too adventurous – but the cooking's not half-bad. Apart, that is,
from the breakfast porridge, where the kitchen hasn't appeared to grasp
the difference between porridge oats and oatmeal. You'll find everything
you need at the Waterside and you'll sleep in comfort.

◐ Open all year; restaurant closed
Sun, Mon eves (grill open every
eve)

⬕ From Aberdeen take the A92 to
Peterhead. At the roundabout
just outside Peterhead, take the
Fraserburgh road – the hotel is 2
miles further on. Private car park

⇌ 108 double (68 with single bed
too), 2 suites; all with bathroom/
WC, TV, room service, baby-

listening; trouser press in deluxe
rooms; hair-dryer on request

◈ 2 restaurants, 2 bars; conference
facilities (max 200 non-
residential, 110 residential);
snooker, sauna, solarium,
swimming-pool, gym at hotel,
other sports nearby. Wheelchair
access to hotel (1 step) and
restaurant, 50 ground-floor
bedrooms

🚫 No dogs in public rooms

▭ Access, Amex, Diners, Visa

💷 Single occupancy of twin/double £56, twin/double/family room

£81, suite £92. Set L £6.50, D £13; alc D £17 (prices till Sept 91). Special breaks available

---

**PORT APPIN** STRATHCLYDE                                **MAP 2**

# The Airds Hotel

PORT APPIN, APPIN, ARGYLL PA38 4DF
TEL: APPIN (063 173) 236   FAX: (063 173) 535

*The high standards of food and service in this tucked-away retreat are impressive.*

The Allens continue to get enthusiastic accolades from their regulars: 'It is bliss. We go there knowing we'll immediately feel relaxed and beautifully cosseted. Every year there is something new – you think it can't be better, yet there is always something extra.' Meticulous attention to detail is the hallmark of Airds' success – complementing the innate charm of the old inn in this tiny village on the edge of Loch Linnhe with high standards of food and service. It is a touch formal and sedate – that is part of the charm – though one guest describes it as 'slightly upmarket of its proper niche'.

There is a conservatory in which to take advantage of the sunshine and two interconnecting sitting-rooms with fires and comfortable armchairs for when the weather is less good. In the dining-room, the tables are angled towards the windows to take full advantage of the view. Betty Allen's food continues to draw nothing but praise; never over-elaborate, always interesting, always delicious. The bedrooms vary considerably in size here but all are comfortable, with bright floral fabrics in the newly redecorated ones. The Allens' refusal to accept credit cards is described as 'in today's circumstances merely an annoying eccentricity' – the more annoying perhaps since they now ask for £100 deposit.

◑ Closed 6 Jan to 6 Mar

🔁 2½ miles off the A828, mid-way between Ballachulish and Connel. Private car park

🛏 1 single, 6 twin, 6 double, 1 suite, most with bathroom/WC, some with shower/WC; TV, room service, hair-dryer, baby-listening; no tea/coffee-making facilities in rooms

◈ Dining-room, bar, 2 lounges, drying room, conservatory;

fishing, riding, water sports nearby

🚫 No wheelchair access; no children under 5; no dogs; no smoking in dining-room

▭ None accepted

💷 Single £79, single occupancy of twin/double £127, twin/double £108 to £138, suite £171; deposit required. Set D £36 (8.30pm); light lunches

# Port Askaig Hotel

PORT ASKAIG, ISLE OF ISLAY, ARGYLL PA46 7RD
TEL: PORT ASKAIG (049 684) 245  FAX: (049 684) 295

*A pleasant, old-fashioned pub in Islay's prettiest village.*

Beyond Port Askaig, the unruffled waters of the Sound of Islay separate the island from the mountains of Jura beyond. Stay in the hotel here and you may be rewarded with wonderful views as the mists clear, tempting you across in the small ferry to explore one of Scotland's wildest islands.

The Port Askaig Hotel is the sort of hotel that everyone occasionally dreams of buying and running, standing at the foot of a hill, with gardens at front and back, and cheerful in its blue and yellow paintwork. It is an old-fashioned hotel, and could do with a facelift, but this would probably be at the expense of spoiling some of the character of the place. The public bar is the local centre and you will hear all the gossip if you park yourself here for an evening or two. Otherwise, there's a residents' lounge on the first floor – old-fashioned in décor, as are the bedrooms, but more than adequate for a night or two's stay. The food is straightforward and unexciting, but good value. The Islay Lifeboat Station, in the hotel's grounds, is reputedly the only RNLI station guarded by a cannon.

| | |
|---|---|
| ◑ | Open all year |
| ⬈ | Overlooking the harbour at Port Askaig. Private car park |
| 🛏 | 2 single, 4 twin, 2 double, 1 family room, 1 self-catering apartment; some with bathroom/WC, some with shower/WC, 3 public bathrooms; TV, room service, hair-dryer in all rooms |
| ◈ | Dining-room, 2 bars, lounge, drying room; fishing, golf, other sports nearby. Wheelchair access to hotel, restaurant and WC, 1 ground-floor bedroom |
| ⊖ | No children under 5 |
| ▭ | None accepted |
| £ | Single £32 to £38, twin/double £46 to £58. Set L, D £15. Special breaks available |

# The Crown Hotel

NORTH CRESCENT, PORTPATRICK, WIGTOWNSHIRE DG9 8SX
TEL: PORTPATRICK (077 681) 261  FAX: (077 681) 551

*An unfussy local inn in a small resort, fresh, airy and good value.*

Portpatrick was once the port for Ireland (only 21 miles distant across the sea), but Stranraer replaced it, leaving Portpatrick as a small fishing and holiday resort on the edge of a peaceful harbour.

The Crown Hotel stands on the quayside – a very typical inn for a place like this. It has plenty of character, with three bars rather than a sitting-room and a pretty, simple dining-room with a conservatory extension in which to take advantage of the sunshine. The bedrooms, with great brass bedsteads in some of them, are well fitted out and feel airy, while the bathrooms are carefully modern. From some rooms you can see over to Ireland on the horizon. The food is more worldly, with steaks and grills, but also with opportunities to indulge in some very fresh seafood.

◑ Open all year, exc 25 Dec

↗ On the harbour side. Follow the A77 from Stranraer. On-street parking

🛏 2 twin, 8 double, 1 family room, 1 suite; all with bathroom/WC, TV, room service, hair-dryer, trouser press, baby-listening

◇ Dining-room, bar, lounge, conservatory; fishing, golf, tennis, other sports nearby. Wheelchair access to dining-room and WC (M,F) only

⊖ None

▭ Access, Visa

£ Single occupancy of twin/double £30, twin/double £56; children under 10 sharing parents' room £10. Alc L, D £9

---

# Knockinaam Lodge

---

**PORTPATRICK, WIGTOWNSHIRE DG9 9AD**
**TEL: PORTPATRICK (077 681) 471   FAX: (077 681) 435**

*A comfortable hidey-hole by the sea, with excellent food.*

You would have trouble finding Knockinaam if it were not for the signs, for the Victorian house lies tucked away in its own little glen, with only the sea and the deer for company.

Marcel Frichot and his wife Corinna run this civilised hotel like clockwork, and guests comment on the friendly and efficient service. 'Two girls came out to collect our luggage even though it was raining.' At first glance, the house seems to be full of clocks: on the landings and in the lounges – and the rooms echo to their gentle chimes. The bar is slightly formal but the rest of the house, including the bedrooms, is prettily furnished, with china lamps, sofas piled with cushions, and plenty of books. Lawns run down to sea where there is a small private beach. You can swim if you are feeling brave.

The food at Knockinaam draws praise: 'As good as we have had anywhere and very well presented.' It is nouvelle in style, with a choice of two main courses and two puddings. The wine list is also commended. Bedrooms vary in size but most of them are comfortably spacious.

◑ Closed 4 Jan to 15 Mar

↗ 3 miles before Portpatrick on the A77 from Stranraer is a turning on the left (well signposted to Knockinaam Lodge). Follow the hotel signs for 3 miles. Private car park

1 single, 3 twin, 6 double; all with bathroom/WC, TV, room service, hair-dryer, baby-listening; no tea/coffee-making facilities in rooms

Dining-room, bar, 2 lounges, drying room; croquet at hotel, fishing, golf, other sports nearby. Wheelchair access to dining-room only

No children under 10 in dining-room eves; no dogs in public rooms; no smoking in dining-room

Access, Amex, Diners, Visa

Single £63, twin/double £92 to £125; deposit required. Set L £18, D £30. Special breaks available

**PORTREE** HIGHLAND                                                    **MAP 1**

# Viewfield House

PORTREE, ISLE OF SKYE IV51 9EU
TEL: PORTREE (0478) 2217

*A house seemingly untouched since the Edwardian era; its charm makes up for what it lacks in modern comforts.*

This hotel is not for everyone. You have to sit on some of the most uncomfortable armchairs in the West Highlands, and put up with bathrooms where the clouds of steam from your bath gather under the 15-foot high ceilings like the mist on the Cuillins. But for many of the guests who come here, these things are part of the charm of Viewfield House, and if they, and the wonderful thunderbox lavatory (the flushing instructions end 'stand well clear') or the array of relics from the days of the Raj don't appeal, then nearby Portree has plenty of more conventional options.

Hugh Macdonald and his wife continue to run Viewfield as a slightly faded but welcoming family home, and guests are treated as one of the family. This means that you gather for a drink before supper in front of the fire, proceed into the dining-room, which shines with silver and is surrounded by portraits of grave ancestors, and eat a five-course dinner, which makes up in value for money what it may lack in sophistication. There's nothing uncomfortable about the bedrooms though – they are spacious and bright. Adventurous single travellers should try the tower room, which is tiny and certainly requires the hot-water bottle provided, but feels like sleeping in a crow's nest, with wonderful views in the bright morning sun.

Closed mid-Oct to Apr

On the southern edge of Portree, just off the A850. Private car park

5 single, 4 twin, 5 double; 4 public bathrooms; hair-dryer, baby-listening on request

Dining-room, lounge, TV room, drying room; fishing, golf, other sports nearby

No wheelchair access; no dogs in public rooms; no smoking in dining-room

None accepted

Single £19 to £20, twin/double £37 to £40; deposit required. Set D £12.50 (7.30pm)

# Isle of Raasay

RAASAY ISLAND, BY KYLE OF LOCHALSH IV40 8PB
TEL: RAASAY (047 862) 222/226

*Away from the tourist traps of Skye, this neat little hotel provides a perfect base on an under-visited island.*

Raasay Island is where Boswell danced a jig on the flat-topped hill which rises to its north, and your companions on the small ferry which wends across from Sconser on Skye are quite likely to contain a Dr Johnson enthusiast or two among their number.

The hotel, the only one on the island, is run by Mr and Mrs Nicolson, but is owned by the Highlands and Islands Development Board. It used to be slightly cramped in its public rooms, but has been much improved by the extension which was added in 1987 – the imaginatively designed Gothic windows throwing light into the lounge and dining-room.

Bedrooms are simply furnished, as indeed is the whole hotel, but immaculate and with good bathrooms. All are a standard size, on the small side if you like to prowl around, but entirely adequate. Dinner is served early, at 7pm, and may include some choice among its four courses. Isobel Nicolson runs the place with a friendly eye on what guests might like to do, and is a fund of local knowledge. Most people spend their time on Raasay walking or gazing at the extensive views of Skye; the Isle of Raasay hotel makes a good place from which to do either.

◑ Closed mid-Oct to end Mar

↗ Easy access to island by ferry from Sconser on Skye. Turn left at top of slipway and follow road north. The hotel is 1 mile from the pier. Private car park

🛏 1 single, 8 twin, 2 double, 1 family room; all with bathroom/WC, exc single with shower/WC; TV in all rooms

◈ Restaurant, bar, 2 lounges, TV room, drying room; fishing nearby. Wheelchair access to hotel (ramp) and restaurant, 6 ground-floor bedrooms, 1 equipped for the disabled

⊖ No dogs in public rooms; no smoking in restaurant and some bedrooms

▭ None accepted

£ Single £30, twin/double £60, children half-price; deposit required. Bar lunches; set D £17 (7pm). Special breaks available

───────────────────────────────

£ *This denotes that the hotel offers especially good value at whatever price level.*

**RUM** HIGHLAND                                             **MAP 1**

# Kinloch Castle

ISLE OF RUM, INVERNESS-SHIRE PH43 4RR
TEL: MALLAIG (0687) 2037

*An exceptional hotel: an industrialist's folly on an isolated island.*

Sir George Bullough, who owned Rum (often spelt Rhum), ran it as a sort of rich man's exclusive hunting paradise, and might have been scandalised by the thought of common-or-garden visitors. His widow left the island to the Nature Conservancy Council, and thanks to the efforts of Ian and Kathleen MacArthur, the remarkable atmosphere of Kinloch Castle has been maintained.

Access to Rum is restricted, and you will need to juggle deftly with ferry timetables to fit a stay here into your holiday. Yet, if you do make it to this rugged island, with its vicious midges and re-introduced sea eagles, you couldn't do better than to stay at the Castle. It is a place in a time-warp, from the balconied Great Hall with its stags' heads to the bedrooms with their old but comfortable beds and amazing showers in the bathroom. Add to this the full-sized billiard table, the music of the automatic organ made for Queen Victoria, the portraits of Napoleon and, to cap it all, excellent food from ingredients shipped in on the ferry, and it is difficult to see what more you could ask for. Guests are seduced by the extraordinary surroundings and a jolly house-party atmosphere quickly develops.

- Closed Oct to end Feb
- The island is reached by ferry from Mallaig on the mainland. Parking at Mallaig
- 2 single, 1 twin, 2 double, 4 four-poster, 6 public bathrooms; also hostel accommodation (13 bedrooms)
- 2 restaurants, 3 lounges, billiard room, library, 2 drying rooms; conference facilities (max 9 people residential); fishing at hotel, other sports nearby
- No wheelchair access; no children under 7; no dogs; smoking in some public rooms only
- None accepted
- Single £66, twin/double/four-poster £132 (rates inc dinner); hostel room £8.50 (room only); deposit required. Set D £22 (7pm); packed lunches £4

---

*If you make a booking using a credit card, and you find after cancelling that the full amount has been charged to your card, raise the matter with your credit card company. They will ask the hotelier to confirm whether the room was re-let, and to justify the charge made.*

---

*Many hotels put their tariffs up in the spring. You are advised to confirm prices when you book.*

**ST ANDREWS** FIFE

MAP 2

# Rufflets

STRATHKINNESS LOW ROAD, ST ANDREWS, FIFE KY16 9TX
TEL: ST ANDREWS (0334) 72594   FAX: (0334) 78703

*A country-house hotel with beautiful gardens, a mile and a half outside St Andrews.*

Rufflets Hotel has been in the hands of the same family for forty years and has gradually been extended over that period from just a few rooms in a manor house to an impressive hotel. Built in 1924 as a private house, the hotel manages to retain an informal atmosphere where guests tend to mingle, and regular visitors, like the golfer Jack Nicklaus (whose photograph joins other family snapshots on a coffee table), are treated as old friends. As part of the hotel's ongoing improvements, several new rooms have been built in one wing of the house. These are smart and comfortable enough, but don't quite match up to those in the older part of the house, especially to the two turret rooms with rounded walls, solid old furniture and loads of space.

The furniture in the public rooms downstairs is the result of a slow accumulation. Where the rooms lack style they excel in comfort (with open fires and Chinese rugs on parquet floors), and in curiosity, like the collection of Russell Flint prints. The Garden Restaurant is a light room with lovely views of the garden, and is popular with non-residents. The menu is good value offering traditional Scottish dishes such as salmon in

- Rufflets -

dill and white wine sauce, along with dishes from south of the border such as venison in Cumberland sauce, and roast beef and Yorkshire pudding. Vegetables and herbs, as well as some fruits, come straight from the hotel's kitchen garden. The remainder of the gardens, ten acres in all, ranges from manicured topiary and tulip beds, to wilderness complete with stream and wild flowers.

◐ *Open all year*

⤢ *On the B939 Ceres/Kirkcaldy road, 1½ miles west of St Andrews. Private car park*

🛏 *4 single, 8 twin, 2 double, 1 four-poster, 2 family rooms, 1 cottage; most with bathroom/ WC, exc 1 twin with shower/ WC; TV, room service, hair-dryer, trouser press, baby-listening in all rooms*

✧ *Restaurant, bar, 2 lounges, drying room; conference facilities (max 20 people residential and non-residential); fishing,*

*golf, other sports nearby. Wheelchair access to hotel, restaurant and WC (M,F), 3 ground-floor bedrooms in cottage*

⊖ *No dogs; no smoking in some bedrooms*

▭ *Access, Amex, Diners, Visa*

💷 *Single from £50, single occupancy of twin/double from £90, twin/double from £100, four-poster £132, family room £120; low-season rate £38 per person. Set L from £11, D from £21. Special breaks available*

---

# Rusacks Hotel

PILMOUR LINKS, ST ANDREWS, FIFE KY16 9JQ
TEL: ST ANDREWS (0334) 74321   FAX: (0334) 77896

*An excellent location for golfers; some treats and a few drawbacks.*

Rusacks Hotel's position, overlooking the 18th green of St Andrews old course, must be its biggest attraction. All rooms at the back of the hotel face the sea and the golf course, and, thanks to their big bay windows, the views are spectacular.

   The rest of the hotel, however, is a strange mix of surprises and disappointments. One curiosity is the Champion's bar, wittily decorated on a 1920s golfing theme with *trompe l'oeil* bookshelves and portraits of famous golfers. The reception rooms are grand with high ceilings and huge marbled pillars, decorated by an interior artist who lists Buckingham Palace and 10 Downing Street amongst his other commissions; while massive windows in the pretty sun-lounge and elegant sitting-room make the most of the views. The restaurant, on the other hand, has no windows at all. At night it is a lovely room – deep green Paisley-style walls create a romantic atmosphere in the candlelight – but it's gloomy and oppressive by day. The food is a real treat, with more than standard Forte fare. An imaginative à la carte menu includes rainbow trout with dry vermouth, saffron and wild rice, as well as local game and seafood dishes. There are eight different standards of room at this hotel, the prices chiefly based on size and whether or not you have a sea view. Some are pretty and some smart; all have luxurious Victorian-style bathrooms with hot towel rails and cosy bathrobes.

◑ Open all year

🅰 Take the A91 to St Andrews from Junction 8 of the M90. Private car park

🛏 7 single, 23 twin, 9 double, 2 suites; all with bathroom/WC, TV, room service, baby-listening; hair-dryer in some rooms

◈ Dining-room, 2 bars, 2 lounges, conservatory; conference facilities (max 140 people non-residential, 40 residential); golf, sauna/solarium at hotel, other

sports nearby. Wheelchair access to dining-room and WC (unisex) only

⊖ No smoking in dining-room

▭ Access, Amex, Diners, Visa

£ Single from £85 to £90, single occupancy of twin/double £85 to £110, twin/double £120 to £130, suite £235. Continental B £6.50, cooked B £9; set L £6 to £7.50, D £25; alc L, D £27 to £31

# St Andrews Old Course Hotel

ST ANDREWS, FIFE KY16 9SP
TEL: ST ANDREWS (0334) 74371   TELEX: 76280
FAX: (0334) 77668

*For golfers with a taste for luxury living, a hotel refurbished with wit and imagination.*

This hotel was built in 1968 on a piece of land formerly owned by a railway company. The architects weren't allowed to encroach upon golfers' territory and hence were confined to a thin strip of land, slightly fatter in the middle where the station platform once stood. The resultant hotel is a rather odd yellow-coloured building, long and narrow, with an incongruous nineteenth-century inn at one end, which is now one of the hotel bars, but was originally the station master's cottage. There's nothing incongruous about the inside, however. Completely refurbished in 1989, when staff were invited to a 'sledgehammer' party and tore many of the walls out themselves, the interior is now grand, distinctive and extremely luxurious. The designers haven't simply thrown money at the job – though some of the antiques and paintings are magnificent – they've used wit and imagination too. If you look carefully in the conservatory, a lovely room with spectacular views over the 17th hole, you'll see why the delicate cane birdcage has its doors left open. Other points of interest include extraordinary light-fittings, beautiful floors and, in the library, used more than once to film *A Question of Sport*'s mystery personality, a hand-painted frieze of anonymous and rather solemn faces.

The bedrooms unfortunately are not so distinctive. But they are still extremely luxurious with stylish grey marble bathrooms and every comfort you'd expect, including (in the huge suites), a few that you wouldn't, like CD players and a bathroom for your visitors! Those with views out over the Old Course and the sea carry a hefty supplement. You can eat in the formal restaurant on the ground floor, or in the rôtisserie upstairs where you watch your meal being prepared. You might have chilled gazpacho followed by steamed trout on leaf spinach, then if you don't want to gorge yourself on fresh cream there are alternative puddings for the health-conscious. Of course, if healthy living is your main reason for staying here, you could always use the spa and leisure centre, jog along the beach, or try a round of golf.

*Open all year; grill restaurant open June to Oct only*

*Take the A91 to St Andrews. The hotel is adjacent to the '17th Road Hole' of the Old Course. Private car park*

*32 twin, 76 double, 17 suites; all with bathroom/WC, TV, room service, hair-dryer, mini-bar, baby-listening; trouser press on request; no tea/coffee-making facilities in rooms*

*2 restaurants, bar, library, conservatory (all air-conditioned); conference facilities (max 250 people non-residential, 125 residential); gym, health spa, heated swimming-pool at hotel, other sports nearby; babysitting on request. Wheelchair access to hotel, restaurant and WC (M,F), lift to bedrooms, 2 specially equipped for the disabled*

*Dogs in bedrooms by arrangement*

*Access, Amex, Diners, Visa*

*Single occupancy of twin/double £92 to £169, twin/double £123 to £189, suite £250; deposit required. Continental B £10, cooked B £12; set L £12, D £25; alc L, D £35 (prices till Mar 92). Special breaks available*

---

**ST FILLANS** TAYSIDE                                           **MAP 1**

# Four Seasons Hotel

ST FILLANS, PERTHSHIRE PH6 2NF
TEL: ST FILLANS (076 485) 333

*A simple, friendly hotel in a lovely village at the eastern end of Loch Earn.*

St Fillans is a small village right on the banks of Loch Earn – an ideal place for those who want to ramble round the loch, explore eastwards to Comrie and Crieff, or maybe do a spot of sailing. The Four Seasons is on the roadside (but it is a fairly quiet road) in the village, and is one of that excellent breed of hotels which makes its guests welcome and feeds and lodges them well without giving itself any unwarranted airs and graces.

There are open fires in the library and bar, a comfortable sitting-room and fine views down the loch. The bedrooms are not luxurious, with plain wooden furniture and bathrooms which are adequate rather than lavish, but they are comfortable. The family rooms (and there are plenty of them) are in the annexe, freeing both parents and other guests from worries about noise. Add to these facilities some very willing and effective service and enjoyable food and you see why the Four Seasons makes an enjoyable stay.

◑ *Closed late Nov to Feb*

⬈ *On the main A85, 13 miles west of Crieff, at the east end of Loch Earn. Private car park*

🛏 *6 twin, 5 double, 7 family rooms (some rooms in annexe); all with bathroom/WC, exc 1 twin with shower/WC; TV, room service, hair-dryer, baby-listening in all rooms*

◈ *Restaurant, 2 bars, 2 lounges, drying room, library; conference facilities (max 30 people non-*

*residential, 18 residential); fishing, golf nearby. Wheelchair access to hotel and restaurant, 3 ground-floor bedrooms*

⊖ *No dogs in public rooms; no smoking in restaurant*

▭ *Access, Visa*

£ *Single occupancy of twin/double £33 to £50, twin/double £58 to £78, family room £67 to £87. Set L £11.50; alc L £15, D £23.50; bar lunches*

---

**SCARISTA** WESTERN ISLES                                    **MAP 1**

# Scarista House

ISLE OF HARRIS, WESTERN ISLES PA85 3HX
TEL: SCARISTA (0859 85) 238

*A heavenly setting on the edge of a deserted beach and the comfort of this converted manse make Scarista special.*

Under the former ownership of the Johnsons, Scarista was something of a pioneer in the now well-established Scottish tradition of comfortable hotels on the edge of nowhere, and a stay here undermined the old cliché that north of Inverness you had to live on white bread and tinned vegetables. Under the ownership of the Callaghans, who came to Scarista in 1989, many of the qualities which first made the hotel well-loved remain. Chief among these is the use of excellent fresh food and an avoidance wherever possible of anything smacking of the factory farm (this includes fish).

Dinners are straightforward no-choice affairs (so you should make your likes and dislikes known in advance) and come in generous helpings. Breakfasts are superb. Scarista is distinctly comfortable: the library is well stocked with books and records and there is a comfortable sitting-room if it gets too full. Bedrooms are individually designed and furnished, including those in the annexe, the furniture being an odd mixture of pieces which have found their way down the long road from Stornoway, some of them rather splendid. The restriction on small children seems rather a pity, since Scarista's setting, on the edge of a great curve of sweeping white sand and surrounded by hills and fields, would seem ideal for family holidays.

🌓 *Closed Nov to Easter*

↗ *15 miles south-west of Tarbert on the A859. Private car park*

🛏 *3 twin, 4 double; all with bathroom/WC, room service (limited), hair-dryer*

◈ *2 dining-rooms, lounge, library; golf, fishing, other sports nearby. Wheelchair access to hotel (1*

step) *and dining-rooms, 4 ground-floor bedrooms*

⊖ *No children under 8; no smoking in dining-rooms*

▭ *None accepted*

£ *Single occupancy of twin/double £41 to £53, twin/double £64 to £80; deposit required. Set D £21.50 (8pm)*

---

## SCONE TAYSIDE                                    MAP I

# Murrayshall

---

SCONE, PERTHSHIRE PH2 7PH
TEL: PERTH (0738) 51171   TELEX: 76197 MURHAL G
FAX: (0738) 52595

*Rather soulless hotel near Perth, but comfortable and with good food.*

This is the sort of hotel which you might find at the end of good golf courses the world over. Despite its distinctively Scottish baronial exterior, with pinkish-grey stone, mullioned windows and creepers, it has that 'international' tinge which high quality but rather bland interior design is apt to produce, and a pianist who tinkles away at the sort of easy-listening melodies you find from Hong Kong to Honolulu.

The guests are likely to be correspondingly international, with a fair proportion of golfers among them. For all that, this is an attractive and comfortable hotel with slick service, a comfortable sitting-room overlooking the golf course which forms a large part of its grounds, and a grand dining-room hung with expensive fabrics. The bedrooms, some on the small side, are well co-ordinated and well kitted-out. The five-course dinners are briskly served and the chef makes the most of the produce supplied by an obviously good butcher. The puddings are well thought of, too. If you want to stay in comfort near Perth and have the time to fit in the odd round of golf, you could do a lot worse than book in to Murrayshall.

🌓 *Open all year, exc 2 weeks early Jan*

↗ *From Perth, take the A94 Coupar Angus road. After 2 miles turn right at the Murrayshall signpost just before New Scone. Private car park*

🛏 *12 twin, 4 double, 3 suites; all with bathroom/WC, TV, room service, hair-dryer, trouser press, baby-listening; no tea/coffee-making facilities in rooms*

◈ *Restaurant, bar, lounge; conference facilities (max 40*

people non-residential, 19 residential); golf, tennis, croquet, bowls at hotel, other sports nearby. Wheelchair access to restaurant and WC (unisex) only

No children under 12; no dogs in public rooms

Access, Amex, Diners, Visa

Single occupancy of twin/double £75 to £90, twin/double £105 to £125, suite from £125; deposit required. Sun L £14; set D £20 to £25; alc D from £30. Special breaks available

## SCOURIE HIGHLAND  MAP 1

# Scourie Hotel

SCOURIE, SUTHERLAND IV27 4SX
TEL: SCOURIE (0971) 2396  FAX: (0971) 2423

*A fishing hotel par excellence, but with other advantages too.*

Scourie is a small town by the sea on one of the most isolated stretches of the Scottish west coast. Apart from its minuscule harbour and the bay on which it stands, there is not a lot to see in the immediate vicinity, but people who come here don't come to sit and gaze at the view. Mostly they come to fish, and since the hotel has plenty of fishing on the surrounding lochs – some reached only by a tramp through the hills – they congregate here. Beats are allocated after dinner, with new arrivals getting the last choice of water to begin with, but gradually moving up the list the longer they stay.

This is just the sort of fishing hotel where, if you are a beginner, you are likely to find plenty of advice and probably some practical help from your fellow guests. If you don't fish, ignore the scales in the porch – you will still be made warmly welcome by the Hays, and there is enough space in the two lounges and the two bars for you to be able to escape from piscatorial conversations. The public rooms are tartan-carpeted and cosy, while the bedrooms have been modernised and are simple but comfortable. Some rooms have brass bedsteads. Food is plain and extremely reasonably priced. It is also well cooked.

Closed end Oct to mid-Mar

On the A894 on the edge of Scourie Bay. Private car park

5 single, 6 twin, 7 double, 2 family rooms; most with bathroom/WC, 1 public bathroom; hair-dryer in all rooms

Dining-room, 2 bars, 2 lounges, drying room; fishing nearby

No wheelchair access; no dogs in public rooms

Access, Amex, Diners, Visa

Single £24 to £36, single occupancy of twin/double £24 to £46, twin/double £43 to £63. Set D £12; bar lunches. Special breaks available

*See the inside front cover for a brief explanation of how to use the* Guide.

# Philipburn House

SELKIRK TD7 5LS
TEL: SELKIRK (0750) 20747   FAX: (0750) 21690

*A good base in the Borders, especially for families. The friendliness
of the welcome is its chief virtue.*

You need to take Philipburn's brochure with a pinch of salt, especially
when it begins to describe its summer lunches as 'lazy poolside barbecues à la Cap Ferrat'. In Selkirk? In fact, Philipburn's style belongs to
Austria rather than the Riviera, which is altogether more appropriate to
its surroundings and climate. The Austrian touches are extensive, from
the room keys to the carved smiling pig which greets you in the dining-
room beneath the painted beam inscribed *Zum Zee*, but are seen at their
best in the bedrooms, where the pine furnishings and stripy fabrics are
cheery and warm. The poolside suites, which are splendid rooms with
plenty of space for families, are the best choice.

Downstairs, there's a smallish lounge with a modern stone fireplace, a
gleaming bar and a kind of conservatory beside the swimming-pool. The
grounds round the mid-eighteenth-century house are not especially
extensive but have been designed for enjoyment, from the garden to the
adventure playground (though softer surfaces beneath the swings would
be appreciated). The food concentrates on local produce, imaginatively
cooked, while the wine list is extensive and comprehensive – especially so
at the cheaper end. Walks in the area are marked on large-scale maps for
all to read, while named photographs of the staff are hung nearby to
dispel any feelings of anonymity.

◐ Open all year

🔁 On the A707 Peebles road, I
mile from Selkirk – the hotel is
well signposted. Private car park

🛏 4 twin, 11 double, I four-poster
(family room, suites available);
all with bathroom/WC, exc 2
doubles with shower/WC; TV,
room service, hair-dryer, trouser
press, baby-listening in all rooms

◈ Restaurant, bar, lounge, games
room, drying room, conservatory;
conference facilities (max 30
people non-residential, 16
residential); table-tennis, heated
outdoor swimming-pool,

badminton at hotel, other sports
nearby; babysitting by
arrangement. Wheelchair access
to hotel, restaurant and WC, I
ground-floor bedroom

⊖ No children in restaurant (eves);
dogs by arrangement only; no
smoking in restaurant

▭ Access, Amex, Diners, Visa

£ Twin/double/four-poster £124 to
£136, single occupancy by
arrangement, suite £136 to
£152 (rates inc dinner); deposit
required. Set L £9, D £22.50;
Sun L £12.50; alc D £25

**SHIELDAIG** HIGHLAND                                                      **MAP 1**

# Tigh an Eilean

SHIELDAIG, BY STRATHCARRON, ROSS-SHIRE IV54 8XN
TEL: SHIELDAIG (052 05) 251    FAX: (052 05) 321

*A small hotel in a beautiful lochside Highland village. The high standards continue to impress.*

'One of the best small simple hotels I have stayed in for a long while,' writes a visitor to this small village on one of the prettiest patches of the West Highland coastline. 'Oh, for more of this type of hotel which gives quality and value for money.' Here, here, we say. How does Tigh an Eilean do it? It is partly to do with the location, it must be said. On the loch's edge with views out to the tiny pine-covered island which gives the hotel its name, it is a glorious site, especially in the evening when other admirers have left. But the hotel's real charm lies in the neatness and freshness with which everything is done.

It seems miniature, but this first impression is confounded by the time you have explored down the long corridor and counted the bedrooms, at which point you start to realise the hotel's skill in retaining a sense of intimacy in what is quite a spacious building. The dining-room, for example, is on different levels to break up any institutional feel there might otherwise be. Callum Stewart's food is the other strong point of the hotel. Three choices at each stage, the food is traditional country cooking and tastes delicious.

◑ Closed end Oct to Easter

↗ In Shieldaig village off the A896. On-street parking

⇌ 3 single, 3 twin, 4 double, 2 family rooms; some with bathroom/WC, some with shower/WC; hair-dryer on request

◇ Dining-room, 2 bars, lounge, TV room, drying room; fishing at hotel, other sports nearby

⊖ No wheelchair access; no dogs in public rooms

▭ Access, Visa

£ Single £29, single occupancy of twin/double £29 to £62, twin/double £55 to £62; children under 8 free; deposit required. Set D £16; bar meals

# Dalmunzie House

SPITTAL OF GLENSHEE, BLAIRGOWRIE, PERTHSHIRE PH10 7QG
TEL: GLENSHEE (025 085) 224   FAX: (025 085) 225

*A comfortable family-run hotel near the top of Glenshee, right in the middle of the hills.*

This is a Highland sporting lodge converted into an hotel. It's not quite in the middle of nowhere, although a long private avenue leads up to it. The nearby skiing facilities at Cairnwell and the little village of Spittal of Glenshee provide some life in the wilderness. The wild hills begin right behind the hotel, and though views from some of the bedrooms are cut off by a long steep hillside, you can still see how well positioned you are.

The hotel itself, a turreted mansion of the Scottish baronial revival style, is pleasantly relaxed and no one is likely to feel inhibited. There's a constant coming and going at the foot of the staircase, where a number of chairs encourage you to sit down and chat. There's also a more peaceful sitting-room. The food comes in ample quantities, with no fanciness. It's designed to appeal to all tastes, especially family ones. Bedrooms are not wildly luxurious but are extremely comfortable all the same.

- ◑ *Open all year, exc Nov to 27 Dec*
- ↗ *On the A93 Perth to Braemar road, 18 miles north of Blairgowrie at Spittal of Glenshee. Private car park*
- 🛏 *9 twin, 7 double; most with bathroom/WC; hair-dryer on request; no tea/coffee-making facilities in rooms*
- ◈ *Dining-room, bar, lounge, TV room, games room, drying room, conference facilities (max 20 people non-residential, 16 residential); fishing, golf, tennis at hotel. Wheelchair access to hotel and restaurant, no ground-floor bedrooms but lift*
- ⊖ *No dogs in public rooms*
- ▭ *Access, Visa*
- 💷 *Single occupancy of twin/double £41 to £46, twin/double £60 to £76; deposit required. Set D £17, bar lunches. Special breaks available*

# Chapeltoun House

IRVINE ROAD, STEWARTON, AYRSHIRE KA3 3ED
TEL: STEWARTON (0560) 82696   FAX: (0560) 85100

*A country-house hotel with lots of comfort and within easy reach of Glasgow or the Ayrshire coast.*

Round here, the big houses usually turn out to have been built on the profits of the Industrial Revolution, and Chapeltoun House, with its rather dour turn-of-the-century exterior built to impress rather than to welcome, is no exception. But industrialists like their peace and quiet too, and the twenty acres of grounds and garden which surround the house quickly allow you to forget that you are in industrial Scotland rather than in some Highland haven.

Chapeltoun is run by Colin and Graeme McKenzie. It manages to combine a strong period atmosphere with the unabashed provision of comfort. This is particularly noticeable in the huge bedrooms, where there is no primping or fussing among the good-quality old furniture – merely the thoughtful provision of everything you might require from sherry to shoe-cleaning kits. The hall and dining-room are panelled, as you might expect, and there is a fire for cold days. There is also a comfortable lounge and an equally comfortable bar.

The food is memorable for its ambition and execution, and the wine list for its wide choice. The set-price menu offers a reasonable choice: soups, including a clear duck consommé with beetroot and spring vegetables may be followed by West Coast mussels with a cider and apple sauce or perhaps monkfish tails in asparagus sauce.

◑ *Open all year*

🡥 *2 miles from Stewarton on the B769 road towards Irvine. Private car park*

🛏 *2 twin, 5 double, 1 four-poster; most with bathroom/WC, some with shower/WC; TV, room service, hair-dryer, trouser press in all rooms; no tea/coffee-making facilities in rooms*

◈ *Dining-room, bar, lounge; conference facilities (max 50 people non-residential, 8*

*residential); fishing at hotel, other sports nearby. Wheelchair access to restaurant only*

⊖ *No children under 12; dogs by arrangement and in bedrooms only; no smoking in dining-room*

▭ *Access, Amex, Visa*

£ *Single occupancy of twin/double £69 to £84, twin/double £99 to £129, four-poster £119 to £129; deposit required. Set L £16, D £23.50*

---

**STIRLING** CENTRAL                                    **MAP 2**

# The Heritage

16 ALLAN PARK, STIRLING FK8 2QG
TEL: STIRLING (0786) 73660    FAX: (0786) 51291

*A well-placed hotel in central Stirling, with the atmosphere of provincial France grafted on to a Scottish town house.*

There is nothing about the exterior of the Heritage to distinguish it from the rest of the substantial Victorian houses which line Allan Park, but the interior is distinctly French and different. It is well placed close to the centre of town (it's a steep walk up to the castle, though), but extremely peaceful. Whether you choose to stay here or in the more opulent Park

Lodge (see entry) will depend on your pocket and whether you would prefer a provincial hotel to a baroque mansion.

Both hotels are run by the Marquetty family: Georges greets you at the Heritage, while his wife runs Park Lodge; and there is a good deal of cross-traffic between the two. The Heritage is the provincial version: the long thin bar, the soft velvet cushions and the flock wallpaper in the downstairs dining-room and lining the staircase. Satirical prints give way to more sentimental scenes as you climb towards the bedrooms, which are spacious and crisply furnished. Some bathrooms are on the small side. The little conference room has finely painted *trompe l'oeil* bookshelves – a style you will see more of at Park Lodge.

◑ Open all year, exc Xmas and New Year; restaurant closed Sun

🔁 In Stirling town centre, around the corner from the cinema. Private car park

🛏 2 twin, 2 double; all with bathroom/WC, TV, room service, hair-dryer; no tea/coffee-making facilities in rooms

◈ Dining-room, bar, lounge, TV room; conference facilities (max 60 people non-residential); golf, tennis nearby. Wheelchair access to restaurant only

⊖ No dogs in public rooms; no smoking in bedrooms

▭ Access, Visa

£ Single occupancy of twin/double from £50, twin/double from £60; deposit required. Set L £12.50, D £19; alc L, D £20

# Park Lodge Hotel

32 PARK TERRACE, STIRLING FK8 2JS
TEL: STIRLING (0786) 74862    FAX: (0786) 51291

*A wonderful exercise in the power of illusion – the creation of a French château in the middle of Stirling.*

The illusion was created by one painter working over several months. The interior walls and doorways of a solidly Scottish late-Georgian town house sprouted baroque panels and pediments. Gilded mouldings and elaborate cornices grew from the paintbrush. Paintwork looks like plaster, plaster looks like grainy wood. If you do not look too closely, you feel yourself to be in a country château – and the impression is reinforced by the heavy swathes of curtaining, the polished parquet of the conservatory floor and the high brass beds.

Beyond the conservatory a small formal walled garden, where a couple of iron deer stand under a tree, manages to suggest that just out of view there is parkland running down to the Loire (in fact there is King's Park golf course instead). In the centre of this remarkable house the small salon is really the bar, but feels designed for a drink before the opera. The dining-room is slightly less formal, with large bay windows and swathes of chintz. If you can't eat here, it is only a short distance to the Marquettys' other Stirling hotel, the Heritage (see above), and the stone

Chinaman in the entrance hall will guard over your possessions while you are away.

◑ Open all year

▨ In Stirling, in front of King's Park golf course. Private car park

🛏 1 single, 7 twin/double, 1 four-poster; all with bathroom/WC, TV, room service, hair-dryer; no tea/coffee-making facilities in rooms

◈ Dining-room, bar, lounge, conservatory; conference facilities (max 80 people non-residential, 9 residential); golf, tennis nearby; babysitting on request. Wheelchair access to hotel (1 step), restaurant and WC, 4 ground-floor bedrooms

⊖ No dogs in public rooms; smoking discouraged in public rooms

▭ Access, Visa

£ Single £45 to £55, single occupancy of twin/double £65 to £75, twin/double £65 to £75, four-poster £75 to £85; deposit required. Set L £12, D £19; alc L, D £22

---

## STRACHUR STRATHCLYDE                          MAP 2

# Creggans Inn

STRACHUR, ARGYLL PA27 8BX
TEL: STRACHUR (036 986) 279   FAX: (036 986) 637

*West Highland inn on the shores of Loch Fyne, fizzing with life and style.*

Loch Fyne, that long stretch of water poking into the heart of Campbell country in Argyll, is famous for kippers, oysters and the Creggans Inn. From the sun lounge at the front of the hotel, it is possible to gaze across the loch towards the sunset and the Duke of Argyll's castle at Inverary.

Creggans is owned by the adventurer and writer Sir Fitzroy Maclean, his wife and their son, Charles, and it is quite obvious that much of the civilised atmosphere, still tinged with adventure, that Creggans Inn exudes is thanks to them. In the MacPhunn (sic) bar, bearded locals chat to bearded hot-air balloonists, or families out from Glasgow for the day tuck into a half-pint of prawns, or trout in oatmeal. Round the front, in the hotel proper, the dining-room is a bit more sober – pink fabrics and flowery wallpaper. Beyond, a large room is being expanded into a coffee shop – no one seems quite certain what it will be like. But it might sell cakes and the T-shirt with a sheep on it which you can find at reception.

The menu is being expanded too, though the old staples of haggis Creggans and oyster stew will remain. Upstairs, bedrooms are peaceful and elegant havens, with gentle colours and relaxing bathrooms.

◑ Open all year

▨ From Glasgow take the A82 north along Loch Lomond to Arrochar. Turn on to the A83, then the A815 – the Inn is on the left. Private car park

🛏 4 single, 11 twin, 6 double; most with bathroom/WC, some with shower/WC; TV, room service in all rooms; hair-dryer on request;

no tea/coffee-making facilities in
rooms

WC (M,F), I ground-floor
bedroom

◈ Dining-room, 2 bars, 2 lounges,
TV room, games room,
conservatory, drying-room;
conference facilities (max 80
non-residential, 21 residential);
fishing, golf, other sports nearby;
babysitting. Wheelchair access to
hotel (3 steps), restaurant and

● No dogs in dining-room

▭ Access, Amex, Diners, Visa

£ Single £35 to £45, single
occupancy of twin/double £45 to
£60, twin/double £90 to £100;
deposit required. Alc L £10, D
£24. Special breaks available

---

**TALLADALE** HIGHLAND                                       **MAP I**

# Loch Maree Hotel

TALLADALE, BY ACHNASHEEN, WESTER ROSS IV22 2HL
TEL: KINLOCHEWE (044 584) 288    FAX: (044 584) 241

*This is one of Scotland's best-known fishing hotels – friendly and
not overpriced.*

Those who remember the Loch Maree Hotel from before 1989 will be
pleasantly surprised at the difference that renovations have made to the
place. Before, 'traditional fishing hotel' was the appropriate epithet. Now
you can add increased comfort, and indeed smartness in places, to your
mental picture. But the hotel remains above all the centre from which
anglers depart for long days on the waters of Loch Maree, and to which
they return laden with success or stiff-lipped with disappointment.

The Ghillies bar has photographs of the sort of catches which are
possible – and you can catch fellow guests eyeing them hopefully over a
warming whisky. The cocktail bar is smartly furnished with green wicker
chairs, and the dining-room, too, is smart but not in the least formal. The
sitting-room is small – most guests will be out until the evening rise in any
event – but adequate for the odd rainy day. Of course, the scenery on the
loch side of the hotel is wonderful. The immensely friendly staff are well
used to the wants and woes of fishermen but extend their hospitality
readily to those who can't tell a silver butcher from a teal and blue. Food
is straightforward and filling. Beware the poor sound insulation in some
rooms.

● Open all year

⎇ On the south-west shore of Loch
Maree, between Achnasheen and
Gairloch. Private car park

🛏 6 single, 8 twin, 4 double, I
family room, I suite; most with
bathroom/WC, some with
shower/WC, TV in all rooms;

hair-dryer, trouser press on
request

◈ Restaurant, 2 bars, 2 lounges,
games room, drying room;
conference facilities (max 35
people non-residential, 20
residential); fishing at hotel,

other sports nearby; babysitting. Wheelchair access to hotel and restaurant, 3 ground-floor bedrooms, one specially equipped for the disabled

● No dogs in public rooms

▭ Access, Visa

£ Single £20 to £35, single occupancy of twin/double £40 to £70, twin/double £40 to £70, family rooms £65 to £95, suite £60 to £80; deposit required. Alc L £11.50; set D £15 (prices till Dec 91). Special breaks available

---

## TARBERT STRATHCLYDE                                    MAP 2

# West Loch Hotel

TARBERT, ARGYLL PA29 6YF
TEL: TARBERT (0880) 820283

*A modest but comfortable hotel; well-suited to voyagers to Islay, Jura and Gigha.*

This old inn is perfectly placed for those travelling on by ferry, for it lies very close to the ferry pier. A black and white three-storey building, which looks like half the pubs of Scotland, it is the sort of place you could easily pass by, thinking it was likely to be shabby. In fact it is fresh, bright and newly furnished, and is an absolutely excellent overnight stop, although it is never likely to be a luxury hotel.

The lounge, with rattan armchairs and a coal fire, dispels all gloom, while the bar next door is equally cheery. The dining-room is rather stiffer and darker, but small bunches of flowers on the tables counter the formality. Upstairs, the bedrooms have been designed to make the most of their limited space. There are electric blankets, duvets, an efficient shower . . . what more do you need? The food is honest but unexciting, and better value if you eat at the bar than if you go for the full 'gourmet' dinner (a bit of a misnomer). Only one caution: infrequent lorries thunder past from Campbeltown in the wee hours and the bedrooms face the road – so if you sleep lightly, bring earplugs.

◑ Open all year

⏏ Leave Tarbert on the A83 Campbeltown road. The hotel is 1 mile outside the village on the left. Private car park

🛏 1 single, 2 twin, 2 double, 2 family rooms; all with bathroom/WC, TV; room service, hair-dryer, baby-listening on request

◈ Restaurant, 2 bars, lounge, drying facilities; fishing, golf, other sports nearby. Wheelchair access to public rooms only

● No smoking in restaurant

▭ Access, Amex, Diners, Visa

£ Single £24 to £26, single occupancy of twin/double £30, twin/double £52, family room £65 to £78; deposit required. Set D £16.50; alc L, D £11; bar meals

# Forss House

FORSS, BY THURSO, CAITHNESS KW14 7XY
TEL: FORSS (0847 86) 201

*The nicest place to stay on Scotland's windswept north coast.*

This is a haven on the gale-battered and largely treeless north coast of
Caithness: in fact Forss House is surrounded by the only substantial
wood for miles. The house is a somewhat disproportionate creation of
the early-nineteenth century, with an incongruous baronial porch stuck
on the front; the kind of house whose tiers of chimneys and grey exterior
let you know it has been designed for, and has seen, a lot of bad weather.

Inside, it is warm, spacious and cared for. Bedrooms are large, neat
and studded with solid wardrobes and chairs. Bathrooms have lots of
space and big towels. The dining-room is distinguished by an Adam
mantelpiece; breakfast is taken in the conservatory extension – light in
the northern morning and cheered up by lots of potted plants on the
windowsill. There's no real lounge as such, though the bar is cosy
enough for most people – especially fishermen, for whom there is a
drying room and rod racks. Food is remarkably good, with a short set
menu and a substantial wine list. Where the River Forss pours down its
last waterfall before reaching the sea, a wooden seat is perched on a rocky
shelf – ideal for romantic poets and salmon watchers alike. The river will
murmur you to sleep too.

- Open all year
- On the A836, 6 miles west of Thurso. Private car park
- 7 twin (2 in cottage); most with bathroom/WC, 1 with shower/WC; TV, hair-dryer in all rooms
- Restaurant, 2 bars, lounge, conservatory, drying room; conference facilities (max 25 people non-residential, 7 residential); fishing in grounds. Wheelchair access to hotel (1 step) and restaurant, 1 ground-floor bedroom
- Dogs by arrangement only
- Access, Amex, Visa
- Single occupancy of twin £40, twin £70. Set D £16 (by arrangement only)

---

*Prices are quoted* per room *rather than* per person.

---

※   *This denotes that the hotel is in an exceptionally peaceful situation where you can be assured of a restful stay.*

**TUMMEL BRIDGE** TAYSIDE                    **MAP I**

# Kynachan Lodge

TUMMEL BRIDGE, BY PITLOCHRY, PERTHSHIRE PH16 5SB
TEL: TUMMEL BRIDGE (088 24) 214; changes to (0882) 634214 early 1992
FAX: (088 24) 316; changes to (0882) 634316 early 1992

*Hydro-electric clutter may mar the scenery for some, but the hotel is good and otherwise well positioned.*

This makes a good base for exploring some of the best scenery in Perthshire, though Loch Tummel itself these days is spoilt by forestry as well as by pylons. However, Kynachan Lodge dates back to before either of these two blots on the scenery, and under the management of Peter and Val Hampson has been turned into a pleasant small hotel, with proportions and decorations belonging to a more expensive place.

The wooden staircase and the hall are distinctly grand; the dining-room shines with silver and cut glass; the bedrooms are thoughtfully designed. Add to this the five-course dinners with Scottish overtones, and you have a very welcoming and comfortable place to stay that represents excellent value.

- ◐ Closed Nov to Easter
- ↗ From Pitlochry take the B8019 to Tummel Bridge. Turn left over the Tummel Bridge towards Aberfeldy for ½ mile. The hotel signs are visible on the left. Private car park
- ⇜ I twin, 2 double, 3 family rooms, all with bathroom/WC, exc I double with shower/WC; TV, hair-dryer, baby-listening in all rooms

- ◈ Dining-room, lounge, drawing-room, library, drying room; fishing at hotel; golf, riding nearby
- ⊖ No wheelchair access; no children under 8; no dogs
- ▭ None accepted
- ⊞ Single occupancy of twin/double £35, twin/double £52; deposit required. Set D £16 (7.30pm)

**TURNBERRY** STRATHCLYDE                    **MAP 2**

# Turnberry Hotel & Golf Courses

TURNBERRY, AYRSHIRE KA26 9LT
TEL: TURNBERRY (0655) 31000   TELEX: 777779 TBERRY G
FAX: (0655) 31706

*Expensive, but with high standards of service, plus two championship golf courses on the doorstep.*

This is a big, luxury hotel built in 1906 and designed to be the obvious place to stay for golfing fanatics with deep pockets. The hotel continues to fulfil this role well. Its position, above the golf course and looking down to the sea and the lumpy rock of Ailsa Craig (also known as Paddy's milestone, from the days when Irish immigrants sailed for Glasgow) is alone worth a substantial percentage of the tariff – and the restaurant, with its marbled pillars, crystal chandeliers and elaborate plasterwork, is the place to take advantage of the view.

With three lounges, two bars and a billiard room, you are not exactly short of space to sit either, though you may find it harder to find somewhere free from the strains of music (the piper who plays on the lawn every night is perhaps the most romantic of the musical offerings). The public rooms are large enough to get lost in, but a bevy of staff ensures that service is punctilious. The nearby leisure centre provides plenty of opportunity to relax after a hard day on the links. The bedrooms, as you might expect, are also luxurious and kitted out with all the extras. The food is traditional or elaborate – the choice is yours. Building is underway on seventeen additional bedrooms above the Country Club that should be completed by November 1991. Here you'll have a choice of more sporting diversions, health/spa facilities and a 60-seater restaurant.

○ *Open all year, exc Xmas*

⊅ *Travel south from Ayr on the A77 until signs for Turnberry. Turn right for ½ mile to the hotel. Private car park*

⊨ *13 single, 98 twin, 9 double, 2 four-poster, 10 suites; all with bathroom/WC, exc 8 twin; TV, room service, hair-dryer, baby-listening in all rooms; mini-bar in some rooms; no tea/coffee-making facilities in rooms*

◇ *Restaurant, 2 bars, 3 lounges, billiard room, drying room, conservatory; conference facilities (max 150 people non-residential, 132 residential); golf,*

*tennis, gym, squash, spa treatment rooms, indoor swimming-pool at hotel, other sports nearby; babysitting. Wheelchair access to hotel, restaurant and WC (M,F), 17 ground-floor bedrooms, 1 specially equipped for the disabled*

● *No dogs in public rooms*

▭ *Access, Amex, Diners, Visa*

£ *Single £120 to £170, twin/double £130 to £195, four-poster £160 to £225, suite £225 to £410; deposit required. Set L £16.50, D £30; alc L, D £40 to £45 (prices till Mar 92)*

**UIG** WESTERN ISLES                                    **MAP 1**

# Baile-na-Cille

TIMSGARRY, UIG, ISLE OF LEWIS PA86 9JD
TEL: TIMSGARRY (085 175) 242

*A refuge at the back of beyond, with a reputation for friendly and high-spirited fun. Good for families.*

'This must be the only hotel in the UK where cricket *after* dinner is more-or-less compulsory,' writes one guest from Joanna and Richard

Gollin's miles-away-from-it-all guesthouse on the very edge of the Outer Hebrides. It is probably also the only hotel to award its guests famous Stornoway black puddings for the best entries in the visitors' book and may be the most isolated hotel to offer conference facilities for business meetings (has anyone taken advantage yet?).

The eighteenth-century manse is modern and comfortable, with plenty of space for children and dogs and some to spare. Everyone eats Joanna's home-cooking (no choice, but tell her your preferences when you book) at round communal tables in the high-ceilinged dining-room. Bedrooms, most with bathroom, are comfortable and spacious. Some account has been taken of Lewis' climate ('The rain at Baile-na-Cille is something to behold/ It soaks straight through your trouser legs and leaves you with a cold'): videos, Dinky toys and gin are readily available. But it need not be like this. 'It could have been the Med – we all swam including Granny aged 80.' If the frenetic, slightly schoolboyish atmosphere gets too much, there are miles and miles of barely populated Hebridean island to explore.

◖ Closed 15 Oct to 1 Mar

🡵 Take the B8011 to Timsgarry. At Timsgarry follow the road to the shore. Private car park

🛏 2 single, 3 twin, 7 double, 2 family rooms; most with bathroom/WC; baby-listening in all rooms

◈ Dining-room, 3 lounges, TV room, library/study, conservatory, drying room; conference facilities (max 12 people residential);

fishing, dinghy at hotel, other sports nearby

⊖ No wheelchair access; no smoking in dining-room, 2 lounges and some bedrooms

▭ None accepted

£ Single £24 to £28, twin/double £48 to £64, family room £80 to £88, annexe room £19 to £21; deposit required. Set D £18 (7.30pm); snacks from £3.50

---

**ULLAPOOL** HIGHLAND

MAP 1

# Altnaharrie Inn

ULLAPOOL, ROSS-SHIRE IV26 2SS
TEL: DUNDONNELL (085 483) 230   FAX: (085 483) 303

*About as far-away-from-it-all as you can get. Altnaharrie maintains its reputation as a stress-relieving, pampering hotel.*

You need to book early these days to have a chance of staying at Altnaharrie in high season, for the numbers of people determined to go back there are always on the increase. What attracts is partly (but only partly) the romance of abandoning your car in Ullapool and being ferried over the loch to the isolated house on the far shore of Loch Broom, where there are only the hills and the sheep for company.

But Altnaharrie's reputation rests equally on Gunn Eriksen's cooking – for despite the isolation, she constantly succeeds in producing five-course dinners that draw rave reviews. Combine this with the friend-liness and comfort of the place, with its two lounges, good library and comfortable bedrooms with excellent views, and it is hardly surprising that people return. Only smokers are banned – but if you can't desist, there are many acres of moorland in which to indulge. Walks over the peninsula to the shore of Little Loch Broom, or to visit the self-sufficient community at Scoraig are perhaps less commonly undertaken than they might be – the temptation to put your feet up and relax is too strong. A stay at Altnaharrie does not come cheap, but you are unlikely to regret the indulgence.

● *Closed Nov to late Mar*

▐⚡ *From Inverness take the A835 to Ullapool, then phone hotel for directions where to meet ferry. Advance booking essential. Private car park in Ullapool*

🛏 *2 twin, 6 double; most with bathroom/WC, some with shower/WC; room service, hair-dryer in all rooms; no tea/coffee-making facilities in rooms*

⬦ *Dining-room, 2 lounges, drying facilities; fishing, tennis nearby*

● *No wheelchair access; no children under 10; dogs by arrangement only; no smoking*

▭ *None accepted*

£ *Single occupancy of twin/double £100 to £160, twin/double £200 to £250 (rates inc dinner); deposit required. Set D £45*

---

# Ceilidh Place                                   ℒ

14 WEST ARGYLL STREET, ULLAPOOL, ROSS-SHIRE IV26 2TY
TEL: ULLAPOOL (0854) 612103   FAX: (0854) 612886

*The cultural centre of Ullapool, and an excellent hotel into the bargain.*

'Ullapool is very lucky to have such a wonderful place . . . I have always found it to be absolutely excellent and Mrs Urquhart an absolute miracle.' So writes one regular visitor to this extraordinary mixture of bookshop, café, restaurant, hotel and concert hall.

When you first come upon the Ceilidh Place, it looks like (indeed is) a collection of cottages, with people taking tea in the front gardens. Only by the time you have penetrated past the bookshop (a number of new arrivals get diverted here long before checking in) and through the bustling café to the conservatory extension, where most people eat at night (good, fresh bistro-style food), and then finally to the upstairs sitting area with its floor cushions and always-on-the-go coffee machine, do you realise just how extensive the place is. Passages ramble off in all directions to the bedrooms, which are furnished with all you might require – some small, others more spacious – and it is easy to get lost if you have spent too long by the bar. Conviviality is the name of the game here, but if it all gets too exhausting, the sitting area is a quiet retreat. On the other hand, if you feel like partying, the events – often folk concerts and dance bands, which happen in the clubhouse a short distance away across the street – will keep you going until dawn (well almost).

◐ *Open all year*

⤴ *In Ullapool, West Argyll Street is the first right past the pier. Private car park*

🛏 *5 single, 4 twin, 6 double in main house, 11 annexe rooms with bunk-beds; some rooms with bathroom/WC, hair-dryer; TV on request; tea/coffee-making facilities in guests' pantry*

◈ *Restaurant, coffee-shop, 2 bars, lounge; conference facilities (max 50 people non-residential,*

*18 residential); fishing, other sports nearby. Wheelchair access to restaurant only*

⊖ *No dogs in public rooms; no smoking in restaurant or bedrooms*

▭ *Access, Amex, Diners, Visa*

£ *Single £23 to £44, twin/double £42 to £84; annexe room £10 per bed (breakfast not inc); deposit required. Set D £17.50; alc D from £12.50; light meals all day. Special breaks available*

---

**UPHALL** LOTHIAN                                    **MAP 2**

# Houstoun House

UPHALL, WEST LOTHIAN EH52 6JS
TEL: BROXBURN (0506) 853831   FAX: (0506) 854220

*An ancient tower house which has survived untouched on the fringes of the brash new town of Livingston.*

The seventeenth-century elegance of Houstoun House is in marked contrast to the clutter of roads, factories and housing which surrounds it. This is not a place to which you would choose to come for a holiday but if business brings you to the area, you are likely to fall upon Houstoun with a cry of delight.

Little has been spoilt: the lawns and surrounding gardens are a haven of peace, while the exterior of the house looks much as it might have done two hundred years ago. In the interior, inevitable compromises have been made, especially in the older rooms where bathrooms have had to be squeezed in, and the small windows in the thick walls give the rooms character but leave them on the dark side. But these are nicer rooms than the somewhat soulless bedrooms in the old steading.

The public rooms reflect the hotel's role as a function centre for the neighbourhood, with a formal dining-room and a lively cocktail bar in the old cellars, but there's nowhere really comfortable to sit and relax. The service is efficient and to the point, food is ambitious and the tariff geared more towards expense-account wielders than to travellers on a budget.

◐ *Open all year*

⤴ *Off the A89 on the A899 – 10 miles west of Edinburgh Airport. Private car park*

🛏 *5 single, 9 twin, 7 double, 9 four-poster; all with bathroom/WC, TV, room service, hair-dryer, trouser press, baby-listening*

◇ Dining-room, bar, lounge; conference facilities (max 50 people non-residential, 30 residential); fishing, golf, other sports nearby; babysitting. Wheelchair access to hotel and 10 ground-floor bedrooms

⊖ No wheelchair access to dining-room; no dogs or smoking in public rooms

▭ Access, Amex, Diners, Visa

£ Single £89, single occupancy of twin/double £89, twin/double £105, four-poster £120. Set L £16, D £29. Special breaks available

**WALKERBURN** BORDERS            **MAP 2**

# Tweed Valley Hotel

WALKERBURN, PEEBLESSHIRE EH43 6AA
TEL: WALKERBURN (089 687) 636    FAX: (089 687) 639

*A fishing hotel by the River Tweed. Its prime virtue is an unassuming friendliness.*

Ask for a room in the main house, for the bedrooms in the annexe are small and don't have the views of the Tweed Valley which you get from the front. Plans are in hand to improve them, but the mills of local authorities grind slowly . . . This was once a house given as a wedding present to the son of a local mill owner in 1906; and the initials of the happy couple are carved above the door.

Curious gargoyles perch on the balustrade of the stairs, and there's an Austrian tinge to the plasterwork in the lounge. The lounge and bar shine with highly polished knick-knacks, and though there's not a great deal of space, there's enough. The best room in the hotel is the restaurant, where the pretty morning-room has been knocked into the panelled formal dining-room, creating a room with two distinct halves, which combine remarkably well.

The food here is substantial, with a touch of daring: gammon steak cooked in honey and kirsch, for example. The atmosphere in the hotel is relaxed – a place where rapturous or despairing anglers can mix happily with tourists or droppers-in, and it is immaculately kept. A nice touch are the special 'teenage' rates (ask).

◑ Open all year, exc 25, 26 Dec

▨ On the A72 on the eastern outskirts of Walkerburn. Private car park

🛏 4 single, 4 twin, 5 double, 1 four-poster, 2 family rooms; most with bathroom/WC, some with shower/WC; TV, room service, hair-dryer, baby-listening in all rooms; trouser press in some rooms

◇ Restaurant, 2 bars, lounge, drying room; conference facilities (max 60 people non-residential, 16 residential); sauna, solarium, gym at hotel, other sports nearby

⊖ No wheelchair access; no dogs or smoking in restaurant

<table>
<tr><td>☐ Access, Visa</td><td>parents' room £10; deposit</td></tr>
<tr><td>£ Single £44, twin/double £74,<br>four-poster £84; children sharing</td><td>required. Set L £7.50 to £9.50, D<br>£16; alc D £25. Special breaks<br>available</td></tr>
</table>

## WEST LINTON BORDERS                          MAP 2

# Medwyn House

MEDWYN ROAD, WEST LINTON, PEEBLESSHIRE EH46 7HB
TEL: WEST LINTON (0968) 60542   FAX: (0968) 60005

*A splendid guesthouse with a lot of style and a very friendly welcome.*

Medwyn House, neatly set back on the edge of the Pentland Hills above West Linton, looks a great deal more like a posh hotel than the welcoming home that it really is. It was once an old coaching-inn but became a private house in 1864. It is surrounded by the specimen trees and fine lawns of the Victorian period.

Anne Waterston welcomes you into the beautiful panelled hall where Victorian craftsmen have created quite a showpiece. Most people sit here too, chatting to Anne (for she usually makes the time to have a good natter with her guests) in front of the blazing fire, although there is a sitting-room too if the hall is too crowded. The bedrooms in the main house are lovely, with spacious bathrooms attached. All are high-ceilinged and fitted out with a mix of modern furniture and older pieces. The overflow bedrooms in the cottage annexe are not quite so opulent but are more than adequate.

Anne's excellent home-cooked four-course dinners are served in the pretty blue dining-room – bring your own wine. She also appreciates being notified in advance if guests require dinner on the night of their arrival. If you hear footsteps suspiciously near your car in the early morning, it will only be Mike Waterston exercising the dog and washing down your windscreen while he is at it. Edinburgh businessmen are in the habit of coming out here to entertain clients – the fact that they prefer to journey to West Linton rather than sit in Edinburgh restaurants speaks for itself.

● Open all year, exc mid-Jan to end Feb

⊘ No wheelchair access; no children under 12; no dogs in public rooms and by arrangement only in bedrooms; smoking in lounges only

▮ Off the A702 in West Linton, signposted Medwyn Road and golf course. Private car park

☐ None accepted

⇤ 1 twin, 2 double, 2 suites (some rooms in annexe); all with bathroom/WC, exc 1 suite with shower/WC; TV on request

£ Single occupancy of twin/double £30 to £44, twin/double £56 to £68. Set D £18 (8pm). Special breaks available

◇ Dining-room, 2 lounges; sauna at hotel, golf, other sports nearby

# Knockie Lodge

WHITE BRIDGE, INVERNESS-SHIRE IV1 2UP
TEL: GORTHLECK (045 63) 276    FAX: (045 63) 389

*A small but comfortable country-house hotel on the 'wrong side' of Loch Ness.*

The country immediately to the east of Loch Ness is often ignored by monster-watchers and more intelligent beings alike. But it is a pleasant area, rich in prehistoric remains and hidden valleys, and without doubt, Knockie Lodge is one of the most comfortable places to stay in the area.

This is Clan Fraser country and the house once belonged to that family. Now it is a country-house hotel, run with friendly panache by Ian and Brenda Milward. There's a billiard room in a newish extension, a very comfortable parquet-floored lounge and a small, bookish sitting-room, with plenty of maps with which to plan outings. The dining-room, half-panelled and formally laid out, is the setting for fine set-price meals of British and French cuisine.

Bedrooms vary in both size and shape; there are no anonymous little boxes here. All are comfortable and there is quite a wide range of interior decoration on display. You pay according to the size of room or the magnificence of the views.

🌓 Closed end Oct to end Apr

↪ Take the A82 north to Fort Augustus, then the B862 for 8 miles. Turn left at the hotel sign down a narrow road for 2 miles to the hotel. Private car park

🛏 2 single, 4 twin, 4 double; all with bathroom/WC; hair-dryer, tea/coffee-making facilities on request

◈ Dining-room, 2 lounges, billiard room, drying room, conservatory; conference facilities (max 10 people residential); fishing, sailing at hotel, other sports nearby

⊖ No wheelchair access; no children under 10; dogs by arrangement only; no smoking in dining-room

▭ Access, Amex, Diners, Visa

£ Single £75, single occupancy of twin/double £89 to £137, twin/double £118 to £182 (rates inc dinner); deposit required. Set D £23

# WALES

**ABERDOVEY** GWYNEDD            **MAP 5**

# Penhelig Arms

ABERDOVEY, GWYNEDD LL35 0LT
TEL: ABERDOVEY (0654) 767215   FAX: (0654) 767690

*An old inn on the seafront with clean, modern rooms and good food.*

Built in the 1700s, the Penhelig Arms was a coaching-inn where, it is said, the much-travelled Charles Dickens was a visitor. The white-washed inn is directly on the busy road which weaves along the seafront at Aberdovey. There's also a railway line behind the hotel where trains rumble by intermittently – you can even take the train to Aberdovey and alight at Penhelig Halt (a request stop). Despite the proximity of road and rail, the noise of the traffic isn't noticeable in the Arms, where the loudest sounds are the chatter of residents and the rattle of cutlery on plates.

Even in mid-winter the Penhelig Arms is popular – visitors come for the restaurant and some stay overnight in the fresh, comfortable rooms with quilt-covered beds. Most of the bedrooms overlook the sea and all have *en suite* bathrooms. The restaurant is panelled and is simply furnished, with several watercolours and prints on the walls. There is also a bar, and a quiet lounge for residents hidden away upstairs. Guests have the benefit of reduced green fees at the local 18-hole golf course.

- ◑ Open all year, exc 25, 26 Dec
- 🖿 From Machynlleth head into Aberdovey, go underneath railway bridge, first hotel on the right. Private car park
- 🛏 1 single, 3 twin, 7 double; some with bathroom/WC, most with shower/WC; TV, room service in all rooms; hair-dryer in some rooms
- ◇ Restaurant, 2 bars, lounge; golf, fishing, other sports nearby
- ● Dogs in public bar only; smoking not encouraged
- ▭ Access, Visa
- £ Single £35, single occupancy of twin/double £35; twin/double £62 to £78; deposit required. Set L from £1.50, D £15.50; Sun L £9.50. Special breaks available

---

*Warning to insomniacs, exercise freaks and late-night lovers: increasing numbers of hotels have infra-red triggered security lamps. To save being embarrassingly illuminated, check before you leave for your late-night or pre-dawn stroll.*

---

*If you are intending to make a lot of phone calls from your room, always check what the hotel is going to charge you per unit. You may be so horrified that you'll prefer to walk to the nearest phone box. Why let them get away with excessive charges?*

**ABERSOCH** GWYNEDD                                    **MAP 5**

# Porth Tocyn Hotel

ABERSOCH, GWYNEDD LL53 7BU
TEL: ABERSOCH (075 881) 3303   FAX: (075 881) 3538

*A relaxed family-run hotel in a lovely position. Good food and a
friendly atmosphere to suit all types.*

Lots of visitors come to this area of Wales for the excellent watersports
but up at Porth Tocyn you can get away from the bustle of Abersoch and
sit quietly in the garden overlooking Cardigan Bay. If you're not keen to
play tennis or swim there are plenty of good walks which start at the hotel.

The Fletcher-Brewer family have run the hotel for the last forty years
and have achieved a good balance of friendliness and efficiency. You
might feel it sometimes gets a bit too relaxed with mother and son
bantering in front of the guests – but it's all part of the flavour of the place
as drinks are served, orders taken and often delivered with one of Nick
Fletcher-Brewer's witty quips.

There's no shortage of places to sit – either in the main comfortable
sitting-room, cosy with a mixture of furnishings, personal bits and lots of
books and magazines – or in one of the four or five smaller, but no less
comfortable rooms. Children are welcome and have their own playroom
with television so they don't irritate those who have come for a quiet,
peaceful time; high teas/early suppers are put on as a matter of course as
only children over seven are allowed in the dining-room in the evening. It
is a very refreshing change to have a choice of five courses or less and be
charged accordingly; the food is very good, so you'll probably end up
eating all five anyway, especially on a summer evening when you can gaze
out of the window across the Bay to Snowdonia. The bedrooms are quite
simply decorated in a traditional style, some with wooden beds, candlewick covers and free-standing wardrobes but all are fully carpeted with
pretty curtains and *en suite* bathrooms.

**◑** *Closed mid-Nov to week before
Easter*

**⤢** *The hotel is 2½ miles beyond
Abersoch, through the hamlets of
Sarn Bach and Bwlchtocyn. On
the outskirts of Abersoch on the
Sarn Bach road is the first of 3
bilingual signs marked 'Gwesty/
Hotel'. Follow these to Porth
Tocyn. Private car park*

**⇌** *3 single, 11 twin, 3 double (most
with extra bed), 1 family room;
all with bathroom/WC, TV, room
service, hair-dryer; tea/coffee-*

*making facilities, baby-listening
on request*

**◈** *Restaurant, bar, 6 lounges, TV/
games room, drying room; tennis
and heated outdoor pool (May to
Sept) at hotel, other sports
nearby. Wheelchair access to
hotel (1 step), restaurant and
WC (unisex), 3 ground-floor
bedrooms; babysitting on request*

**⊖** *No children under 7 in
restaurant eves; no dogs in
public rooms; smoking not
encouraged in restaurant*

▭ Access

£ Single £38 to £49, single occupancy of twin/double £52 to £74, twin/double £68 to £90, family room £68 to £90 (plus

£17 to £24 per child); deposit required. Set D £16.50/£21; Sun L £13 (prices till mid-Nov). Special breaks available

---

**BEAUMARIS** GWYNEDD                                                **MAP 5**

# Ye Olde Bulls Head

---

CASTLE STREET, BEAUMARIS, ANGLESEY, GWYNEDD LL58 8AP
TEL: BEAUMARIS (0248) 810329   FAX: (0248) 811294

---

*A popular inn with better-than-average food and stylish rooms.*

Ye Olde Bulls Head Inn blends innocuously into the shops and buildings of the main street in Beaumaris, but inside it is more special. Parts of the coaching-inn date back to 1617 and it has had a couple of famous guests, including Charles Dickens, who stayed here while reporting on the sinking of the *Royal Charter*. Rooms are named after Dickens' characters: the Artful Dodger is a small room with simple pine furniture (for children who would like to be more independent of their parents); the Sergeant Buzfuz room is formal, with a brass bed, and is decorated in Christmas colours of deep reds and olive green. Each bedroom has been individually styled and co-ordinated. Brass beds abound, matching the brass fittings on showers and baths, and each room has all the facilities you could need.

Downstairs, the bar is a popular meeting place. Green leather seats, gleaming brasses, copper jugs and pewter pots give the bar a sense of history and luxury. There are interesting curios dotted around the bar: in one corner, an innocent-looking chair with a high back, rather like a watchman's sentry box, is in fact an original ducking-stool and a cheerful sign states: 'Time wanes deth claimes.' Reasonably priced bar meals are served in the bar, but there is also a restaurant to the back of the hotel, which is plainly furnished but serves good food. The residents' lounge is slightly quieter than the bar at night and has chintzy chairs which you can sink into.

◑ Open all year

↗ The inn is in the centre of Beaumaris, on the main street. Private car park

⇌ 1 single, 5 twin, 5 double; all with bathroom/WC, TV, limited room service, hair-dryer, baby-listening

◈ Restaurant, bar, lounge; golf, riding, other sports nearby

⊖ No wheelchair access; children under 7 discouraged in restaurant Sun L; dogs in bar only (not at lunchtimes)

▭ Access, Visa

£ Single £40, single occupancy of twin/double £47, twin/double £68. Sun L £18; alc D £27.50; bar lunches. Special breaks available

# Ty Gwyn Hotel

BETWS-Y-COED, GWYNEDD LL24 0SG
TEL: BETWS-Y-COED (0690) 710383/710787

*A roadside inn filled with antiques; the welcome could perhaps be better.*

Ty Gwyn is packed with antiques – a bewildering array of plates, jugs and farming equipment jostles for space with huge dried-flower arrangements. The bar area, at one end of the long narrow building, has a wild mix of chintzy armchairs and wooden chairs smothered in home-made scatter cushions. There is, as one reader noted, 'nowhere to sit other than the bar – which is naturally full of cigarette smoke'.

The dining-room is like an antique curiosity shop – nothing matches. Some of the silverware is labelled with hotel names which have presumably long since gone into liquidation; cut glasses come in various patterns, shapes and sizes, and the silver pepper and salt pots may be from different ages. Beyond the dining-room is an antique shop where any extra antiques are sold. Reports on dinner vary from mediocre to good, though breakfasts are rated as excellent. The bedrooms are as cluttered with antiques as the rest of the inn. They tend to be economical with space but are generally very comfortable. Light sleepers may be disturbed by noise from the bar as much as by the traffic noise (ask for a room at the back to avoid the latter).

-Ty Gwyn-

This year we've had some criticisms of the service, particularly on reception. More reports are welcome.

◑ Open all year

➡ South of the village of Betws-y-coed on the A5, 100 yards south of Waterloo Bridge. Private car park

🛏 I single, 4 twin, 4 double, 2 four-poster, I half-tester, I suite; most with shower/WC, 2 with bathroom/WC, 2 public bathrooms; TV, room service, baby-listening in all rooms; hair-dryer on request

◈ Restaurant, bar, lounge; fishing, riding, other sports nearby. Wheelchair access to hotel (no steps), restaurant and WC (M,F), I ground-floor bedroom

⊖ None

▭ Access, Visa

£ Single £19, twin/double £38 to £56, four-poster £70, suite £75; deposit required. Set D £14; alc L, D £20 (prices till Jan 92). Special breaks available

## BRECHFA DYFED                                            MAP 5

---

# Tŷ Mawr Country Hotel

---

BRECHFA, NR CARMARTHEN, DYFED SA32 7RA
TEL: BRECHFA (0267) 202332   FAX: (0267) 202437

*Small-scale hotel in peaceful setting with a noted restaurant.*

The Brechfa Triangle is the rather fanciful name that the owners Beryl and Dick Tudhope give to the sparsely populated hilly woods behind the hotel. It's certainly quiet and easy to forget that the M4 is only 16 miles away. Everything about the place suggests 'getting away from it all'. The rooms don't have TVs, and newspapers are available only if you're truly desperate.

The hotel is in a sixteenth-century stone-built white-painted building that stands near the River Cothi that runs through the village. Part of the building houses a wholefood bakery which is also run by the Tudhopes. Inside, there is a small bar, also used by locals, with bare stone walls, and in summer you can take your drinks out on to a stone-flagged terrace overlooking a quiet garden, with another small river, the Marlais, tumbling by.

The dining-room is divided in two by a large fireplace. In one half stands an imposing seventeenth-century Welsh dresser and a large table for seating parties. The cooking is done by Mrs Tudhope and the restaurant is gaining a fine reputation. Upstairs, there are five bedrooms all decorated with cotton floral designs. The Tudhopes, who took over the hotel in 1989, would like to impose their own personality on these rooms, so expect some changes.

◑ Open all year, exc last week Nov, last week Jan, first week Feb; restaurant closed Mon eve

➡ Brechfa is 10 miles north-east of

Carmarthen, on the B4310. Private car park

🛏 I twin, 3 double, I family room; all with bathroom/WC, baby-

listening; hair-dryer, trouser
press on request

dogs in public rooms

Access, Amex, Visa

Restaurant, bar, lounge, drying
room; riding, fishing, other sports
nearby; babysitting

Single occupancy of twin/double
£38 to £40, double £58 to £63,
family suite £73 to £78; deposit
required. Set L £12.50, D
£17.50. Special breaks available

No wheelchair access; no
children under 8 at dinner; no

---

**CAPEL COCH** GWYNEDD                                   **MAP 5**

# Tre-Ysgawen Hall

CAPEL COCH, NR LLANGEFNI, ANGLESEY, GWYNEDD LL77 7UR
TEL: BANGOR (0248) 750750   FAX: (0248) 750035

*A formal country-house hotel where guests are pampered.*

Tre-Ysgawen Hall is a stately hotel offering everything from shooting
weekends with days out in a chauffeur-driven Rolls Royce, to deluxe
four-poster and champagne breaks. As one reader comments: 'It's nice
to find a new hotel where the owners with no previous experience
apparently have created a delightful place which was a pleasure to be in!'

The Craigheads have completely renovated the old manor house, built
in 1882, to replace the old family home that mysteriously burnt down. It
is said that a very strong smell of burning permeates the hotel sometimes
– some say it is the phantom smell of the old house burning. There have
also been sightings of the servants who died at the hall through accidents
or suicide. These ghostly goings-on don't interfere with the running of
the hotel which is highly efficient and professional. Your every need is
anticipated: beds are turned down while you are eating dinner, your
shoes are cleaned overnight and should you wake up in the middle of the
night craving a peanut butter sandwich, the 24-hour room service could
probably provide it. If you decide to come by helicopter, you can land in
the grounds, but if you would rather come by train or aeroplane, then you
can be collected at any time of day.

The bedrooms are luxuriously furnished in co-ordinating colours and
fabrics – yards of material are draped over the windows and beds. Dinner
is served in a horse-shoe-shaped extension to the house. Waiters hover
solicitously, bringing steaming dishes from the kitchen, while a pianist
plays old favourites in the hallway. The food is simple with an exotic
edge, for example, salmon mousse with mussels is served with a saffron
sauce.

Open all year

From Llangefni follow road for
Amlwch and Llanerchymedd,
through village of Rhos-meirch to
a house with monkey puzzle
trees outside. Turn right, follow

road for 1 mile, drive is on left.
Private car park

1 single, 7 twin, 8 double, 3
four-poster, 1 suite; all with TV,
room service, hair-dryer, trouser
press, baby-listening; no tea/

coffee-making facilities in rooms

 Dining-room, bar, lounge, drying room; conference facilities (max 120 people non-residential, 26 residential); heated swimming-pool, game and clay-shooting at hotel. Wheelchair access to hotel, restaurant and WC, 3

ground-floor bedrooms

None

Access, Amex, Visa

Single £79, twin/double £105, four-poster £150, suite £200; deposit required. Continental B £5, cooked B £8; set L £14, D £18, £25; alc D £30

---

**CARDIFF** SOUTH GLAMORGAN                    **MAP 5**

# Cardiff International

MARY ANN STREET, CARDIFF, SOUTH GLAMORGAN CF1 2EQ
TEL: CARDIFF (0222) 341441   TELEX: 498005 INTHOT G
FAX: (0222) 223742

*New international-style city-centre hotel, with an unusual lobby.*

This hotel was opened on 7 September 1990 by the Secretary of State for Wales. It stands within walking distance of the main shopping streets and St David's Hall. An underground car park has direct access to the hotel's showpiece, a five-storey-high lobby/atrium which looks like a grand Victorian railway station. In the centre of the floor is the reception and hanging above the desk is a four-sided clock. There are green and gold painted girders and pillars, and the walls are finished to give the impression that you are standing in a square of terraced housing. There is even a park bench where four mannequins sit and watch the goings-on. It's all open-plan, with the lounge and restaurant to the side, which serves continental fare plus some Welsh specialities. The bar is decorated with Art Deco-style stained glass.

Upstairs, the corridors to the bedrooms are decorated in light colours and the odd modern print breaks the monotony. The bedrooms themselves have all the advantages and disadvantages that you would expect of an international hotel. They are neat, well designed and well stocked with mini-bar and so on, but they are also impersonal. Standard furnishings include dark blue carpets and curtains and bedspreads of an intricately patterned red and gold material.

Open all year

Follow signs to city centre, 500 yards from Cardiff Central Station, next to Cardiff World Trade Centre. Private car park

66 twin, 66 double, 8 family rooms, 3 suites; all with bathroom/WC, TV, room service, hair-dryer, trouser press, mini-bar, baby-listening

Restaurant, bar, lounge, 2

conservatories (all air-conditioned); conference facilities (max 40 people residential); fishing, golf, other sports nearby. Wheelchair access to hotel, restaurant and WC (unisex), 8 bedrooms specially equipped for the disabled

No dogs

Access, Amex, Diners, Visa

Single occupancy of twin/double

£30 to £70, twin/double £50 to £80, family room £75 to £100, suite £80 to £125. Cooked B

£8.50, continental B £5.50; set L £14.50, D £15.50; alc L, D £17

**CHIRK** CLWYD                                                          **MAP 6**

# Starlings Castle

BRONYGARTH, NR CHIRK, OSWESTRY, SHROPSHIRE SY10 7NU
TEL: GLYN CEIRIOG (0691) 72464

*A remote hotel with the accent on the kitchen and friendly service.*

As the hotel brochure points out, Starlings Castle is not so much a castle as a solidly built eighteenth-century sandstone farmhouse, though the site used to be a fortification against marauding Englishmen. This is sheep-farming country, and the farmhouse is not easy to find in a maze of Welsh lanes, so you'll need to telephone ahead for instructions.

You can expect a friendly welcome. One reader reports: 'The second time we visited it was like going home. The welcome is low-key and genuine, the whole atmosphere is almost like visiting family and just picking up from where one left off the last time.' Inside, the hotel has eight good-sized bedrooms which are simply and comfortably furnished. All the rooms have washbasins, but otherwise share two public bathrooms. Downstairs, there's a cosy sitting-room in deep reds and greens, with oak dressers, a cat to share your sofa, and a roaring log fire to sit round with a pre-dinner drink. The hotel's strength is undoubtedly its restaurant, which is also open to non-residents. The food is cosmopolitan (the result of Antony Pitt's 18-years' experience as a chef in and around Bath), and includes plaice and grey mullet with coconut, coriander and chilli, and lambs' tongues with a blue cheese dressing. In summer the hotel is busy with specialist weeks for budding painters and mushroom foragers, so book well in advance.

◑ *Open all year*

⤴ *From the A5 north of Oswestry take the exit from the roundabout signed Weston Rhyn. Drive 2 miles to Selattyn, turn right, and drive through the village for 2½ miles. Turn right at the top of the hill and follow signs to Starlings Castle. Private car park*

🛏 *2 single, 2 twin, 4 double; 2 public bathrooms; TV, hair-dryer, baby-listening in all rooms*

◈ *Restaurant, bar, lounge, drying room; conference facilities (max 25 people non-residential, 8 residential); fishing, golf, other sports nearby. Wheelchair access to restaurant and WC (unisex) only*

⊖ *No dogs in public rooms; no smoking in bedrooms*

▭ *Access, Visa*

💷 *Single £18 to £32, single occupancy of twin/double £25, twin/double £32. Cooked B £2.50; alc L, D £22*

**CRICKHOWELL** POWYS   **MAP 5**

# Gliffaes Country Hotel

CRICKHOWELL, POWYS NP8 1RH
TEL: BWLCH (0874) 730371   FAX: (0874) 730463

*Family-run hotel with memorable gardens. A popular hotel with anglers.*

The hotel has been run by the same family, the Brabners, for over 40 years – maybe that's why the atmosphere is so relaxed here.

The hotel is set in 29 acres of grounds and six acres of carefully tended garden, but for many guests that is not as important as the access to a prime trout and salmon fishing stretch on the left bank of the River Usk. The building itself is gradually drowning in ivy, but two brick Italianate campanile stick out like ships' masts. The hotel has a 'lived-in' feel: things are worn and comfortable. The sitting-room, with its wood-panelled walls, is clubby and warm, and well-thumbed magazines lie on the coffee table. But the drawing-room is slightly more formal and liberally furnished with antiques. The bedrooms are all different but of a good size; the best have high ceilings, tiled fireplaces and fine river views. There is a well-appointed restaurant, with pleasant views of the garden.

◐ Closed Jan to mid-Mar

↗ 1 mile off A40, 2½ miles west of Crickhowell. Private car park

🛏 19 twin/double, 3 lodge rooms; most with bathroom/WC, some with shower/WC; limited room service, baby-listening in all rooms; hair-dryer on request

◇ Dining-room, bar, 2 lounges, TV room, billiard room, drying room, conservatory; conference facilities (max 20 people residential); tennis, croquet, putting at hotel, fishing, other sports nearby

⊖ No wheelchair access; dogs in lodge only

▭ Access, Amex, Diners, Visa

💷 Single £35, single occupancy of twin/double £55, twin/double/ lodge £60 to £82. Set L £10.50, D £16.50; alc D £28. Special breaks available

**EGLWYSFACH** DYFED   **MAP 5**

# Ynyshir Hall

EGLWYSFACH, MACHYNLLETH, POWYS SY20 8TA
TEL: GLANDYFI (0654) 781209

*Stunning setting for this individually decorated and comfortable hotel.*

The blurb for this hotel proclaims, 'A country hotel of individuality', and it is right. Ynyshir Hall bears the confident stamp of Rob Reen who runs the hotel along with his wife Joan. They both meet and greet the guests although some reports suggest Mr Reen can be a cool customer. He is an artist and many of his large, Post-Impressionist works in oil and acrylic hang on the walls.

There are clear uncompromising colours throughout the hotel: the bar is painted orange and a large open fire adds to its snugness; the lounge has blue walls and pink hangings and luxuriant potted plants. The building itself is a white Georgian house set in 12 acres of landscaped gardens full of rhododendrons, camellias and azaleas. Nearby are the 365 acres of the Ynyshir bird sanctuary.

The food is imaginative and stylishly presented. A meal could include monkfish and mussels in a herb sauce, or fresh sardines in vine leaves. Bedrooms have bright matching fabrics and only one lacks *en suite* facilities. The hotel's artistic motif is continued by naming the rooms after famous painters and by running painting courses throughout the year. One complaint – the hot water can fail to meet the demands placed on it during the peak early-evening period.

◑ *Open all year*

▱ *6 miles south-west of Machynlleth, 11 miles north-east of Aberystwyth, off the A487. Private car park*

🛏 *1 single, 3 twin, 2 double, 1 four-poster, 2 suites; all (exc 1 double) with bathroom/WC; TV, room service in all rooms*

◈ *Restaurant, bar, lounge, breakfast room; conference facilities (max 25 people non-residential); fishing, riding, other sports nearby. Wheelchair access*

*to hotel (3 steps) and restaurant, 1 ground-floor bedroom*

⊖ *No children under 9; no dogs in public rooms and in some bedrooms only; no smoking in restaurant and bedrooms*

▱ *Access, Amex, Visa*

£ *Single £32 to £45, single occupancy of twin/double £50, twin/double £75 to £90, four-poster £80 to £100, suites £90 to £120; deposit required. Set L, D £19.50 (prices till Apr 92). Special breaks available*

---

**FISHGUARD** DYFED                                                      **MAP 5**

# Plâs Glyn-y-Mêl

LOWER TOWN, FISHGUARD, PEMBROKESHIRE SA65 9LY
TEL: FISHGUARD (0348) 872296

*A good choice of base for the Pembrokeshire Coast: handsome house, beautiful surroundings and friendly, easy-going hosts.*

If you want to explore the wilder parts of the Pembrokeshire coast, or spend a night in Fishguard before catching the ferry to Ireland, you could do far worse than stay at Plâs Glyn-y-Mêl, at the head of the Gwaun Valley. The handsome Georgian residence feels isolated, with green meadows grazed by a few ponies sloping down to the river screened by dense trees. In contrast to the windy clifftops by the sea, it's very sheltered here: a palm tree, fig trees and rhododendrons grow around the hotel.

Inside, the style is easy-going. You might first encounter the owners, Jenny and Michael Moore, with daughter Marianne and dog, returning from a muddy walk. The public rooms are the best: a colonnaded and arched entrance hall with a grandfather clock, a cosy, chintzy sitting-room, overlooking the meadows, with huge gilt-framed mirror and elaborately carved oak dresser (and open fire, of course); and the elegant dining-room, where the bird prints on green walls echo the bird mats on the polished tables. There's also a bar and conservatory downstairs.

The four bedrooms run around a wide landing on the first floor (the Moores live on the top). Carved out of what must have once been large family bedrooms, they're on the small and simple side, but fresh, differently decorated, with thoughtful touches such as dried flowers and fresh milk for morning tea.

- Closed Nov to Easter, dining-room closed Mon eve
- In Fishguard lower town. Private car park
- 2 twin, 2 double; all with bathroom/WC, TV
- Dining-room; heated swimming-pool, fishing at hotel
- No wheelchair access; no dogs in public rooms
- None accepted
- Single occupancy of twin/double £50, twin/double £70. Set D £17.50

## GLYNARTHEN DYFED                                                    MAP 5

# Penbontbren Farm

GLYNARTHEN, NR CARDIGAN, DYFED SA44 6PE
TEL: ABERPORTH (0239) 810248   FAX: (0239) 811129

*Smart motel-style accommodation in converted farm buildings.*

The buildings have been in Nan Humphreys' family for generations and now she runs the hotel with her husband Barrie. The Humphreys are both Welsh speakers and all information and notices in the hotel are printed in Welsh and English. It's a friendly place where other members of the family chip in when they can. At one end of the dining-room stands a harp which is sometimes played by the Humphreys' daughter. They try to give their visitors a taste, albeit sanitised, of Welsh rural life and a lot of effort has gone into converting the farm buildings.

Inside, the bedrooms are furnished with pine fittings and floral duvets; they are clean and fresh but a touch impersonal. Public rooms are on the other side of the courtyard, so you have to brave the weather to go from bedroom to dining-room. What is now the dining-room used to be the cow shed, the bar was the fodder room and the small lounge, a cart shed. The furnishing is modern pine with exposed brickwork. The menu offers hearty Welsh dishes – soups and lamb stew followed by a selection from a sweets trolley. The best way to work up an appetite for this feast is to follow one of the marked walks across the 90 acres of farmland that surround the hotel. The Humphreys are more than willing to point you in the right direction.

○ Open all year

↗ Travelling south from Aberystwyth on the A487 take first left after Sarnau (signposted Penbontbren). Travelling north on A487 from Cardigan take second right 1 mile after Tan-y-groes (signposted Penbontbren). Private car park

🛏 3 twin, 1 double, 6 family rooms; all with bathroom/WC, TV, baby-listening

◇ Dining-room, bar, 2 lounges,

games room; conference facilities (max 20 residential); fishing, riding, water sports nearby. Wheelchair access to hotel (ramp) and restuarant, 6 ground-floor bedrooms

⊖ No dogs in public rooms; no smoking in dining-room

▭ Access, Visa

£ Single occupancy of twin/double £27 to £32, twin/double £48 to £54; deposit required. Alc L, D £12 to £15 (prices till Dec 91)

---

**GOVILON** GWENT                                                        **MAP 5**

# Llanwenarth House

GOVILON, ABERGAVENNY, GWENT NP7 9SF
TEL: GILWERN (0873) 830289

*Smart family home that makes a good base for exploring the Brecon Beacons.*

The handsome grey-stone sixteenth-century house of Bruce and Mandy Weatherill has been restored into a welcoming family home. Perhaps the most interesting feature of the house is its splendid staircase. The bright yellow walls are hung with hunting and bird prints, and an octagonal cupola surrounded by family crests lets the daylight flood in.

You can take a pre-dinner drink in the lounge which is decorated with floral fabric sofas and antiques. There is a mini grand piano on which photographs of the Weatherill children stand. The food is prepared by Mandy Weatherill and there is no choice on the menu, although special dishes will be prepared if advance notice is given. If possible, guests are seated around one large table. 'We like to make every evening a dinner party,' says Bruce. There is a substantial wine list. One reader particularly recommends the generous breakfast with wild mushrooms and home-cured bacon, endless supplies of toast and very good coffee. The Weatherills keep their own pigs (Oxford Sandies), sheep and chickens and grow their own vegetables. The bedrooms are upstairs apart from one on the ground floor that has its own access to the garden. All the rooms are a good size and the main one is massive.

○ Closed mid-Jan to end Feb; restaurant closed some eves

↗ 2 miles west of Abergavenny. From the junction of the A40

from Monmouth, the A465 from Hereford and the A4042 from Newport, east of Abergavenny, follow the A465 towards Merthyr Tydfil for 3½ miles to next roundabout. Take first exit to Govilon; the ½-mile drive is 150 yards on the right-hand side. Private car park

🛏 2 twin, 3 double (family rooms available); some with bathroom/WC, some with shower/WC; TV in all rooms; hair-dryer on request

◈ Dining-room, drawing-room;

croquet at hotel, other sports nearby. Wheelchair access to hotel (1 step) and dining-room, 1 ground-floor bedroom

⊖ No children under 10; no dogs in public rooms; no smoking in dining-room

▭ None accepted

£ Single occupancy of twin/double £49 to £58, twin/double £61 to £70; 10 to 14-year-old sharing parents' room £20 to £24; deposit required. Set D £19.50 to £21 (7.45pm). Special breaks available

---

**GWAUN** DYFED                                                    **MAP 5**

# Tregynon Country Farmhouse

GWAUN VALLEY, NR FISHGUARD, PEMBROKESHIRE SA65 9TU
TEL: NEWPORT (0239) 820531   FAX: (0239) 820808

*A place for those who want to get away from it all.*

Tregynon has all the features you would look for in a farmhouse hotel: it's cheap, comfortable accommodation with good wholesome food. But this doesn't do Tregynon justice. The farm perches on the side of the Gwaun Valley, renowned for its ancient oak woodlands and unspoilt lands where wildlife such as badgers, squirrels and buzzards can be seen, as well as the occasional peregrine falcon and red kite. You can take walks down various tracks into the valley which eventually spills into the sea at Fishguard, or over the Preselis, from where you can see both Ireland and Snowdon on a clear day. Back at the farm, there are two trout ponds and a waterfall which tips down into the valley.

The sixteenth-century stone farmhouse is casual and comfortable with low-beamed ceilings, an inglenook fireplace and a stone-walled dining-room. Some of the bedrooms are in the main house, but the rest are in converted stone cottages across the yard. Each room has a fresh, rustic style with pine furnishings, flowery quilts, *en suite* facilities and television.

Tregynon food is something to look forward to. Peter Heard has his own smoke house where he cures bacon and gammon according to traditional methods. 'It is a very special privilege to eat here,' reports one reader. Everything on the menu is home-made, and, as far as possible, contains no artificial anything. They also make a tremendous effort to suit everybody's needs – vegetarian, vegan, gluten-free diets provide no problems. And one reader described the home-made ice-creams as 'the best I have eaten in my life'.

◐ Open all year

⤢ At intersection of B4313 and B4429, take B4313 towards Fishguard, then take first right and follow signs. Private car park

🛏 4 double, 4 twin/family rooms; most with bathroom/WC, some with shower/WC; TV in all rooms; hair-dryer, baby-listening on request

◈ 2 dining-rooms, bar, lounge; conference facilities (max 25 people non-residential, 8

residential); golf, fishing, other sports nearby. Wheelchair access to hotel and restaurant, all are ground-floor rooms

⊖ No dogs; no smoking in dining-rooms and bedrooms

▭ None accepted

£ Single occupancy of twin/double £40 to £51, twin/double £40 to £51; deposit required. Set D £12.50 (prices till Apr 92). Special breaks available

**HAY-ON-WYE** POWYS                                **MAP 5**

# Old Black Lion          𝒮𝓛

LION STREET, HAY-ON-WYE, HEREFORD HR3 5AD
TEL: HAY-ON-WYE (0497) 820841

*Comfortable rooms above a popular pub.*

The Old Black Lion is a lively pub in the centre of this capital of second-hand books. Parts of the building date from the thirteenth century, so floors have a tendency to slope, ceilings are quite low in places and the restaurant and bar are beamed – all these features add a cosiness to the atmosphere.

The bar is quite lively in the evening and serves bar snacks, or you can have à la carte meals in the small restaurant (not unanimously recommended). There is a small lounge just off the bar area for those who would like a quieter place to sit. The bedrooms are cottagey in style with flowery quilts (sheets and blankets can be requested if preferred) and have televisions. Some of the bathrooms may be in need of refurbishment. More reports, please.

◐ Open all year

⤢ In the centre of Hay-on-Wye, 2 minutes' walk from the castle. Private car park

🛏 1 single, 3 twin, 5 double, 1 family; some with bathroom/WC, most with shower/WC; TV in all rooms; hair-dryer on request

◈ Restaurant, bar, lounge, drying room; fishing, golf nearby. Wheelchair access to restaurant and WC only

⊖ No children under 8 in restaurant; dogs in bar only; no smoking in bedrooms

▭ Access, Visa

£ Single £17, single occupancy of twin/double £26, twin/double £40, family room from £40; deposit required. Sun L £7; alc D £18.50; bar meals. Special breaks available

**LAKE VYRNWY** POWYS                                          **MAP 5**

# Lake Vyrnwy Hotel

LAKE VYRNWY, LLANWDDYN, POWYS SY10 0LY
TEL: LLANWDDYN (069 173) 692   FAX: (069 173) 259

*Outstanding lakeside position for this unpretentious sporting hotel.*

Spectacular Lake Vyrnwy was created in the nineteenth century to
supply water to Liverpool. This hotel, practically the only building to be
seen at the lakeshore, capitalises on its stunning situation, with panoramic views from the public rooms and some bedrooms. It's tempting to sit
all day and drink in the views over the water to the Victorian pumping
tower in the distance, but many sporting activities can be arranged, from
archery to white-water rafting as well as traditional country pursuits like
hunting and fishing.

Inside, the rooms have been restored to their Victorian grandeur, with
stylish furnishings in strong colours. Deep and comfortable leather
chairs give the bar a clubby feel and there's a piano in the yellow and blue
drawing-room. An imposing pitch pine staircase leads to the bedrooms
which vary in size and fittings. Décor is simple, and patterned pastel
fabrics keep the mood light. It's worth paying a little extra for a lakeside
room. Meals are taken in the Regency-style dining-room where the set
three-course meals have inventiveness plus wide appeal and can feature
venison and game, dishes that suit the atmosphere.

Unfortunately the hotel is not undiscovered – a lakeside sign invites
daytrippers to the tavern alongside and on a fine day the place can be
packed, with rock music belting out. Not the peace and tranquillity that
the view suggests.

◑ *Open all year*

🔁 *From Shrewsbury take the A458
road to Welshpool and turn on
to the B4393 signposted 'Lake
Vyrnwy 28 miles'. Private car
park*

🛏 *3 single, 20 twin/double, 2 four-
poster, 2 family rooms, 2 suites;
all with bathroom/WC, TV, room
service, hair-dryer, baby-
listening; no tea/coffee-making
facilities in rooms*

◈ *Restaurant, 2 bars, lounge,
drying room, conservatory;
conference facilities (max 30*

*people residential, 50 non-
residential); fishing, shooting,
tennis, bicycles, canoeing, sailing
at hotel, other sports nearby;
babysitting by arrangement.
Wheelchair access to restaurant
and WC (M,F) only*

⊖ *No dogs in public rooms*

▭ *Access, Amex, Diners, Visa*

£ *Single from £46, single
occupancy of twin/double £46 to
£71, twin/double £55 to £82,
four-poster £82, suite £105. Set
L £9.50, D £19.50. Special
breaks available*

**LLANARMON DYFFRYN CEIRIOG** CLWYD                    **MAP 5**

# West Arms

LLANARMON DYFFRYN CEIRIOG, NR LLANGOLLEN CLWYD LL20 7LD
TEL: LLANARMON DYFFRYN CEIRIOG (069 176) 665   FAX: (069 176) 622

*A comfortable, casual base in the depths of the Welsh Marches.*

As you wind down yet more narrow twisting roads into the heart of North Wales countryside, you wonder for the umpteenth time whether you've really come the right way. Right at the end of one of these roads is Llanarmon Dyffryn Ceiriog, a group of buildings on the bend of the road after a tiny bridge.

The hills rise up either side of the Ceiriog Valley and disappear into the ubiquitous low cloud. It has a Brigadoon feel – the air is damp with mist and the village is unbelievably quaint with whitewashed stone buildings and climbing ivy.

The West Arms is over 400 years old. The warmth from log fires greets you as you enter, and the host ushers you up to one of the comfortable bedrooms with quilt-covered beds and *en suite* facilities. Downstairs, the public rooms have rug-covered slate floors, low-beamed ceilings and huge inglenook fireplaces with hanging copper pans, wood baskets and pewter plates. After dinner, it's only with great reluctance that you finally relinquish your seat in a squashy chintzy chair beside a glowing log fire to wend your way up to bed.

- **◐** Open all year
- **⚡** Turn off the A5 trunk road at Chirk and follow the B4500 along Ceiriog Valley for 11 miles. Private car park
- **⇌** 8 twin, 4 double, 2 suites; all with bathroom/WC, room service; hair-dryer on request; TV in suites only; no tea/coffee-making facilities in rooms
- **◇** Restaurant, 2 bars, 2 lounges, TV room, drying room; conference

facilities (max 70 people non-residential, 14 residential); fishing at hotel, tennis, riding nearby; babysitting. Wheelchair access to hotel and restaurant, 3 ground-floor bedrooms

- **⊖** Some bedrooms non-smoking
- **▭** Access, Amex, Diners, Visa
- **£** Single £50 to £55, twin/double £78 to £88, suite £99; deposit required. Set L £11.50, D £19.50. Special breaks available

---

*If you make a booking using a credit card, and you find after cancelling that the full amount has been charged to your card, raise the matter with your credit card company. They will ask the hotelier to confirm whether the room was re-let, and to justify the charge made.*

## LLANDDEINIOLEN GWYNEDD

MAP 5

# Ty'n Rhos

SEION, LLANDDEINIOLEN, CAERNARFON, GWYNEDD LL55 3AE
TEL: PORT DINORWIC (0248) 670489

*Home-produced food and comfortable bedrooms are to be found at
this farm in the rolling foothills of Snowdonia.*

The Kettles have lived on Ty'n Rhos farm for 18 years. At first they were
full-time farmers, but later they expanded into the accommodation
business and haven't looked back. Ty'n Rhos is still a working farm, with
a lot of the produce, such as home-made cheese and yoghurt, being
diverted to the farmhouse kitchens to feature on the evening menu.

The furnishings inside the long farmhouse building are far removed
from the casual styles generally associated with working farms. The
sitting-room has chintzy chairs, ticking pendulum clocks, gilt mirrors,
and brasses on the fireplace. The bedrooms are co-ordinated in fresh,
bold modern prints and floral patterns, and all have *en suite* facilities.
Some of the bedrooms facing westwards have french windows overlooking undulating farmland towards Anglesey and are flooded with the
evening sun. The restaurant is also a bright room, plainly furnished and
having a wooden dresser at one end.

Breakfast may be home-made yoghurt with honey, kippers or poached
haddock, and the evening meal is a set four-course dinner including
home-made soups and bread rolls. The rates are very reasonable and the
farm is well placed for Snowdonia, Anglesey and Caernarfon.

- ◐ Closed 18 Dec to 8 Jan
- ⬈ In hamlet of Seion off the B4366, 4 miles from Caernarfon. Private car park
- ⇌ 2 single, 4 twin, 2 double, 3 family rooms; all with bathroom/WC, exc 1 family room with shower/WC; TV in all rooms; hair-dryer on request
- ◇ Restaurant, bar, lounge; fishing, golf nearby. Wheelchair access to farm (1 step) and dining-room, 3 ground-floor bedrooms
- ⊖ No children under 6; no dogs in public rooms; smoking in lounge only
- ▭ Access, Visa
- £ Single £29 to £30, single occupancy of twin/double £45 to £51, twin/double £50 to £56, family room £42 to £50; deposit required. Set D £13.50

---

*Many hotels put up their tariffs in the spring. You are advised to confirm
prices when you book.*

# Bodidris Hall

LLANDEGLA, WREXHAM, CLWYD LL11 3AL
TEL: LLANDEGLA (097 888) 434   FAX: (097 888) 335

*An isolated hotel with strong historical connections, set in the wild
moorlands of North Wales.*

Up in the wild moorlands of the Clwydian range, Bodidris Hall is like
something from a Brontë novel. It nestles in the windswept landscape of
bracken and gorse, overlooking a duck pond and the empty valley below.
The Hall creaks with romantic history: Owain Glyndwr, Prince of
Wales, is said to have killed the Bishop of St Asaph at Bodidris, and later,
Elizabeth I is said to have visited her 'favourite', the Earl of Leicester,
here when he used it as a hunting lodge. There is also supposed to be a
phantom knight who wanders the hallways at night, but he hasn't been
spotted for many years.

Bodidris Hall is daunting from the outside, built from craggy grey
stone, with tall chimneys and gargoyles over the doorways, but inside it is
warm and much more friendly. The atmosphere has strong Tudor
overtones: dark oak beams support ceilings and stags' heads hang over
open fireplaces. The panelled dining-room has an impressive banqueting table and the bar, popular with locals, has deep red walls and dark
wood furniture. The feeling of history is reinforced by the upright suit of
armour which guards the entrance to the staircase. Upstairs, you
negotiate the roller-coaster floors and low ceilings to reach the bedrooms. Each room is different in style, size and shape, but some have
hand-made quilt covers and even a spa bath. The Elizabethan suite has a
four-poster bed made from panelling rescued from other parts of the
house.

Bar meals are reasonably priced and range from chicken tikka to
steak-and-kidney pie. The restaurant offers both British and continental
dishes and consists of locally reared meat and game supplemented by
home-produced vegetables, herbs and eggs.

◐ Open all year

⚡ On the A5104, 1 mile east of the
junction with the A525. Private
car park

🛏 6 double, 3 four-poster; all with
bathroom/WC, TV, room service,
baby-listening

◇ Restaurant, bar, lounge, TV
room; conference facilities (max
50 people non-residential, 9
residential); shooting on the
estate, fishing, riding nearby;
babysitting

⊖ No wheelchair access; no dogs

▭ Access, Amex, Visa

£ Single occupancy of double £50,
double £72, four-poster £78;
deposit required. Set L £7.50, D
£12.50; alc L £10.50, D £18.50.
Special breaks available

## LLANDEGLEY POWYS

MAP 5

# Ffaldau Country House and Restaurant

LLANDEGLEY, LLANDRINDOD WELLS, POWYS LD1 5UD
TEL: PENYBONT (059 785) 1421

*A fine restaurant with three rooms attached in a converted farmhouse.*

More of a restaurant-with-rooms than a full-blown hotel, the Ffaldau has only three rooms to choose from. The house was renovated and is run by Leslie and Sylvia Knott who make very friendly hosts. While Sylvia is overseeing the cooking, Leslie serves drinks in the small bar and chats away to guests. The upstairs landing has been converted into the guests' lounge where photos of the Knotts' daughter's wedding and piles of well-thumbed paperbacks are stacked up on either side of the television. Only one of the pink and green bedrooms has an *en suite* shower. The others use a bath down the corridor which could be inconvenient if guests are sitting in the lounge.

The entrance to the dining-room is guarded by an extremely low doorway. Inside, the tables are well spead out over the stone floor. Generous helpings of adventurous combinations like apricot and lentil soup and smoked tuna are served up by Mrs Knott. Don't be misled by the homely, unpretentious style of the rest of the guesthouse – the food is sophisticated and delicious.

- ◑ Open all year
- ⏎ Set back from the A44 in Llandegley, 2 miles south-east of Penybont. Private car park
- 🛏 2 twin, 1 double; shower/WC in the double, 1 public bathroom; hair-dryer in all rooms
- ◈ Restaurant, bar, lounge, drying room, TV; fishing, golf, other sports nearby
- ⊖ No wheelchair access; no children under 10; no dogs; no smoking in bedrooms
- ▭ None accepted
- £ Single occupancy of twin/double £20 to £24, twin/double £32 to £40; deposit required. Set D £15 to £16

---

🍲 *Denotes somewhere you can rely on a good meal – either the hotel features in the 1992 edition of our sister publication,* The Good Food Guide, *or our own inspectors thought the cooking impressive, whether particularly competent home cooking or more lavish cuisine.*

**LLANDRILLO** CLWYD  MAP 5

# Tyddyn Llan Country House

LLANDRILLO, NR CORWEN, CLWYD LL21 0ST
TEL: LLANDRILLO (049 084) 264   FAX: (049 084) 264

*A stylish country hotel with excellent food in a pretty setting.*

Peter and Bridget Kindred run this stylish country house hotel in the pretty vale of Edeyrnion with the Yberwyn mountains rising up in the distance. It is a tranquil spot surrounded by fields where the noisiest elements are birds and sheep. The atmosphere at the hotel is relaxed: you can lounge about on a peach sofa in front of a scented log fire in the winter, or wander about the gardens where tea is served in the summer. If you want to walk further afield, a guide can be arranged.

Upstairs, the bedrooms are individually furnished in a smart but homely style: some have brass beds, others have antique wooden bed-heads. Readers report them as 'firm, with a return to blankets and sweet-smelling linen'. The only television is tucked away in the corner of the lounge; entertainment comes mostly in the form of musical evenings – it could be jazz, or balladeers singing Elizabethan love songs or a Welsh harpist. These mini-concerts take place in the dining-room, where long windows overlook the garden.

The food is highly regarded by readers: 'Peaceful as you say, and comfortable too, but what will remain burnt on our brains are the flavours, the textures, the artistry of dinner. One should never wish one's days away, but in all our travels we cannot recall looking forward more to the perusal and feasting of the evening's menu.'

◐ Open all year

⤢ From the A5 at Corwen take the B4401 through Cynwyd to Llandrillo. Private car park

🛏 4 twin, 6 double, 1 family room; most with bathroom/WC, 2 doubles with shower/WC; room service, hair-dryer, baby-listening in all rooms

◇ 2 restaurants, bar, 2 lounges, drying room; conference facilities (max 10 people residential, 30 non-residential); croquet at hotel, fishing, golf, other sports nearby

⊖ No wheelchair access; no dogs in public rooms

▭ Access, Visa

£ Single occupancy of twin/double £47 to £51, twin/double £74 to £82; deposit required. Snack lunches; Sun L £12.50; set D £20/£25. Special breaks available

*All reports are welcome on any hotel, whether or not it is in the* Guide

**LLANDUDNO** GWYNEDD                                   **MAP 5**

# Bodysgallen Hall

LLANDUDNO, GWYNEDD LL30 1RS
TEL: ABERCONWAY (0492) 584466   TELEX: 837108 HARTH
FAX: (0492) 582519

*A very civilised, peaceful place to stay with quietly efficient staff
and good food.*

Bodysgallen Hall has been skilfully and sympathetically restored by
Historic House Hotels. It is a seventeenth-century house which has
retained its character but includes all the modern facilities that spell
luxurious comfort. Both the first-floor lounge and the large entrance hall
are oak-panelled and have soft sofas and open fireplaces to warm your
feet on cold evenings.

Some of the bedrooms are in the main house; they are large with
Edwardian-style bathrooms, and most have stunning views across parkland or across the ornamental gardens. Other bedrooms are in separate
mini-cottages, equipped with kitchenettes (though not designed for self-
catering) for those people who want to be reclusive. All the bedrooms are
attractively furnished.

A lazy couple of hours can be spent wandering amongst the
seventeenth-century knot-garden of box hedges and the walled rose
garden. There is also a thirteenth-century tower which juts out from the
roof. From here, allowing for the vagaries of Welsh weather, you can see
Conwy Castle and the purple heights of Snowdonia. For the more
energetic there is a croquet lawn and tennis courts. The staff are young
and unobtrusive, and the atmosphere in the hotel is calm and relaxed.
The hotel attracts people for miles around for its moderately priced
Sunday lunches. Dinner is much more expensive with far more choice
but is generally considered worth it.

◐ Open all year

⤴ Take the A55 to its intersection
with the A470, then follow the
A470 towards Llandudno. The
hotel is one mile on the right.
Private car park

🛏 3 single, 15 twin/double, 1 four-
poster, 9 cottage suites; all with
bathroom/WC, TV, hair-dryer,
trouser press; tea/coffee-making
facilities in cottages only

◈ Restaurant, bar, 2 lounges,
library; conference facilities (max
51 people non-residential, 24
residential); tennis, croquet at

hotel, other sports nearby.
Wheelchair access to restaurant
only

⊖ No children under 8; dogs in
cottages only

▭ Access, Amex, Diners, Visa

£ Single £77 to £100, single
occupancy of twin/double £100,
twin/double £102 to £128, four-
poster £146, cottage suites £100
to £197; deposit required.
Continental B £6, cooked B £9;
set L £15.50, D £30 (prices till
Mar 92). Special breaks
available

# St Tudno Hotel

PROMENADE, LLANDUDNO, GWYNEDD LL30 2LP
TEL: LLANDUDNO (0492) 874411   FAX: (0492) 860407

*A smart seaside hotel with an ideal position on the promenade and a welcoming informal atmosphere.*

The St Tudno Hotel is part of a white Victorian terrace and makes a good base from which to explore this genteel resort and the rest of north Wales. Alice Liddell, the model for Lewis Carroll's *Alice*, stayed here in 1861 and many Alice devotees come to retrace her steps. But whatever your reasons for staying you'll warm to the hotel's friendly and welcoming atmosphere. Janette Bland, the owner, makes a point of dropping into the bar to welcome new arrivals, and there's a quarter bottle of fizzy wine waiting for guests in the bedrooms. Some bedrooms, which are decorated with floral fabrics, are rather small for two people and those with a seaview are more expensive.

In the evening, home-made canapés are served to guests in the bar. Opposite the bar is a chintzy residents' lounge with peacock-patterned wallpaper and matching curtains, offset by lots of prints and antiques and a row of mounted plates. The dining-room is decorated with trellises and lots of potted plants and prints. The food, either à la carte or a three- or five-course set menu, is French-based and served with nice attention to detail. A tiny indoor swimming-pool is in a low building at the back for those who don't fancy a dip in the sea.

**◐** Open all year

**↗** On Llandudno's promenade, opposite the pier entrance and ornamental garden. Small private car park and on-street parking

**⇌** 1 single, 6 twin, 9 double, 1 four-poster, 4 family rooms; all with bathroom/WC, exc 2 doubles with shower/WC; TV, room service, hair-dryer, trouser press, baby-listening, fridge in all rooms

**◈** Air-conditioned restaurant, bar, 2 lounges, drying room; conference facilities (max 25 people residential and non-residential); heated indoor swimming-pool at hotel, other sports nearby; babysitting

**⊖** No wheelchair access; dogs at hoteliers' discretion; no smoking in restaurant and 1 lounge

**▭** Access, Amex, Visa

**£** Single £50 to £58, single occupancy of twin/double from £53, twin/double from £72, four-poster £95 to £115; special rates for children. Set L £11.50, D £18.50 and £23.50; bar snacks. Special breaks available

---

*The* Guide *office can quickly spot when a hotelier is encouraging customers to write a recommending inclusion – and sadly, several hotels have been doing this in 1991. Such reports do not further an hotel's cause.*

**LLANGAMMARCH WELLS** POWYS                    **MAP 5**

# The Lake Hotel

LLANGAMMARCH WELLS, POWYS LD4 4BS
TEL: LLANGAMMARCH WELLS (059 12) 202   FAX: (059 12) 457

*In beautiful parkland, this Victorian-cum-mock-Tudor country house offers just the right balance between the relaxed and the formal.*

Well off the beaten track, but well placed for explorers of the Brecon Beacons and the Wye Valley, the Lake is best used as a weekend break destination – the rates for stays of more than a night are much better value, in any case. The hotel's name comes from the trout-stocked lake which is surrounded by beautiful parkland – sloping lawns, woodland, rhododendrons, benches to sit on and admire it all and paths to potter along.

Inside, the experience is similarly pleasant. From the reception hall (more like an elegant lounge than a reception) open creaky stairs lead to the Victorian-feel bedrooms: floral fabrics on pelmets, curtains, blinds, bedspreads and borders. Rooms with names like 'Heron Suite' or 'Pump Room Suite' have a sleeping half and a comfortable sitting half. The chintzy sofas in the large drawing-room (it's as high as it's wide) are just the sort for flopping in at any time of day, but especially at tea-time, with a trolley of home-made cakes by your side and a log fire lit in the fireplace. Not too many cakes, though, as the dinner, served in another beautifully proportioned room, is four-course and delicious, with a good selection of local Welsh cheeses to finish.

Overall, the hotel strikes just the right balance between the formal and the informal: you're expected to dress for dinner, but the rule is readily waived if the hotel isn't full.

◑ *Closed Jan*

🔁 *Leave Junction 24 on M4, follow A449 to Raglan, then the A40 to Abergavenny, signs to Builth Wells up the Wye Valley. A483 to Garth and follow hotel signs. Private car park*

🛏 *8 twin, 8 double, 2 four-poster, 1 family room; all with bathroom/ WC, TV, room service, hair-dryer; trouser press in some rooms*

◇ *Dining-room, bar, 2 lounges, games room, drying room; conference facilities (max 75 people non-residential, 20 residential); golf, tennis, fishing, clay pigeon shooting, riding at hotel. Wheelchair access to hotel, restaurant and WC, 2 ground-floor bedrooms*

⊖ *No children under 8; no dogs in public rooms; no smoking in dining-room*

▭ *Access, Visa*

💷 *Single occupancy of twin/double £75, twin/double/four-poster £130, suite £150 (rates inc dinner); deposit required. Special breaks available*

**LLANGOLLEN** CLWYD                                    **MAP 5**

# Gales of Llangollen

18 BRIDGE STREET, LLANGOLLEN, CLWYD LL20 8PF
TEL: LLANGOLLEN (0978) 860089    FAX: (0978) 861313

*A busy wine bar with reasonably priced accommodation for those who don't want to leave.*

Huddled between buildings along Bridge Street in the centre of Llangollen, Gales is a popular haunt for locals and visitors alike. Previously an antique shop, it now houses a wine bar on two levels with dark oak-panelling and bare wood floors. The good, inexpensive food and large wine selection means that Gales is filled with good-natured chatter even on weekdays; it is wise to annex a table quite early on in the evening.

The menu is chalked up on a blackboard and includes soups, salads and various hot dishes of the day, suiting the needs of carnivores and vegetarians alike. There are also sweets, such as home-made ice-creams. The bedrooms have slightly sloping floors and low ceilings and are furnished with antique beds, some of which have brass bedsteads. A large function room doubles as the breakfast room – a room dominated by a large oak dining-table which seats up to twelve people. Children are welcome here and there are televisions in the bedrooms hooked up to cable and video to keep them occupied in the evenings.

- ◑ Open all year, exc 25 Dec to 1 Jan; restaurant closed Sun eve
- ⤢ 9 miles south-west of Wrexham. Coming from the south on the A5, turn right at the traffic lights in Llangollen and right again before the bridge. The hotel is 50 yards on the right. Private car park
- ⇌ 1 twin, 6 double, 1 family room; some with bathroom/WC, most with shower/WC; TV, hair-dryer, baby-listening in all rooms
- ◈ Restaurant, bar; conference facilities (max 12 people non-residential, 8 residential); fishing, golf, other sports nearby
- ● No wheelchair access; no dogs
- ▭ Access, Visa
- £ Single occupancy of twin/double £30, twin/double £48; deposit required. Alc L £10, D £12

---

*The 1993 Guide will be published before Christmas 1992. Reports on hotels are most welcome at any time of the year, but are extremely valuable in the spring. Send them to* Which? Hotel Guide, FREEPOST, *2 Marylebone Road, London NW1 1YN. No stamp is needed if reports are posted in the UK.*

**LLANSANFFRAID GLAN CONWY GWYNEDD**          **MAP 5**

# The Old Rectory

LLANRWST ROAD, LLANSANFFRAID GLAN CONWY, NR CONWY,
GWYNEDD LL28 5LF
TEL: ABERCONWAY (0492) 580611   FAX: (0492) 584555

*A fine Georgian rectory where evening meals have a dinner-party atmosphere.*

The first thing to say is that hosts Michael and Wendy Vaughan belong to the Wolsey Lodge group, so a stay here is a stay in their elegant home, not an hotel. The house with its terraced gardens is a good vantage point from which to look down on the Conwy estuary.

Roman coins found in the garden are among the interesting things on display in the house, with its panelled drawing-room with deep sofas and chairs, long windows to the garden and watercolours on the walls, and a dining-room with parquet floor and oval mahogany table. The bedrooms are equally well furnished, with half-tester beds draped in lacy frills. In the evening, guests are introduced to each other over cocktails before dinner. As at all Wolsey Lodges, your enjoyment depends on how you get on with the other guests.

The Vaughans are Welsh and keen to use Welsh produce when they can. The menu proudly boasts that only Welsh beef and lamb are served at the table. An interesting selection of Welsh cheeses ends the meal and on occasion the meal is taken to the accompaniment of the Vaughans' sons reading Welsh poetry and playing the harp. None of this comes cheap, but a stay here can be a memorable experience.

- ◑ Closed 7 Dec to 1 Feb
- ⬀ On the A470, ½ mile south of the junction with the A55. Private car park
- ⇔ 2 twin, 2 half-testers; most with bathroom/WC, 1 with shower/WC; TV, room service, hair-dryer in all rooms; ironing facilities on request
- ◈ Restaurant, 2 lounges; golf, fishing, other sports nearby
- ⊖ No wheelchair access; no children under 10; no dogs; no smoking
- ▭ Access, Visa
- ⊞ Twin/half-tester £125 to £135 (rates inc dinner); deposit required. Set D £24.50. Special breaks available

---

*Warning to insomniacs, exercise freaks and late-night lovers: increasing numbers of hotels have infra-red triggered security lamps. To save being embarrassingly illuminated, check before you leave for your late-night or pre-dawn stroll.*

# Abbey Hotel

LLANTHONY, NR ABERGAVENNY, GWENT NP7 7NN
TEL: CRUCORNEY (0873) 890487

*Spartan but memorable accommodation among the ruins of a twelfth-century Augustinian priory.*

The ruins of the Abbey stand in the Black Mountains of Brecon. It's a spooky spot and if the atmosphere starts to get to you, then a night in this hostelry is unlikely to calm your nerves. Some of the walls date from the twelfth century and moss is creeping over the slate roof.

The entrance is via the bar which was originally the Abbot's cellar. Kegs of real ale are lined up behind the small wooden bar and battered kitchen chairs stand on the stone floor. The bar serves as a meeting place for many of the local farmers. There is a separate bar and restaurant for hotel guests in a room with three vaulted bays that used to be the Abbot's conference room. Copper kettles decorate the working fireplace and wine bottles stand on an old and ancient-looking oak cupboard.

Food is regular pub fare, but there is no shirking on the size of the helpings which are dished up with little ceremony. Just the thing after a day's walking. This is a relaxed hostelry, and if you sit in the bar you'll soon be drawn into conversation. The way to the bedrooms is up an extremely narrow and steep stone spiral staircase. Facilities in the rooms could be described as monastic – a chair, a bed, a trunk, a mirror and little else, but they are clean and perfectly adequate. But be warned, access is not easy – the top room is reached by climbing 62 steps and, on the night that our inspector stayed, it was also sheltering a family of bats!

- ◐ Open Easter to Nov; weekends and holidays only Nov to Easter
- ↗ From A465 take B4423 to Llanthony (6 miles). Adjacent car park
- ⊨ 1 twin, 2 double, 2 four-poster, 1 family room; 1 public bathroom
- ◈ Dining-room, bar; fishing, riding nearby
- ⊖ No wheelchair access; no children under 8; no dogs in public rooms
- ▭ None accepted
- £ Single occupancy of twin/double £21, twin/double £41 to £48, family room rate on request; deposit required. Special breaks available

---

*Prices are what you can expect to pay in 1992, except where specified to the contrary. Many hoteliers tell us that these prices can be regarded only as approximations.*

**LLWYNDAFYDD** DYFED  **MAP 5**

# Park Hall

CWMTYDU, LLWYNDAFYDD, NR NEW QUAY, DYFED SA44 6LG
TEL: NEW QUAY (0545) 560306

*A peaceful spot near the bay for this Victorian hotel run by
friendly hosts.*

Cwmtydu Bay is frequented by a herd of seals, a joy after the mysterious
virus that almost wiped them out a couple of years ago. Park Hall
provides another reason, apart from seal watching, for heading for this
quiet corner of Wales. The hotel is run by Pete and Christine McDonnell, a hairdresser and florist respectively, who have made the big break
from London to this two-storey house that stands at the mouth of a tree-
lined valley.

It's a small hotel, thoughtfully restored, and furnished with Victoriana;
bedrooms have large brass beds with white lace covers, and some still
have original tile fireplaces. The interior pine fittings have been stripped,
helping to keep the rooms light. Decoration is obviously something that
Mrs McDonnell enjoys – she scours car-boot sales looking for interesting objects to add to her collection. Hats have been hung up on the walls,
and there are straw pith helmets above the stairs, and a top hat and
bowler in the lounge – an indication that the hosts have a sense of
humour, a prerequisite for a relaxed stay. A conservatory-style dining-
room built on to the side can't compete with the rest of the house's style,
but the views are splendid. Dinner makes use of local produce when
possible, perhaps salmon poached in vermouth or a lobster salad.

🌓 Open all year

↗ Take A487 Aberystwyth to
Cardigan road; at Synod Inn head
towards Cardigan for 1 mile,
turn right at crossroads to
Llwyndafydd and Cwmtydu,
follow for 2½ miles; at
crossroads turn left to
Llwyndafydd, turn right between
the Crown and the shop; after
1½ miles Park Hall is on the
left. Private car park

🛏 2 twin, 2 double, 1 four-poster;
some with bathroom/WC, some

with shower/WC; TV, room
service, hair-dryer in all rooms

◈ Dining-room, bar, 2 lounges, TV
room, conservatory; conference
facilities (max 60 people non-
residential); fishing, tennis, other
sports nearby

⊖ No wheelchair access

▭ Access, Amex, Diners, Visa

£ Single occupancy of twin/double
£30, twin/double £50, four-
poster £60; deposit required. Set
D £13, £15; alc L from £5.50, D
£20. Special breaks available

---

*See the inside front cover for a brief explanation of how to use the* Guide.

# Llangoed Hall

LLYSWEN, BRECON, POWYS LD3 0YP
TEL: BRECON (0874) 754525    FAX: (0874) 754545

*Exceptional and sympathetically restored Edwardian mansion.*

From the moment the butler in morning suit steps out to greet your car outside this Edwardian mansion, you know you are in for something special. Designed by Sir Clough Williams-Ellis, the visionary architect responsible for the Italianate village at Portmeirion, Llangoed Hall stands in ten acres of garden and meadow on the banks of the Wye. The estate was rescued from ruin by Sir Bernard Ashley, widower of Laura. He has done a superb job, adding modern comforts without losing the style of an Edwardian house. The gardens and grounds have also been spruced up: a maze, tennis court and croquet lawn have been added and the vegetable and herb garden now supplies much of the kitchen's needs.

Inside, as you would expect, the fabrics used in the bedrooms and public rooms draw heavily on the Laura Ashley catalogue. Where possible, antique furniture and fittings have been retained. It's the individual touches that impress: the decanter of sherry placed in each room, the interesting *objets d'art* and books that are distributed around the house and the large collection of period paintings. Dinner is a six-course affair: you might have John Dory to start, followed by breast of pigeon. After port, have a game of billiards in a setting that is straight out of the pages of Evelyn Waugh.

- Open all year
- 1 mile north of Llyswen on the A470 towards Builth Wells. Private car park
- 2 single, 11 twin, 10 four-poster (inc 5 suites); all with bathroom/WC, TV, room service, hair-dryer, baby-listening
- Dining-room, 2 lounges, games room, library; conference facilities (max 26 people residential); tennis at hotel, golf, fishing, other sports nearby
- No wheelchair access; no children under 8; no dogs; no smoking in dining-room
- Access, Amex, Diners, Visa
- Single £95, single occupancy of twin/double £115 to £145, twin/double £125 to £185, suites £175 to £215 (in low season these prices inc dinner, B&B); deposit required. Set L £17.50, D £32.50; alc L £25.50, D £37.50

---

*The text of entries is based on unsolicited reports sent in by readers and backed up by inspections. The factual details under the text are from questionnaires the* Guide *sends to all hotels that feature in the book.*

**MILEBROOK** POWYS                                    **MAP 5**

# Milebrook House

MILEBROOK, KNIGHTON, POWYS LD7 1LT
TEL: KNIGHTON (0547) 528632   FAX: (0547) 520509

*Small, family-run hotel with tastefully decorated rooms and home-produced food.*

Just over the border into Wales, Milebrook House is a large, mostly grey-stone building dating from the mid-eighteenth century with some later additions. Set back from the main road between Knighton and Ludlow, the hotel is in three acres of grounds.

The fresh vegetables which accompany the dishes on the menu are home-grown in the kitchen gardens. There is also a formal garden of more exotic plants, a croquet lawn surrounded by rhododendrons and unspoilt meadows full of wild flowers and butterflies, stretching down to the riverside. Inside, the hotel is informal and relaxed. The lounge bar and restaurant is open to non-residents. Rodney Marsden, the genial front-of-house man and owner of Milebrook House, will discuss the merits of different types of brandy, while Beryl Marsden prepares the evening's specialities. The menu features home-made dishes with lo-cally reared meats, including Welsh lamb. There is a peaceful residents' lounge (where coffee can be served), with wood floors and furnishings in deep greens and pinks. Upstairs, there are six clean, spacious bedrooms, each with *en suite* bathrooms. One bedroom has a huge brass bed with a mattress which raises you over three feet off the ground. Each room has pine furnishings and is decorated in soft pastel colours.

◖ Open all year

🡒 2 miles east of Knighton, Powys on the A4113. Private car park

🛏 2 twin, 4 double; twins with bathroom/WC, doubles with shower/WC; TV in all rooms

◈ Restaurant, bar, lounge, drying room; conference facilities (max 36 people non-residential, 6 residential); trout fishing, croquet, badminton at hotel, other sports nearby. Wheelchair access to restaurant and WC (M,F) only

⊖ No children under 6; no dogs; no smoking in bedrooms

▭ Access, Visa

£ Single occupancy of twin/double £41, twin/double £55; deposit required. Set D £15.50; alc L £13.50, D £19 (prices till end 91). Special breaks available

---

*If you are intending to make a lot of phone calls from your room, always check what the hotel is going to charge you per unit. You may be so horrified that you'll prefer to walk to the nearest phone box. Why let them get away with excessive charges?*

# Pen-y-gwryd Hotel

NANTGWYNANT, GWYNEDD LL55 4NT
TEL: LLANBERIS (0286) 870211

*Isolated position in the heart of Snowdonia: famed in walking and climbing circles. Not luxurious, but still memorable.*

The hotel stands at the beginning of the Llanberis Pass and is something of an institution – even maps use it as a landmark. Don't expect to be pampered here, it's very informal and friendly – the bedrooms don't even have keys. Most guests are hill walkers and the hotel with its stone floors, wooden benches and drying room complements that rugged, no-frills activity.

Inside, log fires burn in the public rooms, boots hang from the ceiling and climbing memorabilia clutters the wall. The hotel was also the training base for one of the Everest expeditions. A booming gong summons guests to dinner at 7.30pm. The meals are ideal walkers' fare: chicken pie, veg, rice pud. They are served up by a cheerful crew of Scandinavian waitresses. After dinner, coffee is taken around the table in the snug bar. Tales of the day's walking sound even better by the warm glow of the wood fire.

Upstairs, the bedrooms are functional but scrupulously kept. Most are furnished with a sink, table, chair and a bed (a huge iron-framed thing). The baths are down the corridor, deep as a lake and with those gnarled taps that you can operate with your toes. There is no better way to relax after a day in the hills.

◗ Closed Nov to New Year, and mid-week Jan and Feb

➦ From Betws-y-coed take the A5 west to Capel Curig. Turn left at Capel Curig on to the A4086 – the inn is 4 miles further on at a T-junction, with Pen-y-gwryd lake in front. Private car park

🛏 3 single, 8 twin, 7 double, I four-poster, I family room; the four-poster and family room with bathroom/WC

◈ Dining-room, 4 bars, lounge, games room, drying room; limited conference facilities;

fishing, lake swimming and sports at hotel, other sports nearby. Wheelchair access to hotel, dining-room and WC (M,F), I ground-floor bedroom specially equipped for the disabled.

⊖ Dogs £I per day

▭ None accepted

£ Single £19 to £23, single occupancy of twin/double £37 to £46, twin/double/four-poster £46; deposit required. Set D £10.50; bar lunches £2.50

# Cnapan Country House

EAST STREET, NEWPORT, DYFED SA42 0WF
TEL: NEWPORT (0239) 820575

*Family-run restaurant-with-rooms with imaginative country cooking.*

Make sure that you go to the right Newport; this one is over on the west coast. Once there, the pink-painted Georgian house is easy to spot. The guesthouse is a family-run affair, the work being shared by two generations of the Lloyd family. Immediately through the front door there's a fine Welsh dresser and then on the right a small sitting-room with bar. There's a pleasing bustle to the hotel; the kitchen door may be open, and various members of the Lloyd family pop in and out to see if you need anything.

The country-style restaurant has pink walls, a stone fireplace and white lacy cloths. Tables are well spaced and there are jams, mustards and postcards for sale and a blackboard for the lunch menu. At dinner Mrs Lloyd will chat about any unusual herbs that have found their way into her dishes. When our inspector visited, bay was described as 'flavour of the month' and a fresh leaf even decorated the dessert dish. Your meal might start with some thick spinach soup, followed by poached halibut in mussel sauce or pork in cherries. Desserts are something of a house speciality and the boozy ginger biscuit is particularly good. Family photographs hang from one wall of the upstairs corridor. The five rooms upstairs are all decorated in pastel shades.

◑ Closed Feb, also 25, 26 Dec; restaurant closed Tues eve Apr to Oct

🅿 Centrally located on Newport's East Street (A487). Private car park

🛏 3 twin, 1 double, 1 family room; all with shower/WC, TV, room service, hair-dryer, baby-listening

◈ Restaurant, bar, lounge; drying facilities; fishing, golf, other sports nearby. Wheelchair access to restaurant only

⊖ No dogs; no smoking in dining-room

▭ Access, Visa

£ Single occupancy of twin/double £22 to £27, twin/double £44, family room £60 (4 people); deposit required. Alc L £12.50, D £19

---

*All entries in the* Guide *are rewritten every year, not least because standards fluctuate. Don't trust an out-of-date* Guide.

# Celtic Manor

COLDRA WOODS, NEWPORT, GWENT NP6 2YA
TEL: LLANWERN (0633) 413000   FAX: (0633) 412910

*Large and comfortable hotel with good sporting facilities.*

You can catch a glimpse of the Celtic Manor from the M4 but it's not until you pull up at the reception that the size of the hotel becomes apparent. The original manor, built in light stone, has had various extensions added and now boasts a large indoor swimming-pool, gym, sauna and two restaurants.

The public rooms are in the old part of the hotel and lead off from a sweeping wooden staircase and stained-glass decorated hallway. There's a peach-coloured bar with prints on the walls; a formal restaurant, Hedleys, with yet more stained-glass among oak-panelled walls and a huge fireplace. There's also a golden harp which is played on special occasions.

It's a plush backdrop for chef, Trefor Jones, who was Welsh Chef of the Year from 1989 to 1991. The cuisine is French-based and the wine list extensive. The bedrooms, some of which can be a few minutes' journey via lifts and long anonymous corridors, are of a good size and furnished with standard international hotel fittings. Another restaurant has been built in the glass conservatory and the passageway that leads to it is lined with signed photographs of rich and famous former guests: Tom Jones, Boy George, Terry Wogan . . .

○ *Open all year*

↗ *Leave the M4 at Junction 24 and take the A48 towards Newport. The hotel is 500 yards along this road on the right. Private car park*

🛏 *1 single, 25 twin, 40 double, 2 four-poster, 6 suites; all with bathroom/WC, TV, room service, hair-dryer, trouser-press; some rooms air-conditioned; baby-listening by arrangement; no tea/coffee-making facilities in rooms*

◇ *2 restaurants, 2 bars, lounge; conference facilities (max 300 people non-residential, 74*

*residential); tennis, riding, sauna/solarium, swimming-pool, gym, archery at hotel, other sports nearby. Wheelchair access to hotel and restaurant, 16 ground-level bedrooms*

● *No dogs*

▭ *Access, Amex, Diners, Visa*

£ *Single £84, single occupancy of twin/double £84, twin/double £99, four-poster £115, suite £150; deposit preferred. Continental B £5.50, cooked B £8.50; set L from £14, D from £17*

---

*Report forms are at the back of the book; write a letter if you prefer.*

**NORTHOP** CLWYD     **MAP 5**

# Soughton Hall

NORTHOP, MOLD, CLWYD CH7 6AB
TEL: NORTHOP (035 286) 811   FAX: (035 286) 382

*A stately hotel that is beautifully furnished and surprisingly informal.*

Soughton Hall is an impressive, mainly red-brick building, dating from the early 1700s. It commands a haughty position at the end of a tree-lined driveway. Having been part of the Wynne-Bankes family estate for centuries it was sold to the Rodenhursts in 1986.

The illusion of grandeur is shattered by a bone-rattling ride up the driveway, as you weave carefully between the free range sheep and the pot-holes. But the disgruntled visitor is soon calmed by the unusual style and comfort of the hotel. A great deal of effort has been put into the restoration of Soughton Hall. Each room is stuffed with original antiques and curios, from the French tapestries hanging in the lounge on the first floor, to the Persian carpets on parquet floors, and the mock bookshelf-door which leads to the Justice Room (now a bar). There is great attention to detail: brass coal scuttles gleam in the fireplace and the scent of well-polished wood mingles with that of fresh-cut flowers throughout the hotel.

The bedrooms are individual in character, with features to please all tastes. One bedroom has a cast-iron staircase which leads up to a garden-style bathroom planted with ornamental trees and shrubs. Despite the

-Soughton Hall-

apparent quality of the surroundings, the hotel is family-run and isn't formal. You feel as though you're visiting a lived-in stately home rather than a self-conscious country-house hotel. The meals have won various awards. On Saturdays, a local harpist plays while you eat.

◐ Open all year, exc first half Jan; restaurant closed some Suns

↗ 3 miles north of Mold. Take the A5119 from Mold or Northop; the Hall is off this road. Private car park

⇌ 5 twin, 5 double, 1 four-poster; all with shower/WC, exc four-poster with bathroom/WC; TV, room service, hair-dryer, trouser press in all rooms; no tea/coffee-making facilities in rooms

◈ Restaurant, bar, 2 lounges, library, private dining-room;

conference facilities (max 20 people non-residential, 11 residential); tennis, bicycles, at hotel, other sports nearby

● No wheelchair access; no children under 12; no dogs; no smoking in bedrooms

▭ Access, Amex, Visa

£ Single occupancy rate on request, twin/double £90 to £110, four-poster £110; deposit required. Alc L £15, D £30. Special breaks available

# Penally Abbey

PENALLY, NR TENBY, DYFED SA70 7BY
TEL: TENBY (0834) 3033/4714

*A friendly and hospitable hotel close to Tenby and the Pembrokeshire Coast National Park.*

'Come in, have a seat, would you like a cup of tea?' The Warrens are keen to make you feel welcome in their hotel. Even though you've only just arrived at Penally Abbey, you almost immediately find yourself sitting in the lounge sipping tea and devouring biscuits, swapping journey horror stories with Eileen or Steve Warren.

As our readers report, this is a place 'where the guest is a very special person'. The emphasis is on pleasing yourself, and so mealtimes are a flexible affair, breakfast is a leisurely meal, available almost until lunch-time, and dinner can be served until quite late in the evening. The food is home-cooked, but sometimes a bit slow in coming.

The hotel is a converted stone-walled, ivy-covered mansion beside a steep village green. Inside, the hotel has curiosities such as the Moorish arches above doorways, and more classical features such as the high ceilings and long windows overlooking the grounds. The bedrooms vary in style, some with satin and lace quilt covers, flowery wallpaper and antique furniture and several have four-poster beds.

◐ Open all year

↗ 1½ miles from Tenby, just off

the A4139 Pembroke coast road. Private car park

🛏 *1 single, 1 twin, 2 double, 6 four-poster; all with bathroom/ WC, TV, hair-dryer; limited room service*

◈ *Restaurant, bar, lounge, games room, conservatory, drying room; conference facilities (max 120 people non-residential, 10 residential); heated swimming-pool at hotel, other sports*

*nearby. Wheelchair access to hotel (1 step) and restaurant, 2 ground-floor bedrooms*

⊖ *No children under 7 in restaurant; no dogs; no smoking in restaurant*

▭ *Access, Visa*

💷 *Single £68, twin/double £88, four-poster £60 to £88. Set L £7.50, D £25; alc D £25*

---

**PORTFIELD GATE** DYFED                                                  **MAP 5**

# Sutton Lodge

---

PORTFIELD GATE, HAVERFORDWEST, DYFED SA62 3LN
TEL: HAVERFORDWEST (0437) 768548   FAX: (0437) 760826

*A peaceful bolt-hole for those who want to escape the rat-race without foregoing some luxuries.*

Down a lane in the heart of the Pembrokeshire countryside is a hotel hideaway for tired city dwellers. The hotel was once the home of a colonel who fought with the Duke of Wellington in the Napoleonic Wars and was a friend of Lord Byron.

A pot-pourri of styles has been tastefully stirred to give a relaxed feel. Salmon-pink sofas with pastel cushions, parquet floors and stripped pine doors in the lounge, while wicker chairs and tables are dotted amongst the greenery in the sun-warmed conservatory. The bedrooms have a cottagey feel with pine furniture, and bathrobes and televisions for those who can't completely cut themselves off from the rest of the world. One bedroom has an enormous claw-footed cast-iron bath, deep enough to soak away worries. For those with reclusive tendencies, there are some bedrooms in a converted dairy down a stepping-stone path at the end of the garden.

Meals are served in the main hotel in a rustic kitchen, or in the soft pink dining-room with red-and-black tiled floor and an old kitchen range. The quiet country character of Sutton Lodge is complemented by the more cosmopolitan delights from Stanford Moseley's kitchen, formerly chef at L'Escargot, the Mirabelle and Le Caprice of London. Co-owner Paul Rodwell looks after the business side of things and welcomes guests to the hotel. Fighter planes thundering overhead occasionally shatter the tranquillity during the day.

◑ *Closed Jan, Feb; restaurant closed Sun eve*

↗ *From Haverfordwest take the B4341 Broadhaven road to the village of Portfield. Take the*

*road to Sutton where directions are signposted. Private car park*

🛏 *2 twin, 3 double; all with bathroom/WC, TV, room service; hair-dryer on request*

◇ Dining-room, lounge, drying room, conservatory; golf, tennis, other sports nearby

● No wheelchair access; no

children under 12; no smoking in dining-room

▭ None accepted

£ Single occupancy of twin/double £38, twin/double £75. Set D £19

---

**PORTHKERRY** SOUTH GLAMORGAN                                              **MAP 5**

# Egerton Grey

---

PORTHKERRY, NR CARDIFF, SOUTH GLAMORGAN CF6 9BZ
TEL: RHOOSE (0446) 711666   FAX: (0446) 711690

*Immaculate country hotel and restaurant within striking distance of Cardiff.*

This nineteenth-century former rectory has been restored with care and a fine eye for detail. It stands in a secluded spot in seven acres of gardens, yet Cardiff Airport is only a few minutes away. The library has lemon yellow walls and the deep comfortable sofas are upholstered with confident floral designs – it works well. The Edwardian drawing-room has a polished wooden floor and soft rugs, light pink sofas and a piano.

Each bedroom is individually decorated with carefully considered combinations of bright fabrics and patterned wallpapers. They are very smart, but some may find them a touch impersonal. Meals are taken in a wood-panelled dining-room seated at high-back chairs to the sound of Radio 3. Service is very formal and correct, but it doesn't make for a particularly relaxed atmosphere. However, the food is excellent and immaculately presented. You might have something like kippers in tangy cream sauce to start, followed by lamb in a gentle marsala sauce. Vegetables are crisp and served separately so that the presentation of the main dish is not spoiled. The helpings are designed to make you relish each mouthful. There is an extensive wine list.

● Open all year

↗ Leave M4 at Junction 33 and follow signs to airport. Turn left at small roundabout at airport and left again after 400 yards. Private car park

🛏 1 single, 2 twin, 2 double, 1 four-poster, 2 family rooms, 2 suites; all with bathroom/WC exc 1 single with shower/WC; TV, room service, hair-dryer, trouser press in all rooms

◇ 2 restaurants, drawing-room, library, conservatory; conference facilities (max 30 people non-

residential, 10 residential); tennis, croquet at hotel, other sports nearby; babysitting by arrangement

● No wheelchair access; no dogs in public rooms

▭ Access, Amex, Visa

£ Single £50, single occupancy of twin/double £60 to £70, twin/double £65 to £75, four-poster £95 to £120, family room £75 to £95, suite £95 to £120; deposit required. Cooked B £4; set L, D £22.50 (prices till end 91). Special breaks available

**PRESTEIGNE** POWYS                                              **MAP 5**

# Radnorshire Arms

HIGH STREET, PRESTEIGNE, POWYS LD8 2BE
TEL: PRESTEIGNE (0544) 267406   FAX: (0544) 260418

*An attractive coaching-inn in Welsh border country. Expensive
rates for singles.*

This Elizabethan house has been a coaching-inn since 1792. Latterly
run by the Forte organisation, it is in good condition. The antique
atmosphere the inn exudes is complemented by a string of antique shops
in the High Street and reflected internally by creaking wooden floors,
beams and oak panelling. The bar, in particular, has a cosy, intimate feel
created by the lower-than-average beamed roof, dark oak panelling,
high-backed pews, hanging horse-brasses and copper pans, and furnishings in deep reds and greens. The bar is as popular with the locals as with
visitors, and so a friendly babble of noise rises each evening.

The oak dining-room and sitting-room are brighter rooms altogether
with higher ceilings, and windows which look over the garden to the side
of the hotel. The set evening menu has five courses which can be difficult
to finish, but there is always the option of the carte menu. Cream teas are
served to antique-browsing visitors in the sitting-room, but on warmer
days you can have the walled garden to yourself. The bedrooms in the
main house vary in size and standard, and are priced accordingly. A
couple of the more interesting rooms have beds made from traditional
panelling. The bedrooms in the rather uninspiring annexe aren't as
inviting.

◑ Open all year

🔼 In the centre of Presteigne.
Private car park

🛏 10 twin, 5 double, 1 half-tester
(family rooms available); all with
bathroom/WC, TV, baby-
listening, room service on request

◈ Restaurant, bar, 2 lounges;
conference facilities (max 30
people non-residential, 16
residential); fishing, golf, other
sports nearby; babysitting by
arrangement

⊖ No wheelchair access; no dogs in
public rooms; no smoking in
restaurant or in some bedrooms

▭ Access, Amex, Diners, Visa

£ Single occupancy of twin/double
£65 to £75; twin/double/half-
tester £80 to £85; children
sharing parents' room free;
deposit preferred. Continental B
£6, cooked B £8; Sun L £9; set D
£14; alc L £15. Special breaks
available

---

*If you have a small appetite, or just aren't feeling hungry, check if you can be
given a reduction if you don't want the full menu.*

# Hotel Portmeirion

PORTMEIRION, GWYNEDD LL48 6ET
TEL: PORTHMADOG (0766) 770228   TELEX: 61540 PORTM G
FAX: (0766) 771331

*An out-of-the-ordinary hotel in an Italianate village; set
curiously in the North Wales landscape.*

The village of Portmeirion is one of the most curious sights in Wales.
The brainchild of Sir Clough Williams-Ellis, Portmeirion was built in an
Italianate style to suit what he saw as the Mediterranean-type scenery on
Porthmadog Bay.

The main hotel is down on the quayside below the rest of the village
which is built at various levels up the headland of the rocky peninsula.
From here the magnificent scenery of North Wales unfolds with views
across the estuary to the hills of Snowdonia. Most of the bedrooms are in
the main hotel but others are available in the pastel-coloured buildings in
the village. Each bedroom is luxuriously furnished, most with antique
pieces, some with Chinese and Indian influences. The main hotel burnt
down in 1981 but has been faithfully restored to its former glory, with
some changes in design. 'I think I prefer the reopening-refurbishing of
the hotel,' comments one reader, 'not nearly as crazy as in the 50s and
60s, but a lot cleaner!'

The restaurant is in a bright conservatory-style room with polished
wooden floors and views over the estuary. The Jaipur Bar has solid wood
and brass chairs and low-level glass-topped tables with silk prints of
elephants on the walls. The Mirror room is a replica of the original
elegant sitting-room in cool blues with gilt-framed mirrors, but for
lounging comfort head for the hallway with comfy sofa and chairs and a
wood fire. Fresh flower arrangements throughout the hotel have also
been favourably remarked upon, although one reader didn't agree with
our assessment of the food and service last year: 'We were astonished to
read in your 1991 review of a disappointment with the food and "rather
sharp service". Our experience was the very reverse.'

◐ Open all year, exc 5 to 31 Jan

⤴ Mid-way between
Penrhyndeudraeth and
Porthmadog on the A470. Private
car park

🛏 12 twin, 7 double, 2 four-poster,
4 family rooms, 10 suites (most
rooms in village); all with
bathroom/WC, TV, room service,
hair-dryer

◈ Restaurant, 2 bars, 3 lounges,
drying room, library/study,

conservatory; conference
facilities (max 100 people non-
residential, 35 residential);
tennis, croquet, heated outdoor
swimming-pool (May to Sept) at
hotel, other sports nearby;
babysitting

⊖ No wheelchair access; no dogs;
no smoking in restaurant and
some public rooms

▭ Access, Amex, Diners, Visa

£ Single occupancy of twin/double

£67 to £82, twin/double £87 to
£102, four-poster £97 to £112,
suite £107 to £133, village room
£51 to £71; deposit required.

Continental B £5, cooked B
£7.50; set L £10, D £23. Special
breaks available

## PWLLHELI GWYNEDD                                MAP 5

# Plas Bodegroes

NEFYN ROAD, PWLLHELI, GWYNEDD LL53 5TH
TEL: PWLLHELI (0758) 612363   FAX: (0758) 701247

*An elegant country-house hotel in peaceful surroundings.*

Chris and Gunna Chown regard their hotel as a 'restaurant-with-rooms', but this shouldn't detract from the hotel itself. Plas Bodegroes is a Georgian house with creamy walls and a verandah which skirts the front of the building. Although only a couple of miles from the busy resort of Pwllheli, it is in a quiet spot, slightly inland from the coast.

You can while away a summer afternoon reading a book on the verandah or watching the birds dart across the lawn. Chris is the chef who, using local produce as much as possible, cooks in *nouvelle cuisine* style with delicate combinations of flavours. Gunna takes orders for dinner and serves dinner and drinks with quiet efficiency. The restaurant, like the rest of the house, is unfussy and chic, with fresh-cut flowers and fine china.

The restaurant is well known and open to non-residents, and thus on

-Plas Bodegroes-

some evenings can be very busy. There's a chintzy lounge, a bar and a separate breakfast room which catches the morning sun. The bedrooms have modern furnishings and are decorated in bold floral prints; two have four-poster beds.

◑ *Closed Nov to Feb, and Mons*

⤵ *From Bangor take the A487 and A499 to Pwllheli. Plas Bodegroes is on the A497 Nefyn road, one mile west of Pwllheli. Private car park*

🛏 *3 twin, 3 double, 2 four-poster; all with bathroom/WC, TV, room service, hair-dryer, baby-listening; no tea/coffee-making facilities in rooms*

◈ *2 restaurants, bar, lounge; conference facilities (max 12*

*people non-residential, 8 residential); croquet at hotel, other sports nearby. Wheelchair access to restaurant and WC (unisex) only*

⊖ *No dogs in public rooms; no smoking in restaurant, 1 no-smoking bedroom*

▭ *Access, Visa*

£ *Single occupancy of twin/double £45 to £55, twin/double £50 to £80, four-poster £60 to £90; deposit required. Set D £25*

---

**REYNOLDSTON** WEST GLAMORGAN                               **MAP 5**

# Fairyhill Country House

REYNOLDSTON, GOWER, SWANSEA, WEST GLAMORGAN SA3 1BS
TEL: GOWER (0792) 390139  FAX: (0792) 391358

*A carefully restored country house that manages to remain homely.*

This eighteenth-century stone-built and ivy-covered mansion might well have been a ruin by now if it had not been for the efforts of owners John and Midge Frayne. They restored the place, with the original intention of living there rather than turning it into an hotel. It stands in 24 acres of grounds and some outbuildings still await restoration.

It is a grand house, but much of its appeal rests with the unfussy way the interior has been restored. There's little antique furniture, so you don't feel as if you were staying in a stately home. Instead there are plain white walls, carpets with a swirly design and comfortable modern chairs. Added to this is Ceyln, a collie dog who has a habit of following guests around. Since last year the second lounge has been converted into a second dining-room, proof that the popularity of the restaurant is growing. A meal might include imaginative combinations of pigeon in raisin sauce or duck with strawberries. The bedrooms vary from large rather formal rooms overlooking the garden to small, less-imposing attic rooms above. Two extra bedrooms with a private sitting-room decorated with spears and a shield are available in the converted coach-house. They look out on a walled garden complete with a magnificent magnolia tree.

◑ *Open Mar to Oct; restaurant closed Sun eve, exc during summer*

⤵ *Leave the M4 at Junction 47 and follow sign to Gorseinon. At the main crossroads in Gorseinon* turn left at the lights, following signs to Gowerton. At the lights in Gowerton turn right and take the B4295 North Gower road through to Oldwalls. After passing the Greyhound Inn, Fairyhill is 1 mile further on. Private car park

🛏 3 single, 3 twin, 5 double, 1 cottage suite, 1 self-catering cottage; some with bathroom/WC, most with shower/WC, 1 public bathroom; TV in all

rooms; trouser press in 1 room

◇ 2 restaurants, bar, lounge, conservatory; fishing at hotel, other sports nearby

⊖ No wheelchair access; no dogs in public rooms

▭ Access, Visa

£ Single £65, single occupancy of twin/double £65, twin/double £75 to £85, cottage suite £140 to £170 (max 4 people); deposit required. Sun L £11; alc D £26

---

## ROSSETT CLWYD                                    MAP 5

# Llyndir Hall

LLYNDIR LANE, ROSSETT, CLWYD LL12 0AY
TEL: CHESTER (0244) 571648   FAX: (0244) 571258

*An efficiently run hotel with a lot of sporting facilities, but a rather soulless atmosphere.*

Llyndir Hall is a creamy-coloured country house at the end of a country lane which leads from the main road in Rossett. The hotel is in a fairly quiet setting in grounds surrounded by trees and rhododendron bushes, although some traffic noise can be heard in the distance. The hotel caters for business people, and so you may be asked which company you work for if you book a room on a weekday. Despite this, the hotel has its advantages for the private traveller. The bedrooms have every facility you might, or might not, need and are tastefully decorated in modern furnishings and bright floral patterns. For the energetic, there is a leisure club with a heated swimming-pool, spa pool, steam room, solarium and gym. The price of the rooms reflects the amount of facilities available, but special weekend rates are offered for golfing weekends and winter breaks.

The lounge and bar in rosy pinks and greens overlook the grounds, as does the restaurant with a conservatory-style extension into the garden. The dinner menu has light and delicately flavoured dishes, finishing with home-made chocolates and coffee. Breakfast is mostly self-service with a buffet of cheeses, cereals, an assortment of fruits and juices. Toast and coffee is brought by the waitress.

◑ Open all year

↗ From Chester take the A483 to Wrexham. At the junction with the A55, follow signs to Pulford. Continue through Pulford to Rossett and follow signs for the

hotel on the right. Private car park

🛏 7 single, 15 twin, 15 double, 1 suite (family rooms available); all with bathroom/WC, TV, room service, hair-dryer, trouser press, baby-listening; mini-bar on request

⊖ No dogs; no smoking in restaurant

◇ Restaurant, 2 bars, lounge, drying facilities; conference facilities (max 160 people non-residential, 38 residential); leisure club, gym, swimming-pool, sauna/solarium at hotel, other sports nearby; babysitting. Wheelchair access to hotel and restaurant, 10 ground-floor bedrooms, 1 specially equipped for the disabled

▭ Access, Amex, Diners, Visa

£ Single £70, single occupancy of twin/double £78, twin/double £95, suite £150; deposit required. Set L £14.50 to £17.50, D £14.50 to £26; alc L, D £28 (prices till Apr 92). Special breaks available

---

**RO-WEN** GWYNEDD · · · · · · · · · · · · · **MAP 5**

# Glyn Isa ✒

RO-WEN, NR CONWY, GWYNEDD LL32 8TP
TEL: TYN-Y-GROES (0492) 650242 FAX: (0492) 650063

*A no-frills hotel offering bed and breakfast at a moderate price.*

Glyn Isa is hidden away in the maze of lanes which criss-cross over the gently rolling farmland in the Conwy Valley. Situated on the outskirts of Snowdonia National Park, it's in a peaceful, rural spot near Ro-wen village.

Len and Pat Boud run the hotel and the well-stocked fishing lake, where, if you so choose, you can while away the hours fishing for trout. There is also a farm shop and smokery for fishy products. The hotel is in an eighteenth-century manor surrounded by trees; there are also self-catering cottages to the rear. It's the sort of place where you can take your children without worrying about fragile antique furniture and breakable ornaments.

The bedrooms are roomy, clean and unfussy, with candlewick bed-spreads and pine furniture. There's a lounge for guests which has a large colour television, upright piano, electric fire and magazines on a coffee table. The dining-room is also plainly furnished with wood floors, its large windows overlooking the gardens. Breakfast is served in a smaller room to the front of the house. Dinner is by prior arrangement only, but there are a couple of local pubs and a restaurant close by.

◐ Open all year, exc 2 weeks Xmas and New Year; restaurant closed Mon eve

⤤ From Conwy take the B5106 to Trefriw and turn right for Ro-wen immediately after Groes Inn. Glyn Isa is 1 mile on the right-hand side. Private car park

⇌ 2 twin, 3 double, 4 self-catering cottages; most with bathroom/WC, 1 with shower/WC, 1 public bathroom; room service in all rooms; TV, hair-dryer, trouser press on request

◇ Restaurant, breakfast room,

lounge, TV, drying room; fly-fishing at hotel, other sports nearby; babysitting. Wheelchair access to hotel and restaurant, ground-floor bedrooms in cottages

⊖ Dogs in 2 cottages only; no smoking in breakfast room

▭ None accepted

£ Single occupancy of twin/double £19, twin/double £34 to £38; cottage £153 to £315 per week (sleeps 4). Meals £3 to £6.50 (3pm to 6.30pm)

## TALSARNAU GWYNEDD

MAP 5

# Hotel Maes-y-Neuadd

TALSARNAU, NR HARLECH, GWYNEDD LL47 6YA
TEL: HARLECH (0766) 780200   FAX: (0766) 780211

*Peace and quiet in a fourteenth-century Welsh country house.*

Maes-y-Neuadd is a solid grey-stone building nestling amongst the trees in the hills rising up from Cardigan Bay. The hotel has undergone considerable alterations over the past year: the re-arrangement of the reception area; the addition of a small external lift at the entrance for those who find steps difficult to navigate; and a new conservatory-style lounge where you might find the resident golden labrador snoozing in the corner.

The original building dates from the mid-fourteenth century but the recent additions have been sympathetically co-ordinated. Each of the rooms are packed with Welsh artefacts such as a heavy oak chest, a grandfather clock and original paintings of the area. The bar to the rear of the house is a stone-walled room with leather chesterfields and a cast-iron stove at one end. The lounge is a calming place with peppermint walls and blue and pink chintzy chairs, and shares great views over Cardigan Bay with the restaurant. With the great bonus, one reader commented, of no Muzak in the dining-room. Andrew Taylor, the present chef, has been working at Maes-y-Neuadd for over a year now, and although the response to his creations has been varied, one reader commented: 'The present chef does not make the dishes too rich to enjoy for several days, and his soufflés are splendid.' The chairs in the dining-room have ladder-backs copied from the design of the balustraded banister which dates from the 1720s. The bedrooms are quite luxurious with individually designed rooms in bold colours, filled with antiques and locally crafted furniture. The larger suites are available in the adjoining Coach House block. The hotel is run by two couples, the Slatters and Horsfalls, whom readers commend for being as friendly as ever.

◑ Open all year, exc first 2 weeks Dec

⤢ 3½ miles north of Harlech on the B4573, take the right turn with the hotel sign on the corner.

Follow this lane for ½ mile to the hotel. Private car park

⇌ 1 single, 14 twin/double; 1 four-poster (some rooms in coach-house annexe); most with

bathroom/WC, some with
shower/WC; TV, room service,
hair-dryer in all rooms; baby-
listening on request; no tea/
coffee-making facilities in rooms

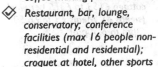 Restaurant, bar, lounge,
conservatory; conference
facilities (max 16 people non-
residential and residential);
croquet at hotel, other sports
nearby. Wheelchair access to
hotel (electric hoist), restaurant

and WC (M,F), 3 ground-floor
bedrooms

No children under 7; no dogs in
public rooms

Access, Amex, Diners, Visa

Single £43, single occupancy of
twin/double £94, twin/double/
four-poster £97; deposit
required. Set L £14, D £24.
Special breaks available

---

**TALYLLYN** GWYNEDD                                    **MAP 5**

# Minffordd Hotel

TALYLLYN, TYWYN, GWYNEDD LL36 9AJ
TEL: CORRIS (0654) 761665

The Minffordd was once a roadside inn and has a history of sheltering
tr elling folk since the 1700s. Sheep drovers, weary travellers and even
convicted criminals, on their way to the gallows in Shrewsbury, have slept
within its walls. Nestling at the foot of Cader Idris, it was once the only
inn for miles around. Today, the Pickles family carry on the ancient
tradition of hospitality. As one of our readers put it: 'It is like coming
home. We are not the only visitors who feel this way of course – all the
residents were returning rather than first-timers.'

   It's a small hotel and the feeling is one of intimacy, informality and
cosiness. The dining-room is in the centre of the house and has
whitewashed walls, beams, and a staircase winding up through the
middle. Jonathon Pickles, the son, is in charge of the kitchen and
produces good-value, home-made dinners, perfect for finishing off a day
after walking in the hills around Talyllyn. Breakfasts are especially
praised, with lots of choice (including porridge, to the delight of a very
small visitor who had his own little pot of brown sugar) and constant
replenishing of toast and tea or coffee.

   There is a bar and two sitting-rooms, one facing the garden, with cane
chairs and a games table, and the other with brown floral-patterned
armchairs. A couple of bedrooms are available on the ground floor for
those who would rather not negotiate stairs. All the bedrooms are *en suite*
(readers tell us a recently dug bore-hole gives a more plentiful water
supply) and have a comfortable cottagey style with pine or white wood
furniture. A holiday here means getting away from it all, with no
television, and newspapers which only arrive three days a week with the
milk deliveries.

○ Closed Jan to mid-Mar

⤴ At the junction of the A487 and

B4405, mid-way between
Dolgellau and Machynlleth.

Private car park

3 twin, 3 double; all with bathroom/WC, exc 1 double with shower/WC; hair-dryer in all rooms

Dining-room, bar, 2 lounges, laundry; fishing nearby

No wheelchair access; no children under 3; no dogs; no smoking in dining-room or bedrooms

Access, Diners, Visa

Single occupancy of twin/double £50 to £59, twin/double £80 to £98 (rates inc dinner); deposit required for stays of 3 days or more. Set D £15.50. Special breaks available

**THREE COCKS** POWYS                                        **MAP 5**

# Three Cocks Hotel

THREE COCKS, NR BRECON, POWYS LD3 0SL
TEL: GLASBURY (049 74) 215   From Nov 1991: GLASBURY (0497) 847215

*A fifteenth-century inn with cobbled forecourt, now a smart hotel with excellent French/Belgian cuisine.*

About ten miles from Brecon and five from Hay-on-Wye, this hotel is in an excellent position for visiting the towns or walking in the National Park. The proprietors, Michael and Marie-Jeanne Winstone, run the place in an efficient and formal way, enquiring after your well-being but not overwhelming you. Inside, the reception area is dominated by a large fireplace. There are a couple of easy chairs here, but the main lounge is up steps to the right. It's a large rectangular room and the pale wood panelling, cream rugs, pastel curtains and plain linen sofas make it light and airy, in contrast to the bare brick décor and leather furniture of the TV room in the basement.

The restaurant is simply decorated, having brick walls and hessian hangings. Food has a French/Belgian slant. Presentation is superb and service flawless, but you may find the helpings a little severe especially after a day tramping the Brecon Beacons. Breakfast is taken in a small room off the bar to the accompaniment of Radio 4.

The bedrooms are furnished with cotton floral duvet covers and matching wallpaper; in contrast to these are the heavy dark woods of the chests and dressers. Through the window you can see the Black Mountains, but a row of modern houses has made the view less splendid than before.

Closed Dec to mid-Feb; restaurant closed Tue

On the A438 between Brecon (11 miles) and Hereford (27 miles). Private car park

3 twin, 3 double, 1 family room; all with shower or bathroom/WC; hair-dryer, baby-listening on request; no tea/coffee-making facilities in rooms

Restaurant, 2 lounges, TV room; conference facilities (max 20 people); fishing, golf, riding, other sports nearby

No wheelchair access; no dogs

Access, Visa

Single occupancy of twin/double £38 to £53, twin/double £53. Set L, D £20; alc L, D £28. Special breaks available

# Parva Farmhouse

TINTERN, CHEPSTOW, GWENT NP6 6SQ
TEL: TINTERN (0291) 689411   FAX: (0291) 279298

*Good-value base in the Wye Valley.*

The magnificent ruins of Tintern Abbey are only a mile away, but you would never know it because it's round a bend in the River Wye. One end of the farmhouse is right on the main road, but the entrance is via a small alley off the road. There is a small car park, but beware, it joins the road on a blind corner so turning right can be quite dicey.

Personal ornaments and knick-knacks decorate Parva Farmhouse and help to convince you that it is not an hotel, but somebody's home. The sitting-room with its stone wall alongside the fireplace, wooden beams in the roof and red leather armchairs all around looks a comfortable and relaxed place. To underline this, there is an honesty bar in one corner, where guests help themselves and keep a tab in a notebook.

The small dining-room has snug alcoves if you want a little extra privacy. There's not a huge choice on the menu but the set-price four-course meal is good value. Upstairs, the rooms are large and furnished with cotton fabrics and pine and dark-wood fittings. Room seven has an unusual feature – a single four-poster bed, popular with children.

- ◑ Open all year
- ↗ On the northern edge of Tintern village on the A466, 50 yards from the banks of the River Wye. Private car park
- 🛏 3 double, 2 four-poster, 4 family rooms; most with bathroom/WC, some with shower/WC; TV, room service, hair-dryer, baby-listening in all rooms
- ◈ Restaurant, bar, lounge, drying room; conference facilities (max 15 people residential); fishing, riding, other sports nearby
- ⊖ No wheelchair access; no dogs in public rooms
- ▭ None accepted
- £ Single occupancy of double £32 to £36, double £42 to £54, four-poster £64, family room £42 to £54 (children under 13 free, others three-quarters rate); deposit required. Set D £15.50; alc D £19. Special breaks available

---

£   *This denotes that the hotel offers especially good value at whatever price level.*

---

✿   *This denotes that the hotel is in an exceptionally peaceful situation where you can be assured of a restful stay.*

**TRECASTLE** POWYS                    **MAP 5**

# Castle Hotel    ℒ

TRECASTLE, POWYS LD3 8UH
TEL: SENNYBRIDGE (0874) 636354

*A busy, family-run inn offering good facilities for families at reasonable rates.*

The Castle Hotel is a small, bustling hive of activity on the main road through the small village of Trecastle. It is on the northern borders of the Brecon Beacons, and the surrounding countryside is magnificent for those keen on walking, fishing, climbing or pony-trekking.

The main bar in the hotel is a haven often frequented by locals and visitors touring the National Park. Bar food is moderate in price and competent – home-cooked ham in freshly cut bread. The bedrooms are plain and simple, with modern and pine furnishings; not all of them are *en suite*. The better rooms are on the upper floors. Efforts have been made to make families welcome; family rooms are available with bunk-beds for the kids, and arrangements can be made for babysitting. The residents' lounge is rather poky, but televisions are provided in all bedrooms. The restaurant is behind the bar to the back of the hotel and is open to the general public – the fare is surprisingly varied for such a small hotel, and reasonably priced.

◑ Open all year; restaurant closed Sun, Mon eves

🔁 On the A40, 12 miles west of Brecon, 7 miles east of Llandovery. Private car park

🛏 3 twin, 4 double, 1 four-poster, 1 family room, 1 suite; some with bathroom/WC, some with shower/WC; TV, baby-listening in all rooms; hair-dryer on request

◈ Restaurant, bar, lounge; conference facilities (max 16 people non-residential, 10 residential); fishing, riding nearby; babysitting. Wheelchair access to restaurant only

⊖ No dogs in public rooms

▭ Access, Visa

£ Single occupancy of twin/double £23 to £33, twin/double/four-poster £36 to £45, family room £36 to £55, suite £55. Alc L £3 to £10, D £8 to £15. Special breaks available

---

*You will find report forms at the back of the Guide – please use them!*

---

*All rooms have tea/coffee-making facilities unless we mention to the contrary.*

# The Crown at Whitebrook

WHITEBROOK, NR MONMOUTH, GWENT NP5 4TX
TEL: MONMOUTH (0600) 860254   FAX: (0600) 860607

*A peaceful spot with fine food served in unpretentious surroundings.*

Set deep in the woods of the Wye Valley, the Crown is an unexceptional white building that hugs the steep valley sides beside a narrow lane. It's a secluded spot and you can hear a babbling brook through an open window at the front of the hotel. The sign that hangs outside the building honestly describes the Crown as a restaurant-with-rooms.

The restaurant is building a fine reputation for itself under the supervision of owners Sandra and Roger Bates. There is a fixed price, three-course menu with over half-a-dozen choices for each course. The cuisine is French and there is a long, predominantly French, wine list, boosted by a few Australian bottles. The public rooms on the ground floor are open-plan. Through the front door is the bar which is comfortable but unremarkable; then a bistro-style restaurant leads to a small breakfast room. The oldest bedrooms are on the first floor – bright, with lightly varnished wood and hessian-decorated furniture and simple cotton fabrics and duvet covers. An extension has been added to the top floor, where again the rooms are cheerful and cosy, although on the small side.

- Closed 3 weeks Jan
- 5 miles south of Monmouth between the A466 and B4293. Private car park
- 3 twin, 8 double, 1 four-poster; all with bathroom/WC, TV, room service, hair-dryer
- Restaurant, bar, lounge; conference facilities (max 20 people non-residential, 12 residential); fishing, riding, other sports nearby. Wheelchair access to restaurant only
- No dogs in restaurant
- Access, Amex, Diners, Visa
- Single occupancy of twin/double £66, twin/double £112, four-poster £125 (rates inc dinner); deposit required. Set L £13, D £22 (prices till Jan 92). Special breaks available

---

*If you have a small appetite, or just aren't feeling hungry, check if you can be given a reduction if you don't want the full menu.*

---

*Many hotels offer special rates for stays of a few nights or more. It is worth enquiring when you book.*

**WOLF'S CASTLE** DYFED                                    **MAP 5**

# Wolfscastle Country Hotel

WOLF'S CASTLE, NR HAVERFORDWEST, DYFED SA62 5LZ
TEL: TREFFGARNE (043 787) 225/688   FAX: (043 787) 383

*An unpretentious and lively hotel and squash club. Popular with non-residents, so it's not particularly peaceful.*

The hotel is close to the Pembrokeshire Coast Path and the Presely Hills. Two large extensions, one a hundred-seater function room and the other consisting of two squash courts, have changed the character of what would otherwise have been a rather sleepy village hotel. This is a bustling, busy meeting place. It's a large, two-storey, stone-fronted building and the extensions have been added on out of sight at the back.

Squash is the theme, and judging by trophies and photographs that hang in the hallway the owner Andrew Stirling is a player of considerable repute. He runs a relaxed place. Freshly showered squash players come for a reviving beer in the bar, easing themselves into one of the deep comfortable chairs. The menu in the restaurant is not particularly adventurous, but the helpings are good-sized and the food well cooked, which is why the place is popular and frequented by local people.

Bedrooms are adequate and decorated with a hotchpotch of furniture styles. Last year we said that it is best to book a room away from the squash courts so the sound of ball on wall does not disturb you. This year we should add that rooms near the function room extension can suffer from the noise of late-night parties.

◐ Open all year

⬕ 6 miles north of Haverfordwest on the A40, in village of Wolf's Castle. Private car park

🛏 3 single, 3 twin, 12 double, 2 four-poster; all with shower or bathroom/WC, TV, room service

◇ Restaurant, bar, lounge, drying room; conference facilities (max 180 people non-residential, 20 residential); tennis, squash at hotel, other sports nearby. Wheelchair access to public areas only

⊖ Dogs in bedrooms by arrangement only

▭ Access, Amex, Visa

£ Single £36, single occupancy of twin/double £42, twin/double £64, four-poster £64. Bar snacks; alc D £17; Sun L £12. Special breaks available

---

*Prices are quoted* per room *rather than* per person.

---

*We mention those hotels that don't accept dogs; guide dogs, however, are almost always an exception. Telephone ahead to make sure!*

# CHANNEL ISLANDS

**HERM** CHANNEL ISLANDS    **MAP 8**

# White House Hotel

HERM, VIA GUERNSEY, CHANNEL ISLANDS
TEL: GUERNSEY (0481) 722159   FAX: (0481) 710066

*Affordable and well-run hotel on a beautiful island; popular, especially with older visitors.*

More people make the 20-minute boat ride to Herm from Guernsey than visit any of Guernsey's own attractions. This tiny, car-free island couldn't be more appealing for a family outing. Come early evening and the glory of one of the most beautiful spots in the Channel Islands reveals itself to the island's handful of inhabitants and the guests of its only hotel.

Standing just up from the harbour, yards from the island's pub, post office and couple of shops, the hotel is in the thick of things. Most of the bedrooms are in the three pastel-coloured cottages in the 'village', perhaps a hundred yards from the main building. That guests can relax under parasols in cushioned sun-loungers on the cottages' neat lawns surrounded by colourful borders somewhat makes up for disappointing interiors – the furniture being modern and plain. Rooms in the main building cost slightly more; some have splendid balconies. The quality of furnishings in the public rooms far surpasses that of the bedrooms.

One reader who has holidayed here for the past four years wrote to urge its inclusion in the Guide for the high standards in the dining-room. Some of the round tables in the light, wooden-block floored room, though set for two, could host a party. Meals are enhanced by a decent wine list, brisk service by young staff over for the summer and dreamy sunsets.

- ◑ Closed from mid-Oct to 2 weeks prior to Easter
- ⤢ Herm is reached by flights or ferries from Guernsey
- ⇌ 2 single, 23 twin/double, 7 family rooms (some rooms in annexe); all with bathroom/WC, baby-listening
- ◈ 2 restaurants, 2 bars, 3 lounges; heated swimming-pool, tennis at hotel, sea-fishing nearby
- ⊖ No wheelchair access; no dogs
- ▤ Access, Visa
- ⊞ Single £43 to £48, single occupancy of twin/double £49 to £72, twin/double £100 to £110 (rates inc dinner); deposit required. Set L £6, £10.50, D £13.50

---

*Are you aware of your rights as a consumer when you book into an hotel? Check them out on page 13.*

---

*Congratulations to Cumbria – our number 1 county with 53 full entries in this year's Guide.*

**ROZEL BAY** JERSEY                                      **MAP 8**

# Château La Chaire

ROZEL BAY, ST MARTIN'S, JERSEY, CHANNEL ISLANDS
TEL: JERSEY (0534) 63354    TELEX: 437334 HATCRT G
FAX: (0534) 65137

*Book well in advance for this remarkably affordable, luxurious
country-house hotel.*

Splendid cliff walks from small bay to bay make the north coast of Jersey
the island's most scenic part. Rozel, in the north east, is one of the
smaller and quieter spots, for its beach is poor. You can walk to the hotel
from the sea front either up the valley road or climb steep steps and
descend to the building through its seven acres of terraced woodland.
Drinking or dining on the suntrapped terrace to the sounds of a bubbling
fountain surrounded by flowers and trees, you feel sea views can be
overrated.

The interior manages to be sumptuous without being overpowering.
The beauty of intricate multicoloured stucco work in the rococo
drawing-room is stunning; the oak-panelled dining-room with ruched-
curtained conservatory provides the right sense of occasion. Bedrooms
are named after flowers and have strong colour schemes and smart
furniture and fabrics. Rooms might have a balcony, a big sofa, curtains
round a chrome-tapped Jacuzzi bath, a pelmeted or four-poster bed; the
sloping attic ceilings of cheaper rooms on the top floor reduce their size.

◑ Open all year

� Approach Rozel village on B38,
take first turning on left; hotel is
100 yards further down the road.
Private car park

🛏 12 twin/double, 1 four-poster; all
with bathroom/WC, TV, room
service, hair-dryer, trouser press;
tea/coffee-making facilities on
request

◈ 3 restaurants, bar, lounge;
conference facilities (max 25

people non-residential, 12
residential); golf, fishing, water
sports nearby

⊖ No wheelchair access; no
children under 7; no dogs

▭ Access, Amex, Diners, Visa

£ Single occupancy of twin/double
£52 to £100, twin/double £74 to
£115, four-poster £95 to £125;
deposit required. Set L £10.50,
£14, D £19.50; alc L, D £25.
Special breaks available

---

*See the back of the* Guide *for an index of hotels listed.*

---

*Hotels in our* Visitors' Book *towards the end of the* Guide *are additional
hotels that may be worth a visit. Reports on these hotels are welcome.*

**ST AUBINS** JERSEY                                    **MAP 8**

# Old Court House Inn

ST AUBINS HARBOUR, JERSEY, CHANNEL ISLANDS
TEL: JERSEY (0534) 46433    FAX: (0534) 45103

*An atmospheric harbourside hotel with a popular restaurant and comfortable rooms.*

The TV series *Bergerac* and Jersey seem to have become inextricably linked. Regular viewers of the programme will instantly recognise the Mizzen mast bar at the Old Court House, with its galleon-style windows as the Royal Barge pub from the series. More importantly it is also where you order dinner. The menu, a large plastic-coated 'steakhouse' affair, does little to inspire confidence but the food, once you've deciphered the large à la carte choice, is excellent. All dishes are lightly and freshly cooked and seafood and fish merit a special mention. For those who dislike the idea of raw oysters the grilled Jersey oysters with Gruyère are a gentle and delicious introduction. Puddings are something of a disappointment. The restaurant is extremely popular and although the hotel is keen to try to accommodate residents it's worth booking a table when you book your room.

Morning clatter and haphazard service are definite weaknesses. As the day goes on, the bars fill with a local yachting crowd quaffing pints – a jovial place for a drink if you're in the mood. At night the harbour is surprisingly quiet so you don't need to worry about noise if you have a room with a view at the front of the hotel. The rooms are some of the most tastefully decorated in the Channel Islands although they lack good chairs.

- ◑ Open all year
- ⚡ At St Aubins on the harbour front. On-street parking difficult
- 🛏 2 single, 7 twin, 1 double, 1 suite; all with bathroom/WC, TV
- ◇ 2 restaurants, 3 bars, lounge, drying room; fishing, golf, other sports nearby
- ⬤ No wheelchair access; no children; no dogs
- ▭ Access, Visa
- £ Single £35 to £45, single occupancy of twin/double £53 to £70, twin/double £80, suite £60 to £75; deposit required. Set D £14.50, Sun L £10.50; alc L £15, D £20 (prices till Easter 92). Special breaks available

---

*Shame on you South Yorkshire, Tyne & Wear and Mid Glamorgan, the only counties without an hotel of merit in this year's Guide.*

**ST BRELADE** JERSEY                                    **MAP 8**

# La Place Hotel

ROUTE DU COIN, LA HAULE, ST BRELADE, JERSEY
TEL: JERSEY (0534) 44261    TELEX: 4192522 LAPLAZ G
FAX: (0534) 45164

*A comfortable, peaceful, well-run hotel taking a mix of business
and holiday trade.*

La Place is part white-rendered, part stone (formerly a seventeenth-
century farmhouse) and was once owned by Françoise de la Place whose
initials are etched in the south courtyard. Now the building is greatly
altered and added to, with modern wings stretching alongside two inner
courtyards. One is flagged, set with spruce gingham-clothed tables for
drinks or lunches amid neat shrub and flower borders; the other contains
a sheltered swimming-pool. The more expensive bedrooms face the pool
terrace, each with its own little hedged patio for sunbathing.

The interior of the hotel is somewhat mixed. The large, well-
proportioned sitting-room, where comfortably upholstered sofas and
armchairs are casually placed around occasional tables strewn with
magazines, resembles a country house. The Cartwheel restaurant has
white monogramed Rosenthal china and stately needlepoint carvers
which don't quite gel with the false timbered ceiling studded with wheel-
like light fittings, or the relentless piped music that drips like some
Chinese water torture over the diners. The cocktail bar belongs to a more
contemporary mode: curved bamboo chairs stained a fierce apple green
with peach cushions spill out towards the pool terrace. Bedrooms are
light and well equipped, furnished in heavy, modern, mostly floral
fabrics. All have peaceful views over gardens or the swimming-pool.

Food is fairly ambitious, with many Frenchified meat and seafood
dishes. There's a firm insistence on 'correct dress' for dinner – out of
deference to the ladies, declares the brochure – but it's hard to assess
whether this is merely an attempt to prevent people from turning up for
dinner in their vests. In the mornings you may have curried kedgeree or
excellent porridge laden with Jersey cream. A pity there's no brown
sugar, and that the jams and marmalades should be from such horridly
wrapped little packs.

◑ *Closed Nov to Mar*

🏊 *4 miles from St Helier, off the
B25 to St Aubin's Bay. Private
car park*

🛏 *36 twin/double, 2 family rooms,
2 suites; all with bathroom/WC,
TV, room service, hair-dryer,
trouser press, baby-listening; no
tea/coffee-making facilities in
rooms*

🍽 *Restaurant, bar, 2 lounges,
laundry room; conference
facilities (max 40 people
residential and non-residential);
sauna, outdoor heated
swimming-pool at hotel, golf,
water sports nearby. Wheelchair
access to hotel and restaurant,
11 ground-floor bedrooms*

⛔ *No children under 7 in*

restaurant eves; dogs by
arrangement only

▭ Access, Amex, Diners, Visa

£ Single occupancy of twin/double
£36 to £56, twin/double £71 to

£120, suite £111 to £150, family
room rate on application; deposit
required. Set L £9, D £18; alc L,
D £29.50. Special breaks
available

---

# Sea Crest

PETIT PORT, ST BRELADE, JERSEY, CHANNEL ISLANDS JE3 8HH
TEL: JERSEY (0534) 46353   FAX: (0534) 47316

*Recently revamped hotel/restaurant still finding its feet under new*
*ownership, but offering ambitious food and accommodation.*

The Sea Crest Hotel is a white, modern building to the north of Corbière
(a rugged peninsula which attracts sightseers on fine days). For many
years under previous ownership it built up an enviable reputation for
carefully prepared and adventurous seafood, and a less than enviable one
for its hideous mustard-coloured, leather-look furnishings. Now, under
the recent new ownership of a husband-and-wife team, Julian and
Martha Bernstein, all the mustard leatherette has been swept away, to be
replaced by smart duck-egg blue contract furnishings in public areas,
and striking, carefully matched yellow and blue modern fabrics with
toning background wallpapers in all the bedrooms.

   Attractive modern prints adorn the restaurant. Unfortunately, something of the old rough magic of the kitchen has also gone out with the
bath water. The food, though ambitious and appetising on the menu, is
not always as carefully presented as it should be. Service, on the other
hand, is constantly solicitous: barely a mouthful is swallowed before yet
another enquiry is made about your enjoyment levels. There's no doubt
that the Bernsteins and their courteous, friendly staff are making a
genuine effort to make guests feel welcome and thoroughly looked after:
names are remembered; bags are carried; everyone gets a personal word
from Julian Bernstein at dinner; and lone diners are attended to with
special care.

   Views from the hotel are not universally remarkable, but the attractively landscaped split-level gardens and pool terrace around the hotel
compensate, and are sensibly hedged against on-shore winds.

◑ Open all year; restaurant closed
Mon eve

🡕 Five minutes' drive from the Red
Houses shopping centre, near
the Corbière lighthouse. Private
car park

🛏 5 twin, 2 double; all with
bathroom/WC, TV, room service,

baby-listening; hair-dryer on
request

◈ Restaurant (air-conditioned); bar,
2 lounges; unheated swimming-
pool at hotel, other sports
nearby; babysitting

⊖ No wheelchair access; no
children under 5; no dogs

▭ Access, Amex, Visa

£ Single occupancy of twin/double
£50 to £53, twin/double £80 to

£85; deposit required. Set L £12;
alc L £20, D £30

---

## ST BRELADE'S BAY JERSEY                              MAP 8

# Hotel L'Horizon

ST BRELADE'S BAY, JERSEY, CHANNEL ISLANDS
TEL: JERSEY (0534) 43101    TELEX: 4192281 ORIZON G
FAX: (0534) 46269

*Well-established upmarket chain hotel, corporately smart but also surprisingly friendly.*

It's easy to see why St Brelade's Bay has attracted such a sizeable proportion of Jersey's holiday business. The beach is a remarkable crescent of golden sand fringed by unspoilt headlands. Most of it is too appealing to leave untouched, however, and L'Horizon occupies a royal box position along the centre of the developed seafront. Its functional modern architecture, while not hideous, does little for the surroundings, but certainly from *inside* the hotel the views are terrific, and there's safe, direct access to the beach with no roads to cross.

Furnishings in its capacious lounges include wing armchairs and matching sofas in needlepoint upholstery, blending into a more contemporary rattan in the bars. The acreages of similar colourings seem a bit wearisome and public rooms too grandiose. L'Horizon's clients are a mix of well-heeled tourists and smart business people. Here you can consume, maybe, a designer sandwich on the terrace, a simple steak or snack in the Brasserie watching activities in the indoor pool and Jacuzzi, a traditional table d'hôte meal in the formal restaurant, or an imaginative business lunch in the sumptuously decorated Star Grill, where oriental bird frescos and boudoir wallpapers in luscious pinks encase a dining area of bamboo chairs. Piped music and foreign accents flow softly among the well-spaced tables. Both service and food are elaborate but extremely good. Staff are obliging rather than superior.

The bedrooms are conventionally spacious, smart and comfortable with expensive modern matching fabrics and well-equipped bathrooms, magic remote-control curtain-opening devices in some rooms, and tremendous views from the balconies at the front.

● Open all year

↗ A 10-minute drive from Jersey
Airport. Private car park

🛏 10 single, 87 twin, 4 double, 1
four-poster, 3 suites; all with
bathroom/WC, TV, room service,
hair-dryer, trouser press, baby-

listening; no tea/coffee-making
facilities in rooms

◈ 3 restaurants, 3 bars, 2 lounges,
library; conference facilities (max
150 people non-residential, 100
residential); heated swimming-
pool, gym, sauna, motor yacht at

hotel, fishing, golf, other sports nearby; babysitting on request. Wheelchair access to hotel, restaurant and WC (M,F), no ground-floor bedrooms but a lift

⊖ No dogs; 1 restaurant is non-smoking

▭ Access, Visa

💷 Single £75 to £85, single occupancy of twin/double £128, twin/double £150 to £170, four poster £170. Set L £14, D £23; alc L £25, D £35. Special breaks available

**ST JOHN** JERSEY                              **MAP 8**

# Idlerocks Hotel

BONNE NUIT BAY, ST JOHN, JERSEY, CHANNEL ISLANDS
TEL: JERSEY (0534) 61633   FAX: (0534) 64800

*A quiet, intimate hotel with views of Jersey's unspoilt north coast, and good bedrooms.*

So low-slung is this modest hotel on the steep cliffs above Bonne Nuit Bay that you might well miss it without the roadside sign. Its most striking exterior feature is a stumpy roundish tower, half stone, half tile-hung, by the entrance door. At the back, café-style blue and white awnings shade the big windows and french doors lead into its small, well-kept gardens. From here, above the sheltering hedges, the eye ranges far and wide over the rocky bay and the fishing boats tethered near the beach. This is a piece of Jersey's least exploited coastline: the green and gorse-splashed headlands unbuilt-up; the tiny rural lanes and cliff paths uncongested except in high season. Just three small hotels and a sprinkling of houses command the views around the bay. Once you're installed at Idlerocks, local entertainment is limited to wholesome hilly walks, afternoon teas on the terrace, or a boat trip.

The street-level entrance is higher than the garden side of the hotel, so you step down an open wooden staircase from the reception desk to its three small public rooms. To your right is a pine-panelled bar of curiously dated green chairs and matching bar-stools, to the left the dining-room of plain modern ladder backed chairs and primly folded pink napkins. In between these at the foot of the stairs, inevitably something of a thoroughfare, is a small sitting-room where three or four people could comfortably watch television, or inspect the bookshelf laden with a variety of holiday paperbacks and *National Geographic* magazines. The furnishings are simple enough, but there's a well-kept and personal air about the ornaments, potted plants and fresh flowers that many similar small hotels on this island lack.

Idlerocks' bedrooms, after the modest introduction of the lower floors, are a pleasant surprise. Neutral creams prevail, but the effect is a positive statement of taste, rather than a mere reluctance to offend. The quality of fabrics and furnishings is high, at least in the best rooms which have sea views and balconies. Keen swimmers should note that Bonne Nuit Bay is not Jersey's best or safest beach. Unless you're content to stay put with lots of books, a car is advisable.

◑ Open all year, exc Oct

⤴ North of the island. Near television mast. Take the A9 to Bonne Nuit Bay. Private car park.

🛏 1 single, 8 twin, 4 double, 1 family; some with bathroom/WC, most with shower/WC; TV, room service in all rooms

◈ Dining-room, bar, lounge, drying-room; heated swimming-pool at

hotel, fishing, riding nearby

⊖ No wheelchair access; no children under 4; no dogs; no smoking in bedrooms

▭ None accepted

£ Single £34 to £36, single occupancy of twin/double £45 to £50, twin/double £68 to £72, family room £102 (rates inc dinner); deposit required

---

**ST MARTIN'S** GUERNSEY                                    **MAP 8**

# Bella Luce

MOULIN HUET, ST MARTIN'S, GUERNSEY, CHANNEL ISLANDS
TEL: GUERNSEY (0481) 38764   FAX: (0481) 39561

*A simple, conventional hotel with few pretensions but lacking style. Located in a beautiful corner of Guernsey.*

The Moulin Huet area of Guernsey is the most attractive part of the island. The Bella Luce, one of the island's original Norman buildings, is set in quiet leafy lanes leading down to Moulin Huet Bay, which has a couple of excellent beaches and dramatic cliff walks and views. The hotel promises much from the outside: well-tended lawns and a pool surrounded by sun-loungers, traditional stone walls and freshly painted windows; but it delivers a little less.

The décor of the corridors and bedrooms is simple (walls freshly emulsioned), but a little bland. Ecclesiastical etchings, subdued prints and drab brown doors line the walls. In the restaurant, the colour scheme livens up and you'll be seeing red: red cloths, red paper napkins, red candles at dinner. Even the waiters and waitresses wear red with natty black bow-ties. Are they trying to carry off some Italian theme? If so, it doesn't extend as far as the food which is plentiful and perfectly adequate if a little stodgy. That the restaurant is so popular on Saturdays speaks volumes for the quality of Guernsey's other hostelries. Perhaps the real attraction is a characterful, lively bar with suits of armour providing a talking point.

◑ Open all year

⤴ From harbour or airport head for St Martin's parish in the south of the island. Private car park

🛏 3 single, 13 twin, 8 double, 7

family rooms; most with bathroom/WC, some with shower/WC; room service, baby-listening in all rooms; no tea/coffee-making facilities in rooms

Restaurant (air-conditioned), bar, lounge; sauna/solarium, heated swimming-pool at hotel, other sports nearby. Wheelchair access to hotel and restaurant, 3 ground-floor bedrooms

 No dogs in public rooms, small dogs only in bedrooms; some

public rooms non-smoking

Access, Visa

Single £22 to £42, single occupancy of twin/double £70, twin/double £40 to £80, family room from £40; deposit required. Set D £10. Special breaks available

# Idlerocks Hotel

JERBOURG ROAD, ST MARTIN'S, GUERNSEY, CHANNEL ISLANDS
TEL: GUERNSEY (0481) 37711   FAX: (0481) 35592

*A smartly renovated, energetically run hotel in a splendid cliff-top location.*

Idlerocks is one of the few Channel Island hotels that take full advantage of their position. Too many fail to live up to the promise of their beautiful settings. But the new husband-and-wife team has lifted this hotel completely above the lacklustre norm of some of its sea-view competitors, with excellent facilities and stylish furnishings. It's as well, though, to specify in advance if you want a view of the sea: the front rooms are definitely the ones to go for, even if they cost a bit more, and these fill up fast.

From these, or the bar-lounge and restaurant, you can see Herm, Alderney and Sark on a clear day. In sea mists the mournful eerie note of the foghorn echoes around this scenic headland to warn shipping off the treacherous coastal rocks. The hotel, smartly painted and renovated within the past couple of years, stands alone above a steeply sloping green hillside on Guernsey's south-east tip. A maze of cliff paths lead along the winding wild coastline where idyllic uncommercialised sandy bays await the dedicated walker who can cope with the gradients. Though isolated, Idlerocks is not cut off. A St Peter Port bus pauses in the turning circle at the end of the drive about every half-hour, and holiday flights are met by the hotel's courtesy minibus.

In sunny weather Idlerocks is a delight, attracting many visitors for terrace teas or bar lunches. Its facilities are good enough to make it a comfortable hideaway in poor weather, too. From most of its public rooms you can enjoy the views through a safe screen of picture window if it's too chilly or damp to be outside. A cosily furnished quiet reading or games room with books and a card table supplements the cheerful colonial-looking Raffles Pavilion bar-lounge with its bamboo screen and potted plants. In the Admiral's Restaurant a smart dark blue and pink scheme of contemporary furnishings sets off the nautical pictures round the walls and the well-spaced opulently decked tables, where a high-chair takes the edge off the formality. It's a family place, and the obedient house dogs are as welcoming as their owners. Bedrooms are well equipped and practical, easy on the eye with matching fabrics and light, modern fittings. The corners have not been cut at Idlerocks, and managerial hands with much experience of hotels and restaurants seem firmly on the tiller.

○ Open all year

🡵 10 minutes' drive from the airport and St Peter Port. Private car park

🛏 2 single, 13 twin, 8 double, 5 family rooms; most with bathroom/WC, some with shower/WC; TV, room service, hair-dryer, baby-listening in all rooms; trouser press in some rooms

◇ Restaurant, bar, lounge, drying room, study; conference facilities (max 130 people non-residential, 28 residential); heated

swimming-pool at hotel, golf, fishing, other sports nearby; babysitting. Wheelchair access to hotel and restaurant, 8 ground-floor bedrooms

● No dogs; no smoking in bedrooms

▭ Access, Amex, Visa

£ Single £23 to £40, single occupancy of twin/double £30 to £55, twin/double from £60 to £110; deposit required. Set D £12.50; alc D £18. Special breaks available

**ST OUEN** JERSEY                                                    **MAP 8**

# The Lobster Pot

L'ETACQ, ST OUEN, JERSEY, CHANNEL ISLANDS
TEL: JERSEY (0534) 82888   FAX: (0534) 81574

*A popular and cheerful restaurant-with-rooms where the seafood is more sophisticated than the décor.*

From the front windows of this well-kept seventeenth-century stone building you get a majestic view of the five-mile surfing beach over the grey-roofed houses of the village. Virtually all its grounds lie under tarmac to accommodate the dozens of cars and coaches that make their way here. At its south end a small walled garden (the 'Floral Patio') of raised flower-beds interspersed with tables and parasols suggests *al fresco* lunches and afternoon teas.

Inside, a universal brushstroke of crimson velveteen and dark wood has been applied through both bars and the restaurant. Shotguns, horse-brasses, copper bric-à-brac, cartwheels and even an eponymous lobster pot decorate the beams. The style is reassuringly familiar – a cosy foil, like the piped music (live with dancing at night), to the important business of this place, which is the food. The bar menu is not too thrilling, and details, such as the coffee, could be improved. Book ahead to avoid disappointment in the restaurant, and try out les homards eight ways, les huîtres Rockefeller, or les coquilles St Jacques parisienne.

The reception lobby and stairway are adorned with pictures of glowing beech forests and improbably static waves. Upstairs is a range of plainish but well-equipped bedrooms, which are light and fresh. The best and most expensive overlook the beach, and the master bedroom has the original granite wall exposed as a feature at one end.

◑ *Open all year*

⤢ *On the west coast of Jersey, overlooking St Ouen's Bay. Private car park*

🛏 *3 twin, 10 double; all with bathroom/WC, TV, room service, hair-dryer, trouser press, mini-bar*

◈ *Restaurant (air-conditioned), bar,*

*lounge; golf, water sports nearby. Wheelchair access to restaurant and WC (M,F) only*

⊖ *No dogs*

▭ *Access, Amex, Diners, Visa*

£ *Single occupancy of twin/double £46 to £64, twin/double £72 to £108; deposit required. Set L £10, D £14. Special breaks available*

---

**ST PETER PORT** GUERNSEY                                      **MAP 8**

# La Collinette

ST JACQUES, ST PETER PORT, GUERNSEY, CHANNEL ISLANDS
TEL: GUERNSEY (0481) 710331   FAX: (0481) 713516

*A family-oriented, well-run hotel with a relaxing air and good facilities.*

This attractive, wistaria-draped white house in a quiet part of the rising land above St Peter Port is the home of the Chambers family. Unusually for a smartly furnished hotel, it welcomes children of any age, not grudgingly, but wholeheartedly, with high teas and free teddy bears. Families may prefer the self-catering units at the back of the garden.

The hotel's exterior attractions include a large swimming-pool (and a children's pool) surrounded by well-kept gardens. The large cantilevered rooms of the modern wings overlook the pool area. All the rooms, though variable in size and style, are very well furnished in traditional styles with restful colour schemes and matching fabrics. The large light bathrooms are a particularly good feature.

Downstairs, public rooms include a quiet lounge furnished with comfortably arranged chairs and burgundy chesterfields. Tartan carpets do not augur well in many hotels, but seem perfectly appropriate in the Bear bar, a civilised and animated room of racing green walls full of cricketing memorabilia and bar games. A jolly menu of simple hot dishes and snacks is available at lunchtimes and evenings. The bear, a stuffed version that presumably once danced or was baited, stands in a corner near the entrance. The restaurant is a split-level room of flame-coloured ruched curtains overlooking the rear gardens. A collection of old jugs and liquor casks fills several shelves.

◑ *Open all year, exc 23 Dec to 2 Jan*

⤢ *Short walk from the centre of town. Private car park*

2 single, 11 twin, 5 double, 5 family suites, 7 cottages; most with bathroom/WC, some with shower/WC; TV, room service, hair-dryer, trouser press, baby-listening in all rooms

Restaurant, bar, lounge, games room, drying room; conference facilities (max 40 people non-residential, 30 residential); sauna/solarium, heated swimming-pool, spa bath at hotel, other sports nearby;

babysitting. Wheelchair access to restaurant only

No dogs; no smoking in restaurant

Access, Amex, Diners, Visa

Single £30 to £38, single occupancy of twin/double £45 to £53, twin/double £60 to £76, family suite £90 to £114, cottages £200 to £500 per week; deposit required. Set L £9, D £11; alc L, D £15. Special breaks available

# Midhurst House

CANDIE ROAD, ST PETER PORT, GUERNSEY, CHANNEL ISLANDS
TEL: GUERNSEY (0481) 724391

*A civilised, quiet guesthouse whose exceptional standards of food and comfort outweigh its limitations of size and public rooms.*

Midhurst House is one of those delightful one-offs that refuses to fit artificial rules about square-footage of bathmats or number of coat-hangers. It's a smallish Regency terraced house, obviously a family home, in a classy residential bit of St Peter Port.

The communal space in the house is limited by its (listed) architecture: the lounge has elegant features (a classically tiled floor, a pine Adam-style fireplace, large ornamental potted plants, restful pictures and comfortable green armchairs), but it is rather a thoroughfare between the small and somewhat cramped dining-area and the garden wing. Bedrooms, all different, vary from the tall-windowed, stately proportioned rooms in the main house where antiques and floor-to-ceiling curtains add opulent touches, to the newer rooms in the garden wing which are smaller, with light modern furnishings. All have good bathrooms.

What makes Midhurst House so constantly popular are its owners, who work very hard to make guests feel welcome and well-fed. Dinners, served at 6.30pm, are four-course meals with two or three choices of freshly prepared ingredients. Attempts are made to suit any special requirements, but orders are expected in advance. Home-made soups, bread, ice-cream and pastries are features. Midhurst is not suitable for boisterousness, nor will it charm people who demand absolute privacy during an hotel stay – social contact is unavoidable.

Closed Nov to Easter

The hotel is adjacent to Candie Gardens and the Beau Séjour leisure centre. Private garaging

3 twin, 3 double, 1 family room; some with bathroom/WC, most with shower/WC; TV in all rooms

◈ Dining-room, lounge

⬤ No wheelchair access; no children under 8; no dogs; no smoking in dining-room

▭ Access

£ Single occupancy of twin/double £30, twin/double £44 to £56, children half price; deposit required. Set D £7.50; alc D £18

---

# Old Government House

---

ANN'S PLACE, ST PETER PORT, GUERNSEY, CHANNEL ISLANDS
TEL: GUERNSEY (0481) 724921   TELEX: 4191144
FAX: (0481) 724429

*A well-established traditional hotel situated above St Peter Port.*

At night, a perplexing blue neon sign lights up the sky on the steeply rising land behind the port. 'OGH' it reads. The uninitiated mind wanders. Some sort of seafarer's institution, perhaps: 'Organisation for Guernsey Harbourmasters'? Not at all. Old Government House, once the official residence of the Governors of Guernsey, reckons it hardly needs spelling out.

It's been much modernised and added to since the old days (1858) when it was first converted to an hotel. It's friendly, though scarcely intimate; the public rooms darkish and clubby, reeking of an insistent application of furniture polish. Reaching a bedroom may involve a maze of corridors, lifts and passageways, so complex is this building. But they haven't stinted on the furnishings; the bedrooms, variable in type and tariff, are stylish and handsomely fitted out. Front rooms overlook the roofs of the town towards the sea. The hotel's facilities include a nightclub called Scarletts, a sheltered pool, dinner dances to live bands and satellite TV. As might be expected from its ambassadorial history, etiquette is observed at OGH, so remember your jacket and tie.

◗ Open all year

🔁 A few minutes' walk from the centre of St Peter Port. Private car park

🛏 26 single, 46 twin/double; all with bathroom/WC, TV, room service, hair-dryer, trouser press, baby-listening; no tea/coffee-making facilities in rooms

◈ Restaurant, 3 bars, lounge; conference facilities (max 120 people non-residential, 72

residential); sauna/solarium, heated outdoor swimming-pool at hotel, other sports nearby; babysitting

⬤ No wheelchair access; no dogs in public rooms

▭ Access, Amex, Diners, Visa

£ Twin/double £87 to £116; deposit required. Set L £7.50, D £12.50; alc L £12, D £17 (prices till end 91). Special breaks available

# St Pierre Park

ST PETER PORT, GUERNSEY, CHANNEL ISLANDS
TEL: GUERNSEY (0481) 728282   TELEX: 4191662 STPPRK G
FAX: (0481) 712041

*A modern luxury hotel in parkland. If you make full use of its
extensive facilities, the pricy tariff could be reasonable value.*

Part of this hotel's 45 acres of parkland includes a nine-hole golf course
designed by Tony Jacklin, and a lake with fountain. Snooker rooms,
tennis courts, gyms, saunas and steam rooms, a fine indoor swimming-
pool and Jacuzzi set the tone. If you like this kind of thing, St Pierre
Park's steep price-tag may seem less awesome, for all the facilities are
free to resident guests.

Inevitably, this type of hotel takes a large chunk of business trade, so
don't expect a conventional holiday hotel. The building rises to four
storeys, with dormer windows in a red-tiled mansard roof. Piped music
whirls round the interior. There are pseudo-classical motifs of moulded
architraves and plush blue carpets. The lounge is full of classy contract
reproduction furniture: curvy clubby chairs and two pianos – or could it
be the same one reflected in a mirror? The Victor Hugo restaurant is
darkish by day, formally intimate by night, with pinnied and authentically
French waiters artfully dodging among the elegant green dining-chairs.
For less daunting dining, the Café Renoir offers an attractive mix of light
lunches, snacks and teas served by pleasant boater-clad young women
amid a haze of subtle pinks and ruched blinds. Instead of fresh flowers on
the tables, little vases contain paintbrushes and feathers.

In the bedrooms, the specially commissioned pastel bedcovers cost
over £800, and the rest, if not particularly interesting, is of a suitably
opulent standard.

◐ Open all year

⏻ The hotel is a few minutes' drive
westwards from central St Peter
Port. Private car park

🛏 79 twin, 50 double, 6 suites; all
with bathroom/WC, TV, room
service, hair-dryer, trouser press,
baby-listening

◈ 2 restaurants, 4 bars, lounge,
games room; air-conditioning
throughout hotel; conference
facilities (max 300 people non-
residential, 135 residential); golf,
tennis, sauna/solarium, heated

swimming-pool, beauty
treatment rooms at hotel;
babysitting. Wheelchair access to
hotel (ramp), restaurant and WC
(unisex), 17 ground-floor
bedrooms

⊖ No dogs

▭ Access, Amex, Diners, Visa

£ Single occupancy of twin/double
£85, twin/double/family room
£125, suite £205 to £240;
deposit required. Set L £10, D
£14.50; alc L £16, D £28.
Special breaks available

*Dog lovers: some hotels not only welcome dogs, but they provide gourmet
meals for them. Ask.*

ST SAVIOUR JERSEY                                   MAP 8

# Longueville Manor

LONGUEVILLE ROAD, ST SAVIOUR, JERSEY JE2 7SA
TEL: JERSEY (0534) 25501   TELEX: 4192306 LMHJY G   FAX: (0534) 31613

*A long-established and successful country-house hotel.*

Longueville is a proper manor in the distinctive Channel Island mode, and the local history book by the bedside is full of fiefdoms and seigneurial anecdotes dating from the thirteenth century. Today, Longueville Manor is smoothly run by two families, the third generation Lewises, and Sue and Malcolm Dufty. The formula is well tested and brings much repeat business, despite the steep tariff.

The house stands only a mile and a half from the traffic-choked heart of St Helier, but you wouldn't guess that from the birdsong in this sheltered dell of fields and gardens. As you sweep into the drive from the suburban Longueville Road, the façade of the house is a motley assortment of styles: part tile-hung, part stone with a seventeenth-century archway, part dull modern rendering on newer extensions. At the back a tall stone tower adds a touch of feudal charm, though the fabric of the building today is much altered from its medieval origins. Inside, the country-house style is consistent. Mostly floral but not ostentatious fabrics and wallpapers prevail, colour schemes tending towards pinks and blues. It feels comfortable and nothing jars; log fires blaze even in May at tea-time, softly upholstered armchairs are loaded with cushions,

-Longueville Manor-

and the tall casement windows overlook the gardens. Bedrooms are carefully and individually decorated in a mixture of traditional furnishings and contemporary fabrics; all are inviting enough to use as sitting-rooms.

A boxer dog or two may greet you in the hallway with such Jeeves-like suavity that you could imagine they ran the place. They may just peep briefly into the bar lounge – 'Did Madam ring?' – but even the most rabid dog-hater could scarcely object to these well-mannered creatures. An aristocratic long-haired cat slumbers on a cushion, obviously considering useful activity ill-bred. Waterfowl and a few interloping seagulls inspect the small lake beyond the oval swimming-pool. Ponies stick their heads over half-doors in a discreetly hidden stable-block beyond. Lawns and ornamental urns crammed with wallflowers or other seasonal offerings lead your eye towards a screen of trees.

The restaurant hums with chic accents as French and German visitors test their discriminating palates and superior bank balances on the food. Andrew Baird dishes up elaborate gourmet menus with unforced panache. A larger section of the dining-room (the smokers' bit, used for breakfast) may lack some of the dusky character of the ancient oak panelling timbers and high-backed carvers of the non-smoking part, but has advantages of garden views.

◗ Open all year

⤤ Take the A3 from Georgetown to Longueville. Private car park

🛏 24 twin, 5 double, 1 four-poster, 2 suites; all with bathroom/WC, TV, room service, hair-dryer; no tea/coffee-making facilities in rooms

◈ Restaurant (air-conditioned), bar, 2 lounges; conference facilities (max 18 people residential and non-residential); heated swimming-pool at hotel, fishing, golf, other sports nearby.

Wheelchair access to hotel, restaurant and WC, 8 ground-floor bedrooms and lift

⊖ No children under 7; no dogs in public rooms

▭ Access, Amex, Diners, Visa

£ Single occupancy of twin/double £115 to £135, twin/double from £115 to £191, four-poster from £147 to £168, suite from £225 to £265; deposit required. Set L £19.50, D £28; alc D £38. Special breaks available

---

**ST SAVIOUR'S** GUERNSEY                                    **MAP 8**

# La Hougue Fouque Farm

BAS COURTILS, ST SAVIOUR'S, GUERNSEY, CHANNEL ISLANDS
TEL: GUERNSEY (0481) 64181

*There are few signs left of the former farm in this safe, unsophisticated hotel.*

An experienced hand (the owners, the Nussbaumers, have been here since the early 1970s) somehow makes La Houque Fouque succeed despite some poor touches: bedrooms are decorated in faded brown floral wallpaper and the backless picture frames reveal wallpaper between picture and wood; there is also a gaudy orange-patterned carpet in the hall.

The stone-and-granite building stands in a quiet inland position surrounded by cultivated fields. Your hosts cater enthusiastically for warm weather with a pleasant small garden, a decent swimming-pool, lots of plastic chairs and parasols, and wooden benches and tables in the courtyard next to a barbecue. The building's odd arrangement means you have to pop in and out to get to some rooms, and a corridor doubles as a sitting-room. The large bar, with tables and wooden round-back chairs, and the long, purple-curtained dining-room with fake-leather-studded chairs (cosily candlelit for dinner, dark for breakfast) absorbs plenty of non-residential trade. An unexceptional dinner comprises a good-value table d'hôte menu and plenty of à la carte choice; expect big platters of food.

◖ Open all year

↗ Near Little Chapel (Les Vauxbelets) heading towards Strawberry Farm. Private car park

🛏 4 twin, 5 double, 4 family rooms, 2 suites; all with bathroom/WC, TV, baby-listening; hair-dryer, trouser press, mini-bar in suites

◇ 2 restaurants, bar, lounge, drying room (air-conditioning in all public rooms); heated swimming-pool at hotel, golf, other sports nearby; babysitting. Wheelchair access to hotel, restaurants and WC (M,F), 2 ground-floor bedrooms

⊖ No dogs

▭ Access, Visa

£ Single occupancy of twin/double £42 to £46, twin/double £44 to £52, suite £64 to £72; deposit required. Set L £8.50, D £12; alc L £12, D £15

# Les Piques Farm

ST SAVIOUR'S, GUERNSEY
TEL: GUERNSEY (0481) 64515   FAX: (0481) 65857

*Well-loved stone farmhouse blending olde-worlde charm with fresh, cottagey bedrooms furnished to a high standard.*

You need a good map to find Les Piques, but if you head for the Strawberry Farm, a popular Guernsey attraction, you won't be far away. Though only a guesthouse, it has a faithful band of admirers, some of whom return regularly for John and Chris Trimby's peaceful brand of rest and recreation.

Les Piques has a reassuring, well-established air: the Trimbys are enterprising folk, and have steadily made alterations over the years to accommodate more visitors and more diners. So, rather sadly, the lovely big stone-fireplaced lounge that was once such a feature of the house is now part of a larger dining-room, and sitting areas are confined to the convivial bar. An elaborate chess set provides some interest in a small waiting-room of a lounge, its pawns fashioned as fully rigged tea-clippers or Spanish galleons.

The lack of a thoroughly appealing lounge seems the only serious drawback to this exceptionally pleasant guesthouse. Outside it's a long, low stone building, skilfully added to in places, with interesting Gothic-style double windows. Parts of the original farmhouse date from the fifteenth century, and the huge stone-beamed fireplaces still make a fine impact (on your head if you're more than averagely tall) in several rooms. Bedrooms are personal but unfussy, individually decorated with matching light spriggy fabrics – poppies in one of the most popular rooms. Most of the bedrooms have views over daisied lawns. Dinner is in the cosy, beamed and stone dining-room with horse-brasses and wheelback chairs; or a conservatory extension beyond with white garden-look furniture and the scent of freesias.

● Closed Nov to Mar

⤴ Head in direction of Strawberry Farm and Woodcarvers, both of which are signposted; Les Piques is very close by. Private car park

🛏 2 single, 9 twin, 14 double; some with bathroom/WC, most with shower/WC; TV in all rooms;

hair-dryer, trouser press in some rooms

◈ 3 dining-rooms, bar, lounge

● No wheelchair access; no children under 10; no dogs

▭ None accepted

£ Single £23 to £31; twin/double £40 to £62; deposit required. Set D £9.50; alc D £10 to £14

---

**SARK** CHANNEL ISLANDS                                   **MAP 8**

# Le Petit Champ

SARK, VIA GUERNSEY, CHANNEL ISLANDS
TEL: SARK (0481) 832046

*A clifftop hotel with stunning views. The welcome and conviviality make it easy to forgive a few minor problems.*

Sark, 45 minutes by boat from Guernsey, has no cars, a population of a little over 500 and 40 miles of coast and cliffs. Le Petit Champ is about five minutes by bike from the village, more like ten going back as it's a fairly steep climb up a bumpy track – entertaining if attempted at night.

Guests return year after year and become firm friends with the hospitable Scott family; new arrivals are just as welcome. It's a modern building although the original stone walls from the turn of the century peak out in places. Décor is dated and a little drab but despite this, the lounges running the length of the house are popular for tea and a good place to enjoy a good book. Le Petit Champ and Sark are all about relaxing and it's easy to forget the lurid carpet in your bedroom and even the slightly over-zealous delivery of early-morning tea to the room next door which ensures that you won't sleep too late.

Over breakfast, the day's weather forecast is handed round making it easy to plan the day. If you're at a loss for where to walk or what to see, ask the Scotts. They request that you order dinner early as this makes life in the kitchen a little easier. A table d'hôte menu comprising three to five dishes for each course is enterprising but not over-ambitious.

◑ Closed Oct to Apr

↗ On the western coast of Sark. No cars allowed on Sark

🛏 3 single, 8 twin, 3 double, 2 family rooms; most with bathroom/WC, some with shower/WC; no tea/coffee-making facilities in rooms

◇ 3 restaurants, bar, 3 lounges, TV room, drying room, library;

fishing, tennis, other sports nearby

⊖ No wheelchair access; no children under 7; no dogs; smoking in specified areas only

▭ Access, Amex, Diners, Visa

£ Single £43, single occupancy of twin/double £60 to £68, twin/double £80 to £90, family room £108 to £135; deposit required. Set D £15.50; alc L, D from £13

# La Sablonnerie

SARK, VIA GUERNSEY, CHANNEL ISLANDS
TEL: SARK (0481) 832061

*La Sablonnerie's idiosyncratically simple but sophisticated charm makes it a Channel Island gem.*

Philip meets you at the boat quay to fetch your luggage by tractor. There are no planes, no trains, no automobiles on Sark, and the roads are mere tracks. To reach La Sablonnerie on Little Sark, you have to cross La Coupée. Mervyn Peake enthusiasts will remember Mr Pye's winged passage across this alarming ridge just the width of a horse-drawn carriage, with suicidal drops to tiny grey beaches on either side.

Little Sark is the quietest and most magical part of this extraordinary island. Here, by the ancient silver mines, is a small cluster of rambling stone farmhouses. La Sablonnerie is one of these, its grey-tiled roof with blue dormer windows sloping down over white-painted, creeper-festooned walls. The gardens behind are an oasis for birds and afternoon teas. La Sablonnerie is owned and run by the Sark-born Perée family, now mostly by son and daughter Philip and Elizabeth. Guests meet and rapidly mingle in the royal blue bar/lounge of the main house, where log fires blaze and you can work up an appetite after healthy walks for a hearty but classy five-course dinner, bustlingly served through a kitchen hatch with a piercingly audible running commentary from staff: 'Has Table Five got its vegetables yet?' Or at breakfast: 'No black pudding for Mrs Jones, please.'

Despite the hideaway locality of Little Sark, La Sablonnerie is not a place for the firmly anti-social. The atmosphere soon develops into something of a house-party, especially since many guests are regular visitors. Some of the bathroom arrangements may startle: one small single requires a trip through both sitting-room and part of the dining-room to reach the nearest loo, so is definitely not for shrinking violets.

○ Closed mid-Oct to mid-Apr

↗ At the southern end of the island. No cars allowed on Sark

🛏 6 single, 14 twin/double, 1 suite; most with bathroom/WC, some with shower/WC; room service, baby-listening in all rooms; no tea/coffee-making facilities in rooms

◇ 2 restaurants, 2 bars, 2 lounges, conservatory; fishing, tennis, riding nearby

● No wheelchair access; no dogs in public rooms and in some bedrooms by arrangement only

▭ Access, Amex, Visa

£ Single £25 to £30, twin/double £50 to £60, suite £55 to £65; deposit required. Set L £15, D £18 (10% service charge added)

# Hotels from our Visitors' Book

Here is a collection of hotels that are worth considering but which we think do not yet merit a full entry. They are marked on the maps at the back of the Guide with an open triangle. Please note that some towns marked with a black triangle (denoting a full entry) also contain one of our 'Visitors' Book' hotels. Not all counties (or regions in Scotland) are represented.

The price given for each hotel is the standard cost of a twin-bedded or double room, and is the latest available as we go to press. Prices may go up sometime in 1992.

We would be particularly pleased to receive reports on these hotels.

## LONDON
**MAPS 10/11**

SW19  **Cannizaro House** West Side   Wimbledon Common
081-879 1464
*Country-house hotel somewhat lacking in individuality but with parkland running up to its back door.   From £110*

SW7  **5 Sumner Place** 5 Sumner Place   071-584 7586
*Spick and span guesthouse in the smartest part of South Kensington.   £89*

E1  **Tower Thistle** St Katharine's Way   071-481 2575
*Massive concrete and glass ziggurat chain hotel wonderfully positioned next to Tower Bridge.   £139*

WC2  **Waldorf** Aldwych   071-836 2400
*A grand Edwardian hotel in Forte style; tea dances in its magnificent Palm Court make up for wear and tear in places.   £155*

SW1  **Wilbraham** Wilbraham Place   071-730 8296
*Benevolent, good-value but fusty hotel with a buttery.   £73 to £80*

## ENGLAND

## Avon
**MAP 9**

Bath  **Bath Spa Hotel** Sydney Road   (0225) 444424
*Newly opened, huge and opulent Forte hotel near the centre with fine decorative detail. Leisure facilities but unappealing grounds.   £150*

Bath  **Cliffe Hotel** Crowe Hill   Limpley Stoke   (0225) 723226
*Country house near Bath. Strong on facilities, weak on personality. £77 to £97*

Bath  **Leighton House** 139 Wells Road   (0225) 314769
*Welcoming Victorian guesthouse on city periphery. Good all-rounder. £52 to £56*

Bath  **Somerset House** 35 Bathwick Hill   (0225) 466451
*Georgian house on busy road. Some cheery, some dour furnishings. £47 to £59*

---

*Prices are quoted per room rather than per person.*

Bristol   **Avon Gorge Hotel** Sion Hill   Clifton˙   (0272) 738955
*Large chain hotel in excellent position overlooking the gorge and suspension bridge.   £105*

# Bedfordshire                                                    MAP 7

Bedford   **Bedford Swan** The Embankment   (0234) 346565
*A straightforward town-centre hotel with luxurious swimming-pool.   £78*
Woburn   **Bell Inn** 21 Bedford Street   (0525) 290280
*A small family-run restaurant-with-rooms that has expanded into Georgian buildings on the other side of the A5130. Noise-conscious guests should ask for rooms at the back.   From £75*

# Berkshire                                                       MAP 9

Windsor   **Aurora Garden** 14 Bolton Avenue   (0753) 868686
*A small, bright and breezy suburban hotel close to the famous Long Walk through Windsor Great Park.   £72*

# Buckinghamshire                                               MAPS 6/9

Marlow Bottom   **Holly Tree House** Burford Close   (0628) 891110
*A modern, immaculate, top-of-the-range B&B with friendly hosts in a slightly soulless satellite suburb of Marlow.   £55 to £60*

# Cambridgeshire                                                  MAP 7

Cambridge   **Cambridge Lodge** 139 Huntingdon Road   (0223) 352833
*Small, comfortable Edwardian house with open fires and a popular restaurant.   £67 to £80*

Cambridge   **University Arms Hotel** Regent Street   (0223) 351241
*Large Edwardian city-centre hotel belonging to the De Vere chain. Grand-scale public rooms. Pretty bedrooms.   £98 to £102*

Wansford   **Haycock Hotel** Peterborough (0780) 782223
*Well-run and busy business/function hotel in old coaching inn. Just off the A1. Excellent bedrooms.   £89*

# Cheshire                                                        MAP 4

Knutsford   **Cottons Hotel** Manchester Road   (0565) 650333
*Distinctive but pricey business hotel with good leisure facilities.   £80 to £113*

# Cornwall                                                        MAP 8

Little Petherick   **Old Mill Country House** nr Padstow   (0841) 540388
*Attractively converted sixteenth-century watermill with homely, inexpensive bedrooms. On a main road.   £37 to £46*

Port Isaac   **Long Cross Victorian Hotel** Trelights (0208) 880243
*Small hotel in a large, Victorian house near restored gardens – done up to Victorian hilt.   £50*

Portscatho    **Roseland House Hotel** Rosevine    (087 258) 644
*Traditional mid-size hotel on a well-known peninsula. Fabulous spot above the sea and friendly hosts.* £70 to £86 (rate inc. dinner)

St Ives    **Garrack Hotel** Burthallan Lane    (0736) 796199
*A family-run hotel set high above the bay at the south end of St Ives.* £53 to £80

St Keyne    **The Old Rectory** Liskeard    (0579) 42617
*Victorian house in lovely isolated spot with some weighty Victorian décor. Several awkwardly shaped bedrooms.    Good value.* £52

# Cumbria                                                    **MAP 3**

Ambleside    **Three Shires Inn** Little Langdale    (096 67) 215
*Beautifully situated inn at the heart of the Lake District. Plain, small bedrooms – the best are those at the front in the old part.* £84 (rate inc. dinner)

Bowness-on-Windermere    **Linthwaite House** Crook Road
(096 62) 88600
*Recently revamped country-house hotel with considerable flair.* £90 to £102

Elterwater    **The Britannia Inn** nr Ambleside    (096 67) 382
*Traditional inn in an exceptionally attractive location. Comfortable rooms.* £37 to £54

Rosthwaite    **Royal Oak Hotel** (076 87) 77214
*Unpretentious, simple but cosy accommodation in a grand location. Great for walkers.* £62 (rate inc. dinner)

Watermillock    **Rampsbeck Country House Hotel**    (07684) 86442
*Traditional country-house hotel in smashing position on the shores of Ullswater.* £60 to £90

Windermere    **Hawksmoor Guesthouse** Lake Road    (096 62) 2110
*Value for money in spruce, well-kept guesthouse that is carefully managed by friendly owners.* £42 to £50

# Derbyshire                                                 **MAP 4**

Hathersage    **Highlow Hall** (0433) 50393
*A large castellated stone manor house at the centre of a working farm. Quite simple accommodation but a very peaceful spot.    B&B only.* £36

Newton Solney    **Newton Park Hotel** (0283) 703568
*An eighteenth-century baronial house that attracts a considerable business clientele and is priced accordingly.* £66 to £95

# Devon                                                      **MAP 8**

Bishop's Tawton    **Downrew House** (0271) 42497
*Expensive rooms, but an unassuming old hotel with good leisure facilities.* £104 (rate inc. dinner)

Branscombe    **The Masons Arms** (029 780) 300
*Nice old village inn done up with style. Rooms vary enormously. Neither cheap nor cosy.* £40 to £70

Chagford    **Thornworthy House**    (064 73) 3297
*Beautifully located and stylish country house. Prices rather steep,
food so-so.*   £65

Clawton    **Court Barn** Holsworthy    (0409 27) 219
*Nicely cluttered Victorian house in quiet grounds. Small and very
friendly.*   £106 (rate inc. dinner)

Kingsbridge    **Buckland-Tout-Saints** Goveton    (0548) 853055
*At the end of a single track road, this Queen Anne manor offers good food and
a peaceful position.*   £105

Lifton    **Arundell Arms** Lifton    (0566) 84666
*Fishermen's hotel on busy road with sophisticated public rooms and good food
but uninspired bedrooms.*   £81

Lydford    **Castle Inn**    (082 282) 242
*Classic but unpretentious village pub with pretty English castle as a
neighbour.*   £35 to £45

Lynton    **Combe Park** Hillsford Bridges    (0598) 52356
*Former hunting lodge in quiet, pretty grounds. Very friendly. Simple, tidy
bedrooms.* £57 to £80

Maidencombe    **Orestone Manor Hotel** Rockhouse Lane
(0803) 328098
*Unremarkably furnished country house with excellent location, very cheery
resident proprietors and super bedrooms.*   £70 to £83

Woolacombe    **Watersmeet Hotel** Mortehoe    (0271) 870333
*Spacious Edwardian hotel with perfect seaside position and good, homely
décor.  No-frills food.*   £94 to £134 (rate inc. dinner)

# Dorset                                               MAP 9

Blandford Forum    **La Belle Alliance** White Cliff Mill Street
(0258) 452842
*Comfortable restaurant-with-rooms on the main road.*   £62

Bournemouth    **Highcliff** St Michael's Road    (0202) 557702
*Huge, staid hotel towering above the sea. Reasonable rates for short breaks.
Now part of the Swallow Group.*   £100 to £120

# Co Durham                                            MAP 3

Durham    **Royal County Hotel** Old Elvet    091-386 6821
*Large, city-centre hotel overlooking River Wear, with leisure and conference
facilities.*   £95

# East Sussex                                          MAP 10

Alfriston    **George Inn**    (0323) 870319
*Lots of fifteenth-century atmosphere and good-value food; noisy front
rooms.*   £60 to £72

Brighton    **The Grand** King's Road    (0273) 21188
*Grand, expensively refitted Victorian seafront hotel.*   £100 to £150

Lewes   **Millers** 134 High Street   (0273) 475631
*Friendly and beautifully decorated old B&B; streetside bedrooms suffer from noise.* £35 to £42

Pevensey   **Priory Court** Pevensey Bay   (0323) 763150
*Old pub next to the castle; decent rooms, unsophisticated food.* £38 to £48

Rushlake Green   **Stone House**   (0435) 830553
*A lovely family manor for nearly 500 years; beautiful grounds; gradually becoming more hotel-like.* £92 to £163

Uckfield   **Hooke Hall** 250 High Street   (0825) 761578
*Cosy Queen Anne house with idiosyncratic furnishings and strong interior design.* £45 to £90

# Essex       **MAPS 7/10**

Coggeshall   **White Hart Hotel** Market End   (0376) 561654
*Well-furnished ancient inn in town centre much used for small conferences. Some bedrooms are too small for their executive goodies.* £82

Dedham   **Dedham Hall** Brook Street   (0206) 323027
*Old country house and restaurant just outside the village. Some dowdiness. New owners since February 1991.* £60

# Gloucestershire       **MAP 6**

Cheltenham   **Lypiatt House** Lypiatt Road   (0242) 224994
*Pretty Victorian villa with elegant public rooms and plainer bedrooms, some suffering from traffic noise. Guests may feel pushed out by corporate business.* £58

Fossebridge   **Fossebridge Inn**   (0285) 720721
*Old coaching inn with pretty gardens next to the River Colne. Good bar food.* £45 to £75

Minchinhampton   **Burleigh Court**   (0453) 883804
*Very friendly family-run Georgian hotel on a hillside overlooking Stroud; problems with housekeeping when we inspected.* £78

# Hampshire       **MAP 9**

Basingstoke   **Audleys Wood** Alton Road   (0256) 817555
*Rather impersonal Thistle-run Victorian country-house hotel; impressive mod cons in the rooms; ambitious food.* £80 to £102+

Lyndhurst   **Parkhill Hotel** Beaulieu Road   (0703) 282944
*A well-furnished Georgian country house surrounded by parkland on the edge of the New Forest.* £93 to £103

Rogate   **Wakeham Wood**   (0730) 821529
*Unexceptional, good-value B&B in a quiet position with views of the Downs.* £34 to £36

Sparsholt   **Lainston House Hotel**   (0962) 63588
*A beautiful, company-owned William and Mary house situated in parkland.* £115 to £145

# Hereford & Worcester                        **MAPS 5/6**

Broadway    **Leasow House** Laverton Meadow    (038 673) 526
*Friendly B&B offering good-value accommodation in an old Cotswold
farmhouse.   £43 to £51*

Weston under Penyard    **Wharton Lodge** Ross-on-Wye    (0989) 81795
*Swish, slightly soulless, country-house-style hotel with developing walled
garden. Attentive service.   £115 to £130*

# Hertfordshire                               **MAPS 7/10**

Harpenden    **Harpenden Moat House** Southdown Road
(0582) 764111
*An attractive Georgian manor house on a village green to the south of
Harpenden. Avoid the dingy rooms in the motel-style annexe.   £70 to £109*

# Isles of Scilly                             **MAP 8**

Bryher    **Hell Bay Hotel**    (0720) 22947
*A farmhouse hotel and hostelry where you can mix with the locals.
£90 to £108 (rate inc. dinner)*

Tresco    **Island Hotel**    (0720) 22883
*Complete refurbishment took place during the winter of 1990 and new
bedrooms have been added. We wait to see if this has changed a comfortable,
friendly hotel. More reports, please.   £122 to £216 (rate inc. dinner)*

Tresco    **The New Inn**    (0720) 22844
*The only pub on Tresco, this hotel is popular with locals and trippers and has
an informal atmosphere in which to enjoy good food.   £74 to £109 (rate inc.
dinner)*

# Kent                                        **MAP 10**

Canterbury    **Thanington Hotel** 140 Wincheap    (0227) 453227
*Smart, commercial B&B ten minutes' walk from the city centre; quiet
bedrooms in a modern block behind main Georgian house.   £55 to £58*

Chartham Hatch    **Howfield Manor** Howfield Lane    (0227) 738294
*Country house with dull furnishings and grounds, but excellent staff and rich,
well-presented food.   £65*

Westerham    **The King's Arms** Market Square    (0959) 629908
*Town hotel with some rather worn bedrooms; pleasant public rooms; good
English food.   £75*

# Lancashire                                  **MAPS 3/4**

Lytham St Anne's    **Grand Hotel** South Promenade    (0253) 721288
*Retains its stately aura of Edwardian seaside splendour despite signs of neglect
in some areas.   £84*

---

*The* Guide *office can quickly spot when a hotelier is encouraging customers
to write a recommending inclusion – and sadly, several hotels have been
doing this in 1991. Such reports do not further a hotel's cause.*

# Lincolnshire        **MAP 4**

Boston    **The White Hart** Bridge Foot    (0205) 364877
*Little character in public rooms but adequate accommodation in an area with few places to stay.* £57

# Merseyside        **MAP 4**

Southport    **Ambassador Hotel** 13 Bath Street    (0704) 543998
*Carefully managed, traditional but comfortable seaside accommodation.* £50

# Middlesex        **MAP 10**

Heathrow    **Sterling Hotel** Terminal 4    Heathrow Airport
081-759 7755
*Futuristic glasshouse with ultra-modern atrium arrangement. Restaurant and service in need of attention when we inspected.* £130

# Norfolk        **MAP 7**

Hunstanton    **Sedgeford Hall** Sedgeford    (0485) 70902
*A lovely house in a very quiet location. As guests in a private home everybody dines together.* £58

South Wootton    **Knights Hill Hotel** Knights Hill Village
(0553) 675566
*Business hotel with good facilities constructed like a mock village. Near a noisy roundabout.* £74

Thorpe St Andrew    **Old Rectory** 103 Yarmouth Road    (0603) 39357
*Patchy food and service in small country house near Norwich. Noisy position. Large bedrooms.* £70

# Northumberland        **MAP 3**

Allendale Town    **Bishop Field**    (0434) 683248
*Friendly, family-run hotel, converted from former farmhouse and cow byres. Lots of outdoor pursuits nearby.* £74

Berwick-upon-Tweed    **Kings Arms Hotel** Hide Hill    (0289) 307454
*Comfortable old eighteenth-century inn with large bedrooms; on one of Berwick's main streets.* £65

# North Yorkshire        **MAPS 3/4**

Askrigg    **The King's Arms Hotel** Market Place    (0969) 50258
*Busy, ancient coaching inn. The village pub from the TV series 'All Creatures Great and Small'. Comfortable bedrooms.* £56 to £80

Bainbridge    **The Rose & Crown Hotel**    (0969) 50225
*Cosy fifteenth-century pub in lovely village.* £62

Clifton    **The Grange**    (0904) 644744
*An attractive Regency house, five minutes' walk from the centre of York. A choice of restaurant or brasserie to eat in and comfortably furnished bedrooms.* £95 to £128

Crathorne   **Crathorne Hall**   (0642) 700398
*Turn-of-the-century country-house hotel in sleepy landscape. The hall is undergoing heavy refurbishment, but positive reports we've had indicate this isn't a problem to guests.   £95*

Gayle   **Rookhurst**   (0969) 667434
*Beautiful Georgian house with friendly hosts; the 100-mile stop on the Pennine Way.   £95 (rate inc. dinner)*

Harrogate   **Hotel St George** 1 Ripon Road   (0423) 561431
*A Swallow Hotel in city centre. Pricey, but good leisure facilities.   £99*

Monk Fryston   **Monk Fryston Hall**   (0977) 682369
*A lovely grey-stone hall with mullioned windows and a rambling garden. Rooms in the new wing are a little cramped and characterless.   £83 to £89*

Nidd   **Nidd Hall**   (0423) 771598
*Self-contained country-house hotel with good sports facilities and lovely grounds. The bedrooms have gorgeous views.   £120*

Staddlebridge   **McCoy's at the Tontine**   (060) 982671
*A restaurant and brasserie with rooms near the North York Moors. One reader who visited for a celebration weekend was very disappointed with room and meal. More reports, please.   £95*

# Oxfordshire                                              MAP 6

Kingston Bagpuize   **Fallowfields** Southmoor   (0865) 820416
*B&B and dinner in an interesting, slightly quirky house once owned by the Aga Khan.   £57*

Shipton-under-Wychwood   **Lamb Inn**   (0993) 830465
*Cosy, friendly pub and restaurant with simply furnished, comfortable bedrooms.   £68*

Woodstock   **Star Inn** 22 Market Place   (0993) 811373
*Amiable, attractive pub in the centre of the village with comfortable, well-equipped bedrooms.   £40 to £55*

# Shropshire                                          MAPS 4/5/6

Bomere Heath   **Fitz Manor**   (0743) 850295
*Fifteenth-century manor house on a remote working farm. Huge rooms are full of antiques. Open fires. Lovely views.   £30*

Hampton Loade   **The Old Forge House** Bridgnorth   (0746) 780338
*Idyllic quiet riverside family home with just three guest bedrooms. From £22*

Shrewsbury   **The Lion** Wyle Cop   (0743) 353107
*Large inn in a good central position. Some bedrooms need a little attention but the public rooms are solidly furnished and cheered by blazing fires.   £80*

---

*Report forms are at the back of the book; write a letter if you prefer.*

# Somerset

Dulverton   **Carnarvon Arms**   (0398) 23302
*Large, friendly fishing and shooting hotel on a minor road. Dignified in parts, drab in others.   £76*

Exford   **The Crown**   (064 383) 554
*Seventeenth-century coaching inn in a pretty town; converted to mid-range hotel. Great location on Exmoor.   £62*

Hatch Beauchamp   **Farthings**   (0823) 480664
*Small, quirky country-house hotel with some worn edges but friendly staff.   £90 to £125*

Wells   **The Swan** Sadler Street   (0749) 678877
*Predictable but fairly priced town-centre inn.   £77*

Withypool   **Westerclose Country House**   (0643) 83302
*Small, casual and relaxing hilltop hotel near village. Space and views are features. New owners as of January 1991.   £58 to £63*

# Staffordshire

**MAP 4**

Alstonefield   **Stanshope Hall** Stanshope   (033 527) 278
*An unusual place with original décor and furnishings, good food and comfortable accommodation.   £39 to £49*

Lichfield   **Oakleigh House** 25 St Chads Road   (0543) 262688
*An Edwardian house with an attractive conservatory restaurant; close to the centre of town.   £54*

Stone   **Stone House Hotel**   (0785) 815531
*An Edwardian residence that has become an efficiently run business hotel in the heart of the Midlands.   £102*

# Suffolk

**MAP 7**

Long Melford   **The Bull** Hall Street   (0787) 78494
*Large, town-centre, half-timbered inn with lots of character but some lacklustre new furniture.   £80*

# Surrey

**MAP 10**

Bagshot   **Pennyhill Park** London Road   (0276) 71774
*Opulent Victorian country house next to country club; run by Prestige Hotels.   From £138*

Dorking   **Burford Bridge Hotel** Box Hill   (0306) 884561
*Good quality Forte hotel with spacious gardens on the edge of Box Hill Park.   £110*

Hampton Wick   **Chase Lodge** 10 Park Road   081-943 1862
*Attractive guesthouse where you'll be left to your own devices.   £46 to £51*

Sanderstead   **Selsdon Park Hotel** Addington Road   081-657 8811
*Massive Victorian mansion; golf course included in vast range of leisure facilities.   £120 to £150*

---

*All reports are welcome on any hotel, whether or not it is in the* Guide.

# Warwickshire                                          MAP 6

Atherstone    **Chapel House** Friars' Gate    (0827) 718949
*Small family-run Georgian townhouse hotel in an area thin on the ground for good hotels.*    £50

Barford    **The Glebe** Church Street    (0926) 624218
*Smart and completely redecorated Georgian house. Lots of facilities.*
£75 to £97

Brandon    **Brandon Hall**    (0203) 542571
*Pleasant position and standard furnishings. It's popular with business clients.*    £80

Henley-in-Arden    **Ashleigh House** Whitley Hill    (0564) 792315
*Spacious turn-of-the-century hotel which has recently changed hands. Lots of antiques and a collection of antique dolls decorate public areas.*    £50

Oxhill    **Nolands Farm**    (0926) 640309
*Genuine working farm offering good-value accommodation with basic en suite bathrooms. Some rooms a little dark.*    £30 to £36

Stratford-upon-Avon    **Welcombe Hotel** Warwick Road    (0789) 295252
*Grand and luxurious Jacobean house. Suites are special, whilst standard rooms are more ordinary. A new golf course has just been built.*    £130

# West Sussex                                          MAPS 9/10

Amberley    **Amberley Castle** Arundel    (0798) 831992
*In the magnificent setting of a medieval castle, complete with suits of armour (see also page 12).*    £130 to £225

Chichester    **Dolphin & Anchor** West Street    (0243) 785121
*Old building opposite the cathedral; Forte-run; poor service when we inspected.*    £86 to £102

Gatwick    **Gatwick Sterling Hotel** Gatwick Airport    (0293) 567070
*A short walkway joins this newly-built, 21st-century atrium-layout hotel to the North Terminal.*    £110

Slinfold    **Random Hall** Stane Street    (0403) 790558
*Sixteenth-century beamed farmhouse converted into an hotel; next to an A-road.*    £83

# Wiltshire                                            MAP 9

Ashton Keynes    **Old Manor Farm**    (0285) 861770
*Good-value B&B in fifteenth-century farmhouse. On minor road. Evening meals by request.*    £28 to £35

Corsham    **Methuen Arms** 2 High Street    (0249) 714867
*Old town-centre inn with average furnishings but very good-humoured and lively owners and staff.*    £56 to £62

Ford    **White Hart Inn** nr Chippenham    (0249) 782213
*Popular waterside inn. Beams, but also many dowdy touches in bedrooms.*    £59

Purton    **Pear Tree at Purton** Church End    (0793) 772100
*A very business-like country hotel. Expanded restaurant-with-rooms.*    £87

Swindon   **Salthrop House** Salthrop   (0793) 812990
*Country-house hotel near Swindon geared to business people. Some dowdy touches but more home-like than hotel-like.* £210

# SCOTLAND

# Dumfries & Galloway     MAP 2

Beattock   **Auchen Castle**   (068 33) 407
*A slightly old-fashioned hotel, praised for its food and the quality of its welcome.* £60 to £66

# Grampian     MAP 1

Aboyne   **Balnacoil Hotel** Rhu-na-Haven Road   (033 98) 86806
*Expensive refurbishment of Edwardian house, still rather raw. Bedrooms comfortable and food promising.* £75

Aboyne   **Hazelhurst Lodge** Ballater Road   (033 98) 86921
*A mixture of guesthouse and restaurant in old stone villa. Bedrooms comfortable and warm; arty atmosphere, but not a strikingly pretty house.* £39

Banchory   **Raemoir House Hotel** Raemoir   (033 02) 4884
*A plush nest in a house of some character. Standards of food and comfort are high, but we have niggles about service and value for money.* £95 to £105

Elgin   **Mansion House** The Haugh   (0343) 548811
*Comfortable Victorian house close to the centre of Elgin. Lots of changes underway as we went to press. More reports, please.* £87 to £115

# Highland     MAP 1

Kingussie   **Homewood Lodge**   (0540) 661507
*Promising reports on this guesthouse in the Spey Valley.* £35

Plockton   **Haven Hotel** Innes Street   (059 984) 223
*A comfortable, if curiously suburban hotel in one of the prettiest villages in the West Highlands. Reports speak well of the food.* £82 to £88 (rate inc. dinner)

# Lothian     MAP 2

Edinburgh   **Caledonian Hotel** Princes Street   031-225 2433
*Huge old station hotel, with renovations almost complete. Quite a lot of character left; bedrooms designed with care and interest. Fairly pricey.* £155 to £195

Edinburgh   **Channings** South Learmonth Gardens   031-315 2226
*High-quality interior design, but rather lacking in individuality. Bedrooms are well conceived, but alcove lounges don't have much space for relaxation.* £93

Edinburgh   **St Bernards Guesthouse** 22 St Bernards Crescent
031-332 2339
*This bright, good-value Edinburgh guesthouse changed hands in the spring of 1991. Reports please.* £30 to £40

Humbie **Johnstounburn House** (087 553) 696
*A well-proportioned baronial house in beautiful grounds. Slickly run, good spot for business meetings; some bedrooms rather old-fashioned.* £115

Kirknewton **Dalmahoy Hotel & Country Club** 031-333 1845
*Golf is a big attraction, but the leisure centre is good too. Otherwise a rather bland conversion of an old house; lots of conference facilities.* £115

# Shetland Islands
MAP I

Walls **Burrastow House** (059 571) 307
*Changes are in the offing at this lovely isolated house. Reports urgently needed.* £102

# Strathclyde
MAPS 1/2

Isle of Arran **Auchrannie Country House** Brodick (0770) 2234
*As long as Muzak (both easy-listening and frisky at breakfast) doesn't drive you mad, you'll have a comfortable, pleasant stay here.* £49 to £75

Isle of Colonsay **Isle of Colonsay Hotel** (095 12) 316
*Promising reports on this isolated island hotel, with smashing hosts and good food into the bargain. Full reports, please.* £88 to £112 (rate inc. dinner)

Oban **King's Knoll Hotel** Dunollie Road (0631) 62536
*Friendly, old-fashioned, family-run hotel being gradually refurbished, but with some way to go yet. The new bedrooms are cramped but nicely done.* £46

Troon **Marine Highland Hotel** Crosbie Road (0292) 314444
*Much praise from one regular for this hotel. Does anyone else agree?* £123

# Tayside
MAPS 1/2

Dunkeld **Stakis Dunkeld House** (035 02) 771
*Old lodge in prime, quiet position on banks of the Tay, done up as sporting and leisure hotel. Excellent leisure facilities. Bedrooms are disappointing.* £122

Killiecrankie **Killiecrankie Hotel** Pass of Killiecrankie (0796) 3220
*Well-positioned, close to Pitlochry, for exploration of the Highlands.* £70 to £84

# Western Isles
MAP I

Lochcarnan **Orasay Inn** South Uist (087 04) 298
*A small, welcoming guesthouse that has a restaurant at the back and three recently added bedrooms.* £42

# WALES

## Dyfed
MAP 5

Cardigan **Crychdu** Nebo Bronwydd (0267) 253640
*Pleasant B&B in isolated hilltop position.* £29

Cardigan **Penralt Ceibwr Farm Guesthouse** Moylegrove
(023 986) 217
*Pink farmhouse with friendly hosts. The doll collection is something of a feature.* £57

Pembroke **Hollyland Hotel** Holyland Road (0646) 681444
*The castle is just visible from the garden of this plush country hotel.* £60

Tenby **Waterwynch House Hotel** Waterwynch Bay (0834) 2464
*A great position facing a semi-private beach. The interior is well worn.* £64 (rate inc. dinner)

Welsh Hook **Stone Hall** (0348) 840212
*A quirky country hotel in a peaceful spot with plain bedrooms and good food.* £53

# Gwynedd

Llanrwst **Meadowsweet Hotel** Station Road (0492) 640732
*A small hotel run by the chef, with moderately priced rooms and good food.* £46 to £66

Penmaenpool **George III Hotel** (0341) 422525
*Peaceful setting by the Mawddach estuary for this pub/hotel converted from a ship chandler's.* £43 to £85

Talyllyn **Tynycornel Hotel** (0654) 782282
*A modernised hotel in a wonderful setting next to Talyllyn. Ideal for walking and fishing.* £80 to £100

# Powys   MAP 5

Caersws **Maesmawr Hall** Newtown (0686) 688255
*A Tudor-style hotel in the Severn Valley, with a period atmosphere in public rooms; the bedrooms aren't as attractive.* £53

Llangynidr **Red Lion** (0874) 730223
*Ivy-covered pub/restaurant with five bedrooms.* £45 to £50

Llanwrtyd Wells **Lasswade Country House** (059 13) 611
*An eccentric pet-loving place with chatty hosts and plain home-made food.* £52

Llyswen **The Griffin Inn** (0874) 754241
*Village pub and restaurant with simple bedrooms.* £50

Three Cocks **Old Gwernyfed Country Manor** Felindre
(049 74) 376
*Elizabethan manor house with minstrels' gallery in lounge, but no central heating.* £42 to £70

# South Glamorgan   MAP 5

Cardiff **Manor Parc Country Hotel** Thornhill Road (0222) 693723
*Smart hotel/restaurant within striking distance of the centre of Cardiff.* £85

Llantwit Major **West House Country House** West Street
(0446) 792406
*Small hotel in pleasant village setting.* £53

# West Glamorgan
MAP 5

Swansea **The Beaumont Hotel** 72 Walter Road   (0792) 643956
*Medium-size town hotel and restaurant, near city centre and with car park that's locked at night.* £60 to £80

Swansea **Windsor Lodge Hotel** Mount Pleasant
(0792) 652744/642158
*Medium-size town hotel; some rooms are decorated in particularly lurid wallpapers.* £56

# CHANNEL ISLANDS
MAP 8

Alderney **Inchalla** St Anne   (048 182) 3220
*Friendly, functional and modern guesthouse-cum-hotel – the best of the island's poor collection.* £26 to £33

Guernsey **La Favorita** Fermain Bay   (0481) 35666
*Well-furnished and comfortable, with good facilities and lush garden and woodland views. Slightly let down by very ordinary bedrooms.* £66 to £84
(rate inc. dinner)

Guernsey **Moore's Central** Le Pollet   St Peter Port   (0481) 724452
*Stylish public areas conflict somewhat with dull bedrooms. A fine position if you like being in the thick of things.* £58 to £66

Guernsey **Pandora Hotel** Hauteville   St Peter Port   (0481) 720971
*Well-kept, comfortable town hotel with peaceful garden views.* £64 to £72
(rate inc. dinner)

Jersey **The Grand** The Esplanade   St Helier   (0534) 22301
*Large and civilised De Vere-run hotel on the sea front.* £115 to £145

Jersey **Greenhill Country Hotel** St Peter's Valley   (0534) 81042
*Stone house in lovely rural setting, with appealing gardens, a pool and modern facilities. Some bedrooms a little bleak.* £70

Jersey **St Brelade's Bay Hotel** St Brelade's Bay   (0534) 46141
*A well-established favourite family seaside hotel with lovely gardens and a good location; a bit dowdy in parts.* £126 to £146

# Index

All full entries are indexed below. For additional ideas, see the Visitors' Book (starting on page 787).

# Maps

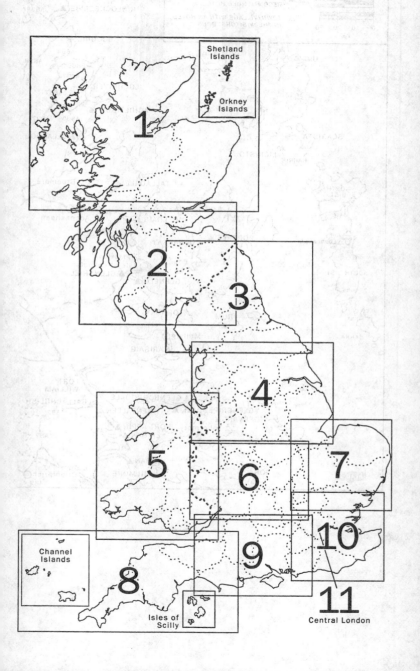

## MAP I  NORTH OF SCOTLAND

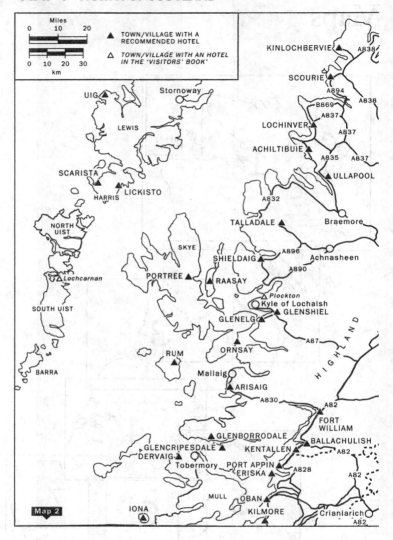

# Scotland

SHETLAND
ISLANDS

BRAE
Walls

ORKNEY
ISLANDS

KIRKWALL

0 Miles 20    40

0 km 20   40   60

THURSO A836
A9
A882
Wick
A882
A895
A9
LYBSTER
A9
Helmsdale
Tongue
A836
A897
A897
A836
LAIRG
A839
Bonar
Bridge
Dornoch
A836
A9

Buckie
Elgin
Fraserburgh
CROMARTY
NAIRN
A96
GRAMPIAN
A95
A98
A947
A92
BUNCHREW
INVERNESS
A941
A96
OLDMELDRUM
PETERHEAD
A82
A9
BALLINDALLOCH
LESLIE
DRUMNADROCHIT
A944
Aberdeen
WHITE BRIDGE
KILDRUMMY
NEWTONMORE
KINGUSSIE
A9
Braemar
Aboyne
A93
A93
BANCHORY
A86
BALLATER
Stonehaven
A93
A94
TAYSIDE
SPITTAL  FETTERCAIRN
OF GLENSHEE
A9
Killiecrankie
A924
A94
Montrose
TUMMEL
BRIDGE
Pitlochry
ABERFELDY
A827
BLAIRGOWRIE
Forfar
A94
DUNKELD
A923
EASSIE
A827
A9  A93
A94
A929
Arbroath
AUCHTERHOUSE
ST FILLANS
SCONE
A85
Dundee
A84
A85
Perth
M90

Map 2

# MAP 2   SOUTH OF SCOTLAND

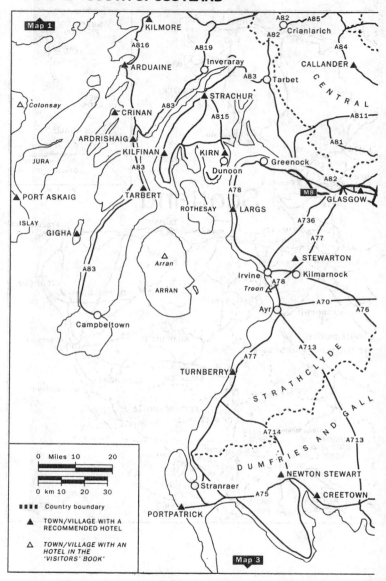

Map 1

KILMORE
A816
ARDUAINE
A819
Inveraray
A83
STRACHUR
CRINAN
A815
ARDRISHAIG
KILFINAN
KIRN
A83
Dunoon
TARBERT
A78
ROTHESAY
PORT ASKAIG
GIGHA
Colonsay
JURA
ISLAY
A83

Crianlarich
A82  A85
A82
CALLANDER
A84
CENTRAL
A811
A81
Greenock
A82
M8
GLASGOW
LARGS
A736
A77
STEWARTON
Irvine
Kilmarnock
A78
Troon
Ayr
A70
A76
A713
TURNBERRY
A77
STRATHCLYDE
DUMFRIES AND GALL
A714
A713
NEWTON STEWART
Stranraer
CREETOWN
A75
PORTPATRICK

Arran
ARRAN
Campbeltown

Map 3

0   Miles  10       20

0 km 10    20    30

▪▪▪▪ Country boundary

▲ TOWN/VILLAGE WITH A
   RECOMMENDED HOTEL

△ TOWN/VILLAGE WITH AN
   HOTEL IN THE
   'VISITORS' BOOK'

Map 1

ST FILLANS  A85  A85  Perth  A85
T A Y S I D E
A9
AUCHTERARDER  A913  ST ANDREWS
KINBUCK  M90  A916  PEAT INN
A91  A914  A915  A917
A91  A911  A915
STIRLING  F I F E
M9  Kincardine  Kirkcaldy
M80  M876
A8911  M9  GULLANE  A198
M73  UPHALL  M8  EDINBURGH  L O T H I A N
Kirknewton  A1  GIFFORD
Humbie
A702  A1
WEST  A701
LINTON  A7  A68
Coldstream
M74  PEEBLES  WALKERBURN  GALASHIELS  KELSO  A697
INNERLEITHEN  A72  A699
A702  ETTRICKBRIDGE  SELKIRK
A70  A74  A698  JEDBURGH
A701  A7  A68
MOFFAT  B O R D E R S
Beattock  SCOTLAND  N O R T H U M B E R L A N D
ENGLAND
A76  A701  A74  A7  A68
O W A Y
Dumfries  CANONBIE
A75  A74  A6071  BRAMPTON  A69
Carlisle  A69
AUCHENCAIRN  M6  C U M B R I A  Allendale Town
A596  CALDBECK  ALSTON
A595  KIRKOSWALD
ST JOHN'S CHAPEL  A689
A591  MOSEDALE  Map 3

# MAP 3  NORTH OF ENGLAND

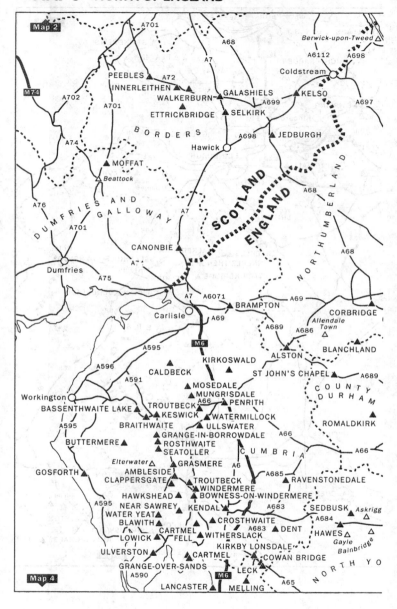

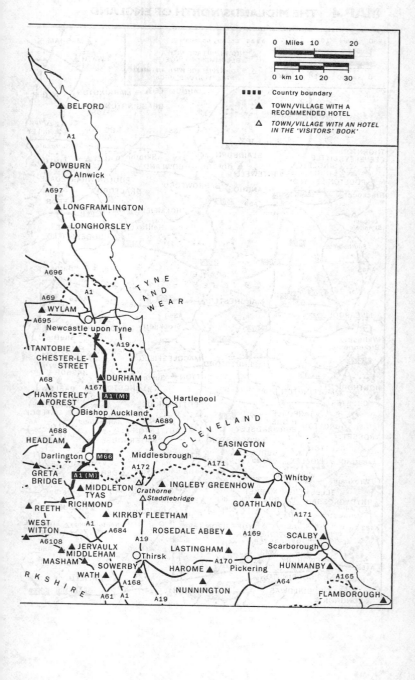

MAP 4   THE MIDDLE NORTH OF ENGLAND

0  Miles  10        20

0 km 10    20    30

▪▪▪▪  Country boundary

▲  TOWN/VILLAGE WITH A
    RECOMMENDED HOTEL

△  TOWN/VILLAGE WITH AN HOTEL
   IN THE 'VISITORS' BOOK'

▲ BELFORD

A1

▲ POWBURN  ○ Alnwick

A697

▲ LONGFRAMLINGTON

▲ LONGHORSLEY

A696

A69    A1

▲ WYLAM

A695

Newcastle upon Tyne

TYNE AND WEAR

TANTOBIE ▲    A19

CHESTER-LE-
STREET

▲ DURHAM

A68

A167

A1 (M)

HAMSTERLEY
▲ FOREST

○ Bishop Auckland

○ Hartlepool

A688

A689

HEADLAM ▲

CLEVELAND

Darlington  M66

▲ EASINGTON

GRETA
BRIDGE ▲

A1 (M)

A172   Middlesbrough  A171

△ Crathorne     ▲ INGLEBY GREENHOW   ○ Whitby

MIDDLETON
TYAS ▲

△ Staddlebridge

▲ REETH

RICHMOND

▲ GOATHLAND

WEST
WITTON ▲

A1   A684

▲ KIRKBY FLEETHAM

A171

ROSEDALE ABBEY ▲   A169

A6108

▲ JERVAULX

A19

LASTINGHAM ▲

SCALBY ▲

▲ MIDDLEHAM

○ Thirsk

Scarborough ○

MASHAM ▲  SOWERBY ▲

HAROME ▲   Pickering ○

HUNMANBY ▲

WATH ▲

A170

A168

Y O R K SHIRE

A61   A1   A19

▲ NUNNINGTON

A64

A165

FLAMBOROUGH ▲

# MAP 4   THE MIDLANDS/NORTH OF ENGLAND

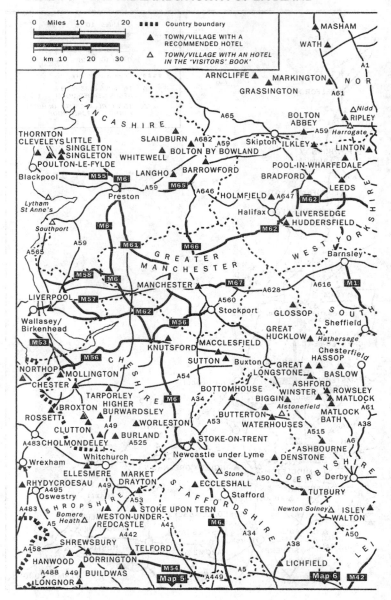

0   Miles   10        20
0   km   10      20      30

▪▪▪▪ Country boundary
▲ TOWN/VILLAGE WITH A RECOMMENDED HOTEL
△ *TOWN/VILLAGE WITH AN HOTEL IN THE 'VISITORS' BOOK'*

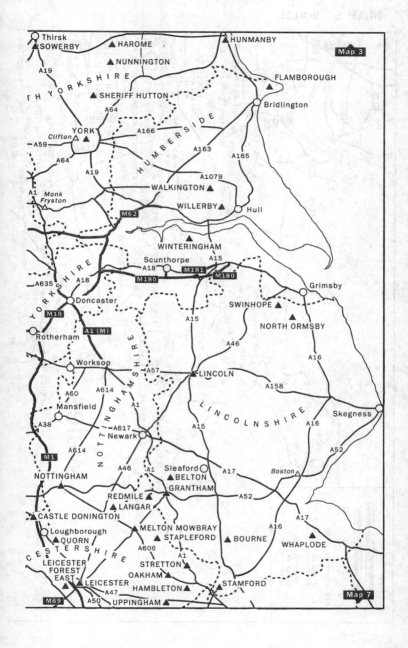

Map 3

Thirsk
▲SOWERBY
▲HAROME
▲HUNMANBY
▲NUNNINGTON
FLAMBOROUGH
A19
TH YORKSHIRE
▲SHERIFF HUTTON
Bridlington
A64
YORK ▲
Clifton △
A166
H U M B E R S I D E
−A59
A64
A163
A165
A19
A1079
Monk
Fryston
WALKINGTON ▲
A1
△
M62
WILLERBY ▲ Hull
WINTERINGHAM ▲
A15
Scunthorpe
M181
A18
▲
M180
M180
Grimsby
Y O R K S H I R E
A635
A18
Doncaster
SWINHOPE ▲
NORTH ORMSBY
M18
A1 (M)
A46
A16
Rotherham
Worksop
A57
LINCOLN ▲
A60
A614
A158
L I N C O L N S H I R E
Skegness
Mansfield
A1
A38
A617
A16
M1
A614
Newark
A15
A52
NOTTINGHAMSHIRE
A46
A1
Sleaford
A17
Boston △
NOTTINGHAM ▲
▲BELTON
REDMILE ▲
GRANTHAM
A52
▲ LANGAR
▲ CASTLE DONINGTON
A17
Loughborough
MELTON MOWBRAY ▲
A16
BOURNE ▲
QUORN
STAPLEFORD ▲
WHAPLODE ▲
CESTERSHIRE
A606
A1
LEICESTER
FOREST
STRETTON ▲
EAST ▲
OAKHAM ▲
LEICESTER ▲
STAMFORD ▲
M69
HAMBLETON ▲
A47
A50
UPPINGHAM ▲

Map 7

## MAP 5 WALES

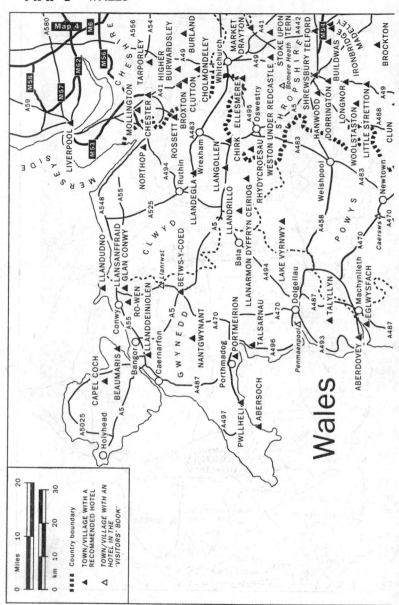

**Scale:**

Miles 0 — 10 — 20

km 0 — 10 — 20 — 30

■■■ Country boundary

▲ TOWN/VILLAGE WITH A RECOMMENDED HOTEL

△ TOWN/VILLAGE WITH AN HOTEL IN THE 'VISITORS' BOOK'

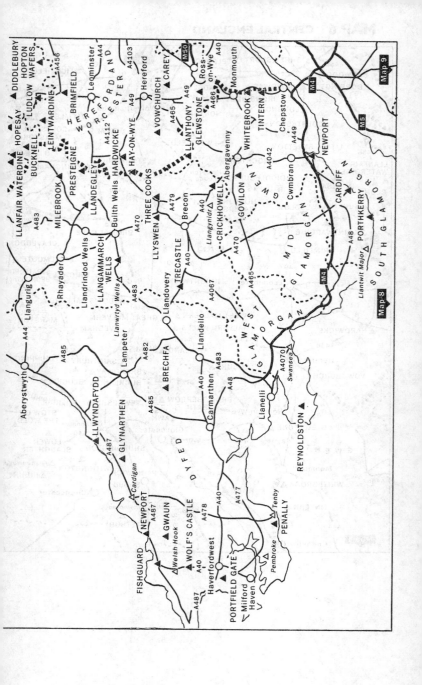

# MAP 6   CENTRAL ENGLAND

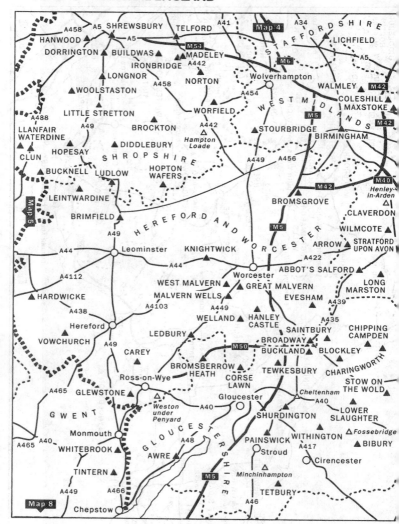

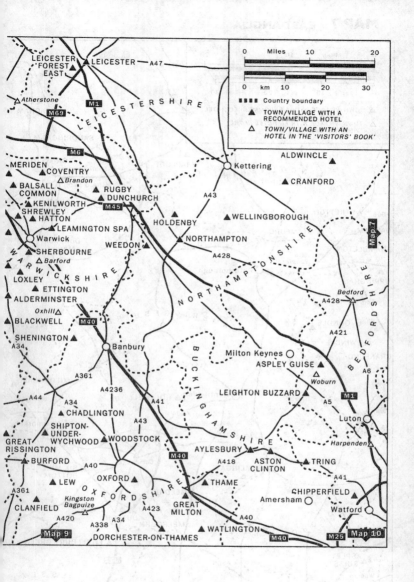

## MAP 7  EAST ANGLIA

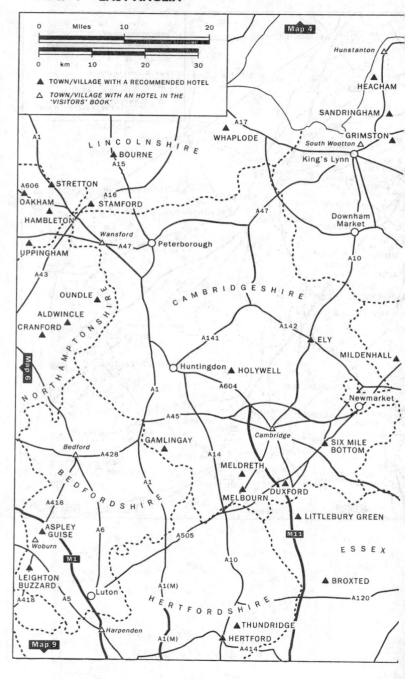

Miles 0 · 10 · 20

km 0 · 10 · 20 · 30

▲ TOWN/VILLAGE WITH A RECOMMENDED HOTEL

△ TOWN/VILLAGE WITH AN HOTEL IN THE 'VISITORS' BOOK'

Map 4

*Hunstanton* △

▲ HEACHAM

SANDRINGHAM ▲

GRIMSTON ▲

*South Wootton* △

King's Lynn ○

▲ WHAPLODE

A17

A1

L I N C O L N S H I R E

▲ BOURNE

A15

STRETTON ▲

A606

OAKHAM ▲

A16

▲ STAMFORD

HAMBLETON ▲

*Wansford* △

A47

Peterborough ○

Downham Market ○

A47

A10

▲ UPPINGHAM

A43

C A M B R I D G E S H I R E

OUNDLE ▲

N O R T H A M P T O N S H I R E

ALDWINCLE ▲

CRANFORD ▲

A142

▲ ELY

MILDENHALL ▲

A141

Huntingdon ○  ▲ HOLYWELL

A604

Newmarket ○

A1

A45

*Cambridge* △

GAMLINGAY ▲

▲ SIX MILE BOTTOM

*Bedford* △

A428

B E D F O R D S H I R E

A1

A14

MELDRETH ▲

▲ DUXFORD

MELBOURN ▲

A418

A6

A505

▲ LITTLEBURY GREEN

ASPLEY GUISE ▲

*Woburn* △

M11

A10

E S S E X

M1

▲ BROXTED

LEIGHTON BUZZARD ▲

A418

A5

Luton ○

A1(M)

H E R T F O R D S H I R E

A120

△ *Harpenden*

Map 9

A1(M)

▲ THUNDRIDGE

HERTFORD ▲

A414

Map 6

MAP 9 · SOUTH-WEST ENGLAND CHANNEL ISLANDS

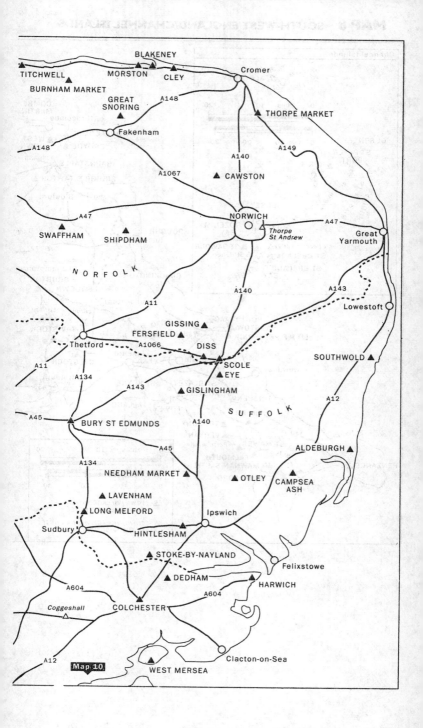

Map 10

## MAP 8  SOUTH-WEST ENGLAND/CHANNEL ISLANDS

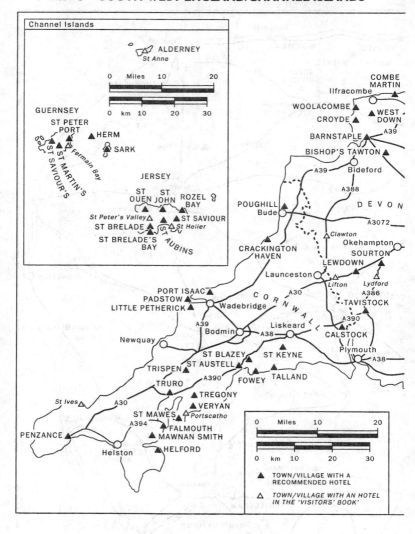

**Channel Islands**

ALDERNEY
*St Anne*

0   Miles   10        20

0   km   10    20    30

GUERNSEY
ST PETER
PORT
▲ HERM
▲ SARK
ST MARTIN'S
ST SAVIOUR'S
*Fermain Bay*

JERSEY
ST
OUEN  ST
JOHN  ROZEL
BAY
*St Peter's Valley*  ST SAVIOUR
ST BRELADE  △ *St Helier*
ST BRELADE'S
BAY        AUBINS

COMBE
MARTIN
Ilfracombe
WOOLACOMBE ▲ ▲ WEST
CROYDE ▲       DOWN
BARNSTAPLE              A39
BISHOP'S TAWTON ▲

A39  Bideford
A388

POUGHILL ▲               D E V O N
Bude
                          A3072
                  *Clawton*  Okehampton
CRACKINGTON               SOURTON
HAVEN          LEWDOWN
        Launceston   *Lifton*   *Lydford*
                              A386
PORT ISAAC ▲   C O R N W A L L   TAVISTOCK
PADSTOW                A30
LITTLE PETHERICK ▲  Wadebridge      A390
                                 CALSTOCK
          A39  Bodmin — A38 — Liskeard
Newquay                          Plymouth
          ST BLAZEY  ST KEYNE       A38
TRISPEN  ST AUSTELL
TRURO        A390  FOWEY  TALLAND
*St Ives*  A30  ▲ TREGONY
                ▲ VERYAN
            ST MAWES △ *Portscatho*
         A394
PENZANCE ▲  FALMOUTH
         MAWNAN SMITH
   Helston  ▲ HELFORD

0   Miles   10        20

0   km   10    20    30

▲ TOWN/VILLAGE WITH A
  RECOMMENDED HOTEL

△ TOWN/VILLAGE WITH AN HOTEL
  IN THE 'VISITORS' BOOK'

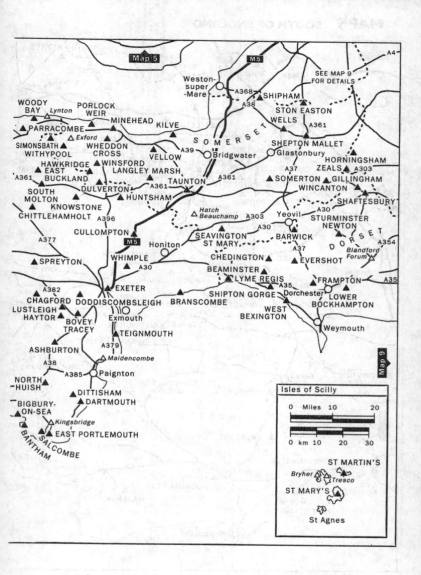

# MAP 9 SOUTH OF ENGLAND

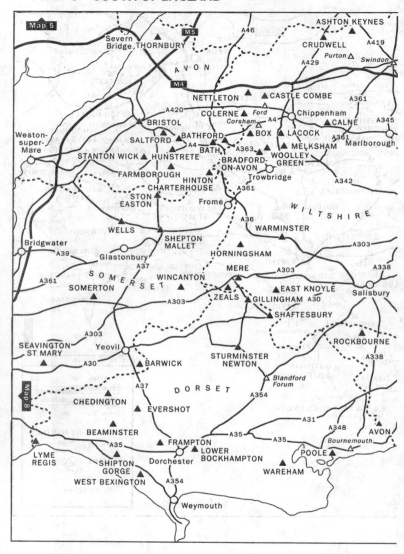

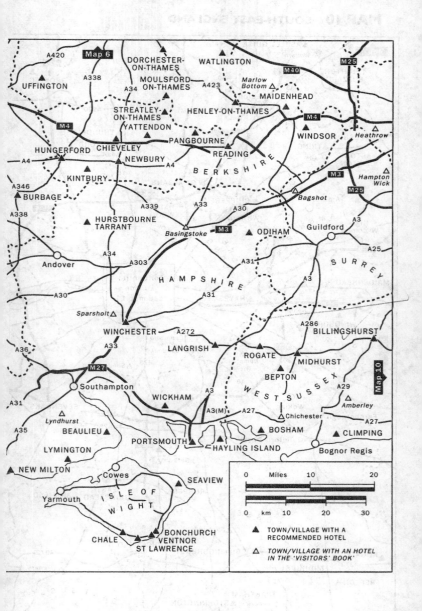

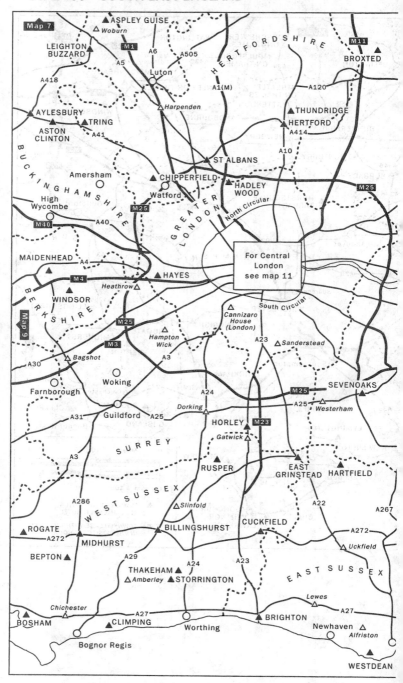

## MAP 10 SOUTH-EAST ENGLAND

Map 7

▲ASPLEY GUISE
△ Woburn

LEIGHTON
BUZZARD

M1

A5    A6    A505

HERTFORDSHIRE

M11

▲ BROXTED

A418

Luton ○

A1(M)    A120

△ Harpenden

▲AYLESBURY    ▲TRING

ASTON
CLINTON

A41

▲THUNDRIDGE
▲HERTFORD

A414

Amersham ○

BUCKINGHAMSHIRE

High
Wycombe ○

M40    A40

St ALBANS

CHIPPERFIELD
Watford ○

A10

M25

▲HADLEY
WOOD

GREATER
LONDON

North Circular

MAIDENHEAD

A4

M4

▲ HAYES

For Central
London
see map 11

BERKSHIRE

Heathrow △

WINDSOR

M25

South Circular

Map 9

M3

Hampton
Wick △

Cannizaro
House
(London) △

A23    △ Sanderstead

A30    △ Bagshot

Woking ○

A3

A24

SEVENOAKS ▲

M25    A25

Farnborough ○

Guildford ○    A25

Dorking △

△ Westerham

A31

HORLEY    M23

A3

SURREY

Gatwick △

RUSPER

EAST
GRINSTEAD    ▲ HARTFIELD

WEST SUSSEX

A286

△ Slinfold

A22    A267

▲ROGATE
A272

▲ BILLINGSHURST

CUCKFIELD ▲

A272

MIDHURST

A29

△ Uckfield

BEPTON ▲

THAKEHAM ▲
△ Amberley  ▲ STORRINGTON

A24    A23

EAST SUSSEX

Chichester △

A27

Lewes △

A27

BOSHAM ○

▲ CLIMPING

Worthing ○

▲ BRIGHTON

Newhaven ○    △
Alfriston

Bognor Regis ○

▲
WESTDEAN

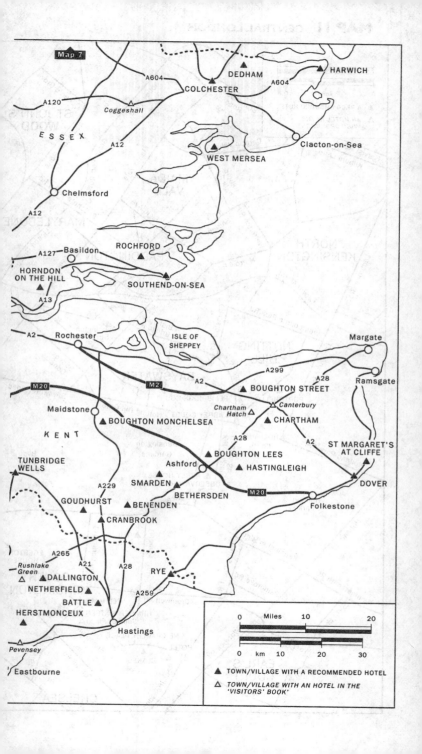

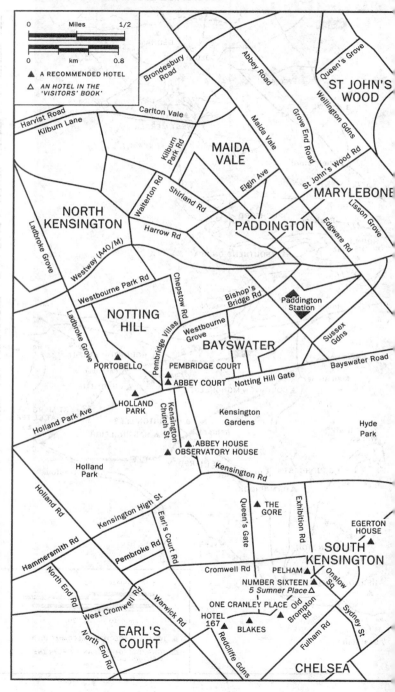

## MAP 11 CENTRAL LONDON

Miles 0 — 1/2
km 0 — 0.8

▲ A RECOMMENDED HOTEL
△ AN HOTEL IN THE 'VISITORS' BOOK'

ST JOHN'S WOOD

MARYLEBONE

MAIDA VALE

NORTH KENSINGTON

PADDINGTON

Paddington Station

NOTTING HILL

BAYSWATER

▲ PORTOBELLO
▲ PEMBRIDGE COURT
▲ ABBEY COURT
▲ HOLLAND PARK
Notting Hill Gate

Kensington Gardens

Hyde Park

▲ ABBEY HOUSE
▲ OBSERVATORY HOUSE

Holland Park

Kensington Rd

▲ THE GORE

EGERTON HOUSE ▲

SOUTH KENSINGTON

PELHAM ▲
NUMBER SIXTEEN ▲
5 Sumner Place △
ONE CRANLEY PLACE ▲
HOTEL 167 ▲   ▲ BLAKES

EARL'S COURT

CHELSEA

Brondesbury Road, Abbey Road, Queen's Grove, Wellington Gdns, Grove End Road, St John's Wood Rd, Lisson Grove, Edgware Rd, Queen's Grove, Maida Vale, Elgin Ave, Harvist Road, Kilburn Lane, Carlton Vale, Kilburn Park Rd, Walterton Rd, Shirland Rd, Harrow Rd, Westway (A40/M), Westbourne Park Rd, Ladbroke Grove, Chepstow Rd, Pembridge Villas, Westbourne Grove, Bishop's Bridge Rd, Sussex Gdns, Bayswater Road, Kensington Church St, Holland Park Ave, Holland Rd, Hammersmith Rd, North End Rd, Kensington High St, Earl's Court Rd, Pembroke Rd, Cromwell Rd, Queen's Gate, Exhibition Rd, Onslow Sq, West Cromwell Rd, Warwick Rd, Redcliffe Gdns, Old Brompton Rd, Fulham Rd, Sydney St, North End Rd

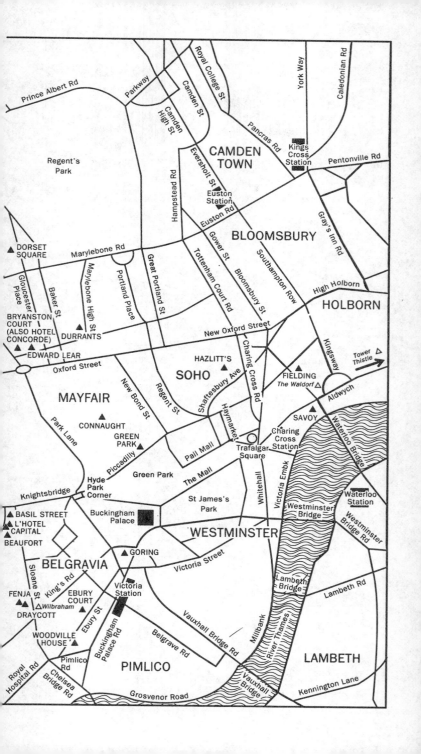

# Report form

Please tell us about a stay at any hotel in Britain, whether or not it appears in this Guide. Write a letter if you would prefer, and send brochures or other material too. Send your forms to: The Editor, *Which? Hotel Guide*, FREEPOST, 2 Marylebone Road, London NW1 1YN

Name of hotel

Address

I visited this hotel on:

My report is:

*(Continue overleaf)*

My name is:

Address:

# Report form

Please tell us about a stay at any hotel in Britain, whether or not it appears in this Guide. Write a letter if you would prefer, and send brochures or other material too. Send your forms to: The Editor, *Which? Hotel Guide*, FREE-POST, 2 Marylebone Road, London NW1 1YN

Name of hotel

Address

I visited this hotel on:

My report is:

*(Continue overleaf)*

My name is:

Address:

# Report form

Please tell us about a stay at any hotel in Britain, whether or not it appears in this Guide. Write a letter if you would prefer, and send brochures or other material too. Send your forms to: The Editor, *Which? Hotel Guide*, FREE-POST, 2 Marylebone Road, London NW1 1YN

Name of hotel

Address

I visited this hotel on:

My report is:

*(Continue overleaf)*

My name is:

Address:

# Report form

Please tell us about a stay at any hotel in Britain, whether or not it appears in this Guide. Write a letter if you would prefer, and send brochures or other material too. Send your forms to: The Editor, *Which? Hotel Guide*, FREEPOST, 2 Marylebone Road, London NW1 1YN

Name of hotel

Address

I visited this hotel on:

My report is:

*(Continue overleaf)*

My name is:

Address:

# Report form

Please tell us about a stay at any hotel in Britain, whether or not it appears in this Guide. Write a letter if you would prefer, and send brochures or other material too. Send your forms to: The Editor, *Which? Hotel Guide*, FREE-POST, 2 Marylebone Road, London NW1 1YN

Name of hotel

Address

I visited this hotel on:

My report is:

*(Continue overleaf)*

My name is:

Address:

# Report form

Please tell us about a stay at any hotel in Britain, whether or not it appears in this Guide. Write a letter if you would prefer, and send brochures or other material too. Send your forms to: The Editor, *Which? Hotel Guide*, FREE-POST, 2 Marylebone Road, London NW1 1YN

Name of hotel

Address

I visited this hotel on:

My report is:

*(Continue overleaf)*

My name is:

Address:

# THE GOOD FOOD GUIDE® 1992
## 40TH ANNIVERSARY EDITION
### Edited by Tom Jaine

In 1951 Raymond Postgate published a pocket-size volume that strongly criticised the mass of British restaurants while bringing the best of them to wider public knowledge. Forty years on THE GOOD FOOD GUIDE is a national institution ('the finest restaurant guide around,' according to *The Independent*), and still campaigning hard on behalf of the consumer. The 1992 guide draws on over 10,000 accounts of meals eaten by consumers and *Guide* inspectors during the previous 12 months, searching out high quality and good-value cooking in restaurants of every kind, from the temples of haute cuisine to humble fish and chip shops. This edition features 1,300 recommendations from the Scilly Isles to the Shetlands, guiding the food-lover to the best on offer.

Paperback   210 × 120mm   720 pages   £12.95
Available from bookshops and from
Consumers' Association, Castlemead,
Gascoyne Way, Hertford X, SG14 1LH

# Which? and Holiday Which?

Published once a month, *Which?* gives you comparative reports on the merits and value for money of many products and services that you buy for yourself, your family and your home.

Because Consumers' Association is an independent organisation our product testing is completely unbiased, so you can be sure you are getting the facts.

As a *Which?* subscriber, you can also get *Holiday Which?*, published 4 times a year in January, March, May and September. It reports on a wide range of holiday destinations in the UK and abroad, with details on food, excursions and sight-seeing as well as background information on climate, scenery and culture.

To claim your free trial subscription to *Which?* and *Holiday Which?* just complete and return the form opposite. No action is necessary if you wish to continue after your free trial: your subscription will bring you *Which?* and *Holiday Which?* for £16.75 a quarter until you cancel by writing to us (and to your bank to cancel your Direct Debiting Mandate), or until we advise you of a change in price. Your subscription becomes due on the first of the month, three months after the date on the mandate. If you do not wish to continue beyond the trial period, simply write and let us know before your first payment is due.

# Gardening from Which?

Published 10 times a year with bumper issues in spring and autumn, this magazine aims to help you in your gardening by sharing the results of our thorough research and the experience of our gardening experts.

Every issue of *Gardening* contains something for everyone, from beginner to expert. The magazine's 80 or so comparative reports a year look at a wide variety of subjects from shrubs, flowers and cacti, fruit and vegetables to tools, techniques and equipment. So whether you've got a few window boxes, a lawn, well-established ornamental borders or a greenhouse, *Gardening* will help you to find ways of improving what you have and save you time and money.

To claim your free trial subscription to *Gardening from Which?* just complete and return the form opposite. No action is necessary if you wish to continue after your free trial: your subscription will bring you *Gardening from Which?* for £11.75 a quarter until you cancel by writing to us (and to your bank to cancel your Direct Debiting Mandate), or until we advise you of a change in price. Your subscription becomes due on the first of the month, three months after the date on the mandate. If you do not wish to continue beyond the trial period, simply write and let us know before your first payment is due.

# Which? way to Health

This lively and authoritative magazine will help you and your family stay healthy. You'll find articles on staying fit, eating the right foods, early detection of any health problems, health products and how to get the best from the NHS.

This magazine is published every two months and, like *Which?*, is completely independent – bringing you unbiased facts about health in Britain today. The magazine takes a close look behind the scenes exposing bad practice and harmful products to help prevent you, the consumer, being deceived. We also report on any medical breakthroughs which could bring relief or cure for victims.

To claim your free trial subscription to *Which? way to Health* just complete and return the form opposite. No action is necessary if you wish to continue after your free trial: your subscription will bring you *Which? way to Health* for £5.75 a quarter until you cancel by writing to us (and to your bank to cancel your Direct Debiting Mandate), or until we advise you of a change in price. Your subscription becomes due on the first of the month, three months after the date on the mandate. If you do not wish to continue beyond the trial period, simply write and let us know before your first payment is due.

Consumers' Association, Castlemead, Gascoyne Way, Hertford X, SG14 1LH.

## FREE TRIAL ACCEPTANCE

Please send me free the next 3 issues of *Which?* and a free issue of *Holiday Which?* as they appear. I understand that I am under no obligation. If I do not wish to continue with *Which?* and *Holiday Which?* after the free trial, I can cancel this order at any time before payment is due on the 1st of the month three months after the date shown. But if I decide to continue I need do nothing – my subscription will bring me *Which?* and *Holiday Which?* for the current price of £16.75 a quarter.

☐ Tick here if you do not wish your name and address to be added to a mailing list to be used by ourselves or third parties for sending you further offers.

KB _

## DIRECT DEBITING MANDATE

I/We authorise you until further notice in writing to charge to my/our account with you unspecified amounts which may be debited thereto at the instance of Consumers' Association by Direct Debit.  Originator's Ref. No. 992338

| Signed | | | | | | Today's date | | | |
|---|---|---|---|---|---|---|---|---|---|
| Bank account in the name of | | | | | | | | | |
| Bank account number | | | | | | | | | |
| Name and address of your bank | | | | | | | | | |
| | | | | | | | Postcode | | |

Banks may decline to accept instructions to charge direct debits to certain types of account other than current accounts.

### YOUR NAME AND ADDRESS

| Name | |
|---|---|
| Address | |
| | Postcode |

---

## FREE TRIAL ACCEPTANCE

Please send me free the next 3 issues of *Gardening* as they appear. I understand that I am under no obligation. If I do not wish to continue with *Gardening* after the free trial, I can cancel this order at any time before payment is due on the 1st of the month three months after the date shown. But if I decide to continue I need do nothing – my subscription will bring me *Gardening* for the current price of £11.75 a quarter.

☐ Tick here if you do not wish your name and address to be added to a mailing list to be used by ourselves or third parties for sending you further offers.

L _ E

## DIRECT DEBITING MANDATE

I/We authorise you until further notice in writing to charge to my/our account with you unspecified amounts which may be debited thereto at the instance of Consumers' Association by Direct Debit.  Originator's Ref. No. 992338

| Signed | | | | | | Today's date | | | |
|---|---|---|---|---|---|---|---|---|---|
| Bank account in the name of | | | | | | | | | |
| Bank account number | | | | | | | | | |
| Name and address of your bank | | | | | | | | | |
| | | | | | | | Postcode | | |

Banks may decline to accept instructions to charge direct debits to certain types of account other than current accounts.

### YOUR NAME AND ADDRESS

| Name | |
|---|---|
| Address | |
| | Postcode |

---

## FREE TRIAL ACCEPTANCE

Please send me free the next 2 issues of *Which? way to Health* as they appear. I understand that I am under no obligation. If I do not wish to continue with *Which? way to Health* after the free trial, I can cancel this order at any time before payment is due on the 1st of the month three months after the date shown. But if I decide to continue I need do nothing – my subscription will bring me *Which? way to Health* for the current price of £5.75 a quarter.

☐ Tick here if you do not wish your name and address to be added to a mailing list to be used by ourselves or third parties for sending you further offers.

E _ XM

## DIRECT DEBITING MANDATE

I/We authorise you until further notice in writing to charge to my/our account with you unspecified amounts which may be debited thereto at the instance of Consumers' Association by Direct Debit.  Originator's Ref. No. 992338

| Signed | | | | | | Today's date | | | |
|---|---|---|---|---|---|---|---|---|---|
| Bank account in the name of | | | | | | | | | |
| Bank account number | | | | | | | | | |
| Name and address of your bank | | | | | | | | | |
| | | | | | | | Postcode | | |

Banks may decline to accept instructions to charge direct debits to certain types of account other than current accounts.

### YOUR NAME AND ADDRESS

| Name | |
|---|---|
| Address | |
| | Postcode |

*Which?* and
*Holiday Which?* –
details overleaf

Consumers' Association, Castlemead,
Gascoyne Way, Hertford X, SG14 1LH.

------------------------------------- ✂ -

*Gardening from
Which?* –
details overleaf

Consumers' Association, Castlemead,
Gascoyne Way, Hertford X, SG14 1LH.

------------------------------------- ✂ -

*Which?* way to
*Health* –
details overleaf

Consumers' Association, Castlemead,
Gascoyne Way, Hertford X, SG14 1LH.